# Essentials of
# **Business**
# **Communication** 12e

**MARY ELLEN GUFFEY**

Emerita Professor of Business
Los Angeles Pierce College
m.e.guffey@cox.net

**DANA LOEWY**

Emerita Lecturer, Business Communication
California State University, Fullerton
dloewy@fullerton.edu

✦ Cengage

Australia • Brazil • Canada • Mexico • Singapore • United Kingdom • United States

***Essentials of Business Communication,***
**12th Edition**
**Mary Ellen Guffey, Dana Loewy**

SVP, Higher Education & Skills Product: Erin Joyner

Product Director: Joe Sabatino

Product Manager: Heather Thompson

Product Assistant: Hannah May

Learning Designer: Megan Guiliani

Content Manager: Kate Begley Reed

Digital Delivery Quality Partner: Amanda Ryan

Director, Marketing: April Danaë

Marketing Manager: Tony Winslow

IP Analyst: Diane Garrity

IP Project Manager: Nick Barrows

IP Project Manager: Kumar Chandrakumar,
Integra Software Services

Production Service: MPS Limited

Designer: Felicia Bennett

Cover Image Source: Tim Robberts/Getty Images;
Delmaine Donson/Getty Images; PeopleImages/
Getty Images; LeoPatrizi/Getty Images; Shannon
Fagan/Getty Images; metamorworks/Getty Images

For product information and technology assistance, contact us at
**Cengage Customer & Sales Support, 1-800-354-9706
or support.cengage.com.**

For permission to use material from this text or product, submit all
requests online at **www.copyright.com.**

Library of Congress Control Number: 2021922995

ISBN: 978-0-357-71497-3

**Cengage**
200 Pier 4 Boulevard
Boston, MA 02210
USA

Cengage is a leading provider of customized learning solutions with
employees residing in nearly 40 different countries and sales in more
than 125 countries around the world. Find your local representative at
**www.cengage.com.**

To learn more about Cengage platforms and services, register or access
your online learning solution, or purchase materials for your course, visit
**www.cengage.com.**

Printed in the United States of America
Print Number: 01     Print Year: 2022

# Essentials of Business Communication 12e

## Dear Business Communication Instructors and Students:

Welcome to the Twelfth Edition of *Essentials of Business Communication*! We are eager to invite you to examine this substantially revised edition that focuses on developing job-ready and future-proof skills for students entering today's complex mobile and social workplace. After leading the business communication textbook market for nearly 30 years, this book has become an even more valuable teaching/learning package.

**Mary Ellen Guffey and Dana Loewy**

Photographer: Barbara D'Allessandro

All the features that made this award-winning book so successful over the decades have been updated with relevant, current research transformed into stimulating content and learning activities. Our goal is to help students develop vital communication skills while also easing the instructor's workload in delivering superior online and classroom resources. A few key features of the Twelfth Edition are listed here:

- **Trusted content.** This new edition reflects the prevalence of communication technologies in today's social and mobile workplace. We have thoroughly revised the book to present best practices for e-mailing, texting, enterprise messaging (Slack), blogging, podcasting, working in face-to-face and remote teams, and using social media professionally.

- **Development of job-ready and future-proof skills.** Students will find special emphasis on emotional intelligence, professionalism, listening, teaming, critical thinking, and other interpersonal skills that cannot be replaced by artificial intelligence, automation, and other technological advances, thus making business graduates recession-proof and future-ready.

- **MindTap.** A multimedia learning experience, MindTap provides a complete ebook combined with unparalleled resources to achieve success in the course. Those resources include abundant grammar/mechanics, chapter assignments with rich feedback, model documents, skills-based activities, and flashcards. This multimedia learning experience seamlessly integrates chapter content with most colleges' preferred learning management systems allowing instructors to customize activities.

- **Latest trends in job searching and interviewing.** True to our goal of making students job ready, Chapters 13 and 14 provide countless tips for today's job search, how to build a personal brand, and how to network. Students benefit from knowing the latest trends in résumé and interview practices, including tips for successful one- and two-way interviewing, whether face-to-face or remotely.

For additional helpful instructor resources such as ready-to-use exercises with solutions, please visit the Guffey Team blog at **https://bizcombuzz.com**, and follow us on Facebook and Twitter (@danaloewy).

Cordially,

*Mary Ellen Guffey & Dana Loewy*

Dr. Mary Ellen Guffey
Emerita Professor of Business
Los Angeles Pierce College
m.e.guffey@cox.net

Dr. Dana Loewy
Emerita Lecturer, Business Communication
California State University, Fullerton
dloewy@fullerton.edu

# Brief Contents

# Contents

# 4 Revising Business Messages 86

# Unit 3 Workplace Communication

# 5 Short Workplace Messages and Digital Media 112

# 6 Positive and Neutral Messages 152

# 7 Bad-News Messages 189

# 8 Persuasive Messages 222

# Unit 4 Business Reports and Proposals— Best Practices

# 9 Informal Reports 258

# 10 Proposals and Formal Reports 292

# Unit 5 Professionalism, Teamwork, Meetings, and Speaking Skills

## 11 Professionalism at Work: Business Etiquette, Teamwork, and Meetings 334

## 12 Business Presentations 369

# Unit 6 Employment Communication

## 13 The Job Search, Résumés, and Cover Messages 406

## **14** Interviewing and Following Up **451**

## Appendixes

## End Matter

# Essentials of Business Communication 12e

This book and this course may well be the most important in your entire college curriculum!

This leading text and MindTap guide you in developing the communication competencies most important for professional success in today's hyperconnected digital age. Refine the skills that employers value most, such as superior writing, speaking, presentation, critical thinking, and teamwork skills.

Survey after survey reveals that employers are seeking new-hires with these key skills:

- Written and oral communication skills
- Critical thinking and analytical reasoning
- Ethical decision making
- Teamwork skills
- Professionalism

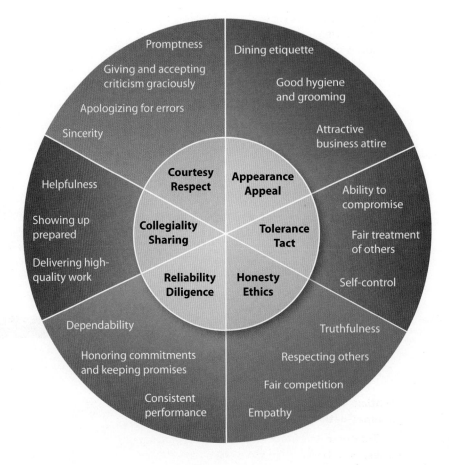

No other college course gives you training in all of these skills at once! Based on interviews with successful practitioners and extensive research into the latest trends, technologies, and practices, this edition offers synthesized advice on building your personal brand, using LinkedIn effectively, and résumé writing. Meaningful assignments, editing opportunities, and digital practice tools further equip you with the communication skills to stand out in business today.

*Essentials of Business Communication*, 12e, covers the following topics you will find indispensable in the digital-age workplace:

- Expert writing techniques geared to developing your writing skills plus Radical Rewrites, authentic model documents, and engaging activities in which you apply your skills—for example, by tackling proofing and revision in each chapter's Editing Challenge

- Presentation skills featuring contemporary examples including coverage of smartphone best practices to prepare you for the realities of workplace communication and technology

- Critical-thinking questions and activities in every chapter to stimulate and develop skills ever more important in a society confronted by disinformation

- Coverage and assignments focusing on ethics, climate change, remote work, and other urgent, timely business subjects

- Teamwork skills with a heavy emphasis on professionalism and etiquette in the workplace so that you will know how to meet employer expectations and excel in teams face-to-face or working from home

- Coverage of social media and mobile technology showing how their explosive growth has not only sparked disruptive new business models in the new sharing economy but also facilitated the dark side of the Internet

- Two updated employment chapters (a) providing tips for a labor market that is more volatile and technology-driven than ever before and (b) accounting for a workplace that's being profoundly transformed in the wake of the COVID-19 pandemic.

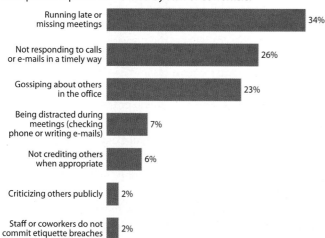

From **senior managers:** Most common breaches of workplace etiquette committed by staff or coworkers:

| | |
|---|---|
| Running late or missing meetings | 34% |
| Not responding to calls or e-mails in a timely way | 26% |
| Gossiping about others in the office | 23% |
| Being distracted during meetings (checking phone or writing e-mails) | 7% |
| Not crediting others when appropriate | 6% |
| Criticizing others publicly | 2% |
| Staff or coworkers do not commit etiquette breaches | 2% |

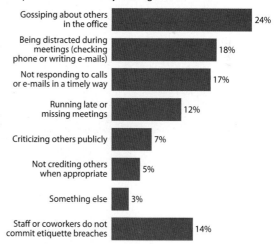

From **workers:** Most common breaches of workplace etiquette committed by colleagues:

| | |
|---|---|
| Gossiping about others in the office | 24% |
| Being distracted during meetings (checking phone or writing e-mails) | 18% |
| Not responding to calls or e-mails in a timely way | 17% |
| Running late or missing meetings | 12% |
| Criticizing others publicly | 7% |
| Not crediting others when appropriate | 5% |
| Something else | 3% |
| Staff or coworkers do not commit etiquette breaches | 14% |

# Premium Online Resources with MindTap

- **MindTap for *Essentials of Business Communication*, 12e, helps you see the importance of communication skills in practice.**

- A comprehensive **Grammar and Mechanics Pre-Course Diagnostic** provides an opportunity to assess your basic language skills in key areas and receive a custom report about your proficiency in each, with options for further review. Upon reviewing your results, you can continue to hone your language skills with targeted Grammar/Mechanics tutorials and put those skills into practice with additional Grammar/Mechanics Checkups.

- Each unit opens with a **"Why Does This Matter to Me?"** activity, showcasing how each part you're learning about connects to your future business success.

- **"Learn It" Concept Check Quizzes** test your knowledge and understanding of the chapter material and provide immediate feedback about your performance.

- **"Apply It" Activities** include the comprehensive **Chapter Assignment** that challenges you to apply what you're learning within examples and business communication scenarios—delivering detailed immediate feedback to underscore chapter concepts in context. Flex your growing communication skills muscle with **Video Presentation activities** challenging you to apply what you're learning in real time.

- The **"Study It" Practice Quiz** enables you to prepare and study for upcoming exams by reinforcing your knowledge, understanding, and application of chapter concepts.

- Each unit ends with a **Writing Assignment** activity that provides the opportunity to learn in context, deepening your understanding of chapter topics and concepts while building your written communication skills and business acumen.

- **Model Documents** included throughout the chapters explain and illustrate many concepts and walk through how to write positive, bad-news, claim adjustment, persuasive, and sales messages.

- The **Cengage Mobile App** empowers you to learn on your terms. Read or listen to your textbook on any mobile device and study with the aid of included tools.

# Social Media Networks and Mobile Technology

The authors address workplace social media and communication technology in a chapter dedicated to best practices on the job. Because these skills are fundamental in the contemporary world of work, social media and communication technology are integrated in each chapter.

Every chapter reflects the pervasive influence of communication technology on business writing. This state-of-the-art coverage makes it clear that writing and speaking are more important than ever in the rapidly changing world of work. Careers are made or thwarted based on one's online digital persona.

- New sections discussing current digital workplace tools are complemented by brand new coverage of social media's disturbing side to help you navigate the complex world of work and hone your critical thinking skills.

- New discussions of workplace messaging are included, particularly the ever popular but controversial app Slack, complete with a guide to Slack etiquette.

- New stimulating coverage of the negative aspects of technology and social media—for example, security breaches, cyberbullying, doxxing, online echo chambers, and disinformation—and how they affect us as businesspeople and citizens has been added.

- New activities, identified with the Social Media and Communication Technology icon, reflect the preeminence of writing in the digital workplace and prompt you to develop your professional social networking skills—frequently using structured role play.

- The coverage in the Grammar/Mechanics Guidebook was expanded to include advice for the use of gender-neutral pronouns and honorifics to reflect changes in the workplace seeking diversity and inclusion.

# Appreciation for Support

No successful textbook reaches a No. 1 position without a great deal of help. We are exceedingly grateful to the reviewers and other experts who contributed their pedagogic and academic expertise in shaping *Essentials of Business Communication*.

We extend sincere thanks to many outstanding professionals at Cengage Learning, including Erin Joyner, senior vice president, Higher Education; Joe Sabatino, product director, Higher Education; Heather Thompson, product manager, Business Communication; Clara Kuhlman, manager, Content Creation, Tony Winslow, marketing manager; Felicia Bennet, designer. Our very special thanks go to Kate Begley Reed, content manager, for her meticulous planning, professional project management, and helpful can-do attitude, as well as to Megan Guiliani, learning designer, for always providing the right polished phrase.

For their expertise in creating superior student assessment and support materials, our thanks go to Nicole Adams, University of Dayton, Susan Schanne, Eastern Michigan University, Anne Sheroff, and Steve Harris.

**Mary Ellen Guffey**
**Dana Loewy**

## Heartfelt Thanks to Reviewers

**Faridah Awang**
*Eastern Kentucky University*

**Joyce M. Barnes**
*Texas A&M University, Corpus Christi*

**Patricia Beagle**
*Bryant & Stratton Business Institute*

**Nancy C. Bell**
*Wayne Community College*

**Ray D. Bernardi**
*Morehead State University*

**Karen Bounds**
*Boise State University*

**Mary Y. Bowers**
*Northern Arizona University*

**Penny A. Braboy**
*Thomas More College*

**Daniel Brown**
*University of South Florida*

**Jean Bush-Bacelis**
*Eastern Michigan University*

**Therese Butler**
*Long Beach City College*

**Cheryl S. Byrne**
*Washtenaw Community College*

**Derrick Cameron**
*Vance-Granville Community College*

**Susan M. Campbell**
*Arkansas Tech University*

**Brennan Carr**
*Long Beach City College*

**Steven V. Cates**
*Averett University*

**Alma Cervantes**
*Skyline College*

**Irene Z. Church**
*Muskegon Community College*

**Debbie Cook**
*Utah State University*

**Lise H. Diez-Arguelles**
*Florida State University*

**Dee Anne Dill**
*Dekalb Technical Institute*

**Dawn Dittman**
*Dakota State University*

**Elizabeth Donnelly-Johnson**
*Muskegon Community College*

**Jeanette Dostourian**
*Cypress College*

**Nancy J. Dubino**
*Greenfield Community College*

**Donna N. Dunn**
*Beaufort County Community College*

**Cecile Earle**
*Heald College*

**Valerie Evans**
*Cuesta College*

**Bartlett J. Finney**
*Park University*

**Westelle Florez**
*Harris-Stowe State University*

**Christine Foster**
*Grand Rapids Community College*

**JoAnn Foth**
*Milwaukee Area Technical College*

**Pat Fountain**
*Coastal Carolina Community College*

**Marlene Friederich**
*New Mexico State University, Carlsbad*

**Gail Garton**
*Ozarks Technical Community College*

**Nanette Clinch Gilson**
*San Jose State University*

**Robert Goldberg**
*Prince George's Community College*

**Margaret E. Gorman**
*Cayuga Community College*

**Judith Graham**
*Holyoke Community College*

Lauren Gregory
*South Plains College*

Bruce E. Guttman
*Katharine Gibbs School, Melville, New York*

Susan E. Hall
*University of West Georgia*

April Halliday
*Georgia Piedmont Technical College*

Tracey M. Harrison
*Mississippi College*

Debra Hawhee
*University of Illinois*

L. P. Helstrom
*Rochester Community College*

Jack Hensen
*Morehead State University*

Rovena L. Hillsman
*California State University, Sacramento*

Karen A. Holtkamp
*Xavier University*

Jodi Hoyt
*Southeast Technical Institute*

Michael Hricik
*Westmoreland County Community College*

Sandie Idziak
*University of Texas, Arlington*

Karin Jacobson
*University of Montana*

Bonnie Jeffers
*Mt. San Antonio College*

Edna Jellesed
*Lane Community College*

Jane Johansen
*University of Southern Indiana*

Laurie J. Johnson
*Manhattan Area Technical College*

Pamela R. Johnson
*California State University, Chico*

Edwina Jordan
*Illinois Central College*

Sheryl E. C. Joshua
*University of North Carolina, Greensboro*

Diana K. Kanoy
*Central Florida Community College*

Ron Kapper
*College of DuPage*

Jan Kehm
*Spartanburg Community College*

Karen Kendrick
*Nashville State Community College*

Lydia Keuser
*San Jose City College*

Linda Kissler
*Westmoreland County Community College*

Deborah Kitchin
*City College of San Francisco*

Frances Kranz
*Oakland University*

Keith Kroll
*Kalamazoo Valley Community College*

Rose Marie Kuceyeski
*Owens Community College*

Richard B. Larsen
*Francis Marion University*

Mary E. Leslie
*Grossmont College*

Ruth E. Levy
*Westchester Community College*

Gary R. Lewis
*Southwest Florida College*

Maryann Egan Longhi
*Dutchess Community College*

Nedra Lowe
*Marshall University*

Elaine Lux
*Nyack College*

Diana Macdonald
*Uintah Basin Applied Technology College*

Elizabeth MacDonald
*Arizona State University*

Margarita Maestas-Flores
*Evergreen Valley College*

Jane Mangrum
*Miami-Dade Community College*

Maria Manninen
*Delta College*

Tim March
*Kaskaskia College*

Paula Marchese
*State University of New York, Brockport*

Tish Matuszek
*Troy University Montgomery*

Kenneth R. Mayer
*Cleveland State University*

Victoria McCrady
*University of Texas at Dallas*

Karen McFarland
*Salt Lake Community College*

Pat McGee
*Southeast Technical Institute*

Patti McMann
*Klamath Community College*

Bonnie Miller
*Los Medanos College*

Mary C. Miller
*Ashland University*

Willie Minor
*Phoenix College*

Nancy Moody
*Sinclair Community College*

Suman Mudunuri
*Long Beach City College*

Nancy Mulder
*Grand Rapids Junior College*

Paul W. Murphey
*Southwest Wisconsin Technical College*

Nan Nelson
*University of Arkansas Phillips Community College*

Lisa Nieman
*Indiana Wesleyan University*

Jackie Ohlson
*University of Alaska, Anchorage*

Richard D. Parker
*Western Kentucky University*

**Martha Payne**
*Grayson County College*

**Catherine Peck**
*Chippewa Valley Technical College*

**Carol Pemberton**
*Normandale Community College*

**Carl Perrin**
*Casco Bay College*

**Jan Peterson**
*Anoka-Hennepin Technical College*

**Susan Peterson**
*Scottsdale Community College*

**Kay D. Powell**
*Abraham Baldwin College*

**Jeanette Purdy**
*Mercer County College*

**Carolyn A. Quantrille**
*Spokane Falls Community College*

**Susan Randles**
*Vatterott College*

**Diana Reep**
*University of Akron*

**Judy A. Reiman**
*Columbia College*

**Ruth D. Richardson**
*University of North Alabama*

**Carlita Robertson**
*Northern Oklahoma College*

**Vilera Rood**
*Concordia College*

**Rich Rudolph**
*Drexel University*

**Rachel Rutledge**
*Carteret Community College*

**Joanne Salas**
*Olympic College*

**Rose Ann Scala**
*Data Institute School of Business*

**Joseph Schaffner**
*SUNY College of Technology, Alfred*

**Daniel Schlittner**
*Phoenix Community College*

**James Calvert Scott**
*Utah State University*

**Laurie Shapero**
*Miami-Dade Community College*

**Lance Shaw**
*Blake Business School*

**Cinda Skelton**
*Central Texas College*

**Estelle Slootmaker**
*Aquinas College*

**Margaret Smallwood**
*The University of Texas at Dallas*

**Clara Smith**
*North Seattle Community College*

**Nicholas Spina**
*Central Connecticut State University*

**Marilyn St. Clair**
*Weatherford College*

**Judy Sunayama**
*Los Medanos College*

**Dana H. Swensen**
*Utah State University*

**James A. Swindling**
*Eastfield College*

**David A. Tajerstein**
*SYRIT College*

**Marilyn Theissman**
*Rochester Community College*

**Zorica Wacker**
*Bellevue College*

**Lois A. Wagner**
*Southwest Wisconsin Technical College*

**Amy Weaver**
*Potomac State College*

**Linda Weavil**
*Elan College*

**William Wells**
*Lima Technical College*

**Gerard Weykamp**
*Grand Rapids Community College*

**Beverly Wickersham**
*Central Texas College*

**Leopold Wilkins**
*Anson Community College*

**Anna Williams**
*College of Central Florida, Ocala*

**Charlotte Williams**
*Jones County Junior College*

**Donald Williams**
*Feather River College*

**Janice Willis**
*College of San Mateo*

**Almeda Wilmarth**
*State University of New York, Delhi*

**Barbara Young**
*Skyline College*

# About the Authors

## Dr. Mary Ellen Guffey

Mary Ellen Guffey

A dedicated professional, Mary Ellen Guffey has taught business communication and business English topics for over 35 years. She received a bachelor's degree, *summa cum laude*, from Bowling Green State University; a master's degree from the University of Illinois, and a doctorate in business and economic education from the University of California, Los Angeles (UCLA). She has taught at the University of Illinois, Santa Monica College, and Los Angeles Pierce College.

Now recognized as the world's leading business communication author, Dr. Guffey corresponds with instructors around the globe who are using her books. She is the founding author of the award-winning *Business Communication: Process and Product*, the leading business communication textbook in the United States. She also wrote *Business English*, which serves more students than any other book in its field; *Essentials of College English*; and *Essentials of Business Communication*, the leading text/workbook in its market. Dr. Guffey is active professionally, serving on the review boards of the *Business and Professional Communication Quarterly* and the *Journal of Business Communication*, publications of the Association for Business Communication. She participates in national meetings, sponsors business communication awards, and is committed to promoting excellence in business communication pedagogy and the development of student writing skills.

## Dr. Dana Loewy

Dana Loewy

Dana Loewy taught business communication at California State University, Fullerton for nearly two decades. She enjoyed introducing undergraduates to business writing and honing the skills of graduate students in managerial communication. Concurrently, she also taught various German courses and was a regular guest lecturer at Fachhochschule Nürtingen, Germany. Dr. Loewy has played an increasingly significant role in collaborating with Dr. Guffey on recent editions of *Essentials of Business Communication* and *Business Communication: Process & Product*.

Dr. Loewy holds a master's degree from Bonn University, Germany, and earned a PhD in English at the University of Southern California. Fluent in several languages, among them German and Czech, her two native languages, Dr. Loewy has authored critical articles in many areas of interest—literary criticism, translation, business communication, and business ethics. Before teaming up with Dr. Guffey, Dr. Loewy worked as a professional translator for 25 years. Active in the Association for Business Communication, Dr. Loewy is now focusing on her consulting practice. Most recently she advised a German bank and a California-based nonprofit organization on communication strategy and effective writing techniques. In addition to a stint in brand-name consulting, she is also a business etiquette consultant certified by The Protocol School of Washington.

# Business Communication in the Information Age

# 1

**Chapter 1**

Thriving in a Digital, Social, and Mobile Workplace

# Thriving in a Digital, Social, and Mobile Workplace

**Learning Outcomes**

After studying this chapter, you should be able to do the following:

**1** Describe how communication skills fuel career success in a challenging digital age marketplace.

**2** Use active listening techniques.

**3** Discuss how effective nonverbal communication can help you build your credibility and advance your career.

**4** Describe the key dimensions of culture and how technology and social media shape intercultural communication.

**5** Identify strategies for enhancing intercultural effectiveness and communication across cultures.

iStockPhoto/Metamorworks

## 1-1 Succeeding With Twenty-First-Century Skills

What will the workplace of the future look like, and will you have the skills to succeed in it? Technologies are rapidly transforming how we work and communicate. Robots, automation, and artificial intelligence (AI) are radically reshaping and even destroying many occupations. Experts estimate that almost half of all present jobs will disappear in the next decade, although new jobs are also likely to emerge.[1] Future-proof occupations will require communication, managing people, creativity, and specialized knowledge.

The COVID-19 pandemic injected high uncertainty into the global labor markets. It has also forced an unprecedented expansion of remote work and, therefore, accelerated the ongoing digital transformation of the workplace. On average, 44 percent of the labor force were able to work from home.[2] Some may do so permanently or continue in some hybrid fashion. In a hyperconnected, always-on environment, communication skills are critical.[3] Your ability to communicate will always be on display.

This first chapter introduces communication in business today. It addresses listening skills, nonverbal communication, the cultural dimensions of communication, and intercultural job skills. The remainder of the book is devoted to developing specific writing and speaking skills.

## 1-1a  Communication Skills and Career Success

Superior communication skills will make you marketable in the workplace of the future regardless of the economic climate. When competition is fierce, excellent communicators immediately stand out. In poll after poll, communication tops recruiters' wish lists.[4] In one recent survey of job postings, written and oral communication ranked first among the five most desirable attributes in job seekers, ahead of management, leadership, problem-solving, and teamwork skills.[5] Your ability to communicate is a stepping-stone to great job opportunities.

Do you know how your skills measure up? The good news is that you can learn effective communication. This textbook and this course may well be the most important in your entire college curriculum because they can equip you with the skills most needed in today's information- and data-driven workplace.

## 1-1b  Why Communication and Other Social Skills Matter

Today's workers communicate more, not less, since information technology, mobile devices, and social media have swept the workplace. According to one survey, the average employee spends almost 12 hours per week answering e-mails at the office and another 5 hours from home.[7] Many office workers also write reports, memos, presentations, instant messages, social media posts, and more. Messages travel instantly to distant locations, reaching potentially huge audiences. Work team members can collaborate virtually, often across vast distances. In such a networked environment, writing, speaking, and other professional skills count more than ever.[8]

In an information-based economy, employers seek workplace-ready employees with a broad range of skills and high levels of knowledge in their field. Researchers warn that to be successful, workers need essential twenty-first-century skills such as oral and written communication, teamwork, analytical thinking, problem solving, and media savvy.[9] Communication plays a leading role, and most Americans know it. Pew Research found that 90 percent of the respondents in one of its studies considered communication the No. 1 skill for a successful life.[10] Furthermore, jobs relying heavily on transferrable skills such as communication are more likely to survive automation and will offer the most opportunities in the future.[11]

Communication and Employability. Not surprisingly, many job listings require excellent oral and written communication skills. An analysis of 142,000 job advertisements revealed that the most highly requested interpersonal skills were oral communication (28 percent) and written communication (23 percent), followed by collaboration (22 percent) and problem solving (19 percent).[13] An earlier study of 2.3 million LinkedIn profiles showed similar results: Oral and written communication skills were the top skills set sought by a large margin.[14]

In addition, as you will learn in later chapters, recruiters will scrutinize your online presence to learn about your communication skills and professionalism. Naturally, they will not hire candidates who write poorly or post inappropriate content.[15] Your reputation and personal credibility are vital assets you must guard.

**OFFICE INSIDER**

"Communication makes the world go round. It facilitates human connections, and allows us to learn, grow and progress. It's not just about speaking or reading, but understanding what is being said—and in some cases what is not being said."[6]

**Richard Branson,** *billionaire entrepreneur, founder of the Virgin Group*

**Note:** Small superscript numbers in the text announce information sources. Full citations are near the end of the book. This edition uses a modified American Psychological Association (APA) reference format.

**Techies Communicate Too.** Yes, accountants and information technology workers must be able to interact and collaborate with others. The COVID-19 pandemic has thrust employees in all job roles into the limelight, as they work remotely and depend on digital meeting tools. Therefore, IT departments are much needed, and techs must possess people skills. An executive for a corporate recruiting firm explains: "The brilliant, introverted developer continues to be in high demand, but we are also seeing an uptick in requirements for relationship building, business acumen and communications in our searches."[16] Technical skills alone are insufficient.

In an economy relying on innovation, generating ideas isn't enough; they must be communicated clearly, often in writing.[17] As one executive coach put it: "Having excellent writing skills can make you an indispensable member of your team or company. And it's one of the best ways to remain consistently employable—no matter your profession."[18] Keeping your skills sharp will allow you to weather any disruption to the economy, even devastating events such as a global pandemic.

**Many Grads Are Not Ready.** With added job responsibilities, you will be expected to make sound decisions and solve complex problems as you advance. Yet in a PayScale survey, half of the employers said new-hires are not workplace ready, mainly lacking critical-thinking and reasoning skills.[19]

In another important study, employers noted that students were adequately trained for entry-level jobs but were not equipped for advancement. In their view, promotable graduates excel at oral communication, critical thinking, ethical judgment, teamwork, independent work, self-motivation, writing, and real-world application of learning. However, only 40 percent are well prepared, said the executives.[20] To make sure you impress future employers, take advantage now of opportunities to strengthen your writing, presentation, and critical-thinking skills.

**Writing Is in Your Future.** Regardless of the field you choose, you probably will be sending many digital messages, such as the e-mail shown in **Model Document 1.1**. Because electronic mail and other digital media have become important channels of communication in today's workplace, all digital business messages must be clear, concise, and professional. Notice that the message in Model Document 1.1 is more businesslike than the quick text or e-mail you might send to friends and family. Learning to write professional digital messages will be an important part of this course.

## 1-1c Employers Want Professionalism

In addition to technical knowledge, your future employer will expect you to show professionalism and possess what are variously called **soft skills**, **people skills**, or **emotional intelligence**. These powerful social skills are anything but "soft" or inferior, however. To reflect their growing importance, we prefer the terms **interpersonal skills** or **professional skills**, which may be defined as a combination of communication, logical reasoning, critical-thinking, teamwork, and management skills.[21]

Not every job seeker is aware of the employer's expectations, even the most basic ones. In some regions of the United States devastated by the opioid crisis, factories struggle to fill openings with candidates who can pass a drug test. One official puts it bluntly: "Employers just want someone who will get up, dress up, show up, shut up, and never give up."[22]

Some new-hires seem surprised that excessive absenteeism or tardiness is grounds for termination, and many employees invite negative attention by sprinkling their speech with *like*, *you know*, and uptalk (making declarative statements sound like questions).

Projecting a professional image can make a real difference in helping you obtain the job of your dreams. Once you get that job, you are more likely to be taken seriously and promoted if you present yourself as professional. Don't send the wrong message and risk losing your credibility with unwitting and unprofessional behavior. **Figure 1.1** reviews areas you will want to check to be sure you are projecting professionalism.

**Model Document 1.1 A Professional E-Mail Message**

Because e-mails have all but replaced business letters and interoffice memos in most workplaces, they must be written carefully, provide complete information, and sound businesslike and professional. Notice that this message is more formal in tone than e-mail messages people might dash off to friends.

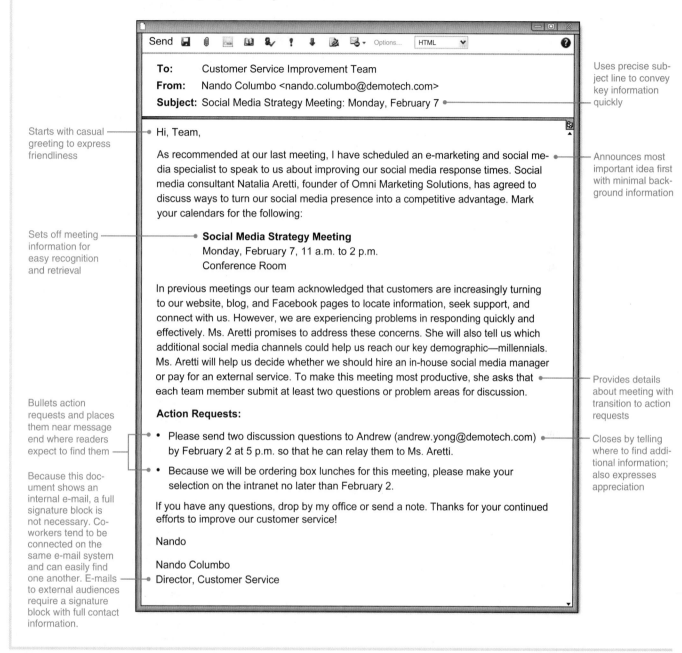

Starts with casual greeting to express friendliness

Sets off meeting information for easy recognition and retrieval

Bullets action requests and places them near message end where readers expect to find them

Because this document shows an internal e-mail, a full signature block is not necessary. Coworkers tend to be connected on the same e-mail system and can easily find one another. E-mails to external audiences require a signature block with full contact information.

Uses precise subject line to convey key information quickly

Announces most important idea first with minimal background information

Provides details about meeting with transition to action requests

Closes by telling where to find additional information; also expresses appreciation

---

Send | Options... | HTML

**To:**      Customer Service Improvement Team
**From:**    Nando Columbo <nando.columbo@demotech.com>
**Subject:** Social Media Strategy Meeting: Monday, February 7

Hi, Team,

As recommended at our last meeting, I have scheduled an e-marketing and social media specialist to speak to us about improving our social media response times. Social media consultant Natalia Aretti, founder of Omni Marketing Solutions, has agreed to discuss ways to turn our social media presence into a competitive advantage. Mark your calendars for the following:

**Social Media Strategy Meeting**
Monday, February 7, 11 a.m. to 2 p.m.
Conference Room

In previous meetings our team acknowledged that customers are increasingly turning to our website, blog, and Facebook pages to locate information, seek support, and connect with us. However, we are experiencing problems in responding quickly and effectively. Ms. Aretti promises to address these concerns. She will also tell us which additional social media channels could help us reach our key demographic—millennials. Ms. Aretti will help us decide whether we should hire an in-house social media manager or pay for an external service. To make this meeting most productive, she asks that each team member submit at least two questions or problem areas for discussion.

**Action Requests:**

* Please send two discussion questions to Andrew (andrew.yong@demotech.com) by February 2 at 5 p.m. so that he can relay them to Ms. Aretti.

* Because we will be ordering box lunches for this meeting, please make your selection on the intranet no later than February 2.

If you have any questions, drop by my office or send a note. Thanks for your continued efforts to improve our customer service!

Nando

Nando Columbo
Director, Customer Service

---

You will learn more about interpersonal skills and professionalism in Chapter 11. The Communication Workshop at the end of this chapter will help you explore your future career and the need for professional skills.

## 1-1d The Economic Benefit of Your College Education

As college tuition rises steeply and student debt mounts, you may wonder whether going to college is still a good investment. The American public seems to share this skepticism, as a Gallup poll suggests. Fewer than half of adults in the United States expressed confidence in higher education.[24] Yet the effort and money you invest in

**Figure 1.1** Projecting Professionalism When You Communicate

| Unprofessional | | Professional |
|---|---|---|
| *Uptalk*, a singsong speech pattern, making sentences sound like questions; *like* used as a filler; *go* for *said*; slang; poor grammar and profanity. | **Speech habits** | Recognizing that your credibility can be seriously damaged by sounding uneducated, crude, or adolescent. |
| Sloppy messages with incomplete sentences, misspelled words, exclamation points, IM slang, and mindless chatter. E-mail addresses such as *partyanimal@gmail.com, snugglykitty@icloud.com,* or *hotmama@outlook.com.* | **E-mail** | Messages with subjects, verbs, and punctuation, free from IM abbreviations; messages that are concise and spelled correctly even when brief. E-mail addresses that include a name or a positive, businesslike expression. |
| Suggestive Twitter handles and user names that point to an immature, unhealthy lifestyle. Posts that reveal political, religious, and other personal leanings. | **Internet, social media** | Real name Twitter handles and user names that don't sound cute or like chatroom nicknames. Posts in good taste, fit for public consumption. |
| An outgoing message with strident background music, weird sounds, or a joke message. | **Voice mail** | An outgoing message that states your name or phone number and provides instructions for leaving a message. |
| Soap operas, thunderous music, or a TV football game playing noisily in the background when you answer the phone. | **Telephone presence** | A quiet background when you answer the telephone, especially if you are expecting a prospective employer's call. |
| Using electronics during business meetings for unrelated purposes or during conversations with fellow employees; raising your voice (cell yell); forcing others to overhear your calls. | **Cell phones, tablets** | Turning off phone and message notification, both audible and vibrate, during meetings; using your smart devices only for meeting-related purposes. |
| Sending and receiving text messages during meetings, allowing texting to interrupt face-to-face conversations, or texting when driving. | **Texting** | Sending appropriate business text messages only when necessary (perhaps when a cell phone call would disturb others). |

earning your college degree will most likely pay off. Depending on the demand for their major, college graduates earn more, suffer less unemployment, and can choose from a wider variety of career options than workers without a college education.[25] As **Figure 1.2** shows, graduates with bachelor's degrees and higher earn nearly three times as much as people with less than a high-school education and are more than three times less likely to be unemployed.

As we have seen, interpersonal skills are highly prized but often in short supply. Workers who lack them may lose their jobs. One researcher even claims that half of all terminations are attributable to poor "soft" skills.[26] A survey of employers confirms that interpersonal skills such as communication ability can tip the scales in favor of one job applicant over another.[27] Your ticket to winning in a competitive job market and launching a successful career is good communication skills.

**Figure 1.2** The Education Bonus: Higher Income, Lower Unemployment

| Education | Median Weekly Earnings | Unemployment Rate |
|---|---|---|
| High school not completed | $ 619 | 11.7% |
| High school diploma | 781 | 9.0% |
| Some college, no degree | 877 | 8.3% |
| Associate's degree | 938 | 7.1% |
| Bachelor's degree | 1,305 | 5.5% |
| Master's degree or higher (average) | 1,774 | 3.2% |

Source: U.S. Bureau of Labor Statistics, Current population survey. (2021, April 21). Employment Projections: Unemployment rates and earnings by educational attainment, 2020.
Note: The COVID-19 pandemic doubled the average unemployment rate. However, job seekers with a college degree and excellent resilient skills such as communication will remain employable.

## 1-1e Meeting the Challenges of the Information Age Workplace

As a businessperson and as a business communicator, you will be affected by many trends. Some of these trends include new, disruptive technologies, expectations of around-the-clock availability, and teamwork. Other trends include flattened management hierarchies, global competition, and a renewed emphasis on ethics. The following overview reveals how communication skills are closely tied to your success in a constantly evolving information age workplace.

- **Disruptive technologies and social media**. The new **sharing economy** (think Uber or Lyft) emerged thanks to platforms accessible with **smartphone apps** and have radically transformed whole industries. The sharing of bikes, cars, and e-scooters has changed urban transportation; similarly, Airbnb has disrupted the hospitality industry. Social media continue to connect people around the world. Positive or negative word of mouth travels at the speed of a few taps on a smartphone. The undeniable advantages of social media also come with downsides (e.g., data breaches, invasion of privacy, identity theft, manipulation, and disinformation). Nevertheless, businesses are unlikely to thrive without digital media. Once employed, you will need to keep up. **Figure 1.3** illustrates many technologies you will encounter in today's workplace.

- **Remote work and 24/7/365 availability**. Even before the COVID-19 pandemic forced 66 percent of U.S. employees to work from home at least part-time, high-speed and wireless Internet access had freed 30 percent of workers from conventional jobs in physical offices.[28] As most employees (83 percent) embrace remote work,[29] flexible arrangements may continue reshaping workplaces and office real estate. However, constant connectedness has also blurred the line between work and leisure. Employees in the United States work long hours without extra compensation and receive the shortest paid vacations among their international counterparts. According to one study, they spend eight hours a week on average answering work e-mails after hours.[30] Experts caution that "digital overload" is a major stressor, leading to burnout.[31] Global studies in the wake of the pandemic have found that remote work may be bad for employees' mental health.[32] Be that as it may, the office today and in the future is mobile, social, and always on.

- **Collaboration and teams**. Teamwork has become a reality in business. Many companies have created cross-functional teams to empower employees and boost

**OFFICE INSIDER**

"In a survey conducted by PwC, CEOs cited 'curiosity' and 'open-mindedness' as traits that are becoming increasingly critical. Today's star employees need the full package: hard or technical skills backed up with soft skills and emotional intelligence. It isn't enough to say you're good with people, a resume catchphrase that's become empty jargon."[23]

**Dennis Yang,** *technology entrepreneur, former CEO of Udemy*

**Figure 1.3** Communication and Collaborative Technologies

# Communication Technologies at Work

Becoming familiar with communication technology in business will help you succeed on the job. Today's digital workplace is shaped by mobile devices, mobile apps, social media, superfast broadband and wireless access, and other technologies that allow workers to share information, work from remote locations, and be more productive in or away from the office. With today's tools you can exchange ideas, solve problems, develop products, forecast future performance, and complete team projects any time of the day or night anywhere in the world.

## Cloud Computing and Beyond: A Social, Mobile, and Smart Future

Increasingly, applications and data are stored in remote locations online, *in the cloud*. This ability to access data on remote servers with a computer or mobile device is called *cloud computing*, and it has helped fuel unparalleled mobility and information sharing. All social media platforms are cloud-based, as are typical workplace applications such as Microsoft's Office 365 or Adobe's Creative Suite.

More changes on the horizon will transform our lives and communication; they include intelligent devices and appliances—the *Internet of things*—*artificial intelligence* (AI), *augmented reality* (AR) and *virtual reality* (VR), voice-activated digital assistants such as Alexa or Siri, and self-driving vehicles. The emergence of the digital currency Bitcoin has introduced *blockchain technology*, a decentralized network of shared and continuously reconciled information, a vast database hosted by millions of computers at once. Some believe that blockchain will revolutionize the Internet.

## VoIP Phone Systems

Savvy businesses are switching from traditional phone service to voice over Internet protocol (VoIP). This technology allows callers to communicate using a broadband Internet connection, thus eliminating long-distance and local

telephone charges. Higher-end VoIP systems now support unified voice mail, e-mail, click-to-call capabilities, and softphones (Internet-based applications or mobile apps, such as Google Voice, for calling and messaging). Other free or low-cost options include Skype and FaceTime. Most messaging apps—such as WhatsApp and Facebook Messenger—now offer wireless voice calling and recorded voice messages.

## Open Offices and Home Offices

The widespread use of smart devices, wireless technology, and VoIP has led to more fluid, flexible, and open workspaces. Smaller computers and flat-screen monitors enable designers to save space with boomerang-shaped workstations and cockpit-style work surfaces rather than space-hogging corner work areas. Smaller breakout areas for impromptu meetings are taking over some cubicle space, and digital databases are replacing file cabinets. Mobile technology allows workers to be fully connected and productive on the go. The COVID-19 pandemic has accelerated the shift to remote-based work—a change that may become permanent in some business sectors, mainly tech and insurance.

## Smart Mobile Devices and Digital Convergence

Lightweight, ever-smaller devices provide phone, e-mail, Web browsing, and calendar options anywhere there is a cellular or Wi-Fi network. Tablets and smartphones such as Android devices and the iPhone and iPad allow workers to tap into corporate databases and intranets from distant locations. Users can check customers' files, complete orders, collect payment, and send out receipts remotely.

The need for separate electronic gadgets is waning as digital smart devices are becoming multifunctional. With streaming video, connectivity between smart TVs and computers, and networked mobile devices, technology is converging, consolidating into increasingly more powerful devices. Many smart devices today can replace digital still photography and video cameras. Mobile smart devices are also competing with TVs and computers for primacy. Mobile apps rival the capabilities of full-fledged software applications on laptops, on desktops, and in the cloud.

## Wearable Devices: Smartwatches, AR and VR Headsets

A growing trend in mobile computing is *wearable devices*. Activity trackers such as Fitbit, Apple Watch, and similar accessories do more than record fitness activities. They are powerful mobile devices that can sync with other smart electronics. Google Glass failed to capture a larger consumer market; however, with Google Lens, the company continues to pursue innovative augmented-reality head-mounted devices. More affordable virtual-reality goggles, for example, Oculus Rift, are popular with gamers, but VR headsets are also used in simulators, in training, and in patient therapy.

Panuwat Phimpha/Shutterstock.com

## Speech Recognition

Computers and mobile devices equipped with speech-recognition software enable users to dictate hands-free with accurate transcription. Speech recognition is particularly helpful to workers with disabilities and professionals with heavy dictation loads, such as physicians and attorneys. Users can create documents, enter data, compose and send e-mails, search the Web, and control their notebooks, laptops, and desktops—all by voice. Smart devices can also execute tasks with voice command apps—for example to dial a call, find a route, or transcribe voice mail.

Monty Rakusen/Getty images

## Electronic Presentations and Data Visualization

Business presentations in PowerPoint, Prezi, or Keynote can be projected from a laptop or tablet, or posted online. Sophisticated presentations may include animation, sound effects, digital photos, video clips, or hyperlinks. In some industries, PowerPoint and other electronic slides (decks) are replacing or supplementing traditional hard-copy reports. Data visualization tools such as SAS can help businesses make sense of large amounts of complex data.

## Social Media for Business

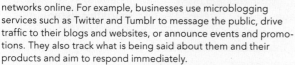

Oleksiy Mark/Shutterstock.com

The term *social media* describes technology that enables participants to connect and share in social networks online. For example, businesses use microblogging services such as Twitter and Tumblr to message the public, drive traffic to their blogs and websites, or announce events and promotions. They also track what is being said about them and their products and aim to respond immediately.

Similarly, organizations use social networks such as Facebook, Instagram, and others to interact with customers and build their brands. Companies may also prospect for talent using social media networks, LinkedIn foremost among them. Many companies are using *corporate social networks* for messaging, collaboration, project management, and data storage. Various popular enterprise-grade platforms behind corporate firewalls include Yammer, Asana, Atlassian HipChat, and SharePoint.

## Blogs, Podcasts, and Wikis

Source: Polycom, Inc.

Businesses use *blogs* to keep customers and employees informed and to receive feedback. Company news can be posted, updated, and categorized for easy cross-referencing. *Podcasts* are popular audio files played back from a website or downloaded to a digital audio player, typically a smart device. A *wiki* is an Internet or intranet site that allows multiple users to collaboratively create, edit, and store digital files. Wikipedia is the best-known public-facing example. In companies, information can get lost in e-mails and chat threads, but wikis provide easy access to important organizational documents and serve as a knowledge management tool. Wikis for business are often integrated within powerful enterprise social and messaging networks, for instance, in Slack.

## Web Conferencing and Videoconferencing

iStockPhoto/Relif

During the COVID-19 pandemic, Zoom grew explosively to become the most popular video conferencing tool for homebound remote workers. With Zoom and other services such as WebEx, GoToMeeting, and Skype for Business, users need only a computer or smart device and an Internet connection to hold a meeting (*webinar*) with customers or colleagues in real time. Although the functions are constantly evolving, Web conferencing incorporates screen sharing, chats, slide presentations, text messaging, and application sharing. All services also provide voice and video, making them videoconferencing tools as well. Best of all, they can be accessed across all devices.

Some companies have invested in sophisticated videoconferencing rooms equipped with HD video cameras and large video screens. Two to 200 individuals can see each other and interact in real time, although they may be far apart.

## Gamification

*Gamification* is the application of game design techniques to increase motivation and engagement. Much like computer games, gamification platforms in business are designed to be fun and in turn increase productivity as well as revenue. Gamification techniques include using badges or points to tap into workers' natural desires for competition, status, and achievement but also altruism and collaboration. Gamification is used in marketing, sales, customer retention, and training, allowing employers to collect large amounts of productivity data.

their involvement in decision making. You can expect to collaborate with a team in gathering information, finding and sharing solutions, implementing decisions, and managing conflict. You may even become part of a virtual team whose members are in remote locations.

Increasingly, organizations are also forming **ad hoc teams** to solve problems. Such project-based teams disband once they have accomplished their objectives. Moreover, parts of our future economy may rely on free agents who will be hired on a project basis in what has been dubbed the **gig economy**, a far cry from traditional full-time, relatively steady jobs.

- **Flattened management layers**. To better compete and to reduce expenses, businesses have for years been trimming layers of management. This means that as a frontline employee, you will have fewer managers. You will be making decisions and communicating them to customers, to fellow employees, and to executives.

- **Global competition and cultural diversity**. American companies continue to expand beyond domestic markets. At the same time, growing workforce diversity at home means that you may be interacting with people from many cultures. To be a successful business communicator, you will need to learn about other cultures. You will also need to develop intercultural skills including sensitivity, flexibility, patience, and tolerance.

- **Emphasis on ethics**. Business ethics continue to grab headlines and cause heated debate. Corporate scandals such as Wells Fargo's systemic consumer abuses or *Dieselgate*, Volkswagen's massive diesel emissions scam, prompted multi-year lawsuits and billion-dollar fines. Harvey Weinstein's sexual indiscretions destroyed his film production company; public outrage triggered the #MeToo movement and led to the firing of other prominent figures. Each new tale of misconduct erodes public trust and feeds into the perception that all business is dishonest. Americans want change. Millennials prefer sustainable and ethical brands; activist shareholders no longer overlook executives' malfeasance; and almost half of Americans want dishonest CEOs to be fired or sent to prison.[33]

These trends mean that in a hyperconnected always-on professional environment, your communication skills will constantly be noticed. In addition, you will need to nurture your reputation and safeguard your *brand* online and off. You will learn more about interpersonal skills and professionalism in Chapter 11.

## 1-2 Practicing Active Listening

**LEARNING OUTCOME 2**

Use active listening techniques.

The famous American entrepreneur Malcolm Forbes wrote, "The art of conversation lies in listening."[34] In an age that relies on information and communication technology, listening is an important leadership skill.[35] You may think that everyone knows how to listen. Most of us believe that listening is an automatic response to noise. We do it without thinking. Perhaps that explains why so many of us are poor listeners. Experts say that most people recall only between 25 and 50 percent of what they hear. Expect your boss, your coworkers, and your customers to retain only half or less of the conversation.[36]

Numerous studies suggest that good listeners make good managers; in fact, good listeners achieve success at all stages of their careers.[37] Active, **empathic listening**—when we sincerely strive to understand others' viewpoints—is the most effective form of listening, researchers tell us.[38] Only when we are **mindful**, meaning fully present, can we truly listen to build trust and gain respect.

Poor listening habits are costly in business. Messages must be rewritten, shipments redirected, appointments rescheduled, contracts renegotiated, and directions restated. Listening skills are important for career success, organization effectiveness, and worker satisfaction.

To develop better listening skills, we must first recognize barriers that prevent effective listening. Then we need to focus on techniques for improving listening skills.

## 1-2a  Identifying Barriers to Effective Listening

Bad habits and distractions can interfere with effective listening. Have any of the following barriers and distractions prevented you from hearing what has been said?

- **Physical barriers**. You cannot listen if you cannot hear what is being said. Physical impediments include hearing disabilities, poor acoustics, and noisy surroundings. It is also difficult to listen if you are ill, tired, or uncomfortable.

- **Psychological barriers**. Everyone brings to the communication process a unique set of cultural, ethical, and personal values. Each of us has an idea of what is right and what is important. If other ideas run counter to our preconceived thoughts, we tend to tune out speakers and thus fail to receive their messages.

- **Language problems**. Unfamiliar words can destroy the communication process because they lack meaning for the receiver. In addition, emotion-laden, or charged, words can adversely affect listening. If the mention of words such as *fraud* or *stock market crash* has an intense emotional impact, a listener may be unable to focus on the words that follow.

- **Nonverbal distractions**. Many of us find it hard to listen if a speaker is different from what we view as normal. Unusual clothing or speech mannerisms, body twitches, or a radical hairstyle can cause enough distraction to prevent us from hearing what the speaker has to say.

- **Thought speed**. Because listeners can process 450 words per minute, but in reality speakers talk about 125 to 175 words per minute,[40] we can become bored and allow our minds to wander. Experts call this lag time the **speech-thought differential**.[41]

- **Faking attention**. Most of us have learned to look as if we are listening even when we are not. Such behavior was perhaps necessary as part of our socialization. Faked attention, however, seriously threatens effective listening because it encourages the mind to engage in flights of unchecked fancy. Those who fake attention often find it hard to concentrate even when they want to.

- **Grandstanding**. Would you rather talk or listen? Naturally, most of us would rather talk. Because our own experiences and thoughts are most important to us, we often want to grab the limelight in conversations. We may fail to listen carefully when we are just waiting politely for the next pause so that we can have our turn to speak.

## 1-2b  Building Powerful Listening Skills

Good listeners on the job must remember that their goal is to listen carefully and to *understand* what is being said so that they can do their work well. The following recommendations will help you become an active and effective listener:

- **Stop talking**. If you are the brash chatty type who dominates conversations, try to break the habit by letting others talk without interrupting. Concentrate on the speaker's words, not on your response. Don't signal nonverbal disagreement or impatience by rolling your eyes, sarcastic snorting, or audible sighs.

Smart devices connect us with others potentially across vast distances, but they can also separate us from those closest to us. A person holding a smartphone signals unavailability for a conversation and listening.

- **Control the listening environment**. Whenever possible, remove competing sounds. Close windows or doors, turn off TVs and smartphones, and move away from loud people, noisy appliances, or engines. Choose a quiet time and place for listening.

- **Adopt an empathic attitude**. Effective listening requires *empathy*, the ability to understand other people's perspectives and emotionally respond to their experiences.[43] Expect to learn something by listening. Strive for a receptive mindset. Be accepting of people who are different from you or don't look like you.

- **Distinguish between facts and opinions**. Facts are truths known to exist; for example, *Apple is headquartered in Cupertino, California*. Opinions are statements of personal judgments or preferences; for example, *Apple stock is always a good investment*. Opinions are not always easy to identify in the absence of phrases such as *I think*, *It seems to me*, or *In my view*.

- **Capitalize on lag time**. Make the speech-thought differential work for you by silently organizing, reviewing, and summarizing the speaker's key points. Anticipate what is coming next without getting distracted. Evaluate evidence the speaker has presented. Don't allow yourself to daydream.

- **Listen between the lines and validate emotion**. Listen for feelings as well as for facts. Observe nonverbal cues and interpret the feelings of the speaker: What is really being said? Acknowledge the feelings even if you disagree on substance.

- **Take selective notes**. If you are hearing instructions or important data, record the major points; then revise your notes immediately or verify them with the speaker. Resist the temptation to type your notes or risk becoming distracted. Moreover, research shows that handwritten notes are more memorable.[44]

- **Provide encouraging feedback**. Let the speaker know that you are listening. Nod your head and maintain eye contact. Ask clarifying questions at appropriate times. Rephrase and summarize the message in your own words to make sure you understand the speaker. Getting involved improves the communication process for both the speaker and the listener.

## 1-3 Communicating Nonverbally

Understanding messages often involves more than merely listening to spoken words. Nonverbal cues, in fact, can speak louder than words. These cues include eye contact, facial expression, body movements, time, space, territory, and appearance. All these nonverbal cues affect how a receiver interprets, or decodes, a message.

Defining Nonverbal Communication. **Nonverbal communication** includes all unwritten and unspoken messages, whether intended or not. These silent signals have a strong effect on receivers. However, understanding them is not simple. Does a downward glance indicate modesty? Fatigue? Does a constant stare reflect coldness? Dullness? Aggression? Do crossed arms mean defensiveness, withdrawal, or just that the person is shivering?

Reconciling Words and Nonverbal Cues. Messages are even harder to decipher when the verbal and nonverbal cues do not agree. What will you think if Soren says he is not angry, but he slams the door when he leaves? What if Rosa assures the host that the meal is excellent, but she eats very little? The nonverbal messages in these situations speak louder than the words. Researchers have long held that humans resolve such clashes between verbal and nonverbal messaging by trusting the nonverbal component more than the words spoken.[45]

Cues broadcast by body language can help receivers understand the feelings and attitudes of senders. Be careful, however, before attaching specific meanings to gestures or actions because behavior and its interpretations strongly depend on context and on one's cultural background, as you will see.

## 1-3a  Your Body Sends Silent Messages

Psychologist and philosopher Paul Watzlawick famously said that *we cannot not communicate*.[46] In other words, it's impossible not to communicate. This means that every behavior is sending a message even if we don't use words. The eyes, face, and body convey meaning without a single syllable being spoken. Let's look at the silent nonverbal messages our bodies send.

Eye Contact. The eyes have been called the windows to the soul. Even if they don't reveal the soul, the eyes are often the best predictor of a speaker's true feelings and attitudes. Most of us cannot look another person straight in the eyes and lie. As a result, in North American culture, we tend to believe people who look directly at us. Sustained eye contact suggests trust and admiration; brief eye contact signals fear or stress. Prolonged eye contact or staring, though, can be intrusive and intimidating.

Good eye contact enables the message sender to see whether a receiver is paying attention, showing respect, responding favorably, or feeling distress. From the receiver's perspective, good eye contact, in North American culture, reveals the speaker's sincerity, confidence, and truthfulness.

Facial Expression. The expression on a person's face can be almost as revealing of emotion as the eyes. Experts estimate that the human face can display over 250,000 expressions.[47] To hide their feelings, some people can control these expressions and maintain so-called poker faces. In North America, however, most of us display our emotions openly and often unintentionally. Raising or lowering the eyebrows, squinting the eyes, swallowing nervously, clenching the jaw, smiling broadly—these voluntary and involuntary facial expressions can enhance or entirely replace verbal messages.

Posture and Gestures. An individual's posture can convey anything from presumed social status and self-confidence to shyness and submissiveness. Leaning toward a speaker suggests attentiveness and interest; pulling away or shrinking back denotes fear, distrust, anxiety, or disgust. Similarly, gestures can communicate entire thoughts via simple movements. However, the meanings of some of these movements differ in other cultures. In the United States and Canada, for example, forming the thumb and forefinger in a circle means everything is OK. But in parts of South America, the OK sign is considered obscene.

In the workplace you can make a good impression by controlling your posture and gestures. When speaking, make sure your upper body is aligned with the person to whom you are talking. Erect posture can send a message of confidence, competence, diligence, and strength. Avoid tilting your head to the side when listening or making an important point. This gesture is thought to undermine a person's perceived self-confidence.[48]

## 1-3b  Time, Space, and Territory Send Silent Messages

In addition to nonverbal messages transmitted by your body, three external elements convey information in the communication process: time, space, and territory.

Time. How we structure and use time tells observers about our personality and attitudes. For example, when Warren Buffett—industrialist, investor, and philanthropist—gives a visitor an extensive interview, he signals his respect for, interest in, and approval of the visitor or the topic to be discussed. On the other hand, when a colleague twice arrives late for a meeting, it could mean that the meeting has low priority in his view, that he is a self-centered, perhaps hostile person or that he has poor time-management skills. These are assumptions that typical North Americans might make. In other cultures, though, punctuality is viewed differently.

**Space.** How we organize the space around us reveals something about us and our objectives. Whether the space is a bedroom, a dorm room, or an office, people express themselves in the design and grouping of their furniture. Generally, the more formal the arrangement, the more formal and closed the communication style. An executive who seats visitors in a row of chairs across from the desk sends a message of aloofness and a desire for separation. A team leader who arranges chairs informally in a circle rather than in straight rows conveys the desire for a more open exchange of ideas.

**Territory.** Each of us has a certain area that we feel is our own territory, whether it is a specific spot or just the space around us. Your loved ones may have favorite chairs in which they are most comfortable, a cook might not tolerate intruders in the kitchen, and veteran employees may feel that certain work areas and tools belong to them. We all maintain zones of privacy in which we feel comfortable.

**Figure 1.4** categorizes the four zones of social interaction among Americans, as formulated by anthropologist Edward T. Hall.[49] Notice that North Americans are a bit standoffish; only intimate friends and family may stand closer than about 1.5 feet. If someone violates that territory, North Americans feel uncomfortable and may step back to reestablish their space. In the workplace be aware of the territorial needs of others and don't invade their space. Of course, mandatory physical distancing rules during the COVID-19 pandemic preempted personal expressions of territorial behavior.

## 1-3c  Appearance Sends Silent Messages

Much like the personal appearance of an individual, the physical appearance of a business document transmits immediate and important nonverbal messages. Ideally, these messages should be pleasing to the eye.

**Eye Appeal of Business Documents.** The way an e-mail, letter, memo, or report looks can have either a positive or a negative effect on the receiver. Sloppy e-mails send a nonverbal message that the writer is in a terrific hurry or does not care about the receiver. Envelopes—through their postage, paper quality, and printing—can suggest that the messages they carry are routine, important, or junk mail. Letters and reports can look neat, professional, well organized, and attractive—or just the opposite.

In subsequent chapters you will learn how to create business documents that send positive nonverbal messages through their appearance, format, organization, readability, and correctness.

**Figure 1.4  Four Space Zones for Social Interaction**

During the COVID-19 pandemic, physical distancing between masked individuals was set at a minimum of 6 feet to prevent the spread of the virus.

| Intimate Zone (1 to 1½ feet) | Personal Zone (1½ to 4 feet) | Social Zone (4 to 12 feet) | Public Zone (12 or more feet) |

**Personal Appearance.** The way you look—your clothing, grooming, and posture—transmits an instant nonverbal message about you. Based on what they see, viewers make quick judgments about your status, credibility, personality, and potential. If you want to be considered professional, think about how you present yourself. One management consultant prefers bright-colored dresses, stiletto heels, and bling. But to be perceived as professional, she adopts a more conservative look to match the occasion and the customer: "The success I dress for is that of my *client*."[51]

As a businessperson, you will want to think about what your appearance says about you. Although the rules of business attire have loosened up, some workers show poor judgment. You will learn more about professional attire and behavior in later chapters.

## 1-3d Mastering Nonverbal Skills

Nonverbal communication can outweigh words in the way it influences how others perceive you. You can harness the power of silent messages by reviewing the following tips for improving nonverbal communication skills:

- **Establish and maintain eye contact**. Remember that in North America appropriate eye contact signals interest, attentiveness, confidence, and credibility.

- **Use posture to show interest**. Encourage interaction by leaning forward, sitting or standing erect, and looking alert.

- **Reduce or eliminate physical barriers**. Move out from behind a desk or lectern; arrange meeting chairs in a circle.

- **Improve your decoding skills**. Watch facial expressions and body language to understand the complete verbal and nonverbal messages being communicated.

- **Probe for more information**. When you perceive nonverbal cues that contradict verbal meanings, politely seek additional cues (*I'm not sure I understand*, *Please tell me more about . . .*, or *Do you mean that . . .?*).

- **Interpret nonverbal meanings in context**. Make nonverbal assessments only when you understand a situation or a culture.

**OFFICE INSIDER**

"Like it or not, your clothes and presentation communicate volumes about you as a person. The question is not whether you care about fashion, it's more about what you're communicating intentionally or unconsciously through your fashion choices. Just as the actor in the right costume moves and speaks differently, so does the everyday person."[50]

**Molly St. Louis,** *creative content producer, writer, and spokesperson*

**WORKPLACE IN FOCUS**

The popularity of tattoos in some U.S. populations and around the world shows no signs of waning. A market research firm reports that 46 percent of Americans have one or more tattoos. Globally, respondents age 14 to 29 have a lower rate of body art (32 percent) than people age 30 to 49 (45 percent) but higher than people over 50 (28 percent). Worldwide, a majority of people (72 percent) don't regret getting inked.[52] Despite these figures, U.S. companies can still legally impose no-tattoo policies, and psychologists confirm that negative attitudes toward tattoos persist.[53] A top human resources expert reveals a "sliding scale of acceptability" depending on the industry as well as the type and placement of the tattoos.[54] Conspicuous body art may make people feel distinctive and edgy, but could they be putting their careers at risk?

- **Associate with people from different cultures**. Learn about other cultures to widen your knowledge and tolerance of intercultural nonverbal messages.

- **Appreciate the power of appearance**. Keep in mind that the appearance of your business documents, your business space, and yourself sends immediate positive or negative messages to others.

- **Observe yourself on video**. Ensure that your verbal and nonverbal messages are in sync by recording and evaluating yourself making a presentation.

- **Enlist friends and family**. Ask friends and family members to monitor your conscious and unconscious body movements and gestures to help you become a more effective communicator.

## 1-4 Understanding Culture and Communication

Even when communicators share the same culture, comprehending the verbal and nonverbal meanings of a message can be difficult. When different cultures come together, special sensitivity and skills are necessary. Global business, communication technologies, and social media span the world, reducing distances. However, cultural differences persist in the increasingly multiethnic United States—and can cause significant misunderstandings.

Defining Culture. For our purposes, **culture** may be defined as the complex system of values, traits, morals, and customs shared by a society. Culture is a powerful operating force that molds the way we think, behave, and communicate. The objective of this section is to broaden your view of culture and open your mind to flexible attitudes so that you can avoid frustration when cultural adjustment is necessary. Globalization, growing diversity, and social networking demand that we adjust and adopt new attitudes.

To help you better understand your culture and how it contrasts with other cultures, we describe five key dimensions of culture: context, individualism, time orientation, power distance, and communication style. The section closes with a look at the interaction between culture and social media.

### 1-4a High and Low Context

**Context** is probably the most important cultural dimension and also the most difficult to define. In a model developed by cultural anthropologist Edward T. Hall, context refers to the stimuli, environment, or ambience surrounding an event. Hall arranged cultures on a continuum, shown in **Figure 1.5**, from low to high in relation to context.[55] This figure also summarizes key comparisons for today's business communicators.

Communicators in low-context cultures (such as those in North America, Scandinavia, and Germany) depend little on the context of a situation and shared experience to convey their meaning. They assume that messages must be explicit, and listeners rely exclusively on the written or spoken word. Low-context cultures tend to be linear, analytical, and action oriented. Business communicators stress clearly articulated messages that they consider to be objective, professional, and efficient. Words are taken literally.

Communicators in high-context cultures (such as those in China, Japan, and Middle Eastern countries) assume that the listener does not need much background information.[56] High-context cultures are more likely to be intuitive and contemplative. Communicators in these cultures pay attention to more than the spoken or written word. They emphasize interpersonal relationships, nonverbal expression, physical settings, and social context. For example, Japanese communicators might say *yes* when they really mean *no*. From the context of the situation, the Japanese speaker would

### Figure 1.5  Comparing Low- and High-Context Cultures

Culture has a powerful effect on business communicators. The following observations point out selected differences. However, these are simplifications, and practices within a given culture vary considerably. Moreover, as globalization expands, low- and high-context cultures are experiencing change, and differences may be less pronounced.

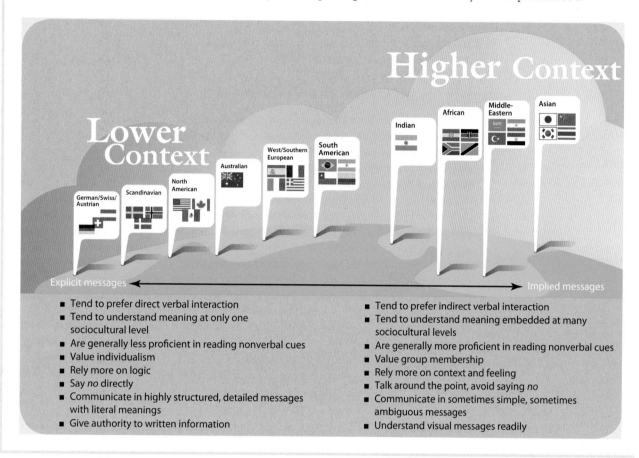

- Tend to prefer direct verbal interaction
- Tend to understand meaning at only one sociocultural level
- Are generally less proficient in reading nonverbal cues
- Value individualism
- Rely more on logic
- Say *no* directly
- Communicate in highly structured, detailed messages with literal meanings
- Give authority to written information

- Tend to prefer indirect verbal interaction
- Tend to understand meaning embedded at many sociocultural levels
- Are generally more proficient in reading nonverbal cues
- Value group membership
- Rely more on context and feeling
- Talk around the point, avoid saying *no*
- Communicate in sometimes simple, sometimes ambiguous messages
- Understand visual messages readily

indicate whether *yes* really meant *yes* or whether it meant *no*. The context, tone, time taken to answer, facial expression, and body cues would convey the meaning of *yes*.[57] Thus, in high-context cultures, communication cues tend to be transmitted by posture, voice inflection, gestures, and facial expression.

## 1-4b  Individualism and Collectivism

An attitude of independence and freedom from control characterizes **individualism**. Members of low-context cultures, particularly North Americans, tend to value individualism. They believe that initiative and self-assertion result in personal achievement. They believe in individual action and personal responsibility, and they desire much freedom in their personal lives.

Members of high-context cultures are more **collectivist**. They emphasize membership in organizations, groups, and teams; they encourage acceptance of group values, duties, and decisions. They typically resist independence because it fosters competition and confrontation instead of consensus. In group-oriented cultures, such as those in many Asian societies, self-assertion and individual decision making are discouraged. "The nail that sticks up gets pounded down" is a common Japanese saying.[58] Business decisions are often made by all who have competence in the matter under discussion. Similarly, in China managers also focus on the group rather than on the individual, preferring a consultative management style over an autocratic style.[59]

Cultures are complex, of course, and cannot be characterized as totally individualistic or group oriented. To complicate things, group differences may be lessening over time. For example, Americans of European descent are generally quite individualistic, whereas African Americans are less so, and Americans with a Latinx or Hispanic heritage are closer to the group-centered dimension. Newer research suggests **cultural convergence**, a trend toward greater global similarity particularly in higher individualism and lower power distance.[60] **Figure 1.6** shows selected countries ranked according to their expression of collectivism and individualism as well as power distance.

## 1-4c Time Orientation

The perception of time and its use are culturally learned. In some cultures, time is perceived sequentially. North Americans, for example, tend to consider time a precious commodity. They correlate time with productivity, efficiency, and money. Keeping people waiting for business appointments is considered a waste of time and rude. E. T. Hall called this time orientation **monochronic time** or *M-Time*, that is, time perceived as if it were running on a single, linear track.

In other cultures (e.g., most Asian, South American, and Native American), time may be perceived as an unlimited resource to be enjoyed; it is open and flexible. This is defined by Hall as **polychronic time** or *P-Time*. Time is viewed as abundant and nonlinear. Relationships are more important than tasks. People in monochronic Western cultures may schedule appointments at 15- to 30-minute intervals. Businesspeople in polychronic cultures may plan fewer but longer meetings without a defined end time. People in monochronic cultures may look at time as formal and task oriented. In polychronic cultures, time is seen as an opportunity to develop interpersonal relationships.

A group of North American businesspeople, for example, was kept waiting two hours past a scheduled appointment time in South America. The executives weren't

**Figure 1.6** Selected Countries' Ranking in Collectivism, Individualism, and Power Distance

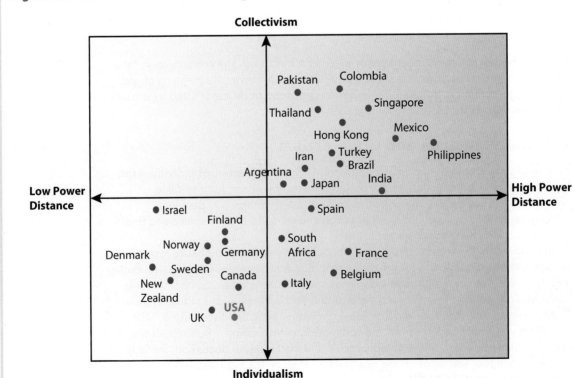

offended, though, because they were familiar with South Americans' more polychronic concept of time. When it comes to attitudes toward time, again, cultures are complex and cannot be neatly divided into monochronic or polychronic. In some countries both tendencies may coexist.

## 1-4d Power Distance

One important element of culture is **power distance**, which was first introduced by influential social psychologist Geert Hofstede. The Power Distance Index measures how people in different societies cope with inequality—in other words, how they relate to more powerful individuals. In high-power-distance countries, subordinates expect formal hierarchies and embrace relatively authoritarian, paternalistic power relationships. In low-power-distance cultures, however, subordinates consider themselves as equals of their supervisors. They confidently voice opinions and participate in decision making. Relationships between high-powered individuals and people with little power tend to be more democratic, egalitarian, and informal.

As you have probably guessed, in most Western cultures people are more relaxed about social status and the appearance of power.[61] Deference is not generally paid to individuals merely because of their wealth, position, seniority, or age. In many Asian cultures, however, these characteristics are important. A strict top-down management structure allows for faster decision making, but it also prevents subordinates from speaking up due to fear or resignation, researchers say. Employee silence can be costly. For example, it has been blamed for such disasters as the Sanlu milk powder scandal in China and the Fukushima nuclear power plant explosion in Japan.[62] The degree of power distance in selected countries is illustrated in Figure 1.6.

## 1-4e Communication Style

People in low- and high-context cultures tend to communicate differently with words. To Americans and Germans, for example, words are very important, especially in contracts and negotiations. People in high-context cultures, on the other hand, place more emphasis on the surrounding context than on the words describing a negotiation. Greek businesspeople may see a contract as a formal statement announcing the intention to build a business for the future. The Japanese may treat contracts as statements of intention, and they assume changes will be made as projects develop. Mexican managers may perceive contracts as approximations of what might be accomplished in an ideal world. They do not necessarily expect contracts to apply consistently in the real world. Some Arab cultures may be insulted by the mere mention of a contract; a person's word is more binding.[63]

In communication style North Americans value straightforwardness, are suspicious of evasiveness, and distrust people whom they perceive as having a hidden agenda or playing their cards too close to the chest.[64] North Americans also tend to be uncomfortable with silence and impatient with delays. Some Asian businesspeople have learned that the longer they drag out negotiations, the more concessions impatient North Americans are likely to make.

## 1-4f Technology and Social Media Affect Intercultural Communication

Few would question the connectedness and networking provided by social media and communication technology today. With minimal resources, communicators can interact instantly across vast distances with larger and more varied audiences than ever before. Not surprisingly, social media may potentially bridge cultural differences or reinforce them, depending on their users.

Whether social media networks will allow business communicators to engage across cultures and bridge intercultural differences will depend on the users' attitudes and openness.

**Social Media: Blurring Boundaries?** What we make of the potential for positive intercultural connectedness online is as much up to us as it would be at a dinner party where we don't know any of the other guests. Some authors believe that social media used mindfully can benefit mental health, blur cultural gaps, reduce hierarchies, and empower people to change their circumstances.[65] At the same time, the online environment may deepen feelings of social isolation, leading to depression and the much debated **loneliness epidemic**, only made worse by the COVID-19 pandemic.[66]

Online, as in real life, we gravitate toward people who seem like us, believes social entrepreneur Rajiv Vinnakota. Social media divide us because we inhabit "echo chambers" online instead of "bridging social capital" and interacting with people not like us as we used to do offline, he says.[67] However, shared causes can mobilize social media users halfway across the globe—for example, the international climate movement Friday for Future or the pro-democracy student protesters in Hong Kong—as they try to win the hearts and minds of the public.[68]

**Social Media: Global and Local?** Despite cultural convergence—the equalizing influence of globalization on cultures around the world—regional and cultural differences persist, as those who design media for markets in other countries know. Adobe Inc., for example, is represented by 30 corporate websites that are adapted to local country-specific tastes and expectations.

Knowledge of color symbolism across cultures is indispensable for designers lest they commit cultural blunders. Consider that yellow—a hue with generally positive connotations in Western cultures, but one that also represents cowardice—stands for courage in Japan. Orange, the signature color of the Dutch royal court, epitomizes the harvest and fall in North America and Europe. Likewise, in Asia, orange is an auspicious hue; however, in the Middle East, orange signifies mourning and loss.[69]

More serious differences nationally as well as globally are now caused by geopolitical turmoil, cyberattacks by foreign powers, and restricted access to the Internet in authoritarian countries around the world—a trend that has been called **digital nationalism**. Some predictions foresee a so-called **Splinternet**, a fragmentation of the Internet, once viewed as a unified global network.[70] It remains to be seen whether the deep divides will dissipate or continue to grow.

## 1-5  Ensuring Intercultural Effectiveness

Being aware of your own culture and how it contrasts with others is a first step in learning intercultural skills. Another step involves recognizing barriers to intercultural accommodation and striving to overcome them. The digital age economy needs workers who can thrive on diverse teams and interact effectively with customers and clients at home and abroad. This section addresses how to overcome barriers to productive intercultural communication, develop strong intercultural skills, and capitalize on workplace diversity.

### 1-5a  Avoiding Ethnocentrism and Stereotyping

The process of understanding and interacting successfully with people from other cultures is often hampered by two barriers: ethnocentrism and stereotyping. These barriers, however, can be overcome by developing tolerance and empathy, two powerful and effective aids to communication.

**Ethnocentrism.** The belief in the superiority of one's own ethnic group is known as **ethnocentrism**, an attitude found in all cultures. Ethnocentrism causes us to judge others by our own values. If you were raised in North America, values such as punctuality and directness probably seem right to you, and you may wonder why the rest of the world doesn't function in the same "sensible" fashion. A North American businessperson in an Arab or Asian country might be upset at time spent over coffee or other social rituals before any *real* business is transacted. In these cultures, however, personal relationships must be established and nurtured before negotiations may proceed.

**Stereotypes.** Our perceptions of other cultures sometimes cause us to form stereotypes about groups of people. A **stereotype** is an oversimplified, rigid perception of a behavioral pattern or characteristic applied uncritically to groups. For example, the Swiss are hardworking, efficient, and neat; Germans are formal, reserved, and blunt; Americans are loud, friendly, and impatient; Asians are gracious, humble, and inscrutable. These attitudes may or may not accurately describe cultural norms. When applied to individual business communicators, however, such stereotypes may be hurtful and cause misunderstandings. Look beyond superficial labels to discover individuals' unique qualities.

**Tolerance and Open-Mindedness.** As global markets expand and as our society becomes increasingly multiethnic, mutual tolerance is critical. **Tolerance** here means learning about those who are not like us; it means being open-minded and receptive to new experiences. With greater knowledge, patience, and compassion, tolerance may lead to *understanding* and *acceptance*.[72] One of the best ways to become tolerant is to practice **empathy**, defined as trying to see the world through another's eyes. It means being less judgmental and more eager to seek common ground.

One way of promoting greater understanding is to work toward a common goal. An environmental studies center in Israel brings together Jews, Muslims, and Christians to tackle water scarcity in the Middle East, home to 10 of the 15 most water-starved countries in the world. The diverse student body is Jewish Israeli, Arab, and non–Middle Eastern. Aside from caring for the environment, the students attend peace-building forums to discuss race, religion, culture, and politics. The center develops one of the region's scarcest resources—trust.[73]

Getting along with others is always a good policy, but doubly so in the workplace. Frequently job descriptions include statements such as *Must be able to communicate with diverse audiences*. The suggestions in the following section can help you prevent miscommunication in oral and written interactions across cultures.

## 1-5b Successful Oral Communication With Intercultural Audiences

When you have a conversation with someone from another culture, you can reduce misunderstandings by following these tips:

- **Use simple English**. Speak in short sentences (under 20 words) with familiar, short words. Eliminate puns, sport and military references, slang, and jargon (special business terms). Be especially alert to idiomatic expressions that can't be translated, such as *face the music* and *hit a home run*.

- **Speak slowly and enunciate clearly**. Avoid fast speech, but don't raise your voice. Overpunctuate with pauses and full stops. Always write and display numbers for all to see.

- **Encourage accurate feedback**. Ask probing questions, and encourage the listener to paraphrase what you say. Don't assume that a *yes*, a nod, or a smile indicates comprehension.

**OFFICE INSIDER**

"[E]mployers are looking for people who have experienced the world and can bring a global perspective helping us to recognize our common engineering challenges and find solutions together. One way I have become a global citizen is through 'voluntourism.' The term describes trips encompassing both volunteer work and tourism."[71]

**Rebecca Delaney,**
*engineering team leader, associate director, Skidmore, Owings & Merrill*

- **Check frequently for comprehension**. Avoid waiting until you finish a long explanation to request feedback. Instead, make one point at a time and pause.

- **Observe eye messages**. Be alert to a glazed expression or wandering eyes. These tell you the listener is lost.

- **Accept blame**. If a misunderstanding results, graciously take responsibility for not making your meaning clear.

- **Listen without interrupting**. Curb your desire to finish sentences or to fill out ideas for the speaker. Keep in mind that North Americans abroad are often accused of listening too little and talking too much.

- **Smile when appropriate**. The smile is often considered the single most understood and most useful form of communication. In some cultures, however, excessive smiling may seem insincere.

- **Follow up in writing**. After conversations or oral negotiations, confirm the results and agreements with written messages. For proposals and contracts, hire a professional translator.

## 1-5c Successful Written Communication With Intercultural Audiences

When you write to someone from a different culture, you can improve your chances of being understood by following the following suggestions:

- **Consider local styles and conventions**. Learn how documents are formatted and how letters are addressed and developed in the intended reader's country. Decide whether to use your organization's preferred format or adjust to local styles.

- **Observe titles and rank**. Use last names, titles, and other signals of rank and status. Send messages to higher-status people; avoid sending copies to lower-rank people.

- **Hire a translator**. Engage a professional translator if (a) your document is important, (b) your document will be distributed to many readers, or (c) you must be persuasive.

- **Use short sentences and short paragraphs**. Sentences with fewer than 20 words and paragraphs with fewer than 8 lines are most readable.

- **Avoid ambiguity**. Include relative pronouns (*that, which, who*) for clarity in introducing clauses. Stay away from contractions (especially ones such as *Here's the problem*). Replace two-word verbs with clear single words (*return* instead of *bring back; delay* instead of *put off; maintain* instead of *keep up*. Avoid idioms (*once in a blue moon*), slang (*my presentation really bombed*), acronyms (*ASAP* for *as soon as possible*), abbreviations (*DBA* for *doing business as*), jargon (*input, bottom line*), and sports references (*ballpark figure, slam dunk*). Use action-specific verbs (*buy a printer* rather than *get a printer*).

- **Cite numbers carefully**. In international trade most nations use the metric system. In citing numbers, use figures (*12*) instead of spelling them out (*twelve*). Always convert dollar figures into local currency. Spell out the month when writing dates. In North America, for example, *March 5, 2022*, might be written as *3/5/2022*, whereas in Europe the same date might appear as *5.3.2022*.

## 1-5d Growing Workforce Diversity

While North American companies are expanding global operations and adapting to a variety of emerging markets, the domestic workforce is also becoming more diverse. This *diversity* has many dimensions—race, ethnicity, age, religion, gender, national origin, disability, sexual orientation, and others. No longer, say the experts, will the workplace be predominantly Anglo-oriented or male-centered.

Today, people of color (individuals with African, Latinx or Hispanic, Asian, or Native American heritage) already comprise 39 percent of the U.S. population. New projections indicate that 2045 will be the year when communities of color will represent the majority of the U.S. population at 50.3 percent.[74] Women comprise nearly 50 percent of the workforce. Moreover, the share of the population over 65 will jump from 15 percent now to almost 22 percent in 2050. By 2030 one in five residents will have reached retirement age, outnumbering children for the first time in U.S. history.[75] Many of these older people will remain in the workforce. Thanks to technological advances, more disabled individuals are also joining the workforce.

What do all these changes mean for you? Simply put, your job may require you to interact with coworkers and customers from around the world. You will need to cooperate with individuals and teams. What's more, your coworkers may differ from you in race, ethnicity, gender, age, and other ways.

## 1-5e Understanding the Benefits of Diversity at Work

As society and the workforce become more diverse, successful communication among the various identity groups brings distinct advantages in three areas.

**Consumers.** Consumers want to deal with companies that respect their values and look like them. A diverse staff is better able to respond to the increasingly diverse customer base in local and world markets. The CEO of a PR firm embraces a diverse staff and customers: "Our team consists of more than 40 people who collectively speak 20 different languages." A CEO in PR urges fellow executives to "Tap into the diversity of your workplace to gain a deep understanding of your workforce and your potential customer base."[77]

**Work Teams.** Leadership experts agree that diversity enhances creativity because inclusive teams bring novel perspectives to the table, resulting in better decision making and problem solving. One leadership consultant says that a culturally diverse group "can create an esprit de corps" and "a feeling of camaraderie among team members" resulting in successful cooperation. Aside from creativity and cohesion, diverse teams are 45 percent more likely to increase market share and 70 percent more likely to capture a new market.[78]

**Businesses.** Organizations gradually realize that inclusivity is a critical bottom-line strategy to increase revenue, engage employees, and spur innovation. A McKinsey report found that gender and ethnically diverse executive teams were 33 percent more likely to lead their industry in profitability.[79] Researchers say that inclusion not only makes business sense but also benefits all workers. "The best workplaces forge bonds among co-workers of different political views, different backgrounds, different job titles," says Ann Nadeau, chief people officer at Great Place to Work.[80]

Developing a diverse staff that can work together cooperatively is one of the biggest challenges and opportunities facing business organizations today.

## 1-5f Communicating in a Diverse Workplace

Acceptance and harmony do not happen automatically when dissimilar people work together. This means that organizations must commit to diversity. Harnessed effectively, diversity and inclusion can enhance productivity and propel a company to success. Mismanaged, it can become a drain on a company's resources. How companies deal with diversity will make all the difference in how they compete in a technology-driven global environment. The following suggestions can help you find ways to improve communication and interaction.

- **Seek training**. Especially if an organization is experiencing diversity problems, awareness-raising sessions or training programs may be helpful. Spend time learning

**OFFICE INSIDER**

"Everyone can and should be adept at interacting with people from other cultures. Do research. Be curious. Don't make assumptions. For organizations, diversity works when there is commitment from the top, education programs and appointments made of people who are experienced at managing change across cultures."[76]

**Johann Xavier,** *managing partner, O2 advisory Inc., Canada* about workforce diversity and how it can benefit organizations. Look upon diversity and inclusion as opportunities, not threats. Intercultural communication, team building, and conflict resolution are skills that can be learned.

- **Understand the value of difference**. Diversity makes an organization innovative and creative. Sameness fosters an absence of critical thinking called **groupthink**. Diversity can be a powerful antidote. Some researchers believe that if Wall Street had been more diverse, the financial crisis of 2008 could have been less severe.[81] Economist and banker Mark Carney concurs: "Almost all decisions in finance are taken under uncertainty, making it especially important that decision makers are exposed to a range of views and engage in open debates with people whose perspectives challenge the prevailing wisdom."[82]

- **Learn about your cultural self**. Begin to think of yourself as a product of your culture, and understand that your culture is just one among many. Take any opportunity to travel or study abroad, if possible. You will learn much, not only about other cultures but also about your own. Try to look at yourself from the outside. Do you see any reflex reactions and automatic thought patterns that are a result of your upbringing? These may be invisible to you until challenged by difference. Be sure to keep what works and yet be ready to adapt as environments change. Flexibility is an important survival skill.

- **Make fewer assumptions**. Be careful of seemingly insignificant, innocent workplace assumptions. For example, don't assume that everyone wants to observe the holidays with a Christmas party and a decorated tree. Celebrating only Christian holidays in December, January, and February excludes those who honor Hanukkah, Kwanzaa, Yule, and the Lunar New Year. Moreover, in workplace discussions don't assume anything about others' sexual orientations or attitudes toward marriage. For invitations, avoid phrases such as *managers and their wives*. *Spouses* or *partners* is inclusive. Valuing diversity means making fewer assumptions that everyone is like you or wants to be like you.

- **Build on similarities**. Look for areas in which you and others not like you can agree or at least share opinions. Be prepared to consider issues from many perspectives, all of which may be valid. Accept that there is room for various points of view to coexist peacefully. Although you can always find differences, it can be harder to find similarities. Look for common ground in shared experiences, mutual goals, and similar values.[83] Concentrate on your objective even when you may disagree on how to reach it.

## Summary of Learning Outcomes

1 **Describe how communication skills fuel career success in a challenging digital age marketplace.**
   - In an era of automation, augmented reality, and artificial intelligence, communication and other interpersonal skills can future-proof well-trained workers.
   - Workers communicate more than ever; many collaborate in teams, which means that even technical fields require excellent communication skills.
   - Employers expect new-hires and other employees to project a professional image and possess superior interpersonal skills, including oral and written communication.
   - Information age job challenges include rapid technological change and uncertainty, 24/7 availability, flatter management, an emphasis on teams, global competition, and a renewed focus on ethics.

## 2 Use active listening techniques.

- Organizational success and careers greatly depend on active listening, but most of us are poor listeners; to improve, we can remove physical and psychological barriers, overlook language problems, ignore nonverbal distractions, and curb our thought speed.
- A significant lag in language processing speed, called speech-thought differential, allows us to let our minds wander; as a result, we fake attention and prefer to talk rather than to listen.
- We can improve listening skills if we stop talking, focus fully on others, limit noise, adopt an empathic attitude, and distinguish facts from opinions.
- Capitalizing on lag time, listening for feelings and validating them, taking selective notes, and providing encouraging feedback are other methods for building listening skills.

## 3 Discuss how effective nonverbal communication can help you build your credibility and advance your career.

- Study nonverbal cues such as eye contact, facial expression, and posture that send silent, highly believable messages.
- Understand that how you use time, space, and territory is interpreted by the receiver, who also reads the eye appeal of your business documents and your personal appearance.
- Master nonverbal skills by keeping eye contact, using posture to signal interest, reducing physical barriers, improving your decoding skills, and probing for more information.
- Interpret nonverbal meanings in context, learn about other cultures, and consider the impact of appearance—of documents, your office space, and yourself.

## 4 Describe the key dimensions of culture and how technology and social media shape intercultural communication.

- Culture is a complex system of values, traits, ethics, and customs shared by a society; culture molds the way we think, behave, and communicate both offline and online.
- Culture can be described using key dimensions such as context, individualism, time orientation, power distance, and communication style.
- Today's communicators need to be aware of low- and high-context cultures, individualistic versus collectivist societies, differing attitudes toward time, clashing perceptions of power, and varying degrees of reliance on the written word.
- Whether social media can bridge cultural divides and erase differences or will lead to greater isolation will depend on the users as much as it would among strangers who meet at a dinner party.

## 5 Identify strategies for enhancing intercultural effectiveness and communication across cultures.

- Beware of ethnocentrism and stereotyping; instead, embrace tolerance and keep an open mind.
- In oral communication, use simple English, speak distinctly, check for comprehension, observe eye messages, accept responsibility for miscommunication, smile when appropriate, don't interrupt, and follow up in writing.
- When writing, consider local styles and conventions, hire a translator, use short sentences, avoid ambiguous wording, and cite numbers carefully.
- As the domestic workforce becomes more diverse, appreciate diversity as a critical business strategy.
- To communicate well with diverse audiences, seek training, understand the value of diversity, learn about your own culture, make fewer assumptions, and look for similarities.

## Key Terms

| | | |
|---|---|---|
| soft skills 4 | smartphone apps 7 | nonverbal communication 12 |
| people skills 4 | ad hoc teams 10 | culture 16 |
| emotional intelligence 4 | gig economy 10 | context 16 |
| interpersonal skills 4 | empathic listening 10 | individualism 17 |
| professional skills 4 | mindful 10 | collectivist 17 |
| sharing economy 7 | speech-thought differential 11 | cultural convergence 18 |

monochronic time 18
polychronic time 18
power distance 19
loneliness epidemic 20

digital nationalism 20
Splinternet 20
ethnocentrism 21
stereotype 21

tolerance 21
empathy 21
groupthink 24

## Chapter Review

1. What will the workplace of the future look like, and what skills does the labor force need to adapt to rapid change and uncertainty? (L.O. 1)

2. What does it mean that the office of the future is mobile and always on? (L.O. 1)

3. List six trends in the information age workplace that can pose a challenge for business communicators. (L.O. 1)

4. List bad habits and distractions that can act as barriers to effective listening. (L.O. 2)

5. List eight techniques for improving your listening skills. Be prepared to discuss each. (L.O. 2)

6. Explain nonverbal communication and its components. What do we believe more when they seem to clash—words or nonverbal cues? (L.O. 3)

7. What did communication theorist Paul Watzlawick mean when he said that we cannot not communicate? Are the nonverbal signals we are sending easy to read? (L.O. 3)

8. What is culture, and what are five key dimensions that can be used to describe it? (L.O. 4)

9. List at least five techniques to successfully communicate with intercultural audiences orally and at least five tips for written messages. Be prepared to explain each. (L.O. 5)

10. List five recommendations for communicating successfully in a diverse and inclusive workplace. Be prepared to discuss each. (L.O. 5)

## Critical Thinking

11. Reflect on the comments about communication made by business tycoons and billionaire investors Richard Branson and Warren Buffett. You will find them in the *Office Insider* features at the beginning of this chapter. What lessons can you glean from the two quotations? (L.O. 1)

12. Do you think executives and managers spend more time listening than do workers? Why? (L.O. 2)

13. What arguments could you give for or against the idea that body language is a science with principles that can be interpreted accurately by specialists? (L.O. 3)

14. When Procter & Gamble launched its Pampers brand in Japan, the diaper package confused and disturbed customers. As in the United States, the package featured the picture of a stork delivering a baby. Why were Japanese parents perturbed? It turns out that the myth of a stork carrying babies to expectant parents is unknown in Japan. Instead, according to Japanese lore, giant floating peaches deliver offspring.[84] Can you explain what may have caused the intercultural blunder? How could Procter & Gamble have avoided it? (L.O. 4, 5)

15. You know that it's not acceptable to make ethnic jokes, least of all in the workplace, but a colleague of yours keeps invoking the worst ethnic and racial stereotypes. How do you respond? Do you remain silent and change the subject, or do you speak up? What other options do you have in dealing with such a coworker? Consider whether your answer would change if the offender were your boss. [L.O. 5]

## Activities and Cases

### 1.1 First Things First: Introductions (L.O. 1)

> **Communication Technology**  >  **E-Mail**  >  **Social Media**

Your instructor wants to know more about you, your motivation for taking this course, your career goals, and your writing skills.

**YOUR TASK.** Send an e-mail or write a memo of introduction to your instructor. See Chapter 5 for formats and tips on preparing e-mails. In your message include the following:

a. Your reasons for taking this class
b. Your career plans and goals (both temporary and long term)
c. A brief description of your employment, if any, and your favorite activities
d. An evaluation and discussion of your current communication skills, including your strengths and areas that need improvement

Alternatively, your instructor may ask you to create a profile within a learning-management system (e.g., Blackboard, Canvas, Moodle, or Brightspace) to introduce yourself to your classmates as well. Your instructor may challenge you to compose your introduction in 140–280 or fewer characters (see Chapter 5 for tips on writing tweets and other microblogging messages). As an option, your instructor may ask you to create a brief business-like video introduction.

## 1.2 Small-Group Presentation: Introducing Teammates (L.O. 1, 2)

> **Team**

Teamwork is the lifeblood of many business organizations today. To help you develop coveted speaking, listening, and teamwork skills, your instructor may assign team projects. One of the first jobs in any team is selecting members and becoming acquainted.

**YOUR TASK.** Your instructor will divide your class into small groups or teams. At your instructor's direction, either (a) interview another group member and introduce that person to the group or (b) introduce yourself to the group. Think of this as an informal interview for a team assignment or a job. You may want to prepare notes from which to speak. Your introduction should include information such as the following:

a. Where did you grow up?
b. What work and extracurricular activities have you engaged in?
c. What are your interests and talents? What are you good at doing?
d. What have you achieved?
e. How involved and familiar are you with communication technology and social media?
f. What are your professional and personal goals? Where do you expect to be five years from now?
g. Name one thing about you that others might not guess when they first meet you.

To develop listening skills, team members should practice the listening techniques discussed in this chapter and take brief notes when other students are presenting. Teams should be prepared to discuss three important facts as well as remember details about each speaker.

In virtual classes, you may form groups in the forum or discussion board of your course management system. Your instructor may assign other means by which you can introduce one or more teammates.

## 1.3 Facing Serious Screen Time (L.O. 1, 3, 4)

> **Communication Technology** > **E-Mail** > **Social Media** > **Team** > **Web**

Are you a *digital native*? If you were born after 1985, you do not remember a time without computer technology and cell phones in wide use. People born in the 1990s have only known a society that depends on the Internet and mobile technology.

Very likely you live, learn, work, play, network, and shop in the digital world. Even if you are not crazy about the latest gadgets and gizmos, your daily life depends on technology. Your smartphone, smart TV, gaming console, and other electronics wouldn't exist without it and are increasingly networked.

To prepare for this assignment, reflect on your Internet, social media, and other technology use. First establish useful criteria—for example, categories such as consumer electronics, social networking sites, preferred modes of communication with friends and family, and so forth. Within each category, list the technology or application you use most frequently. For instance, for social media networks and messaging, indicate your use of Instagram, YouTube, Facebook, Messenger, WhatsApp, Twitter, Snapchat, LinkedIn, and more. Estimate how often you access these sites per day, and indicate the tools you use (e.g., smartphone, tablet, laptop). How much do you text every day?

**YOUR TASK.** Create at least three categories of communication technology and record your responses in writing. Then compare your three lists within a group of five classmates or in assigned teams. Share your results individually or in teams, either verbally or in writing. Your instructor may ask you to summarize your observations about how plugged in you and your classmates are in a post on a discussion board or in an e-mail.

**Note**: Users of newer Apple devices can monitor their digital habits with Screen Time; Digital Wellbeing is the equivalent for Android devices. Research shows that teens average 7 hours 22 minutes on screen media a day, not counting using screens for school or homework.[85] How has the COVID-19 pandemic changed your media use? Have your parents ever "digitally grounded" you, that is, limited your screen use?

## 1.4 Interpersonal Skills: Are You a People Person? (L.O. 1)

When hiring future workers, employers look for technical skills, which are those we learn such as mastery of software applications or accountancy procedures. However, as we have seen in this chapter, businesses are desperate for job candidates equipped with interpersonal skills; some recruiters value interpersonal skills even more than technical skills. Recall that these interpersonal skills include strengths such as communication, social skills, and other psychological assets a person possesses. Studies have divided interpersonal skills into four categories:

- Thinking and problem solving
- Oral and written communication
- Personal qualities and work ethic
- Social skills and teamwork

**YOUR TASK.** Using the four categories to guide you, identify your own interpersonal skills, paying attention to those attributes you think a potential employer would value. Prepare lists of at least four items in each of the four categories. For example, as evidence of problem solving, you might list a specific workplace or student problem you recognized and solved. You will want to weave these words and phrases into cover letters and résumés, which are covered in Chapter 13.

## 1.5 Listening Skills Self-Assessment (L.O. 2)

> **Web**

By completing this brief self-assessment, you can test whether your listening skills are excellent or may need work.

**YOUR TASK.** Take this self reflection quiz that you will find among the accompanying student resources on **www.cengage.com**.

## 1.6 Listening Habits Survey: How Good a Listener Are You? (L.O. 3)

> **Team**

"The simple fact is that nobody ever learned anything by listening to themselves speak," believes Richard Branson, billionaire businessman and founder of the Virgin Group.[86] Psychologists say that listening is an act of connection. Even if we can't touch or see others, we feel connected hearing their voices. In relationships, listening is an act of love, we are told.[87]

In business, assertiveness and strong opinions tend to rule and drown out other voices. Leaders wishing to exude decisiveness speak more than they listen and are not even aware of their domineering behavior. Yet researchers note that active, empathic listening is key to being successful in teams and in leadership roles. They advise businesspeople to examine their bad habits, validate opinions of others, verify what is being said, watch for speakers' nonverbal cues, and control their own reactions and body language.[88]

How do you measure up? Do you know how good your listening skills are? Try this self-assessment:[89]

Score yourself on each question as 1 (the statement is not true for me at all), 2 (I mildly disagree), 3 (I partly agree and partly disagree with the statement), 4 (I mildly agree), or 5 (the statement is totally true for me).

_____ 1.  I prefer talking to listening to what others may say.

_____ 2.  It mostly doesn't occur to me to ask questions.

_____ 3.  When others are talking, I'm often thinking about what I'll say next.

_____ 4.  The main point of talking is to impress people, or at least to entertain them.

_____ 5.  My perspective is usually right, so if others disagree, I convince them to see it my way.

_____ 6.  It bothers me when people get their facts wrong.

_____   7.   It's important to point out when people are wrong about something.

_____   8.   Most people are boring, so I usually do most of the talking.

_____   9.   When my body tries to talk to me with pain or other discomforts, I tune my body out.

_____        Total Score

**YOUR TASK.** Record your score. Your instructor will share the interpretation of the results with you. Did you score high or low? Try the following experiment at home with your loved ones: Select an object, a "listening stick" or a "listening stone," that will indicate turn-taking. Only the person in possession of the listening object will be allowed to speak. Not until the speaker is ready to give up the stick or stone can another person talk. Is it difficult for you to remain silent until you get your hands on the listening object? Are you truly present during the conversation? Do you listen without waiting impatiently to speak? Share your observations in class. The instructor may ask you to submit your findings and/or report in writing. What could you do to further improve your listening skills?

## 1.7 Becoming a Better Listener With TED (L.O. 2)

> **Communication Technology** ▸ **E-Mail** ▸ **Social Media** ▸ **Team**

Reading this chapter, did you wonder how much you are able retain from a conversation—50 percent? Twenty-five percent without notes?

TED Talks are opportunities to learn from the best minds in tech, entertainment, and design. With this assignment you can practice listening and retention. Julian Treasure is one of several authorities on active, conscious listening, silence, quiet, and noise in our hectic lives.

**YOUR TASK.** Choose any one of Treasure's five popular TED Talks on YouTube or the TED site. Find a quiet space free from distractions. Turn off your notifications to avoid interruptions. Watch Julian Treasure's entire talk attentively without taking notes. After it ends, jot down what you recall from the presentation. Alone or with teammates, review your notes. Watch the TED talk again to establish what important points you may have left out. In class or on your learning-management platform, chat about your observations. Estimate how much you remembered from the talk. Discuss your insights from Treasure's presentation. Share his recommendations, and comment on your ability to recall his main points. You may be asked to summarize your findings in a memo or a social media post. Other experts could be assigned for this activity.

## 1.8 Deciphering Nonverbal Cues: Is It a Cinch? (L.O. 3)

Can body language be accurately interpreted? Take eye contact. Many people think that avoiding eye contact means a person is lying, but nonverbal language expert Steven Keyl explains that depending on context, eye contact can be ambiguous. For example, shy or nervous people may avert their eyes. In some cultures, locking eyes with an authority figure is viewed as disrespectful. Paradoxically, brazen liars tend to engage in more eye contact than normal to *appear* truthful. Too much eye contact, therefore, might raise suspicions.[90] Prolonged eye contact, i.e., staring, can seem threatening or it can indicate romantic interest.

**YOUR TASK.** What attitudes do the following nonverbal signals suggest to you? Do these nonverbal signals always mean the same thing? What part does context play in your interpretations?

a. Leaning back in a chair, figure four leg cross, hands cupping the back of the head
b. Bowed posture, twiddling thumbs
c. Steepled hands, sprawling sitting position
d. Rubbing hand through hair
e. Chin up, forehead back, looking down one's nose
f. Wringing hands, tugging ears
g. Twitching, sweating
h. Fidgeting, darting eyes

## 1.9 Nonverbal Communication: Casual Attire at Work (L.O. 3)

**Communication Technology** ▸ **E-Mail** ▸ **Social Media** ▸ **Team** ▸ **Web**

Although many employers allow casual attire, not all employers and customers are happy with the results. To learn more about the implementation, acceptance, and effects of casual-dress programs, select one of the following activities, all of which involve some form of interviewing.

**YOUR TASK.**

a.  In teams, gather information from human resources directors to determine which companies allow casual or dress-down days, how often, and under what conditions. The information may be collected by personal interviews, e-mail, telephone, or instant messaging.
b.  In teams, conduct inquiring-reporter interviews. Ask individuals in the community how they react to casual dress in the workplace. Develop a set of standard interview questions.
c.  Compare and contrast the effects of business-dress standards on such factors as the projected image of the company, the nature of the interactions with customers and with fellow employees, the morale of employees, and the productivity of employees. What generalizations can you draw from your findings?

## 1.10 Nonverbal Communication Around the World (L.O. 3, 4)

**Intercultural** ▸ **Web**

Whenever people communicate, gestures play an important role. Because culture shapes the meaning of gestures, miscommunication and misunderstanding can easily result in international situations.

**YOUR TASK.** Use the Internet to research the meanings of selected gestures. Make a list of ten gestures (other than those discussed in the text) that have different meanings in different countries. Consider the fingertip kiss, nose thumb, eyelid pull, nose tap, head shake, and other gestures. How are the meanings different in other countries? Can you name neutral symbols that have changed meaning because they were appropriated by a certain political group (think the index-finger-thumb pinch—the OK sign)? Which gestures that are innocent in the United States are considered vulgar and offensive in other countries?

## 1.11 Intercultural Communication: Watching Those Corporate Clichés (L.O. 4)

**Intercultural**

The language of business is rife with jargon and clichés—once-fashionable idiomatic expressions that become stale and lose meaning. They sound particularly murky to the uninitiated.

**YOUR TASK.** Translate the annoying buzzwords into plain English.[91] Assume that you are explaining them to nonnative speakers of English.

a.  low-hanging fruit
b.  circle back
c.  move the needle
d.  bite the bullet
e.  at the end of the day
f.  think outside the box
g.  peel back (the layers of) the onion
h.  par for the course
i.  throw someone under the bus

## 1.12 Intercultural Communication: Analyzing Cultural Stereotypes (L.O. 4, 5)

**Intercultural** ▸ **Team** ▸ **Web**

Almost all of us at some point in our lives are subject to stereotyping by others, whether we are immigrants, communities of color, women, members of certain professions, or Americans abroad. Negative stereotypes sting. However, even presumably positive stereotypes can offend or embarrass because they deny people's individuality and uniqueness. If we remain open to new experiences, we won't be limited by rigid, stereotypical perceptions of other cultures.

**YOUR TASK.** Think about a nation or culture about which you have only a hazy idea. Jot down a few key traits that come to mind. For example, you may not know much about the Netherlands and the Dutch people. You can probably think of gouda cheese, wooden clogs, Heineken beer, tulips, and windmills. Anything else? Then consider a culture with which you are very familiar, whether it is yours or that of a country you visited or studied. In one column, write down a few stereotypical perceptions that are positive. Then, in another column, record negative stereotypes you associate with that culture. Share your notes with your team or the whole class, as the instructor may direct. How do you respond to others' descriptions of your culture? Which stereotypes irk you and why? For a quick fact check and overview at the end of this exercise, google the *CIA World Factbook* or *BBC News Country Profiles*.

## 1.13 Learning From Epic Intercultural Fails (L.O. 4, 5)
Intercultural

As business organizations become increasingly global in their structure and marketing, they face communication problems resulting from cultural misunderstandings. They also must deal with culture clashes and radically different values around the world.

**YOUR TASK.** Based on what you have learned in this chapter, describe several broad principles that could be applied in helping the individuals involved understand what went wrong in the following events. What suggestions could you make for remedying the problems?

a. Social media leaders are not immune to intercultural missteps that go viral. Twitter CEO Jack Dorsey landed in hot water in India for posing with a group of female activists and holding a controversial sign. The slogan "Smash Brahminical Patriarchy" caused outrage because it is calling for the dismantling of the Hindu caste system and male dominance with it. Many Twitter users called it hate speech and were furious. Twitter publicly apologized but then reaped criticism for caving in to the ruling class and silencing marginalized voices.[92]

b. When Susan Kramer served as the British transportation minister, she faced embarrassment after presenting the mayor of Taipei, Taiwan, Ko Wen-je, with a watch—a taboo in Chinese culture. Ko remarked to reporters that he would "sell it to a scrap dealer" because a watch would be useless to him. *Giving a clock* and *attending an old person's funeral* sound very similar in Chinese.[93]

c. During a state dinner for a delegation from Singapore visiting the government of the Czech Republic, the conversation turned to the tasty main course they were eating. One of the Czech hosts explained to the inquiring foreign guests that they were enjoying a Czech specialty, rabbit, known for its light white meat. The Singaporeans' faces mirrored shock, embarrassment, and irritation. As inconspicuously as possible, they put down their silverware. Only later did the Czech hosts learn that rabbit is a pet in Singapore much like the house cat in European or North American households.[94]

d. More than half of Japanese hotels do not allow guests with tattoos in their *onsens*, or hot spring bathing facilities. Some operators do, but only if the guests cover up their body art. In Japan tattoos are associated with organized crime. The bans were put in place to keep yakuza gangsters out and to prevent complaints from Japanese guests. A controversy erupted when a Māori woman (a member of the Indigenous Polynesian People from New Zealand) was barred from a public bath in Hokkaido for her traditional face tattoos.[95] Critics of the restrictive Japanese policies pointed out the pervasive presence of tattoos in many Western countries.

## 1.14 Intercultural Missteps and Bias Amplified on Social Media (L.O. 4, 5)
Intercultural     Social Media

Once a gaffe blows up on social media, it is difficult to contain. Consider the worst, most embarrassing intercultural mistake or bigotry incident, and then imagine it amplified a thousandfold or millionfold for everyone to see. What follows is a list of diversity and inclusion blunders as well as awkward social media slip-ups with intercultural implications.[96]

**YOUR TASK.** Consider the gravity of each offense; then, individually or in groups, discuss each for its take-away, the lesson to be learned from it.

a. In a case of awful timing, WW, formerly Weight Watchers, released a New Year's campaign #ThisIsMyWW on Twitter just as the United States launched a targeted drone strike that killed Iran's top general, Qasem Soleimani in Iraq, causing international consternation. Thus, WW's promoted trend campaign clashed with the unfortunate trending hashtag WWIII (for World War III). The company immediately pulled its campaign and Twitter helped by removing the promoted trend within one hour of its launch. Even so, more than 870,000 people would belabor the topic over the course of three days on Twitter alone.[97]

b. Papa John's pizza company forced out its founder and CEO, John Schnatter, after he had used a racial slur and made other racially tinged comments during a conference call with executives and the company's advertising agency. Predictably, his remarks made it onto social media, and Papa John's sales dropped 10.5 percent in the following weeks.

c. Two African American men were arrested at a Philadelphia Starbucks, the victims of apparent racial bias. The two men were waiting for an associate and asked to use the restroom without making a purchase. The situation escalated, and police were called. Social media blew up with negative tweets. Starbucks' brand perception among customers plummeted to its lowest in ten years. Starbucks closed 8,000 U.S. stores for sensitivity training.

## 1.15 Intercultural Communication: Fired for Being French? (L.O. 4, 5)

> E-Mail > Intercultural > Team >

Guillaume Rey was dismissed from his Vancouver restaurant job after warnings that he was being "combative and aggressive" toward other staff. When he reduced a fellow server to tears over a disagreement, he was let go for violating workplace policy. The Milestones restaurant admitted that Rey was professional and friendly with guests and often served as shift lead. The waiter filed a complaint with British Columbia's Human Rights Tribunal. He alleged discrimination and claimed that French culture "tends to be more direct and expressive." He insisted he was let go for having acquired high standards in France along with a "direct, honest and professional personality."

An employment consultant in British Columbia agrees that most French-speaking people from Europe tend to be direct, whereas Canadians are steeped in a non-conflict culture, particularly on the job. A French expatriate living in London believes that many French dislike chitchat such as talking about the weather. They get to the point. Talking or even smiling at strangers strikes them as intrusive, she says.[98]

**YOUR TASK.** Critically analyze the scenario in small teams or as a class. If your instructor directs, write a discussion forum post or an e-mail evaluating the intercultural encounter. Consider questions such as the following to get to the bottom the controversy:

What is the fundamental conflict here? Was Guillaume Rey a competent waiter? Do you find his claims and his defense credible? Does his official complaint have merit? Did the restaurant act reasonably? In how far is the incident an intercultural one? Is it the result of a cultural misunderstanding?

## Grammar/Mechanics Checkup 1

These checkups are designed to improve your grammar and mechanics skills, which include punctuation, spelling, capitalization, and number use. The checkups systematically review all sections of the Grammar/Mechanics Handbook. Answers are provided at the bottom of the page. You can find accompanying student resources at **www.cengage.com**.

### NOUNS

Review Sections 1.02–1.06 in the Grammar/Mechanics Handbook. Then select the correct form to complete each of the following statements. Record the appropriate Grammar/Mechanics section to illustrate the principle involved. When you finish, compare your responses with those at the bottom of the page. If your answers differ, study carefully the principles shown in parentheses.

___b___ ___(1.05b)___   **EXAMPLE**  The delivery driver arrived in the afternoon and unloaded the (a) box's, (b) boxes.

_____   1.  In Spanish Buenos Aires means *good air*, but the beautiful capital of Argentina is among the ten most polluted big (a) *citys*, (b) *cities*.

_____   2.  The (a) *CPAs* (b) *CPA's* we hired to do our taxes work tirelessly during tax season.

_____   3.  The two freshly minted (a) *attornies*, (b) *attorneys* lost their case although they had mounted a masterful defense.

_____   4.  Are you available to coach basketball on (a) *Mondays*, (b) *Monday's*?

_____   5.  (a) *Turkies*, (b) *Turkeys* bred rapidly in factory farms can barely walk.

_____   6.  The Garzas and the (a) *Ramirez's*, (b) *Ramirezes* prefer to take the whole family to the park instead of the beach.

_____   7.  The United States Environmental Protection Agency was established in the (a) *1970's*, (b) *1970s*.

_____   8.  (a) Mothers-in-law, (b) Mother-in-laws don't deserve the negative reputation attributed to them in popular culture.

_____   9.  Iron (a) *benchs*, (b) *benches* are not comfortable without cushions, but they last a long time.

_____   10. The IRS requested copies of all documents showing the company's assets and (a) *liabilitys*, (b) *liabilities*.

_____ 11. The department decided to send the newlyweds a large bouquet of (a) *peonys*, (b) *peonies*, their favorite flowers.

_____ 12. With Google Earth you can visit any mountains and (a) *valleys* (b) *vallies* on this planet.

_____ 13. Credit (a) *inquirys*, (b) *inquiries* help banks determine whether to grant loans to applicants.

_____ 14. When it's sunny and I'm outside, I can't tell the difference between (a) *i's and I's*, (b) on my tablet.

_____ 15. My sister-in-law joined several (a) *woman*, (b) *women* in her circle who were inspired by Greta Thunberg to fight against climate change.

## Editing Challenge 1

Every chapter provides an editing exercise to fine-tune your grammar and mechanics skills. These are the skills that employers frequently find lacking in employees. In this e-mail look for errors in proofreading, grammar, spelling, punctuation, capitalization, word use, and number form. Study the guidelines in the Grammar/Mechanics Handbook in Appendix D, including the lists of Confusing Words and Frequently Misspelled Words.

**YOUR TASK.** Edit the following by (a) inserting corrections in your textbook or on a photocopy using the proofreading marks in Appendix C or (b) downloading the message from **www.cengage.com** and correcting at your computer. **Hint:** You should make about 30 edits. Your instructor may ask you to use **Track Changes** in MS Word as you edit. See the Communication Workshop in Chapter 4 for more information about using **Track Changes**.

---

**To:**      Shannon Heymans <sheymans@siriussales.com>

**From:**    René Xanthopoulos <rxanthopoulos@siriussales.com>

**Subject:** Suggestions as Your Work From Home

---

Hi, Shannon,

Congratulations! I'm happy for you that you were granted permission to work remotely for the foreseeable future, here are some tips on how to be productive working from home.

- **Establish a defined workspace.** Creating a dedicated workspace sends a clear message to others in your house hold that you are doing work.

- **Respond to e-mail and texts.** Check your e-mail and other messages at least 3 times a day. Answer all message promply, and send copys of relevant messages to the appropriate office staff.

- **Transmit all work orders to Parker.** Parker will analyze each weeks activitys and update all sales assignments and inventorys.

- **Prepare an end of week report.** Send a summery of your weeks work to me indicating the major accounts you managed.

If you any questions about these tips do let me know as soon as possible. Please shoot e-mails to any staff member. When you need clarification on a project, or if you just want to keep us updated.

We will continue to hold once a week staff meetings on Friday s at 9 a.m. in the morning. Join us for 1 or 2 of these meeting. The next one is on Friday June 9th.

You're sure to enjoy working from home Shannon. Following these basic guideline should help you complete your work efficintly and provide the office with adequate communication.

Best wishes,

René

Director, Personnel | Sirius Sales | byoung@siriussales.com | 909-848-9043

## Letting LinkedIn Help You Land a Job

Where are the jobs? The COVID-19 pandemic upended one of the best job markets in decades. The resulting economic slump has led to greater competition for fewer positions.[99] Without traditional face-to-face networking with contacts whom job seekers know, LinkedIn and other online job search tools have become even more critical places where to find and be found. Even before the pandemic, polls revealed that more than 95 percent of recruiters use LinkedIn regularly to locate and vet job candidates.[100]

Although it has significantly fewer monthly active users than Facebook, LinkedIn is the go-to professional social networking site. One reason for its popularity is the 20 million companies and 20 million job openings listed there.[101] Other social media platforms, such as Facebook, Twitter, and Glassdoor, as well as popular job boards, are additional job-search tools you can literally manage in the palm of your hand. All are also available as mobile apps. LinkedIn is an excellent place for any job seeker to learn what is available, what qualifications are necessary, and what salaries are being offered. If you haven't done so already, you will need to develop an effective, professional LinkedIn profile sooner or later.

**CAREER APPLICATION.** It is never too soon to explore potential career opportunities. Assume that you are about to graduate, and you are now looking for a job. At the direction of your instructor, study online job advertisements in your field. What's available? How much is the salary? What are the requirements?

**YOUR TASK**

- **Visit LinkedIn.** If you haven't created a profile yet, sign up to conduct your search. Once you're signed in, click the Jobs icon on top of the browser page or on the bottom of the mobile app.

- **Study the opening page.** Once you have joined LinkedIn and created at least a first basic profile, your search results will be relevant to the information you have provided in it.

- **Select keyword, category, city, and state.** Decide whether you want to search by a job title (such as *nurse, accountant, project manager*) or a category (such as *Accounting/Finance, Administrative/Clerical, Advertising/Marketing*). Enter your keyword job title or select a category—or do both. Enter a city, state, or region. Click Search.

- **Study the job listings.** Click the links to read more about the job openings.

- **Explore popular job boards.** Try Indeed, the No. 1 job site, offering millions of job listings gathered from company job postings and career sites. Other big boards are CareerBuilder, Monster, and CollegeRecruiter. These sites allow you to search by location and type of job. Become familiar with the sites' search tools, and look for jobs in your field.

- **Select the best ads.** In your targeted career field and desired geographical area, select the three best ads and save or print them out.

- **Analyze the skills required.** How often do the ads you viewed mention *communication, teamwork, computer skills,* or *professionalism*? What tasks do the ads mention? What is the salary range identified in these ads for the positions they feature? **Tip:** Glassdoor offers an insider's look at many companies and positions. Because posts are anonymous, you will find confidential salary data. Your instructor may ask you to submit your findings and/or report to the class.

Communication Workshops (such as the one on this page) provide insight into special business communication topics and skills not discussed in the chapters. Topics include ethics, technology, career skills, and collaboration. Each workshop includes a career application to extend your learning and help you develop skills relevant to the workshop topic.

# The Writing Process in the Digital Era  2

**Chapter 2**

Planning Business Messages

**Chapter 3**

Organizing and Drafting Business Messages

**Chapter 4**

Revising Business Messages

# Planning Business Messages

## Learning Outcomes

After studying this chapter, you should be able to do the following:

**1** List the steps in the communication process.

**2** Describe the goals of business writers and three phases of the writing process.

**3** Identify the intended purpose and audience of a message to select the best communication channel.

**4** Discuss expert writing techniques that improve business messages.

**5** Apply writing techniques that improve the tone, clarity, and effectiveness of a message.

ESB Basic/Shutterstock.com

## 2-1 Exploring the Communication Process

Communication technology and digital media dominate nearly all aspects our lives—the way we work, play, learn, socialize, conduct business, and connect with each other. As the world becomes increasingly interconnected, people are communicating more than ever. They are sending and receiving a staggering number of digital messages through many channels. However, even as we routinely connect and exchange information via e-mail, texts, instant messages, tweets, Slack, Zoom, and other interactive media, the basic elements of the communication process remain largely unchanged.

## Figure 2.1 The Communication Process

Noise and barriers often disrupt the communication process. Success requires communicators to choose words carefully and plan strategies to overcome barriers and noise.

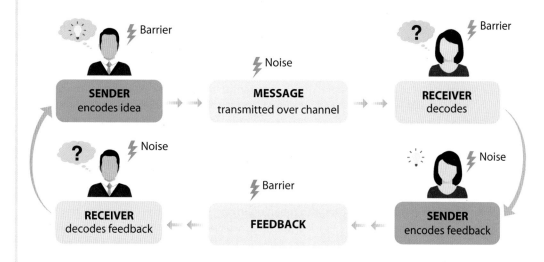

In its simplest form, **communication** may be defined as the *transmission of information and meaning from a sender to a receiver*. The crucial element in this definition is **meaning**. The process is successful only when the receiver understands an idea as the sender intended it. How does an idea travel from one person to another? It involves a sensitive circular process, shown in **Figure 2.1**. This process can easily be sidetracked, resulting in miscommunication. The process of communication achieves its purpose when both the sender and receiver understand the process and how to make it work. In our discussion we are most concerned with professional communication in the workplace so that you can be successful as a business communicator in your career.

## 2-1a Sender Has Idea

The communication process begins when the sender has an idea. The form of the idea may be influenced by complex factors surrounding the sender. These factors include mood, frame of reference, background, culture, and physical makeup, as well as the context of the situation and many other factors. Senders shape their ideas based on their own experiences and assumptions. When senders know their purpose and anticipate the expected response, they are better able to shape successful messages.

## 2-1b Sender Encodes Idea

The next step in the communication process involves **encoding**. This means converting the idea into words or gestures that will convey meaning. A major problem in communicating any message verbally is that words have different meanings for different people. Recognizing how easy it is to be misunderstood, skilled communicators choose familiar, concrete words. In choosing proper words and symbols, senders must be alert to the receiver's communication skills, attitudes, background, experiences, and culture. Including a smiley face in an e-mail announcement to stockholders may turn them off.

International messages require even more caution. In the United Kingdom, *scheme* is a neutral word describing an officially organized plan or system. In the United States, however, *scheme* means deceit. Successful messages are conveyed with appropriate words, gestures, and symbols that match the situation. Effective messages also make it easy for the receiver to respond.

**OFFICE INSIDER**

In explaining the need for plain English in a new Securities and Exchange Commission rule, Congressman Sean Casten sagely observed, "The simplest test of communication is whether the person you're communicating with understands it."[1]

**Sean Casten,**
*scientist, clean-energy entrepreneur, author, Congressman from Illinois*

### 2-1c  Sender Selects Channel and Transmits Message

The medium over which the message travels is the **channel**. Messages may be delivered by e-mail, SMS text, instant message, social media post, letter, memorandum, report, announcement, picture, spoken word, fax, Web page, or some other channel. Messages carried over digital networks face much opportunity for distraction and communication breakdown. Receivers may be overloaded with incoming messages or distracted by the many other functions of their devices. Only well-crafted messages may be accepted, understood, and acted on.

Anything that interrupts the transmission of a message in the communication process is called **noise**. Channel noise may range from a weak Wi-Fi signal to sloppy formatting and typos in e-mail messages. Noise may even include the annoyance a receiver feels when the sender chooses an improper channel for transmission or when the receiver is jammed with messages and information.

### 2-1d  Receiver Decodes Message

The individual for whom the message is intended is the **receiver**. Translating the message from its symbol form into meaning involves **decoding**. Only when the receiver understands the meaning intended by the sender—that is, successfully decodes the message—does communication take place. Such success is often difficult to achieve because of a number of barriers that block the process.

No two people share the same life experiences or have the same skills. Decoding can be disrupted internally by the receiver's lack of attention, by bias against the sender, or by competing messages. It can be disrupted externally by loud sounds or illegible words. Decoding can also be sidetracked by semantic obstacles, such as misunderstood words or emotional reactions to certain loaded terms. Alert receivers decode successfully with a receptive attitude while minimizing distractions.

### 2-1e  Feedback Returns to Sender

The verbal and nonverbal responses of the receiver create **feedback**, a vital part of the communication process. Feedback helps the sender know that the message was received and understood. Senders can encourage feedback by asking questions such as *Am I making myself clear?* and *Is there anything you don't understand?* Senders can further improve feedback by timing the delivery appropriately and by providing only as much information as the receiver can handle.

Receivers improve the communication process by providing clear and complete feedback. In business one of the best ways to advance understanding is to paraphrase the sender's message with comments such as *Let me see if I understood you correctly.*

## 2-2  Applying the 3-x-3 Writing Process to Business Messages

**LEARNING OUTCOME 2**
Describe the goals of business writers and three phases of the writing process.

Digital technologies enable you to choose from innumerable communication channels to create, transmit, and respond to messages. Regardless of channel, nearly all communication revolves around writing. Because writing is central to nearly all business communication, this chapter presents a systematic plan for preparing business messages in the digital era.

### 2-2a  Understanding the Goals of Business Writers

One thing you should immediately recognize about business writing is that it differs from other writing you have done. In preparing high school or college compositions and term papers, you probably focused on discussing your feelings or displaying your knowledge. Your instructors wanted to see your thought processes, and they wanted assurance that you had internalized the subject matter. You may have been required to meet a minimum word count. Business writing is definitely not like that! It also differs from personal messages you may exchange with your friends and family. Those messages enabled you to stay connected and express your feelings. In the workplace, however, writing should be:

- **Purposeful.** Your goal will be to solve problems and convey information. Each message should have a definite strategy.

- **Economical**. You will try to present ideas clearly but concisely. Length is not rewarded.

- **Audience centered.** You will look at a problem from the perspective of the audience instead of seeing it from your own.

These distinctions actually ease your task. No more searching your imagination for creative topic ideas. No stretching your ideas to make them appear longer. Writing consultants and businesspeople complain that many college graduates entering the workplace have a conscious—or perhaps unconscious—perception that quantity enhances quality. Wrong! Get over the notion that longer is better. Whether you are presenting your ideas in print, online, or in person, conciseness and clarity are what counts in business.

The ability to prepare purposeful, concise, and audience-centered messages does not come naturally. Very few people, especially beginners, can sit down and draft an effective e-mail message, letter, or report without training. However, following a systematic process, studying model messages, and practicing the craft can make nearly anyone a successful business writer or speaker.

## 2-2b Following the 3-x-3 Writing Process

Regardless of what you are writing, the process will be easier if you follow a systematic plan. The 3-x-3 writing process breaks the entire task into three phases: *prewriting*, *drafting*, and *revising*, as shown in **Figure 2.2**.

To illustrate the writing process, let's say you own a popular fast-food restaurant that's part of a large franchise. Corporate management recently installed digital kiosks to automate ordering. You aren't happy with the new plan because customers are confused, and many refuse to use the digital kiosk. To assist customers, an employee must stand nearby to help. After placing an order, a customer often must still go to a cashier to pay. You fail to see how kiosk ordering is boosting your profit. Your customers clearly prefer cashiers to kiosk ordering, especially when they are ordering more than one item.

You want to convince other franchise owners in the district to join you in protesting this unwanted change. To convince others, you could make a lot of telephone calls or send many text messages. However, you want to present a serious argument with compelling points that the recipients will remember and be willing to act on when they gather for their next district meeting. Texting doesn't enable you to make a serious argument. You decide to send a persuasive e-mail that you hope will win their support.

Prewriting. The first phase of the writing process prepares you to write. It involves *analyzing* the audience and your purpose for writing. The audience for your message will be other franchise owners, some highly educated and others not. Your purpose in writing is to convince them that rolling back the new policy would restore customer service and please patrons. Creating a single-line system, such as that used in banks, may reduce the chaos.

Prewriting also involves *anticipating* how your audience will react to your message. You are sure that some of the other owners will agree with you, but others might fear that customers seeing a long single line might go elsewhere. In *adapting* your message to the audience, you try to think of the right words and the right tone that will win approval.

Drafting. The second phase involves researching, organizing, and then drafting the message. In *researching* information for this message, you would probably investigate

**OFFICE INSIDER**

Author David Silverman blasts "an educational system that rewards length over clarity." Students learn to over-write, he says, in hopes that at least some of their sentences "hit the mark." Once on the job, they continue to act as if they were paid by the word, a perception that must be unlearned.[2]

**David Silverman,**
*entrepreneur and business teacher*

**Figure 2.2** The 3-x-3 Writing Process

**1 Prewriting**

**Analyze**
- What is your purpose?
- What do you want the receiver to do or believe?
- What channel should you choose: face-to-face conversation, group meeting, e-mail, memo, letter, report, blog, Slack, tweet?
- What are the benefits or barriers of each channel?

**Anticipate**
- What is the audience profile?
- What does the receiver already know?
- Will the receiver's response be neutral, positive, or negative? How will the response affect your organizational strategy?

**Adapt**
- What techniques can you use to adapt your message to its audience?
- How can you promote feedback?
- What can you do to ensure positive, conversational, and courteous language?

**2 Drafting**

**Research**
- Gather data to provide facts.
- Review previous correspondence.
- Search company files for background information.
- Talk with the boss and colleagues.
- Search the Internet.
- What do you need to know to write this message?

**Organize**
- Organize direct messages with the big idea first, followed by an explanation in the body and an action request in the closing.
- For persuasive or negative messages, use an indirect problem-solving strategy.

**Draft**
- Prepare a first draft usually writing quickly.
- Focus on short, clear sentences using the active voice.
- Build paragraph coherence by repeating key ideas, using pronouns, and incorporating appropriate transitional expressions.

**3 Revising**

**Edit**
- Edit your message to be sure it is clear, concise, conversational, and readable.
- Revise to eliminate wordy fillers, long lead-ins, redundancies, and trite business phrases.
- Consider using headings and numbered and bulleted lists for quick reading.

**Proofread**
- Take the time to read the message carefully.
- Look for errors in spelling, grammar, punctuation, names, and numbers.
- Check to be sure the format is consistent.

**Evaluate**
- Will this message achieve its purpose?
- Does the tone sound pleasant and friendly rather than curt?
- Have you thought enough about the audience to be sure this message is appealing?
- Did you encourage feedback?

other kinds of businesses that use kiosks and single lines. You might check your competitors. What are McDonald's, Wendy's, and Burger King doing? You might do some calling to see whether other franchise owners are concerned about the new kiosks and chaotic lines. Before writing to the entire group, you might brainstorm with a few owners to see what ideas they have for solving the problem.

Once you have collected enough information, you would focus on *organizing* your message. Should you start out by offering your solution? Or should you work up to it slowly, describing the problem, presenting your evidence, and then ending with the solution? The final step in the second phase of the writing process is actually *drafting* the letter. At this point many writers write quickly, knowing that they will polish their ideas when they revise.

Revising. The third phase of the process involves editing, proofreading, and evaluating your message. After writing the first draft, you will spend considerable time *editing* the message for clarity, conciseness, tone, and readability. Could parts of it be rearranged to make your point more effectively? This is the time when you look for ways to improve the organization and tone of your message. Next, you will spend time *proofreading* carefully to ensure correct spelling, grammar, punctuation, and format. The final phase involves *evaluating* your message to decide whether it accomplishes your goal.

## 2-2c Pacing the Writing Process

The time you spend on each phase of the writing process varies depending on the complexity of the problem, the purpose, the audience, and your schedule. On average, you should expect to spend about 25 percent of your time prewriting, 25 percent drafting, and 50 percent revising, as shown in **Figure 2.3**.

**Figure 2.3** Scheduling the Writing Process

Although the writing process looks like a linear set of steps, it actually is recursive, enabling writers to revise their work continually as they progress. However, careful planning can avoid wasted time and frustration caused by rethinking and reorganizing during drafting.

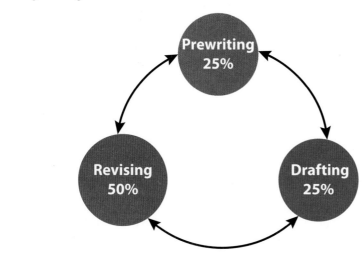

These are rough guidelines, yet you can see that good writers spend most of their time on the final phase of revising and proofreading. Much depends, of course, on your project, its importance, and your familiarity with it. What is critical to remember, though, is that revising is a major component of the writing process even if the message is short.

It may appear that you perform one step and progress to the next, always following the same order. Most business writing, however, is not that rigid. Although writers perform the tasks described, the steps may be rearranged, abbreviated, or repeated. Some writers revise every sentence and paragraph as they go. Many find that new ideas occur after they have begun to write, causing them to back up, alter the organization, and rethink their plan. Beginning business writers often follow the writing process closely. With experience, though, they will grow like other good writers and presenters who alter, compress, and rearrange the steps as needed.

## 2-3 Analyzing the Purpose and Anticipating the Audience

Have you ever started to write a message and discovered toward the end that your purpose changed? Were you frustrated at the wasted time? If you analyze your purpose before you begin, you can avoid having to backtrack and start over. The remainder of this chapter covers the first phase of the 3-x-3 writing process: (a) analyzing the purpose for writing, (b) anticipating how the audience will react, and (c) adapting the message to the audience.

**LEARNING OUTCOME 3**

Identify the intended purpose and audience of a message to select the best communication channel.

### 2-3a Determining Your Purpose

As you begin to compose a workplace message, ask yourself two important questions: (a) Why am I sending this message? and (b) What do I hope to achieve? Your responses will determine how you organize and present the information.

Your message may have primary and secondary purposes. For college work your primary purpose may be merely to complete the assignment; secondary purposes might be to make yourself look good and to earn an excellent grade. The primary purposes for sending business messages are typically to inform and persuade. A secondary purpose is to promote goodwill. You and your organization want to look good in the eyes of your audience.

Many business messages do nothing more than *inform*. **Informational messages** explain procedures, announce meetings, answer questions, and transmit findings. Such messages are usually developed directly, as discussed in Chapter 3. Some business messages, however, are meant to *persuade*. **Persuasive messages** attempt to sell products, convince managers, motivate employees, and win over customers. Persuasive messages are often developed indirectly, as presented in Chapter 3 and subsequent chapters.

## 2-3b Anticipating the Audience

Before writing any message, spend a moment thinking about the audience who will receive it. What is the reader or listener like? How will that person react to the message? Although one can't always know exactly who the receiver is, it is possible to imagine some of that person's characteristics. A copywriter at a major retailer imagines his sister-in-law whenever he writes product descriptions for the catalog.

Identifying your audience is a pivotal step in the writing process. The questions in **Figure 2.4** will help you understand your audience.

How much time you devote to answering these questions depends on your message and its context. An analytical report that you compose for management or an oral presentation before a big group would, of course, demand considerable time identifying the audience. An e-mail message to a coworker or a message to a familiar supplier might require only a few moments of planning.

Preparing a blog post on an important topic to be published to a company website would require you to think about the local, national, and international audiences that might read that message. Even posting brief personal messages on Facebook, Twitter, or Tumblr should make you think about who will read them. How much of your day and life do you want to share? Will customers and business partners be reading your posts?

No matter how short your message is, spend some time thinking about the people in your audience so that you can tailor your words to them. Remember that your receivers will be thinking, *What's in it for me? (WIIFM)*. One of the most important writing tips you can take away from this book is remembering that every message you write should begin with the notion that your audience is thinking *WIIFM*.

### Figure 2.4  Questions to Help You Identify Your Audience

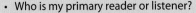

**Primary Audience**

- Who is my primary reader or listener?
- What are my personal and professional relationships with this person?
- How much does this person know about the subject?
- What do I know about this person's education, beliefs, culture, and abilities?
- Should I expect a neutral, positive, or negative response to my message?

**Secondary Audience**

- Who might see or hear this message in addition to the primary audience?
- How do these people differ from the primary audience?
- Do I need to include more background information?
- How must I reshape my message to make it understandable and accessible to others to whom it might be forwarded?

## 2-3c Tailoring Your Message to the Audience

Identifying your audience helps you make decisions about shaping the message. You will discover what language is appropriate, whether you are free to use specialized technical terms, whether you should explain the background, and so on. Identifying the audience helps you decide whether your tone should be formal or informal. When you identify the audience, you are better able to anticipate whether the receiver is likely to respond positively or negatively to your message, or be neutral about it.

Another consideration in identifying your audience is the possibility of a secondary audience. Let's say, for example, that you start to write an e-mail message to your manager, Keira, describing a problem you are having. Halfway through the message, you realize that Keira will probably forward this message to her boss, the vice president. Super-efficient Keira will probably not want to rewrite what you said; instead, she may take the easy route and merely forward your e-mail. When you realize that the vice president may see this message, you decide to use a more formal tone. You remove your inquiry about Keira's family, you reduce your complaints, and you tone down your language about why things went wrong. Instead, you provide more background information, and you are more specific in identifying items the vice president might not recognize. Analyzing the task and anticipating the audience help you adapt your message so it will be effective for both primary and secondary receivers.

## 2-3d Choosing the Best Channel

After identifying the purpose and the audience of your message, you will want to choose the most appropriate communication channel as illustrated in **Figure 2.5**. Your decision to use a live chat, send an e-mail message, schedule a videoconference, or select some other channel depends on some of the following factors:

- Available technology
- Importance of the message
- Amount and speed of feedback and interactivity required
- Necessity of a permanent record
- Cost of the channel
- Degree of formality desired
- Confidentiality and sensitivity of the message
- Receiver's preference and level of technical expertise

**Figure 2.5 Comparing Rich and Lean Communication Channels**

**LEARNING OUTCOME 4**

Discuss expert writing techniques that improve business messages.

In addition to these practical issues, you will also need to consider how rich the channel is, shown in Figure 2.5. The **richness** of a channel involves the extent to which a channel or medium recreates or represents all the information available in the original message. A richer medium, such as a face-to-face conversation or a live video chat, permits more interactivity and feedback. A leaner medium, such as a letter or an e-mail, presents a flat, one-dimensional message. Richer media enable the sender to provide more verbal and visual cues as well as to tailor the message to the audience.

Choosing the wrong medium can result in a message that is less effective or even misunderstood. If, for example, marketing manager Eli must motivate the sales force to increase sales in the fourth quarter, he is unlikely to achieve his goal if he merely posts an announcement on the office bulletin board, writes a memo, or sends an e-mail. Eli could be more persuasive with a richer channel, such as individual face-to-face conversations or a group meeting to stimulate sales. For sales reps on the road, a richer medium would be a videoconference (i.e., a virtual meeting). In choosing channels, keep in mind two tips: (a) Use the richest media available, and (b) employ richer media for more persuasive or personal communication.

## 2-4 Employing Expert Writing Techniques to Adapt to Your Audience

After analyzing the purpose and anticipating the audience, writers begin to think about how to adapt a message to the task and the audience. Adaptation is the process of creating a message that suits the audience. Skilled communicators employ a number of expert writing techniques such as featuring audience benefits, cultivating a "you" view, and sounding conversational but professional.

### 2-4a Focusing on Audience Benefits

Spotlighting the needs of the audience sounds like a modern idea, but actually one of America's early statesmen and authors recognized this fundamental writing principle more than 200 years ago. In describing effective writing, Ben Franklin observed, "To be good, it ought to have a tendency to benefit the reader."[3] This wise insight has become an essential guideline for today's business communicators.

Expanding on Franklin's counsel, a contemporary communication consultant gives this solid advice to his business clients: "Always stress the benefit to the audience of whatever it is you are trying to get them to do. If you can show them how you are going to save them frustration or help them meet their goals, you have the makings of a powerful message."[4] Remember, WIIFM!

Adapting your message to the receiver's needs means putting yourself in that person's shoes. This ability to share someone else's feelings is called **empathy**. Empathic senders think about how a receiver will decode a message. They try to give something to the receiver, solve the receiver's problems, save the receiver's money, or just understand the feelings and position of that person. Which version of each of the following messages is more appealing to the audience?

| Sender Focus | Audience Focus |
|---|---|
| All employees are herewith instructed to fill out the attached survey so that we can allocate our limited training resource funds to selected employees. | By filling out the attached survey, you can be one of the first employees to sign up for our limited training funds. |
| Our one-year warranty becomes effective only when we receive the owner's registration. | Your one-year warranty begins working for you as soon as you return your owner's registration. |

## 2-4b Cultivating the "You" View

Notice that many of the previous audience-centered messages had included the word "you." In focusing on audience benefits, skilled communicators naturally develop the *"you" view*. They emphasize second-person pronouns (*you, your*) instead of first-person pronouns (*I/we, us, our*). Whether your goal is to inform, persuade, or promote goodwill, the catchiest words you can use are *you* and *your*. Compare the following examples.

| "I/We" View | "You" View |
|---|---|
| I need your account number before I can do anything about your claim. | Would you mind giving me your account number so that I can locate your records and help you solve this problem? |
| Our experienced staff has created a webinar that teaches how to use Instagram more productively. | Join an upcoming webinar to learn which of your Instagram photos are generating the most engagement to promote your business. |

A survey revealed that *you* phrasing was more effective than *we* phrasing for conveying ideas related to interest and intent, such as in sales and marketing messages. Researchers argued that *you* phrasing does a better job of subconsciously grabbing attention and transferring ownership to the receiver.[6]

Although you want to focus on the reader or listener, don't overuse or misuse the second-person pronoun *you*. Readers and listeners appreciate genuine interest; on the other hand, they resent obvious attempts at manipulation. The authors of some sales messages, for example, are guilty of overkill when they include *you* dozens of times in a direct-mail promotion. What's more, the word can sometimes create the wrong impression. Consider this statement: *You cannot return merchandise until you receive written approval.* The word *you* appears twice, but the reader may feel singled out for criticism. In the following version, the message is less personal and more positive: *Customers may return merchandise with written approval.*

Another difficulty in emphasizing the "you" view and de-emphasizing *we/I* is that it may result in overuse of the passive voice. For example, to avoid writing *We will give you* (active voice), you might write *You will be given* (passive voice). *You will receive*, though, is active voice and a better option here. The active voice in writing is generally preferred because it identifies who is doing the acting. You will learn more about active and passive voice in Chapter 3.

In recognizing the value of the "you" view, however, you don't have to sterilize your writing and totally avoid any first-person pronouns or words that show your feelings. You can convey sincerity, warmth, and enthusiasm by the words you choose. Don't be afraid of phrases such as *I'm happy* or *We're delighted*, if you truly are. When speaking face-to-face, you can show sincerity and warmth with nonverbal cues such as a smile and a pleasant voice tone. In e-mails, letters, memos, and digital messages in general, only expressive words and phrases can show your feelings. These phrases suggest a pleasing secondary meaning that says *You are important, I hear you,* and *I'm honestly trying to please you.*

## 2-4c Sounding Conversational but Professional

Most business messages replace conversation. That's why an informal, conversational tone is usually more effective than a formal, pretentious tone. Just how informal you can be depends greatly on the workplace. At Google, writing skews casual. In a short message to users describing changes in its privacy policies, Google staff members wrote, "We believe this stuff matters."[7] In more traditional organizations, that message probably would have been more formal. The dilemma for you, then, is knowing how

Once signaling incompetency and unprofessionalism, emojis are enjoying greater acceptance in the workplace. Messages with playful emojis build positive emotional associations and help create team spirit. In clipped e-mail and smartphone messages, they introduce warmth and reduce misunderstandings. However, seemingly harmless images such as winky faces, tearful eyes, and blowing kisses can also send unclear messages. Are they flirtatious or just good-humored fun? Although increasingly seen in personal chats and text messages, emojis in the workplace must be used cautiously and sparingly.[8] If you were asked to advise recent grads about how to use emojis in workplace messages, what restrictions would you suggest?

casual to be in your writing. We suggest that you strive to be conversational but professional, especially until you learn what your organization prefers.

E-mail, instant messaging, chat, Twitter, and other short messaging channels enable you and your coworkers to have spontaneous conversations. Don't, however, let your messages become sloppy, unprofessional, or even dangerous. You will learn more about the potential risks of e-mail and other digital channels later. At this point, though, we focus on the tone of the language.

To project a professional image, you want to sound educated and mature. The overuse of expressions such as *super, totally awesome, insanely, you know,* and *like,* as well as a reliance on unnecessary abbreviations (*BTW* for *by the way*), may make a businessperson sound immature. Emojis are fun to pop into casual personal messages, but think twice before using them at work. See the Workplace in Focus to learn how emojis can send ambiguous messages on the job. Professional messages do not include texting-style abbreviations, slang, sentence fragments, and chitchat. We urge you to adopt a warm, conversational tone and diction. As shown in **Figure 2.6**, levels of diction range from unprofessional to formal. Most business messages fall in the middle.

Your goal is a warm, friendly tone that sounds professional. Although some writers are too casual, others are overly formal. To impress readers and listeners, they use big words, long sentences, legal terminology, and third-person constructions. Stay away from expressions such as *the undersigned, the writer,* and *the affected party.* You will sound friendlier with familiar pronouns such as *I, we,* and *you.* The following examples illustrate a professional yet conversational tone:

### Figure 2.6  Levels of Diction and Tone

| Unprofessional | Conversational | Formal |
|---|---|---|
| badmouth | criticize | denigrate |
| guts | nerve | courage |
| pecking order | line of command | dominance hierarchy |
| ticked off | upset | provoked |
| rat on | inform | betray |
| rip off | steal | expropriate |

| Unprofessional | Professional |
|---|---|
| Hey, boss, Gr8 news! Firewall now installed!! BTW, check with me b4 blasting the news. | Ms. Williams, our new firewall software is now installed. Please check with me before announcing it. |
| Look, dude, this report is totally bogus. And the figures don't look kosher. Show me some real stats. Got sources? | Because the figures in this report seem questionable, please submit the source statistics. |

| Overly Formal | Conversational |
|---|---|
| All employees are herewith instructed to return the appropriately designated contracts to the undersigned. | Please return the contracts to me. |
| Pertaining to your order, we must verify the sizes that your organization requires prior to consignment of your order to our shipper. | We will send your order as soon as we confirm the sizes you need. |

## 2-5 Improving the Tone and Clarity of a Message

**LEARNING OUTCOME 5**

Apply writing techniques that improve the tone, clarity, and effectiveness of a message.

As you continue to improve your writing skills, you can use additional expert techniques that improve the tone, clarity, and effectiveness of a message. These valuable techniques include using a positive and courteous tone, bias-free language, plain words, and precise terms. Take a look at **Model Document 2.1** to see how you can improve an e-mail message by applying several professional writing techniques.

### 2-5a Choosing to Be Positive Rather Than Negative

You can improve the clarity, tone, and effectiveness of a message choosing positive rather than negative language. Positive language generally conveys more information than negative language does. Moreover, positive messages are uplifting and pleasant to read. Positive wording tells what *is* and what *can be done* rather than what *isn't* and what *can't be done*. For example, *Your order cannot be shipped by January 10* is not nearly as informative as *Your order will be shipped January 15*.

An office supply store adjacent to an ice cream parlor in Portland, Maine, posted a sign on its door that reads: *Please enjoy your ice cream before you enjoy our store.* That sounds much more positive and inviting than *No food allowed!*[10]

Using positive language also involves avoiding negative words that create ill will. Some words appear to blame or accuse your audience. For example, opening a letter to a customer with *You claim that* suggests that you don't believe the customer. Other loaded words that can get you in trouble are *complaint, criticism, defective, failed, mistake,* and *neglected.* Also avoid phrases such as *you apparently are unaware of, you did not provide, you misunderstood,* and *you don't understand.* Often you may not realize the effect of these words. Notice in the following examples how you can revise the negative tone to create a more positive impression.

**OFFICE INSIDER**

"Positive tone is clearer and helps us get things done because its phrasing is simpler and it uses fewer words. By phrasing messages positively, you encourage people to buy into your ideas and establish good relationships for the future. Positive tone is a credibility builder."[9]

**Leigh Geraghty,**
*communication skills trainer, Wavelength*

| Negative | Positive |
|---|---|
| Our request for a fitness center will never be approved without senior management support. | Our request for a fitness center could be approved if we obtain senior management support. |
| You failed to include your credit card number, so we can't mail your order. | We look forward to completing your order as soon as we receive your credit card number. |

*(Continued)*

# Model Document 2.1  Improving the Tone and Clarity of an E-Mail Message

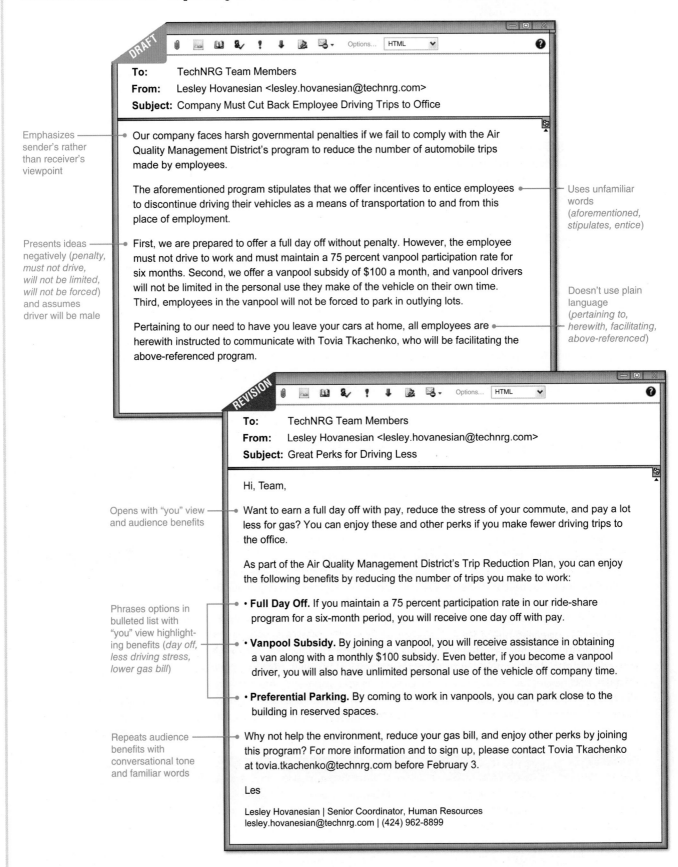

**DRAFT**

To: TechNRG Team Members
From: Lesley Hovanesian <lesley.hovanesian@technrg.com>
Subject: Company Must Cut Back Employee Driving Trips to Office

*Emphasizes sender's rather than receiver's viewpoint* →

Our company faces harsh governmental penalties if we fail to comply with the Air Quality Management District's program to reduce the number of automobile trips made by employees.

The aforementioned program stipulates that we offer incentives to entice employees to discontinue driving their vehicles as a means of transportation to and from this place of employment.

← *Uses unfamiliar words (aforementioned, stipulates, entice)*

*Presents ideas negatively (penalty, must not drive, will not be limited, will not be forced) and assumes driver will be male* →

First, we are prepared to offer a full day off without penalty. However, the employee must not drive to work and must maintain a 75 percent vanpool participation rate for six months. Second, we offer a vanpool subsidy of $100 a month, and vanpool drivers will not be limited in the personal use they make of the vehicle on their own time. Third, employees in the vanpool will not be forced to park in outlying lots.

← *Doesn't use plain language (pertaining to, herewith, facilitating, above-referenced)*

Pertaining to our need to have you leave your cars at home, all employees are herewith instructed to communicate with Tovia Tkachenko, who will be facilitating the above-referenced program.

**REVISION**

To: TechNRG Team Members
From: Lesley Hovanesian <lesley.hovanesian@technrg.com>
Subject: Great Perks for Driving Less

Hi, Team,

*Opens with "you" view and audience benefits* →

Want to earn a full day off with pay, reduce the stress of your commute, and pay a lot less for gas? You can enjoy these and other perks if you make fewer driving trips to the office.

As part of the Air Quality Management District's Trip Reduction Plan, you can enjoy the following benefits by reducing the number of trips you make to work:

*Phrases options in bulleted list with "you" view highlighting benefits (day off, less driving stress, lower gas bill)* →

- **Full Day Off.** If you maintain a 75 percent participation rate in our ride-share program for a six-month period, you will receive one day off with pay.

- **Vanpool Subsidy.** By joining a vanpool, you will receive assistance in obtaining a van along with a monthly $100 subsidy. Even better, if you become a vanpool driver, you will also have unlimited personal use of the vehicle off company time.

- **Preferential Parking.** By coming to work in vanpools, you can park close to the building in reserved spaces.

*Repeats audience benefits with conversational tone and familiar words* →

Why not help the environment, reduce your gas bill, and enjoy other perks by joining this program? For more information and to sign up, please contact Tovia Tkachenko at tovia.tkachenko@technrg.com before February 3.

Les

Lesley Hovanesian | Senior Coordinator, Human Resources
lesley.hovanesian@technrg.com | (424) 962-8899

| Negative | Positive |
|---|---|
| Your e-mail of June 9 claims that you returned a defective headset. | Your June 9 e-mail describes a headset you returned. |
| Employees cannot park in Lot H until April 1. | Employees may park in Lot H starting April 1. |

## 2-5b Expressing Courtesy

Maintaining a courteous tone involves not just guarding against rudeness but also avoiding words that sound demanding or preachy. Expressions such as *you should, you must,* and *you have to* cause people to instinctively react with *Oh, yeah?* One remedy is to turn these demands into rhetorical questions that begin with *Will you please . . . .* Giving reasons for a request also softens the tone.

Even when you feel justified in displaying anger, remember that losing your temper or being sarcastic will seldom accomplish your goals as a business communicator: to inform, to persuade, and to create goodwill. When you are irritated, frustrated, or infuriated, keep cool and try to defuse the situation. In dealing with customers in phone conversations, use polite phrases such as these: *I would be happy to assist you with that, Thank you for being so patient,* and *It was a pleasure speaking with you.* The following examples show a courteous and helpful attitude:

| Less Courteous | More Courteous and Helpful |
|---|---|
| Jaylen, you must complete all performance reviews by April 1. | Jaylen, will you please complete all performance reviews by April 1. |
| Why can't you people get anything right? This is the second time I've had to write to you! | Please credit my account for $250. The latest update of my account shows that the error noted in my e-mail of January 4 has not yet been corrected. |
| Have you tried reading the operating manual, or am I the only one who can do that? | Let's review the operating manual together so that you can get your documents to print correctly next time. |
| You should organize a carpool in this department. | Organizing a carpool will reduce your transportation costs and help preserve the environment. |

To make a positive impression and show respect, use good manners in person and in writing. For example, don't be presumptuous by issuing orders or setting the time for a meeting with a supervisor. Use first names only if given permission to do so. Even if your boss or manager sends error-filled messages, don't let such errors creep into your own writing.

## 2-5c Avoiding Gender-, Age-, and Disability-Biased Language

In adapting a message to its audience, be sure your language is sensitive and bias-free. Few writers set out to be offensive. Sometimes, though, we may say things that could be hurtful. Awareness and sensitivity are key. The real problem is that we don't think about words and phrases that stereotype groups of people, such as *the boys in tech support* or *the girls in the front office.* Be cautious about expressions that might be biased in terms of gender, race, ethnicity, age, and disability.

Generally, you can avoid gender-biased language by choosing alternate language for words involving *man* or *woman,* by using plural nouns and pronouns, or by changing

**OFFICE INSIDER**

"What's my problem with 'No problem'? Why do I pine so for 'You're welcome'? Is it just sentimental nostalgia? Nothing of the kind. It's the informality! ... There's an implicit, albeit unintentional, condescension in the 'No problem' come-back. As if to say 'You're interrupting my busy life, but I'll make a little time for you because I'm just that magnanimous.' Not to mention, it's negative."[11]

**Gregg Opelka,** *musical theater composer-lyricist*

to a gender-free word (*person* or *representative*). Avoid the *his or her* option. It's wordy and conspicuously perpetuates the exclusion of other gender identities. With a little effort, you can usually find a construction that is graceful, grammatical, and unselfconscious.

Specify age only if it is relevant, and avoid expressions that are demeaning or subjective such as *spry old codger*. Avoid patronizing references such as *one of the lovely office ladies will help you*. Instead, try *one of the administrative assistants will help you*.

To avoid disability bias, do not refer to an individual's disability unless it is relevant. When necessary, use terms that do not stigmatize disabled persons. Never use *cripple* or *crippled* when talking about people with disabilities. Moreover, don't refer to them as specially courageous, brave, or superhuman. Doing so makes it seem unexpected that they can be successful or live life like anyone else.

Below are just a few examples of bias and their possible replacements. More categories of bias exist, for example, language stigmatizing the LGBTQ+ community. Skilled business writers avoid any form of language that diminishes or disparages others. The key to bias-free communication lies in awareness and commitment. Be on the lookout to be sure that your messages do not exclude, stereotype, or offend people.

| Gender-Biased | Improved |
| --- | --- |
| female doctor, woman attorney, cleaning lady | doctor, attorney, cleaner |
| waiter/waitress, authoress, stewardess | server, author, flight attendant |
| mankind, man-hour, man-made | humanity, working hours, artificial |
| office girl, office lady | office worker, administrative assistant |
| the doctor . . . he | doctors . . . they |
| the teacher . . . she | teachers . . . they |
| executives and their wives | executives and their spouses |
| foreman, flagman, workman, craftsman | lead worker, flagger, worker, artisan |
| businessman, salesman | businessperson, sales representative |
| Each employee had his picture taken. | Each employee had a picture taken. All employees had their pictures taken. |

| Racially Or Ethnically Biased | Improved |
| --- | --- |
| A Hispanic accountant was hired. | An accountant was hired. |
| Derek Jones, an African American, applied. | Derek Jones applied. |
| A small group of joyous Black students gathered near the statue of an Indian on horseback. | A small group of students gathered before the statue of a Native American on horseback. |

| Age-Biased | Improved |
| --- | --- |
| The law applied to old people. | The law applied to people over 65. |
| Sally Kay, 55, was transferred. | Sally Kay was transferred. |
| a sprightly old gentleman | a man, an old man |
| a little old lady | a woman, an old woman |

| Disability-Biased | Improved |
|---|---|
| afflicted with arthritis, crippled by arthritis | has arthritis |
| confined to a wheelchair | uses a wheelchair |
| is mentally retarded, slow | is cognitively disabled |

## 2-5d Preferring Plain Language and Familiar Words

In adapting your message to your audience, use plain language and familiar words that you think audience members will recognize. Don't, however, avoid a big word that conveys your idea efficiently and is appropriate for the audience. Your goal is to reject pompous and pretentious language. If you mean *begin,* don't say *commence* or *initiate.* If you mean *pay,* don't write *compensate.* By substituting everyday, familiar words for unfamiliar ones, as shown here, you help your audience comprehend your ideas quickly.

| Unfamiliar | Familiar |
|---|---|
| implement | begin, start |
| subsequent to | after |
| commensurate | equal |
| interrogate | question |
| materialize | appear |
| obfuscate | confuse |
| remuneration | pay, salary |

**OFFICE INSIDER**

In a letter to the editor, a teacher criticized an article in *USA Today* on autism because it said "autistic child" rather than "child with autism." She championed "people-first" terminology, which avoids defining individuals by their ability or disability.[12] Can language change perceptions?

At the same time, be selective in your use of jargon. **Jargon** describes technical or specialized terms within a field. These terms enable insiders to communicate complex ideas quickly, but to outsiders they mean nothing. Human resources professionals, for example, know precisely what's meant by *cafeteria plan* (a benefits option program), but most of us would be thinking about lunch. Geologists refer to *plate tectonics,* and physicians discuss *metastatic carcinomas.* These terms mean little to most of us. Such specialized language is appropriate only when the audience will understand it. In addition, don't forget secondary audiences: Will those potential receivers understand any technical terms used?

## 2-5e Using Precise, Vigorous Words

Strong verbs and specific nouns give receivers more information and keep them interested. Don't overlook the thesaurus (available in print, online, and on your computer) for expanding your word choices and vocabulary. Whenever possible, use precise, specific words, as shown here:

| Imprecise, Dull | More Precise |
|---|---|
| to get | to receive, buy, grab, bring, pick up |
| | to earn, obtain, capture, secure, snag |
| a change in profits | a 25 percent hike in profits |
| | a 10 percent plunge in profits |
| to say | to promise, confess, understand |
| | to allege, assert, assume, judge |
| to think about | to identify, diagnose, analyze |
| | to probe, examine, inspect |

## Summary of Learning Outcomes

**1  List the five steps in the communication process.**
- A sender has an idea.
- The sender encodes (converts) the idea into words or symbols to express the idea in a message.
- The message travels over a channel (such as an e-mail, text, letter, report, announcement, image, tweet, spoken word, Web page).
- "Noise" (loud sounds, misspelled words, an inappropriate channel, or other distractions) may interfere with the transmission.
- The receiver decodes (interprets) the message and may respond with feedback.

**2  Describe the goals of business writers and three phases of the writing process.**
- Business writing should be purposeful, economical, and audience-centered.
- Phase 1 of the 3-x-3 writing process (prewriting) involves analyzing the message, anticipating the audience, and considering how to adapt the message to the audience.
- Phase 2 (drafting) includes researching the topic, organizing the material, and drafting the message.
- Phrase 3 (revising) consists of editing, proofreading, and evaluating the message.
- The 3-x-3 writing process provides a systematic plan describing what to do in each step of creating efficient and effective messages.

**3  Identify the intended purpose and audience of a message to select the best communication channel.**
- Before drafting, decide why you want to write and what you hope to achieve.
- Define your purpose, whether to inform, persuade, or communicate goodwill.
- After identifying the purpose, visualize both the primary and secondary audiences.
- Remember that receivers will usually be thinking, "What's in it for me (WIIFM)?"
- Choose the best channel by considering the (a) importance of the message, (b) amount and speed of feedback needed, (c) necessity of a permanent record, (d) cost of the channel, (e) degree of formality desired, (f) confidentiality and sensitivity of the message, and (g) receiver's preference and level of technical expertise.

**4  Discuss expert writing techniques that improve business messages.**
- Shape the message from the receiver's, not the sender's, view by focusing on audience benefits.
- Apply the "you" view without attempting to manipulate.
- Use conversational but professional language. Strive to convey a warm, friendly tone.
- Avoid expressions such as *totally awesome, you know,* and *like;* use emojis sparingly.

**5  Apply writing techniques that improve the tone, clarity, and effectiveness of a message.**
- Use positive language that tells what can be done rather than what can't be done (*With your support, the project will succeed* rather than *The project won't succeed without your support*).
- Be courteous rather than rude, preachy, or demanding.
- Provide reasons for a request to soften the tone of a message.
- Avoid biased language that excludes, stereotypes, or offends people (*lady lawyer, spry old gentleman, confined to a wheelchair*).
- Choose plain language (*equal* instead of *commensurate*), familiar terms (*end* instead of *terminate*), and precise words (*analyze* instead of *think about*).

## Key Terms

| | | |
|---|---|---|
| communication 39 | receiver 40 | richness 46 |
| meaning 39 | decoding 40 | empathy 46 |
| encoding 39 | feedback 40 | jargon 53 |
| channel 40 | informational messages 44 | |
| noise 40 | persuasive messages 44 | |

## Chapter Review

1. Define *communication*. When is it successful? (L.O. 1)

2. Describe the five steps in the process of communication. What can disrupt this process? (L.O. 1)

3. In what ways is business writing different from school essays and private messages? (L.O. 2)

4. Describe the components in each stage of the 3-x-3 writing process. Approximately how much time is spent on each stage? (L.O. 2)

5. What eight factors should writers consider in selecting an appropriate channel to deliver a message? What is the difference between a rich and a lean channel? (L.O. 3)

6. How does anticipating and identifying the audience help a business communicator prepare a message? (L.O. 3)

7. What is the "you" view? When can the use of *you* backfire? (L.O. 4)

8. What three techniques for developing a warm, friendly, and conversational tone can communicators use in business messages? (L.O. 4)

9. What are three ways to avoid biased language? Give an original example of each. (L.O. 5)

10. Name five gender-biased words and their improved versions. (L.O. 5)

## Critical Thinking

11. Have you ever read something complex and blamed yourself for not understanding it? Fergal McGovern, CEO of VisibleThread, argues that it's not your fault, particularly if the subject is investing. He blames "turgid" and "dense" writing. He thinks that even complex ideas can be expressed in natural, plain language.[13] Do you agree? If so, how can writers do this? (L.O. 4)

12. Digital communication channels have overtaken face-to-face and voice-to-voice communication in the workplace. How has this shift changed the fundamental process of communication? (L.O. 1)

13. Do short messages also require that communicators follow a writing process? Why or why not? (L.O. 2)

14. Writers sometimes use abbreviations such as *FYI* (*for your information*) and *ASAP* (*as soon as possible*). Others sometimes use *LOL* (*laughing out loud*), *4 u* (*for you*), and *gr8* (*great*). Where would these abbreviations most likely be found, and how do they contribute to one's professional image? (L.O. 4)

15. How would knowing that your manager might forward your e-mail to higher-ups affect how you write your e-mail message? Which characteristics of your e-mail might change? (L.O. 3)

## Writing Improvement Exercises

### Audience Benefits and the "You" View (L.O. 4)

**YOUR TASK.** Revise the following sentences to emphasize the perspective of the audience and the "you" view.

16. Because we have automated our mobile worker trip forms, we need all employees to use the SmartTrip travel reimbursement mobile app. This is the fastest way to be reimbursed.

17. We are issuing all our customers new chip-enabled credit cards to replace expired or lost cards and prevent increasingly costly payouts we have suffered from cyberfraud.

18. Our strict safety policy does not allow us to rent power equipment to anyone who cannot demonstrate sufficient skill in its use.

19. We're asking that all employees fill out the online survey by April 1 so that we may develop a master schedule for summer vacations more efficiently.

20. Our app developers are excited to announce a new free app called FanMile that we believe will entice fans to share, like, and subscribe to your content.

21. To minimize the cost of having our coaches set up your team training sessions in our limited office space, we suggest conducting customized team training for your employees right in your own building.

22. We take pride in our national policy of selling name brands at discount prices. That's why we can allow store credit, but we cannot give cash refunds on returned merchandise.

## Conversational but Professional (L.O. 4)

**YOUR TASK.** Revise the following to make the tone conversational yet professional.

23. BTW, Madison blew a gasket when the manager accused the whole department of ripping off pricey office supplies.

24. As per your recent request, the undersigned is happy to inform you that we are sending you forthwith the procedure manuals you requested.

25. Kindly be informed that it is necessary for you to designate the model number of the laser cutting machine before we can ship your order.

26. Pursuant to your e-mail of the 4th, please be advised that your shipment was sent March 6.

27. R head honcho wz like totally raggety kuz I wz sick n stuff n mist the team meet. Geez!

28. The undersigned respectfully reminds affected individuals that employees desirous of changing their health plans must do so before December 31.

## Positive and Courteous Expression (L.O. 5)

**YOUR TASK.** Revise the following statements to make them more positive and courteous.

29. We are sorry to let you know that we can offer the 30 percent rebate only to the first 25 buyers, so hurry up!

30. Construction on your building is at a standstill because the contractor is unable to pour footings until the soil is no longer soggy.

31. A travel visa cannot be issued until an application is completed and a recent photo is included.

32. Your message of June 1 claims that the blade in your food processor malfunctioned. Although you apparently failed to read the operator's manual, we are sending you a replacement blade PLUS another manual. Next time read page 18 carefully so that you will know how to attach this blade.

33. Customers are ineligible for the 25 percent discount if they fail to provide the discount code at the time of purchase.

34. As team leader, you apparently failed to remember that you have already assigned me two gigantic and complex research tasks, and now you have dumped another big job on me—one that I can't possibly begin until after I finish the other two jobs.

## Bias-Free Language (L.O. 5)

**YOUR TASK.** Revise the following sentences to reduce bias (e.g., gender, racial, ethnic, age, and disability).

35. The conference in Honolulu offers special side trips for the wives of executives.

36. Sports Research International hired Demarcus Jones, an African American, for the position of social media coordinator.

37. In the past a skilled assistant would proofread her boss's documents and correct any errors he made.

38. Douglas Luna is crippled with arthritis, but his crippling rarely interferes with his work.

39. Recently elected to the city council are a lady lawyer, an Indian CPA, and two businessmen.

## Plain Language and Familiar Words (L.O. 5)

**YOUR TASK.** Revise the following sentences to use plain language and familiar words.

40. Civil Service exams were once required for federal government jobs, but they were phased out subsequent to the passage of antidiscrimination laws.

41. To expedite ratification of the agreement, we beseech you to vote in the affirmative.

42. Although the remuneration for the position of social media consultant seems low, it is commensurate with other pay packages for similar positions.

43. The attorney tried to obfuscate the issue with extraneous and superfluous data.

44. Although researchers dialogued with individual students on campus, subsequent group interviews proved fruitless.

## Precise, Vigorous Words (L.O. 5)

**YOUR TASK.** From the choices in parentheses, select the most precise, vigorous words.

45. If you receive two job offers at once, you can probably (*get, land, negotiate*) a better deal.

46. Dakota's outstanding report contains (*a lot of, loads of, reams of*) helpful data.

47. The CEO said that we must (*review, change, reduce*) overtime hours to (*fix, balance, rework*) the budget.

48. Our operations manager demanded a (*substantial, 20 percent, big*) reduction in staff travel expenditures.

49. In the courtroom the attorney (*said, alleged, thought*) that the car was stolen.

50. As you suggested, we will (*question, interrogate, probe*) our accountant.

## Selecting Communication Channels (L.O. 3)

**YOUR TASK.** Using Figure 2.5, suggest the best communication channels for the following messages. Assume that all channels are available. Be prepared to explain your choice.

51. You want to know what team members are available immediately for a quick video conference. They are all workaholics and glued to their mobile devices.

52. As a manager during a company reorganization, you must tell nine workers that their employment is being terminated.

53. You need to know whether Miguel in Reprographics can produce a rush job for you in two days.

54. A prospective client in France wants price quotes for a number of your products—*vite, vite*!

55. As vice president for community relations, you want to explore the possibility of developing service learning programs with several nearby colleges and universities.

56. You must respond to a letter from the Internal Revenue Service informing you that your company did not pay the correct amount for last quarter's employer's taxes.

## Radical Rewrites

**Note:** Radical Rewrites are provided at **www.cengage.com** for you to download and revise. Your instructor may show a suggested solution.

From Chapter 2 through Chapter 7, you will find Radical Rewrite cases. These are poorly written messages that invite you to apply the writing techniques you have been learning. Rewriting is an excellent way to help you build writing skills. It enables you to focus on revising and not on supplying a context or generating imaginary facts. Your instructor's feedback regarding your strengths and challenges will speed your growth as a business communicator. Note that this exercise emphasizes *revising*, not correcting grammar and mechanics.

### 2.1 Radical Rewrite: Salvaging a Negative, Unprofessional Message (L.O. 4, 5)

The following e-mail from Avianca Keller, the vice president of employee relations, seeks to help supervisors and managers write safe and helpful performance reviews.

**YOUR TASK.** Analyze the problematic e-mail. List at least five weaknesses. Pay special attention to its tone. Your instructor may ask you to revise the e-mail so that it reflects some of the writing techniques you learned in this chapter. How can you make this e-mail more courteous, positive, concise, precise, and audience centered? Your instructor may ask you to revise this message as a collaboration project using Google Docs or Word's Track Changes and Comment features.

**To:** All Supervisors and Departmental Managers
**From:** Avianca Keller <akeller@rubin.com>
**Subject:** Legally Risky Employee Evaluations

All,

Although it pains me to do this, I must warn you all that recently one of our employees filed a lawsuit against the company because of comments a supervisor made during a performance evaluation. This did not have to happen. Look, people, you must be smarter!

Because none of you are dense, here are suggestions you must share with all supervisors and managers regarding company-wide evaluations:

- It goes without saying that you cannot accurately evaluate an employee's performance unless you have a system to measure that performance. That's why the obvious very first step is developing performance standards and goals for each employee. To be effective, these standards and goals must be shared with the employee. However, don't do it orally. Do it in writing.

- The performance of each employee must be monitored throughout the year. Keep a log for each worker. Note memorable incidents or projects in which he was involved. But don't just keep favorable comments. I know that many of you are understandably averse to placing negative comments in an employee's file. However, MAN UP! Even negative comments must be included as part of the evaluation process.

- Once a year each employee must be formally evaluated in a written performance appraisal—yes, I do mean written! In a face-to-face meeting, let the employee know what you think they did well and in what areas the employee may be able to improve. Be specific, give deadlines, be honest, and be realistic.

Giving evaluations can be difficult. With careful preparation, however, the process can be smooth and safe. Don't allow yourself or the company to get involved in any more legal ramifications.

Avianca Keller
Vice President, Employee Relations
akeller@rubin.com


List at least five weaknesses.


## Activities

## 2.2 Analyzing Primary and Secondary Audiences (L.O. 3)

**YOUR TASK.** Using the questions in Figure 2.4, write a brief analysis of the audience for each of the following communication tasks. What kind of reaction should you expect from the primary reader and any secondary readers? What tone should you convey?

a. As a soon-to-graduate senior, you are writing a profile that you will post to LinkedIn. You hope it will land you a job offer.
b. As an administrator of your city water department, you must write a letter to water users explaining that the tap water may taste and smell bad; however, it poses no threats to health.
c. You are a member of an organization promoting Earth Day. You have been asked to encourage your office to save paper, and you know of several tips for doing that. You want to persuade your boss to send a message to employees with several tips that you will provide.
d. You are about to send an e-mail to your regional sales manager describing your visit to a new customer who is demanding special discounts.
e. You are preparing an unsolicited sales message to a targeted group of executives promoting part-time ownership in a corporate jet plane.
f. You are planning to write an e-mail to your manager to try to persuade her to allow you to attend a leadership training program that will require two hours of weekly release time for ten weeks.

## 2.3 Is Plain Writing a Civil Right? (L.O. 5)

E-Mail | Team

As an intern at VisibleThread, the compliance and clarity experts, you and several other interns have been assigned the task of researching the history of the plain writing/plain language movement. Many of its principles are embodied in the business model of VisibleThread. Your training manager Fiona McBride thinks that this research will help you better understand the company goals. She found a stirring quotation from Annetta Cheek, who kicked off the Plain Language Symposium in Washington, D.C., some years ago. Ms. Cheek claimed that "plain writing is a civil right."[14] Do you agree?

**YOUR TASK.** As part of your intern training, Ms. McBride asks you and other interns to prepare a brief history of the movement. Explain how it got started, who must comply, and whom it benefits. She also asks that you list and illustrate at least five of its guidelines with original examples. Individually or as a team, prepare a one-page report as an e-mail directed to Fiona.McBride@ vthread.com but submitted to your instructor.

## Grammar/Mechanics Checkup 2

## Pronouns

Review Sections 1.07–1.09 in the Grammar Review section of the Grammar/Mechanics Handbook. Select the correct form to complete each of the following statements. Record your answer and the appropriate Grammar/Mechanics section to illustrate the principle involved. When you finish, compare your responses with those at the bottom of the page. If your answers differ, study carefully the principles in parentheses.

|     |     |
| --- | --- |
| a     (1.09d) | **EXAMPLE**   The Ride Share Committee will introduce (a) *its*, (b) *their* employee carpool program soon. |
| _____ | 1.   (a) *Who*, (b) *Whom* in this department have you considered for promotion? |
| _____ | 2.   When parking your car facing uphill, turn (a) *it's*, (b) *its* front wheels away from the curb and let it roll back a few inches. |
| _____ | 3.   Every text message sent between the CEO and (a) *he*, (b) *him* was revealed during the discovery phase before the deposition. |
| _____ | 4.   I was expecting to meet with Neta. Was it (a) *she*, (b) *her* who called to explain the delay? |
| _____ | 5.   It looks as if (a) *yours*, (b) *your's* is the only financial report that discusses global markets. |
| _____ | 6.   Send the sales figures to (a) *whoever*, (b) *whomever* requests them. |
| _____ | 7.   My sister and (a) *I*, (b) *me*, (c) *myself* responded to the same casting call at The Walt Disney Studios. |
| _____ | 8.   Every player on the women's soccer team must wear (a) *her*, (b) *their* uniform to be able to play. |
| _____ | 9.   Amandeep asked Otilia and (a) *I*, (b) *me*, (c) *myself* to help him finish a presentation on retirement benefits. |
| _____ | 10.   Everyone except the budget director and (a) *I*, (b) *me*, (c) *myself* heard the fire alarm. |
| _____ | 11.   No one knows that potential building site better than (a) *she*, (b) *her*, (c) *herself*. |
| _____ | 12.   If neither Ellis nor I receive our vaccination in time, (a) *him and me*, (b) *he and I* cannot make the trip. |
| _____ | 13.   One of the mothers visiting the zoo left (a) *their*, (b) *her* smartphone on the bus. |
| _____ | 14.   Yeong and (a) *I*, (b) *myself*, (c) *me* are planning our community service day. |
| _____ | 15.   A proposed change to the bylaws was sent to (a) *we*, (b) *us* owners before the vote. |

**1.** b (1.08!) **2.** b (1.08d) **3.** b (1.08c) **4.** a (1.08b) **5.** a (1.08d) **6.** a (1.08b) **7.** a (1.08!) **8.** a (1.08a) **9.** b (1.08c) **10.** b (1.08c) **11.** a (1.08f) **12.** b (1.08a) **13.** b (1.08c) **14.** a (1.08a) **15.** b (1.08g)

## Editing Challenge 2

Every chapter provides an editing exercise to build your grammar and mechanics skills. The following e-mail is a short report about beverage sweeteners from a researcher to his boss. In this message look for errors in proofreading, grammar, spelling, punctuation, capitalization, word use, and number form. Be especially alert to problems with noun plurals, pronouns, and *then/than* and *there/their*. Study the guidelines in the Grammar/Mechanics Handbook (Appendix D), including the lists of Confusing Words and Frequently Misspelled Words. **Hint:** You should make about 30 edits.

**YOUR TASK.** Edit the following by (a) inserting corrections in your textbook or on a photocopy using proofreading marks in Appendix C or (b) downloading the message from **www.cengage.com** and correcting at your computer using the MS Word feature Track Changes.

---

**To:** Cruz Wayan <cwayan@interbev.com>
**From:** Yuuki Tamandani <ytamandani@interbev.com>
**Subject:** PepsiCo and Coca-Cola Introduce New Sweeteners

Cruz:

As you requested, herewith is the initial report from Ron and I on the topic of beverage sweeteners. As you may all ready know, PepsiCo and Coca-Cola launched two drinks using sweeteners that are new to the market.

Last week Pepsi announced Pepsi True, it's first mid-calorie soda since the failed launch of Pepsi Next more then two years ago. Sweetened with a blend of sugar and stevia, which is a plant-derived sugar substitute Pepsi True contains only 60 calories. Thats 30 percent fewer calorys then regular cola. As sales of low-calorie diet sodas like Diet Pepsi drop, mid-calorie alternatives blend sugar with other sweetners. According to inside information obtained by Ron and I, Pepsi True was tested on the shelves of grocerys, mass merchants, and convenience stores in 5 cities in Florida.

Last month Coca-Cola rolled out Coca-Cola Life which is also sweetened with sugar and stevia. It was successfully tested in the U.K. and South America. In our own in-house research, all of the office gals really liked Life.

BTW, approval from the Food and drug administration did not materialize automatically for these new sweeteners. FDA approval was an issue because studys conducted in the early 1990s suggested that their were possible adverse health affects from the use of stevia-based products. However the herb has been approved for use in 12 countrys.

Both PepsiCo and Coca-Cola eventually received FDA approval, and there products are all ready on the market. Ron and I cannot submit our full report until after him and I complete our investigation in October.

Yu
Yuuki Tamandani
Senior Investigator | Research and Development | ytamandani@interbev.com
Office: (424) 644-1080 | Cell: (562) 851-8937

---

## Practicing Your Problem-Solving and Decision-Making Skills

Browsing job postings on Indeed, you will see ads in the hundreds of thousands explicitly asking for critical-thinking skills (133,170); decision-making skills (210,600); and, most coveted, problem-solving skills (403,300). It's not a coincidence. These crucial professional skills are vital in a workplace that needs employees who can think, work independently, and make sound decisions.

Much of this book is devoted to helping you solve problems and communicate those decisions to management, fellow workers, clients, the government, and the public. Facing a challenge, most of us do a lot of worrying before identifying the concerns or making a decision. You can convert all that worrying to directed critical thinking by following these steps:

1. **Identify and clarify the problem.** Your first task is to recognize that a problem exists. Some problems are big and unmistakable, such as failure of a shipping company to deliver packages to customers on time. Other problems may be continuing annoyances, such as regularly running out of toner for a networked office printer in heavy use. The first step in reaching a solution is pinpointing the problem.

2. **Gather information.** Learn more about the problem or situation. Look for possible causes and solutions. This step may mean checking files, calling suppliers, or brainstorming with fellow workers. For example, the shipping company might analyze personnel workloads and traffic patterns in the city at various times of the day to determine the causes of the delays.

3. **Evaluate the evidence.** This is where you apply your critical thinking: Where did the information come from? Does it represent various points of view? What biases could be expected from each source? How accurate is the information? Is it fact or opinion? For example, it is a fact that packages are missing; it is an opinion that they are merely lost, it's not a big deal, and they will turn up eventually.

4. **Consider alternatives and implications.** Draw conclusions from the gathered evidence and propose solutions. Then weigh the advantages and disadvantages of each solution. What are the costs, benefits, and consequences? What are the obstacles, and how can they be handled? Most important, what solution best serves your goals and those of your organization? Here is where your creativity is especially important.

5. **Choose the best alternative and test it.** Select an alternative, and try it out to see if it meets your expectations. If it does, put your decision into action. If it doesn't, rethink your alternatives. The shipping company decided to give its unhappy customers free delivery service to make up for the lost packages and downtime. Be sure to continue monitoring and adjusting the solution to ensure its effectiveness over time.

**CAREER APPLICATION.** As a manager of a much frequented Burger King restaurant, you have a problem. Customers are unhappy with multiple lines for counter service because they don't seem to know where to stand to be the next served. Tempers flare when aggressive customers cut in line, and other customers spend so much time protecting their places in line that they are not ready to order. As the manager, you want to solve this problem. Any new procedures, however, must be approved by a majority of Burger King owners in your district. You know that Burger King's management favors the multiline system because the executives believe that this configuration accommodates higher volumes of customers more quickly than a single-line system does. In addition, customers are turned off when they see a single long line.

### YOUR TASK

- Individually or with a team, use the critical-thinking steps outlined here. Begin by clarifying the problem.

- Where could you gather information? Would it be wise to see what your competitors are doing? How do banks handle customer lines? Amusement parks? Airlines?

- Evaluate your findings and consider alternatives. What are the pros and cons of each alternative?

- With your team, choose the best alternative. Present your recommendation to your class and give your reasons for choosing it.

# Organizing and Drafting Business Messages

**Learning Outcomes**

After studying this chapter, you should be able to do the following:

**1** Compare two forms of research that begin Phase 2 of the 3-x-3 writing process.

**2** Demonstrate methods for organizing ideas to show relationships.

**3** Write effective sentences that avoid fragments, run-ons, and comma splices.

**4** Demonstrate methods for emphasizing ideas, using active and passive voice, developing parallelism, and placing modifiers correctly.

**5** Explain how to create well-organized, coherent paragraphs.

Fizkes/Shutterstock.com

## 3-1 Drafting Workplace Messages Begins With Research

With today's ever-present technology, you may believe or hope that you will never be required to write on the job. The truth is, however, that business, technical, and professional people in this digital age are exchanging more messages than ever before. The faster you can articulate your ideas and the more efficiently you can explain what needs to be said, the more successful and content you will be in your career.

Being able to write efficiently and clearly is also critical to promotions. That's why we devote three chapters to teaching you a tried-and-true writing process, summarized in **Figure 3.1**. This process guides you through the steps necessary to write confidently, but more important, clearly. Instead of struggling with a writing assignment and not

**Figure 3.1  The 3-x-3 Writing Process**

### 1  Prewriting

**Analyze:** Decide on the message purpose. What do you want the receiver to do or believe?

**Anticipate:** What does the audience already know? How will it receive this message?

**Adapt:** Think about techniques to present this message most effectively. Consider how to elicit feedback.

### 2  Drafting

**Research:** Gather background data by searching files and the Internet.

**Organize:** Arrange direct messages with the big idea first. For persuasive or negative messages, use an indirect, problem-solving strategy.

**Draft:** Prepare the first draft, using active-voice sentences, coherent paragraphs, and appropriate transitional expressions.

### 3  Revising

**Edit:** Eliminate wordy fillers, long lead-ins, redundancies, and trite business phrases. Strive for parallelism, clarity, conciseness, and readability.

**Proofread:** Check carefully for errors in spelling, grammar, punctuation, and format.

**Evaluate:** Will this message achieve your purpose? Is the tone pleasant? Did you encourage feedback?

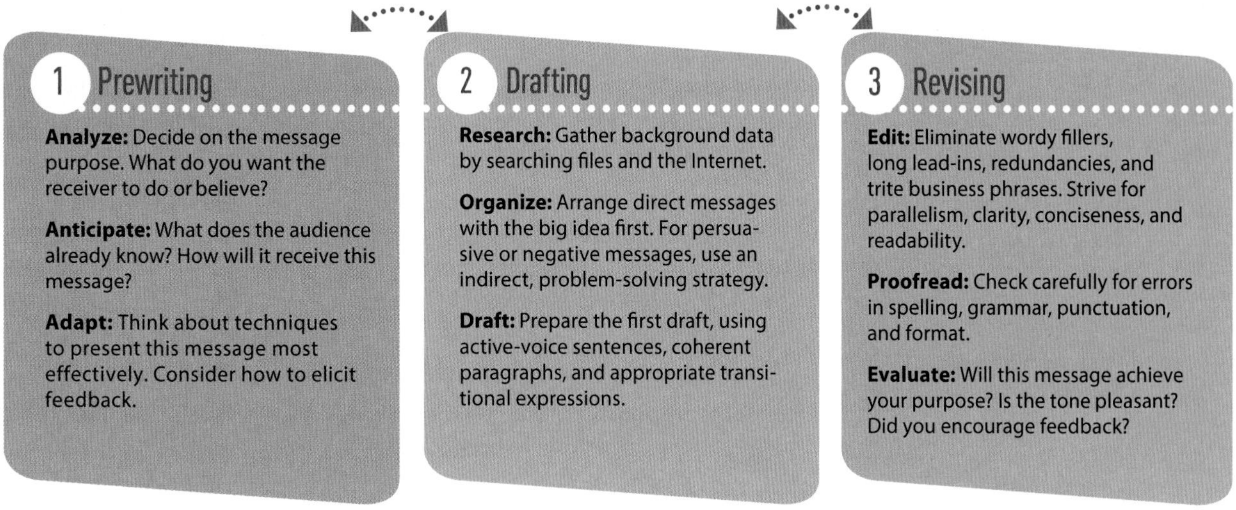

knowing where to begin or what to say, you can use this effective process both in college and on the job.

Chapter 2 focused on the prewriting stage of the writing process. You studied the importance of using a conversational tone, positive language, plain and courteous expression, and familiar words. This chapter addresses the second stage of the process: researching, organizing, and drafting.

**LEARNING OUTCOME 1**

Compare two forms of research that begin Phase 2 of the 3-x-3 writing process.

## 3-1a  The Writing Process Begins With Background Information

No savvy businessperson would begin drafting a message before gathering background information. We call this process *research*, a rather formal-sounding term. For our purposes, however, **research** simply means collecting information about a topic. This is an important step in the writing process because that information helps you shape your message. Discovering significant information after you have almost completed a message often means starting over and reorganizing your thoughts. To avoid annoying second starts and inaccurate messages, thoughtful writers collect information that answers several questions:

- What does the receiver need to know about this topic?

- What is the receiver to do?

- How is the receiver to do it?

- When must the receiver do it?

- What will happen if the receiver doesn't do it?

Whenever your communication task requires more information than you have in your head or at your fingertips, you must conduct research. This research may be informal or formal.

## 3-1b  Informal Research

Many routine tasks—such as drafting e-mails, memos, letters, informational reports, and oral presentations—require information that you can collect informally. Where can you find information before starting a project? The following techniques are useful in informal research:

- **Search your company's files**. If you are responding to an inquiry or drafting a routine message, you often can find background information such as previous correspondence in your own files or those of the company. You might consult the company wiki or other digital and print files. You might also ask colleagues.

- **Talk with the boss**. Get information from the individual giving you the assignment. What does that person know about the topic? What slant should you take? What other sources would that person suggest?

- **Interview the target audience**. Consider talking with individuals at whom the message is aimed. They can provide clarifying information that tells you what they want to know and how you should shape your remarks. Suggestions for conducting more formal interviews are presented in Chapter 10.

- **Create an informal survey**. Gather unscientific but helpful information through questionnaires and telephone or online surveys. In preparing a report predicting the success of a proposed company fitness center, for example, circulate a questionnaire asking for employee reactions.

- **Brainstorm for ideas**. Alone or with others, discuss ideas for the writing task at hand, and record at least a dozen ideas without judging them. Small groups are especially fruitful in brainstorming because people spin ideas off one another. Use your laptop or tablet for a quick, erasable surface to record ideas.

### 3-1c Formal Research

Information for long reports and proposals may be obtained through formal research using primary or secondary sources:

- **Primary sources**. **Primary data** come from firsthand experience. This information might be generated from surveys, interviews, observation, and experimentation. Scientific researchers conduct experiments with controlled variables to produce information that helps solve problems. Because formal research is particularly necessary for reports, you will study resources and research techniques beginning in Chapter 10.

- **Secondary sources**. **Secondary data** come from reading what others have experienced or observed and written about. Books, magazines, journals, and online resources are all considered secondary sources. Most writers conducting research begin with secondary sources. These topics and research techniques are covered in Chapters 9 and 10.

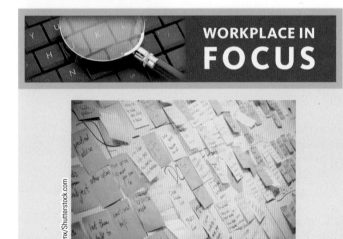

**WORKPLACE IN FOCUS**

Traditionally, teams have generated ideas by **brainstorming**, the spontaneous contribution of ideas by team members. A facilitator records these ideas. The emphasis is on quantity, not quality. Judgment is discouraged because the goal is to think freely. Critics charge that the practice may enable one noisy extrovert to dominate the conversation.[2]

Like brainstorming, **mind mapping** is a process for generating and sorting ideas. However, mind mapping emphasizes visual concepts, beginning with a single concept drawn as an image in the center of a blank page. Associated words and images branch out treelike showing the relationship between the ideas and the central concept. What idea-generating method works for you?

SkyLynx/Shutterstock.com

## 3-2 Organizing Ideas to Show Relationships

After collecting data and generating ideas, business communicators must find a way to organize their information. Skilled writers group similar items together. Then they place ideas in a strategic sequence that helps the reader understand relationships and accept the writer's views.

**LEARNING OUTCOME 2**

Demonstrate methods for organizing ideas to show relationships.

Unorganized messages proceed free-form, jumping from one thought to another. Such messages fail to emphasize important points. Puzzled readers can't see how the pieces fit together, and they become frustrated and irritated. Many communication experts regard poor organization as the greatest failing of business writers. Two simple techniques can help you organize data: the scratch list and the outline.

### 3-2a Creating Lists and Outlines

To develop simple messages, some writers make a quick scratch list of the topics they wish to cover. Next they compose a message directly from the scratch list. Most writers, though, need to organize their ideas—especially if the project is complex—into a hierarchy, such as an outline. The beauty of preparing an outline is that it gives writers a chance to organize their thoughts before becoming bogged down in word choice and sentence structure. **Model Document 3.1** shows the format for a typical outline.

### 3-2b Typical Document Components

How you group ideas into components depends on your topic and your channel of communication. Business documents usually contain typical components arranged in traditional strategies, as shown in **Figure 3.2**. Notice that an e-mail, memo, or letter generally is organized with an opening, body, and closing. Instructions for writing a procedure, such as how to apply for an audit, would proceed through several steps. The organizational plan for an informational report usually includes an introduction, facts, and a summary. However, the plan for an analytical report includes an introduction/problem, facts/findings, conclusions, and recommendations (if requested). The plan for a proposal includes an introduction, a proposed solution, staffing, a schedule and/or costs, and authorization.

These document outlines may seem like a lot to absorb at this time. Later in this book, you will be introduced to all the business documents outlined here, and you will learn how to expertly draft all their parts.

---

**Model Document 3.1 Format for an Outline**

Title: Major Idea or Purpose

I. First major component
   A. First subpoint
      1. Detail, illustrations, edvidence
      2. Detail, illustrations, edvidence
      3. Detail, illustrations, edvidence
   B. Second subpoint
      1.
      2.
II. Second major component
   A. First subpoint
      1.
      2.
   B. Second subpoint
      1.
      2.
      3.

**Tips for Making Outlines**

- Define the main topic in the title.
- Divide the main topic into major components or classifications (preferably three to five).
- Break the components into subpoints.
- Don't put a single item under a major component; if you have only one subpoint, integrate it with the main item above it or reorganize.
- Strive to make each component exclusive (no overlapping).
- Use details, illustrations, and evidence to support subpoints.

---

## Figure 3.2 Typical Major Components in Business Outlines

**E-Mail, Memo, Letter**
I. Opening
II. Body
III. Closing

**Procedure**
I. Step 1
II. Step 2
III. Step 3
IV. Step 4

**Informational Report**
I. Introduction
II. Facts
III. Summary

**Analytical Report**
I. Introduction/problem
II. Facts/findings
III. Conclusions
IV. Recommendations (if requested)

**Proposal**
I. Introduction
II. Proposed solution
III. Staffing
IV. Schedule, costs
V. Authorization

## 3-2c Structuring Ideas Into Strategies

Thus far, you have seen how to collect information, generate ideas, and prepare an outline. How you order the information in your outline, though, depends on the strategy you choose. Two organizational strategies provide plans of action for typical business messages: the direct strategy and the indirect strategy.

The primary difference between the two strategies is where the main idea is placed. In the **direct strategy**, the main idea comes first, followed by details, explanation, or evidence. In the **indirect strategy**, the main idea follows the details, explanation, and evidence. The strategy you select is determined by how you expect the audience to react to the message.

Direct Strategy for Receptive Audiences. In preparing to write any message, you need to anticipate the audience's reaction to your ideas and frame your message accordingly. When you expect the reader to be pleased, mildly interested, or neutral—use the direct strategy. That is, put your main point—the purpose of your message—in the first or second sentence. Dianna Booher, renowned writing consultant, pointed out that typical readers begin any message by thinking, "So what am I supposed to do with this information?"

In business writing you need to signal clearly to the reader: Here is my point! As quickly as possible, tell why you are writing. Compare the direct and indirect strategies in the following e-mail openings. Notice how long it takes to get to the main idea in the indirect opening.

| Indirect Opening | Direct Opening |
|---|---|
| As you may remember, our company has been contemplating strategies to attract better-qualified prospective job candidates. As a result, the Management Council is actively gathering information about a possible internship program that might attract college students. After considerable discussion and investigation, we have voted to launch a pilot program starting next fall. **We are asking for your help in organizing it.** | **Please help us organize a college internship pilot program that the Management Council voted to begin next fall.** Our company has been concerned with attracting better-qualified prospective job candidates. For this reason, the Management Council has been gathering information about an internship program for college students. |

Explanations and details follow the direct opening. Getting to the main idea quickly is important. This direct method, also called **frontloading**, offers at least three advantages:

- **Saves the reader's time**. Many of today's businesspeople can devote only a few moments to each message. Messages that take too long to get to the point may lose their readers along the way.

- **Sets a proper frame of mind**. Learning the purpose up front helps the reader put the subsequent details and explanations in perspective. Without a clear opening, the reader may be thinking, "Why am I being told this?"

- **Reduces frustration**. Readers forced to struggle through excessive verbiage before reaching the main idea become frustrated. They may begin to resent the writer. Poorly organized messages create a negative impression of the writer.

Typical business messages that follow the direct strategy include routine requests and responses, orders and acknowledgments, nonsensitive memos, e-mails, informational reports, and informational oral presentations. All these tasks have one element in common: they do not address a sensitive subject that will upset the reader.

**Indirect Strategy for Unreceptive Audiences.** When you expect the audience to be uninterested, unwilling, displeased, or perhaps even hostile, the indirect strategy is more appropriate. In this strategy you reveal the main idea only after you have offered an explanation and evidence. This approach works well with three kinds of messages: (a) bad news, (b) ideas that require persuasion, and (c) sensitive news, especially when being transmitted to superiors. The indirect strategy has these benefits:

- **Respects the feelings of the audience**. Bad news is always painful, but its negative impact can be lessened by preparing the receiver for it.

- **Facilitates a fair hearing**. Messages that may upset the reader are more likely to be read when the main idea is delayed. Beginning immediately with a piece of bad news or a persuasive request, for example, may cause the receiver to stop reading or listening.

- **Minimizes a negative reaction**. A reader's overall reaction to a negative message is generally improved if the news is delivered gently.

Business messages that could be developed indirectly include e-mails, memos, and letters that refuse requests, deny claims, and disapprove credit. Persuasive requests, sales letters, sensitive messages, and some reports and oral presentations may also benefit from the indirect strategy. You will learn more about using the indirect strategy in Chapters 7 and 8.

In summary, business messages may be organized directly (with the main idea first) or indirectly (with the main idea delayed), as illustrated in **Figure 3.3**.

**Figure 3.3  Audience Response Determines Direct or Indirect Strategy**

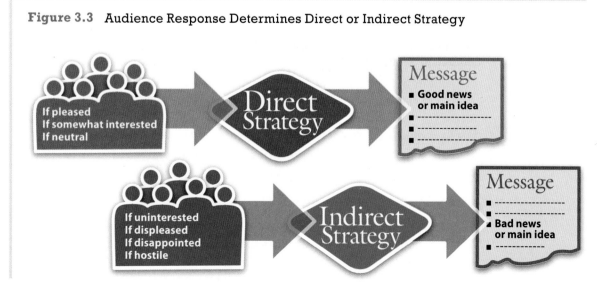

If pleased
If somewhat interested
If neutral

**Direct Strategy**

Message
- **Good news or main idea**
- ----------------
- ----------------
- ----------------

If uninterested
If displeased
If disappointed
If hostile

**Indirect Strategy**

Message
- ----------------
- ----------------
- **Bad news or main idea**
- ----------------

Although these two strategies cover many communication problems, they should be considered neither universal nor absolute. Every business transaction is distinct. Some messages are mixed: part good news, part bad; part goodwill, part persuasion. In upcoming chapters you will practice applying the direct and indirect strategies in typical situations. Then you will have the skills and confidence to evaluate communication problems and vary these strategies depending on your goals and your audience.

# 3-3 Writing a First Draft With Powerful Sentences

After you have researched your topic, brainstormed for fresh ideas, and selected a strategy to organize the data, you are ready to begin drafting sentences. However, at this point many writers suffer from writer's block and can't get started. Organizing your ideas and working from an outline are very helpful in overcoming writer's block. Composition is also easier if you have a quiet environment in which to concentrate. Businesspeople with messages to compose set aside a given time and allow no calls, visitors, or other interruptions. This is a good technique for students as well.

As you begin writing, think about what style fits you best. Some experts suggest **freewriting**. This technique involves getting your thoughts down quickly and refining them in later versions. As you take up each idea, imagine that you are talking to the reader. If you can't think of the right word, insert a substitute or type *find perfect word later*. Freewriting works well for some writers, but others prefer to move more slowly and think through their ideas more deliberately. Whether you are a speedy or a deliberate writer, keep in mind that you are writing the first draft. You will have time later to revise and polish your sentences.

## 3-3a Adding Interest and Variety With Four Sentence Types

To avoid monotony and to add spark to your writing, use a variety of sentence types. You have four sentence types from which to choose: simple, compound, complex, and compound-complex. In the following examples, a single underscore identifies the subject and a double underscore identifies the verb.

**Simple Sentence**

Contains one complete thought (an independent clause) with a subject and predicate verb:

*Our company lacked a social media presence.*

**Compound Sentence**

Contains two complete but related thoughts. May be joined by (a) a conjunction such as *and, but,* or *or*; (b) a semicolon; or (c) a conjunctive adverb such as *however, consequently,* and *therefore*:

*Our company lacked a social media presence, and it hired a specialist.*

*Our company lacked a social media presence; it hired a specialist.*

*Our company lacked a social media presence; therefore, it hired a specialist.*

**Complex Sentence**

Contains an independent clause (a complete thought) and a dependent clause (a thought that cannot stand by itself). Dependent clauses are often introduced

by words such as *although, since, because, when,* and *if.* When dependent clauses precede independent clauses, they always are followed by a comma: *Because our <u>company</u> <u>lacked</u> a social media presence, <u>it</u> <u>hired</u> a specialist.*

**Compound-Complex Sentence**

Contains at least two independent clauses and one dependent clause:

*Because our <u>company</u> <u>lacked</u> a social media presence, <u>it</u> <u>hired</u> a specialist; however, our <u>brand</u> <u>required</u> time to build.*

## 3-3b Avoiding Three Common Sentence Faults

As you craft your sentences, beware of three common traps: fragments, run-on (fused) sentences, and comma-splice sentences. If any of these faults appears in a business message, the writer immediately loses credibility.

One of the most serious sentence errors in English a writer can make is punctuating a fragment as if it were a complete sentence. A **fragment** is usually a broken-off part of a complex sentence. Fragments often can be identified by the words that introduce them— words such as *although, as, because, even, except, for example, if, instead of, since, such as, that, which,* and *when.* These words introduce dependent clauses, as italicized in the following fragment examples. They should not be punctuated as sentences. Make sure such clauses always connect to independent clauses, as shown in the revisions.

| Fragment | Revision |
|---|---|
| *Because most transactions require a permanent record.* Good writing skills are critical. | Because most transactions require a permanent record, good writing skills are critical. |
| The recruiter requested a writing sample. *Even though the candidate seemed to communicate well.* | The recruiter requested a writing sample even though the candidate seemed to communicate well. |

A second serious writing fault is the **run-on (fused) sentence**. A sentence with two independent clauses must be joined by a coordinating conjunction (*and, or, nor, but*), by a semicolon (;), or separated into two sentences. Without a conjunction or a semicolon, a run-on sentence results.

| Run-On Sentence | Revision |
|---|---|
| One candidate sent an e-mail résumé another sent a link to an online portfolio. | One candidate sent an e-mail résumé, and another sent a link to an online portfolio. |
| | One candidate sent an e-mail résumé. Another sent a link to an online portfolio. |
| | One candidate sent an e-mail résumé; another sent a link to an online portfolio. |

A third sentence fault is a **comma splice**. It results when a writer joins (splices together) two independent clauses with a comma. Independent clauses may be joined with a coordinating conjunction (*and, or, nor, but*) or a conjunctive adverb (*however, consequently, therefore,* and others). Notice that clauses joined by coordinating conjunctions require only a comma. Clauses joined by a conjunctive adverb require a semicolon and a comma. To rectify a comma splice, try one of the possible revisions shown here:

| Comma Splice | Revisions |
|---|---|
| Be sure to include keywords from the job description, also include variations of the job title. | Be sure to include keywords from the job description, but also include variations of the job title. |
| | Be sure to include keywords from the job description; however, also include variations of the job title. |
| | Be sure to include keywords from the job description; also include variations of the job title. |

### 3-3c Choosing Short Sentences

Because your goal is to communicate clearly, try to form sentences that average 20 words. Some sentences will be shorter; some will be longer. The American Press Institute established that reader comprehension drops off markedly as sentences become longer.[5] Therefore, in crafting your sentences, think about the relationship between sentence length and comprehension.

| Sentence Length | Comprehension Rate |
|---|---|
| 8 words | 100% |
| 15 words | 90% |
| 19 words | 80% |
| 28 words | 50% |

Instead of stringing together clauses with *and, but,* and *however,* break some of those complex sentences into separate segments. Business readers want to grasp ideas immediately. They can do that best when thoughts are separated into short sentences. On the other hand, too many short sentences will sound monotonous and choppy; they may bore or even annoy the reader. Strive for a balance between longer sentences and shorter ones. Your grammar-checker and spell-checker can show you readability statistics that flag long sentences and give you an average sentence length.

WORKPLACE IN FOCUS

Friedgreenbeans/iStock/Getty Images

When SeaWorld announced it was ending its controversial policy of breeding captive killer whales, the message needed to be clear and precise. Skillful writers emphasize major ideas by placing them front and center, and the blog post announcing the major policy turnaround at the marine theme park did just that: *We're making historic announcements at SeaWorld, including ending orca breeding, introducing new, inspiring and natural orca encounters, and launching new partnerships to protect oceans and marine animals.* The sentence structure highlights the main news immediately and uses the stylistic writing technique of parallelism to create balance and symmetry.[6] What other strategies can you employ to improve your writing techniques?

## 3-4 Mastering Four Helpful Writing Techniques

Business writers can significantly improve their messages by learning to use a few helpful techniques. In this section we focus on (a) emphasizing and de-emphasizing ideas, (b) using active and passive voice strategically, and (c) ensuring parallelism. Writers must also beware of dangling and misplaced modifiers.

### 3-4a Creating Emphasis

When you are talking with someone, you can emphasize your main ideas by saying them loudly or by repeating them slowly. You could even pound the table if you wanted to show real emphasis! Another way you could signal the relative importance of an idea is by raising your eyebrows, shaking your head, or whispering. But when you write, you must rely on other means to tell your readers which ideas are more important than others. Emphasis in writing can be achieved primarily in two ways: mechanically and stylistically.

**Achieving Emphasis Visually.** To emphasize an idea, a writer may use any of the following mechanical devices:

| | |
|---|---|
| **Underlining** | <u>Underlining</u> draws the eye to a word. |
| **Italics and boldface** | Using *italics* or **boldface** conveys special meaning. |
| **Font changes** | Selecting a large, small, or *different* font draws interest. |
| **All caps** | Printing words in ALL CAPS is like shouting them. |
| **Dashes** | Dashes—used sparingly—can be effective. |
| **Tabulation** | Listing items vertically makes them stand out: |
| | 1. First item |
| | 2. Second item |
| | 3. Third item |

Other means of achieving mechanical emphasis include the arrangement of space, color, lines, boxes, columns, titles, headings, and subheadings. Today's software applications (and color printers) provide an array of capabilities for setting off ideas. More tips on achieving emphasis are given in Chapter 4, in which we cover document design.

**Achieving Emphasis Through Style.** Although visual devices are occasionally appropriate, more often a writer achieves emphasis stylistically. That is, the writer chooses words carefully and constructs sentences skillfully to emphasize main ideas and de-emphasize minor or negative ideas. Here are four suggestions for emphasizing ideas stylistically:

- **Use vivid, not general, words**. Vivid words are emphatic because the reader can picture ideas clearly.

| General | Vivid |
|---|---|
| The way we seek jobs has changed. | Technology has dramatically changed how job hunters search for positions. |
| Someone will contact you as soon as possible. | Ms. Rivera will call you before 5 p.m. tomorrow, May 3. |

- **Label the main idea**. If an idea is significant, tell the reader.

| Unlabeled | Labeled |
|---|---|
| Consider looking for a job online, but also focus on networking. | Consider looking for a job online, but, *most important*, focus on networking. |
| We shop here because of the customer service and low prices. | We like the customer service, but the *primary reason* for shopping here is the low prices. |

- **Place the important idea first or last**. Ideas have less competition from surrounding words when they appear first or last in a sentence. Observe how the concept of productivity can be emphasized by its position in the sentence:

| Main Idea Lost | Main Idea Emphasized |
|---|---|
| Profit-sharing plans are more effective in increasing *productivity* when they are linked to individual performance rather than to group performance. | *Productivity* is more likely to be increased when profit-sharing plans are linked to individual performance rather than to group performance. |

- **Give the important idea the spotlight**. Place the main idea in a simple sentence or in an independent clause.

| Main Idea Lost | Main Idea Clear |
|---|---|
| Although you are the first trainee we have hired for this program, we had many candidates and expect to expand the program in the future. (The main idea is lost in a dependent clause.) | You are the first trainee we have hired for this program. (Simple sentence) |

De-Emphasizing When Necessary. To de-emphasize an idea, such as bad news, try one of the following stylistic devices:

- **Use general words**.

| Emphasizes Harsh Statement | De-Emphasizes Harsh Statement |
|---|---|
| Our records indicate that you were recently fired. | Our records indicate that your employment status has recently changed. |

- **Subordinate the bad news**. Place the bad news in a dependent clause connected to an independent clause that contains something positive.

| Emphasizes Bad News | De-Emphasizes Bad News |
|---|---|
| We cannot issue you credit at this time, but we have a special plan that will allow you to fill your immediate needs on a cash basis. | Although credit cannot be issued at this time, you can fill your immediate needs on a cash basis with our special plan. |

## 3-4b Using the Active and Passive Voice Effectively

In a sentence in the **active voice**, the subject (also called the actor) performs the action. In a sentence in the **passive voice**, the subject receives the action. Active-voice sentences are more direct because they reveal the performer immediately. They are easier to understand and usually shorter. Most business writing should be in the active voice. However, passive voice is useful to (a) emphasize an action rather than a person, (b) de-emphasize negative news, and (c) conceal the doer of an action.

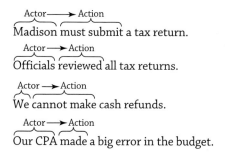

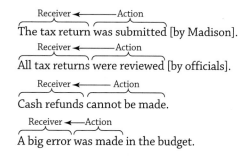

**Active Voice**

Actor → Action
Madison must submit a tax return.

Actor → Action
Officials reviewed all tax returns.

Actor → Action
We cannot make cash refunds.

Actor → Action
Our CPA made a big error in the budget.

**Passive Voice**

Receiver ← Action
The tax return was submitted [by Madison].

Receiver ← Action
All tax returns were reviewed [by officials].

Receiver ← Action
Cash refunds cannot be made.

Receiver ← Action
A big error was made in the budget.

## 3-4c Creating Parallelism

**Parallelism** is an excellent writing technique that produces balanced writing. Sentences written so that their parts are balanced, or parallel, are easy to read and understand. To achieve parallel construction, use similar structures to express similar ideas. For example, the words *computing, coding, recording,* and *storing* are parallel because the words all end in *-ing*. To express the list as *computing, coding, recording,* and *storage* is disturbing because the last item is not what the reader expects. Try to match nouns with nouns, verbs with verbs, and clauses with clauses. Avoid mixing active-voice verbs with passive-voice verbs. Your goal is to keep the wording balanced in expressing similar ideas.

| Lacks Parallelism | Illustrates Parallelism |
|---|---|
| A conference organizer must arrange for the venue, the hospitality, and a person to give the keynote speech. | A conference organizer must arrange for the venue, the hospitality, and a *keynote speaker*. (Matches nouns.) |
| Our primary goals are to increase productivity, reduce costs, and the improvement of product quality. | Our primary goals are to increase productivity, reduce costs, and *improve product quality*. (Matches verbs.) |
| We are scheduled to meet in Baltimore on February 4, we are meeting in Boston on the 18th of March, and in Detroit on June 3. | We are scheduled to meet in Baltimore on February 4, *in Boston on March 18*, and in Detroit on June 3. (Matches phrases.) |
| Darian audits all accounts lettered A through L; accounts lettered M through Z are audited by Jaya. | Darian audits all accounts lettered A through L; *Jaya audits accounts lettered M through Z*. (Matches clauses.) |
| Our Super Bowl ads have three objectives:<br>1. We want to increase product use.<br>2. Introduce complementary products.<br>3. Our corporate image will be enhanced. | Our Super Bowl ads have three objectives:<br>1. *Increase* product use<br>2. *Introduce* complementary products<br>3. *Enhance* our corporate image<br>(Matches verbs in listed items.) |

## 3-4d Dodging Dangling and Misplaced Modifiers

For clarity, modifiers must be close to the words they describe or limit. A **dangling modifier** occurs when the word or phrase it describes is missing from its sentence—for example, *Driving through Malibu Canyon, the ocean came into view.* This sentence says that the ocean was driving through Malibu Canyon. Revised, the sentence contains a logical subject: *Driving through Malibu Canyon, we saw the ocean come into view.*

A **misplaced modifier** occurs when the word or phrase it describes is not close enough to be clear—for example, *Firefighters rescued a dog from a burning car that had a broken leg.* Obviously, the car did not have a broken leg. The solution is to position the modifier closer to the word(s) it describes or limits: *Firefighters rescued a dog with a broken leg from a burning car.*

Introductory verbal phrases are particularly dangerous; be sure to follow them immediately with the words they logically describe or modify. Try this trick for detecting and remedying many dangling modifiers. Ask the question *Who?* or *What?* after any introductory phrase. The words immediately following should tell the reader who or what is performing the action. Try the *Who?* test on the first three danglers here:

| Dangling or Misplaced Modifier | Clear Modification |
| --- | --- |
| Skilled at 3-D printing, the manga character was easily copied by Blake. | Skilled at 3-D printing, Blake easily copied the manga character. |
| Working together as a team, the project was finally completed. | Working together as a team, we finally completed the project. |
| To meet the deadline, all paperwork must be sent by May 2. | To meet the deadline, applicants must send all paperwork by May 2. |
| The recruiter interviewed candidates who had excellent computer skills in the morning. | In the morning the recruiter interviewed candidates with excellent computer skills. |
| As a newbie in our office, we invite you to our Friday after-hours get-together. | As a newbie in our office, you are invited to our Friday after-hours get-together. |

# 3-5 Building Well-Organized Paragraphs

**LEARNING OUTCOME 5**

Explain how to create well-organized, coherent paragraphs.

A **paragraph** is a group of sentences about one idea. The following types of sentences may be organized to express ideas in a well-organized paragraph:

**Topic sentence:** *Expresses the primary idea of the paragraph; often, but not always, comes first in a paragraph.*

**Supporting sentences:** *Illustrate, explain, or strengthen the primary idea.*

## 3-5a Crafting Topic Sentences

A paragraph is unified when it develops a single main idea. That idea is usually expressed in a **topic sentence**, which may appear at the beginning, in the middle, or at the end of the paragraph. Business writers generally place the topic sentence first in the paragraph. It tells readers what to expect and helps them understand the paragraph's central thought immediately.

## 3-5b Developing Supporting Sentences

**Supporting sentences** illustrate, explain, or strengthen the topic sentence. One of the hardest things for beginning writers to remember is that all support sentences in the paragraph must relate to the topic sentence. Any other topics should be treated separately. Supporting sentences provide specific details, explanations, and evidence. The following example starts with a topic sentence about flexible work scheduling and is followed by three supporting sentences that explain how flexible scheduling could work. Transitional expressions are italicized.

**Topic sentence:** Flexible work scheduling could immediately increase productivity and enhance employee satisfaction in our entire organization.

**Supporting sentences:** Managers would maintain their regular hours. For many other employees, *however,* flexible scheduling provides extra time to manage family responsibilities. Feeling less stress, employees are able to focus their attention better at work; *therefore,* they become more relaxed and more productive.

## 3-5c  Creating Paragraph Coherence

Paragraphs are **coherent** when ideas stick together, and one idea leads logically to the next. When the author skips from Step 1 to Step 3 and forgets Step 2, coherence is lost, and most likely the reader is lost, too. Several techniques will help you keep the reader in step with your ideas.

**Sustaining the Key Idea.** Repeating a key expression or using a similar one throughout a paragraph helps sustain a key idea. In the following example, notice that the repetition of *guest* and *VIP* connects ideas.

> Our philosophy holds that every customer is really a guest. All new employees are trained to treat *guests* in our theme parks as *VIPs.* We take great pride in respecting our guests. As *VIPs,* they are never told what they can or cannot do.

**Dovetailing Sentences.** Sentences are **dovetailed** when an idea at the end of one connects with an idea at the beginning of the next. Dovetailing sentences is especially helpful with dense, difficult topics. It is also helpful with ordinary paragraphs, such as the following:

> New hosts and hostesses learn about the theme park and its *facilities.* These *facilities* include telephones, food services, bathrooms, and attractions, as well as the location of *offices.* Knowledge of *offices* and the internal workings of the company is required of all staffers.

**Including Pronouns.** Familiar pronouns, such as *we, they, he, she,* and *it,* help build continuity, as do demonstrative pronouns, such as *this, that, these,* and *those.* These words confirm that something under discussion is still being discussed. However, be careful with such pronouns. They often need a noun with them to make their meaning clear. In the following example, notice how confusing the pronoun *this* would be if the word *training* were omitted.

> All new park employees receive a two-week orientation. They learn that every staffer has a vital role in preparing for the show. *This training* includes how to maintain enthusiasm.

**Employing Transitional Expressions.** Transitional expressions are another excellent device for showing connections and achieving paragraph coherence. These words, some of which are shown in **Figure 3.4**, act as verbal road signs to readers and listeners. **Transitional expressions** enable the receiver to anticipate what's coming, reduce uncertainty, and speed comprehension. They signal that a train of thought is moving forward, being developed, possibly detouring, or ending. As Figure 3.4 shows, transitions can amplify or strengthen a thought, show time or order, clarify ideas, show cause and effect, contradict thoughts, and contrast ideas. Remember that coherence in communication rarely happens spontaneously; it requires effort and skill.

## 3-5d  Controlling Paragraph Length

Although no rule regulates the length of paragraphs, business writers recognize that short paragraphs are less intimidating and more readable than long ones. Paragraphs with eight or fewer printed lines look inviting. Long, solid chunks of print appear formidable. If a topic can't be covered in eight or fewer printed lines (not sentences), consider breaking it into smaller segments.

**Figure 3.4** Transitional Expressions That Build Coherence

| To Amplify or Strengthen | To Show Time or Order | To Clarify | To Show Cause and Effect | To Contradict | To Contrast |
|---|---|---|---|---|---|
| additionally | after | for example | accordingly | actually | as opposed to |
| accordingly | before | for instance | as a result | but | at the same time |
| again | earlier | I mean | consequently | however | by contrast |
| also | finally | in other words | for this reason | in fact | conversely |
| beside | first | put another way | hence | instead | on the contrary |
| indeed | meanwhile | that is | so | rather | on the other hand |
| likewise | next | this means | therefore | still | previously |
| moreover | now | thus | because | yet | similarly |

## Summary of Learning Outcomes

**1  Compare two forms of research that begin Phase 2 of the 3-x-3 writing process.**

- Apply the second phase of the writing process (prewriting) by researching, organizing, and drafting.
- Begin the writing process by researching background information.
- Collect information by answering questions about what the receiver needs to know and what the receiver is to do.
- Conduct informal research for routine tasks by reviewing the company's digital and other files, talking with the boss, interviewing the target audience, conducting informal surveys, and brainstorming for ideas.
- Conduct formal research for long reports and complex problems by searching digital sources or manually, investigating primary sources, and constructing scientific experiments.

**2  Demonstrate methods for organizing ideas to show relationships.**

- For simple messages, make a quick scratch list of topics; for more complex messages, create an outline.
- To prepare an outline, divide the main topic into three to five major components.
- Break the components into subpoints consisting of details, illustrations, and evidence.
- Organize the information using the direct strategy (with the main idea first) when audiences will be pleased, mildly interested, or neutral.
- Organize information using the indirect strategy (with explanations preceding the main idea) for audiences that will be unwilling, displeased, or hostile.

**3  Write effective sentences that avoid fragments, run-ons, and comma splices.**

- Decide whether to compose quickly (*freewriting*) or to write more deliberately—but remember that you are writing a first draft.
- Employ a variety of sentence types including simple (one independent clause), complex (one independent and one dependent clause), compound (two independent clauses), and compound-complex (two independent clauses and one dependent clause).
- Avoid fragments (broken-off parts of sentences), run-on sentences (two clauses fused improperly), and comma splices (two clauses joined improperly with a comma).
- Remember that sentences are most effective when they are short (20 or fewer words).

**4  Demonstrate methods for emphasizing ideas, using active and passive voice, developing parallelism, and placing modifiers correctly.**

- Emphasize an idea visually by using underlining, italics, boldface, font changes, all caps, dashes, tabulation, and other devices.
- Emphasize an idea stylistically by using vivid words, labeling it, making it the sentence subject, placing it first or last, and removing competing ideas.

- De-emphasize ideas by using general words or by placing the idea in a dependent clause.
- For most business writing, use the active voice by making the subject the doer of the action (*the company hired the recent graduate*).
- Use the passive voice (*The recent graduate was hired*) to de-emphasize negative news, to emphasize an action rather than the doer, or to conceal the doer of an action.
- Employ parallelism for balanced construction (*researching, analyzing, and tabulating* rather than *researching, analyzing, and to tabulate*).
- Avoid dangling modifiers (*sitting at my computer, the words would not come*) and misplaced modifiers (*I have the report you wrote in my office*).

## 5 Explain how to create well-organized, coherent paragraphs.
- Build well-organized, unified paragraphs by focusing on a single idea.
- Always include a topic sentence that states the main idea of the paragraph.
- Develop support sentences to illustrate, explain, or strengthen the topic sentence.
- Build coherence by repeating a key idea, using pronouns to refer to previous nouns, and showing connections with transitional expressions (*however, therefore, consequently*).
- Control paragraph length by striving for eight or fewer lines.

## Key Terms

research 63
primary data 64
secondary data 64
brainstorming 64
mind mapping 64
direct strategy 66
indirect strategy 66
frontloading 66

freewriting 68
fragment 69
run-on (fused) sentence 69
comma splice 69
active voice 72
passive voice 72
parallelism 73
dangling modifier 73

misplaced modifier 74
paragraph 74
topic sentence 74
supporting sentences 74
coherent 75
dovetailed 75
transitional expressions 75

## Chapter Review

1. Describe the three parts of the second phase of the writing process. (L.O. 1)

2. What is research, and what activities does it involve? (L.O. 1)

3. What is the difference between a scratch list and an outline? (L.O. 2)

4. When is the indirect strategy appropriate, and what are the benefits of using it? (L.O. 2)

5. What is the difference between a compound and a complex sentence? Provide an original example of each. (L.O. 3)

6. What writing fault is illustrated in the following groups of words, and how can it be remedied? *Because they have been hobbled by government regulations, privacy issues, and internal bureaucracy. Giant banks are struggling to find the magic formula for using social media.* (L.O. 3)

7. When should business writers use active-voice sentences? When should they use passive-voice sentences? Give an original example of each. (L.O. 4)

8. What is the difference between emphasis achieved with *mechanical* means as opposed to emphasis achieved with *stylistic* devices? (L.O. 4)

9. What is a topic sentence, and where is it usually found? (L.O. 5)

10. What is paragraph coherence, and how is it achieved? (L.O. 5)

11. How long should paragraphs be? (L.O. 5)

## Critical Thinking

12. Why are short sentences and short paragraphs appropriate for business communication? (L.O. 4, 5)

13. How can bad writing waste a businessperson's time? A researcher asked that question of workers who read business material an average of 25 hours per week (about half of which was e-mail).[8] What writing flaws do you think they named? Should new employees be trained in writing effectively on the job? (L.O. 1–5)

14. A much-quoted PayScale survey revealed a significant gap in perception between managers and recent graduates. "Overall, the majority of workers (87 percent) feel well prepared (immediately or within 3 months) for their job upon graduation from college. In contrast, only about half of managers (50 percent) feel that employees who recently graduated from college are well prepared for the workforce."[9] The skill most lacking, said the managers, was writing proficiency. What could explain this gap in perception between managers and recent college graduates? (L.O. 1–5)

15. How are speakers different from writers in the way they emphasize ideas? (L.O. 4)

16. Is the indirect strategy of organization ethical, or is it manipulative to delay the presentation of the main idea in a message? (L.O. 2)

## Writing Improvement Exercises

### Sentence Types (L.O. 3)

**YOUR TASK.** For each of the numbered sentences, select the letter that identifies its type:

a. Simple sentence
b. Compound sentence
c. Complex sentence
d. Compound-complex sentence

17. Bottled water consumption rose 2.2 percent in volume last year. _____

18. Because Americans are increasingly health conscious, they are drinking more bottled water than ever before. _____

19. Americans are drinking fewer soft drinks, and heavy-hitters Coca-Cola and PepsiCo are affected negatively. _____

20. Calorie-counting Americans are backing away from sugary soda, but they are also fleeing diet soda. _____

21. Sales volume across the entire beverage industry slid last year; however, smaller players such as Monster Beverage and Red Bull expanded their market share because they appealed to younger consumers. _____

### Sentence Faults (L.O. 3)

**YOUR TASK.** In the following, identify the sentence fault (fragment, run-on sentence, comma splice). Then revise to remedy the fault.

22. Although PepsiCo signed Beyoncé to endorse its soft drinks. Sales continued to plummet.

23. In the beverage industry, the latest sales declines are astonishing. But not surprising.

24. Sugar-filled soft-drink sales have been declining for nine straight years, however diet drinks are not far behind.

25. Coca-Cola hired a creative director PepsiCo tried a new bottle design.

26. Health concerns are not the only problem, soft-drink makers are also facing a boom in alternative beverages.

### Emphasis (L.O. 4)

**YOUR TASK.** For each of the following sentences, circle (a) or (b). Be prepared to justify your choice.

27. Which sentence is more emphatic? Why?

   a. Artisanal, small-batch burgers will compete well against the burger giants.
   b. Although many new burger restaurants are opening, ours will be unique because we plan to feature artisanal, small-batch burgers that we expect will compete well against the burger giants that have controlled the burger restaurant business for decades.

28. Which sentence is more emphatic? Why?

   a. The new restaurant will attract foot traffic and also serve unique burgers.
   b. The new restaurant will attract foot traffic and, most important, will serve unique burgers.

29. Which sentence is more emphatic? Why?

   a. For many reasons hamburgers are definitely American.
   b. Hot, fast, and affordable hamburgers are a uniquely American triumph.

30. Which sentence emphasizes the writer of the report?

   a. Emma wrote a report about the emergence of fast casual restaurants such as Panera Bread and Chipotle Mexican Grill.
   b. A report about the emergence of fast casual restaurants such as Panera Bread and Chipotle Mexican Grill was written by Emma.

31. Which sentence places more emphasis on the seminar?

   a. A training seminar for all new managers starts June 1.
   b. We are pleased to announce that starting June 1 a training seminar for all new managers will include four prominent speakers who own famous restaurants.

32. Which sentence is more emphatic?

   a. Because he has experience in the restaurant business, the new CEO comes highly recommended and is expected to appear at the next meeting of the management board on January 17, which has been rescheduled because of room conflicts.
   b. The new, experienced CEO comes highly recommended. He will appear at the next meeting of the management board on January 17.

33. Which sentence is more emphatic?

   a. Three burger restaurants compete for business: (1) McDonald's, (2) Burger King, and (3) Shake Shack.
   b. Three burger restaurants compete for business:
      (1) McDonald's
      (2) Burger King
      (3) Shake Shack

34. Which sentence is *less* emphatic?

   a. One of our global brand's profits decreased last quarter.
   b. Profits in Esso-branded fuels, services, and lubricants dropped 15 percent last quarter.

35. Which sentence *de-emphasizes* the refusal of government funding?

   a. Pfizer said no to research and development money from the government.
   b. Although Pfizer appreciated potential government funding, the American multinational pharmaceutical corporation financed its R&D independently instead.

36. Which sentence gives more emphasis to emotional intelligence?

   a. She has many admirable qualities, but most important is her emotional intelligence.
   b. She has many admirable qualities, including emotional intelligence, good judgment, and leadership skills.

## Active-Voice Verbs (L.O. 4)

**YOUR TASK.** Business writing is more forceful when it uses active-voice verbs. Revise the following sentences so that verbs are in the active voice. Put the emphasis on the doer of the action. Add subjects if necessary.

   **EXAMPLE**   Laws were passed to protect homeowners from scams.
   **REVISION**   Governments passed laws to protect homeowners from scams.

37. Workers were asked to wear badges with tiny sensors to monitor their communication and activity patterns at Bank of America.

38. Tracking devices are being installed by many companies to gather real-time information on how employees interact.

39. Reliable data about how workers do their jobs are difficult to collect.

40. Concern was expressed by some workers about the difference between Big Data and Big Brother.

## Passive-Voice Verbs (L.O. 4)

**YOUR TASK.** When indirectness or tact is required, use passive-voice verbs. Revise the following sentences so that they are in the passive voice.

**EXAMPLE** Kendall did not submit the report before the deadline.
**REVISION** The report was not submitted before the deadline.

41. Kendall made a serious error in our annual tax figures.

42. We discovered the error too late to correct the annual report.

43. The Federal Trade Commission targeted deceptive diet advertisements by weight-loss marketers.

44. We issue refunds only for the amount of the purchase; we are unable to include shipping and handling charges.

45. An embarrassing mishap was caused because someone misinterpreted the procedures somehow.

## Parallelism (L.O. 4)

**YOUR TASK.** Revise the following sentences so that their parts are balanced.

46. (**Hint:** Match verbs.) Critics complain that young people today are obsessed with playing video games, taking selfies, and they are constantly checking their social media pages.

47. (**Hint:** Match adjectives.) To be hired, an applicant must be reliable, creative, and show enthusiasm.

48. (**Hint:** Match verb phrases.) Job seekers use the Internet to find job opportunities, market themselves to companies, showcase their skills, and they hope to be able to land that dream job.

49. (**Hint:** Match adjectives.) Recent graduates are seeking jobs that are stimulating and a challenge.

50. LinkedIn can help college graduates by sending job alerts, by leveraging their networks, they can research a company, and LinkedIn can take the awkwardness out of asking for recommendations.

51. A company's website might contain valuable information such as you might find current job openings, the company's mission statement might be there, and the names of key hiring managers could be available.

52. When you want to complain about something, sending an e-mail or a letter is better than to make a telephone call.

53. The NSF application for a grant requires this information: proposed funds required for staff salaries, how much we expect to spend on equipment, and what is the length of the project.

## Dangling and Misplaced Modifiers (L.O. 4)

**YOUR TASK.** Revise the following sentences to avoid dangling and misplaced modifiers.

54. While interviewing applicants, questions are often asked by recruiters about qualifications.

55. To be reimbursed, the enclosed application must be filled out and returned.

56. Skilled at social networking, the marketing contract was won by ReachOut.

57. Susan made a presentation about workplace drug problems in our boardroom.

## Organizing Paragraph Sentences (L.O. 5)

**YOUR TASK.** In a memo to the college president, the athletic director argues for a new stadium scoreboard. One paragraph will describe the old scoreboard and why it needs to be replaced. Study the following list of ideas for that paragraph.

1. *The old scoreboard is a tired warhorse that was originally constructed in the 1970s.*

2. *It is now hard to find replacement parts when something breaks.*

3. *The old scoreboard is not energy efficient.*

4. Coca-Cola has offered to buy a new sports scoreboard in return for exclusive rights to sell soft drinks on campus.

5. The old scoreboard should be replaced for many reasons.

6. It shows only scores for football games.

7. When we have soccer games or track meets, we are without a functioning scoreboard.

58. Which sentence should be the topic sentence? _____

59. Which sentence(s) should be developed in a separate paragraph? _____

60. Which sentences should become support sentences? _____

## Building Coherent Paragraphs (L.O. 5)

**YOUR TASK.** Organize the following sentences into coherent paragraphs.

61. Use the information from the previous activity **Organizing Paragraph Sentences** to write a coherent paragraph about replacing the sports scoreboard. Strive to use three devices to build coherence: (a) repetition of key words, (b) pronouns that clearly refer to previous nouns, and (c) transitional expressions.

62. Use the following facts to construct a coherent paragraph with a topic sentence and appropriate transitional expressions in the supporting sentences. Strive for conciseness.

   - Car dealers and lenders offer a variety of loan terms.
   - To get the best deal, shop around when buying a new or used car.
   - You have two payment options: you may pay in full or finance over time.
   - You should compare offers and be willing to negotiate the best deal.
   - If you are a first-time buyer—or if your credit isn't great—be cautious about special financing offers.
   - Buying a new or used car can be challenging.
   - Financing increases the total cost of the car because you are also paying for the cost of credit.
   - If you agree to financing that carries a high interest rate, you may be taking a big risk. If you decide to sell the car before the loan expires, the amount you get from the sale may be far less than the amount you need to pay off the loan.
   - If money is tight, you might consider paying cash for a less expensive car than you originally had in mind.

63. Revise the following wordy and poorly organized paragraph. Add a topic sentence. Correct problems with pronouns, parallelism, and misplaced or dangling modifiers. Add transitional expressions if appropriate.

   *You may be interested in applying for a new position within the company. The Human Resources Department maintains these lists, and you may see which jobs are available immediately. The positions are at a high level. Current employees may apply immediately for open positions in production, for some in marketing, and jobs in administrative support are also available. To make application, these positions require immediate action. Come to the Human Resources Department. On the company intranet you can see the lists showing the open positions, what the qualifications are, and job descriptions are shown. Many of the jobs are now open. That's why we are sending this now. To be hired, an interview must be scheduled within the next two weeks.*

## Radical Rewrites

**Note:** Radical Rewrites are provided at **www.cengage.com** for you to download and revise. Your instructor may show a suggested solution.

Radical Rewrites provide messages that need to be rewritten. Rewriting is an excellent way to help you build writing skills. It enables you to focus on revising and not on supplying a context or generating imaginary facts. Your instructor's feedback regarding your strengths and challenges will speed your growth as a skilled business communicator.

## 3.1 Radical Rewrite: Improving a Faulty E-Mail Message (L.O. 4, 5)

**YOUR TASK.** Study the numbered sentences in the following poorly written e-mail message. In teams or in a class discussion, identify specific sentence faults. **Hint:** You should find five sentence fragments, one dangling modifier, one passive-voice sentence, and one parallelism fault. Your instructor may ask you to revise the message to remedy these writing faults.

**To:** Sierra.Maldonado@gmail.com
**From:** Justin.Corona@premierefinances.com
**Subject:** Responding to Your Question About eBay Profits

Hi, Sierra,

¹As your CPA, I'm happy to respond to your request for clarification of the tax status of profits from eBay. ²Or one of the other online sellers such as Etsy, Amazon, and Bonanza.

³As you are probably already aware, you can use eBay or one of the other sellers to clean out your closets or to run a small business. ⁴Tax liabilities should definitely be clarified. ⁵Although no clear line separates fun from profit or a hobby from a business. ⁶One thing is certain: the IRS taxes all income.

⁷A number of factors will help you determine whether your hobby is a business. ⁸To use eBay safely, the following questions should be considered:

- ⁹Do you run the operation in a businesslike manner? ¹⁰That is, do you keep records, is your profit and loss tracked, and how about keeping a separate checking account?

- ¹¹Do you devote considerable time and effort to your selling? ¹²If you spend eight or more hours a day trading on eBay. ¹³The IRS would tend to think you are in a business.

- ¹⁴Some people depend on the income from their eBay activities for their livelihood. ¹⁵Do you?

- ¹⁶Are you selling items for more than they cost you? ¹⁷If you spend $5 for a garage sale vase and sell it for $50. ¹⁸The IRS would probably consider this a business transaction.

¹⁹All profits are taxable. ²⁰Even for eBay sellers who are just playing around. ²¹If you wish to discuss this further, please call me at 213-456-8901.

Justin Corona
[Full contact information]

## Grammar/Mechanics Checkup 3

## Verbs

Review Sections 1.10–1.15 in the Grammar Review section of the Grammar/Mechanics Handbook. Underline any incorrect form in statements 1–11 below. In the space provided, write the correct form (or C if correct) and the number of the Grammar/Mechanics principle illustrated. For statements 12–15 follow the instructions. When you finish, compare your responses with those at the bottom of this page. If your responses differ, study carefully the principles in parentheses.

| has | (1.10c) | **EXAMPLE** Every one of the top salespeople _have_ been awarded stellar bonuses. |

_____    1. The invitation-only business council _provide_ an opportunity to learn from other executives.

_____    2. Our virtual team _have_ been paving the way to enable more employees to work remotely.

_____    3. Everyone except the new-hires onboarded this year _has_ been issued crisp new uniforms.

_____    4. On the next bus _is_ the quality assurance staff and the logistics team members.

_____    5. Are you sure that your password management software storing login data and your personal profiles _are_ secure?

_____    6. If you _was_ surrounded by noisy machinery for hours each day, you would eventually damage your hearing.

_____ 7. Nationwide, along with most other large national lenders, *offer* a variety of mortgages.

_____ 8. Some of the board members *insists* that the evidence presented in support of the merger was flimsy.

_____ 9. The angry worker's letter of resignation had *laid* on the boss's desk for a week before anyone noticed it.

_____ 10. Either of the surfacings (porous or fine-textured) *are* more cost effective than noise barriers or noise insulation and offer the highest noise reduction.

_____ 11. By now all managers should have *went* to the diversity and inclusion training.

In the space provided, write the letter of the sentence that illustrates consistency in subject, voice, tense, and mood.

_____ 12. a. First, evaluate the attributes of the grinding tools; then, select the machine best suited for the application.
   b. First, evaluate the attributes of the grinding tools; then, the machine best suited for the application must be selected.

_____ 13. a. All visitors must sign in as they enter; only then will you be admitted.
   b. All visitors must sign in as they enter; only then will they be admitted.

_____ 14. a. By adding overhead digital cameras, projectors, and control software, an ideal cutting solution can be achieved.
   b. By adding overhead digital cameras, projectors, and control software, users can achieve an ideal cutting solution.

_____ 15. a. Our manager was a kind joker who always cheered us up.
   b. Our manager was a kind joker who always cheers us up.

1. provides (1.10i) 2. has (1.10i) 3. C (1.10l) 4. are (1.10h) 5. is (1.10e) 6. were (1.10c) 7. offers (1.10d) 8. insist (1.10d) 9. lain (1.15)
10. is (1.10h) 11. gone (1.15) 12. a (1.15c—matches active voice) 13. b (1.15c—matches subjects) 14. b (1.15c—matches active voice)
15. a (1.14b—matches verb tense)

Every chapter provides an editing exercise to build your grammar and mechanics skills. The following letter requires edits in proofreading, grammar, spelling, punctuation, capitalization, and writing techniques covered in this chapter. Study the guidelines in the Grammar/Mechanics Handbook (Appendix D), including the lists of Confusing Words and Frequently Misspelled Words.

**YOUR TASK.** Edit the following by (a) inserting corrections in your textbook or on a photocopy using the proofreading marks in Appendix C or (b) downloading the message from **www.cengage.com** and correcting at your computer.

---

**Gymzo Total Body**
**TRAINING | MASSAGE | WELLNESS**
244 Brickyard Avenue, Detroit, MI 48205 (313) 588-3248

June 8, 2022

Peyton R. Yassin
662 Marquette Drive
Detroit, MI 92695

Dear Peyton Yassen:

You probably choose Gymzo Total Body because it has became one of the top-rated gyms in the Detroit Metro area. Making your work out enjoyable has always been our principle goal. To continue to provide you with the best equipment and programs, your  feedback is needed by my partner and myself.

We have build an outstanding program with quality equipment, excellent training programs, and our support staff is very helpful. We feel, however, that we could have a more positive affect and give more individual attention if we could extend our peak usage time. You have probable noticed that attendance at the gym raises from 4 p.m. to 8 p.m. We wish it was possible to accommodate all our customers on their favorite equipment during those hours. Although we can't stretch an hour. We would like to make better use of the time between 8 p.m. and 11 p.m. With more members' coming later, we would have less crush from 4 to 8 p.m. Our exercise machines and strength-training equipment is lying idle later in the evening.

To encourage you to stay later, security cameras for our parking area are being considered by us. Cameras for some inside facilitys may also be added. We have gave this matter a great deal of thought. Although Gymzo Total Body have never had an incident that endangered a member. We have went to considerable trouble to learn about security cameras. Because we think that you will feel more comfortable with them in action.

Please tell us what you think, fill out the enclosed questionnaire, and drop it in the ballot box during your next visit at the desk. We are asking for your feed back about scheduling your workouts, selecting your equipment, and if you would consider coming later in the evening. If you have any other suggestions for reducing the crush at peak times. Please tell us on the enclosed form.

Cordially,

*Finley Trinidad*

Finley Trinidad, Manager
Enclosure

---

NOTE: When writing to a recipient with a gender-neutral name and you cannot be sure of the person's gender of identity, omit the honorific (Ms., Mrs., or Mr.) and address the individual by the full name, first and last, as in these examples: *Dear Carson Brown, Dear Sawyer Miller,* or *Dear Phoenix Holt.*

# Communication Workshop: Social Media

## Eight Tips for Safe Social Networking

Despite the undeniable upsides of social networking, social media sites track users and sell their information. After all, that's their business model. All this data is not always used legitimately, for instance, for annoying but harmless ad targeting. Savvy business communicators can protect themselves with the following safeguards:

- **Beware of privacy settings.** Many sites promise users control over their privacy. Don't rely on the default settings, which are devised to extract a maximum of data and other information about your device, location, and Internet behavior. Read the site's privacy policy and use its settings to control who sees your basic information, personal information, photos, contact lists, and postings. Not every app needs to know your location or be able to access your photos and camera. Revisit your privacy choices periodically because social media sites can change settings anytime without notice. Don't rely solely on privacy settings. Always use discretion in what you post.

- **Check before you click.** Never let your guard down when presented with hyperlinks in e-mails, messages, texts, or on unfamiliar websites. A scam called *phishing* is still ensnaring unsuspecting users. Even if a message looks as if it's from your bank, visit the organization's website instead of following a link in an e-mail. Beware of videos forwarded from friends on Messenger, for example. The media could infect your device with malware as hackers may have cracked that person's account. Use an alternate method to confirm the message and the media forwarded to you.

- **Realize that Big Data never goes away.** Whether you are making business contacts or visiting fun sites, you are leaving a digital trail practically forever when you have a smart device and browse the Internet—even in incognito mode! Be mindful of the digital "bread crumbs" (cookies) you are leaving behind when you search. Seek out tips from reputable online sources and trustworthy forums suggesting steps toward avoiding nonessential cookies, targeted advertising, and location tracking.

- **Beware of oversharing.** If your employer visits your Instagram page and notices a flurry of activity while you should be working, you might land in the hot seat. If you call in sick and then allow Facebook to show your location, you could reveal that you're playing hooky. Additionally, never give details of upcoming travel or post pictures from your trip while you're away. Criminals scour social networks to find empty houses to burgle.

- **Think twice before friending.** Don't reject friend requests from some coworkers while accepting them from others. Snubbed workers may harbor ill feelings. Don't friend your managers unless they friend you first. Send friend requests only once. On the flip side, don't accept every friend or follow request you receive. Connect only with people you know in real life. Criminals create fake online accounts to befriend others and harvest personal information for nefarious purposes.

- **Be careful of third-party apps.** Polls, quizzes, and games often look innocent, but signing up for them may be giving scammers permission to access your profile. And if you decide to pay for admission or added perks, you may be providing your credit card and private information to cyber criminals.

- **Limit your LinkedIn info.** Think carefully before posting your full résumé to LinkedIn. Yes, you do want to include enough information to help in a job search, but don't make it easy for identity thieves to use that information, for instance, to fill out a loan application.

- **Don't link accounts.** Many websites and apps allow you to log in with Facebook, Gmail, etc., rather than creating a separate account. Doing so enables the social network to share all the information it holds about you, including the date and place of your birth and other personal information. Is the temporary convenience worth the risk?

**CAREER APPLICATION.** Office workers and businesspeople are steeped in technology. Best practices are a key concern in IT and HR departments. We've presented eight salient tips here for the safe use of social media.

**YOUR TASK.** In teams discuss the tips presented here. From your own experience, add more suggestions that can make social media use safer. What risky behavior have you experienced or observed? What violations of decorum and civility have you witnessed? Prepare a list of additional helpful tips. Present them using the format shown here, with each statement a command. Submit your list to your instructor and discuss it in class. Consider making a PowerPoint presentation summarizing your findings and offering cautionary tales for illustration.

# Revising Business Messages

**Learning Outcomes**

After studying this chapter, you should be able to do the following:

**1** Apply techniques to achieve conciseness as part of revision, Phase 3 of the writing process.

**2** Apply revision techniques that simplify and clarify business messages.

**3** Explain how to improve readability with effective document design.

**4** Describe proofreading techniques allowing writers to catch errors in both routine and complex business documents.

**5** Analyze a business message to evaluate its effectiveness.

gpointstudio/Shutterstock.com

## 4-1  Revising: Applying Phase 3 of the Writing Process

In this 24/7 world of work, who has the time to review every message? Proofreading and editing the endless stream of e-mails and other messages business people dash off daily may seem crazy. However, sending quick but sloppy business messages may achieve just the opposite of boosting productivity. Those rushed messages can be confusing and frustrating. They often set into motion a maddening series of back-and-forth queries and responses seeking clarification. To avoid messages that waste time, create confusion, and reduce your credibility, take time to slow down and revise—even short messages.

The final phase of the 3-x-3 writing process focuses on editing, proofreading, and evaluating. **Editing** means improving the content and sentence structure of your message. **Proofreading** involves correcting its grammar, spelling, punctuation, format, and mechanics. **Evaluating** is the process of analyzing whether your message achieves its purpose.

Rarely is the first or even second version of a message satisfactory. Only amateurs expect writing perfection on the first try. The revision stage is your chance to make sure your message says what you mean and makes you look good. Renowned mystery writer Stephen King wisely observed, "To write is human; to edit is divine."[1]

Many professional writers compose the first draft quickly without worrying about language, precision, or correctness. Then they revise and polish extensively. Other writers, however, prefer to revise as they go—particularly for shorter business documents.

Whether you revise immediately or after a break, you will want to examine your message critically. You should be especially concerned with improving its conciseness, clarity, and readability.

## 4-1a  Revising for Conciseness

In business, time is indeed money. Translated into writing, this means that concise messages save reading time and, thus, money. In addition, messages that are written directly and efficiently are easier to read and comprehend. In the revision process, look for shorter ways to say what you mean. Examine every sentence you write. Could the thought be stated in fewer words? Your writing will be more concise if you slash wordy expressions, purge long lead-ins, drop fillers, reject redundancies, and eliminate empty words.

**Slashing Wordy Expressions.** As you revise, focus on eliminating wordy expressions. This takes conscious effort. For example, notice the wordiness in this sentence: *In view of the fact that sales are booming, in all probability profits will increase.* It could be said more concisely: *Because sales are booming, profits will probably increase.* Many vague, wordy expressions can be clarified and shortened as shown here and illustrated in **Figure 4.1**. Notice in this figure how you can revise digital documents with strikethrough formatting and color. If you are revising print documents, use popular proofreading marks.

**Purging Long Lead-Ins.** Concise sentences are free from unnecessary introductory words also called **long lead-ins.** Consider this sentence: *We are using this e-mail to*

**LEARNING OUTCOME 1**
Apply techniques to achieve conciseness as part of revision, Phase 3 of the writing process.

| Wordy | Concise |
|---|---|
| as a means to, in order to | to |
| at a later date | later |
| at this point in time | now, presently |
| despite the fact that | although |
| due to the fact that, inasmuch as, in view of the fact that | because |
| feel free to | please |
| for the period of, for the purpose of | for |
| in addition to the above | also |
| in all probability | probably |
| in the event that | if |
| in the near future | soon |
| in very few cases | seldom, rarely |
| until such time as | until |
| with regard to | about |

**Figure 4.1** Revising Digital and Print Documents

**Revising Digital Documents Using Strikethrough and Color**

~~This is a short note to let you know that, as~~ As you requested, I ~~made an~~ ~~investigation of~~ investigated several of our competitors' websites. Attached ~~hereto~~ is a summary of my findings.~~of my investigation.~~ I was ~~really~~ most interested in ~~making a comparison of the employment of~~ ~~strategies for~~ comparing marketing strategies as well as ~~the use of~~ navigational graphics ~~used~~ to guide visitors through the sites. ~~In view of~~ ~~the fact that~~ Because we will be revising our own website ~~in the near~~ ~~future~~ soon, I was ~~extremely~~ intrigued by the organization, ~~kind of~~ marketing tactics, and navigation at each ~~and every~~ site I visited.

When revising digital documents, you can use simple word processing tools such as strikethrough and color. In this example, strikethroughs in red identify passages to be deleted. The strikethrough function is located on the Font tab. We used blue to show inserted words, but you may choose any color you prefer.

**Revising Printed Documents Using Proofreading Symbols**

When revising printed documents, use standard symbols to manually show your revisions.

~~This is a short note to let you know that,~~ as you requested, I ~~made an~~ investigation of ^ed several of our competitors' websites. Attached ~~hereto~~ is a summary of my findings.~~of my investigation.~~ I was ~~really~~ most interested in ~~making a comparison of the employment of~~ ^comparing strategies for ~~marketing~~ ^marketing as well as ~~the use of~~ navigational graphics ~~used~~ to guide visitors through the sites. ~~In view of the fact that~~ ^Because we will be revising our own website ~~in the near~~ ^soon ~~future,~~ I was ~~extremely~~ intrigued by the organization, ~~kind of~~ marketing tactics, and navigation at ~~each and~~ ^every site I visited.

| Popular Proofreading Symbols | |
|---|---|
| Delete | ℱ |
| Capitalize | ≡ |
| Insert | ∧ |
| Insert comma | ⋀ |
| Insert period | ⊙ |
| Start paragraph | ¶ |

*announce that we are considering a flex work schedule.* Cutting the long lead-in results in a more concise and direct version: *We are considering a flex work schedule.* The meat of the sentence often follows the word *that* or *because,* as shown in the following:

| Wordy | Concise |
|---|---|
| This early announcement is being made at this time because it is now possible for you to sign up for vacation slots. | You may now sign up for vacation slots. |
| We would like to inform all customers that lower airfares may be available at our website. | Lower airfares may be available at our website. OR: You may find lower airfares on our website. |
| I am writing this letter because Dr. Erin Blocher disclosed that your organization was hiring trainees. | Dr. Erin Blocher told me that your organization was hiring trainees. |

**Dropping There is/are and It is/was Fillers.** In many sentences the expressions *there is/are* and *it is/was* function as **unnecessary fillers**. In addition to taking up space, these fillers delay getting to the point of the sentence. Eliminate them by recasting the sentence. Many—but not all—sentences can be revised so that fillers are unnecessary.

| Wordy | Concise |
|---|---|
| *There is* a referee to determine the winner. | A referee determines the winner. |
| *It was* a Facebook post that revealed the news. | A Facebook post revealed the news. |

Rejecting Redundancies. **Redundancies** are expressions that repeat meaning or include unnecessary words. Saying *new innovations* means expressing the same idea twice because *innovation* already describes a *new* process, method, or product. Excessive adjectives, adverbs, and phrases often create redundancies and wordiness. Redundancies do not add emphasis, as some people think. Instead, they identify a writer as inexperienced. As you revise, look for redundant expressions such as the following:

| Redundant | Concise |
|---|---|
| added bonus | bonus |
| adequate enough | adequate |
| basic fundamentals | fundamentals *or* basics |
| collaborate together | collaborate |
| exactly identical | identical |
| each and every | each *or* every |
| final outcome | outcome |
| fewer in number | fewer |
| new beginning | beginning |
| refer back | refer |
| repeat again | repeat |
| small in size | small |
| true facts | facts |

Eliminating Empty Words. Familiar phrases roll off the tongue easily, but many contain expendable parts. Be alert to these empty words and phrases: *case, degree, the fact that, factor, instance, nature,* and *quality.* Notice how much better the following sentences sound when we remove all the empty words:

~~In the case of~~ Google~~, it~~ poured money into augmented-reality glasses.
Because of the ~~degree of~~ research required, the investment was enormous.
~~We are aware of the fact that n~~New products soar when pushed on social media ~~platforms~~.
Except for ~~the instance of~~ Amazon, sales tanked.
Kerry chose a career in a field that was analytical ~~in nature~~. [*OR: Kerry chose a career in an analytical field.*]
Student writing in that class is excellent ~~in quality~~.

Also avoid saying the obvious. In the following examples, notice how many unnecessary words we can cut through revision:

~~When it arrived,~~ I cashed your check immediately. (*Announcing the check's arrival is unnecessary. That fact is assumed in its cashing*.)
As consumers learn more about ingredients ~~and as they become more knowledgeable~~, they are demanding fresher foods. (*Avoid repeating information.*)

**OFFICE INSIDER**

"Clutter is the disease of American writing. We are a society strangling in unnecessary words, circular constructions, pompous frills, and meaningless jargon."[3]

**William Zinsser,**
*renowned writer, literary critic, and author of the classic* On Writing Well

Look carefully at clauses beginning with *that, which*, and *who*. They can often be shortened without loss of clarity. Search for phrases such as *it appears that*. These phrases often can be reduced to a single adjective or adverb such as *apparently*.

~~It appears that~~ Apparently, communal working spaces are popular with remote ~~who work remotely.~~ employees.

If you are offered a new title ~~that seems impressive~~ impressive but it comes without a pay raise, you should respond with a ~~wisely considered~~ wise answer.

The final offer~~, which was submitted in its final form,~~ had been substantially altered.~~in many substantial ways.~~

## 4-1b Writing Concise Social Media Messages

*Microblogging* is a term you probably won't hear very often, but chances are you have posted a short message today. As its name suggests, **microblogging** refers to messaging on sites such as Twitter, Tumblr, or Plurk; some would include Facebook's status update feature, Snapchat, and other services.

Businesses monitor social media to see what's being said about them and their brands. They can respond immediately and often solve customer problems. Companies are also using short messaging to make announcements, promote their products, and build goodwill.

Although Twitter doubled the number of characters allowed for tweets, most users still keep their messages under 140 characters because brevity is expected on services such as Twitter, and attention spans are short.

**Examples of Business Twitter Messages.** Regardless of the short messaging platform, conciseness is critical. Your messages must be short—without straying too far from conventional spelling, grammar, and punctuation. Sound difficult? It is, but it can be done, as shown in the following 140-character examples of business tweets:

Source: JetBlue

**Replying to Customer**
**@JetBlue**
**@RMLazo 13 Your flight is currently scheduled to leave at 11 a.m. Hang in there. We'll have you on your way as soon as possible**

Source: British Gas

**Sharing Useful Information**
**@BritishGas**
**@CleverMom Some boilers can be confusing. Please check our boiler manual to help you figure it out. Try http://po.st/BoilerManual Sarah**

Source: HubSpot

**Presenting Fresh Facts**
**@HubSpot**
**72.6% of salespeople using social media actually outperformed their colleagues who were not on social media: hub.am/14ikdDS**

Source: SUBWAY

**Promoting Products**
**@SUBWAY**
**It's #FridayThe 13th! It might be an old wive's tale but we hear a Bacon, Egg & Cheese w/Avocado counteracts bad luck.**

Source: Zappos

**Announcing Closure for Company Party**
**@Zappos**
**Hi all! We are closed for our annual Vendor Party! We will reopen at 7am PST tommorrow. We can still be reached at cs@zappos.com if needed.**

**Tips for Writing Concise, Effective Business Tweets.** Your short messages will be most effective if you follow these tips:

- Include only main ideas focused on useful information.
- Choose descriptive but short words.
- Personalize your message if possible.
- Use hashtags so that your tweets are categorized around topics and easier to find.
- Be prepared to draft several versions striving for conciseness, clarity, and, yes, correctness.

It's like playing a game: can you get your message across in only 140 characters? You'll learn more about communication technology in Chapter 5.

# 4-2 Ensuring Message Clarity

"Clarity is the most important characteristic of good business writing," insists Grammar Girl podcaster Mignon Fogarty—and we agree![5] A clear message is one that is immediately understood. Today's employees, customers, and investors want to be addressed in a clear and authentic way. Fuzzy, long-winded, and careless writing hinders comprehension.

Readers understand better when information is presented clearly and concisely. A Dartmouth study found a huge advantage in presenting drug facts concisely, as **Figure 4.2** shows. Several techniques can improve the clarity of your writing: applying the **KISS** formula (Keep It Short and Simple), dumping trite business phrases, scrapping clichés and buzzwords, rescuing buried verbs, curbing exuberance, and opting for precise words.

**LEARNING OUTCOME 2**

Apply revision techniques that simplify and clarify business messages.

## 4-2a Keeping It Short and Simple

To achieve clarity, resist the urge to show off or be fancy. Remember that your goal is not to impress a reader. As a business writer, your goal is to *express*, not *impress*. Be guided by KISS: *Keep it short and simple.* Use active-voice verbs to avoid unclear, pompous language as shown here:

| Wordy and Unclear | Improved |
|---|---|
| High-quality environments for children are a necessary precondition for facilitation and enhancement of the ongoing learning process. | To learn properly, children need good schools. |
| In regard to the matter of obtaining optimal results, it is essential that employees be given the implements that are necessary for their work to be completed satisfactorily. | For best results, give employees the tools they need to do their work. |

### Figure 4.2  Concise Drug Facts Win With Consumers

 **People who correctly quantified a heart drug's benefits after reading concise fact box.** 72%

 **People who correctly quantified a heart drug's benefits after reading the company's long ad.** 9%

Consumers understand drug effects better when the information is presented concisely and clearly. A Dartmouth University study revealed that concise fact boxes were superior to the tiny-type, full-page DTC (direct-to-consumer) advertisements that drug manufacturers usually publish.

## 4-2b Dumping Trite Business Phrases

In an attempt to sound businesslike, some business writers repeat **trite expressions**. These are stale overused phrases that have lost their vigor. Your writing will sound fresher if you eliminate these trite phrases or find more original ways to convey the idea.

| Trite Phrase | Improved |
| --- | --- |
| as per your request | as you requested |
| pursuant to your request | at your request |
| enclosed please find | enclosed is |
| every effort will be made | we'll try |
| in accordance with your wishes | as you wish |
| in receipt of | have received |
| please do not hesitate to | please |
| under separate cover | separately |
| respond forthwith | respond immediately |
| with the exception of | except |
| with reference to | about |

## 4-2c Cutting Clichés

**Clichés** are expressions that have become exhausted by overuse. Many cannot be explained, especially to those who are learning the language or are new to writing. Clichés lack not only freshness but also clarity. Instead of repeating clichés such as the following, try to find another way to say what you mean.

| | |
| --- | --- |
| below the belt | last but not least |
| better than new | make a bundle |
| beyond a shadow of a doubt | pass with flying colors |
| easier said than done | quick as a flash |
| exception to the rule | shoot from the hip |
| fit the bill | stand your ground |
| first and foremost | think outside the box |
| good to go | true to form |

## 4-2d Shunning Slang and Buzzwords

**Slang** is composed of informal words with arbitrary and extravagantly changed meanings. These words quickly go out of fashion because they are no longer appealing when everyone begins to understand them. If you want to sound professional, avoid expressions such as *snarky, lousy, blowing the budget, bombed, trashed,* and social media slang such as *b/c* (because), *FOMO* (fear of missing out), *ICYMI* (in case you missed it), and *br* (best regards).

Equally unprofessional and imprecise are **buzzwords**. These are technical expressions that have become fashionable and often are meant to impress rather than express. Business buzzwords to avoid include empty terms such as *optimize, incentivize, impactful, leveraging, right-size,* and *paradigm shift*. Other vague expressions to stay away from are buzzwords such as *cost effective, positioned to perform, solutions-oriented,* and *value-added services with end-to-end fulfillment*.

**OFFICE INSIDER**

In a survey of 547 workers who write on the job, a majority said that "what they read is frequently ineffective because it's too long, poorly organized, unclear, filled with jargon, and imprecise. . . . Entry-level employees get little training in how to write in a brief, clear, and incisive way."[6]

**Josh Bernoff,** *author of business writing books including* Groundswell

**WORKPLACE IN FOCUS**

Girts Ragelis/ Shutterstock.com

Buzzwords abound in business. The COVID-19 pandemic has given us *coronacation* (a forced stay-at-home vacation), *WFH* (abbreviation of *work from home*), and *Zooming* (videoconferencing software Zoom used as a verb). Other common expressions are *blue sky thinking* (brainstorming without limits), *at the end of the day* (essentially, finally), *circle back* (rehash an issue), and *core competency* (distinguishable capability). Business jargon is much criticized as being overused, annoying, and meaningless. Some, however, argue that "buzzwords create a common language in the workplace and help foster collaboration and a sense of belonging."[7] What if your boss and colleagues use expressions that others condemn as buzzwords? Should you use them to fit in?

## 4-2e Rescuing Buried Verbs

**Buried verbs** are those that are needlessly converted to wordy noun expressions—nominalizations. Verbs such as *acquire, establish,* and *develop* are made into nouns such as *acquisition, establishment,* and *development.* Such nouns often end in *-tion, -ment,* and *-ance.* Sometimes called **zombie nouns** because they cannibalize and suck the life out of active verbs,[8] these nouns increase sentence length, slow the reader, and muddy the thought. Notice how you can make your writing cleaner and more forceful by avoiding buried verbs and zombie nouns:

| Buried Verbs | Unburied Verbs |
|---|---|
| take action on | act |
| perform an analysis of | analyze |
| engage in the preparation of | prepare |
| give consideration to | consider |
| make an assumption | assume |
| make a discovery | discover |
| conduct a discussion of | discuss |
| reach a conclusion that | conclude |
| create a reduction in | reduce |

## 4-2f Curbing Exuberance

Occasionally, inexperienced writers show their **exuberance**—over-the-top intensity or enthusiasm—with words such as *very, definitely, quite, completely, extremely, really, actually,* and *totally.* These intensifiers can emphasize and strengthen meaning. Overuse, however, sounds unbusinesslike. Punctuation marks (e.g., multiple exclamation points) can also indicate excessive exuberance. Restrain your enthusiasm and guard against excessive use.

| Excessive Exuberance | Businesslike |
|---|---|
| The manufacturer was *extremely* upset to learn that its smartphones were *definitely* being counterfeited!!! | The manufacturer was upset to learn that its smartphones were being counterfeited. |
| We *totally* agree that we *actually* did not give his proposal a *very* fair trial. | We agree that we did not give his proposal a fair trial. |

### 4-2g Choosing Clear, Precise Words

As you revise, make sure your words are precise so that the audience knows exactly what you mean. Clear writing creates meaningful images in the mind of the reader. Such writing is sparked by specific verbs, concrete nouns, and vivid adjectives. Foggy messages are marked by sloppy references that may require additional inquiries to clarify their meaning.

| Less Precise | More Precise |
|---|---|
| She requested that everyone help out. | Our manager begged each team member to volunteer. |
| They will consider the problem soon. | Our steering committee will consider the recruitment problem on May 16. |
| We received many responses. | The Sales Division received 28 job applications. |
| Someone called about the meeting. | Russell Vitello called about the June 13 sales meeting. |

## 4-3 Improving Readability With Strategic Document Design

LEARNING OUTCOME **3**
Explain how to improve readability with effective document design.

Want to make your readers think you are well organized and intelligent? You can accomplish this by cleverly using document design. Doing so will also enhance the readability of your messages. In the revision process, you have a chance to adjust formatting and make other changes so that readers grasp your main points quickly. Significant design techniques to improve readability include the strategic use of white space, margins, typefaces, fonts, numbered and bulleted lists, and headings for visual impact.

### 4-3a Making White Space Work for You

Empty space on a page is called **white space**. A page crammed full of text or graphics appears busy, cluttered, and unreadable. You can make white space work for you by using headings, bulleted or numbered lists, and effective margins. Remember that short sentences (20 or fewer words) and short paragraphs (8 or fewer printed lines) improve readability and comprehension. As you revise, think about shortening long sentences. Consider breaking up long paragraphs into shorter chunks.

### 4-3b Understanding Margins and Text Alignment

**Margins** determine the white space on the left, right, top, and bottom of a block of type. They define the reading area, provide important visual relief, and enhance readability. Business letters and memos usually have side margins of 1 to 1.5 inches.

Your word processing software probably offers four forms of margin alignment: (a) lines align only at the left, (b) lines align only at the right, (c) lines align at both left and right, and (d) lines are centered. When letter and word-spacing is adjusted so that lines are aligned at both left and right margins, the margins are said to be **justified**. The text in books, magazines, and other long works is often justified on the left and right for a formal appearance. Take a look at this book. Notice that the right margin is uneven, that is, not justified. If the right margin is unjustified (e.g., in report manuscripts), it is said to be **ragged right**.

Justified text may require more attention to word spacing and hyphenation to avoid awkward empty spaces or rivers of spaces running through a document. When right margins are ragged—that is, without alignment or justification—they provide more white space and improve readability. Therefore, you are best served by using left-justified text and ragged-right margins without justification. Centered text is appropriate for headings and short announcements but not for complete messages.

## 4-3c Choosing Appropriate Typefaces

Business writers today may choose from a number of typefaces provided by their word processing software. A typeface defines the shape of text characters. A wide range of typefaces, as shown in **Figure 4.3**, is available for various uses. Some are decorative and useful for special purposes. For most business messages, however, you should choose from *serif* or *sans serif* categories.

**Serif** typefaces have small features at the ends of strokes. The most common serif typeface is Times New Roman. Other popular serif typefaces are Century, Cambria, Georgia, and Palatino. Serif typefaces suggest tradition, maturity, and formality. They are frequently used for body text in business messages and longer documents. Because books, newspapers, and magazines favor serif typefaces, readers are familiar with them.

**Sans serif** typefaces include Arial, Calibri, Gothic, Tahoma, Helvetica, and Univers. These clean characters are widely used for headings, signs, and material that does not require continuous reading. Web designers often prefer sans serif typefaces for simple, pure pages. For longer documents, however, sans serif typefaces may seem colder and less appealing than familiar serif typefaces.

For less formal messages or special decorative effects, you might choose one of the happy fonts such as Comic Sans or a bold typeface such as Impact. You can simulate handwriting with a script typeface. Despite the wonderful possibilities provided by

### Figure 4.3  A Typeface for Any Occasion

| All-Purpose Sans Serif | Traditional Serif | Happy, Creative Script/Funny | Assertive, Bold Modern Display | Plain Monospaced |
|---|---|---|---|---|
| Arial | Century | Brush Script | Britannic Bold | Courier |
| Calibri | Garamond | Comic Sans | Broadway | Letter Gothic |
| Helvetica | Georgia | Gigi | Elephant | Monaco |
| Tahoma | Goudy | Jokerman | Impact | Prestige Elite |
| Univers | Palatino | Lucinda | Bauhaus 93 | |
| Verdana | Times New Roman | Kristen | SHOWCARD | |

your word processing software, don't get carried away with fancy typefaces. All-purpose sans serif and traditional serif typefaces are most appropriate for your business messages. Generally, use no more than two typefaces within one document.

## 4-3d Selecting Type Fonts and Sizes

**Font** refers to a specific style (such as *italic*) within a typeface family (such as Times New Roman). Here are examples of font styles in the Verdana font family:

| | |
|---|---|
| CAPITALIZATION | <u>underline</u> |
| SMALL CAPS | Outline |
| **boldface** | Shadow |
| *italics* | |

Font styles are a mechanical means of adding emphasis to your words. ALL CAPS, SMALL CAPS, and **bold** are useful for headings, subheadings, and single words or short phrases in the text. ALL CAPS, HOWEVER, SHOULD NEVER BE USED FOR LONG STRETCHES OF TEXT BECAUSE ALL THE LETTERS ARE THE SAME HEIGHT. This makes it difficult for readers to differentiate words. In addition, excessive use of all caps feels like shouting and irritates readers.

**Boldface,** *italics*, and <u>underlining</u> are effective for calling attention to important points and terms. Be cautious, however, when using fancy or an excessive number of font styles. Don't use them if they will confuse, annoy, or slow down readers.

During revision, think about type size. Readers are generally most comfortable with 10- to 12-point type for body text. Smaller type enables you to fit more words into a space. Tiny type, however, makes text look dense and uninviting. Slightly larger type makes material more readable. Overly large type (14 points or more) looks amateurish and out of place for body text in business messages. Larger type, however, is appropriate for headings.

## 4-3e Enhancing Comprehension With Numbered and Bulleted Lists

One of the best ways to ensure rapid comprehension is through the use of numbered or bulleted lists. Lists provide high **skim value**. This means that readers can browse quickly and grasp main ideas. By breaking up complex information into smaller chunks, lists improve readability, understanding, and retention. They also force the writer to organize ideas and write efficiently.

When revising, look for ideas that could be converted to lists, and follow these techniques to make your lists look professional:

- **Numbered lists**: Use for items that represent a sequence or reflect a numbering system.

- **Bulleted lists**: Use to highlight items that don't necessarily show a chronology.

- **Capitalization**: Capitalize the initial word of each line.

- **Punctuation**: Add end punctuation only if the listed items are complete sentences.

- **Parallelism**: Make all the lines consistent; for example, start each with a verb.

In the following examples, notice that the list on the left presents a sequence of steps with numbers. The bulleted list does not show a sequence of ideas; therefore, bullets are appropriate. Also notice the parallelism in each example. In the numbered list, each item begins with a verb. In the bulleted list, each item follows an adjective/noun sequence. Business readers appreciate lists because they focus attention. Be careful, however, not to use so many that your messages look like grocery lists.

Chapter 4: Revising Business Messages

| Numbered List | Bulleted List |
|---|---|
| Our recruiters follow these steps when hiring applicants:<br><br>1. Examine the application.<br>2. Interview the applicant.<br>3. Check the applicant's references. | To attract fashion-conscious customers, we feature the following:<br><br>■ Quality fashions<br>■ Personalized service<br>■ Generous return policy |

## 4-3f Improving Business Messages With Headings

Headings are an effective tool for highlighting information and improving readability. They encourage the writer to group similar material together. Headings help the reader separate major ideas from details. They enable a busy reader to skim familiar or less important information. They also provide a quick preview or review. Headings appear most often in reports, which you will study in greater detail in Chapters 9 and 10. However, main headings, subheadings, and category headings can also improve readability in e-mails, memos, and letters. In the following example, they are used with bullets to summarize categories:

**CATEGORY HEADINGS**

Our company focuses on the following areas in the employment process:

■ **Attracting applicants**. We advertise for qualified applicants, and we also encourage current employees to recommend good people.

■ **Interviewing applicants**. Our specialized interviews include simulated customer encounters as well as scrutiny by supervisors.

■ **Checking references**. We investigate every applicant thoroughly. We contact former employers and all listed references.

In **Model Document 4.1** the writer converts a dense, unappealing e-mail message into an easier-to-read version by applying professional document design. Notice that the all-caps font in the first paragraph makes its meaning difficult to decipher. In the revised version, the writer changed the all-caps font to upper- and lowercase. One of the best document design techniques in this message is the use of headings and bullets to help the reader see chunks of information in similar groups. All of these improvements are made in the revision process. You can make any message more readable by applying the document design techniques presented here.

# 4-4 Catching Errors With Careful Proofreading

Alas, none of us are perfect, and even the best writers sometimes make mistakes. The problem, however, is not making the mistakes; the real problem is not finding and correcting them. Documents with errors affect your credibility and the success of your organization, as illustrated in **Figure 4.4**.

Once the message is in its final form, it's time to proofread. Don't proofread earlier because you may waste time checking items that eventually will be changed or omitted. Important messages—such as those you send to management or to customers or turn in to instructors for grades—deserve careful revision and proofreading.

When you finish a first draft, plan for a cooling-off period. Put the document aside and return to it after a break, preferably after 24 hours or longer. Proofreading is especially difficult because most of us read what we *thought* we wrote. That's why it's important to look for specific problem areas.

**LEARNING OUTCOME 4**

Describe proofreading techniques allowing writers to catch errors in both routine and complex business documents.

## Model Document 4.1 Greater Readability Through Document Design

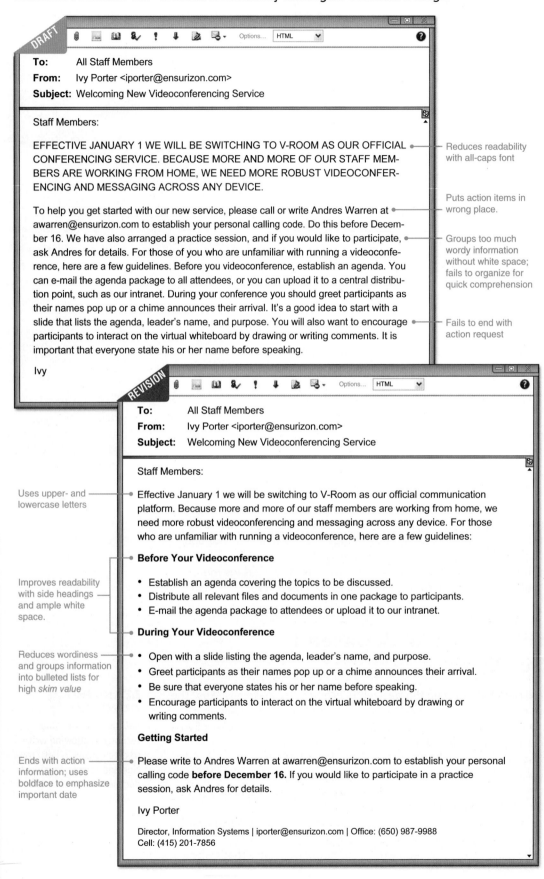

**DRAFT**

**To:** All Staff Members
**From:** Ivy Porter <iporter@ensurizon.com>
**Subject:** Welcoming New Videoconferencing Service

Staff Members:

EFFECTIVE JANUARY 1 WE WILL BE SWITCHING TO V-ROOM AS OUR OFFICIAL CONFERENCING SERVICE. BECAUSE MORE AND MORE OF OUR STAFF MEMBERS ARE WORKING FROM HOME, WE NEED MORE ROBUST VIDEOCONFERENCING AND MESSAGING ACROSS ANY DEVICE.

To help you get started with our new service, please call or write Andres Warren at awarren@ensurizon.com to establish your personal calling code. Do this before December 16. We have also arranged a practice session, and if you would like to participate, ask Andres for details. For those of you who are unfamiliar with running a videoconference, here are a few guidelines. Before you videoconference, establish an agenda. You can e-mail the agenda package to all attendees, or you can upload it to a central distribution point, such as our intranet. During your conference you should greet participants as their names pop up or a chime announces their arrival. It's a good idea to start with a slide that lists the agenda, leader's name, and purpose. You will also want to encourage participants to interact on the virtual whiteboard by drawing or writing comments. It is important that everyone state his or her name before speaking.

Ivy

*Reduces readability with all-caps font*

*Puts action items in wrong place.*

*Groups too much wordy information without white space; fails to organize for quick comprehension*

*Fails to end with action request*

**REVISION**

**To:** All Staff Members
**From:** Ivy Porter <iporter@ensurizon.com>
**Subject:** Welcoming New Videoconferencing Service

Staff Members:

Effective January 1 we will be switching to V-Room as our official communication platform. Because more and more of our staff members are working from home, we need more robust videoconferencing and messaging across any device. For those who are unfamiliar with running a videoconference, here are a few guidelines:

**Before Your Videoconference**

- Establish an agenda covering the topics to be discussed.
- Distribute all relevant files and documents in one package to participants.
- E-mail the agenda package to attendees or upload it to our intranet.

**During Your Videoconference**

- Open with a slide listing the agenda, leader's name, and purpose.
- Greet participants as their names pop up or a chime announces their arrival.
- Be sure that everyone states his or her name before speaking.
- Encourage participants to interact on the virtual whiteboard by drawing or writing comments.

**Getting Started**

Please write to Andres Warren at awarren@ensurizon.com to establish your personal calling code **before December 16.** If you would like to participate in a practice session, ask Andres for details.

Ivy Porter

Director, Information Systems | iporter@ensurizon.com | Office: (650) 987-9988
Cell: (415) 201-7856

*Uses upper- and lowercase letters*

*Improves readability with side headings and ample white space.*

*Reduces wordiness and groups information into bulleted lists for high skim value*

*Ends with action information; uses boldface to emphasize important date*

**Figure 4.4** Why Proofread?

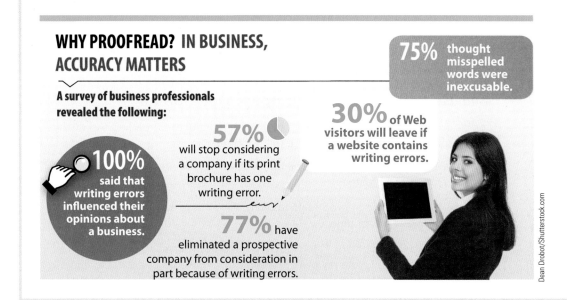

## 4-4a What to Watch for in Proofreading

Careful proofreaders check for problems in the following areas:

- **Spelling**. Now is the time to consult the dictionary. Is *recommend* spelled with one or two *c*'s? Do you mean *affect* or *effect*? Use your spell-checker, but don't rely on it totally.

- **Grammar**. Locate sentence subjects; do their verbs agree with them? Do pronouns agree with their antecedents? Review the principles in the Grammar/Mechanics Handbook if necessary. When using a grammar-checker, be suspicious. It's not always correct.

- **Punctuation**. Make sure that introductory clauses are followed by commas. In compound sentences put commas before coordinating conjunctions (*and, or, but, nor*). Double-check your use of semicolons and colons.

- **Names and numbers**. Compare all names and numbers with their sources because inaccuracies are not always visible. Especially verify the spelling of the names of individuals receiving the message. Most of us immediately dislike someone who misspells our name.

- **Format**. Be sure that your document looks balanced on the page. Compare its parts and format with those of the standard documents shown in Appendix A. If you indent paragraphs, be certain that all are indented and that their spacing is consistent.

## 4-4b How to Proofread Routine Documents

Most routine documents require a light proofreading. If you read on screen, use the down arrow to reveal one line at a time. This focuses your attention at the bottom of the screen. A safer proofreading method, however, is reading from a printed copy. Regardless of which method you use, look for typos and misspellings. Search for easily confused words, such as *to* for *too* and *then* for *than*. Read for missing words and inconsistencies.

For handwritten or printed messages, use standard proofreading marks, some of which are shown in **Figure 4.5**; for a complete list, see Appendix C. For digital documents simply use the **Font** strikethrough and color presented in Figure 4.1 or the **Track Changes** feature of your word-processing application. For collaborative projects, apply the editing techniques presented in the Communication Workshop at the end of this chapter.

## 4-4c How to Proofread Complex Documents

Long, complex, or important documents demand careful proofreading. Apply the previous suggestions but also add the following techniques:

- Print a copy, preferably double-spaced, and set it aside for at least a day. You will be more alert after a breather.

- Allow adequate time to proofread carefully. A common excuse for sloppy proofreading is lack of time.

- Be prepared to find errors. One student confessed, "I can find other people's errors, but I can't seem to locate my own." Psychologically, we don't expect to find errors, and we don't want to find them. You can overcome this obstacle by anticipating errors and congratulating, not criticizing, yourself each time you find one.

- Read the message at least twice—once for word meanings and once for grammar and mechanics. For very long documents (book chapters and long articles or reports), read a third time to verify consistency in formatting.

- Reduce your reading speed. Concentrate on individual words rather than ideas.

### Figure 4.5 Most Common Proofreading Marks

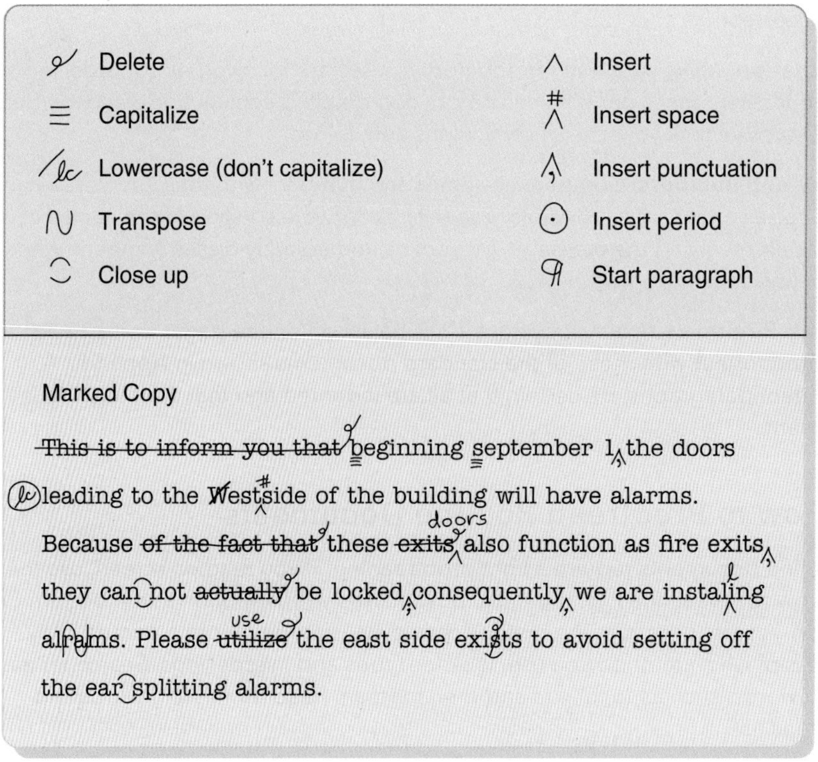

- For documents that must be perfect, enlist a proofreading buddy. Have someone read the message aloud, spelling names and difficult words, noting capitalization, and reading punctuation.

- Use the standard proofreading marks shown in Appendix C to indicate changes.

Many of us struggle with proofreading our own writing because we are seeing the same information over and over. We tend to see what we expect to see as our eyes race over the words without looking at each one carefully. We tend to know what is coming next and glide over it. To change the appearance of the text you are reading, you might print it on a different-colored paper or change the font and line spacing. If you are proofing on screen, enlarge the page view or change the background color of the screen.

## 4-5 Evaluating the Effectiveness of Your Message

**LEARNING OUTCOME 5**
Analyze a business message to evaluate its effectiveness.

As you apply finishing touches, take a moment to evaluate your messages and documents. Remember that everything you write, whether for yourself or someone else, takes the place of a personal appearance. If you were meeting in person, you would be certain to dress appropriately and professionally. The same standard applies to your writing. Evaluate what you have written to be sure that it attracts the reader's attention in a positive way. Is it polished and clear enough to convince the reader that you are worth listening to? How successful will this message be? Does it say what you want it to? Will it achieve its purpose? How will you know whether it succeeds?

The best way to judge the success of your communication is through feedback. For this reason you should encourage the receiver to respond to your message. This feedback will tell you how to modify future efforts to improve your communication technique.

Your instructor will also be evaluating some of your writing. Although any criticism is painful, try not to be defensive. Look on these comments as valuable advice tailored to your specific writing challenges—and strengths. Many businesses today spend thousands of dollars bringing in communication consultants to improve employee writing skills. You are getting the same training in this course. Take advantage of this opportunity—one of the few you may have—to improve your skills. The best way to improve your skills, of course, is through instruction, practice, and evaluation.

In this class you have all three elements: instruction in the writing process, practice materials, and a competent guide to evaluate your efforts. Those three elements are the reasons this book and this course may be the most valuable in your entire curriculum. Because it's almost impossible to improve your communication skills alone, take advantage of this opportunity.

## Summary of Learning Outcomes

1 **Apply techniques to achieve conciseness as part of revision, Phase 3 of the writing process.**
   - Eliminate wordy expressions (*at this point in time, for the purpose of, in the event that, this is to inform you*).
   - Cut long lead-ins (*this is to inform you that*), fillers (*there is/are*), redundancies (*basic essentials*), and empty words (*in the case of, the fact that*).
   - In short messages such as posts and tweets, include only main ideas, choose precise words, and strive for conciseness, clarity, and correctness.

**2  Apply revision techniques that simplify and clarify business messages.**

- Apply the KISS formula (Keep It Short and Simple) to improve message clarity.
- Dump trite business phrases (*pursuant to your request, enclosed please find, in receipt of*), clichés (*fill the bill, good to go*), slang (*snarky, lousy, bombed*), and buzzwords (*optimize, paradigm shift, incentivize*).
- Rescue buried verbs and zombie nouns (*to investigate* rather than *to conduct an investigation* and *to analyze* rather than *perform an analysis*).
- Beware of unbusinesslike exuberance (*totally, actually, very, definitely*).
- Choose precise words (*the report was well organized* rather than *the report was great*).

**3  Explain how to improve readability with effective document design.**

- Provide ample white space, appropriate side margins, and ragged-right (not justified) margins to improve message readability and comprehension.
- For body text, use serif typefaces such as Times New Roman, Cambria, and Palatino; for headings and signs, use sans serif typefaces such as Arial, Helvetica, and Calibri.
- Choose font styles and sizes that are appropriate for business messages.
- Ensure high skim value and comprehension with numbered and bulleted lists.
- Include headings to add visual impact and aid readability in business messages as well as in reports.

**4  Describe proofreading techniques allowing writers to catch errors in both routine and complex business documents.**

- In proofreading be especially alert to spelling, grammar, punctuation, names, numbers, and document format.
- Proofread routine documents immediately after completion line by line on the computer or device screen or, better yet, from a printed draft.
- Proofread more complex documents from a printed copy after a breather.
- Allow adequate time, reduce your reading speed, and read the document at least three times—for word meanings, grammar and mechanics, and formatting.

**5  Analyze a business message to evaluate its effectiveness.**

- Encourage feedback from the receiver so that you can determine whether your communication achieved its goal.
- Be open to any advice from your instructor on how to improve your writing skills.

## Key Terms

| | | |
|---|---|---|
| editing 86 | clichés 92 | justified 95 |
| proofreading 86 | slang 92 | ragged right 95 |
| evaluating 86 | buzzwords 92 | serif 95 |
| long lead-ins 87 | buried verbs 93 | sans serif 95 |
| unnecessary fillers 88 | zombie nouns 93 | font 96 |
| redundancies 89 | exuberance 93 | skim value 96 |
| microblogging 90 | white space 94 | |
| trite expressions 92 | margins 94 | |

## Chapter Review

1. What's involved in the revision process? Is revision still feasible and necessary in the 24/7 digital era when workplace messages fly back and forth in a split second? (L.O. 1)

2. What's wrong with expressions such as *collaborate together* and *fewer in number*? (L.O. 1)

3. What's wrong with a message that begins, *I am writing this announcement to let everyone know that . . .* ? (L.O. 1)

4. Why should writers avoid expressions such as *first and foremost, last but not least,* and *think outside the box*? (L.O. 2)

5. What are buried verbs and zombie nouns? Give an original example. Why should writers avoid buried verbs? (L.O. 2)

6. Why are bulleted and numbered lists useful? (L.O. 3)

7. What is white space, and why is it important for readability? (L.O. 3)

8. What are five items to check in proofreading? Be ready to discuss methods you find useful in spotting errors. (L.O. 4)

9. List four or more effective techniques for proofreading complex documents. (L.O. 4)

10. How can you overcome defensiveness when your writing is criticized constructively? (L.O. 5)

## Critical Thinking

11. Consider the case of Taylor, who is serving as interim editor of the company newsletter. She receives an article written by the company president describing, in abstract and pompous language, the company's goals for the coming year. Taylor believes the article will need considerable revising to be readable. Attached to the president's article are complimentary comments by two of the company vice presidents. What action should Taylor take? (L.O. 1–5)

12. You have just submitted a beautifully researched report. But your supervisor focused on the two or three little errors that you missed and gave none of the praise you expected. Was this fair of your supervisor? (L.O. 4, 5)

13. In this digital era of rapid-fire communication, how can you justify the time it takes to stop and revise a message? (L.O. 1–5)

14. Because business messages should have high skim value, why not write everything in bulleted or numbered lists? (L.O. 3)

15. Conciseness is valued in business, but can messages be too short? (L.O. 1)

## Writing Improvement Exercises

### Wordy Expressions (L.O. 1)

**YOUR TASK.** Revise the following sentences to eliminate wordy phrases.

16. We cannot complete the report at this point in time due to the fact that we encountered difficulties in our research and lost a collaborator to serious illness.

17. In the normal course of events, we would probably buy a larger building; however, in view of the fact that the economic outlook has dimmed, we cannot.

18. In very few cases do the new names of merged corporations signal clearly what the companies actually do.

19. Inasmuch as our tax and regulatory policies hamper a return of manufacturing to the United States, they should be reformed.

20. Despite the fact that forced shutdowns during the COVID-19 pandemic caused huge job losses in manufacturing, 63 percent of executives polled by Deloitte are optimistic about the future.

### Long Lead-Ins (L.O. 1)

**YOUR TASK.** Revise the following to eliminate long lead-ins.

21. This is an announcement to inform the public that the New York Stock Exchange reversed its decision to delist China's three largest telecommunications companies.

22. We are sending this message to notify all staff that anyone who wants to work from home may apply immediately.

23. I am writing this e-mail to inform you that your new account executive is Aubrey Lee.

24. This is to let all our staff members know that hackers exploit weak employee passwords to enter IT systems.

### There is/are and It is/was Fillers (L.O. 1)

**YOUR TASK.** Revise the following to avoid unnecessary *there is/are* and *it is/was* fillers.

25. There are hackers who distribute malware that blocks access to a target's systems and then demand ransom payment to release the digital hostages.

26. It is large corporations and local governments that struggle to devote the resources and expertise necessary to establish basic defenses against ransomware attacks.

27. There are phishing attempts that many e-mail users don't recognize even if it is obvious how crude they are.

28. If there are any questions that you have about computer safety, please call us.

## Redundancies (L.O. 1)

**YOUR TASK.** Revise the following to avoid redundancies.

29. Because her smartphone was bright red in color, she could always find it in the clutter of her home office.

30. The basic fundamentals of computer safety are to avoid using the names of pets, one's birth date, the number sequence 1234567, and the word *password* to log into accounts.

31. The IT manager repeated again and again that we must use strong passwords and change them frequently.

32. Although the two reports look exactly identical, we need to proofread each and every page.

## Trite Business Phrases (L.O. 2)

**YOUR TASK.** Revise the following sentences to eliminate trite business phrases.

33. Pursuant to your inquiry, I will e-mail you the buyer's residential preference sheet immediately.

34. Enclosed please find the directory of our most recent corporate clients.

35. As per your request, our payables staff is sending the check under separate cover.

36. Every effort will be made by our collections staff to extract payment from customers with overdue invoices.

## Jargon, Slang, Clichés, Wordiness (L.O. 2)

**YOUR TASK.** Revise the following sentences to avoid confusing jargon, slang, clichés, and wordiness.

37. To pull ourselves up by our bootstraps from this recession, we must think outside the box.

38. Although we made a bundle whenever our response was quick as a flash, we can't keep shooting from the hip.

39. In comparison with our lousy competitors, we have passed with flying colors and will ignore their snarky claims.

40. Please circle back to me about the proposal and we will be good to go.

## Buried Verbs and Zombie Nouns (L.O. 2)

**YOUR TASK.** Revise the following to recover buried verbs and convert zombie nouns.

41. After conducting an investigation, the legal department reached the conclusion that fraud had been committed.

42. Our board promised to give consideration to the proposed acquisition at its next meeting.

43. The Consumer Financial Protection Bureau issued a warning to borrowers that an important provision will face expiration effective January 1.

44. One of the lending provisions under the Dodd-Frank Act extends liability protection to borrowers who have a higher debt load but meet standards set by Fannie Mae and Freddie Mac.

45. Under the current legislation, lenders are provided incentives to issue loans to borrowers who may not meet the strictest standards but are a relatively safe credit risk.

46. In order to receive an adequate assessment of the home insurance amount, homeowners must make a determination of the total value of their furnishings.

## Precise, Direct Words (L.O. 2)

**YOUR TASK.** Revise the following sentences to improve clarity and precision. Use your imagination to add appropriate words.

**EXAMPLE** They said it was a long way off.

**REVISION** The executives announced that the HQ relocation would not take place for two years.

47. One of the employees told me that it would be available soon.

48. Please get in touch with the company in the near term.

49. An employee from that organization announced the change in date for the event.

50. She said that the film she worked on was not very good.

## Microblogging: Replying to Tweets (L.O. 1)

**YOUR TASK.** Read the following authentic Twitter messages and write a reply of no more than 280 characters to each. Be selective in what you include. Your instructor may show you the actual responses that the company wrote.

51. **@HTWilson94 asks whether grocer Whole Foods stocks Whole Trade certified flowers all year long.** Prepare a response (preferably 140 or fewer characters) based on the following information: Yes, at Whole Foods stores we are happy to offer Whole Trade certified flowers the entire year. We strongly advocate and support the Whole Trade movement, which strives to promote quality, premium price to the producer, better wages and working conditions, and the environment. However, we can't tell you exactly which certified flowers will be available at our stores and when. You would have to check with your local store for its specific selection.

52. **@AmyJean64 sent Bank of America a tweet saying she was frustrated with a real estate short sale. "Have a contract on a house and cannot get them to return calls to finalize."** Prepare a response based on the following information: You work for Bank of America, and you would very much like to help her, but you can't without certain information. You need her to send you the property address along with her name and phone number so that you can call to see how you can help. She should probably DM (direct message) you with this crucial information.

53. **@VickiK wrote to JetBlue: "I have booked a flt in July, CA-VT. Wondering about flying my wedding dress w/me. Is there a safe place to hang it on the plane?"** Prepare a response based on the following information: We congratulate you on your coming wedding! We bet your wedding dress is beautiful. We don't have special closets on our planes and certainly nothing big enough for a wedding dress. But here's a suggestion. Have you considered having it shipped ahead of time? All the best wishes on your upcoming happy event!

54. **@ChrisC sent a message to Southwest Airlines saying, "This is extremely frustrating, how is it possible for your website to be down the entire day?"** Prepare a response based on the following information: Southwest is very, very sorry! It's extremely frustrating to us also. We realize that you are accustomed to using this site to book flights. Our IT people tell us that the website functionality is getting better. We are not sure exactly what that means in terms of availability, but we are very hopeful that customers will be able to book their flights soon.

55. **@JamesR. sent a message to the delivery service UPS complaining, "Holy XXX. It's after 6 pm and UPS still hasn't delivered my pkg yet."** Prepare a response based on the following information: UPS makes every effort to deliver all packages promptly. For packages destined for offices, we must deliver by 3 p.m. However, for packages going to residences, our goal is to deliver by 7 p.m. But we can't always make it, so our drivers can sometimes run later. We're sorry about the wait.

## Lists, Bullets, and Headings (L.O. 3)

**YOUR TASK.** Revise the following sentences and paragraphs using lists, bullets, and category headings, if appropriate. Improve parallel construction and readability while reducing wordiness.

56. Revise the following paragraph about three Twitter best practices by using a bulleted list.

*There are three simple ways you can build an online following, drive your reputation, and develop customers' trust by using these uncomplicated and simple Twitter practices. First off, share some of your photos and information about your business from behind the scenes. Sharing is so important! Next, listen. That is, you should regularly monitor the comments about your company, what's being said about your brand, and any chatter about your products. And, of course, you should respond. In real time it is necessary to respond to statements that are compliments as well as just general feedback.*

57. Revise the following by incorporating a numbered list.

*Computer passwords are a way of life at this point in time. In the creation of a strong password, you should remember a few things. First, you should come up with an eight-word phrase that is easy to remember, such as my favorite uncle was a firefighter in Cleveland. Then take each of those words and the first letter should be selected, such as mfuwafic. The last step for creating a really strong password is to exchange—that is, swap out—some of those letters for characters and capital letters, such as Mf@w&%iC.*

58. Revise the following by incorporating a bulleted list with category headings.

*Auto accidents account for a high number of accidental deaths. The most common causes of these accidents are due to the following causes. In all probability, the most common cause is distracted drivers. Talking on smartphones, applying makeup, texting, eating food, and reading the morning newspaper are all common ways that drivers are being distracted. Another cause is most assuredly impaired driving. Alcohol and drugs impair judgment and reaction times. This obviously results in accidents. Another cause has got to be aggressive drivers. Being an aggressive driver instead of a defensive driver puts you at risk for getting involved in an accident. Finally, road rage is a significant cause. Drivers who get angry easily and then take it out on other drivers are one of the leading causes of accidents.*

59. Revise the following by incorporating a bulleted list with category headings.

*There are many people today who want to improve their credit scores. Some simple tips for bumping up your score are obvious. For one thing, you should immediately fix mistakes. If you check your credit report (you should do this at least once a year) and there are errors, you can dispute these and have them investigated. Another way to improve your credit score is to pay on time. At least 35 percent of your score is a direct result of your payment history. Next, you should make an effort to lower and reduce your balances. It may be difficult, but you should keep your personal credit balances as low as possible. The less you're using, the better for your score. Finally, making a habit of keeping older accounts will improve your score. This means that you should keep your older cards so that you have a longer history to share. It also shows stability.*

## Radical Rewrites

**Note:** Radical Rewrites are provided at **www.cengage.com** for you to download and revise. Your instructor may show a suggested solution.

## 4.1 Radical Rewrite: Manager's Wordy Malware Warning (L.O. 1–5)

**YOUR TASK.** Study the following ineffective message from a manager to employees and staff. It suffers from numerous wordy constructions covered in this chapter. Study the message and list at least five weaknesses. Then revise to avoid excessive wordiness and repetition.

**To:** Employees and Staff
**From:** Zach Brogdon <zbrogdon@fisher.com>
**Subject:** Computer Attacks

I am sending this message because hackers using malware spread by e-mail are targeting many organizations, I think it's a good time to give consideration to five incredibly important tips that are really helpful in preventing infection on your machine. Following are the tips:

Tip 1: Before opening an incoming e-mail, check the address of the person who sent the message. This is usually in the header. If it looks suspicious, don't open.

Tip 2. Look carefully at the subject line. Does it claim your account will be suspended or your account suffered an unauthorized login attempt? Attempts at urgency often are clues to malicious e-mail.

Tip 3. Do you see that the sender doesn't seem to know your name and that you are addressed anonymously as "Valued Customer"? Senders who are legitimate in all probability know your name.

Tip 4. In the matter of attachments, click only on those from senders that you know. There is danger in attachments because that's where viruses may hide or lurk.

Tip 5. Don't believe everything you see in an e-mail. Scammers are spectacularly clever at spoofing brands that we all know.

As a final note, if an incoming e-mail looks fishy, please use **Shift Delete**, which will permanently delete the e-mail. Don't just delete, which does not remove it permanently. I hope these tips are useful!!

Zach B.
[Full contact information]

## Adjectives and Adverbs

Review Sections 1.16 and 1.17 of the Grammar/Mechanics Handbook. Then select the correct form to complete each of the following statements. Record the appropriate Grammar/Mechanics section to illustrate the principle involved. When you finish, compare your responses with those at the bottom of the page. If your answers differ, study carefully the principles in parentheses.

__b__ (1.17e)    **EXAMPLE**   Shockingly, 40 percent of the Air Force's active fleet is at least 25 years old; corrosion and fatigue are reducing the (a) *quarter century old,* (b) *quarter-century-old* aircrafts' availability.

_____ 1. After the (a) *end of life,* (b) *end-of-life* military aircraft have been stripped of all components, the Department of Defense auctions them off as scrap metal.

_____ 2. The CH-47F Chinook helicopter's twin rotors were running (a) *smooth,* (b) *smoothly* after they had been rebuilt.

_____ 3. Offshore wind farms prefer the more (a) *cost-effective,* (b) *cost effective* larger wind turbines to offset their high installation costs.

_____ 4. I hope I won't regret my (a) *spur of the moment,* (b) *spur-of-the-moment* decision to move overseas for a new job.

_____ 5. Of the two health plans, which is (a) *more,* (b) *most* expensive?

_____ 6. Throughout the pandemic the Occupational Safety and Health Administration (OSHA) required employers to record confirmed (a) *work-related,* (b) *work related* cases of COVID-19.

_____ 7. Many business students go to college because they want to open (a) *there,* (b) *their* own business.

_____ 8. When they called to offer me a job overseas, I decided on the (a) *spur of the moment,* (b) *spur-of-the-moment* to accept.

_____ 9. How is the Shazam app able to identify a song so (a) *quick,* (b) *quickly*?

_____ 10. The credit union had to abandon its (a) *well-thought-out,* (b) *well thought out* plan to revamp its home banking application.

_____ 11. To sign up for mail forwarding, a business must complete a (a) *change of address,* (b) *change-of-address* form when it moves.

_____ 12. Our sales figures may get (a) *worse,* (b) *worst* before they pick up again.

_____ 13. I could be more productive if my printer were (a) *more closer,* (b) *closer to* my computer.

_____ 14. If you reject his offer to help, Jack will feel (a) *bad,* (b) *badly*.

_____ 15. Although purchased 30 years ago, the polished fire engine still looked (a) *brightly,* (b) *bright*.

**1.** b (1.17e) **2.** b (1.17d) **3.** a (1.17d) **4.** a (1.17e) **5.** a (1.16) **6.** a (1.17e) **7.** b (1.17e) **8.** b (1.17g) **9.** b (1.17e) **10.** a (1.17d) **11.** b (1.17e) **12.** a (1.16) **13.** b (1.17b) **14.** a (1.17c) **15.** b (1.17c)

## Editing Challenge 4

The following message from a district manager to her boss submits recommendations for launching an employee suggestion plan. However, her enthusiastic message suffers from excessive exuberance, wordiness, lack of parallelism in its list, poor proofreading, a dangling modifier, and other writing faults that require correction.

**YOUR TASK.** Edit the following by (a) inserting corrections in your textbook or on a photocopy using the proofreading marks in Appendix C or (b) downloading the message from **www.cengage.com** and correcting at your computer. Your instructor may show you a possible solution.

---

**To:**      Kenzie Fitzgerald <kfitzgerald@peterson.com>
**From:**    Corinne Yu <cyu@peterson.com>
**Subject:** Launching an Incredibly Successful Employee Suggestion Program!

Kenzie,

Due to the fact that you recently asked me to provide ideas for encouraging employees to make suggestions, I am absolutely delighted to submit the following. You noted that a high level of employee engagement is linked to increased profitability, productivity, and employees are retained longer. I agree totally and completely! After conducting research and interviews, the following ideas came to me on how to make a start for such a program:

- **Obtain senior management buy-in.** To make any suggestion program successful, we must first gain the support of the CEO and all upper management. They must get behind the program and help communicate why it is important to employees as well as to the business.
- **A promotion plan must be developed.** Next we must give the program a name and create initial buzz with a fun launch. Perhaps including a party.
- **Agree on incentive.** A basic fundamental of any suggestion program is the right mix of incentives to encourage employees to share there ideas. Some employees respond to cash prizes, others like perks such as a month of free parking near the front door. One company found that a hand written thank you message from a manger or a mention on the intranet provided sufficient reward for ideas that were good.
- **Educate employees.** The program will never be successful if we are not able to train employees about what types of ideas are sought. A pilot program would be a good idea.
- **A suggestion review team must be set up.** All key departments need to be represented with members to review those ideas and evaluate them as well.

I have many more incredible ideas for launching a suggestion program because I feel that such a program could be very, very successful for our organization. May I make an appointment to discuss these ideas with you farther? I suggest that we actually give serious consideration to taking initial steps to launching a suggestion program.

Best,

Corinne Yu
District Manager

## Collaborate, Revise, and Edit With Google Docs

Collaborative writing and editing projects are challenging. Fortunately, several cloud-based productivity applications are available that enable teams to draft and edit documents in real time. Students will probably be most familiar with the free service Google Docs. This Google platform allows users to import or create, share, revise, and comment on an evolving document—from any device. More useful than file-hosting sites such as Dropbox, Google Docs lets writers not only privately share cloud-based documents, but also edit them. Moreover, team members can message via e-mail from within the program.

At present, Google Docs works seamlessly with MS Word documents that can be imported. Also, files created in Google Docs can be downloaded as Word documents. Edits are recorded in different colors—one for each reviewer. Content to be deleted appears as strikethrough text; new edits match the editor's assigned color, as you can see in **Figure 4.6**. The collaborators can subsequently accept or reject proposed changes. Clicking on a marginal comment or the corresponding crossed-out text activates horizontal brackets in the editor's color to call attention to the phrase or word under review. In the **Suggesting** mode, team members can point out problematic passages or errors, ask or answer **Suggesting** questions, and share ideas without changing or adding text. The original writer may accept or reject these changes. The multicolored comments are identified by the individual writers' names and date/time stamps.

One of the notable features is **See revision history,** which enables users not only to view a log of earlier versions of the document, but also to return to and work with those earlier versions. Google Docs automatically saves all changes. Collaborators can choose free storage space on Google Drive.

**CAREER APPLICATION.** On the job, you will likely be working with others on projects that require written documents. During employment interviews, employers may ask whether you have participated in team projects using collaboration tools. To be able to answer that question favorably, take advantage of this opportunity to work collaboratively on a document using the revising and commenting features provided in the **Editing** and **Suggesting** modes in Google Docs.

**YOUR TASK.** In pairs, practice collaborative editing. Use Google Docs to revise the Radical Rewrite or Editing Challenge document in this chapter. One team member imports the document into Google Docs, makes the first edits in **Editing** or **Suggesting** mode, and notifies the other team member with the convenient **Share** (or **Email collaborators**) feature that the file is ready for further editing. The team then submits the final document to the instructor—with or without edits showing, depending on the instructor's preference.

**Figure 4.6  Google Docs Aids Collaboration**

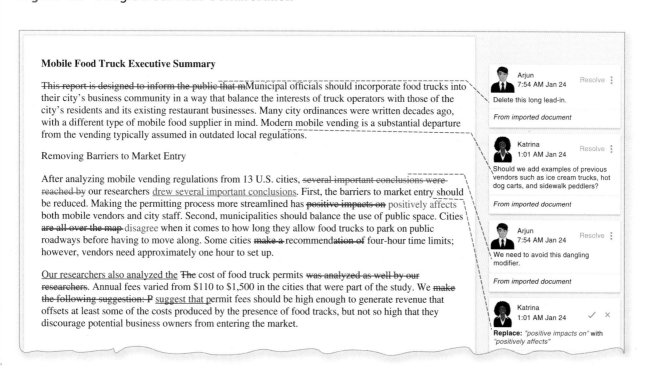

# Workplace Communication 3

# Short Workplace Messages and Digital Media

ESB Professional/Shutterstock.com

## Learning Outcomes

After studying this chapter, you should be able to do the following:

**1** Examine the professional usage, structure, and format of e-mails and memos in the digital era workplace.

**2** Explain workplace messaging and texting including their liabilities and best practices.

**3** Identify professional applications of business podcasts and the professional standards underpinning them.

**4** Describe how businesses use blogs to connect with internal and external audiences.

**5** Discuss business organizations' external and internal social media practices as well as the risks inherent in Internet use today.

## 5-1 Communicating in the Digital Age With E-Mails and Memos

Enabled by technology, our lives have become social and mobile. Social media such as Facebook, YouTube, Instagram, and Twitter have transformed communication from one-on-one online conversations to one-to-many transmissions. Users create, edit, and consume content, review products, and share information as well as media. The distinction between online and offline is becoming blurry as our virtual and real-life connectedness intertwine. As we engage socially almost all the time, our reliance on smartphones and other electronic devices only keeps growing.

In many businesses ever-smaller laptops, netbooks, smartphones, and tablets are making desktop computers obsolete. Powerful mobile devices largely access data and applications stored in the **cloud**—in remote networks—not on individual computers in an office. **Virtual private networks** (VPNs) offer secure access to organizations' information from any location in the world that provides an Internet connection. For better or for worse, businesspeople are increasingly connected 24/7.

Even if you are Internet and social media savvy, you may need to know how businesses use communication technologies to transmit and share information. This chapter discusses short forms of workplace communication, beginning with e-mail, which many workers love to hate, and memos, which are fading away but still necessary in many organizations.

Furthermore, you will learn about workplace messaging, interoffice chat applications, and comprehensive internal communication platforms. You will study business podcasts, corporate blogs, and professional social media use before exploring many contemporary cyberthreats. Familiarizing yourself with workplace technologies and best practices can save you time, reduce blunders, and boost your credibility as a professional.

## 5-1a  E-Mail: Going Strong at Fifty

Workplace e-mail is unlikely to go away. Roughly 50 years after the first e-mail was sent, total e-mail traffic keeps growing 4 percent a year worldwide.[1] Office workers receive on average 120 messages a day; globally, 125 billion business e-mails are exchanged daily.[2] Despite chat, texting, and mobile messaging of all kinds, most business messages are still sent by e-mail.[3] Moreover, when it comes to marketing, e-mail is very much alive and kicking, as we will see in Chapter 8. Tech expert Alexis Madrigal is one of many staunch defenders of e-mail. "You can't kill email!" he claims. "It's the cockroach of the Internet, and I mean that as a compliment. This resilience is a good thing."[4]

Neither social media, augmented reality, and video chatting, nor phishing, hacking, and spam have diminished the high importance of e-mail in the workplace. Not even popular workplace applications such as the team communication and collaboration tool Slack are likely to replace e-mail anytime soon.[5] One e-mail proponent argues that e-mail is technologically far superior to social media, messaging, and collaboration platforms; he offers advice on turning e-mail into the biggest, "least-distracting," and most sophisticated social network, but one that is offering greater privacy.[6]

E-mail has replaced paper memos for many messages inside organizations and some letters to external audiences. Most businesspeople (85 percent) now first open their e-mail on mobile devices.[7] Because you can expect to use e-mail extensively to communicate at work, it's smart to learn how to do it expertly. You may have to adjust the messaging practices you currently follow for texting, chatting, and posting on Instagram, Snapchat, or Facebook, but turning out professional e-mails is an easily attainable goal.

## 5-1b  Common Complaints About E-Mail

Although e-mail is recognized as the mainstay of business communication, it's not always done well. Business journalist Suzy Welch is emphatic that sloppiness and mistakes are not an option: "You may like to write off-the-cuff, train-of-thought messages, because it's fast and easy," she says, "but no one wants to receive them, OK? No one."[9] Author Vicky Oliver insists that more than one typo per e-mail is unprofessional. She also complains about impersonal "one-line emails that are so transactional they sound like an automaton is responding."[10] Goldman Sachs CEO David Solomon is eager to hire graduates with liberal arts backgrounds because writing skills in general are increasingly harder to find, he laments.[11]

**LEARNING OUTCOME 1**
Examine the professional usage, structure, and format of e-mails and memos in the digital era workplace.

**OFFICE INSIDER**

"I can see email lasting tens of thousands of years, as preposterous as that sounds. If email is ever killed, it will be replaced with something that has all its virtues and all its problems as well. It's an open system that anyone can participate in and that has a global name space. It's a protocol that's decades old and has thousands of clients that support it."[8]

Stewart Butterfield, *CEO of Slack Technologies*

**E-Mail Overload.** In addition to the complaints about confusing and poorly written e-mails, many people are overwhelmed with too many messages. Workers report that they spend about five hours a day reading and writing e-mail—approximately three hours on work e-mail and two hours on personal messages.[12] Social computing expert Gloria Mark says that e-mail use is about being in control, stressing out workers who struggle in vain to bring down their clogged inboxes to zero. For a study Mark cut off participants from e-mail for a week and found significant reductions in stress levels.[13] Each day more than 4 billion global e-mail users exchange almost 310 billion e-mails.[14]

Some of those messages are unnecessary, such as those that merely confirm receipt of a message or ones that express thanks. The use of *Reply all* adds to the inbox, irritating those who have to skim and delete dozens of messages that barely relate to them. Others blame e-mail for eliminating the distinction between work life and home life—now more than ever in the wake of the COVID-19 pandemic because employees working remotely feel an urgency to be available 24/7 and respond immediately.

**The Scary Permanence of Digital Messages.** Still other e-mail senders fail to recognize how dangerous e-mail can be. After deletion, e-mail files still leave trails on servers within and outside organizations. Long-forgotten messages may turn up in court cases as damaging and costly evidence—for example, BP engineer Brian Morel's e-mail to a colleague before the disastrous explosion of the Deepwater Horizon oil platform off the coast of Louisiana that killed 11 workers: "This has been a nightmare well which has everyone all over the place." This and other incriminating e-mails prompted BP to agree to a decade-long compensation process totaling $65 billion to settle 300 lawsuits.[16]

Organizations can legally monitor their staff's personal e-mail accounts too if the workers access them on the company's computer network. Moreover, if employees set up their company's e-mail on their smartphones, they have given their employer the right to remotely delete all personal data on that mobile device.[17] Even writers with nothing to hide should be concerned about what may come back to haunt them. Your best bet is to put nothing in an e-mail message that you wouldn't post on your office door. Also be sure that you know your organization's e-mail policy before sending personal messages or forwarding work-related information to your personal e-mail account. Estimates suggest that almost 30 percent of bosses have fired an employee for Internet or e-mail-related misuse.[18]

Despite its dark side, e-mail has many advantages and remains a prime communication channel. Therefore, it's to your advantage to learn when and how to use it efficiently and safely.

## 5-1c Knowing When E-Mail Is Appropriate

Short informal messages mostly travel by text, instant message, or chat. In comparison, e-mail is appropriate for longer, more involved, and well-organized messages that may provide or request information and respond to inquiries. It is especially effective for messages to multiple receivers and messages that must be archived (saved). An e-mail is also appropriate as a cover document when sending longer attachments.

E-mail, however, is not a substitute for face-to-face conversations or telephone calls. These channels are much more successful if your goal is to convey enthusiasm or warmth, explain a complex situation, present a persuasive argument, or smooth over disagreements. One expert advises delivering messages in person when they "require a human moment"—that is, those that are emotional, require negotiation, and relate to personnel.[19] Researchers have found that people are 34 times more likely to comply with in-person requests than those sent by e-mail; the scholars also established that most office workers overestimate the persuasiveness of e-mail.[20]

## 5-1d Composing Professional E-Mails

Professional e-mails are quite different from messages you may send to friends. Instead of casual words tossed off in haste, professional e-mails are well-considered messages that involve all three stages of the writing process. They have compelling subject lines, appropriate greetings, well-organized bodies, and complete closing information. The following writing plan will help you create information e-mails quickly.

## Information E-Mails

**SUBJECT LINE:** Summarize the main idea in condensed form.

**OPENING:** Reveal the main idea immediately but in expanded form (complete sentences).

**BODY:** Explain and justify the main idea using headings, bulleted lists, and other high-skim techniques when appropriate.

**CLOSING:** Include (a) action information, dates, or deadlines; (b) a summary of the message; or (c) a closing thought.

Draft a Compelling but Concise Subject Line. A crucial part of an e-mail is its subject line—not surprising when writers can expect that their messages will be viewed on mobile devices by busy people. Avoid meaningless statements such as *Help, Urgent,* or *Meeting.* Summarize the purpose of the message clearly and make the receiver want to open the message. Try to include a verb (*Need You to Attend Las Vegas Trade Show*). In some instances the subject line can be the entire message (*Meeting Location Changed to Conference Room II*). Also be sure to adjust the subject line if the topic changes after a thread of replies emerges. Subject lines should appear as a combination of uppercase and lowercase letters—never in all lowercase letters or all caps.

| Poor Subject Lines | Improved Subject Lines |
|---|---|
| Budget Report | Need You to Prepare a Budget Report |
| Division Meeting | Middle Atlantic Division Meeting Rescheduled for April 22 |
| Important! | Please Schedule Your OSHA Safety Training |
| Parking Permits | New Employee Parking Permits Available From HR |

Include a Greeting. To help receivers see the beginning of a message and to help them recognize whether they are the primary or secondary receiver, include a greeting, also called a **salutation**. The greeting sets the tone for the message and reflects your audience analysis. For friends and colleagues, try friendly greetings (*Hi, Lara; Thanks, Lara; Good morning, Lara;* or *Greetings, Lara*). For more formal messages and those to outsiders, include an honorific and last name (*Dear Ms. Ingram*). When a given name is gender-neutral (unisex), and the gender of identity is not known, omit the honorific. Use the full name of the recipient instead (*Dear Robin Gray*).

Organize the Body for Readability and Tone. In the revision phase, ask yourself how you could make your message more readable. Did you start directly? Did you group similar topics together? Could some information be presented with bulleted or numbered lists? Could you add headings—especially if the message contains more than a few paragraphs? Do you see any phrases or sentences that you could condense? Get rid of wordiness, but don't sacrifice clarity. If a longer sentence is necessary for comprehension, then keep it. To convey the best tone, read the message aloud. If it sounds curt, it probably is.

**Close Effectively.** At the end of your message, include an action statement with due dates and requests. Although complimentary closes are unnecessary, you might include a friendly closing such as *Many thanks* or *Warm regards.* Do include your name because messages without names become confusing when forwarded or when they are part of a long thread of responses.

For most messages, include full contact information in a signature block, which your e-mail application can insert automatically. **Model Document 5.1** illustrates a typical information e-mail that starts directly and displays proper formatting. It also illustrates how a draft can be revised to improve readability.

## 5-1e  Keeping Your Inbox in Check

Instead of letting your inbox consume your time and crimp your productivity, you can control it by observing a few time-management strategies. The most important strategy is checking your e-mail at set times, such as first thing in the morning and again after lunch or at 4 p.m. To avoid being distracted, be sure to turn off your audio and visual alerts. No fair peeking! If mornings are your best working times, check your e-mail later in the day. Discuss with our boss your schedule for responding and share it with your colleagues.

Another excellent time-saver is the two-minute rule. If you can read and respond to a message within two minutes, then take care of it immediately. For messages that require more time, add them to your to-do list or schedule them on your calendar. To be polite, send a quick note telling the sender when you plan to respond. Blogger and podcaster Merlin Mann suggests that "Your job is not to read an email and then read it again." Instead, he recommends taking one of five steps right away: delete, delegate, respond, defer, or do.[22]

## 5-1f  Replying Efficiently With Down-Editing

When answering e-mail, a useful skill to develop is **down-editing**. This involves inserting your responses to parts of the incoming message. After a courteous opening, your reply message will include only the parts of the incoming message to which you are responding. Delete the sender's message headers, signature, and all unnecessary parts. Your responses can be identified with your initials if more than one person will be seeing the response. Another efficient technique is to use a different font color for your down-edits. It takes a little practice to develop this skill, particularly formatting the e-mail, but the down-edited reply reduces confusion, saves writing and reading time, and makes you look professional. **Figure 5.1** shows additional best practices for managing your e-mail.

## 5-1g  Writing Interoffice Memos

In addition to e-mail, you should be familiar with another workplace document type, the interoffice memorandum. Although e-mail has largely replaced memos, you may still be called on to use the memo format in specific instances. Memos are necessary for important internal messages that (a) are too long for e-mail, (b) require a permanent record, (c) demand formality, or (d) inform employees who may not have work e-mail, such as those in manufacturing or construction. Within organizations, memos deliver changes in procedures, official instructions, and reports.

The memo format is particularly necessary for complex, lengthy internal messages. Prepared as memos, long messages are then delivered as attachments to e-mail cover messages. Memos seem to function better as permanent records than e-mail messages because the latter may be cumbersome to store and may contain a long thread of confusing replies. E-mails also may change the origination date whenever the file is accessed, thus making it impossible to know the original date of the message.

## Model Document 5.1 Creating an Information E-Mail

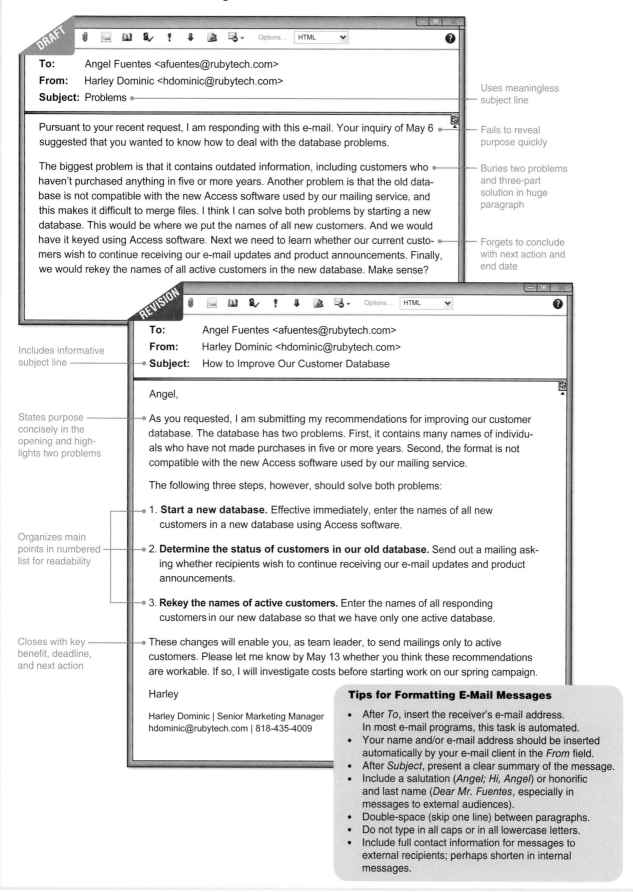

**DRAFT**

Options... | HTML

**To:** Angel Fuentes <afuentes@rubytech.com>
**From:** Harley Dominic <hdominic@rubytech.com>
**Subject:** Problems •———

Uses meaningless subject line

Pursuant to your recent request, I am responding with this e-mail. Your inquiry of May 6 suggested that you wanted to know how to deal with the database problems.

Fails to reveal purpose quickly

The biggest problem is that it contains outdated information, including customers who haven't purchased anything in five or more years. Another problem is that the old database is not compatible with the new Access software used by our mailing service, and this makes it difficult to merge files. I think I can solve both problems by starting a new database. This would be where we put the names of all new customers. And we would have it keyed using Access software. Next we need to learn whether our current customers wish to continue receiving our e-mail updates and product announcements. Finally, we would rekey the names of all active customers in the new database. Make sense?

Buries two problems and three-part solution in huge paragraph

Forgets to conclude with next action and end date

**REVISION**

Options... | HTML

**To:** Angel Fuentes <afuentes@rubytech.com>
**From:** Harley Dominic <hdominic@rubytech.com>
**Subject:** How to Improve Our Customer Database

Includes informative subject line

Angel,

States purpose concisely in the opening and highlights two problems

As you requested, I am submitting my recommendations for improving our customer database. The database has two problems. First, it contains many names of individuals who have not made purchases in five or more years. Second, the format is not compatible with the new Access software used by our mailing service.

The following three steps, however, should solve both problems:

Organizes main points in numbered list for readability

1. **Start a new database.** Effective immediately, enter the names of all new customers in a new database using Access software.

2. **Determine the status of customers in our old database.** Send out a mailing asking whether recipients wish to continue receiving our e-mail updates and product announcements.

3. **Rekey the names of active customers.** Enter the names of all responding customers in our new database so that we have only one active database.

Closes with key benefit, deadline, and next action

These changes will enable you, as team leader, to send mailings only to active customers. Please let me know by May 13 whether you think these recommendations are workable. If so, I will investigate costs before starting work on our spring campaign.

Harley

Harley Dominic | Senior Marketing Manager
hdominic@rubytech.com | 818-435-4009

### Tips for Formatting E-Mail Messages

- After *To*, insert the receiver's e-mail address. In most e-mail programs, this task is automated.
- Your name and/or e-mail address should be inserted automatically by your e-mail client in the *From* field.
- After *Subject*, present a clear summary of the message.
- Include a salutation (*Angel; Hi, Angel*) or honorific and last name (*Dear Mr. Fuentes*, especially in messages to external audiences).
- Double-space (skip one line) between paragraphs.
- Do not type in all caps or in all lowercase letters.
- Include full contact information for messages to external recipients; perhaps shorten in internal messages.

**Figure 5.1  Best Practices for a Better E-mail**

### Getting Started

- Don't write if another channel—such as IM, tweet, or a phone call—might work better.
- Send only content you would want to be published.
- Write compelling subject lines, possibly with names and dates: *Jake: Can You Present at January 10 Staff Meeting?*

### Replying

- Scan all e-mails, especially those from the same person. Answer within 24 hours or say when you will.
- Change the subject line if the topic changes. Check the threaded messages below yours.
- Practice down-editing; include only the parts from the incoming e-mail to which you are responding.
- Start with the main idea.
- Use headings and lists.

### Observing Etiquette

- Obtain approval before forwarding.
- Soften the tone by including a friendly opening and closing.
- Resist humor and sarcasm. Absent facial expression and tone of voice, humor can be misunderstood.
- Avoid writing in all caps, which is like SHOUTING.

### Closing Effectively

- End with due dates, next steps to be taken, or a friendly remark.
- Add your full contact information including social media addresses.
- Edit your text for readability. Proofread for typos or unwanted auto-corrections.
- Double-check before hitting Send.

When preparing e-mail attachments, be sure that they carry sufficient identifying information. Because the attachment may become separated from the cover e-mail message, it must be named thoughtfully. Preparing the e-mail attachment as a memo provides a handy format that identifies the date, sender, receiver, and subject.

**Comparing Memos and E-Mails.** Memos have much in common with e-mails. Both usually carry nonsensitive information that may be organized directly with the main idea first. Both have guide words calling for a subject line, a dateline, and the identification of the sender and receiver. To enhance readability, both should be organized with headings, bulleted lists, and enumerated items whenever possible.

**Similarities.** E-mails and memos both generally close with (a) action information, dates, or deadlines; (b) a summary of the message; or (c) a closing thought. An effective memo or e-mail closing might be *Please create a slideshow featuring our new product line by April 20 so that we are prepared for the trade show in May.* In more detailed messages, a summary of main points may be an appropriate closing. If no action request is made and a closing summary is unnecessary, you might end with a simple concluding thought (*I'm glad to answer your questions* or *This sounds like a worthwhile project*).

**Differences.** You need not close messages to coworkers with goodwill statements such as those found in e-mails or letters to customers and clients. However, some closing thought is often necessary to avoid sounding abrupt. Closings can show gratitude or encourage feedback with remarks such as *I sincerely appreciate your help* or *What are your ideas on this proposal?* Other closings look forward to what's next, such as *How would you like to proceed?* Avoid closing with overused expressions such as *Please let me know if I may be of further assistance.* This ending sounds mechanical and insincere.

In **Model Document 5.2**, notice how interoffice memos are formatted and how they can be created to improve readability with lists, tables, and white space.

## Model Document 5.2  Formatting an Interoffice Memo

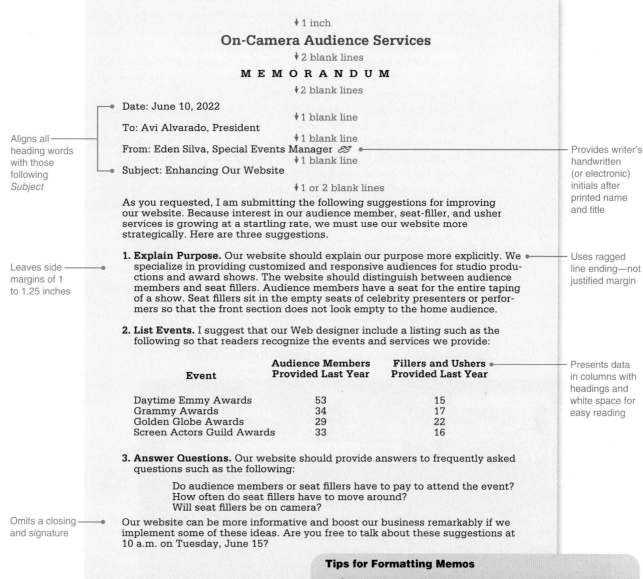

**↓ 1 inch**

### On-Camera Audience Services

**↓ 2 blank lines**

### M E M O R A N D U M

**↓ 2 blank lines**

Date: June 10, 2022

**↓ 1 blank line**

To: Avi Alvarado, President

**↓ 1 blank line**

From: Eden Silva, Special Events Manager 𝓔𝓢

**↓ 1 blank line**

Subject: Enhancing Our Website

**↓ 1 or 2 blank lines**

*Aligns all heading words with those following Subject*

*Provides writer's handwritten (or electronic) initials after printed name and title*

As you requested, I am submitting the following suggestions for improving our website. Because interest in our audience member, seat-filler, and usher services is growing at a startling rate, we must use our website more strategically. Here are three suggestions.

1. **Explain Purpose.** Our website should explain our purpose more explicitly. We specialize in providing customized and responsive audiences for studio productions and award shows. The website should distinguish between audience members and seat fillers. Audience members have a seat for the entire taping of a show. Seat fillers sit in the empty seats of celebrity presenters or performers so that the front section does not look empty to the home audience.

*Leaves side margins of 1 to 1.25 inches*

*Uses ragged line ending—not justified margin*

2. **List Events.** I suggest that our Web designer include a listing such as the following so that readers recognize the events and services we provide:

| Event | Audience Members Provided Last Year | Fillers and Ushers Provided Last Year |
|---|---|---|
| Daytime Emmy Awards | 53 | 15 |
| Grammy Awards | 34 | 17 |
| Golden Globe Awards | 29 | 22 |
| Screen Actors Guild Awards | 33 | 16 |

*Presents data in columns with headings and white space for easy reading*

3. **Answer Questions.** Our website should provide answers to frequently asked questions such as the following:

Do audience members or seat fillers have to pay to attend the event?
How often do seat fillers have to move around?
Will seat fillers be on camera?

*Omits a closing and signature*

Our website can be more informative and boost our business remarkably if we implement some of these ideas. Are you free to talk about these suggestions at 10 a.m. on Tuesday, June 15?

**Tips for Formatting Memos**

- Set 1-inch top and bottom margins.
- Set left and right margins of 1 to 1.25 inches.
- Include the optional word *MEMO or MEMORANDUM* as the heading.
- Set one tab to align entries evenly after *Subject*.
- Single-space all but the shortest memos.
- Double-space between paragraphs.
- For a two-page memo, use a second-page heading with the addressee's name, page number, and date.
- If you print a hard copy, handwrite your initials after your typed name. Alternatively, in Adobe Acrobat add your electronic initials.
- Place bulleted or numbered lists flush left or indent them 0.5 inches.

## 5-2 Messaging and Texting at Work

**Instant messaging** (IM) has become a powerful communication tool in the office and on the go. IM enables two or more individuals to communicate in real time by exchanging brief text-based messages. Companies large and small now provide live online chats staffed with customer service representatives during business hours, in addition to the usual contact options, such as telephone and e-mail. Increasingly, AI-powered automated chat bots are replacing humans for routine inquiries 24/7. Facebook Messenger, WhatsApp, WeChat, Skype, and Snapchat and some browsers have built-in instant messaging (chat) functions. Slack is the most popular enterprise instant messaging and group chat tool.

**Text messaging**, or texting, is another popular means for exchanging brief messages in real time. Usually exchanged via smartphone, texting requires a **short message service** (SMS) supplied by a wireless service provider. A new system, **rich communication services** (RCS), promises advanced features such as multimedia-enhanced texts that can be customized for more appealing opt-in text alerts and mobile marketing. Increasingly, both instant and text messages are sent from mobile devices as 81 percent of Americans now own smartphones and many depend on them for Internet access.[23]

Fueled by online security and legal compliance concerns, business enterprises are combining multiple communication functions behind corporate firewalls. For example, Adobe Systems has developed Unicom. The Unified Communications Tool is an all-in-one internal communication platform connecting coworkers anywhere by chat, Twitter-like microblogging, and employee directory access, as well as by e-mail and phone. **Figure 5.2** shows a screenshot of such an integrated internal communication

**Figure 5.2  All-in-One Messaging on an Internal Enterprise Network**

To create a platform for secure and legally compliant internal communication, large companies have introduced powerful networks behind corporate firewalls that combine various capabilities in one: e-mail, chat, Twitter-like short messaging, and directory access by phone. All workers need to be professional; they are always on display. Everyone from from rookie coder to CEO is on the system.

system. Another great benefit is **presence functionality**. Coworkers can locate each other online, thus avoiding wild goose chases hunting someone who is out of the office. Messaging avoids phone tag and eliminates the downtime associated with personal telephone conversations. The immediacy of instant and text messaging has created many fans, not least because users know right away whether a message was delivered.

## 5-2a Benefits of Instant Messaging and Texting

The major attraction of instant messaging is real-time communication with colleagues anywhere in the world—if a cell phone signal or a Wi-Fi connection is available. Facebook's Messenger and WhatsApp, Apple's iMessage, and Snapchat are popular consumer messaging apps that can also be spotted on the job. Because IM allows people to share information immediately and make decisions quickly, its impact on business communication has been dramatic. Slack's group chat capability enables coworkers on far-flung project teams to communicate instantly or review the chat history afterward.

Like instant messaging, texting can substitute for voice calls, delivering messages between mobile phone users quickly and discreetly. Organizations around the world provide news alerts, financial information, and promotions to customers via text. Credit card accounts can be set up to notify account holders by text or e-mail of approaching payment deadlines. Embracing opt-in text marketing, Airbnb, DoorDash, Lyft, Nordstrom, Subway, and hundreds of other businesses engage consumers with coupons, games, and other offers. Text alerts sent by Old Navy are shown in **Figure 5.3**. Some businesses (e.g., Target and Domino's Pizza) use SMS for recruitment, first by inviting applicants to opt in with a short code so that they may receive text updates at each stage of the hiring process.

**OFFICE INSIDER**

"Texting is not the venue to convey delicate or difficult information. As with other digital communication, be careful about what you type—remember that your words can live on forever in a screenshot. Once you hit send, it's out of your control. . . . Every piece of communication [reflects] your professionalism, including a simple text. . . . As with every form of communication, spelling and punctuation count."[24]

**Diane Gottsman,**
*etiquette expert, owner of The Protocol School of Texas*

**Figure 5.3   Old Navy Uses SMS Marketing**

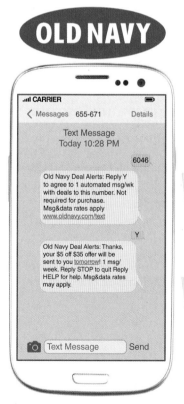

Old Navy Deal Alerts: Reply Y to agree to 1 automated msg/wk with deals to this number. Not required for purchase. Msg&data rates apply www.oldnavy.com/text

Old Navy Deal Alerts: Thanks, your $5 off $35 offer will be sent to you tomorrow! 1 msg/week. Reply STOP to quit Reply HELP for help. Msg&data rates may apply.

Old Navy encourages consumers to sign up for its mobile alert program. Once customers opt in by texting their nearest store's dedicated short code 653-689 (old-navy), they receive text messages announcing sneak peeks at new merchandise, rebates, and exclusive offers. Marketers report faster response times and increased engagement over other communication channels such as e-mail.

## 5-2b Risks of Messaging Apps and Texting

Despite their popularity among workers, some organizations forbid employees to use texting and instant messengers unless these tools are job-relevant and enterprise-grade. Employers consider chat and messaging yet another distraction in addition to phone calls, e-mail, and the Internet. Some organizations also fear that employees using free consumer-grade instant messaging apps could reveal privileged information and company records. Fearing charges of impropriety such as insider trading or interest rate manipulation following the Libor scandal, firms ranging from JPMorgan Chase, Barclays, and Citigroup to Deutsche Bank have restricted or completely banned messaging and chat apps.[25]

**Compliance Requirements and Security.** The SEC and other regulators require that financial services firms track and store all written business communication. Banks monitor e-mails and chats on company devices and limit personal phones and messaging. However, the task may be overwhelming and onerous to some, which is why many employees are eluding oversight by communicating via encrypted apps such as WhatsApp, iMessage, and WeChat.[26] Messages on Signal or Snapchat can be set to disappear altogether, causing regulators and employers compliance headaches and fear of fraud. Bring-your-own-device (BYOD) policies may give employers access to workers' personal devices.

Companies also worry about **phishing** (fraudulent schemes), viruses, and **malware** (malicious software programs). Like e-mail, any type of message and all other electronic records are subject to **discovery** (disclosure); that is, they can become evidence in lawsuits.

**Liability Burden.** A worker's improper use of mobile devices while on company business can expose the organization to staggering legal liability. The CDC reports that even a nonfatal injury crash at work caused by distraction costs businesses on average almost $72,500. Citing growing evidence, the agency also warns that hands-free devices are just as distracting as handheld phones.[27] When workers use messaging apps or texts to harass other workers, the employer may be culpable unless explicit rules and enforcement measures exist.

Organizations are fighting back to raise awareness and diminish liability. They are instituting detailed media use policies, now covering encrypted and ephemeral messaging apps. Businesses also protect themselves with formal employee training and technology tools such as monitoring, filtering, and blocking.

## 5-2c Best Practices for Instant Messaging and Texting

Before messaging on the job, be sure to seek approval. Because unsolicited text messages might seem invasive, ask permission first. Do not download and use third-party apps without checking with your supervisor. If your organization does allow messaging or texting for work, you can use it efficiently and professionally by following these guidelines:

- Comply with company policies: social media use, code of conduct, and ethics guidelines, as well as harassment and discrimination policies.

- Don't disclose sensitive financial, company, customer, employee, or executive data, and don't say anything that could damage your reputation or that of your organization.

- Avoid harassment and discriminatory content against classes protected by law (race, color, religion, sex, sexual orientation, national origin, age, and disability).

- Don't forward or link to inappropriate photos, videos, and art.

**OFFICE INSIDER**

"Slack is a compulsion, a distraction. A burden. Often, though, our complaints about it carry a note of aggrieved resignation. They're delivered in the same tone used for laments regarding air travel, Facebook, or Time Warner. Slack has become another utility we both rely on and resent."[29]

**Molly Fischer,** *editor and feature writer,* New York Magazine's *The Cut*

- Don't text or chat while driving a car; pull over if you must read or send a message.

- Separate business contacts from family and friends; limit personal messaging.

- Avoid unnecessary chitchat and know when to say goodbye. If personal messaging is allowed, keep it to a minimum.

- Ensure your presence status is up-to-date so that people trying to reach you don't waste their time. Make yourself unavailable when you need to meet a deadline.

- Use good grammar and correct spelling; beware of jargon, slang, and abbreviations, which can be confusing and appear unprofessional.

## 5-2d Text Messaging Etiquette

Texting is quick and unobtrusive, and for simple routine messages it is often the best alternative to a phone call or e-mail. Given the popularity of SMS, etiquette experts offer valuable advice.[28] **Figure 5.4** summarizes the suggestions they offer for the considerate and professional use of texting.

## 5-2e Enterprise Messaging—Slack

As we have seen, texting and instant messaging are convenient alternatives to routine phone calls and have all but replaced e-mail for short internal communication. All the major players in tech—Facebook, Google, Apple, IBM, and Microsoft—provide instant messaging software, mostly rolled out as mobile-friendly apps, reflecting growing smartphone access. Primarily for security reasons, but also to entice businesses to

### Figure 5.4  Texting Etiquette

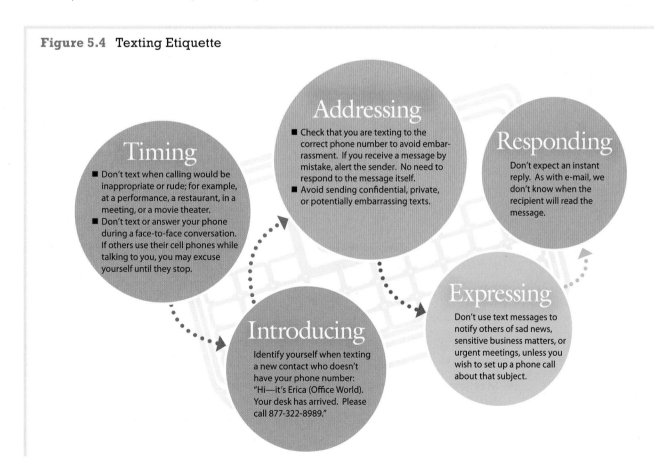

**Timing**
- Don't text when calling would be inappropriate or rude; for example, at a performance, a restaurant, in a meeting, or a movie theater.
- Don't text or answer your phone during a face-to-face conversation. If others use their cell phones while talking to you, you may excuse yourself until they stop.

**Addressing**
- Check that you are texting to the correct phone number to avoid embarrassment. If you receive a message by mistake, alert the sender. No need to respond to the message itself.
- Avoid sending confidential, private, or potentially embarrassing texts.

**Responding**
Don't expect an instant reply. As with e-mail, we don't know when the recipient will read the message.

**Introducing**
Identify yourself when texting a new contact who doesn't have your phone number: "Hi—it's Erica (Office World). Your desk has arrived. Please call 877-322-8989."

**Expressing**
Don't use text messages to notify others of sad news, sensitive business matters, or urgent meetings, unless you wish to set up a phone call about that subject.

commit to their complete cloud-based environment, Google, Microsoft, Adobe, and others offer popular office suite bundles that generally include personal productivity, communication, collaboration, and content management tools. Microsoft 365 (Skype, Teams), Google's G Suite (Hangouts), and Salesforce (Quiq) dominate the workplace. As of now, though, Slack is outperforming the giants.

**The Upside.** At 10 million daily users, Slack is popular mostly with small businesses and start-ups—so much so that it has become a verb: *Slack me* or *Yes, we Slacked.*[30] Enterprise group chat apps such as Slack appeal to many workers because they declutter e-mail inboxes, simplify workplace communication, and function as digital water coolers with chat rooms (channels) to socialize in. One of Slack's main benefits is increased camaraderie as workers collaborate on main channels but also congregate in private channels to chat about mundane topics. Slack facilitates conversations across dispersed teams and time zones. Software developers, for example, tend to be heavy users. Reviewers of Slack uniformly praise its intuitive interface and ease of use for local and remote teams. They also like the seamless integration of other productivity tools with Slack, such as G Suite and Dropbox.[31]

Unlike e-mail, Slack is ideal for quick answers and efficient back-and-forth exchanges, but it is not suited for information dumps or lengthy discussions. Employers approve of Slack because they can securely monitor, log, and archive all communication.

**The Downside.** Slack critics cite three major problem areas: distraction, spillover of workplace messaging into home life, and rude behavior on the platform. Often businesses deploy Slack expecting that collaboration will happen magically without providing guidance how to use the platform. Some workers find Slack so distracting that they refuse to use it, while others cannot disengage from it. Training sessions and snoozing Slack notifications help doubters focus on work. Silencing channel notifications during downtime reduces the pressure to respond instantly and thus fosters a better work-life balance.[32] Without clear rules, workers can get overwhelmed. A recent spate of class action lawsuits has centered on the use of digital workplace and mobile apps during rest periods and outside of business hours, as Slack and similar apps are erasing the line between work and leisure.[33]

As for misconduct, the reviews are mixed. Some executives praise Slack for having a positive effect on workplace culture by providing workers with a platform to share professional and personal information. However, it's precisely the informality of Slack chat, experts say, that can also be "an incubator for misbehavior" because distinctions between professional and personal can blur.[34]

## 5-2f Slack Etiquette

Because Slack has the look and feel of a social media network like Facebook or Twitter, users easily slip into iMessage lingo, slang, and informal conversations. Also, chat platforms foster friendships at work, and friends tend to be casual with each other. Slack is much less formal than e-mail. To avoid the danger of accidental oversharing and forgetting you are at work, follow this "ultimate Slack etiquette guide"[35]:

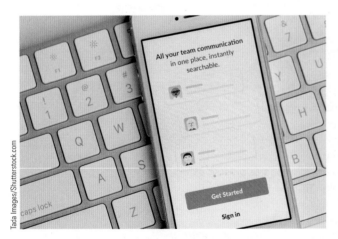

Slack is ideal for quick and efficient back-and-forth exchanges. Its interface is intuitive and easy to use. Employers like Slack because they can monitor, log, and archive all communication. Some users complain that Slack is distracting.

- **Stay away from slang and acronyms with swear words in them**. Experts agree, swearing still has no place at work. Anticipate future readers on Slack who might dislike an ill-mannered style. Slang and trendy words grow stale quickly and aren't always understood.

- **Avoid talking about job hunting, illness, finances, or hating coworkers**. The company reads your Slack messages. It can legally access any content that passes through work devices. Keep personal issues to yourself. All chats are saved on Slack. Oversharing is forever.

- **Shun arguments.** Through a false sense of familiarity, encrypted and ephemeral apps induce people to talk in ways they wouldn't in person. Slack may enable passive-aggressive speech and bullying. Avoid embarrassment when meeting the person in the lunchroom.

- **Compliment your coworkers.** Highlight accomplishments of colleagues when deserved. In your team's main chatroom, such positive messages live on for weeks, where management may see the good work your team is doing.

- **Curb the emojis.** The occasional thumbs up or smiley face sends a friendly message, but a string of emojis is too cutesy for the workplace. Be professional; hold off on emojis in serious messages or when communicating with senior leaders at your company.

- **Use miscellaneous channels to make friends.** Aside from the main channel, companies often keep miscellaneous channels for specific groups, such as remote workers. Don't share in your first week on the job, unless it's a "fun" channel for cat lovers or NBA fanatics. Observe first.

- **Adjust your tone to your audience.** You can be colloquial with coworkers at happy hour but not with the CEO. Be professional with your boss and other executives. Leave the *LOL* for chatting with a close coworker. Follow the cues of your office.

## 5-3 Making Podcasts Work for Business

Professional podcasts can be elaborate productions and require quality hardware, which may explain why their use is lagging that of other corporate digital media channels. However, podcasts have their place among contemporary communication technology tools, and businesses may finally be catching on to the huge potential of podcasting as an engagement tool. In addition to discussing the role of podcasts in business today, this section includes several podcaster categories, and identifies a few valuable business podcasts.

**LEARNING OUTCOME 3**
Identify professional applications of business podcasts and the professional standards underpinning them.

### 5-3a The Growing Popularity of Podcasts

**Podcasts** are digital audio programs resembling radio shows. They tend to be series of episodes that generally feature a host, sometimes two, often in an interview format. They are distributed regularly—daily, weekly, or monthly—as audio programs that can be played on demand in a Web browser or with a mobile app on various digital devices. The terms *podcast* and *podcasting* originate from combining the words *broadcasting* and *iPod*, the Apple MP3 player. Podcasts can cover topics as diverse as news, politics, business, sports, popular culture, and self-help. Most are pre-recorded, but some are live.

The growth in smartphone use and other technological advances have boosted the reach and popularity of podcasting. In the last five years alone, awareness of podcasting has grown from 50 percent to 70 percent among Americans 12 years old and up; more than half have ever listened to at least one podcast (up from a third).[36] Estimates suggest that 850,000 shows with more than 30 million episodes may be vying for listeners' attention today.[37]

One huge benefit of podcasting is portability. Podcasts encoded as MP3, ACC, or WMA files can be downloaded to a computer, a smartphone, a tablet, or an MP3 player to be enjoyed offline. Unlike watching video that requires some focused attention, listening to a recording allows busy professionals to learn, keep informed, and be entertained while maximizing their limited time on their commute or in the gym.

## 5-3b  The Main Players in Podcasting

Podcasts can be categorized by genre (subject) and by producers and their purpose. Business is our focus; however, a clear majority of podcasts is devoted to entertainment. At 36 percent, comedy leads the weekly podcast consumption in the United States, followed by news (23 percent), society and culture (22 percent), sports (15 percent), and true crime (12 percent). Business podcasts are "consumed" only by 10 percent of weekly listeners.[38] Among podcast providers, we will focus on business organizations, podcasting entrepreneurs, news media, and podcasting in education.

**Corporations and Other Businesses.** Many companies are eager to jump into making a podcast series. Marketing experts estimate that half of all brands are about to launch or plan to launch their own podcasts. The advantage to companies is independence from social media algorithms and the ability to diversify their media channels.[39]

Companies as varied as Caterpillar, IBM, and Walmart are on board with public, professionally produced podcasts. Beyond the Iron is a podcast series created by Caterpillar devoted to the company's "corporate roots and iconic products" as well as its "other brands and offerings."[40] IBM distributes a whole range of podcasts clustered around its products and tech topics. The podcasts address various audiences, external and internal, and are often paired with blogs. Walmart Radio, the self-described "biggest retail radio show in the world,"[41] also publishes a series of podcast episodes featuring interviews, company news, and more.

Internally, podcasts can be used to inform, engage, and train staff. A podcast series can help convey authenticity by featuring the voices of employees and personalizing executives. Because they can broadcast repetitive information that does not require interaction, podcasts often replace costlier live teleconferences. Alternatively, teleconferences or webcasts are later provided as podcasts to those who missed the live event. Human resources policies can also be presented in the form of podcasts or videos for on-demand consumption.

**Entrepreneurs and Enterprising Individuals.** For the purpose of attracting listeners, it helps if the podcast host is a well-known businessperson or TV personality, whether it be sports columnist Bill Simmons or the "Matriarch of Money," Suze Orman.[42] Her Women and Money show confirms that Orman is a no-nonsense authority preaching financial literacy, and people gladly listen. Then there are those who become wealthy and Internet famous through shrewd investments and loud self-promotion on social media, entrepreneurs such as Gary Vaynerchuk and Tim Ferriss. They author best-selling self-help books, blogs, and podcasts with a loyal following.

Although he has been called a fake expert,[43] Tim Ferriss is one of America's most successful podcasters, as shown in **Figure 5.5**. Ferriss provides podcasts on many self-improvement topics, but his interviews with businesspeople, scientists, and celebrities appear to be the most intriguing feature. Countless such self-described business experts issue podcasts and amass sizable fan communities.

**News and Media Organizations.** Perhaps because they have the necessary technical and journalistic expertise, major news organizations and media outlets podcast radio shows. National Public Radio (NPR), *Harvard Business Review, The Wall Street Journal,* and *The New York Times,* just to name a few, each distribute not one but several podcast series. Two noteworthy business and tech podcasts are WSJ Secrets of Wealthy Women and WSJ's The Future of Everything.

Another notable podcast series worth exploring is the TED Radio Hour by NPR, "a narrative journey through fascinating ideas, astonishing inventions, fresh approaches to

**Figure 5.5  A Weekly Hit Podcast: The Tim Ferriss Show**

A bestselling author, Tim Ferriss is also the host of an award-winning podcast series on leadership and entrepreneurship—500+ episodes and almost 700 million downloads at this count. On his weekly Tim Ferriss Show, he interviews an eclectic mix of leaders, such as Disney's Bob Iger, psychologists Brené Brown and Esther Perel, filmmaker Ken Burns, or scientist and media personality Neil deGrasse Tyson. Ferriss is a master of media, whether on Instagram (1.1 million followers) or Twitter (1.7 million followers). He maintains a popular blog, sends out a weekly newsletter to his 1.5 million subscribers, and has been dubbed "the Oprah of Audio" (*The Observer*) for his show.

Source: The Tim Ferriss Show

old problems, and new ways to think and create."[44] In addition to its famous TED Talks on YouTube, the nonprofit organization produces daily audio TED Talks.

**Education Podcasts.** Podcasts are increasingly common in education. Some instructors started recording their own to facilitate accessible learning for students with disabilities, to benefit auditory learners, and create an archive of lessons. The portability of podcasts allows students to listen to instructors' lectures, interviews, sporting events, and other content anytime and anywhere.

Apple's iTunes U is likely the best-known example of free educational programs from hundreds of renowned universities across the globe. Open University on iTunes covers a vast amount of learning resources in categories such as business and economics, engineering, history, languages, science, and many more. An Internet search reveals many options for education podcasts.

## 5-3c  Can Podcasts Make Money and Do They Last?

The biggest names in podcasting who command sizable audiences will attract advertisers, usually those that offer related brands and covet the listenership demographic of the show. Advertisers go where the ears are. The 2,000 most popular podcasts draw the likes of GEICO, Capital One, Progressive, Procter & Gamble brands, and TrueCar—the top five most prolific podcast advertisers among more than 9,000 brands buying podcast ads.[45] Sought-after podcasters also have sponsors and get paid for product endorsements.

As a personal finance guru, Suze Orman plugs federal credit unions on her podcast website. However, promotion deals have been criticized as inevitably leading to biased recommendations.[46] Consumers should always know whether a trusted authority is being paid for endorsements.

Of course, video is a much bigger draw on the Internet than audio. Videos range from millions of cat videos, myriad how-to instructions, and shaky user-generated smartphone footage to slick professional videos, movie previews, and entire feature films. YouTube, Vimeo, and TikTok are examples of popular video hosting and sharing services. Most companies and brands maintain video channels as part of their overall media strategy. More coverage of YouTube is included in our discussion of social media.

## 5-4 Telling Stories With Blogs and News Sites

**LEARNING OUTCOME 4**

Describe how businesses use blogs to connect with internal and external audiences.

A **blog** is a website or social media platform with generally well-crafted articles or commentaries on topics such as new products or services, media coverage, industry news, human resources, and philanthropy. Businesses use blogs to keep customers, employees, and the public at large informed. The two biggest advantages of external business blogs are that they can accumulate a far-flung, vast audience and allow companies to shape the brand story in a longer narrative form. Blogs are another tool for public relations and brand building—one channel in a multichannel social media strategy.

Employees and executives at companies as varied as Allstate, Caterpillar, Exxon Mobil, General Motors, Patagonia, Southwest Airlines, and Target maintain blogs. They use blogs to communicate internally with employees and externally with the public. At present, 270 (54 percent) of Fortune 500 companies in the United States maintain a public-facing corporate blog.[48] However, blog adoption varies across industries. Research shows that the top five sectors most likely to embrace blogs are commercial banks, specialty retailers, semiconductors and electronics makers, gas and electric utilities, and pharmaceuticals.[49]

In this section you will learn how businesses use blogs. You will also find guidance on professional blogging practices.

**OFFICE INSIDER**

"For companies and entrepreneurs, gaining online visibility is one of the best ways to grow subscribers, leads and ultimately revenue. This can't be achieved with a static corporate website. Creating blog content that is valuable, helpful, and/or entertaining is an effective way to grow your website's authority, online rankings, and traffic."[47]

**Gary Dekmezian,**
*entrepreneur, digital marketer, professional blogger*

### 5-4a How Companies Tell Stories

Like social media platforms, corporate blogs may be used to create virtual communities. Companies use blogs for public relations, customer relations, market research, internal communication, online community building, and recruiting. Internal blogs accessible to employees on a corporate intranet serve as information hubs, encourage discussion, create a sense of community, and foster engagement.

**Public Relations and Customer Relations.** One of the prominent uses of blogs is to provide up-to-date

company information to the media, employees, and the public. Blogs can be written by rank-and-file employees or by top managers. An avid longtime blogger, executive chairman Bill Marriott addressed the COVID-19 pandemic-related furloughs and layoffs his hotel chain was forced to undertake. In his Marriott on the Move blog, the longtime executive spoke very sincerely to the public ("We were forced to . . . postpone weddings, bar mitzvahs, anniversary parties and so many once-in-a-lifetime events the world holds dear") but also spoke empathically about "our beloved associates, many of whom have been with Marriott for 20, 30, and even 40 years." His voice sounded heartfelt and authentic.

Predictably, tech companies rely heavily on blogs. The GE Aviation blog is just one of several General Electric news and media hubs; it highlights key employees and the company's latest aerospace and flight news. The GE Digital division operates the futuristic Industrial Insights IoT blog. Prominent features include information about GE's many software products and the company's technical assistance.

Many retailers blog as well. In its Best Buy Influencer Network, the electronics retailer is inviting **influencers**, loyal fans with a large social media following, to create a profile and blog on its platform. Quirky online shoe retailer Zappos in its Beyond the Box blog faithfully conjures up the image as an entrepreneurial company that strives for "The Power of WOW" by focusing on dedicated customer service.

Business blogs can be extremely lucrative. Some bloggers with a huge online following turn their writing into perks or cash through promotion. Well-known **brand ambassadors** such as former Apple exec and entrepreneur Guy Kawasaki **evangelize** (i.e., advocate) for brands and are well compensated; for example, Mercedes-Benz loaned Kawasaki an AMG GTS super car.

**Engagement and Viral Marketing.** The engagement aspect of blogging appears to be waning. Starbucks shut down its long-lasting My Idea community blog it had used for crowdsourcing. The coffee retailer still solicits creative ideas from the public, just not as visibly as a running tally listing thousands of suggestions on a website. Similarly, Frito-Lay pulled the plug on its long-running Crash the Super Bowl contest which lured thousands of fans to create a humorous Doritos commercial. Entrants competed for a $1 million prize. Insiders point to a demographic shift from millennial to Gen Z consumers who prefer to engage with brands via social media, not blogs, where they create content, for example, on the popular short video platform TikTok.[50]

Marketers realize the potential of getting the word out about their brands in channels such as blogs and social media in general. They hope their messages will be picked up by those well-connected brand advocates or influencers mentioned earlier, who appeal to large audiences. The hope is that buzz will develop and even go viral. The term **viral marketing** refers to the rapid spread of messages online, much like the spread of infectious diseases. Viral messages must be authentic and elicit an emotional response, but for that very reason they are difficult to orchestrate. Large companies employ teams of social media experts and marketers who scrutinize social media for buzz and positive or negative posts about their organizations and products.

**Online Communities.** Like Instagram, YouTube, Snapchat, Facebook, and Twitter, company blogs can draw a loyal core following to businesses and brands. Such followers want to keep informed about company events, product updates, offers, freebies, and other news. The Coca-Cola Company has transformed its Conversations blog to a News site with rich stories about its many brands. In one article chairman and CEO James Quincey reflects on Coke's century of accomplishments as a public company. The soft drink maker also maintains interactive pages with offers to earn perks by connecting with its brands, for example, tie-ins with March Madness and

**Blogs can draw a loyal core following to businesses and brands. Such followers want to keep informed about company events, product updates, offers, freebies, and other news.**

AMC Theaters or games to win gift cards and vacations. A Coca-Cola smartphone app invites users to create custom Coca-Cola mixes.

**Internal Communication and Recruiting.** Internally, blogs can be used to keep virtual teams on track and share updates on the road. Members in remote locations can stay in touch by smartphone and other mobile devices, exchanging documents, images, audio, and video clips. In many companies, blogs have replaced hard-copy publications in offering late-breaking news or tidbits of interest to employees. Such blogs can help build communities, prompt the sharing of expertise, and stimulate employee involvement. In addition, internal corporate blogs serve as searchable archives of company knowledge.

Public-facing blogs mirror the company culture and present an invaluable opportunity for job candidates to size up a potential employer and the people working there. Public-facing blogs mirror the company culture and present an invaluable opportunity for job candidates to size up a potential employer and the people working there. The explicit purpose of Target's Pulse Blog, for example, is to "help our candidates get a sneak peek into what it's like to work at Target."[51]

Early blogs were attempts to show the human face of a company, its executives, and employees. Some continue this mission to connect on a more personal level. However, as blogs mature, fewer encourage commentary, or they require registering and logging in behind corporate firewalls. Many blogs today publish news items written by PR professionals, and their slick posts typically remain nameless.

## 5-4b Mastering Blogging: Seven Tips

Much advice is freely accessible online, but this section offers guidelines culled from experienced bloggers and communication experts that will lead you to successful online writing. As with any public writing, your posts will be scrutinized; therefore, you want to make the best impression.

Lev dolgachov/Syda Productions/AGE Fotostock

**WORKPLACE IN FOCUS**

**Wearable devices (wearables)**—such as heart rate monitors and skin response sensors—enable companies to monitor worker productivity and lifestyle. Much like fitness devices worn by athletes, wearables can measure brain activity, record movement, and even monitor posture. Very soon sensors will be embedded in smart work clothes; think touch-screen sleeves or collars changing color based on mood.[52] Bio-sensing wearables are entering the mining, construction, and oil and gas industries, mainly to monitor workers' health and safety.

Employers love wearables because they believe the devices can help them save on health-care costs. They feel justified in tracking workers' behavior even outside the workplace. They argue that lifestyle choices—including alcohol and caffeine intake, exercise, sleep, eating habits, and smoking—affect job performance. They want to measure stress levels and productivity. Critics fear poor morale and pushback if workers don't know how information is used and fear that their data are not private and secure. They also worry about the accuracy of the devices used. How do you feel about these types of workplace monitoring? Would you want to opt out?

**Craft a Catchy but Concise Title.** The headline is what draws online readers to even click to go your post. Some will be intriguing questions or promises. Bloggers often use numbers to structure their posts. Here are some examples of captivating blog post titles: *9 Tips on How to Scale Your Business; Six Apps You Don't Want to Miss; 5 Tips to Keep Hackers Out of Your Accounts; Create Powerful Imagery in Your Writing; How Financially Sexy Is Your Household?* An analysis of 100 million blog post titles revealed that the most successful headline included the phrase "Will Make You," followed by "This Is Why," and "Can We Guess."[53] Success was measured by user engagement in the form of a like, share, or comment. Here are two examples: "These 3 Warren Buffett Rules Will Make You a Better Investor" and "13 Travel Tips That Will Make You Feel Smart."

**Ace the Opening Paragraph.** The lead must deliver on the promise of the headline. Identify a need and propose to solve the problem. Ask a relevant question. Tell an anecdote or use an analogy to connect with the reader. Say something startling. The Direct2Dell blog author of "Do You Have What It Takes? Top 20 Most Rugged Jobs in America" opened with this:

> *Have you ever scaled a 20-foot tree, hung off the side of a skyscraper, been 700 meters underground, or labored on a ship for 36 hours straight? It's hard to imagine that this is a normal day of work for some people. . . .*[54]

**Provide Details in the Body.** Mind the *So what?* and *What's in it for me?* questions. Use vivid examples, quotations and testimonials, or statistics. Structure the body with numbers, bullets, and subheadings. Use expressive action verbs *(buy* for *get; own* for *have; travel* or *jet* for *go)*. Use conversational language to sound warm and authentic. Use contractions *(can't* for *cannot; doesn't* for *does not; isn't* for *is not)*.

**Consider Visuals.** Add visual interest with relevant images and diagrams. Keep paragraphs short and use plenty of white space around them. Aim to make the look simple and easy to scan.

**Include a Call to Action.** Call on readers to do something or provide a take-away and gentle nudge at the end.

> *Here's a tip you can use right away. You'll have vastly better copy on your website in 20 minutes by following these two simple steps:*
>
> *Go look at your web copy right now.*
>
> *Take out every word that doesn't contribute something new.*
>
> *Come back here and tell us about the before-and-after. I bet you'll have something to say!*[55]

Asking open-ended questions is another effective closing: "Those are two of XYZ Company's ideas about where business-to-business marketing is heading. How about you? Have you developed some new strategies of your own? What exciting ideas are fueling your own marketing—and how are you applying them? Let us know in the comments."

**Edit and Proofread.** Follow the revision tips in Chapter 4 of this book. Cut any unneeded words, sentences, and irrelevant ideas. Fix awkward, wordy, and repetitious sentences. Edit and proofread as if your life depended on it—your reputation might. The best blogs are error free.

**Respond to Posts Respectfully.** Build a positive image online by posting compelling comments on other bloggers' posts. Politely and promptly reply to comments on your site. This reply to Jamie Spencer's blogging advice post[56] makes a positive comment and asks a question. The exchange is cordial, albeit marred by punctuation errors:

**OFFICE INSIDER**

"When it comes to the biggest trends in marketing today, our industry is obsessed with channels such as social, voice, and augmented reality as the means for reaching today's modern audience. And while each plays an important role in the customer journey, new research from Adobe finds a more traditional form of marketing—email—is very much holding its own among newer channels and technologies."[57]

Giselle Abramovich, *executive editor, Enterprise Thought Leadership, Adobe*

**Figure 5.6** Writing a Captivating Blog

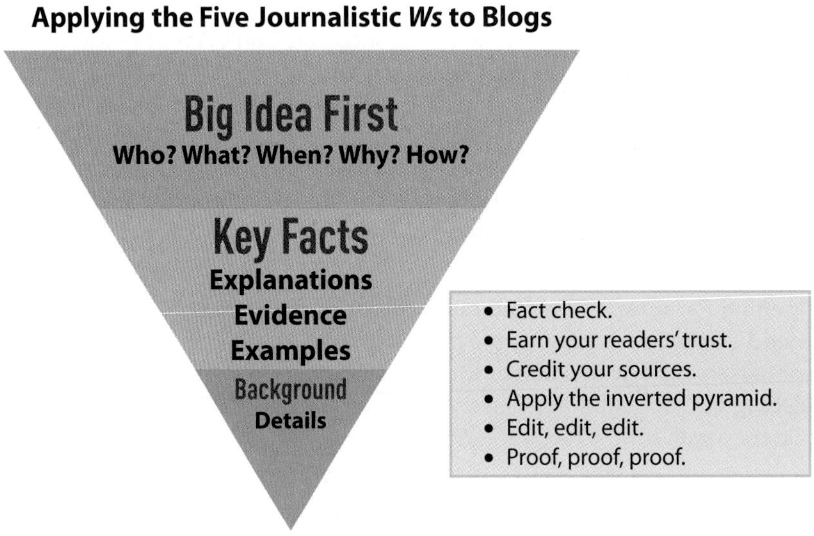

**Applying the Five Journalistic *Ws* to Blogs**

**Big Idea First**
Who? What? When? Why? How?

**Key Facts**
Explanations
Evidence
Examples
Background
Details

- Fact check.
- Earn your readers' trust.
- Credit your sources.
- Apply the inverted pyramid.
- Edit, edit, edit.
- Proof, proof, proof.

**Alice M:** *Thank you for all your helpful information. I've found this website so useful! I'm about to start my first blog. The blog is basically music reviews and I was just wondering if you knew whether I'm allowed to copy videos off YouTube for example?*

**Jamie:** *As long as you use the relevant embed codes from YouTube to add videos to your site you should be ok to do that. I wouldn't recommend ripping any content from a YouTube video and then hosting it yourself, this could be a copyright issue.*

If you disagree with a post, do so respectfully. Don't ramble. Your blog posts can benefit from the journalistic pattern shown in **Figure 5.6** by emphasizing the big news up front, supported by specifics and background information.

## 5-5 Navigating Social Networking for Business

**LEARNING OUTCOME 5**
Discuss business organizations' external and internal social media practices as well as the risks inherent in Internet use today.

Popular social networking sites such as Instagram, Facebook, and Twitter are used by businesses for similar reasons and in much the same way as podcasts and blogs. Social media enable businesses to connect with customers and employees, share company news, promote goods and services, and exchange ideas. Social online communities for professional audiences (e.g., LinkedIn), discussed in Chapter 13, help recruiters find talent and encounter job candidates before hiring them. Today, LinkedIn occupies the No. 1 spot as 99 percent of businesses use the platform for business networking and recruiting.[58] Seven in ten (70 percent) of hiring managers scour social media as part of their screening processes.[59]

### 5-5a Tapping Into Social Media

Business interest in social media is not surprising if we consider that online is where—in marketing speak—the consumer eyeballs are. Nearly three-fourths (72 percent) of American adults use some type of social media.[60] The most avid social media users, however, are the millennials (85 percent), the cohort born 1981–1996. Their smartphone ownership is highest at 93 percent, although older age groups are gaining on them in tech adoption.[61] At the same time, millennials are now the largest generation in the workforce (35 percent).[62] No wonder, then, that businesses are eager to connect on social media with this particular demographic but also precisely target the other age groups wherever they may congregate online.

**The Most Popular Social Media.** Knowing how various cohorts and consumer segments in the United States use technology and which social media they favor is invaluable to marketers for building and promoting their brands. YouTube is the most popular online platform as it draws 73 percent of U.S. adults, followed by Facebook (69 percent), Instagram (37 percent), Pinterest (28 percent), LinkedIn (27 percent), Snapchat (24 percent), Twitter (22 percent), and WhatsApp (20 percent).[63] Overall, social media adoption is still growing, with a slight drop-off or leveling out among Gen X and boomer Facebook users perhaps linked to Facebook's privacy and disinformation stumbles.

**Where Businesses Go Social.** As can be expected, a staggering 95 percent of the Fortune 500 companies have a presence on Facebook, up 6 percent over the previous year. With engaging word-of-mouth content, corporate Twitter accounts (96 percent in the Fortune 500) can drive e-mail subscriptions and increase sales overall. YouTube's 1 billion global users may be the reason that 90 percent of the Fortune 500 have a YouTube presence. Instagram is gaining momentum; 73 percent of the largest companies use Instagram, up 10 points from the previous year. Companies understand that to be successful, they need to embrace a multichannel media strategy as part of their broader business goals.[64]

The newest kid on the block is TikTok, the quirky short video-sharing platform featuring "Real People. Real Videos." Advertisers love the creativity of the wildly popular teen-dominated network and see an opportunity to win credibility with a young age group ranging from 14 to 26. Teen favorite Chipotle garnered 3.9 billion views with its viral #boorito hashtag challenge. ELF Cosmetics composed a TikTok song now appearing in 1.7 million videos. Teenage influencers like Charli D'Amelio, who has 80 million fans, have become early sensations.[65] However, because TikTok is owned by a Chinese company, U.S. authorities suspect it of delivering American user data to the Chinese government. Like 5G innovator Huawei, TikTok is perceived as a potential national security threat.[66]

**Figure 5.7** shows the three most popular brands on Facebook.

## Figure 5.7 The Brands That Rule on Facebook

The biggest global social network, Facebook has reached more than 2.7 billion monthly active users (MAU) worldwide, followed by YouTube with 2 billion MAU. Since buying WhatsApp, Facebook saw the messaging app's popularity soar to 2 billion MAU. Another Facebook-owned brand, Instagram, boasts more than 1.15 billion global MAU; relative newcomer TikTok reports 689 million MAU; LinkedIn has 766 million registered users but only 310 million are active per month; and monthly active users on Twitter now number 340 million. On Facebook, the top three product brands with the most fans are Facebook itself (211 million followers), Samsung (1620 million), and Coca-Cola (106 million).

## 5-5b Enterprise Social Networking

Mirroring social media sites but securely located behind corporate firewalls, Connections, created by tech giant IBM, is an internal social networking platform to help organizations share knowledge, improve decision making, and foster innovation. Companies launching comprehensive enterprise networking platforms, such as Connections, Jive, or Microsoft's Yammer, are investing in what they hope will lead to greater employee engagement and productivity. The platforms promise seamless networking away from e-mail, connecting workers one-on-one, in small teams, and across the entire company in one secure environment.

Connections, for example, combines an array of functions (e.g., project management, up-to-the-minute microblogging updates across the network, profiles of people in the organization, collaborative space, crowdsourcing tools, blogging, task management, content storage, and forums). The hope is that these tools will flatten the corporate hierarchy and empower individual employees at all levels. The advantage of enterprise social media networks is that they are searchable, enabling workers to tag, follow, view activity feeds, and more. Users can access and send information much more efficiently than by e-mail alone.[67]

**Nimble Damage Control and Responding to Grievances.** Insurance and financial services firm Nationwide uses internal social networking to quickly respond to disasters such as hurricanes. Agents in Florida used the platform to record customers' pressing needs during a major storm, which led to improved service in subsequent natural disasters when Nationwide trucks headed into disaster zones equipped with the right essentials.[68]

Over at IBM, after an employee posted a petition against a new company policy that would ban reimbursement for ride-sharing services such as Uber, within hours the post had drawn hundreds of comments and more than 1,200 views. IBM's social analytics picked up the network traffic, and Diane Gherson, senior vice president for human resources, responded directly to the employee on the Connections platform and explained that the company would reverse the ban. The post and the swift response to it led to positive change, and the goodwill of the unhappy employee was most likely restored.[69]

**Connecting Dispersed Workers.** Because social networks are about connections, they also enable companies to match up and connect off-site employees. The Goodyear Tire & Rubber Company uses the Microsoft 365 suite that includes Yammer to ensure

WORKPLACE IN FOCUS

Arguably the world's most famous department store, Harrods suffered an embarrassing website blunder. The upscale UK retailer caused a run on its Aspinal of London designer handbags once some of these luxury items, typically costing £250 ($325) to £950 ($1,240), were advertised online for £2.13 ($2.80) to £8.08 ($10.54). The upscale department store blamed a supplier's computer pricing error for the glitch. Representatives personally contacted customers to apologize "for any inconvenience caused"[70] but refused to deliver the merchandise at the incorrect price. Was Harrods obligated to honor the offer?

its associates around the world work effectively together as a team. Chief information officer Sherry Neubert explains that Goodyear's virtual teams conduct meetings with Skype for Business, exchange instant messages to quickly resolve problems, and participate in enterprise social networking to contribute creative ideas.[71]

**Crowdsourcing Employees to Achieve Buy-In.** Internal social networks and blogs can help companies invite employee input to effect change and solve business problems. Gathering and sharing input on Yammer, the Red Robin restaurant chain motivates its workers with incentives to propose cost-saving ideas.[72] Similarly, when IBM realized it had to do something about its hated performance management system, the tech firm decided to solicit employee feedback using Connections. At first the crowdsourcing initiative met with skepticism; however, during the first 24 hours of the comment period, IBM received a whopping 2,000 responses. Online debates and polling followed. Within a few months, the company developed a new evaluation system prototype, called Checkpoint, and deployed it to 375,000 employees.[73]

## 5-5c Social Media and Risk Management

Public-facing social networks hold great promise for businesses while also presenting potential risk. Most managers desire plugged-in employees with strong tech skills and fantasize about their brands becoming overnight sensations thanks to viral marketing. Managers like to imagine their workers as enthusiastic brand evangelists. However, businesses also fret about lost productivity, reputational damage, and legal issues (e.g., violations of privacy laws, workplace harassment, and defamation). To minimize risk, companies rely on social media policies, approve and oversee employees' use of social media, and mandate training.[74]

Experts are divided on accessing private social media accounts on-site. Advocates cite authentic promotion of the business, improved morale, and new client relationship building. Skeptics denounce oversharing and the leaking of confidential information. They believe only trained social media professionals should speak for an organization.[75] Businesses vary in their approaches to personal social media use. Some, such as Zappos, take a hands-off approach and encourage employee online activity. Others, such as IBM, have crafted detailed Social Computing Guidelines that allow "incidental personal use" as long as it "is limited in duration, does not violate company policies, and does not distract us or others from the work we do."[76]

Although more than half of U.S. employers block social media at work,[77] such efforts can be circumvented when employees use their personal smartphones, virtual private networks, or work from home in the wake of the COVID-19 pandemic, as 66 percent of U.S. employees do at least some of the time.[78] Data security scientists fear that hackers may deliver malware through Twitter, LinkedIn, Facebook, or Instagram by hijacking accounts; however, they also acknowledge that banning social media is an extreme measure that may breed resentment among current workers and deter future talent. In addition, employees may need to access social media as part of their job duties.[79]

The best advice to workers is to follow company policies; assume that privacy doesn't exist, and avoid sharing sensitive information, least of all risqué photographs. Furthermore, refusing friend requests or unfriending individuals could jeopardize professional relationships. Consider the dos and don'ts in **Figure 5.8** if you want to use social media and keep your job.

## 5-5d The Dark Side of Technology and Social Media

Internet access nearly for all has meant that in cyberspace users can bypass gatekeepers who filter content in the traditional print and visual media. This open marketplace of ideas online was once hailed as democratic and empowering. However, user anonymity has displaced accountability, and public discourse has descended into disrespect, hate speech, and worse. Even extreme views may reach audiences of thousands or even millions. The dangers are obvious. Fact checking often falls by the

**OFFICE INSIDER**

"The major new challenge in reporting news is the new shape of truth. Truth is no longer dictated by authorities but is networked by peers. For every fact there is a counterfact and all these counterfacts and facts look identical online, which is confusing to most people."[80]

**Kevin Kelly,** *co-founder,* Wired *magazine*

**Figure 5.8** Using Digital Media Like a Pro: Dos and Don'ts

**DON'TS** — Avoid questionable content, personal documents, and file sharing

**Don't spread rumors, gossip, and negative defamatory comments.** Because all digital information is subject to discovery in court, avoid unprofessional content and conduct, including complaints about your employer, customers, and employees.

**Don't download and share cartoons, video clips, photos, and art.** Businesses are liable for any recorded digital content regardless of the medium used.

**Don't open unfamiliar attachments.** Attachments with executable files or video files may carry viruses, spyware, or other malware (malicious programs).

**Don't download free software and utilities to company machines.** Employees can unwittingly introduce viruses, phishing schemes, and other cyber bugs.

**Don't store your music and photos on a company machine (or server) and don't watch streaming videos.** Capturing precious company bandwidth for personal use is a sure way to be shown the door.

**Don't share files, and avoid file-sharing services.** Clarify whether you may use Google Docs and other services that offer optional file sharing. Stay away from distributors or pirated files such as LimeWire.

**DOs** — Know workplace policies and use media only for work-related purposes

**Learn your company's rules.** Some companies require workers to sign that they have read and understand Internet and digital media use policies. Being informed is your best protection.

**Avoid sending personal e-mail, instant messages, or texts from work.** Even if your company allows personal use during lunch or after hours, keep it to a minimum. Better yet, wait to use your own electronic devices away from work.

**Separate work and personal data.** Keep information that could embarrass you or expose you to legal liability on your personal storage devices, on hard drives, or in the cloud, never on your office computer.

**Be careful when blogging, tweeting, or posting on social networking sites.** Unhappy about not receiving a tip, a Beverly Hills waiter lost his job for tweeting disparaging remarks about an actress. Forgetting that his boss was his Facebook friend, a British employee was fired after posting, "OMG, I HATE MY JOB!" and calling his supervisor names.

**Keep sensitive information private.** Use privacy settings, but don't trust the "private" areas on Facebook, Twitter, Flickr, and other social networks.

**Avoid pornography, sexually explicit jokes, or inappropriate screen savers.** Anything that might poison the work environment is a harassment risk and, therefore, prohibited.

---

wayside, buzz becomes more important than truth, and a few keystrokes can threaten a reputation. Americans fear for their privacy yet increasingly trust information on social media more than mainstream media sources. This section addresses several cyberthreats that affect all of us as businesspeople and citizens.

Privacy Fears. Our smartphones spy on us. Location services in most apps allow users to be tracked with pinpoint precision. Tracking is enabled by default and most people don't know that practically all their movements can be followed, as a disturbing *New York Times* exposé revealed.[81] Our personal data from every account or profile we create online ends up in the cloud where it exists indefinitely. Once there, our data can be hacked, viewed by unauthorized personnel, or sold to advertisers. Sometimes it ends up on the dark web in the hands of criminals. The **Dark Web** is the black market of the Internet, a mostly illicit network of websites that cannot be accessed by standard search engines and browsers.

Sensitive financial information and our medical data are stored in networks that are frequently breached. Wearable devices track our vital signs, exercise frequency, and lifestyle patterns. The end user doesn't know where all the massive data are stored, as U.S. consumers are largely unprotected in a yet barely regulated market.

Future trends are no less worrisome to privacy advocates. The sophistication of artificial intelligence and facial recognition technology is growing. In China, a huge surveillance apparatus will soon enable the repressive regime to keep track of millions of people and identify protesters and dissidents. In the United States a small secretive company, Clearview AI, has devised a pioneering facial recognition app allowing users to match the image of an individual against all public photos of this person already existing on the Internet, revealing the target's identity and attached personal information in seconds. What has been a boon to law enforcement may soon land in the hands of everyday users—not just advertisers, but stalkers and other bad actors. True privacy and anonymity may be a thing of the past for consumers who use smart electronic devices, maintain social media profiles, and pay with credit cards—that is, nearly all of us.

**Disinformation and Election Tampering.** Researchers tell us that social media have changed how we consume information and form opinions. More than 90 percent of users access their news online; some 50 to 68 percent of them rely solely on social media.[82] Online, people tend to seek out so-called **echo chambers** of like-minded individuals and embrace narratives that confirm their existing views while rejecting contradicting information. The resulting polarization carries with it a negative emotional charge.[83] As Pew Research suggests, such charged information environments make people vulnerable to misinformation. False news stories and doctored narratives, including targeted **disinformation** (i.e., propaganda originating primarily in Russia and China), confuse the public.[84] A BuzzFeed survey found that 75 percent of American adults can't spot fake news.[85]

Even more troubling, though, is stealthy interference by foreign agents who use large bot armies to disseminate fake news stories on social media and incite conflict to deepen sharp divisions among the American public. Fake news planted by bots has risen to the level of potentially tampering with U.S. elections thus undermining democratic institutions. Bots are also used to steal social identities of people by impersonating them. Our carefree sharing on social media can provide criminals with clues.

**Deepfakes, Doctored Videos.** It has been said that we live in a **post-truth era**; in other words, we now exist in "circumstances in which objective facts are less influential in shaping public opinion than appeals to emotion and personal belief."[86] The urgent need for critical thinking now extends even to visual information—video content we don't question because, after all, instinctively we tend to believe what we see. Advances in AI could soon make creating fake video and audio a lot easier, permitting ever more sophisticated disinformation.

The ability to manipulate video footage to make people seem to say or do something they did not do is so worrisome to the U.S. government that it has begun to combat **deepfakes**. Altering photos and videos to distort the truth is not new, but deepfake technology takes deception to a whole new level. Computers can be trained to synthesize facial features and create composites of realistic-looking humans. It's easy to see how such tampering could be weaponized before an election or might threaten national security; likewise, people could claim that real videos are fake.[87] Alarmingly, this is already happening as sizable Internet communities aggressively proclaim the moon landing in 1969 was staged, the Earth is flat, and the terror attacks of 9/11 were "an inside job."[88]

**Incivility, Trolling, and Cyberbullying.** The anonymity of the Internet facilitates toxic behavior. **Trolls** are users who fake their identity, provoke skirmishes, and disrupt discussions on social media. They can be vicious bullies who thrive on denigrating others. Social media may originally have been idealized as a public square which guaranteed participants a practically unlimited freedom of expression. However, even

former proponents of an unregulated Internet, such as Jack Dorsey, the Twitter founder and CEO, have second thoughts. Dorsey now admits that social media cannot be neutral, passive platforms because of threats of violence, **doxxing** (public shaming and harassment), and troll armies bent on silencing others.[89] Facebook too has long been criticized for allowing demagogues and bigots to go unchecked; then it banned a few of them from the site, triggering suspicions of bias.[90]

**Cyberbullying** is a particularly devastating form of online harassment through the sharing of embarrassing information online, persistent messaging, and other digital nastiness. Nearly all states have passed anti-cyberbullying laws, but critics contend that social media companies aren't doing enough to combat the practice.[91] In extreme cases, cyberbullying on social media—via texts, e-mails, and other electronic means—has driven victims, many of them teenagers, to despair.

Data Security. Spyware. Ransomware attacks. Phishing. Data breaches. Romance scammers on dating sites. Fake bot accounts. Hacking of connected security networks. Vulnerabilities in smart speakers and connected cars. These are but a few problems ranging from annoying to highly problematic and downright fraudulent. Businesses face a huge expenditure of time and money combatting cybercrime and ensuring safe data storage. The average total cost of a data breach stands at $3.9 million; in the most recent year, an average 25,575 records were compromised per breach, and it took 279 days on average to identify and contain the breach.[92]

One of the biggest weaknesses enabling common security threats is human. According to Pew Research, Americans' knowledge of digital topics, such as cybersecurity or the advertising business model of social media companies, is inadequate.[93] Too many Internet users are lax with their credentials and still choose the word *password* to log in, not to mention *qwerty* or the infamous number sequence *123456* that enabled 23 million victim accounts to be hacked across the globe in one recent year.[94] Instead of adopting a password manager such as LastPass to generate and keep track of strong passwords, many Internet users log in with Facebook or reuse the same password. However, the adoption of VPNs is spreading, adding a layer of security by shielding browsing activity. More people, too, prefer browsers that don't track them, such as DuckDuckGo.

Americans seem to slowly realize that their electronic devices may be keeping tabs on them and that their personal data are frequently collected without their knowledge. Convenience comes at the cost of privacy and security. Aided by fact-checking websites, people are learning that they must take news sources on the Internet with a grain of salt and not believe everything they read or see. A recent Pew study shows that Americans don't trust social media for political and election news although many primarily rely on social media for such information.[95] Growing concern has led to efforts to introduce privacy protections. The awareness seems to be spreading that technology, the Internet, and social media in particular can be a mixed blessing.

## Summary of Learning Outcomes

**1** **Examine the professional usage, structure, and format of e-mails and memos in the digital era workplace.**

- Even after five decades, e-mail remains a heavily used communication channel in most workplaces.
- Office workers still send paper-based messages when they need a permanent record; wish to maintain confidentiality; or need to convey formal, long, and important messages.

- E-mail is the lifeblood of businesses, but messaging apps are gaining popularity. All digital workplace messages are permanent because they must be stored. They can be used as evidence in court.
- E-mail and memo subject lines summarize the central idea, which is restated in the opening. The body provides details. The closing includes (a) action information and deadlines, (b) a summary, or (c) a closing thought.
- Memos are still used for internal messages that are too long for e-mail, require a lasting record, demand formality, or inform workers who don't have e-mail.

## 2  Explain workplace messaging and texting including their liabilities and best practices.

- Instant messaging and real-time chat apps such as Slack as well as texting are best suited for brief text-based exchanges.
- Benefits of messaging apps and texting are their speed, allowing quick decisions; Slack's group chat connects distant as well as local project teams; SMS marketing is growing.
- Risks include productivity losses, leaked trade secrets, and legal liability from workers' improper use of digital media; fraud, malware, and spam pose additional risks.
- Best practices include following company policies, avoiding sensitive information, not sending inappropriate digital content, and using correct grammar and spelling.
- Text messages should observe proper timing, be addressed to the correct person, and identify the sender; savvy workers don't send sensitive news or expect an instant reply.
- Slack is beloved by many as an e-mail alternative and team chat tool; the downsides include distraction and incivility.

## 3  Identify professional applications of business podcasts and the professional standards underpinning them.

- Business podcasts are digital audio files ranging from short clips to long media files.
- Applications that do not require a human presence (e.g., training videos) lend themselves to podcast recordings that users can stream or download on the go.
- Podcasts are a growing channel for informing, advising, and engaging with customers; businesses, entrepreneurs, the media, and educational organizations create podcasts.
- Some entrepreneurial podcasters are able to monetize their large, devoted following.

## 4  Describe how businesses use blogs to connect with internal and external audiences.

- Blogs help businesses to keep customers, employees, and suppliers informed and to receive feedback.
- Businesses tell stories with blogs to engage with their customers and the public, for public relations, to grow online communities, and for internal communication and recruiting.
- Advice for masterful blogs includes crafting a catchy title, acing the first paragraph, providing details, using visuals, including call to action, careful editing, and responding respectfully.

## 5  Discuss business organizations' external and internal social media practices as well as the risks inherent in Internet use today.

- Social media such as Facebook and Twitter allow firms to share company news; exchange ideas; and connect with customers, employees, other stakeholders, and the public.
- Companies boost their brand recognition by engaging customers on the social media platforms where they congregate; enterprise social networks provide secure internal communication.
- Productivity losses, legal liability, leaking of trade secrets, and angry Internet users are potential risks of social media use at work.
- Workers should share only appropriate, work-related information, not post questionable content; they should activate and monitor their privacy options on social media sites.
- Technology and social media have a dark side, which includes threats to privacy, disinformation, deepfakes, incivility, and trolling, as well as threats to data security.

## Key Terms

| | | |
|---|---|---|
| cloud 113 | text messaging 120 | malware 122 |
| virtual private networks 113 | short message service 120 | discovery 122 |
| salutation 115 | rich communication services 120 | podcasts 125 |
| down-editing 116 | presence functionality 121 | blog 128 |
| instant messaging 120 | phishing 122 | influencers 129 |

## Chapter Review

1. List and concisely describe at least five electronic communication channels used most commonly by businesspeople today. (L.O. 1–4)

2. Why is workplace e-mail unlikely to go away anytime soon? (L.O. 1)

3. Why do many workers complain about e-mail? (L.O. 1)

4. Name at least five reasons some organizations forbid employees to use instant and text messaging. (L.O. 2)

5. How can you show professionalism and respect for your receivers in writing business instant messages and texts? (L.O. 2)

6. How do organizations use podcasts, and how are they accessed? (L.O. 3)

7. Explain why companies use blogs. (L.O. 4)

8. List the eight best practices for master bloggers. (L.O. 4)

9. How do businesses try to tap the vast potential of social networking? (L.O. 5)

10. Why do you need to critically evaluate all information that engulfs you daily? (L.O. 5)

## Critical Thinking

11. You have seen that e-mail is not universally loved although it is here to stay, despite the advent of real-time chat apps, texting, and other workplace short-form messaging. "Email is the last great unowned technology," said the Harvard law professor Jonathan Zittrain, "and by unowned, I mean there is no CEO of email . . . it's just a shared hallucination that works." Others believe that e-mail, though much maligned, "is still a cornerstone of the open web."[96] Interpret these statements. What points are they making, about openness in particular? (L.O. 1, 5)

12. Despite laws dictating a 40-hour workweek, many young Chinese tech workers endure the dreaded 9-9-6 schedule: 9 a.m. to 9 p.m., six days a week. What role does technology play here? How do you feel about work-life balance? (L.O. 3)

13. Are conversational Internet acronyms and slang—such as *AFAIK, G2G, HIFW, ICYMI,* and *NSFW*—as well as all-lowercase writing acceptable in e-mail, texting, or instant messaging for business? (L.O. 1, 2)

14. Traditional mainstream media act as so-called gatekeepers that vet the news and decide what kind of content gets published. However, social media networks have changed the game. Now anyone with an Internet connection can publish anything, even fake news and hate speech, and reach vast audiences in mere seconds. What are the benefits and dangers of this unprecedented access and speed of distribution? (L.O. 5)

15. In many workplaces employers are introducing game-like competitions and tracking of workers' vital functions with wearable devices. Consider the potential impact of gamification and wearable devices on your career. How do you feel about such tracking of employees and monitoring on the job and outside the workplace? Can you think of other vulnerable technologies? What advice would you give someone who is not sure how to handle invasive technologies that may threaten privacy and security? (L.O. 1–5)

## Writing Improvement Exercises

### Message Openers and Subject Lines (L.O. 1)

**YOUR TASK.** Compare the following sets of message openers. Circle the letter of the opener that illustrates a direct opening. Write an appropriate subject line for each opening paragraph.

16. An e-mail announcing a study:

   a. We have noticed recently a gradual but steady decline in the number of customer checking accounts. We are disturbed by this trend, and for this reason I am asking our Customer Relations Department to conduct a study and make recommendations regarding this important problem.
   b. Our Customer Relations Department will study the gradual but steady decline of customer checking accounts and recommend potential solutions.
   **Subject line:**

17. An e-mail announcing a new procedure:

   a. It has come to our attention that increasing numbers of staff members are using IM to send business messages. We realize that IM saves time and gets you fast responses, and we are prepared to continue to allow its use, but we have developed some specific procedures that we want you to use to make sure it is safe as well as efficient.
   b. The following new procedures for using instant messaging at work will enable staff members to continue to use it safely and efficiently.
   **Subject line:**

18. An e-mail inquiring about software:

   a. Please answer the following questions about your voice-recognition software. We would like to know how reliable the machine transcription is and whether the software can be trained to recognize various voices.
   b. We are interested in your voice-recognition software that we understand allows users to dictate and copy text without touching a keyboard. We are interested in answers to a number of questions, such as the reliability of the machine transcription. We also want to know whether the software can be trained to recognize various voices.
   **Subject line:**

19. An e-mail announcing introducing a new manager:

   a. Please welcome our new HR manager, Kristi Bostock, who comes from our Chicago office. Kristi is a 17-year management veteran with a strong focus on diversity and inclusion. Please join us in warmly welcoming our new HR manager.
   b. This is a message to bring you good news. You will be pleased to learn that our long wait is over. After going without an HR chief for many weeks, we are finally able to welcome our new manager, Kristi Bostock, who comes from our Chicago office.
   **Subject line:**

## Bulleted and Numbered Lists (L.O. 1)

E-mails and memos frequently contain numbered lists (for items in a sequence) or bulleted lists. Study how the following wordy paragraph was revised into a more readable format with a list:

**Before Revision:**
Our office could implement better environmental practices such as improving energy efficiency and reducing our carbon footprint. Here are three simple things we can do to make our daily work practices greener. For one thing, we can power down. At night we should turn off monitors, not just log off our computers. In addition, we could "Light Right." This means installing energy-efficient lighting throughout the office. A final suggestion has to do with recycling. We could be recycling instantly if we placed small recycling bins at all workstations and common use areas.

**After Revision:**
Our office could use energy more efficiently and reduce our carbon footprint in three simple ways:
- **Power down:** Turn off monitors rather than just logging off our computers.
- **Light right:** Install energy-efficient lighting throughout the office.
- **Recycle instantly:** Place small recycling bins at all workstations and common use areas to encourage recycling.

**YOUR TASK.** Revise the following wordy, unorganized paragraphs. Include an introductory statement followed by a bulleted or numbered list. Look for ways to eliminate unnecessary wording.

20. In writing to customers granting approval for loans, you should follow four steps that include announcing that loan approval has been granted. You should then specify the terms and limits. Next, you should remind the reader of the importance of making payments that are timely. Finally, a phone number should be provided for assistance.

21. The National Crime Prevention Council made a statement about crime in the workplace. It also provided some tips for improving workplace safety and preventing crime at work. It says that crime prevention and safety measures are just as important at work as they are at home. Some of the ways you can improve safety and prevent crime including changing locks

before you move into a new office. When doors, windows, and locks are broken or not working, someone should report this immediately. Lighting is another important factor. Many organizations leave some interior lights on even when the business may be closed. Dark places around a building should have lights, and shrubs can be a problem.

22. Producing excellent digital prints that equal what you see on your computer monitor is the most frustrating aspect of digital photography. You don't have to be frustrated, however. If you follow three steps, you can improve your prints immensely. We recommend that you first calibrate your screen. You should use the Datacolor Spyder X to do that. Next you should edit your photo so that your image looks natural and balanced. The final step involves configuring your printer. At the same time you should, of course, select the correct type of paper.

23. Our attorney made a recommendation that we consider several things to avoid litigation in regard to sexual harassment. The first thing he suggested was that we take steps regarding the establishment of an unequivocal written policy prohibiting sexual harassment within our organization. The second thing we should do is make sure training sessions are held for supervisors regarding a proper work environment. Finally, some kind of official procedure for employees to lodge complaints is necessary. This procedure should include investigation of complaints.

## Radical Rewrites

**Note:** Radical Rewrites are provided at **www.cengage.com** for you to download and revise. Your instructor may show a suggested solution.

## 5.1 Radical Rewrite: Weak Request Response Requires Your Revision (L.O. 1)

Blog writer Brian Drummond needs examples and information for a blog he plans to publish on the Online Voices platform. He writes to Nadya DeAlba, office manager at a high-tech firm, requesting information and examples. He met Ms. DeAlba at a conference and believes that she could be a willing source of information for his blog. Ms. DeAlba's advice is valuable, but her message is poorly organized, contains writing and grammar errors, and is hard to read.[97]

**YOUR TASK.** Analyze the following poorly written message from Nadya DeAlba. Identify its weaknesses including sentence fragments, wordiness, grammar faults, misspellings, and other writing problems you have studied. Include examples. Then revise if your instructor advises. Your instructor may provide a possible revision. Remember that you can download these documents at **www.cengage.com**

**To:** Brian Drummond <brian.drummond@gmail.com>
**From:** Nadya DeAlba <Nadya.dealba@techsolutions.com>
**Subject:** Your Request

Brian,

Thanks for this opportunity to make a contribution to your blog post for Online Voices. You ask that I confine my remarks to five main and important points. Which I will try to do. However, I could share many more annoying habits that create tension in the workplace. They interrupt workflow, reduce productivity, and lead to stress. Here's my top five annoying tech habits that drive coworkers crazy. I have observed these in our open office.

The first has to do with cc abuse. Todays e-mail programs make it to easy to copy people who may be unrelated to the discussion. Before clicking the cc field, writers should ask themselves whether it's critical to ask all receivers specific questions such as who wants the vegan or the barbecue lunch. Another annoying habit is what I call "radio silence." This occurs when receivers fail to respond to e-mails within 24 hours. It's not that I expect responses to every Slack message, tweet, DM, text message, voice mail, or Facebook post. As a writer, however, it is annoying when important e-mail messages are ignored.

One of my coworkers complains about notification overload. Offices today are awash with chirps, dings, and rings of countless devices that are allowed to ring and echo through the sweeping open space. The constant ding, ding, dinging is not only annoying to the intended recipients. But also to nearby colleagues.

Another annoying habit has to do with jumbled threads. When writers do not observe the conventions of threading their comments on Slack or e-mail. The structure of the conversation becomes garbled. This really annoying behavior is one of the many tech irritants that aggravate coworkers.

A final irritant is channel hopping. I've heard a lot of complaining about coworkers who pursue the recipient from channel to channel, following an e-mail with repeated Slack messages or a text. It would be advantageous if people let there coworkers know their preferred method of staying in touch.

Hope this is helpful!

Best,

Nadya DeAlba
[Full contact information]

List at least five weaknesses.

## 5.2 Radical Rewrite: Information E-Mail—Tips for Video Conferencing (L.O. 5)

Bailey Owens, an IT and teleconferencing expert, responds to a request from Mareli Barajas, who wants advice for an internal networking manual she is writing. Bailey's advice is good, but his message is poorly organized, contains grammar and other errors, and is hard to read.

**YOUR TASK.** Analyze the following message and list at least five weaknesses. Then revise it if your instructor advises.

**To:**      Mareli Barajas <mbarajas@trevipublications.com>
**From:**    Bailey Owens <bowens@a-z-conferencing.com>
**Subject:** Your Request

Dear Mrs. Barajas:

Hey, thanks for asking me to provide some help with the networking manual about teleconferencing that you are preparing and working up for Trevi Publications. Appreciate this opportunity! Although you asked me to keep it brief, I could give you an extensive, comprehensive list of dos and don'ts for videoconferencing. If you want this, let me know.

As an alternative to on-site meetings, virtual meetings became a necessity during the COVID-19 pandemic. Here's a bunch of tips for your manual. First and foremost, plan ahead. All participants should be notified well ahead of time of things like the date, time, and duration. It's your job to send log-ins and passwords by e-mail. Zoom, for example, generates all necessary information automatically and you can distribute the invitation by e-mail.

If you have documents that are needed during the conference, send them by e-mail ahead of time or prepare them to be shared onscreen during the meeting. Be very careful with the log-in credentials if you don't want to be "Zoom-bombed." This means that anyone with the password and meeting ID can hijack your meeting and cause all kinds of mischief. For the same reason, use a waiting room approximately 10 minutes before admitting attendees to your meeting at the appointed time. That way you can control admission.

Another tip has to do with muting (silencing) your microphone. Believe me, there's nothing worse than barking dogs, side conversations. And worst of all is the sound of toilets flushing during a video conference. Ick! Also, check your camera before the meeting! Activate it once the meetings is about to begin. If you use headphones, make sure they work too.

You should play with your microphone, speakers or headphones, and camera until you sound and look good. And of course, don't shuffle papers. Don't eat. Don't move things while your speaking. You may have heard that some people love to wear pajama bottoms and shorts with their suit jacket. Don't do it. Resist the temptation. Look good, feel good, but don't overdo it. Business casual will suffice.

My final tip involves using a waiting room before admitting participants to the meeting. They will see a slide that tells the meeting details. Such as the start time, audio and video information, and the agenda. This waiting-room slide should go up about 10 minutes before the meeting begins.

Hope this helps!
Bailey

Bailey Owens | A-Z Conferencing and IT | bowens@a-z-conferencing.com

List at least five weaknesses.

### 5.3 Instant Messaging: Live Chat Training at TransAvia Airlines (L.O. 2)

> **Communication Technology** ⟩ **E-Mail** ⟩ **Team** ⟩ **Web** ⟩

Live chat operators who help customers by exchanging instant messages with them in real time play an important role in customer service. The goal of providing such direct communication online is to inform and troubleshoot, but also to build a lasting relationship with customers. Ideally, by being cordial, professional, and helpful, live chat operators can contribute significantly to turning customers into fans of the company or brand. Representatives must sound authentic and human. TransAvia Airlines is training its representatives with hypothetical customer service scenarios. Following are two logs of chats by trainees who were asked to respond to a customer, Victor, in an online chat.

**YOUR TASK.** Carefully review the logs of the conversations between Victor and Representative 1 as well as Representative 2. Individually or as a team, critique Rep 1 and Rep 2 in class or in an e-mail to your instructor summarizing your observations. Support your views with examples. For instance, you could comment on the representatives' courtesy, helpfulness, tone, or writing skills. Then, if your instructor asks you to rewrite this chat, try your hand at being Representative 3 and apply some of the lessons you have learned in this chapter and Chapter 4.

**Tip:** Create a table to approximate the dialogue in an online chat. Note that sometimes the same person may write two or more comments in a row instead of waiting for a reply to the first one.

| Representative 1 | Representative 2 |
|---|---|
| **Rep:** Hey, Victor, what's shakin' in Atlanta? What do you need? | **Rep:** Good day, dear sir! We are honored to serve esteemed customers like you. |
| **Victor:** Hi. | **Victor:** Hi. |
| **Rep:** Perf to have you here. Hiw can I hlep? | **Rep:** How can we be of assistance? |
| **Victor:** Your award-travel system sucks!! I'm so tired of wasting time on your website! | **Victor:** Your award-travel system sucks!! I'm so tired of wasting time on your website! |
| **Rep:** Whoa! Chill!?. Why diss our system. What trasnpired | **Rep:** We are so very sorry to hear that your customer experience is less than stellar, sir! |
| **Victor:** What happened is that I keep getting an error message just before I click Purchase. I tried many times. | **Victor:** What happened is that I keep getting an error message just before I click Purchase. I tried many times. |
| **Victor:** What point are award miles when they can't be redeemed?? | **Victor:** What point are award miles when they can't be redeemed?? |
| **Rep:** Where… what Just a sec I'm on another chat. Whats wrong? | **Rep:** Would you be so kind and describe the precise nature of your issue? |
| **Victor:** I am planning a business trip to London with some of my 500k frequent flyer miles. Whenever I choose the itinerary, fill in payment information for the taxes etc, I hit Purchase and an Error !!! pops up. I can't finish the booking. So annoying! Who has the time?? | **Victor:** I am planning a business trip to London with some of my 500k frequent flyer miles. Whenever I choose the itinierary, fill in payment information for the taxes etc, I hit Purchase and an Error !!! pops up. I can't finish the booking. So annoying! Who has the time?? |
| **Rep:** How v nice to be able to go to London Wow, 500k miles? I can see your search in our systm. Lemme try it for you. Leave technology to a milenial! [Pause] | **Rep:** When you visited our website, we saw your credentials and search parameters. I shall attempt to complete the booking in your stead. [Pause] |
| **Rep:** Nope! it doesn't work Sorry. System is new and has glitches. | **Rep:** I'm truly inconsolable, sir. It appears that I am unable to complete the transaction using our new system. I might need to escalate the problem to my supervisor. |
| **Victor:** Why on earth do you roll out something that's full of bugs, why waste my time?? | **Victor:** Why on earth do you roll out something that's full of bugs, why waste my time?? |
| **Rep:** Yasss, good question tbh. Listen I can try to get on this and will let you go now. When I make the booking I will give you a buzz first. then shoot you an email. Our tech boss has a blog for complaints. You should give him an earful there!! He says he wants to hear from our ticked off customers. Will send you the link too. Oh and I will save you money, no live booking fees. | **Rep:** Please stay calm, sir. We are trying our best to serve you. As one of America's most respected airlines, we take customer service very seriously. Allow me to keep trying to complete the transaction gratis, without live booking fees. I shall telephone you and communicate via e-mail once the booking is completed. You will also receive a link that will allow you to share your experience with our CTO. |

**Representative 1**

**Victor:** Okay. That's a relief. Thanks. I'll be awaiting your call and e-mail.

**Rep:** Anything else I can do??

**Victor:** No, gotta run! Bye

**Rep:** Cheers!

**Representative 2**

**Victor:** Okay. That's a relief. Thanks. I'll be awaiting your call and e-mail.

**Rep:** May we do even more to provide excellent service, sir?

**Victor:** No, gotta run! Bye

**Rep:** Have an enjoyable day, sir. Goodbye!

## 5.4 Instant Messaging: Practicing Your Professional Real-Time Chat Skills (L.O. 2)

Communication Technology    Social Media    Team    Web

Your instructor will direct this role-playing group activity. Using instant messaging, you will simulate one of several typical business scenarios—for example, responding to a product inquiry, training a new-hire, troubleshooting with a customer, or making an appointment. For each scenario, two or more students chat professionally with only a minimal script to practice on-the-spot, yet courteous, professional interactions by real-time chat. Your instructor will determine which client software or app you will need and provide brief instructions to prepare you for your role.

If you don't have instant messaging software on your computer or smart device yet, download the application first—for example, Slack, WhatsApp, Facebook Messenger, or Skype. All messaging software enables users to share photos and media files. These advanced features turn messaging apps into a simple conferencing tool and video phone. You can make voice calls and use webcam video as well. Zoom and FaceTime are other videoconferencing options. Contrary to calling landlines or cell phones, you can connect for free on Wi-Fi with people all around the world, as long as you're both connecting by the same app. You may want to use a computer because downloading chat sessions is easier on a computer than on a smartphone.

**YOUR TASK.** Open the messaging or chat app your instructor chooses. Follow your instructor's directions closely as you role-play the business situation you were assigned with your partner or team. The scenario involves two or more people who communicate by real-time chat.

## 5.5 Discovering Your Favorite Business Podcast Series (L.O. 3)

Communication Technology    E-Mail    Social Media    Team    Web

Podcasting done right is hard work. Most podcasts (80 percent) fail or no longer publish.[98] Experts advise business podcasters first to provide quality content with an authentic voice to build value, and to consider money making second.[99] To browse and learn from popular favorites, search for *iTunes Charts US Podcasts* or *Top US Podcasts Insights (Apple Podcasts Top Charts)*. These sites rank the top 100 most popular podcasts, some business-related (e.g., The $100 MBA, Freakonomics Radio, The Indicator from Planet Money, How I Built This, and HBR Ideacast). Podcast Awards, an annual ranking of favorites selected by listeners and podcasters, is another resource for finding valuable podcasts in various categories, including business, science, and technology. Past winners include the irreverent, chatty Big Girl Money show and Ellen on the Go featuring Ellen DeGeneres.

**YOUR TASK.** Using the rankings mentioned above or other podcast sources, individually or as a small team find a highly rated business-related podcast series that sparks your interest. Scan the topics covered. Listen to several episodes and jot down notes. Evaluate the show's format (e.g., frequency of publication, duration, number of presenters or hosts, music use, interviews, formality of tone, professionalism, and other characteristics).

Categorize the content of your chosen podcast series (topics covered, invited guests, value of the information presented, your level of interest, and more). Look up the producer's credentials. Are the hosts competent subject experts? Find out what other authorities say about the podcast you selected and its producers. Then consider the overall value and credibility of the show. Would you recommend the podcast series to your classmates? Why or why not? Summarize your findings in a well-organized e-mail or classroom presentation. Alternatively, create an informative but brief social media post for an audience that doesn't know the podcast series or tweet an intriguing tidbit about the show.

## 5.6 Analyzing a Podcast (L.O. 3)

Communication Technology    E-Mail    Social Media    Web

Browsing the podcasts at iTunes, you stumble across the Quick and Dirty Tips series, specifically Money Girl, who has been dispensing financial advice since 2008. You sign up for the free podcasts that cover a variety of business topics. You can also visit the website Quick and Dirty Tips or interact with Laura D. Adams on her Money Girl Facebook page. Alternatively, examine the advice conveyed via podcast, the Web, Facebook, and Twitter by clever Grammar Girl Mignon Fogarty.

**YOUR TASK.** Choose a Money Girl podcast that interests you. Listen to it or obtain a transcript on the website and study it for its structure. Is it direct or indirect? How is it presented? What style does the speaker adopt? How useful is the information provided? At your instructor's request, write an e-mail that discusses the podcast you analyzed. Alternatively, if your instructor allows, you could also send a very concise summary of the podcast by text message from your smartphone or tweet to your instructor. Try limiting yourself to no more than 280 characters to practice conciseness.

## 5.7 Creating a Simple Business Podcast (L.O. 3)

**Communication Technology** ▸ **Social Media** ▸ **Web**

Do you want to try your hand at producing a podcast? Businesses rely on a host of social media and communication technologies when reaching out to the public or internally to their workers. As you have seen, some companies produce such short audio or video clips on focused, poignant subjects. The following process describes how to create a simple podcast.

**Select software.** The best software for newbies is Audacity and GarageBand (Mac only). One step up is Adobe Audition. They allow recordings within a Web browser or from a smartphone. Most can also be accessed as mobile apps.

**Obtain hardware.** For high sound quality, you may need a sophisticated microphone and other equipment. The recording room must be properly shielded against noise, echo, and other interference. Many universities and some libraries provide recording booths. In the absence of fancy recording locations, a quiet room at home will do.

**Organize the message.** Make sure your broadcast has a beginning, middle, and end. Build in some redundancy. Previews, summaries, and transitions are important to help your audience follow the message.

**Choose an extemporaneous or scripted delivery.** Extemporaneous delivery means that you prepare, but you use only brief notes. It usually sounds more spontaneous and natural than reading from a script, but it can also lead to rambling, repetition, and flubbed lines.

**Prepare and practice.** Practice before recording. Editing audio or video is difficult and time consuming. Try to get your recording right, so that you won't have to edit much.

**Publish your message.** Once you post the MP3 podcast to your course website or blog, you can introduce it and request feedback.

**YOUR TASK.** Create a short podcast about a business-related subject you care about. Producing a simple podcast does not require sophisticated equipment. With free or inexpensive recording, editing, and publishing software such as Audacity, you can inform customers, mix your own music, or host interviews. Any digital recorder can be used to create a no-frills podcast if the material is scripted and well-rehearsed. If all fails, even voice mail recordings can be used for this purpose.

## 5.8 Blogging: Learning From the Best (L.O. 4)

**Communication Technology** ▸ **E-Mail** ▸ **Social Media** ▸ **Web**

Examine the blogs of Seth Godin, Chris Brogan, Guy Kawasaki, Bill Marriott, and other acclaimed bloggers. See what tricks of the trade you can adopt and make work for you.

**YOUR TASK.** You may be asked to write a blog post detailing your analysis of the professional blogs you have examined. Apply the best practices for professional business blogs outlined in this chapter. Remember to offer a catchy title that will attract browsers or, in this case, your peers in class and your instructor. Share helpful advice in easy-to-read numbered items and, if applicable, provide links to other relevant articles. To motivate readers to respond, ask questions at the end of your blog entry.

## 5.9 Blogging: Writing a Blog Post (L.O. 4)

**Communication Technology** ▸ **E-Mail** ▸ **Social Media** ▸ **Web**

Review the guidelines for professional blogging in this chapter. Find a recent social media–related study or survey, and target an audience of business professionals who may wish to know more about social networking. Search for studies conducted by respected organizations and businesses such as Pew Research Center, Robert Half International, Burson-Marsteller, ePolicy Institute, and U.S. government agencies, as applicable. As you plan and outline your post, follow the advice provided in this chapter. Although the goal is usually to offer advice, you could also weigh in with your opinion regarding a controversy. For example, do you agree with companies that forbid employees to use company computers to access their social media accounts? Do you agree that millennials and Gen Z are losing social skills because of excessive online connectivity?

**YOUR TASK.** Compose a one-page blog entry in MS Word. Post it to the discussion board on the class course-management platform, or e-mail it to your instructor, as appropriate. Because you will be drawing on other people's ideas, be careful to paraphrase correctly and not to copy from your sources. Visit Chapter 10 to learn how to put ideas into your own words with integrity.

## 5.10 Epic Twitter Blunders (L.O. 5)

Communication Technology    E-Mail    Social Media

The modern workplace is a potential digital minefield. The imprudent use of practically any online tool—whether e-mail, real-time messaging, texting, tweeting, blogging, or posting to Instagram—can land workers in hot water and even lead to dismissal. Here are five ways Twitter can get you canned for showing poor judgment:[100]

a. **Sending hate tweets about the boss.** Example: *My idiot boss said he put in for raises. I think he lies. He is known for that. His daddy owns the company.*

b. **Lying to the boss and bragging about it.** Example: *I so lied to my boss . . . I was late but I said I forgot my badge and got away with it.*

c. **Romancing the boss (kissing and telling).** Example: *I give the boss what he wants, and the fringe benefits are amazing.*

d. **Announcing the desire to quit.** Example: *So close to quitting my job right now. Sometimes I can't [expletive] stand this place [expletive] moron assistant plant manager I'm about to deck him.*

e. **Blocking your boss.** Example: *i kept my promise . . . my boss thought she was gonna follow me on here . . . i BLOCKED her [expletive] ASAP.*

**YOUR TASK.** Discuss each violation of Twitter best practices, or summarize in general why these tweets are potentially damaging to their authors. How could the Twitter users have handled their grievances more professionally? Should they have refrained altogether? Comment on the style of these questionable tweets. If your instructor requests, summarize your observations in an e-mail message or an online post.

## 5.11 Social Media: Following the Top 10 Most Plugged-in CEOs (L.O. 5)

E-Mail    Social Media    Team    Web

If you are a budding entrepreneur and future tycoon, you may be looking to successful business leaders for inspiration. Learning about and connecting with chief executives has never been easier thanks to social media. Consulting firm Brunswick Group examined the digital profiles of 790 CEOs in the U.S. and U.K. for their social media presence on Facebook, Instagram, Twitter, and LinkedIn. Additionally, Brunswick surveyed thousands of employees in both countries for its study. After crunching 100,000+ data points, the firm established a ranking of CEOs based not only on connectedness, that is, the presence of accounts, but also on their owners' active engagement. The ranking extends from the lowest score of 536 for Flutter Entertainment CEO Peter Jackson, who placed 100th, to No.1-ranked Walmart CEO Doug McMillon and his score of 829. The study also confirmed that Twitter and LinkedIn are the CEOs' preferred networking sites.[101]

Social media are "an unfiltered forum for corporate leaders to listen to their communities and to connect by sharing their successes and challenges," Nasdaq president and CEO Adena Friedman says. The fourth-ranked CEO believes that "Social media projects the human side of the corporate world."[102] The Brunswick study revealed that most workers check a CEO's social media accounts before joining a company. The candidates also consult Glassdoor, a popular platform where current and former employees submit anonymous company reviews, including otherwise hard-to-come-by salary information. A top Glassdoor score means high job approval among employees. Highly connected CEOs on average scored better than their less connected peers on Glassdoor (+5 percent), as did their companies (+3 percent).

**YOUR TASK.** Search for the *Connected Leadership* report by Brunswick on the Web. Peruse or download a PDF copy. You will find that the top five executives are Doug McMillon (Walmart), Brent Saunders (Allergan), Ramon Laguarda (PepsiCo), Adena Friedman (Nasdaq), and Dan Schulman (PayPal). Mary Barra (GM), Hans Vestberg (Verizon), and Ed Bastian (Delta Air Lines) are also among the top 10 CEOs. Individually or as a team, select a CEO who interests you. Analyze the executives' presence and influence on their social media networks of choice. Find out how many followers they have, how often they post, what topics they discuss (strictly business or personal), how they come across to you (approachable and friendly or formidable and tough), and more. Correlate these observations with the executives' Glassdoor scores. Does the approval score match your CEO's Brunswick survey rating? Discuss your findings as a group or in class. If asked, summarize your research in a cogent e-mail or memo.

## 5.12 Social Media: Serious Withdrawal? (L.O. 5)

Communication Technology    Social Media    Web

Could you give up your electronic toys for 24 hours without withdrawal symptoms? How about quitting social media cold turkey for a week? Thirty days? Would you be able to survive unplugged from all media? Headlines decrying social media addiction litter the Internet. Self-declared social media junkies detail the lessons they learned after renouncing their gadgets for a "detox," "sabbatical," "purge," or "dramatic spree." Those who go offline describe feelings of emptiness, boredom, loneliness, depression, and anxiety. Some are baffled by their digital friends reacting to their abstinence with coercion, cajoling—even scorn![103]

In one study a class of 200 students at the University of Maryland, College Park, went media free for 24 hours and then blogged about the experience.[104] Some did sound like addicts going cold turkey: *In withdrawal. Frantically craving. Very anxious. Extremely antsy. Miserable. Jittery. Crazy.* One student lamented: *I clearly am addicted and the dependency is sickening.* In the absence of technology that anchors them to friends and family, students felt bored and isolated. One wrote: *I felt quite alone and secluded from my life. Although I go to a school with thousands of students, the fact that I was not able to communicate with anyone via technology was almost unbearable.*

The study reveals a paradigm shift in human interaction. Some users are viscerally wedded to electronic toys, so much so that technology has become an indispensable part of their lives. Electronically abstinent students stated that they spent more time on course work, took better notes, and were more focused. As a result, they said they learned more and became more productive. They also reported that they spent more time with loved ones and friends face-to-face. Life slowed down and the day seemed much longer to some.

**YOUR TASK.** Discuss in class, in a chat, or in an online post the following questions: Have you ever unplugged? What was that experience like? Could you give up your smartphone, iPod, TV, car radio, online magazines and newspapers, and computer (no texting, no Facebook, or IM) for a day or longer? What would you do instead? Is there any harm in not being able to unplug?

## Grammar/Mechanics Checkup 5

## Prepositions and Conjunctions

Review Sections 1.18 and 1.19 in the Grammar Review section of the Grammar/Mechanics Handbook. Then select the correct form to complete each of the following statements. Record the appropriate Grammar/Mechanics section and letter to illustrate the principle involved. When you finish, compare your responses with those at the bottom of the page. If your answers differ, study carefully the principles in parentheses.

| | |
|---|---|
| b    (1.18a) | **EXAMPLE** a. When do you expect your daughter to graduate high school?<br>b. When do you expect your daughter to graduate from high school? |
| _____ | 1. a. Instant messages should be respectful, professional, and written with brevity in mind.<br>b. Instant messages should be respectful, professional, and brief. |
| _____ | 2. a. Don't you hate when you must write a clarifying e-mail because you couldn't understand someone's message?<br>b. Don't you hate it when you must write a clarifying e-mail because you couldn't understand someone's message? |
| _____ | 3. a. If the boss urgently wants to see you, than you must be in trouble.<br>b. If the boss urgently wants to see you, then you must be in trouble. |
| _____ | 4. a. Ethnocentrism is when you think your culture is better than any other.<br>b. Ethnocentrism is the idea that your culture is better than any other. |
| _____ | 5. a. The new marketing trainee is more experienced than the last.<br>b. The new marketing trainee is more experienced then the last. |
| _____ | 6. a. What type of smartphone do you prefer—iPhone or Android?<br>b. What type smartphone do you prefer—iPhone or Android? |
| _____ | 7. a. Can you tell me where the cafeteria is at?<br>b. Can you tell me where the cafeteria is? |
| _____ | 8. a. Did you apply to the subsidiary in Chicago or to the headquarters in Boston?<br>b. Did you apply to the Chicago subsidiary or the Boston headquarters? |
| _____ | 9. a. The job candidate said she graduated college last year.<br>b. The job candidate said she graduated from college last year. |
| _____ | 10. a. Myra had a great interest, as well as a profound respect for, environmental activism.<br>b. Myra had a great interest in, as well as a profound respect for, environmental activism. |

_____  11. a. A behavioral interview question is when the recruiter says, "Tell me about a time. . . ."
        b. A behavioral interview question is one in which the recruiter says, "Tell me about a
           time. . . ."

_____  12. a. Connor's slide presentation was too long, as we feared it would be.
        b. Connor's slide presentation was too long, like we feared it would be.

_____  13. a. An ethics code is where a set of rules spells out appropriate behavior standards.
        b. An ethics code is a set of rules spelling out appropriate behavior standards.

_____  14. a. Please store coffee pods and sugar near the espresso machine.
        b. Please store coffee pods and sugar near to the espresso machine.

_____  15. a. Plant visitors must wear hard hats, bring protective eye wear, and caution needs to be
           exercised.
        b. Plant visitors must wear hard hats, bring protective eye wear, and exercise caution.

1. b (1.19a) 2. b (1.19a) 3. b (1.19c) 4. b (1.19d) 5. a (1.19c) 6. a (1.19d) 7. b (1.18a) 8. b (1.18c) 9. b (1.18c) 10. b (1.18a) 11. a (1.18e) 12. a (1.19c) 13. b (1.19b) 14. a (1.18b) 15. b (1.19a)

Chapter 5: Short Workplace Messages and Digital Media                                    **149**

## Editing Challenge 5

Every chapter provides an editing exercise to fine-tune your grammar and mechanics skills.

The following e-mail requires edits that address grammar, punctuation, conciseness, lead-ins, parallelism, listing techniques, and other writing issues. Study the guidelines in the Grammar/Mechanics Handbook (Appendix D), including the lists of Confusing Words and Frequently Misspelled Words.

**YOUR TASK.** Edit the following by (a) inserting corrections in your textbook or on a photocopy using the proofreading marks in Appendix C or (b) downloading the message from **www.cengage.com** and correcting at your computer.

---

**To:**      Department Heads, Managers, and Supervisors
**From:**    Tristan Garcia <tristan.garcia@dl-industrial.com>
**Subject:** Submitting Appraisals of Performance by May 2

---

This is just a reminder to all of you to say that performance appraisals for all you employees must be submitted by May second. These appraisal are especially important and essential this year because of job changes, new technologys, and because of office reorganization.

To complete your performance appraisal in the most effective manner, you should follow the procedures described in our Employee Manual. Let me briefly make a review of those procedures;

- Be sure each and every employee has a performance plan with three or 4 main objective.
- For each objective make an assessment of the employee on a scale of 5 (consistently exceeds requirements) to 0 (does not meet requirements.
- You should identify three strengths that he brings to the job.
- Name three skills that he can improve. These should pertain to skills such as Time Management rather then to behaviors such as habitual lateness.
- You should meet with the employee to discuss the appraisal.
- Then be sure to obtain the employees signature on the form.

We look upon appraisals as a tool for helping each worker assess his performance. And enhance his output. Please submit and send each employees performance appraisal to my office by May second. If you would like to discuss this farther, please do not hesitate to call me.

Tristan Garcia, Director
Human Resources | tristan.garcia@dl-industrial.com | Office: 555-555-5555 | Cell: 555-555-5555

# Communication Workshop: Social Media

## Being Astute in the Information Age

In college you are learning to think, read, and ask questions to function in a complex networked world. The avalanche of information that engulfs you daily requires you to evaluate sources critically because not all news outlets were created equal. Some engage in deliberate disinformation as they pursue hidden political agendas. Others may be purposely manipulated by hostile powers engaging in a cyber war. Bots and fake accounts have been found to spread **propaganda**—untruths planted to divide Americans, disrupt public discourse, and even interfere in democratic elections—via social media.

## Disinformation and Fake News

As a discerning businessperson and voter in a democracy, you will be challenged to stay informed, detect fake news stories, confront conspiracy narratives, and withstand attempts at manipulation. However, even the very definition of the catch phrase **fake news** is complex. After all, many types of **misinformation** (accidental untruth) and disinformation (intentional untruth) exist. Two U.S. economists have presented research defining fake news as "news stories that have no factual basis but are presented as facts."[105] In partisan politics, the term *fake news* has also been used to describe unwelcome evidence that some people find uncomfortable because it clashes with their convictions.

## Conspiracy Myths*

Although it's easy to laugh off conspiracy narratives, too many people believe (1) the COVID-19 pandemic was caused by a biological war, (2) the disease was at least partially spread by 5G cell towers, or (3) the COVID-19 vaccine syringes implant tracking RFID chips in people's bodies. Adherents believing such outrageous claims went so far as to vandalize cell towers and refuse life-saving vaccinations. The 5G conspiracy tale began in an obscure Belgian newspaper that cited a wholly unqualified physician and slapped a sensationalist headline on the article. His claims went viral. Yet radio frequency waves emanating from cellphone towers and smartphones are so low energy that they can't heat body tissues or damage human DNA.[106] The microchip conspiracy is based on a poor understanding of science and on fear. RFID chips are used widely in logistics to guard against counterfeiting and to monitor expiration. Such microchips remain on the outside of the syringe; they are not injectable. Private information is not stored on the microchips affixed to syringes, nor are specific people being tracked.[107]

In one episode of his popular HBO show Last Week Tonight—available on YouTube—comedian John Oliver addressed conspiracy myths and the harm they are causing.[108] He usefully covered three points: (1) why conspiracy narratives are popular, (2) how to detect them, and (3) how to stop them. Then he offered three questions to help debunk a conspiracy myth: (1) Is there a rational non-conspiracy explanation? (2) Has this narrative held up to scientific or expert scrutiny? and (3) How plausible is this conspiracy as a practical matter?

**CAREER APPLICATION.** In an age of automation that will devour millions of jobs, positions that require thinking, brainpower, and decision-making skills are likely to remain plentiful. To be successful in these jobs, you will need to be able to think critically, make well-founded decisions, and communicate those decisions. All workers, from executives to subordinates, need the ability to think creatively and critically. When your boss or team leader says, "What do you think we ought to do?" you want to be able to supply good ideas and demonstrate that you can **think critically**. This means voicing opinions that are backed by solid reasons and evidence.

**YOUR TASK.** Choose a popular conspiracy myth—preferably a business-related one—and subject it to the kind of scrutiny proposed by John Oliver. You may want to watch the 22-minute YouTube video of Last Week Tonight before applying John Oliver's critical-thinking questions to an actual conspiracy narrative. As a critical thinker, don't forget to ask *why*, as Oliver does, to illuminate the question what makes conspiracies so very appealing and so resistant to rational thought and debunking. Summarize your research in a memo or e-mail at the direction of your instructor.

---

* We purposely avoid using the words *conspiracy theory* because they describe a paradox. A theory is a scientific construct; the belief in an unproven, absurd, even patently false conspiracy is not.

# Positive and Neutral Messages

Roman Samborskyi/Shutterstock.com

## Learning Outcomes

After studying this chapter, you should be able to do the following:

**1** Identify the channels through which positive and neutral messages— e-mails, memos, and business letters—travel in the digital era workplace.

**2** Write direct messages that make requests, respond to inquiries via any channel, and deliver step-by-step instructions.

**3** Prepare contemporary messages that make direct claims and voice complaints, including those posted online.

**4** Compose adjustment messages that restore customers' trust and promote further business.

**5** Create special messages that convey goodwill and kindness.

## 6-1 Routine E-Mails, Memos, and Letters

Most workplace messages convey positive or neutral information that helps workers conduct everyday business. Because positive or neutral messages are routine and straightforward, they are direct and to the point. Such routine messages include simple requests for information or action, replies to customers, and explanations to coworkers. Other types of routine messages are instructions, direct claims, and complaints.

E-mail is the channel most frequently used, but memos and letters still play a role in the digital workplace. In addition, businesses must listen and respond to social media buzz. In some industries, memos continue to be an important channel of communication within organizations. Memos are also used as attachments sent with brief cover e-mails when formatting matters and the memo is important enough that it might be printed and displayed. Letters are a vital channel typically used for external communication, either in hard copy or in electronic form.

Chapter 5 discussed e-mail and social media used to communicate within organizations as well as with outside audiences. You also learned how to format and use memos safely and professionally. This chapter focuses on routine neutral and positive messages. They will make up the bulk of your workplace communication.

The direct writing plans that follow will help you get started fast. First, though, you will learn when writing a business letter is appropriate and how to format it.

## 6-1a Understanding Business Letters

Despite e-mail, workplace instant messaging, and social networking, in certain situations letters are still the preferred channel of communication for delivering messages *outside* an organization. Such letters go to suppliers, government agencies, other businesses, and, most important, customers.

You may think that everybody is online, but even with an Internet penetration rate in North America of nearly 95 percent,[1] a small portion of the U.S. population is still unplugged. Just as they are eager to connect with a majority of consumers online, businesses continue to give letters to customers a high priority because these messages, too, encourage product feedback, project a favorable image of the organization, promote future business, and signal greater formality. In addition, the sheer volume of daily e-mails can let important messages go unnoticed. Even a form letter mailed to consumers gets more attention than an e-mail does.[2]

Whether you send a business letter will depend on the situation and the preference of your organization. Business letters are necessary when the situation (a) calls for a permanent record; (b) requires confidentiality; (c) calls for formality and sensitivity; and (d) favors a persuasive, well-considered presentation.

**Providing a Permanent Record.** Many business transactions require a permanent record. For example, when a company enters into an agreement with another company, business letters introduce the agreement and record decisions and points of understanding. Business letters deliver contracts, explain terms, exchange ideas, negotiate agreements, answer vendor questions, and maintain customer relations. Increasingly, though, contracts are transmitted and signed electronically, not printed and sent in hard copy or by fax.

**Safeguarding Confidentiality.** Business letters are confidential. They are less likely than digital media to be intercepted, misdirected, forwarded, retrieved, or otherwise inspected by unintended recipients. Today's business communicators know how risky it is to entrust confidential and sensitive information to digital channels.

**Conveying Formality and Sensitivity.** Business letters presented on company stationery communicate formality and importance not possible with e-mail. They look

OFFICE INSIDER

"The old-fashioned personal business letter—written on pristine, high-quality paper, sealed in an envelope, and delivered by post or by hand—remains the single most impressive written ambassador for your company. A letter has a dignity that cannot be equaled by electronic mail or faxed correspondence."[4]

**The Emily Post Institute,** *etiquette experts, "Effective Business Letters"*

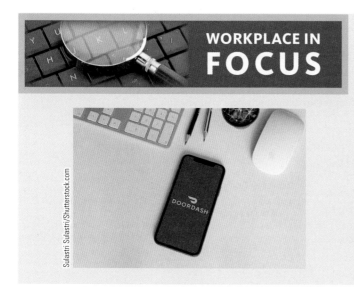

WORKPLACE IN FOCUS

Sulastri Sulastri/Shutterstock.com

Certain situations call for a more permanent and confidential record that requires a letter. Businesses may mail letters to vendors, other businesses, the government, or customers. When food-delivery service DoorDash discovered that hackers had accessed the user data of 4.9 million of its customers, the company posted a security notice on its blog site, sent e-mails, and also mailed letters to customers. The letter clearly laid out the types of information that may have been compromised as well as DoorDash's response to the attack. It directed those affected to a 24/7 support hotline and ended with a sincere apology.[3] Why do you think DoorDash also sent letters to its customers?

important, as illustrated in **Model Document 6.1**. Letters carry a nonverbal message that the writer considered the message to be significant and values the recipient.

*Delivering Persuasive, Well-Considered Messages.* Business letters deliver deliberate, thoughtful communication. Letters can persuade people to change their actions, adopt new beliefs, make donations, contribute their time, and try new products. Direct-mail letters remain a powerful tool to promote services and products, boost e-commerce and retail traffic, and enhance customer relations. You will learn more about writing persuasive and sales messages in Chapter 8.

**Model Document 6.1  Formatting a Direct Response Letter—Block Style**

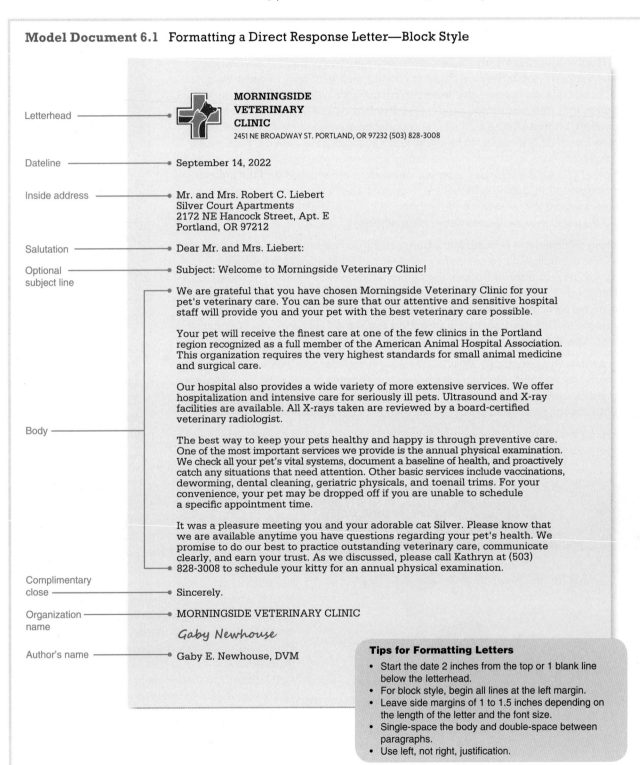

Letterhead

**MORNINGSIDE VETERINARY CLINIC**
2451 NE BROADWAY ST. PORTLAND, OR 97232 (503) 828-3008

Dateline

September 14, 2022

Inside address

Mr. and Mrs. Robert C. Liebert
Silver Court Apartments
2172 NE Hancock Street, Apt. E
Portland, OR 97212

Salutation

Dear Mr. and Mrs. Liebert:

Optional subject line

Subject: Welcome to Morningside Veterinary Clinic!

We are grateful that you have chosen Morningside Veterinary Clinic for your pet's veterinary care. You can be sure that our attentive and sensitive hospital staff will provide you and your pet with the best veterinary care possible.

Your pet will receive the finest care at one of the few clinics in the Portland region recognized as a full member of the American Animal Hospital Association. This organization requires the very highest standards for small animal medicine and surgical care.

Our hospital also provides a wide variety of more extensive services. We offer hospitalization and intensive care for seriously ill pets. Ultrasound and X-ray facilities are available. All X-rays taken are reviewed by a board-certified veterinary radiologist.

Body

The best way to keep your pets healthy and happy is through preventive care. One of the most important services we provide is the annual physical examination. We check all your pet's vital systems, document a baseline of health, and proactively catch any situations that need attention. Other basic services include vaccinations, deworming, dental cleaning, geriatric physicals, and toenail trims. For your convenience, your pet may be dropped off if you are unable to schedule a specific appointment time.

It was a pleasure meeting you and your adorable cat Silver. Please know that we are available anytime you have questions regarding your pet's health. We promise to do our best to practice outstanding veterinary care, communicate clearly, and earn your trust. As we discussed, please call Kathryn at (503) 828-3008 to schedule your kitty for an annual physical examination.

Complimentary close

Sincerely.

Organization name

MORNINGSIDE VETERINARY CLINIC

*Gaby Newhouse*

Author's name

Gaby E. Newhouse, DVM

**Tips for Formatting Letters**
- Start the date 2 inches from the top or 1 blank line below the letterhead.
- For block style, begin all lines at the left margin.
- Leave side margins of 1 to 1.5 inches depending on the length of the letter and the font size.
- Single-space the body and double-space between paragraphs.
- Use left, not right, justification.

## 6-1b Formatting Business Letters

A letter's appearance and format reflect the writer's carefulness and experience. A short letter bunched at the top of a sheet of paper, for example, looks as though it were prepared in a hurry or by a person unfamiliar with letter-writing conventions.

For your letters to make a good impression, select an appropriate format. The block style shown in Model Document 6.1 is a popular format. In this style the parts of a letter—dateline, inside address, optional subject line, body, and so on—are set flush left on the page. The letter is arranged on the page so that it is framed by white space. Most letters have margins of 1 to 1.5 inches.

In preparing business letters, use ragged-right margins; that is, don't allow your computer to justify the right margin and make all lines end evenly. Unjustified margins improve readability, say experts, by providing visual stops and by making it easier to tell where the next line begins. Although book publishers use justified right margins, your letters should be ragged right as shown in this book. Study Model Document 6.1 for more tips on making your letters look professional. If you have questions about letter formats, see Appendix A.

## 6-2 Typical Request, Response, and Instruction Messages

Neutral and positive messages take the form of e-mails, memos, and letters. Brief neutral or positive messages are also delivered by instant messaging, texting, tweets, and other social media posts. When you need information from a team member in another office, you might send an e-mail or dash off a Slack message. If you must explain new safety measures to plant workers who do not have company e-mail, you would write a memo for posting in a shared space such as the lunchroom. When you welcome a new customer or respond to a customer letter, you would match the customer's communication channel and prepare a letter.

Most of your business messages will involve routine requests and responses to requests, which are organized directly. You might, for example, receive an inquiry via Twitter, Instagram, or Facebook about an upcoming product launch. You may need to request information from a resort as you plan a company retreat. These kinds of routine requests and replies follow a similar pattern, as shown in the following writing plan.

**LEARNING OUTCOME 2**

Write direct messages that make requests, respond to inquiries via any channel, and deliver step-by-step instructions.

### Direct Request Messages

**WRITING PLAN**

**OPENING:** Ask the most important question, express a polite command, or state the main idea.

**BODY:** Explain the request logically and courteously. Ask other questions if necessary.

**CLOSING:** Request a specific action with an end date, if appropriate, and express appreciation.

## 6-2a Writing Requests

When you write messages that request information or action and you think your request will be received positively, **frontload** your message, which means start with the main idea. The most emphatic positions in a message are the opening and closing. Readers tend to look at them first. As a writer, you should capitalize on this tendency by putting the most significant statement first. The first sentence of a direct request is usually a question or a polite command.

**Big Idea First.** The e-mail in **Model Document 6.2** inquiring about hotel accommodations begins immediately with the most important idea: Can the hotel provide meeting rooms and accommodations for 150 people and their guests? If several questions must be asked, you have two choices. You can ask the most important question first, as shown in Model Document 6.2. An alternate opening begins with a summary statement, such as *Please answer the following questions about providing meeting rooms and accommodations for 150 people from March 9 to March 12.* If written as a letter, this direct request would most commonly be attached to an e-mail or in some cases perhaps faxed.

**Providing Details.** The body of a message that requests information or action provides necessary details. Remember that the quality of the information obtained

**Model Document 6.2   Customer Direct Request E-Mail**

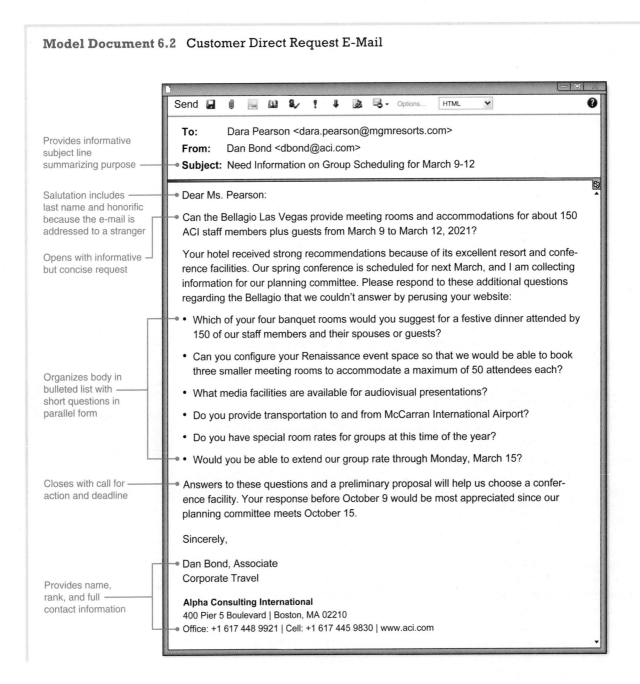

*Provides informative subject line summarizing purpose*

> **To:** Dara Pearson <dara.pearson@mgmresorts.com>
> **From:** Dan Bond <dbond@aci.com>
> **Subject:** Need Information on Group Scheduling for March 9-12

*Salutation includes last name and honorific because the e-mail is addressed to a stranger*

Dear Ms. Pearson:

*Opens with informative but concise request*

Can the Bellagio Las Vegas provide meeting rooms and accommodations for about 150 ACI staff members plus guests from March 9 to March 12, 2021?

Your hotel received strong recommendations because of its excellent resort and conference facilities. Our spring conference is scheduled for next March, and I am collecting information for our planning committee. Please respond to these additional questions regarding the Bellagio that we couldn't answer by perusing your website:

*Organizes body in bulleted list with short questions in parallel form*

- Which of your four banquet rooms would you suggest for a festive dinner attended by 150 of our staff members and their spouses or guests?
- Can you configure your Renaissance event space so that we would be able to book three smaller meeting rooms to accommodate a maximum of 50 attendees each?
- What media facilities are available for audiovisual presentations?
- Do you provide transportation to and from McCarran International Airport?
- Do you have special room rates for groups at this time of the year?
- Would you be able to extend our group rate through Monday, March 15?

*Closes with call for action and deadline*

Answers to these questions and a preliminary proposal will help us choose a conference facility. Your response before October 9 would be most appreciated since our planning committee meets October 15.

Sincerely,

*Provides name, rank, and full contact information*

Dan Bond, Associate
Corporate Travel

**Alpha Consulting International**
400 Pier 5 Boulevard | Boston, MA 02210
Office: +1 617 448 9921 | Cell: +1 617 445 9830 | www.aci.com

from a request depends on the clarity of the inquiry. If you analyze your needs, organize your ideas, and frame your request logically, you are likely to receive a meaningful answer that doesn't require a follow-up message. Whenever possible, focus on benefits to the reader (*To ensure that you receive the exact sweater you want, please send us your color choice*). To improve readability, itemize the appropriate information in bulleted or numbered lists. Notice that the questions in Model Document 6.2 are bulleted, and they are parallel. That is, they use the same balanced construction.

Closing With Appreciation and a Call for Action. In the closing of your message, tell the reader courteously what is to be done. If the request is time sensitive, set a deadline and explain why. You can save the reader time by spelling out the action to be taken. Avoid overused endings such as *Thank you for your cooperation* (trite), *Thank you in advance for . . .* (trite and presumptuous), and *If you have any questions, do not hesitate to call me* (suggests that you didn't make yourself clear).

Showing appreciation is always appropriate, but try to do so in a fresh and efficient manner. For example, you could hook your thanks to the deadline (*Thanks for taking our Qualtrics survey before May 5, when we will begin tabulation*). You might connect your appreciation to a reader benefit (*We are grateful for the information you will provide because it will help us serve you faster and better*). You could briefly describe how the information will help you (*I appreciate this information that will enable me to. . .*). When possible, make it easy for the reader to comply with your request (*Follow the link to the fillable PDF form; once completed, your response will be automatically sent to us* or *Join our Slack workspace IOdesignteam.slack.com so that you can reach us quickly*).

## 6-2b Responding to Requests

Most of your replies to requests for information or action will be favorable and, therefore, direct. A customer wants information about a product, a supplier asks to arrange a meeting, an employee inquires about a procedure, or a manager requests your input on a marketing campaign. In complying with such requests, apply the same direct strategy you used in making requests, as shown in the following writing plan.

### Direct Request Messages

**SUBJECT LINE:** Summarize the main information from your reply. (A subject line is optional in letters.)

**OPENING:** Start directly by responding to the request with a summary statement.

**BODY:** Provide additional information and details in a readable format.

**CLOSING:** Add a concluding remark, summary, or offer of further assistance.

A customer reply letter that starts with an effective (optional) subject line, as shown in Model Document 6.1, helps the reader recognize the topic immediately. Subject lines refer in abbreviated form to previous correspondence and/or summarizes a message (*Subject: Providing Information You Requested About Alta Vista Golf Resort*).

In the first sentence of a direct reply, deliver the information the reader wants. Avoid wordy, drawn-out openings (*I am responding to your e-mail of December 1, in which you request information about. . .*). More forceful and more efficient is an opener that answers the inquiry directly (*Here is the information you wanted about . . .*). When agreeing to a request for action, announce the good news promptly (*Yes, I will be happy to speak to your business communication class about conciseness. . .*).

When answering several questions or providing considerable data, arrange the information logically and make it readable by using graphic devices such as lists, tables, headings, boldface, or italics. When customers or prospective customers inquire about products or services, your response should do more than merely supply helpful answers. Try to promote your organization and products, as Model Document 6.1 does. Be sure to present the promotional material with attention to the "you" view and reader benefits (*Your pet will receive the finest care at one of the few hospitals in the Portland region recognized as a full member of the American Animal Hospital Association*).

In concluding a response message, refer to enclosures if they are provided (*The attached list summarizes our recommendations. We wish you all the best in redesigning your social media presence.*). If further action is requested or required, help the reader with specifics as Model Document 6.1 shows (*Please call Kathryn at (503) 828-3008 to schedule your kitty for an annual physical examination*). To prevent abruptness, include a pleasant closing remark that shows your willingness to help. Tailor your remarks to fit the message and the reader. Avoid signing off with clichés (*If I may be of further assistance, don't hesitate to. . .*). In an e-mail provide your full contact information to enable the reader to follow up, as the writer in Model Document 6.2 does.

### 6-2c Reacting to Customer Comments on Social Media

We live in an age when vocal individuals can start a firestorm of criticism online or become powerful brand ambassadors who champion certain products. Therefore, businesses must listen to social media comments about them and, if necessary, respond. You may ask, how do companies know when to respond, and how? After all, in the era of bots, some reviewers may not even be real, and their reviews may require validation.

However, social media marketing experts have developed guidelines to provide organizations with tools for strategic decision making in various situations. Businesses can't control the conversation without disabling public comments on their Facebook walls or blogs, but they can respond in a way that benefits customers, prevents the problem from snowballing, and shines a positive light on the organization.

**Welcoming Customer Comments.** Customer reviews on social media platforms are opportunities for savvy businesses to improve their products or services and may serve as a free and efficient crowdsourced quality-control system. Companies such as JetBlue, Nike, Starbucks, T-Mobile, and Whole Foods use powerful social media

WORKPLACE IN FOCUS

Canbedone/Shutterstock.com

Eager to make a buck, shoppers-for-hire recruited in dubious Facebook reviewer groups keep flooding Amazon with fraudulent reviews. Although Amazon lists reviews only if they result from a verified purchase, unscrupulous vendors issue refunds or other incentives to buyers in exchange for positive reviews. Five-star reviews are pure marketing gold because brands with the best reviews land at the top of search results. Amazon and Facebook have been criticized for not doing enough to stamp out this practice.[6] How seriously should companies and consumers take the threat of fraudulent reviews?

monitoring software to sift through billions of posts and product reviews. The data offer real-time feedback that may help clear up supply chain bottlenecks, expose product flaws, and improve operating instructions.[7] For example, when a customer complained to Procter & Gamble that her Bounce Dryer Bar broke from its plastic base, the Bounce brand manager mailed her a cordial personal letter with a replacement. The company then fixed the problem by increasing the length of tape on the back of the dryer bar holder and improving the installation instructions.[8]

In fact, customers take a prompt response for granted. In the United States, 75 percent of consumers expected that businesses respond to social media questions or complaints fast—on the same day (31 percent), within an hour (24 percent), or immediately (20 percent).[9]

*Adopting Best Practices for Replying to Social Media Posts.* Most experts would agree that not every snarky comment on social media merits an answer. In fact, marketers recommend responding to posts only when businesses can add value—for example, by correcting false information or providing customer service. Additional guidelines for professional responses to customer comments are summarized in **Figure 6.1**.

## 6-2d Composing Instruction Messages

Instruction messages describe how to complete a task. You may be asked to write instructions about how to use annotation and drawing markup tools in PDFs, order supplies, file a grievance, or hire new employees. Instructions are different from policies and official procedures, which establish rules of conduct to be followed within an organization. We are most concerned with creating messages that clearly explain how to complete a task.

*Creating Step-by-Step Instructions.* Before writing instructions for a process, be sure you understand the process completely. Practice doing it yourself. Like requests and responses, instruction messages follow a straightforward, direct approach. Instructions must use plain English and be especially clear. This writing plan will get you started:

**OFFICE INSIDER**

Whether it's a critical issue that needs to be addressed by a service agent, or a customer commenting: 'I really love your products'—in which case a simple 'Thank you!' will do—every interaction deserves attention. Employees need to be enabled to respond quickly to these comments and questions without the need to run everything past a PR or legal department first.'[10]

**Nicole Klemp,**
*Salesforce.com blog author*

---

**Figure 6.1  Responding to Customers Online**

In an era of consumer-centric, omnichannel customer service, businesses must listen and be ready to respond swiftly to social media comments and complaints.

| Be positive. | Be transparent. | Be honest. | Be timely. | Be helpful. |
|---|---|---|---|---|
| • Respond in a friendly, upbeat, yet professional tone. <br>• Correct mistakes politely. <br>• Do not argue, insult, or blame others. | • State your name and position with the business. <br>• Personalize and humanize your business. | • Own up to problems and mistakes. <br>• Tell customers when and how you will improve the situation. | • Respond to e-mail in less than 24 hours, as fast as possible on social media. | • Point users to valuable information on your website or other approved websites. <br>• Follow up with users when new information is available. |

## Instruction Messages

**SUBJECT LINE:** Summarize the content of the message.

**OPENING:** Expand the subject line by stating the main idea concisely in a full sentence.

**BODY:** List the steps in the order in which they are to be carried out. Arrange the items vertically with numbers. Begin each step with an action verb using the imperative (command) mood.

**CLOSING:** Request a specific action, summarize the message, or present a closing thought. If appropriate, include a deadline and a reason. If applicable, try to tie following the instructions to benefits to the organization or individual.

The most effective way to list directions is to use command language, which is called the **imperative mood**. Think recipes, owner manuals, and assembly instructions. The imperative mood differs from the **indicative mood** in that it requests an action, whereas the indicative mood describes a statement; both are shown here:

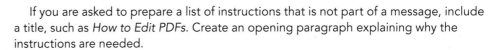

| Indicative Mood | Imperative (Command) Mood |
|---|---|
| The contract must be signed immediately. | Sign the contract immediately. |
| The first step involves downloading the app. | Download the app first. |
| A survey of employees is necessary to learn what options they prefer. | In a survey find out what options employees prefer. |

If you are asked to prepare a list of instructions that is not part of a message, include a title, such as *How to Edit PDFs*. Create an opening paragraph explaining why the instructions are needed.

**Revising a Message Delivering Instructions.** **Model Document 6.3** shows the first draft of an interoffice memo written by Andre Quincy. His memo was meant to announce a new method for employees to follow in requesting equipment repairs. However, the tone was negative, the explanation of the problem rambled, and the new method was unclear. Finally, Andre's first memo was wordy and filled with clichés (*do not hesitate to call*). By explaining clearly and changing his tone, Andre was able to improve his memo.

**Provide clear explanations.** Andre realized that his original explanation of the new procedure was confusing. To clarify the instructions, he itemized and numbered the steps. Each step begins with an action verb in the imperative (command) mood (*Log in, Indicate, Select, Identify*, and *Print*). It is sometimes difficult to force all the steps in a list into this kind of command language. Andre struggled, but he finally found verbs that worked.

Why should you go to so much trouble to make lists and achieve parallelism? Because readers can comprehend what you have said much more quickly. Parallel language also makes you look professional and efficient.

**Watch your tone.** In the revision Andre improved the tone considerably. The frontloaded idea is introduced with a *please*, which softens an order. The subject line specifies the purpose of the memo. Instead of dwelling on past procedures and failures (*we are no longer using* and *many mix-ups in the past*), Andre revised his message to explain constructively how reporting should be handled.

**OFFICE INSIDER**

"To get others to read your product's or service's instructions, first design and write them so that they are as simple and as appealing as possible. Tell readers up front the benefits of reading the guides—maybe even offer an incentive to those completing the instructions. The payoff might be worth the savings in customer service's time down the road."[11]

Leslie Stum, *implementation manager, Learning Stream*

## Model Document 6.3 Memo Delivering Instructions

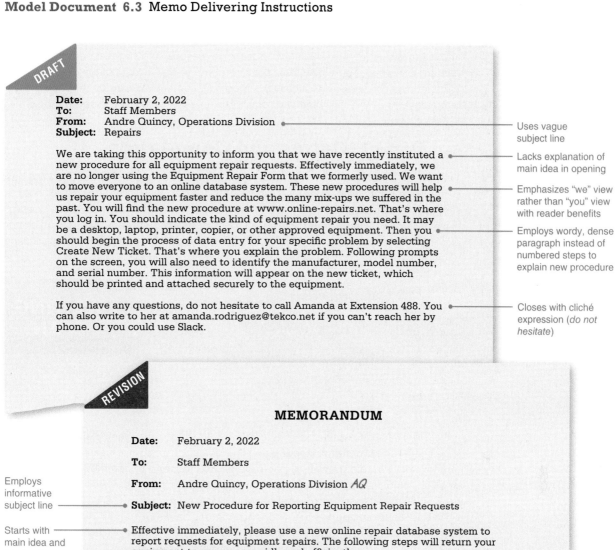

**DRAFT**

**Date:** February 2, 2022
**To:** Staff Members
**From:** Andre Quincy, Operations Division
**Subject:** Repairs

We are taking this opportunity to inform you that we have recently instituted a new procedure for all equipment repair requests. Effectively immediately, we are no longer using the Equipment Repair Form that we formerly used. We want to move everyone to an online database system. These new procedures will help us repair your equipment faster and reduce the many mix-ups we suffered in the past. You will find the new procedure at www.online-repairs.net. That's where you log in. You should indicate the kind of equipment repair you need. It may be a desktop, laptop, printer, copier, or other approved equipment. Then you should begin the process of data entry for your specific problem by selecting Create New Ticket. That's where you explain the problem. Following prompts on the screen, you will also need to identify the manufacturer, model number, and serial number. This information will appear on the new ticket, which should be printed and attached securely to the equipment.

If you have any questions, do not hesitate to call Amanda at Extension 488. You can also write to her at amanda.rodriguez@tekco.net if you can't reach her by phone. Or you could use Slack.

- Uses vague subject line
- Lacks explanation of main idea in opening
- Emphasizes "we" view rather than "you" view with reader benefits
- Employs wordy, dense paragraph instead of numbered steps to explain new procedure
- Closes with cliché expression (*do not hesitate*)

**REVISION**

### MEMORANDUM

**Date:** February 2, 2022

**To:** Staff Members

**From:** Andre Quincy, Operations Division *AQ*

**Subject:** New Procedure for Reporting Equipment Repair Requests

Effective immediately, please use a new online repair database system to report requests for equipment repairs. The following steps will return your equipment to you more rapidly and efficiently:

1. Log in to www.online-repairs.net.

2. Indicate the kind of repair you need, such as a desktop, laptop, printer, copier, or other approved equipment.

3. Select Create New Ticket and explain the specific problem.

4. Identify the manufacturer, model number, and serial number of the equipment.

5. Print the new ticket and attach it securely to the equipment.

If you have questions, call Amanda at Extension 488, write to her at amanda.rodriguez@tekco.net, or message her on Slack. Following this new procedure should vastly improve turnaround time and reduce mix-ups.

- Employs informative subject line
- Starts with main idea and emphasizes how the new procedure benefits the receiver
- Lists easy-to-follow steps, beginning each numbered step with a verb
- Closes with follow-up information and reinforces reader benefits

**Tips for Writing Instructions**
- Arrange steps in the order in which they should be completed.
- Start each step with an action verb in the imperative (command) mood.
- Be careful of tone in writing messages that give orders.
- Strive to show reader benefits if you are encouraging the use of the procedure.

When writing messages that deliver instructions, be careful of tone. Today's managers and team leaders seek employee participation and cooperation. These goals can't be achieved, though, if the writer sounds like a dictator. Avoid making accusations and fixing blame. Rather, explain changes, give reasons, and suggest benefits to the reader. Assume that employees want to contribute to the success of the organization and to their own achievement. Notice in the Model Document 6.3 revision that Andre tells readers that they will save time and reduce mix-ups if they follow the new method.

# 6-3 **Direct Claims and Complaints**

The wheels of commerce turn smoothly for millions of transactions, but even the best systems are not failsafe—promised shipments are late, warrantied goods fail, and service is disappointing. When consumers must write to identify or correct a wrong, the message is called a **claim**. Because straightforward claims are those to which you expect the receiver to agree readily, use a direct approach, as shown in the following writing plan.

## Direct Claim

WRITING PLAN

**OPENING:** Describe the desired action clearly.

**BODY:** Explain the claim, tell why it is justified, and provide details describing the desired action.

**CLOSING:** End pleasantly with a goodwill statement, and include an end date and action request, if appropriate.

Increasingly, consumers resort to telephone calls, they e-mail their claims, or—as we have seen—they vent their peeves in online posts. Large companies can afford to employ social media specialists who monitor and respond to comments. However, small and midsized businesses often have few options other than Google Alerts and their own limited forays into social networking.

This is why in an age of digital communication, claims written as letters of complaint still play an important role even as they are being replaced by telephone calls, e-mails, and social media posts. Depending on the circumstances, letters more convincingly establish a record of what happened. Some business communicators opt for letters they can either attach to e-mail messages or fax. Regardless of the channel, straightforward claims use a direct approach. Claims and responses to them that require persuasion are presented in Chapter 8.

## 6-3a **Stating a Clear Claim in the Opening**

Smart businesses want to hear from their customers. They know that retaining a customer is far less costly than recruiting a new customer. When you, as a consumer, have a legitimate claim, you can expect a positive response from a company.

Open your claim with a compliment, a point of agreement, a statement of the problem, a brief review of action you have taken to resolve the problem, or a clear statement of the action you want. You might expect a replacement, a refund, a new product, credit to your account, correction of a billing error, free repairs, or cancellation of an order. When the remedy is obvious, state it immediately (*Please correct multiple charges for my single card-based cryptocurrency purchase. My VISA card was charged 17 times for the same transaction*).

When the remedy is less obvious, you might ask for a change in policy or procedure or simply for an explanation (*Because three of our employees with confirmed reservations were refused rooms September 16 in your hotel, please clarify your policy regarding reservations and late arrivals*).

## 6-3b Supporting a Claim

In the body of a claim message, explain the problem and justify your request. Provide the necessary details so that the issue can be resolved without further correspondence. Avoid becoming angry or trying to fix blame. Bear in mind that the person reading your message is seldom responsible for the problem. Instead, state the facts logically, objectively, and unemotionally; let the reader decide on the causes.

If you choose to send a letter by postal mail, include copies of all pertinent documents such as invoices, sales slips, catalog descriptions, and repair records. Of course, those receipts and other documents can also be scanned and attached to an e-mail. If using paper mail, send copies and *not* your originals, which could be lost.

When service is involved, cite the names of individuals you spoke to and the dates of calls. Assume that a company honestly wants to satisfy its customers—because most do. When an alternative remedy exists, spell it out (*If a refund for your return is not an option, please issue a store credit, and apply it to our next order*).

## 6-3c Concluding With an Action Request

End a claim message with a courteous statement that promotes goodwill and summarizes your action request. If appropriate, include an end date (*I hope you understand that mistakes in ordering online sometimes occur. Because I have enjoyed your prompt service in the past, I hope that you will be able to issue a refund or store credit by May 2*). In making claims, act promptly. Delaying claims makes them appear less important. Delayed claims are also more difficult to verify.

By taking the time to put your claim in writing, you indicate your seriousness. A written claim starts a record of the problem, should later action be necessary. Save a copy of your message, whether paper or digital.

## 6-3d Completing the Message and Revising

When Nick Arthur received a statement showing a charge for a three-year service warranty that he did not purchase, he was furious. He called the store but failed to get satisfaction. Nick decided against voicing his complaint online because he wished for a quick resolution and doubted that the independent retail business would notice his social media post. He chose to write an e-mail to the customer service address featured prominently on the Maxtronics website.

You can see the first draft of Nick's direct claim e-mail in **Model Document 6.4**. This draft gave him a chance to vent his anger, but it accomplished little else. The tone was belligerent, and the writer assumed that the company intentionally mischarged him. Furthermore, Nick failed to tell the reader how to remedy the problem. The revision, also shown in Model Document 6.4, tempered the tone, described the problem objectively, and provided facts and figures. Most important, it specified exactly what Nick wanted to be done.

## 6-3e Posting Complaints and Reviews on Social Media

Social media experts advise that consumers exhaust all other options for complaints with the company before venting online.[13] Just as you probably wouldn't complain to the Better Business Bureau without giving a business at least one chance to respond, you shouldn't express dissatisfaction just to let off steam. Although it may feel good temporarily to rant, most businesses want to please their customers and welcome an opportunity to right a wrong.

Large companies employ social media specialists who track chatter about their brands and respond or troubleshoot. This type of social data gathering to improve business strategy and customer service is called **social listening**.[14] Travelers frequently get attention faster on social media 24/7 than by calling. Delta employs more than 40 staff members who address thousands of daily tweets. At Southwest, nearly

**OFFICE INSIDER**

"E-venting is particularly risky. We think it's private because we can do it in a secluded place, like our bed while we're in our pajamas. We have our phones with us all the time so we often e-vent before we've had a chance to calm down. A rant put out via the Internet is a click away from being shared. And shared. And shared."[12]

**Elizabeth Bernstein,**
*columnist,* The Wall Street Journal

## Model Document 6.4 Direct Claim E-Mail

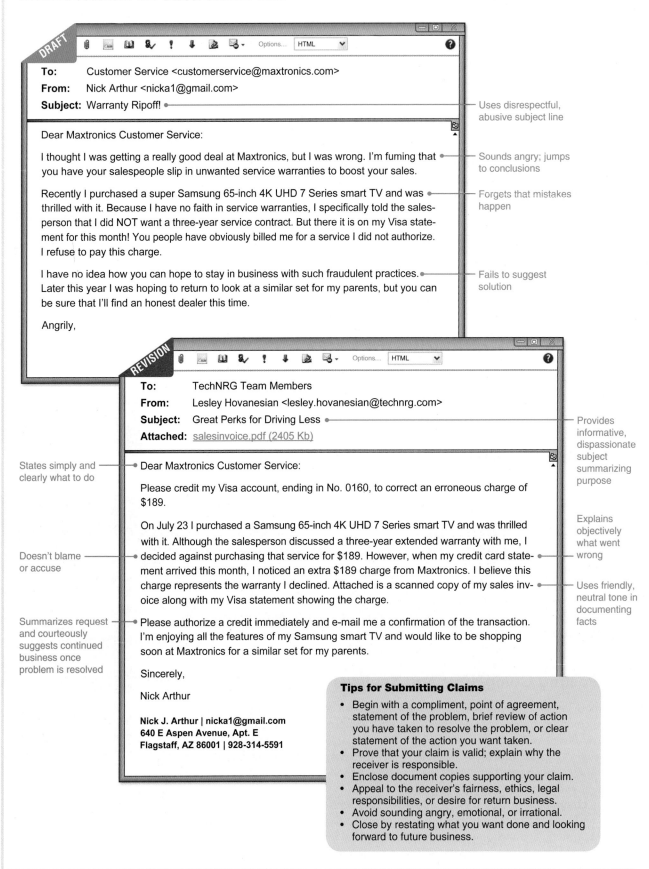

**DRAFT**

**To:** Customer Service <customerservice@maxtronics.com>
**From:** Nick Arthur <nicka1@gmail.com>
**Subject:** Warranty Ripoff! ●————— Uses disrespectful, abusive subject line

Dear Maxtronics Customer Service:

I thought I was getting a really good deal at Maxtronics, but I was wrong. I'm fuming that ●—— Sounds angry; jumps to conclusions
you have your salespeople slip in unwanted service warranties to boost your sales.

Recently I purchased a super Samsung 65-inch 4K UHD 7 Series smart TV and was ●—— Forgets that mistakes happen
thrilled with it. Because I have no faith in service warranties, I specifically told the salesperson that I did NOT want a three-year service contract. But there it is on my Visa statement for this month! You people have obviously billed me for a service I did not authorize.
I refuse to pay this charge.

I have no idea how you can hope to stay in business with such fraudulent practices. ●—— Fails to suggest solution
Later this year I was hoping to return to look at a similar set for my parents, but you can
be sure that I'll find an honest dealer this time.

Angrily,

**REVISION**

**To:** TechNRG Team Members
**From:** Lesley Hovanesian <lesley.hovanesian@technrg.com>
**Subject:** Great Perks for Driving Less ●————— Provides informative, dispassionate subject summarizing purpose
**Attached:** salesinvoice.pdf (2405 Kb)

States simply and clearly what to do ———● Dear Maxtronics Customer Service:

Please credit my Visa account, ending in No. 0160, to correct an erroneous charge of
$189.

On July 23 I purchased a Samsung 65-inch 4K UHD 7 Series smart TV and was thrilled    Explains objectively what went wrong
with it. Although the salesperson discussed a three-year extended warranty with me, I
Doesn't blame ———● decided against purchasing that service for $189. However, when my credit card state- ●—— what went wrong
or accuse        ment arrived this month, I noticed an extra $189 charge from Maxtronics. I believe this
charge represents the warranty I declined. Attached is a scanned copy of my sales inv- ●—— Uses friendly, neutral tone in documenting facts
oice along with my Visa statement showing the charge.

Summarizes request ———● Please authorize a credit immediately and e-mail me a confirmation of the transaction.
and courteously      I'm enjoying all the features of my Samsung smart TV and would like to be shopping
suggests continued   soon at Maxtronics for a similar set for my parents.
business once
problem is resolved  Sincerely,

Nick Arthur

**Nick J. Arthur | nicka1@gmail.com**
**640 E Aspen Avenue, Apt. E**
**Flagstaff, AZ 86001 | 928-314-5591**

### Tips for Submitting Claims

- Begin with a compliment, point of agreement, statement of the problem, brief review of action you have taken to resolve the problem, or clear statement of the action you want taken.
- Prove that your claim is valid; explain why the receiver is responsible.
- Enclose document copies supporting your claim.
- Appeal to the receiver's fairness, ethics, legal responsibilities, or desire for return business.
- Avoid sounding angry, emotional, or irrational.
- Close by restating what you want done and looking forward to future business.

40 employees tackle about 2,300 tweets and 1,900 Facebook posts a day. The company's Listening Center responds within minutes.[15]

Angry Posts Are Out of Your Control. Social media posts have a way of ending up in the wrong hands, making vicious complainers seem irrational. As always, consider whether people you respect and prospective employers would approve. Even anonymous posts can be traced back to the writer. No workplace wants to be associated with off-color, racist, sexist, or otherwise inappropriate comments in violation of company policy.[16] Employees who take a sick day but to go to the beach and are foolish enough to post evidence online get the boot promptly. A junior developer at a small startup was canned after tweeting all day how he hated the company and his job fixing software bugs.[17]

Public Criticism Can Cost You. Businesses and professionals can take individuals to court for negative comments online. A Florida man who complained on Yelp about his dog's death was sued by the animal hospital for defamation. A doctor in New York sued a patient for $1 million for posting negative reviews. A Kansas man faced a lawsuit for giving three stars to a theme park on Tripadvisor. Such so-called "strategic lawsuits against public participation" (SLAPP) are criticized as chilling to free speech. The Federal Trade Commission (FTC) is beginning to crack down on the silencing of critical reviewers under the Consumer Review Fairness Act of 2016.[18]

Commenting Responsibly. Shoppers read online comments on sites such as Yelp, Tripadvisor, Angi, and Amazon. A solid 36 percent of U.S. consumers *always* read user reviews when researching a product category, and a whopping 82 percent check out reviews of local businesses.[19] Even if posting does not achieve your objective, your well-written complaint or review may help others. You have a responsibility. Use it wisely.

Gleaned from *Consumer Reports*, the tips in **Figure 6.2** will allow you to exercise your right to free speech while staying safe when critiquing a product or service on social media.

## Figure 6.2 Guidelines for Writing Online Reviews and Complaints

### Establish your credibility.

- Zero in on your objective and make your comment as concise as possible.
- Focus only on the facts and be able to support them.

### Consider the reach and permanence of posts.

- Know that your review may be posted indefinitely, even if you change your mind and modify a post later.
- Be open; even anonymous comments can be tracked down. Privacy policies do not protect writers from subpoenas.

### Check posting rules.

- Understand what's allowed by reading the terms and conditions on the site.
- Keep your complaint clean, polite, and to the point.

### Accept offers to help.

- Reply if a business offers to help or discuss the problem; update your original post as necessary.

### Provide balanced reviews.

- To be fair, offset criticism with positives to show that you are a legitimate consumer.
- Suggest improvements even in glowing reviews; all-out gushing is suspicious and not helpful.

### Refuse payment for favorable critiques.

- Never accept payment to change your opinion or your account of the facts.
- Comply with requests for a review if you are a satisfied customer.

# 6-4 Adjustment Messages

**LEARNING OUTCOME 4**

Compose adjustment messages that restore customers' trust and promote further business.

Even the best-run and best-loved businesses occasionally receive claims or complaints from consumers. When a company receives a claim and decides to respond favorably, the message is called an **adjustment**. Most businesses make adjustments promptly: they replace merchandise, refund money, extend discounts, send coupons, and repair goods. In fact, social media have shortened the response time drastically to mere minutes or hours, not days.

Businesses make favorable adjustments to legitimate claims for two reasons. First, contractual and tort law protects consumers for recovery of damages. If, for example, you find an insect in a package of frozen peas, the food processor of that package is bound by contractual law to replace it. If you suffer injury, the processor may be liable for damages. Second and more obviously, most organizations genuinely want to satisfy their customers and retain their business.

In responding to customer claims, you must first decide whether to grant an adjustment. Unless the claim is obviously fraudulent or excessive, you will probably comply with it. When you say *yes*, your adjustment message will be good news to the reader. Deliver that good news by using the direct strategy. When your response is *no*, the indirect strategy might be more appropriate. Chapter 7 discusses the indirect strategy for conveying negative news. You have three goals in adjustment messages:

- Rectifying the wrong, if one exists
- Regaining the confidence of the customer
- Promoting further business

A positive adjustment message follows the direct strategy described in the following writing plan.

## Adjustment Messages

**WRITING PLAN**

| | |
|---|---|
| **SUBJECT LINE:** | Identify the previous correspondence and refer to the main topic. |
| **OPENING:** | Grant the request or announce the adjustment immediately. |
| **BODY:** | Provide details about how you are complying with the request. Try to regain the customer's confidence. Apologize, if appropriate, but don't admit negligence. |
| **CLOSING:** | End positively with a forward-looking thought; express confidence about future business relations. Include a sales promotion, if appropriate. Avoid referring to unpleasantness. |

## 6-4a Revealing Good News Up Front

Instead of beginning with a review of what went wrong, present the good news in an adjustment message immediately. When Leslie Bartolme-Williams responded to the claim of customer Daramis Services about a missing shipment, her first draft, shown at the top of **Model Document 6.5**, was angry. No wonder. Daramis Services apparently had provided the wrong shipping address, and the goods were returned. Once Leslie and her company decided to send a second shipment and comply with the customer's claim, however, she had to give up the anger. Her goal was to regain the goodwill and the business of the customer. The improved version of her letter announces that a new shipment will arrive shortly.

If you decide to comply with a customer's claim, let the receiver know immediately. Don't begin your message with a negative statement (*We are very sorry that you are having trouble with your dishwasher*). This approach reminds the reader of the problem and may rekindle the heated emotions or unhappy feelings experienced when the

## Model Document 6.5 Customer Adjustment Letter

**Dear Sir:**

Your complaint letter dated May 17 has reached my desk. I assure you that we take all inquiries about missing shipments seriously. However, you failed to supply the correct address.

*Fails to reveal good news immediately and blames customer*

After receiving your complaint, our investigators looked into your problem shipment and determined that it was sent immediately after we received the order. According to the shipper's records, it was delivered to the warehouse address given on your stationery: 5261 Motor Avenue SW, Lakewood, WA 98433. Unfortunately, no one at that address would accept delivery, so the shipment was returned to us. I see from your current stationery that your company has a new address. With the proper address, we probably could have delivered this shipment.

*Creates ugly tone with negative words and sarcasm*

Although we feel that it is entirely appropriate to charge you shipping and restocking fees, as is our standard practice on returned goods, in this instance we will waive those fees. We hope this second shipment finally catches up with you at your current address.

*Sounds grudging and reluctant in granting claim*

Sincerely,

---

**ACT** | **Allied Control Technology**
4166 SE Stanley Avenue
Portland, OR 97206

Phone: (503) 777-3183
Fax: (503) 777-5167
Web: www.act-or.com

May 23, 2022

Mr. Elias Vysocky
Daramis Services
2749 Ninth Street SW
Lakewood, WA 98499

Dear Mr. Vysocky:

*Uses customer's name in salutation*

Subject: Your May 17 Letter About Your Purchase Order

*Announces good news immediately*

Your second shipment of the Blu-ray players, video game consoles, and other electronics that you ordered April 18 is on its way and should arrive on May 29.

*Regains confidence of customer by explaining what happened and by suggesting plans for improvement*

The first shipment of this order was delivered May 3 to 5261 Motor Avenue SW, Lakewood, WA 98433. When no one at that address would accept the shipment, it was returned to us. Now that I have your letter, I see that the order should have been sent to 2749 Ninth Street SW, Lakewood, WA 98499. When an order is undeliverable, we usually try to verify the shipping address by telephoning the customer. Somehow the return of this shipment was not caught by our normally painstaking shipping clerks. You can be sure that I will investigate shipping and return procedures with our clerks immediately to see if we can improve existing methods.

*Closes confidently with genuine appeal for customer's respect*

Your respect is important to us, Mr. Vysocky. Although our rock-bottom discount prices have enabled us to build a volume business, we don't want to be so large that we lose touch with valued customers like you. Over the years our customers' respect has made us successful, and we hope that the prompt delivery of this shipment will retain yours.

Sincerely,

*Leslie Bartolome-Williams*

Leslie Bartolome-Williams
Distribution Manager

c    Steve Richman
     Shipping Department

claim was written. Instead, focus on the good news. The following openings for various messages illustrate how to *frontload* the good news:

*You're right! We agree that the warranty on your Whirlpool 500 Series dishwasher should be extended for six months.*

*You will be receiving shortly a new LG smartphone to replace the one that shattered when dropped recently.*

*Please take your portable Panasonic EM835 microwave oven to Argus Appliance Service, 360 Chapman Avenue, Orange, where it will be repaired at no cost to you.*

In announcing that you will make an adjustment, do so without a grudging tone—even if you wonder whether the claim is legitimate. Once you decide to comply with the customer's request, do so happily. Avoid halfhearted or reluctant responses (*Although the Whirlpool 500 Series dishwasher works reliably for many years when used correctly as specified in the user's manual, you may take yours to Argus Appliance Service for repair at our expense*).

## 6-4b Explaining Compliance in the Message Body

In responding to claims, most organizations sincerely want to correct a wrong. They want to stand behind their products and services and do what is right.

In the body of the message, explain how you are complying with the claim. In all but the most routine claims, also seek to regain the customer's trust. You might reasonably expect that a customer who has experienced difficulty with a product, with delivery, with billing, or with service has lost faith in your organization. Rebuilding that faith is important for future business.

How to rebuild lost confidence depends on the situation and the claim. If procedures need to be revised, explain what changes will be made. If a product has defective parts, tell how the product is being improved. If service is faulty, describe genuine efforts to improve it. Notice in Model Document 6.5 that the writer promises to investigate shipping procedures to see whether improvements might prevent future mishaps.

Sometimes the problem is not with the product but with the way consumers use it. In other instances customers misunderstand warranties or inadvertently cause delivery and billing mix-ups. Remember that rational and sincere explanations will do much to regain the confidence of unhappy customers. In your explanation avoid emphasizing negative words such as *trouble, regret, misunderstanding, fault, defective, error, inconvenience,* and *unfortunately.* Keep your message positive and upbeat.

## 6-4c Deciding Whether to Apologize

Whether to apologize is debatable. Attorneys generally discourage apologies fearing that they admit responsibility and will trigger lawsuits. However, both judges and juries tend to look on apologies favorably. Thirty-six U.S. states have passed **apology laws** that allow an expression of regret without fear that such a statement would be used as a basis for liability in court.[21] Some business writing experts advise against apologies, contending that they are counterproductive and merely remind the customer of the unpleasantness related to the claim. If, however, apologizing seems natural, do so.

People like to hear apologies. A well-timed, sincere apology is essential for repairing relationships on the job. It shows that you value the relationship and respect the other person's perspective.[22] Don't, however, fall back on the familiar phrase *I'm sorry for any inconvenience we may have caused.* It sounds mechanical and insincere. Instead, try something like this: *We understand the frustration our delay has caused you* or *We're sorry you didn't receive better service.* If you feel that an apology is appropriate, apologize early and briefly. You will learn more about delivering effective apologies in Chapter 7, when we discuss negative messages.

The primary focus of an adjustment message is on how you are complying with the request, how the problem occurred, and how you are working to prevent its recurrence.

**OFFICE INSIDER**

"'I'm sorry' is good yet often used in place of 'I apologize.' But 'I'm sorry' is when we step on someone's toes. Or someone passes away. 'I apologize' is a stronger and better word when something has gone wrong in the business world. . . . If we mishandle a situation, it's 'I apologize.' [The phrase 'no problem'] tops the list of words that annoy customers and clients. 'Thank you' and 'You're welcome' are not used enough. The importance of each is underrated."[20]

**Nancy Friedman,** *author of popular books on customer service*

## 6-4d Using Sensitive Language

The language of adjustment messages must be particularly sensitive, because customers are already upset. Here are some don'ts:

- Don't use negative words or phrases.
- Don't blame customers—even when they may be at fault.
- Don't blame individuals or departments within your organization; it's unprofessional.
- Don't make unrealistic promises; you can't guarantee that the situation will never recur.

To regain the confidence of your customer, consider including resale information. Describe a product's features and any special applications that might appeal to the customer. Promote a new product if it seems appropriate.

## 6-4e Showing Confidence in the Closing

End positively by expressing confidence that the problem has been resolved and that continued business relations will result. You might mention the product in a favorable light, recommend a new product, express your appreciation for the customer's business, or anticipate future business. It's often appropriate to refer to the desire to be of service and to satisfy customers. Notice how the following closings illustrate a positive, confident tone:

*You were most helpful in informing us of this situation and permitting us to correct it. We appreciate your thoughtfulness in writing to us.*

*Thanks for writing. Your satisfaction is important to us. We hope that this refund check convinces you that service to our customers is our No. 1 priority. Our goals are to earn your confidence and continue to justify that confidence with quality products and excellent service.*

*For your patience and patronage, we are truly grateful.*

*Your Acer Chromebook 514 will come in handy whether you are doing your homework, video chatting with friends, streaming music, watching movies, or playing games. What's more, you can add a Total Defense Premium Security package and a deluxe carrying bag for a little more. Take a look at the enclosed booklet detailing the big savings for essential technology on a budget. We value your business and look forward to your future orders.*

Although the direct strategy works for many requests and replies, it obviously won't work for every situation. With more practice and experience, you will be able to alter the pattern and apply your skills to other communication scenarios.

# 6-5 Goodwill Messages

**LEARNING OUTCOME 5**
Create special messages that convey goodwill and kindness.

Finding the right words to express feelings is often more difficult than writing ordinary business documents. Many communicators are intimidated when they must write goodwill messages expressing thanks, recognition, and sympathy. That is why writers tend to procrastinate when it comes to goodwill messages. Sending a ready-made card or picking up the telephone is easier than writing a heartfelt message. Remember, though, that the personal sentiments of the sender are always more expressive and more meaningful to readers than printed cards or oral messages. Taking the time to write gives more importance to our well-wishing. Personal notes also provide a record that can be reread, savored, and treasured.

In expressing thanks, recognition, or sympathy, you should always do so promptly. These messages are easier to write when the situation is fresh in your mind. They also mean more to the recipient. A prompt thank-you note carries the hidden message that you care and that you consider the event to be important. Instead of learning

writing plans for each goodwill message—whether thanks, congratulations, praise, or sympathy—we recommend that you concentrate on the five Ss. Goodwill messages should have the following characteristics:

- **Selfless.** Focus the message solely on the receiver, not the sender. Don't talk about yourself; avoid such comments as *I remember when I. . . .*

- **Specific.** Personalize the message by mentioning specific incidents or characteristics of the receiver. Telling a colleague *Great speech* is much less effective than *Great story about McDonald's marketing in Moscow.* Take care to verify names and other facts.

- **Sincere.** Let your words show genuine feelings. Rehearse in your mind how you would express the message to the receiver orally. Then transform that conversational language to your written message. Avoid pretentious, formal, or flowery language (*It gives me great pleasure to extend felicitations on the occasion of your firm's twentieth anniversary*).

- **Spontaneous.** Keep the message fresh and enthusiastic. Avoid canned phrases (*Congratulations on your promotion, Good luck in the future*). Strive for directness and naturalness, not creative brilliance.

- **Short.** Although goodwill messages can be as long as needed, try to accomplish your purpose in only a few sentences. Remembering an individual is most important. Such caring does not require documentation or wordiness. Individuals and business organizations often use special note cards or stationery for brief messages.

## 6-5a Saying Thank You

In business as in our personal lives, we need to say thanks or show appreciation when someone has done us a favor or when an action deserves praise. Letters of appreciation may be written to customers for their orders, to hosts for their hospitality, to individuals for kindnesses performed, to employees for a job well done, and especially to customers who complain. After all, whether in social media posts, by e-mail, or on paper, customer gripes can be opportunities to improve your business and turn "complaints into compliments."[24]

Because the receiver will be pleased to hear from you, you can open directly with the purpose of your message. The writer of **Model Document 6.6** thanks a speaker who addressed a group of marketing professionals. Although such thank-you notes can be short, this one is a little longer because the writer wants to lend importance to the receiver's efforts. Notice that every sentence relates to the receiver and offers specific, enthusiastic praise. By using the receiver's name along with contractions and positive words, the writer makes the letter sound warm and conversational.

Written notes that show appreciation and express thanks are significant to their receivers. Although messages that express thanks may be as long as the letter shown in Model Document 6.6, businesspeople generally write a short note on special notepaper or heavy card stock. The following messages provide models for expressing thanks for a gift, for a favor, for hospitality, and for employee contributions.

**Expressing Thanks for a Gift.** When expressing thanks, tell what the gift means to you. Use sincere, simple statements.

> *Thanks, Alice, to you and the other team members for honoring me with the elegant Bohemia crystal vase at the party celebrating my retirement after twenty-five years with the company. The height and shape of the vase are perfect to hold roses and other bouquets from my garden. Each time I fill it, I'll remember your thoughtfulness in choosing this lovely gift for me.*

# Global Marketing Association

9654 MISSION CENTER ROAD, SUITE 2350-600
SAN DIEGO, CA 92109
WWW.GLOBALMARKETINGASSOCIATION.COM

October 28, 2022

Ms. Liza Hausman
Vice President, Industry Marketing
Houzz
285 Hamilton Avenue, 4th Floor
Palo Alto, CA 94301

Dear Ms. Hausman:

The San Diego chapter of the Global Marketing Association extends its sincere •——— Opens directly with the purpose of message and thanks
thanks to you for a most entertaining and enlightening presentation on
October 25.

Personalizes the message with specific references to the presentation ———• Your description of the unusual expansion of Houzz into India mesmerized our
memers, particularly when you told us about the dizzying variety of Indian
culture. We were fascinated by how India came to Houzz, not the other way
around. Your Houzz site draws 40 million visitors monthly, and over time you
noticed that a million customers and service providers among those monthly
visitors had signed up from India. Houzz was compelled to launch a custom
Indian site.

In addition to your good advice about entering the Indian market, we enjoyed •——— Spotlights the reader's talents
your sense of humor and jokes—as you must have recognized from the uproar-
ious laughter. What a great routine you do on faulty translations!

Concludes with compliments and gratitude ———• We are grateful, Ms. Hausman, for the stimulating and instructive evening you
provided for our marketing professionals.

Cordially,

*R. Dearborn*

Russ K. Dearborn
Program Chair, GMA

Reference initials ———• RKD:fam

**Sending Thanks for a Favor.** In showing appreciation for a favor, explain the
importance of the gesture to you.

> *I sincerely appreciate your filling in for me last week when I was too ill to attend the
> planning committee meeting for the spring exhibition. Without your participation,
> much of my preparatory work would have been lost. Knowing that competent
> and generous individuals like you are part of our team, Craig, is a great comfort.
> Moreover, counting you as a friend is my very good fortune. I'm grateful to you.*

**Saying Thank-You for Hospitality.** When you have been a guest, send a note that compliments the fine food, charming surroundings, warm hospitality, excellent host, and good company.

> *Robert and I want you to know how much we enjoyed the dinner party for our department that you hosted Saturday evening. Your charming home and warm hospitality, along with the lovely dinner and sinfully delicious chocolate dessert, combined to create a truly memorable evening. Most of all, though, we appreciate your kindness in cultivating togetherness in our department. Thanks, Linda, for being such a special person.*

**Recognizing Employees for Their Contributions.** A letter that recognizes specific employee contributions makes the person feel appreciated even if it is not accompanied by a bonus check.

> *Gregorio, I am truly impressed by how competently you led your team through the complex AutoLive project. Thanks to your leadership, team members stayed on target and met their objectives. Your adept meeting facilitation, use of an agenda, and quick turnaround of meeting minutes kept the project on track. However, most of all I appreciate the long hours you put in to hammer out the final report.*

## 6-5b Replying to Goodwill Messages

Should you respond when you receive a congratulatory note or a written pat on the back? By all means! These messages are attempts to connect personally; they are efforts to reach out, to form professional and/or personal bonds. Failing to respond to notes of congratulations and most other goodwill messages is like failing to say *You're welcome* when someone says *Thank you.* Responding to such messages is simply the right thing to do. Do avoid, though, minimizing your achievements with comments that suggest you don't really deserve the praise or that the sender is exaggerating your good qualities.

**Answering a Congratulatory Note.** In responding to congratulations, keep it short and simple.

> *Thanks for your kind words regarding my award, and thanks, too, for forwarding me the link to the article online. I truly appreciate your warm wishes.*

**Responding to Praise.** When acknowledging a pat-on-the-back note, use simple words in conveying your appreciation.

> *Your note about my work made me feel good. I'm grateful for your thoughtfulness.*

## 6-5c Expressing Sympathy and Condolences

Most of us can bear misfortune and grief more easily when we know that others care. Sympathy notes, though, are probably more difficult to write than any other kind of message. Commercial sympathy cards make the task easier—but they are far less meaningful than personal notes. Grieving friends want to know what you think—not what Hallmark's card writers think.

**Conveying Sympathy.** To help you get started, you can always glance through cards expressing sympathy. They will supply ideas about the kinds of thoughts you might wish to convey in your own words. In writing a sympathy note, (a) refer to the death or misfortune sensitively, using words that show you understand what a crushing blow it is; (b) in the case of a death, praise the deceased in a personal way; (c) offer assistance without going into excessive detail; and (d) end on a reassuring, forward-looking note. Sympathy messages may be typed, although handwriting seems more personal. In either case, use quality paper stock or personal stationery.

**Writing Condolences.** As you write your condolence note, mention the loss tactfully, recognize good qualities of the deceased, assure the receiver of your concern, offer assistance, and conclude on a reassuring note.

> *We are deeply saddened, Maria, to learn of the death of your husband. Bob's kind nature and friendly spirit endeared him to all who knew him. He will be missed. Although words seem empty in expressing our grief, we want you to know that your friends at Isotronics extend their profound sympathy to you. If we may help you or lighten your load in any way, you have but to call.*
>
> *We know that the treasured memories of your many happy years together, along with the support of your family and many friends, will provide strength and comfort in the months ahead.*

Like other goodwill messages, personal expressions of sympathy should be acknowledged by the recipient. If the grieving person is not able to respond, a family member or a friend can take on the task of expressing thanks.

## 6-5d Using E-Mail for Goodwill Messages

In expressing thanks or responding to goodwill messages, handwritten notes are most impressive and personal. However, if you frequently communicate with the receiver by e-mail and if you are sure your note will not get lost in a cluttered inbox, then sending an e-mail goodwill message is acceptable, according to the Emily Post Institute and other experts.[25]

To express sympathy immediately after learning of a death or accident, you might precede a phone call or a handwritten condolence message with an e-mail. E-mail is a fast and nonintrusive way to show your feelings. However, advises the Emily Post Institute, immediately follow with a handwritten note: "A single sincere line expressing the genuine feeling you had for the deceased is all you need to write."[26] Remember that e-mail messages are quickly gone and forgotten. Handwritten or printed messages remain and can be savored. Your thoughtfulness is more lasting if you take the time to prepare a handwritten or printed message on quality card stock or personal stationery.

## Summary of Learning Outcomes

**1 Identify the channels through which positive and neutral messages—e-mails, memos, and business letters—travel in the digital era workplace.**

- When writing neutral and positive messages—e-mails, interoffice memos, or business letters—you can be direct because they convey routine, nonsensitive information.
- Write a business letter when the situation (a) demands a permanent record; (b) requires confidentiality; (c) calls for formality; and (d) favors a persuasive, well-considered presentation.
- Using company stationery, format your letters carefully. Select the block style, leave enough white space, and set margins of 1 to 1.5 inches. Don't justify the right margin.

**2 Write direct messages that make requests, respond to inquiries via any channel, and deliver step-by-step instructions.**

- In requests, frontload key information because readers look at the opening and closing first; explain the request in the body; express any questions or lists in a parallel, grammatically balanced form; and close with appreciation and a call for action.
- When complying with requests, be direct; explain and provide additional information in the body; and write a cordial, personalized closing that tells the reader how to proceed if action is needed.
- When responding to posts on the Internet, follow the example of businesses that strive to be positive, transparent, honest, timely, and helpful. Respond to benefit customers, prevent escalation, and present your organization in a positive light.
- Be direct and divide instructions into steps in the correct order, arrange items vertically with numbers, and begin each step with an action verb in the imperative mood.

**3** **Prepare contemporary messages that make direct claims and voice complaints, including those posted online.**

- When you compose a message to identify a wrong and request a correction, you are writing a *claim*; direct claims are requests to which receivers are expected to readily agree.
- Open a claim by describing the desired action; in the body explain and justify your claim. Conclude pleasantly with a goodwill statement, a date, and an action request, if appropriate.
- In making claims, act promptly. Delaying claims makes them appear less important and makes them difficult to verify; include copies or relevant documents to support your claim.
- Take your complaint online only after exhausting all other options with the business in question; keep your post concise and clean; focus on your objective; and be prepared to support the facts.

**4** **Compose adjustment messages that restore customers' trust and promote further business.**

- When granting a customer's claim, you are providing an *adjustment*, which has three goals: (a) rectifying the wrong if one exists, (b) regaining the confidence of the customer, and (c) promoting further business.
- In the opening immediately grant the claim without sounding grudging; in the body explain what went wrong and how the problem will be corrected; avoid acknowledging potential liability.
- When appropriate, apologize early and briefly. Don't use negative language, don't blame customers or coworkers, and don't make unrealistic promises.
- Show confidence in the closing; end positively by expressing confidence that the problem has been resolved and that continued business relations will result.

**5** **Create special messages that convey goodwill and kindness.**

- Write goodwill messages to express thanks, recognition, and sympathy; dispatch goodwill notes promptly to show that the reader is important to you.
- Make your goodwill messages selfless, specific, sincere, spontaneous, and short.
- Answer congratulatory notes and respond to praise in simple words that convey your appreciation.
- When expressing condolences, mention the loss tactfully, recognize good qualities of the deceased, assure the receiver of your concern, offer assistance, and end on a reassuring note.
- Sending an e-mail goodwill message is acceptable; however, follow up with a handwritten note.

## Key Terms

frontload 155
imperative mood 160
indicative mood 160

claim 162
social listening 163
adjustment 166

apology laws 168

## Chapter Review

1. What communication channels are used for routine messages in organizations today? (L.O. 1)

2. When are letters still the preferred channel of communication despite the advent of e-mail, social networking, and other electronic communication? (L.O. 1)

3. What are the most emphatic positions in a message, and what goes there? (L.O. 2)

4. Why should businesses welcome customer comments online? (L.O. 2)

5. How should instructions be written? Give an example. (L.O. 2)

6. What is a claim? When should it be straightforward? (L.O. 3)

7. What are a writer's three goals in composing an adjustment message? (L.O. 4)

8. Why is it debatable whether business communicators should apologize? (L.O. 4)

9. What are five characteristics of goodwill messages? (L.O. 5)

10. Name four groups of people to whom business communicators might write letters of appreciation. (L.O. 5)

## Critical Thinking

11. In this chapter you learned that badmouthing businesses online can have costly consequences. Some companies have used so-called SLAPP laws to sue consumers for writing negative reviews on the Internet. The acronym stands for *Strategic Lawsuit Against Public Participation*. Opponents consider such lawsuits frivolous and believe they threaten the public's free speech rights under the First Amendment. Therefore, 30 states and the District of Columbia currently have anti-SLAPP laws allowing early dismissal of meritless lawsuits brought to intimidate and silence reviewers and other public critics. Is trying to silence reviewers on social media fair, or are businesses within their rights to protect from illegitimate damaging complaints? (L.O. 3)

12. Why is it smart to remain cool when making a claim, and how should you go about it? (L.O. 3)

13. Why is it important to regain the trust of a customer in an adjustment message? How can it be done? (L.O. 4)

14. A writer compared letters and social media posts: "What is special about a letter is the time that is taken in creating a letter—that someone went to the trouble of finding a piece of paper, sitting down, crafting their thoughts, putting them on paper, and that they created this document really just for me. A letter is a very singular expression, it's a unique document, and for that reason, to get it in the mail feels almost like a gift. . . . It's a piece of paper that I can feel. . . . There's a physical connection."[27] How might these observations apply to business letters? What other special traits can you identify? (L.O. 1, 5)

15. Consumers in the United States and the United Kingdom enjoy some of the world's most generous merchandise return policies. It is no wonder, perhaps, that a few shoppers presumably buy clothes and return them afterward, no questions asked. Some people may be tempted to wear, post photos on Instagram, and then return the clothes. Is this so-called renting, or wardrobing, wrong? Italian clothing brand Diesel created an ad campaign dubbed "Enjoy Before Returning," poking fun at the practice by showing young people wearing the company's duds with tags still attached.[28] Why might Diesel be mocking wardrobing? Do retailers invite such behavior with their liberal policies? (L.O. 3)

## Writing Improvement Exercises

### Improving Subject Lines and Opening Sentences (L.O. 2)

**YOUR TASK.** Revise the following wordy openings for messages so that they are more direct and concise. Write an appropriate subject line and opening sentence for each one.

16. My name is Daryl Davidson, and I am assistant to the director of Human Resources at MicroSinergie. Our company has a Yammer-based enterprise social platform, which we would like to use more efficiently to elicit feedback on employee issues and concerns. I understand you have a software product called Opinionware that might do this, and I need to ask you some questions about it.

    **Subject line:**

    **Opening sentence:**

17. Thank you for your e-mail of February 8 in which you inquired about the availability of the best-selling OWC Mercury Pro external USB Blu-ray reader/writer.

    **Subject line:**

    **Opening sentence:**

18. I have received your message of May 6 asking whether or not our company was able to manufacture custom metric fasteners for you. You inquired about whether we could provide a custom solution to your metric fastener demands or let you know whether we currently have any metric fasteners in stock. I can answer in the affirmative to both queries! We do indeed have a variety of metric fasteners in stock because most of our customers require standard precision manufactured metric screws. Of course, custom solutions are available in many materials. Check out our Metric Fastener Inventory page. If you can't find what you need, we will manufacture custom fasteners to any provided specification.

    **Subject line:**

    **Opening sentence:**

19. This will acknowledge receipt of your inquiry of November 14 in which you ask whether we will be hosting the next edition of PACK EXPO International in Chicago, October 23–26, 2022. After canceling the 2021 in-person PACK EXPO in Chicago due to the COVID-19 pandemic, we are confident that we can return to McCormick Place in October 2022.

    **Subject line:**

    **Opening sentence:**

20. Your complaint about our recent shipment of MESA 12AX7 preamp tubes that were broken in transit to you has been directed to me for response. Thank you for telling us immediately about this mishap with your Order No. 008976. We also thank you for your thoughtfulness in noting the damage carefully on the express receipt. That information is very helpful. We are sending a replacement shipment of your entire order by prepaid express and expect that it will arrive by March 15 to replace your stock of guitar and bass amp tubes.

**Subject line:**

**Opening sentence:**

# Writing Instructions (L.O. 2)

**YOUR TASK.** Revise each of the following wordy, dense paragraphs into a set of concise instructions. Include a short introductory sentence.

21. Who wouldn't want to hide a messy room during a Zoom session? Millions of people were using video chat during the COVID-19 pandemic as they were working and studying from home. Some discovered they could customize the video background using stock images, their own photos, or even videos. Here is how to use virtual backgrounds. Of course, one's system must have the right requirements. You should select **Virtual Background** on the menu to the left after clicking your profile and then **Settings**. People can choose a default option, for example, an image of outer space or a green screen. Or they can upload their own background photos by clicking the plus icon on the **Virtual Background Page**. A pop-up box will let users upload a picture from their computers. By clicking the one they may want, they can see it alongside the stock pictures. To remove photos, users just need to tap the **X** in the top left corner. These instructions are for laptop and desktop computers, but mobile devices can be set up in a similar way. Zoom users shouldn't forget to experiment with a beauty filter to soften their appearance!

22. Customer service today is omnichannel and customer-driven, so when someone wants to reach out to you on social media, you need to be there, ready to respond. Of course, having an official response for major concerns or inquiries is an advantage. Companies must always respond and do it quickly. Many organizations fail to respond to many (or *any*) of their social media interactions. They say they aren't exactly sure how to respond to social media comments and questions. But consistency is key when responding. It's also important to listen to the competition and to track every mention on social media to find out what people are saying about you, even if they don't know that you're listening. Measuring the effectiveness of organizations' social media response is crucial too, as is hanging out where your customers are. Social listening also means to be friendly and personable. It helps to coordinate responses with executives and others who are visible on social media.[29]

23. Obtaining credit and keeping good credit can be difficult, especially for people beginning their professional journeys. Here are five suggestions that will help you obtain credit and maintain a good credit score. One thing I like to suggest first is getting a gas store card. These cards are easier to get than regular credit cards. What's great about them is that you can establish a credit history by making small payments in full and on time. To maintain good credit, you should always pay your bills on time. Delinquencies are terrible. They create the biggest negative effect on a credit score. If you already have credit cards, your balance should be paid down. If you can't afford to do that, you might take a loan from a family member or friend. If you have unused credit card accounts, don't close them. I know it sounds as if you should, but actually, canceling a card can lower your score. Don't do it! Finally, never max out your credit cards. A good rule of thumb to follow is to keep your balance below 30 percent of your credit limit.

## Radical Rewrites

## 6.1 Radical Rewrite: Poor Direct Request—Planning Accessible Conference (L.O. 2)

As a member of the planning committee for an upcoming conference, you have been asked to draft a message requesting information about whether the venue is accessible for all participants.

**YOUR TASK.** Analyze this message and list its writing weaknesses. Does this message apply the advice in this chapter for writing requests? If your instructor directs, revise the message using the suggestions you learned in this and previous chapters. Strive to arrange the information in an orderly bulleted list.

| | |
|---|---|
| **To:** | Angela.Marakot@capitalhilton.com |
| **From:** | Carol.Frazier@gmail.com |
| **Cc:** | Nanci.Masri@gmail.com; Jason.Nadir@hotmail.com; Lori.Petuno@gmail.com |
| **Subject:** | Need Information |

Dear Angela:

How is your day going? I hope well! I need some information, and I found your name at the Capital Hilton booking site. I'm on the planning committee for our upcoming Accessibility For All (AFA) conference that we would like to hold in Washington next fall. Will you please answer the following questions that need answers? The Capital Hilton comes highly recommended.

Does your hotel provide assistive listening systems? Such as the induction-loop system that bypasses acoustical conditions and delivers sound directly to listeners? Does the hotel have accessible parking? We would need level parking nearby with drop-off availability up close to the building. In the matter of accessible restrooms, are ADA restrooms available on the meeting room floors? Some of our attendees might bring service animals. Do you provide a comfortable space for them to rest during an event? Do you also have accessible nearby toileting and watering facilities for service animals? Finally, do your meeting rooms have ample accessible electrical outlets? Do they accommodate laptops, adaptive devices, and other electronics?

Thank you.

Carol.Frazier@gmail.com

AFA Fall Conference, Washington

## 6.2 Radical Rewrite: Direct Request—Protecting Medical Information (L.O. 2)

The following serious message requests information, but its poor organization and other writing faults prevent it from accomplishing its goal.

**YOUR TASK.** Analyze this message and list at least five writing weaknesses. If your instructor directs, revise the message using the suggestions you learned in this and previous chapters.

**To:** vjgallagher@safecybernetics.com
**From:** scott.woo@vistalinda-internists.com
**Subject:** Inquiry

Dear Sir:

I am a physician in a small medical practice, and I am worried about protecting patients' medical information. Your website (SafeCybernetics.com) looks quite promising but I found it overwhelming. I could not find answers to my specific questions, so I am writing this message to ask them. Could you call me within the next two days? I'm usually in surgery until 4 p.m. most days and try to leave at 6 p.m.

First, as I mentioned heretofore, my practice is small. Do you have experience in working with small medical practices? We may already have experienced a security breach. When you investigate, if you find out that privacy laws have been broken, do you report them to government agencies immediately?

We're really extremely interested in how you investigate an incident that may have taken place. If you discover a privacy breach, do you help your client make notification to his patients who are affected? Additionally, are you discreet about it?

I look forward to hearing from you.

Scott Woo, M.D.

## 6.3 Radical Rewrite: Direct Response—Data Breach Query (L.O. 2)

> **E-Mail**

The following message responds to the inquiry in Activity 6.2. Dr. Woo asks for information about dealing with a data breach at his medical office. Mr. Gallagher, representing Safe Cybernetics, wants to respond briefly and answer more fully in a telephone conversation with Dr. Woo. However, the following direct response is disorganized and needs revision to be effective in achieving its goal.

To:       scott.woo@vistalinda-internists.com
From:     vjgallagher@safecybernetics.com
Subject:  Data Breaches

Dear Dr. Woo:

We have received your inquiry, which has been directed to me for response. I can assure you that our company can do what you want in the way of cyber security, data breach response, and incident analysis solutions. We are specialists. You asked some specific questions, such as having experience with smaller medical establishments. I can assure you that, yes, we certainly do have such experience. Even with limited resources, smaller companies will benefit from basic security awareness training in a manner related to how to properly handle, store, and the processing of patient health information.

In regard to any incident that may have already occurred, we are experienced at investigating incidents, we analyze clues, and we can quickly and defensively uncover critical information. In regard to notifying patients of any breach, we assure you that we can give discreet breach notification that is prompt and we also customize it for your business. However, I must warn you in advance that if we become aware of any wrongdoing, we must notify any applicable government or law enforcement agencies because we are obligated to do so. But I can assure you that such notification is hardly ever necessary. We can discuss your concerns more extensively by telephone. Thank you for your interest in Safe Cybernetics.

Van Jim Gallagher
[Full contact information]

## 6.4 Radical Rewrite: Faulty Instruction E-Mail (L.O. 2)

The following wordy and poorly expressed e-mail from a CEO discusses a growing problem for organizations: how to avoid the loss of valuable company data to hackers.

YOUR TASK. Study the message, list its weaknesses, and then rewrite it in the form of an instruction message. Is it better to use bullets or numbers for an internal list?

To:       Staff Members
From:     Paul Salzman <paul.salzman@pacificsavings.com>
Subject:  Vital Warning!

Valued Staff Members:

I am writing this message to let you know that, like other banks, we are extremely concerned about the possibility of hackers gaining access to sensitive information. We fear that employees will expose valuable information without realizing what they are doing. Because of our fear, we have consulted cybersecurity experts, and they gave us much good advice with new procedures to be followed. Following are some of the procedures suggested by experts:

1. Phishing links seem to be the worst problem. Any request for password information or any requests to click links should be viewed with suspicion. Never click them. Even messages that seem to be from high-level officials or the human resources department within our own company can be sophisticated, realistic fakes. Examples include a request to click a link to receive a package or to download a form from within the company.

2. Be aware of URLs. You should read all URLs from right to left. The last item is the true domain. If it is not the address of the purported sender, it is probably a phishing attempt.

3. Please don't leave out-of-office messages. These voice mails or e-mails might explain when you will be away. Such messages are a red flag to hackers telling them that your computer is vacant and not being monitored.

4. Because smartphones can be lost or stolen, don't snap photos of company documents. Phones may be lost or stolen, and our data might be compromised.

5. Although small memory devices (thumb drives) are handy and easy to use, you may be inclined to store company files or information on these drives. Don't do it. They can easily be lost, thus exposing our company information.

6. Using work e-mail addresses for social media is another problem area. When you post details about your job, hackers can figure out an organization's best target.

We want to let you all know that within the next two months, we plan to begin implementing a program that will educate and train employees with regard to what to avoid. The program will include fake phishing messages. The program will be explained and you will learn more from your managers in training workshops that are scheduled to begin January 3.

Paul Salzman, CEO
[Full contact information]

## Activities and Cases

### 6.5 Responding to Social Media Posts (L.O. 2, 3)

Social Media    Web

**YOUR TASK.** Decide whether to respond to the following online posts.[30] If you believe you should respond, compose a concise Facebook reply following the guidelines in this chapter. Your instructor may also direct that you rewrite some of the posts themselves, if necessary.

a.  Jackie posted this to the Grocery Barn Facebook site: *So sad!! Ran to my store to pick up Pumpkin Yippee Pie mix and it's all sold out. (And all sold out online also! Bummer. I knew I should've bought more! LOL)….*
b.  Angel posted this comment on the Shoes Galore Facebook site: *I ordered a few things on the 20th and opted for next day shipping… but UPS says expected delivery date is the 30th! -:-(*
c.  Tyrone wrote the following to upscale men's clothing purveyor Joss Brothers: *I first began shopping at Joss Brothers about six years ago. I had read a book on menswear called "Style" by Jamal Klein. He made mention to brass collar stays. I could not find them in Canada. I wandered into a Joss Brothers store in Michigan and asked, "You don't sell brass collar stays do you?" The salesman said, "Of course." I bought collar stays, shirts and pajamas that day. A devoted customer I became. You can imagine how happy I am that Joss Brothers has come to Canada. Bienvenue! Welcome!*
d.  Katie posted this message on EsureSafe's Facebook page: *I just wanted to thank EsureSafe for all your support on a claim I filed. The service was excellent at one of your body repair shops and also, your customer service is top notch: calls, emails, and not to mention the site which gives you all details possible like pictures, status of the claim, easy contact us section, upload of files. GREAT WEBSITE and SERVICE. EsureSafe has me in GOOD HANDS, not Allstate :-)*
e.  Kendra posted this request for information on the Facebook page of her favorite resort hotel, Encore at Wynn in Las Vegas: *Will the pool still be opened this weekend?*

### 6.6 Direct Message—Memo Relaxing Strict Dress Codes in Banking (L.O. 1, 2)

J.P. Morgan Chase, the largest U.S. bank based on assets, stunned the usually conservative financial sector when it parted with long-standing tradition and started allowing business-casual attire on most occasions, except in client meetings. The move away from pinstripes to pullovers signals a larger trend, perhaps driven by wealthy clients who are increasingly shedding their ties. Even the Chairman and CEO, Jamie Dimon, started dressing down after meetings with more casual Silicon Valley executives. Young talent, for whom banking is competing with the IT sector, may also favor more comfortable garb. A Robert Half International survey found that approximately 50 percent of senior managers stated that employees are wearing less-formal attire than they did just five years earlier. Among office workers, 31 percent said they favor a workplace with a business-casual dress code. The most common dress-code violations are overly casual clothes, followed by revealing clothing, according to the survey.[31] This suggests that workers need help understanding business-casual policies.

The J.P. Morgan memo that announced the new policy outlined the dos and don'ts. Not allowed is athletic clothing (i.e., sweatpants, leggings, and yoga pants; halter tops; flip-flops; hats or hoods). "Distracting, tight, revealing or exceptionally loose or low-cut clothing" is also verboten. On the flip side, casual slacks, capris, polo shirts, and dress sandals are acceptable. Jeans and sneakers aren't considered business casual in most circumstances and job sites. The key guideline is to match clients in formality of dress. "Business casual is not weekend casual," the memo states. Unacceptable attire or appearance can lead to reprimand and disciplinary action including dismissal. Critics contend that some "decoding" of ambiguous items listed in the policy, especially for women, is needed.[32] If gray capris are acceptable, how about bright floral ones? Are women wearing denim viewed differently than men? What exactly is "tasteful" jewelry? And will judging "appropriate" hairstyles be left to managers' perception of race?[33]

**YOUR TASK.** Your boss in HR, Erin Schmidt, asks you to draft a memo modeled on J.P. Morgan's casual-dress policy for your traditional community bank, Willowbrook Financial. Mr. Hamdi, the CEO, realizes that your financial institution must go with the times. At the same time, he believes that Willowbrook employees need clear guidelines to understand the new policy and reduce ambiguity. Ms. Schmidt has instructed you to flesh out more detail in Willowbrook's policy. Consider including a table with dress code dos and don'ts.

## 6.7 Direct Request: Planning a Winter Retreat in Whistler, British Columbia (L.O. 2)

> **E-Mail**    **Web**

Your employer, Engineerian Services of Columbus, Ohio, has had an excellent year, and the CEO, Sydney Owen, would like to reward the troops for their hard work with a rustic yet comfortable winter retreat but also provide a team-building opportunity. The CEO wants Engineerian Services to host a four-day combination conference/retreat/vacation for the company's 55 engineering and tech professionals with their spouses or significant others at some spectacular winter resort.

One of the choices is Whistler, British Columbia, a famous ski resort town and former Winter Olympics venue with steep slopes and dramatic mountain views. As you investigate the options in Whistler, you are captivated by the Westin Resort and Spa, a four-star property with an outdoor pool, indoor and outdoor hot tubs, ski-in/ski-out access, a ski concierge, an acclaimed gourmet restaurant, and an amply equipped gym and fitness center. Other amenities include an on-site spa with massage and treatment rooms, a sauna, and facial and body treatments. For business travelers, the hotel offers complimentary wired high-speed Internet access, complimentary wireless Internet access, and multiline phones as well as the use of two desktop computers.

The website of the Westin Resort and Spa, Whistler is not very explicit on the subject of business and event facilities, so you decide to jot down a few key questions. You estimate that your company will require about 50 rooms. You will also need two conference rooms (to accommodate 25 participants or more) for one and a half days. You want to know about room rates, conference facilities, A/V equipment in the conference rooms, Internet access, and entertainment options for families. You have two periods that would be possible: December 15–19 or January 12–16. You realize that both are peak times, but you wonder whether you can get a discounted group rate. You are interested in entertainment in Whistler, and in tours to the nearby national parks. You wonder how your group would travel from Vancouver Airport. Also, one evening the CEO will want to host a banquet for about 85 people. Ms. Owen wants a report from you by September 12.

**YOUR TASK.** Write a well-organized direct request letter or e-mail to Teagan Smith, Sales Manager, 4090 Whistler Way, Whistler, V0N 1B4, British Columbia, Canada.

## 6.8 Direct Response: Falmouth Sail & Canvas Slammed on Yelp (L.O. 2)

> **Social Media**    **Web**

Yelp, the social network for consumer reviews and local searches, logs approximately 104 million monthly unique mobile visitors and 74 million monthly unique desktop visitors. The platform has listed 205 million reviews at this time.[34] Many users rely on what they hope to be real reviews by real people, as the company claims. They wish to make more informed buying decisions based on Yelp reviews. Businesses would do well to monitor their status on Yelp because anything less than a four- or five-star rating might be a blemish costing them sales.

Richard Hall, owner of Falmouth Sail & Canvas in Falmouth, Maine, watches his Yelp reviews. Currently, he has six reviews, all five stars. Imagine his surprise when he recently received a rating of one star from Annabelle T.:

> *Falmouth Sail & Canvas does good work, but it seems to have become a casualty of its own success. The company is unresponsive when you call and e-mail. I will take my business elsewhere because after 3 weeks, I still haven't heard about that estimate for new sails and weather cloths. I had left a voice mail message and sent an e-mail. No response. I called again and was received as if my request were outlandish when I expressed the hope of getting a quote that same week. Since then, silence. Not cool. And I am a repeat customer. … People, fortunately there are other businesses out there!*

The writer says she is a returning customer. Richard sighs because he is really shorthanded. His administrative assistant has been sick a lot lately, and inquiries have gone unanswered; communication has not been flowing well. Business is booming, and he does not have enough qualified installers; as a result, weeks elapse before his small crew gets around to completing a job. Barry searches his files and finds the job the company completed for Annabelle four years earlier. Falmouth had made a dodger, sail cover, and other smaller canvas items for Annabelle's 30-foot Catalina sailboat.

**YOUR TASK.** Consider Richard's options. Should he respond to the one negative review? What could be the consequences of ignoring it? If you believe that Richard should respond, discuss first how. He has the disgruntled customer's e-mail, phone number, and street address. He could post a reply on Yelp to provide a commentary to the bad review. If your instructor directs, plan a strategy for Richard and respond to the customer in the way you believe is best for Richard and his business.

## 6.9 Direct Response: Interviewing at Forrest + Partners (L.O. 2)

> **E-Mail**

Nathan Forrest, founder and CEO of Forrest + Partners, is a busy architect. As he expands his business, he is looking for ecologically conscious designers who can develop sustainable architecture that minimizes the negative environmental impact of buildings. His company has an open position for an environmental architect/designer. Three candidates were scheduled to be interviewed on April 12. However, Mr. Forrest now finds he must be in Houston during that week to consult with the builders of a 112-unit planned golf course community. He asks you, his office manager, to call the candidates, reschedule for April 19 or April 20, and prepare an e-mail with the new times as well as a brief summary of the candidates' backgrounds.

Fortunately, you were able to reschedule all three candidates. Paula Larson will come on April 19 at 2 p.m. Ms. Larson specializes in passive solar energy and has two years of experience with GigaSolar, Inc. She has a bachelor's degree from the University of California, Los Angeles. Rubie Gaul has a master's degree from Arizona State University and worked for five years as an architect planner for Phoenix Builders, with expertise in sustainable building materials. She will come on April 19 at 11 a.m. Without a degree but with ten years of building experience, Sanford Clayton is scheduled for April 19 at 9 a.m. He is the owner of LEED Consulting and has experience with energy efficiency, sustainable materials, domes, and earth-friendly design. You are wondering whether Mr. Forrest forgot to include Fred Dittman, his partner, who usually helps make personnel selections.

**YOUR TASK.** Prepare an e-mail to Mr. Forrest with all the information he needs in the most readable format. Consider using a three-column table format for the candidate information.

## 6.10 Instruction Message Needs Revision: Explaining the Office Move (L.O. 2)

> **E-Mail**

The following message, which originated in an international technology company, was intended to inform new team members about their upcoming move to a different office location. But its stream-of-consciousness thinking and jumbled connections leave the receiver confused as to what is expected and how to respond.

**YOUR TASK.** Study the complete message. Then revise it with (a) a clear introduction that states the purpose of the message, (b) a body with properly announced lists, and (c) a conclusion that includes a call to action and a deadline. Improve the organization by chunking similar material together. What questions must be answered? What tasks should be performed? Should this message show more of a "you" view? In addition, make it easy for recipients to respond. Recipients will be down-editing—that is, returning the message with their responses (in another color) interspersed among the listed items.

Hello everyone,

We'll be moving new team members into a new location next week so there are things we need you to do to be ready for the move. For one thing, let me know which Friday you want your personal items moved. The possibilities are November 12 and 19. Also, if you have an ergonomic desk or chair you want moved, let me know. By the way, we'll be sending boxes, labels, tape and a move map four or five days before the move date you choose, so let me know if this time frame allows you enough time to pack your office tools and personal belongings. And if you are bringing office equipment from your current team to the new team, let me know. Remember that company policy allows you to take a workstation/laptop from your current team to the new workstation. So check with your admin and let me know what office equipment you will be bringing. Incidentally, your new workstation will have a monitor and peripherals.

You'll need to do some things before the movers arrive. Make sure you put foam pads around your valuable, fragile items and then box them up. This includes things such as IT plaques, glass, or anniversary glass sculptures. If the glass things break, replacing them is expensive and the cost center is responsible for replacement. You may want to move them yourself and not have the movers do it.

Another thing—make sure you pack up the contents of all gray filing cabinets because movers do not move those. Also, write on the move map the number and delivery location of whiteboards, corkboards, and rolling cabinets. Most important, make sure you add a name label to all your work tools and furniture, such as desk phones, docking stations, peripherals, monitors, tables, ergonomic desks, ergonomic chairs, etc. If you see old move labels on recycled boxes, remove them or cross them out.

Get back to me ASAP. And by the way, the movers will arrive between 4 p.m. and midnight on the move date.

Thank you

## 6.11 Instruction Message: Copying Pictures and Text From PDF Files (L.O. 2)

> **E-Mail**

As a summer intern in the Marketing Department at Garrison Scientific, Inc., in Waltham, Massachusetts, you have been working on the company's annual catalog. You notice that staffers could save a lot of valuable time by copying images and text from the old edition and inserting them into the new digital document. Your boss, Marketing Director Kierra Moyer, has received numerous inquiries from staffers asking how to copy text and images from previous editions. You know that this can be done, and you show a fellow worker how to do it using a PDF feature in Adobe Acrobat called Take a Snapshot. Marketing Director Moyer decides that you are quite a tech-savvy student. Because she has so much confidence in you, she asks you to draft a memo detailing the steps for copying images and text passages from portable document format (PDF) files.

You start by viewing the **Edit** pull-down menu in an open PDF document. Depending on the Acrobat version, a feature called **Take a Snapshot** can be seen. It is preceded by a tiny camera icon and a check mark when the tool is activated. To copy content, you need to select the part of the PDF document that you want to capture. The cursor will change its shape once the feature is activated. Check what shape it acquires. With the left mouse button, click the location where you want to copy a passage or image. At the same time, you need to drag the mouse over the page in the direction you want. A selected area appears that you can expand and reduce, but you can't let go of the left mouse button. Once you release the left mouse button, a copy of the selected area will be made. You can then paste the selected area into a blank Microsoft Office document, whether Word, Excel, or PowerPoint. You can also take a picture of an entire page.

**YOUR TASK.** Prepare a memo or e-mail addressed to Marketing Department staff members for the signature of Kierra Moyer. Practice the steps described here in abbreviated form, and arrange all necessary instructions in a logical sequence. You may need to add steps not noted here. Remember, too, that your audience may not be as computer literate as you are, so ensure that the steps are clear and easy to follow.

## 6.12 Direct Claim: Smart TV Fail (L.O. 3)

> E-Mail

You run a popular restaurant for owner Joseph Grimes, and patrons have been telling you that they would like it if you installed a television in the dining area. After some hesitation, you decide to buy a late-model ultra HD 4K TV. You conduct research to compare prices and decide on a Samsung QLED Q90R 65" 4K UHD TV (QN65Q90RAFXZA). You spot the TV at Commander Electronics for $2,597.99 plus tax, the lowest price you could find for the model *PC Magazine* has selected as "Best for high-end home theaters." Although the closest Commander Electronics store is a 35-minute drive, the price is so good you decide it's worth the trip. You and one of the servers spend a good hour mounting the new QLED TV on the wall and setting it up. It works perfectly, but the next day when you turn it on, nothing happens. You check all connections, but no matter what you do, you can't get a picture. You're irritated! You are without a TV and have wasted time hooking up the Samsung. Assuming it's just a faulty set, you pack up the TV and drive back to Commander Electronics. You have no trouble returning the item and drag a second Samsung, the same model, into your dining room.

Again you set up the TV, hook it up to the restaurant's cable receiver, and are pleased with the new purchase. Your customers seem to enjoy the TV that plays on mute with captions. But a few days later, you have no picture for a second time. Now you are fuming! Not looking forward to your third trip to Commander Electronics, you repack the Samsung television and return it. The customer service representative tries to offer you another Samsung TV, but you decline. You point out all the trouble you have suffered and ask for a more reliable TV from a different manufacturer in the same price range and size as the Samsung. Commander Electronics is selling a comparable LG 65" 4K UHD HDR Smart OLED TV (OLED65C8PUA) and carries a larger Sony 75" 4K Ultra HD Smart LED TV (XBR75X940E) that also fits your criteria. However, at almost $3,000 both sets cost more than you had budgeted.

You feel that after all the problems you have endured, Commander Electronics should sell you the Sony or the LG at the same price as the defective Samsung. However, when you call to discuss the matter, you learn that the local sales manager isn't authorized to make this decision. You are told to submit a written request to the regional office.

**YOUR TASK.** Write a direct claim e-mail to Louis Estrada, Regional Manager at Commander Electronics, in Atlanta, Georgia, asking him to provide your restaurant with one of the alternative TV sets for less than the advertised price.

## 6.13 Direct Message: Encouraging Employees to Catch More Zs (L.O. 1, 2)

Sleep deprivation is very common among executives and rank-and-file workers in most organizations. Hard-charging business leaders pull all-nighters or sleep only a few hours a night. When Tesla chief Elon Musk turned 47, he spent the full 24 hours of his birthday at work. However, sleep researchers tell us that tired workers are less effective and make more mistakes. People tend to become irritable and abusive; productivity suffers. Lack of sleep causes impulsive behavior, impairs decision making, and stifles creativity. Chronic sleep deprivation has serious repercussions for our mental, emotional, and physical health.[35]

Your human resources manager wants to spread the awareness that sleep is key to long-term health and productivity. She knows that the choice is between having a normal, full workday of high-quality work or an extremely long workday of deficient work. Getting a good night's sleep will ultimately make the staff more productive. She has read Arianna Huffington's *The Sleep Revolution*. The best-selling book details how this once-driven businesswoman, author, and editor-in-chief of the *Huffington Post*—who passed out from exhaustion more than a decade ago—has become a crusader for quality shut-eyes. Huffington says sleep deprivation is "the new smoking," suggesting that employers will eventually be forced recognize the harm of sleep deprivation and overwork. Then workers might be able to take walks and nap at work, perhaps.

Many businesspeople think they are indispensable and don't sufficiently delegate work to team members who could relieve their workloads. Not developing a team that could step up can lead to a dangerous spiral of unsustainable frenzy and stress. Experts believe that planning the workday with a focus on getting out of the office by a certain time and prioritizing tasks accordingly will help disengage from work and lead to better sleep. One red flag is heavy caffeine consumption. It can mask the problem of sleep deprivation.[36]

**YOUR TASK.** On the Internet, search for Arianna Huffington's recommendations for sound sleep hygiene. Using the steps advanced by the sleep guru and the information presented here, write a memo from HR manager Gloria Sanchez to all staff, encouraging healthy sleep habits. This memo will be sent to all employees as an e-mail attachment, posted on the intranet, and displayed in the lunchroom and other common areas.

## 6.14 Direct Claim: The Unkindest Cut (L.O. 3)

> **E-Mail**

The owner of Millennium Interiors, Dominique Reese, recently worked on the custom Malibu home of an NBA basketball player. He requested an oversized 12-foot mahogany entry door. Dominique ordered by telephone the solid mahogany door ("Nantucket") from Union Wood Products on April 19. When it arrived on May 18, her carpenter and installer gave her the bad news. Magnificent as it was, the huge door was cut too small. Instead of measuring a total of 12 feet 2 inches, the door measured 11 feet 10 inches. In Dominique's carpenter's words, "No way can I stretch that door to fit this opening!" Dominique had waited four weeks for this hand-crafted custom door, and her client wanted it installed immediately. Dominique's carpenter said, "I can rebuild this opening for you, but I'm going to have to charge you for my time." His extra charge came to $1,250.

Sue feels that the people at Union Wood Products should reimburse her for this amount since it was their error. In fact, Dominique saved them a bundle of money by not returning the door. She has decided to write to Union Wood Products and enclose a copy of her carpenter's bill. She wonders whether she should also include a copy of the invoice, even though it does not show the exact door measurements. Millennium Interiors is a good customer of Union Wood Products, having used its quality doors and windows on many other jobs. Dominique is reasonably confident that the company will grant this claim.

**YOUR TASK.** Draft a claim letter for Dominique Reese's signature. Address it to Andres McMillan, Operations Manager, Union Wood Products, 44 High Noon Street, Unit 120, Redondo Beach, CA 90278. Ms. Reese may ask you to fax or e-mail the letter. Or, if your instructor directs, write a cover e-mail instead, attach a PDF copy of the letter, and mention the scanned documents you are sending.

## 6.15 Direct Claim: Iron Gate Is a Drag (L.O. 3)

You work for Ledlow Property Management in Boise, Idaho. Your employer specializes in commercial real estate. Yesterday one of your business tenants in the tony East End neighborhood complained about problems with an iron gate you had installed by Cormier Iron Foundry just six months earlier, on August 13. Apparently, the two wings of the double wing gate have settled and don't match in height. The gate gets stuck. It takes much force to open, close, and lock the gate. The iron gate was painted, and in some spots rust is bleeding onto the previously pristine white paint. The tenant at 4820 E Mill Station Drive, Boise, ID 83716 is a petite shop owner, who complained to you about struggling with the gate at least twice a day when opening and closing her store.

You realize that you will have to contact the installer, Cormier Iron Foundry, and request that the company inspect the gate and remedy the problem. Only six months have passed, and you recall that the warranty for the gate was for one year. To have a formal record of the claim, and because Cormier Iron Foundry does not use e-mail, you decide to write a claim letter.

**YOUR TASK.** Address your letter to Irvin Windham at Cormier Iron Foundry, 3050 W Businesspark Lane, Unit 7, Boise, ID 83709. To jog his memory, you will enclose a copy of the company's proposal and invoice. Your business address is 290 S Fifth Street, Level 2, Boise, ID 83702, phone (208) 335-5444 and fax (208) 335-5646.

## 6.16 Direct Claim: Disappointed? Let the Business Know (L.O. 3)

> **E-Mail**

Like most consumers, you have probably occasionally been unhappy with service or with products you have used.

**YOUR TASK.** Select a product or service that has disappointed you. Write a claim letter requesting a refund, replacement, explanation, or whatever seems reasonable. Generally, such letters are addressed to customer service departments. For claims about food products, be sure to include bar code identification from the package, if possible. Your instructor may ask you to mail this letter or attach a digital copy to a cover e-mail addressed to the company. Remember that smart companies want to know what their customers think, especially if a product could be improved. Share your ideas for improvement. When you receive a response, show it to your class.

## 6.17 Adjustment: Resolving a TV Claim (L.O. 4)

**E-Mail**

Louis Estrada is Regional Manager at Commander Electronics in Atlanta, Georgia. He received an e-mail from Joseph Grimes, a frustrated restaurant owner who is demanding a steep price match for all his trouble with two new 4K Ultra HD televisions that both malfunctioned (see **Activity 6.12**). He had bought a Samsung QLED Q90R 65" 4K UHD TV (QN65Q90RAFXZA) at Commander Electronics for $2,597.99 plus tax. After installing it, he found, much to his chagrin, that the TV set failed the very next day. Wanting a new TV as soon as possible, he drove 30 minutes to the same Commander Electronics store to exchange the faulty model for another Samsung QLED Q90R 65" 4K UHD TV.

A few days later, this TV also conked out. Again Joseph had to return the TV set, but this time he insisted on exchanging it for a different brand, a comparable LG 65" 4K UHD HDR Smart OLED TV (OLED65C8PUA) or a larger Sony 75" 4K Ultra HD Smart LED TV (XBR75X940E) that also fit Joseph's criteria. However, at almost $3,000 both sets cost more than he had budgeted.

The e-mail landed in Mr. Estrada's inbox because the lower-level sales managers were not authorized to grant an adjustment of such magnitude.

Mr. Estrada empathizes with the customer, but the price difference is too great. He decides to grant the adjustment as long as Mr. Grimes instead accepts the older, soon-to-be-discontinued model of the LG TV that Mr. Estrada would be able to provide in a swap. Alternatively, Mr. Estrada can offer the customer a substantially reduced smaller Sony 65" TV, a floor model for only $100 more than what the customer had paid for the Samsung. Of course, Mr. Grimes could also try his luck with another Samsung QLED Q90R 65" 4K UHD TV that would require no additional payment.

**YOUR TASK.** Because he wants to respond promptly to the frustrated customer, Mr. Estrada asks you to write an adjustment e-mail to Joseph Grimes (jogrimes@gmail.com) and explain his options. Copy the store manager, Norah Reyes, who has called Mr. Estrada about Mr. Grimes's request.

## 6.18 Adjustment: Responding to Unkindest Cut (L.O. 4)

**E-Mail**

As Andres McMillan, operations manager, Union Wood Products, you have a problem. Your firm manufactures quality precut and custom-built doors and frames. You have received a letter from Dominique Reese (described in **Activity 6.14**), an interior designer. Her letter explained that the custom mahogany door ("Nantucket") she received was cut to the wrong dimensions. She ordered an oversized door measuring 12 feet 2 inches. The door that arrived was 11 feet 10 inches.

Ms. Reese kept the door because her client, an NBA basketball player, insisted that the front of the house be closed up as soon as possible. Therefore, she had her carpenter resize the door opening. He charged $1,250 for this corrective work. She claims that you should reimburse her for this amount, since your company was responsible for the error. You check her April 19 order and find that the order was filled correctly. In a telephone order, Ms. Reese requested the Nantucket double-entry door measuring 11 feet 10 inches, and that is what you sent. Now she says that the door should have been 12 feet 2 inches.

Your policy forbids refunds or returns on custom orders. Yet you remember that around April 15 you had two new people working the phones taking orders. It is possible that they did not hear or record the measurements correctly. You don't know whether to grant this claim or refuse it. But you do know that you must look into the training of telephone order takers and be sure that they verify all custom order measurements. It might also be a good idea to confirm all phone orders by e-mail, IM, or text message.

Ms. Reese is a successful interior designer who has provided Union Wood Products with a number of orders. You value her business but aren't sure how to respond. You would like to remind her that Union Wood Products has earned a reputation as a premier manufacturer of wood doors and frames. Your doors feature prime woods, meticulous craftsmanship, and award-winning designs. What's more, the engineering is ingenious. You also have a wide range of classic designs.

**YOUR TASK.** Decide how to treat this claim and then respond to Dominique Reese, Millennium Interiors, 518 Crestview Drive, Beverly Hills, CA 90210. You might mention that you have a new line of energy-efficient windows that are available in three sizes. Include a brochure describing these windows. Alternatively, at your instructor's discretion, you could write an e-mail and refer Ms. Reese to your website (www.union-wood-products.com), which features the new line of windows.

## 6.19 Goodwill Message: Microsoft's Letter to a Newborn (L.O. 5)

Microsoft shared with *Business Insider* the template of the goodwill letter it sends to new parents, or, more precisely, to their babies.[37]

**YOUR TASK.** Evaluate the strengths and weaknesses of this message—in writing if your instructor assigns a written analysis.

Date
Dear [Name],

While you've been busy getting ready for the world, we've been busy doing our part to get the world ready for you. You represent the most important thing we've all been working toward—the future.

Enclosed are some special gifts we selected just for you. The Welcome Baby Box is lovingly put together by AtWork!, a non-profit organization whose mission is to help people with disabilities be productive, integrated, and contributing members of their communities. One of our favorite gifts is the Nanny and Webster blanket. Not only will this blanket keep you warm, but also, all profits from Nanny and Webster blankets support children's charities. Please be sure to share these gifts with your parents.

Ask your parents to familiarize themselves with the great benefits that Microsoft offers, like Back-Up Care, subsidized child care, new mothers' rooms, and family resources from the Microsoft CARES Employee Assistance Program. All can be found under Work & Life—Children & Family on benefits.me.microsoft.com.

We look forward to watching you grow and seeing what you'll achieve.
Sincerely,

Fred Thiele
GM, Global Benefits

## 6.20 Goodwill Message: Sending a Sympathy Note to a Spouse (L.O. 5)

**YOUR TASK.** Imagine that the spouse of a coworker recently died from an infectious disease. Write the coworker a letter of sympathy.

## 6.21 Goodwill Message: Saying Thanks for a Recommendation (L.O. 5)
> **E-Mail**

One of your instructors has complied with your urgent request for a letter of recommendation and has given you an enthusiastic endorsement. Regardless of the outcome of your application, you owe thanks to all your supporters. Respond promptly after receiving this favor. Also, you can assume that your instructors are interested in your progress. Let them know whether your application was successful.

**YOUR TASK.** Write an e-mail or, better yet, a letter thanking your instructor. Remember to make your thanks specific so that your words are meaningful. Once you know the outcome of your application, use the opportunity to build more goodwill by writing to your recommender again.

## 6.22 Goodwill Message: Cherishing Good Wishes and Saying Thanks (L.O. 5)

**YOUR TASK.** Write a short note thanking a friend who sent you good wishes when you recently completed your degree or reached a similar milestone.

## Commas 1

Review the Grammar Review section of the Grammar/Mechanics Handbook Sections 2.01–2.04. Then select the correctly punctuated sentences and record their letters in the space provided. Also record the appropriate G/M guidelines to illustrate the principles involved. When you finish, compare your responses with those at the end bottom of the page. If your answers differ, study carefully the principles in parentheses.

_____a_____ (2.01)   **EXAMPLE**   a. The auto manufacturer considered moving its headquarters to Nashville, Spartanburg, or Canton.
b. The auto manufacturer considered moving its headquarters to Nashville, Spartanburg or Canton.

_____   1.  a. The engineer assured us however that the bridge was now safe.
b. The engineer assured us, however, that the bridge was now safe.

_____   2.  a. We are certain Mr. Sexton, that your custom-made shoes will be ready for pick-up by 10 a.m. tomorrow.
b. We are certain, Mr. Sexton, that your custom-made shoes will be ready for pick-up by 10 a.m. tomorrow.

_____   3.  a. Our alarm system is affordable user-friendly and 100 percent secure.
b. Our alarm system is affordable, user-friendly, and 100 percent secure.

_____   4.  a. The real-estate website listed hotels in South Bend, Indiana, and Fayetteville, North Carolina, to sell to interested corporate buyers.
b. The real-estate website listed hotels in South Bend, Indiana and Fayetteville, North Carolina to sell to interested corporate buyers.

_____   5.  a. By the way, how is the geological survey report coming?
b. By the way how is the geological survey report coming?

_____   6.  a. The last East Coast regional association meeting was held on June 7, 2021 in Tallahassee.
b. The last East Coast regional association meeting was held on June 7, 2021, in Tallahassee.

_____   7.  a. Mr. Mack, Ms. Ortiz and Ms. Hanna were all promoted.
b. Mr. Mack, Ms. Ortiz, and Ms. Hanna were all promoted.

_____   8.  a. The shipment addressed to CogCity Technology, 9242 Paris Street, Rockaway, NJ 07866, was misdirected to Jamaica, NY 11432.
b. The shipment addressed to CogCity Technology, 9242 Paris Street, Rockaway, NJ, 07866, was misdirected to Jamaica, NY 11432.

_____   9.  a. He was very tired. Nevertheless, he continued to work on his speech.
b. He was very tired. Nevertheless he continued to work on his speech.

_____   10. a. U.S. companies succeed globally because they operate in a world language, come from a risk culture and exist in a vast home market.
b. U.S. companies succeed globally because they operate in a world language, come from a risk culture, and exist in a vast home market.

**1.** b (2.03) **2.** b (2.02) **3.** b (2.01) **4.** a (2.04c) **5.** a (2.03) **6.** b (2.04b) **7.** b (2.01) **8.** a (2.04b) **9.** a (2.03) **10.** b (2.01)

## Editing Challenge 6

Every chapter provides an editing exercise to fine-tune your grammar and mechanics skills.

The following e-mail requires edits that address proofreading, grammar, spelling, punctuation (especially commas), capitalization, word use, and other writing issues. Study the guidelines in the Grammar/Mechanics Handbook (Appendix D), including the lists of Confusing Words and Frequently Misspelled Words.

**YOUR TASK.** Edit the following by (a) inserting corrections in your textbook or on a photocopy using the proofreading marks in Appendix C or (b) downloading the message from **www.cengage.com** and correcting at your computer.

**To:** Lauryn Vincent <lvincent@weldsy-machining.com>
**From:** Alexander Yoder <alexander.yoder@framasoft.com>
**Subject:** Your October 11 Inquiry About Computador Software

Dear Mr. Vincent:

Yes we do offer personel record-keeping software specially designed for medium-sized businesses like your's. Here's answers to your three questions about this software,

1.  Our Computador software provide standard employee forms so that you are always in compliance with current goverment regulations.
2.  You recieve an interviewers guide for structured employee interviews and you also receive a scripted format for checking references by telephone.
3.  Yes, you can up date your employees records easy without the need for additional software, hardware or training. As a matter of fact everything you need is immediately available.

Our Computador software was professionally designed to provide you with expert forms for interviewing, verifying references, recording attendance, evaluating performance and tracking the status of your employees. We even provide you with step by step instructions, and suggested procedures. You can treat your employees as if you had a Professional human resources specialist right on your staff.

Because important changes in laws and regulations are constantly being made every business needs to have details in one place. One major step toward compliance is having these details clearly accessible.

To try out Computador in your office for 30 days risk-free just make an appointment by clicking here. We look forward Ms. Vincent to demonstrating Computador to you personal in the comfort of your office.

Best wishes,

Alexander Yoder
alexander.yoder@framasoft.com | Product Development | 455-309-2091
www.framasoft.com

# Knowing How to Do the Right Thing

It's easy to commit ethical lapses because of natural self-interest and the desire to succeed. In writing business messages or engaging in other activities on the job, business communicators can't help being torn between conflicting loyalties. Do we tell the truth and risk our jobs? Do we show loyalty to friends even if it means bending the rules? Should we be tactful or totally honest? Is it our duty to make a profit or be socially responsible?

Acting ethically means doing the right thing *given the circumstances*. Each set of circumstances requires analyzing issues, evaluating choices, and acting responsibly. Resolving ethical issues is never easy, but the task can be made less difficult if you know how to identify key issues. The following questions may be helpful.

- **Is the action legal?** No matter who asks you to do it or how important you feel the result will be, avoid anything that is prohibited by law. Bribing a buyer to secure a large order is illegal, even if you suspect that others in your field do it and you know that without the kickback you will lose the sale.

- **Would you do it if you were on the receiving end of the action?** Looking at both sides of an issue helps you gain perspective. By weighing both sides of an issue, you can arrive at a more equitable solution.

- **Can you rule out a better option?** Would the alternative be more ethical? Under the circumstances, is the alternative feasible?

- **Would a trusted advisor agree?** Suppose you feel ethically bound to report accurate information to a client—even though your boss has ordered you not to do so. Talking about your dilemma with a coworker or with a colleague in your field might give you helpful insights and lead to possible alternatives.

- **Would your family, friends, employer, or coworkers approve?** If the thought of revealing your action publicly produces cold sweats, your choice is probably not a wise one. Losing the faith of your friends or the confidence of your customers is not worth whatever short-term gains you might realize.

**CAREER APPLICATION.** One of the biggest accounting firms uses an ethical awareness survey that includes some of the following situations. You may face similar situations with ethical issues on the job or in employment testing.

**YOUR TASK.** In teams or individually, decide whether each of the following ethical issues is (a) very important, (b) moderately important, or (c) unimportant. Then decide whether you (a) strongly approve of, (b) are undecided about, or (c) strongly disapprove of the action taken. Apply the ethical tools presented here to determine whether the course of action is ethical. What alternatives might you suggest?

- **Recruiting.** You are a recruiter for your company. Although you know company morale is low, the turnover rate is high, and the work environment in many departments is deplorable, you tell job candidates that it is a great place to work.

- **Training program.** Your company is offering an exciting training program in Hawaii. Although you haven't told anyone, you plan to get another job shortly. You decide to participate in the program anyway because you have never been to Hawaii. One of the program requirements is that participants must have "long-term career potential" with the firm.

- **Thievery.** As a supervisor, you suspect that one of your employees is stealing. You check with a company attorney and find that a lie detector test cannot be legally used. Then you decide to scrutinize the employee's records. Finally, you find an inconsistency in the employee's records. You decide to fire the employee, although this inconsistency would not normally have been discovered.

- **Downsizing.** As part of the management team of a company that makes potato chips, you face the rising prices of potatoes. Rather than increase the cost of your chips, you decide to decrease slightly the size of the bag. Consumers are less likely to notice a smaller bag than a higher price.

# Bad-News Messages

Fizkes/Shutterstock.com

**Learning Outcomes**
After studying this chapter, you should be able to do the following:

**1** Explain the strategies of business communicators in conveying negative news.

**2** Describe the direct and indirect strategies in communicating unfavorable news.

**3** Identify the components of effective bad-news messages.

**4** Analyze effective techniques for presenting bad news to customers and refusing requests or claims.

**5** Evaluate effective techniques for delivering negative news within organizations.

## 7-1 Communicating Negative News Strategically

Bad things happen in all businesses. Products fail to perform as expected, goods are not delivered, service is poor, billing gets mixed up, or customers are misunderstood. You may have to write messages ending business relationships, declining proposals, explaining service outages, admitting data breaches, announcing price increases, refusing requests for donations, terminating employees, turning down invitations, or responding to unhappy customers. You might have to apologize for mistakes in orders or pricing, the rudeness of employees, overlooked appointments, substandard service, faulty accounting, defective products, or jumbled instructions. As a company representative, you may have to respond to complaints posted for the world to see on Twitter, Instagram, Facebook, or complaint websites.

Unfortunately, everyone occasionally must deliver bad news in business. Because bad news disappoints, irritates, and sometimes angers the receiver, such messages must be written carefully. The bad feelings associated with disappointing news can generally be reduced if the receiver (a) knows the reasons for the letdown, (b) feels that the news was revealed sensitively, and (c) believes that the matter was treated seriously and fairly.

189

**LEARNING OUTCOME 1**

Explain the strategies of business communicators in conveying negative news.

In this chapter you will learn when to use the direct strategy and when to use the indirect strategy to deliver unfavorable news. You will study the goals of business communicators in working with negative news and learn techniques for achieving those goals.

## 7-1a Setting Goals in Communicating Negative News

Sending bad news is not the easiest communication task you may have, but it can be gratifying if you do it effectively. As a business communicator working with bad news, you will have many goals. The most important of them are summarized here:

- **Explain clearly and completely**. Your goal is to make your readers understand and, in the best case, accept the unfavorable news. Recipients do not have to call or write to clarify your message.

- **Convey empathy and sensitivity**. You use language that respects the receiver and attempts to reduce bad feelings. When appropriate, you accept blame and apologize without creating legal liability for your organization or yourself.

- **Project a professional image**. Even when irate customers sound threatening and overstate their claims, you strive to stay calm, use polite language, and respond with clear explanations of why a bad-news message was necessary.

- **Be fair**. If you try to show sincerely that the decision was fair, impartial, and rational, receivers will be far more likely to accept the negative news.

- **Maintain friendly relations**. A final goal is to demonstrate your desire to continue pleasant relations with the receivers and to regain their confidence.

These goals are ambitious, and, frankly, we are not always successful in achieving them all. However, many writers have found the strategies and techniques you are about to learn helpful in communicating disappointing news sensitively. With experience, you will be able to vary these strategies and adapt them to your organization's specific communication tasks.

## 7-2 Examining Bad-News Strategies

**LEARNING OUTCOME 2**

Describe the direct and indirect strategies in communicating unfavorable news.

Unfavorable news in business doesn't always fall into neat categories. To successfully convey bad news, writers must carefully consider the audience, purpose, and context. Experienced business communicators understand that their approaches to negative news must be flexible.[1] However, as a business writer in training, you have at your disposal two basic strategies for delivering negative news: direct and indirect, as compared in **Figure 7.1**.

Which approach is best suited for your particular message? One of the first steps you need to take before communicating negative news is analyzing how your receiver will react to this news. In earlier chapters we discussed applying the **direct strategy** to positive and neutral messages. The **indirect strategy**, on the other hand, tends to work best when the audience might be unwilling, uninterested, disappointed, or hostile. In this chapter we expand on that advice and offer additional considerations to help you decide which strategy to use.

## 7-2a Using the Direct Strategy to Convey Negative News

The direct strategy saves time and is preferred by some who consider it to be more professional and even more ethical than the indirect strategy. The direct strategy may be more effective in situations such as the following:

- **When the bad news is not damaging**. If the bad news is insignificant (such as a small increase in cost) and doesn't personally affect the receiver, then the direct strategy makes sense.

**Figure 7.1** Comparing the Direct and Indirect Strategies for Bad-News Messages

- **When the receiver may overlook the bad news**. Changes in service, new policy requirements, legal announcements—these critical messages may require boldness to ensure attention.

- **When the organization or receiver prefers directness**. Some companies and individuals expect all internal messages and announcements—even negative news—to be straightforward and presented without frills.

- **When firmness is necessary**. Messages that must demonstrate determination and strength should not use delaying techniques. For example, the last in a series of collection letters that seek payment on an overdue account may require a direct opener.

Security breach messages provide a good example of how to employ the direct strategy in delivering bad news. Notice in **Model Document 7.1** that the writer, Cyril Cenek, is direct in announcing that consumer identity information was lost at Uniox Federal Credit Union.

Although he does not blurt out "your information has been compromised," the writer does announce a potential identity theft problem in the first sentence. He then explains that a hacker attack has compromised roughly a quarter of customer accounts. In the second paragraph, he recommends that credit union customer Petru Ramakrishna take specific corrective action to protect his identity and offers helpful contact information. The tone is respectful and serious. The credit union's letter is modeled on an FTC template that was praised for achieving a balance between a direct and indirect opening.[2]

## 7-2b Using the Indirect Strategy to Convey Negative News

The indirect strategy does not reveal the bad news immediately. This strategy, at least theoretically, enables you to keep the reader's attention until you have been able to explain the reasons for the bad news. Some writing experts have claimed that the indirect strategy "ill suits today's skeptical, impatient, even cynical audience."[4]

## Model Document 7.1   Announcing Negative News Directly: Security Breach Letter

8878 CHESTNUT RD.  FRAMINGHAM, MA 01701
www.unioxfcu.com                    508.288.3101

September 8, 2022

Mr. Petru Ramakrishna
30 South Marvon Street
Phoenixville, PA 19460

Dear Mr. Ramakrishna:

*Uses modified direct strategy because urgent action is needed to prevent identity theft*

We are contacting you about a potential problem involving identity theft. On August 30, names, encrypted social security numbers, birth dates, and e-mail addresses of fewer than 25 percent of accounts were compromised in an apparent hacker attack on our website. Outside data security experts are working tirelessly to identify the causes of the breach as well as prevent future intrusions into our system. Immediately upon detecting the attack, we notified the local police authorities as well as the FBI. We also alerted the three major credit-reporting agencies.

We recommend that you place a fraud alert on your credit file. A fraud alert tells creditors to contact you before they open any new accounts or change your existing accounts. Please call any one of the three major credit bureaus. As soon as one credit bureau confirms your fraud alert, the others are notified to place fraud alerts. All three credit reports will be sent to you, free of charge.

*Suggests recommended steps and provides helpful information about credit-reporting agencies*

| Equifax | Experian | TransUnion |
|---|---|---|
| 800-685-1111 | 888-397-3742 | 800-680-7289 |

*Gives reasons for the recommended action, provides contact information, and offers additional pointers*

Even if you do not find any suspicious activity on your initial credit reports, the Federal Trade Commission (FTC) recommends that you check your credit reports periodically. Victim information sometimes is held for use or shared among a group of thieves at different times. Checking your credit reports periodically can help you spot problems and address them quickly.

If you find suspicious activity on your credit reports or have reason to believe your information is being misused, call 518-584-5500 and file a police report. Get a copy of the report; many creditors want the information it contains to absolve you of the fraudulent debts. You also should file a complaint with the FTC at www.ftc.gov/idtheft or at 1-877-ID-THEFT (877-438-4338).

*Ends by providing more helpful information, company phone number, and offer of one year of free credit monitoring*

Please visit our website at www.unioxfcu.com/databreach for updates on the investigation, or call our privacy hotline at 800-358-4422. Affected customers will receive free credit-monitoring services for one year.

Sincerely,

Cyril Cenek

Cyril Cenek
Customer Service

---

Others have argued the relative advantages of both approaches and their effects on the receiver.[5] To be sure, in social media, bluntness seems to dominate public debate. Directness is equated with honesty; hedging, with deceit.

Regardless, many communicators prefer to use the indirect strategy to soften negative news. Whereas good news can be revealed quickly, bad news may be easier to accept when broken gradually. Here are typical instances in which the indirect strategy works well:

- **When the bad news is personally upsetting**. If the negative news involves the receiver personally, such as a layoff notice, the indirect strategy makes sense. Telling

## WORKPLACE IN FOCUS

DUAL OS PLATFORMS

Julie Jacobson/AP Photo

Two years before his ouster, Intel chief Brian Krzanich sent an e-mail to employees announcing a "restructuring initiative." In the buffer paragraph, Krzanich described Intel's successful pivot from PC to cloud, mobile, and smart computing during his tenure. This strategy was working, he said, but it was time "to accelerate our momentum and build on our strengths." He foreshadowed "some difficult decisions" as he presented the reasons for the restructuring. Finally, in the fourth paragraph, Krzanich broke the bad news: "We expect that this initiative will result in the reduction of up to 12,000 positions globally."[3] What helps determine the choice to use the indirect strategy to deliver bad news? How might the audience react to such buffered news?

employees that they no longer have a job is probably best done in person and by starting indirectly and giving reasons first. When a company has made a mistake that inconveniences or disadvantages a customer, the indirect strategy also makes sense.

- **When the bad news will provoke a hostile reaction**. When your message will irritate or infuriate the recipient, the indirect method may be best. It begins with a buffer and reasons, thus encouraging the reader to finish reading or hearing the message. A blunt announcement may make the receiver stop reading.

- **When the bad news threatens the customer relationship**. If the bad-news message may damage a customer relationship, the indirect strategy may help salvage the customer bond. Beginning slowly and presenting reasons that explain what happened can be more helpful than directly announcing bad news or failing to adequately explain the reasons.

- **When the bad news is unexpected**. Readers who are totally surprised by bad news tend to have a more negative reaction than those who expected it. If a company suddenly closes an office or a plant and employees had no inkling of the closure, that bad news would be better received if it were revealed cautiously with reasons first.

Whether to use the direct or indirect strategy depends largely on the situation, the reaction you expect from the audience, and your goals. The indirect approach does not guarantee that recipients will be pleased, because, after all, bad news is just that—bad. However, many communicators prefer to use it because they believe that revealing bad news slowly and indirectly shows sensitivity to the receiver. By preparing the receiver, you tend to soften the impact. Moreover, although social media users may favor the direct approach, most bad-news messages are still conveyed indirectly. To apply the indirect strategy effectively, you may use four parts, as shown in **Figure 7. 2**.

## 7-2c  Keeping the Indirect Strategy Ethical

If you worry that the indirect strategy is unethical or manipulative because the writer deliberately delays the main idea, consider the alternative. Breaking bad news bluntly can cause pain and hard feelings. By delaying bad news, you soften the blow somewhat, as well as ensure that your reasoning will be read while the receiver is still receptive. One psychologist recognized that the indirect strategy depends on a clear explanation: "If the *why* of my *no* is clear and understandable, it's less likely that

**Figure 7.2** Four-Part Indirect Strategy for Negative News

| Buffer | Reasons | Bad News | Closing |
|---|---|---|---|
| Open with a neutral but meaningful statement that does not mention the bad news. | Explain the causes of the bad news before disclosing it. | Reveal the bad news without emphasizing it. Provide an alternative or compromise, if possible. | End with a personalized, forward-looking, pleasant statement. Avoid referring to the bad news. |

the other person will take it as being a *no* to them."[6] In using the indirect strategy, your motives are not to deceive the reader or hide the news. Rather, your goal is to be a compassionate, yet effective, communicator.

The key to ethical communication lies in the motives of the sender. Unethical communicators *intend to deceive*. Although the indirect strategy provides a setting in which to announce negative news, it should not be used to avoid or misrepresent the truth. For example, the Internet is rife with bogus offers such as skin care products promising to deliver the fountain of youth. Teeth-whitening systems Snow and iSmile fraudulently used the FDA logo. MyPillow touted a sham sleep study. The world's largest retailer, Amazon, is promoting and profiting from falsely marketed brain supplements. These are but a few of the most recent scams, says Truth in Advertising, a nonprofit dedicated to stamping out deceptive advertising.[7] As you will see in Chapter 8, misleading, deceptive, and unethical claims are never acceptable. In fact, many are simply illegal.

## 7-3 Composing Effective Bad-News Messages

**LEARNING OUTCOME 3**

Identify the components of effective bad-news messages.

No one is happy to receive negative news, but you can reduce bad feelings by structuring your message sensitively. Most bad-news messages contain some or all these parts: buffer, reasons, bad news, and closing. **Figure 7.3** presents these four components of the indirect strategy in greater detail. This section also discusses apologies and how to convey empathy in delivering bad news.

### 7-3a Opening Indirect Messages With a Buffer

To reduce the shock or pain of negative news, most writers use a buffer. They begin with a neutral but meaningful statement that makes the reader continue reading. The buffer should be relevant and concise and provide a natural transition to the

**Figure 7.3** Delivering Bad News Sensitively

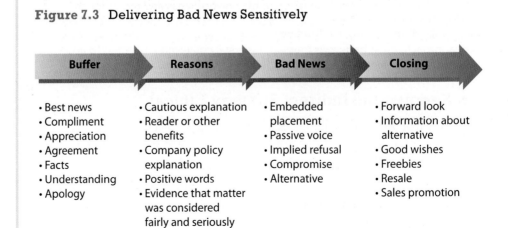

| Buffer | Reasons | Bad News | Closing |
|---|---|---|---|
| • Best news | • Cautious explanation | • Embedded placement | • Forward look |
| • Compliment | • Reader or other benefits | • Passive voice | • Information about alternative |
| • Appreciation | • Company policy explanation | • Implied refusal | • Good wishes |
| • Agreement | • Positive words | • Compromise | • Freebies |
| • Facts | • Evidence that matter was considered fairly and seriously | • Alternative | • Resale |
| • Understanding | | | • Sales promotion |
| • Apology | | | |

explanation that follows. The situation, of course, will help determine what you should put in the buffer. Avoid trite buffers such as *Thank you for your e-mail.*

Not all business communication authors agree that buffers increase the effectiveness of bad-news messages. However, in many cultures softening bad news is appreciated. Following are buffer possibilities.

**Best News.** Start with the part of the message that represents the best news. For example, a message to customers who purchased mobile device insurance announced a progressive rate increase that was tied to the replacement value of each smart device. Only customers with very expensive handsets will experience price increases. You might start by reminding customers about the value of insuring a mobile device: *As a reminder, your MobilePeer Protection provides the benefit of a replacement device when your smartphone is accidentally damaged, including liquid damage, loss, theft, and malfunction. Although devices are becoming increasingly expensive, no changes will be made to your deductible amount or coverage.*

**Compliment.** Praise the receiver's accomplishments, organization, or efforts, but do so with honesty and sincerity. For instance, in a message declining an invitation to speak, you could write: *The Karegiverz have my sincere admiration for their fund-raising projects on behalf of hungry children. I am honored that you asked me to speak Friday, November 11.*

**Appreciation.** Express thanks for doing business, for sending something, for showing confidence in your organization, for voicing their feelings, or simply for providing feedback. Suppose you had to draft a letter that refuses employment. You could say: *I appreciated learning about the occupational therapist program at USC and about your qualifications in our interview last Friday.* Avoid thanking the reader, however, for something you are about to refuse.

**Agreement.** Make a relevant statement with which both you and the receiver can agree. A letter that rejects a loan application might read: *We both realize how much falling crude oil prices on the world market have devastated domestic oil production.*

**Facts.** Provide objective information that introduces the bad news. For example, in a memo announcing cutbacks in the hours of the employee cafeteria, you might say: *During the past five years, the number of employees eating breakfast in our cafeteria has dropped from 32 percent to 12 percent.*

**Understanding.** Show that you care about the reader. Notice how in the following e-mail to customers announcing a product defect, the writer expresses concern: *We know that you expect superior performance from all the products you purchase from SupplyPlex. That's why we are writing personally about the InkMeister printer cartridges you recently ordered.*

## 7-3b Apologizing

An **apology** is defined as an "admission of blameworthiness and regret for an undesirable event."[9] Apologies to customers are especially important if you or your company erred. You learned about making apologies in adjustment messages in Chapter 6. We expand that discussion here because apologies are often part of bad-news messages. Genuine expressions of remorse are thought to promote healing, influence perceptions of the offending party's character, and invite victims to empathize with the offender, leading to forgiveness.[10]

The truth is that sincere apologies work and may even affect the bottom line. A study of 130 press releases showed that businesses blaming external factors instead of taking responsibility for their failing tend to experience ongoing financial decline. Those who own up to their poor performance see their finances recover and improve.[11] The following pointers can help you apologize effectively in business messages:

- **Apologize promptly and sincerely.** Credibility suffers when a public figure delays an apology and responds only after causing an outrage. Also, people dislike

**OFFICE INSIDER**

"Answer negative feedback as soon as you see it. It's an opportunity to show the human side of your business. Customers forgive if they feel their concerns are heard and taken seriously. For negative feedback, simply apologize, offer a solution or an investigation, and provide direct contact information for a human being should they wish to take it further. 'Sorry' goes a long way."[8]

**Freya Smale,**
*The Millennium Alliance*

"The purpose of an apology is not to restore trust, but to confirm to others that we deserve it," says best-selling author and speaker Joseph Grenny.[13]

OFFICE INSIDER

"We all know empathy is the right thing to do, but empathy is not just good for the world (and our own sanity). It can also bring a competitive advantage in business. Our ability to see the world from the perspective of others is one of the most crucial tools in our business toolbox."[14]

**Maria Ross,**
*brand strategist, author, and speaker*

apologies that sound hollow (*We regret that you were inconvenienced* or *We are sorry that you are disturbed*). Focusing on your regret does not convey sincerity; explaining what you will do to prevent recurrence of the problem does.

- **Accept responsibility**. One CEO has this advice for leaders who make a mistake: "Never try to cover up or blame others for what went wrong. If you messed up, admit it and own it. It doesn't have to be a big deal—simply acknowledge your responsibility and move on. Admitting your mistakes earns you the respect of those you lead and makes your leadership human."[12]

- **Use good judgment**. Before admitting blame, it might be wise to consult a supervisor or the company legal counsel to avoid litigation.

Consider these poor and improved apologies:

**Poor apology:** *We are sorry that mistakes were made in filling your order.*

**Improved apology:** *You are right to be concerned. We sincerely apologize for the mistakes we made in filling your order. To prevent recurrence of this problem, we are introducing. . . .*

**Poor apology:** *We regret that you are unhappy with the price of frozen yogurt purchased at one of our self-serve scoop shops.*

**Improved apology:** *We are genuinely sorry that you were disappointed in the price of frozen yogurt recently purchased at one of our self-serve scoop shops. Your opinion is important to us, and we appreciate your giving us the opportunity to investigate the problem you describe.*

### 7-3c Showing Empathy

One of the hardest things to do in apologies is to convey empathy. As discussed in Chapter 2, **empathy** means "understanding our emotional impact on others and making change as a result." The Empathy Business, a UK-based consulting firm, has established a so-called **empathy quotient** and ranked 170 large companies on metrics such as corporate culture, leadership, brand perception, ethics, carbon footprint, and social media presence. Facebook took first place, followed by Alphabet (Google) and LinkedIn.[15] Business leaders are catching on. Some U.S. employers have started providing empathy training. In a recent survey of CEOs, more than 90 percent said empathy was key to success.[16]

Here are examples of ways to express empathy in written messages:

- In writing to an unhappy customer: *We did not intentionally delay the shipment, and we sincerely regret the disappointment and frustration you must have suffered.*

- In laying off employees: *It is with great regret that we must take this step. Rest assured that I will be more than happy to write letters of recommendation for anyone who asks.*

- In responding to a complaint: *I am deeply saddened that our service failure disrupted your sale, and we will do everything in our power to respond to any future outages promptly.*

- In showing genuine feelings: *You have every right to be disappointed. I am truly sorry that . . . .*

## 7-3d Presenting the Reasons

Without sound reasons for denying a request, refusing a claim, or revealing other bad news, a message will fail, no matter how cleverly it is organized or written. Providing an explanation reduces feelings of ill will and improves the chances that readers will accept the bad news. For example, if you must deny a customer's request, as part of your planning before writing, you analyze the request and decide to refuse it for specific reasons. Where do you place your reasons? In the indirect strategy, the reasons appear before the bad news. In the direct strategy, the reasons appear immediately after the bad news.

**Explaining Clearly.** If the reasons are not confidential and if they will not create legal liability, you can be specific: *Growers supplied us with a limited number of our popular hydrangeas, and our demand this year was twice that of last year.* In responding to a billing error, explain what happened: *After you informed us of an error on your May statement, we realized the mistake was ours. Until our new automated billing system is fully online, we are still subject to human error. Rest assured that you will see a credit on your next bill.* In refusing a speaking engagement, tell why the date is impossible: *On February 18 I will be out of the country, attending a strategic planning summit.* Don't, however, make unrealistic or dangerous statements in an effort to be the good guy: *Although we can't contribute now, we expect increased revenues next year and promise a generous gift then.*

**Citing Reader or Other Benefits, if Plausible.** Readers are more open to bad news if in some way, even indirectly, they may benefit. When *The New York Times* announced a first-ever price hike to its 4 million digital subscribers, the e-mail included lofty words: "These rates will help us sustain and strengthen our coverage at a time when independent journalism is under great pressure. Your support allows us to go wherever the story is, no matter the danger, hardship or cost. . . . That would not be possible without subscribers like you. Thank you again for supporting *The Times* in our pursuit of the truth, without fear or favor."[17]

Readers also accept bad news more readily if they recognize that someone or something else benefits, such as the environment or other workers: *Although we would like to consider your application, we prefer to fill managerial positions from within.* Avoid trying to show reader benefits, though, if they appear insincere: *To improve our service to you, we are increasing our brokerage fees.*

**Explaining Company Policy.** Readers resent blanket policy statements prohibiting something: *Company policy prevents us from making cash refunds* or *Contract bids may be accepted from local companies only.* Instead of hiding behind a vague company policy, gently explain why the policy makes sense: *We prefer to promote from within because it rewards the loyalty of our employees. In addition, we have found that people familiar with our organization instantly start contributing to our team effort.* By offering explanations, you demonstrate that you care about readers and are treating them as important individuals.

**Choosing Positive Words.** Because the words you use can affect a reader's response, choose carefully. Remember that the objective of the indirect strategy is holding the reader's attention until you have had a chance to explain the reasons justifying the bad news. To keep the reader in a receptive mood, avoid expressions with punitive, demoralizing, or otherwise negative connotations. Stay away from such words

gg-foto/Shutterstock.com

A luxury resort in French Polynesia attempted to soothe disappointed customers with a discount after an Internet price goof: "Please note that our website contained an unfortunate misprint offering $850-per-night Bora Bora bungalows at $85. Although we cannot honor that rate, we are offering a special half-price rate of $425 to those who responded."

as *cannot, claim, denied, error, failure, fault, impossible, mistaken, misunderstand, never, regret, rejected, unable, unwilling, unfortunately,* and *violate.*

**Showing Fairness and Serious Intent.** In explaining reasons, show the reader that you take the matter seriously, have investigated carefully, and are making a reasonable decision. Receivers are more accepting of disappointing news when they feel that their requests have been heard and that they have been treated fairly. In canceling funding for a program, board members provided this explanation: *As you know, the publication of ArtWorks was funded by a renewable annual grant from the National Endowment for the Arts. Recent cutbacks in federally sponsored city arts programs have left us with few funds. Because our grant has been discontinued, we have no alternative but to cease publication of ArtWorks. Our board has searched long and hard for some other viable funding but was not able to find a workable path forward. Accordingly, the June issue will be our last.*

## 7-3e Cushioning the Bad News

Although you can't prevent the disappointment that bad news brings, you can reduce the pain somewhat by breaking the news sensitively. Be especially considerate when the reader will suffer personally from the bad news. Several thoughtful techniques can cushion the blow.

**Positioning the Bad News Strategically.** Instead of spotlighting it, sandwich the bad news between other sentences, perhaps among your reasons. Don't let the refusal begin or end a paragraph; the reader's eye will linger on these high-visibility spots. Another technique that reduces shock is putting a painful idea in a subordinate clause: *Although another candidate was hired, we appreciate your interest in our organization and wish you every success in your job search.* Subordinate clauses often begin with words such as *although, as, because, if,* and *since.*

**Using the Passive Voice.** Passive-voice verbs enable you to depersonalize an action. Whereas the active voice focuses attention on a person (*We don't give cash refunds*), the passive voice highlights the action (*Cash refunds are not given because. . .*). Use the passive voice for the bad news. In some instances you can combine passive-voice verbs and a subordinate clause: *Although franchise scoop shop owners cannot be required to lower their frozen yogurt prices, we are happy to pass along your comments for their consideration.*

**Highlighting the Positive.** As you learned earlier, messages are far more effective when you describe what you can do instead of what you can't do. Rather than *We will no longer allow credit card purchases,* try a more positive appeal: *Although credit card purchases are no longer allowed, we are now selling gasoline at discount cash prices.*

**Implying the Refusal.** It is sometimes possible to avoid a direct refusal. Often your reasons and explanations leave no doubt that a request has been denied. Explicit refusals may be unnecessary and at times cruel. In this refusal to contribute to a charity, for example, the writer never actually says *no: Because we will soon be moving into new offices in Eagle Rock, all our funds are earmarked for relocation costs. We hope that next year we will be able to support your worthwhile cause.* The danger of an implied refusal, of course, is that it is so subtle that the reader misses it. Be certain that you make the bad news clear, thus preventing the need for further correspondence. If you raise hopes for possible future support, mean it.

**Suggesting a Compromise or an Alternative.** A refusal is not so depressing—for the sender or the receiver—if a suitable compromise, substitute, or alternative is available. In denying permission to a group of students to visit a historical private residence, for instance, this writer softens the bad news by proposing an alternative: *Although private tours of the grounds are not given, we do open the house and its gardens for* *one charitable event in the fall.* You can further reduce the impact of the bad news by refusing to dwell on it. Present it briefly (or imply it) and move on to your closing.

### 7-3f Closing Pleasantly

After explaining the bad news sensitively, close the message with a pleasant statement that promotes goodwill. The closing should be personalized and may include a forward look, an alternative, good wishes, freebies, resale information, or a sales promotion. **Resale** refers to mentioning a product or service favorably to reinforce the customer's choice or, depending on the context, suggesting a different model that might suit the receiver's needs better. For example, *you chose our best-selling model* or *The rugged model DiveX-35, rated for water depths of up to 1,000 feet, might be a better companion on your next diving adventures.*

**Forward Look.** Anticipate future relations or business. A letter that refuses a contract proposal might read: *Thanks for your bid. We look forward to working with your talented staff when future projects demand your special expertise.*

**Alternative.** If an alternative exists, you might end your letter with follow-through advice. For example, in a letter rejecting a customer's demand for replacement of landscaping plants, you might say: *I will be happy to give you a free inspection and consultation. Please call 301-746-8112 to arrange a date for my visit.* In a message to a prospective home buyer: *Although the lot you saw last week is now sold, we do have two excellent lots available at a slightly higher price.*

**Good Wishes.** A letter rejecting a job candidate might read: *We appreciate your interest in our company, and we extend to you our best wishes in your search to find the perfect match between your skills and job requirements.*

**Freebies.** When customers complain—primarily about food products or small consumer items—companies often send coupons, samples, or gifts to restore confidence and promote future business. In response to a customer's complaint about a frozen dinner, you could write: *Your loyalty and your concern about our frozen entrées are genuinely appreciated. Because we want you to continue enjoying our healthy and convenient dinners, we are enclosing a coupon for your next nutritious Town Foods entrée that you can redeem at your local market.*

**Resale or Sales Promotion.** When the bad news is not devastating or personal, references to resale information or promotion may be appropriate: *The military-grade laptops you ordered for your field staff are unusually popular because of their rigid, robust cases. To help you locate hard-to-find accessories for these laptops, we invite you to visit our online catalog for a huge selection of USB-C hubs, Pelican cases, laptop bags, power banks, and charging stations.*

Avoid endings that sound canned, insincere, inappropriate, or self-serving. Don't invite further correspondence (*If you have any questions, do not hesitate. . .*), and don't refer to the bad news. Figure 7.3. summarizes these suggestions for delivering bad news sensitively.

## 7-4 Refusing Typical Requests and Claims

As you advance in your career, you may receive requests for favors or contributions. You may have to say *no* to customer claims or invitations to give presentations. You may also deal with disappointment and anger. When you must refuse typical requests, first think about how the receiver will react to your refusal and decide whether to use the direct or the indirect strategy. If you have any doubt, use the indirect strategy and the following writing plan:

**OFFICE INSIDER**

"The most pressing need of angry customers is to be heard. Listen to them without interrupting. Then show you understand their situation by finding common points of frustration."[18]

**Jonathan Rick,**
*director, Levick Strategic Communications*

**LEARNING OUTCOME 4**

Analyze effective techniques for presenting bad news to customers and refusing requests or claims.

## Refusing Typical Requests and Claims

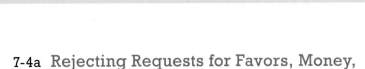

**WRITING PLAN**

**BUFFER:** Start with a neutral statement on which both reader and writer can agree, such as a compliment, appreciation, a quick review of the facts, or an apology. Try to include a key idea or word that acts as a transition to the reasons.

**REASONS:** Present valid reasons for the refusal, avoiding words that create a negative tone.

**BAD NEWS:** De-emphasize the bad news, use the passive voice, accentuate the positive, or imply a refusal. Suggest a compromise, alternative, or substitute, if possible. The alternative may be part of the bad-news section or part of the closing.

**CLOSING:** Renew good feelings with a positive statement. Avoid referring to the bad news. Include resale or sales promotion material, if appropriate. Look forward to continued business.

### 7-4a Rejecting Requests for Favors, Money, Information, and Action

Requests for favors, money, information, and action may come from charities, friends, or business partners. Many are from people representing worthy causes, and you may wish you could comply. However, resources are usually limited. In a letter from Manteau Management Associates, shown in **Model Document 7.2**, the company must refuse a request for a donation to a charity.

Following the indirect strategy, the letter begins with a buffer acknowledging the request. It also praises the good works of the charity and uses those words as a transition to the second paragraph. In the second paragraph, the writer explains why the company cannot donate. Notice that the writer reveals the refusal without explicitly stating it (*Because of internal restructuring and subsequent cutbacks in charitable giving, we are forced to take a much harder look at funding requests that we receive this year*). This gentle refusal makes it unnecessary to be blunter in stating the denial.

In some donation refusal letters, the reasons may not be fully explained: *Although we can't provide financial support at this time, we all unanimously agree that the Make-A-Wish Foundation contributes a valuable service to sick children*. The emphasis is on the foundation's good deeds rather than on an explanation for the refusal. Refusal messages can often be tactfully handled by showing appreciation for the inquiry and respect for the writer. Businesses that are required to write frequent refusals might prepare a form letter, changing a few variables as needed.

### 7-4b Dealing With Disappointed Customers in Print and Online

All businesses must occasionally respond to unhappy customers. Whenever possible, problems should be addressed immediately and personally. Most business professionals strive to control the damage and resolve such problems in the following manner:

- Call or e-mail the disappointed customer immediately or reply to the individual's online post within 24 hours.

- Describe the problem and apologize.

- Explain why the problem occurred, what they are doing to resolve it, and how they will prevent it from happening again.

**OFFICE INSIDER**

"[W]hat people recall most of all is not what went wrong but how you handled it. Don't miss out on these golden opportunities to show your integrity, reduce the drama, and improve the way your business operates. That's how you make 'my bads' good."[19]

**Michael Houlihan,**
*author and cofounder,*
*Barefoot Cellars*

**Model Document 7.2   Refusing a Donation Request**

Opens with praise and compliments

Transitions with repetition of key ideas (*good work and worthy projects*)

Closes graciously with praise and a forward look

**manteau**

819 Proctor Street, Suite 800
Anoka, MN 55303
www.manteaumanagement.com

February 16, 2022

Ms. Alexandra Milan
PuppyTale Guide Dog Foundation
7543 Spring Court
Pickerington, OH 43147

Dear Ms. Milan:

Here at Manteau Management Associates, we are pleased that over the years we were able to partner with the PuppyTale Guide Dog Foundation and assist in its admirable program that provides guide and service dogs to blind or visually impaired individuals. We appreciate your recent letter describing the exceptionally worthwhile Dogs for Vets program that offers trained animals to America's returning heroes needing service dogs.

Supporting the good work and worthy projects of your organization and others, although unrelated to our business, is a luxury we have enjoyed in the past. Because of internal restructuring and subsequent cutbacks in charitable giving, we are forced to take a much harder look at funding requests that we receive this year. We feel that we must focus our charitable contributions on areas that relate more directly to our business.

We are hopeful that in the future we will be able to again partner with the PuppyTale Guide Dog Foundation to help defray the costs of breeding, training, and placing guide and service dogs. You provide an admirable service, and Manteau salutes you.

Cordially,

MANTEAU MANAGEMENT ASSOCIATES

*Victor Maquinna*

Victor Maquinna
Vice President

Doesn't say *yes* or *no*

Explains cutback in gifts, thus revealing refusal without actually stating it

- Promote goodwill by following up with a message that documents the phone call or acknowledges the online exchange of posts.

**Responding by E-Mail and in Hard Copy.** Written messages are important (a) when personal contact is impossible, (b) to establish a record of the incident, (c) to formally confirm follow-up procedures, and (d) to promote good relations. Dealing with problems immediately is very important in resolving conflict and retaining goodwill.

A bad-news follow-up letter is shown in **Model Document 7.3**. Consultant Natalia Lelise found herself in the embarrassing position of explaining why she had given out the name of her client to a salesperson. The client, Jarvis & Chantel International, had hired her firm, Maxence & Collen Consulting, to help find an appropriate service

**Model Document 7.3   Bad-News Follow-Up Message**

**MAXENCE & COLLEN CONSULTING**

500 Henry Road, Suite 100          (260) 842-0971
Fort Wayne, IN 46804               www.mcconsulting.com

May 10, 2022

Mr. Reilly Ellington
Director, Administrative Operations
Jarvis & Chantel International
210 North Illinois Street, Suite 1640
Indianapolis, IN 46204

Dear Mr. Ellington:

*Opens with agreement and apology* → You have every right to expect complete confidentiality in your transactions with an independent consultant. As I explained in yesterday's telephone call, I am very distressed that you were called by a salesperson from Gragson Payroll, Inc. This should not have happened, and I apologize to you again for inadvertently mentioning your company's name in a conversation with a potential vendor, Gragson Payroll, Inc.

*Takes responsibility and promises to prevent recurrence* → All clients of Maxence & Collen Consulting are assured that their dealings with our firm are held in the strictest confidence. Because your company's payroll needs are so individual and because you have so many contract workers, I was forced to explain how your employees differed from those of other companies. Revealing your company name was my error, and I take full responsibility for the lapse. I can assure you that it will not happen again. I have informed Gragson Payroll that it had no authorization to call you directly and that its actions have forced me to reconsider using its services for my future clients. ← *Explains what caused the problem and how it was resolved*

*Closes with forward look* → A number of other payroll services offer outstanding programs. I'm sure we can find the perfect partner to enable you to outsource your payroll responsibilities, thus allowing your company to focus its financial and human resources on its core business. I look forward to our next appointment when you may choose from a number of excellent payroll outsourcing firms.

Sincerely,

*Natalia Lelise*

Natalia Lelise
Partner

---

**Tips for Resolving Problems and Following Up**

- Whenever possible, call or see the individual involved.
- Describe the problem and apologize.
- Explain why the problem occurred.
- Take responsibility, if appropriate.
- Explain what you are doing to resolve it.
- Explain what you are doing to prevent recurrence.
- Follow up with a message that documents the personal contact.
- Look forward to positive future relations.

---

for outsourcing its payroll functions. Without realizing it, Natalia had mentioned to a potential vendor (Gragson Payroll, Inc.) that her client was considering hiring an outside service to handle its payroll. An overeager salesperson from Gragson Payroll immediately called on Jarvis & Chantel, thus angering the client.

Natalia Lelise first called her client to explain and apologize. She was careful to control her voice and rate of speaking. She also followed up with the letter shown in Model Document 7.3. The letter not only confirms the telephone conversation but also adds the right touch of formality. It sends the nonverbal message that the writer takes the matter seriously and that it is important enough to warrant a hard-copy letter.

Many consumer problems are handled with letters, either written by consumers as complaints or by companies in response. However, e-mail and social media are now common channels for delivering complaints and bad-news messages.

**Managing Negative News Online.** The phone and e-mail remain the preferred channels for customer complaints.[21] However, today's impatient, hyperconnected consumers often take their gripes to social media rather than calling customer service. Internet sites (e.g., HissingKitty or GripeO) encourage consumers to quickly share complaints about stores, products, and services that disappoint. Twitter, Facebook, Angie's List, Tripadvisor, Yelp, and other social media allow consumers to make public their ire, often without giving the business an opportunity to fix the problem first.

Online complaints are gaining momentum for many reasons. Consumers may receive faster responses to tweets than to customer service calls.[22] More than 50 percent of users who complain on Twitter expect an answer from customer service within an hour or less. Almost 60 percent of consumers think the response time should always be the same, including weekends.[23] The pressure is on for businesses, as 88 percent of consumers say they are less likely to buy from companies that don't answer complaints on social media.[24]

Airing grievances in public also helps other consumers avoid the same problems and may improve the complainer's leverage in solving the problem. In addition, dashing off a tweet is much easier than navigating endless phone menus to reach an agent. Businesses can employ some of the following effective strategies to manage negative news on social media:

- **Recognize social media as an important feedback channel**. Instead of fearing social networks, smart companies embrace these channels as opportunities to reveal the true mindset of customers and receive free advice on how to improve.

- **Verify the situation**. Investigate to learn what happened. If the complaint is legitimate and your organization messed up, it's best to fess up. Admit the problem and try to remedy it.

- **Become proactive**. Social media help companies listen to their customers as well as spread the word about their own good deeds. Marketing experts believe that 96 percent of unhappy customers don't complain to companies directly but tell 15 friends about their bad experience.[25] This means anticipating trouble and exceeding consumers' expectations is key. American Airlines has set a 30-minute average response time goal for 4,500 daily tweets.[26] JetBlue, Virgin America, and AlaskaAir have won praise for responding in less than 5 minutes on average.[27]

- **Monitor comments**. Many large companies employ social media customer service representatives to monitor online traffic 24/7 and respond immediately whenever possible. At Southwest Airlines and other carriers, such social care teams listen online to what people are saying about their companies. Their policy is to engage the positive and address the negative as fast as possible, ideally in real time.

- **Accept the inevitable**. Recognize that nearly every business will experience some negativity, especially on today's readily accessible social media. Do what you can to respond constructively, and then move on.

For advice on answering online comments, see Chapter 6.

## 7-4c Denying Claims

When customers are unhappy with a product or service, they often are emotionally involved. Messages that say *no* to emotionally involved receivers will probably be your most challenging communication task. As publisher Malcolm Forbes observed, "To be agreeable while disagreeing—that's an art."[28]

**OFFICE INSIDER**

"Responding within 24 hours is a good rule of thumb, depending on the situation. But be careful when handling negative reviews on social media. Once you post, it's in writing, forever. That said, addressing the customer on their turf, through their preferred mode of communication, is a good idea, but use private messages and encourage a phone conversation if it's a complicated issue."[20]

**Brandie Claborn,**
*McAfee*

Fortunately, the reasons-before-refusal plan helps you be empathic and artful in breaking bad news. Obviously, in denial messages you will need to adopt the proper tone. Don't blame customers, even if they are at fault. Avoid *you* statements that sound preachy (*You would have known that cash refunds are impossible if you had read your contract*). Use neutral, objective language to explain why the claim must be refused. Consider offering resale information to rebuild the customer's confidence in your products or organization.

In **Model Document 7.4** the writer denies the customer's claim for the difference between the price the customer paid for speakers and the price he saw advertised online (which would have resulted in a refund of $100). Although the retailer does match any advertised lower price, the price-matching policy applies only to exact models. This claim must be rejected because the advertisement the customer submitted showed a different, older speaker model.

## Model Document 7.4    E-Mail Denying a Claim

| | |
|---|---|
| **To:** | Florian Alva <falva@outlook.com> |
| **From:** | Ayden Hartwin <ayden.hartwin@beosocal.com> |
| **Subject:** | Your Inquiry About Beolab 8000 Speakers |

Dear Mr. Alva:

*Buffer* — You're absolutely right. We sell the finest surround sound speakers that are also acoustic works of art. The Bang & Olufsen Beolab 8000 stereo speakers that you purchased last month are premier concert hall speakers that sound every bit as good as they look.

*Combines agreement with resale*

*Reasons* — We have such confidence in our products and prices that we offer the price-matching policy you mention in your e-mail of March 15. That policy guarantees a refund of the price difference if you see one of your purchases offered at a lower price for 30 days after your purchase. To qualify for that refund, customers are asked to send us an advertisement or verifiable proof of the product price and model. As our website states, this price-matching policy applies only to exact models with USA warranties.

*Explains price-matching policy and how reader's purchase is different from lower-priced model*

*Implied refusal* — The Bang & Olufsen Beolab 8000 speaker set sells for $1,199.99. You sent us a local advertisement showing a price of $699.95 for Beolab speakers. This advertisement, however, describes an earlier version, the Beolab 6000. The set you received has a wider dynamic range and smoother frequency response than the Beolab 6000 set. It is also 20 percent more compact than the Beolab 6000. Naturally, the advanced model you purchased costs more than the older Beolab 6000 model.

*Without actually saying no, shows why reader's claim cannot be honored*

*Builds reader's confidence in wisdom of purchase*

*Positive closing* — You bought the finest compact speakers on the market, Mr. Alva. If you haven't installed them yet, you may be interested in ceiling or wall mounts and other accessories, shown on our website at www.beosocal.com/beolab8000 and available at competitive prices. We value your business and invite your continued comparison shopping.

*Continues resale; looks forward to future business*

Sincerely,

Ayden Hartwin, Senior Product Manager
BANG & OLUFSEN La Jolla

**8518 Girard Avenue | La Jolla, CA 92038 | phone 858-835-1012 | www.beosocal.com**

The e-mail to Florian Alva opens with a buffer in which the writer agrees with a statement in the customer's e-mail. Ayden Hartwin repeats the key idea of product confidence as a transition to the second paragraph. Next comes an explanation of the price-matching policy. Ayden does not assume that the customer is trying to deceive. Nor does he suggest that the customer didn't read or understand the price-matching policy. The safest path is a neutral explanation of the policy along with precise distinctions between the customer's speakers and the older ones. The writer also gets a chance to resell the customer's speakers and demonstrate what a quality product they are. By the end of the third paragraph, it is evident to the reader that his claim is unjustified.

Internal bad news is conveyed face-to-face or in writing. The anticipated audience reaction determines whether a direct or indirect strategy is appropriate.

# 7-5 Managing Bad News Within Organizations

A reasons-first approach and a tactful tone help preserve friendly relations with customers. These same techniques are also useful when delivering bad news within organizations. Interpersonal bad news might involve telling the boss that something went wrong or confronting an employee about poor performance. Organizational bad news might involve declining profits, lost contracts, harmful lawsuits, public relations controversies, and policy changes. Whether you use a direct or an indirect strategy in delivering that news depends primarily on the anticipated reaction of the audience. Generally, bad news is better received when reasons are given first. Within organizations, you may find yourself giving bad news in person or in writing.

## 7-5a Delivering Bad News in Person

The unhappy responsibility of delivering bad news may fall on supervisors and employees alike. First, decide whether the negative information is newsworthy. For example, minor mistakes or one-time bad behaviors are best left alone. However, fraudulent travel claims, consistent hostile behavior, or failing projects must be reported.[30] For example, you might have to tell the boss that the team's computers picked up malware that caused them to infect the company's computer network. Similarly, as a team leader or supervisor, you might be required to confront an underperforming employee.

If you know that the news will upset the receiver, the reasons-first strategy is most effective. When the bad news involves one person or a small group nearby, you should generally deliver that news in person. Here are pointers on how to do so tactfully, professionally, and safely:[31]

- **Gather all information**. Cool down and have all the facts before marching in on the boss or confronting someone. Remember that most stories have two sides.

- **Prepare and rehearse**. Outline what you plan to say so that you are confident, coherent, and dispassionate.

**OFFICE INSIDER**

"A difficult conversation is often better received when delivered using a 'bad news sandwich,' where the 'buns' of the sandwich include positive words of praise, and the 'meat' in the middle deals with the heart of the matter. This method allows you to share good news along with hard-to-share news—ideal for those of us who dread conflict."[29]

**Virginia Franco,**
*Virginia Franco Resumes*

**LEARNING OUTCOME 5**

Evaluate effective techniques for delivering negative news within organizations.

- **Explain: past, present, future**. If you are telling the boss about a problem such as the malware infestation, explain what may have caused the problem, the current situation, and how and when it can be fixed.

- **Consider taking a partner**. If you fear a shoot-the-messenger reaction, especially from your boss, bring a colleague with you. Each person should have a consistent and credible part in the presentation of facts. If possible, take advantage of your organization's internal resources. To lend credibility to your view, call on auditors, inspectors, or human resources experts.

- **Think about timing**. Don't deliver bad news when someone is already stressed or grumpy. Experts also advise against giving bad news on Friday afternoon when people have the weekend to dwell on it and can't resolve the situation.

- **Be patient with the reaction**. Give the receiver time to vent, think, recover, and act wisely.

### 7-5b Refusing Workplace Requests

Occasionally, managers must refuse requests from employees. In **Model Document 7.5** you see the first draft and revision of a message responding to a request from a key specialist, Tashi McNiven. The tech expert wants permission to attend a conference. However, the timing of the request is bad; Tashi must be present at budget planning meetings scheduled for the same two weeks. Normally, this matter would be discussed in person. However, Tashi has been traveling among branch locations and hasn't been in the office recently.

The vice president's first inclination was to dash off a quick e-mail, as shown in the Model Document 7.5 draft, and tell it like it is. However, Lindy realized that this message was going to hurt and that it had possible danger areas. Moreover, the message misses a chance to give Tashi positive feedback. Notice that Lindy's revision carefully employs a buffer, gives a rational explanation, and closes positively with an alternative and gratitude.

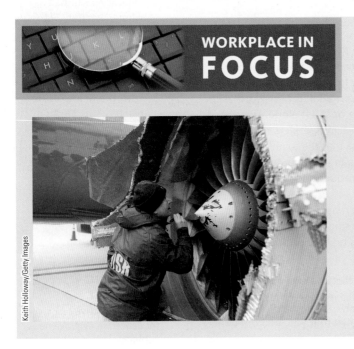

**WORKPLACE IN FOCUS**

Keith Holloway/Getty Images

Carrying 144 passengers and 5 crew, Dallas-bound Southwest flight 1380 suffered an engine rupture at cruising altitude. Shrapnel shattered a window, killing a passenger and injuring several others. In Dallas, senior executives launched the airline's well-rehearsed emergency-response plan. Southwest's social media team kept the executives informed, as it was picking up terrified passengers' tweets and a livestream from the disabled plane. When the aircraft safely landed, CEO Gary Kelly delivered a sincere video apology and condolences. Behind the scenes, Southwest worked hard to assist passengers. The airline won praise for handling this difficult situation.[32] In a social and mobile world, what challenges do businesses face when crisis hits?

**Model Document 7.5   Refusing an Internal Request**

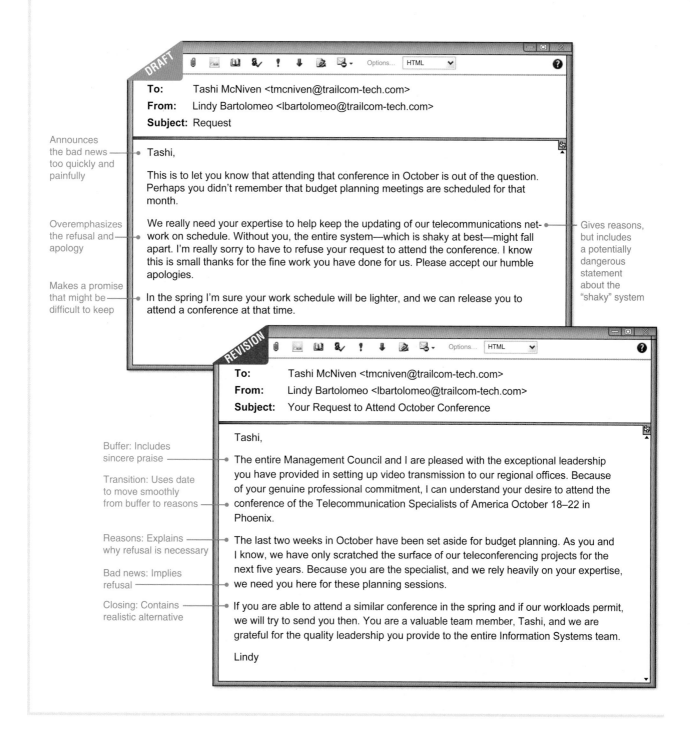

Announces the bad news too quickly and painfully

Overemphasizes the refusal and apology

Makes a promise that might be difficult to keep

**DRAFT**

To:      Tashi McNiven <tmcniven@trailcom-tech.com>
From:   Lindy Bartolomeo <lbartolomeo@trailcom-tech.com>
Subject: Request

Tashi,

This is to let you know that attending that conference in October is out of the question. Perhaps you didn't remember that budget planning meetings are scheduled for that month.

We really need your expertise to help keep the updating of our telecommunications net-work on schedule. Without you, the entire system—which is shaky at best—might fall apart. I'm really sorry to have to refuse your request to attend the conference. I know this is small thanks for the fine work you have done for us. Please accept our humble apologies.

In the spring I'm sure your work schedule will be lighter, and we can release you to attend a conference at that time.

Gives reasons, but includes a potentially dangerous statement about the "shaky" system

**REVISION**

To:      Tashi McNiven <tmcniven@trailcom-tech.com>
From:   Lindy Bartolomeo <lbartolomeo@trailcom-tech.com>
Subject:  Your Request to Attend October Conference

Buffer: Includes sincere praise

Transition: Uses date to move smoothly from buffer to reasons

Reasons: Explains why refusal is necessary

Bad news: Implies refusal

Closing: Contains realistic alternative

Tashi,

The entire Management Council and I are pleased with the exceptional leadership you have provided in setting up video transmission to our regional offices. Because of your genuine professional commitment, I can understand your desire to attend the conference of the Telecommunication Specialists of America October 18–22 in Phoenix.

The last two weeks in October have been set aside for budget planning. As you and I know, we have only scratched the surface of our teleconferencing projects for the next five years. Because you are the specialist, and we rely heavily on your expertise, we need you here for these planning sessions.

If you are able to attend a similar conference in the spring and if our workloads permit, we will try to send you then. You are a valuable team member, Tashi, and we are grateful for the quality leadership you provide to the entire Information Systems team.

Lindy

## 7-5c  Announcing Bad News to Employees and the Public

In an age of social media, damaging information can rarely be contained for long. Executives can almost count on it to be leaked. Corporate officers who fail to communicate effectively and proactively may end up on the defensive and face an uphill battle trying to limit the damage. Many of the techniques used to deliver bad news personally are useful when organizations face a crisis or must deliver bad news to their workers and other stakeholders.

**Keeping Communication Open and Honest.** Smart organizations involved in a crisis prefer to communicate the news openly to employees and other stakeholders. A crisis might involve serious performance problems, a major relocation, massive layoffs, a management shakeup, or public controversy. Instead of letting rumors distort the truth, managers ought to explain the organization's side of the story honestly and promptly.

**Choosing the Best Communication Channel.** Morale can be destroyed when employees learn of major events affecting their jobs through the grapevine or from news accounts—rather than from management. When bad news must be delivered to individual employees, management may want to deliver the news personally. With large groups, however, this is generally impossible. Instead, organizations deliver bad news through multiple channels, ranging from hard-copy memos to digital media. Such messages travel over multiple channels and can take the form of intranet posts, e-mails, videos, webcasts, internal as well as external blogs, and voice mail.

## Announcing Negative News to Employees

**BUFFER:** Start with a neutral or positive statement that transitions to the reasons for the bad news. Consider opening with the best news, a compliment, appreciation, agreement, or solid facts. Show understanding.

**REASONS:** Explain the logic behind the bad news. Provide a rational explanation using positive words and displaying empathy. If possible, mention reader benefits.

**BAD NEWS:** Position the bad news so that it does not stand out. Be positive, but don't sugarcoat the bad news. Use objective language.

**CLOSING:** Provide information about an alternative, if one exists. If appropriate, describe what will happen next. Look forward positively.

**Draft of Intranet Post.** The draft of the intranet blog post shown in **Model Document 7.6** announces a substantial increase in the cost of employee health care benefits. However, the message suffers from many problems. It announces jolting news bluntly in the first sentence. Worse, it offers little or no explanation for the steep increase in costs. It also sounds insincere (*We did everything possible. . .*) and arbitrary. In a final miscue, the writer fails to give credit to the company for absorbing previous health cost increases.

**Revision of Intranet Post.** The revised bad-news message shows the indirect strategy and a much-improved tone. Notice that it opens with a relevant, upbeat buffer regarding health care—but says nothing about increasing costs. For a smooth transition, the second paragraph begins with a key idea from the opening (*comprehensive package*). The reasons section discusses rising costs with explanations and figures. The bad news (*you will be paying $119 a month*) is clearly presented but embedded within the paragraph. Throughout, the writer strives to show the fairness of the company's position. The ending, which does not refer to the bad news, emphasizes how much the company is paying and what a wise investment it is.

The entire message demonstrates a kinder, gentler approach than that shown in the first draft. Of prime importance in breaking bad news to employees is providing clear, convincing reasons that explain the decision. Parallel to this intranet post, the message was also sent by e-mail. In smaller companies in which some workers do not have company e-mail, a hard-copy memo would be posted prominently on bulletin boards and in the lunchroom.

Chapter 7: Bad-News Messages

## Model Document 7.6   Announcing Bad News to Employees

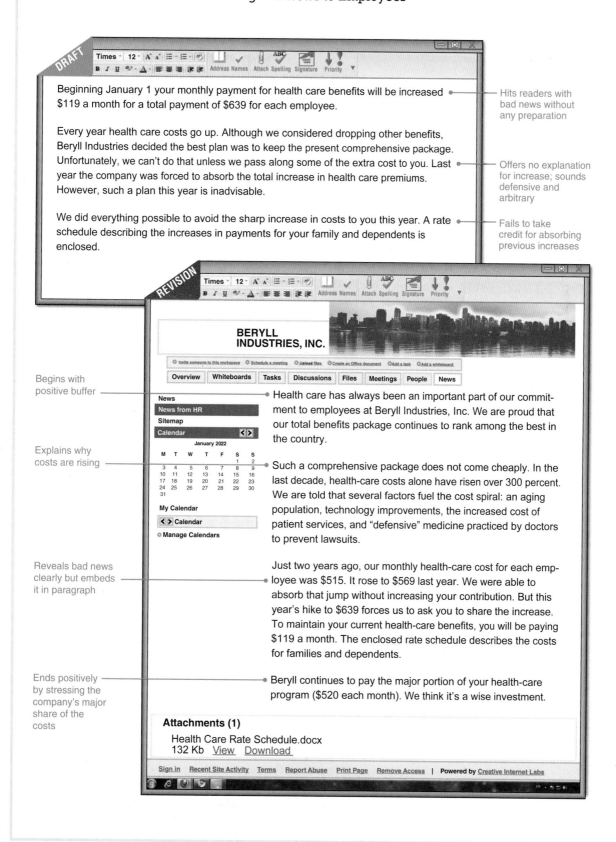

**DRAFT**

Beginning January 1 your monthly payment for health care benefits will be increased ●———— Hits readers with bad news without any preparation
$119 a month for a total payment of $639 for each employee.

Every year health care costs go up. Although we considered dropping other benefits,
Beryll Industries decided the best plan was to keep the present comprehensive package.
Unfortunately, we can't do that unless we pass along some of the extra cost to you. Last ●———— Offers no explanation for increase; sounds defensive and arbitrary
year the company was forced to absorb the total increase in health care premiums.
However, such a plan this year is inadvisable.

We did everything possible to avoid the sharp increase in costs to you this year. A rate ●———— Fails to take credit for absorbing previous increases
schedule describing the increases in payments for your family and dependents is
enclosed.

**REVISION**

### BERYLL INDUSTRIES, INC.

Invite someone to this workspace · Schedule a meeting · Upload files · Create an Office document · Add a task · Add a whiteboard

| Overview | Whiteboards | Tasks | Discussions | Files | Meetings | People | News |

**News**

News from HR

Sitemap

Calendar

**January 2022**

| M | T | W | T | F | S | S |
|---|---|---|---|---|---|---|
|   |   |   |   |   | 1 | 2 |
| 3 | 4 | 5 | 6 | 7 | 8 | 9 |
| 10 | 11 | 12 | 13 | 14 | 15 | 16 |
| 17 | 18 | 19 | 20 | 21 | 22 | 23 |
| 24 | 25 | 26 | 27 | 28 | 29 | 30 |
| 31 |   |   |   |   |   |   |

**My Calendar**

◄ ► Calendar

○ Manage Calendars

Begins with positive buffer ———— ● Health care has always been an important part of our commitment to employees at Beryll Industries, Inc. We are proud that our total benefits package continues to rank among the best in the country.

Explains why costs are rising ———— ● Such a comprehensive package does not come cheaply. In the last decade, health-care costs alone have risen over 300 percent. We are told that several factors fuel the cost spiral: an aging population, technology improvements, the increased cost of patient services, and "defensive" medicine practiced by doctors to prevent lawsuits.

Reveals bad news clearly but embeds it in paragraph ———— ● Just two years ago, our monthly health-care cost for each employee was $515. It rose to $569 last year. We were able to absorb that jump without increasing your contribution. But this year's hike to $639 forces us to ask you to share the increase. To maintain your current health-care benefits, you will be paying $119 a month. The enclosed rate schedule describes the costs for families and dependents.

Ends positively by stressing the company's major share of the costs ———— ● Beryll continues to pay the major portion of your health-care program ($520 each month). We think it's a wise investment.

**Attachments (1)**

Health Care Rate Schedule.docx
132 Kb  View  Download

Sign in  Recent Site Activity  Terms  Report Abuse  Print Page  Remove Access  |  Powered by Creative Internet Labs

## Summary of Learning Outcomes

**1 Explain the strategies of business communicators in conveying negative news.**

- Two important goals of business communicators working with bad news are to explain clearly and completely while projecting a calm, polite, professional image.
- In addition, communicators strive to convey empathy and sensitivity and show the receiver that the decision was fair, impartial, and rational.
- A final goal is to maintain friendly relations aiming to regain the confidence of the receiver.

**2 Describe the direct and indirect strategies in communicating unfavorable news.**

- Use the direct strategy, with the bad news first, when the news is not damaging, when the receiver may overlook it, when the organization or receiver prefers directness, or when firmness is necessary.
- Use the indirect strategy, with a buffer and explanation preceding the bad news, when the bad news is personally upsetting, when it may provoke a hostile reaction, when it threatens the customer relationship, and when the news is unexpected.
- To avoid being unethical, never use the indirect method to deceive or manipulate the truth.

**3 Identify the components of effective bad-news messages.**

- To soften bad news, start with a buffer such as the best news, a compliment, appreciation, agreement, facts, understanding, or an apology.
- If you apologize, do it promptly and sincerely. Accept responsibility but don't admit blame without consulting a supervisor or company counsel. Strive to project empathy.
- In explaining the reasons for the bad news, cite reader or other benefits if plausible, explain company policy if necessary, choose positive words, and aim to show fairness and serious intent.
- Strive to cushion the bad news with strategic positioning by (a) sandwiching it between other sentences, (b) presenting it in a subordinating clause, (c) using passive-voice verbs, (d) highlighting anything positive, (e) implying the refusal, and (f) suggesting a compromise or an alternative.
- Close pleasantly by (a) suggesting a means of following through on an alternative, (b) offering freebies, (c) extending good wishes, (d) anticipating future business, or (e) providing resale information or a sales promotion.

**4 Analyze effective techniques for presenting bad news to customers and refusing requests or claims.**

- In rejecting requests for favors, money, information, and action, follow the bad-news strategy: (a) begin with a buffer, (b) present valid reasons, (c) explain the bad news and possibly an alternative, and (d) close with good feelings and a positive statement.
- To deal with disappointed customer, (a) call or e-mail the individual immediately; (b) describe the problem and apologize when the company is to blame; (c) explain why the problem occurred, what you are doing to resolve it, and how you will prevent it from happening again; and (d) promote goodwill with a follow-up message.
- To handle negative posts and reviews online, (a) verify the situation, (b) respond quickly and constructively, (c) consider giving freebies such as refunds or discounts, (d) learn from negative comments, and (e) be prepared to accept the inevitable and move on.
- To deny claims, (a) use the reasons-before-refusal plan, (b) don't blame customers (even if they are at fault), (c) use neutral objective language to explain why the claim must be refused, and (d) consider offering resale information to rebuild the customer's confidence in your products or organization.

**5 Evaluate effective techniques for delivering negative news within organizations.**

- To deliver workplace bad news in person, (a) gather all the information; (b) prepare and rehearse; (c) explain the past, present, and future; (d) consider taking a partner; (e) think about timing; and (f) be patient with the reaction.
- In announcing bad news to employees and to the public, strive to keep the communication open and honest, choose the best communication channel, and consider applying the indirect strategy, but give clear, convincing reasons.
- Be positive, but don't sugarcoat the bad news; use objective language.

## Key Terms

## Chapter Review

1. Name the goals of business communicators in conveying negative news, and explain how they can achieve these goals. (L.O. 1)

2. When delivering bad news, how can a communicator reduce the bad feelings of the receiver? (L.O. 1)

3. What are the major differences between the direct and indirect strategies in delivering bad news? (L.O. 2)

4. When is the direct strategy more effective than the indirect strategy in delivering bad news? (L.O. 2)

5. What does expressing empathy mean in delivering apologies? (L.O. 3)

6. What are some tips for business writers wishing to apologize effectively? (L.O. 3)

7. Describe the writing plan for refusing typical requests and claims. (L.O. 4)

8. What are some strategies to manage unfavorable news on social media effectively? (L.O. 4)

9. Explain how a subordinate can tactfully, professionally, and safely deliver upsetting news in person to a superior. (L.O. 5)

10. Name some of the channels that large organizations may use to deliver bad news to employees. (L.O. 5)

## Critical Thinking

11. Mike Michalowicz, author of *Profit First* and CEO of Provendus Group, quotes a famous American poet to illustrate how he refuses unpleasant potential clients: "Emily Dickinson said speak the truth but with slant. You don't have to say something so coldly it starts an argument. We usually tell the client we don't have resources to support your specific needs," he says.[33] Discuss this strategy, its advantages, and disadvantages. (L.O. 3)

12. Consider this view voiced by Robert Bies, professor of management at Georgetown University: "Bad news should never come as a surprise. Failure to warn senior leadership of impending bad news, such as poor sales or a loss of a major client, is a cardinal sin. So is failure to warn subordinates about mistakes in their performance and provide an opportunity for them to make corrections and improve."[34] Do you agree or disagree? Give reasons for your position. (L.O. 1–3)

13. Recall a situation during which you chose to remain silent instead of revealing what would have been unfavorable news or negative feedback to the recipient. Why did you keep the negative news or feedback to yourself, and what may be the consequences of such reticence? (L.O. 1–5)

14. Consider times when you have been aware that others were using the indirect strategy in writing or speaking to you. How did you react? (L.O. 2)

15. At a sustainability conference, Levi Strauss CEO Chip Bergh caused a viral sensation by revealing he had never laundered his two-year-old Levi's in a washing machine. Instead, he hand-washed and line-dried his jeans every few months. His point was that jeans shouldn't be washed all the time, but people thought it meant Bergh *never* washed them. The fallout from this one quip continues even years later: "Today, if you type 'CEO Levi's' into Google, 'don't wash jeans' comes up," Bergh says. "I expect that my supposed anti-laundry stance will be mentioned in my obituary."[35] Can you think of other, more negative examples of executives' offhand public comments causing consternation and worse? (L.O. 4)

## Writing Improvement Exercises

### Passive-Voice Verbs (L.O. 3)

Passive-voice verbs may be preferable in breaking bad news because they enable you to emphasize actions rather than personalities. Compare these two refusals:

| EXAMPLE | Active voice: | We cannot send any executives to the World Economic Forum Annual Meeting in Davos, Switzerland, this year. |
|---|---|---|
| | Passive voice: | No executives can be sent to the World Economic Forum Annual Meeting in Davos, Switzerland, this year. |

Revise the following refusals so that they use passive-voice instead of active-voice verbs. If possible, present the bad news positively.

16. Because we are retooling our production line, we are postponing requests for company tours until the fall.

17. We cannot examine new patients until we have verified their insurance coverage.

18. Company policy prevents us from offering health and dental benefits until employees have been on the job for 12 months.

19. The manager and I have arranged for the investors to have lunch after the tour.

20. Unfortunately, we cannot offer free shipping after January 1. Act now!

## Subordinate Clauses (L.O. 3)

You can further soften the effect of bad news by placing it in an introductory subordinate clause that begins with *although, since,* or *because.* The emphasis in a sentence is on the independent clause. Instead of saying *Unfortunately, we no longer print and mail a catalog, but we offer all catalog selections on our website,* try *Although a print catalog is no longer available, you will find all catalog selections on our website.* Revise the following so that the bad news is de-emphasized in a dependent clause that precedes an independent clause.

21. We are sorry to disappoint you, but our nine-day boat excursion to the Galápagos Islands has filled up quickly and is now fully booked. We can place you on a wait list that would make you only the second in line.

22. Your frequent flyer miles expire on December 31 because you have earned no qualifying segments during this calendar year. However, you could keep your miles if you apply for our Northeastern credit card and spend $2,000 in the next three months.

23. We are pleased by your interest in our firm, but we are unable to extend an employment offer to you at this time.

24. Regretfully, we cannot supply you with the cabinet hinge you requested. The manufacturer no longer offers it. A new hinge should work for you, and we are sending it to you.

## Implying Bad News (L.O. 3)

Bad news can be de-emphasized by *implying* a refusal instead of stating it directly. Compare these refusals:

**EXAMPLE**    **Direct refusal:**    We cannot send you a price list, nor can we sell our spas directly to consumers. We sell exclusively through distributors, and your local distributor is SpaWorld.

**Implied refusal:**    Our spas are sold exclusively through local distributors, and your distributor is SpaWorld.

Revise the following refusals so that the bad news is implied. If possible, use passive-voice verbs and subordinate clauses to further de-emphasize the bad news.

25. We cannot ship our fine steaks and hamburgers c.o.d. Your order was not accompanied by payment, so we are not shipping it. We have it ready, though, and will rush it to your home if you call us with your credit card number.

26. Unfortunately, we cannot contribute to your worthy charitable cause this year. At present we need all the funds of our organization to lease new equipment and offices for our new branch in Clearwater. We hope to be able to support this endeavor in the future.

27. Because our government contract has run out, we must disband the task force managing the project. Some of you will be reassigned; unfortunately, we will also have to let a few team members go.

## Radical Rewrites

**NOTE:** Radical Rewrites are provided at **www.cengage.com** for you to download and revise. Your instructor may show a suggested solution.

### 7.1 Radical Rewrite: Request Refusal—*No* to Taste of the Beach (L.O. 1, 2, 4)

The following blunt refusal from a restaurant owner rejects a previously agreed-to favor. To avoid endangering a friendship and losing community goodwill, the writer needs to revise this message.

**YOUR TASK.** Analyze the message. List at least five weaknesses and suggest ways to improve this message. If your instructor directs, revise the letter.

Current date

Ms. Sally Segovia
Taste of the Beach
310 Ocean Avenue, Suite 304
Carmel-by-the-Sea, CA 93521

Dear Ms. Segovia:

Unfortunately, we cannot participate in this summer's Taste of the Beach event. This may be particularly disappointing to you because, merely as a friendly gesture, I had earlier agreed to provide a selection of tasty hors d'oeuvres from my restaurant, The Zodiac. I'm sorry to let you down like this. We have participated in the past, but we just can't do it this year because our aging kitchen facilities require major and extensive remodeling.

I heard that this year's Taste of the Beach is really going to be a blast with new and old food, wine, music, and artistic offerings. How did you get so many prized vintners and all those well-known chefs, artists, and music groups to participate and perform?

This is probably quite disappointing to you (and to me) because the event supports Big Brothers Big Sisters of America. I know that BBBSA is simply the very best as a youth mentoring organization.

Let me repeat—I'm sorry we can't participate. Don't bother to beg me. But for your silent raffle we can offer you a coupon for a dinner for two. Of course, this could not be used until October when our renovations are completed.

Sincerely,

## 7.2 Radical Rewrite: Bad News to Customers—Guard Payment Systems Was Hacked (L.O. 1, 2, 4)

The following poorly written e-mail tells customers that their e-mail addresses have been hacked. However, the message is clumsy and fails to include essential information in revealing security breaches to customers.

**YOUR TASK.** Analyze the message and list at least five weaknesses. If your instructor directs, revise it using the suggestions you learned in this chapter about security breach messages.

**To:** Detlev Max <detlev.max@alpha.com>
**From:** Fanny Bettino <fbettino@guardpayment.net>
**Subject:** Security Incident at Guard Payment Systems

Companies and individuals across the country are experiencing more and more security breaches. This is just to let you know that you are receiving this e-mail because of a recent unfortunate security breach at Guard Payment Systems. Rest assured, however, that as a customer of Guard Payment, your privacy was never at risk. We promise to guard your privacy around the clock.

Hackers last week were able to maliciously exploit a new function that we were trying to use to make the customer log-in process faster for you and our other customers. The hackers were ingenious and malicious, going to extreme lengths to gain access to some customer addresses at Guard Payment. You should now beware of scams that may result from your address being used in phishing scams. To learn more, go to https://www.fdic.gov/consumers/consumer/alerts/phishing.html.

To provide even more information about this incident, the U.S. Postal Service will bring you a letter with more information. Taking your privacy very seriously, e-mail addresses are heavily protected here at Guard Payment. Within hours of the hacker break-in, the log-in mechanism was disabled, and a new procedure was established. The user is now required to enter their e-mail address and their password before they can log in successfully. E-mail addresses were the only information the hackers got. Other information such as account information and other personal information were never risked.

We appreciate you being a Guard Payment customer.

Sincerely,

## 7.3 Request Refusal: Walk With Love Stopped in Its Tracks (L.O. 1-4)

> E-Mail    > Web >

Having enjoyed a meteoric rise, CompuBotics Incorporated prides itself on its commitment to employees who receive generous benefits and are steeped in a supportive corporate culture. This core value may have contributed to the company's high ranking among *Fortune* magazine's 50 Best Startups. The software company wants to be known for its community involvement and corporate social responsibility. This is why, like most successful companies, CompuBotics receives many requests for sponsorships of charity events and community projects. True to its innovative spirit, the software company has streamlined the application process by providing an online sponsorship request form on its website.

You work in Corporate Affairs/Community Relations at CompuBotics and periodically help decide which nonprofits obtain support. Just yesterday you received an e-mail from Walk With Love, the largest fundraising vehicle of the Dr. Susan Love Foundation. Since 2008, Walk With Love has raised millions of dollars to support groundbreaking breast cancer research. Both *Charity Navigator* and *Medical News Today* ranked the Dr. Susan Love Foundation the top breast cancer research organization in the United States for its stewardship of resources and impact. The organization hosts annual fundraising walks in Pacific Palisades, Palm Springs, and Santa Barbara, California.

The walk organizers would like CompuBotics to sponsor its fundraising walks in California taking place in less than a month, three events potentially drawing at least 6,000 participants. Your company is already funding several cancer charities and has a policy of sponsoring many causes. Naturally, no corporate giving program has infinite funds, nor can it green-light every request. The team judging the sponsorship entries wants to ensure that each proposal reaches audiences affiliated with CompuBotics. Most important, applicants must submit their requests at least six weeks before the event.

**YOUR TASK.** As a junior staff member in Corporate Affairs/Community Relations, write an e-mail to Walk With Love event director Michelle Chang (*mchang@wwl.org*) refusing her initial request and explaining the CompuBotics sponsorship philosophy and submission rules.

## 7.4 Request Refusal: No Support for Kaboom! This Time (L.O. 1, 2, 4)

As a vice president of a financial services company, you serve many clients, and they sometimes ask your company to contribute to their favorite charities. You recently received a letter from Mia Takeshi asking for a substantial contribution to Kaboom!, a charity devoted to making playgrounds safe for everyone, including children with disabilities. On visits to your office, Ms. Takeshi has told you about her organization's efforts to update existing playgrounds as well as install new play areas around the nation to make playground equipment completely safe and accessible to all kids. She herself is active in your town as a Kaboom! volunteer, helping identify outdated playgrounds, finding sites for new playgrounds, and allocate construction funds.

You have a soft spot in your heart for children and especially for those with disabilities. You sincerely want to support Kaboom! and its good work. But times are tough, and you can't be as generous as you have been in the past. Ms. Takeshi wrote a special letter to you asking you to become a Key Contributor, with a pledge of $2,000.

**YOUR TASK.** Write a refusal letter that maintains good relations with your client. Address it to Ms. Mia Takeshi, 47 Beach Street, Lynchburg, VA 24502.

## 7.5 Request Refusal: No Disclosure of Sensitive Data (L.O. 1, 2, 4)

> E-Mail >

A well-known financial blogger, Dora Wieland, is doing research for her industry blog In the Know. Specifically, she seeks information about salary and commission information of the star salespeople at PharmaCore, a large pharmaceutical firm, for an article comparing compensation levels and diversity across several large pharmaceutical companies. She also wants to know the star salespeople's demographic information, such as ages, ethnicities, and genders.

Allan Gottschalk, director of public affairs and communication, must deny Dora's request because of privacy concerns and fear of litigation. Each salesperson works under an individual contract as a result of salary negotiations conducted several years ago. At the time, agreement was reached that both the sales staff and management would keep the terms of the individual contracts confidential. The communication director remembers that three of the top salespeople are currently under the age of thirty-five.

Allan acknowledges that an article juxtaposing salaries and commissions with age, gender, and ethnicity of the salesforce could be interesting to industry insiders. PharmaCore boasts many diverse salespeople of various ages, several rising starts among them, who command top salaries.

**YOUR TASK.** Draft a tactful reply for an e-mail to be signed and sent by Allan Gottschalk denying Dora's request; the message should maintain the goodwill of this influential writer. PharmaCore cannot disclose salaries and commission rates. However, the company is willing to share a list with the names of the top salespeople for a period of the past five years and a few short bios of current stars.

## 7.6 Request Refusal: Thank You, But I Can't Give a Talk (L.O. 1–4)

As an assistant to body language expert and author Tonya Reiman, you must help her politely decline an invitation to speak at the University of South Carolina in Columbia. The business associations on campus pooled their resources and decided to invite Ms. Reiman to give a talk about nonverbal communication. A sought-after TV commentator and consultant, Ms. Reiman is the author of three books, *The Power of Body Language, The YES Factor,* and *The Body Language of Dating.*

In their invitation, the students demonstrated they had done their homework. They knew Ms. Reiman's books and were fascinated by her focus on proxemics, power gestures, projecting the best image, building rapport, and reading microexpressions. Ms. Reiman likes to speak to young students, mostly pro bono or for a nominal fee, but during the spring semester she is too busy writing a new book and providing training to several domestic and international companies. She could, however, send her deputy director and senior trainer, Tinashe Efe.

**YOUR TASK.** In Ms. Reiman's name, refuse the invitation but suggest an alternative. Send your letter to Celeste Gunvaldsen, Associated Students, University of South Carolina, 1244 Blossom Street, Suite 206, Columbia, SC 29208. Note that Celeste is a gender-unspecific name. How will you handle the honorific (Ms., Mr., etc.) in your letter?

## 7.7 Request Refusal: No Eviction for Noise (L.O. 1–4)
> **Web**

As the owner of the Corporate Center in Springfield, Illinois, you must respond to the request of Troy E. Washko, one of the tenants in your two-story office building. Mr. Washko, a CPA, demands that you immediately evict a neighboring tenant who plays loud music throughout the day, interfering with Mr. Washko's conversations with clients and with his concentration. The noisy tenant, Robert Murphy, seems to operate an entertainment booking agency and spends long hours in his office.

You know you can't evict Mr. Murphy because, as a legal commercial tenant, he is entitled to conduct his business. However, you might consider adding soundproofing, an expense that you would prefer to share with Mr. Murphy and Mr. Washko. You might also discuss limiting the time of day that Mr. Murphy could make noise.

**YOUR TASK.** Before responding to Mr. Washko, you decide to find out more about commercial tenancy. Use the Web to search the keywords *commercial eviction.* Then develop a course of action. In a letter to Mr. Washko, deny his request but retain his goodwill. Tell him how you plan to resolve the problem. Write to Troy Washko, CPA, Suite 300, Corporate Center, 3631 South 6th Street, Springfield, IL 62703. Your instructor may also ask you to write an appropriate message to Robert Murphy occupying Suite 350.

## 7.8 Claim Denial: Expensive Glasses Lost on the Plane (L.O. 1–4)

Atlantic Southern Airlines (ASA) had an unhappy customer. Casey Segal-Jain flew from Baltimore, Maryland, to Seattle, Washington. The flight stopped briefly at Detroit Metropolitan Airport, where Ms. Segal-Jain got off the plane for half an hour. When she returned to her seat, her $400 prescription reading glasses were gone. She asked the flight attendant where the glasses were, and the attendant said they probably were thrown away since the cleaning crew had come in with big bags and tossed everything in them. Ms. Segal-Jain tried to locate the glasses through the airline's lost-and-found service, but she failed.

Then she wrote a strong letter to the airline demanding reimbursement for the loss. She felt that it was obvious that she was returning to her seat. The airline, however, knows that an overwhelming number of passengers arriving at hubs switch planes for their connecting flights. The airline does not know who is returning. What's more, flight attendants usually announce that the plane is continuing to another city and that passengers who are returning should take their belongings. Cabin cleaning crews speed through planes removing newspapers, magazines, leftover food, and trash. Airlines feel no responsibility for personal items left in cabins.

**YOUR TASK.** As a staff member of the Customer Relations Department of Atlantic Southern Airlines, deny the customer's claim but retain her goodwill using techniques learned in this chapter. The airline never refunds cash, but it might consider travel vouchers for the value of the glasses. Remember that apologies cost nothing. Write a claim denial to Casey Segal-Jain, 999 3rd Avenue, Apt. 45, Seattle, WA 98104.

## 7.9 Claim Denial: Consumers Empowered by Social Media (L.O. 1–4)
> **E-Mail**    **Social Media**    **Web**

The growth of social media has spawned many platforms dedicated to customer reviews and complaints—for example, Angi, which profiles local service companies, contractors, and professionals—or Yelp, a site with user reviews of eateries, bars, doctors, dentists, and hair salons. For travelers, Tripadvisor has become a force to be reckoned with, featuring reviews, price comparisons, and booking options. More specifically, sites such as Cruise Critic focus solely on vacations by ship or CarComplaints takes aim at automobiles. Alternatively, visit Sitejabber, Ripoff Report, or another complaint site. Study ten or more complaints about products or companies (e.g., iPhone, Starbucks, Delta Air Lines). Of course, examples of official complaint sites include the Better Business

Bureau and government agencies such as Consumer Complaint Database, Federal Trade Commission, state attorneys general, USAGov, Federal Communications Commission, and more.

**YOUR TASK.** Select one complaint and, as a company representative, respond to it employing some of the techniques presented in this chapter. Submit a copy of the complaint along with your response to your instructor. Your instructor may request that you write an e-mail or a letter.

## 7.10 Customer Bad News: Announcing a Price Increase (L.O. 1–4)

> E-Mail   >   Web

Select a product or service that you now use (e.g., Internet or cable service, water or electricity, propane or natural gas, smartphone or landline, or car insurance). Assume that the provider must raise its rates and that you are the employee who must notify customers. Should you use an e-mail, a letter, company website, or blog? Decide whether you should use the direct or indirect strategy. Gather as much information as you can about the product or service. What, if anything, justifies the increase? What benefits can be cited?

For inspiration study the example below. Netflix announced the most recent increase in its subscription price to existing customers via e-mail.

---

Hi Gabby,

We hope you have been enjoying your Netflix membership. We are writing to let you know about an upcoming change.

Your monthly price is increasing to $12.99 on Tuesday, May 21. Why? We're hard at work improving Netflix so that you can have even more great TV shows and movies to enjoy.

Here's to watching what you want, when you want, where you want.

You can **change your plan**, or if you do not wish to continue your membership, as always you can cancel any time at **netflix .com/cancel**.

We're here to help if you need it. Visit the **Help Center** for more info or **contact us**.

—The Netflix Team

---

**YOUR TASK.** Analyze the Netflix e-mail announcing the price hike. Does the message follow the practices recommended in this chapter? Prepare your own rate increase announcement. Submit it along with a memo explaining your rationale for the strategy you chose and include your analysis of the Netflix example.

## 7.11 Bad News to Applicants: "Human Error" Admits Rejected Students (L.O. 1–4)

> E-Mail

The University of South Florida St. Petersburg recently made a big mistake. It inadvertently welcomed 430 rejected applicants. The e-mail said, "Once again congratulations on your admission to USFSP! We are excited to welcome you to the university and are very proud of all that you have accomplished so far! I also wanted to provide you with your next steps." The message then provided instructions for students to obtain their university IDs, pay a tuition deposit, apply for housing, and more.[36]

That message was intended to be sent to the 250 students who had been accepted. Instead, it went to a subset of students whose applications were still under review or denied. Chancellor Martin Tadlock blamed human error in the admissions office for the mistake. "We regret it," Tadlock said in an interview. "We pride ourselves on our relationship with the community, and this doesn't represent that. It was an error and a mistake."[37]

One applicant who had received the acceptance e-mail in error, Alexandria Rizzotto, was very disappointed: "I was very, very let down because I've been waiting for a final decision from them since November now."[38] What could the university do to correct this massive slip-up?

**YOUR TASK.** For Chancellor Martin Tadlock, write an appropriate bad-news message to the students who received the message in error. Many applicants will be wondering what their real admission status is.

## 7.12 Customer Bad News: Which Elliptical for 24-Hour Fitness? (L.O. 1–4)

You are happy to receive a large order from Finn Valentino at 24-Hour Fitness gym. This order includes two Olympic Benches (at $349 each), three Stamina Power Towers (at $249 each), three sets of Premier Dumbbells (at $105 each), and two Titanic 20 Ellipticals (at $1,099 each).

You could ship immediately except for one problem. The Titanic 20 Elliptical, as rated by *Consumer Reports*, is intended for home use, not for gym or club use. More and more fitness lovers are purchasing ellipticals because they have better track records than treadmills and stair climbers for aerobic exercise. The Titanic 20 is effective for personal use. However, this is not the model you would recommend for club use. The Titanic 90 is larger, sturdier, and safer for commercial gyms. It also has extras such as a built-in cooling fan, water bottle holder, and speakers that allow users to hook up to any smartphone or MP3 player for easy listening. You believe that Mr. Valentino should order the Titanic 90 Elliptical. It's solidly built, comes with a chest-strap heart-rate monitor, has 20 resistance levels, and features a lifetime warranty on its frame. For gym use, the Titanic 90 is clearly better. The bad news is that it is considerably more expensive at $3,100 per machine.

You get no response when you try to telephone Mr. Valentino to discuss the problem. Should you ship what you can, or hold the entire order until you learn whether he wants the Titanic 20 or the Titanic 90 Elliptical? Another option is to substitute the Titanic 90 and send only one of them. Another possibility is sending one of the home models and one of the gym models.

**YOUR TASK.** Decide what to do and then send an e-mail to Finn Valentino (fvalentino@24hourfitness.com).

## 7.13 Customer Bad News: Pay Day Delayed (L.O. 1–4)

> **Team**

Carlos Felix, a printing company sales manager, must tell one of his clients that the payroll checks her company ordered are not going to be ready by the date Carlos had promised. The printing company's job scheduler overlooked the job and didn't get the checks into production in time to meet the deadline. As a result, Carlos's client, a major insurance company, is going to miss its pay run.

Carlos meets with internal department heads. They decide on the following plan to remedy the situation: (a) move the check order to the front of the production line; (b) make up for the late production date by shipping some of the checks—enough to meet their client's immediate payroll needs—by air freight; (c) deliver the remaining checks by truck.

**YOUR TASK.** Form groups of three or four students. Discuss the following issues about how to present the bad news to Jeanine Pradip, Carlos's contact person at the insurance company.

a. Should Carlos call Jeanine directly or delegate the task to his assistant?
b. When should Jeanine be informed of the problem?
c. What is the best procedure for delivering the bad news?
d. What follow-up would you recommend to Carlos?

Be prepared to share your group's responses during a class discussion. Your instructor may ask two students to role-play the presentation of the bad news, and request that you write a follow-up message to Jeanine.

## 7.14 Employee Bad News: No to Tuition Assistance (L.O. 1–5)

> **E-Mail**

Naomi Emery, a hardworking auto damage adjuster, has sent an e-mail request asking that her employer create a program to reimburse the tuition and book expenses for employees taking college courses. Naomi knows that some companies have such a program, for example, GEICO, but Ensurit Mutual Insurance has not felt that it could indulge in such an expensive employee perk. Moreover, the CEO is not convinced that companies see any direct benefit from such programs. Employees improve their educational credentials and skills, but what is to keep them from moving that education and those skill sets to other employers? Ensurit Mutual has over 200 employees. If even a fraction of them started classes, the company could see a huge bill for the cost of tuition and books.

Because the insurance is facing stiff competition and its profits are sinking, the expense of such a program makes it out of the question. In addition, it would involve administration—applications, monitoring, and record keeping. It is just too much of a hassle. When employees were hard to hire and retain, companies had to offer employment perks. With a fluctuating job market, however, such inducements are unnecessary.

**YOUR TASK.** As director of Human Resources, send an individual e-mail response to Naomi Emery. The answer is a definite *no*, but you want to soften the blow and retain the loyalty of this conscientious employee.

## 7.15 Employee Bad News: No Time Off for Infant.ly Foundation Volunteer (L.O. 1, 2, 4, 5)

Oscar Cassandra is a dedicated volunteer who has served Infant.ly Foundation for several years. The charity has raised millions of dollars to make a difference in the lives of young children and babies, particularly premature ones. Oscar's employer, Outlays Financials, is the worldwide leader in on-demand financial planning and reporting software. In the past Oscar's firm made generous contributions to Infant.ly's annual animal parade/luncheon, which also included Oscar's paid time off to coordinate the popular fundraiser.

This time the situation is different. The economy has entered a downturn, and Outlays Financials is in the midst of releasing its important client Planning Guide 3.0. The company needs Oscar's technical expertise. He is to interview clients, make video testimonials, and seek stories about customer successes for the new corporate website to launch within six weeks. Outlays Financials had to dismiss staff to save money and is now short-handed. Oscar can't possibly be granted time off now.

**YOUR TASK.** Draft a professionally written e-mail for financial director Kim Henning to send to Oscar Cassandra. Let him down gently. Explain why Outlays Financial cannot commit any resources to the Infant.ly Foundation, including time off for the charity's fundraiser that Oscar coordinates.

## Grammar/Mechanics Checkup 7

## Commas 2

Review the Grammar/Mechanics Handbook Sections 2.05–2.09. Then select the correctly punctuated sentence and record its letter in the space provided. Record also the appropriate Grammar/Mechanics guideline to illustrate the principle involved. When you finish, compare your responses with those at the bottom of the page. If your answers differ, study carefully the principles in parentheses.

| | |
|---|---|
| _____a_____ (2.06a) | **EXAMPLE** a. When the president arrives in Omaha, the local staff will be waiting at the airport. |
| | b. When the president arrives in Omaha the local staff will be waiting at the airport. |

_____ 1. a. The scrappy disruptive ride-hailing startup launched in Singapore on May 1.
                    b. The scrappy, disruptive ride-hailing startup launched in Singapore on May 1.

_____ 2. a. Our shipping department works with time zones around the world, and the staff members keep several clocks set to different zones in the office.
                    b. Our shipping department works with time zones around the world and the staff members keep several clocks set to different zones in the office.

_____ 3. a. Dealing with bureaucracy is less challenging if you are patient, and if you can avoid becoming irritated at unexpected delays.
                    b. Dealing with bureaucracy is less challenging if you are patient and if you can avoid becoming irritated at unexpected delays.

_____ 4. a. Zypp, an electric scooter sharing app that has over 500,000 users in India alone, is helping many people across the subcontinent.
                    b. Zypp, an electric scooter sharing app that has over 500,000 users in India alone is helping many people across the subcontinent.

_____ 5. a. If you are based in Denver, and working with a manufacturer in Shanghai you will be dealing with a 15-hour time difference.
                    b. If you are based in Denver and working with a manufacturer in Shanghai, you will be dealing with a 15-hour time difference.

_____ 6. a. Any Infraspeak user in an organization who identifies a failure in an electric system, can report the technical failure instantly to the relevant technicians.
                    b. Any Infraspeak user in an organization who identifies a failure in an electric system can report the technical failure instantly to the relevant technicians.

_____ 7. a. Maxi Donovan, who was recently transferred to the European subsidiary in Germany, quickly became fluent in German.
                    b. Maxi Donovan who was recently transferred to the European subsidiary in Germany, quickly became fluent in German.

_____ 8. a. In less than a month our vice president made several trips to Morocco and Kenya to prospect for new business.
                    b. In less than a month, our vice president made several trips to Morocco and Kenya to prospect for new business.

9.  a. When you are working with overseas clients who are nonnative speakers of English you may have to speak slowly and avoid idioms.
    b. When you are working with overseas clients who are nonnative speakers of English, you may have to speak slowly and avoid idioms.

10. a. To succeed in international business, you must read between the lines and learn to pick up on different cultural vibes.
    b. To succeed in international business, you must read between the lines, and learn to pick up on different cultural vibes.

1. b (2.08) 2. a (2.05) 3. b (2.05) 4. a (2.09) 5. b (2.06a) 6. b (2.06a) 7. a (2.06c) 8. b (2.07) 9. b (2.06a) 10. a (2.07)

# Editing Challenge 7

Every chapter provides an editing exercise to fine-tune your grammar and mechanics skills. The following letter requires edits that address grammar, concise wording, sentence structure, punctuation (especially commas), and other writing issues. Study the guidelines in the Grammar/Mechanics Handbook (Appendix D), including the lists of Confusing Words and Frequently Misspelled Words.

**YOUR TASK.** Edit the following by (a) inserting corrections in your textbook or on a photocopy using the proofreading marks in Appendix C or (b) downloading the message from **www.cengage.com** and correcting at your computer, using the MS Word feature **Track Changes**.

## SINERGI ELECTRIC COMPANY

November 15, 2022

Ms. Laurie Dyer-Haroldson
7163 Bradford Dr.
Antioch, CA 94509

Dear Mr. Dyer-Haroldson:

This is to let you know that our top priority at the Sinergi Electric Company is to provide safe and reliable power to over 93,000 people here in the East Bay region. Providing accurate regular electricity bills to our customers homes and businesses' every month is an integral part of our service. Since the launch of a new billing system we have experienced problems in delivering bills in a manner that is timely. We apologize for the inconvenience and frustration this may have caused you. However we want you to know that we are doing everything we can to resolve this billing issue as quick as possible.

About two years ago we began researching new billing systems in response to our customers requests for more flexible convenient payment methods. Such as online billing and the ability to make credit card payments. Customers also expressed interest in improved access to electricity use information and online tools. After an extensive vendor search and vetting process we engaged Excel Power Management to implement a new billing system to meet our customers needs.

Unfortunately since making the transition we have experienced unexpected and unacceptable implementation challenges. We are extremely disapointed and frustrated with the impact that the new billing plan has had on our customers. Without question some of our customers has not received the reliably scheduled billing service that they expect, and that we are committed to providing.

Please be assured that we are working in a diligent manner to fix these problems to protect our customers interests, keep our costs low and provide electricity bills on a timely basis.

We appreciate you ongoing patience and understanding while we work to resolve this billing issue. If you are interested in following our efforts please visit our website for regular progress updates, www.sinergielectric.com.

Sincerely,

Melvin E. McCrae, Manager

## Communication Workshop: Intercultural Skills

### Delivering Bad News Across Cultures

As you have learned in this chapter, Americans generally prefer to present negative news indirectly to minimize disappointment. Other cultures may treat bad news differently, as illustrated in the following:

- British writers tend to be straightforward with bad news, seeing no reason to soften its announcement.

- In Germany business communicators occasionally use buffers but tend to present bad news bluntly.

- In Latin American countries, the question is not how to organize bad-news messages but whether to present them at all. It is considered disrespectful and impolite to report bad news to superiors. Therefore, reluctant employees may fail to report accurately any negative situations to their bosses.

- In Thailand the negativism represented by a refusal is completely alien; the word *no* does not exist. In many cultures negative news is offered with such subtlety or in such a positive light that it may be overlooked or misunderstood by literal-minded Americans.

- Mannerisms and communication may vary among ethnic groups, but most South Africans exhibit a direct communication style. They speak confidently and get straight to the point.

- In many Asian and some Latin American cultures, one must look beyond an individual's actual words to understand what is really being communicated. One must weigh the communication style, the culture, and especially the context. Consider the following phrases and their possible meanings:

| Phrase | Possible Meaning |
| --- | --- |
| I agree. | I agree with 15 percent of what you say. |
| We might be able to... | Not a chance! |
| We will consider... | *We* will consider, but the real decision maker will not. |
| That is a little too much. | That is outrageous! |
| Yes. | Yes, I'm listening. *OR*: Yes, you have a good point. *OR*: Yes, I understand, but I don't necessarily agree. |

**CAREER APPLICATION.** Interview fellow students or work colleagues who were born in other countries, have lived abroad, or are familiar with cultures that are different from those represented in North America. Collect information by asking the following questions:

- How is negative news commonly handled in your culture?

- How would typical business communicators refuse a request for a business favor (such as a contribution to a charity)?

- How would typical business communicators refuse a customer's claim?

- How would an individual be turned down for a job?

**YOUR TASK.** Report the findings of your interviews in class discussion or in a memo report. In addition, collect samples of foreign business letters. You might search the Internet for sample business letters in other languages with the help of international students or your peers who speak other languages. Alternatively, you might ask your campus admissions office or local export/import companies whether they would be willing to share business letters written in English from other countries. Compare letter styles, formats, tone, and writing strategies. How do these elements differ from those in typical North American business letters?

# Persuasive Messages

Prostock-studio/Shutterstock.com

## Learning Outcomes

After studying this chapter, you should be able to do the following:

**1** Identify digital age persuasion as well as time-proven persuasive techniques.

**2** Craft persuasive messages that request actions.

**3** Write compelling claims and successful complaints.

**4** Compose persuasive messages within organizations demonstrating your knowledge of interpersonal persuasion at work.

**5** Create effective and ethical direct-mail and e-mail sales messages.

## 8-1 Understanding Persuasion in the Contemporary Workplace

Flatter corporate hierarchies, teamwork, collaboration across divisions, and blurred lines of authority characterize business today. As managers and teams are abandoning the traditional command structure, solid persuasive skills are becoming ever more important at work. Businesspeople must try to *influence* others. Likewise, pushy hard-sell techniques are waning because today's consumers are well-informed, have many choices, and can be fickle.[1] However, getting others to do what we want isn't easy. Persuasion is needed when we are making more than routine demands and facing skeptical audiences.

Although we are subjected daily to a flood of print and electronic persuasive messages, we often fail to recognize the techniques of persuasion and its evil cousin, manipulation. As citizens and consumers, we need to be alert to persuasive practices and how they influence behavior. Being informed is our best defense. However, trusting information sources has become trickier in the age of bots and trolls that spread disinformation and downright propaganda, often from abroad, with ill intent. As we have seen in Chapter 5, social media users have the tendency to congregate with like-minded people online and, as a result, may be susceptible to confirmation bias typical of echo chambers or **opinion bubbles**.

You have already studied techniques for writing routine request messages that require minimal persuasion. This chapter focuses on messages that require deliberate and skilled persuasion in the workplace. It also addresses selling, both offline and online.

## 8-1a Defining Persuasion

As communication scholar Richard M. Perloff defines it, **persuasion** is "a symbolic process in which communicators try to convince other people to change their attitudes or behaviors regarding an issue through the transmission of a message in an atmosphere of free choice."[3] Helping us understand how persuasion works, Perloff's definition has five components, which are outlined in the following sections.

*Persuasion Is a Symbolic Process.* Symbols can take the form of lofty words, signs, and images infused with rich meaning—for example, words such as *liberty*, signs such as national flags, and images such as a red cross for rescue or an apple for computers. An ethical persuader understands the power of symbols and does not use them to trick others. Because people's attitudes change slowly, persuasion takes time.

*Persuasion Involves an Attempt to Influence.* Persuasion involves a conscious effort to influence another person with the understanding that change is possible. For instance, when you ask your boss for permission to work from home, you intend to achieve a specific outcome and assume that your boss can be swayed. This deliberate attempt to change another person's mind doesn't always succeed.

*Persuasion Is Self-Persuasion.* Ethical communicators give others the choice to accept their arguments by making compelling, honest cases to support them. They plant the seed but do not push. They leave it to others to "self-influence"—that is, to decide whether to make the change. In the case of remote work, you would want to present to your boss clear benefits of working off-site but definitely not use pressure, not least because your boss has more power.

*Persuasion Involves Transmitting a Message.* Persuasive messages can be verbal or nonverbal, and they can be conveyed face-to-face or via the Internet, TV, radio, and other media. Persuasive messages are not always rational. They often appeal to our emotions. Consider the car commercial playing your favorite tune and showing pristine landscapes, not a gridlocked interstate during rush hour.

*Persuasion Requires Free Choice.* Although *free* is a difficult term to define, we can perhaps agree that people are free when they are not forced to comply, when they can refuse the idea suggested to them, and when they are not pressured to act against their own preferences. In fact, most people respond to pressure with what psychologists call **reactance**, a defensive strategy of resistance that humans adopt when feeling cornered, robbed of their autonomy, or restricted in their options by others.

Many smart thinkers have tried to explain how savvy persuaders influence others. They agree, however, that it's not easy to change entrenched views. It's a gradual, slow process. One classic model illustrating persuasion is shown in **Figure 8.1**. In the definitive book *Influence*,[4] Robert B. Cialdini outlined six psychological triggers that prompt us to act and believe: *reciprocation, commitment, social proof, liking, authority,* and *scarcity.* Each "weapon of automatic influence" motivates us to say *yes* or *no* without much thinking or awareness. Our complex world forces us to resort to these shortcuts. Needless to say, such automatic responses make us vulnerable to manipulation.

**OFFICE INSIDER**

"Persuasion isn't convincing someone that you are something that you're not. Persuasion is about finding an authentic story that will change beliefs or behaviors. So don't promise innovation if you're just meeting a need. Don't tell your date you love dogs if you really don't....If there's a perception gap between how you see yourself and how the person you are trying to persuade sees you, you will have a problem."[2]

**Lee Hartley Carter,**
*consultant and communication expert*

**Figure 8.1  Six Psychological Triggers That Aid Persuasion**

### Reciprocation
"The Old Give and Take … and Take"

Humans seem to be hardwired to give and take. If someone does us a favor, most of us feel obligated to return the favor. This rule is so binding that it may lead to a *yes* to a request we might otherwise refuse. This explains the "gifts" that accompany requests for money.

### Commitment
"Hobgoblins of the Mind"

We believe in the correctness of a difficult choice once we make it. We want to keep our thoughts and beliefs consistent with what we have already decided. Fundraisers may ask for a small amount at first, knowing that we are likely to continue giving once we start.

### Social Proof
"Truths Are Us"

To determine correct behavior, we try to find out what other people think is correct. We see an action as more acceptable when others are doing it. Advertisers like to tell us that a product is "best-selling"; the message is that it must be good because others think so.

### Liking
"The Friendly Thief"

We are more likely to accept requests of people we know and like or those who say they like us. Tupperware capitalizes on this impulse to buy from a friend. Strangers are persuasive if they are likable and attractive. Also, we favor people who are or appear to be like us.

### Authority
"Directed Deference"

We tend to obey authority because we learn that a widely accepted system of authority is beneficial to the orderly functioning of society. People exuding authority, even con artists, can trigger our mechanical, blind compliance. Testimonials bank on this response to authority.

### Scarcity
"The Rule of the Few"

We tend to regard opportunities as more valuable when their availability is restricted. Scarce items seem more appealing to us. The idea of potential loss greatly affects our decisions. Marketers may urge customers not to miss out on a "limited-time offer."

---

Once you become aware of these gut-level mechanisms that trigger decisions, you will be able to resist unethical and manipulative persuasion more easily. In turn, this knowledge might make you a successful persuader. The delivery channels may change over time, but the proven principles of successful and ethical persuasion outlined in **Figure 8.2** still apply.

When you want your ideas to prevail, start thinking about how to present them. Listeners and readers will be more inclined to accept what you are offering if you focus on important strategies, as outlined in Figure 8.1 and further discussed throughout this chapter.

## 8-2 Planning and Writing Persuasive Requests

**LEARNING OUTCOME 2**
Craft persuasive messages that request actions.

Direct request and claim messages, such as those you wrote in Chapter 6, are straightforward and, therefore, can be direct. Persuasive requests, on the other hand, are generally more effective when they are indirect. Reasons and explanations should precede the main idea. To overcome possible resistance, the writer lays a logical foundation before delivering the request. A writing plan for persuasive requests requires deliberate development.

In this chapter you will learn to apply the preceding writing plan to (a) messages that request actions, (b) claims and adjustment requests that may meet with opposition, (c) messages intended to persuade subordinates and supervisors, and (d) direct-mail and e-mail sales messages.

## Figure 8.2 Effective Persuasion Techniques

**Establish credibility**
- Show that you are truthful, experienced, and knowledgeable.
- Use others' expert opinions and research to support your position.

**Make a reasonable, specific request**
- Make your request realistic, doable, and attainable.
- Be clear about your objective. Vague requests are less effective.

**Tie facts to benefits**
- Line up plausible support such as statistics, reasons, and analogies.
- Convert the supporting facts into specific audience benefits.

**Recognize the power of loss**
- Show what others stand to lose if they don't agree.
- Know that people dread losing something they already possess.

**Expect and overcome resistance**
- Anticipate opposition from conflicting beliefs, values, and attitudes.
- Be prepared to counter with well-reasoned arguments and facts.

**Share solutions and compromise**
- Be flexible and aim for a solution that is acceptable to all parties.
- Listen to people and incorporate their input to create buy-in.

## 8-2a Crafting an Effective Persuasive Message

Convincing someone to change a belief or to perform an action when that person is reluctant requires planning and skill—and sometimes a little luck. A written request may require more preparation than a face-to-face request, but it can be more effective. For example, you may ask a well-known businessperson to make a presentation to your club. You may ask a company to encourage its employees to participate in a charity drive. Such messages require skill in persuasion.

**Model Document 8.1** shows a persuasive request from Lois Bailey. Her research firm seeks to persuade other companies to complete a questionnaire revealing salary data. In most organizations, salary information is strictly confidential. What can Lois do to convince strangers to part with such private information?

## Persuasive Requests

**OPENING:** Capture the reader's attention and interest. Describe a problem, make an unexpected statement, suggest reader benefits, offer praise or compliments, or ask a stimulating question.

**BODY:** Build interest. Explain logically and concisely the purpose of the request. Prove its merit. Use facts, statistics, expert opinion, examples, and specific details. Focus on the reader's direct and indirect benefits. Reduce resistance. Elicit a desire to comply. Anticipate objections, offer counterarguments, establish credibility, demonstrate competence, and show the value of your proposal.

**CLOSING:** Motivate action. Ask for a particular action. Make the action easy to take. Show courtesy, respect, and gratitude.

## Model Document 8.1  Persuasive Request

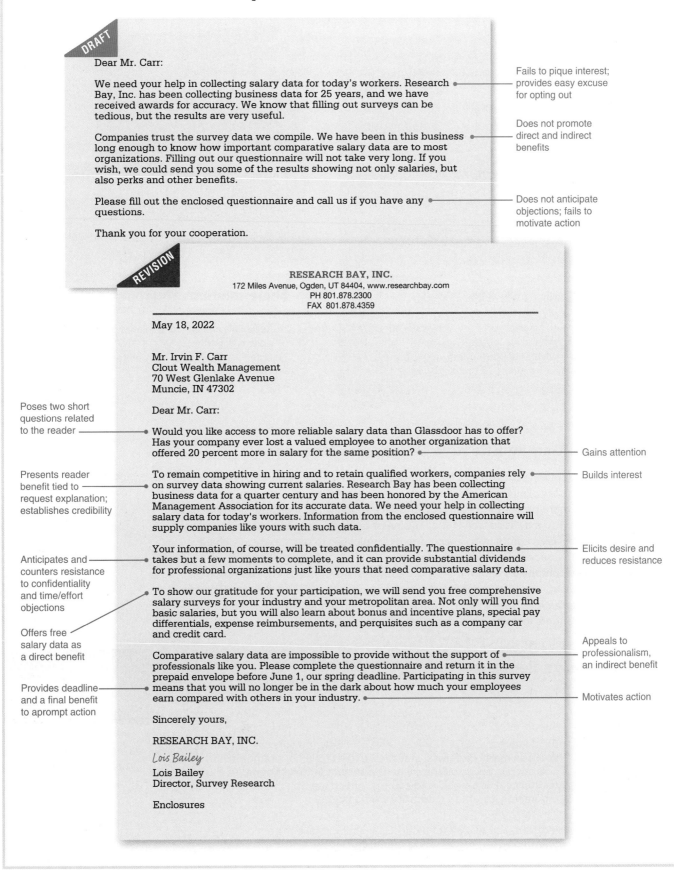

**DRAFT**

Dear Mr. Carr:

We need your help in collecting salary data for today's workers. Research Bay, Inc. has been collecting business data for 25 years, and we have received awards for accuracy. We know that filling out surveys can be tedious, but the results are very useful.

*Fails to pique interest; provides easy excuse for opting out*

Companies trust the survey data we compile. We have been in this business long enough to know how important comparative salary data are to most organizations. Filling out our questionnaire will not take very long. If you wish, we could send you some of the results showing not only salaries, but also perks and other benefits.

*Does not promote direct and indirect benefits*

Please fill out the enclosed questionnaire and call us if you have any questions.

*Does not anticipate objections; fails to motivate action*

Thank you for your cooperation.

---

**REVISION**

**RESEARCH BAY, INC.**
172 Miles Avenue, Ogden, UT 84404, www.researchbay.com
PH 801.878.2300
FAX  801.878.4359

May 18, 2022

Mr. Irvin F. Carr
Clout Wealth Management
70 West Glenlake Avenue
Muncie, IN 47302

Dear Mr. Carr:

*Poses two short questions related to the reader*

Would you like access to more reliable salary data than Glassdoor has to offer? Has your company ever lost a valued employee to another organization that offered 20 percent more in salary for the same position?

*Gains attention*

*Presents reader benefit tied to request explanation; establishes credibility*

To remain competitive in hiring and to retain qualified workers, companies rely on survey data showing current salaries. Research Bay has been collecting business data for a quarter century and has been honored by the American Management Association for its accurate data. We need your help in collecting salary data for today's workers. Information from the enclosed questionnaire will supply companies like yours with such data.

*Builds interest*

*Anticipates and counters resistance to confidentiality and time/effort objections*

Your information, of course, will be treated confidentially. The questionnaire takes but a few moments to complete, and it can provide substantial dividends for professional organizations just like yours that need comparative salary data.

*Elicits desire and reduces resistance*

*Offers free salary data as a direct benefit*

To show our gratitude for your participation, we will send you free comprehensive salary surveys for your industry and your metropolitan area. Not only will you find basic salaries, but you will also learn about bonus and incentive plans, special pay differentials, expense reimbursements, and perquisites such as a company car and credit card.

*Provides deadline and a final benefit to aprompt action*

Comparative salary data are impossible to provide without the support of professionals like you. Please complete the questionnaire and return it in the prepaid envelope before June 1, our spring deadline. Participating in this survey means that you will no longer be in the dark about how much your employees earn compared with others in your industry.

*Appeals to professionalism, an indirect benefit*

*Motivates action*

Sincerely yours,

RESEARCH BAY, INC.

*Lois Bailey*

Lois Bailey
Director, Survey Research

Enclosures

Analyzing the First Draft. The hurriedly written first version of the request in Model Document 8.1 suffers from many faults. It fails to pique the interest of the reader in the opening. It also provides an easy excuse for Mr. Carr to refuse (*filling out surveys can be tedious*). In the body, Mr. Carr doesn't receive any incentive to accept the request. The writing is self-serving and offers few specifics. In addition, the draft does not anticipate objections and fails to suggest counterarguments. Last, the closing does not motivate action by providing a deadline or a final benefit.

Revising the First Draft. In the revised version shown in Model Document 8.1, to gain attention, Lois poses two short questions that spotlight the need for salary information. To build interest and establish trust, she states that Research Bay, Inc. has been collecting business data for a quarter century and has received awards. She ties her reasonable request to audience benefits.

## 8-3 Writing Effective Persuasive Claims and Complaints

As their name suggests, complaints deliver bad news. Some complaint messages just vent anger. However, if the goal is to change something (and why bother to write except to motivate change?), then persuasion is necessary. Persuasive claim and complaint messages may involve damaged products, mistaken billing, inaccurate shipments, warranty problems, limited return policies, insurance snafus, faulty merchandise, and so on. Generally, the direct strategy is best for requesting straightforward adjustments (see Chapter 6). When you can assume that your request is justified and will be granted, use the direct strategy. However, if a past request has been refused or ignored, or if you anticipate reluctance, then the indirect strategy is appropriate.

An effective claim message makes a reasonable and valid request, presents a logical case with clear facts, and has a moderate tone. Anger and emotion are not effective persuaders.

### 8-3a Developing a Logical Claim Message

Strive for logical development in a claim message. You might open with sincere praise, an objective statement of the problem, a point of agreement, or a quick review of what you have done to resolve the problem. Then you can explain precisely what happened or why your claim is legitimate. Don't provide a blow-by-blow chronology of details; just hit the highlights. Be sure to enclose copies of relevant invoices, shipping orders, warranties, and payments. Close with a clear statement of what you want done: a refund, replacement, credit to your account, or other action. Be sure to think through the possibilities and make your request reasonable.

### 8-3b Using a Moderate Tone

The tone of your message is important. Don't suggest that the receiver intentionally deceived you or intentionally created the problem. Rather, appeal to the receiver's sense of responsibility and pride in the company's good name. Calmly express your disappointment in view of your high expectations of the product and of the company. Communicating your feelings without resentment is often the strongest appeal.

Jen Sims's e-mail, shown in **Model Document 8.2**, follows the persuasive strategy as she seeks credit for two VoIP (voice over Internet protocol) office systems. Actually, she was quite upset because her company was counting on these new Internet systems to reduce its phone bills. Instead, the handsets produced so much static that incoming and outgoing calls were all but impossible to hear. The full setup also proved to be too complex for the small business.

What's more, Jen was frustrated that the Return Merchandise Authorization form she filled out at the company's website seemed to sink into a dark hole in cyberspace. She had reason to be angry! However, Jen resolved to use a moderate tone in writing her complaint e-mail because she knew that a calm, unemotional tone would be more effective. She opted for a positive opening, a well-supported claim, and a request for specific action in the closing.

**LEARNING OUTCOME 3**

Write compelling claims and successful complaints.

OFFICE INSIDER

"Complaining for the purpose of resolving a concern or grievance is helpful for mental health, as it is a way to channel your needs into actionable outcomes. This can lead to positive experiences like self-awareness (mindfulness) and happiness."[5]

**Shadeen Francis,** *psychologist practicing in Philadelphia*

## Model Document 8.2  Persuasive Claim (Complaint) E-Mail

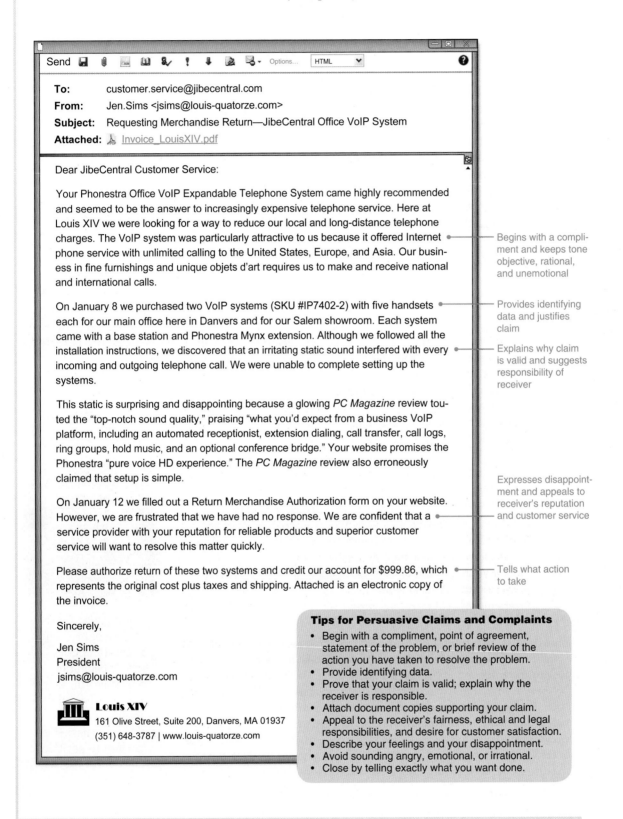

**Send**  Options...  HTML

**To:**  customer.service@jibecentral.com
**From:**  Jen.Sims <jsims@louis-quatorze.com>
**Subject:**  Requesting Merchandise Return—JibeCentral Office VoIP System
**Attached:**  Invoice_LouisXIV.pdf

Dear JibeCentral Customer Service:

Your Phonestra Office VoIP Expandable Telephone System came highly recommended and seemed to be the answer to increasingly expensive telephone service. Here at Louis XIV we were looking for a way to reduce our local and long-distance telephone charges. The VoIP system was particularly attractive to us because it offered Internet phone service with unlimited calling to the United States, Europe, and Asia. Our business in fine furnishings and unique objets d'art requires us to make and receive national and international calls.

*Begins with a compliment and keeps tone objective, rational, and unemotional*

On January 8 we purchased two VoIP systems (SKU #IP7402-2) with five handsets each for our main office here in Danvers and for our Salem showroom. Each system came with a base station and Phonestra Mynx extension. Although we followed all the installation instructions, we discovered that an irritating static sound interfered with every incoming and outgoing telephone call. We were unable to complete setting up the systems.

*Provides identifying data and justifies claim*

*Explains why claim is valid and suggests responsibility of receiver*

This static is surprising and disappointing because a glowing *PC Magazine* review touted the "top-notch sound quality," praising "what you'd expect from a business VoIP platform, including an automated receptionist, extension dialing, call transfer, call logs, ring groups, hold music, and an optional conference bridge." Your website promises the Phonestra "pure voice HD experience." The *PC Magazine* review also erroneously claimed that setup is simple.

On January 12 we filled out a Return Merchandise Authorization form on your website. However, we are frustrated that we have had no response. We are confident that a service provider with your reputation for reliable products and superior customer service will want to resolve this matter quickly.

*Expresses disappointment and appeals to receiver's reputation and customer service*

Please authorize return of these two systems and credit our account for $999.86, which represents the original cost plus taxes and shipping. Attached is an electronic copy of the invoice.

*Tells what action to take*

Sincerely,

Jen Sims
President
jsims@louis-quatorze.com

**Louis XIV**
161 Olive Street, Suite 200, Danvers, MA 01937
(351) 648-3787 | www.louis-quatorze.com

**Tips for Persuasive Claims and Complaints**
- Begin with a compliment, point of agreement, statement of the problem, or brief review of the action you have taken to resolve the problem.
- Provide identifying data.
- Prove that your claim is valid; explain why the receiver is responsible.
- Attach document copies supporting your claim.
- Appeal to the receiver's fairness, ethical and legal responsibilities, and desire for customer satisfaction.
- Describe your feelings and your disappointment.
- Avoid sounding angry, emotional, or irrational.
- Close by telling exactly what you want done.

# 8-4 Crafting Persuasive Messages in Digital Age Organizations

The lines of authority are blurry in today's information age workplaces, and the roles of executives are changing. Technology has empowered rank-and-file employees who can turn to their companies' intranets and don't need their managers to be information providers—formerly a crucial managerial role. Starbucks employees are called *partners*, suggesting equal footing but also equal responsibility for the customer experience.[7] Offering benefits such as health insurance, flexible hours, and tuition-free college, Starbucks has been successful in reducing **churn** (i.e., turnover) so common in the industry. At productivity company Evernote, the organizational structure is open and egalitarian, too. Individual offices and other perks suggesting seniority or status don't exist in the modern sweeping HQ space in Redwood City, California.[8]

This shift in authority is affecting the writing strategies and the tone of workplace persuasive messages. You may still want to be indirect if you hope to persuade your supervisors to do something they will be reluctant to do; however, your bosses, in turn, are less likely to be toxic autocrats who rely on the power of position and just issue commands. Rather, today's executives increasingly bank on persuasion to achieve buy-in from subordinates.[9]

This section focuses on messages flowing downward and upward within organizations. Horizontal messages exchanged among coworkers resemble the persuasive requests discussed earlier in requesting actions.

## 8-4a Persuading Employees: Messages Flowing Downward

Employees need to know how to perform their jobs and what is expected of them; therefore, instructions or directives moving downward from supervisors to subordinates usually require little persuasion. Messages such as information about procedures, equipment, or customer service still use the direct strategy, with the purpose immediately stated.

However, some organizations encourage employees to join programs to stop smoking, lose weight, or start exercising. Organizations may ask employees to participate in capacities outside their work roles—such as spending their free time volunteering for charity projects. In such cases, the writing plan for persuasive requests introduced earlier provides a helpful structure.

**Paying Attention to Tone.** Because many executives today rely on buy-in instead of exercising raw power, messages flowing downward require attention to tone. Warm words and a conversational tone convey a caring attitude. Persuasive requests coming from trusted supervisors are more likely to be accepted than demands from dictatorial executives who rely on threats and punishments to secure compliance.

**Presenting Honest, Accurate Evidence.** The goal is not to manipulate employees or to seduce them with trickery. Rather, the goal is to present a strong but honest argument, emphasizing points that are important to the receiver or the organization. In business, honesty is not just the best policy—it's the only policy. People see right through puffery and misrepresentation. For this reason, the indirect strategy is effective only when supported by accurate, honest evidence.

## 8-4b Persuading the Boss: Messages Flowing Upward

Managers are just as resistant to change as others are. Convincing management to adopt a procedure or invest in a product or new equipment requires skillful communication. Providing facts, figures, and evidence is critical when submitting a recommendation to your boss. When pitching an idea to decision makers, strive to make a strong dollars-and-cents case.[11] A request that emphasizes how the proposal saves money or benefits the business is more persuasive than one that simply announces a good deal or tells how a plan works.

**LEARNING OUTCOME 4**

Compose persuasive messages within organizations demonstrating your knowledge of interpersonal persuasion at work.

**OFFICE INSIDER**

"Leaders with character are highly effective. They have no need to pull rank or resort to command and control to get results. Instead, they're effective because they're knowledgeable, admired, trusted, and respected. This helps them secure buy-in automatically, without requiring egregious rules or strong oversight designed to force compliance."[6]

**Frank Sonnenberg,** *author of* Follow Your Conscience

To commemorate World Water Day, this expensive, selectively targeted mailpiece, Green Belgium Mailing, drives home a memorable and nearly irresistible message about the importance of clean water. The message can be read only if submerged in water. In an example of ingenious branding, the ad agency behind this creative campaign, Duval Guillaume of Antwerp, Belgium, subscribes to this scrappy motto: "We are a small global agency with big brave clients."

**GREEN BELGIUM MAILING**
**WITHOUT WATER, KNOWLEDGE CAN'T FLOW.**

To mark World Water Day, this mailing was sent out to companies and the press.
The letter inside can only be read when held under water - proving that water really is the source of all knowledge.

Duval Guillaume

**LEARNING OUTCOME 5**

Create effective and ethical direct-mail and e-mail sales messages.

Persuasive messages traveling upward require a special sensitivity to tone. When asking supervisors to change views or take action, use phrases such as *we suggest* and *we recommend* rather than *you must* or *we should*. Avoid sounding pushy or argumentative. Strive for a conversational, yet professional tone that conveys warmth, competence, and confidence. When Marketing Assistant Winston Collins wanted his boss to authorize the purchase of a multifunction color laser copier, he knew he had to be persuasive. His memo, shown in **Model Document 8.3**, illustrates an effective approach.

Notice that Winston's memo isn't short. A successful persuasive message typically takes more space than a direct message because proving a case requires evidence. In the end, Winston chose to send his memo as an e-mail attachment accompanied by a polite, short e-mail message because he wanted to keep the document format in MS Word intact. He also felt that the message was too long to paste into his e-mail program. The subject line announces the purpose of the message without disclosing the actual request.

The strength of the persuasive document in Model Document 8.3 is in the clear presentation of comparison figures showing how much money the company can save by purchasing a remanufactured copier.

## 8-5 Creating Effective Sales Messages in Print and Online

The best sales messages, whether delivered by postal mail or by e-mail, have much in common. They use persuasion to promote products and services. Marketing professionals analyze and perfect every aspect of a sales message to encourage consumers to read and act on the message. This section presents techniques developed by experts for drafting effective sales messages, in print and online.

Sales letters and other physical mailpieces, such as postcards, flyers, self-mailers, product samples, and brochures, are called **direct mail**. Usually part of multichannel marketing campaigns, these promotional messages are a powerful means to make sales, generate leads, boost retail traffic, solicit donations, and direct consumers to websites.

Direct mail is an ideal channel for personalized, tangible, three-dimensional messages that are less invasive than telephone solicitations and less reviled than **spam**, unsolicited and often unwanted promotional e-mail. Neuroscience-based studies show that physical direct mail appears to have a greater emotional impact than digital ad content. Brain scans in a USPS-sponsored neuromarketing study suggested that

## Model Document 8.3 Persuasive Message Flowing Upward

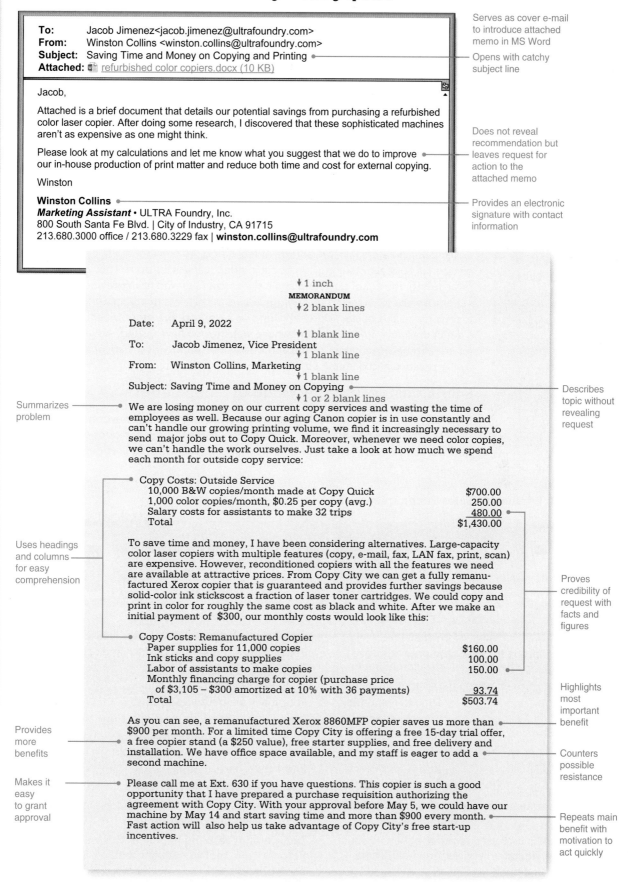

**To:** Jacob Jimenez<jacob.jimenez@ultrafoundry.com>
**From:** Winston Collins <winston.collins@ultrafoundry.com>
**Subject:** Saving Time and Money on Copying and Printing
**Attached:** 📄 refurbished color copiers.docx (10 KB)

Serves as cover e-mail to introduce attached memo in MS Word

Opens with catchy subject line

Jacob,

Attached is a brief document that details our potential savings from purchasing a refurbished color laser copier. After doing some research, I discovered that these sophisticated machines aren't as expensive as one might think.

Please look at my calculations and let me know what you suggest that we do to improve our in-house production of print matter and reduce both time and cost for external copying.

Does not reveal recommendation but leaves request for action to the attached memo

Winston

**Winston Collins**
*Marketing Assistant* • ULTRA Foundry, Inc.
800 South Santa Fe Blvd. | City of Industry, CA 91715
213.680.3000 office / 213.680.3229 fax | **winston.collins@ultrafoundry.com**

Provides an electronic signature with contact information

↓ 1 inch
**MEMORANDUM**
↓ 2 blank lines

Date:     April 9, 2022
↓ 1 blank line
To:       Jacob Jimenez, Vice President
↓ 1 blank line
From:     Winston Collins, Marketing
↓ 1 blank line
Subject:  Saving Time and Money on Copying
↓ 1 or 2 blank lines

Describes topic without revealing request

Summarizes problem

We are losing money on our current copy services and wasting the time of employees as well. Because our aging Canon copier is in use constantly and can't handle our growing printing volume, we find it increasingly necessary to send  major jobs out to Copy Quick. Moreover, whenever we need color copies, we can't handle the work ourselves. Just take a look at how much we spend each month for outside copy service:

Uses headings and columns for easy comprehension

Copy Costs: Outside Service
   10,000 B&W copies/month made at Copy Quick          $700.00
   1,000 color copies/month, $0.25 per copy (avg.)      250.00
   Salary costs for assistants to make 32 trips         480.00
   Total                                              $1,430.00

To save time and money, I have been considering alternatives. Large-capacity color laser copiers with multiple features (copy, e-mail, fax, LAN fax, print, scan) are expensive. However, reconditioned copiers with all the features we need are available at attractive prices. From Copy City we can get a fully remanufactured Xerox copier that is guaranteed and provides further savings because solid-color ink stickscost a fraction of laser toner cartridges. We could copy and print in color for roughly the same cost as black and white. After we make an initial payment of  $300, our monthly costs would look like this:

Proves credibility of request with facts and figures

Copy Costs: Remanufactured Copier
   Paper supplies for 11,000 copies                   $160.00
   Ink sticks and copy supplies                        100.00
   Labor of assistants to make copies                  150.00
   Monthly financing charge for copier (purchase price
      of $3,105 – $300 amortized at 10% with 36 payments)  93.74
   Total                                              $503.74

Highlights most important benefit

As you can see, a remanufactured Xerox 8860MFP copier saves us more than $900 per month. For a limited time Copy City is offering a free 15-day trial offer, a free copier stand (a $250 value), free starter supplies, and free delivery and installation. We have office space available, and my staff is eager to add a second machine.

Provides more benefits

Counters possible resistance

Makes it easy to grant approval

Please call me at Ext. 630 if you have questions. This copier is such a good opportunity that I have prepared a purchase requisition authorizing the agreement with Copy City. With your approval before May 5, we could have our machine by May 14 and start saving time and more than $900 every month. Fast action will  also help us take advantage of Copy City's free start-up incentives.

Repeats main benefit with motivation to act quickly

physical materials "leave a longer lasting impact for easy recall when making a purchase decision."[12] A UK Royal Mail study attributed the enduring effectiveness of direct mail to its tactile heft: "Giving, receiving and handling tangible objects remain deep and intuitive parts of the human experience."[13] **Figure 8.3** juxtaposes the most relevant features of traditional direct-mail and digital sales messages.

## 8-5a Betting on Highly Targeted, Relevant Direct Mail

Professionals who specialize in traditional direct-mail campaigns have made it a science. They analyze a market, develop an effective mailing list, study the product, prepare a sophisticated campaign aimed at a target audience, and motivate the reader to act. You have probably received direct mail, often derisively called **junk mail**. Although not as flashy as social media campaigns, direct mail still works as long as it is well targeted and personalized.[14] Experts know that most recipients do look at their direct mail and respond to it; in fact, 79 percent of consumers act on direct mail immediately, whereas only 45 percent deal with e-mail right away.[15] Chances are direct mail will keep coming, but it will be a lot more relevant to you and your spending habits.

Today's marketers take advantage of technology to connect digital leads and direct-mail appeals, resulting in a boost in effectiveness for both. They call this synergy **retargeting**, the act of targeting again the consumers who have previously visited a brand's website. Tracking technology allows advertisers to match website visitors to their name and postal address.[16] Don't be surprised, therefore, when you receive a direct mailpiece from the brand whose website you have visited. Advertisers like retargeting because it links online and offline marketing. Privacy advocates are alarmed by the practice and demand stricter control over user data.[17]

## 8-5b Considering the Value of Sales Letters

Because sales letters are usually written by specialists, you may never write one on the job. Why learn how to write a sales letter? Learning the techniques of sales writing will help you be more successful in any communication that requires persuasion and

**Figure 8.3** Persuasive Sales Techniques in the Digital Age

| **Traditional Direct Mail (Sales Letter)** | **E-Commerce (E-Mail, Social Media Messages)** |
|---|---|
| Creating static content (hard copy) | Creating dynamic digital content |
| Anticipating a single response (inquiry, sale) | Creating engagement instead of selling overtly |
| Resorting to "spray and pray" approach rather than building communities | Building one-to-one relationships and communities around brands |
| Single communication channel | Multiple communication channels |
| Limited response | Potentially unlimited responses |
| Monologue | Dialogue, potential for mass diffusion |
| Private response | Public, shared response |
| Asynchronous (delayed) response | Instant, real-time response possible |
| Passive | Interactive, participatory |
| Promoter-generated content | User-generated content |
| The needs of target groups must be anticipated and met in advance. | Consumers expect that brands understand their unique needs and deliver. |
| **Direct mail is preferred for information about insurance, financial services, and health care; excellent channel for offline customers.** | **Savvy brands respond nimbly to customer participation; today's sophisticated consumers dislike "hard sell."** |

promotion. What's more, you will recognize sales strategies directed at you, which will make you a more perceptive consumer of ideas, products, and services.

Your primary goal in writing a sales message is to get someone to devote a few moments of attention to it. You may be promoting a product, a service, an idea, or yourself. In each case the most effective messages follow the classic indirect strategy known by the acronym **AIDA** illustrated in **Figure 8.4**: (a) gain **a**ttention, (b) build **i**nterest, (c) elicit **d**esire and reduce resistance, and (d) motivate **a**ction. In Chapter 6 you learned that if you are asking for something that you know will be approved, you would make a direct request. However, when you expect resistance or when you need to educate the receiver, the indirect strategy often works better.

## Sales Messages: AIDA

**OPENING:** Gain *attention*. Offer something valuable; promise a benefit to the reader; ask a question; or provide a quotation, fact, product feature, testimonial, startling statement, or personalized action setting.

**BODY:** Build *interest*. Describe central selling points and make rational and emotional appeals. Elicit *desire* in the reader and reduce resistance. Use testimonials, money-back guarantees, free samples, or performance tests.

**CLOSING:** Motivate *action*. Offer a gift, promise an incentive, limit the offer, set a deadline, or guarantee satisfaction.

**Gaining Attention in Sales Messages.** One of the most critical elements of a sales message is its opening paragraph. This opener should be short (one to five lines), honest, relevant, and stimulating. Marketing pros have found that eye-catching typographical arrangements or provocative messages can hook a reader's attention. Consider these examples:

- **Offer:** *Sign up now and get a free iPad to enjoy your programming on the go!*

- **Promise:** *Now you can raise your sales income by 50 percent or even more with the proven techniques found in....*

- **Question:** *Why wait in the Starbucks line for a pitiful paper cup when for $20 you can have the Chiseled Chrome Coffee Cup, a handsome stylish tumbler of your own to refill every morning?*

- **Quotation or proverb:** *Automotive pioneer Henry Ford once said, "A business that makes nothing but money is a poor business."*

**Figure 8.4** The AIDA Strategy for Sales Messages

| | STRATEGY | CONTENT | SECTION |
|---|---|---|---|
| **A** | **Attention** | Captures attention, creates awareness, makes a sales proposition, prompts audience to read on | Opening |
| **I** | **Interest** | Describes central selling points, focuses not on features of product/service but on benefits relevant to the reader's needs | Body |
| **D** | **Desire** | Reduces resistance, reassures the reader, elicits the desire for ownership, motivates action | Body |
| **A** | **Action** | Offers an incentive or gift, limits the offer, sets a deadline, makes it easy for the reader to respond, closes the sale | Closing |

- **Fact:** *The Greenland Eskimos ate more fat than anyone in the world. And yet . . . they had virtually no heart disease.*

- **Product feature and its benefit:** *The Atlas sock is made from cotton, polyester, and carbonized coffee. Yup! Coffee helps filter odor, but equally important, we use pressure mapping and thermal imaging to create a ridiculously comfortable sock!*

- **Startling statement:** *Bigger houses cost less.*

- **Personalized action setting:** *It's 4:30 p.m. and you've got to make a decision. You need everybody's opinion, no matter where they are. Before you pick up your phone and call them one at a time, call a Cisco Webex Meeting.*

Other openings calculated to capture attention include a solution to a problem, an anecdote, a personalized statement using the receiver's name, or a relevant current event.

**Building Interest With Rational and Emotional Appeals.** In this phase of your sales message, you should clearly describe the product or service. In simple language emphasize the central selling points that you identified during your prewriting analysis. Those selling points can be developed using rational or emotional appeals.

**Rational appeals** are associated with reason and intellect. They translate selling points into references to making or saving money, increasing efficiency, or making the best use of resources. In general, rational appeals are appropriate when a product is expensive, long-lasting, or important to health, security, and financial success.

**Emotional appeals** relate to status, ego, and sensual feelings. Appealing to the emotions is sometimes effective when a product is inexpensive, short-lived, or nonessential. Many clever sales messages, however, combine emotional and rational strategies for a **dual appeal**. Consider these examples:

### Rational Appeal

*You can buy the things you need and want, pay household bills, pay off higher-cost loans and credit cards—as soon as you are approved and your ChoiceCredit card account is opened.*

### Emotional Appeal

*Leave the urban bustle behind and escape to sun-soaked Bermuda! To recharge your batteries with an injection of sun and surf, all you need is your bathing suit, a little suntan lotion, and your ChoiceCredit card.*

**Dual Appeal**

*New ChoiceCredit cardholders are immediately eligible for a $200 travel certificate and additional discounts at fun-filled resorts. Save up to 40 percent while lying on a beach in picturesque, sun-soaked Bora Bora, the year-round luxury destination.*

A physical description of your product is not enough, however. Zig Ziglar, thought by some to be America's greatest salesperson, pointed out that no matter how well you know your product, no one is persuaded by cold, hard facts alone. In the end, people buy because of product benefits.[20] Your job is to translate those cold facts into warm feelings and reader benefits.

A **feature** is what your product is or does; a **benefit** is how the audience can use it. Let's say a sales message promotes a hand cream made with aloe and cocoa butter extracts, along with vitamin A. Those facts become *Nature's hand helpers—including soothing aloe and cocoa extracts, along with firming vitamin A—form invisible gloves that protect your sensitive skin against the hardships of work, harsh detergents, and constant environmental assaults.*

**Reducing Resistance and Building Desire.** Marketing specialists use a number of techniques to overcome resistance and build desire. When price is an obstacle, consider these suggestions:

- Delay mentioning price until after you have created a desire for the product.

- Show the price in small units, such as the price per issue of a magazine.

- Demonstrate how the reader saves money—for instance, by subscribing for two or three years.

- Compare your prices with those of a competitor.

In addition, you need to anticipate objections and questions the receiver may have. When possible, translate these objections into selling points (*If you are worried about training your staff members on the new software, remember that our offer includes $1,000 worth of on-site one-on-one instruction*). Be sure, of course, that your claims are accurate and do not stretch the truth. Other techniques to overcome resistance and prove the credibility of the product include the following:

- **Testimonials:** *"I never stopped eating, yet I lost 107 pounds."—Tina Rivers, Greenwood, South Carolina*

- **Names of satisfied users (with permission, of course):** *Enclosed is a partial list of private pilots who enthusiastically subscribe to our service.*

- **Money-back guarantee or warranty:** *We offer the longest warranties in the business—all parts and service on-site for five years!*

- **Free trial or sample:** *We are so confident that you will like our new accounting program that we want you to try it absolutely free.*

- **Performance tests, polls, or awards:** *Our TP-3000 was named Best Internet Phone, and Etown.com voted it Smartphone of the Year.*

**Motivating Action at the Conclusion of a Sales Message.** All the effort put into a sales message goes to waste if the reader fails to act. To make it easy for readers to act, you can provide a reply card, a stamped and preaddressed envelope, a toll-free telephone number, a smartphone-readable matrix barcode, a simple Web address, or a promise of a follow-up call. Because readers often need an extra push, consider including additional motivators, such as the following:

- **Offer a gift:** *You will receive a free iPad mini with the purchase of any new car.*

- **Promise an incentive:** *With every new paid subscription, we will plant a tree in one of America's Heritage Forests.*

OFFICE INSIDER

"Even though I've been in the business of selling complex, million dollar projects to Fortune 500 companies, no matter how long the proposal itself was, I always insisted that page one include the top three reasons our solution was the best. I was always battling sales people who wanted to stack the features and benefits higher and higher. I knew that if you had the right reasons, three were enough."[21]

**Kevin Kruse,**
*CEO of LEADx and author of Great* Leaders Have No Rules

- **Limit the offer:** *Call now! The first 100 customers receive free travel mugs.*

- **Set a deadline:** *You must act before June 1 to take advantage of these low prices.*

- **Guarantee satisfaction:** *We will return your full payment if you are not entirely satisfied—no questions asked.*

The final paragraph of the sales message carries the punch line. This is where you tell readers what you want them to do and give them reasons for doing it. Most sales messages also include postscripts because they make irresistible reading. Even readers who might skim over or bypass paragraphs are drawn to a PS. Therefore, use a postscript to reveal your strongest motivator, to add a special inducement for a quick response, or to reemphasize a central selling point.

## 8-5c Putting Together All the Parts of a Sales Message

A direct-mail sales letter is the No. 2 preferred marketing medium right behind e-mail[22] because it can be personalized, directed to very specific target audiences, and filled with a more complete message than other advertising media can. However, direct mail is more expensive than e-mail. That's why crafting and assembling all the parts of a sales message are so critical.

**Model Document 8.4** shows a sales letter addressed to individuals and families who may need health insurance. To prompt the reader to respond to the mailing, the letter incorporates the effective four-part AIDA strategy. The writer first establishes the need for health coverage. Then she develops a rational central selling point (a variety of affordable health plans for every budget offered without sales pressure and medical jargon) and repeats this selling point in all the components of the letter. This sales letter saves its strongest motivator—a free heart-rate monitor for the first 30 callers—for the high-impact PS line.

Although you want to be persuasive in sales letters, you must guard against overstepping legal and ethical boundaries. Be sure to check out the Communication Workshop at the end of this chapter to see examples of what is legal and what is not.

## 8-5d Writing Successful E-Mail Sales Messages

Much like traditional direct mail, e-mail marketing can attract new customers, keep existing ones, encourage future sales, cross-sell, and cut costs. However, e-marketers can create and send a promotion in half the time it takes to print and distribute a traditional message. To reach today's consumer, marketers must target their e-mails well if they wish to even get their messages opened. "Customers want to hear from you, but their expectations are rising. They increasingly demand emails that are personalized, contextual, and relevant," says one marketing specialist.[24]

**Analyzing the Purpose: Knowing What You Want to Achieve.** Meet Chef James Barry and his nutritionist wife and business partner Margaret Barry. The owners of Eat Naked Kitchen—a customized, one-on-one whole-food coaching and lifestyle service—understand contemporary persuasive techniques. A former personal chef for celebrities, Chef James and nutrition expert Margaret recognize that all their customers want to feel special. Both know that to achieve success today, they must cultivate relationships, not just push products.[25] Margaret and James provide value by giving away free recipes, sharing cooking techniques, and offering lifestyle recommendations. They engage their well-heeled clients by maintaining an attractive website, tweeting updates, and posting curated advice on their Facebook, Instagram, and Pinterest pages.

Eat Naked Kitchen also has a YouTube channel presenting how-to cooking tips and tricks. Margaret Barry typically authors the opt-in advice e-newsletter such as the one shown in **Model Document 8.5** along with social media screenshots, and she signs off with greetings on behalf of her whole family. Sales pitches are conspicuously absent, so is any mention of program cost because the audience is not price sensitive.

**Model Document 8.4   HealthMatch Sales Letter**

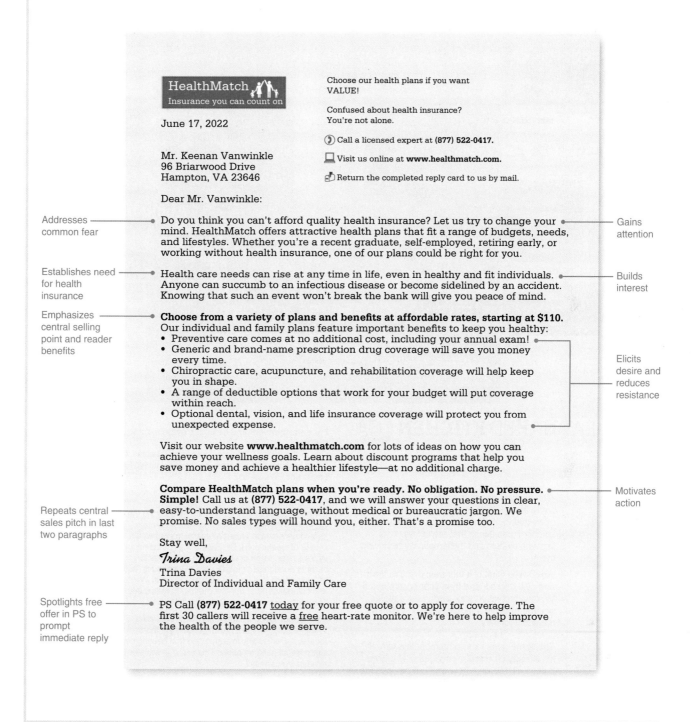

**HealthMatch**
Insurance you can count on

June 17, 2022

Mr. Keenan Vanwinkle
96 Briarwood Drive
Hampton, VA 23646

Dear Mr. Vanwinkle:

Choose our health plans if you want VALUE!

Confused about health insurance? You're not alone.

Call a licensed expert at **(877) 522-0417.**

Visit us online at **www.healthmatch.com.**

Return the completed reply card to us by mail.

*Addresses common fear*

Do you think you can't afford quality health insurance? Let us try to change your mind. HealthMatch offers attractive health plans that fit a range of budgets, needs, and lifestyles. Whether you're a recent graduate, self-employed, retiring early, or working without health insurance, one of our plans could be right for you.

*Gains attention*

*Establishes need for health insurance*

Health care needs can rise at any time in life, even in healthy and fit individuals. Anyone can succumb to an infectious disease or become sidelined by an accident. Knowing that such an event won't break the bank will give you peace of mind.

*Builds interest*

*Emphasizes central selling point and reader benefits*

**Choose from a variety of plans and benefits at affordable rates, starting at $110.** Our individual and family plans feature important benefits to keep you healthy:
- Preventive care comes at no additional cost, including your annual exam!
- Generic and brand-name prescription drug coverage will save you money every time.
- Chiropractic care, acupuncture, and rehabilitation coverage will help keep you in shape.
- A range of deductible options that work for your budget will put coverage within reach.
- Optional dental, vision, and life insurance coverage will protect you from unexpected expense.

*Elicits desire and reduces resistance*

Visit our website **www.healthmatch.com** for lots of ideas on how you can achieve your wellness goals. Learn about discount programs that help you save money and achieve a healthier lifestyle—at no additional charge.

*Repeats central sales pitch in last two paragraphs*

**Compare HealthMatch plans when you're ready. No obligation. No pressure. Simple!** Call us at **(877) 522-0417**, and we will answer your questions in clear, easy-to-understand language, without medical or bureaucratic jargon. We promise. No sales types will hound you, either. That's a promise too.

*Motivates action*

Stay well,

*Trina Davies*

Trina Davies
Director of Individual and Family Care

*Spotlights free offer in PS to prompt immediate reply*

PS Call **(877) 522-0417** today for your free quote or to apply for coverage. The first 30 callers will receive a free heart-rate monitor. We're here to help improve the health of the people we serve.

**Adapting to the Audience to Make Your Message Heard.** In addition to identifying the purpose of a persuasive message, you also need to concentrate on the receiver. Zorba the Greek wisely observed, "You can knock forever on a deaf man's door." A persuasive message is futile unless it meets the needs of its audience. In a broad sense, you want to show how your request helps the receiver achieve some of life's major goals or fulfills key needs: money, power, comfort, confidence, importance, friends, peace of mind, and recognition, to name a few.

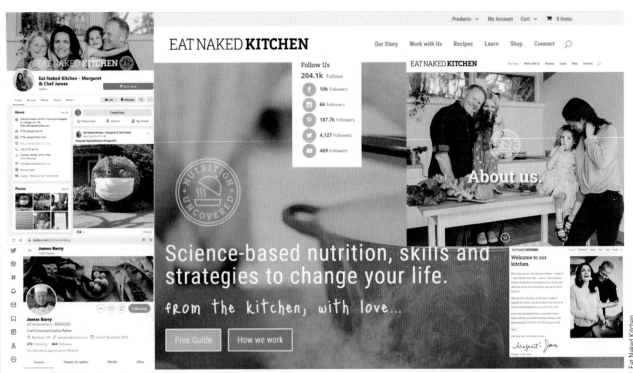

Eat Naked Kitchen

Personalizes the e-mail newsletter to connect with customers

**Hi Linda,**

With all eyes on our immune health as we battle the novel coronavirus pandemic, an often-overlooked but essential strategy is to identify those things that are taxing your immune system and systematically removing them.

Captures attention with references to current events, addressing the reader's concerns

Why? Well think of it this way: if you're tired and overworked, and then your boss plops a big new project on your desk, how capable are you of doing a fabulous job on that new project? Not very.

Empathizes with the recipient and builds interest in boosting the immune system and removing stressors in trying times

The same goes for your immune system. If it's already chronically engaged in low-level battles all day long, how well is it equipped to fight a big new battle like the coronavirus? Not very.

Shifts to we to identify with the reader and to establish expertise

One of the most important things we can do right now is identify the things in our life that are engaging that immune system, and systematically removing or reducing these stressors. This is a core strategy I use with all clients - whether we're thinking of prepping for exposure to a gnarly virus or working to bring an Autoimmune disease into remission.

Provides link to more tips; mostly uses you view

Here are five things you can do right now ... continue reading.

**For entrepreneurs and business owners during this time....**
One of the things I've found exceptionally helpful is a 2-part podcast that Brendon Burchard did called Fear, Focus and Forecasting. Part 1. Part 2.

**Replay of one-day mini-summit....**
Coronavirus - Voices of Reason Mini- Summit - How to Keep Yourself and Your Family Safe during the COVID-19 Pandemic. Featuring Tom Moorcroft (Infectious disease expert Margaret interviewed a couple of weeks ago); Dr. Elisa Song (Pediatrician who's written some of our favorite resources for parents during this time); Dr. Joan Rosenburg (author of 90 seconds to a Life You Love); Dr. Terry Wahls; and several other of our favorite health rock stars. The replay is free and well worth a listen.

Offers information and curated advice; does not engage in overt selling

**For deeper sleep in these high anxiety times...**
Weighted blankets are proving to be very therapeutic for sleep. Particularly in supporting that healing deep sleep we all need so badly! This brand is well reviewed and priced.

Here's to removing the stressors,

Margaret, Chef James and family

Spreads good cheer; again personalizes the newsletter, signing off as a family sending greetings to the recipient's family

Follow. Share.Tag. Together we can do so much good.

Positive call to action and unity; invites reader to connect on social media

On a more practical level, you want to show how your persuasive message solves a problem, achieves a personal or work objective, or just makes life easier for your audience. During the anxiety-inducing COVID-19 pandemic, Eat Naked Kitchen gently reminded its customers and social media followers that wholesome food and a healthy lifestyle nourish the immune system.

When adapting persuasive requests to your audience, consider these questions that receivers will very likely be asking themselves: *Why should I? What's in it for me? What's in it for you? Who cares?*

## 8-5e Selling by E-Mail

The goal of a persuasive message is to convert the receiver to your ideas and motivate action. To accomplish this feat in the age of social media, persuaders seek to build relationships with their audiences. Even so, a message without a clear purpose is doomed. Too often, inexperienced writers reach the end of the first draft of a message before discovering exactly what they want the receiver to think or do.

The first rule of e-marketing is to communicate only with those who have given permission. By sending messages only to opt-in folks, you greatly increase your open rate—e-mails that will be opened and perhaps read. E-mail users detest spam. However, receivers are highly receptive to offers tailored specifically to them. Remember that today's customer is somebody—not just anybody.

Some differences between traditional sales messages and e-marketing are obvious when you study Model Document 8.5. Online sales messages are shorter than direct-mail messages, feature colorful graphics, and occasionally even come with sound or video clips. They offer a richer experience to readers who can click hyperlinks at will to access content that interests them. When such messages are sent out as ads or periodic e-newsletters, they may not have salutations or closings. Rather, they may resemble Web pages.

Here are a few guidelines that will help you create effective e-mail sales messages:

- **Craft a catchy subject line**. Include an audience-specific location (*Emporium in Vegas Opens Soon!*); ask a meaningful question (*What's Your Dream Vacation?*); and use no more than 50 characters. Promise realistic solutions. Offer discounts or premiums.

- **Place the main information within the first screen**. E-mails should be top heavy. Primary points should appear early in the message (before the reader begins to scroll) so that they capture the reader's attention. In physical letters, this principle means placing key information "above the fold," that is, before the first fold in a letter about to be mailed in an envelope.

- **Make the message short, conversational, and focused**. Because on-screen text is taxing to read, be brief. Focus on one or two central selling points only.

- **Sprinkle testimonials throughout the copy**. Authentic consumers' own words are the best sales copy. These comments can serve as callouts or be integrated into the copy.

- **Provide a means for opting out**. It's a legal requirement and polite business policy to include a statement that tells receivers how to unsubscribe from the sender's marketing e-mails.

## 8-5f Writing Short Persuasive Messages Online

Increasingly, writers are turning to social networks to promote their businesses, further their causes, and build their online personas. As we have seen, social media are not primarily suited for overt selling; however, tweets and other online posts can be used to influence others and project a professional, positive online presence.

Typically, organizations and individuals with followers post updates of their events, exploits, thoughts, and experiences. In persuasive tweets and posts, writers try to

**Figure 8.5** Analyzing Persuasive Tweets

 **jonah berger** ✓ @j1berger · Feb 1
Have something you want to change?
Check out my new book, The Catalyst.
All about how to change minds, organizations, and the world.
Here's more information ow.ly/UxR550y5flx

 **Aéropostale** ✓ @Aeropostale · Apr 29
Look like sunshine, feel like sunshine. Shop now and save 60% (or more) off site wide: bit.ly/3f4UTu0

 **JetBlue** ✓ @JetBlue · Jan 17
It's almost #BlueMonday, the gloomiest day of the year. Share your winter view with us using #JetBlueMondayContest and @JetBlue—the most creative submissions will win round-trip flights* to PHX. No purch nec 48US/DC, 18+ Ends 11:59:59pmET 1/20/20 Rules@https://bit.ly/2u3riOK

 **REI** ✓ @REI · Apr 25
Save 50% or more on all clothing at REI Outlet! Includes jackets, pants, tops, workout wear & more, thru 4/27. Online only.

 **UPS** ✓ @UPS · Mar 24
Moving your business online? We can help. Sign up for a free UPS My Choice® for business account to get started. #ecommerce

 **Arianna Huffington** ✓ @ariannahuff · Feb 22
This weekend, I write about deathbed photography, beauty in Bentonville and Billie Eilish's decision to unplug. Sign up to read my Weekly Thoughts: buff.ly/38QAIBX

 **Bill Gates** ✓ @BillGates · Jun 18, 2019
I encourage software developers, inventors, and scientists to consider how they can use their skills to fight inequity.

 **jonah berger** ✓ @j1berger · Mar 7
Want to change minds using social media?
Check out this new podcast with @Mike_Stelzner at @SMExaminer on the Catalyst.

 **Los Angeles Ronald McDonald House** @LosAngelesRMH · May 1
Our families are LOVING the tasty treats from @ClifBar ! Thank you for providing an easy, portable, and nutritious snack for families to enjoy throughout their busiest of days 🍫 #LARMH #KeepingFamiliesClose

 **Apple** ✓ @Apple
Introducing the new iPad Pro. The world's most advanced mobile display. Faster than most PC laptops. Featuring Wide and Ultra Wide Pro cameras and LiDAR Scanner.

 **Susan G. Komen** ✓ @SusanGKomen · Jan 31
Did you know you can help bring an end to #breastcancer by putting your feet to the pavement? Join @The3Day and walk an inspiring 60 miles in 3 days to show your commitment. Sign up now and save $20. Hurry, early bird pricing ends February 7! bit.ly/2RFvA8f

 **Deloitte** ✓ @Deloitte · Jan 22
Are leaders prepared to fight global financial crime in the 4IR? Join LIVE from #WEF20 as Bob Contri, Deloitte's Global Financial Services Industry Leader, leads a panel of industry experts to discuss via #Periscope 📹: deloi.tt/2NLy2Yw

 **Publix** ✓ @Publix · Sep 30, 2019
The Publix Stories Podcast is back for #InternationalPodcastDay! Our Dietitians provided great info on making better choices and the benefits of family meals. Tweet us some things your family does to make better food choices. spr.ly/601418QaA

 **Teach For America** ✓ @TeachForAmerica · Dec 23, 2019
Are you interested in gaining policy experience on the national level? Apply now to join our 2020 Capitol Hill Fellows Program, which places alumni in year-long, paid Congressional staff positions.

 **suzeormanshow** ✓ @SuzeOrmanShow · 1h
Today's the day to listen in to another #AskSuzeAnything podcast where I'm answering your questions. Listen in!

 **Mashable** ✓ @mashable · 4m
The end of aging: Are you ready to live to 150?

 **Team Robert Cialdini** @RobertCialdini · Feb 18
The ability to ethically influence the decisions and behaviors of others is incredibly useful. So, how is successful ethical persuasion best achieved? You can't afford to scroll past this post. ow.ly/XfiT50ypGDe

 **Team Robert Cialdini** @RobertCialdini · Jan 31
Happy Friday! Did you know we have a youtube channel with loads of informative and entertaining videos? Watch a video or 2 over lunch or during your commute. Have a great and safe weekend. - Team C #influence #persuasion #watch #youtube youtube.com/influenceatwork

 **Guy Kawasaki** ✓ @GuyKawasaki · Apr 28
How will you weather the storm? I shared The Art of Perseverance on my podcast to help you your business and answer some questions I've been getting. bit.ly/2yM45mx #remarkablepeople

*Twitter*

pitch offers, prompt specific responses, or draw the attention of their audiences to interesting events, sales, and media links. Figure 8.5 displays a sampling of persuasive tweets.

Note that the compact format of a tweet requires extreme conciseness and efficiency. Don't expect the full four-part AIDA strategy to be represented in a 140- or 280-character Twitter message. Instead, you may see attention-getters and calls for action, both of which must be catchy and intriguing. Regardless, many of the principles of persuasion discussed in this chapter apply even to micromessages.

## Summary of Learning Outcomes

**1 Identify digital age persuasion as well as time-proven persuasive techniques.**

- Business communicators need to use persuasion when making more than routine demands and facing a skeptical audience.
- Persuasion is a symbolic process in which communicators try to convince other people to change their attitudes or behaviors regarding an issue through the transmission of a message in an atmosphere of free choice.
- Six psychological triggers, or "weapons of automatic influence," assist in persuasion: reciprocation, commitment, social proof, liking, authority, and scarcity.
- Communicators able to recognize unethical and manipulative persuasion might in turn become successful persuaders.
- Effective persuaders establish credibility, make a specific request, tie facts to benefits, recognize the power of loss, expect and overcome resistance, share solutions, and compromise.

**2 Craft persuasive messages that request actions.**

- Convincing a reluctant person requires planning and skill and sometimes a little luck.
- Persuasive requests are generally most effective when indirect, that is, when reasons and explanations precede the main idea.
- The writing plan for persuasive requests consists of an opening that captures the reader's attention; a body that establishes credibility, builds interest, and proves the merit of the request by using specific details; and a closing that motivates action while showing courtesy.

**3 Write compelling claims and successful complaints.**

- Complaints and some persuasive claims deliver bad news; some vent anger, yet persuasion is necessary to effect change.
- Persuasive claims and complaints may involve damaged products, billing errors, wrong shipments, warranty problems, limited return policies, or insurance mix-ups.
- Employing a moderate tone, claim/complaint messages need to be logical and open with praise, a statement of fact or agreement, and a quick review of what was done to resolve the problem.
- In the body, writers highlight what happened and why the claim/complaint is legitimate; they enclose supporting documents such as invoices, shipping orders, warranties, and payments.
- The closing specifies what is to be done (e.g., a refund, replacement, or credit).

**4 Compose persuasive messages within organizations demonstrating your knowledge of interpersonal persuasion at work.**

- Today's executives rely on persuasion and buy-in from employees, not so much on the power of their position.
- When asking workers to volunteer for projects or make lifestyle changes, businesses use a conversational tone and warm words; they rely on honest, accurate evidence.
- Messages to management should provide facts, figures, and evidence and make strong dollars-and-cents cases for proposed ideas using a warm, professional tone.

**5 Create effective and ethical direct-mail and e-mail sales messages.**

- Whether delivered by postal mail or by e-mail, marketers design sales messages to encourage consumers to read and act on the message.
- Sales letters and other physical direct mail are still an important part of multichannel marketing campaigns that can make sales, generate leads, boost retail traffic, solicit donations, and direct consumers to websites.
- The AIDA writing plan consists of an opening that gains attention, a body that builds interest and elicits desire, and a closing that motivates action by setting a deadline or presenting an incentive or a limited offer.
- Skilled e-marketers create catchy subject lines, start with the most important points, make the message conversational and focused, use testimonials, and allow readers to opt out.
- Short persuasive posts and tweets concisely pitch offers, prompt responses, and draw attention to events and media links. Principles of persuasion apply even to micromessages.

## Key Terms

| | | |
|---|---|---|
| opinion bubbles 223 | retargeting 232 | ethos 246 |
| persuasion 223 | AIDA 233 | pathos 246 |
| reactance 223 | rational appeals 234 | logos 246 |
| churn 229 | emotional appeals 234 | kairos 246 |
| direct mail 230 | dual appeal 234 | puffery 255 |
| spam 230 | feature 235 | hyperbole 255 |
| junk mail 232 | benefit 235 | |

## Chapter Review

1. List and explain the five components that make up Richard M. Perloff's definition of persuasion. (L.O. 1)

2. List effective persuasion techniques. (L.O. 1)

3. Describe the writing plan for persuasive requests and its components. (L.O. 2)

4. What do claim/complaint messages typically involve, and how should they be crafted? (L.O. 3)

5. How can you ensure that your claim/complaint message is developed logically? (L.O. 3)

6. How have shifts in authority in digital age organizations affected the strategies for creating goodwill and the tone of workplace persuasive messages? (L.O. 4)

7. What is the four-part AIDA writing plan for sales messages, and what does the acronym stand for? (L.O. 5)

8. Name eight or more ways to attract attention in the opening of a sales message. (L.O. 5)

9. Name the best practices for e-marketers hoping to write effective e-mail sales messages. (L.O. 5)

10. Describe the purpose and characteristics of persuasive tweets and other online posts. (L.O. 5)

## Critical Thinking

11. *Sit back in your first-class seat and sip a freshly stirred drink while letting 12 channels of superb audio wash over you—or snooze* is an example of what type of persuasive appeal? How does it compare to the following: *Take one of four daily direct flights to South America on our modern Airbus aircraft, and enjoy the most legroom of any airline. If we're ever late, you will receive coupons for free trips.* (L.O. 5)

12. Many consumers rely on product reviews posted online, presumably by ordinary citizens describing their authentic experiences. Unfortunately, though, Amazon and Yelp, the most prominent of the many Internet review sites, have been called out for fake and paid-for reviews. Amazon has threatened to sue people posting fake public reviews.[26] Why is it important that online reviews or testimonials be trustworthy? (L.O. 1, 5)

13. Direct marketers sometimes resort to scare tactics—for example, to make us purchase alarm systems or subscribe to monitoring services. They may also appeal to our compassion and guilt before the holidays in soliciting money for the less fortunate. Are such emotional appeals ethical? (L.O. 1, 5)

14. How are direct-mail and e-mail sales messages similar, and how are they different? (L.O. 5)

15. Microtargeting is a controversial persuasive technique. Advertisers are trying to sweet-talk Internet users into allowing them to harvest their location information, browser history, and other personal behavior data. They argue it's to users' advantage to see ads tailored to their lifestyles and preferences. An even bigger problem than threats to privacy are narrowly focused political ads. Critics worry that misleading information cannot be rebutted if it's narrowly targeted. What are the risks of microtargeted political ads on social media and tailored ads curated by automation? (L.O. 1, 5)

## Writing Improvement Exercises

## Direct and Indirect Strategies

**YOUR TASK.** For each of the following situations, check the appropriate writing strategy.

| Direct Strategy | Indirect Strategy | |
|---|---|---|
| _____ | _____ | 16. A request by management asking employees to commit to volunteering at one of more than 100 local nonprofits during an annual community service day |
| _____ | _____ | 17. A request from an agent to confirm an appointment for a private real estate showing |
| _____ | _____ | 18. An e-mail message to employees telling them to expect an emergency preparedness drill within the next 10 days |
| _____ | _____ | 19. An e-mail announcing the opportunity of receiving the COVID-19 vaccine during work hours and urging employees to participate |
| _____ | _____ | 20. A safety talk to a construction crew about the dangers of asbestos |
| _____ | _____ | 21. A safety talk to a production team in a foundry about lifestyle choices that may interfere with workers' ability to perform their jobs |

| Direct Strategy | Indirect Strategy | |
|---|---|---|
| _____ | _____ | 22. A request for a refund by a QuickBooks user who failed to deactivate the software within the 30-day trial period |
| _____ | _____ | 23. A message to your accountant asking her to reconsider her fee, which you think is excessive, considering that it was a bad year for your business |
| _____ | _____ | 24. A letter from a property owner to a nearby business asking it to prohibit mobile catering service trucks from gathering outside the business at lunchtime |
| _____ | _____ | 25. A memo to employees announcing a new procedure for choosing or switching health insurance plans |

## Radical Rewrites

**NOTE:** Radical Rewrites are provided at **www.cengage.com** for you to download and revise. Your instructor may show a suggested solution.

### 8.1 Radical Rewrite: A Poor Invitation to a Chef to Speak (L.O. 1, 2)

The following letter from a program chair strives to persuade a well-known chef to make a presentation before a local restaurant association. But the letter is not very persuasive. How could this message be more effective? What reader benefits could it offer? What arguments could be made to overcome resistance? How should a persuasive message conclude?

**YOUR TASK.** Analyze the following invitation and list its weaknesses. If your instructor directs, revise the letter.

Current date

Ms. Cassidee Dabney
Executive Chef, The Barn
Blackberry Farm
1471 West Millers Cove Road
Walland, TN 37886-2649

Dear Ms. Dabney:

We know you are a very busy hospitality professional as chef at The Barn, but we would like you to make a presentation to the Atlanta chapter of the National Restaurant Association. I was asked to write you since I am program chair.

I heard that you made a really good presentation at your local chapter in Knoxville recently. I think you gave a talk called "Avoiding the Seven Cardinal Sins in Food Service" or something like that. Whatever it was, I'm sure we would like to hear the same or a similar presentation. All restaurant operators are interested in doing what we can to avoid potential problems involving discrimination, safety at work, how we hire people, etc. As you well know, operating a fast-paced restaurant is frustrating—even on a good day. We are all in a gigantic rush from opening the door early in the morning to shutting it again after the last customer has gone. It's a rat race and easy to fall into the trap with food service faults that push a big operation into trouble.

Enclosed please find a list of questions that our members listed. We would like you to talk in the neighborhood of 45 minutes. Our June 10 meeting will be in the Carnegie Room of the St. Regis Atlanta and dinner begins at 7 p.m.

How can we get you to come Atlanta? We can only offer you an honorarium of $200, but we would pay for any travel expenses. You can expect a large crowd of restaurateurs who are known for hooting and hollering when they hear good stuff! As you can see, we are a rather informal group. Hope you can join us!

Sincerely,

## 8.2 Radical Rewrite: Persuasive Message Flowing Upward: Saving Money on Shirts (L.O. 1, 2, 4)

> E-Mail

In the following message, Anton tries to convince his boss, the vice president of marketing, that their company could save money by sourcing T-shirts from El Salvador. However, his message could be improved by employing several strategies for persuasion.

**YOUR TASK.** Analyze the following e-mail and list its weaknesses. If your instructor directs, revise the message.

**To:**     Janelle Edwards <bryanna@ultrafit-international.com>
**From:**   Anton Sheppard <anton@ultrafit-international.com>
**Subject:** Possible Chance for Saving Money

We always try our best to meet customers and sell UltraFit International equipment at numerous trade shows. But instead of expanding our visits to these trade shows, the company continues to cut back the number that we attend. And we have fewer staff members attending. I know that you have been asking us to find ways to reduce costs, but I don't think we are going about it right.

With increased airfare and hotel costs, my staff has tried to find ways to live within our very tight budget. Yet, we are being asked to find other ways to reduce our costs. I'm currently thinking ahead to the big Orlando trade show coming up in September.

One area where we could make a change is in the gift that we give away. In the past we have presented booth visitors with a nine-color T-shirt that is silk-screened and gorgeous. But it comes at a cost of $23 each and every one of these beauties from a top-name designer.

To save money, I suggest that we try a $6 T-shirt made in El Salvador, which is reasonably presentable. It's got our name on it, and, after all, folks just use these shirts for workouts. Who cares if it is a fancy silk-screened T-shirt or a functional Salvadoran one that has "UltraFit International" plastered on the chest? Because we give away 2,000 T-shirts at our largest show, we could save big bucks by dumping the designer shirt. But we have to act quickly. I'm sending a cheap one for you to see. Oh, we have found a source that would guarantee sustainable production and no child labor.

Let me know what you think.
Anton

[Full contact information]

## 8.3 Radical Rewrite: LinkedIn Favor Request (L.O. 1, 2, 5)

> Social Media   > E-Mail

A student chose LinkedIn to request a recommendation from his professor. The following message suffers from many writing faults, including poor tone and flawed persuasive strategy.

**YOUR TASK.** Analyze the LinkedIn message and list at least five weaknesses. If your instructor directs, revise the message. Decide whether to use LinkedIn, of which the receiver is a member, or an e-mail to make this request.

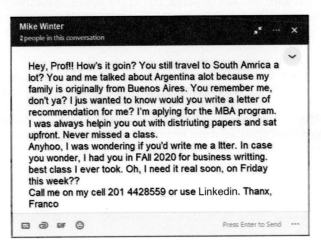

## 8.4 Analyzing Tweets: Finding Persuasive Techniques in Tweets (L.O. 1, 2, 5)

Communication Technology  >  E-Mail  >  Social Media  >  Web

As you have learned in this chapter, the time-tried AIDA sales technique is alive and well even in short Twitter messages. Of course, we can't expect to find all four parts in a single tweet.

**YOUR TASK.** Study the following tweets and describe the persuasive techniques they employ. For additional tweets to study, especially if you have no Internet access, see Figure 8.5.

**HINT:** You may find that Twitter users rely on attention getters, calls for action, emotional appeals, incentives, and testimonials. They may also create urgency to stoke readers' interest. Chat about your findings in class or on your favorite course-management platform. Your instructor may ask you to collect your own examples of persuasive tweets or other social media posts and discuss their frequency as well as effectiveness. After you have collected a sample large enough to allow you to generalize, compose an e-mail or post about your observations.

a.
**Coca-Cola** ✔ @CocaCola · Dec 16
Help us recognize the out-of-the-ordinary students who graduated in an out-of-the-ordinary situation. Share a kind comment with a graduate to celebrate all of their hard work. #TogetherTastesBetter

b.
**Campbell Soup Co** ✔ @CampbellSoupCo · Feb 18
New Farmhouse Thin & Crispy Butter Pecan cookies are on shelves this month—they're rich and buttery with fresh-from-the-oven taste. #CampbellSnacks

c.
**DIRECTV** ✔ @DIRECTV · Feb 18
Who will walk away a 2021 #AusOpen champion? 🏆 Catch the tournament's final matches on @espn and our interactive sports mix on Ch 906 🎾 ☀

d.
**John Deere** ✔ @JohnDeere · Apr 2, 2020
Running out of activities for the kids? Have them color these pages and dedicate it to someone they love—then share it here! Download here: bit.ly/2JuH21P

e.
**Harley-Davidson** ✔ @harleydavidson · Jan 28
"To me, la dolce vita is right here, right now." Learn why Davide got back on a motorcycle and the sense of freedom he feels on the open road. Experience the #HarleyDavidson 2021 Virtual Event ▶ live.harley-davidson.com

f.
**DreamWorks Animation** ✔ @Dreamworks · Feb 26
Perfect family fun! Take your pack on an adventure they'll enjoy again and again when you own #CroodsNewAge. Get it on Amazon @PrimeVideo today. uni.pictures/Croods2AMZ

g.
**McDonald's** ✔ @McDonalds · Apr 21
📣 Friends. Family. Community. WE NEED YOU! ❤ Please help us help our frontline workers. We want to give them a FREE thank you meal. If you know anyone who could use one, please like, tag in comment or retweet to let them know. We'd truly be proud to take their order.

h.
**Starbucks News** ✔ @StarbucksNews · Jan 11
When you purchase an eGift card by the end of today from our Recognition category, Starbucks will donate $5 to support @NAMICommunicate and the mental wellness of front-line responders helping our communities during COVID-19. Shop now: sbux.co/eGiftRecogniti...

i.
**REI** ✔ @REI · Feb 17
"On sunny winter days, I always have a run planned. It's so tranquil and quiet when it's cold. Yesterday, I passed an eagle just chilling in a tree. I get to pause and just be. Those moments on winter runs always leave me feeling refreshed. " Renee P., #REImember since 2002.

j.
**Southwest Airlines** ✔ @SouthwestAir · Feb 22
Hey Writers! Have you submitted your entry to the Storytellers On The Rise Contest on Wattpad yet? This is your last week to tell us a story of kindness rooted in travel. Enter at the link below!

## 8.5 Writing Persuasive Tweets and Other Social Media Posts (L.O. 1, 5)

> Communication Technology  >  Social Media  >  Web

Build your professional online persona with effective and concise micromessages (tweets) and other social media posts.

**YOUR TASK.** Brainstorm to identify a special skill you have, an event you want others to attend, a charitable cause dear to your heart, or a product you like. Applying what you have learned about short persuasive messages online, write your own persuasive tweet of no more than 280 characters or create a brief persuasive Instagram or Facebook post. Use Figure 8.5 as a starting point and model.

## 8.6 The Art of Persuasion—As Old as Aristotle's *Rhetoric* (L.O. 1)

> Social Media  >  Web

Besides the persuasive models introduced in this chapter, many more exist. One of the oldest and best-known modes of persuasion comes from Aristotle (384–322 BC). The Greek philosopher identified four components of persuasion: **ethos, pathos, logos,** and **kairos.**[27]

**Ethos** describes the merit, character, and expertise of a speaker. Persuasion is possible when the audience believes that the persuader is credible and has a good reputation. For instance, we tend to believe a successful coach speaking about training methods. Testimonials in advertising by people we respect are an example of ethos.

**Pathos** describes an emotional appeal. It means the style of delivery—for example, when a speaker exhibits passion and uses colorful metaphors, language, attention getters, and more. When successful, pathos triggers feelings in the audience intended by the speaker, such as empathy or outrage.

**Logos** describes a rational appeal. It is the persuasive technique of an argument based in logic and appealing to the audience's intellect. Logos requires us to support our ideas with sound reasons, relevant statistics, and other solid evidence.

**Kairos** suggests that persuaders consider the timing and setting of an argument, that is, the "right moment."

As experts point out, most persuaders skillfully weave all four tactics into a seamless, effective persuasive message.[28] In reputable publications such as *The Wall Street Journal* and *The New York Times*, and highly regarded news media such as CBS, ABC, and PBS, expect logos to dominate the generally "civilized" debate. Contributors featured in these media generally rank high on ethos. On the political fringes, however, be they left- or right-leaning, pathos dominates over logos. Similarly, expect a lot more pathos than logos in advertising.

**YOUR TASK.** Look for persuasive messages: speeches on YouTube or opinion pieces such as editorials or blog entries. Examine them for ethos, pathos, and logos. The discussion of rational and emotional appeals in this chapter might be helpful. Jot down your observations and bring your notes to class. If your instructor directs, submit a written interpretation discussing the ethos, pathos, logos, and kairos of a speech, an ad, or an opinion piece.

## 8.7 Requesting a Letter of Recommendation From a Busy Prof (L.O. 1, 2)

> E-Mail

As a student, you will need letters of recommendation to find a job, to apply for a scholarship or grant, or to enter graduate school. Naturally, you will consider asking one or several of your college instructors. You talk to Andy, a senior you know, to find out how to get a busy professor, whose memory of you may be hazy, to write you an effective letter. Andy has the following advice:

- Ask only instructors who have had the opportunity to observe your performance and may recall your performance if you jog their memory a little. Two to five years after you attended a course of 20 to 40 students, your teachers may not recall you at all.
- Contact only professors who can sing your praises. If your grades were poor, the endorsement won't be glowing. Some instructors refuse to write recommendations for mediocre students.

Make it easy for your instructors to agree to your request and to write a solid letter promptly by following these guidelines:

- Make the first request in person, if possible; your former instructor will be more likely to remember you.
- Introduce yourself by name and try to point out something memorable you did to help your professor recall your performance.
- Have a hard copy of the job description, scholarship information, grant requirements, or graduate school application ready, or direct the instructor to a website.
- Carry a copy of a recent polished résumé, or promise to e-mail these documents and any other information to help your recommender recall you in a professional setting and understand what you need.
- Confirm any agreement by e-mail promptly, and set a firm yet reasonable deadline by which the letter must be received. Don't expect to get a letter if you ask at the last minute.
- Gently nudge by e-mail to remind the recommender when the deadline is approaching.

**YOUR TASK.** Write a persuasive request by e-mail asking your instructor (or supervisor or manager) to write you a letter of recommendation for a job application, grant, scholarship, or graduate school application. Provide all relevant information to make it easy for your reader to write a terrific letter. Explain any attachments.

## 8.8 Persuasive Request: Making a Case for Tuition Reimbursement (L.O. 1, 2, 4)

**Communication Technology** ❯ **E-Mail** ❯ **Team**

After working a few years, you would like to extend your college education on a part-time basis. You know that your education can benefit your employer, but you can't really afford the tuition, fees, and books. You have heard that many companies offer reimbursement for tuition and books when employees complete approved courses with a grade of C or higher.

**YOUR TASK.** In teams discuss the best way to approach an employer whom you wish to persuade to start a tuition and books reimbursement program. How could such a program help the employer? Remember that the most successful requests help receivers see what's in it for them. What objections might your employer raise? How can you counter them? After discussing strategies in teams face-to-face or online, write a team memo or individual memos (or e-mail) to your boss (at a company where you now work or one with which you are familiar). Persuade your manager to act on your persuasive request.

## 8.9 Persuasive Claim: Pricy Toner for Tony Myrtle Beach Country Club (L.O. 1, 3)

Nanette was new to her job as administrative assistant at the Barefoot Resort & Golf in Myrtle Beach, South Carolina. Alone in the office one morning, she answered a phone call from Chas, who said he was the country club's copier contractor. "Hey, look, Babydoll," Chas purred, "the price on the toner you use is about to go way up. I can offer you a great price on this toner if you order right now." Nanette knew that the copy machine regularly needed toner, and she thought she should go ahead and place the order to save the country club some money. Ten days later two bottles of toner arrived, and Nanette was pleased at the perfect timing. The copy machine needed it right away. Three weeks later Erika, the bookkeeper, called to report a bill from The Toner People for $960.43 for two bottles of toner. "What's going on here?" asked Erika. "We don't purchase supplies from this company, and this price is totally off the charts!"

Nanette spoke to the manager, Forrest Vartanian, who immediately knew what had happened. He blamed himself for not training Nanette. "Never, never order anything from a telephone solicitor, no matter how fast-talking or smooth he sounds," warned Forrest. He outlined an office policy for future supplies purchases. Only certain people can authorize or finalize a purchase, and purchases require a confirmed price including shipping costs settled in advance. But what to do about this $960.43 bill? The country club had already begun to use the toner, although the current copies were looking faint and streaked.

**YOUR TASK.** As Forrest Vartanian, decide how to respond to this obvious scam. Should you pay the bill? Should you return the unused bottles? Write a persuasive claim to The Toner People, 1218 Sam Rittenberg Boulevard, Suite 100, Charleston, SC 29407. Supply any details necessary.

## 8.10 Persuasive Claim: Contesting Steep Legal Costs (L.O. 1, 2, 3)

Over the last decade, the popularity of Mediterranean and Middle Eastern cuisines has soared in the United States. Seattle's downtown, popular with young urban professionals eager to eat healthier fare, is no exception. A casual Lebanese eatery, Beqaa Café, located there has taken off so promisingly that the owners, Adel and Zalfa Mahshi, opened a second restaurant in the district. They managed to stay open even during the COVID-19 pandemic for takeout and delivery because their patrons couldn't get enough of the always-fresh wholesome dishes.

Assume that you are the business manager for Beqaa Café's owners. They were approached by an independent vendor who wants to use the Beqaa Café name and the delicious secret recipes to distribute frozen Lebanese dishes through grocery and convenience stores. As business manager, you worked with a law firm Hempelmann, Kanji, Rosato & Sturm, LLP. This firm was to draw up contracts regarding the use of Beqaa Café's name and quality standards for the product. When you received the bill from Jayson Hempelmann, you were flabbergasted. It itemized 38 hours of attorney preparation, at $400 per hour, and 55 hours of paralegal assistance, at $100 per hour. The bill also showed $415 for telephone calls, which might be accurate because Mr. Hempelmann had to talk with the owners, who were vacationing in Beirut at the time. You seriously doubt, however, that an experienced attorney would require 38 hours to draw up the contracts in question. When you began checking, you discovered that excellent legal advice could be obtained for $200 an hour.

**YOUR TASK.** Decide what you want to request, and then write a persuasive request to Jayson Hempelmann, Attorney at Law. The address is Hempelmann, Kanji, Rosato & Sturm, LLP, 1111 3rd Avenue, Suite 3000, Seattle, WA 98101. Include an end date and a reason for it.

## 8.11 Persuasive Organizational Message Flowing Upward: Keep the Apples! (L.O. 1, 4)

> E-Mail

Omni Hotels ranks at the top in "Highest in Guest Satisfaction Among Upscale Hotel Chains," according to J. D. Power. The chain operates 60 luxury hotels and resorts in leading business gateways and leisure destinations across North America. From exceptional golf and spa retreats to dynamic business settings, each Omni showcases the local flavor of the destination while featuring four-diamond services. One signature amenity it has offered for years is a bowl of free apples in its lobbies. However, providing apples costs hundreds of thousands of dollars a year. Always seeking out efficiencies, executives are debating whether to cut out apples as a way to save money with minimal impact on guests.

Omni Hotels prides itself on delivering superior service through The Power of One, a service program that provides associates the training and authority to make decisions that exceed the expectations of guests. The entire culture of the hotel creates a positive, supportive environment that rewards associates through the Omni Service Champions program. As an Omni associate, you are disturbed that the hotel is considering giving up its free apples. You hope that executives will find other ways to trim costs, such as purchasing food in smaller amounts to reduce waste or cutting the hours of its lobby cafés.[29]

**YOUR TASK.** In the true sense of The Power of One, you decide to express your views to management. Write a persuasive message to Richard Johnson (*rjohnson@omni.com*), Vice President, Operations, Omni Hotels, 420 Decker Drive, Irving, TX 75062. Should you write a letter or an e-mail? In a separate note to your instructor, explain your rationale for your channel choice and your message strategy.

## 8.12 Persuasive Organizational Message Flowing Upward: A Four-Day Workweek Sounds Divine! (L.O. 1, 4)

> E-Mail    Team    Web

You have heard that some companies and municipalities are switching to a four-day workweek to reduce traffic congestion, air pollution, and stressed employees. Compressing the workweek into four 10-hour days sounds pretty good to you. You would much prefer having Friday free to schedule medical appointments and take care of family business, in addition to leisurely three-day weekends.

As a manager at Nitroglow, a mineral-based skin care products and natural cosmetics company, you are convinced that the company's 200 employees could switch to a four-day workweek with many resulting benefits. For one thing, they would save on gasoline and commute time. You know that many cities and companies have already implemented a four-day workweek with considerable success. You took a quick poll of immediate employees and managers and found that 80 percent thought that a four-day workweek was a good idea. One said, "This would be great! Think of what I could save on babysitting and lunches!"

**YOUR TASK.** With a group of other students, conduct research on the Internet and discuss your findings. What are the advantages of a four-day workweek? What organizations have already tried it? What appeals could be used to persuade management to adopt a four-day workweek? What arguments could be expected, and how would you counter them?

Individually or as a group, prepare a one-page persuasive e-mail or memo addressed to the Nitroglow Management Council. Decide on a goal. Do you want to suggest a pilot study? Should you meet with management to present your ideas? How about starting a four-day workweek immediately?

## 8.13 Persuasive Organizational Message Flowing Upward: Pitching an Idea (L.O. 1, 4)

> E-Mail

In your own work or organization experience, identify a problem for which you have a solution. Should a procedure be altered to improve performance? Would a new or different piece of equipment or software help you perform your work better? Could some tasks be scheduled more efficiently? Are employees being used most effectively? Could customers be better served by changing something? Do you want to work other hours or perform other tasks? Do you deserve a promotion? Do you have a suggestion to improve profitability?

**YOUR TASK.** Once you have identified a situation requiring persuasion, write a memo or an e-mail to your boss or organization head. Use actual names and facts. Employ the concepts and techniques in this chapter to help you convince your boss that your idea should prevail. Include concrete examples, anticipate objections, emphasize reader benefits, and end with a specific action to be taken.

## 8.14 Persuasive Organizational Message Flowing Downward: Saving on Shipping (L.O. 1, 4)

As office manager of a Phoenix footwear and apparel company, write a memo persuading your shipping employees to reduce express delivery fees. Your FedEx and other shipping bills have been sky high, and you feel that staff members are overusing these services to please their favorite distributors. They don't consider less expensive options, such as sharing shipping costs with the recipient.

If shipping staff members plan ahead and allow enough time, they can use UPS or FedEx ground service, which takes three to five days and is much cheaper. Do staff members even consider whether the recipient would mind waiting a few days longer for the merchandise in exchange for prices remaining low? When is overnight shipment justified? You would like to reduce overnight delivery services voluntarily by 50 percent over the next two months. Unless a sizable reduction occurs, the CEO threatens severe restrictions in the future.

**YOUR TASK.** Address your memo to all staff members. What other ways could help employees reduce shipping costs?

## 8.15 Persuasive Organizational Message Flowing Downward: Getting Into Urban Farming (L.O. 1, 4)

> **E-Mail**     **Web**

As employee relations manager of The Clorox Company based in Oakland, California, one of your tasks is to promote Urban Farming, a global organization that has established more than 66,000 gardens in nearly 40 cities. Originating in the Detroit area, Urban Farming is a combined effort of major corporations. You must recruit 12 coworkers who will volunteer to plant gardens and teach community families about healthy eating.

Your task is to find volunteers in your company to start a community garden and in turn recruit other Clorox volunteers. The greater San Francisco area offers more than 5,000 vacant lots to choose from, and 40 gardens already exist in the region. Clorox volunteers will be expected to attend training sessions and then to supervise and instruct participating members of the community. In return, employees will receive two hours of release time per week to work on their Urban Farming projects. The program has been very successful thus far, and the interest in community gardens is strong.

**YOUR TASK.** Learn more about Urban Farming by searching the Web. Then write a persuasive memo or e-mail with convincing appeals that will bring you 12 volunteers to work with Urban Farming.

## 8.16 Persuasive Organizational Message Flowing Downward: Volunteering at NuStar Energy (L.O. 1, 4)

> **E-Mail**

NuStar Energy in San Antonio, Texas, is big on giving back to the community. The liquids terminal and pipeline operator considers volunteering a core value and supports it with up to 60 hours (7.5 days) of paid time per worker per year. NuStar has a pet philanthropic project, the Annual Charity Golf Tournament, the proceeds of which benefit Haven of Hope, a local organization helping the homeless.

As employee relations manager of NuStar Energy, you are tasked with finding employees willing to organize the tournament, obtain sponsorships, create decorations, paint fences and other objects, assemble gift bags, direct the event, coordinate a welcome dinner for more than 1,000 guests, and more. In the last eight years NuStar has helped raise more than $27 million for Haven of Hope.[30] Although volunteers keep getting paid by their employer, participating in activities such as the golf fundraiser is not everyone's cup of tea because workers must pause important projects, or they may perhaps favor other causes. You cannot take them for granted.

**YOUR TASK.** Write a persuasive memo or e-mail with convincing appeals that will attract as many company volunteers as possible to put on and staff the next charity golf tournament.

## 8.17 Can You Spot the AIDA Strategy in Sales Messages? (L.O. 1, 5)

> **E-Mail**

**YOUR TASK.** Select a one- or two-page sales letter or promotional e-mail from a business or a charitable organization received by you or a friend. If you are unable to find a sales message, your instructor may have a collection. Study the sales message and then answer these questions:

1. What techniques capture the reader's attention?
2. Is the opening effective? Explain.
3. What is the central selling point?
4. Does the message use rational, emotional, or a combination of appeals? Explain.
5. What reader benefits are suggested?
6. How does the message build interest in the product or service?
7. How is price handled?
8. How does the message anticipate reader resistance and offer counterarguments?
9. What action is the reader to take? How is the action made easy?
10. What motivators spur the reader to act quickly?

## 8.18 Selling With Audience Benefits (L.O. 1, 5)

> Web

Audience benefits sell. People are more likely to be persuaded when they see a direct or indirect benefit of a product, service, idea, or cause. Features may describe a product or service, but they don't tell a story. To be persuasive, writers must convert features into benefits. They must tell the audience how they can best use the item to benefit from it.

**YOUR TASK.** Online or offline find a product or service that you admire. Be sure to locate a detailed description of the item's unique features. Identify a suitable audience for the product or service. Create a table and in the left column list the item's features. In the right column, convert the features into benefits by matching them to the needs of your target audience.

## 8.19 Sales Message: Conquering Reactance While Promoting an Electric Car (L.O. 1, 5)

> Social Media     Team     Web

Perhaps you have been eying an electric vehicle (EV). Here is your opportunity to conduct minor research to understand your chosen EV's features and then write a direct-mail message to pitch the car to a well-defined audience. Here is information about the Nissan Leaf, for example:

> *The Nissan Leaf is the best-selling electric vehicle of all time; more than 400,000 cars have been delivered worldwide. Nissan completely redesigned the Leaf for the 2018 model year. In 2019 the automaker added a long-range Leaf Plus option. New features were added in 2020.*
>
> *With an MSRP of $31,600, the Leaf offers an attractive price for an EV. It features a generous interior, huge cargo capacity, composed handling, and lively acceleration. However, other compact cars offer more upscale interiors and better predicted reliability ratings.*
>
> *According to the EPA, the standard Leaf delivers 149 miles of range, while the Leaf Plus can travel up to 226 miles. The Leaf Plus starts at an MSRP of $38,200. These aggressive base prices are complemented by attractive lease deals.*
>
> *The Leaf comes standard with an 8-inch touch screen, Android Auto, Apple CarPlay, Bluetooth, and satellite radio. Standard safety features include forward collision warning, automatic emergency braking, blind spot monitoring, rear cross traffic alert, and lane departure warning. The Leaf Plus offers a more powerful electric motor.[31]*

Obviously, no one runs out to buy a car, not even after reading an eloquent sales letter. Purchases of big-ticket items typically take a long time to develop. They involve research and don't happen spontaneously. Before you can start, you will need to analyze your audience and your purpose.

**YOUR TASK.** Choose a currently available electric car that you will pitch in a sales letter to be mailed to an audience of recent college graduates. *Your target group is defined as follows*: gender neutral; mostly unmarried, no kids; late millennial and early Gen Z cohort; primarily an urban dweller with a first job out of college, receiving a steady paycheck and building credit; cares deeply about the environment and takes climate change very seriously.

*Challenges you can expect*: Many members of the ecologically minded age groups you're targeting don't feel the need to own a car. Walkability of their neighborhoods is more important to them. They have public transport options and may bike to work. Even the least expensive electric cars are pricier than their gasoline-burning counterparts. People contemplating electric vehicles experience range anxiety; they fear running out of power, sometimes irrationally so. Gasoline in the United States continues to be a lot cheaper than it is in other developed countries. Tuition debt could be a crushing burden.

*What is your purpose?* The best you can hope for is to build awareness and potentially prompt a social media response to measure the effectiveness of your campaign—for example, liking a page, encouraging a post of some kind, making a TikTok video on a related topic, or similar activities. You have a budget of $2,000 to buy items that might serve as inducements to raffle off among a certain number of those who respond first, create the best submission in a contest, or visit the dealership to test drive the EV.

## 8.20 Sales Message: Organic Produce, Home-Delivered (L.O. 1, 5)

> E-Mail

Many Americans care deeply about what they eat and feed their family. They fear conventional factory farming, wish to be good stewards of the environment, and desire a sustainable lifestyle. Wholesome organic food can increasingly be found on the shelves of mainstream supermarkets. Even big-box stores such as Costco—not just health food stores such as Mother's Market, Sprouts Farmers Market, and Whole Foods Market—are capitalizing on the farm-to-table trend. Weekly farmers' markets selling local produce and fruit are common across America.

Home delivery services have skyrocketed during the COVID-19 pandemic, and most people have gotten used to shopping online even for groceries. Home-bound during lockdown, consumers didn't need to forego healthy fare because they could subscribe to farm-fresh veggies and fruit online to be delivered to their doorstep. Services such as Farmhouse Delivery in Texas, founded by Stephanie Scherzer in 2009, partner with local organic farms to offer customizable boxes with several service and delivery options. Because these co-op-type outfits benefit from economies of scale, their prices, although higher than those of conventional markets, are not excessive. Subscribers can customize their boxes on the Farmhouse Delivery website, or they can let the service select seasonal offerings for them.

The advantages of receiving weekly boxes filled with healthy seasonal produce, groceries, or meal kits are many: they include fresh, delicious taste, wholesome food that's free of herbicides and pesticides, and convenience. In addition, subscribers are supporting small family farms that supply "hyper-local," in-season fruit and veggies instead of buying greens that are flown halfway around the world. Depending on location, subscribers receive their boxes on Tuesday or Wednesday if they order a box by 10 a.m. on Sunday. For Thursday or Friday delivery, orders must be placed by 10 a.m. on Tuesday. New members receive 20 percent off their first order.

**YOUR TASK.** Write a sales message—a letter or an e-mail—for the signature of Founder and Marketer-in-Chief Stephanie Scherzer, Farmhouse Delivery, 9715 Burnet Road, Suite 400, Austin, TX 78758. Provide an enticing but accurate explanation of the service, and invite your reader to subscribe. Focus on audience benefits.

## 8.21 Sales Message: Applying Your Persuasive Skills (L.O. 1, 5)

> E-Mail

Identify a situation in your current job or a previous one in which a sales message is or was needed. Using suggestions from this chapter, write an appropriate sales message that promotes a product or service. Use actual names, information, and examples. If you have no work experience, imagine a business you would like to start, such as data processing, pet grooming, car detailing, cleaning, tutoring, specialty knitting, balloon decorating, delivery service, child or elder care, gardening, or lawn care.

**YOUR TASK.** Write a sales letter or an e-mail marketing message selling your product or service to be distributed to your prospective customers. Be sure to tell them how to respond. You don't need to know HTML or have a Constant Contact account to craft a concise and eye-catching online sales message. Try designing it in Microsoft Word and saving it as a Web page (go to the **File** tab and select **Save as**; then in the **Save as type** line, select **Web page**). Consider adding graphics or photos—either your own or samples borrowed from the Internet. As long as you use them for this assignment and don't publish them online, you are not violating copyright laws.

## 8.22 Phony Online Reviews: Cutting Through "Opinion Spam" (L.O. 1, 5)

A Cornell University study demonstrated that humans are really bad at spotting fake reviews. The study participants might as well have tossed a coin. This is why the researchers used machine learning and developed an algorithm that was said to be 90 percent accurate in flagging fake reviews of Chicago area hotels. The researchers called the tool Review Skeptic and made it available to the public.[32] The other three prominent apps designed to spot fake reviews are Fakespot, ReviewMeta, and The Review Index. Fakespot examines webpages for their trustworthiness and spits out a reliability grade; ReviewMeta works in similar ways but checks only Amazon reviews. The Review Index likewise determines whether a product score has been inflated by fake reviews.[33]

Aside from algorithms, the Cornell researchers identified these three tell-tale signs that a review is probably fake to help shoppers base their buying decisions on more solid evidence: (1) *lacks detail*: offers general praise instead of specifics; (2) *includes more first-person pronouns*: fraudsters resort to a lot of *I* and *me* to appear sincere; and (3) *contains more verbs than nouns*: genuine reviews rely more on nouns than the swindlers who use verbs to write their bogus positive (or negative) stories.[34] In addition, watch out for extremes, either very positive (five-star) or very negative (one-star) reviews that don't provide much detail. If several of them were posted at the same time, they are probably unreliable.[35]

**YOUR TASK.** Visit Amazon, Yelp, Tripadvisor, BestBuy, or Walmart. Look up a product or service you might buy or are interested in. Choose a brand that has a number of reviews and critically examine them using the guidelines provided above. To check your accuracy, run your page through one of the apps designed to spot fakes. Compare your results with those of the review robots. Compile your notes and present your findings to the class or in writing if your instructor directs.

## 8.23 The Coolest of All? Puffery in Advertising (L.O. 1, 5)

> Communication Technology ⟩ Social Media ⟩ Web

As discussed in the Communication Workshop at the end of this chapter, puffery in advertising may be tacky, but it is not illegal. Few of us take claims seriously that shout *the best pastry on the planet, the performance of a lifetime, the most accurate watch in the world, nothing outlasts an Eveready battery, anything is possible after coffee,* or *coldest beer in Colorado.* After all, such exaggerated claims, called hyperbole, cannot be proven and do not fool anyone.

Serious, quantifiable claims, however, must be backed up with evidence or they could mean litigation: "Our chicken has less fat than a hamburger. It's better for you."[36] This bold claim was investigated, and the fried chicken restaurant had to stop using it in its advertising. Yes, the fried chicken had a little less total fat than a hamburger, but it contained more harmful trans fat, sodium, and cholesterol, making it higher in calories—a decidedly unhealthy alternative. As the Federal Trade Commission points out, a restaurant can compare itself to others, but it must tell the truth.

**YOUR TASK.** Look for examples of puffery and find ads that would need to prove their claims—whether online, on TV, on social media, or on the radio. How can you tell hyperbole from deception? Discuss examples in class or in an online forum set up for your class.

## Grammar/Mechanics Checkup 8

## Commas 3

Review the Grammar/Mechanics Handbook Sections 2.10–2.15. Then select the correct responses and record your responses in the space provided. Also record the appropriate Grammar/Mechanics guideline to illustrate the principle involved. When you finish, compare your responses with those provided at the bottom of the page. If your answers differ, study carefully the principles in parentheses.

| | | |
|---|---|---|
| __b__ (2.12) | **EXAMPLE** | a. It was a weak password, not a sophisticated attack that helped hackers breach the company's IT system.<br>b. It was a weak password, not a sophisticated attack, that helped hackers breach the company's IT system. |
| _____ | 1. | a. We are required at this time to check ID and verify eligibility.<br>b. We are required, at this time, to check ID and verify eligibility. |
| _____ | 2. | a. "The best way to predict your future" said David Drucker, "is to create it."<br>b. "The best way to predict your future," said David Drucker, "is to create it." |
| _____ | 3. | a. We purchased the new steel fasteners on July 1 didn't we?<br>b. We purchased the new steel fasteners on July 1, didn't we? |
| _____ | 4. | a. The longer I worked on the project, the more the original idea began to shift and change.<br>b. The longer I worked on the project the more the original idea began to shift and change. |
| _____ | 5. | a. Average retail investors snapped up $6.6 billion in U.S. equities, and remained bullish on stocks with the biggest losses such as, Apple and Tesla.<br>b. Average retail investors snapped up $6.6 billion in U.S. equities and remained bullish on stocks with the biggest losses, such as Apple and Tesla. |

# Review Commas 1, 2, 3

_____ 6. a. We believe, however, that mobile vaccination sites will serve the elderly, and other eligible members of the community better.

b. We believe, however, that mobile vaccination sites will serve the elderly and other eligible members of the community better.

_____ 7. a. As ambitious efforts to vaccinate Americans ramped up doctors suggested that people make appointments prepare to wait in line and rest afterwards.

b. As ambitious efforts to vaccinate Americans ramped up, doctors suggested that people make appointments, prepare to wait in line, and rest afterwards.

_____ 8. a. An influential study of productivity that was conducted by reputable researchers claimed that workers in the United States are more productive than workers in Europe or Japan.

b. An influential study of productivity, that was conducted by reputable researchers, claimed that workers in the United States are more productive than workers in Europe or Japan.

_____ 9. a. Managers of vaccine sites which were created ad hoc carefully considered precautions beyond floor decals, strict masking or capacity limits.

b. Managers of vaccine sites, which were created ad hoc, carefully considered precautions beyond floor decals, strict masking, or capacity limits.

_____ 10. a. As a matter of fact customers who are happy with their return process are 71 percent more likely to become devoted loyal customers.

b. As a matter of fact, customers who are happy with their return process are 71 percent more likely to become devoted, loyal customers.

1. a (2.15) 2. b (2.15) 3. b (2.14a) 4. a (2.12) 5. b (2.15) 6. b (2.03) 7. b (2.06a, 2.01) 8. a (2.15) 9. b (2.06c, 2.01) 10. b (2.03, 2.08)

# Editing Challenge 8

Every chapter provides an editing exercise to fine-tune your grammar and mechanics skills.

The following letter requires edits that address proofreading, grammar, concise wording, punctuation (especially commas), capitalization, word use, and other writing issues. Study the guidelines in the Grammar/Mechanics Handbook (Appendix D), including the lists of Confusing Words and Frequently Misspelled Words.

**YOUR TASK.** Edit the following by (a) inserting corrections in your textbook or on a photocopy using the proofreading marks in Appendix C or (b) downloading the message from **www.cengage.com** and correcting at your computer.

May 9, 2022

Mr. Rick Steves, General Manager
Warren's Lobster House
11 Water Street, Route 1
Kittery, ME 03904

Dear Mr. Steves:

I'm writing this letter to let you know that the waitstaff at the Maine coasts best lobster house would like to bring to your attention a serious problem. Even when us servers have gave good service some customer's leave no tip. Many of us have gotten together and decided to bring the problem and a possible solution to your attention per this letter.

Some of the countries finest restaurants which cater to tour groups and well-off tourists, have been adding a 20 percent automatic charge to the bill for years. All such service charges go to the house and every one is paid wages from that. Other restaurants are also printing gratuity guidelines on checks. In fact American Express now provides a calculation feature on it's terminals so that restaurants can chose the tip levels they want printed. In Europe a service charge of 10-15 percent is often auto calculated, and added to a check.

Us servers are of the opinion that a suggested tip printed on checks would work good here at Warren's Lobster House. We know that we give good service but some customers forget to tip. By printing a suggested tip on the check we remind them so that they won't forget. A printed suggested tip also does the math for them which is a advantage for customer's who are not to good with figures. In addition many of our customers are tourists from Europe. Who don't understand our more generous tipping system.

Printing suggested tips on checks not only helps customers but also proves to the staff that you support them in there goal to recieve decent wages for the hard work they do. A few customers might resist, however these customers can always cross out the printed tip if they wish. If you have any doubts about the plan we could try it for a 6-month period, and monitor customers reactions.

We erge you to begin printing a suggested 20 percent service charge on each customers bill. Our American express terminals are all ready equipt to do this. Please let us know your feelings about this proposal because its a serious concern to us.

Sincerely,

*Darren Fisher*
Darren Fisher
Server, Warren's Lobster House

# Communication Workshop: Ethics

## Legal and Ethical Jeopardy in Sales Messages and Online Reviews

In promoting products and writing sales messages, be careful about the words you use and the claims you make. Watch out for paid reviews. How far can marketers go in praising and selling their products?

- **Puffery.** You might see advertisements that make proclamations such as *We have the perfect car for you!* or *Our coffee will blow your mind!* Called **puffery**, such promotional claims are not taken literally by reasonable consumers. Such subjective statements are accepted as puffery because they puff up, or exaggerate. They are considered **hyperbole**. Surprisingly, this kind of sales exaggeration is not illegal. However, when sales claims consist of objective statements that cannot be verified (*Our cars are the most reliable vehicles in town* they become deceptive advertising.

- **Deceptive advertising.** If you write that your coffee is organic and responsibly sourced, you had better have solid evidence to support the claim. Such a claim goes beyond puffery and requires proof. This is why reputable businesses often seek certification from government or independent oversight organizations. Dietary supplements are regulated as food, not drugs, by the U.S. Food and Drug Administration (FDA). They are not subject to approval or testing as long as they make only general "structure/function claims" about how a nutrient affects the body (e.g., "calcium builds strong bones"). However, manufacturers are not allowed to say their products treat diseases such as Alzheimer's or osteoporosis.[37] Goop, Gwyneth Paltrow's lifestyle company, settled a lawsuit by ten California counties for advertising women's health products without competent and reliable scientific evidence.[38]

- **Celebrities.** The unauthorized use of a celebrity's name, likeness, or nickname is not permitted in sales messages. Celebrity chef Cat Cora won a $565,000 judgment against the Fatbird restaurant group in New York for misusing Cora's name, image, and recipes without compensation.[39] Pop star Ariana Grande sued clothing company Forever 21 seeking $10 million over Instagram posts that in her view depict a "look-alike model" dressed like the singer. The lawsuit alleged that Forever 21 was falsely insinuating an affiliation with Ariana Grande.[40] The so-called right of publicity allows claims when a person's name, likeness, or voice—that is, any identifiable traits—are used for commercial purposes without permission and/or pay.

- **Misleading promises.** Multilevel marketing companies such as Herbalife frequently invite scrutiny. In a $200 million settlement, the Federal Trade Commission (FTC) forced the company to pay back consumers it had wooed with false promises of a lucrative business opportunity and big bucks from retail sales of Herbalife products. Moreover, the FTC forced the company to change its business model of rewarding distributors who buy products and recruit others to join and themselves buy products.[41] On its webpages the FTC debunks preposterous claims in ads for weight-loss supplements, warning consumers of potentially harmful drugs or chemicals not listed on the product label.[42] Devices such as electronic muscle stimulators are overseen by the FDA. The agency not only exposes promises that regular use will produce "rock hard abs" without working out, but it warns about "shocks, burns, bruising, skin irritation, and pain" caused by shoddy, noncompliant devices.[43]

- **Paid online reviews.** The FTC also mandates full disclosure when a merchant and a promoter have a financial relationship. Lumos Labs not only made bogus claims about the benefits of its Lumosity brain-training games, but the company also failed to disclose that it had used testimonials from customers who had received iPads, free trips, and other incentives for their reviews.[44] Skin-care brand Sunday Riley recently settled with the FTC for writing fake Sephora reviews for two years. The company got off with a warning.[45] The FTC also sued the marketer of the garcinia cambogia weight-loss supplement for using fake paid reviews to maintain a high Amazon rating and boost its sales. Fake reviews shake the public's trust. "People rely on reviews when they're shopping online," Andrew Smith, director of the FTC's Bureau of Consumer Protection, said. "When a company buys fake reviews to inflate its Amazon rating, it hurts both shoppers and companies that play by the rules."[46]

**CAREER APPLICATION.** Bring to class at least three promotional e-mails, sales letters, social media posts, or advertisements that may represent issues described here. What examples of puffery can you identify? Are claims substantiated by reliable evidence? What proof is offered? Do any of your examples include names, images, or nicknames of celebrities? How likely is it that the celebrity authorized this use? Have you ever received unwanted merchandise as part of a sales campaign? What were you expected to do with it?

# Business Reports and Proposals— Best Practices

# 4

Gaudi Lab/Shutterstock.com

# Informal Reports

## Learning Outcomes

After studying this chapter, you should be able to do the following:

**1** Define informational and analytical report functions, strategies, and writing styles.

**2** Describe typical report formats and effective report headings.

**3** Explain the report writing process starting with defining the problem and collecting data.

**4** Write short informational reports that describe routine tasks.

**5** Compose short analytical reports that solve business problems.

Marvent/Shutterstock.com

## 9-1 Writing Reports in the Digital Age

Nearly all businesses create reports. Efficient reporting plays a critical role in helping digital age organizations sift through huge amounts of data to make decisions. Whether a company decides to launch a new product, expand into new markets, reduce expenses, improve customer service, or increase its social media presence, decisions are usually based on information submitted in reports. Routine reports keep managers informed about work in progress. Focused, in-depth reports help managers analyze the challenges they face before recommending solutions.

**Business reports** range widely in length, purpose, and delivery mode. Some are short, informal bulleted lists with status updates. Others are formal 100-page financial

**WORKPLACE IN FOCUS**

Never Settle Media/Shutterstock.com

Suddenly electric scooters multiplied on sidewalks and street corners across the country. Bird and Lime, two companies pushing the shareable dockless vehicles, seemingly had hit upon a potentially huge market. Electric scooters could transform urban transportation. But had the investors done the research necessary to ensure acceptance and profitability? In many cities, vandals, pedestrians, and infuriated merchants rebelled by destroying unwanted scooters littering walkways. Scooter companies were accused of dumping the vehicles while ignoring local regulations. Although the companies may become profitable, some researchers expect to see many go bankrupt.[1] What kinds of primary and secondary research could have prevented the backlash and potential bankruptcy?

forecasts. Routine reports may be generated weekly or monthly, whereas focused reports cover specific problems or situations. Report findings may be presented orally in a meeting or shared online. Reports today are delivered digitally in e-mail messages, PDF (portable document format) files, websites, or slide decks. Report files can be accessed on a company's intranet or saved on cloud servers off-site.

This chapter examines the functions, strategies, writing styles, and formats of typical business reports. It also introduces the report-writing process and discusses methods of collecting, documenting, and illustrating data. Some reports provide information only; others analyze and make recommendations. Although reports vary greatly in length, content, form, and formality level, they all have one or more of the following purposes: *to convey information, answer questions,* and *solve problems.*

**LEARNING OUTCOME 1**
Define informational and analytical report functions, strategies, and writing styles.

## 9-1a Basic Report Functions

In terms of what they do, most reports fit into one of two broad categories: informational reports and analytical reports.

**Informational Reports.** **Informational reports** present data without analysis or recommendations. For such reports, writers collect and organize facts, but they do not analyze the facts for readers. A trip report describing an employee's visit to a trade show, for example, simply provides factual information. Weekly bulleted status reports distributed by e-mail to a team summarize the activities of each group member and are shared with supervisors. Other reports that present information without analysis include monthly sales reports, progress reports, and government compliance reports.

**Analytical Reports.** In addition to reporting data and findings, **analytical reports** provide analysis and conclusions. If requested, writers also supply recommendations. Analytical reports may intend to persuade readers to act or change their beliefs. For example, if you were writing a yardstick report that compares several potential manufacturing locations for a new automobile plant, you would compare the locations using the same criteria and then provide a recommendation. Other reports that provide recommendations are feasibility studies (e.g., for expansion opportunities) and justification reports (e.g., for buying equipment or changing procedures).

## 9-1b Organizational Strategies

Like other business messages, reports may be organized directly or indirectly. The reader's anticipated reaction and the content of a report determine its organizational strategy, as illustrated in **Figure 9.1**. In long reports, such as corporate annual reports, some parts may be organized directly whereas other parts are arranged indirectly.

Analytical reports may also be organized directly, especially when readers are supportive of or familiar with the topic. Many busy executives prefer this strategy because it gives them the results of the report immediately. They don't have to spend time wading through the facts, findings, discussion, and analyses to get to the two items they are most interested in—the conclusions and recommendations.

**Direct Strategy.** When you place the purpose for writing close to the beginning of a report, the organizational strategy is direct. Informational reports, such as the safety compliance report shown in **Model Document 9.1**, are usually arranged directly. They open with an introduction, which is followed by the facts and a summary. In Model Document 9.1 the writer sends this report to respond to a request for information about complying with job safety procedures. The report opens with an introduction followed by a bulleted list of compliance data. The report ends with a summary and a forward look.

**Indirect Strategy.** The organizational strategy is indirect when the conclusions and recommendations, if requested, appear at the end of the report. Such reports usually begin with an introduction or description of the problem, followed by facts and explanations. They end with conclusions and recommendations. This strategy is helpful when readers are unfamiliar with the problem or when they must be persuaded. When readers may be disappointed in or hostile toward the report's findings, an indirect strategy works best. The writer is more likely to retain the reader's interest by first explaining, justifying, and analyzing the facts and then making recommendations. This

**Figure 9.1 Audience Analysis and Report Organization**

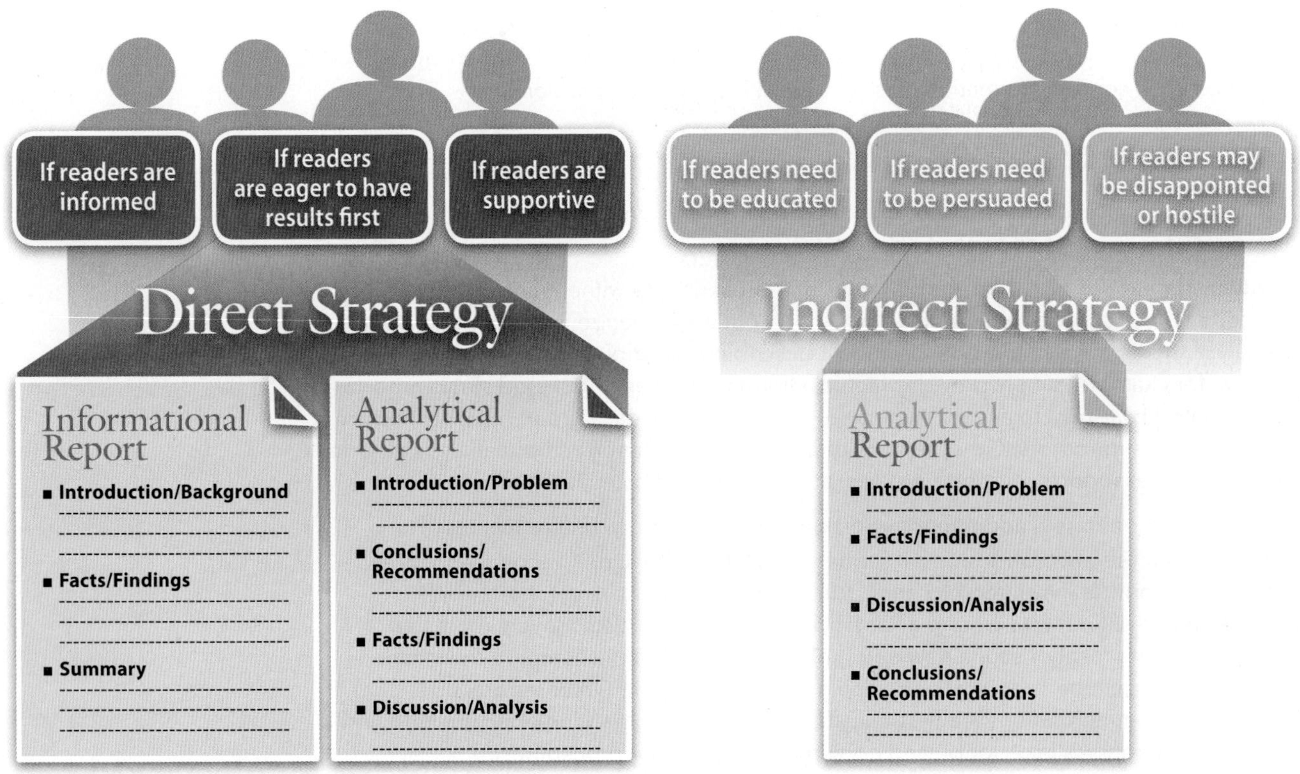

If readers are informed

If readers are eager to have results first

If readers are supportive

If readers need to be educated

If readers need to be persuaded

If readers may be disappointed or hostile

## Direct Strategy

### Informational Report

- **Introduction/Background**
- **Facts/Findings**
- **Summary**

### Analytical Report

- **Introduction/Problem**
- **Conclusions/Recommendations**
- **Facts/Findings**
- **Discussion/Analysis**

## Indirect Strategy

### Analytical Report

- **Introduction/Problem**
- **Facts/Findings**
- **Discussion/Analysis**
- **Conclusions/Recommendations**

**Model Document 9.1** Informational Safety Compliance Report—Letter Format

---

**ARKEMA MANUFACTURING CO.**
8937 WEST MARLBOROUGH AVENUE
WEST HEMPSTEAD, NY 11552

August 10, 2022

Mr. Tyson Roth
New York Public Employee Safety Bureau
401 New Karner Road, Suite 300
Albany, NY 12205

Dear Mr. Roth:

Subject: Job Safety and Standard Operating Procedures at Arkema Manufacturing Co.

Here is the report you requested regarding our job safety and operating procedures. As you suggested, we followed your instructions to outline plant safety responsibilities for all personnel. This report, along with diagrams and manuals, is now available at each workstation. It has also been circulated to all employees and is posted on all department bulletin boards.

As instructed, we hired a firm to translate our safety manuals into the languages spoken on the plant floor. In addition, we are working on a plan to ensure regular updating of the manuals. Specific procedures are as follows:

- The binding manager will stand in front of the department near the binding equipment to observe employees operating the equipment and working near the machinery. The manager will direct employees out the employee entrance or through the main office, in case of a fire.

- The fabrication manager will be responsible for the proper shutdown of all equipment before shifts end. Press operators and injection operators will perform shutdown of ovens and extruders.

- The production supervisor will go to the junction at the binding and finishing cells to ensure that (a) work areas are clutter free, (b) proper attire is worn, and (c) safety equipment is working properly.

- In the supplies room, the forklift operator on each shift will inspect the forklift for any visible damage.

- In the assembly area, the shift supervisor will ensure that employees are directed out of the building through the east hallway.

We hope these procedures are satisfactory since we seek the utmost safety for our employees. Should you have any questions or further suggestions, please call me at 518-464-3053 or send an e-mail to tspears@arkemamfg.com. With these measures now in place, we trust that we will pass the September inspection with flying colors.

Sincerely,

*Tiara Spears*

Tiara Spears
Vice President, Operations

**Annotations (left margin):**
- Includes subject line for quick comprehension
- Organizes information into bulleted segments to concisely present an overview of separate safety concerns

**Annotations (right margin):**
- Uses letterhead stationery for informal report addressed to an outsider
- Presents facts without analysis or recommendations
- Closes politely with contact information and a look forward

**Tips for Writing Letter Reports**
- Use letter format for short informal reports sent to outsiders.
- Organize the report into an introduction, body, and summary closing.
- Single-space the body.
- Double-space between paragraphs.
- Create side margins of 1 to 1.25 inches.

---

strategy also seems most rational to readers because it follows the normal thought process: problem, alternatives (facts), solution.

## 9-1c Informal and Formal Writing Styles

Like other business messages, reports can range from informal to formal depending on their purpose, audience, and setting. An **informal writing style** is conversational. It is appropriate for familiar audiences and noncontroversial topics. Characterized by a

**Figure 9.2** Report-Writing Styles

| | INFORMAL WRITING STYLE | FORMAL WRITING STYLE |
|---|---|---|
| **Appropriate Use** | • Short, routine reports<br>• Reports for familiar audiences<br>• Noncontroversial reports<br>• Internal use reports<br>• Internal announcements and invitations | • Lengthy, formal reports and proposals<br>• Research studies<br>• Controversial or complex reports<br>• External use reports<br>• Formal invitations |
| **Overall Effect** | • Friendly tone<br>• Relationship building<br>• Casual | • Objectivity and accuracy<br>• Sense of professional distance between writer and reader |
| **Writing Style Characteristics** | • Use of first-person pronouns *(I, we, me, my, us, our)*<br>• Use of contractions *(can't, don't)*<br>• Emphasis on active-voice verbs *(I conducted the study)*<br>• Shorter sentences<br>• Familiar words<br>• Conversational language | • Use of third person *(the researcher, the writer)* (depends on the circumstances)<br>• Absence of contractions *(cannot, do not)*<br>• Use of passive-voice verbs *(the study was conducted)*<br>• Professional, respectful language<br>• Absence of humor and figures of speech<br>• Elimination of "editorializing" (author's opinions and perceptions) |

friendly tone, first-person pronouns, and shorter sentences, an informal writing style is often used for short internal business reports.

A **formal writing style** is characterized by objectivity, authority, and impartiality. It is appropriate for proposals and long research reports. A report from a consultant informing executives about the feasibility of moving to a new location would tend to be formal.

An office worker once called a grammar hotline service with this problem: "We've just sent a report to our headquarters, and it was returned with this comment, 'Put it in the third person.' What do they mean?" The hotline experts explained that management apparently wanted a more formal writing style, using third-person constructions (*the company* or *the researcher* instead of *we* and *I*). **Figure 9.2**, which compares the characteristics of formal and informal report-writing styles, can help you decide which style is appropriate for your reports. Formal reports writers today increasingly use contractions and active-voice verbs. They try to avoid awkward third-person references to themselves as *the researchers* or *the authors* because it sounds stilted and outdated.

## 9-2 Formats and Heading Levels

**LEARNING OUTCOME 2**
Describe typical report formats and effective headings.

The overall design of a formatted report should be visually appealing and professional looking. Reports in the conventional workplace may be presented in a number of formats. Their design should include a hierarchy of meaningful headings that highlight major points, allowing readers to see the flow of ideas. Many corporations use templates or reporting software to standardize the look of their report in terms of formats and heading levels.

## 9-2a  Typical Report Formats

Reporting in organizations remains a key need in business today. Many types of reports coexist and vary greatly by sector or industry. The format of a report depends on its length, topic, audience, and purpose. After considering these elements, you will probably choose from among the following formats.

**Digital Formats and PDF Files.** Writers routinely save and distribute reports as **portable document format (PDF)** files. This file type, invented by Adobe, condenses documents while preserving the formatting and graphics. A report created with Microsoft Word, Excel, or PowerPoint can easily be saved as a PDF file. A PDF report might include links to external websites, a nice advantage over printed reports. Web-based reports may feature engaging multimedia effects, such as interactive charts and video.

**Digital Slide Decks.** Many business writers deliver their report information in a digital slideshow, also called a **slide deck**. These slides can be sent by e-mail, posted on the Web, or accessed on a company intranet. When used in reporting, slide decks may have more text than typical presentation slides. Photographs, tables, charts, and other visuals make slide decks more inviting to read than print pages of dense report text. Not surprisingly, communicators in marketing, technology, media, entertainment, and consulting are fond of using slide deck reports to summarize their statistics and other findings.

**Figure 9.3** illustrates a Facebook slide deck reporting on topics and trends recently gaining momentum. The slides present the key elements of a report: introduction,

### Figure 9.3  Facebook Slide Deck

Facebook presents the culmination of a year's research and insights in a visually appealing slide deck. The report validates the findings of its research tracking conversations of its users in six categories: Art and Design, Beauty and Fashion, Entertainment, Food and Drink, Mind and Body, and Travel and Leisure. The slide deck follows a typical report format with a title page, table of contents, introduction, executive letter, methodology, and sections devoted to findings including statistics and charts—all properly footnoted.

methodology, concise descriptions, statistics, and even footnotes. From the myriad conversations of Facebook users, this report documents developments in people's attitudes, expectations, and behaviors. This valuable information is of particular interest to Facebook advertisers as well as to other marketers looking for future consumer behavior.

**Infographics.** **Infographics**, short for information graphics, are visual representations of data or information. They can display complex information quickly and clearly, and they are easier to understand than written text. Infographics are also affordable and effortlessly shared on social media platforms. In fact, good infographics can go viral when viewers embed and spread the word about them in their blogs and on their social media networks. Infographics can tell compelling stories that help all types of businesses attract and inform consumers.

**E-Mail and Memo Formats.** Many reports are attached to e-mails, posted online, or, if short, embedded in the body of e-mails. For short informal reports that stay within organizations, the **memo format** may still be appropriate. Memo reports begin with essential background information, using standard headings: *Date, To, From,* and *Subject.* Memo reports differ from regular memos in length, use of headings, and deliberate organization. Today, memo reports are rarely distributed in hard copy; more likely they are shared electronically as PDF files.

**Forms and Templates.** Office workers use digital forms that are usually made available on the company intranet or the Internet. Such electronic **templates** are suitable for repetitive data, such as monthly sales reports, performance appraisals, merchandise inventories, and personnel and financial reports. Employees can customize and fill in the templates and forms. Then they distribute them electronically or print them. Using standardized formats and headings saves a writer time and ensures that all necessary information is included.

**Letter Format.** The **letter format** for short informal reports (usually eight or fewer pages) addressed outside an organization can still be found in government agencies, real estate, and accounting firms. Prepared on office stationery, a letter report contains a date, inside address, salutation, and complimentary close, as shown earlier in Model Document 9.1. Although they may carry information similar to that found in correspondence, letter reports usually are longer and show more careful organization than typical letters. They also may include headings to guide the reader through the content and may come with attachments. Like memo reports, letter reports are also likely to be sent to clients as PDF files.

**Manuscript Format.** For longer, more formal reports, use the **manuscript format**. These reports are usually printed on plain paper without letterhead or memo header. They begin with a title followed by systematically displayed headings and subheadings. You will see examples of proposals and formal reports using the manuscript format in Chapter 10.

## 9-2b Effective Report Headings

Descriptive headings are structural cues that assist readers in comprehending the organization of a report. They highlight major ideas, allowing busy readers to see the big picture at a glance. Moreover, headings provide resting points for the mind and for the eye, breaking up large chunks of text into manageable and visually inviting segments.

Report writers may use functional or talking headings, examples of which are shown in **Figure 9.4**. **Functional headings** are one- or two-word labels that show the outline of a report but provide little insight about the contents. Functional headings are useful for routine reports. By keeping the headings general, experienced writers hope to minimize reader opposition or reaction to controversial subjects.

**Figure 9.4** Distinguishing Among Functional, Talking, and Combination Headings

| Functional Headings | Talking Headings | Combination Headings |
|---|---|---|
| • Background | • More Colleges Offer Sustainability Courses | • Introduction: Students Increasingly Proactive About Sustainability |
| • Findings | • Survey Shows Support for Campus Recycling Program | • Sustainability Recommendation: Switching to Drought-Resistant Landscaping |
| • Personnel | | |
| • Production Costs | | |

**Talking headings** provide more information and spark interest. Unless carefully written, however, talking headings can fail to reveal the organization of a report. With some planning, though, headings can combine the best attributes of both functional and talking, as Figure 9.4 shows. The best strategy for creating helpful talking headings is to write a few paragraphs first and then generate a talking heading that covers those paragraphs. To create the most effective report headings, follow a few basic guidelines:

- **Use logical heading levels**. Some reports have one level of heading and others may have three. The position and format of a heading indicate its level of importance and relationship to other points. **Model Document 9.2** illustrates and discusses a commonly used heading format for business reports. Reports are easier to follow when they use no more than three heading levels.

- **Capitalize and emphasize carefully**. Most writers use all capital letters (without underlines) for main titles, such as report, chapter, and unit titles. For first- and second-level headings, they capitalize only the first letter of main words such as nouns, verbs, adjectives, adverbs, names, and so on. Do not capitalize articles (*a, an, the*), conjunctions (*and, but, or, nor*), and prepositions with three or fewer letters (*in, to, by, for*) unless they are the first or last words in the heading. For additional emphasis, headings generally appear in bold font, as shown in Model Document 9.2.

- **Balance headings within levels**. Although it may not be always possible, try to create headings that are grammatically similar or parallel, within the same level. For example, *Developing Product Teams* and *Presenting Plan to Management* are balanced, parallel headings; they both begin with an action word ending in *-ing*. *Development of Product Teams* and *Presenting Plan to Management* are not parallel headings.

- **For short reports use one or two heading levels**. Many business reports contain only one or two levels of headings. For such reports, use first-level headings (centered, bolded) and, if needed, second-level headings (flush left, bolded). See Model Document 9.2.

- **Include at least one heading per report page, but don't end the page with a stand-alone heading**. Headings increase the readability and add visual appeal to report pages. Use at least one heading per page to break up blocks of text. If a heading at the bottom of a page gets separated from the text that follows, move that heading to the top of the following page.

- **Apply punctuation correctly**. Omit end punctuation in first- and second-level headings. End punctuation is required in third-level headings because they are capitalized and punctuated like sentences. Proper nouns (names) are capitalized in third-level headings as they would in a sentence.

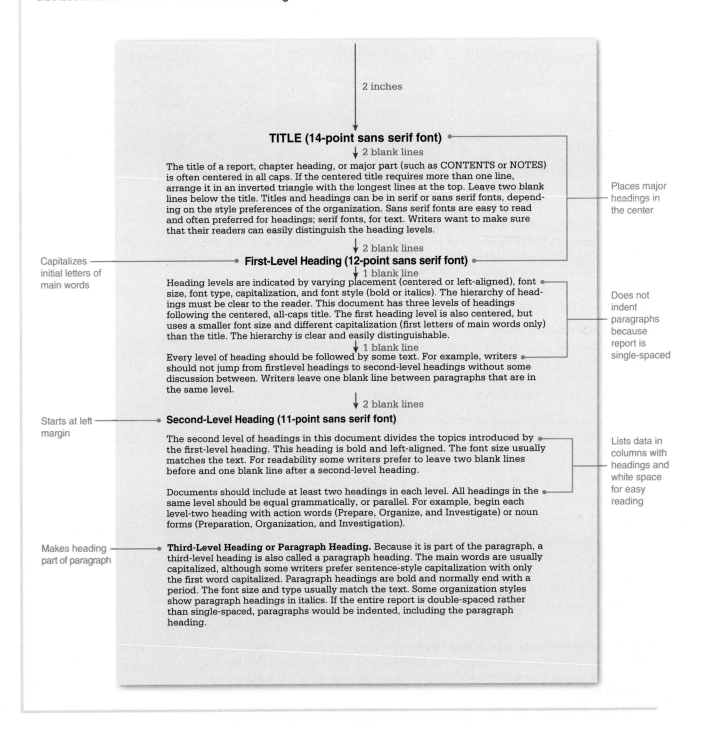

2 inches

**TITLE (14-point sans serif font)** ●

↓ 2 blank lines

The title of a report, chapter heading, or major part (such as CONTENTS or NOTES) is often centered in all caps. If the centered title requires more than one line, arrange it in an inverted triangle with the longest lines at the top. Leave two blank lines below the title. Titles and headings can be in serif or sans serif fonts, depending on the style preferences of the organization. Sans serif fonts are easy to read and often preferred for headings; serif fonts, for text. Writers want to make sure that their readers can easily distinguish the heading levels.

↓ 2 blank lines

**First-Level Heading (12-point sans serif font)** ●

↓ 1 blank line

Heading levels are indicated by varying placement (centered or left-aligned), font size, font type, capitalization, and font style (bold or italics). The hierarchy of headings must be clear to the reader. This document has three levels of headings following the centered, all-caps title. The first heading level is also centered, but uses a smaller font size and different capitalization (first letters of main words only) than the title. The hierarchy is clear and easily distinguishable.

↓ 1 blank line

Every level of heading should be followed by some text. For example, writers should not jump from firstlevel headings to second-level headings without some discussion between. Writers leave one blank line between paragraphs that are in the same level.

↓ 2 blank lines

**Second-Level Heading (11-point sans serif font)**

The second level of headings in this document divides the topics introduced by the first-level heading. This heading is bold and left-aligned. The font size usually matches the text. For readability some writers prefer to leave two blank lines before and one blank line after a second-level heading.

Documents should include at least two headings in each level. All headings in the same level should be equal grammatically, or parallel. For example, begin each level-two heading with action words (Prepare, Organize, and Investigate) or noun forms (Preparation, Organization, and Investigation).

**Third-Level Heading or Paragraph Heading.** Because it is part of the paragraph, a third-level heading is also called a paragraph heading. The main words are usually capitalized, although some writers prefer sentence-style capitalization with only the first word capitalized. Paragraph headings are bold and normally end with a period. The font size and type usually match the text. Some organization styles show paragraph headings in italics. If the entire report is double-spaced rather than single-spaced, paragraphs would be indented, including the paragraph heading.

Annotations:
- Capitalizes initial letters of main words
- Starts at left margin
- Makes heading part of paragraph
- Places major headings in the center
- Does not indent paragraphs because report is single-spaced
- Lists data in columns with headings and white space for easy reading

- **Keep headings short but clear.** One-word headings are emphatic but not always clear. For example, the heading *Budget* does not adequately describe figures for a summer project involving student interns for a Texas oil company. A better heading would be *OilGrove's Internship Program Budget*. Keep your headings brief (no more than eight words), but make them meaningful and understandable. Clarity is more important than brevity. Experiment with headings that concisely tell who, what, when, where, and why.

## 9-3 Analyzing the Problem, Defining the Purpose, and Collecting Data

Because business reports are systematic attempts to compile data, answer questions, and solve problems, you'll want to be methodical in achieving those goals. Following are guidelines that will help you identify the report problem and purpose as well as gather relevant data.

**LEARNING OUTCOME 3**

Explain the report writing process starting with defining the problem and collecting data.

### 9-3a Determine the Problem and Purpose

The first step in writing a report is clearly understanding the problem or assignment. Preparing a written **problem statement** helps clarify the task. Suppose a pharmaceutical company wants to investigate the problem of high transportation costs for its sales representatives. Some sales reps visit clients using company-leased cars; others drive their own cars and are reimbursed for expenses. The leasing agreements for 12 cars expire in three months. The company wants to investigate the transportation choices and report the findings before the leases are renewed. The following problem statement helps clarify the reason for the report:

> **Problem statement:** *The leases on all company cars will expire in three months. The company must decide whether to renew them or develop a new policy regarding transportation for sales reps. Expenses and reimbursement paperwork for employee-owned cars seems excessive.*

A statement of purpose further defines the report's purpose and scope. To begin, develop questions that help clarify the purpose: Is the problem that the company spends too much money on leased vehicles? Should the company invest in owning a fleet of cars instead? Should the company gather current data on reimbursement costs for reps driving personal cars? Will the report writers evaluate the data and recommend a course of action? Should the sales reps' reactions be considered? Then write a statement of purpose that answers the questions.

> **Statement of purpose:** *To recommend a plan that provides sales reps with cars to be used in their calls. The report will compare costs for three plans: outright ownership, leasing, and compensation for employee-owned cars. Data will include the sales reps' reactions to each plan.*

Preparing a written **purpose statement** is a good idea because it defines the focus of a report and provides a standard that keeps the project on target. In writing useful purpose statements, choose action verbs telling what you intend to do: *analyze, choose, investigate, compare, justify, evaluate, explain, establish, determine,* and so on. Notice that the preceding purpose statement uses the action verbs *recommend* and *compare.*

Some reports require only a simple statement of purpose (e.g., *to investigate expanded teller hours, to select a manager from among four candidates, to describe the position of accounts supervisor*). Many assignments, though, require expanded purpose statements.

### 9-3b Collect Information From Secondary and Primary Sources

One of the most important steps in writing a report is that of collecting information (research). A good report is based on solid, accurate, verifiable facts. This factual information falls into two broad categories: primary and secondary. **Primary data** result from firsthand experience and observation. **Secondary data** come from reading what others have experienced or observed and recorded. Typical sources of both primary and secondary factual information for informal reports are (a) company records, (b) printed material, (c) electronic resources, (d) observation, (e) surveys and questionnaires, and (f) interviews.

**Company Records.** Many business reports begin with an analysis of company records and files. These records reveal past performance and methods used to solve previous problems. You can collect pertinent facts that will help determine a course of action.

**Printed Material.** Although some print resources are also available online, libraries should not be overlooked as an excellent source for many types of print resources. Some information in libraries is available only in print. Print sources include books, newspapers, and periodicals, such as magazines and journals.

**Digital Resources.** An extensive source of current and historical information is available from digital resources. From a computer or mobile device, you can access information provided by government sites, news media, periodicals, nonprofits, and businesses. As a student, you most likely have access to several business-related library databases, to which your college or university may subscribe. For short informal reports, you will probably gather most of your data from digital resources. Chapter 10 provides more detailed suggestions about digital resources and Web search tools.

**Observation.** In the absence of secondary sources, a primary source of data for many problems comes from personal observation and experience. For example, if you were writing a report on the need for a comprehensive policy on the use of social media, you might observe employees to see whether they are checking their social networks during the workday or sharing potentially damaging company information on social media. Observation might yield incomplete results, but it is nonetheless a valid form of data collection.

**Surveys and Questionnaires.** When a report requires current user or customer feedback, you can collect the data efficiently and economically by using surveys and questionnaires. This is another primary source of information. For example, if you were part of a committee investigating the success of an employee carpooling program, you might gather data by asking the employees themselves to fill out questionnaires. See Chapter 10 for more information about surveys.

**Interviews.** Talking with individuals directly concerned with the problem produces excellent firsthand information if published sources are not available. For example, if you would like to find ways to improve the hiring process of your company, you might interview your company's human resources director or several of the department hiring managers for the most accurate and relevant information. Interviews allow you to gather data from experts in their fields.

**WORKPLACE IN FOCUS**

Christopher Penler/Shutterstock.com

Music-streaming service Spotify is part of the industry trend of providing both free and paid access to a huge inventory of music. Unlike Internet radio app Pandora, however, Spotify allows listeners to choose an unlimited number of songs to share with friends or to listen to at any time. The Swedish-based service partners with broadcasters, festivals, blogs, and nongovernmental organizations to bring music to their constituents. As a public company, Spotify must issue regular financial reports. Its July 2019 quarterly report, for example, includes information about user data, financial metrics, and new products and services.[3] What types of information would business communicators need to include in these reports?

# 9-4 **Preparing Short Informational Reports**

Now that you are familiar with the basics of gathering data, you are ready to organize that information into short informational or analytical reports. Informational reports often describe periodic, recurring activities (such as monthly sales or weekly customer calls) as well as situational, nonrecurring events (such as trips, conferences, and special projects). Short informational reports may include safety compliance reports, such as that illustrated in Model Document 9.1, and summaries of longer publications. Most informational reports have one thing in common: a neutral or receptive audience. The readers of informational reports do not need to be persuaded; they simply need to be informed.

As an entry-level or middle-management employee, you can expect to write many informational reports. These reports generally deliver nonsensitive data and are therefore written directly. Although the writing style is usually conversational and informal, the report contents must be clear to all readers. All headings, lists, and graphics should help readers grasp major ideas immediately.

The principles of conciseness, clarity, courtesy, and correctness discussed in earlier chapters apply to report writing as well. Your ability to write effective reports can boost your visibility in a business organization and result in advancement.

## 9-4a Trip, Convention, and Conference Reports

Employees traveling on business to conventions and conferences typically must submit **trip reports**, also referred to as **conference reports**, when they return. Organizations want to know that their money was well spent in funding the travel. These reports often inform management about business trends, new procedures, innovative equipment, legal requirements, or other information that would affect their products, operations, and service.

The hardest parts of writing these reports are selecting the most relevant material and organizing it coherently. Generally, it is best not to use chronological sequencing (*in the morning we did X, at lunch we heard Y, and in the afternoon we did Z*). Instead, you should focus on three to five topics in which your reader will be interested. These items become the body of the report. Then simply add an introduction and a closing, and your report is organized. Here is a general outline for trip, conference, and convention reports:

- Begin by identifying the event (name, date, and location) and previewing the topics that were discussed.

- In the body summarize the three to five main topics that might benefit the reader. Use headings and bullets to enhance readability.

- Close by expressing appreciation, suggesting action to be taken, or synthesizing the value of the trip or event.

- Itemize your expenses, if requested, on a separate sheet.

Adelyn Richards was encouraged by her boss Dan Preston to attend a two-day conference in Tucson, Arizona, focused on social marketing. Adelyn's report, shown in **Model Document 9.3**, emphasizes two main points that could help her company use social media to improve customer service.

## 9-4b Progress/Interim Reports

Continuing projects often require **progress reports**, also known as **interim reports**, to describe their status. These reports may be external (notifying customers about the headway of their projects) or internal (informing management of the status of activities). Progress reports typically follow this pattern of development:

- In the opening specify the purpose and nature of the project.

**Model Document 9.3   Conference Report—Memo Format**

**Date:**     March 16, 2022

**To:**       Dan Preston, Marketing Manager

**From:**     Adelyn Richards, Marketing Specialist AR

*SmartBaud*

**Subject:** Conference on Social Customer Service—February 2022

I attended the Social Customer Service conference in Tucson, Arizona, on
February 24–25, sponsored by Social Partners, Inc. The conference emphasized
the importance of delivering excellent customer service in social spaces (social
media gathering places). As we prepare to increase our social media involvement, this report summarizes two topics that would benefit our employees: (a)
the rising expectations of customers in social media networks, and (b) the role
of customer service specialists.

*Identifies the topic and previews the report's contents*

**Customer Expectations of Social Marketers**

Conference presenters emphasized the following customer service expectations:
• Customers expect social business connections to be helpful and friendly
  —always.
• Online customers expect that you're listening and will remember what they
  said to you last time.
• Before buying, customers are powerfully influenced by user reviews,
  Facebook comments, Twitter feeds, and forum messages.
• Customers expect honest and prompt responses when they have complaints.

*Sets off major topics with bold headings in the same font*

**The Role of Social Marketers**

Whether a company hires a social media management service or uses in-house
personnel, the responsibilities of social customer service specialists are the same:
• Monitor customer feedback and respond promptly to questions and complaints.
• Check social media platforms for mention of their businesses. Send text
  message responses to the right people immediately.
• Examine the company's Facebook activity and create dialogue on Twitter.
• When problems occur, own up to them and explain publicly what you're doing
  to make things right.

*Covers the main ideas that will benefit the reader*

**Conference Highlights**

Companies realize the importance of communicating with customers promptly
and personally, especially in social spaces. Since our company is heavily
invested in social media platforms, the conference topics seemed especially
relevant. I would be happy to share highlights from the conference at our next
management meeting. Let me know what date and time work best.

*Concludes with an offer to share information*

---

**Tips for Formatting Memo Reports**
• Use memo stationery or plain paper with "Memorandum"
  centered 1 or 2 inches from the top.
• Leave side margins of 1 to 1.25 inches.
• If distributing hard copies, sign your initials on the *From line*.
• Use an informal, conversational style.
• Include headings and bulleted lists to enhance readability.
• Consider sending long memo reports as an e-mail attachment.

---

■ Provide background information if the audience requires filling in.

■ Describe the work completed so far.

■ Explain the work currently in progress, including personnel involved, activities,
  methods, and locations.

- Describe current and potential problems and possible remedies.

- In the closing discuss future activities and provide the expected completion date.

As a location manager for Cinefil Productions, Lexie Barnes frequently writes progress reports, such as the one shown in **Model Document 9.4**. Producers want to know what she is doing, and a phone call does not provide a permanent record.

## Model Document 9.4 Progress Report

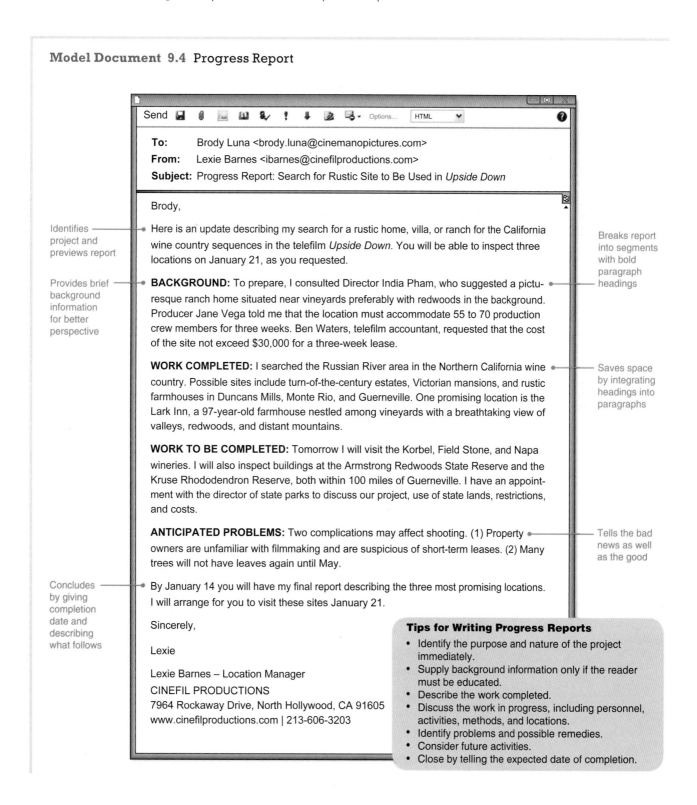

Identifies project and previews report

Provides brief background information for better perspective

Concludes by giving completion date and describing what follows

Breaks report into segments with bold paragraph headings

Saves space by integrating headings into paragraphs

Tells the bad news as well as the good

**To:** Brody Luna <brody.luna@cinemanopictures.com>
**From:** Lexie Barnes <ibarnes@cinefilproductions.com>
**Subject:** Progress Report: Search for Rustic Site to Be Used in *Upside Down*

Brody,

Here is an update describing my search for a rustic home, villa, or ranch for the California wine country sequences in the telefilm *Upside Down*. You will be able to inspect three locations on January 21, as you requested.

**BACKGROUND:** To prepare, I consulted Director India Pham, who suggested a picturesque ranch home situated near vineyards preferably with redwoods in the background. Producer Jane Vega told me that the location must accommodate 55 to 70 production crew members for three weeks. Ben Waters, telefilm accountant, requested that the cost of the site not exceed $30,000 for a three-week lease.

**WORK COMPLETED:** I searched the Russian River area in the Northern California wine country. Possible sites include turn-of-the-century estates, Victorian mansions, and rustic farmhouses in Duncans Mills, Monte Rio, and Guerneville. One promising location is the Lark Inn, a 97-year-old farmhouse nestled among vineyards with a breathtaking view of valleys, redwoods, and distant mountains.

**WORK TO BE COMPLETED:** Tomorrow I will visit the Korbel, Field Stone, and Napa wineries. I will also inspect buildings at the Armstrong Redwoods State Reserve and the Kruse Rhododendron Reserve, both within 100 miles of Guerneville. I have an appointment with the director of state parks to discuss our project, use of state lands, restrictions, and costs.

**ANTICIPATED PROBLEMS:** Two complications may affect shooting. (1) Property owners are unfamiliar with filmmaking and are suspicious of short-term leases. (2) Many trees will not have leaves again until May.

By January 14 you will have my final report describing the three most promising locations. I will arrange for you to visit these sites January 21.

Sincerely,

Lexie

Lexie Barnes – Location Manager
CINEFIL PRODUCTIONS
7964 Rockaway Drive, North Hollywood, CA 91605
www.cinefilproductions.com | 213-606-3203

**Tips for Writing Progress Reports**
- Identify the purpose and nature of the project immediately.
- Supply background information only if the reader must be educated.
- Describe the work completed.
- Discuss the work in progress, including personnel, activities, methods, and locations.
- Identify problems and possible remedies.
- Consider future activities.
- Close by telling the expected date of completion.

She provides background information because a director does not always know or remember exactly what instructions she was given for a location search. She then includes information about what she has completed and what she plans to do next. Lexie is up front about possible complications and concludes by giving a completion date. She chose to use bold paragraph headings with caps followed by colons to make the report's sequence easy to follow.

## 9-4c Minutes of Meetings

**Meeting minutes** summarize the proceedings of meetings. Most businesses post team meeting minutes to intranet sites soon after the meeting ends. The notes are then accessible to all attendees and absent team members. Companies often use in-house templates for recording meeting minutes. Formal, traditional minutes, illustrated in **Model Document 9.5**, are written for more formal meetings and legislative bodies. If you are assigned to take minutes, you will want to follow this general pattern:

- Begin with the name of the group, as well as the date, time, and place of the meeting.

- Identify the names of attendees and absentees.

- State whether the previous minutes were approved or revised.

- Record briefly the discussions of old business, new business, announcements, and committee reports.

- Include the precise wording of motions; record the votes and actions taken.

- Conclude with the name of the person recording the minutes. Formal minutes may require a signature.

## 9-4d Summaries

A **summary** compresses the main points from a book, report, article, website, meeting, or convention. A summary saves time by reducing a report or article by 85 to 95 percent. Employees are sometimes asked to write summaries that condense technical reports, periodical articles, or books so that their staff or superiors may grasp the main ideas quickly. Students may be asked to write summaries of articles, chapters, or books to sharpen their writing skills and confirm their knowledge of reading assignments.

CEO Stephen Page asked his administrative assistant Destiny Schwartz to search for current information on CEO involvement in social networks. Destiny found an article that identified the social profiles of every CEO on the Fortune 500 list and their participation in the six most popular networks: Twitter, Facebook, LinkedIn, Instagram, and YouTube. Shown in **Model Document 9.6**, her summary includes headings to highlight the article's main ideas. Destiny concluded with her overall reaction to the article. Summary reports of all types follow these general guidelines:

- State the main idea or purpose as well as the source of the document being summarized. Why was it written?

- Highlight the research methods (if appropriate), findings, conclusions, and recommendations.

- Omit illustrations, examples, other details, and references.

- Organize for readability by including headings and bulleted or enumerated lists.

## Model Document 9.5 Formal Meeting Minutes

Shows attendees and absentees

Notes approval of agenda and describes disposition of previous minutes

Describes discussion; does not record every word

Highlights motions showing name of person making motion and person seconding it

Describes new business and announcements

Records meeting adjournment and next meeting date

Includes name and signature of person recording minutes

**International Association of Administrative Professionals**
**Planning Committee Meeting**
**March 14, 2022, 10 a.m.**
**Conference Room B, Hilton Gardens Hotel**

**Present:** Lauren Harmon, Emanuel Schroder, Ignacio Malone, Quintin Brock, Desirae Powers, Eliana Boyle, Lizbeth Nguyen
**Absent:** Maurice Gallegos

**Call to Order/Approval of Agenda/Approval of Minutes**

The meeting was called to order by Chair Eliana Boyle at 10:05 a.m. The agenda was unanimously approved as distributed. Minutes from the February 1 meeting were read and approved.

**Reports of Officers and Committees**

Lizbeth Nguen reported on convention exhibits and her desire to involve more companies and products during this year's international convention. Discussion followed regarding how this might be accomplished.

MOTION: That IAAP office staff develop a list of possible convention exhibitors. The list should be submitted at the next meeting. (Harmon/Brock). PASSED 7-0

**Unfinished Business.**

Lauren Harmon and Emanuel Schroder reviewed the information distributed at the last meeting about hotels for the Denver conference. Lauren said that the Brown Palace Hotel has ample conference rooms and remodeled interiors. Emanuel reported that the Adams Mark Hotel also has banquet facilities for 200, meeting facilities, and rooms at $169 per night.

MOTION: To recommend that IAAP hold its International Convention at the Adams Mark Hotel in Denver, July 20–23, 2022. (Malone/Powers). PASSED 6-1.

**New Business**

The chair announced three possible themes for the convention, all of which focused on technology and the changing role of administrative assistants. Quintin Brock suggested the title "Vision Without Boundaries." Lauren Harmon proposed an intercultural communication theme. Several other possibilities were discussed. The chair appointed a subcommittee of Quintin and Lauren to bring two or three concrete theme ideas to the next meeting.

Emanuel Schroder thinks that IAAP should be doing more to offer professional development opportunities for members. He suggested workshops to polish skills in document design, project management, Web search tools, presentation software, and scheduling software.

MOTION: To recommend to IAAP that it investigate offering fee-based technology workshops at the national and regional conventions. (Powers/Nguyen). PASSED 5-2.

**Adjournment**

There being no further business, it was moved, seconded, and carried that the meeting be adjourned. The meeting was adjourned at 11:50 a.m. by Eliana Boyle. The next meeting will be held on April 15 at 10 a.m. at the Hilton Gardens Hotel.

Respectfully submitted,

*Emanuel Schroder*
Emanuel Schroder, Secretary

- Paraphrase accurately from memory without copying passages.

- Include your reaction or an overall evaluation of the document if asked to do so.

An **executive summary** summarizes a long report, proposal, or business plan. It concentrates on what management needs to know about the full report. You can see an executive summary of a formal report in Chapter 10.

## Model Document 9.6  Article Summary

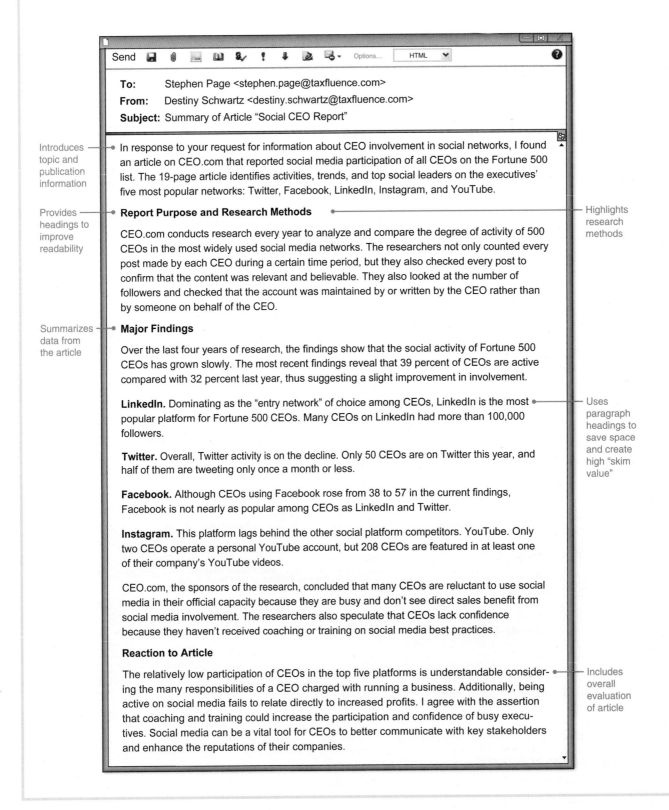

Send    Options...    HTML

**To:**      Stephen Page <stephen.page@taxfluence.com>

**From:**    Destiny Schwartz <destiny.schwartz@taxfluence.com>

**Subject:** Summary of Article "Social CEO Report"

*Introduces topic and publication information →*

In response to your request for information about CEO involvement in social networks, I found an article on CEO.com that reported social media participation of all CEOs on the Fortune 500 list. The 19-page article identifies activities, trends, and top social leaders on the executives' five most popular networks: Twitter, Facebook, LinkedIn, Instagram, and YouTube.

*Provides headings to improve readability →*

### Report Purpose and Research Methods

*← Highlights research methods*

CEO.com conducts research every year to analyze and compare the degree of activity of 500 CEOs in the most widely used social media networks. The researchers not only counted every post made by each CEO during a certain time period, but they also checked every post to confirm that the content was relevant and believable. They also looked at the number of followers and checked that the account was maintained by or written by the CEO rather than by someone on behalf of the CEO.

*Summarizes data from the article →*

### Major Findings

Over the last four years of research, the findings show that the social activity of Fortune 500 CEOs has grown slowly. The most recent findings reveal that 39 percent of CEOs are active compared with 32 percent last year, thus suggesting a slight improvement in involvement.

**LinkedIn.** Dominating as the "entry network" of choice among CEOs, LinkedIn is the most popular platform for Fortune 500 CEOs. Many CEOs on LinkedIn had more than 100,000 followers.

*← Uses paragraph headings to save space and create high "skim value"*

**Twitter.** Overall, Twitter activity is on the decline. Only 50 CEOs are on Twitter this year, and half of them are tweeting only once a month or less.

**Facebook.** Although CEOs using Facebook rose from 38 to 57 in the current findings, Facebook is not nearly as popular among CEOs as LinkedIn and Twitter.

**Instagram.** This platform lags behind the other social platform competitors. YouTube. Only two CEOs operate a personal YouTube account, but 208 CEOs are featured in at least one of their company's YouTube videos.

CEO.com, the sponsors of the research, concluded that many CEOs are reluctant to use social media in their official capacity because they are busy and don't see direct sales benefit from social media involvement. The researchers also speculate that CEOs lack confidence because they haven't received coaching or training on social media best practices.

### Reaction to Article

The relatively low participation of CEOs in the top five platforms is understandable considering the many responsibilities of a CEO charged with running a business. Additionally, being active on social media fails to relate directly to increased profits. I agree with the assertion that coaching and training could increase the participation and confidence of busy executives. Social media can be a vital tool for CEOs to better communicate with key stakeholders and enhance the reputations of their companies.

*← Includes overall evaluation of article*

# 9-5 **Preparing Short Analytical Reports**

Analytical reports differ significantly from informational reports. Although the authors of both seek to collect and present data clearly, writers of analytical reports also evaluate the data and typically try to persuade the reader to accept the conclusions and act on the recommendations. Informational reports emphasize facts; analytical reports emphasize reasoning and conclusions. This section describes three common types of analytical business reports: (a) justification/recommendation reports, (b) feasibility reports, and (c) yardstick reports. These reports involve collecting and analyzing data, evaluating the results, drawing conclusions, and making recommendations.

For some situations you may organize analytical reports directly with the conclusions and recommendations near the beginning. Directness is appropriate when the reader has confidence in the writer, based on either experience or credentials. Frontloading the recommendations also works when the topic is routine or familiar and the reader is supportive.

Directness can backfire, though. If you announce the recommendations too quickly, the reader may immediately object to a single idea. Once the reader has an unfavorable mind-set, changing it may be difficult or impossible. A reader may also believe that you have oversimplified or overlooked something noteworthy if you provide your recommendations before explaining how you arrived at them. When you must lead the reader through the process of discovering the solution, use the indirect strategy: present conclusions and recommendations last.

Most analytical reports answer questions about specific problems and aid in decision making (e.g., *How can we use LinkedIn most effectively? Should we close the Brownsville plant? Should we purchase or lease a fleet of electric cars? How can we improve customer service?*). Analytical reports provide conclusions that help management answer these questions.

**LEARNING OUTCOME 5**
Compose short analytical reports that solve business problems.

## 9-5a Justification/Recommendation Reports

Both managers and employees must occasionally write reports that justify or recommend actions, such as buying equipment, changing a procedure, filling a position, consolidating departments, or investing funds. These reports are called **justification reports** or **recommendation reports**. They may also be called **internal proposals** because their persuasive nature is similar to that of external proposals (presented in Chapter 10). Large organizations sometimes prescribe how these reports should be organized and formatted; they often use forms with conventional headings. When you are free to select an organizational plan yourself, however, let your audience and topic determine your choice of the direct or indirect strategy.

**Direct Strategy.** For nonsensitive topics and recommendations that will be agreeable to readers, you can organize directly according to the following order:

1. Identify the problem or need briefly.
2. Announce the recommendation, solution, or action concisely and with action verbs.
3. Explain more fully the benefits of the recommendation or steps necessary to solve the problem.
4. Include a discussion of pros, cons, and costs.
5. Conclude with a summary specifying the recommendation and necessary action.

**Indirect Strategy.** When a reader may oppose a recommendation or when circumstances suggest caution, do not rush to reveal your recommendation. Consider using the following sequence for an indirect approach to your recommendations:

1. Refer to the problem in general terms, not to your recommendation, in the subject line.

2. Describe the problem or need your recommendation addresses. Use specific examples, supporting statistics, and authoritative quotes to lend credibility to the seriousness of the problem.

3. Discuss alternative solutions, beginning with the least likely to succeed.

4. Present the most promising alternative (your recommendation) last.

5. Show how the advantages of your recommendation outweigh its disadvantages.

6. Summarize your recommendation. If appropriate, specify the action it requires.

7. Ask for authorization to proceed if necessary.

Nash Floyd, an executive assistant at a large petroleum and mining company in Irving, Texas, received a challenging research assignment. His boss, the director of Human Resources and Welfare, asked him to investigate ways to persuade employees to quit smoking. Here is how Nash described his task: "We banned smoking many years ago inside our buildings and on the premises, but we never tried very hard to get smokers to actually kick their habits. My job was to gather information about the problem and learn how other companies have helped workers stop smoking. The report would go to my boss, but I knew she would pass it along to the management council for approval."

Continuing his explanation, Nash said, "If the report were just for my boss, I would put my recommendation up front, because I'm sure she would support it. However, the management council may need to be persuaded because of the costs involved—and because some of them are smokers. Therefore, I put the alternative I favored last. To gain credibility, I footnoted my sources. I had enough material for a ten-page report, but I kept it to two pages in keeping with our company report policy." As you can see in **Model Document 9.7**, Nash chose APA style to document his sources. Although he prepared the report as a memo, he sent it as an attachment to an e-mail message.

## 9-5b Feasibility Reports

**Feasibility reports** examine the practicality and advisability of following a course of action. They answer this question: Will this plan or proposal work? Feasibility reports typically are internal reports written to advise on matters such as switching to solar energy, offering a wellness program to employees, or hiring an outside firm to handle a company's accounting or social media presence. These reports may also be written by consultants called in to investigate a problem. The focus of these reports is on the decision: rejecting or proceeding with the proposed option. Your role as a report writer is usually not to persuade the reader to accept the decision; your role is to present information objectively. In writing feasibility reports, consider these suggestions:

- Announce the decision immediately.

- Provide a description of the background and problem necessitating the proposal.

- Discuss the benefits of the proposal.

- Describe the problems that may result.

- Calculate the costs associated with the proposal, if appropriate.

- Show the time frame necessary for implementing the proposal.

- Conclude with an action request if appropriate.

Raven Acevedo, human resources director for a large financial services firm in Evansville, Indiana, wrote the feasibility report shown in **Model Document 9.8**. Because she discovered that the company was losing time and money as a result of personal e-mail and Internet use by employees, she talked with vice president Julian Rasmussen about employee-monitoring software. Rather than take time away from Raven's regular duties to have her investigate software programs, the vice president suggested that she hire a consultant to analyze the situation and present a plan. When the consultant's work was completed, the vice president wanted to know whether the consultant's plan was feasible. Although Raven's feasibility report is only one page long, it provides all the necessary information: background, benefits, employee acceptance, costs, and time frame.

## 9-5c Yardstick Reports

**Yardstick reports** examine problems with two or more solutions. To determine the best solution, the writer establishes criteria by which to compare the available options.

**Model Document 9.7   Justification/Recommendation Report, APA Style**

**Date:**      November 17, 2022

**To:**        Nia Young, Vice President, Human Resources

**From:**    Nash Floyd, Executive Assistant *NF*

**Subject:**  Analysis of Employee Smoking Cessation Programs

At your request, I have examined measures that encourage employees to quit smoking. As company records show, approximately 23 percent of our employees still smoke, despite the antismoking and clean-air policies we adopted in 2015. To collect data for this report, I studied professional and government publications; I also inquired at companies and clinics about stop-smoking programs.

*Introduces purpose of report, tells method of data collection, and previews organization*

This report presents data describing the significance of the problem, three alternative solutions, and a recommendation based on my investigation.

*Avoids revealing recommendation immediately*

**Significance of Problem: Health Care and Productivity Losses**

*Uses headings that combine function and description*

Employees who smoke are costly to any organization. The following statistics show the effects of smoking for workers and for organizations:

- Absenteeism is 40 to 50 percent greater among smoking employees.
- Accidents are two to three times greater among smokers.
- Bronchitis, lung and heart disease, cancer, and early death are more frequent among smokers (Arhelger, 2022, p.4).

Although our clean-air policy prohibits smoking in the building, shop, and office, we have done little to encourage employees to stop smoking. Many workers still go outside to smoke at lunch and breaks. Other companies have been far more proactive in their attempts to stop employee smoking. Many companies have found that persuading employees to stop smoking was a decisive factor in reducing their health insurance premiums. Following is a discussion of three common stop-smoking measures tried by other companies, along with a projected cost factor for each (Rindfleisch, 2021, p. 4).

*Documents data sources for credibility, uses APA style citing author and year in the text*

**Alternative 1: Literature and Events**

The least expensive and easiest stop-smoking measure involves the distribution of literature, such as "The Ten-Step Plan" from Smokefree Enterprises and government pamphlets citing smoking dangers. Some companies have also sponsored events such as the Great American Smoke-Out, a one-day occasion intended to develop group spirit in spurring smokers to quit. "Studies show, however," says one expert, "that literature and company-sponsored events have little permanent effect in helping smokers quit." (Mendel, 2020, p.108).

Cost: Negligible

**Model Document 9.7**  *Continued*

### Alternative 2: Stop-Smoking Programs Outside the Workplace

Local clinics provide treatment programs in classes at their centers. Here in Houston we have the Smokers' Treatment Center, ACC Motivation Center, and New-Choice Program for Stopping Smoking. These behavior-modification stop-smoking programs are acknowledged to be more effective than literature distribution or incentive programs. However, studies of companies using off-workplace programs show that many employees fail to attend regularly and do not complete the programs.

Cost: $1,200 per employee, three-month individual program — *Highlights costs for easy comparison*
(Your-Choice Program)
$900 per employee, three-month group session

### Alternative 3: Stop-Smoking Programs at the Workplace

Many clinics offer workplace programs with counselors meeting employees — *Arranges alternatives so that most effective is last* in company conference rooms. These programs have the advantage of keeping a firm's employees together so that they develop a group spirit and exert pressure on each other to succeed. The most successful programs are on company premises and also on company time. Employees participating in such programs had a 72 percent greater success record than employees attending the same stop-smoking program at an outside clinic (Honda, 2020, p. 35). A disadvantage of this arrangement, of course, is lost work time—amounting to about two hours a week for three months.

Cost: $900 per employee, two hours per week of release time for three months

### Conclusions and Recommendation — *Summarizes findings and ends with specific recommendation*

Smokers require discipline, counseling, and professional assistance to kick the nicotine habit, as explained at the American Cancer Society website ("Guide to Quitting Smoking," 2021). Workplace stop-smoking programs on company time are more effective than literature, incentives, and off-workplace programs. If our goal is to reduce health care costs and lead our employees to healthful lives, we should invest in a workplace stop-smoking program with release time for smokers. Although the program temporarily reduces productivity, we can expect to recapture that loss in lower health care premiums and healthier employees.

*Reveals recommendation only after discussing all alternatives*

Therefore, I recommend that we begin a stop-smoking treatment program on company premises with two hours per week of release time for participants for three months.

*Lists all references in APA Style*

### References

*Magazine* — Arhelger, Z. (2021, November 5). The end of smoking. *The World of Business*, 3–8.

*Website article* — Guide to quitting smoking. (2021, October 17). Retrieved from the American Cancer Society https://www.cancer.org

*Journal article* — Honda, E. M. (2020). Managing anti-smoking campaigns: The case for company programs."*Management Quarterly*, *32*(2), 29–47. Retrieved from https://search.ebscohost.com

*Book* — Mendel, I. A. (2020). *The puff stops here.* Chicago: Science Publications, p. 108.

*Newspaper article* — Rindfleisch, T. (2021, December 4). Smoke-free workplaces can help smokers quit, expert says." *Evening Chronicle*, 4.

## Model Document 9.8 Feasibility Report

**LARSSON FINANCIAL SERVICES LLP**
**MEMORANDUM**

**Date:** October 3, 2022

**To:** Julian Rasmussen, Vice President

**From:** Raven Acevedo, Director, Human Resources *RA*

**Subject:** Feasibility of Installing an Internet Monitoring Program

*(margin note: Explains reason for report and outlines its organization)*

As you suggested, we hired a consultant to investigate the feasibility of a plan to monitor employee Internet use. The consultant reports that such a plan is workable and could be fully implemented by February 1. This report discusses the background, benefits, problems, costs, and time frame of the plan.

*(margin note: Reveals decision immediately)*

**Background: Current Misuse of Internet Privileges.** Currently we allow employees Internet access for job-related tasks. Many use social media—specifically, Facebook, Twitter, and LinkedIn—to communicate with clients and the public. However, some employees use this access for personal reasons, resulting in lowered productivity, higher costs, and a strain on the network. Therefore, we hired an outside consultant who suggested an Internet-monitoring program.

*(margin note: Describes problem and background)*

**Benefits of Plan: Appropriate Use of Social Media and the Internet.** The proposed plan calls for installing Internet-monitoring software such as NetGuard or eMonitor. We would fully disclose to employees that this software will be tracking their online activity. We would also teach employees what social media and Internet use is appropriate. In addition to increased productivity, lowered costs, and improved network performance, this software will also help protect our company against loss of intellectual property, trade secrets, and confidential information.

*(margin note: Evaluates positive and negative aspects of proposal objectively)*

**Employee Acceptance.** One of the biggest challenges will be convincing employees to accept this new policy without feeling that their privacy is being violated. However, proper training will help employees understand the appropriate use of social media and the Internet.

**Costs.** Implementing the monitoring plan involves two direct costs. The first is the initial software cost of $500 to $1,100, depending on the package we choose. The second cost involves employee training and trainer fees. However, the expenditures are within the project's budget.

*(margin note: Presents costs and schedule; omits unnecessary summary)*

**Time Frame.** Selecting the software package will take about two weeks. Preparing a training program will require another three weeks. Once the program is started, the breaking-in period will take at least three months. By February 1 the Internet-monitoring program will be fully operational resulting in increased productivity, decreased costs, lowered liability, and improved network performance.

Please let me know by October 14 whether you would like additional information about monitoring social media and Internet use.

*(margin note: Concludes with action request)*

---

The criteria then act as a yardstick against which all the options are measured, as shown in **Model Document 9.9**. The yardstick approach is effective for companies that must establish specifications for equipment purchases and then compare each manufacturer's product with the established specs. The yardstick approach is also effective when exact specifications cannot be established.

For example, a yardstick report might help a company decide on an inexpensive job perk. Perks are nontraditional benefits that appeal to current and future employees. Popular job perks include free food and beverages, flexible scheduling and remote-work options, on-site gyms, and fitness classes. A yardstick report may help a company decide what job perks make the most sense. If the company wants to encourage long-term wellness, it might consider offering employees discounted fitness club memberships, on-site yoga classes, or ergonomic workstations. The yardstick report would describe and compare the three options in terms of (a) costs, (b) long-term benefits, and (c) expected participation level. After interviewing employees and talking to people whose companies offer similar benefits, report writers would compare the options and recommend the most workable job perk.

The real advantage to yardstick reports is that the available options can be measured consistently using the same criteria. Writers using a yardstick approach typically do the following:

- Begin by describing the problem or need.

## Model Document 9.9 Yardstick Report

**Date:** March 2, 2022
**To:** Harish Mitra, Director, Operations
**From:** Aubrey Fortin, Benefits Administrator *AF*
**Subject:** Choosing Outplacement Plan

Here is the report you requested investigating the possibility of CompuTech's use of outplacement services. It discusses the problem of counseling services for discharged staff and establishes criteria for selecting an outplacement agency. It then evaluates three prospective agencies and presents a recommendation based on that evaluation.

> *Introduces purpose and gives overview of report organization*

### Problem: Counseling Discharged Staff

In an effort to reduce costs and increase competitiveness, CompuTech will begin a program of staff reduction that will involve releasing up to 20 percent of our workforce over the next 12 to 24 months. Many of these employees have been with us for ten or more years, and they are not being released for performance faults. These employees deserve a severance package that includes counseling and assistance in finding new careers.

> *Discusses background briefly because readers already know the problem*

### Solution and Alternatives: Outplacement Agencies

Numerous outplacement agencies offer discharged employees counseling and assistance in locating new careers. This assistance minimizes not only the negative feelings related to job loss but also the very real possibility of litigation. Potentially expensive lawsuits have been lodged against some companies by unhappy employees who felt they were unfairly released.

In seeking an outplacement agency, we should find one that offers advice to the sponsoring company as well as to dischargees. The law now requires certain procedures, especially in releasing employees over forty. CompuTech could unwittingly become liable to lawsuits because our managers are uninformed of these procedures. I have located three potential outplacement agencies appropriate to serve our needs: Gray & Associates, Right Access, and Careers Plus.

> *Uses dual headings, giving function and description*

> *Announces solution and the alternative it presents*

### Establishing Criteria for Selecting Agency

In order to choose among the three agencies, I established criteria based on professional articles, discussions with officials at other companies using outplacement agencies, and interviews with agencies. Here are the four groups of criteria I used in evaluating the three agencies:

> *Tells how criteria were selected*

1. Counseling services—including job search advice, résumé help, crisis management, corporate counseling, and availability of full-time counselors

2. Administrative and research assistance—including availability of administrative staff, librarian, and personal computers

3. Reputation—based on a telephone survey of former clients and listing with a professional association

4. Costs—for both group programs and executive services

> *Creates four criteria for use as yardstick in evaluating alternatives*

- Explain possible options and solutions.

- Establish criteria for comparing the options; explain how the criteria were selected or developed.

- Discuss and evaluate each option in terms of the criteria.

- Draw conclusions and make recommendations.

Aubrey Fortin, benefits administrator for computer manufacturer CompuTech, was called on to write the report in Model Document 9.9 comparing outplacement agencies. These agencies counsel discharged employees and help them find new

---

**Model Document 9.9** *Continued*

Director Mitra                    Page 2                    March 2, 2022

**Discussion: Evaluating Agencies by Criteria**

Each agency was evaluated using the four criteria just described. Data comparing the first three criteria are summarized in Table 1.

Table 1
A COMPARISON OF SERVICES AND REPUTATIONS
FOR THREE LOCAL OUTPLACEMENT AGENCIES

*[Places table close to spot where it is first mentioned]*

| | Gray & Associates | Right Access | Careers Plus |
|---|---|---|---|
| Counseling services | | | |
| Résumé advice | Yes | Yes | Yes |
| Crisis management | Yes | No | Yes |
| Corporate counseling | Yes | No | No |
| Full-time counselors | Yes | No | Yes |
| Administrative, research assistance | | | |
| Administrative staff | Yes | Yes | Yes |
| Librarian, research library | Yes | No | Yes |
| Personal computers | Yes | No | Yes |
| Listed by National Association of Career Consultants | Yes | No | Yes |
| Reputation (telephone survey of former clients) | Excellent | Good | Excellent |

*[Summarizes complex data in table for easy reading and reference]*

**Counseling Services**
All three agencies offered similar basic counseling services with job-search and résumé advice. They differed, however, in three significant areas.

Right Access does not offer crisis management, a service that puts the discharged employee in contact with a counselor the same day the employee is released. Experts in the field consider this service especially important to help the dischargee begin "bonding" with the counselor immediately. Immediate counseling also helps the dischargee learn how to break the news to family members. Crisis management can be instrumental in reducing lawsuits because dischargees immediately begin to focus on career planning instead of concentrating on their pain and need for revenge. Moreover, Right Access does not employ full-time counselors; it hires part-timers according to demand. Industry authorities advise against using agencies whose staff members are inexperienced and employed on an "as-needed" basis.

*[Highlights the similarities and differences among the alternatives]*

In addition, neither Right Access nor Careers Plus offers regular corporate counseling, which I feel is critical in training our managers to conduct terminal interviews. Careers Plus, however, suggested that it could schedule special workshops if desired.

**Administrative and Research Assistance**
Both Gray & Associates and Careers Plus offer complete administrative services and personal computers. Dischargees have access to staff and equipment to assist them in their job searches. These agencies also provide research libraries, librarians, and databases of company information to help in securing interviews.

*[Does not repeat obvious data from table]*

**Model Document 9.9** *Continued*

Director Mitra                              Page 3                              March 2, 2022

**Reputation**

*(Discusses objectively how each agency meets criteria)*

To assess the reputation of each agency, I checked its listing with the National Association of Career Consultants. This is a voluntary organization of outplacement agencies that monitors and polices its members. Gray & Associates and Careers Plus are listed; Right Access is not.

For further evidence I conducted a telephone survey of former agency clients. The three agencies supplied me with names and telephone numbers of companies and individuals they had served. I called four former clients for each agency. Most of the individuals were pleased with the outplacement services they had received. I asked each client the same questions so that I could compare responses.

**Costs**

All three agencies have two separate fee schedules, summarized in Table 2. The first schedule is for group programs intended for lower-level employees. These include off-site or on-site single-day workshop sessions, and the prices range from $1,200 a session (at Right Access) to $1,700 per session (at Gray & Associates). An additional fee of $50 to $60 is charged for each participant.

*(Selects most important data from table to discuss)*

The second fee schedule covers executive services. The counseling is individual and costs from 10 percent to 18 percent of the dischargee's previous year's salary. Since CompuTech will be forced to release numerous managerial staff members, the executive fee schedule is critical. Table 2 shows fees for a hypothetical case involving a manager who earns $100,000 a year.

Table 2

A COMPARISON OF COSTS FOR THREE AGENCIES

| | Gray & Associates | Right Access | Careers Plus |
|---|---|---|---|
| Group programs | $1,700/session $55/participant | $1,200/session $50/participant | $1,600/session $60/participant |
| Executive services | 15% of previous year's salary | 10% of previous year's salary | 18% of previous year's salary plus $1,000 fee |
| Manager at $100,000/year | $15,000 | $10,000 | $19,000 |

**Conclusions and Recommendations**

*(Gives reasons for making recommendation)*

Although Right Access charges the lowest fees, it lacks crisis management, corporate counseling, full-time counselors, library facilities, and personal computers. Moreover, it is not listed by the National Association of Career Consultants. Therefore, the choice is between Gray & Associates and Careers Plus. Because they offer similar services, the deciding factor is costs. Careers Plus would charge $4,000 more for counseling a manager than would Gray & Associates. Although Gray & Associates has fewer computers available, all other elements of its services seem good. Therefore, I recommend that CompuTech hire Gray & Associates as an outplacement agency to counsel discharged employees.

*(Narrows choice to final alternative)*

positions; fees are paid by the former employer. Aubrey knew that downsizing and outsourcing would take place in the next two years. Her task was to compare outplacement agencies and recommend one to management.

Aubrey gathered information about three outplacement agencies and wanted to organize it systematically using a yardstick report. She chose to evaluate each agency using the following categories: counseling services, administrative and research assistance, reputation, and costs. Aubrey showed the results of her research in Table 1 and Table 2 in Model Document 9.9. She used the criteria as headings and discussed how each agency met, or failed to meet, each criterion. Making a recommendation was easy once Aubrey had created the tables and compared the agencies.

## Summary of Learning Outcomes

**1   Define informational and analytical report functions, strategies, and writing styles.**

- Informational reports—such as monthly sales reports, status updates, and compliance reports—present data without analysis or recommendations.
- Analytical reports provide findings, analyses, conclusions, and recommendations when requested. Examples include justification, recommendation, feasibility, and yardstick reports.
- Audience reaction and content determine whether a report is organized directly or indirectly.
- Reports organized directly reveal the purpose and conclusions immediately; reports organized indirectly place the conclusions and recommendations last.
- Like other business messages, reports can range from informal to formal, depending on their purpose, audience, and situation.

**2   Describe typical report formats and effective report headings.**

- Report formats vary, depending on the report's length, topic, audience, and purpose.
- Common report formats include e-mail, letter, memo, and manuscript; digital reports can be created and shared as slide decks and infographics.
- Report headings add visual appeal and readability; they reveal the report's organization and flow of ideas.
- The hierarchy of heading levels should be clear to a reader; headings in the same level should use the same font size and style, placement, and capitalization.

**3   Explain the report writing process starting with defining the problem and collecting data.**

- Clarifying the problem the report will address is the first step in writing a report.
- A purpose statement states the reasons for the report and answers the questions that prompted the report.
- Typical sources of secondary information used in reports are company records, books, journals, magazines, newspapers, and Web resources.
- Typical sources of primary, or firsthand, information used in reports are personal observations, surveys, questionnaires, and interviews with subject experts.

**4   Write short informational reports that describe routine tasks.**

- Trip, convention, and conference reports present information about a business trip or event, focusing on topics that will benefit the organization.
- Progress, or interim, reports describe a job or project, including background information, work completed, work in progress, problems encountered, and future plans.
- Meeting minutes include the names of attendees and absentees, a discussion of old and new business, committee reports, and decisions made.
- Summaries of longer publications include the name, date, and author of the publication plus an outline of the main ideas along with a description of research methods, findings, conclusions, and recommendations.

**5   Compose short analytical reports that solve business problems.**

- Analytical reports, such as justification/recommendation, feasibility, and yardstick reports, evaluate information, draw conclusions, and make recommendations.
- Justification/recommendation reports are organized directly when the reader is supportive and indirectly when the reader needs persuasion to accept the recommendations.
- Feasibility reports are written directly and examine the practicality and advisability of following a course of action.
- Yardstick reports examine problems by using a standard set of criteria to compare several available options before recommending a solution.

## Key Terms

| | | |
|---|---|---|
| business reports 258 | formal writing style 262 | memo format 264 |
| informational reports 259 | portable document format (PDF) 263 | templates 264 |
| analytical reports 259 | slide deck 263 | letter format 264 |
| informal writing style 261 | infographics 264 | manuscript format 264 |

## Chapter Review

1. What role do reports play in business today? (L.O. 1)

2. Describe seven formats used for reports. Be prepared to discuss each. (L.O. 2)

3. Explain the difference between primary and secondary data. (L.O. 3)

4. What sources of factual information for informal reports can report writers consult? (L.O. 3)

5. Why is it important to write a purpose statement before composing a report? (L.O. 3)

6. What is the purpose of the following informational reports? (L.O. 4)
   a. **Trip or conference report**
   b. **Progress report**
   c. **Minutes of meetings**
   d. **Summary**

7. What is the purpose of the following analytical reports? (L.O. 5)
   a. **Justification/recommendation report**
   b. **Feasibility report**
   c. **Yardstick report**

8. Your supervisor wants you to find a reputable official source explaining how to spot counterfeit KN-95 face masks. What report category and format would be appropriate? (L.O. 2, 4)

9. Your team was assigned to write a report explaining how your company, a medical device manufacturer, can comply with the FDA's regulations and secure premarket approval before Class III devices can go into production. Your boss wants to know what you have done thus far. What report category and format would be appropriate? (L.O. 2, 4)

10. You represented your company at the AeroDef Manufacturing Conference, the nation's premier aerospace and defense manufacturing conference and trade show, in Fort Worth, Texas. Your supervisor asked for information about innovative processes to reduce costs, expedite production, and maintain global competitiveness typically exchanged at this convention. What report category and format would be appropriate? (L.O. 2, 4)

## Critical Thinking

11. Outline the considerations leading report writers to adopt either the direct strategy or the indirect strategy for any company report they are writing. (L.O. 1)

12. Why do most report writers start their research with secondary data rather than gathering primary data first? (L.O. 3)

13. Explain the differences between an informal writing style and a formal writing style in reporting. When would each be appropriate? (L.O. 1)

14. Explain how report writers can ensure objectivity and credibility. (L.O. 1–5)

15. Describe the three heading types discussed in this chapter and their purposes. (L.O. 2)

## Activities and Cases

### 9.1 Engaging Readers With Report Headings (L.O. 2)

**YOUR TASK.** Identify the following report headings and titles as *functional, talking,* or *combination*. Discuss the usefulness and effectiveness of each.

a. Guarding Against Online Identity Theft
b. Project Costs
c. Disadvantages
d. Using the Intranet to Convey Employee Benefits
e. Case Study: America's Most Sustainable College Campuses
f. Recommendations: Identifying Non-Compliance Risks
g. Comparing Costs of AI Recruiting Platforms
h. Budget

## 9.2 Informational Report: Recording Information From Your Work Experience (L.O. 4)

Select a position you now hold or one that you have held in the past. If you have not been employed, choose a campus, professional, or community organization to which you belong. You may also select an internship or a volunteer experience.

**YOUR TASK.** Write an informational memo report to your instructor describing your current or former employment, an internship or volunteer experience, or your involvement in a professional or community group. Introduce the report by describing the organization's products or services, its history and leadership, and its primary location. In the body of the report, add your title and job responsibilities, including the skills you need or needed to perform the job. Then describe the value and skills you gained from this experience. Your memo report should be single-spaced and 1 1/2 to 2 pages long. Add a meaningful subject line and descriptive headings for each section of the report.

## 9.3 Informational Report: Researching Potential Employers (L.O. 4)
> Web

You are preparing a targeted résumé and cover message for a Fortune 500 company. You've spoken with a friend who works there, but you now want to do your own research.

**YOUR TASK.** If available, use your campus library research options to access Hoover's company profile database and other resources for company records and other facts. Then take a look at the company's website; check its background, news releases, and annual report. Learn about its major product, service, or emphasis. Find its Fortune 500 ranking, its current stock price (if listed), and its high and low range for the year. Look up its profit-to-earnings ratio. Track its latest marketing plan, promotion, or product. Identify its home office, major officers, and number of employees. In a memo report to your instructor, summarize your research findings. Explain why this company would be a good or bad employment choice for you.

## 9.4 Summary: Keeping the Boss in the Loop (L.O. 4)
> Web

Like many executives, your boss is too rushed to read long journal articles. She asks you to submit one summary to her every month on an article of interest to help her stay abreast of relevant research in various business disciplines.

**YOUR TASK.** In your field of study, select a professional journal, such as the *Journal of Marketing, Journal of Management, Journal of Accountancy,* or *Harvard Business Review*. Using a research database or a Web search, look for articles in your target journal. Select an interesting article that is approximately 2,000 words long, and write an executive summary in memo format. Include an introduction that might begin with *As you requested, I am submitting this executive summary of . . . .* Identify the author, article title, journal, and date of publication. Start with the main idea of the study or article. Summarize three or four of the most important findings of the study or article in approximately 200 words, or 10 percent of the original article. Use descriptive rather than functional headings. Your boss would also like a concluding statement indicating your response to the article in a separate paragraph below your summary.

## 9.5 Progress Report: Closing in on Your Goal? (L.O. 4)

You have promised your parents (spouse, partner, relative, or friend) that you would submit a progress report at this time.

**YOUR TASK.** Prepare a progress report in letter format in which you do the following: (a) describe your headway toward your educational goal (such as employment, degree, or certificate); (b) summarize the work you have completed thus far; (c) discuss the work currently in progress, including your successes and anticipated obstacles; and (d) outline what you have left to complete.

## 9.6 Progress Report: How Is That Project Coming? (L.O. 4)

**E-Mail**   **Team**

Consider a research project, service-learning assignment, or an experiential learning opportunity you are currently completing. Perhaps you are doing research for the long report assignment in Chapter 10 or another course. In any case, you will want to keep your instructor informed of your progress.

**YOUR TASK.** Write a progress report informing your instructor of your work. Briefly describe the project—its purpose, assigned team member roles, work completed, work yet to be completed, problems encountered, future activities, and expected completion date. Address the e-mail report to your instructor.

## 9.7 Justification/Recommendation Report: Cash Available for Good Deeds (L.O. 5)

**Web**

Terrific news! MegaTech, the start-up company where you work, has become enormously successful. Now the owner wants to support some kind of philanthropic program. He does not have time to investigate the possibilities, so he asks you, his assistant, to conduct research and report to him and the board of directors.

**YOUR TASK.** The owner wants you to investigate the charitable projects at 20 high-profile companies of your choice. Visit their websites and study programs such as volunteerism, cause-related marketing, matching funds, and charitable donations. In a recommendation report, discuss five of the best programs and recommend one that could serve as a philanthropic project model for your company.

## 9.8 Informational or Analytical Report: Examining Tweets and Other Social Media Posts (L.O. 4, 5)

**E-Mail**   **Social Media**   **Web**

Select a Fortune 500 company that appeals to you, and search recent tweets and Facebook posts about it. Soon you will recognize trends and topic clusters that may help you organize the report content by criteria. For example, if you use the hashtag to conduct a subject search on Coca-Cola (i.e., *#Coca-Cola*), you will obtain a huge number of tweets about the company and brand. They will range from fan posts, buying tips, exhortations to recycle plastic, and specious cleaning tips involving Coke all the way to urban legends (e.g., the acid in Coke will completely dissolve a T-bone steak in two days). Many returned tweets will be only marginally interesting because they show up just because *#Coca-Cola* is mentioned.

If you explore Facebook, you will mostly find official pages and fan sites, most of which display favorable posts. You would have to look hard to find negative posts, partly because companies moderate discussions and often remove offensive posts according to their user agreements.

**YOUR TASK.** Write either an informational or analytical report about the company you chose. In an informational report to your instructor, you could summarize your findings in memo form or as an e-mail. Describe how the tweets about the company are trending. Are they overwhelmingly positive or negative? Organize the report around the subject areas you identify (criteria). Alternatively, you could write an analytical report detailing the strategies your chosen company adopts in responding to tweets and Facebook posts. Your analytical report would evaluate the organization's social media responses and provide specific examples to support your claims.

## 9.9 Feasibility Report: International Student Club on Campus (L.O. 5)

**Intercultural**

To fulfill a senior project in your department, you have been asked to submit a letter report to the dean evaluating the feasibility of starting an organization of international students on campus.

**YOUR TASK.** Find out how many international students are on your campus, what nations they represent, how one goes about starting an organization, and whether a faculty sponsor is needed. Assume that you conducted an informal survey of international students. Of the 39 who filled out the survey, 31 said they would be interested in joining.

## 9.10 Feasibility Report: Encouraging Healthy Habits (L.O. 5)

Your company is considering ways to promote employee fitness and morale.

**YOUR TASK.** Select a fitness/teambuilding program that seems reasonable for your company. Consider a softball league, bowling teams, a basketball league, lunchtime walks, lunchtime fitness speakers and demos, company-sponsored health club memberships, a workout room, a fitness center, or a fitness director. Assume that your boss has tentatively agreed to the program you select and has asked you to write a memo report investigating its feasibility.

## 9.11 Examining Meeting Minutes (L.O. 4)

Attend an organized meeting at your school, in your community, in city government, or for a professional organization. Alternatively, view records of virtual meetings in public governance available online.

**YOUR TASK.** After your on-site visit, write the meeting minutes including all the data necessary and following the instructions in this chapter. Focus on committee reports, old and new business, motions and votes, decisions made, and action items for future meetings. Include the organization's name and the date, time, and location of the meeting in the heading.

Alternatively, after locating minutes of virtual meetings in public governance, examine posted minutes, staff reports, and other documents. Carefully compare them to what you have learned about meeting minutes in this chapter. Write a brief summary to your instructor describing differences and similarities, such as formatting, included items, number of people involved, and more.

## 9.12 Meeting Minutes: Keeping Your Team on Track (L.O. 4)

> Team

When working on a formal report with a team, volunteer to take notes at a team meeting and be prepared to share the meeting minutes with your instructor, if requested. Follow the instructions in this chapter for meeting minutes.

**YOUR TASK.** Record the proceedings of a team meeting for a group project. Record the date and time of the meeting, the attendees' names, discussion items, decisions made, and the date of the next meeting.

## 9.13 Yardstick Report: Office Equipment Options (L.O. 5)

You recently complained to your boss that you were unhappy with a piece of equipment you use (printer, computer, copier, scanner, or the like). After some thought, the boss decided that your complaint is valid and greenlighted new purchases. But first you must do research.

**YOUR TASK.** Compare at least three manufacturers' models and recommend one. Because the company will be purchasing ten or more units, and because several managers must approve the purchase, write a careful report documenting your findings. Establish at least five criteria for comparing the models. Submit a memo report to your boss.

## 9.14 Yardstick Report: Finding the Best Live Chat Solution (L.O. 5)

> Web

Your company would like to add a live chat feature on its website to improve customer service with online shoppers. Your boss is aware that these shoppers frequently accept invitations to chat live when they need help or have questions. What's more, they often turn into buyers. Your boss asks you to research the most popular live chat software options, compare the features and monthly costs, and recommend one that the company could implement quickly.

**YOUR TASK.** Write a memo yardstick report to Vice President of Marketing Jada Delgado that compares the options. Search online for live chat support software, and look at several sources that list the most popular options for small and midsized companies. Choose five of the most frequently mentioned options, and compare them in terms of (a) monthly or yearly costs, (b) main features, and (c) ratings or reviews. Follow the instructions in this chapter for writing yardstick reports. Briefly discuss the background for the report, list the live chat options, and compare them using the established criteria. Your comparison data may work best in a table. Draw conclusions and recommend a live chat solution that you believe will best meet the needs of the company.

## 9.15 Yardstick Report: Improving Workplace Procedures (L.O. 5)

Even the best workplaces face challenges or have downsides awaiting positive change. Companies spend much money on *optimizing* their processes and procedures (i.e., on making them as effective as possible).

**YOUR TASK.** Identify a problem or procedure that must be changed at your work or in an organization you know. Consider challenges such as poor scheduling of employees, outdated equipment, slow order processing, failure to encourage employees to participate fully, restrictive rules, inadequate training, or disappointed customers. Consider several solutions or courses of action (retaining the present status could be one alternative). Develop criteria that you could use to evaluate each alternative. Write a report measuring each alternative by the yardstick you have created. Recommend a course of action to your boss or to the organization head.

## 9.16 Article or Infographic Summary: Social Marketing Trends (L.O. 4)

> Social Media     Web

Your supervisor wants to stay abreast of the latest social media marketing trends. You are tasked with researching *social marketing* and list the hot trends with a brief explanation of each. You will format this document as an article summary.

**YOUR TASK.** Search for an article or infographic that addresses current or trending social marketing trends. In a memo report addressed to your boss, Maxie Yong, summarize the main ideas presented in the article or infographic. Be sure to identify the author, article title, publication name, and date of the article. If your source is an infographic, follow a similar procedure and identify the title, sponsoring website, source, and date, if available. Conclude with your overall opinion of the article or infographic.

## 9.17 Report Topics for Informal Reports (L.O. 4, 5)

> Team     Web

A list of over 100 report topics is available at the accompanying student site. The topics are divided into the following categories: accounting, finance, human resources, marketing, information systems, management, and general business/education/campus issues. You can collect information for many of these reports by using electronic research databases and the Web. Your instructor may assign them as individual or team writing projects. All require critical thinking in collecting and organizing information into logical reports.

**YOUR TASK.** As directed by your instructor, select a topic from the report list at **www.cengage.com**.

## Grammar/Mechanics Checkup 9

## Semicolons and Colons

Review Sections 2.16–2.19 in the Grammar/Mechanics Handbook. Then select the correctly punctuated sentence and record its letter in the space provided. Also record the appropriate Grammar/Mechanics guideline to illustrate the principle involved. When you finish, compare your responses with those at the bottom of the page. If your answers differ, study carefully the principles in parentheses.

| | | |
|---|---|---|
| <u>a</u>    (2.16b) | **EXAMPLE** | a. Ma Modular founder Chris Krager has a master's degree in architecture; he also holds a bachelor's degree in business administration. |
| | | b. Ma Modular founder Chris Krager has a master's degree in architecture, he also holds a bachelor's degree in business administration. |

_____  1.  a. *Passive house* is a rigorous energy-efficient building standard, consequently, homeowners can save up to 80 percent on heating and cooling.

                                      b. *Passive house* is a rigorous energy-efficient building standard; consequently, homeowners can save up to 80 percent on heating and cooling.

_____  2.  a. Heat recovery ventilation comes with filters that remove pollen, dust mites, mold, and bacteria; therefore, the higher upfront cost may be well worth it.

                                      b. Heat recovery ventilation comes with filters that remove pollen, dust mites, mold, and bacteria, therefore, the higher upfront cost may be well worth it.

_____  3.  a. Zero energy home design incorporates the following elements: triple-glazed windows, double low-emissivity window film, and high-efficiency doors.

                                      b. Zero energy home design incorporates the following elements; triple-glazed, windows, double low-emissivity window film, and high-efficiency doors.

4. a. Two well-known builders of green modular houses in California are: Clever Homes and Living Homes.

   b. Two well-known builders of green modular houses in California are Clever Homes and Living Homes.

5. a. Prefab homes once were thought to be a low-quality building option,  in recent years, however, modular homes have come a long way.

   b. Prefab homes once were thought to be a low-quality building option;  in recent years, however, modular homes have come a long way.

6. a. In addition to the kit house, expect three types of fixed cost: lot preparation, septic well installation, and building a foundation.

   b. In addition to the kit house, expect three types of fixed cost; lot preparation, septic well installation, and building a foundation.

7. a. Top talent will speak about modular homes: Ray Kappe, architect, Living Homes, Chris Corson, owner, Ecocor, Jennifer Siegal, professor, USC.

   b. Top talent will speak about modular homes: Ray Kappe, architect, Living Homes; Chris Corson, owner, Ecocor; and Jennifer Siegal, professor, USC.

8. a. The firm has completed many custom prefab homes; for example, in California, Nevada, Colorado, Georgia, and North Carolina.

   b. The firm has completed many custom prefab homes: for example, in California, Nevada, Colorado, Georgia, and North Carolina.

9. a. Principal Leo Marmol lectures widely about the following topics: architecture, sustainability, and restoration.

   b. Principal Leo Marmol lectures widely about the following topics; architecture, sustainability, and restoration.

10. a. The new Laguna Beach homes are certifiable green buildings, they use the most efficient form of wood-frame modular construction.

    b. The new Laguna Beach homes are certifiable green buildings; they use the most efficient form of wood-frame modular construction.

## Editing Challenge 9

Every chapter provides an editing exercise to fine-tune your grammar and mechanics skills. The following progress report requires edits that address proofreading, grammar, spelling, punctuation, concise wording, parallelism, and other writing issues. Study the guidelines in the Grammar/Mechanics Handbook (Appendix D), including the lists of Confusing Words and Frequently Misspelled Words.

**YOUR TASK.** Edit the following by (a) inserting corrections in your textbook or on a photocopy using the proofreading marks in Appendix C or (b) downloading the message from **www.cengagebrain.com** and correcting at your computer. Your instructor may show you a possible solution.

**To:** Ignacio Castaneda <icastaneda@northstar-realty.com>
**From:** Lilliana Stanton <lstanton@unitedcontractors.com>
**Subject:** Progress Report on Construction of Jacksonville Beach Branch Office

Dear Mr. Castaneda:

Construction of Northstar Realtys Jacksonville Beach branch office has entered Phrase 3. Although we are one week behind the contractors original schedule the building should be already for occupancy on April 1.

**Past Progress**

Phase 1 involved development of the architects plans, this task was completed on July 1. Phase two involved submission of the plans for county building department approval. A copy of the plans were then given to the following two contractors for the purpose of obtaining an estimate, Declan Stark Contractors and Abernathy Builders. The lower bidder was Declan Stark Contractors, consequently this firm began construction on August 15.

**Present Status**

Phase three includes initial construction work. We have completed the following work as of November 9

- Demolition of the existing building at 4460 Majestic Bluff Drive North
- Excavation of foundation footings for the building and for the surrounding wall
- Steel reinforcing rods installed in building pad and wall
- Pouring of the concrete foundation

Declan Stark Contractors indicated that it was one week behind schedule for several reasons. The building inspectors required more steel reinforcement then was showed on the architects blueprings. In addition excavation of the footings required more time then the contractor anticipated because the 18-inch footings were all below grade.

**Future Schedule**

In spite of the fact that we lost time in Phrase 3 we are substantially on target for the completion of this office building by March 1. Phase 4 includes the following activities, framing, drywalling, and installation of plumbing. If you have questions call me at 904-945-7213.

Lilliana Stanton
Project Manager
United Contractors | lstanton@unitedcontractors.com | 8370 Kinkaid Street |
Jacksonville, FL 32210 | 904-945-7213

# Communication Workshop: Mastering Team Writing Projects

## Best Practices for Writing in Teams

Participating in group presentations and collaborating on written reports will help you develop the kinds of teamwork skills that employers prize. Although sometimes frustrating, team projects can be highly successful and rewarding when members follow best practices such as those presented here.

## Preparing to Work Together

Before beginning the project, meet as a team and establish roles and ground rules by doing the following:

- Select a team leader to coordinate and manage the project.
- Choose a recorder to write and distribute the ground rules and take notes on each meeting's accomplishments.
- Decide whether your team will be governed by consensus (everyone must agree) or by majority rule.
- Compare team members' schedules, gather contact information, and agree on meeting times.
- Decide how to involve collaborators who miss a meeting.
- Discuss the value of sharing diverging opinions. When multiple viewpoints are shared, a better product results. Talk openly about conflict and how it should focus on issues, not on people.
- Discuss how to deal with members who do miss deadlines or fail to do their part; in a team charter, determine a scale of steps ranging from written censure to specific penalties.

## Planning the Document

Once you have established ground rules, you are ready to discuss the project and resulting document.

- Establish the document's specific purpose and identify the main issues involved.
- Discuss the audience(s) for the document and what appeal would help it achieve its purpose.
- Write a detailed outline of the report. What parts will be assigned to each team member? What graphics and visuals are needed?
- Develop a work plan. Set deadlines for submitting the early drafts, for integrating the parts into one document, and for proofreading the final draft.
- Decide what fonts and format you will use in the final document. Will the report need a cover sheet, a table of contents, or a list of citations?

## Collecting Information

- As a group, brainstorm ideas for gathering relevant information.
- Establish deadlines for collecting information from secondary and primary sources.
- Discuss ways to ensure the accuracy and currency of the information collected.

## Organizing, Writing, and Revising

As the project progresses, your team may wish to modify some of its earlier decisions.

- Review the proposed outline and adjust if necessary.
- Share the first drafts and have all members review them. Make sure all writers are using the same format, heading styles, and font sizes.
- Appoint the strongest writer to integrate all the parts, striving for a consistent voice. The report should read as if it were written by one person.

## Editing and Evaluating

- Review the document's overall design, format, and heading levels. Is the report organized so that it is easy to follow?
- Although all members should review and suggest edits to the final document, assign a strong writer to copyedit the report for grammar and punctuation correctness and consistency.
- Evaluate the final document. Discuss whether it fulfills its purpose and meets the needs of the audience.

## Using Online Collaboration Tools

Consider using Google Docs or another document management and editing tool. Some writers prefer to create drafts in Microsoft Word and use the **Track Changes** feature to gather comments from multiple readers. Search online or ask educators and project managers what document-sharing platforms they prefer.

**CAREER APPLICATION.** Select a topic from the suggested activities in this chapter or from Report Topics at **www .cengage.com**. Assume that you are preparing the report as a team project. If you are working on a long report, your instructor may ask you to prepare individual progress reports as you develop your topic.

**YOUR TASK**

- Form a team of two to five members, and prepare to work together by following the suggestions in this workshop.
- Plan your report by establishing its purpose, analyzing the audience, writing a detailed outline, developing a work plan, and deciding how you want the final document to look.
- Collect information, organize it, and write the first draft.
- Offer to proofread and comment on the drafts of team members.

Your instructor may assign grades not only for the final report but also for team effectiveness and your individual contribution, as evaluated by fellow team members.

# Proposals and Formal Reports

## Learning Outcomes

After studying this chapter, you should be able to do the following:

**1** Explain the purpose of informal and formal proposals and their basic components.

**2** Outline the steps in the process of writing formal business reports.

**3** Describe primary and secondary research and how to evaluate its credibility.

**4** Discuss the importance and methods of ethically documenting information from business report sources.

**5** Incorporate meaningful visual aids and graphics in business reports.

**6** Identify the components of typical formal business reports.

Fizkes/Shutterstock.com

## 10-1 Crafting Winning Business Proposals

Proposals can mean life or death for an organization. Why are they so important? Let's begin by defining what they are. A **proposal** is a written offer to solve a problem, provide a service, pitch a project, or sell equipment. A well-written proposal can generate billion-dollar contracts for big companies. The public-private partnership of space agency NASA with aerospace manufacturer SpaceX may be the most prominent example. People running smaller businesses—such as electricians, contractors, plumbers, and interior designers—also rely on proposals to sell their services and products. Equally dependent on proposals are many nonprofit organizations whose funding hinges on successful grant proposals.

## 10-1a Types of Business Proposals

Some business proposals are brief; some are lengthy and complex. A proposal recipient could be a manager inside your company or a potential client outside your company. All types of proposals share two significant characteristics: (a) they use easy-to-understand language, and (b) they show the value and benefits of the product or service being recommended. Proposals may be classified as (a) informal or formal, (b) internal or external, and (c) solicited or unsolicited.

Informal or Formal. Informal proposals are short reports, often formatted as memos or letters. Proposal sections can vary, but an informal proposal might include the following parts: (a) an introduction or description of the problem, (b) pertinent background information or a statement of need, (c) the proposal benefits and schedule for completion, (d) the staffing requirements, (e) a budget analysis, and (f) a conclusion that may include an authorization request. **Model Document 10.1** illustrates an informal letter proposal to a Nebraska dentist who sought to improve patient satisfaction. The research company submitting the proposal describes the benefits of a patient survey to gather data about the level of patient satisfaction. As you can see, the proposal contains the basic components of an informal proposal.

Formal proposals differ from informal proposals not in style but in size and format. Formal proposals respond to big projects and may range from 5 to 200 or more pages. In addition to the six basic parts of informal proposals, formal proposals may contain some or all of these additional parts: (a) a copy of a request for proposal (RFP), (b) a letter of transmittal, (c) an abstract or executive summary, (d) a title page, (e) a table of contents, (f) a list of figures, and (g) an appendix. **Figure 10.1** shows the typical sections included in informal and formal proposals.

Internal or External. Proposal writers may submit internal proposals to management when they see benefits in changing a company policy, purchasing equipment, or adding new products and services. A company decision maker will review the proposal and accept or reject the idea. Internal proposals may resemble justification and recommendation reports, as discussed in Chapter 9. Most proposals, however, are external and addressed to clients and customers outside the company. An external sales proposal to a client would show how the company's goods or services would solve a problem or benefit the client.

Another type of external proposal is a **grant proposal**, written to obtain funding from agencies that support worthwhile causes. The Robert Wood Johnson Foundation, for example, receives many funding requests in the form of grant proposals from organizations seeking support for their research and charitable causes. The accompanying Workplace in Focus describes some of the foundation's current support goals.

### Figure 10.1 Components of Informal and Formal Proposals

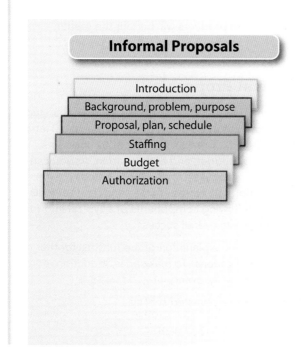

**Informal Proposals**

- Introduction
- Background, problem, purpose
- Proposal, plan, schedule
- Staffing
- Budget
- Authorization

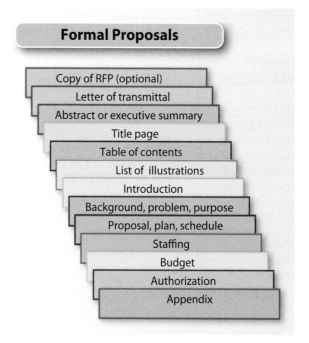

**Formal Proposals**

- Copy of RFP (optional)
- Letter of transmittal
- Abstract or executive summary
- Title page
- Table of contents
- List of illustrations
- Introduction
- Background, problem, purpose
- Proposal, plan, schedule
- Staffing
- Budget
- Authorization
- Appendix

Solicited (RFP) or Unsolicited. When government organizations or businesses have a specific need, they prepare a **request for proposal (RFP)**, a document that specifies their requirements. A **solicited proposal** is the response to an RFP. Government agencies as well as private businesses use RFPs to invite competitive bids from vendors. RFPs ensure that bids are comparable and that funds are awarded fairly, using consistent criteria. For example, the California city of Hermosa Beach was seeking bids for an audiovisual system for its city council chambers. Its RFP included details of how and when the application should be made.[2] Companies responding to requests for proposals are careful to follow the RFP instructions explicitly, which might include following a specific proposal format.

Enterprising companies looking for work or special challenges might submit **unsolicited proposals**, that is, bids that had not been explicitly requested. For instance, the Center for the Advancement of Science in Space (CASIS), which runs the International Space Station U.S. National Laboratory, continuously accepts innovative unsolicited proposals to develop groundbreaking technologies and products.[3] Both large and small companies are likely to use RFPs to solicit bids on their projects, so that the businesses can compare prices from various bidders. They also want the legal protection offered by proposals, which are considered legal contracts.

When writing proposals, remember that they must be persuasive, not merely mechanical descriptions of what you can do. Like the persuasive sales messages discussed in Chapter 8, effective proposals must (a) get the reader's attention, (b) emphasize how the proposed methods and products will benefit the reader, (c) showcase the bidding firm's expertise and build credibility, and (d) present ideas clearly and logically, making it easy for the reader to understand.

## 10-1b  Components of Informal Proposals

Informal proposals may be presented in manuscript format (usually no more than ten pages) with a cover page, or they may take the form of short (two- to four-page) letters. Sometimes called **letter proposals**, they usually contain six principal components: introduction, background, proposal, staffing, budget, and authorization. As you can see in Figure 10.1, both informal and formal proposals contain these six basic parts. The titles, or headings, of the components of informal proposals may vary, but the goals of the components are standard. Each of the following components of a typical informal proposal serves a purpose and contributes to its overall success.

Introduction. Most proposals begin with a brief explanation of the reasons for the proposal and then highlight the writer's qualifications. To make an introduction more persuasive, strive to provide a hook, such as the following:

- Hint at extraordinary results with details to be revealed shortly.

OFFICE INSIDER

"When it comes to proposal formatting, it's better to follow traditions than to think outside the box. Sponsors are used to seeing key information structured in a specific way. Tinkering with it will just cause confusion."[4]

**Sylvia Moses,**
*graphic designer,*
*workamajig.com*

- Promise low costs or speedy results.

- Mention a remarkable resource (e.g., well-known authority, new computer program, well-trained staff) available exclusively to you.

- Identify a serious problem (worry item) and promise a solution, to be explained later.

- Specify a key issue or benefit that you feel is the heart of the proposal.

Before writing the proposal shown in Model Document 10.1, Antoine Gibson analyzed the request of Nebraska dentist Caroline Foley and decided that she was most interested in improving service to her patients. However, Antoine did not hit on this hook until he had written a first draft and had come back to it later. It's not a bad idea to put off writing the proposal introduction until after you have completed other parts. In longer proposals the introduction also describes the scope and limitations of the project, as well as outlining the organization of the material to come.

**Background, Problem, and Purpose.** The background section identifies the problem and discusses the goals or purposes of the project. In an unsolicited proposal, your goal is to convince the reader that a problem exists. Therefore, you must present the problem in detail, discussing such factors as revenue losses, failure to comply with government regulations, or decreased customer satisfaction.

In a solicited proposal, your aim is to persuade the reader that you understand the problem completely and that you have a realistic solution. If responding to an RFP, follow its requirements precisely and use the soliciting company's language in your description of the problem. For example, if the RFP asks for *the design of a maintenance program for wireless communication equipment,* don't call it a *customer service program for wireless products.* The background section might include segments titled *Statement of Need, Basic Requirements, Most Critical Tasks,* or *Important Secondary Problems.*

**Proposal, Plan, and Schedule.** In the proposal section itself, you would explain your plan for solving the problem. In some proposals this is tricky because you want to disclose enough of your plan to secure the contract, without giving away so much information that your services will not be needed. Without specifics, though, your proposal has little chance, so you must decide how much to reveal.

The proposal section often includes an implementation plan. If research is involved, state what methods you will use to gather the data. Remember to be persuasive by showing how your methods and products will benefit the reader. For example, show how the initial investment will pay off later. The proposal might even promise specific **deliverables**—tangible things your project will produce for the customer. A proposal deliverable might be a new Web design or a digital marketing plan. To add credibility, also specify how the project will be managed and how its progress will be audited. Most writers also include a schedule or timetable of activities showing the proposal's benchmarks for completion.

**Staffing.** The staffing section of a proposal describes the qualifications of the team that will complete the work as well as the credentials and expertise of the project leaders. In other words, this section introduces all participating staff members and their qualifications. This section is a good place to endorse and promote your staff. The client sees that qualified people will be on board to implement the project. Although full résumés might be attached to a proposal, busy decision makers will appreciate a summary highlighting the credentials of the key players. Each summary might describe that person's expertise, certifications, and a few examples of experience on similar projects.[5]

**Budget.** A central item in most proposals is the **budget**, a list of proposed project costs. You need to prepare this section carefully because it represents a contract; you cannot raise the project costs later—even if your costs increase.

**OFFICE INSIDER**

"My years at the United Nations made me the Grand Mistress of report writing. We wrote daily, weekly, monthly and annual reports. A couple of years in the UN and you can write reports in your sleep. Because I cared so deeply about the people I was writing about, I wanted to be sure the people in Kabul or New York who read my reports were paying attention. So I taught myself to tell a good story in every report. People pay attention and keep reading for a good story."[6]

**Marianne Elliott,**
*New Zealand-based author and human rights advocate*

In the proposal shown in Model Document 10.1, Antoine Gibson decided to justify the budget for his firm's patient satisfaction survey by itemizing the costs. Whether the costs in a proposal are itemized or presented as a lump sum depends on the reader's needs and the proposal's objectives.

**Conclusion and Authorization.** The closing section should remind the reader of the proposal's key benefits and make it easy for the reader to respond. It might also include a project completion date as well as a deadline beyond which the proposal offer will no longer be in effect. Writers of informal proposals often refer to this as a request for approval or authorization. The conclusion of the proposal in Model Document 10.1 states a key benefit as well as a deadline for approval.

## Model Document 10.1   Informal Letter Proposal

6300 O Street
Lincoln, NE 68510
(402) 747-6300
www.corepoll.com

May 27, 2022

Caroline Foley, DDS
7880 Cobblestone Street
Lincoln, NE 68506

Dear Dr. Foley:

*(Uses opening paragraph in place of introduction)*

Understanding the views of your patients is the key to meeting their needs. CorePoll Research is pleased to propose a plan to help you become even more successful by learning what patients expect of your practice, so that you can improve your services.

*(Grabs attention with hook that focuses on key benefit)*

**Background and Goals**

We know that you have been incorporating a total quality management system in your practice. Although you have every reason to believe that your patients are pleased with your services, you may want to give them an opportunity to discuss what they like and possibly don't like about your office. Specifically, your purposes are to survey your patients to (a) determine the level of their satisfaction with you and your staff, (b) elicit their suggestions for improvement, (c) learn more about how they discovered you, and (d) compare your preferred and standard patients.

*(Identifies four purposes of survey)*

*(Announces heart of proposal)*

**Proposed Plan**

On the basis of our experience in conducting many local and national customer satisfaction surveys, CorePoll proposes the following plan:

**Survey.** We will develop a short but thorough questionnaire probing the data you desire. Although the survey instrument will include both open-ended and close-ended questions, it will concentrate on the latter. Close-ended questions enable respondents to answer easily; they also facilitate systematic data analysis. The questionnaire will gauge patients' views of courtesy, professionalism, billing accuracy, friendliness, and waiting time. After you approve it, the questionnaire will be sent to a carefully selected sample of 300 patients whom you have separated into groupings of preferred and standard.

*(Describes procedure for solving problem or achieving goals)*

*(Divides total plan into logical segments for easy reading)*

**Analysis.** Survey data will be analyzed by demographic segments, such as patient type, age, and gender. Using state-of-the art statistical tools, our team of seasoned experts will study (a) satisfaction levels, (b) the reasons for satisfaction or dissatisfaction, and (c) the responses of your preferred compared to standard patients. Moreover, our team will give you specific suggestions for making patient visits more pleasant.

**Report.** You will receive a final report with the key findings clearly spelled out, Dr. Foley. Our expert staff will draw conclusions based on the results. The report will include tables summarizing all responses, divided into preferred and standard clients.

**Model Document 10.1**   *Continued*

Includes second-page heading

Dr. Caroline Foley                    Page 2                    May 27, 2022

**Schedule.** With your approval, the following schedule has been arranged for your patient satisfaction survey:

| | |
|---|---|
| Questionnaire development and mailing | August 2–6 |
| Deadline for returning questionnaire | August 16 |
| Data tabulation and processing | August 16–18 |
| Completion of final report | September 3 |

*Uses past-tense verbs to show that work has already started on the project*

**Staffing**

Promotes credentials and expertise of key people

CorePoll is a nationally recognized, experienced research consulting firm specializing in survey investigation. I have assigned your customer satisfaction survey to Joel Palmer, PhD, our director of research. Dr. Palmer was trained at Emory University and has successfully supervised our research program for the past nine years. Before joining CorePoll, he was a marketing analyst with T-Mobile.

*Builds credibility by describing outstanding staff and facilities*

Assisting Dr. Palmer will be a team headed by Elizabeth Avila, our vice president for operations. Ms. Avila earned a BS degree in computer science and an MA degree in marketing from the University of Florida. She supervises our computer-aided telephone interviewing (CAT) system and manages our 30-person professional staff.

**Budget**

Itemizes costs carefully because a proposal is a contract offer

| | Estimated Hours | Rate | Total |
|---|---|---|---|
| Professional and administrative time | | | |
| Questionnaire development | 3 | $175/hr. | $525 |
| Questionnaire mailing | 4 | 50/hr. | 200 |
| Data processing and tabulation | 12 | 50/hr. | 600 |
| Analysis of findings | 15 | 175/hr. | 2,625 |
| Preparation of final report | 5 | 175/hr. | 875 |
| Mailing costs | | | |
| 300 copies of questionnaire | | | 150 |
| Postage and envelopes | | | 300 |
| Total costs | | | $5,275 |

**Authorization**

Closes by repeating key qualifications and main benefits

We are convinced, Dr. Foley, that our professionally designed and administered patient satisfaction survey will enhance your practice. CorePoll Research can have specific results for you by September 2 if you sign the enclosed duplicate copy of this letter and return it to us with a retainer of $2,500 so that we may begin developing your survey immediately. The rates in this offer are in effect only until October 1.

Makes response easy

*Provides deadline*

Sincerely,

*Antoine Gibson*

Antoine Gibson
Senior Researcher

Enclosure

## 10-2   Preparing Formal Business Reports

A **formal report** may be defined as a document in which a writer analyzes findings, draws conclusions, and makes recommendations intended to solve a problem. Formal business reports are similar to formal proposals in length, organization, and tone. Instead of making an offer, however, formal reports are the product of thorough investigation and analysis. They present ordered information to decision makers in business, industry, government, and education. Informal and formal business reports have similar components, as shown in **Figure 10.2**, but, as might be expected, formal reports have more sections.

**LEARNING OUTCOME 2**

Outline the steps in the process of writing formal business reports.

**Figure 10.2  Components of Informal and Formal Reports**

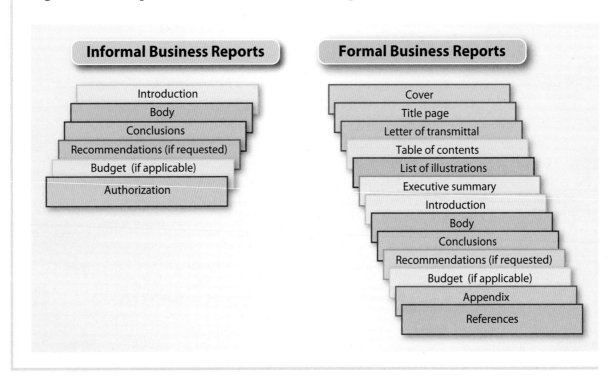

| Informal Business Reports |
|---|
| Introduction |
| Body |
| Conclusions |
| Recommendations (if requested) |
| Budget  (if applicable) |
| Authorization |

| Formal Business Reports |
|---|
| Cover |
| Title page |
| Letter of transmittal |
| Table of contents |
| List of illustrations |
| Executive summary |
| Introduction |
| Body |
| Conclusions |
| Recommendations (if requested) |
| Budget  (if applicable) |
| Appendix |
| References |

## 10-2a  Steps to Follow in Writing Formal Business Reports

Writing a formal report is a difficult task. It requires planning, researching, and organizing. Because this is a complex process, writers are most successful when they follow specific steps, as outlined in the following sections.

**Determine the Purpose and Scope of the Report.** Like proposals and informal reports, formal reports begin with a purpose statement. Preparing a written **purpose statement** is helpful because it defines the focus of the report and provides a standard that keeps the project on target. Study the following purpose statement and notice the use of action words (*adding, writing,* and *establishing*):

> **Simple purpose statement:** *To recommend adding three positions to our sales team, writing a job description for the sales team leader, and establishing recruitment guidelines for sales team hiring.*

Next you will need to determine the scope of the report. The **scope statement** prepares the audience by clearly defining which problem or problems will be researched and analyzed. As part of the scope statement, the **limitations** further narrow the subject by focusing on constraints or exclusions. You might consider these questions: How much time do I have to complete the report? How accessible is the data I need? How thorough should my research be, and what boundaries will help me limit the scope of this report? If interviews or surveys are appropriate, how many people should I contact, and what questions should I ask?

**Anticipate the Needs of the Audience.** Your goal is to present key findings that are relevant to your audience. Keep in mind that the audience may or may not be familiar with the topic. If you were reporting to a targeted audience of human resources managers, the following facts gathered from an employee survey would be considered relevant: *According to the company survey completed by 425 of our 515 employees, 72 percent of employees are currently happy with their health benefits package.*

**Decide on a Work Plan and Appropriate Research Methods.** A **work plan** is a tentative schedule that guides the investigation. This plan includes a clear **problem statement,**

a purpose statement, and a description of the research methods to be used. A good work plan also involves a tentative outline of the report's major sections and a logical work schedule for completion of major tasks, as illustrated in **Model Document 10.2**.

**Conduct Research Using Primary and Secondary Sources.** Formal report writers conduct most of their research using **secondary sources**—that is, information that has been previously compiled, analyzed, and, in most cases, published. Books and e-books,

---

**Model Document 10.2   Work Plan for a Formal Report**

**WORK PLAN FOR LEE JEANS ONE TRUE FIT LINE**

*Defines purpose, scope, limits, and significance of report*

**Statement of Problem.** Many women between the ages of 18 and 34 have trouble finding jeans that fit. Lee Jeans hopes to remedy that situation with its One True Fit line. We want to demonstrate to Lee that we can create a word-of-mouth campaign that will help it reach its target audience.

**Statement of Purpose.** The purpose of this report is to secure an advertising contract from Lee Jeans. We will examine published accounts about the jeans industry and Lee Jeans in particular. In addition, we will examine published results of Lee's current marketing strategy. We will conduct focus groups of women in our company to generate campaign strategies for our pilot study of 100 BzzAgents. The report will persuade Lee Jeans that word-of-mouth advertising is an effective strategy to reach women in this demographic group and that advertising contract with Lee Jeans would help our company grow significantly in size and stature.

**Research Strategy (Sources and Methods of Data Collection)**

*Describes primary and secondary data*

We will gather information about Lee Jeans and the product line by examining published marketing data and conducting focus group surveys of our employees. In addition, we will gather data about the added value of word-of-mouth advertising by examining published accounts and interpreting data from previous marketing campaigns, particularly those toward similar age groups. Finally, we will conduct a pilot study of 100 BzzAgents in the target demographic.

**Tentative Outline**
I. How effectively has Lee Jeans marketed to the target population?
    A. Historically, who has bought Lee Jeans products? How often? Where?
    B. How effective are the current marketing strategies for the One True Fit line?
II. Is this product a good fit for our marketing strategy and our company?

*Factors problem into manageable chunks*

    A. What are the reactions of our staff and sample survey?
    B. How well does our pool of BzzAgents correspond to the target demo graphic in terms of age and geographic distribution?
III. Why should Lee Jeans engage BzzAgent to advertise its One True Fit line?
    A. What are the benefits of word of mouth in general and for this demo-graphic in particular?
    B. What previous campaigns have we engaged in that demonstrate our company's credibility?

**Work Schedule**

*Estimates time needed to complete report tasks*

| | |
|---|---|
| Investigate the current marketing strategy of One True Fit | July 15–25 |
| Test product using focus groups | July 15–22 |
| Create campaign materials for BzzAgents | July 18–31 |
| Run a pilot test with a selected pool of 100 BzzAgents | August 1–21 |
| Evaluate and interpret findings | August 22–25 |
| Compose draft of report | August 26–28 |
| Revise draft | August 28–30 |
| Submit final report | September 1 |

---

news and scholarly articles, podcasts, videos, correspondence, and annual reports are examples of secondary sources. In contrast, writers may conduct some of their research using **primary sources**—information and data they gather themselves from firsthand experience. Interviews, observations, surveys, questionnaires, and meetings are examples of primary research. Research methods are discussed later in this chapter in the section *Collecting Information Through Primary and Secondary Research*.

**Organize, Analyze, and Draw Conclusions.** Formal report writers should organize their information logically and base their recommendations on solid facts to impress decision makers. They should analyze the findings and make sure they are relevant to the report's purpose.

When organizing your ideas, arrange your main topics and subtopics into an **outline** as shown in **Model Document 10.3**.

As you sort through your information, decide what information is substantiated and credible. Give readers only the information they need. Then assemble that information using one of the strategies shown in **Figure 10.3**. For example, if a company wants to design its own online surveys, management may request a report that compares the best survey software solutions. In this case, the compare/contrast strategy helps the report writer organize the data and compare the features and costs of each survey tool.

Conclude the report by summarizing your findings, drawing conclusions, and making recommendations. The way you conclude depends on the purpose of your

### Model Document 10.3  Outline Format

**FORMS OF BUSINESS OWNERSHIP**

I. **Sole proprietorship**
   A. Advantages of sole proprietorship
      1. Minimal capital requirements
      2. Control by owner
   B. Disadvantages of sole proprietorship
      1. Unlimited liability
      2. Limited management talent
II. **Partnership**
   A. Advantages of partnership
      1. Access to capital
      2. Management talent
      3. Ease of formation
   B. Disadvantages of partnership
      1. Unlimited liability
      2. Personality conflicts

### Figure 10.3  Strategies for Organizing Report Findings

| Strategy Type | Data Arrangement | Useful Application |
| --- | --- | --- |
| **Chronological** | Arrange information in a time sequence to show history or development of topic. | Useful in showing time relationships, such as five-year profit figures or a series of events leading to a problem |
| **Geographical** | Organize information by geographic regions or locations. | Appropriate for topics that are easily divided into locations, such as East Coast, Northwest, etc. |
| **Topic/Function** | Arrange by topics or functions. May use a prescribed, conventional format. | Works well for topics with established categories or for recurring reports |
| **Compare/Contrast** | Present problem and show alternative solutions. Use consistent criteria. Show how the solutions are similar and different. | Best used for "before and after" scenarios or when comparing alternatives |
| **Importance** | Arrange from least to most important, lowest to highest priority, or lowest to highest value, etc. | Appropriate when persuading the audience to take a specific action or change a belief |
| **Simple/Complex** | Proceed from simple to more complex concepts or topics. | Useful for technical or abstract topics |
| **Best Case/Worst Case** | Describe the best and the worst possible scenarios. | Useful when dramatic effect is needed to achieve results; helpful when audience is uninterested or uninformed |

report and what the reader needs. A well-organized report with conclusions based on solid data will impress management and other decision makers.

**Design Graphics to Clarify the Report's Message.** Presenting numerical or quantitative data visually helps your reader understand information readily. Trends, comparisons, and cycles are easier to comprehend when they are expressed graphically. These visual elements in reports draw attention, add interest, and often help readers grasp information quickly. Visuals include drawings, graphs, maps, charts, photographs, and tables. This topic is covered in more depth in the section *Incorporating Meaningful Visual Aids and Graphics* later in this chapter.

## 10-2b  Reviewing and Editing Formal Business Reports

The final step in preparing a formal business report involves editing and proofreading. Because the reader is the one who determines the report's success, review the report as if you were the intended audience. Pay particular attention to the following elements:

- **Format**. Look at the report's format and assess the report's visual appeal.

- **Consistency**. Review the report for consistency in margins, page numbers, indents, line spacing, and font style.

- **Graphics**. Make sure all graphics have meaningful titles, are clear, and are placed in the report near the words that describe them.

- **Heading levels**. Check the heading levels for consistency in font style and placement. Headings and subheadings should be meaningful and help the reader follow the report's logic.

- **Accuracy**. Review the content for accuracy and clarity. Make sure all facts are documented.

- **Mechanics**. Correct all grammar, punctuation, capitalization, and usage errors. Such errors could damage your credibility and might cause the reader to mistrust the report's content.

## 10-3  Conducting Primary and Secondary Research

Research is one of the most important steps in writing a business report. **Research** may be defined as the methodical search for information relevant to the report topic. As we have seen, research is usually divided into two categories. **Primary research** is the act of generating or gathering firsthand data, say, by conducting interviews, surveys, or systematic observation. **Secondary research** involves the use of existing data that result from reading what others have published, experienced, or observed.

As you begin collecting data, you will answer questions about your objectives and audience: Will your readers need a lot of background information? Will they value or trust statistics, case studies, or expert opinions? Will they want to see data from interviews or surveys?

## 10-3a  Collecting Information Through Secondary Research

Instead of collecting and analyzing primary data, most report writers begin with secondary research. With the sheer volume and breadth of data publicly available today, you are likely to find that something has already been written about your topic. Why reinvent the wheel?

**LEARNING OUTCOME 3**
Describe primary and secondary research and how to evaluate its credibility.

Reviewing secondary sources can save time and effort because typically the data have already been organized and stored in an electronic format. But where to begin? Following is information about the most valuable secondary resources, including library databases, books, periodicals, and encyclopedias.

**Library Databases.** Most writers conducting secondary research quickly turn to library databases because they are fast and easy to use. You can use your computer to conduct detailed searches without ever leaving your office, home, or dorm room.

A **database** is a collection of searchable information stored digitally so that it is accessible by computer or mobile devices. Libraries subscribe to databases that provide bibliographic information (titles of documents and brief abstracts) and links to full-text documents. Databases accessed through libraries contain a rich array of magazine, newspaper, and journal articles, as well as newsletters, business reports, company profiles, government data, reviews, and directories. The databases most useful to business writers are ABI/INFORM Complete Collection (ProQuest), Business Source Premier (EBSCO), JSTOR, Factiva (Dow Jones), and Google Scholar. Many more databases exist. **Figure 10.4** shows screenshots of ABI/INFORM and EBSCO search results.

**Books and E-Books.** Print and e-books provide excellent historical, in-depth data. Check the book's table of contents or index to find information relevant to your project. You may also find helpful citations to other resources in the book's bibliography. Although books can become swiftly outdated, they provide a broad background.

By the way, if you are an infrequent library user, begin your research by talking with a reference librarian about your project. Librarians won't do your research for you, but they will steer you in the right direction. Many librarians help you understand their computer, cataloging, and retrieval systems by providing advice, brochures, handouts, and workshops. As one wise person observed, "Google can bring you back 100,000 answers; a librarian can bring you back the right one."[9]

**Periodicals.** Publications that are produced on a set schedule are called **periodicals**. Three kinds of periodicals may be helpful in your research:

- **Scholarly journals** publish peer-reviewed articles usually written by academics, experts, or researchers. The in-depth articles are likely to be scientifically valid, contain original research, and reach reasonable conclusions. Examples include *The Journal of Business and Professional Communication*, *Journal of Management*, and *Technology and Culture*.

- **Trade publications offer** *practical articles written to appeal to individuals interested in a specific trade or industry. Examples include Advertising Age, Beverage and Industry, and Women's Wear Daily.* Although trade publication articles are not peer-reviewed, they provide specialized information that may not be available elsewhere.

- **Newspapers, magazines, and other popular periodicals** *include, for example, The Wall Street Journal, Bloomberg Businessweek, and Money.* Their primary purpose is to produce a profit, entertain, persuade, or inform the general public. Newspapers and magazines are excellent for up-to-date information on current events and for opinion pieces. However, like trade publications, articles in popular periodicals are not peer-reviewed. Therefore, they must be cited cautiously in reports.

In conducting digital research, one must be selective, guarding against distractions and information overload.

**Figure 10.4  Library Database Search Result**

Business Source Premier (EBSCO) provides full text for more than 2,300 periodicals, including 1,100 peer-reviewed journals. ABI/INFORM (ProQuest) indexes more than 6,800 journals and features more than 5,510 full-text documents about business topics. Users can access newspapers, magazines, reports, dissertations, book reviews, scholarly journals, and trade publications. Figure 10.4 shows that the search terms solar energy and energy efficiency brought up 203 full-text, peer-reviewed search results in EBSCO and only 26 full-text, peer-reviewed search results in ABI/ INFORM after a more focused search. When retrieving too many results, savvy researchers further narrow their search to retrieve a more manageable number.

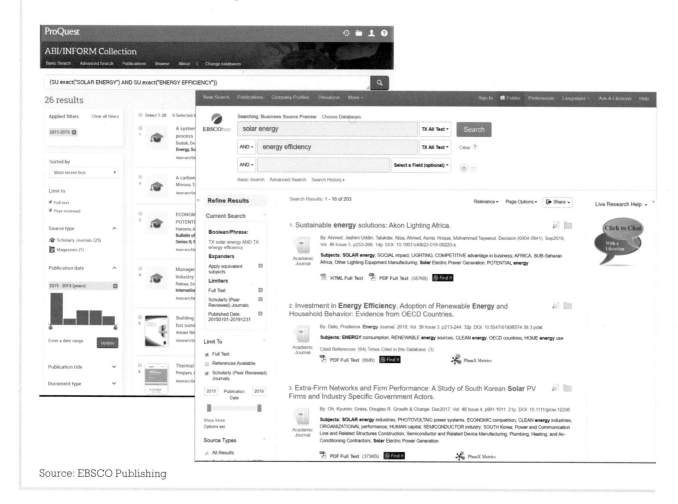

Source: EBSCO Publishing

## 10-3b  Searching the Internet

Finding what you are seeking on the Internet is hopeless without powerful search tools such as browsers and search engines. When you enter a search term, you usually do so in a browser such as (Google) Chrome, (Mozilla) Firefox, (Apple) Safari, or (Microsoft) Edge. A **browser** is a software application that connects to servers and displays their webpages. When you enter keywords or search terms into a browser, a **search engine** scans hundreds of millions of webpages to locate the desired content. Some of the best-known search engines are Google, Bing, Baidu, and DuckDuckGo.

**Web Search Tools.** Using your keywords, a search engine sends out software robots, known as spiders or crawlers, to locate the requested content. These bots scour the Web searching for documents, images, videos, PDFs, and other files. The search engine then sorts and organizes the content and ranks it from most to least relevant. Your Web browser allows you to see the results of this search. Most search engines list the results

**Figure 10.5** Useful Internet Search Techniques

**DEFINE YOUR SEARCH QUESTION**

Frame your search in a question, for example:
*is it economic to go green in constructing an apartment complex?*

**USE NATURAL LANGUAGE**

AI helps search engines understand questions as people speak them:
*what is the ROI for going green in constructing an apartment complex?*

**BOOKMARK USEFUL REFERENCES**

Even if you aren't sure you will use it, bookmark anything that just might be helpful. Removing a bookmark is easy, but tracking down a lost reference is maddening.

**CHOOSE EFFECTIVE KEYWORDS**

Distill your topic into four to five words, for example:
*green building, net-zero homes, ecofriendly construction, LEED certification, sustainability cost*

**TRY SCHOLARLY WEB SEARCHES**

Focus and limit your search with Google Scholar and Google Advanced Search for more nuanced results.

**PUT QUOTES AROUND KEYWORDS**

Send the search engine straight to an exact match.
Avoid marginal, irrelevant hits.
*"LEED certification"*
*"net-zero homes"*

**TRY BOOLEAN OPERATORS**

AND – *green building* AND *ROI*
OR – *green building* OR *sustainability*
NOT – *green construction* NOT *color*
Near – *green building* NEAR *costs*
(target word is to close to another)

**KEEP TRYING**

If you get no hits, check your spelling. Ensure your Boolean operators are used correctly. Try synonyms.
If you get too many hits, try to be more specific. Use many keywords.

based on how frequently users access them. Therefore, you shouldn't just rely on the links on top of the first browser page.

To get the most from Google, try the Advanced search feature. It resembles the query fields in research databases and allows you to narrow your searches more effectively than you can when you rely on a simple search and thus obtain only the most popular results that Google displays first.

**Internet Search Strategies and Techniques.** To use Google casually to find a restaurant menu or trivia answers is easy. However, using the Internet to find factual, rigorous, reliable data requires skill. **Figure 10.5** outlines several effective search techniques.

**Wikipedia and Other Encyclopedias.** College-level research requires you to use general encyclopedia information only as a starting point for more in-depth research. That means you will not cite nor copy from Wikipedia, general encyclopedias, search engines, or similar reference works in your writing. Because most online encyclopedias are crowdsourced, their information is too uneven in quality and too general. However, these information-packed sites often provide their own references (bibliographies) that you can employ in your research. Locate the original sources of information rather than condensed reference articles. Both the American Psychological Association (APA) and the Modern Language Association (MLA) encourage the use of original source material.

## 10-3c Evaluating the Credibility of Internet Sources

Most Internet users tend to assume that any information located by a search engine has somehow been evaluated as part of a valid selection process. Wrong! Unlike library-based research, information at many sites has not undergone the editing or scrutiny of scholarly publication procedures. Anyone can publish anything, truthful or not. That's what makes the Internet treacherous.

Information on the Internet is much less reliable than information from traditional sources. Blogs and discussion forum entries illustrate this problem. They change constantly and may disappear fast, so that your source can't be verified. Many don't provide any references, or they list sources that are either obscure or suspect. Academic researchers prefer lasting, scholarly sources.

To use the Internet meaningfully, you must scrutinize the information you find and check who authored and published it. The Communication Workshop at the end of this chapter provides a comprehensive list of questions to ask when checking the currency, authority, content, and accuracy of a website.

## 10-3d Conducting Primary Research

As we have seen, most writers of workplace and academic reports begin their investigation with secondary research. However, problems that require current information often make primary, firsthand data necessary. If, for example, management wants to discover the cause of increased employee turnover in its Seattle office, it might investigate employment trends in Seattle, prepare an employee survey about job satisfaction, and interview management for another perspective. Writers typically generate primary data through surveys, interviews, observation, or experimentation.

Surveys. A **survey** is a method of gathering information from a sample of people, usually with the goal of generalizing the results to a larger audience. Before developing new products, for example, companies often survey consumers to learn about their needs. Surveys help businesses stay attuned to employees, customers, and markets. By using surveys, researchers can gather information quickly and efficiently whether respondents are nearby or far away.

Mailed or e-mailed surveys, of course, have disadvantages. Because most of us rank them with junk mail or spam, response rates may be low. Furthermore, respondents may not represent an accurate sample of the overall population, thus invalidating generalizations from the group. Let's say, for example, that an insurance company sends out a questionnaire asking about provisions in a new policy. If only older people respond, the questionnaire data cannot be used to generalize what people in other age groups might think. If a survey is e-mailed, it may be overlooked and deleted without being read.

A final problem with surveys has to do with truthfulness. Some respondents exaggerate their incomes or distort other socially desirable facts, thus causing the results to be unreliable. Nevertheless, surveys may be the best way to generate data for business and academic reports. In preparing surveys, consider these pointers:

Gathering and analyzing survey data for business reports has never been easier. One cloud-based tool has turned the task of conducting surveys into a lot of monkey business—literally. SurveyMonkey provides online templates and easy methodologies so that anyone can create a survey and get results quickly. Yet it's so powerful that more than 20 million people around the world, including 99 percent of the Fortune 500 companies, have used it to gather survey-related information. One human resources manager said that the "360 degree feedback survey we created is sent to employees, managers, and even customers. The insights it provides are invaluable."[10] What other uses of surveys are commonly found in business?

- **Choose the best media channel for your survey**. Consider your time frame, budget, and goals in deciding how to do it. You could conduct your survey in person, by telephone, or online. Low-cost cloud-based applications such as SurveyMonkey can help you automate the collection of data.

- **Select the survey population carefully**. Many surveys question a small group of people (a sample) and project the findings to a larger population. Let's say that a survey of your class reveals that nearly everyone favors reusable, refillable water bottles to reduce plastic waste. Can you then say that all students on your campus (or in the nation) prefer refillable bottles? To be able to generalize from a survey, you need to make the sample large and varied enough to represent the larger population. Serious researchers use scientific sampling methods.

- **Prepare a cover letter or introductory paragraph explaining the survey purpose**. Strive to show how the survey benefits the receiver or someone other than you. If appropriate, offer to send recipients a report of the findings.

- **Limit the number of questions**. Resist the temptation to ask for too much. Request only information you will use. Don't, for example, include demographic questions (income, gender, age, and so forth) unless the information is necessary to evaluate responses.

- **Use questions that produce quantifiable answers**. Check-off, multiple-choice, yes–no, and/or rank-order (scale) questions, some of which are illustrated in **Figure 10.6**, provide quantifiable data that are easily tabulated. When questions elicit variable data, give interviewees a list of possible responses, as shown in item 4.

- **Avoid leading or ambiguous questions**. The wording of a question can dramatically affect responses. When respondents were asked, "Are we spending too much, too little, or about the right amount on *assistance to the poor?*" 13 percent responded *Too much.* When the same respondents were asked, "Are we spending too much, too little, or about the right amount on *welfare?*" 44 percent responded *Too much.* Because words have different meanings for different people, strive to use objective language. Ask neutral, unbiased questions (*Do CEOs earn too much, too little, or about the right amount?*).

- **Make it easy for respondents to return the survey**. Researchers often provide prepaid

**Figure 10.6  Preparing a Survey Using SurveyMonkey**

STUDENT ACTIVITY FEE ALLOCATION COMMITTEE SURVEY

1. What year are you?
   ○ First year   ○ Sophomore   ○ Junior   ○ Senior

2. How many units are you carrying this semester?
   ○ 6 or fewer units   ○ 7–10 units   ○ 11–16 units   ○ 17 or more units

3. Have you attended any events sponsored by your Student Activity Fee?
   ○ Yes   ○ No

4. How should your student activity fee be spent? Please rank in order of importance to you, 1 being the most important.
   ○ Lectures and special speakers on campus   ○ Fitness Center equipment and extended hours   ○ Entertainment events
   ○ Diversity programs   ○ Support of clubs
   ○ Other (please specify) [          ]

5. When do you prefer entertainment events to be scheduled?
   ○ Lunchtimes   ○ Late evening   ○ Early evening   ○ Weekends

6. Rank in level of importance the following entertainment events, 1 being most important.
   ○ Movie nights   ○ Dances   ○ Karaoke   ○ Cultural events
   ○ Musical and novelty performances   ○ Other [          ]

7. Indicate your position on the following alternatives.

| | Agree | Undecided | Disagree |
|---|---|---|---|
| The current Student Activity fee should be reduced or eliminated. | ○ | ○ | ○ |
| The current fee should be increased to support more and better student activities and events. | ○ | ○ | ○ |
| The current fee is about right. | ○ | ○ | ○ |

8. What would you like to see changed or improved in relation to the Student Activity fee? [          ]

*Thank you for helping the Student Activity Fee Allocation Committee decide how to distribute its funds.*

self-addressed envelopes or business-reply envelopes. Survey software such as SurveyMonkey helps users develop simple, template-driven questions and allows respondents to take the survey online.

**Interviews.** One of the best research tools is the **interview**. Interviews of subject experts can generate excellent information, particularly on topics about which little has been written. Consider both in-house and outside experts for business reports. Tapping these competent sources will call for in-person, telephone, or video interviews. To elicit the most useful data, try these techniques:

- **Locate an expert**. Ask managers and individuals who are considered to be most knowledgeable in their fields. Check membership lists of professional organizations, and consult articles about the topic. Most people enjoy being experts or at least recommending them. You could also *crowdsource* your question on social media, that is, you could pose the query to your network to get referrals and tips from your contacts.

- **Prepare for the interview**. Learn about the individual you will interview, and make sure you can pronounce the interviewee's name. Research the background and terminology of the topic. Let's say you are interviewing a corporate communication expert about producing an in-house newsletter. You ought to be familiar with terms such as *font* and software such as MS Publisher and InDesign or know about platforms such as Mailchimp or Constant Contact. In addition, be prepared by creating a list of questions that pinpoint your focus on the topic. Ask the interviewee if you may record the talk. Familiarize yourself with a reliable recording tool beforehand.

- **Maintain a professional attitude**. Call or e-mail before the interview to confirm the arrangements, and then arrive on time, whether in person or by video call. Be prepared to take notes if your recorder fails (and remember to ask permission beforehand if you want to record). Use your body language to convey respect.

- **Make your questions objective and unbiased**. Adopt a courteous and respectful attitude. Don't get into a debating match with the interviewee, and don't interrupt. Remember that you are there to listen, not to talk! Use open-ended questions to draw experts out.

- **Watch the time**. Tell interviewees in advance how much time you expect to need for the interview. Don't overstay your appointment. If your subjects ramble, gently try to draw them back to the topic; otherwise, you may run out of time before asking all your questions.

- **End graciously**. Conclude the interview with a general question, such as *Is there anything you would like to add?* Express your appreciation, and ask permission to contact your interviewee later if you need to verify points.

**Observation and Experimentation.** Some kinds of primary data can be obtained only through firsthand **observation** and investigation. If you decide you need observational data, then plan carefully what or whom to observe and how often those observations are necessary. For example, if you wanted to learn more about an organization's live chat customer service, you would probably need to conduct an observation (along with interviews and perhaps even surveys). You would want to answer questions such as *How long does a typical customer wait before a chat service rep responds?* and *How many chat sessions can a service rep handle in a given amount of time?*

To observe, arrive early enough to introduce yourself and set up any equipment. If you are recording, secure permissions beforehand. In addition, take notes, not only of the events or actions but also of the settings. Changes in environment, even the presence of an observer, often affect actions. Starbucks chief Howard Schultz long resisted surveys and sophisticated marketing research. Instead, he would visit 25 Starbucks locations a week to learn about his customers and Starbucks operations.[11]

**Experimentation** produces data suggesting causes and effects. Informal experimentation might be as simple as a pretest and posttest in a college course. Did students learn in the course? Scientists and professional researchers undertake more formal experimentation. They control variables to test their effects. Assume, for example, that Hershey's wants to test the hypothesis (a tentative assumption) that chocolate provides an emotional lift. An experiment testing the hypothesis would separate depressed people into two groups: the chocolate eaters (the experimental group) and the chocolate deprived (the control group). Such experiments are not done haphazardly, however. Valid experiments require sophisticated research designs with careful matching of control and experimental groups.

Rudiruzt/Shutterstock.com

**LEARNING OUTCOME 4**

Discuss the importance and methods of ethically documenting information from business report sources.

OFFICE INSIDER

"Plagiarism reaches its full blown status as a moral problem and disciplinary (possibly expellable or fireable) offense when the plagiarist uses the other person's uncited work for personal and professional gain—to earn credits or a college degree, to get ahead at work, to win a Pulitzer Prize, to sell a book or an article."[12]

**Pat McGuire,**
*president, Trinity Washington University*

## 10-4   Documenting Information

In writing business reports, you will often build on the ideas and words of others. In Western culture, whenever you borrow the ideas of others, you must give credit to your information sources. This is called **documentation**.

### 10-4a   The Purposes of Documentation

As a careful writer, you should take pains to document report data properly for the following reasons:

- **To strengthen your argument**. Including good data from reputable sources will convince readers of your credibility and the logic of your reasoning.

- **To protect yourself against charges of plagiarism**. Acknowledging your sources keeps you honest. **Plagiarism**, which is unethical and in some cases illegal, is the act of using others' ideas without proper documentation.

- **To instruct the reader**. Citing references enables readers to pursue a topic further and make use of the information themselves.

- **To save time**. The world of business moves so quickly that words and ideas must often be borrowed—which is very acceptable when you give credit to your sources.

### 10-4b   Intellectual Theft: Plagiarism

Plagiarism of words or ideas is a serious offense and can lead to loss of a job. Famous historians, politicians, journalists, and even college professors have suffered grave consequences for copying from unnamed sources.[13] Your instructor may use a commercial plagiarism detection service such as Turnitin, which cross-references much of the information on the Web, looking for documents with identical phrasing. The result, an "originality report," shows the instructor whether students have been accurate and honest.

You can avoid charges of plagiarism as well as add clarity to your work by knowing what to document and by developing good research habits. First, however, let's consider the differences between business and academic writing with respect to documentation.

### 10-4c   Academic Documentation and Business Practices

In the academic world, documentation is critical. Especially in the humanities and sciences, students are taught to cite sources by using quotation marks, parenthetical citations, footnotes, and bibliographies. College term papers require full documentation to demonstrate that a student has become familiar with respected sources and can cite them properly in developing an argument. Giving credit to the authors is extremely important. Students who plagiarize risk a failing grade in a class and even expulsion from school.

In business, however, documentation and authorship are sometimes viewed differently. Business communicators on the job may find that much of what is written does not follow the standards they learned in school. In many instances individual authorship is unimportant. For example, employees may write for the signature of their bosses. The writer receives no credit. Similarly, teams turn out documents for which none of the team members receive individual credit. Internal business reports, which often include chunks of information from previous reports, also don't give credit. Even information from outside sources may lack detailed documentation. However, if facts are questioned, business writers must be able to produce their source materials.

Although both internal and external business reports are not as heavily documented as school assignments or term papers, business communication students are well advised to learn proper documentation methods. In the workplace, stealing the ideas of others and passing them off as one's own can be corrosive to the business because it leads to resentment and worse. One writer suggests that in addition to causing businesses to lose the public's trust, unethical practices undermine free markets and free trade.[14] Moreover, copyright and trademark violations are criminal offenses and can lead to severe punishment.

## 10-4d  What to Document

When you write reports, especially in college, you are continually dealing with other people's ideas. You are expected to conduct research, synthesize ideas, and build on the work of others. But you are also expected to give proper credit for borrowed material. To avoid plagiarism, you must give credit whenever you use the following:[15]

- Another person's ideas, opinions, examples, or theory

- Any facts, statistics, graphs, and drawings that are not common knowledge

- Quotations of another person's actual spoken or written words

- Paraphrases of another person's spoken or written words

- Visuals, images, and any kind of electronic media

Information that is common knowledge requires no documentation. For example, the statement The Wall Street Journal *is a popular business newspaper* would require no citation. Statements that are not common knowledge, however, must be documented. The following statement would require a citation because most people do not know this fact: *Phoenix, Arizona, is the nation's fastest-growing U.S. city with a population of 50,000 or more.*[16] More important, someone went to the trouble and expense of assembling this original work and now *owns* it. Cite sources for such proprietary information—in this case, statistics reported by a newspaper or magazine. Even if you summarize data in your own words, you must cite the source.

## 10-4e  The Fine Art of Paraphrasing

In writing reports and using the ideas of others, you will probably rely heavily on **paraphrasing**, which means restating an original passage in your own words and in your own style. To do a good job of paraphrasing, follow these steps:

1. Read the original material intently to comprehend its full meaning.

2. Write your own version without looking at the original.

3. Avoid repeating the grammatical structure of the original and merely replacing words with synonyms.

4. Reread the original to be sure you covered the main points but did not borrow specific language.

To better understand the difference between plagiarizing and paraphrasing, study the following passages. Notice that the writer of the plagiarized version uses the same grammatical construction as the source and often merely replaces words with synonyms. Even the acceptable version, however, requires a reference to the source author.

**Source**
*Once Web enterprises figured out their business models and how to securely process credit cards, clicks turned to dollars, forging some of the most powerful companies in the world, companies that have since become titans in distribution, media, and even space travel. [17]*

**Plagiarized version**
*When Web businesses finally developed their business models and learned how to safely transact credit cards online, they were able to convert clicks to big bucks and create many of the most successful enterprises in the world, enterprises that have become leaders in media, distribution, and even space exploration. (Evans, 2018)*

**Acceptable paraphrase**
*The ability to securely process credit cards online enabled Web entrepreneurs to convert clicks to profits, thus propelling the growth of many of today's most successful enterprises in media, distribution, and even space exploration. (Evans, 2018)*

## 10-4f   When and How to Quote

On occasion, you will want to use the exact words of a source, but beware of overusing quotations. Documents that contain pages of spliced-together quotations suggest that writers have few ideas of their own. Wise writers and speakers use direct quotations for three purposes only:

- To provide objective background data and establish the severity of a problem as seen by experts

- To repeat identical phrasing because of its precision, clarity, or aptness

- To duplicate exact wording before criticizing

When you must use a long quotation, try to summarize and introduce it in your own words. Readers want to know the gist of a quotation before they tackle it. For example, to introduce a quotation describing the impact of secure credit cards, you could precede the quotation with your words: *In describing the explosive growth of online enterprises as a result of secure online credit cards, in her book* Broad Band, *Evans observed that. . . .* To introduce quotations or paraphrases, use wording such as the following:

*According to Evans, . . .*

*Evans argues that . . .*

*In her book, Evans reported . . .*

Use quotation marks to enclose exact quotations, as shown in the following: The Internet, a *"technology that began as a networked hypertext system for particle physicists,"* writes Clare Evans, *"became the world's gossip page, multimedia art gallery, and library, in a feverish burst of cultural activity the likes of which the world has never seen"* (2018, p. 204).

## 10-4g   Citation Formats

You can direct readers to your sources with parenthetical notes inserted into the text and with bibliographies. The

most common **citation formats** are presented by the Modern Language Association (MLA), the American Psychological Association (APA), and the Chicago Manual of Style (CMS). Learn more about using MLA and APA formats in Appendix B.

# 10-5 Creating Meaningful Graphics

Whether you are presenting a business report in person, in print, or digitally, you can create visual interest and clarify the data with meaningful graphics. If your report contains complex data and numbers, you may want to consider graphics such as tables and charts. By simplifying complex ideas and emphasizing key data, well-constructed graphics make key information easier to remember. However, the same data can be shown in many forms, for example, in a chart, table, or graph. The following guidelines will help you match the graphic with your objective and how to incorporate it into your report.

**LEARNING OUTCOME 5**
Incorporate meaningful visual aids and graphics in business reports.

## 10-5a Matching Graphics and Objectives

In developing the best graphics, you must decide what data you want to highlight and which graphics are most appropriate given your objectives. Tables? Bar charts? Pie charts? Line charts? Surface charts? Flowcharts? Organization charts? Pictures? **Figure 10.7** summarizes appropriate uses for each type of graphic. The following sections discuss each type in more detail.

Tables. Probably the most frequently used graphic in reports is the **table**. Because a table presents quantitative or verbal information in systematic columns and rows, it can clarify large quantities of data in small spaces. Although tables do not readily display trends, they enable you to effectively organize raw data collected from surveys or interviews. The following tips help will help you produce effective tables, one of which is shown in **Figure 10.8**.

- Place titles and labels at the top of the table.

- Arrange items in a logical order (alphabetical, chronological, geographical, highest to lowest), depending on what you need to emphasize.

- Provide clear headings for the rows and columns.

- Identify the units in which figures are given (percentages, dollars, units per worker hour) in the table title, in the column or row heading, with the first item in a column, or in a note at the bottom.

**Figure 10.7** Matching Graphics to Objectives

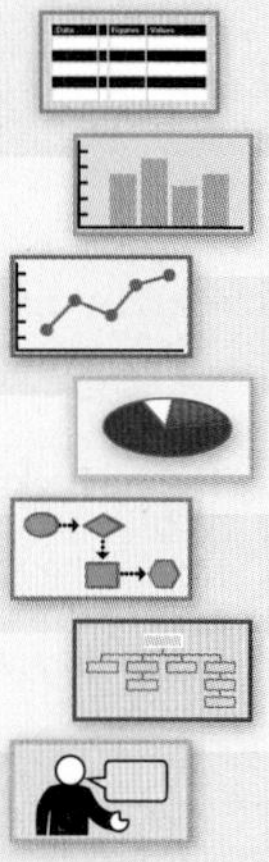

Table
**To show exact figures and values**

Bar Chart
**To compare one item with others**

Line Chart
**To demonstrate changes in quantitative data over time**

Pie Chart
**To visualize a whole unit and the proportions of its components**

Flowchart
**To display a process or procedure**

Organization Chart
**To define a hierarchy of elements**

Photograph, Map, Illustration
**To create authenticity, to spotlight a location, and to show an item in use**

**Figure 10.8  Table Summarizing Precise Data**

| Figure 1<br>MPM ENTERTAINMENT COMPANY<br>Income by Division (in millions of dollars) | | | | |
|---|---|---|---|---|
| | Theme Parks | Motion Pictures | Streaming Media | Total |
| 2019 | $15.8 | $39.3 | $11.2 | $66.3 |
| 2020 | 18.1 | 17.5 | 15.3 | 50.9 |
| 2021 | 23.8 | 21.1 | 22.7 | 67.6 |
| 2022 | 32.2 | 22.0 | 24.3 | 78.5 |
| 2023 (projected) | 35.1 | 21.0 | 26.1 | 82.2 |

- Make long tables easier to read by shading alternate lines or by leaving a blank line after groups of five.

- Place tables as close as possible to the place where they are mentioned in the text.

Figure 10.7 shows the purposes of various graphics. The table in Figure 10.8 presents data about the MPM Entertainment Company over several years, making it easy to compare several divisions. **Figures 10.9 through 10.12** illustrate how some of the data for MPM can be displayed in various chart formats.

**Bar Charts.** Although they lack the precision of tables, **bar charts** enable you to make emphatic visual comparisons by using horizontal or vertical bars of varying lengths. Bar charts are useful for comparing related items, illustrating changes in data over time, and showing segments as a part of the whole. Note how the bars in **Figures 10.9** and **10.10** present information in differing ways. Many techniques for constructing tables also hold true for bar charts. Here are a few more tips:

- Keep the length and width of each bar and segment proportional.

- Include a total figure in the middle or at the end of the bar if the figure helps the reader and does not clutter the chart.

- Start dollar or percentage amounts at zero.

- Place the first bar at some distance (usually half the amount of space between bars) from the y-axis.

- Avoid showing too much information, to avoid clutter and confusion.

- Place each bar chart as close as possible to the place where it is mentioned in the text.

**Line Charts.** The major advantage of **line charts** is that they show changes over time, thus indicating trends. The vertical axis is typically the dependent variable, and the horizontal axis, the independent one. Multiple line charts compare items, such as two or more data sets, using the same variable (Figure 10.11). **Segmented line charts**

**Figure 10.9  Horizontal Bar Chart**

Figure 2
TOTAL MPM INCOME, 2019 TO 2023

| Year | Millions of Dollars |
|---|---|
| 2019 | $66.3 |
| 2020 | 50.9 |
| 2021 | 67.6 |
| 2022 | 78.5 |
| 2023* | 82.2 |

*Projected

Source: *Industry Profiles* (New York, DataPro, 2022).

**Figure 10.10  Segmented 100 Percent Bar Chart**

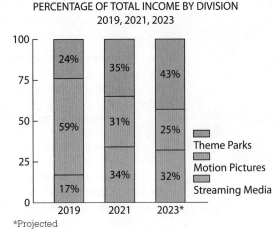

Figure 3
PERCENTAGE OF TOTAL INCOME BY DIVISION
2019, 2021, 2023

| | 2019 | 2021 | 2023* |
|---|---|---|---|
| Theme Parks | 24% | 35% | 43% |
| Motion Pictures | 59% | 31% | 25% |
| Streaming Media | 17% | 34% | 32% |

*Projected

Source: *Industry Profiles* (New York, DataPro, 2022).

Chapter 10: Proposals and Formal Reports

**Figure 10.11  Multiple Line Chart**

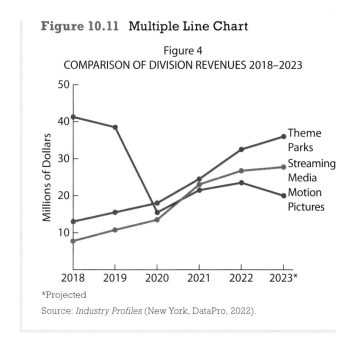

Figure 4
COMPARISON OF DIVISION REVENUES 2018–2023

*Projected

Source: *Industry Profiles* (New York, DataPro, 2022).

**Figure 10.12  Segmented Line (Area) Chart**

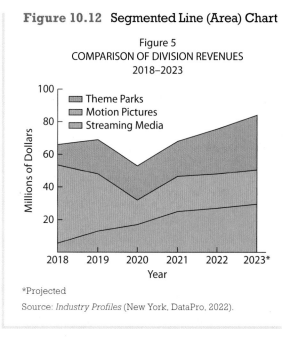

Figure 5
COMPARISON OF DIVISION REVENUES
2018–2023

*Projected

Source: *Industry Profiles* (New York, DataPro, 2022).

(Figure 10.12), also called **area charts**, illustrate how the components of a whole change over time. To prepare a line chart, follow these tips:

- Begin with a grid divided into squares.

- Arrange the time component (usually years) horizontally across the bottom; arrange values for the other variable vertically.

- Draw small dots at the intersections to indicate each value at a given year.

- Connect the dots and add color if desired.

- To prepare a segmented (area) chart, plot the first value (say, streaming media income) across the bottom; add the next item (say, motion picture income) to the first figures for every increment; for the third item (say, theme park income), add its value to the total for the first two items. The top line indicates the total of the three values.

Pie Charts. **Pie charts**, or circle graphs, enable readers to see a whole and the proportion of its components, or wedges. Although less flexible than bar or line charts, pie charts are useful for showing percentages, as **Figure 10.13** illustrates. They are very effective for lay, or nonexpert, audiences. Notice that a wedge can be exploded, or popped out, for special emphasis, as seen in Figure 10.13. MS Excel and other spreadsheet programs provide a selection of three-dimensional pie charts. For the most effective pie charts, follow these suggestions:

- Make the biggest wedge appear first. Computer spreadsheet programs correctly assign the biggest wedge first (beginning at the 12 o'clock position) and arrange the others in order of decreasing size as long as you list the data representing each wedge on the spreadsheet in descending order.

- Include, if possible, the actual percentage or absolute value for each wedge.

- Use four to six segments for best results; if necessary, group small portions into a wedge called *Other*.

- Draw radii from the center.

**Figure 10.13  Pie Chart**

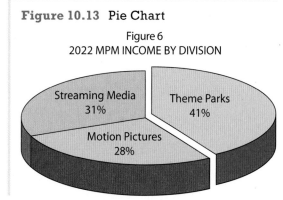

Figure 6
2022 MPM INCOME BY DIVISION

- Distinguish wedges with color, shading, or cross-hatching.

- Keep all the labels horizontal.

Flowcharts. Procedures are simplified and clarified by diagramming them in a **flowchart**, as shown in **Figure 10.14**. Whether you need to describe the procedure for handling a customer's purchase, highlight steps in solving a problem, or display a problem with a process, flowcharts help the reader visualize the process. Traditional flowcharts use the following symbols:

- Ovals to designate the beginning and end of a process

- Diamonds to designate decision points

- Rectangles to represent major activities or steps

Organization Charts. Many large organizations are so complex that they need charts to show the chain of command, from the boss down to the line managers and employees. **Organization charts** provide such information as who reports to whom, how many subordinates work for each manager (the span of control), and what channels of official communication exist. These charts may illustrate a company's structure—for example, by function, customer, or product. They may also be organized by the work being performed in each job or by the hierarchy of decision making.

Photographs, Maps, and Illustrations. Some business reports include photographs, maps, and illustrations to serve specific purposes. Photos, for example, add authenticity and provide a visual record. An environmental engineer may use photos to document hazardous waste sites. Maps enable report writers to depict activities or concentrations geographically, such as dots indicating sales reps in states across the country. Illustrations and diagrams are useful in indicating how an object looks or operates. A drawing showing the parts of a printer with labels describing their functions, for example, is more instructive than a photograph or verbal description.

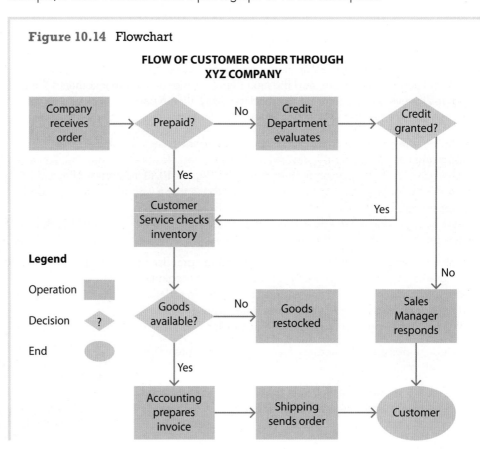

**Figure 10.14  Flowchart**

Infographics. An **infographic** is a visual representation of complex information in a format that is easy to understand. Compelling infographics tell a story by combining words, figures, and graphics such as charts and diagrams. More than compelling pictures, infographics are designed with a purpose. They offer a visual shorthand to deliver a message that presents information with few words. Many infographics include a call to action.

As shown in **Figure 10.15**, Michael Anderson created stylized charts in his infographic résumé to display his experience, education, and skills as a graphic designer. Infographics are frequently built around basic types of graphical elements such as bar, line, and pie charts. Although art makes an infographic visually appealing, the most important element of an infographic is accuracy: the data must be accurate and presented fairly. Because infographics tend to be complex and colorful, they are commonly shared in digital form online.

## 10-5b Incorporating Graphics in Reports

Used appropriately, graphics make reports more interesting and easier to understand. In putting graphics into your reports, follow these suggestions for best effects:

- **Evaluate the audience**. Consider the reader, the content, your schedule, and your budget. Because graphics take time to create and can be costly to print in color, think carefully before deciding how many to use. Six charts in an internal report to an executive may seem like overkill; however, in a long technical report to outsiders, six may be too few.

**Figure 10.15** Infographic Résumé

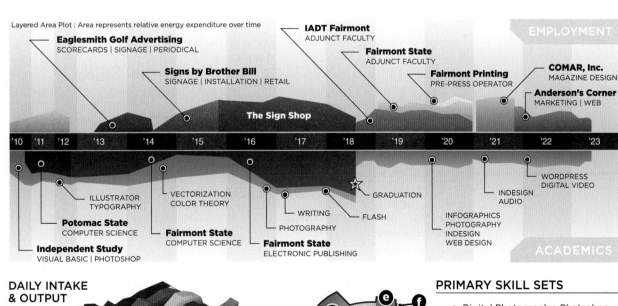

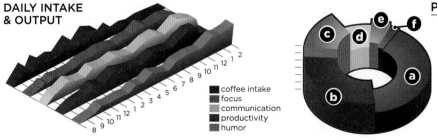

- **Use restraint**. Don't overuse color or decorations. Although color can effectively distinguish bars or segments in charts, too much color can be distracting and confusing. Remember, too, that colors themselves sometimes convey meaning: in North America red suggests deficits or negative values; blue suggests calmness and authority; yellow may suggest warning.

- **Be accurate and ethical**. Double-check all graphics for accuracy of figures and calculations. Be certain that your visuals aren't misleading—either accidentally or intentionally. Manipulation of a chart scale can make trends look steeper and more dramatic than they really are. Moreover, be sure to cite sources when you use someone else's facts.

- **Introduce a graph meaningfully**. Refer to every graphic in the text, and place the graphic close to the point where it is mentioned. Most important, though, help the reader understand the significance of the graphic. You can do this by telling your audience what to look for or by summarizing the main point of the graphic. Don't assume the reader will automatically reach the same conclusions you reached from a set of data. Instead of saying, *The findings are shown in Figure 3*, tell the reader what to look for: *Two thirds of the responding employees, as shown in Figure 3, favor a flextime schedule.* The best introductions for graphics interpret them for readers.

- **Choose an appropriate caption or title style**. Like reports, graphics may use talking titles or generic, descriptive titles. Talking titles are more persuasive; they suggest to the reader what to think. Descriptive titles describe the facts more objectively.

## 10-6 Assembling and Completing Formal Business Reports

In many ways formal business reports are longer versions of the analytical business reports presented in Chapter 9. Because of their length and complexity, formal business reports include more sections than routine informal business reports do. To compare the components of informal and formal reports, see Figure 10.2. In this section, the focus is on formal report components.

### 10-6a Front Matter Components of Formal Reports

The **front matter** of a formal report refers to the preliminary sections before the body section. Some front matter components are optional, but they typically appear in the following order: (a) report cover (optional), (b) title page, (c) letter or memo of transmittal (optional), (d) table of contents, (e) list of figures or tables (optional), and (f) executive summary. Writers often number these sections with lowercase Roman numerals; the title page, however, is normally not numbered. These components make it easy for the reader to find specific information quickly.

Title Page. The format of title pages may vary, but title pages often include the following elements:

- *Name* of the report, often in uppercase letters (no underscore and no quotation marks)

- *Presented to* (or *Submitted to*) followed by the name, title, and organization of the individual receiving the report

- *Prepared by* (or *Submitted by*) followed by the author's name and title

- Date of submission

Letter or Memo of Transmittal. Generally written on organization stationery, a letter or **memorandum of transmittal** introduces a formal report. A transmittal letter or memorandum follows the direct strategy and is usually less formal than the report itself.

The transmittal document typically (a) announces the topic of the report and tells how it was authorized; (b) briefly describes the project; (c) highlights the report's findings, conclusions, and recommendations; and (d) closes with appreciation for the assignment, acknowledgment of help from others, or instruction for the reader's follow-up actions. If a report is going to various readers, a special transmittal letter or memo should be prepared for each, anticipating how each reader will use the report.

Table of Contents. The **table of contents** shows the headings in the report and their page numbers. It gives an overview of the report topics and helps readers locate them. The table of contents includes front matter items, the body section's main headings and subheadings, and back matter sections, such as the appendix. Major headings are left-aligned, and leaders (spaced dots) help guide the eye to the page numbers.

List of Illustrations. For reports with many figures or tables, you may wish to include a list to help readers locate them. This list may appear on the same page as the table of contents, space permitting. For each figure or table, include a title and page number. Some writers distinguish between tables and all other illustrations, which they call figures. In that case they prepare separate lists of tables and figures.

Executive Summary. The purpose of an **executive summary** is to present an overview of a longer report to people who may not have time to read the entire document. Generally, an executive summary is prepared by the author of the report. However, you might be asked to write an executive summary of a published report or article written by someone else. In either case, the writer's goal is to summarize the report's major sections, such as the purpose, background, conclusions, and recommendations. Readers often go straight to the executive summary and look for the recommendations before glancing at the full report.

## 10-6b Body Components

Body components of formal reports typically include the introduction and body sections. In the introduction, the writer briefly describes the report's contents. In the body, the longest and most substantive section, the writer discusses the problem and findings before presenting analyses, conclusions, and recommendations.

Introduction. Formal reports begin with an introduction that sets the stage and announces the subject. A good report introduction typically covers the following elements, although not necessarily in this order:

- **Background:** Describe events leading up to the problem or need.

- **Problem or purpose:** Explain the report topic, and specify the problem or need that motivated the report.

- **Significance:** Tell why the topic is important. You may wish to quote experts or cite newspapers, journals, books, Internet resources, and other secondary sources to establish the importance of the topic.

- **Scope:** Clarify the boundaries of the report, defining what will be included or excluded.

- **Organization:** Orient readers by previewing the structure of the report.

Beyond these minimal introductory elements, consider adding any of the following information that may be relevant to your readers:

- **Authorization:** Identify who commissioned the report. If no letter of transmittal is included, also tell why, when, by whom, and to whom the report was written.

- **Literature review:** Summarize what other authors and researchers have published on this topic, especially for academic and scientific reports.

- **Sources and methods:** Describe your secondary sources (periodicals, books, Internet sources). If applicable, explain how you collected primary data.

- **Definitions of key terms:** Define words that may be unfamiliar to the audience.

**Report Body (Findings and Analyses).** The body is the main section in a formal report. It discusses, analyzes, interprets, and evaluates the research findings or solution to the initial problem. This is where you show the evidence that justifies your conclusions. Organize the body into main categories following your original outline.

The body section contains clear headings that explain each major section. Headings may be functional or talking. Functional heads (such as *Results of the Survey, Analysis of Findings,* or *Discussion*) help readers identify the purpose of the section but do not reveal what is in it. Such headings are useful for routine reports or for sensitive topics that may upset readers. Talking heads (for example, *Anatomy of a Market Crash* or *Your Money as a Force for Good*) are more descriptive and informative.

**Conclusions and Recommendations.** This important section tells what the findings mean, particularly in terms of solving the original problem. Some writers prefer to intermix their conclusions with the analysis of the findings—instead of presenting the conclusions separately. Other writers place the conclusions before the body so that busy readers can examine them immediately. Still other writers combine the conclusions and recommendations. Most writers, though, present the conclusions after the body because readers expect this structure. To improve readability, you may present the conclusions in a numbered or bulleted list.

## 10-6c Back Matter Components

The **back matter** of most reports includes a reference section and one or more appendixes. The reference section includes a list of sources, and the appendix contains supplemental information or source documents. In organizing the back matter sections, use standard Arabic numerals to number the pages.

**Appendixes.** Incidental or supplemental materials belong in **appendixes** at the end of a formal report. These materials are relevant to some readers but not to all. They may also be too bulky to include in the text. Appendixes may include survey forms, copies of other reports, tables of data, large graphics, and related correspondence. If multiple appendixes are necessary, they are named *Appendix A, Appendix B,* and *Appendix C.*

**Works Cited, References, or Bibliography.** If you use the **MLA** (Modern Language Association) citation format, list all sources of information alphabetically in a section titled **Works Cited.** If you use the **APA** (American Psychological Association) format, your list is called **References.** Your listed sources must correspond to in-text citations in the report whenever you are borrowing words or ideas from published and unpublished resources.

Regardless of the documentation format, you must include the author, title, publication, date of publication, page number, and other significant data for all ideas or quotations used in your report. For digital references include the Internet address, or URL, leading to the citation according to the guidelines of your chosen documentation format or your company's preference. Appendix B of this textbook contains documentation models and information.

## 10-6d Model Formal Report With MLA Format

Formal reports in business generally aim to study problems and recommend solutions. To see a complete formal report illustrating nearly all the parts, visit the Student Companion Website at **www.cengage.com**.

In this formal report, Keyla Wright, senior research consultant with Pueblo Development Company, was asked to study the economic impact of a local industrial park on the city of Flagstaff, Arizona.

The city council hired consultants to evaluate Coconino Industrial Park and to assess whether future commercial development would stimulate further economic growth. Keyla Wright subdivided the economic impact into three aspects: Revenues, Employment, and Indirect Benefits. The report was compiled from survey data as well as from secondary sources that Keyla consulted.

Keyla's report illustrates many of the points discussed in this chapter. Although it is a good example of the typical report format and style, it should not be viewed as the only way to present a report. Wide variation exists in business and academic reports. This model report illustrates MLA in-text citations and references (*Works Cited*).

For an overview of selected pages from the model formal report, see **Model Document 10.4**.

---

## Model Document 10.4 Selected Pages From the Formal Report

### Page 1 (Title page)

ECONOMIC IMPACT OF COCONINO INDUSTRIAL PARK
ON THE CITY OF FLAGSTAFF

Prepared for
The Flagstaff City Council
Flagstaff, Arizona

Prepared by
Keyla Wright
Senior Research Consultant
Sedona Development Company

January 12, 2022

### Page 2 (Letter of transmittal)

**SEDONA DEVELOPMENT COMPANY**
425 Saddle Rock Circle     www.sedonadevco.com
Sedona, Arizona 86340     928.450.3348

January 12, 2022

City Council
City of Flagstaff
211 West Aspen Avenue
Flagstaff, AZ 86001

Dear Council Members:

The attached report, requested by the Flagstaff City Council in a letter to Goldman-Lyon & Associates dated October 20, describes the economic impact of Coconino Industrial Park on the city of Flagstaff. We believe you will find the results of this study useful in evaluating future development of industrial parks within the city limits.

This study was designed to examine economic impact in three areas:

- Current and projected tax and other revenues accruing to the city from Coconino Industrial Park
- Current and projected employment generated by the park
- Indirect effects on local employment, income, and economic growth

Primary research consisted of interviews with 15 Coconino Industrial Park (CIP) tenants and managers, in addition to a 2021 survey of over 5,000 CIP employees. Secondary research sources included the Annual Budget of the City of Flagstaff, county and state tax records, government publications, periodicals, books, and online resources. Results of this research, discussed more fully in this report, indicated that Coconino Industrial Park exerts a significant beneficial influence in the Flagstaff metropolitan economy.

We would be pleased to discuss this report and its conclusions with you at your request. My firm and I thank you for your confidence in selection our company to prepare this comprehensive report.

Sincerely,

*Keyla Wright*

Keyla Wright
Senior Research Consultant

KW:coe
Attachment

### Page 3 (Table of Contents)

TABLE OF CONTENTS

### Page iv (Executive Summary)

**EXECUTIVE SUMMARY**

The city of Flagstaff can benefit from the development of industrial parks like the Coconino Industrial Park. Both direct and indirect economic benefits result, as shown by this in-depth study conducted by Sedona Development Company. The study was authorized by the Flagstaff City Council when Goldman-Lyon & Associates sought the City Council's approval for the proposed construction of a G-L industrial park. The City Council requested evidence demonstrating that an existing development could actually benefit the city.

Our conclusion that the city of Flagstaff benefits from industrial parks is based on data supplied by a survey of 5,000 Coconino Industrial Park employees, personal interviews with managers and tenants of CIP, city and state documents, and professional literature.

Analysis of the data revealed benefits in three areas:

- **Revenues.** The city of Flagstaff earned over $3 million in tax and other revenues from the Coconino Industrial Park in 2020. By 2025 this income is expected to reach $5.4 million (in constant 2018 dollars.)

- **Employment.** In 2020, CIP businesses employed a total of 7,035 workers, who earned an average wage of $56,579. By 2025, CIP businesses are expected to employ directly nearly 15,000 employees who earn salaries totaling over $998 million.

- **Indirect benefits.** Because of the multiplier effect, by 2025 Coconino Industrial Park will directly and indirectly generate a total of 38,362 jobs in the Flagstaff metropolitan area.

On the basis of these findings, it is recommended that development of additional industrial parks be encouraged to stimulate local economic growth. The city would increase its tax revenues significantly, create much-needed jobs, and thus help stimulate the local economy in and around Flagstaff.

iv

### Page 1 (Introduction)

**INTRODUCTION: COCONINO AND THE LOCAL ECONOMY**

This study was designed to analyze the direct and indirect economic impact of Coconino Industrial Park on the city of Flagstaff. Specifically, the study seeks answers to these questions:

- What current tax and other revenues result directly from this park? What tax and other revenues may be expected in the future?

- How many and what kinds of jobs are directly attributable to the park? What is the employment picture for the future?

- What indirect effects has Coconino Industrial Park had on local employment, incomes, and economic growth?

**BACKGROUND: THE ROLE OF CIP IN COMMERCIAL DEVELOPMENT**

The development firm of Goldman-Lyon & Associates commissioned this study of Coconino Industrial Park at the request of the Flagstaff City Council. Before authorizing the development of a proposed Goldman-Lyon industrial park, the city council requested a study examining the economic effects of an existing park. Members of the city council wanted to determine to what extent industrial parks benefit the local community, and they chose Coconino Industrial Park as an example.

For those who are unfamiliar with it, Coconino Industrial Park is a 400-acre industrial park located in the city of Flagstaff about 4 miles from the center of the city. Most of the land lies within a specially designated area known as Redevelopment Project No. 2, which is under the jurisdiction of the Flagstaff Redevelopment Agency. Planning for the park began in 2001; construction started in 2003.

The original goal for Coconino Industrial Park was development for light industrial users. Land in this area was zoned for uses such as warehousing, research and development, and distribution. Like other communities, Flagstaff was eager to attract light industrial users because such businesses tend to employ a highly educated workforce, are relatively quiet, and do not pollute the environment (Cohen C1). The city of Flagstaff recognized the need for light industrial users and widened an adjacent highway to accommodate trucks and facilitate travel by workers and customers coming from Flagstaff.

1

### Page 6 (Works Cited)

**WORKS CITED**

Arizona State Board of Equalization. *Bulletin.* Phoenix State Printing Office, 2019, pp. 26–29.

Badri, Joseph, H. Jose Rivera, and Michael E. Kussk. "A Comparison of Sustainability and Economic Development in Urban Industrial Parks." *Journal of Industrial Ecology,* vol. 24, no. 4. Jan. 2019, pp. 233–268, https://doi .org/10.1078/0366-6133.25.335.

Cohen, Andrew P. "Industrial Parks Invade Suburbia." *The New York Times.* 14 Dec. 2019: C1.

Fighting Poverty and Protecting the Environment: Development of a Sustainable Technologies Industrial Park, 15 Nov. 2019, www.smart-communities.ncat.org /success/northam.shtml.

Miller, Aaron M. *Redevelopment Projects: Future Prospects.* Rincon Press.

Pearson, Sophie. "Travel to Work Characteristics for the 50 Largest Metropolitan Areas by Population in the United States." *The Wall Street Journal,* 30 June 2019.

U.S. Department of Labor, Bureau of Labor Statistics. *Overview of the 2010–2020 Projections,* 2019.

iStockPhoto/Prostock-Studio

## Summary of Learning Outcomes

**1  Explain the purpose of informal and formal proposals and their basic components.**

- Proposals are written offers that solve problems, provide services, or sell products.
- Proposals may be internal, such as a request to change a company policy or to purchase equipment; or they may be external, such as a grant proposal requesting funding from agencies that support worthwhile causes.
- Proposals may be solicited (requested by an organization) or unsolicited (written to offer a service, request funding, or solve a problem).
- Requests for proposals (RFPs) specify what a proposal should include.
- Standard parts of informal proposals include (a) a persuasive introduction explaining the purpose of the proposal; (b) background identifying the problem and project goals; (c) a proposal, plan, or schedule outlining the project; (d) a section describing staff qualifications; (e) expected costs; and (f) a request for approval or authorization.
- Formal proposals may include additional parts not found in informal proposals: (a) a copy of the RFP (request for proposals); (b) a letter of transmittal; (c) an abstract or executive summary; (d) a title page; (e) a table of contents; (f) a list of illustrations; and (g) an appendix.

**2  Outline the steps in the process of writing formal business reports.**

- In a formal report, the author analyzes findings, draws conclusions, and makes recommendations intended to solve a problem.
- Writers determine the purpose and scope of the report, anticipate the needs of the audience, prepare a work plan, decide on appropriate research methods, conduct research using secondary and primary sources, organize findings, draw conclusions, and design graphics.
- Writers proofread and edit formal reports by reviewing the format, spacing and font consistency, graphics placement, heading levels, data accuracy, and mechanics.

**3  Describe primary and secondary research and how to evaluate its credibility.**

- Nearly every research project begins with secondary data, including print books or e-books and periodicals (scholarly journals, trade publications, newspapers, and magazines).
- Library databases (such as ProQuest, EBSCO, JSTOR, and Factiva) enable researchers to access in-depth data remotely.
- The most successful researchers know their Internet search tools and apply advanced Internet search strategies.
- Writers and researchers need to be able to evaluate the credibility of each Web resource by scrutinizing it for its currency (last update), author or sponsoring organization, content, purpose, and accuracy.
- Report writers gather data from primary sources by distributing surveys, conducting interviews, and collecting data from firsthand observation or systematic experimentation.

**4  Discuss the importance and methods of ethically documenting information from business report sources.**

- Documenting sources means giving credit to information sources to avoid plagiarism, strengthen an argument, and instruct readers.
- In the academic world, documentation is critical. In business, reports are less heavily documented; however, writers still may need to cite their sources.-
- Paraphrasing involves putting another's ideas into one's own words.
- Common citation formats include the Modern Language Association (MLA), the American Psychological Association (APA), and the Chicago Manual of Style (CMS).

**5  Incorporate meaningful visual aids and graphics in business reports.**

- Graphics clarify data, add visual interest, and make complex data easy to understand; they should be placed close to where they are referenced.
- Tables show quantitative information in systematic columns and rows; they require meaningful titles, bold column headings, and logical arrangement (alphabetical, chronological, etc.).
- Bar charts and line charts enable data to be compared visually; line charts are especially helpful in showing changes over time.
- Pie charts show a whole and the proportion of its components; flowcharts diagram processes and procedures.
- To incorporate graphics into reports, evaluate the audience, use restraint in colors and decorations, be accurate and ethical, introduce a graph meaningfully, and choose an appropriate caption or title style.
- Infographics combine images and graphic elements to visually illustrate information in an easy-to-understand format.

## 6 Identify the components of typical formal business reports.

- Front matter components of formal reports often include a title page, letter or memo of transmittal, table of contents, list of figures, and an executive summary that explains key points.
- Typical components of formal reports include the introduction, the body, and the conclusions and recommendations.
- The main section of a formal report is the body; it discusses, analyzes, interprets, and evaluates the research findings or solution to a problem before drawing conclusions.
- Back matter components of a formal report include a bibliography, which may be a works-cited or reference page, and any appendix(es).

## Key Terms

| | | |
|---|---|---|
| proposal 292 | primary research 301 | area charts 313 |
| grant proposal 293 | secondary research 301 | pie charts 313 |
| request for proposal (RFP) 294 | database 302 | flowchart 314 |
| solicited proposal 294 | periodicals 302 | organization charts 314 |
| unsolicited proposals 294 | browser 303 | infographic 315 |
| letter proposals 294 | search engine 303 | front matter 316 |
| deliverables 295 | survey 305 | memorandum of transmittal 316 |
| budget 295 | interview 307 | table of contents 317 |
| formal report 297 | observation 307 | executive summary 317 |
| purpose statement 298 | experimentation 308 | back matter 318 |
| scope statement 298 | documentation 308 | appendixes 318 |
| limitations 298 | plagiarism 308 | MLA 318 |
| work plan 298 | paraphrasing 309 | works cited 318 |
| problem statement 298 | citation formats 311 | APA 318 |
| secondary sources 299 | table 311 | references 318 |
| primary sources 300 | bar charts 312 | contract cheating 322 |
| outline 300 | line charts 312 | |
| research 301 | segmented line charts 312 | |

## Chapter Review

1. Why are formal and informal proposals written? (L.O. 1)

2. Why do government agencies and other organizations make requests for proposals (RFPs)? (L.O. 1)

3. Name five possible parts of a work plan for a formal report. (L.O. 2)

4. Why are formal reports written in business? Give an example of what a business report might investigate. (L.O. 2)

5. If the Internet is one of the greatest sources of information, why must researchers be cautious when using its sources? (L.O. 3)

6. What are the differences between primary and secondary sources? Which should a researcher seek first? Give an example of each. (L.O. 3)

7. What is the difference between plagiarizing and paraphrasing? What techniques can a writer employ to paraphrase effectively? (L.O. 4)

8. Briefly compare the advantages and disadvantages of illustrating data with charts (bar and line) versus tables. (L.O. 5)

9. What should be included in the introduction to a formal business report? (L.O. 6)

10. What should the report writer strive to include in the body of a formal business report? (L.O. 6)

## Critical Thinking

11. Why do researchers trust the information obtained from scholarly journals, major newspapers, and well-known magazines? Why should researchers use caution when accessing information from anonymous blogs, Wikipedia, and other crowdsourced content? (L.O. 3)

12. What is the difference between conclusions and recommendations in a report? (L.O. 2)

13. Some people say that business reports never contain footnotes. If you were writing your first report for a business and you did considerable research, what would you do about documenting your sources? (L.O. 4)

14. An infographic is far more effective at conveying statistics than any bar graph or pie chart, claims Dallas marketing firm Frozen Fire.[18] Do you agree or disagree? How could infographics be useful in your field? (L.O. 5)

15. Plagiarism detection software such as Turnitin makes cheating by copying easy to spot. This explains why ghostwritten assignments are booming online. The old paper mills have morphed into global enterprises and brazenly market their services in slick YouTube videos but also offline. Students cite time pressure and stress as reasons for resorting to **contract cheating**. Some rationalize buying written-to-order papers online by falling back on the old saw that "everyone is doing it." In a recent NPR story, a student made this argument: "Technically, I don't think it's cheating. Because you're paying someone to write an essay, which they don't plagiarize, and they write everything on their own." When pressed, the student acknowledged that perhaps it's "a difficult question to answer," verging on "a gray area" or being "on the edge, kind of." How do you feel about this type of growing academic dishonesty? Do you think it is common on college campuses? (L.O. 4)

## Activities and Cases

### 10.1 Proposal: Never too Soon to Plan for Retirement (L.O. 1)

As a financially literate business student, you know about the magic of compound interest. Conventional wisdom and Suze Orman tell us that college grads will have a tidy sum as senior citizens if they start socking away for retirement even a small sum each month and letting it grow in stock mutual funds for decades. Unlike you, few of your peers worry about retirement savings; they are busy looking for a good job fresh out of college. Now, imagine you are working for a small but growing construction company. Your boss insists the company can't afford to offer an IRA or 401(k) plan to you and the other ten employees. You do some digging and find that providing a SIMPLE IRA (Savings Incentive Match Plan for Employees Individual Retirement Account) would generate tax savings for your boss's small company, not to mention give you a head start on investing in mutual funds.

**YOUR TASK.** Search for articles that explain SIMPLE IRA rules. Check out the Department of Treasury, Internal Revenue Service website. Once you are well informed about the plan, think through your persuasive strategy. What arguments are most likely to sway your boss? Write a memo proposal to your boss (use your current supervisor's or your instructor's name) arguing for the benefits of introducing a SIMPLE IRA. Apply what you have learned about unsolicited informal proposals in this chapter.

### 10.2 Proposal: Be a Problem Solver at Work (L.O. 1)

Most managers welcome workers who are able to spot problems before they turn into serious risks. Drawing on your internship and work experience, can you identify a problem that could be solved with a small to moderate financial investment? Look for issues such as a lack of lunch or break rooms for staff; badly needed health initiatives such as gyms or sport club memberships; replacing low-gas-mileage, high-emission company vehicles; or introducing a recycling program.

**YOUR TASK.** Discuss with your instructor the workplace problem you have identified. Make sure you choose a relatively weighty problem that can be lessened or eliminated with a modest expenditure. Be sure to explain how the benefits merit the cost. Address your unsolicited letter or memo proposal to your current or former boss and copy your instructor.

### 10.3 Proposal: Are You a Tycoon in the Making? (L.O. 1)
> **Web**

Perhaps you have fantasized about one day owning your own company, or maybe you have already started a business. Proposals are offers to a very specific audience whose business you are soliciting. Think of a product or service that you like or know something about. Search the Internet or research databases, and study the market so that you understand going rates, prices, and costs. Search the Small Business Administration's website (**https://www.sba.gov**) for valuable tips on how to launch, run, and manage a successful business.

**YOUR TASK.** Choose a product or service you would like to offer to a particular audience, such as a dating consulting service, a window cleaning business, a bakery specializing in your favorite cakes, an online photography business, a distributor of e-bikes, or a new specialized hair care line. Discuss products and services as well as target audiences with your instructor. Write an informal letter proposal promoting your chosen product or service to the target audience you have identified.

## 10.4 Proposal: Helping a Friend Find Samples to Study (L.O. 1, 2)

E-Mail        Web

Many new companies with services or products to offer would like to land corporate or government contracts. However, they are intimidated by the proposal and RFP processes. Your friend Jocelyn, who has started her own designer uniform company, has asked you for help. Her goal is to offer her colorful yet functional uniforms to hospitals and clinics. Before writing a proposal, however, she wants to see examples and learn more about the process.

**YOUR TASK.** Search the Internet to find at least two examples of business proposals. Try search terms such as *small business proposals* or *small business proposal examples*. Don't waste time on sites that want to sell templates or books. Find actual examples. Try **https://www.bplans.com/samples/sba.cfm**. Then prepare an e-mail or memo to Jocelyn in which you do the following:

a. Identify two sample business proposals.
b. Outline the parts of each proposal.
c. Compare the strengths and weaknesses of each proposal.
d. Draw conclusions. What can Jocelyn learn from these examples?

## 10.5 Proposal: Pitching Ortopedica Sports Medicine (L.O. 1)

Team

Sports medicine is increasingly popular, especially in university towns. A new medical clinic, Ortopedica Sports Medicine, is opening its doors in your community. A friend recommended your small business to the administrator of the clinic, and you received a letter asking you to provide information about your service. The new medical clinic specializes in sports medicine, physical therapy, and cardiac rehabilitation services. It is interested in retaining your company, rather than hiring its own employees to perform the service your company offers.

**YOUR TASK.** Working in teams, first decide what service you offer. It could be landscaping, uniforms, uniform laundering, general cleaning, a cloud-based storage system, online medical supplies, patient transportation, supplemental hospice care, temporary office support, social media guidance, or food service. As a team, develop a letter proposal outlining your plan, staffing, and budget.

Use persuasion to show why contracting your services is better than hiring in-house employees. In the proposal letter, request a meeting with the administrative board. In addition to a written proposal, you may be expected to make an oral presentation that includes visual aids and/or handouts. Send your proposal to Dr. Sven Rasmussen, Director, Ortopedica Sports Medicine. Supply a local address.

## 10.6 Grant Writing: Nonprofits' Lifeblood (L.O. 1, 2)

Web

Nonprofit organizations are always seeking grant writers, and you would like to gain experience in this area. You've heard that they earn high salaries, and one day you might even decide to become a professional grant/proposal writer. However, you first need experience. On a website belonging to The Actors Theatre Workshop you saw an ad for a grant writer to "seek funding for general operating expenses and program-related funding." A grant writer would "develop proposals, generate boilerplates for future applications, and oversee a writing team." This listing sounds good, but you need a local position.

**YOUR TASK.** Search the Internet for local nonprofits. Alternatively, your instructor may already know of local groups seeking grant writers, such as a United Way member agency, an educational institution, or a faith-based organization. Perhaps your university maintains a service-learning or experiential learning program. Talk with your instructor about an assignment. Your instructor may ask you to submit a preliminary memo report outlining ten or more guidelines you expect to follow when writing proposals and grants for nonprofit organizations.

## 10.7 Service Learning: Better Your Community! (L.O. 1–6)

E-Mail        Web

Your school may be one that encourages service learning, a form of experiential learning. You could receive credit for a project that bridges academic and nonacademic communities. Because writing skills are in high demand, you may have an opportunity to simultaneously apply your skills, contribute to the community, and expand your résumé. The National Service-Learning

Clearinghouse describes service learning as "a teaching and learning strategy that integrates meaningful community service with instruction and reflection to enrich the learning experience, teach civic responsibility, and strengthen communities."[19] You can access thousands of Clearinghouse resources at **https://www.community-wealth.org**. The Internet offers many sites devoted to examples of students engaging in service-learning projects.

**YOUR TASK.** Research possible service-learning projects in this class or another. Your instructor may ask you to submit a memo or e-mail message analyzing your findings. Describe at least four completed service-learning projects that you found in your Web search. Draw conclusions about what made them successful or beneficial. What kinds of similar projects might be possible for you or students in your class? Your instructor may use this as a research project or turn it into a hands-on project by having you find a service organization in your community that needs trained writers.

## 10.8 Formal Business Report: Planning an International Launch (L.O. 2–6)

> **Intercultural** > **Team** > **Web**

U.S. businesses are expanding into foreign markets with manufacturing plants, sales offices, and branches abroad. Many Americans, however, have little knowledge of or experience with people from other cultures. To prepare for participation in the global marketplace, you are to collect information for a report focused on an Asian, Latin American, European, or African country where English is not regularly spoken. Before selecting the country, though, consult your campus international student program for volunteers who are willing to be interviewed. Your instructor may make advance arrangements with international student volunteers.

**YOUR TASK.** In teams of three to five, collect information about your target country from research databases, the Internet, and other sources. Then invite an international student representing your target country to be interviewed by your group. Alternatively, you could interview a faculty member who hails from another country. Prepare and know your interview questions and be courteous; people like to talk about themselves, but no one wants to waste time.

As you conduct primary and secondary research, investigate the topics listed in **Figure 10.16** Confirm what you learn in your secondary research by talking with your interviewee. When you complete your research, write a report for the CEO of your company (make up a name and company). Assume that your company plans to expand its operations abroad. Your report should advise the company's executives of the social customs, family life, attitudes, religions, education, and values of the target country. Remember that your company's interests are business oriented; do not dwell on tourist information. Write your report individually or in teams.

## 10.9 Preparing a Work Plan (L.O. 2)

Any long report project requires a structured work plan. In fact, any complex assignment can benefit from a plan that structures the various phases until completion.

**YOUR TASK.** Select a report topic from activities presented at the ends of Chapters 12 and 13. For that report prepare a work plan that includes the following:

a. Statement of the problem
b. Expanded statement of purpose (including scope, limitations, and significance)
c. Research strategy to answer the questions
d. Tentative outline of key questions to answer
e. Work schedule (with projected completion dates)

## 10.10 Conducting Primary Research by Exploring Campus Food Delivery Options (L.O. 2)

> **Communication Technology** > **E-Mail** > **Team** > **Web**

The COVID-19 pandemic has made food delivery apps such as GrubHub, DoorDash, UberEats, Postmates, or Instacart household names. Some universities have even created their own mobile apps for delivery from a few available campus cafés and commons. However, hungry students staying in residence halls dislike delivery fees and wait time for outside dining orders, despite their greater variety.

Planning ahead to in-person classes, your University Business Club (UBC) sees an opportunity to put its business expertise to work by sponsoring a small student-run restaurant in the campus food court. But what food should it dish out? Is it true that college students overwhelmingly prefer food high in salt, sugar, and fat? Your fellow club members have chosen you to create an online survey to poll fellow students, staff, and faculty about their preferences. You hope to generate data that will support the feasibility of the eatery and help UBC create winning menu choices.

**Figure 10.16   Intercultural Interview Topics and Questions**

## Social Customs

- How do people react to strangers? Are they generally friendly? Hostile? Reserved?
- How do people greet each other?
- What are the appropriate manners when you enter a room? Bow? Nod? Bump elbows? The COVID-19 pandemic has all but nixed handshaking.
- How are names used for introductions? Is it appropriate to inquire about one's occupation or family?
- What are the attitudes toward touching?
- How does one express appreciation for an invitation to another's home? Bring a gift? Send flowers? Write a thank-you note? Are any gifts taboo?
- Are there any customs related to how or where one sits?
- Are any facial expressions or gestures considered rude?
- What is the attitude toward punctuality in social situations? In business situations?
- What are acceptable eye contact patterns?
- What gestures indicate agreement? Disagreement?

## Family Life

- What is the basic unit of social organization? Basic family? Extended family?
- Do women work outside of the home? In what occupations?

## Housing, Clothing, and Food

- Are there differences in the kinds of housing used by different social groups? Differences in location? Differences in furnishings?
- What occasions require special clothing?
- Are some types of clothing considered taboo?
- What is appropriate business attire for men? For women?
- How many times a day do people eat? What are some of the staples, that is, typical foods?
- What types of places, food, and drink are appropriate for business entertainment? Where is the seat of honor at a table?

## Class Structure

- Into what classes is society organized?
- Do racial, religious, or economic factors determine social status?
- Are there any minority groups? What is their social standing?

## Political Patterns

- Are there any immediate threats to the political survival of the country?
- How is political power manifested?
- What channels are used for expressing political opinions?
- What information media are important?
- Is it appropriate to talk politics in social situations?

## Religion and Folk Beliefs

- To which religious groups do people belong? Is one predominant?
- Do religious beliefs influence daily activities?
- Which places are considered sacred? Which objects? Which events?
- How do religious holidays affect business activities?

## Economic Institutions

- What are the country's principal products and industries?
- Are workers organized in unions?
- How are businesses owned? By family units? By large public corporations? By the government?
- What is the standard work schedule and work week?
- Is it appropriate to do business by telephone? By computer?
- How has technology affected business procedures?
- Is participatory management used?
- Are there any customs related to exchanging business cards?
- How is status shown in an organization? Private office? Secretary? Furniture?
- Are businesspeople expected to socialize before conducting business?

## Value Systems

- Is competitiveness or cooperation more prized?
- Is thrift or enjoyment of the moment more valued?
- Is politeness more important than bluntness?
- What are the attitudes toward education?
- Do women own or manage businesses? If so, how are they treated?
- What are your people's perceptions of Americans? Do Americans offend you? What has been hardest about adjusting to life in the United States? How could Americans make this adjustment easier for you?

The main provider of online survey software, SurveyMonkey, makes creating questionnaires fast, fun, and easy. After signing up for the free no-frills basic plans, you can create brief online questionnaires and e-mail the links to your targeted respondents. The programs analyze and display the results for you—at no charge.

**YOUR TASK.** In pairs or teams of three, design a basic questionnaire to survey students on your campus about food options in the campus cafeteria. Visit SurveyMonkey, which offers a free basic plan limited to ten questions. After creating the online survey, start by polling students in your course and potentially in similar business classes. Interpret the results. As a team, write a memo that you will e-mail to the campus food services administrator advocating for a student-run eatery featuring the top-scoring national or regional foods.

Your instructor may ask you to complete this activity as a report or proposal assignment for the campus food services administrator and support your advocacy with the survey results.

## 10.11 Secondary Research: Where Are Teens Heading After Facebook? (L.O. 2)

**Communication Technology** ▸ **E-Mail** ▸ **Web**

As an assistant market researcher, you have been asked by your boss, Kym Koenig, to explore marketing opportunities targeting teens. Understanding teen preferences in this notoriously fickle consumer group is key to success of any promotional or ad campaign. Recent studies suggest that, although some teens still use Facebook, they prefer to spend their time on Instagram, Snapchat, YouTube, or TikTok. They also love to try new apps recommended by friends. Most important, 95 percent of teens have a smartphone or access to one, and 45 percent admit that they are online nearly constantly.

For a full picture to emerge, you will need to consult several recent studies. The best candidates for your research are surveys by Pew Research Center, Common Sense Media, and similar reputable sources of data.

**YOUR TASK.** Ms. Koenig has requested a brief informational e-mail report summarizing your main findings. Paraphrase correctly and don't just copy from the online source. Ms. Koenig may ask you later to analyze more comprehensive data in an analytical report and create a media use profile of American teens and young adults. You may be called on to create graphs to illustrate your findings.

## 10.12 Citing Secondary Sources: Apply the MLA Format (L.O. 4)

**E-Mail**

You will want to stay up-to-date on your career field by reading, saving current articles, and bookmarking valuable resources. Think about a current business topic related to your professional field that you would like to learn more about. This is your chance to learn more about, gather tips and strategies about, and follow current trends in your field of interest.

**YOUR TASK.** Look for three current (within the last two years) secondary research sources on a topic related to your field of study. In a memo or e-mail to your instructor, write a one-paragraph summary of each article or resource. Then list the citations for your three sources using the MLA style. The citations should follow the format used on a Works Cited page with citations in alphabetical order and using the hanging indent style.

## 10.13 Plagiarism and Cheating: The Fraudulent Paper That Keeps Killing Children (L.O. 4)

**Team** ▸ **Web**

Occasionally we read about people who plagiarize their work, try to cheat their way through college, invent news features, copy from others, or fabricate research results. Have you ever wondered who gets hurt when students, teachers, journalists, scientists, and other authors are dishonest researchers and writers?

One of the most notorious and prolific medical miscreants was Japanese anesthesiologist Yoshitaka Fujii, who wrote 172 bogus scientific papers, 126 of which were based on imaginary research studies. Two other shocking cases in medical research rival Fujii's fabrications in gravity and scope. Former British surgeon Andrew Wakefield published an article in the reputable medical journal *The Lancet* that seemed to provide evidence that a common immunization against measles, mumps, and rubella (MMR) could cause autism. However, Wakefield had fabricated evidence and was found guilty of professional misconduct. He lost his license to practice as a medical doctor. His fraudulent research, however, caused a precipitous drop in vaccinations in the United Kingdom and Ireland. In the words of one pediatrician, "That paper killed children"; to this day the fraud continues to cause harm by sowing mistrust of other vaccines, for example, those for COVID-19.[20] Many American parents still refuse to vaccinate their kids and are causing the spread of diseases that had been eradicated in the United States.[21]

A Harvard researcher's purposely nonsensical research paper, consisting of randomly generated text accompanied by two fake authors, was accepted by 17 of 37 medical journals. Journals publishing such bogus research are called predatory publishers. A prominent bioethicist calls such practices "publication pollution."[22]

**YOUR TASK.** If your instructor directs, individually or as a team, investigate the cases of Andrew Wakefield, Joachim Boldt, Stephen Ambrose, Jayson Blair, Doris Kearns Goodwin, Jonah Lehrer, Kaavya Viswanathan, or other infamous plagiarists. Alternatively, you could focus on the case of 200 professors from 50 universities implicated in a massive publishing scam in South Korea.[23] Consider the authors' transgressions, their excuses, and the consequences of their actions. As a team, gather your individual research results, compare notes, and summarize your insights in a memo report to your instructor. This assignment could also be turned into a formal report if the investigation is expanded to include more detailed discussions and more cases.

## 10.14 Plagiarism, Paraphrasing, and Citing Sources (L.O. 4)

One of the biggest challenges for student writers is paraphrasing secondary sources correctly to avoid plagiarism.

**YOUR TASK.** For each of the following, read the original passage. Analyze the paraphrased version. List the weaknesses in relation to what you have learned about plagiarism and the use of references. Then write an improved version.

a. **Original Passage**

The abbreviation AI is used to refer both to present-day technology like Siri, Google Translate, and IBM's Watson and to transformative future technologies that surpass human capabilities in all areas. That means surveying people about "risks from AI" is a fraught project—some of them will be thinking about Facebook's News Feed, and some of them, like Stephen Hawking, about technologies that exceed our intelligence "by more than ours exceeds that of snails."[24]

**Paraphrased Passage**

The term AI [Artificial Intelligence] is used to describe current technologies like Siri, Google Translate, and IBM's Watson. It also refers to future technologies that may exceed our ability to understand them. That means that asking people what they think about "risks from AI" is a worrisome project. Some may think about Facebook's News Feed, and others, such as Stephen Hawking, will imagine technologies that surpass our intelligence "by more than ours exceeds that of snails."

b. **Original Passage**

When the Tesla Model S launched four years ago, the all-electric luxury sedan certainly had its critics. Many of them were executives at German luxury carmakers, quick to dismiss the upstart American carmaker as a quixotic but doomed effort. But as the Model S won plaudits, achieved respectable sales, and captured the public's imagination, that attitude has changed. And that was before Tesla racked up nearly 400,000 reservations for its Model 3 sedan, which is expected to compete with German mainstays like the Audi A4 and BMW 3-Series. Now, Audi, BMW, Mercedes-Benz, and Porsche are downright worried about Tesla. "Tesla has promised a lot but has also delivered most of it," Dieter Zetsche—chairman of Mercedes parent Daimler—said earlier this month.[25]

**Paraphrased Passage**

Upon the launch of its Model S, Tesla had many detractors; most were executives at German car companies selling luxury cars. They dismissed the new California-based carmaker as a doomed effort. That attitude has changed as the Model S won praise, racked up considerable sales, and impressed the general public. Most recently, Tesla secured 400,000 early reservations for its Model 3, which will compete with German luxury cars such as the Audi A4 and the BMW 3-Series. Now that Tesla has promised a lot but has also delivered most of it, said Daimler chairman Dieter Zetsche, the German carmakers Audi, Mercedes-Benz, Porsche, and BMW are pretty worried about Tesla.

c. **Original Passage**

American Dream, the most expensive U.S. mall ever built, opened Friday. It is the first in the U.S. to devote more space to entertainment, restaurants and theme-park rides than to traditional retail. Given that more than a few people have declared the mall dead, the entire industry is glued to the spectacle to see if its formula could save the American shopping center from oversupply and the rise of online shopping.[26]

**Paraphrased Passage**

The most expensive U.S. mall ever built, American Dream, opened Friday. It is the first in this country to give more space to theme-park rides, entertainment, and restaurants than it gives to traditional retail. The complete industry is fascinated by the spectacle to see if its model could save the American shopping center from online shopping and oversupply.

## 10.15 Picking Suitable Graphics (L.O. 5)

**YOUR TASK.** Identify the best graphics forms to illustrate the following data.

a. Figure showing the tracking and fulfillment of an e-commerce order
b. Annual restaurant industry sales figures for meatless hamburgers
c. Government unemployment data by industry and sector, in percentages
d. Figures showing COVID-19 infection rates by state
e. Figures showing the process of delivering water to a metropolitan area
f. Information showing which U.S. states have enacted laws banning handheld phone conversations while driving.
g. Figures showing what proportion of every state tax dollar is spent on education, social services, transportation, debt, and other expenses
h. Academic, administrative, and operation divisions of a college, from the president to department chairs and division managers
i. Figures comparing the sales of smartphones, tablets, and laptops over the past five years

## 10.16 Analyzing Graphics (L.O. 5)

> **E-Mail** > **Web**

Being able to make sense of figures and graphics is important in business. Test your ability to interpret and explain visuals found in typical business publications.

**YOUR TASK.** Select four graphics from newspapers or magazines in hard copy or online. Look in *The Wall Street Journal*, *USA Today*, *Bloomberg Businessweek*, *U.S. News & World Report*, *Fortune*, *Forbes*, or other business news publications. Add the title and the source of each graphic. In an e-mail or memo to your instructor, critique each graphic based on what you have learned in this chapter. Do you think the graphic could have been expressed more effectively in text? How effective are the labels and headings used in this graphic? Did color add clarity? If used, describe the placement and effectiveness of a legend. Is the appropriate graphic form used? What is your overall impression of the effectiveness of the graphic?

## 10.17 Creating Bar Charts and Line Graphs (L.O. 5)

> **Web**

Practice creating your own bar charts and line graphs with figures provided by Internet World Stats.

**YOUR TASK.** Create a bar chart comparing the current number of Internet users (by millions) in the following countries: United States, India, Japan, Brazil, Indonesia, China, United Kingdom, and Russia. Find statistics within the last year and name the source of your information. Arrange the bars according to the country with the highest number of users to the lowest. Add a chart title and appropriate labels. Alternatively, create the appropriate graphic that illustrates the growth of Internet use in the population by continent (Africa, Asia, Europe, Latin America/Caribbean, Middle East, North America, Oceania/Australia).

## 10.18 Proposals and Formal Reports: Find Topics to Write About (L.O. 1–6)

> **Team** > **Web**

A list of more than 100 **Report Topics** is available at the accompanying student site. The topics are divided into the following categories: accounting, finance, personnel/human resources, marketing, information systems, management, and general business/education/campus issues.

You can collect information for many of these reports by using library databases and searching the Internet. Your instructor may assign topics as individual or team projects. All involve critical thinking in organizing information, drawing conclusions, and making recommendations. The topics are appropriate for proposals and formal business reports.

**YOUR TASK.** As directed by your instructor, select a topic from the report list at **www.cengage.com**.

## Grammar/Mechanics Checkup 10

## Apostrophes

Review Sections 2.20–2.22 in the Grammar/Mechanics Handbook. In the space provided, write the letter of the correctly punctuated sentence. Also record the appropriate Grammar/Mechanics guideline for the principle involved. When you finish, compare your responses with those provided at the bottom of the page. If your answers differ, study carefully the principles in parentheses.

| | | |
|---|---|---|
| b (2.20b) | **EXAMPLE** | In just three to five (a) *months,* (b) *months'* time, you could obtain your real-estate license. |
| _____ | 1. | My new (a) boss's, (b) bosses, (c) boss' keynote address received a standing ovation. |
| _____ | 2. | During job interviews candidates are often asked where they see themselves in five (a) years, (b) year's, (c) years' time. |
| _____ | 3. | Several of my colleagues missed (a) Lucas', (b) Lucas's, (c) Lucas important and entertaining IT workshop. |

_____    4. CIO (a) Ramirez's, (b) Ramirezes, (c) Ramirezes' frequent warnings urging employees to use strong passwords and change them often fell on deaf ears.

_____    5. Several (a) employees', (b) employee's, (c) employees e-mail accounts were hacked after the workers had fallen victim to phishing e-mails.

_____    6. So far several of (a) Elon Musks' (b) Elon Musk's, (c) Elon Musks daring objectives to revolutionize space travel have been reached.

_____    7. (a) Luisa, (b) Luisas', (c) Luisa's intelligence and people skills helped her get promoted ahead of more senior employees.

                   8. We always visit a new (a) citys, (b) city's, (c) cities most famous museums first.

_____    9. Following the COVID-19 pandemic, at least 340 (a) companies, (b) company's, (c) companies' in the United States went out of business.

_____   10. Within one (a) years, (b) year's, (c) years' time we plan to expand overseas.

## Editing Challenge 10

Every chapter provides an editing exercise to fine-tune your grammar and mechanics skills. The following executive summary requires edits that address spelling, grammar, punctuation, concise wording, and other issues. Study the guidelines in the Grammar/Mechanics Handbook (Appendix D), including the lists of Confusing Words and Frequently Misspelled Words.

**YOUR TASK.** Edit the following by (a) inserting corrections in your textbook or on a photocopy using the proofreading marks in Appendix C or (b) downloading the message from **www.cengage.com** and correcting at your computer.

### EXECUTIVE SUMMARY

#### Problem

Approximately 21 percent of employee's still smoke, despite our industrys antismoking efforts and our clean-air policies adapted in 2020.

Employees who smoke are costly to there organizations'. The following statistics show the affects of smoking for workers and organizations:

- Absenteeism is more then 50 percent higher among smoking employees.
- Accidents are 2 to 3 times greater among smokers.
- Bronchitis, lung and heart disease, cancer, and early death are more frequent among smokers.

Although our clean-air policy prohibits smoking in the building, shop, and offices. We have done little to encourage employees to stop smoking. Many workers still go outside to smoke at lunch and during break's.

#### Summary of Findings

Many companys have found that persuading employee's to stop smoking was the decisive factor in reducing health insurance premiums.

The least expensive and easiest stop-smoking measure involves the distribution of literature, such as "The Ten-Step Plan" from Smokefree Enterprises, and government pamphlets citing smoking dangers. Some companys sponsor group events such as the Great American Smoke-Out to spur smokers to quit.

Local clinics provide treatment programmes in classes at their centers. These behavior-modification stop-smoking programs have been shown to be more effective than literature distribution or incentive programs, however, many workers do not attend regularly and many drop out.

Some clinics offer workplace programs with counselors meeting employees in company's conference rooms. These on-sight programs our most successful. However, participant miss a lot of werk hours.

#### Conclusions and Recommendation

Smokers require discipline, counseling and professional assistance to kick the nicotin habit, as explained on the American Cancer Society website. If our goal is to reduce health care costs and lead our employees to healthful lives. We should invest in a workplace smoking-sessation program with release time for smokers. The program temporarily reduces productivity, nevertheless we can expect to recapture that loss in lower health care premiums and healthier employee.

We recommend a stop-smoking treatment program on company premises with two hour's a week of release time for participants' for three months'.

## Examining the Credibility of Websites: Reader Beware

Evaluating a website's credibility requires critical thinking and a good eye. Savvy Internet users start the evaluation process by thinking about how they found the site in the first place. They may have accessed the site from the results page of a search engine or by following a link from a reputable site. Perhaps the site was recommended by a friend, which would add credibility as long as the friend is knowledgeable and cautious. The processes for finding information on the Internet may vary, but the reader alone is responsible for determining the validity, truthfulness, and integrity of that information. Because anyone with a computer and an Internet connection can publish on the Internet, the reader must beware and wisely question all content found online.

Unlike the content of journals, magazines, and newspapers found in research databases, the content of most websites has not been reviewed by skilled editors. Some Web pages do not show authorship, credentials, or sponsoring organizations. The content cannot be verified. These sites have low credibility.

As a frequent Internet user, you must learn to critically examine all information on the Internet for credibility. Here we are focusing on your Web search results. The following checklist of questions about authorship, publisher or sponsor, currency, content quality, accuracy, and organization will help you critically assess the validity of information you will find on the Web. You may also want to adapt the checklist to vetting the social media news stream that you may be consuming daily.

### Authorship

- Who authored this page or article?
- Are the author's credentials easily found? If not, check the author's credentials online.
- Is the author affiliated with a reputable organization?
- Is the author's contact information, such as an e-mail address, easily found?
- Are the About page and the Contact page easy to spot?

### Publisher or Sponsor

- What organization publishes or sponsors this Web page? Is the publisher reputable?
- What domain is used in the URL? The domain name gives clues about who published the document (e.g., .com, .org, .edu, .gov, .net).
- Is the site published or sponsored in another country? Look for a two-letter code in the URL: .uk, .au, .br, .hu, .mx, .ca, .in.
- Is there evidence that the site is a parody or spoof page? Could it be fraudulent or fake?
- Have you found any reputable sources discussing the website or its sponsoring organization?

### Currency

- When was the Web page published or last updated? Readers expect copyright year or most recent update information at the bottom of the page.

- Is this a website that requires current, updated information (e.g., science, medicine, current events)?
- Are all links on this Web page current and working? Broken links are red flags.

### Content Quality

- What is the purpose of the Web page? For example, does the page entertain, inform, persuade, sell, or express satire?
- Who is the intended audience of the page, based on its content, tone, and style?
- Do you see evidence of bias, and does the author acknowledge the bias?
- Does the site link to other reputable sites? Do those sites in turn link back to the site in question?
- Does the page contain distracting graphics or fill the screen with unwanted ads and pop-ups?

### Accuracy and Organization

- Does the information appear to be well researched?
- If the site contains statistics and facts, are sources, dates, and/or citations provided?
- Is the information well organized with main points clearly presented?
- Is the site well designed and easy to navigate? Good design adds credibility.
- Does the page have broken links or graphics that don't load?
- Are the graphics appropriately placed and clearly labeled?
- Does the site have spelling, grammar, or usage errors? Careless errors are red flags.

**CAREER APPLICATION.** As interns in a news-gathering service, you have been asked to assess the credibility of the following websites. Think about whether you would recommend these sites as trustworthy sources of information.

- Beef. It's What's For Dinner. (**https://www.beefitswhatsfordinner.com**)
- Edmunds (**https://www.edmunds.com**)
- EarthSave (**https://www.earthsave.org**)
- The White House (**https://www.whitehouse.net**)
- The White House (**https://www.whitehouse.gov**)
- The Anaheim White House Restaurant (**https://www.anaheimwhitehouse.com**)
- National Anti-Vivisection Society (**https://www.navs.org**)
- PETA (**https://www.peta.org**)
- WebMD (**https://www.webmd.com**)
- Mayo Clinic (**https://www.mayoclinic.org**)
- Goop (**https://goop.com**)
- Petrol Direct (**https://www.petroldirect.com**)
- Smithsonian (**https://www.si.edu**)
- Hootsuite (**https://hootsuite.com**)

- Bureau of Sasquatch Affairs (**https://zapatopi.net/bsa**)
- The Royal Mint (**https://www.royalmint.com**)
- DHMO.org (**https://www.dhmo.org**)
- Lonely Planet (**https://www.lonelyplanet.com**)
- Drudge Report (**https://www.drudgereport.com**)
- Children's Wish Foundation International (**https://childrenswish.org**)
- Make-A-Wish Foundation (**http://www.wish.org**)
- The Onion (**https://www.theonion.com**)
- Pacific Northwest Tree Octopus (**https://zapatopi.net/treeoctopus**)

**YOUR TASK.** If you decide to use teams, divide the preceding list among team members. If you are working individually, select four of the sites. Analyze each site using the checklist of questions in each category. Then summarize your evaluation of each site in a memo or e-mail report addressed to your boss (your instructor). Your report may also become part of a team presentation or a class discussion. Add a comment about whether you would recommend this site for researchers of news articles. Be careful—even a hoax site can seem reputable and trustworthy at first glance. Try not to label sites as good or bad. Even biased sites may have large audiences and some merit. Tip: If you wish to examine nonprofits and charities, look them up on Charity Navigator for their ratings.

# Professionalism, Teamwork, Meetings, and Speaking Skills

# 5

**Chapter 11**

Professionalism at Work: Business Etiquette, Teamwork, and Meetings

**Chapter 12**

Business Presentations

Fizkes/Shutterstock.com

# Professionalism at Work: Business Etiquette, Teamwork, and Meetings

Dotshock/Shutterstock.com

## Learning Outcomes

After studying this chapter, you should be able to do the following:

**1** Discuss how developing professionalism and business etiquette skills can boost your credibility and improve your competitive advantage.

**2** Name techniques for successful face-to-face communication on the job.

**3** List techniques for improving telephone skills to project a positive image.

**4** Explain why teamwork is important in the digital era workplace and how you can contribute to excellent team performance.

**5** Identify effective practices and technologies for planning and participating in face-to-face meetings and virtual meetings.

## 11-1 Developing Professionalism and Business Etiquette Skills On-Site and Online

As you have seen in Chapter 1, interpersonal skills are the hallmark of a professional. Your future employer will expect you to possess interpersonal skills in addition to your technical training. Besides complex communication skills, important twenty-first-century attributes include curiosity, creativity, adaptability, resilience, and critical thinking, as well as the ability to collaborate and thrive in diverse environments.[1]

Consulting firm McKinsey identifies "cognitive skills, creativity, social and emotional skills" as safeguards—along with a college degree—against job loss from AI, machine learning, and automation.[2] In the digital age, professionalism also means maintaining *personal credibility* and a *positive online presence*, discussed in Chapters 1 and 7 as well as in Unit 6, Employment Communication.

**Business etiquette** is more than formal or rigid rules of behavior. It is an attitude, a desire to show others consideration, courtesy, and respect. It includes a desire to make others feel comfortable and acknowledge our shared humanity. Good manners and a businesslike, professional demeanor are among the top interpersonal skills that employers seek in job candidates. Good manners can also be career-relevant: A Robert Half/Accountemps survey of 300 senior managers found that 65 percent believe being courteous to coworkers positively affects advancement.[3]

But can you really learn how to be professional, civil, and courteous? Of course! This section gives you a few pointers.

## 11-1a Understanding Professionalism and the Cost of Incivility

What exactly is professionalism? The term **professionalism** and its synonyms, such as business etiquette or business protocol, soft skills, social intelligence, emotional intelligence, polish, and civility, all have one element in common. They describe **desirable workplace behavior**. Businesses have an interest in employees who get along and deliver positive results that enhance profits and boost the company's image.

As workloads increase and face-to-face meetings decline, bad behavior is becoming alarmingly common in the American workplace and may exact a high cost.[5] Researchers found that even low-level rude exchanges spread like contagion; they taint a worker's entire day.[6] Employers, of course, suffer from the resulting drop in productivity and exodus of talent. Employees, too, suffer. They are more likely to disengage or quit and experience stress responses such as digestive problems, sleeplessness, and headaches.[7] Workplace rudeness also turns customers away.[8]

Not surprisingly, businesses are responding to increasing incidents of **desk rage** and **cyberbullying** in American workplaces by establishing policies to enforce civility.[9] In short, it is not hard to understand why employers are looking for people who are courteous, polite, respectful, and well mannered. Following are a few traits and skills that define professional behavior to foster positive workplace relations.

**Civility.** **Civility** is generally understood to mean courtesy or politeness. Management professor Christine Porath, who has studied workplace behavior for more than two decades, defines rising incivility at work as "any rude, disrespectful or insensitive behavior that people feel runs counter to the norms of their workplace."[10] The need to combat uncivil behavior gave rise to two important nonprofit organizations:

The Civility Initiative at Johns Hopkins University, cofounded by the late civility advocate P. M. Forni, defined its mission as "assessing and promoting the significance of civility, manners, and politeness in contemporary society."[11] Professor Forni argued that civility meant less stress, better driving, and higher workplace productivity. He also believed that acts of violence often resulted from acts of rudeness that escalated out of control.[12]

The Institute for Civility in Government was founded in response to a heated, polarized political climate in the United States.

**Polish.** You may hear businesspeople refer to someone as being *polished* or displaying *polish* when dealing with others. In her book with the telling title *Buff and Polish: A Practical Guide*

**OFFICE INSIDER**

"Live the reputation you want to see online. These days, everything you do or say, even in a moment of weakness or in private, ends up online. It's impossible to live one life and project another, so remember your current or future business before posting that provocative picture on Facebook. The Internet sees the good, the bad and the ugly."[4]

**Martin Zwilling,** *start-up mentor, angel investor*

Businesses are responding to increasing incidents of desk rage and cyberbullying by establishing policies to enforce civility.

to Enhance Your Professional Image and Communication Style, corporate trainer Kathryn J. Volin explains that **polish** includes making positive first impressions, shaking hands, improving one's voice quality, listening, presenting well, dining skills, and more.

In two newer volumes, both called Polished, Calvin Purnell Jr. addresses, among other things, appearance, character, and focus but also keeping one's digital footprint clean. You will find pointers on developing many of these valuable traits of a polished business professional in this textbook and also in the Communication Workshop at the end of this chapter.

**Business and Dining Etiquette.** Business etiquette, proper business attire, and **dining etiquette** are just a few aspects of your professional self-presentation that could sabotage your prospects, for instance, in an interview over lunch or dinner. Even a seemingly harmless act such as sharing a business meal can have a huge impact on your career. In the immortal words of "Miss Manners," Judith Martin, "Eating is not an executive skill . . . but it is especially hard to imagine why anyone negotiating a rise to the top would consider it possible to skip mastering the very simple requirements necessary to get food directly into the mouth. What else did they skip learning?"[14]

Business meals are almost always strategic; your dining partner may want to see how you treat the waitstaff and whether you might embarrass yourself during client visits. "Etiquette is thinking about the other people you're with," says etiquette consultant Dennis Cornell. "It's about respecting them."[15] In short, you will be judged on more than your college-bred expertise.

**Social Intelligence and Emotional Intelligence.** Occasionally you may encounter the expression **social intelligence**. In the words of one of its modern proponents, it is "the ability to get along well with others and to get them to cooperate with you."[16] Social intelligence points to a deep understanding of culture and life that helps us negotiate interpersonal and social situations. This type of intelligence can be much harder to acquire than simple etiquette. Social intelligence requires us to interact well, be perceptive, show sensitivity toward others, and grasp a situation quickly and accurately.

Put simply, **emotional intelligence** or emotional quotient is the ability to identify one's emotions as well as those of other people, empathize with others, and use emotional cues to guide thinking and behavior. Daniel Goleman's bestselling book Emotional Intelligence: Why It Can Matter More Than IQ established a whole new view of intelligence, focusing on empathy, self-awareness, and self-discipline, and a whole range of other emotional skills that can have a greater impact on professional success than purely rational intelligence as measured by IQ.

**Soft Skills.** Perhaps the most common definition of important interpersonal habits is soft skills, as opposed to **hard skills**, a term for the technical knowledge in your field. **Soft skills** are commonly defined as interpersonal or social skills, professional skills, or, more broadly, emotional intelligence. As we have established in Chapter 1, these powerful skills are not "soft" or somehow less. On the contrary! In today's collaborative, hyperconnected workplaces and in the approaching age of automation, they are indispensable. Therefore, we prefer to call them social skills, interpersonal skills, or professional skills.

Employers want managers and employees who are comfortable with diverse coworkers, listen actively to customers and colleagues, make eye contact, and display good workplace manners. Your long-term success depends on how well you communicate with your boss, coworkers, and customers and whether you can be an effective and contributing team member.

To sum up, all these attempts to explain proper behavior at work aim at identifying traits that make someone a good employee and a compatible coworker. You will want to achieve a positive image on the job and online to maintain a solid reputation.

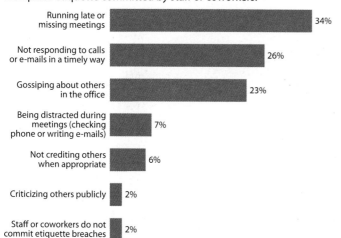

**From senior managers:** Most common breaches of workplace etiquette committed by staff or coworkers:

- Running late or missing meetings — 34%
- Not responding to calls or e-mails in a timely way — 26%
- Gossiping about others in the office — 23%
- Being distracted during meetings (checking phone or writing e-mails) — 7%
- Not crediting others when appropriate — 6%
- Criticizing others publicly — 2%
- Staff or coworkers do not commit etiquette breaches — 2%

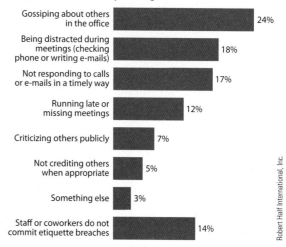

**From workers:** Most common breaches of workplace etiquette committed by colleagues:

- Gossiping about others in the office — 24%
- Being distracted during meetings (checking phone or writing e-mails) — 18%
- Not responding to calls or e-mails in a timely way — 17%
- Running late or missing meetings — 12%
- Criticizing others publicly — 7%
- Not crediting others when appropriate — 5%
- Something else — 3%
- Staff or coworkers do not commit etiquette breaches — 14%

Robert Half International, Inc.

A survey of 300 senior managers and 1,000 workers in the United States by Robert Half/Accountemps established the most common complaints about poor workplace etiquette by these two groups.

## 11-1b Relating Professional Behavior to Ethics

A broad definition of professionalism also encompasses another crucial quality in a businessperson: ethics and personal integrity. Simply put, **ethics** is a set of moral principles or virtues. **Integrity** means following a code of moral values and being incorruptible. You may have a negative view of business after learning of corporate scandals swirling around well-established businesses such as Wells Fargo, Volkswagen, GM, or Mylan, maker of the EpiPen. However, for every company that captures the limelight for misconduct, hundreds or even thousands of others operate honestly and serve their customers and the public well. The overwhelming majority of businesses wish to recruit ethical and polished graduates.

The difference between ethics and etiquette is minimal in the workplace. Ethics professor Douglas Chismar—and Harvard professor Stephen L. Carter before him— suggested that no sharp distinction between ethics and etiquette exists. How we approach the seemingly trivial events of work life reflects our character and attitudes when we handle larger issues. Our conduct should be consistently ethical and professional. Professor Chismar believes that "Unprofessional conduct around the office will eventually overflow into official duties. Few of us have mastered the rare art of maintaining multiple personalities."[18] He calls on all of us to treat each other with respect and sensitivity every day.

**Figure 11.1** summarizes the many components of professional workplace behavior and identifies six main dimensions that will ease your entry into the world of work.[19]

## 11-1c Gaining an Etiquette Edge in a Networked World

An awareness of courtesy and etiquette can give you a competitive edge in the job market. Etiquette, civility, and goodwill efforts may seem out of place in today's fast-paced offices. However, when two candidates have equal qualifications, the one who appears to be more polished and professional is more likely to be hired and promoted.

In the professional environment of the digital era, you must manage and guard your reputation—at the office and online. How you present yourself in the virtual world, meaning how well you communicate and protect your brand, may very well determine how successful your career will be. Thoughtful blog posts, astute comments on LinkedIn and Facebook, as well as competent e-mails will enhance your credibility and show your professionalism. Conversely, bad behavior can be recorded practically

OFFICE INSIDER

"While some Fortune 100 executives have gone to jail trying to deliver financial results at all costs, others have pushed their businesses forward with decisions rooted in integrity and a commitment to employees, customers, and shareholders. . . . If leaders do not operate from a place of integrity, it sets the tone for everything and everyone else and directly and negatively impacts the bottom line."[17]

**Nicole Alvino,** *cofounder and CSO of SocialChorus*

**Figure 11.1** The Six Dimensions of Professional Behavior

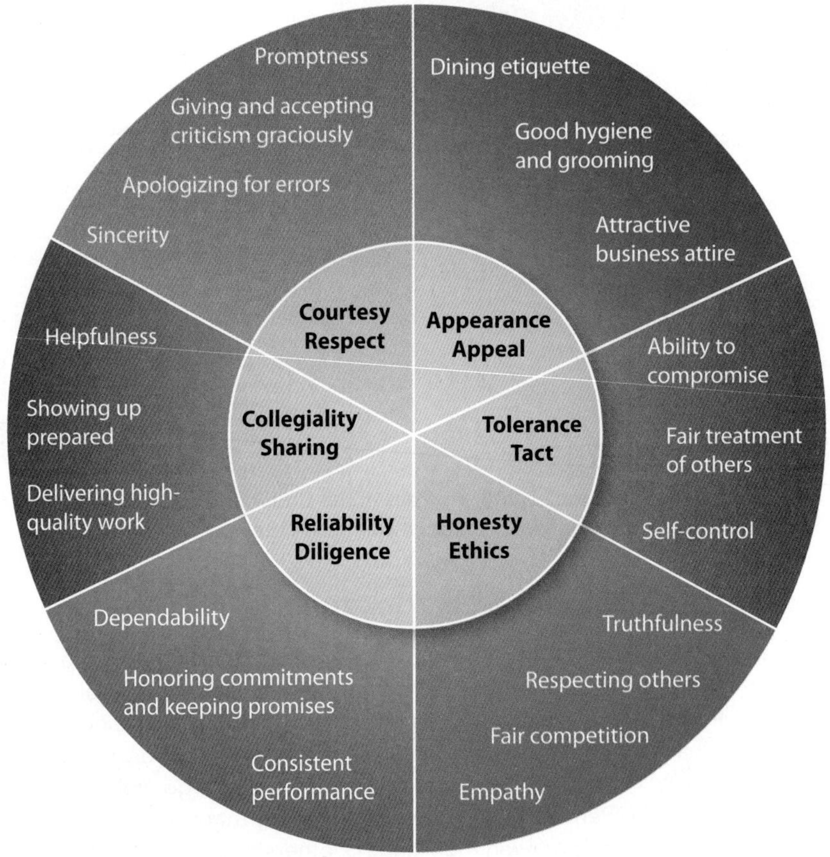


forever, sometimes coming back to haunt people years later, as inappropriate tweets by *Teen Vogue* staff members recently did.[20]

This chapter focuses on developing interpersonal skills, telephone and voice mail etiquette, teamwork proficiency, and meeting management skills. These are some of the interpersonal skills employers seek in the hyperconnected competitive work environments of the digital age.

## 11-2 Communicating Face-to-Face on the Job

**LEARNING OUTCOME 2**
Name techniques for successful face-to-face communication on the job.

You have learned that e-mail is the preferred communication channel at work because it is faster, cheaper, and more convenient than telephone, mail, or fax. You also know that businesspeople have embraced instant messaging, texting, and social media. However, despite its popularity and acceptance, communication technology can't replace the richness or effectiveness of face-to-face communication if you wish to build or maintain a business relationship.[21] Imagine that you want to tell your boss how you solved a problem. Would you settle for a one-dimensional phone call, a text message, or an e-mail when you could step into her office and explain in person?

Face-to-face conversation has many advantages. It is the richest communication channel because you can use your voice and body language to make a point, convey warmth, and build rapport. You are less likely to be misunderstood because you can read feedback and make needed adjustments. In conflict resolution, you can reach a solution with fewer misunderstandings and cooperate to create greater levels of mutual benefit when communicating face-to-face.[22] Communicating in person remains the most effective of all communication channels, as you can see in **Figure 11.2**.

**Figure 11.2  Media Richness and Communication Effectiveness**

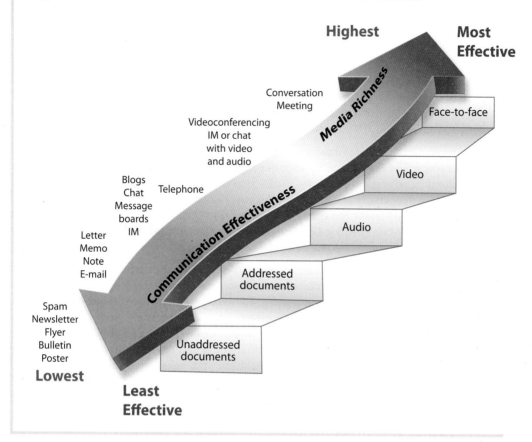

In this section you will explore professional interpersonal speaking techniques, starting with viewing your voice as a communication tool.

## 11-2a  Using Your Voice as a Communication Tool

Studies suggest a strong correlation between voice and perceived authority and trust. Respondents typically favor lower-pitched voices in men and higher but not "shrill" female voices.[23] A voice carries so much nonverbal meaning that celebrities, actors, business executives, and others consult coaches and speech therapists to help them shake bad habits or avoid sounding less intelligent than they are. You too can pick up valuable tips for using your voice most effectively by learning how to control your pronunciation, voice quality, pitch, volume, rate, and emphasis.

**Pronunciation.** Proper pronunciation involves saying words correctly and clearly with the accepted sounds and accented syllables. You will have a distinct advantage in your job if you pronounce words correctly. How can you improve your pronunciation? The best ways are to listen carefully to educated people and acclaimed broadcasters, to look words up in the dictionary, and to practice. Many online dictionaries provide audio files so you can hear words pronounced correctly.

**Voice Quality.** The quality of your voice sends a nonverbal message to listeners. It identifies your personality and your mood. Some voices sound enthusiastic and friendly, conveying the impression of an upbeat person who is happy to be with the listener. However, voices can also sound controlling, patronizing, slow-witted, angry, bored, or childish. This does not mean that the speaker necessarily has these attributes. It may mean that the speaker is merely carrying on a family tradition or pattern learned in childhood. To check your voice quality, record your voice and listen to it critically. Is it projecting a positive quality about you? Do you sound professional?

Young women in particular have been criticized for **vocal fry**, a creaky, raspy sound at the end of drawn-out sentences. This speech habit occurs in men, too, but it is generally perceived more favorably, suggesting gender bias.[24] Negative perceptions of vocal fry appear to be generational.[25] Nevertheless, if you want to impress a recruiter, avoid this affectation.

Pitch. Effective speakers use a relaxed, controlled, well-pitched voice to attract listeners to their message. **Pitch** refers to sound vibration frequency, that is, the highness or lowness of a sound. Voices are most engaging when they rise and fall in conversational tones. Flat, monotone voices are considered boring and ineffectual.

Volume and Rate. The **volume** of your voice is the loudness or the intensity of sound. Just as you adjust the volume on your headphones or television set, you should adjust the volume of your speaking to the occasion and your listeners. **Rate** refers to the pace of your speech. If you speak too slowly, listeners can become bored and their attention can wander. If you speak too quickly, listeners may not be able to understand you. Most people normally talk at about 125 words a minute. Monitor the nonverbal signs of your listeners and adjust your volume and rate as needed.

Emphasis and Verbal Tics. By emphasizing or stressing certain words, you can change the meaning you are expressing. To make your message interesting and natural, use emphasis appropriately. Some speakers today are prone to **uptalk**. This is a habit of using a rising inflection at the end of a sentence resulting in a singsong pattern that makes statements sound like questions. Uptalk makes speakers seem weak and tentative. Their messages lack authority. On the job, managers wishing to sound confident and competent avoid uptalk. Moreover, employees don't realize that they are sabotaging their careers when they sprinkle their conversation with annoying fillers such as *like, you know, actually,* and *basically.*

How well you handle workplace conversations helps determine your career success.

## 11-2b Making Workplace Conversation Matter

Face-to-face conversation helps people work together harmoniously and feel that they are part of the larger organization. Workplace conversations may involve giving and taking instructions, providing feedback, exchanging ideas, brainstorming, participating in performance appraisals, or engaging in small talk about such things as families and sports. Following are several business etiquette guidelines that promote positive workplace conversations, both in the office and at work-related social functions.

Use Correct Names and Titles. Although the world seems increasingly informal, it is still wise to use titles and last names when addressing other professionals (*Ms. Grady, Mr. Schiano*). In some organizations senior staff members speak to junior employees on a first-name basis, but the reverse may not be encouraged. Probably the safest plan is to ask your supervisors and colleagues how they want to be addressed. Customers and others outside the organization should always be addressed initially by title (honorific) and last name. Wait for an invitation to use first names. Don't hesitate to ask about an individual's chosen gender pronouns.

When you meet strangers, do you have trouble remembering their names? You can improve your memory considerably if you associate the person with an object, place, color, animal, job, adjective, or some other memory hook. For example, *tech wiz Sophia, L.A. Gustavo, silver-haired Mr. Schulz, baseball fan Albert, programmer Lori, traveler Ms. Kim.* The person's name will also be more deeply imbedded in your memory if you use it immediately after being introduced, in subsequent conversation, and when you part.

**Choose Appropriate Topics.** In some workplace activities, such as social gatherings and interviews, you will be expected to engage in small talk. Stay away from controversial topics. Avoid politics, religion, and controversial current events that can trigger heated arguments. To initiate appropriate conversations, follow news sites such as NPR, the BBC, CNN, Apple News, Google News, and major newspapers online. Subscribe to e-newsletters that deliver relevant news to you via e-mail. Listen to podcasts as well as reputable radio and TV shows discussing current events. Try not to be defensive or annoyed if others present information that upsets you.

Watch out for dubious websites and be skeptical of news items on Facebook, Twitter, and other social media as too many have been shown to be planted, fake stories. Check several trustworthy publications or media outlets to evaluate the accuracy of a news story. Be particularly wary of unverified Twitter posts.

Active listening is an important, yet underused workplace skill.

**Avoid Negative Remarks.** Workplace conversations are not the proper avenue to complain about your colleagues, your friends, the organization, or your job. No one enjoys listening to whiners. What's more, your criticism of others may come back to haunt you. A snipe at your boss or a complaint about a coworker may reach him or her, sometimes embellished or distorted with meanings you did not intend. Be circumspect in all negative judgments. It goes without saying that workplace grievances should never be posted online.

**Listen to Learn.** In conversations with managers, colleagues, subordinates, and customers, train yourself to expect to learn something. Being attentive is not only instructive but also courteous. Being receptive and listening with an open mind means not interrupting or prejudging. Let's say you wish to work at home for part of your workweek. You try to explain your idea to your boss, but he cuts you off, saying, *It is out of the question; we need you here every day.* Suppose instead he had said, *I have strong reservations about your working from home, but maybe you will change my mind,* and then settles in to listen to your presentation. In this case, even if your boss refuses your request, you will feel that your ideas were heard.

**Give Sincere and Specific Praise.** The Greek philosopher Xenophon once said, "The sweetest of all sounds is praise." Probably nothing promotes positive workplace relationships better than sincere and specific praise. Whether the compliments and appreciation are traveling upward to management, downward to workers, or horizontally to colleagues, everyone responds well to recognition. Organizations run more smoothly and morale is higher when people feel appreciated. In your workplace conversations, look for ways to recognize good work and good people. Try to be specific. Instead of *You did a great job in running that Zoom meeting,* say something more specific, such as *Your excellent leadership skills certainly kept that Zoom meeting short, focused, and productive.*

**Act Professionally in Social Situations.** You will likely attend many work-related social functions during your career, including dinners, picnics, holiday parties, and other events. It is important to remember that your actions at these events can help or harm your career. Dress appropriately and avoid or limit alcohol consumption. Choose appropriate conversation topics, and make sure that your voice and mannerisms communicate that you are glad to be there.

## 11-2c Receiving Workplace Criticism Gracefully

Most of us hate giving criticism, but we dislike receiving it even more. However, giving and receiving criticism on the job is normal. The criticism may be given informally—for example, during a casual conversation with a supervisor or coworker. Sometimes the criticism is given formally—for example, during a performance evaluation. You need to accept and respond professionally when receiving criticism.

When being criticized, you may feel that you are being attacked. Your heart beats faster, your temperature shoots up, your face reddens, and you respond with the classic fight-flight-or-freeze reflex. You want to instantly retaliate or escape from the attacker. However, focusing on your feelings distracts you from hearing what is being said and prevents you from responding professionally. The following suggestions can help you respond positively to criticism so that you can benefit from it:

- **Listen without interrupting.** Even though you might want to protest, hear the speaker out.

- **Determine the speaker's intent.** Unskilled communicators may throw verbal bricks with unintended negative-sounding expressions. If you think the intent is positive, focus on what is being said rather than reacting to poorly chosen words.

- **Acknowledge what you are hearing.** Respond with a pause, a nod, or a neutral statement such as *I understand you have a concern*. This buys you time. Don't disagree, counterattack, or blame, which may escalate the situation and harden the speaker's position.

- **Paraphrase what was said.** In your own words, restate objectively what you are hearing.

- **Ask for more information if necessary.** Clarify what is being said. Stay focused on the main idea rather than interjecting side issues.

- **Agree—if the comments are accurate.** If an apology is in order, give it. Explain what you plan to do differently. If the criticism is on target, the sooner you agree, the more likely you will be to receive respect from the other person.

- **Disagree respectfully and constructively—if you feel the comments are unfair.** After hearing the criticism, you might say, *May I tell you my perspective?* Alternatively, you could say, *How can we improve this situation in a way you believe we can both accept?* If the other person continues to criticize, say, *I want to find a way to resolve your concern. When do you want to talk about it next?*

- **Look for a middle position.** Search for a middle position or a compromise. Be genial even if you don't like the person or the situation.

- **Learn from criticism.** Most work-related criticism is given with the best of intentions. You should welcome the opportunity to correct your mistakes and to learn from them. Responding positively to workplace criticism can help you improve your job performance. In the words of a career coach, if you make a mistake on the job, "own it and hone it."[26] Learn from it.

## 11-2d Providing Constructive Criticism on the Job

Today's workplace often involves team projects. As a team member, you will be called on to judge the work of others. In addition to working on teams, you can also expect to become a supervisor or manager one day. As such, you will need to evaluate subordinates. Good employees want and need timely, detailed observations about their work to reinforce what they do well and help them overcome their personal challenges. However, making that feedback constructive is not always easy. Depending on your situation, you may find the following suggestions helpful:

- **Mentally outline your conversation.** Think carefully about what you want to accomplish and what you will say. Find the right words and deliver them at the right time and in the right setting.

- **Generally, use face-to-face communication.** Most constructive criticism is best delivered in person. Personal feedback offers an opportunity for the listener to ask questions and give explanations. Occasionally, however, complex situations may require a different strategy. You might write out your opinions and deliver them by telephone or in writing. A written document enables you to organize your thoughts, include all the details, and be sure of keeping your cool. Remember, though, that written documents create permanent records—for better or worse.

- **Focus on improvement.** Instead of attacking, use language that offers alternative behavior. Use phrases such as *Next time, perhaps you could . . . .*

- **Offer to help.** Criticism is accepted more readily if you volunteer to help eliminate or solve the problem.

- **Be specific.** Instead of a vague assertion such as *Your work is often late*, be more specific: *The specs on the Riverside job were due Thursday at 5 p.m., and you didn't hand them in until Friday.* Explain how the person's performance jeopardized the entire project.

- **Avoid broad generalizations.** Don't use words such as *should, never, always,* and other sweeping expressions because they may cause the listener to shut down and become defensive.

- **Discuss the behavior, not the person.** Instead of *You seem to think you can come to work anytime you want,* focus on the behavior: *Coming to work late means that we have to fill in with someone else until you arrive.*

- **Use the word *we* rather than *you*.** Saying *We need to meet project deadlines* is better than saying *You need to meet project deadlines.* Emphasize organizational expectations rather than personal ones. Avoid sounding accusatory.

- **Encourage two-way communication.** Even if well planned, criticism is hard to deliver. It may hurt the feelings of the employee. Consider ending your message like this: *It can be hard to hear this type of feedback. If you would like to share your thoughts, I'm listening.*

When giving or receiving criticism at work, stay calm. Plan what you will say. Keep criticism factual and deliver it in a low, controlled voice.

- **Avoid anger, sarcasm, and a raised voice.** Criticism is rarely constructive when tempers flare. Plan in advance what you will say and deliver it in low, controlled, and sincere tones.

- **Keep it private.** Offer praise in public; offer criticism in private. "Setting an example" through public criticism is never a wise management policy. Human resources experts warn executives that the only morale-saving, courteous way to fire a worker is in private and face-to-face—not, for example, by letter, e-mail, voice mail, and least of all by text. Otherwise, the remaining employees will be afraid to trust the boss.[27]

## 11-3 Following Telephone and Voice Mail Best Practices

The skill of presenting yourself well on the telephone is still very important in today's workplace. Despite the continuing reliance on e-mail, the telephone remains a crucial piece of equipment, whether in offices or on the go, thanks to mobile technology. Business communication experts advise workers to pick up the phone when they have a lot of information to convey or when the topic is sensitive. In these cases a quick call is

**LEARNING OUTCOME 3**

List techniques for improving telephone skills to project a positive image.

a lot more efficient than e-mailing back and forth. As a business communicator, you can be more productive, efficient, and professional by following a few simple guidelines. This section focuses on telephone techniques and voice mail etiquette.

## 11-3a Making Telephone Calls Professionally

Before making a telephone call, decide whether the intended call is really necessary. Could you find the information yourself? If you wait a while, will the problem resolve itself? Perhaps your message could be delivered more efficiently by some other means. Some companies have found that telephone calls are often less important than the work they interrupt. Alternatives to phone calls include instant messaging, texting, e-mail, and calls to automated voice mail systems. If you must make a telephone call, consider using the following suggestions to make it productive:

- **Plan a mini-agenda.** Have you ever been embarrassed when you had to make a second telephone call because you forgot an important item the first time? Before calling, jot down notes regarding all the topics you need to discuss.

- **Use a three-point introduction.** When placing a call, immediately (a) name the person you are calling, (b) identify yourself and your affiliation, and (c) give a brief explanation of your reason for calling. For example: *May I speak to Gino Suarez? This is Gwyn Roundtree of Waldman Enterprises, and I'm seeking information about a software program called ZoneAlarm Internet Security.*

- **Be brisk if you are rushed.** For business calls when your time is limited, avoid questions such as *How are you?* Instead, say, *Emily, I knew you would be the only one who could answer these two questions for me.* Another efficient strategy is to set a contract with the caller: *Look, Emily, I have only ten minutes, but I really wanted to get back to you.*

- **Be cheerful and accurate.** Let your voice show the same kind of animation that you radiate when you greet people in person. Try to envision the individual answering the telephone. A smile can certainly affect the tone of your voice, so smile at that person. Speak with an enthusiastic, attentive, and respectful tone. Moreover, be accurate about what you say. *Hang on a second; I will be right back* rarely is true. It is better to say, *It may take me two or three minutes to get that information.*

- **Be professional and courteous.** Remember that you are representing yourself and your company when you make phone calls. Use professional vocabulary and courteous language. Say *thank you* and *please* during your conversations. Don't eat, drink, or chew gum while talking on the phone. Don't shuffle papers, loudly close drawers, or make noise of any kind. Focus entirely on the conversation.

- **End the call politely.** The responsibility for ending a call lies with the caller. This is sometimes difficult to do if the other person rambles on. You may need to use the following tactful cues: (a) *I have enjoyed talking with you*; (b) *I have learned what I needed to know, and now I can proceed with my work*; (c) *Thanks for your help*; (d) *I must go now, but may I call you again if I need . . .?*; or (e) *Should we talk again in a few weeks?*

- **Avoid telephone tag.** If you call someone who's not in, ask when it would be best to call again. State that you will call at a specific time—and do it. If you ask a person to call you, give a time when you can be reached, and then make yourself available at that time.

- **Leave complete voice mail messages.** Always enunciate clearly and speak slowly when leaving your telephone number or spelling your name. Provide a complete message, including your name, telephone number, and the time and date of your call. Briefly explain your purpose so that the receiver can be ready with the required information when returning your call.

## 11-3b Receiving Telephone Calls Professionally

With a little forethought, you can present a professional image and make your telephone a productive, efficient work tool. Developing good telephone manners and techniques, such as the following, will reflect well on you and your organization.

- **Pick up and identify yourself immediately.** In answering your telephone or someone else's, provide your name, title or affiliation, and, possibly, a greeting. For example, *Gino Suarez, MetaDigital. How may I help you?* Train yourself to speak clearly and slowly. The caller may be unfamiliar with what you are saying and fail to recognize slurred syllables.

- **Be responsive and helpful.** If you are in a support role, be sympathetic to callers' needs. Instead of *I don't know*, try *That's a good question; let me investigate.* Instead of *We can't do that*, try *That's a tough one; let's see what we can do.* Avoid *No* at the beginning of a sentence. It sounds harsh because it suggests rejection.

- **Practice telephone confidentiality.** When answering calls for others, be courteous and helpful, but don't give out confidential information. It is better to say, *She's away from her desk* or *He's out of the office* than to report a colleague's exact whereabouts. Also be tight-lipped about sharing company information with strangers.

- **Take messages carefully.** Few things are as frustrating as receiving a potentially important phone message that is illegible. Repeat the spelling of names and verify phone numbers. Write messages legibly and record their time and date. Promise to give the messages to intended recipients, but don't guarantee return calls.

- **Leave the line respectfully.** If you must put a call on hold, let the caller know and give an estimate of how long you expect the call to be on hold. Give the caller the option of holding (e.g., *Would you prefer to hold, or would you like me to call you back?*).

- **Explain what you are doing when transferring calls.** Give a reason for transferring and identify the extension to which you are directing the call in case the call is disconnected.

## 11-3c Using Smartphones in Business

Business is unthinkable without cellular phones. We're mobile and always on: The vast majority of Americans (96 percent) own a cell phone today. Smartphone ownership stands at 81 percent, up from 35 percent just a decade ago.[30] Aside from posture problems resulting from the so-called **text neck** as we hang our heads while staring at screens, smartphones also make us antisocial, experts say.[31] No wonder! On average U.S. adults are now spending nearly half their day (11 hours and 45 minutes) connected to media, according to Nielsen.[32]

Constant connectivity is posing new challenges in social settings and is perceived as distracting to group dynamics, a Pew study found.[33] However, people's views on acceptable cell phone use vary. More than three quarters don't object to using a cell phone while walking down the street, on public transport, and when waiting in line. Even in restaurants, smartphone use is acceptable to 38 percent. However, respondents strongly condemned cell phone use during meetings, in movie theaters, and in places of worship. Although Americans view cell phones as distracting and annoying, many *do* access their own devices in group settings.

**OFFICE INSIDER**

"Mobile devices are the mother of inattentional blindness. That's the state of monomaniacal obliviousness that overcomes you when you're absorbed in an activity to the exclusion of everything else."[29]

**Henry Alford,** author of *Would It Kill You to Stop Doing That: A Modern Guide to Manners*

Because so many people depend on their mobile devices, it is important to understand proper use and etiquette. Most of us have experienced thoughtless and rude smartphone behavior. Researchers say that the rampant use of mobile electronic devices has increased workplace incivility. Most employees consider texting and compulsive e-mail checking while working and during meetings disruptive, even insulting. Employers may question workers' commitment and productivity if they are among the 20 percent who check their phones at least once every 20 minutes at work.[34] To avoid offending, smart business communicators practice professional mobile phone etiquette, as outlined in **Figure 11.3**.

## 11-3d Making the Best Use of Voice Mail

Because telephone calls can be disruptive, many businesspeople make extensive use of voice mail to intercept incoming calls. Voice mail also eliminates telephone tag, inaccurate message taking, and time zone barriers. Both receivers and callers can use the following guidelines to make voice mail work most effectively for them.

**On the Receiver's End.** Your voice mail should project professionalism and provide an easy way for your callers to leave messages for you. Here are some voice mail etiquette tips:

- **Don't overuse voice mail.** Don't hide behind voice mail to avoid taking phone calls. Individuals who screen all incoming calls cause irritation, resentment, and needless

**Figure 11.3  Courteous and Responsible Mobile Phone Use**

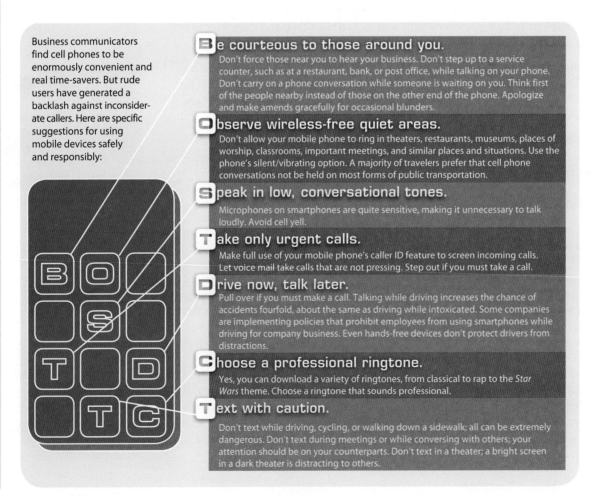

Business communicators find cell phones to be enormously convenient and real time-savers. But rude users have generated a backlash against inconsiderate callers. Here are specific suggestions for using mobile devices safely and responsibly:

**B**e courteous to those around you.
Don't force those near you to hear your business. Don't step up to a service counter, such as at a restaurant, bank, or post office, while talking on your phone. Don't carry on a phone conversation while someone is waiting on you. Think first of the people nearby instead of those on the other end of the phone. Apologize and make amends gracefully for occasional blunders.

**O**bserve wireless-free quiet areas.
Don't allow your mobile phone to ring in theaters, restaurants, museums, places of worship, classrooms, important meetings, and similar places and situations. Use the phone's silent/vibrating option. A majority of travelers prefer that cell phone conversations not be held on most forms of public transportation.

**S**peak in low, conversational tones.
Microphones on smartphones are quite sensitive, making it unnecessary to talk loudly. Avoid cell yell.

**T**ake only urgent calls.
Make full use of your mobile phone's caller ID feature to screen incoming calls. Let voice mail take calls that are not pressing. Step out if you must take a call.

**D**rive now, talk later.
Pull over if you must make a call. Talking while driving increases the chance of accidents fourfold, about the same as driving while intoxicated. Some companies are implementing policies that prohibit employees from using smartphones while driving for company business. Even hands-free devices don't protect drivers from distractions.

**C**hoose a professional ringtone.
Yes, you can download a variety of ringtones, from classical to rap to the *Star Wars* theme. Choose a ringtone that sounds professional.

**T**ext with caution.
Don't text while driving, cycling, or walking down a sidewalk; all can be extremely dangerous. Don't text during meetings or while conversing with others; your attention should be on your counterparts. Don't text in a theater; a bright screen in a dark theater is distracting to others.

follow-up calls. It is better to answer calls yourself than to let your voice mail box fill up so that callers can't leave messages.

- **Prepare a professional, concise, friendly greeting.** Make your voice mail greeting sound warm and inviting, both in tone and content. Your greeting should be in your own voice, not a computer-generated voice. Identify yourself, thank the caller, and briefly explain that you are unavailable. Invite the caller to leave a message or, if appropriate, to call back. Here's a typical voice mail greeting: *Hi! This is Jenny Schwartz of Kerberos Software, and I appreciate your call. I'm either working with customers or talking on another line at the moment. Please leave your name, number, and reason for calling so that I can be prepared when I return your call.* If you screen your calls as a time management technique, try this message: *I'm not near my phone right now, but I should be able to return calls after 1 p.m.*

- **Test your message.** Call your number and assess your message. Does it sound sincere? Professional? Are you pleased with your tone? If not, record your message again until it conveys the professional image you want.

- **Respond to messages promptly.** Check your messages regularly and try to return all voice mail messages within one business day.

- **Plan for vacations and other extended absences.** If you will not be picking up voice mail messages for an extended period, let callers know how they can reach someone else if needed.

On the Caller's End. When leaving a voice mail message, follow these tips:

- **Be prepared to leave a message.** Before calling someone, be prepared for voice mail. Decide what you are going to say and what information you are going to include in your message. If necessary, write your message down before calling.

- **Leave a concise, thorough message.** When leaving a message, always identify yourself using your complete name and affiliation. Mention the date and time you called and a brief explanation of your reason for calling. Always leave a complete phone number, including the area code. Tell the receiver the best time to return your call. Don't ramble.

- **Speak slowly and clearly.** Make sure that your receiver will be able to understand your message. Speak slowly and pronounce your words carefully, especially when providing your phone number. If you suspect a poor connection, repeat the number before saying goodbye. The receiver should be able to write information down without having to replay your message.

- **Be careful with confidential information.** Don't leave confidential or private information in a voice mail message. Remember that anyone could gain access to this information.

- **Don't make assumptions.** If you don't receive a call back within a day or two after leaving a message, don't get angry or frustrated. Assume that the message wasn't delivered or that it couldn't be understood. Call back and leave another message or send the person an e-mail.

## 11-4 Excelling in Professional Teams

LEARNING OUTCOME 4
Explain why teamwork is important in the digital era workplace and how you can contribute to excellent team performance.

As we discussed in Chapter 1, collaboration is the rule today, and an overwhelming majority of white-collar professionals (85 percent) need to partner with others to complete their work.[36] In addition, 84 percent of U.S. employees are members of so-called **matrixed teams**. This means that their job tasks are spread out across multiple teams and they don't always work with the same people or report to the same manager.[37] Research by design company Gensler shows that just before the COVID-19 pandemic, the 6,000 knowledge workers surveyed nationally spent on average about 30 percent of their time collaborating in person and 14 percent virtually.[38]

When physically in the office, workers collaborate not only at their desks but also informally in hallways and unassigned workspaces or in rooms equipped with the latest teleconferencing tools. Needless to say, solid communication and professional skills rule in face-to-face as well as far-flung remote teams.

## 11-4a Understanding the Purpose of Teams

The workplace is teeming with teams: diverse, dispersed, digital, and dynamic (4-D) teams.[39] You might find yourself a part of a work team, project team, customer support team, supplier team, design team, planning team, functional team, cross-functional team, or some other group. All of these teams are formed to accomplish specific goals.

It's no secret that one of the most important objectives of businesses is finding ways to do jobs better at less cost. This objective helps explain the popularity of teams, which are formed for the following reasons:

- **Better decisions.** Decisions are generally more accurate and effective because group and team members contribute different expertise and perspectives.

- **Faster responses.** When action is necessary to respond to competition or to solve a problem, small groups and teams can act rapidly.

- **Increased productivity.** Because they are often closer to the action and to the customer, team members can see opportunities for improving efficiency.

- **Greater buy-in.** Decisions arrived at jointly are usually better received because members are committed to the solution and are more willing to support it.

- **Less resistance to change.** People who have input into decisions are less hostile, aggressive, and resistant to change.

- **Improved employee morale.** Personal satisfaction and job morale increase when teams are successful.

- **Reduced risks.** Responsibility for a decision is diffused, thus carrying less risk for any individual.

Regardless of their specific purpose, teams normally go through predictable phases as they develop. The psychologist B. W. Tuckman identified four phases: *forming*, *storming*, *norming*, and *performing*. Later he and Mary Ann Conover Jensen added a fifth stage, *adjourning* or *mourning*, describing the potentially emotional disbanding of a project team.[40] Some groups move quickly from *forming* to *performing*. Other teams may never reach the stage of *performing*. However, most struggle through disruptive, although ultimately constructive, team-building stages as illustrated in **Figure 11.4**.

## 11-4b Working Remotely: The Rise of Virtual Teams

Working from home used to be the privilege of a few highly paid knowledge workers and other affluent professionals (7 percent of the workforce).[41] Then suddenly the COVID-19 pandemic propelled 42 percent of the U.S. labor force into the home office. Fortunately, most people welcome the flexibility of telework, at least part time.[42] Over half of U.S. respondents in one poll now favor a **hybrid model**, balancing remote work and on-site presence.[43] By 2025, according to one forecast, 22 percent of the American workforce will be full-time teleworkers, 87 percent more than before the pandemic; up to 70 percent of the workforce will work remotely at least five days a month.[44] These changes are profound, so much so that a Stanford scholar believes the United States has entered a new **working-from-home economy**; a Spotify executive calls our time the **Distributed Age**.[45]

**Figure 11.4** Five Phases of Project Team Development

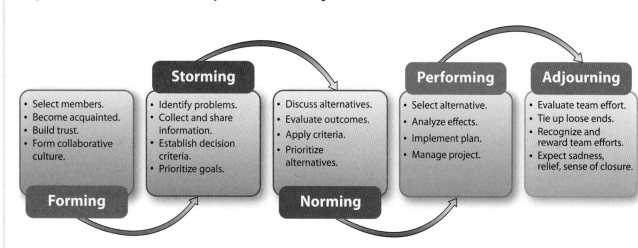

**Forming**
- Select members.
- Become acquainted.
- Build trust.
- Form collaborative culture.

**Storming**
- Identify problems.
- Collect and share information.
- Establish decision criteria.
- Prioritize goals.

**Norming**
- Discuss alternatives.
- Evaluate outcomes.
- Apply criteria.
- Prioritize alternatives.

**Performing**
- Select alternative.
- Analyze effects.
- Implement plan.
- Manage project.

**Adjourning**
- Evaluate team effort.
- Tie up loose ends.
- Recognize and reward team efforts.
- Expect sadness, relief, sense of closure.

Given these trends, you can expect to collaborate with coworkers located anywhere, whether in the same town or in other cities and even in other countries. Such collaborations are referred to as **virtual teams**. This is a group of people who, aided by information technology, must accomplish shared tasks largely without face-to-face contact across geographic boundaries, sometimes on different continents and across time zones.[46]

Research suggests that the advantages of remote work and virtual collaboration outweigh its disadvantages. Happier employees, fewer absences, less attrition, a larger potential talent pool, cost savings, and more collaboration options are just a few of the benefits cited. The consensus among large businesses such as Best Buy, Dow Chemical, American Express, and others is that remote workers are 35 to 40 percent more productive than on-site workers.[47] No wonder, then, that more than ever businesses are enthusiastic about a permanent shift to remote work.

In some organizations, remote coworkers may be employees from the same office or may be specialists called together for temporary projects. Regardless of the assignment, virtual teams can benefit from shared views, a mix of skills, and diversity.

## 11-4c Recognizing Positive and Negative Team Behavior

By displaying positive behavior, team members show their commitment to achieving the group's purpose. How can you be a high-performing team member? The most effective groups have members who are willing to establish rules and abide by them. Effective team members are able to analyze tasks and define problems so that they can work toward solutions. Helpful team members strive to resolve differences and encourage a warm, supportive climate by praising and agreeing with others. When agreement is near, they move the group toward its goal by summarizing points of understanding. These and other positive traits are shown in **Figure 11.5**.

Not all groups, however, have members who contribute positively. Negative behavior emerges when some constantly put down the ideas and suggestions of others. They may waste the group's time with unnecessary recounting of personal achievements or irrelevant topics. Also disturbing are team members who withdraw and refuse to be drawn out. To be a productive and welcome member of a group, be prepared to perform the positive tasks described in Figure 11.5. Avoid the negative behaviors.

Not surprisingly, tech companies have embraced remote work—some of them 100 percent (Google, Twitter, Square, Facebook, Spotify, and others)—at least until the end of the COVID-19 global pandemic. Outdoor retailer REI decided to sell its brand-new but never-used corporate campus in Bellevue, Washington, as the popular co-op began to shift to remote work.

**Figure 11.5** Positive and Negative Group Behaviors

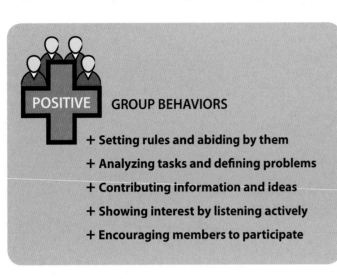
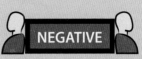

**POSITIVE GROUP BEHAVIORS**

+ Setting rules and abiding by them
+ Analyzing tasks and defining problems
+ Contributing information and ideas
+ Showing interest by listening actively
+ Encouraging members to participate

**NEGATIVE GROUP BEHAVIORS**

− Blocking the ideas of others
− Insulting and criticizing others
− Making improper jokes and comments
− Failing to stay on task
− Withdrawing, failing to participate

## 11-4d Defining Successful Teams

The use of teams has been called the solution to many ills in the current workplace.[49] It's an old saw in business to claim that TEAM means Together, Everyone Achieves More.[50] However, teams that do not work well together can actually increase frustration, lower productivity, and create employee dissatisfaction. Experts who have studied team dynamics and decisions have discovered that effective teams share some or all of the following characteristics.

**Stay Small and Embrace Diversity.** Teams may range from two to 25 members, although four to six is an optimal number for many projects. Teams smaller than ten members tend to agree more easily on a common objective and form more cohesive units.[51] Jeff Bezos, executive chairman and founder of Amazon, reportedly said: "If you can't feed a team with two pizzas, the size of the team is too large."[52] For the most creative decisions, teams generally have members who differ in gender, age, ethnicity, race, social background, training, and experience. The key business advantage of diversity is the ability to view a project from multiple perspectives.[53] Many organizations are finding that diverse teams can produce innovative solutions with broader applications than homogeneous teams can.

**Agree on a Purpose.** An effective team begins with a purpose. Working from a general purpose to specific goals typically requires a huge investment of time and effort. Meaningful discussions, however, motivate team members to buy into the project. Responding to an aging workforce and wishing to boost its hiring, construction company TDIndustries teamed up with United Way of Greater Houston to train and recruit female candidates. The partnership resulted in a 12-week program geared to easing skilled female workers into the male-dominated profession. Despite a few initial challenges, the collaboration was so successful that TDIndustries plans to extend the program to its other divisions in Texas and Arizona.[54]

**Establish Procedures.** The best teams develop procedures to guide them. They set up intermediate goals with deadlines. They assign roles and tasks, requiring all members to contribute equivalent amounts of real work. They decide how they will make decisions, whether by majority vote, consensus, or other methods. Procedures are continually evaluated to ensure movement toward the team's goals.

**Confront Conflict.** Poorly functioning teams avoid conflict, preferring sulking, gossiping, or backstabbing. A better plan is to acknowledge conflict and address the root of the problem openly using the six-step plan outlined in **Figure 11.6**. Although it may feel emotionally risky, direct confrontation saves time and enhances team commitment in the long run. To be constructive, however, confrontation must be task oriented, not person oriented. An open airing of differences, in which all team members have a chance to speak their minds, should center on the strengths and weaknesses of the various positions and ideas—not on personalities. After hearing all sides, team members must negotiate a fair settlement, no matter how long it takes.

**Communicate Effectively.** The best teams exchange information and contribute ideas freely in an informal environment often facilitated by technology. Team members speak and write clearly and concisely, avoiding generalities. They encourage feedback. Listeners become actively involved, read body language, and ask clarifying questions before responding. Tactful, constructive disagreement is encouraged. Although a team's task is taken seriously, successful teams are able to inject humor into their interactions.

**Collaborate Rather Than Compete.** Effective team members are genuinely interested in achieving team goals instead of receiving individual recognition. They contribute ideas and feedback unselfishly. They monitor team progress, including what is going right, what is going wrong, and what to do about it. They celebrate individual and team accomplishments.

**Accept Ethical Responsibilities.** Teams as a whole have ethical responsibilities to their members, to their larger organizations, and to society. Members have a number of specific responsibilities to each other. As a whole, teams have a responsibility to represent the organization's view and respect its privileged information. They should not discuss with outsiders any sensitive issues without permission. In addition, teams have a broader obligation to avoid advocating actions that would endanger members of society at large.

**Share Leadership.** Effective teams often have no formal leader. Instead, leadership rotates to those with the appropriate expertise as the team evolves and moves from one phase to another. Many teams operate under a democratic approach. This approach can achieve buy-in to team decisions, boost morale, and create fewer hurt feelings and less resentment. In times of crisis, however, a strong team member may need to step up as a leader.

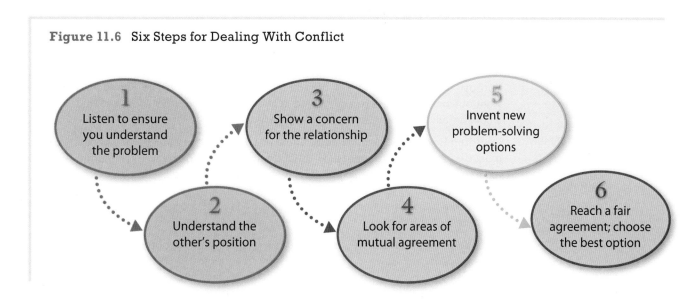

**Figure 11.6  Six Steps for Dealing With Conflict**

1. Listen to ensure you understand the problem
2. Understand the other's position
3. Show a concern for the relationship
4. Look for areas of mutual agreement
5. Invent new problem-solving options
6. Reach a fair agreement; choose the best option

The skills that make you a valuable and ethical team player will serve you well when you run or participate in professional meetings.

## 11-5 Making the Most of Face-to-Face and Virtual Meetings

**LEARNING OUTCOME 5**

Identify effective practices and technologies for planning and participating in face-to-face meetings and virtual meetings.

"In a co-located meeting, there are social norms: You don't get up and walk around the room, not paying attention. Virtual meetings are no different: You don't go on mute and leave the room to get something. In a physical meeting, you would never make a phone call and 'check out' from the meeting. So in a virtual meeting, you shouldn't press mute and respond to your emails, killing any potential for lively discussion, shared laughter and creativity."[55]

**Keith Ferrazzi,** *CEO of consulting and training company Ferrazzi Greenlight*

As you prepare to join the workforce, expect to attend meetings—lots of them! One conservative estimate suggests that workers on average spend more than a fifth of their work time in meetings and consider more than half of that time as wasted.[56] Top managers spend even more time in meetings. A U.S. study of chief executives reveals that CEOs devote 72 percent of their workweeks to meetings with the average meeting taking an hour or less, but 17 percent exceeded two hours.[57] In one survey, managers considered more than a third of meeting time unproductive and reported that two thirds of meetings fell short of their stated objectives.[58]

Business meetings consist of three or more people who assemble to pool information, solicit feedback, clarify policy, seek consensus, and solve problems. However, as the number of employees working remotely has exploded in the wake of the COVID-19 pandemic, meetings have changed. Many workers have come to rely on video conferencing, predominantly facilitated by the popular Zoom platform and app. To be able to exchange information effectively and efficiently, you will need to know how to plan and participate in face-to-face as well as virtual meetings.

Although meetings are disliked, they can be career-critical. Meeting participation, if well played, can bring you favorable status and help build your reputation.[59] Therefore, instead of treating meetings as thieves of your valuable time, try to see them as golden opportunities to demonstrate your leadership, communication, and problem-solving skills. To help you make the most of these opportunities, this section outlines best practices for running and contributing to meetings.

### 11-5a Preparing for the Meeting

A face-to-face meeting provides the most nonverbal cues and other signals that help us interpret the intended meaning of words. Therefore, an in-person meeting is the richest of available media. Yet meetings are also costly, draining the productivity of all participants. If you are in charge of a meeting, determine your purpose, decide how and where to meet, choose the participants, invite them using a digital calendar, and organize an agenda.

**Determining the Purpose of the Meeting.** No meeting should be called unless it is important, can't wait, and requires an exchange of ideas. If people are merely being informed, it's best to send an e-mail, text message, or memo. Pick up the phone or leave a voice mail message, but don't call a costly meeting. To decide whether the purpose of the meeting is valid, consult the key people who will be attending. Ask them what outcomes they desire and how to achieve those goals. This consultation also sets a collaborative tone and encourages full participation.

**Deciding How and Where to Meet.** Once you are sure that a meeting is necessary, you must decide whether to meet face-to-face or virtually. If you decide to meet in person, reserve a conference room. If you decide to meet virtually, select the appropriate media and make any necessary arrangements for your voice/audio conference or videoconference. Commonly used communication technologies are discussed in Chapter 1.

**Selecting Meeting Participants.** The purpose of the meeting determines the number of participants, as shown in **Figure 11.7**. If the meeting purpose is motivational, such as an awards ceremony for sales reps of cosmetics giant Avon or nutrition supplement seller Herbalife, then the number of participants is potentially unlimited. However, for effective decision making, experts recommend limiting the session to fewer than eight

## WORKPLACE IN FOCUS

**Zoom fatigue** is real, Stanford researchers say. Jeremy Bailenson and his team have identified four main factors causing remote workers to feel exhausted after hours on Zoom and other video calls. (1) The close proximity to a screen showing large faces staring at each other causes overstimulation. (2) Gazing at oneself for many hours can trigger self-critical feelings and stress. (3) The camera's narrow field of vision forces us to sit still unnaturally, stressing the mind and body. (4) Not being able to read body language, we need to work harder to communicate. The researchers recommend shrinking face size, turning off self-view, moving away from the screen, and taking breaks off camera.[60] How would you describe your virtual experience?

participants.[61] Other meetings may require a greater circle of stakeholders and those who will implement the decision.

Let's consider Timberland's signature employee volunteer program. Company executives might meet with managers, employee representatives, and community leaders to decide how best to improve school grounds, give back to veterans, or maintain community gardens.[62] Inviting key stakeholders who represent various interests, perspectives, and competencies ensures valuable input and, therefore, is more likely to lead to informed decisions.

**Using Digital Calendars to Schedule Meetings.** Finding a time when everyone can meet is often difficult. Fortunately, digital calendars make the task quick and efficient. Popular programs and mobile apps are Google Calendar, Apple Calendar, and the business favorite, Outlook Calendar, shown in **Figure 11.8**. Online calendars and mobile apps enable users to make appointments, schedule meetings, and keep track of daily activities.

To schedule meetings, you enter a meeting request and add the names of attendees. You select a date, enter a start and end time, and list the meeting subject and location. Then the meeting request goes to each attendee. Later you check the attendee availability tab to see a list of all meeting attendees. As the meeting time approaches, the program automatically sends reminders to invitees. The free Web-based meeting scheduler and mobile app Doodle is growing in popularity because it helps users poll participants to determine the best date and time for a meeting.

**Figure 11.7**    Meeting Purpose and Number of Participants

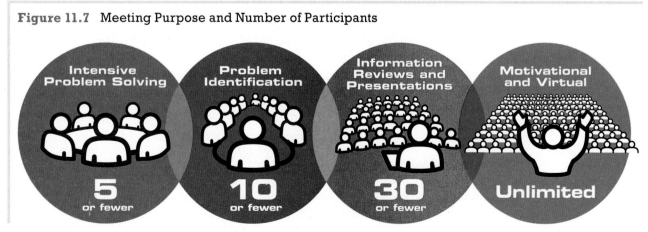

## Figure 11.8 Using Calendar Programs

Calendar programs ease the frustration of scheduling meetings for busy people. The program allows you to check colleagues' calendars (if permission is given), locate a free time, schedule a meeting, send out an initial announcement, and follow up with reminders.

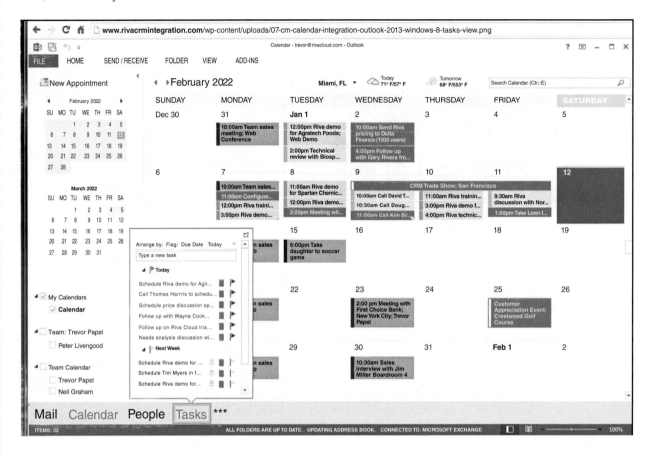

**Distributing an Agenda and Other Information.** At least two days before a meeting, distribute an agenda of topics to be discussed. Also include any reports or materials that participants should read in advance. For continuing groups, you might also include a copy of the minutes of the previous meeting. To keep meetings productive, limit the number of agenda items. Remember, the narrower the focus, the greater the chances for success. A good agenda, as illustrated in **Figure 11.9**, covers the following information:

- Date and place of meeting
- Start time and end time
- Brief description of each topic, in order of priority, including the names of individuals who are responsible for performing some action
- Proposed allotment of time for each topic
- Any premeeting preparation expected of participants

## 11-5b Managing the Meeting

Whether you are the leader or a participant, it is important to act professionally during the meeting. Meetings can be more efficient and productive if leaders and participants recognize how to get the meeting started, establish ground rules, move the meeting along, and handle conflict.

## Figure 11.9 Typical Meeting Agenda

**AGENDA**
Smart Global Travel
Staff Meeting
September 5, 2022
10 to 11 a.m.
Conference Room

|  |  | Person | Proposed Time |
|---|---|---|---|
| I. | Call to order; roll call | | |
| II. | Approval of agenda | | |
| III. | Approval of minutes from previous meeting | | |
| IV. | Committee reports | | |
| | A. Social media news update | Mason | 5 minutes |
| | B. Tour packages | Minerva | 10 minutes |
| V. | Old business | | |
| | A. Equipment maintenance | Scott | 5 minutes |
| | B. Client escrow accounts | Olivia | 5 minutes |
| | C. Internal e-newsletter | Evelyn | 5 minutes |
| VI. | New business | | |
| | A. New accounts | Javier | 5 minutes |
| | B. Pricing policy for Asian tours | Thanh | 15 minutes |
| VII. | Announcements | | |
| VIII. | Chair's summary, adjournment | | |

**Getting Started and Establishing Ground Rules.** Even if some participants are missing, start meetings promptly to avoid wasting time and irritating attendees. For the same reasons, don't give quick recaps to latecomers.[63] Open the meeting with a three- to five-minute introduction that includes the following:

- Goal and length of the meeting

- Background of topics or problems

- Possible solutions and constraints

- Tentative agenda

- Ground rules to be followed

Typical ground rules include communicating openly, being supportive, listening carefully, participating fully, confronting conflict frankly, silencing cell phones and other digital devices, and following the agenda. More formal groups follow parliamentary procedures based on Robert's Rules. The next step is to assign one participant to take minutes and one to act as a recorder. The recorder uses a computer and projector or stands at a flipchart or whiteboard to list the main ideas being discussed and agreements reached.

**Moving the Meeting Along.** An effective leader lets others talk and tries to involve all participants. If the group has one member who dominates, the leader might say, *Thanks, Tom, for that perspective, but please hold your next point while we hear how Alana would respond to that.* This technique also encourages quieter participants to speak up.

**OFFICE INSIDER**

"The finger shouldn't necessarily be pointed at meetings; it's multitasking that you should be throwing the book at. When we multitask, our IQs fall by 10 points. Our errors increase by 50%. And according to a study by multi-project management software company Realization, multi-tasking is costing organizations $450 billion globally each year."[64]

**Kathleen Owens,** *senior executive, board member, Epicor Software*

To avoid allowing digressions to sidetrack the group, try generating a parking lot list, a list of important but divergent issues that should be discussed later. Another way to handle digressions is to say, *Folks, we're drifting astray here. Please forgive me for pressing on, but let's return to the central issue of* . . . . It is important to adhere to the agenda and the schedule. Equally important, when the group seems to have reached a consensus, is to summarize the group's position and see whether everyone agrees.

**Handling Conflict in Meetings.** As you learned earlier, conflict is natural and even desirable. However, it can also cause awkwardness and uneasiness. In meetings, conflict typically develops when people feel unheard or misunderstood. If two people clash, the best approach is to encourage each to make a complete case while group members give their full attention. Let each one question the other. Then, the leader should summarize what was said, and the participants should offer comments. The group may modify a recommendation or suggest alternatives before reaching consensus on a direction to follow.

## 11-5c  Concluding the Meeting and Following Up

End the meeting at the agreed time or sooner. The leader should summarize all decisions, assigned tasks, and deadlines. It may be necessary to ask attendees to volunteer for completing action items. All participants should understand what was accomplished. One effective technique that encourages participation is **round-robin**, in which people take turns summarizing briefly their interpretations of what was decided and what happens next. Of course, this closure technique works best with smaller groups. The leader should conclude by asking the group to set a time for the next meeting. He or she should assure the group that a report will follow. Finally, the leader should thank participants for attending.

If minutes were taken, they should be distributed within a couple of days of the meeting. Meeting management programs and mobile apps offer a structured template such as that shown in **Figure 11.10**, which includes brief meeting minutes, key points and decisions, and action items. The leader needs to ensure that decisions are executed. The leader may need to contact participants to remind them of their assignments and solicit help if necessary.

## 11-5d  Interacting in Zoom, Teams, and Other Virtual Meetings

**Virtual meetings** are real-time gatherings of dispersed participants who connect with communication technology. These meetings have many purposes, including training employees, making sales presentations, coordinating team activities, and talking to customers. As we have seen, the COVID-19 pandemic instantly banned a majority of office workers to the home office, and both employees and employers have embraced the advantages of remote working. The traditional five-day work week is unlikely to make a full comeback.

Once employers sort out the new, post-COVID workplace, perhaps employees will successfully retain the new-found flexibility of telework while drawing stronger boundaries between their work and leisure. Employers favor remote work because it significantly boosted productivity during the pandemic, but this gain may have come at the cost of teleworkers' longer hours in the home office.[65] Be it as it may, virtual meetings are in your future.

Although the same good meeting management techniques discussed for face-to-face meetings apply, additional skills and practices are important in virtual meetings. The following best practices recommended by experienced meeting facilitators will help you address premeeting issues such as technology glitches, scheduling across time zones, and language challenges.[66] Creating ground rules, anticipating limited media richness, managing turn-taking, and humanizing the interaction with remote members all achieve the best results during virtual meetings.

## Figure 11.10  E-Mail Meeting Minutes

Meeting proceedings are efficiently recorded in a summary distribution template that provides subject, date, time, participant names, absentee names, meeting documents and files, key points, decisions, and action items.

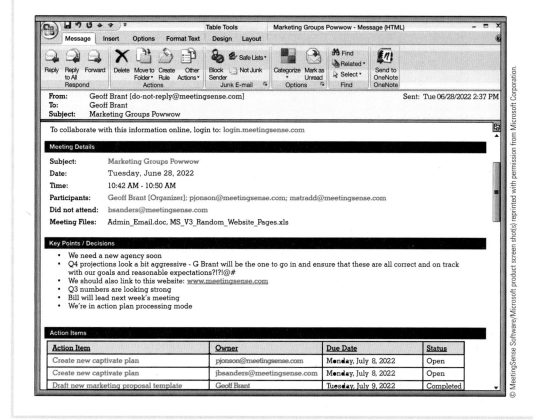

- **Select the most appropriate technology.** Decide whether audio- or video conferencing is needed. Choose the appropriate program or application. Zoom and Teams are two applications in heavy use.

- **Ensure that all participants are able to use the technology.** Coach attendees who may need help before the session begins.

- **Encourage participants to log in 15 minutes early.** Some programs require downloads and installations that can cause immense frustration if not done early.

- **Be aware of different time zones.** Use Coordinated Universal Time (UTC) to minimize confusion resulting from mismatched local times. Avoid spanning a lunch hour or holding someone overtime.

- **Rotate your meeting time to be fair to all dispersed group members.** Ensure that everyone shares the burden of an inconvenient time.

- **Decide what language to use.** If the meeting language may be difficult for some participants, think about using simple expressions and repeating major ideas. Always follow up in writing.

- **Explain how questions may be asked and answered.** Many meeting programs allow participants to virtually raise their hands using an icon on the computer screen and to type in their questions.

- **Ensure that it is clear who is speaking in audioconferences.** Ask participants to always say their names before beginning to comment.

- **Remind the group to silence all electronic alerts and alarms.** Ask participants to mute their microphones when not speaking. Ask the group to silence all ringers and buzzers and control background noise, or disruptions such as dogs barking, telephones ringing, and toilets flushing will follow.

- **Don't multitask.** Giving your full attention is critical. That includes texting and checking e-mail.

- **Anticipate the limitations of virtual technology.** Given the lack of nonverbal cues, be as precise as possible. Use simple language and summarize the discussion often. Confirm your understanding of the discussion. Project an upbeat, enthusiastic, and strong voice.

- **Manage turn-taking.** Ask questions of specific people. Invite each participant to speak for 30 seconds without interruption. Avoid asking vague questions such as *Does everyone agree?*

- **Humanize virtual meetings.** Build camaraderie and trust. Leave time for small talk to establish a warm environment. Build trust and interest by logging in early and greeting others as they join in.

Companies with a global reach or a distributed domestic workforce could not function without teleconferencing. For Mozilla's Chief Innovation Officer Katharina Borchert, 70 percent of her daily meetings are video calls because her company has many remote employees: "I cannot imagine a world without video calls anymore. Video is equally important for my professional communication and for staying in touch with friends and family back in Europe."[67] **Figure 11.11** shows how athletic gear company EverSports used video conferencing to meet virtually and design a new activity tracker.

Although many acknowledge that virtual meetings may not be as effective as face-to-face meetings, virtual meetings are here to stay.[68] Learning to plan and participate in them professionally will enhance your career as a business communicator.

**Figure 11.11** Understanding Video Conferencing

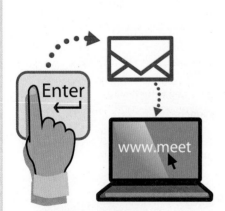

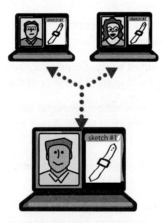

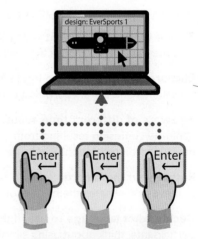

**1. E-Mail Contact:**
Mark K., president of EverSports, an athletic gear company in Seattle, WA, sends an e-mail to Jen S., chief designer at Digital Interactive Partners in Tucson, AZ, to discuss a new fitness tracker. The e-mail includes meeting date and time and a link to launch the session.

**2. Virtual Meeting:**
When the video conference begins, participants see live video of each other's faces on their screens. They look at photos of fitness trackers, share ideas, sketch designs on a shared "virtual whiteboard," and review contract terms.

**3. Design Collaboration:**
Digital Interactive artists and EverSports managers use peer-to-peer software that allows them to share spaces on each other's computers. The software enables them to take turns modifying the designs, and it also tracks all the changes.

## Summary of Learning Outcomes

**1** **Discuss how developing professionalism and business etiquette skills can boost your credibility and improve your competitive advantage.**

- Professionalism, good business etiquette, developed interpersonal skills, social intelligence, polish, and civility are desirable workplace behaviors that are complemented by a positive online presence.
- Employers most want employees who can prioritize their work, work in teams, and exhibit a positive attitude in addition to displaying good workplace manners and other interpersonal skills.
- Professionalism means having integrity and being ethical; experts believe that no sharp distinction between ethics and etiquette exists. Businesspeople should always treat others with respect.
- Practicing business etiquette on the job and online can put you ahead of others who lack polish.

**2** **Name techniques for successful face-to-face communication on the job.**

- In-person communication is the richest communication channel; use your voice effectively by honing your pronunciation, voice quality, pitch, volume and rate, and emphasis.
- To excel in face-to-face conversations, use correct names and titles, choose appropriate topics, be positive, listen to learn, give sincere praise, and act professionally in social situations.
- When receiving criticism, avoid interrupting, paraphrase what you are hearing, agree if the criticism is accurate, disagree respectfully, look for compromise, and learn from criticism.
- When criticizing, plan your remarks, do it in person, focus on improvement, offer help, be specific, use the word *we*, encourage two-way communication, stay calm, and keep it private.

**3** **List techniques for improving telephone skills to project a positive image.**

- Effective callers plan a mini-agenda, use a three-point introduction (name, affiliation, and purpose), practice sounding cheerful and courteous, and use closing language.
- In answering calls, workers identify themselves immediately, show a helpful attitude, don't give out confidential information when answering for others, and take careful messages.
- Workers need to follow proper etiquette when using their smartphone for business.
- Skilled businesspeople prepare a concise, friendly voice mail greeting, respond to messages promptly, and plan for extended absences.
- Callers should be prepared to leave a concise message, speak slowly and clearly, and not reveal confidential information.

**4** **Explain why teamwork is important in the digital era workplace and how you can contribute to excellent team performance.**

- Teams are popular because they lead to better decisions, faster responses, increased productivity, greater buy-in, less resistance, improved morale, and reduced risks.
- The five phases of team development are forming, storming, norming, performing, and adjourning (or mourning).
- Virtual teams are collaborations among remote coworkers connecting with technology.
- Positive group behaviors include establishing and following rules, resolving differences, being supportive, praising others, and summarizing points of understanding.
- Negative behaviors include showing contempt for others, wasting the team's time, and withdrawing.
- Successful teams are small and diverse, agree on a purpose and procedures, confront conflict, communicate well, don't compete but collaborate, are ethical, and share leadership.

**5** **Identify effective practices and technologies for planning and participating in face-to-face meetings and virtual meetings.**

- Before a meeting businesspeople determine its purpose and location, choose participants, use a digital calendar, and distribute an agenda.
- Experienced meeting leaders establish ground rules, move the meeting along, and confront any conflict; they end the meeting on time, ensure everyone is heard, and distribute meeting minutes promptly.
- Virtual meetings save costs but require attention to communication technology and to the needs of dispersed participants regarding issues such as different time zones and language barriers.
- Virtual meetings demand specific procedures to handle questions, noise, lack of media richness, and turn-taking. Because they are impersonal, virtual meetings benefit from building camaraderie and trust.

## Key Terms

business etiquette 335
professionalism 335
desirable workplace behavior 335
desk rage 335
cyberbullying 335
civility 335
polish 336
dining etiquette 336
social intelligence 336
emotional intelligence 336

hard skills 336
soft skills 336
ethics 337
integrity 337
vocal fry 340
pitch 340
volume 340
rate 340
uptalk 340
text neck 345

matrixed teams 347
hybrid model 348
working-from-home economy 348
Distributed Age 348
virtual teams 349
Zoom fatigue 353
round-robin 356
virtual meetings 356

## Chapter Review

1. Define the traits and skills listed in the chapter that demonstrate professionalism. (L.O. 1)

2. Explain the difference between ethics and etiquette. (L.O. 1)

3. Explain the advantages of face-to-face conversation over other communication channels. (L.O. 2)

4. Name several business etiquette guidelines that promote positive workplace conversations, both in the office and at work-related social functions. (L.O. 2)

5. Name at least six recommendations to ensure that your calls at work are productive. (L.O. 3)

6. Which practices should courteous cell phone users adopt to avoid offending others? List at least three. (L.O. 3)

7. List at least five reasons explaining the popularity of workplace teams. (L.O. 4)

8. Name the four (plus one) phases of team development as defined by psychologist B. W. Tuckman, who later added a fifth phase in collaboration with Mary Ann Conover Jensen. Explain what happens at each stage. (L.O. 4)

9. What is the best approach to address conflict in meetings? (L.O. 5)

10. List five behaviors you consider most important to participate actively in workplace meetings. (L.O. 5)

## Critical Thinking

11. Cal Newport, computer scientist and author, blames open-office layouts and relentless collaboration for a decline in concentrated deep thinking. He cites research suggesting that even short interruptions significantly increase the total time needed to complete a task. Other studies show that multitasking not only drags out work but reduces its quality. One researcher believes that jumping from one task to another reduces efficiency because of "attention residue." As the mind turns to a new task, it is still thinking about the old task.[69] Are you easily distracted? What techniques help you concentrate? (L.O. 4, 5)

12. Employers try to screen for and encourage professional skills such as excellent communication, promptness, a positive attitude, good teamwork skills, and civility. On this difficult mission, they try novel approaches. A recruiter would intentionally drop a piece of trash by his office door just before an interview. He then would hire anyone who picked it up.[70] One gas station manager rewarded his workers by relieving them of bathroom cleaning duty if they started their shifts on time. Discuss these techniques. Do you believe they are effective? (L.O. 1, 2, 4)

13. "Weathering the professional effects of COVID-19 together has introduced an authenticity to digital communication that can strengthen how we relate at work, even—or perhaps especially—in remote environments," says Jon Friedman, VP of design and research at Microsoft. He believes that remote work has allowed "humanizing glimpses into areas of our lives that may have previously been walled off from our coworkers, and it's ironic that this is happening through tools not traditionally known for deep human connection!"[71] Having worked remotely in the pursuit of your education, discuss Friedman's claim that the virtual environment shows us as more human and thus enables a greater connection among coworkers. Do you agree? (L.O. 5)

14. As any salesperson will tell you, some people (not only customers) seem to believe that if they vent their anger and make a scene, bullying and intimidating others, they are more likely to get their way. Indeed, some customer service staff may cave in, wishing to defuse the ruckus. Evaluate such behavior in the light of what you have learned in this chapter about business etiquette and professionalism. (L.O. 1–3)

15. In his book *The Ideal Team Player*, management consultant Patrick Lencioni describes what he calls the three virtues that effective team members possess: They are *humble*, *hungry*, and *smart*, he believes. Humble means little ego and giving credit to others. Hungry describes the drive to get things done. Smart refers to emotional intelligence, to being interpersonally aware and appropriate. How does the emphasis on humility square with the conspicuous, hard-driving bosses like Elon Musk or Jerry Jones, the brash owner of the Dallas Cowboys? (L.O. 4).

## Activities and Cases

### 11.1 Workplace Conflict Resolution: Putting the Six-Step Procedure to Work (L.O. 1, 4, 5)

> Team

Although conflict is a normal part of every workplace, if unresolved, it can create hard feelings and reduce productivity.

**YOUR TASK.** Analyze the following scenarios. In teams, discuss each scenario and apply the six-step procedure for dealing with conflict outlined in Figure 11.6. Choose two of the scenarios to role-play, with two of your team members taking roles.

a. During an important meeting, several agenda items require actions that are crucial to the success of a current project. They require that key decisions be made—fast! As usual, John is telling entertaining anecdotes without regard for the meeting's urgency. Jill is becoming impatient and irritated. She doesn't understand why the other meeting participants, and the boss in particular, don't stop John's antics.

b. Kacey, an accountant, cannot complete her report until Rashawn, a salesperson, provides her with all the necessary numbers and documentation. Kacey thinks that Rashawn is a procrastinator who forces her to deliver a rush job, thus causing her great stress and increasing the likelihood of error. Rashawn believes that Kacey is exerting pressure on both of them and setting unrealistic deadlines. As the conflict intensifies, productivity decreases.

c. A company policy manual is posted and updated on the company intranet. Employees must sign that they have read and understand the manual. A conflict arises when team member Alvaro insists that employees should sign electronically. Fellow team member Hallie thinks that a paper form should be signed by employees so that better records may be kept.

d. The author of a lengthy report refuses to collaborate with a colleague on future projects because she believes that her colleague's review of her document was superficial, short, and essentially useless. The report author is angry at the lack of attention her 25-page report received.

e. A manager and her assistant plan to attend a conference together at a resort location. Six weeks before the conference, the company announces a cutback and limits conference attendance to one person. The assistant, who has developed a presentation specifically for the conference, feels that he should be the one to attend. Travel arrangements must be made immediately.

### 11.2 Interpersonal Skills: What Employers Want (L.O. 1)

> Communication Technology > Social Media > Team > Web

What interpersonal skills do employers request when they list job openings in your field?

**YOUR TASK.** Individually or in teams, check the listings at an online job board. Visit Indeed, CareerBuilder, Monster, Job.com, or Glassdoor. Follow the instructions to search job categories and locations. Study many job listings in your field. Print or otherwise save the results of your search. How often do the ads mention communication, teamwork, and computer skills? What tasks do the ads mention? Discuss your findings with your team members. Then prepare a list of the most frequently requested interpersonal skills. Your instructor may ask you to submit your findings and/or report to the class. If you are not satisfied with the job selection at any job board, choose ads posted on the websites of companies you admire or on LinkedIn.

### 11.3 Interpersonal Skills: Taking Stock of Personal Strengths (L.O. 1)

> Web

When hiring future workers, employers look for *hard skills* (technical skills, such as mastery of software applications or accountancy procedures) and *interpersonal skills* typically defined as emotional intelligence, people skills, positive character traits, and other personal strengths.

Studies have divided interpersonal skills into four categories:

- Thinking and problem solving
- Oral and written communication
- Personal qualities and work ethic
- Interpersonal and teamwork

Chapter 11: Professionalism at Work: Business Etiquette, Teamwork, and Meetings

**YOUR TASK.** Using the preceding categories to guide you, identify your own interpersonal skills, paying attention to those you think a potential employer would value. Prepare lists of at least four items in each of the four categories. For example, as evidence of problem solving, you might list a specific workplace or academic problem you recognized and solved. You will want to weave these words and phrases into cover letters and résumés, which are covered in Chapter 13.

## 11.4 Voice Quality: Sounding Like a Pro (L.O. 2)

> **Team**

Recording your voice allows you to learn how you sound to others and provides an opportunity to use your voice effectively. Don't be surprised if you fail to recognize your own voice or if it sounds strange to your ears.

**YOUR TASK.** Record yourself reading a news or business article.

a. If you think your voice sounds a bit high, practice speaking slightly lower.
b. If your voice is low or expressionless, practice speaking slightly louder and with more inflection.
c. Ask a colleague, teacher, or friend to provide feedback on your pronunciation, pitch, volume, rate, and professional tone.

## 11.5 Constructive Criticism on the Job (L.O. 2)

No one likes to give it or receive it, but sometimes criticism is unavoidable, even desirable. Constructive criticism in the workplace is necessary when team members need feedback and managers must assess team effectiveness.

**YOUR TASK.** To remedy each of the following unprofessional actions, supply the appropriate solution following the guidelines provided in this chapter.

a. Supervisor Abel hates any kind of conflict and is tempted to send his negative feedback of a team member by e-mail.
b. Regional manager Miranda delivered a stern lecture to an underperforming sales rep who was clearly stunned and hurt.
c. Manager Tyson has a hot temper. He exploded when Adam, one of his subordinates, came late to a staff meeting. Tyson told Adam that he hated his tardiness and that Adam was always late.
d. Hot-headed manager Tyson loudly confronted Miranda in her cubicle within earshot of staff. Miranda had requested time off as an important deadline was looming, and the project was already late.
e. Rylie provided feedback to a dysfunctional team by spontaneously approaching team members in the hallway. Face-to-face with the argumentative team, she was at a loss for words and felt that she did not convey her points fully.

## 11.6 Practicing Professional Telephone Skills (L.O. 3)

> **Team**

Acting out the roles of telephone caller and receiver is an effective technique for improving skills. To give you such practice, your instructor will divide the class into pairs.

**YOUR TASK.** For each scenario take a moment to read and rehearse your role silently. Then play the role with your partner. If time permits, repeat the scenarios, changing roles.

**Partner 1**

a. You are the personnel manager of Blu Cellular, Inc. Call Daria Alameda, office manager at Tactical IT Corporation. Inquire about a job applicant, Adeline Chung, who listed Ms. Alameda as a reference.
b. Call Ms. Alameda again the following day to inquire about the same job applicant, Adeline Chung. Ms. Alameda answers today, but she talks on and on, describing the applicant in great detail. Tactfully close the conversation.
c. You are now the receptionist for Nicolas Sarikakis, of Sarikakis Imports. Answer a call for Mr. Sarikakis, who is working in another office, at Ext. 2219, where he will accept calls.
d. You are now Nicolas Sarikakis, owner of Sarikakis Imports. Call your attorney, Jacqueline Goodman-Heine, about a legal problem. Leave a brief, incomplete message.
e. Call Ms. Goodman-Heine again. Leave a message that will prevent telephone tag.

**Partner 2**

a. You are the receptionist for Tactical IT Corporation. The caller asks for Daria Alameda, who is home sick today. You don't know when she will be able to return. Answer the call appropriately.
b. You are Ms. Alameda, office manager. Describe Adeline Chung, an imaginary employee. Think of someone with whom you have worked. Include many details, such as her ability to work with others, her professionalism, her skills at computing, her schooling, her ambition, and so forth.
c. You are an administrative assistant for attorney Jacqueline Goodman-Heine. Call Nicolas Sarikakis to verify a meeting date Ms. Goodman-Heine has with Mr. Sarikakis. Use your own name in identifying yourself.
d. You are the receptionist for attorney Jacqueline Goodman-Heine. Ms. Goodman-Heine is skiing in Vail and will return in two days, but she does not want her clients to know where she is. Take a message.
e. Take a message again.

## 11.7 Voice Mail: Recording a Professional Greeting (L.O. 3)

**Communication Technology** ▸ **E-Mail** ▸ **Team** ▸ **Web**

To present a professional image, smart businesspeople carefully prepare their outgoing voice mail greetings and announcements. After all, they represent their companies and want to be perceived as polished and efficient. Before recording a greeting, most workers plan and perhaps even jot down what they will say. To be concise, the greeting should not run longer than 25 seconds.

**YOUR TASK.** Use the guidelines in this chapter to plan your greeting. Invent a job title and the name of your company. Indicate when and how callers can reach you. Individually or as a team, record a professional voice mail greeting using a smartphone or another digital recording device. If the instructor directs, share your recording by sending it via e-mail to a designated address for evaluation. Alternatively, team members may be asked to exchange their recorded greetings for a peer critique. Download a free voice recorder app such as Voice Memos (for iOS and Android) that allows voice recordings. These mobile applications are easy to use, and when the recording is completed, you have the option of sharing it by e-mail, by Bluetooth, on Facebook, and so forth.

## 11.8 Voice Mail: Leaving a Message Like a Pro (L.O. 3)

**Communication Technology** ▸ **Web**

Voice mail messages can be very effective communication tools as long as they are professional and make responding to them easy.

**YOUR TASK.** If your instructor allows, call his or her office number after hours or within a specified time frame. Plan what you will say; if needed, jot down a few notes. Leave a professional voice mail message as described in this chapter. Start by introducing yourself by name, then give your telephone number, and finally, leave a brief message about something you discussed in class, read in the chapter, or want the instructor to know about you. Speak slowly, loudly enough, and clearly, so your instructor won't need to replay your message.

## 11.9 Scheduling a Meeting With a Doodle Poll (L.O. 5)

**Communication Technology** ▸ **Team**

Have you ever planned an event for multiple invitees? If yes, then you know how difficult it is to find a date and time that works for most participants. Businesspeople use Outlook and other calendar apps that allow them to call a meeting, but even then, picking the right day and time can be a challenge and occasionally a hit-and-miss proposition. Enter Doodle. This free Web-based poll generator will help you schedule the best date and time for your group.

**YOUR TASK.** Your instructor may divide the class into teams and ask a representative of each team to call a study group meeting or a social event for your business society. As the designated group leader, you will open a free account with Doodle (go to **https:// doodle.com**). You won't need to input much personal information and can start sending out free basic scheduling polls almost instantly.

Follow these steps: After creating your free account, name your event. Add a location and an optional note. Follow the on-screen options. Suggest several dates and times in the calendar. Invite participants by typing their e-mail addresses. If you synced your address book, the e-mail addresses will appear automatically. Or e-mail the link you generate at the end of the poll to your group members. After your invitees fill in their available slots, confirm the date and time that works best for most if not all participants. If possible, rotate the responsibilities within the team; share the scheduling duties with the other group members and in class.

## 11.10 Making Meetings Productive (L.O. 5)

**E-Mail** ▸ **Team**

As you have learned, facilitating a productive meeting requires skills that may be critical to your career success.

**YOUR TASK.** Individually or as a team, describe how you would deal with the following examples of unproductive or dysfunctional behavior and other challenges in a team meeting that you are running. Either report your recommendations verbally, or, if your instructor directs, summarize your suggestions in an e-mail or memo.

a. Andy likes to make long-winded statements and often digresses to unrelated subjects.
b. Gemma keeps interrupting other speakers and dominates the discussion.
c. Nathan and Oswaldo are hostile toward each other and clash over an agenda item.
d. Shania arrives 15 minutes late and noisily unpacks her briefcase.
e. Maria, Emilee, and Dennis are reading e-mails and texting under the table.
f. Nora is quiet, although she is taking notes and seems to be following the discussion attentively.
g. Dennis, a well-known office clown, is telling off-color jokes while others are discussing the business at hand.
h. The meeting time is up, but the group has not met the objective of the meeting.

## 11.11 Mastering Meetings That Don't Suck (L.O. 5)

> Team    Web

"Meetings are indispensable when you don't want to do anything," observed the late economist John Kenneth Galbraith, and management guru Peter Drucker claimed: "Meetings are a symptom of a bad organization. The fewer meetings, the better."[72] More recently, Tesla and SpaceX founder and CEO Elon Musk grumbled that "Excessive meetings are the blight of big companies and almost always get worse over time."[73] Before the COVID-19 pandemic, Amazon chief executive Jeff Bezos railed against unproductive meetings and kept them small by employing his two pizza rule. He never invited more people than could be fed by two pizzas.[74]

Much venomous ink has been spilled decrying meetings, but they won't go away because—despite their potential shortcomings—many workplace gatherings are necessary.

**YOUR TASK.** Examine the preceding quotations and perhaps other statements deriding meetings. Are they exaggerations or accurate assessments? If the assertions of wastefulness are true, what does that mean for the health of organizations conducting large numbers of lengthy meetings? Individually or as a team, search the Internet for information in defense of meetings. (a) Begin by discussing your own and classmates' experience with workplace meetings. (b) Interview your parents, other relatives, and friends about meetings. (c) Finding gripes is easy, but search the Web for advice on making meetings more effective. What information beyond the tips in this book can you find? In a class discussion or individually—perhaps in writing or in a slide presentation, such as PowerPoint, if your instructor directs—introduce your findings.

## 11.12 Five-Minute Meetings: The Answer to Meeting Bloat? (L.O. 5)

> E-Mail    Team

Tired of long, boring meetings, some companies have embraced five-minute huddles or desk "drive-bys" for minor decision making. The CEO of a New York digital agency likes to cut people short when they talk too long by resorting to being "politely blunt." Brief daily check-in meetings are common in marketing, e-commerce, advertising, and related fields.[75] These mini meetings are so short that PowerPoint is out. So are long-winded speeches. Participants learn to boil down their contributions or they risk being cut off—brutally.

An account director at a digital agency in Phoenix says that the resulting bluntness "feels like having the wind knocked out of you." An executive creative director tactfully concludes: "You sort of need to check your ego at the door." Some companies limit even video meetings to five minutes. A Boston software developer holds lightning meetings that he praises for their energy and fast action. This breakneck efficiency leaves no time for idle chitchat about the kids or the weather.

**YOUR TASK.** As a team, brainstorm all possible applications of quick meetings. What types of businesses could benefit from such meetings? How would you ensure on-time arrival, participation and order during the meeting, and turn-taking? What type of sanctions would you impose for violations? What are some potential drawback of the five-minute scrum? If your instructor directs, write an e-mail (see Chapter 7) to persuade your current or past boss to adopt or reject five-minute meetings.

## 11.13 Virtual Meetings: Keeping the Team Engaged (L.O. 5)

> Communication Technology    Team    Web

Amelia Russo works at the headquarters for a large HMO that contracts with physician groups across the nation. Her position requires her to impose organizational objectives and systems on smaller groups that often resist such interference. Amelia recently needed to inform regional groups that the home office was introducing a systemwide change to hiring practices. She set up a teleconference between her office in Charleston, South Carolina, and others in Madison, Wisconsin; Denver, Colorado; and Seattle, Washington. Amelia set the meeting for 9 a.m. Eastern Standard Time.

At the designated date and hour, she found that the Seattle team was not logged in; she paused and delayed the session. When the Seattle team finally did log in, Amelia launched into her presentation. She explained the reasons behind the hiring change in a PowerPoint presentation that contained complex data she had not distributed prior to the video call. Amelia heard cell phone ringtones and typing in the background as she spoke. Still, she pushed through her one-hour presentation without soliciting feedback.

**YOUR TASK.** In teams, discuss ways Amelia might have improved the virtual meeting. Prepare a list of recommendations from your team.

## 11.14 Virtual Meeting to Clarify an Order (L.O. 5)

> Communication Technology    Social Media    Internet

TRUE Fitness, Inc., a commercial strength equipment manufacturer in O'Fallon, Missouri, contracts with several distributors overseas who exclusively sell weight machines to gyms and fitness studios, not to the general public. The distributor in the United Kingdom,

Blake Luca, has sent a confusing order by e-mail containing incorrect item numbers and product names as well as inconsistent quantities of items. Mr. Luca doesn't respond to telephone calls or e-mail requests for clarification. You remember that you conversed with Mr. Luca via Skype and notice to your delight that your distributor seems to be online.

**YOUR TASK.** Using Skype, FaceTime, Zoom, or Teams, call a classmate designated to play Mr. Luca and request clarification of the rather large order. Improvise the details of the order in a Skype, FaceTime, Zoom or Teams call to your peer (with or without a camera) applying the tips for virtual meetings in this chapter. Alternatively, your instructor may introduce a short background fact sheet or script for each participant, guiding your conversation and defining your roles and the particulars of the order. To use teleconferencing apps with or without a camera, select a laptop, computer lab desktop computer, smartphone, or iPad. This exchange can occur in the classroom or computer lab where the image can be projected onto a screen. The person playing the remote partner should leave the room and connect from a quiet place outside. Fellow students and your instructor will evaluate your virtual meeting with Mr. Luca.

## 11.15 Visiting Your Instructor's Virtual Office Hours (L.O. 2, 5)

> Communication Technology    Social Media

In distance courses in particular, some instructors hold virtual office hours. When using course-management systems such as Blackboard, Moodle, or Canvas, your professors can create class chat rooms. At appointed times, you may join your instructor and your peers in the online chat room and ask questions, request clarification, or comment on the class and the teaching material. Some of your professors may offer video chat—for example, by Skype.

**YOUR TASK.** During virtual office hours, practice professional demeanor and courtesy. Your class is a workshop environment in which you are practicing appropriate workplace etiquette. Impress your instructor by following the guidelines in this chapter—for example, by offering a friendly, respectful greeting, introducing yourself, communicating clearly, writing correct prose, being an active participant in group meetings, providing and accepting constructive criticism, and exhibiting a positive can-do attitude. Plan your virtual visit as you would a professional phone conversation, also described in this chapter. Your instructor may give you informal feedback or decide to use a more formal assessment such as a performance appraisal.

## Grammar/Mechanics Checkup 11

## Other Punctuation

Although this checkup concentrates on Sections 2.23–2.29 in the Grammar/Mechanics Handbook, you may also refer to other punctuation principles. In the space provided, write the letter of the correctly punctuated sentence. Also record the appropriate Grammar/Mechanics section for the principle involved. When you finish, compare your responses with those provided at the bottom of the page. If your answers differ, study carefully the appropriate principles.

| a    (2.26a) | **EXAMPLE** | (Emphasize.) |

a. The biggest citrus-growing states—Florida, California, and Arizona— enjoy a warm climate well suited for citrus growth.
b. The biggest citrus-growing states (Florida, California, and Arizona) enjoy a warm climate well suited for citrus growth.
c. The biggest citrus-growing states, Florida, California, and Arizona, enjoy a warm climate well suited for citrus growth.

1. (Emphasize.)
   a. The study abroad committee has invited three applicants (Maxim Moreno, Niko Wang, and Esther Trevino) to a final interview.
   b. The study abroad committee has invited three applicants—Maxim Moreno, Niko Wang, and Esther Trevino—to a final interview.
   c. The study abroad committee has invited three applicants—Maxim Moreno, Niko Wang, and Esther Trevino, to a final interview.

2. a. "Why not buy an electric vehicle," said the consultant, "if you care about the planet?"
   b. "Why not buy an electric vehicle, said the consultant, "if you care about the planet?"
   c. "Why not buy an electric vehicle, said the consultant, if you care about the planet?"

_____ 3. a. I wondered whether the tax deadline really was May 17 or April 15?
b. I wondered whether the tax deadline really was May 17 or April 15.
c. I wondered, whether the tax deadline really was May 17 or April 15?

_____ 4. a. The three most affordable U.S. cities for young adults: Austin, Salt Lake City, and Durham, beckon with jobs, ample entertainment, and low rents.
b. The three most affordable U.S. cities for young adults, Austin, Salt Lake City, and Durham, beckon with jobs, ample entertainment, and low rents.
c. The three most affordable U.S. cities for young adults—Austin, Salt Lake City, and Durham—beckon with jobs, ample entertainment, and low rents.

_____ 5. a. The Jeep Wrangler posted the best-ever first-quarter retail sales (see Appendix A), following the best-ever fourth-quarter sales in the previous year.
b. The Jeep Wrangler posted the best-ever first-quarter retail sales—see Appendix A—following the best-ever fourth-quarter sales in the previous year.
c. The Jeep Wrangler posted the best-ever first-quarter retail sales, see Appendix A, following the best-ever fourth-quarter sales in the previous year.

_____ 6. a. The word complement means "an enhancement."
b. The word "complement" means "an enhancement."
c. The word _complement_ means "an enhancement."

_____ 7. a. Will Ms Melendez attend the Zoom meeting at 3 p.m?
b. Will Ms. Melendez attend the Zoom meeting at 3 p.m.?
c. Will Ms. Melendez attend the Zoom meeting at 3 PM?

_____ 8. a. Wow! Our company is considering a four-day work week.
b. Wow, our company is considering a four-day work week.
c. Wow. Our company is considering a four-day work week!

_____ 9. a. Have you read the "Bloomberg" article titled "Rivian Takes On Tesla"?
b. Have you read the _Bloomberg_ article titled "Rivian Takes On Tesla"?
c. Have you read the "Bloomberg" article titled _Rivian Takes On Tesla?_

_____ 10. a. Ms. Phelps said she had received MS and PhD degrees, didn't she?
b. Ms. Phelps said she had received M.S. and Ph.D. degrees didn't she?
c. Ms Phelps said she had received MS and PhD degrees, didn't she?

## Editing Challenge 11

Every chapter provides an editing exercise to fine-tune your grammar and mechanics skills. The following meeting minutes have errors in spelling, grammar, punctuation, number form, concise wording, and other writing faults. Study the guidelines in the Grammar/Mechanics Handbook (Appendix D), including the lists of Confusing Words and Frequently Misspelled Words.

**YOUR TASK.** Edit the following by (a) inserting corrections in your textbook or on a photocopy using the proofreading marks in Appendix C or (b) downloading the message from **www.cengage.com** and correcting at your computer.

*State of Hawai'i*
*Business Development and Support Division*
Room 15, 250 South Hotel Street, Honolulu
February 11, 2022

**Present:** Stephanie Mahelona, Scott Saiki, Mazie Moana, Josh Greene, Kai Kahele, and
Edward Case

**Absent:** Ron Kouchi

The meeting was call to order by Chair Kai Kahel at 9:02 a.m. in the morning. Minutes from the January 10th meeting was read and approve.

**Old Business**

Stephanie Mahelona discussed the cost of the annual awards luncheon that honors outstanding employees. The ticket price does not cover all the expenses incured. Major expenses include: awards, leis, and complementary lunches for the judges, VIP guests and volunteers. Business Development and Support Division can not continue to make up the difference between income from tickets and costs for the luncheon. Ms. Mahelona reported that it had come to her attention that other agencies relied on members contributions for their awards' programs.

**MOTION:** To send a letter to agency members asking for there contributions to support the annual awards luncheon. (Mahelonna/Moana). PASSED 6-0.

**Reports**

Josh Greene reported that the homeland defense committee sponsored a get acquainted meeting in September. More then eighty people from various agencys attended.

**New Business**

The chair announced a Planing Meeting to be held in March regarding revising the emergency dismissal plan. In other New Business, Edward Case recommended that the staff read an article titled Enhancing Local Government Resources that recently appeared in the Hawaii Tribune-Herald.

**Next Meeting**

The next meeting will be held in early Aprl at the Fleet and Industrial Supply Center, Pearl harbor. The meeting will include a tour of the Red Hill under ground fuel storage facility.

The meeting was adjourned at 10:25 am by Kei Kahele.

Respectfully submitted,

## Business Etiquette: Managing Gadgets in Meetings

Smartphones and other mobile electronic devices have become indispensable extensions of our professional and private selves. No wonder then that some businesspeople compulsively eyeball their smartphones and tablets to read e-mail, search the Internet, and check their social media accounts during meetings. As ubiquitous and helpful as smartphones may be, however, most professionals dislike disruptions caused by electronic gadgets during face-to-face and virtual meetings. In one poll of managers, 94 percent felt strongly that it's never acceptable to check one's smartphone during a meeting unless it's an emergency and the attendee leaves the room. At the same time, the managers admitted to having broken this rule themselves on occasion.[76] A Harris Poll revealed that 49 percent of employers considered the distractions caused by texting and cell phone use the biggest productivity killers.[77]

Career advisors concede that smartphones may be used for legitimate, meeting-related purposes—for example, to add items to the calendar, look up a relevant statistic, or take notes. However, the experts warn that it's never okay to text, check social media feeds, post status updates, or play games.[78] Executives are trying various tactics to minimize distractions in meetings. One IT manager made participants stand for the rest of the meeting if their phones went off. Subsequently he reported improved conversations and greater respect among team members. A frustrated CEO blew up in a meeting in which most participants were fiddling with their smartphones. He then banned all phones only to find that meeting participants would arrive wearing smartwatches or bringing laptops, which were equally distracting.[79] How could businesspeople encourage responsible, legitimate smartphone use?

**CAREER APPLICATION.** Assume that you have been asked to develop a policy discussing the use of mobile electronic devices in meetings. Your boss can't decide whether to ask you to develop a short policy or a more rigorous one. Keep in mind that meeting participants could have legitimate reasons for using mobile electronic devices—for example, to take notes, look up calendar items, or fact-check a disputed point. How could this conflict between disruptive and productive uses of mobile devices in meetings be resolved?

**YOUR TASK.** As an individual or with a team, compose two documents: (a) a short statement that treats employees as grown-ups who can exercise intelligent judgment and (b) a more complete set of guidelines that spell out exactly what should and should not be done.

# Business Presentations

iStockPhoto/alvarez

**Learning Outcomes**
After studying this chapter, you should be able to do the following:

**1** Discuss two important first steps in preparing for business presentations.

**2** Explain how to organize your business presentations to build audience rapport.

**3** List contemporary visual aids and design practices that help presenters overcome the monotony of bullet points.

**4** Create a memorable error-free multimedia presentation that shows a firm grasp of basic visual design principles.

**5** Name delivery techniques for use before, during, and after a presentation to keep the audience engaged.

## 12-1 Creating Effective Business Presentations

It's called **glossophobia** by experts and means fear of public speaking. Many of us suffer bouts of intense anxiety at the thought of having to speak or present in front of an audience. We admire public personalities such as Tony Robbins, Earvin "Magic" Johnson, Suze Orman, Oprah Winfrey, or best-selling author Malcolm Gladwell, who speak in front of multitudes with apparent ease. Don't be fooled. As you will see, making a business presentation look seamless requires many hours of intense preparation and practice.

At some point all businesspeople have to inform others or sell an idea. Such informative and persuasive presentations are often conveyed in person and involve audiences of various sizes. The good news is that you can conquer the fear of public speaking and hone your skills with instruction and practice. Good speakers are made, not born.

### 12-1a Speaking Skills and Your Career

Aspiring businesspeople take advantage of opportunities in college to develop their speaking skills. As you have seen in Chapters 1 and 11, social and emotional skills play an important role in professional success: Interpreting information through speaking, listening, and observing is part of the skill set that will robot-proof your career.[1] In one much-cited survey, 39 percent of managers found new graduates lacking in public

LEARNING OUTCOME **1**

Discuss two important first steps in preparing for business presentations.

**OFFICE INSIDER**

"Poor presentation skills mean that leaders fail to inspire their teams, products fail to sell, entrepreneurs fail to attract funding, and careers fail to soar. That seems like a big price to pay for neglecting such a basic skill that anyone can improve upon."[5]

**Carmine Gallo,**
*communication coach, keynote speaker, author*

speaking; 46 percent would like to see better overall communication skills.[2] Speaking skills are useful at every career stage. You might, for example, have to make a sales pitch before customers, speak to a professional gathering, or describe your company's expansion plans to your banker.

When you are in the job market, remember that speaking skills rank high on recruiters' wish lists. According to an annual survey of career services professionals, almost 70 percent of the respondents named verbal communication as a key attribute they seek in an applicant's résumé; being well-spoken ranks among the top ten employability skills.[3] A Harris poll for presentation software service Prezi revealed that 70 percent of professionals who give presentations consider them "critical to their success at work."[4]

This chapter prepares you to use speaking skills in making professional oral presentations, whether alone or as part of a team, whether face-to-face or virtually. Before we dive into the specifics of how to become an excellent presenter, the following section addresses the types of business presentations you may encounter in your career.

## 12-1b  Understanding Presentation Types

A common part of a business professional's life is making presentations. Some presentations are informative, whereas others are persuasive. Some are face-to-face; others, virtual. Some are performed before big audiences, whereas others are given to smaller groups. Some presentations are elaborate; others are simple. **Figure 12.1** shows a sampling of business presentations you may encounter in your career.

## 12-1c  Knowing Your Purpose

Regardless of the type of presentation, you must prepare carefully to ensure that it is effective. The most important part of your preparation is deciding what you want to accomplish. Do you want to sell a health care program to a prospective client? Do you want to persuade management to increase the social media marketing budget?

**Figure 12.1  Types of Business Presentations**

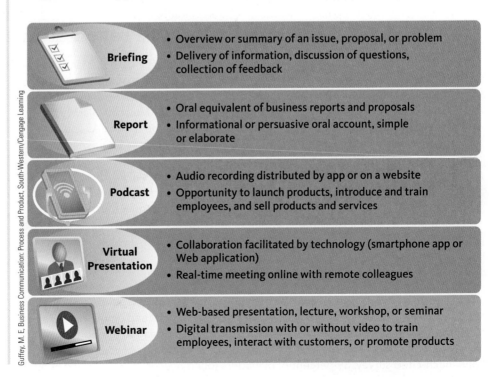

- **Briefing**
  - Overview or summary of an issue, proposal, or problem
  - Delivery of information, discussion of questions, collection of feedback

- **Report**
  - Oral equivalent of business reports and proposals
  - Informational or persuasive oral account, simple or elaborate

- **Podcast**
  - Audio recording distributed by app or on a website
  - Opportunity to launch products, introduce and train employees, and sell products and services

- **Virtual Presentation**
  - Collaboration facilitated by technology (smartphone app or Web application)
  - Real-time meeting online with remote colleagues

- **Webinar**
  - Web-based presentation, lecture, workshop, or seminar
  - Digital transmission with or without video to train employees, interact with customers, or promote products

Guffey, M. E. Business Communication: Process and Product, South-Western/Cengage Learning

Whether your goal is to persuade or to inform, you must have a clear idea of where you are going. At the end of your presentation, what do you want your listeners to remember or do?

Sheri Valdez, a loan officer at Credit Federation, faced such questions as she planned a talk for a class in small business management. (You can see the outline for her talk in **Model Document 12.1**.) Sheri's former business professor had asked her to return to campus and give the class advice about borrowing money from banks to start new businesses. Because Sheri knew so much about this topic, she found it difficult to extract a specific purpose statement for her presentation. After much thought she narrowed her purpose to this: *To inform potential entrepreneurs about three important factors that loan officers consider before granting start-up loans to launch small businesses.* Her entire presentation focused on ensuring that the students understood and remembered three main ideas.

### 12-1d Knowing Your Audience

As in any type of communication, a second key element in preparation is analyzing your audience, anticipating the reactions of audience members, and adjusting to their needs if necessary. Audiences may fall into four categories, as summarized in **Figure 12.2**. By anticipating your audience, you have a better idea of how to organize your presentation. A friendly audience, for example, will respond to humor and personal experiences. A hostile audience requires an even, controlled delivery style with objective data and expert opinion. Whatever type of audience you will face, remember to plan your presentation so that it focuses on audience benefits. People in your audience will want to know what's in it for them.

Other elements, such as the age, gender, education level, experience, and size of the audience, will affect your style and message. Analyze the following questions to determine your organizational pattern, delivery style, and supporting material:

- How will this topic appeal to this audience?

- How can I relate this information to my listeners' needs?

- How can I earn respect so that they accept my message?

- What would be most effective in making my point? Facts? Statistics? Personal experiences? Expert opinion? Humor? Cartoons? Graphic illustrations? Demonstrations? Case histories? Analogies?

- What measures must I take to ensure that this audience remembers my main points?

After considering these questions, you will be able to start organizing the content and planning the features that will help you build rapport with your audience.

## 12-2 Organizing Presentations to Connect With Audiences

After determining your purpose and analyzing the audience, you are ready to collect information and organize it logically. Good organization and intentional repetition are the two most powerful tools in ensuring audience comprehension and retention. In fact, many speech experts recommend the following admittedly repetitious, but effective, plan:

**Step 1:** Tell them what you are going to tell them.

**Step 2:** Tell them.

**Step 3:** Tell them what you have told them.

In other words, repeat your main points in the introduction, body, and conclusion of your presentation. Although it is redundant, this strategy is necessary in oral

**OFFICE INSIDER**

"Engaging your audience can mean telling stories with which people can identify, using illustrations or exercises that engage all their senses, asking rhetorical questions, using 'you' rather than 'I' phrasing, polling the audience for their opinion, telling hero stories about audience members, and so forth."[6]

**Dianna Booher,**
*communication consultant and author*

**LEARNING OUTCOME 2**

Explain how to organize your business presentation to build audience rapport.

**Figure 12.2 Succeeding With Four Audience Types**

| Audience Members | Organizational Pattern | Delivery Style | Supporting Material |
|---|---|---|---|
| **Friendly** | | | |
| They like you and your topic. | Use any pattern. Try something new. Involve the audience. | Be warm, pleasant, and open. Use eye contact and smiles. | Include humor, personal examples, and experiences. |
| **Neutral** | | | |
| They are calm, rational; their minds are made up, but they think they are objective. | Present both sides of the issue. Use pro/con or problem/solution patterns. Save time for audience questions. | Be controlled. Do nothing showy. Use confident, small gestures. | Use facts, statistics, expert opinion, and comparison and contrast. Avoid humor, personal stories, and flashy visuals. |
| **Uninterested** | | | |
| They have short attention spans; they may be there against their will. | Be brief—include no more than three points. Avoid topical and pro/con patterns that seem lengthy to the audience. | Be dynamic and entertaining. Move around. Use large gestures. | Use humor, cartoons, colorful visuals, powerful quotations, and startling statistics. |
| **CAUTION!** **Avoid** darkening the room, standing motionless, providing handouts, using dull visuals, or asking the audience to participate. | | | |
| **Hostile** | | | |
| They want to take charge or to ridicule the speaker; they may be defensive, emotional. | Organize using a noncontroversial pattern, such as a topical, chronological, or geographical strategy. | Be calm and controlled. Speak evenly and slowly. | Include objective data and expert opinion. Avoid anecdotes and humor. |
| **CAUTION!** **Avoid** a question-and-answer period, if possible; otherwise, use a moderator or accept only written questions. | | | |

Guffey, M. E, Business Communication: Process and Product, South-Western/Cengage Learning

presentations. Let's examine how to construct the three parts of an effective presentation: introduction, body, and conclusion.

## 12-2a Getting Off to a Good Start in the Introduction

How many times have you heard a speaker begin with, *It's a pleasure to be here.* Or, *Today I'm going to talk about . . . .* Boring openings such as these get speakers off to a dull start. Avoid such banalities by striving to accomplish three goals in the introduction to your presentation:

- Capture listeners' attention and get them involved.

- Identify yourself and establish your credibility.

- Preview your main points.

If you are able to appeal to listeners and involve them in your presentation right from the start, you are more likely to hold their attention until the finish. Consider some of the techniques you used to open sales letters: a question, a startling fact, a joke, a story, or a quotation. Some speakers achieve engagement by opening with a question or command that requires audience members to raise their hands or stand up. Additional techniques to gain and keep audience attention are presented in **Figure 12.3**.

To establish your credibility, you need to describe your position, knowledge, or experience—whatever qualifies you to speak. The way you dress, the self-confidence you display, and your direct eye contact can also build credibility. In addition, try to connect with your audience. Listeners respond particularly well to speakers who reveal something of themselves and identify with them. A consultant addressing office workers might reminisce about how he started as an administrative assistant; a CEO might tell a funny story in which the joke is on her. With American audiences, use humor if you can pull it off (not everyone can); self-effacing humor may work best for you.

## Figure 12.3 Gaining and Keeping Audience Attention

iStockPhoto/PeopleImages

Experienced speakers know how to capture the attention of an audience and how to maintain that attention throughout a presentation. You can spruce up your presentations by trying these twelve proven techniques.

- **A promise.** Begin with a realistic promise that keeps the audience expectant (for example, *By the end of this presentation, you will know how you can increase your sales by 50 percent!*).

- **Drama.** Open by telling an emotionally moving story or by describing a serious problem that involves the audience. Throughout your talk include other dramatic elements, such as a long pause after a key statement. Change your vocal tone or pitch. Professionals use high-intensity emotions such as anger, joy, sadness, or excitement.

- **Eye contact.** As you begin, command attention by surveying the entire audience to take in all listeners. Give yourself two to five seconds to linger on individuals to avoid fleeting, unconvincing eye contact. Don't just sweep the room and the crowd.

- **Movement.** Leave the lectern area whenever possible. Walk around the conference table or down the aisles of the presentation room. Try to move toward your audience, especially at the beginning and end of your talk.

- **Questions.** Keep listeners active and involved with rhetorical questions. Ask for a show of hands to get each listener thinking. The response will also give you a quick gauge of audience attention.

- **Demonstrations.** Include a member of the audience in a demonstration (for example, *I'm going to show you exactly how to implement our four-step customer courtesy process, but I need a volunteer from the audience to help me*).

- **Samples/props.** If you are promoting a product, consider using items to toss out to the audience or to award as prizes to volunteer participants. You can also pass around product samples or promotional literature. Be careful, though, to maintain control.

- **Visuals.** Give your audience something to look at besides yourself. Use a variety of visual aids in a single session. Also consider writing the concerns expressed by your audience on a flipchart, a whiteboard, or a smart board as you go along.

- **Attire.** Enhance your credibility with your audience by dressing professionally for your presentation. Professional attire will help you look competent and qualified, making your audience more likely to listen and take you seriously.

- **Current events/statistics.** Mention a current event or statistic (the more startling, the better) that is relevant to your topic and to which the audience can relate.

- **A quote.** Quotations, especially those made by well known individuals, can be powerful attention-getting devices. The quotation should be pertinent to your topic, short, and interesting.

- **Self-interest.** Review your entire presentation to ensure that it meets the critical *What's-in-it-for-me* audience test. People are most interested in things that benefit them.

After capturing your audience's attention and establishing your credibility, you will want to preview the main points of your topic, perhaps with a visual aid.

Take a look at Sheri Valdez's introduction, shown in Model Document 12.1, to see how she integrated all the elements necessary for a good opening.

## 12-2b Organizing the Body of the Presentation

The most effective oral presentations focus on a few central ideas. Therefore, the body of your short presentation (20 minutes or shorter) should include a limited number of main points—say, two to four. Develop each main point with adequate, but not

**Model Document 12.1** Outlining an Oral Presentation

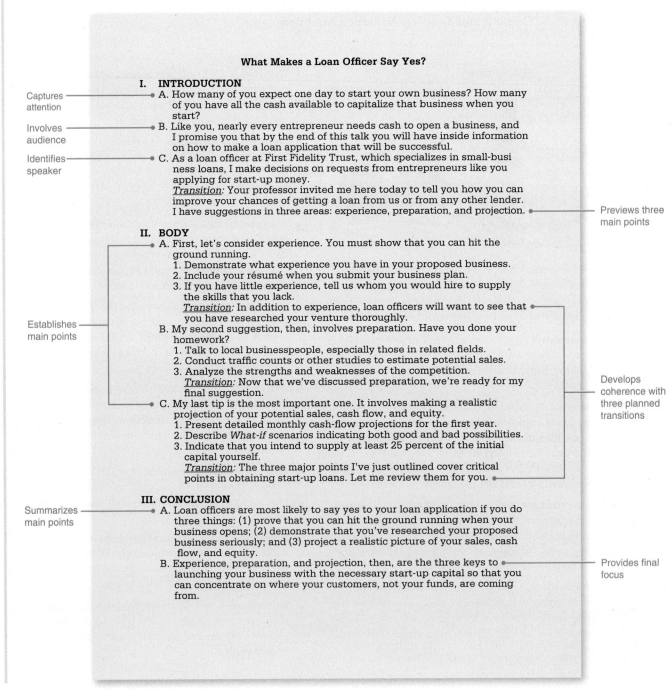

**What Makes a Loan Officer Say Yes?**

**I. INTRODUCTION**

*Captures attention* —
A. How many of you expect one day to start your own business? How many of you have all the cash available to capitalize that business when you start?

*Involves audience* —
B. Like you, nearly every entrepreneur needs cash to open a business, and I promise you that by the end of this talk you will have inside information on how to make a loan application that will be successful.

*Identifies speaker* —
C. As a loan officer at First Fidelity Trust, which specializes in small-business loans, I make decisions on requests from entrepreneurs like you applying for start-up money.
*Transition:* Your professor invited me here today to tell you how you can improve your chances of getting a loan from us or from any other lender. I have suggestions in three areas: experience, preparation, and projection. — *Previews three main points*

**II. BODY**

*Establishes main points* —
A. First, let's consider experience. You must show that you can hit the ground running.
1. Demonstrate what experience you have in your proposed business.
2. Include your résumé when you submit your business plan.
3. If you have little experience, tell us whom you would hire to supply the skills that you lack.
*Transition:* In addition to experience, loan officers will want to see that you have researched your venture thoroughly.

B. My second suggestion, then, involves preparation. Have you done your homework?
1. Talk to local businesspeople, especially those in related fields.
2. Conduct traffic counts or other studies to estimate potential sales.
3. Analyze the strengths and weaknesses of the competition.
*Transition:* Now that we've discussed preparation, we're ready for my final suggestion.

C. My last tip is the most important one. It involves making a realistic projection of your potential sales, cash flow, and equity.
1. Present detailed monthly cash-flow projections for the first year.
2. Describe *What-if* scenarios indicating both good and bad possibilities.
3. Indicate that you intend to supply at least 25 percent of the initial capital yourself.
*Transition:* The three major points I've just outlined cover critical points in obtaining start-up loans. Let me review them for you. —

*Develops coherence with three planned transitions*

**III. CONCLUSION**

*Summarizes main points* —
A. Loan officers are most likely to say yes to your loan application if you do three things: (1) prove that you can hit the ground running when your business opens; (2) demonstrate that you've researched your proposed business seriously; and (3) project a realistic picture of your sales, cash flow, and equity.

B. Experience, preparation, and projection, then, are the three keys to — *Provides final focus*
launching your business with the necessary start-up capital so that you can concentrate on where your customers, not your funds, are coming from.

excessive, explanation and details. Too many details can obscure the main message, so keep your presentation simple and logical. Remember, listeners have no pages to refer to should they become confused.

When Sheri Valdez began planning her presentation, she realized immediately that she could talk for hours on her topic. She also knew that listeners are not good at separating major and minor points. Therefore, instead of drowning her listeners in information, she sorted out a few main ideas. In the banking industry, loan officers generally ask the following three questions of each budding entrepreneur: (a) Are you ready to hit the ground running in starting your business? (b) Have you done your homework? and (c) Have you made realistic projections of sales, cash flow, and equity investment? These questions would become her main points, but Sheri wanted to streamline them further so that her audience would be sure to remember them. She encapsulated the questions in three words: *experience, preparation,* and *projection.* As you can see in Model Document 12.1, Sheri prepared a sentence outline showing these three main ideas. Each is supported by examples and explanations.

How to organize and sequence main ideas may not be immediately obvious when you begin working on a presentation. The following methods, which review and amplify those discussed in Chapter 10, provide many possible strategies and examples to help you organize a presentation:

- **Chronology:** A presentation describing the history of a problem, organized from the first sign of trouble to the present.

- **Geography/space:** A presentation about the changing diversity of the workforce, organized by regions in the country (East Coast, West Coast, and so forth).

- **Topic/function/conventional grouping:** A presentation discussing on-time performance, organized by names of airlines.

- **Comparison/contrast (pro/con):** A presentation comparing e-marketing with traditional direct mail.

- **Journalistic pattern (the six Ws):** A presentation describing the prevention of identity theft and how to recover after identity thieves strike. Organized by who, what, when, where, why, and how.

- **Value/size:** A presentation describing fluctuations in housing costs, organized by home prices.

- **Importance:** A presentation describing five reasons a company should move its headquarters to a specific city, organized from the most important reason to the least important.

- **Problem/solution:** A presentation offering a solution to a problem of declining sales, such as reducing staff.

- **Simple/complex:** A presentation explaining the genetic modification of crops such as corn, organized from simple seed production to complex gene introduction.

- **Best case/worst case:** A presentation analyzing whether two companies should merge, organized by the best-case results (improved market share, profitability, employee morale) as opposed to the worst-case results (devalued stock, lost market share, poor employee morale).

In the presentation outline shown in Model Document 12.1, Sheri arranged the main points by importance, placing the most important point last, where she believes it has maximum effect. When organizing any presentation, prepare a little more material than you think you will actually need. Savvy speakers always have something useful in reserve such as an extra handout, slide, or idea—just in case they finish early. At the same time, most speakers go about 25 percent over the time they spent practicing at home in front of the mirror. If your speaking time is limited, as it usually is in your classes, aim for less than the limit when rehearsing, so that you don't take time away from the next presenters.

## 12-2c Summarizing in the Conclusion

Nervous speakers often rush to wrap up their presentations because they can't wait to flee the stage. However, listeners will remember the conclusion more than any other part of a talk or speech. That's why you should spend some time to make it as effective as you can. Strive to achieve three goals:

- Summarize the main themes of the presentation.

- Leave the audience with a specific and memorable take-away.

- Include a statement that allows you to exit the podium gracefully.

A conclusion is like a punch line and must stand out. Think of it as the high point of your presentation, a valuable kernel of information to take away. The valuable kernel of information, or take-away, should tie in with the opening or present a forward-looking idea. Avoid merely rehashing, in the same words, what you said before, but ensure that you will leave the audience with very specific information or benefits and a positive impression of you and your company. The **take-away** is the value of the presentation to the audience and the benefit audience members believe they have received. The tension that you built in the early parts of the talk now culminates in the close. Compare these poor and improved conclusions:

> **Poor conclusion:** *Well, I guess that's about all I have to say. Thanks for your time.*
> **Improved:** *In bringing my presentation to a close, I will restate my major purpose. . . .*
> **Improved:** *In summary, my major purpose has been to . . . .*
> **Improved:** *In conclusion, let me review my three major points. They are . . . .*

Notice how Sheri Valdez, in the conclusion shown in Model Document 12.1, summarized her three main points and provided a final focus to listeners.

If you are making a recommendation, you might end as follows: *In conclusion, I recommend that we retain Envoy Marketing to conduct a telemarketing campaign beginning September 1 at a cost of X dollars. To do so, I suggest that we (a) finance this campaign from our operations budget, (b) develop a persuasive message describing our new product, and (c) name Lucius Roy to oversee the project.*

In your conclusion you could use an anecdote, an inspiring quotation, or a statement that ties in the opener and offers a new insight. Whatever you choose, be sure to include a closing thought that indicates you are finished without having to ineffectively say, *That's it!*

## 12-2d Establishing Audience Rapport

Excellent speakers are adept at building audience **rapport**. This means they establish a connection with the audience, creating a harmonious relationship in which people feel they have something in common. Speakers form a bond with the audience, often entertaining as well as informing. How do they do it? From observations of successful and unsuccessful speakers, we have learned that the good ones use a number of verbal and nonverbal techniques to connect with their audiences. Their helpful techniques include providing effective imagery, supplying verbal signposts, and using body language strategically.

**Effective Imagery.** You will lose your audience quickly if you fill your talk with abstractions, generalities, and dry facts. To enliven your presentation and enhance comprehension, try using some of the techniques presented in **Figure 12.4**. However, beware of exaggeration or distortion. Keep your imagery realistic and credible.

**Figure 12.4** Engaging the Audience With Effective Imagery

| **Metaphor** | **Comparison between dissimilar things without the words *like* or *as*** |
|---|---|
| | • Our competitor's CEO is a snake when it comes to negotiating.<br>• My desk is a garbage dump. |

| **Analogy** | **Comparison of similar traits between dissimilar things** |
|---|---|
| | • Product development is similar to conceiving, carrying, and delivering a baby.<br>• Downsizing is comparable to an overweight person's regimen of dieting and exercising. |

| **Personalized Statistics** | **Statistics that affect the audience** |
|---|---|
| | • Look around you. Only three out of five graduates will find a job right after graduation.<br>• One typical meal at a fast-food restaurant contains all the calories you need for an entire day. |

| **Worst- or Best-Case Scenario** | **The worst or best that could happen** |
|---|---|
| | • If we don't back up now, a crash could wipe out all customer data.<br>• If we fix the system now, we can expand our customer files and also increase sales. |

| **Personal Anecdote** | **A personal story** |
|---|---|
| | • Let me share a few personal blunders online and what I learned from my mistakes.<br>• I always worried about my pets while I was away. That's when I decided to start a pet hotel. |

| **Simile** | **Comparison that includes the words *like* or *as*** |
|---|---|
| | • Our critics used our report like a drunk uses a lamppost—for support rather than illumination.<br>• She's as happy as someone who just won the lottery. |

**Verbal Signposts.** Speakers must remember that listeners, unlike readers of a report, cannot control the rate of presentation or read through pages to review main points. As a result, listeners get lost easily. Knowledgeable speakers help the audience recognize the organization and main points in an oral message with verbal signposts. They keep listeners on track by including helpful previews, summaries, and transitions, such as these:

- **Previewing**
  *The next segment of my talk presents three reasons for . . . .*
  *Let's now consider the causes of . . . .*

- **Summarizing**
  *Let me review with you the major problems I have just discussed….*
  *You see, then, that the most significant factors are . . . .*

- **Switching directions**
  *Thus far we have talked solely about . . . ; now let's move to . . . .*
  *I have argued that . . . and . . . , but an alternate view holds that . . . .*

You can further improve any oral presentation by including appropriate transitional expressions such as *first, second, next, then, therefore, moreover, on the other hand, on the contrary,* and *in conclusion.* These transitional expressions build coherence, lend emphasis, and tell listeners where you are headed. Notice in Sheri Valdez's outline in Model Document 12.1 the specific transitional elements designed to help listeners recognize each new principal point.

Nonverbal Messages. Although what you say is most important, the nonverbal messages you send can also have a powerful effect on how well your audience receives your message. How you look, how you move, and how you speak can make or break your presentation. The following suggestions focus on nonverbal tips to ensure that your verbal message resonates with your audience.

- **Look terrific!** Like it or not, you will be judged by your appearance. For everything but small in-house presentations, be sure to dress professionally. The rule of thumb is that you should dress at least as well as the best-dressed person in the audience.

- **Animate your body**. Be enthusiastic and let your body show it. Stand with good posture to show confidence. Emphasize ideas to enhance points about size, number, and direction. Use a variety of gestures, but, if you want to look natural, don't plan them in advance.

- **Punctuate your words**. You can keep your audience interested by varying your tone, volume, pitch, and pace. Use pauses before and after important points. Allow the audience to take in your ideas.

- **Get out from behind the podium**. Avoid standing rigidly behind a podium. Movement makes you look natural and comfortable, unless you pace nervously. You might pick a few places in the room to walk to calmly. Even if you must stay close to your visual aids, make a point of leaving them occasionally so that the audience can see your whole body.

- **Vary your facial expression**. Begin with a smile, but change your expressions to correspond with the thoughts you are voicing. You can shake your head to show disagreement, roll your eyes to show disdain, look heavenward for guidance, or wrinkle your brow to show concern or dismay. It is important to note that this advice to be an animated speaker applies to most North American audiences. Some intercultural audiences may be accustomed to a more measured delivery.

Whenever possible, beginning presenters should have an experienced speaker watch them and give them tips as they rehearse. Your instructor is an important coach who can provide you with invaluable feedback. In the absence of helpers, record yourself and watch your nonverbal behavior on camera. Are you doing what it takes to build rapport?

## 12-3 Understanding Contemporary Visual Aids

**LEARNING OUTCOME 3**

List contemporary visual aids and design practices that help presenters overcome the monotony of bullet points.

Your goals as a speaker are to make listeners understand, remember, and act on your ideas. To get them interested and engaged, include effective visual aids. Why? The developmental biologist John Medina tells us that "vision is probably the best single tool we have for learning anything" and urges readers to "toss your PowerPoint presentations" because they can be text-heavy and thus inefficient by design.[9] Information conveyed in images is more memorable than text alone; scientists call this phenomenon **pictorial superiority**.[10] Therefore, an oral presentation that incorporates visual aids is far more likely to be understood and retained than one lacking a meaningful visual component.

Good visual aids serve many purposes. They emphasize and clarify main points, thus improving comprehension and retention. They increase audience interest, and they make the presenter appear more professional, better prepared, and more persuasive. Well-designed visual aids illustrate and emphasize your message more effectively than words alone; therefore, they may help shorten a meeting or achieve your goal faster. Good visuals also serve to jog the memory of a speaker, thus improving self-confidence, poise, and delivery.

**Figure 12.5** Pros and Cons of Visual Aid Options

| Media: High Tech | Pros | Cons |
|---|---|---|
| Multimedia slides | Create professional appearance with many color, art, graphic, and font options. Allow users to incorporate video, audio, and hyperlinks. Offer ease of use and portability via thumb drives, cloud storage, or e-mail attachment. Are inexpensive to update. | Present potential incompatibility issues. Require costly projection equipment and practice for smooth delivery. Tempt user to include razzle-dazzle features that may fail to add value. Can be too one-dimensional and linear. |
| Zoom presentations | Enable presenter to zoom in on and out of content to show the big picture or specific details in nonlinear, 3D quality. Provide attractive templates. Allow users to insert rich media. Offer an interactive, cinematic, and dynamic experience. | Require Internet access because they are cloud based. Don't allow editing of images. Offer limited font choices. Can be difficult to operate for some presenters used to individual slides; can make moving around the canvas challenging. Zooming can be distracting and even nauseating. |
| Video | Gives an accurate representation of the content; strongly indicates forethought and preparation. | Creates potential for compatibility issues related to computer video formats. Is generally expensive to create and update. |

| Media: Low Tech | Pros | Cons |
|---|---|---|
| Handouts | Encourage audience participation. Are easy to maintain and update. Enhance recall because audience keeps reference material. | Increase risk of unauthorized duplication of speaker's material. Can be difficult to transport. May cause speaker to lose audience's attention. |
| Flipcharts or whiteboards | Provide inexpensive option available at most sites. Enable users to (a) create, (b) modify or customize on the spot, (c) record comments from the audience, and (d) combine with more high-tech visuals in the same presentation. | Require graphics talent. Can be difficult for larger audiences to see. Can be cumbersome to transport. Easily wear with use. |
| Props | Offer a realistic reinforcement of message content. Increase audience participation with close observation. | Lead to extra work and expense in transporting and replacing worn objects. Are of limited use with larger audiences. |

Andrey Yurlov/Shutterstock.com
Elena Elisseeva/Shutterstock.com
Marko Rupena/Shutterstock.com
Mykola Komarovskyy/Shutterstock.com
Andrey_Popov/Shutterstock.com

## 12-3a Types of Visual Aids

Speakers have many forms of media at their fingertips if they wish to enhance their presentations. **Figure 12.5** describes the pros and cons of several visual aids, both high-tech and low-tech, that can guide you in selecting the best one for any speaking occasion. Two of the most popular visuals for business presentations are multimedia slides and handouts. Zoom presentations, an alternative to multimedia slides, are growing in popularity.

Multimedia Slides. With today's excellent presentation software—such as Microsoft PowerPoint, Apple Keynote, Google Slides, and Adobe Presenter—you can create or enhance dynamic, colorful presentations with your desktop, laptop, tablet, or smartphone. The output from these programs is generally shown on a computer screen, a smart TV, an LCD (liquid crystal display) panel, or a projection screen. With a little expertise and the right equipment, you can create multimedia presentations that

"New, dynamic presentation tools like Prezi allow us to communicate design ideas with our clients in highly engaging and dynamic ways, liberating interesting conversations from the boredom of one-way presentations."[11]

**Randy Howder,**
*design strategist with Gensler*

include audio, videos, images, animation, and hyperlinks, as described shortly in the discussion of multimedia presentations.

Multimedia slides can also be created by cloud-based apps that are either free with limited functionality or require a tiered subscription as **software as a service (SaaS)** applications. MS PowerPoint, too, is now in the cloud as part of Office 365. Check whether your college has an education license with the big software companies, for example, Microsoft and Adobe. You might be able to use their latest apps free of charge while you are a student.

**Handouts.** You can enrich and complement your presentations by distributing pictures, outlines, brochures, articles, charts, summaries, or other supplements. Speakers who use presentation software often prepare a set of their slides along with notes to hand out to viewers. To avoid distractions and to keep control, announce and discuss handouts during the presentation, but delay distributing them until after you finish.

**Zoom Presentations.** Many business presenters feel limited by multimedia slides, which tend to be linear. As a result, some communicators prefer more dynamic visual aids. Using software such as Prezi, a cloud-based presentation and storytelling tool, they work with a single large digital canvas. This canvas enables the speaker to zoom in on and out of text blocks or images to help the audience understand and remember content, details, and relationships. Prezi zoom presentations allow speakers to communicate their ideas in a more exciting, creative way. Audience members also seem to appreciate the cinematic, interactive quality of these presentations. **Figure 12.6** shows what a typical Prezi canvas looks like during the design process. Hyatt, TED, Vodafone, and Avon are just a few among the many businesses that have adopted the software. Prezi the company claims to support more than 100 million users.

### Figure 12.6   Prezi Zoom Presentation

Prezi uses one canvas for a presentation rather than individual slides arranged in a linear fashion. Here is an example of the main canvas of a zoom presentation. Clicking on any section of this canvas will zoom in on detailed information. For example, if you click on the area around the tree roots, you will zoom in on a quote about thinking positively, as shown in the thumbnail images in the left pane.

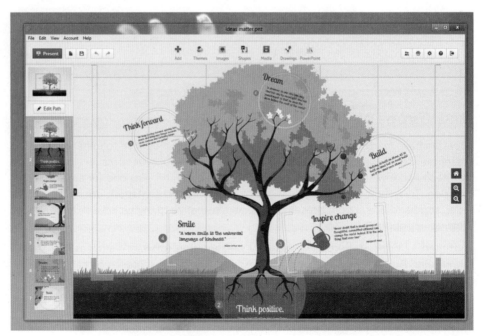

Source: http://prezi-a.akamaihd.net/presskit/Prezi%20Desktop/PreziDesktop_Windows.png

## 12-3b Moving Beyond PowerPoint Bullets

Slideshows created using PowerPoint in particular are a staple of business presentations. However, overuse or misuse may be the downside of the ever-present PowerPoint slideshow. Over more than three decades of the software program's existence, millions of poorly created and badly delivered presentations have tarnished PowerPoint's reputation as an effective communication tool. Tools are helpful only when used properly.

More than a decade ago, several communication experts set out to show businesspeople how they can move beyond bullet points to avoid **chartjunk** and **PowerPoint Phluff**.[12] The experts recommend creating slideshows that tell a story and send a powerful message with much less text and more images.[13] Presentation guru Garr Reynolds urges readers to unleash their creativity: "Do not rely on technology or other people to make your choices. Most of all, do not let mere habit—and the habits of others—dictate your decisions on how you prepare, design, and ultimately deliver your presentations."[14]

However, not all content—think complex financial or technical data—is equally suitable to being presented in images, as attractive as such slideshows may be. Communication consultant Nancy Duarte believes that such data don't belong on slides in the first place but should be provided on handouts. In her classic book *Slide:ology*, she too advocates for simplicity and clarity.

Expect a learning curve if you are new to presentation programs. Even much-touted alternatives to PowerPoint, such as Prezi, Canva, and Google Slides, require some knowledge of the solid design principles covered in the next section. **Figure 12.7** shows some of the tools that Canva provides to create a visually rich presentation. The goal is to abandon boring bulleted lists.

### Figure 12.7  Canva Presentation

Like most applications today, the basic version of Canva is a free cloud-based presentation software. Like PowerPoint, it allows users to create slides, but it takes the emphasis off bullet points. Canva's strength is in offering appealing slide templates, ready-made customizable graphic design elements, and many tools to help users create visually rich slides and social media graphics, such as eye-catching YouTube thumbnails, Instagram stories, or Facebook covers.

Source: Canva

## 12-4 Preparing Engaging Multimedia Presentations

**LEARNING OUTCOME 4**

Create a memorable error-free multimedia presentation that shows a firm grasp of basic visual design principles.

When operated by proficient designers and skillful presenters, PowerPoint, Keynote, or Prezi can add visual impact to any presentation. Of course, gaining expertise with a software program requires an investment of time and effort. You could take a course, or you could teach yourself through an online tutorial.

Some presenters prefer to create their visuals first and then develop the narrative around them. Others prepare their content first and then create the visual component. The risk associated with the first approach is that you may be tempted to spend too much time making your visuals look good and not enough time preparing your content. Remember that great-looking slides never compensate for thin content.

The following sections explain how to adjust your visuals to the situation and your audience. You will also receive how-to instructions for creating engaging and visually appealing PowerPoint, Keynote, Canva, or Prezi presentations.

### 12-4a Analyzing the Situation and Purpose

Making the best design choices for your presentation depends greatly on your analysis of the situation and the purpose of your slideshow. Will your slides be used during a live presentation? Will they be part of a self-running presentation such as in a store kiosk? Will they be saved on a cloud server so that users can watch the presentation online at their convenience? Will they be sent as a PowerPoint show or a PDF slide deck to a client instead of a hard-copy report? Will your presentation mainly run on smartphones or tablets?

If you are e-mailing the presentation or posting it online as a self-contained file or slide deck, it should feature more text than one that you would deliver orally. If, on the other hand, you are creating slides for a live presentation, you will likely rely more on images than on text.

### 12-4b Adjusting Slide Design to Your Audience

Think about how you can design your presentation to get the most positive response from your audience. Audiences respond, for example, to the colors, images, and special effects you use. Primary ideas are generally best conveyed with bold colors such as blue, green, and purple. Because the messages that colors convey can vary from culture to culture, presenters must choose colors and other design elements carefully.

**The Meaning of Color.** In the United States, blue is the color of credibility, tranquility, conservatism, and trust. Therefore, it is the background color of choice for many business presentations and social media sites. Green relates to interaction, growth, money, and stability. It can work well as a background or an accent color. Purple can also work as a background or accent color. It conveys spirituality, royalty, dreams, and humor.[15] As for text, adjust the color to provide high contrast so it is readable. White or yellow, for example, usually works well on dark backgrounds.

Adapt the slide colors based on where you will give the presentation. Use light text on a dark background for presentations in darkened rooms. Use dark text on a light background for presentations in lighted rooms. Avoid using a dark font on a dark background, such as red text on a dark blue background. In the same way, avoid using a light font on a light background, such as white text on a pale blue background. Keep in mind that colors that look vibrant on your monitor may look washed out when projected onto a screen.

**The Power of Images.** Adapt the amount of text on your slide to how your audience will use the slides. The traditional guideline for slide design is to follow the **6-x-6 rule**: "Six bullets per screen, max; six words per bullet, max."[17] You may find, however, that breaking this rule is sometimes necessary, particularly when your users will be viewing

## Figure 12.8 Revising and Enhancing Slides for Greater Impact

The slide on the left contains bullet points that are not parallel. Two unnecessarily repeat "Great presenters." The first and the last bullets are needlessly long. The contrast of white on gray is poor. In the revised slide, the title avoids the overused word "great." The short sentences begin with a verb for parallelism and an emphasis on action. The icons add interest.

**Before Revision**

**Great Presentations**

- Great presenters should use fewer slides—and fewer words.
- Great presenters don't use bullet points.
- Enhancing vocal delivery.
- Creating "wow" moments.
- If you want to be a great presenter, rehearse.

**After Revision**

**The Best Presenters**

Use fewer slides—and fewer words.

Don't use bullet points.

Enhance vocal delivery.

Create "wow" moments.

Rehearse.

Source: Microsoft Corporation

the presentation on their own with no speaker assistance. For most purposes, though, strive to break free from bulleted lists whenever possible and minimize the use of text.

When using presentation software such as PowerPoint, try to avoid long, boring bulleted lists. You can alter layouts by repositioning, resizing, or changing the fonts for the placeholders in which your title, bulleted list, organization chart, video clip, photograph, or other elements appear. **Figure 12.8** shows how to make your slides visually more appealing and memorable even with relatively small changes. The advice illustrated here comes from communication consultant Carmine Gallo.[18]

Notice that the bulleted items on the Before Revision slide in Figure 12.8 are not parallel. The first and the last bullet points are needlessly long; the first two bullets repeat "Great presenters." On the After Revision slide, the former bullets almost serve as captions that accompany illustrations. Notice that the captions are short and well within the 6-x-6 rule, although they are complete sentences. The illustrations in the revised slide add interest and highlight the message. You may use icons and stock photos that you can download from the Internet for personal or school use without penalty, or consider taking your own digital pictures.

You can also use other PowerPoint features, such as SmartArt, to add variety and pizzazz to your slides. Converting pure text and bullet points to graphics, charts, and other images will keep your audiences interested and help them retain the information you are presenting. Newer versions of PowerPoint now offer helpful design assistance, converting bulleted lists into more attractive slides.

**The Impact of Special Effects.** Just as you anticipate audience members' reactions to color, you can usually anticipate their reactions to special effects. Using animation and sound effects—flying objects, swirling text, clashing cymbals, and the like—only because they are available is not a good idea. Special effects distract your audience, drawing attention away from your main points. Add animation features only if doing so helps convey your message or adds interest to the content. When your audience members leave, they should be commenting on the ideas you conveyed—not on the wild swivels and sound effects. The zooming effect of Prezi presentations can add value to your presentation as long as it helps your audience understand connections and remember content. The motion should not make your listeners dizzy, however.

**OFFICE INSIDER**

"Frequently in good presentations, photos serve well in a metaphorical or conceptual sense, or to set a backdrop tone for what the audience is hearing from the presenter, and not necessarily to communicate actual content. . . . TED's most viewed talk of all time hasn't a single slide, and many of TED's most successful talks have a focus on what's said, not seen."[16]

**Aaron Weyenberg,**
*creator of TED conference slides*

## 12-4c  Building Your Business Presentation

After considering design principles and their effects, you are ready to start putting together your presentation. In this section you will learn how to organize and compose your presentation, which templates to choose, and how to edit, proofread, and evaluate your work.

**Organizing Your Presentation.** When you prepare your presentation, translate the major headings in your outline into titles for slides. Then build bullet points using short phrases. In Chapter 4 you learned to improve readability by using document design techniques, including bullets, numbers, and headings. In preparing a PowerPoint, Keynote, or Prezi presentation, you will use those same techniques.

The slides (or canvas) you create to accompany your spoken ideas can be organized with visual elements that will help your audience understand and remember what you want to communicate. Let's say, for example, that you have three points in your presentation. You can create a **blueprint slide** that captures the three points in a visually appealing way, and then you can use that slide several times throughout your presentation. Near the beginning, the blueprint slide provides an overview of your points. Later, it provides transitions as you move from point to point. For transitions, you can direct your audience's attention by highlighting the next point you will be talking about. Finally, the blueprint slide can be used near the end to provide a review of your key points.

**Composing Your Presentation.** During the composition stage, many users fall into the trap of excessive formatting and programming. They waste precious time fine-tuning their slides or canvas and don't spend enough time on what they are going to say and how they will say it. To avoid this trap, set a limit for how much time you will spend making your slides or canvas visually appealing. Your time limit will be based on how many "bells and whistles" (a) your audience expects and (b) your content requires to make it understandable.

Not every point nor every thought requires a visual. In fact, it's smart to switch off the presentation occasionally and direct the focus to yourself. Darkening the screen while you discuss a point, tell a story, give an example, or involve the audience will add variety to your presentation.

Create a slide or canvas only if it accomplishes at least one of the following purposes:

- Generates interest in what you are saying and helps the audience follow your ideas

- Highlights points you want your audience to remember

- Introduces or reviews your key points

- Provides a transition from one major point to the next

- Illustrates and simplifies complex ideas

Consider perusing the Help articles built into your presentation software, purchasing one of many inexpensive guides to electronic slide presentations, or learning from online teaching manuals and tips. Your presentations will be more appealing, and you will save time if you know, for example, how to design with master slides and how to create your own templates.

**Working With Templates.** All presentation programs require you to (a) select or create a template that will serve as the background for your presentation and (b) make each slide by selecting a layout that best conveys your message. Novice and even advanced users often choose existing templates because they are designed by professionals who know how to combine harmonious colors, borders, bullet styles, and fonts for pleasing visual effects. If you prefer, you can alter existing templates so they better suit your needs. Adding a corporate logo, adjusting the color scheme to better match the colors used on your organization's website, or selecting a different font are just some of the

**Figure 12.9** Designing More Effective Slides

The slide on the left uses a difficult-to-read font style on a busy background. In addition, the slide includes too many words per bullet and violates most of the slide-making rules it covers. After revision, the slide on the right provides an appealing color combination, uses short phrases in a readable font style, and creates an attractive list using PowerPoint design features.

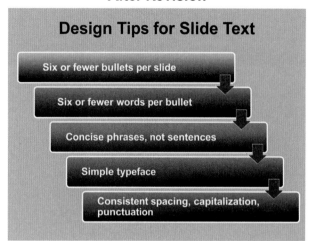

ways you can customize existing templates. One big advantage of templates is that they get you started quickly.

Be careful, though, of what experts call **visual clichés**.[19] Overused templates and clip art that come preinstalled with PowerPoint, Canva, and Prezi can weary viewers who have seen them repeatedly in presentations. Instead of using a standard template, search for *PowerPoint template*, *Keynote template*, or *Prezi template* in your favorite search tool. You will see hundreds of templates available as free downloads. Unless your employer requires that presentations all have the same look, your audience will appreciate fresh templates that complement the purpose of your presentation and provide visual variety.

**Revising and Proofreading Your Presentation.** Use the PowerPoint slide sorter view to rearrange, insert, and delete slides during the revision process. You can use the Prezi editor to make any necessary changes to your canvas. This is the time to focus on making your presentation as clear and concise as possible. If you are listing items, be sure they all use parallel grammatical form. **Figure 12.9** shows how to revise a PowerPoint slide to improve it for conciseness, parallelism, and other features. Study the design tips described in the first slide, and determine which suggestions their author did not follow. Then compare it with the revised slide.

As you are revising, check carefully to find spelling, grammar, punctuation, and other errors. Use the PowerPoint, Keynote, or Prezi spell-check feature, but don't rely on it solely. Careful proofing, preferably from a printed copy of the slideshow, is a must. Nothing is as embarrassing as projecting errors on a huge screen in front of an audience. Also, check for consistency in how you capitalize and punctuate points throughout the presentation.

**Evaluating Your Presentation.** Finally, critically evaluate your slideshow. Is your message presented in a visually appealing way? Have you tested your slides on the equipment and in the room you will be using during your presentation? Do the colors you selected work in this new setting? Are the font styles and sizes readable from the back of the room? **Figure 12.10** shows examples of PowerPoint slides that incorporate what you have learned in this discussion.

## Figure 12.10 PowerPoint Slides That Illustrate Multimedia Presentations

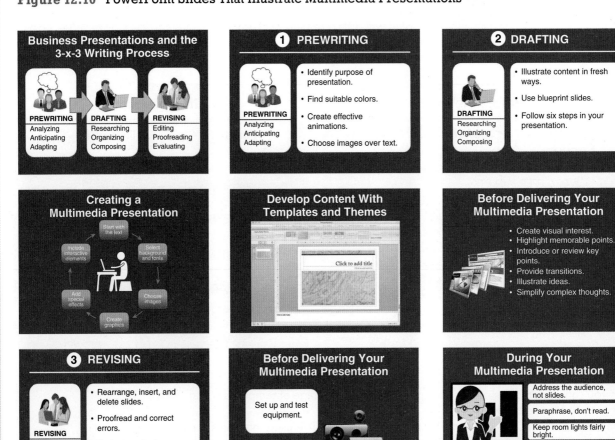

The blue background and the matching hues in the slideshow shown in Figure 12.10 are standard choices for many business presentations. With an unobtrusive dark background, white fonts are a good option for maximum contrast and, hence, readability. The creator of the presentation varied the slide design to break the monotony of bulleted or numbered lists. Images and sparsely animated diagrams add interest and zing to the slides.

Some presenters allow their PowerPoint slides, Keynote slides, or Prezi canvases to upstage them. Advertising mogul David Ogilvy once observed, "Most people use PowerPoint like a drunk uses a lamppost—for support rather than for illumination."[20] Although multimedia presentations can supply terrific sizzle, they cannot replace the steak. In developing a presentation, don't expect your slides to carry the show. You can avoid being upstaged by not relying totally on your slides or canvas. Remember that you are still the main attraction!

### 12-4d Seven Steps to a Powerful Multimedia Presentation

We have now discussed many suggestions for making effective PowerPoint, Keynote, and Prezi presentations, but you may still be wondering how to put it all together. **Figure 12.11** presents a step-by-step process for creating a powerful multimedia presentation.

**Figure 12.11 Seven Steps to a Powerful Multimedia Presentation**

**1 Start with the text.**

What do you want your audience to believe, do, or remember? Organize your ideas into an outline with major and minor points.

**2 Select background and fonts.**

Choose a template or create your own. Focus on consistent font styles, sizes, colors, and backgrounds. Try to use no more than two font styles in your presentation. The point size should be between 24 and 36, and title fonts should be larger than text font.

**3 Choose images that help communicate your message.**

Use relevant clip art, infographics, photographs, maps, or drawings to illustrate ideas. Access Microsoft Office 365 from within PowerPoint and choose from thousands of images and photographs, most of which are in the public domain and require no copyright permissions. Before using images from other sources, determine whether permission from the copyright holder is required. Canva, Prezi, and other apps also offer these features.

**4 Create graphics.**

When possible, transform boring bulleted items into appealing graphics and charts. PowerPoint's SmartArt feature can be used to create organization charts, cycles and radials, time lines, pyramids, matrixes, and Venn diagrams. Use PowerPoint's Chart feature to develop types of charts including line, pie, and bar charts. In PowerPoint follow the guidance of the built-in Designer feature that will "suggest" design options.

**5 Add special effects.**

To keep the audience focused, use animation and transition features to control when text or objects appear. With motion paths, 3D, and other animation options, you can move objects to various positions on the slide and zoom in on and out of images and text on your canvas. To minimize clutter, you can dim or remove them once they have served their purpose. But use with care! Some experts discourage the use of special effects.

**6 Create hyperlinks.**

Make your presentation more interactive and intriguing by connecting to videos, spreadsheets, or websites.

**7 Move your presentation online.**

Make your presentation available by posting it to the Internet or an organization's intranet. Even if you are giving a face-to-face presentation, attendees appreciate electronic handouts if you don't want to give away your entire slideshow. To discourage copying, convert your presentations to PDF documents—if needed with a watermark and in black and white. Your multimedia presentation can be shared in a Web conference or broadcast. Slide presentations can also be converted to video, still photos, decks, and other formats.

Guffey, M. E, Business Communication: Process and Product, South-Western/Cengage Learning

## 12-5 Refining Delivery, Rehearsing, and Performing Your Talk

Once you have organized your presentation and prepared visuals, you are ready to practice delivering it. You will feel more confident and appear more professional if you know more about delivery methods and techniques to use before, during, and after your presentation.

**LEARNING OUTCOME 5**

Name delivery techniques for use before, during, and after a presentation to keep the audience engaged.

## WORKPLACE IN FOCUS

When the founders of the microlending nonprofit organization Kiva make business presentations around the world, audiences respond with enthusiastic applause and even tears. Kiva's online lending platform connects personal lenders with poverty-stricken individuals in developing nations, enabling villagers to start tomato farms, carpet kiosks, and other small ventures that improve their lives. Lindiwe in rural Zimbabwe operates three small businesses in her village and mentors other young women in her community. Kiva's presentations include heartwarming stories and videos about village entrepreneurs to show that small loans can make a big difference.[21] What tips can communicators follow to deliver powerful, inspirational presentations?

## 12-5a  Choosing a Delivery Method

Inexperienced speakers often hold on to myths about public speaking. They may believe that they must memorize an entire presentation or read from a manuscript to be successful. Let's debunk the myths and focus on effective delivery techniques.

**Avoid Memorizing Your Presentation.** Unless you are an experienced performer, you will sound robotic and unnatural if you try to recite your talk by heart. What's more, forgetting your place can be disastrous! That is why we don't recommend memorizing an entire oral presentation. However, memorizing significant parts—the introduction, the conclusion, and perhaps a meaningful quotation—can make your presentation dramatic and impressive.

**Don't Read From Your Notes.** Reading your business presentation to an audience from notes or a manuscript is boring, and listeners will quickly lose interest. Because reading suggests that you don't know your topic well, the audience loses confidence in your expertise. Reading also prevents you from maintaining eye contact. You can't see audience reactions; consequently, you can't benefit from feedback.

**Deliver Your Presentation Extemporaneously.** The best plan for delivering convincing business presentations, by far, is extemporaneous delivery, especially when you are structuring your talk with a multimedia presentation such as a PowerPoint slideshow, Keynote presentation, Google Slides, Adobe Presenter, or Prezi canvas. **Extemporaneous** delivery means speaking freely, generally without notes, after preparing and rehearsing. You comment on the multimedia visuals you have prepared. Reading from notes or a manuscript in addition to a PowerPoint slideshow, Keynote slides, or a Prezi canvas will damage your credibility. Unlike extemporaneous delivery, **impromptu** speaking describes improvised, unrehearsed, spontaneous spur-of-the-moment delivery.

**Know When Notes Are Appropriate.** If you give a talk without multimedia technology, you may use note cards or an outline containing key sentences and major ideas, but beware of reading from a script. By preparing and then practicing with your notes, you can use them while also talking to your audience in a conversational manner. Your notes should be neither entire paragraphs nor single words. Instead, they should contain a complete sentence or two to introduce each major idea. Below the topic sentence(s), outline subpoints and illustrations. Note cards will keep you on track and prompt your memory, but only if you have rehearsed the presentation thoroughly.

## 12-5b Combating Stage Fright

Even pros experience some **stage fright** when performing before an audience. World-renowned singer-songwriter Adele is terrified of huge arenas and has said she may never tour again: "I have anxiety attacks, constant panicking on stage; my heart feels like it's going to explode because I never feel like I'm going to deliver, ever."[22] Celebrated soprano Renee Fleming confessed in her biography, "Stage fright makes you feel as if you will die if you go out on the stage."[23] And Laurence Olivier, considered one of the greatest actors of the twentieth century, acquired **performance anxiety** late in life. It filled him with dread. Performing in a London theater, he had a manager push him onstage every night.[24]

Being afraid is quite natural and results from actual physiological changes occurring in your body. Faced with a frightening situation, your body responds with the **fight-flight-freeze response**. This physical reflex provides your body with increased energy to deal with threatening situations. It also creates those sensations—dry mouth, sweaty hands, increased heartbeat, and stomach butterflies—that we associate with stage fright. **Figure 12.12** offers tips for combating the fear of public speaking.

### Figure 12.12 Conquering Stage Fright

Ever get nervous before making a presentation? Everyone does! And it's not all in your head, either. When you face something threatening or challenging, your body reacts in what psychologists call the *fight-flight-freeze response*. This involuntary reflex readies your body for action—in this case, making a presentation.

Because everyone feels some form of apprehension before speaking, it's impossible to eliminate the physiological symptoms altogether. However, you can reduce their effects with the following techniques:

- **Breathe deeply.** Use deep breathing to ease your fight-or-flight symptoms. Inhale to a count of ten, hold this breath to a count of ten, and exhale to a count of ten. Concentrate on your counting and your breathing; both activities reduce your stress.

- **Convert your fear.** Don't view your sweaty palms and dry mouth as evidence of fear. Interpret them as symptoms of exuberance, excitement, and enthusiasm to share your ideas.

- **Know your topic and come prepared.** Feel confident about your topic. Select a topic that you know well and that is relevant to your audience. Prepare thoroughly and practice extensively.

- **Use positive self-talk.** Remind yourself that you know your topic and are prepared. Tell yourself that the audience is on your side—because it is! Moreover, most speakers appear to be more confident than they feel. Make this apparent confidence work for you.

- **Take a sip of water.** Drink some water to alleviate your dry mouth and constricted voice box, especially if you're talking for more than 15 minutes.

- **Shift the spotlight to your visuals.** At least some of the time the audience will be focusing on your slides, transparencies, handouts, or whatever you have prepared—and not totally on you.

- **Ignore any stumbles.** If you make a mistake, ignore the stumble and keep going. Don't apologize or confess your nervousness. The audience will forget any mistakes quickly.

- **Feel proud when you finish.** You will be surprised at how good you feel when you finish. Take pride in what you have accomplished, and your audience will reward you with applause and congratulations. Your body, of course, will call off the fight-flight-freeze response and return to normal!

When Apple CEO Tim Cook continues the tradition started by the late Steve Jobs and headlines one of his spectacular product launches, the world is listening. Striking graphics and Cook's commentary work together seamlessly. Making his keynote presentations look effortless requires countless hours of practice and rehearsals.

**OFFICE INSIDER**

"You're never really comfortable. Even though you may think you are . . . you really aren't." But in time, "you learn how to open, how to sustain, how to pace . . ." and you will get more comfortable.[25]

**Jerry Seinfeld,**
*comedian, actor, writer, producer*

You can learn to control and reduce performance anxiety as well as to incorporate techniques for effective speaking, by using the following strategies and techniques before, during, and after your presentation.

## 12-5c Before Your Presentation

Speaking in front of a group will be less daunting if you allow for adequate preparation, sufficient practice, and rehearsals. Interacting with the audience and limiting surprises such as malfunctioning equipment will also enhance your peace of mind. Consider the following tips for a smooth start:

**Prepare Thoroughly.** One of the most effective strategies for reducing stage fright is knowing your subject thoroughly. Research your topic diligently and prepare a careful sentence outline. Those who try to wing it usually suffer the worst butterflies—and give the worst presentations.

**Rehearse Repeatedly.** When you rehearse, practice your entire presentation. In PowerPoint you may print out speaker's notes, an outline, or a handout featuring miniature slides, which are excellent for practice. If you don't use an electronic slideshow, place your outline sentences on separate note cards. You may also wish to include transitional sentences to help you move to the next topic as you practice. Rehearse alone or before friends and family. Also consider making an audio or video recording of your rehearsals so you can evaluate your effectiveness.

**Time Yourself.** Most audiences tend to get restless during longer talks. Therefore, try to complete your presentation in 20 minutes or less. If you have a time limit, don't go over it. Set a simple kitchen timer or the timer app on your smartphone during your rehearsal to keep track of time. Better yet, use the PowerPoint function Rehearse Timings in the Slide Show tab to measure the length of your talk as you practice. Other presentation software packages offer similar features.

**Dress Professionally.** Dressing professionally for a presentation will make you look more credible to your audience. You will also feel more confident. If you are not used to professional attire, practice wearing it so you appear comfortable during your presentation.

**Check the Room and the Equipment.** If you are using a computer, a projector, or sound equipment, be certain they are operational. Before you start, check the lighting, the electrical outlets, and the position of the viewing screen. Ensure that the seating arrangement is appropriate to your needs. Make sure that all video or Web links are working and that you know how to operate all features the first time you try.

**Greet Members of the Audience.** Try to make contact with a few members of the audience when you enter the room, while you are waiting to be introduced, or when you walk to the podium. Your body language should convey friendliness, confidence, and enjoyment.

**Practice Stress Reduction.** If you feel tension and fear while you are waiting your turn to speak, use stress-reduction techniques, such as deep breathing. Additional techniques to help you conquer stage fright are presented in Figure 12.12.

No matter how much time you put into preshow setup and testing, you still have no guarantee that all will go smoothly. Therefore, always bring backups of your presentation. Transferring your presentation to a CD, DVD, or a USB flash drive that could run from any available computer might prove useful. Likewise, copying your file to the cloud (e.g., Dropbox or Google Drive) or sending it to yourself as an e-mail attachment can be beneficial.

## 12-5d During Your Presentation

To stay in control during your talk, build credibility, and engage your audience, follow these time-tested guidelines for effective speaking:

**Start With a Pause and Present Your First Sentence From Memory.** When you first approach the audience, take a moment to make yourself comfortable. Establish your control of the situation. By memorizing your opening, you can immediately develop rapport with the audience through eye contact. You will also sound confident and knowledgeable.

**Maintain Eye Contact.** If the size of the audience overwhelms you, pick out two individuals on the right and two on the left. Talk directly to these people. Don't ignore listeners in the back of the room. Even when presenting to a large audience, try to make genuine, not fleeting eye contact with as many people as possible during your presentation.

**Control Your Voice and Vocabulary.** This means speaking in moderated tones but loudly enough to be heard. Eliminate verbal static, such as *ah, er, like, you know,* and *um.* Silence is preferable to meaningless fillers when you are thinking of your next idea.

**Show Enthusiasm.** If you are not excited about your topic, how can you expect your audience to be? Show passion for your topic through your tone, facial expressions, and gestures. Adding variety to your voice also helps keep your audience alert and interested.

**Skip the Apologies.** Avoid weak openings, such as *I know you have heard this before, but we need to review it anyway.* Or: *I had trouble with my computer and the slides, so bear with me.* Unless the issue is blatant, such as not being able to load the presentation or make the projector work, apologies are counterproductive. Focus on your presentation.

**Slow Down and Know When to Pause.** Many novice speakers talk too rapidly, displaying their nervousness and making it very difficult for audience members to understand their ideas. Put the brakes on and listen to what you are saying. Pauses give the audience time to absorb an important point. Silence can be effective especially when you are transitioning from one point to another. Paraphrase and elaborate on what the listeners have seen. Don't read verbatim from the slides.

**WORKPLACE IN FOCUS**

You may know Apple's trademarked slogan *There's an app for that.* Now imagine that an app could help you lower your public speaking anxiety and eliminate annoying fillers such as *um, uh, er, basically,* or *you know.* One such app is Ummo. When activated as a presentation begins, it tracks users' speech patterns, pace, and volume. It logs pauses and fillers. A handy transcript can be displayed on screen showing the problem areas that will require more practice. To improve, users can set a beep to alert them to pesky speech mannerisms.[26] Why is it a good idea to work on improving speech habits?

**Move Naturally.** If you have a lectern, don't hide behind it. Move about casually and naturally. Avoid fidgeting with your clothing, hair, or items in your pockets. Do not roll up your sleeves or put your hands in your pockets. Learn to use your body to express a point.

**Control Visual Aids With Clickers, Pointers, and Blank Screens.** Discuss and interpret each visual aid for the audience. Move aside as you describe it so people can see it fully. Learn to use a clicker to advance your slides remotely. Use a laser pointer if necessary, but steady your hand if it is shaking. Dim the slideshow when not discussing the slides. In Slide Show view in PowerPoint, press *B* on the keyboard to blacken the screen or *W* to turn the screen white. In Prezi, remember to zoom back out when necessary.

**Avoid Digressions.** Stick to your outline and notes. Don't suddenly include clever little anecdotes or digressions that occur to you on the spot. If it is not part of your rehearsed material, leave it out so you can finish on time.

**Summarize Your Main Points and Drive Home Your Message.** Conclude your presentation by reiterating your main points or by emphasizing what you want the audience to think or do. Once you have announced your conclusion, proceed to it directly.

## 12-5e After Your Presentation

As you are concluding your presentation, handle questions and answers competently and provide handouts, if appropriate. Try the following techniques:

**Distribute Handouts.** If you prepared handouts with data the audience will not need during the presentation, pass them out when you finish to prevent any distraction during your talk.

**Encourage Questions but Keep Control.** If the situation permits a question-and-answer period, announce it at the beginning of your presentation. Then, when you finish, ask for questions. Set a time limit for questions and answers. If you don't know the answer to a question, don't make one up or panic. Instead, offer to find the answer within a day or two. If you make such a promise, be sure to follow through. Don't allow one individual to dominate the Q&A period. Keep the entire audience involved.

**Repeat Questions.** Although you may have heard the question, some audience members may not have. Begin each answer by repeating the question. This also gives you thinking time. Then, direct your answer to the entire audience.

**Reinforce Your Main Points.** You can use your answers to restate your primary ideas (*I'm glad you brought that up because it gives me a chance to elaborate on . . .*). In answering questions, avoid becoming defensive or debating the questioner.

**Avoid *Yes, but* Answers.** The word *but* immediately cancels any preceding message. Try replacing it with *and*. For example, *Yes, X has been tried. And Y works even better because . . . .*

**End With a Summary and Appreciation.** To signal the end of the session before you take the last question, say something like *We have time for just one more question.* As you answer the last question, try to work it into a summary of your main points. Then, express appreciation to the audience for the opportunity to present.

## Summary of Learning Outcomes

**1** **Discuss two important first steps in preparing for business presentations.**

- Excellent presentation skills are sought by employers and will benefit you at any career stage.
- Presentations can be informative or persuasive, face-to-face or virtual, performed in front of big audiences or small groups, and elaborate or simple.
- Business professionals give a variety of business presentations including briefings, reports, podcasts, virtual presentations, and webinars.
- Savvy speakers know what they want to accomplish and are able to adjust to friendly, neutral, uninterested, as well as hostile audiences.

**2** **Explain how to organize your business presentations to build audience rapport.**

- In the introduction capture the audience's attention, introduce yourself, establish your credibility, and preview the main points.
- Organize the body around two to four main points; arrange them according to chronology, space, function, comparison/contrast, a journalistic pattern, value/size, importance, problem/solution, simple/complex, or best case/worst case.
- In the conclusion summarize the main topics of your talk, leave the audience with a memorable take-away, and end with a statement that provides a graceful exit.
- Build rapport by using effective imagery, verbal signposts, and positive nonverbal messages.

**3** **List contemporary visual aids and design practices that help presenters overcome the monotony of bullet points.**

- Your audience is more likely to retain your talk if you use well-prepared visual aids because images are more memorable than text; this phenomenon is called pictorial superiority.
- Good visuals emphasize and clarify main points, increase audience interest, prove you are professional, illustrate your message better than words alone, and serve to jog your memory.
- Common types of visual aids are multimedia slides, zoom presentations, videos, handouts, flipcharts and whiteboards, as well as props.
- In good hands presentation software such as PowerPoint, Apple Keynote, or Google Slides is helpful; aspire to using more images and less text.
- Whenever possible, expert speakers move beyond boring bulleted text and choose relevant vivid images.

**4** **Create a memorable error-free multimedia presentation that shows a firm grasp of basic visual design principles.**

- The purpose and the audience determine the slide design, which includes color, images, and special effects.
- Building a presentation involves organizing and composing slide content; avoiding overused templates; and revising, proofreading, and evaluating the final product.
- The seven steps to creating impressive multimedia slides are as follows: start with the text, select a template, choose images, create graphics, add special effects, create hyperlinks, and post online.

**5** **Name delivery techniques for use before, during, and after a presentation to keep the audience engaged.**

- When delivering a business presentation, don't memorize your talk or read from notes; rather, speak extemporaneously and use notes only when you're not using presentation software.
- When enduring a fight-flight-freeze response due to performance anxiety, note that this involuntary reflex is normal in stress situations such as public speaking; even professional performers experience stage fright.
- Before your presentation prepare and rehearse, time yourself, dress professionally, check the room and equipment, greet members of the audience, and practice stress reduction.
- During the presentation deliver your first sentence from memory, maintain eye contact, control your voice, show enthusiasm, slow down, move naturally, use visual aids skillfully, and stay on topic.
- After the presentation distribute handouts, invite and repeat questions, reinforce your main points, avoid *Yes, but* answers, and end with a summary and appreciation.

## Key Terms

glossophobia 369

take-away 376

rapport 376

pictorial superiority 378

software as a service (SaaS) 380

chartjunk 381

PowerPoint Phluff 381

6-x-6 rule 382

blueprint slide 384

visual clichés 385

extemporaneous 388

impromptu 388

stage fright 389

performance anxiety 389

fight-flight-freeze response 389

## Chapter Review

1. Why are analyzing an audience and anticipating its reactions particularly important before business presentations, and how would you adapt to the four categories of listeners? (L.O. 1)

2. List and describe five types of presentations a business professional might make. (L.O. 1)

3. Name at least eight techniques that can help you gain and keep audience attention. (L.O. 2)

4. List six techniques for creating effective imagery in a presentation. Be prepared to discuss each. (L.O. 2)

5. List suggestions that would ensure that your nonverbal messages reinforce your verbal messages. (L.O. 2)

6. Good visual aids have many purposes. List five of these purposes. (L.O. 3)

7. Name specific advantages and disadvantages of multimedia presentation software such as PowerPoint, Apple Keynote, and Prezi. (L.O. 3)

8. What is the 6-x-6 rule, and what might prompt a presentation slide creator to break it? (L.O. 4)

9. Which delivery method is best for persuasive business presentations? Explain why. (L.O. 5)

10. How can speakers overcome stage fright? Name at least six helpful techniques. (L.O. 5)

## Critical Thinking

11. Can expert speakers save time and just "wing it"?

12. Corporate communication consultant Dianna Booher believes that enthusiasm is infectious and "boredom is contagious."[27] What does this mean for you as a presenter? How can you avoid being a boring speaker? (L.O. 2, 4, 5)

13. Why do many communication consultants encourage businesspeople to move beyond bullet points? What do they recommend instead and why? (L.O. 3)

14. How can you prevent multimedia presentation software from upstaging you? (L.O. 4)

15. Etiquette expert Jacqueline Whitmore offers this advice to aspiring speakers: "A long, dry presentation of facts is sure to be a yawn-inducer, so consider your presentation as a conversation with your audience. . . . Ask questions, incorporate teambuilding exercise, and ask for volunteers to come up to the front to help you demonstrate a point. . . . Ask the group to stand, clap, or raise their hands, and give you frequent feedback. And remember, a little humor goes a long way."[28] Consider what you've learned in this chapter and the book as a whole. Is this good advice for all audiences? (L.O. 4, 5)

## Activities and Cases

### 12.1 Studying Famous Speeches (L.O. 1, 2, 5)

> Web

**YOUR TASK.** Select a speech by a significant businessperson or a well-known public figure. Consider watching the following iconic political speeches, considered to be among the best in the twentieth century: Martin Luther King Jr.'s "I Have a Dream" speech, President Kennedy's inaugural address, and Franklin Delano Roosevelt's Pearl Harbor Address to the Nation.[29]

If you prefer business tycoons dispensing advice, search for the best-known commencement speeches—for example, Steve Jobs' legendary "Stay Hungry, Stay Foolish" Stanford address, Salman Khan's "Live Your Life Like It's Your Second Chance" speech at MIT, or Sheryl Sandberg's "Rocketship" commencement speech at Harvard Business School. Transcripts of these and other well-known speeches are also available online.[30] Write a memo report or give a short presentation to your class critiquing the speech you have selected in terms of the following:

a. Effectiveness of the introduction, body, and conclusion
b. Evidence of effective overall organization
c. Use of verbal signposts to create coherence
d. Emphasis of two to four main points
e. Effectiveness of supporting facts (use of examples, statistics, quotations, and so forth)
f. Focus on audience benefits
g. Enthusiasm for the topic
h. Body language and personal mannerisms

## 12.2 Audience Analysis First (L.O. 1, 2, 4)

> Web

The key to a captivating business presentation or speech is adapting both the information and delivery to one's audience.

**YOUR TASK.** Select a recent issue of *Fortune, The Wall Street Journal, Bloomberg Businessweek, The Economist, Money, Forbes,* or another business periodical approved by your instructor. Based on an analysis of your peer audience, select an article that will appeal to them and that you can relate to their needs. Submit to your instructor a one-page summary that includes the following: (a) the author, article title, source, issue date, and page reference; (b) a one-paragraph article summary; (c) a description of why you believe the article will appeal to your classmates; and (d) a summary of how you can relate the article to their needs.

## 12.3 Seeking Inspiration and Charisma: Hiring a Speaker (L.O. 1, 2)

> Communication Technology   Social Media   Team   Web

Have you ever wondered why famous entrepreneurs, politicians, athletes, and other celebrities can command high speaking fees? How much are they really making per appearance, and what factors may justify their high fees? You may also wonder how a motivational speaker or corporate trainer might benefit you and your class or your campus community. Searching for and selecting an expert is easy with several commercial speaker bureaus vying for clients. All bureaus provide detailed speaker bios, areas of expertise, and fees. One even features video previews of its clients.

The preeminent agencies for booking talent are All American Speakers, BigSpeak Speakers Bureau, Speakerpedia, and Brooks International Speakers & Entertainment Bureau. Speakerpedia represents the likes of real estate Mogul Barbara Corcoran, investor Mark Cuban, Netflix founder and CEO Reed Hastings, and futurist Samantha Radocchia. Brooks International features casino mogul Stephen Wynn, entrepreneur and philanthropist Richard Branson, and polar explorer Robert Swan, among others. BigSpeak would allow you to hire, for example, personal finance expert Suze Orman, tech whiz Tan Le, and Apple co-founder Steve Wozniak—due to the COVID-19 pandemic all as *virtual keynote speakers*.

**YOUR TASK.** Imagine that you have a budget of up to $100,000 to hire a well-known public speaker. In teams or individually, select a business-related category of speaker by searching one of the speaker bureaus online. For example, choose several prominent personal finance gurus (Suze Orman, Terry Savage, and others) or successful entrepreneurs, managers, and venture capitalists (Elon Musk, Ursula Burns, Jack Dorsey). Other categories are motivational speakers, philanthropists, and inspiring women of color in STEM careers (search AAE Speakers). Study their bios for clues about their expertise and accomplishments.

Comparing at least three speakers, come up with a set of qualities that apparently make these individuals sought-after speakers. Consider how those qualities could enlighten you and your peers. To enrich your experience and enhance your knowledge, watch videos of your chosen speakers on YouTube or the TED website, if available. Check talent agencies, personal websites, and Facebook for further information. Write a memo report about your speaker group, or present your findings face-to-face or virtually, with or without a slide presentation. If your instructor directs, recommend your favorite speaker and give reasons for your decision.

## 12.4 Following a Preeminent STEM Scientist or Entrepreneur on Twitter (L.O. 1–5)

> Communication Technology   Social Media   Web

We learn best from emulation, that is, by observing experts in their field and trying to imitate what they do best—ideally under their guidance, benefiting from their feedback. You may know some of the most famous Twitter users such as Elon Musk, Richard Branson, Suze Orman, Guy Kawasaki, and other well-known businesspeople. But why not learn from accomplished women in science? Consider rocket scientist Aprille Ericsson-Jackson, geochemist and oceanographer Ashanti Johnson, video game artist Lisette Titre-Montgomery, robotics professor Ayanna Howard, or mechanical engineer and science reporter Shini Somara.

**YOUR TASK.** On Twitter, in the Search window on top of the page, enter the name of the public figures, STEM scientists, or businesspeople whose tweets you wish to follow.

Over the course of a few days, read the tweets of your favorite VIPs. After a while, you should be able to discern some trends and areas of interest. Note whether and how your subjects respond to queries from followers. What are their favorite topics? Report your findings to the class, verbally with notes or virtually using PowerPoint or Prezi. If you find particularly intriguing tweets and links, share them with the class. Your instructor may ask you to summarize your observations in an e-mail or a presentation—face-to-face or virtual.

## 12.5 Speaking Anxiety Be Banned! (L.O. 5)

Communication Technology 〉 E-Mail 〉 Social Media 〉 Team 〉

What scares you the most about making a presentation in front of a group of people? Being tongue-tied? Fearing all eyes on you? Messing up? Forgetting your ideas and looking unprofessional?

**YOUR TASK.** Discuss the previous questions as a class. Then, in groups of three or four, talk about ways to overcome these fears. Have you come across strategies that have worked for you and you can pass on to others? Your instructor may ask you to write a memo, an e-mail, a discussion board contribution or social media post (individually or collectively) summarizing your suggestions. If your instructor prefers, you may break out of your small groups and report your best ideas to the entire class—if virtually then by using your learning-management system (e.g., Moodle, Blackboard, or Canvas).

## 12.6 Will You Get by Without Public Speaking in Your Field? Not Likely (L.O. 1, 4, 5)

Communication Technology 〉 Social Media 〉 Team 〉 Web 〉

Do you believe you won't need to speak publicly in your chosen field? It's unlikely because ambitious people communicate more, not less, when advancing up the career ladder. Speaking and presenting to groups is commonplace. So, grapple with your fear of speaking now, in college; this way you will be confident once you enter the workplace.

**YOUR TASK.** Interview one or two individuals in your professional field—in person, by e-mail, using social media (e.g., LinkedIn), or via Zoom, if your interviewee agrees. How is oral communication important in this profession? Does the need for oral skills change as one advances? What suggestions can your interviewees make to newcomers to the field for developing proficient oral communication skills? Discuss your findings with your class. Your instructor may ask you to complete your research as a team and prepare a written or oral report to be presented in class.

## 12.7 Outlining an Oral Presentation (L.O. 1, 2, 4)

One of the hardest parts of preparing an oral presentation is developing the outline.

**YOUR TASK.** Select an oral presentation topic from the list in Activity 12.15, or suggest an original topic. Prepare an outline for your presentation using the following format:

**Title**
**Purpose**

|  | I. INTRODUCTION |
| --- | --- |
| **State your name** | A. |
| **Gain attention and involve the audience** | B. |
| **Establish credibility** | C. |
| **Preview main points** | D. |
| **Transition** | |
| | II. BODY |
| **Main point** | A. |
| **Illustrate, clarify, contrast** | 1. |
| | 2. |
| | 3. |
| **Transition** | |
| **Main point** | B. |
| **Illustrate, clarify, contrast** | 1. |
| | 2. |
| | 3. |
| **Transition** | |
| **Main point** | C. |
| **Illustrate, clarify, contrast** | 1. |
| | 2. |
| | 3. |

**Transition**

|                                   | III. CONCLUSION |
| --------------------------------- | --------------- |
| **Summarize main points**         | A.              |
| **Provide final focus or take-away** | B.           |
| **Encourage questions**           | C.              |

## 12.8 Life After Death by PowerPoint and Beyond (L.O. 1–3)

> **Web**

Much hate has been leveled at the mainstay of business presentations, PowerPoint. Rightly so? At least one comic has been able to cast a humorous eye on the ever-present presentation software.

**YOUR TASK.** Watch Don McMillan's YouTube classic "Life After Death by PowerPoint." Which specific PowerPoint sins is McMillan satirizing? Write a brief summary of the short clip for discussion in class. With your peers discuss whether the bad habits the YouTube video parodies correspond with design principles introduced in this chapter.

## 12.9 Analyzing a TED Talk (L.O. 1–5)

> **Communication Technology**     **E-Mail**     **Social Media**     **Web**

Communication consultant Nancy Duarte dispenses this useful piece of advice in her classic guide to business presentations, *Slide:ology*: "Keep yourself visually and conceptually fed by watching films, visiting museums, and reading design-related publications."[31] Duarte suggests that we can develop expertise by learning from and emulating outstanding examples.

To learn from the presentation skills of the best speakers today, visit the TED channel on YouTube or the TED website. Watch one or more of the 3,700+ TED talks (motto: Ideas worth spreading) available online. Standing at more than three billion views worldwide, the presentations cover topics from the fields of technology, entertainment, and design (TED).

**YOUR TASK.** If your instructor directs, select and watch one of the TED talks and outline it. You may also be asked to focus on the selected speaker's presentation techniques based on the guidelines you have studied in this chapter. Jot down your observations either as notes for a classroom discussion or to serve as a basis for an informative memo or e-mail. If directed by your instructor, compose a concise yet informative tweet directing Twitter users to your chosen TED talk and commenting on it.

## 12.10 Showcasing Your Job (L.O. 1–5)

> **Communication Technology**

Could you describe the multiple tasks you perform at work or when volunteering? Could you do it in a five-minute PowerPoint, Keynote, or Prezi presentation?

Your instructors, for example, may wear many hats. Most academics (a) teach; (b) conduct research to publish; and (c) provide service to the department, college, university, and community. Can you see how those aspects of their profession lend themselves to an outline of primary slides (teaching, publishing, service) and second-level slides (instructing undergraduate and graduate classes, presenting workshops, and giving lectures under the teaching label)?

**YOUR TASK.** Now it's your turn to introduce the duties you perform (or performed) in a current or past job, volunteer activity, or internship in a brief, simple, yet well-designed slide presentation. Your goal is to inform your audience of your job duties in a three- to five-minute talk. Use animation features and graphics where appropriate. Your instructor may show you a completed example of this project.

**Instructor: You will find a model PowerPoint presentation for Chapter 12 in the Cengage Instructor Center.**

## 12.11 Preparing a Perfect Elevator Pitch (L.O. 1, 2)

"Can you pass the elevator test?" asks presentation whiz Garr Reynolds in a new twist on the familiar scenario.[32] He suggests that this technique will help you sharpen your core message. In this exercise you need to pitch your idea in a few brief moments instead of the 20 minutes you had been granted with your vice president of product marketing. You arrive at her door for your appointment as she is leaving, coat and laptop bag in hand. Something has come up.

This meeting is a huge opportunity for you if you want to get the OK from the executive team. Could you sell your idea during the elevator ride and the walk to the parking lot? Reynolds asks. Although this scenario may never happen, you will possibly be asked to shorten a presentation, say, from an hour to 30 minutes or from 20 minutes to 5 minutes. Could you make your message tighter and clearer on the fly?

**YOUR TASK.** Take a business idea you may have, a familiar business topic you care about, or a promotion or raise you wish to request. Create a two- to five-minute speech making a good case for your core message—impromptu or with minimal preparation. Even though you won't have much time to think about the details of your speech, you should be sufficiently familiar with the topic to boil it down and yet be persuasive.

## 12.12 Making Sense of *Fortune* Lists (L.O. 1, 2)

> Web

**YOUR TASK.** Using a research database, perform a search to learn how *Fortune* magazine determines which companies make its annual lists. Research the following lists. Then organize and present a five- to ten-minute informative talk to your class.

a. Fortune 500
b. Global 500
c. 100 Best Companies to Work For
d. World's Most Admired Companies

## 12.13 Presenting an Intriguing Business Topic (L.O. 1–3)

> Social Media > Web

Peruse any business website—for example, *The Wall Street Journal, Forbes,* or *Bloomberg Businessweek*—to search for a topic of interest to you and your peers.

**YOUR TASK.** Select an interesting business article, and verbally present it to the class with or without notes. You could record your talk for a virtual on-demand presentation. Summarize the article and explain why you have chosen it and why you believe it's valuable. Another option is to select a short business-related video clip. First introduce the video and summarize it. Time permitting, show the video in class or post it to the learning management system your course is using. If your instructor directs, compose a tweet recommending or commenting on your article or video clip. Of the available 280 characters, leave at least 10 for retweeting.

## 12.14 Advocating for a Worthy Cause (L.O. 1–5)

> Communication Technology > Social Media > Web

Do you care deeply about a particular nonprofit organization or cause? Perhaps you have donated to a cancer charity or volunteered for a local faith-based nonprofit. The Red Cross, Greenpeace, and the World Wildlife Fund (WWF) may be household names, but thousands of lesser-known nonprofit organizations are also trying to make the world a better place.

Professional fund-raiser and nonprofit service expert Sarah W. Mackey encourages volunteers-to-be to become ambassadors for their favorite organizations. Much like brand ambassadors, advocates for nonprofits should wear the nonprofit's logo, invite friends, tell their families, raise money, volunteer, and spread the word on social media, Mackey says.[33] Some nonprofits—for example, the California-based environmental group Heal the Bay—are proactive. They offer speakers bureau training to volunteers eager to reach out to their communities and raise awareness.[34] Ambassadors do good, become professional speakers, and acquire valuable skills to put on their résumés, a win-win-win!

**YOUR TASK.** Select your favorite charity. If you need help, find your charity or cause by visiting GuideStar, a nongovernmental watchdog that monitors nonprofits, or simply google *list of nonprofits*. Learn as much as you can from the organization's website and from articles written about it. Also, vet your charity by checking it out on GuideStar. Then assemble your information into a logical outline, and create a persuasive oral presentation using presentation software. Your goal is not only to introduce the charity but also to inspire your peers to seek more information and to volunteer. **Tip:** Focus on the benefits, direct and indirect, of volunteering for this charity. Finally, if your instructor asks, practice writing tweets advocating for your organization and calling the public to action.

## 12.15 Selecting Business Presentation Topics (L.O. 1, 2, 5)

> Communication Technology > Web

Consider yourself an expert who has been called in to discuss a business topic before a group of interested people. Because your time is limited, prepare a concise yet powerful presentation with effective visual aids.

**YOUR TASK.** Select a report topic from the following suggestions or from the expanded list of Report Topics available at the accompanying student site. Prepare a five- to ten-minute oral presentation.

a. What options (think aid, grants, and scholarships) do students have to finance their college tuition and fees as costs continue to rise?

b. Which is financially more beneficial to a business, leasing or buying company cars?

c. Tablet computers and other mobile devices are eroding the market share previously held by laptops and netbooks. Which brands are businesses embracing, and why? Which features are a must-have for businesspeople?

d. What kind of marketing works best with students on college campuses? Word of mouth? Internet banner advertising? Social media? Free samples? How do students prefer to get information about goods and services?

e. How can your organization appeal to its members to prevent them from texting while driving or from driving under the influence?

f. Some brands are not afraid to poke fun at themselves. Take Buick, maker of vehicles many associate with older drivers. The company leveraged this perception into a discussion of what Buick is today in a successful series of "Experience the New Buick" ads. Find three or more examples of companies admitting weaknesses, and draw conclusions from their strategies. Would you recommend this as a smart marketing ploy?

g. How can students and other citizens contribute to conserving gasoline and other fossil fuel to save money and address the global climate crisis?

h. What is the career outlook in a field of your choice? Consider job growth, compensation, and benefits. What kind of academic or other experience is typically required in your field?

i. What is the economic outlook for a given product, such as electric cars, laptop computers, digital cameras, fitness equipment, or a product of your choice?

j. What kinds of workers can most easily work from home? Examine how the COVID-19 pandemic has changed telecommuting.

k. What are the Webby Awards, and what criteria do the judges use to evaluate websites? Alternatively, examine the Clio Awards or Cannes Lions Awards. Consider evaluation criteria and several of the most recent winners.

l. What franchise would offer the best investment opportunity for an entrepreneur in your area?

m. What should a guide to proper smartphone etiquette include?

n. Why should a company have a written e-mail, Web use, and social media policy?

o. Where should your organization hold its next convention?

p. What is the outlook for real estate (commercial or residential) investment in your area?

q. What do the personal assistants for celebrities do, and how does one become a personal assistant? (Investigate the Association of Celebrity Personal Assistants.)

r. What kinds of gifts are appropriate for businesses to give clients and customers during the holiday season?

s. What rip-offs are on the Federal Trade Commission's list of top ten consumer scams, and how can consumers avoid falling for them?

t. How can your organization or institution improve its image?

u. What are the pros and cons of using Prezi zoom presentations? Would they be appropriate in your field?

v. How can consumers protect themselves against identity theft?

w. How could people be persuaded to start saving for retirement, considering the magic of compound interest, which allows even small contributions to grow substantially over long periods of time? How could very young people who may not give much thought to retiring be motivated to start?

x. What are the differences among casual, business casual, and business formal attire?

y. What is a sustainable business? What can companies do to become sustainable?

z. What smartphone apps are available that will improve a businessperson's productivity?

## 12.16 Creating a Multimedia Presentation (no additional research required) (L.O. 1–5)
**Communication Technology**

You are a consultant and have been hired to improve the effectiveness of corporate trainers. These trainers frequently make presentations to employees on topics such as conflict management, teamwork, time management, problem solving, performance appraisals, and employment interviewing. Your goal is to teach these trainers how to make better presentations.

**YOUR TASK.** Create six visually appealing slides based on the following content, which will be spoken during your presentation titled *Effective Employee Training*. The comments shown here are only a portion of a longer presentation.

Trainers have two options when they make presentations. The first option is one-way communication in which the trainer basically dumps the information on the audience and leaves. The second option is a two-way approach that involves the audience. The benefits of the two-way approach are that it helps the trainer connect with the audience and reinforce key points, it increases audience retention rates, and it changes the pace and adds variety to the presentation. The two-way approach also encourages audience members to get to know each other. Because today's employees demand more than just a talking head, trainers must engage their audiences by involving them in a dialogue.

If you decide to interact with your audience, you need to choose an approach that suits your delivery style. Also, think about which options your audience would be likely to respond to most positively. Let's consider some interactivity approaches now. Realize, though, that these ideas are presented to help you get your creative juices flowing. After reading the list, think about situations in which these options might be effective. You could also brainstorm to come up with creative ideas to add to this list.

• Ask employees to guess at statistics before revealing them.

- Ask an employee to share examples or experiences.
- Ask a volunteer to help you demonstrate something.
- Ask the audience to complete a questionnaire or worksheet.
- Ask the audience to brainstorm or list things as fast as possible.
- Ask a variety of question types to achieve different purposes.
- Invite the audience to work through a process or examine an object.
- Survey the audience.
- Pause to let the audience members read something to themselves.
- Divide the audience into small groups to discuss an issue.

## Grammar/Mechanics Checkup 12

## Capitalization

Review Sections 3.01–3.16 in the Grammar/Mechanics Handbook. In the space provided, write the letter of the sentence with correct capitalization. Also record the appropriate Grammar/Mechanics section for the principle involved. When you finish, compare your responses with those provided at the bottom of the page. If your answers differ, review the appropriate principles.

<u>  b  </u>  (3.16, 3.05)

**EXAMPLE:**
  a. In the Spring Kaitlin took sociology, English, and Journalism courses.
  b. In the spring Kaitlin took sociology, English, and journalism courses.
  c. In the Spring Kaitlin took Sociology, English, and Journalism courses.

_____

1. a. The Secretary of our Graduate Studies Committee convinced the Librarian to serve.
   b. The secretary of our Graduate Studies Committee convinced the librarian to serve.
   c. The secretary of our graduate studies committee convinced the librarian to serve.

_____

2. a. The Marketing Professor explained that German consumers shop for food often and buy in small quantities.
   b. The marketing professor explained that German consumers shop for food often and buy in small quantities.
   c. The Marketing professor explained that German Consumers shop for food often and buy in small quantities.

_____

3. a. During the summer the new grad applied for an analyst position in the federal government.
   b. During the summer the new grad applied for an analyst position in the Federal Government.
   c. During the Summer the new grad applied for an analyst position in the federal government.

_____

4. a. Driving West on Interstate 70 last August, my Niece and Nephew had a flat tire.
   b. Driving west on Interstate 70 last August, my Niece and Nephew had a flat tire.
   c. Driving west on Interstate 70 last August, my niece and nephew had a flat tire.

_____

5. a. All southwest airlines passengers will board the Aircraft at gate B2.
   b. All Southwest Airlines Passengers will board the Aircraft at Gate B2.
   c. All Southwest Airlines passengers will board the aircraft at Gate B2.

_____

6. a. At a City College in the rural South, the most popular photography apps are Adobe Lightroom, Flickr, Instagram, and Google Photos.
   b. At a city college in the rural South, the most popular photography apps are Adobe Lightroom, Flickr, Instagram, and Google Photos.
   c. At a City College in the rural south, the most popular photography apps are adobe lightroom, flickr, Instagram, and google photos.

_____ 7. a. Please see figure 1.6 in chapter 3 for U.S. bureau of labor statistics unemployment figures among spanish-speaking residents.

b. Please see Figure 1.6 in Chapter 3 for U.S. Bureau of Labor Statistics unemployment figures among Spanish-speaking residents.

c. Please see figure 1.6 in chapter 3 for U.S. Bureau of Labor Statistics unemployment figures among Spanish-speaking residents.

_____ 8. a. I bought the newest iPad Pro model, but you may choose any tablet on the market.

b. I bought the newest iPad Pro Model, but you may choose any Tablet on the market.

c. I bought the newest iPad Pro model, but you may choose any Tablet on the market.

_____ 9. a. In the Fall our College Recruiter will travel to china, thailand, and india to meet with new Graduate Students.

b. In the Fall our College Recruiter will travel to China, Thailand, and India to meet with new Graduate Students.

c. In the fall our college recruiter will travel to China, Thailand, and India to meet with new graduate students.

_____ 10. a. Did you read _The Wall Street Journal_ article titled "Dow passes 34,000 on strong earnings data"?

b. Did you read _The wall street journal_ article titled "Dow passes 34,000 on strong earnings data"?

c. Did you read _The Wall Street Journal_ article titled "Dow Passes 34,000 on Strong Earnings Data"?

1. b (3.06e, 3.09) 2. b (3.01, 3.02) 3. a (3.16, 3.10) 4. c (3.08, 3.06g) 5. c (3.04, 3.07) 6. b (3.01, 3.08) 7. b (3.07, 3.04, 3.15) 8. a (3.11)
9. c (3.16, 3.06e, 3.01) 10. c (3.12)

Every chapter provides an editing exercise to fine-tune your grammar and mechanics skills. The following executive summary requires edits that address capitalization, punctuation, parallelism, concise wording, and other writing issues. Study the guidelines in the Grammar/Mechanics Handbook (Appendix D), including the lists of Confusing Words and Frequently Misspelled Words.

**YOUR TASK.** Edit the following (a) by inserting corrections in your textbook or on a photocopy using the proofreading marks in Appendix C or (b) by downloading the summary from the accompanying student site and correcting it on your computer.

### EXECUTIVE SUMMARY
#### Purpose of Report

The purposes of this report are to: (1) Determine the Gold Coast University campus communitys awareness of the campus recycling program and (2) Recommend ways to increase participation. Gold Coasts recycling program was intended to respond to the increasing problem of waste disposal, to fulfill it's social responsibility as an educational institution and to meet demands of legislation that made it a requirement for individuals and organizations to recycle.

A Survey was conducted in an effort to learn about the campus communitys recycling habits and to make an assessment of the participation in the recycling program that is current. A total of 220 individuals responded to the Survey, but 27 Surveys could not be used. Since Gold coast universitys recycling program now include only aluminum, glass, paper and plastic, these were the only materials considered in this Study.

#### Recycling at Gold coast

Many Survey respondents recognized the importance of recycling, they stated that they do recycle aluminum, glass, paper and plastic on a regular basis either at home or at work. However most respondents displayed a low level of awareness of the on-campus program. At least half of the respondants were unfamiliar with the location of the bins around campus, therefore, they had not participated in the Recycling Program. Other responses indicated that the bins were not located in convenent locations.

#### Reccommendations for increasing recycling participation

To increase participation in the recycling Program, we recommend the following:

1. Relocate the Recycling Bins for greater visibility.

2. Development of incentive programs to gain the participation of on-campus groups.

3. Training student volunteers to give on-campus presentations that give an explanation of the need for Recycling, and the benefits of such a Program.

4. We should increase Advertising in regard to the program.

# Communication Workshop: Collaboration Is King

## Effective Team Presentations

If you have been part of any team effort before, you know that such projects can be frustrating—particularly when some team members don't carry their weight or produce poor-quality work. Very often members struggle to resolve conflict. On the other hand, team projects can be harmonious and productive when members establish ground rules and follow these steps:

- **Prepare to work together.** First, you should (a) compare team members' schedules to set up the best meeting times, (b) plan regular face-to-face and virtual meetings, and (c) discuss how you will deal with team members who are not contributing to the project or are submitting shoddy work. Such ground rules should be put in writing much like a contract. A team charter, signed by all members, can be used in your class to spell out responsibilities, specific roles, deadlines, meeting frequency, communication, and more.

- **Plan the presentation.** Your team will need to agree on (a) the specific purpose of the presentation, (b) your audience, (c) the length of the presentation, (d) the types of visuals to include, and (e) the basic structure and content of the presentation.

- **Assign duties.** Once you decide what your presentation will cover, give each team member a written assignment that details his or her responsibilities, such as researching content, producing visuals, developing handouts, building transitions between segments, and showing up for team meetings and rehearsals.

- **Collect information.** To gather or generate information, teams can brainstorm together, conduct interviews, or search databases or the Internet. The team should set deadlines for collecting information and should discuss how to ensure the accuracy and currency of the information collected. Team members should exchange periodic progress reports on how their research is coming along.

- **Organize and develop the presentation.** Once your team has completed the research, start working on the presentation. Determine the organization of the presentation, compose a draft in writing, and prepare presentation slides and other visual aids. The team should meet often in person or virtually to discuss the presentation and to decide which members are responsible for delivering what parts of the presentation. Each member should build a transition to the next member's topic and strive for logical connections between segments.

- **Edit, rehearse, and evaluate.** Before you deliver the presentation, rehearse several times as a team. Make sure transitions from speaker to speaker are smooth. For example, a speaker might say, *Now that I have explained how to prepare for the meeting, Pete is going to discuss how to get the meeting started.* Decide who will be responsible for advancing slides during the presentation (either on the computer or using a remote). Practice fielding questions if you plan to have a question-and-answer session. Decide how you are going to dress to look professional and competent. Run a spell-checker and proofread your presentation slides to ensure that the design, format, and vocabulary are consistent.

- **Deliver the presentation.** Show up on time for your presentation and wear appropriate attire. Deliver your part of the presentation professionally and enthusiastically. Remember that your audience is judging the team on its performance, not the individuals. Do what you can to make your team shine!

**CAREER APPLICATION.** Your boss named you to a team that is to produce an organizational social media communication strategy for your company. You know this assignment will end with an oral presentation to management. Your first reaction is dismay. You have been on teams before in the classroom, and you know how frustrating they can be. However, you want to give your best, and you resolve to contribute positively to this team effort.

**YOUR TASK.** In small groups or with the entire class, discuss effective collaboration. How can members contribute positively to teams? How should teams deal with members who aren't contributing or who have negative attitudes? What should team members do to ensure that the final presentation is professional and well-coordinated? How can the team use technology to improve collaboration? If your instructor directs, summarize your findings in writing or in a brief presentation.

# Employment Communication 6

Fizkes/Shutterstock.com

# The Job Search, Résumés, and Cover Messages

## Learning Outcomes

After studying this chapter, you should be able to do the following:

**1** Describe how digital age technology will enhance the four major steps in your job search.

**2** List search strategies that explore the open job market.

**3** Identify job-search strategies that unlock the hidden job market.

**4** Explain how to organize your qualifications and skills into effective categories for résumés and an engaging LinkedIn profile.

**5** Describe digital tools that can enhance your job search and résumé.

**6** Analyze the importance and construction of customized cover messages.

Alexander Supertramp/Shutterstock.com

## 13-1 Harnessing Technology in Today's Challenging Job Market

The COVID-19 pandemic shattered the best job market in decades. A strong economy screeched to a halt and unemployment soared. In the wake of the pandemic, recent college graduates face a highly competitive job outlook, even in traditionally sought-after STEM (science, tech, engineering, and math) fields.[1] However, as we have discussed in Chapter 1, transferable skills such as excellent communication, creativity, problem solving, teamworking, and flexibility will help you thrive in any economic climate. To get ready for a potentially slow post-pandemic recovery, you can build important marketable skills now while in college, which remains a sound investment in your future despite rising education costs.[2]

If you fear entering a highly competitive job market, think of the advantages your college training, current skills, and resilient attitude provide. Yet another recent survey confirms that the top five attributes employers look for in résumés are—in this order—teamwork, problem solving, analytical/quantitative skills, verbal communication, and writing skills.[3] This means you are taking a very important class. In addition, you have this book with the latest research, invaluable advice, and helpful model documents to guide you in your job search. Think positively!

A successful job search today requires perseverance and a blend of old and new job-hunting skills. Traditional techniques are still effective, but job candidates must also take advantage of technology tools and know current trends, some of which are presented in **Figure 13.1**. Job boards, social media, and mobile technologies have all become indispensable tools in hunting for a job. However, even in the digital age, networking and referrals are the way most candidates find a job.

**LEARNING OUTCOME 1**

Describe how digital age technology will enhance the four major steps in your job search.

## 13-1a  Using Technology in Your Job Search

Technology is an integral part of the job-search process. Nearly every job hunter today has at least one mobile device, and an overwhelming number of apps on them. You can download apps to plan your career, manage the job hunt, scour multiple job boards, receive instant job alerts, and arrange lunch dates to network and meet others in your field. Working from a smartphone, you can create, store, and send a résumé as soon as a promising opening pops up.

*Organizations Rely on Technology.* Beyond mobile devices, technology has greatly affected the way organizations announce jobs, select candidates, screen résumés, and conduct interviews. Companies of all sizes now employ AI-enabled applicant tracking systems (ATS) to automatically post openings, select résumés, rank candidates, and generate interview requests. Automated texts inform candidates about the status of their applications. With all the digital options in job searching, candidates more than

**Figure 13.1  Current Trends in Job Searching**

**It's all digital.**

Today's candidates search job boards, apply online, research employers, e-mail and post their résumés, and develop a personal brand online.

**A positive social media presence is a must.**

Presenting a positive social media presence to the world, particularly a professional profile on LinkedIn, is key when competing for scarce jobs.

**Mobile technology and social media rule.**

Job seekers use apps to receive job listings and respond rapidly to openings; recruiters post jobs and solicit applications on social media and increasingly communicate with candidates by text on their smart devices.

**Networking—it's whom you know and who knows you.**

Recruiters say their best job candidates come from referrals. Now more than ever, candidates need to be proactive in making professional connections.

**Interpersonal skills are in high demand.**

E-commerce and other remote jobs are in high demand, and these positions crucially require writing, speaking, and team skills.

**Résumés must please scanners and skimmers.**

Overwhelmed with candidates, recruiters skim résumés scanned and preselected by AI-based applicant tracking systems (ATS).

ever need guidance in crafting their job search and résumés. Tips in this chapter will help you to adapt your job search and résumé to take advantage of tracking systems and other technologies.

Just as candidates are eager to find the right fit, organizations are eager to hire people who will fit into their culture. A candidate today should be prepared for a longer interview process, perhaps enduring as many as four different interviews as companies strive to find the perfect someone who fits their culture.

**Has Technology Killed the Résumé?** The résumé is still important, but it may not be the document that introduces you as a job seeker. Instead, the résumé may come only after you have established a virtual or face-to-face relationship. What's more, chances are that your résumé and cover letter will be read digitally rather than in print. However, although some attention-grabbing publications scream that the print résumé is dead, the truth is that every job hunter needs one. Whether offered online or in print, your résumé should be always available and current. Later in this chapter we will present résumé styles, formats, and online posting tips.

It's natural to think that the first step in finding a job is writing a résumé. However, that's a mistake. The job-search process begins long before you are ready to prepare your résumé. Regardless of the kind of employment you seek, you must invest time and effort in getting ready. As illustrated in **Figure 13.2**, your best plan for completing a successful job search involves a four-step process.

## 13-1b Starting Your Job Search With Self-Analysis

The first step in a job search is analyzing your interests and goals and evaluating your qualifications. This means looking inside yourself to explore what you like and dislike so that you can make good employment choices. For guidance in choosing a career that eventually proves to be satisfying, ask yourself the following questions:

- What are you passionate about? Can you turn this passion into a career?

- Do you enjoy working with people, data, or things?

- How important are salary, benefits, technology support, and job stimulation?

- Must you work in a specific city, geographical area, or climate?

- Are you looking for security, travel opportunities, money, power, or prestige?

- How would you describe the perfect job, boss, and coworkers?

If you need assistance in your self-analysis, numerous online tools help measure personalities, interests, skills, and values. One of the best known is the **Myers–Briggs Type Indicator**. It divides people into four temperaments (guardian, idealist, rational,

**Figure 13.2  Four Steps in an Effective Job Search**

**Analyze Yourself**
- Identify your interests and goals.
- Assess your qualifications.
- Explore career opportunities.

**Explore the Open and Hidden Job Markets**
- Search online job boards.
- Look for jobs on social media.
- Start building your personal network.
- Create your personal brand.

**Create a Customized Résumé and Cover Letter**
- Choose a résumé style.
- Tailor your résumé to each position.
- Optimize for digital technology.
- Prepare a LinkedIn profile.

**Know the Hiring Process**
- Submit your résumé, application, or e-portfolio.
- Undergo screening and hiring interviews.
- Accept an offer or reevaluate your progress.

and artisan). A similar tool is **Big Five**, which groups people into five personality types (openness, conscientiousness, extraversion, agreeableness, and neuroticism).

## 13-1c  Evaluating Your Qualifications

Once you have analyzed your interests and goals, it's time to take a hard look at your qualifications. Remember that today's job market is fiercely competitive. How will your qualifications measure up against those of other candidates? What assets can you offer? Your responses to the following questions will target your thinking as well as prepare a foundation for your résumé. Always keep in mind, though, that employers seek more than empty assurances; they will want proof of your qualifications.

- What technology skills can you present? What specific software programs have you mastered, what Internet research skills do you have, and what social media savvy can you offer?

- Do you communicate well in speech and in writing? Do you speak another language? How can you illustrate and verify these abilities?

- What other skills have you acquired in school, on the job, in an internship, or through leisure activities and volunteer work? How can you demonstrate these skills?

- Do you work well with people? Do you enjoy teamwork? What proof can you offer? Consider extracurricular activities, clubs, class projects, and jobs.

- Are you a leader, self-starter, or manager? What evidence can you provide? What leadership roles have you held?

- Do you learn quickly? Can you think critically? How can you demonstrate these characteristics?

## 13-1d  Preparing for Career Opportunities

The job picture in the United States is dynamic and you will need to be flexible. In a U.S. Bureau of Statistics 37-year longitudinal survey, individuals between the ages of 28 and 52 averaged 12.3 jobs with nearly half of these jobs held before the age of 25.[4] If the past is any indication of the future, you can expect to have as many as six different jobs before you reach 25. Older workers can also expect to hold many different positions during their working lives. Not only are people changing jobs, but they often are working in new ways: flexibly, remotely, and part time in the gig economy.

In the past workers expected to develop skills and remain in their careers for life. Today, **reskilling**, that is, continuous education and (re)training, is required to remain relevant and employable. Because you can expect to hold numerous jobs in your future, now is the time to explore career opportunities so that you can make the best decisions when job possibilities arise. Where can you find the best career data? Here are some suggestions:

- **Visit your campus career center.** Most campus career centers have vast resources on their websites. You can access job search information, inventories, career-related software programs, and employment or internship databases that allow you to explore such fields as accounting, finance, office technology, information systems, and hotel management.

- **Search for career apps.** Many job-search sites—such as Indeed, CareerBuilder, and Monster—offer career-planning information and resources. Popular sites and apps are Glassdoor or PathSource, tools that suggest careers, give salaries, provide anonymous company reviews, and help you build a résumé.

- **Check government data in your library and online.** Consult O*NET OnLine, *Dictionary of Occupational Titles, Occupational Outlook Handbook,* and *Jobs Rated Almanac* for information about job requirements, qualifications, salaries, and employment trends.

**LEARNING OUTCOME 2**

List search strategies that explore the open job market.

- **Take a summer job, internship, or part-time position in your field.** Nothing is better than trying out a career. Many companies offer internships and temporary or part-time jobs to begin training college students and to develop relationships with them. Most interns are hired into full-time positions—almost 67 percent in one study—despite the pandemic during which 72 percent of internships were held virtually.[5]

- **Interview someone in your chosen field.** People are usually flattered when asked to describe their careers. Inquire about needed skills, required courses, financial and other rewards, benefits, working conditions, future trends, and entry requirements.

- **Volunteer with a nonprofit organization.** Many colleges and universities encourage service learning. In volunteering their services, students gain valuable experience, and nonprofits appreciate the fresh ideas that students bring.

- **Monitor classified ads.** Early in your college career, begin monitoring want ads and the websites of companies in your career area. Check job availability, qualifications sought, duties, and salary ranges. Don't wait until you are about to graduate to explore the job market.

## 13-2 Exploring the Open Job Market

Candidates for jobs will quickly become aware of two distinct job markets. The **open job market** consists of jobs that are advertised or publicly listed. The **hidden job market** consists of jobs that are never advertised or listed. Some analysts and authors claim that between 50 and 80 percent of all jobs are never listed or are filled before they even make it to online job boards or advertisements.[7] Those openings are in the hidden job market, which we will explore shortly. First, let's start where most job seekers start—in the open job market.

### 13-2a Surveying the Big Boards and Beyond

To many candidates, Internet job boards may seem like a giant swamp that swallows résumés. Yet job boards can provide valuable job-search information such as résumé, interviewing, and salary tips. Job boards also serve as a jumping-off point in most searches. They inform candidates about the kinds of jobs available and the skill sets required. Recruiters are primarily listing jobs on social media sites as you can see in **Figure 13.3**, and job seekers are turning to LinkedIn, Facebook Jobs, and Twitter to

**Figure 13.3  How Recruiters Find Their Best Talent**

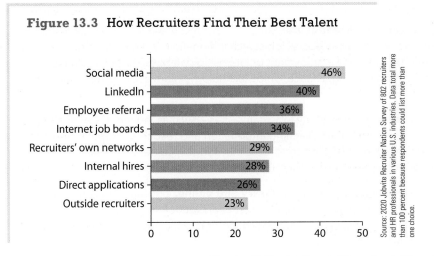

Source: 2020 Jobvite Recruiter Nation Survey of 802 recruiters and HR professionals in various U.S. industries. Data total more than 100 percent because respondents could list more than one choice.

find them. One large study found that online sources (career sites, job search engines, job boards, and social media) by far exceed offline sources (recruiting agencies, campus events, and job fairs) in leading to interviews (86 percent) and hires (72 percent).[8] Many job hunters begin their search with job boards.

**Four Top Job Sites.** As Figure 13.3 indicates, the number of jobs found through job boards is respectable, with a solid third of jobs filled this way. Following are four of the best job sites for both traditional and nontraditional college students:

- **Indeed** offers millions of job listings aggregated from thousands of websites. Whether you are looking for your first real job, changing careers, or seeking career advancement, Indeed presents extensive listings from company career pages.

- **CareerBuilder** lets you filter by several criteria such as location, degree required, and pay range.

- **Monster** permits you to upload your résumé and offers company profiles, a résumé review service, and a mobile app.

- **CollegeRecruiter** strives to be the premier information and job source for recent grads who are seeking employment, continuing education, or business opportunities. It focuses on positions that generally require zero to three years of work experience.

**Niche Sites for Specialized Fields.** If you seek a job in a particular field, look for a niche site, such as **Dice** for technology jobs, **Advance Healthcare Network** for jobs in the medical field, and **Accountemps** for temporary accounting positions. Niche websites also exist for job seekers with special backgrounds or needs, such as **GettingHired** for disabled workers and **Workforce50** for older workers. If you are looking for a short-term job, check out **CoolWorks**, which specializes in seasonal employment. If you yearn for a government job, try **USAJOBS**, a website for students and recent graduates interested in federal service.

**Company Websites for the Best Leads.** As Figure 13.3 indicates, a good quarter of applicants find jobs by applying directly on a company website. Many companies post job openings only on their own sites to avoid being inundated by the hordes of applicants—many unqualified—responding to postings on online job boards. A company's website is the first place to go if you have a specific employer in mind. You might find vision and mission statements, a history of the organization, and the names of key hiring managers. Possibly you will see a listing for a position that doesn't fit your qualifications. Even though you're not right for this job, you have discovered that the company is hiring. Don't be afraid to send a résumé and cover letter expressing your desire to be considered for future jobs.

**Newspapers, Career Fairs, and Other Sources.** Despite the rush to social media and mobile technology, some organizations still list openings in newspapers online and in print. Don't overlook this possibility, especially for local jobs. Craigslist can be a haven for people looking for part-time or even full-time work. Some jobs can also be found through career fairs (once it is safe to host them again) and university and college alumni contacts.

## 13-2b Gaining an Edge With Mobile Apps

Job seekers are embracing smartphone apps to gain an edge in the job search. With many of the following mobile apps, you can access and vet job openings as soon as they are listed—even when you are on the go. Like its full website, the **Indeed Job Search** app lets you filter your search results based on your field, desired salary, and location. **Intro** is an app that connects you to people in your field or in your social media network. **JobAware** allows you to integrate all your Internet job-search activity including LinkedIn. **JobCompass** helps you narrow the search to your zip code. **LinkUp Job Search Engine, Monster, Reach, Simply Hired, Snagajob,** and **Switch** all offer

**OFFICE INSIDER**

"A referral is never a sure-fire way to a new job; however, they can improve your odds of a hiring manager or recruiter reviewing your application. A referral from a former colleague or professional connection is an endorsement for a particular position. Securing a referral will require more legwork, but in today's job market, it is worth the extra effort."[10]

**Matthew Bennett,**
*digital marketing manager,*
*Johnson Service Group*

**Figure 13.4  Protecting Your Personal Data When Posting on Internet Job Boards**

- **Use reputable, well-known sites** and never pay to post your résumé.

- **Don't divulge personal data** such as your date of birth, social security number, or home address. Use your city and state or region in place of your home address.

- **Set up a separate e-mail account** with a professional-sounding e-mail address for your job search.

- **Post privately** if possible. Doing so means that you can control who has access to your e-mail address and other information.

- **Keep careful records** of every site on which you posted. At the end of your job search, remove all posted résumés.

- **Don't include your references** or reveal their contact information without permission.

- **Don't respond to blind job postings** (those without company names or addresses). Unfortunately, scammers use online job boards to post fake job ads to gather your personal information.

mobile links to job listings from a variety of sources.[9] Best of all, most apps let you set up e-mail or text alerts that will notify you if a job matching your criteria becomes available.

When posting job-search information online, it's natural to want to put your best foot forward and openly share information that will get you a job. The challenge is to strike a balance between supplying enough information and protecting yourself. To avoid some of the risks involved, study the cautions described in **Figure 13.4**.

## 13-3  Unlocking the Hidden Job Market

**LEARNING OUTCOME 3**

Identify job-search strategies that unlock the hidden job market.

Not all available positions are announced or advertised in the open job market. As mentioned earlier, between 50 and 80 percent of jobs are estimated to be in the hidden job market. Companies prefer to avoid publicizing job announcements widely for many reasons. They don't welcome a deluge of unqualified candidates. What's more, companies dislike hiring unknown quantities. According to one manager, "If someone is willing to stick their neck out and recommend a candidate, putting their reputation on the line, a recruiter will likely take a look at your resume. If you receive a good referral, you can expect your resume to be put on top of the pile."[11] A vice president at SilkRoad, a talent management software company, praises employee referrals because they make hiring fast and less costly, helping to "secure top talent to fill hard-to-fill positions."[12]

The most successful job candidates seek to transform themselves from unknown into known quantities through networking whether online or offline. Referrals and person-to-person contacts continue to be employers' top source of hires. That's because people trust what they know. Therefore, your goal is to become known to a large network of people, and this means going beyond close friends.

### 13-3a  Building a Personal Network

Because most candidates find jobs today through networking, be prepared to work diligently to build your personal networks. Just what is **networking**? In the context of job searching, networking means developing a supportive system of individuals with a common interest who are willing to share information and services. If you are looking for a job, networking involves meeting people and talking to them about your field or industry so that you can gain information and possibly open doors to job vacancies.

Not only are many jobs never advertised, but some positions aren't even contemplated until the right person appears. One recent college graduate underwent three interviews for a position, but the company hired someone else. After being turned down, the grad explained why she thought she was perfect for this company but perhaps in a different role. Apparently, the hiring manager agreed and decided to create a new job (in social media) because of the skills, personality, and perseverance of this determined young grad. Traditional networking pays off, but it requires dedication. Here are three steps that will help you establish your own network:

**Step 1. Develop a contact list.** Make a list of anyone who would be willing to talk with you about finding a job. **Figure 13.5** suggests possibilities. Even if you haven't talked with people in years, reach out to them in person or online. Consider asking your campus career center for alumni willing to talk with students. Also dig into your social networking circles, which we will discuss shortly.

**Step 2. Make contacts in person and online.** Call the people on your list or connect online. To set up a meeting in person, say, *Hi,_____. I'm looking for a job and I wonder if you could help me out. When could I schedule a Zoom meeting to talk about it?* During your virtual meeting be friendly, well organized, polite, and interested in what your contact has to say. Provide a copy of your résumé, and try to keep the conversation centered on your job search. Your goal is to get two or more referrals. In pinpointing your request, ask, *Do you know of anyone who might have an opening for a person with my skills?* If the individual does not, ask, *Do you know of anyone else who might know of someone?*

**Step 3. Follow up on your referrals.** Call or contact the people on your list. You might say something like, *Hello. I'm Cyrus Freeman, a friend of Isabelle Vazquez. Isabelle suggested that I ask you for help. I'm looking for a position as a marketing trainee, and she thought you might be willing to spare a few minutes and steer me in the right direction.* Don't ask for a job. During such referral interviews, ask how the individuals got started in their line of work, what they like best (or least) about the work, what career paths exist in the field, and what problems a novice must overcome. Most important, ask how a person with your background and skills might get started in the field. Send an informal thank-you note to anyone who helps you in your job search, and

**Figure 13.5  Whom to Contact in Networking**

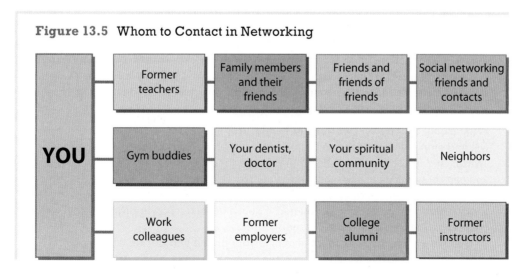

keep in touch with the most promising people. Ask whether you could stay in contact every three weeks or so during your job search.

Unfortunately, many new grads are reluctant to engage in person-to-person networking because it feels pushy, and it requires much effort. As uncomfortable as speaking with acquaintances or even cold contacts might be, this is the time to build confidence and start practicing skills that will be useful on the job.

### 13-3b Searching for Jobs on Social Media

As digital technology permeates our lives, job candidates have powerful tools at their disposal: social media networks. One of the most important networks is LinkedIn, which

has become critical in a job search. If you just send out your résumé randomly, not much will happen. However, if you have a referral, your chances of landing an interview multiply. Social media are a principal path to developing those coveted referrals.

**Letting LinkedIn Help You Find a Job.** If you are seriously looking for a job, it's extremely important that you create an engaging LinkedIn profile and keep it current. With almost 760 million members (675 million monthly active users), LinkedIn is more than a networking site for professionals. It has become a top social media site—the most trusted one to boot.[13] LinkedIn dominates the world of job searching and recruiting. As discussed in Chapter 5, surveys have shown that as many as 99 percent of recruiting and staffing professionals use LinkedIn to locate and vet job candidates.[14]

LinkedIn is truly the place to find and be found, especially for new graduates. The network is vast, currently listing 57 million companies and 15 million open jobs; LinkedIn claims that three people are hired on its platform every minute.[15] Developing a credible presence on LinkedIn enables you to post information about yourself in one central place where it's available to potential employers, graduate schools, future colleagues, and people you will want to stay connected to. A LinkedIn page tells the working world that you are a professional, and it remains significant even after you obtain a position.

One of the best ways to use LinkedIn is to search for a company in which you are interested. Try to find company employees who are connected to other people you know. Then use that contact as a referral when you apply. You can also send an e-mail to everyone in your LinkedIn network asking for help or for people they could put you in touch with. Don't be afraid to ask an online contact for advice on getting started in a career and for suggestions to help a newcomer break into that career. Another excellent way to use a contact is to have that person look at your résumé and help you tweak it. Like Facebook, LinkedIn has status updates, and it's critical to update yours regularly so that your connections know what is happening in your career search and afterward.

LinkedIn can aid your job search in at least five ways, as shown in **Figure 13.6**. Because LinkedIn functions in many ways as a résumé, you will find tips for preparing your LinkedIn profile in the next pages.

**What About Facebook, Twitter, and Instagram?** In addition to LinkedIn, job seekers will find employment opportunities on other social media sites, such as Facebook, Twitter, and Instagram. If you are in the market for a job, these sites are places where you can showcase your skills, highlight your experience, and possibly land that dream job. Because organizations may post open jobs to their Facebook or Twitter pages prior to advertising them elsewhere, you might gain a head start on applying by following these organizations on their social media sites.

If you use a Facebook account, examine your profile and decide what you want prospective employers to see—or not see. Create a simple profile with minimal

OFFICE INSIDER

"Think of LinkedIn as your resume that never sleeps. But a lot more. It's your professional brand in the world. It's the result you actually want up top when someone Googles you (which they will!). . . . If you're not on LinkedIn, you simply don't exist in the working world."[16]

**Omar Garriott,**
*head of global education at Qualtrics, career coach*

**Figure 13.6** Harnessing the Power of LinkedIn

**Five Ways LinkedIn Can Help You Find a Job**

1. **Receiving Job Alerts.** LinkedIn notifies you of recommended jobs.

2. **Leveraging Your Network.** You may start with two connections, but you can leverage those connections to thousands.

3. **Researching a Company.** Before applying to a company, you can check it out on LinkedIn and locate valuable inside information.

4. **Getting Recommendations.** LinkedIn helps you take the awkwardness out of asking for recommendations. It's so easy!

5. **Helping Companies Find You.** Many companies are looking for skilled college grads, and your strong profile on LinkedIn can result in inquiries.

graphics, widgets, and photos. Post only content relevant to your job search or career, and choose your friends wisely.

Employers often visit social media to keep tabs on and vet candidates before an interview. Make sure your social media profiles represent you professionally. You can make it easy for your potential employer to learn more about you by including an informative bio in your Twitter or Facebook profile that has a link to your LinkedIn profile. Posting thoughtful blog posts and tweets on topics related to your career goal makes you even more discoverable.

## 13-3c Building Your Personal Brand

A large part of your job-search strategy involves building a brand for yourself. You may be thinking, *Who me? A brand?* Yes, absolutely! Even college graduates should seriously consider branding because finding a job in a competitive market is tough. Before you get into the thick of the job hunt, focus on developing your brand so that you know what you want to emphasize.

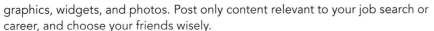

WORKPLACE IN **FOCUS**

PK Studio/Shutterstock.com

Employers routinely refer to job applicants' social networking sites to discover indiscretions. Perhaps less commonly known, however, is that Facebook now allows employers to post jobs directly to their pages. This enables employers to run the postings as ads and target potential employees. The good news for job hunters is that many already have Facebook accounts and can fill out job applications automatically with their profile information. However, when using Facebook as part of a job search, candidates must be extremely careful to separate personal friends from professional contacts. The professional contacts list becomes a way for job seekers to reach out by posting industry-related content and personal work-related status updates.[17] How can you build your personal brand on Facebook?

Personal branding involves deciding what makes you special and desirable in the job market. What is your unique selling point? What special skill set or trait makes you stand out among all job applicants? What would your instructors or employers say is your greatest strength? Think about your intended audience. What are you promoting about yourself?

Experts suggest that you create a tagline that describes what you do, who you are, and what's special about you. A nurse wrote this fetching tagline:

*Tireless, caring Registered Nurse who helps pediatric cancer patients and their families feel at ease throughout treatment and recovery*

If you prefer a shorter tagline for your business card, consider the sample taglines for new grads in **Figure 13.7**. It's OK to shed a little modesty and strut your stuff. However, do keep your tagline simple, short, and truthful so that it's easy to remember.

Once you have a tagline, prepare a professional-looking business card with your name and tagline. Include an easy-to-remember e-mail address such as *firstname. lastname@domain.com.* Consider using an app such as SnapDat, Haystack, SwitChit, or CamCard that creates a digital business card to connect with new contacts and help you be remembered.

Now that you have your tagline and business card, work on an **elevator pitch**. This is a concise speech that you can give in 60 seconds or less describing who you are and what you can offer. Tweak your brief speech for your audience, and practice until you can say it naturally. Here are suggestions to help you prepare your own authentic elevator pitch depending on your situation:

*Hi, my name is _____, and I am about to graduate from _____ with a degree in _____. I'm looking to _____ because I enjoy _____. Recently I _____ where I was able to develop skills such as _____. I'm most confident about my skills in _____. I'm inspired by the field (or position of) _____ because _____. My ultimate aim is to _____. I'm looking for a position in _____. Do you have any suggestions or advice on how I can _____?*

## Figure 13.7  Branding YOU

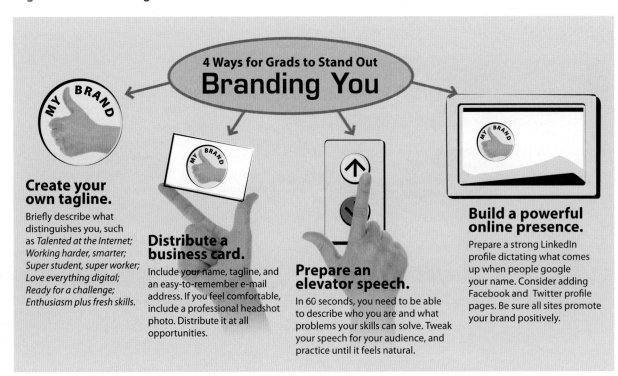

**4 Ways for Grads to Stand Out**
# Branding You

**Create your own tagline.**
Briefly describe what distinguishes you, such as *Talented at the Internet; Working harder, smarter; Super student, super worker; Love everything digital; Ready for a challenge; Enthusiasm plus fresh skills.*

**Distribute a business card.**
Include your name, tagline, and an easy-to-remember e-mail address. If you feel comfortable, include a professional headshot photo. Distribute it at all opportunities.

**Prepare an elevator speech.**
In 60 seconds, you need to be able to describe who you are and what problems your skills can solve. Tweak your speech for your audience, and practice until it feels natural.

**Build a powerful online presence.**
Prepare a strong LinkedIn profile dictating what comes up when people google your name. Consider adding Facebook and Twitter profile pages. Be sure all sites promote your brand positively.

# 13-4 Customizing Your Résumé

**LEARNING OUTCOME 4**

Explain how to organize your qualifications and skills into effective categories for résumés and an engaging LinkedIn profile.

In today's highly competitive job market, you must customize your résumé for every position you seek. The competition is so stiff today that you cannot get by with a generic, one-size-fits-all résumé. Although you can start with a basic résumé, you should customize it to fit each company and position if you want to stand out from the crowd.

The Internet makes it almost too easy to apply for jobs. Result: Recruiters are swamped with applications. As a job seeker, you have approximately ten seconds to catch the recruiter's eye—if your résumé is even read by a person. It may very well first encounter an **applicant tracking system (ATS)**. This software acts as a database for job applicants and helps businesses manage job postings, screen résumés, rank candidates, and generate interview requests.

These automated systems make creating your résumé doubly challenging. Although your goal is to satisfy a recruiter or hiring manager, that person may never see your résumé unless it is selected by the ATS—now used by a whopping 99 percent of the Fortune 500 companies![19] Because so many mid-size and large organizations are using ATS software today, this chapter provides you with the latest advice on how to get your résumé ranked highly—so that it will then proceed to the real human beings who will call you for an interview.

## 13-4a Selecting a Résumé Style

The first step in preparing a winning, customized résumé that appeals to both the human reader and the ATS screening device is to decide what style to use. Résumés usually fall into two categories: chronological and functional. This section presents basic information as well as insider tips on how to choose an appropriate résumé style, determine its length, and arrange its parts. You will also learn about adding a summary of qualifications, which many busy hiring managers welcome. In the upcoming pages, we present several examples for you to use as basic models.

**What Is a Chronological Résumé?** The most popular résumé format is the chronological format, shown in **Model Documents 13.3**, **13.4**, and **13.6**. The **chronological résumé** lists work history job by job but in reverse order, starting with the most recent position. Recruiters favor the chronological format because they are familiar with it and because it quickly reveals a candidate's education and experience. The chronological style works well for candidates who have experience in their field of employment and for those who show steady career growth, but it is less helpful for people who have changed jobs frequently or who have gaps in their employment records. For college students and others who lack extensive experience, the functional résumé format may be preferable.

**What Is a Functional Résumé?** The **functional résumé**, shown in **Model Document 13.5**, focuses on a candidate's skills rather than on past employment. Like a chronological résumé, a functional résumé begins with the candidate's name, contact information, job objective, and education. Instead of listing jobs, though, the functional résumé groups skills and accomplishments in special categories, such as Supervisory and Management Skills or Retailing and Marketing Experience. This résumé style highlights accomplishments and can de-emphasize a negative employment history.

Workers who have changed jobs frequently, who have gaps in their employment records, or who are entering an entirely different field may prefer the functional résumé. Recent graduates with little or no related employment experience often find the functional résumé useful. Older

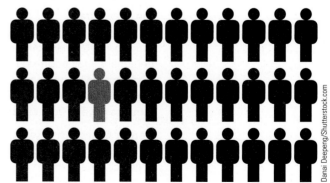

job seekers who want to downplay a long job history and job hunters who are afraid of appearing overqualified may also prefer the functional format. Be aware, though, that online job boards may box you in and insist on the chronological format.

### 13-4b How Long Should a Résumé Be?

Experts disagree on how long a résumé should be. Conventional wisdom has always held that recruiters prefer one-page résumés. However, recruiters who are serious about candidates often prefer the kind of details that can be provided in a two-page or longer résumé. What's more, with today's digital résumés, page length is no longer restricted. The best advice is to make your résumé as long as needed to present your skills to recruiters and hiring managers.

Individuals with more experience will naturally have longer résumés. Workers with fewer than ten years of experience, those making a major career change, and those who have had only one or two employers will likely have one-page résumés. Those with ten years or more of related experience may have two-page résumés. Finally, some senior-level managers and executives with a lengthy history of major accomplishments might have résumés that are three pages or longer.[20]

### 13-4c Organizing Your Information Into Effective Résumé Categories

Although résumés have standard categories, their arrangement and content should be strategically planned. A customized résumé emphasizes skills and achievements aimed at a particular job or company. It shows a candidate's most important qualifications first, and it de-emphasizes weaknesses. In organizing your qualifications and information, try to create as few headings as possible; more than six looks cluttered. No two résumés are ever exactly alike, but most writers include all or some of these customary categories as headings: Career Objective, Summary of Qualifications, Education, Work Experience, Capabilities and Skills, and Awards and Activities. First, however, you will create a header with your contact information.

**Résumé Header With Contact Information.** Your résumé, whether chronological or functional, should start with an uncluttered and simple header, sometimes still called a letterhead. The first line should always be your name; add your middle initial for an even more professional look. Format your name so that it stands out on the page. Following your name, include your e-mail address and social media handle (LinkedIn), personal website, or blog, if relevant. Some candidates omit their street addresses to protect their privacy and for safety reasons.

Your telephone number should be one where you can receive text and voice mail messages. Consider using Google Voice, the voice over internet protocol (VoIP) phone service that allows you to protect your real smartphone number as well as your privacy. All outgoing messages at any number you list should be in your voice, it should state your full name, and it should be concise and professional. If you are expecting an important call from a recruiter, pick up only when you are in a quiet environment and can concentrate.

Your e-mail address should sound professional instead of something like *snugglykitty@gmail.com* or *sixpackguy@outlook.com*. Also be sure that you are using a personal e-mail address. Putting your work e-mail address on your résumé announces to prospective employers that you are consuming your current employer's resources to look for another job. If you have a LinkedIn profile or a website where an e-portfolio or samples of your work can be viewed, include the link in the résumé header.

**Career Objective or Job Title.** Although experts disagree about whether to include an objective or a job title on a résumé, nearly all agree that if you do, it should be very specific. A well-written objective—customized for the job opening—makes sense, especially for new graduates with fresh training and relevant skills. Most important:

Strive to include strategic keywords from the job listing because these will help tracking systems select your résumé. Focus on what you can contribute to the organization, not on what the organization can do for you.

**Poor objective:** *To obtain a position with a well-established organization that will lead to a lasting relationship in the field of marketing.* (Sounds vague and self-serving.)

**Improved objective:** *To obtain a position that capitalizes on my recent training in business writing and marketing to boost customer contacts and expand brand penetration using my social media expertise.* (Names specific skills and includes nouns that might be picked up by an applicant tracking system.)

If you decide to use a job title instead of an objective, consider including the words *Target Job Title* as shown here:

*Target Job Title: Medical Administrative Assistant*

Using a customized objective or a job title makes it clear that you have taken the time and made the effort to prepare your résumé for the position. If you decide to omit a career objective, be sure to discuss your career goals in your cover letter.

Optional Summary of Qualifications. Over the past decade, the biggest change in résumés has been a shift from a career objective to a **summary of qualifications** at the top. Also called a **résumé summary** or **profile statement**, this list presents a snapshot of your most notable work experience, achievements, and skills.[22] Once a job is advertised, a hiring manager may receive hundreds or even thousands of résumés. A summary ensures that your most impressive qualifications are not overlooked by a recruiter who is skimming résumés quickly.

A summary also enables you to present a concentrated list of many relevant keywords for a tracking system to pick up, thus boosting your chance of selection. Additionally, because résumés today may be viewed on tablets and smartphones, the summary spotlights your most compelling qualifications in a highly visible spot.

Your summary might consist of a list of three to eight bulleted statements demonstrating that you are the ideal candidate for the position. When formulating these statements, consider your experience in the field, your education, your unique skills, awards you have won, certifications you hold, and any other accomplishments. Strive to quantify your achievements wherever possible. Target the most important qualifications an employer will be looking for in the person hired for this position. Focus on nouns that might be selected as keywords by an applicant tracking system. Examples of summaries of qualifications appear in Model Documents 13.3 and 13.5.

Education. The next component in a chronological résumé is your education—if it is more noteworthy than your work experience. In this section you should include the name and location of schools, dates of attendance, major fields of study, and degrees earned. By the way, once you have attended college, you should not list high school information on your résumé.

Your grade point average (GPA) and/or class ranking may be important to prospective employers in certain fields. In accounting, education, finance, health, and law, GPA is an important qualification. A high GPA is generally proof that you can complete tasks, are organized, and can handle stress. If your GPA is not stellar, one way to enhance it is to calculate it in your major courses only (for example, *3.6/4.0 in major*). Doing so is not unethical if you clearly show that your GPA is in the major only.

Under Education you might be tempted to list all the courses you took, but such a list makes for dull reading and consumes valuable space. Include a brief list of courses only if you can relate them to the position you seek. When relevant, include certificates earned, seminars attended, workshops completed, scholarships awarded, and honors earned. If your education is incomplete, include such statements as *BS degree expected 6/2023* or *80 units completed in 120-unit program*. Title this section Education, Academic Preparation, or Professional Training. If you are preparing a

**OFFICE INSIDER**

"If crafted well, your resume is one of the most valuable marketing tools you have. In a matter of seconds, it can make or break your chances of moving along the hiring journey with a company. That's why it's important to be proactive with your resume and avoid embellishments or mistakes. Take advantage of the tools available to you—the worst thing you can do is send a generic copy out to employers and then sit and hope for a response."[21]

**Rosemary Haefner,**
*chief human resources officer, CareerBuilder*

functional résumé, you will probably put the Education section below your skills summary, as in Model Document 13.5.

**Work Experience or Employment History.** When your work or volunteer experience is significant and relevant to the position sought, this information should appear before your education. List your most recent employment first and work backward, including only those jobs that you think will help you win the targeted position. A job application form may demand a full employment history, but your résumé may be selective. Be aware, though, that time gaps in your employment history will probably be questioned in the interview. For each position show the following:

- Employer's name, city, and state

- Dates of employment (month and year)

- Most important job title

- Significant duties, activities, accomplishments, and promotions

Be sure to include relevant volunteer work. A survey conducted by LinkedIn revealed that 41 percent of LinkedIn hiring managers consider volunteer work experience as respectable as paid work experience when evaluating candidates.[24]

Your employment achievements and job duties will be easier to read if you place them in bulleted lists. Rather than list every single thing you have done, customize your information so that it relates to the targeted job. Your bullet points should be concise but not complete sentences, and they usually do not include personal pronouns (*I, me, my*). Strive to be specific:

**Poor:** *Worked with customers*

**Improved:** *Developed superior customer service skills by successfully interacting with 40+ customers daily*

Whenever possible, quantify your achievements:

**Poor:** *Did equipment study and report*

**Improved:** *Conducted research and wrote final study analyzing equipment needs of 100 small businesses in Houston*

**Poor:** *Was successful in sales*

**Improved:** *Personally generated orders for sales of $90,000 annually*

As we have emphasized many times before, in addition to technical skills, employers seek job candidates with communication, management, and interpersonal capabilities. This means you will want to select work experiences and achievements that illustrate your initiative, dependability, responsibility, resourcefulness, flexibility, and leadership. But above all, employers want people who can work in teams.

**Poor:** *Worked effectively in teams*

**Improved:** *Enjoyed collaborating with five-member interdepartmental team in developing ten-page handbook for temporary workers*

**Poor:** *Joined in team effort on campus*

**Improved:** *Headed 16-member student government team that conducted most successful voter registration in campus history*

Statements describing your work experience should include many nouns relevant to the job you seek. These nouns may match keywords sought by the ATS. To appeal to human readers, your statements should also include action verbs, such as those in **Figure 13.8**. Starting each of your bullet points with an action verb helps ensure that your bulleted lists are parallel.

**Capabilities and Skills.** Recruiters want to know specifically what you can do for their companies. List your special skills, including many nouns that relate to the targeted

**Figure 13.8**  Action Verbs for a Powerful Résumé

| Communication Skills | Teamwork, Supervision Skills | Management, Leadership Skills | Research Skills | Clerical, Detail Skills | Creative Skills |
|---|---|---|---|---|---|
| clarified | advised | analyzed | assessed | activated | acted |
| collaborated | coordinated | authorized | collected | approved | conceptualized |
| explained | demonstrated | coordinated | critiqued | classified | designed |
| interpreted | developed | directed | diagnosed | edited | fashioned |
| integrated | evaluated | headed | formulated | generated | founded |
| persuaded | expedited | implemented | gathered | maintained | illustrated |
| promoted | facilitated | improved | interpreted | monitored | integrated |
| resolved | guided | increased | investigated | proofread | invented |
| summarized | motivated | organized | reviewed | recorded | originated |
| translated | set goals | scheduled | studied | streamlined | revitalized |
| wrote | trained | strengthened | systematized | updated | shaped |

position. Highlight your familiarity with Internet research, software programs, social media networking or marketing, office equipment, and communication technology tools. Use expressions such as *proficient in, competent in, experienced in,* and *ability to* as illustrated in the following:

**Poor:** *Have payroll experience*

**Improved:** *Proficient in preparing federal, state, and local payroll tax returns as well as franchise and personal property tax returns*

**Poor:** *Trained in computer graphics*

**Improved:** *Certified in graphic design including infographics through an intensive 350-hour classroom program*

**Poor:** *Have writing skills*

**Improved:** *Competent in writing, editing, and proofreading reports, tables, letters, memos, e-mails, manuscripts, and business forms*

You will also want to showcase exceptional aptitudes, such as working well under stress, learning computer programs quickly, and interacting with customers. If possible, provide details and evidence that back up your assertions. Include examples of your writing, speaking, management, organizational, interpersonal, and presentation skills—particularly those that are relevant to your targeted job. For recent graduates, this section can be used to give recruiters evidence of your potential and to highlight successful college projects.

**Awards, Honors, and Activities.** If you have three or more awards or honors, highlight them by listing them under a separate heading. If you have fewer, put them in the Education or Work Experience section if appropriate. Include awards, scholarships (financial and other), fellowships, dean's list, honors, recognition, commendations, and certificates. Be sure to identify items clearly. Your reader may be unfamiliar, for example, with Greek organizations, honors, and awards; tell what they mean.

**Poor:** *Recipient of Star award*

**Improved:** *Recipient of Star award given by Pepperdine University to outstanding graduates who combine academic excellence and leadership in extracurricular activities*

It's also appropriate to include campus, community, volunteer, and professional activities. Employers are interested in evidence that you are a well-rounded person.

This section provides an opportunity to demonstrate leadership and interpersonal skills. Strive to use action statements.

**Poor:**   *Treasurer of business club*

**Improved:**   *Collected dues, kept financial records, and paid bills while serving as treasurer of 35-member business management club*

Personal Data. Résumés in the United States omit personal data, such as birth date, marital status, height, weight, national origin, health, disability, and religious affiliation. Such information doesn't relate to genuine occupational qualifications, and recruiters are legally barred from asking for such information. Some job seekers do, however, include hobbies or interests (such as skiing or photography) that might grab the recruiter's attention or serve as conversation starters. For example, let's say you learn that your hiring manager enjoys distance running. If you have run a marathon, you may want to mention it. Many executives practice tennis or golf, two sports highly suitable for networking. You could also indicate your willingness to travel or to relocate, since many companies will be interested.

Including References—Yes or No? Listing references directly on a résumé would take up valuable space. Moreover, references are not normally instrumental in securing an interview—few companies check them before the interview. Instead, recruiters prefer that you e-mail or bring to the interview a list of individuals willing to discuss your qualifications. Therefore, you should prepare a list separate from the résumé, such as the one in **Model Document 13.1**, when you begin your job search. Consider three to five individuals, such as instructors, your current employer or previous employers, colleagues or subordinates, and other professional contacts. First, though, ask whether they would be willing to answer inquiries regarding your qualifications for employment. Be sure to provide them with an opportunity to refuse. No reference is better than

**Model Document 13.1   Sample Reference List**

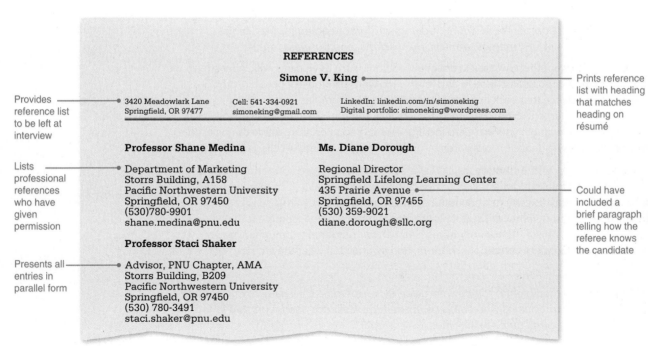

Provides reference list to be left at interview

Lists professional references who have given permission

Presents all entries in parallel form

**REFERENCES**

**Simone V. King**

3420 Meadowlark Lane          Cell: 541-334-0921          LinkedIn: linkedin.com/in/simoneking
Springfield, OR 97477          simoneking@gmail.com          Digital portfolio: simoneking@wordpress.com

**Professor Shane Medina**

Department of Marketing
Storrs Building, A158
Pacific Northwestern University
Springfield, OR 97450
(530)780-9901
shane.medina@pnu.edu

**Professor Staci Shaker**

Advisor, PNU Chapter, AMA
Storrs Building, B209
Pacific Northwestern University
Springfield, OR 97450
(530) 780-3491
staci.shaker@pnu.edu

**Ms. Diane Dorough**

Regional Director
Springfield Lifelong Learning Center
435 Prairie Avenue
Springfield, OR 97455
(530) 359-9021
diane.dorough@sllc.org

Prints reference list with heading that matches heading on résumé

Could have included a brief paragraph telling how the referee knows the candidate

a negative one. Better yet, to avoid rejection and embarrassment, ask only those contacts who you are confident will give you a glowing endorsement.

Do not include personal or character references, such as friends, family, or neighbors, because recruiters rarely consult them. One final note: Most recruiters see little reason for including the statement *References available upon request*. It is unnecessary and takes up precious space.

## 13-4d Creating a LinkedIn Profile

LinkedIn is usually the first place hiring managers and recruiters go to look for candidates. Preparing a LinkedIn profile takes a little effort, but it's well worth the investment. To ease your task, LinkedIn provides a template with standard résumé categories in which you fill in your qualifications. Compared with a print résumé, LinkedIn offers many advantages. You have ample space to expand the description of your skills and qualifications, and you can add media such as images, hyperlinks, and more. Your LinkedIn page also allows you to be more conversational and personal than you can be within the limits imposed by a traditional résumé. You can even use the pronoun *I* to tell your story more naturally and passionately. Include your LinkedIn URL such as **www.linkedin.com/in/simoneking**.

**Professional Headline.** To stand out, prepare an informative headline that appears below your name. In a LinkedIn profile, a **headline** is a type of tagline or branding slogan, a short phrase that sums up your professional self. It should include keywords in your field and a brief description of what you want, such as the following:

*Marketing Grad and Social Media Branding Specialist Seeking Internship*
*Recent Grad With Billing and Coding Training in Medical Insurance Field*
*Seeking Recruiter/Human Resources Assistant Position in Health Services*
*Finance and Management Grad Looking for Position as Analyst Trainee*

Some experts suggest that you write an even longer headline that takes full advantage of the 220-character LinkedIn space to promote yourself. Check out this recent grad's professional headline:

*Communication Graduate Specializing in Millennial and Mobile Marketing Interested in Survey Research and Data Analysis*

Because the headline is important, LinkedIn won't let you leave it blank. Use the headline to highlight your expertise and field of interest.

**Photo.** To increase your chance of being selected, definitely include a photo. Profiles with photos are known to score up to 21 times more views and nine times more connection requests than those without.[25] Your photo should be a head-and-shoulder shot in work-appropriate attire. Should you smile? A study by New York University researchers revealed that people who looked a "little" happy in their photos made the best impression.[26]

**Profile.** In your profile/summary, use keywords and phrases that appear in the job descriptions you are targeting. Include quantifiable achievements and specifics that reveal your skills. Unsurprisingly, listing your skills on LinkedIn makes you 13 times more likely to be viewed.[27] You can borrow much of this information from your résumé, but don't make it sound as terse as a résumé. In the Work Experience and Education fields, include all of your experience, not just your current position. Follow the tips provided earlier for presenting information in these résumé fields.

**Recommendations.** Ask your instructors and employers to recommend you. Having recommendations in your profile makes you look more credible, trustworthy, and reliable.

Career coach Susan Adams even encourages job seekers to offer to write the draft for the recommender; in the world of LinkedIn, she says, this is perfectly acceptable.[28] **Model Document 13.2** shows a portion of a new graduate's LinkedIn page.

**Model Document 13.2 LinkedIn Profile for New Graduate**

On LinkedIn Simone King presents a more personal description of her background, education, and experience than on her résumé. She includes a photo and a professional headline, "Honors graduate in e-marketing with social expertise." Her summary briefly describes her skills and experience. One expert warns candidates not to cut corners on the summary statement. Describe what motivates you and use first-person pronouns, unlike what you would do on a résumé. LinkedIn gives you an opportunity to be more conversational than you can be in a résumé. You may be asked to present this same kind of personalized résumé information on job boards.

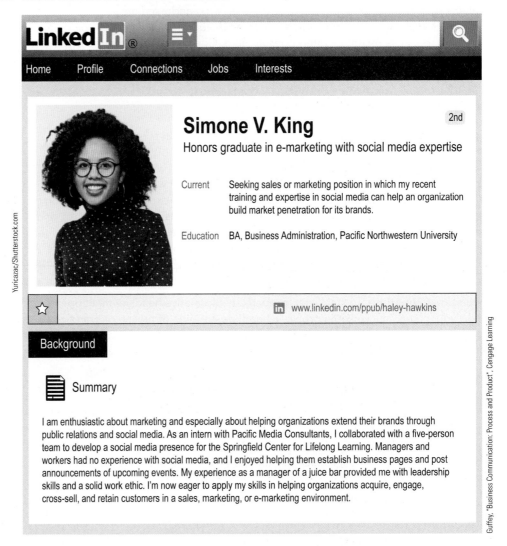

Yuricazac/Shutterstock.com

Guffey, "Business Communication: Process and Product", Cengage Learning

## 13-4e Perfecting Your Résumé and Keeping It Honest

As you continue to work on your résumé, look for ways to improve it. For example, consider consolidating headings. By condensing your information into as few headings as possible, you will produce a clean, professional-looking document. Study other résumés for valuable formatting ideas. Ask yourself what graphic highlighting techniques you can use to improve readability: capitalization, underlining, indenting, and bulleting. Experiment with headings and styles to achieve a pleasing, easy-to-read message. Moreover, look for ways to eliminate wordiness. For example, instead of *Supervised two employees who worked at the counter*, try *Supervised two counter employees*. Review Chapter 4 for more tips on writing concisely.

A résumé is expected to showcase a candidate's strengths and minimize weaknesses. For this reason, recruiters expect self-promotion. Some résumé writers, however, step over the line that separates honest self-marketing from deceptive half-truths and flat-out lies. Distorting facts on a résumé is unethical; lying may be illegal.

## Model Document 13.3  Chronological Résumé: Recent University Graduate With Limited Experience

Recent grad Simone King used MS Word to design a traditional chronological résumé that she plans to give to recruiters during interviews. She will also save it as a PDF for easy e-mailing and posting online. The two-column format enables recruiters and hiring managers to immediately follow the chronology of her education and experience. This format is easy to create by using the Word table feature and removing the borders so that no lines show.

Simone's objective is specific in describing what she seeks but broad enough to fit many possible positions. Her summary of qualifications highlights her experience and education. Because she has so little experience, she lists related courses to indicate her areas of interest and training. Although she has limited paid experience that relates to the position she seeks, she is able to capitalize on the accomplishments and transferable skills she gained as an intern.

---

**Simone V. King**

3420 Meadowlark Lane
Springfield, OR 97477
Cell: 541-334-0921

E-mail: simoneking@gmail.com
LinkedIn: www.linkedin.com/in/simoneking
Digital portfolio: https://simoneking,wordpress.com

**OBJECTIVE**
Position in sales, marketing, or e-marketing in which my marketing, communication, and social media expertise can help an organization build market penetration for its brands

**SUMMARY OF QUALIFICATIONS**
- Graduated with honors from Pacific Northwestern University
- Applied e-marketing and public relations training as an intern
- Experienced with Twitter, Facebook, Instagram, and other platforms
- Keep up-to-date with evolving technologies in social networking
- Developed strong work ethic with part-time jobs that financed more than 50 percent of my education
- Honed leadership skills as vice president of award-winning chapter of American Marketing Association

**EDUCATION AND RELATED COURSE WORK**
BA in Business Administration, Pacific Northwestern University, Cum Laude                                                    **May, 2022**
  **Major:** Business Administration, e-marketing emphasis.
  **Minor:** Organizational Communication
  **GPA:** Major, 3.7; overall 3.5 (A = 4.0)

Marketing Research and Analysis          Social Relations in the Workplace
Marketing Communication                   Writing for the Web and Social Media
Professional Public Relations             Organizational Behavior

**PROFESSIONAL EXPERIENCE**
**Social Media Intern**                                    09/2021–02/2022
Pacific Media Consultants, Springfield, Oregon
- Collaborated with five-person team to develop social media presence for Center for Lifelong Learning
- Introduced clients to LinkedIn and established Facebook and Twitter accounts for Lifelong Learning staff
- Demonstrated how to boost social media presence with announcements and tweets of upcoming activities
- Prepared brochure, handouts, name tags, and press kit to promote a Saturday community event
- Handled over 40 client calls with the account management team, ranging from project check-ins to inbound client inquiries

**Manager**                                                06/2019–08/2021
Juice Zone, Eugene, Oregon
- Developed management skills in assuming all responsibilities in absence of store owners including finances and scheduling
- Supervised daily store operations, maintained store security, and managed a team of 5–10 employees

**HONORS ACTIVITIES**
- Received prestigious Brooks Award as the outstanding graduate in marketing based on academic excellence and community service
- Served as vice president of Pacific Northwestern University chapter of the American Marketing Association providing monthly marketing forums, events, and competitions

---

## Model Document 13.4   Chronological Résumé: Student Seeking Internship

Although Sofia has had one internship, she is seeking another as she is about to graduate. To aid her search, she prepared a chronological résumé that emphasizes her education and related course work. She left out her mailing address because she prefers digital communication and phone contact. Instead of a career objective, she states exactly the internship position she seeks.

Notice that in her résumé Amy uses standard headings that would be easily recognized by an ATS. She skipped a summary of qualifications because she has little to offer yet. Instead, she focused on her work and internship experience and related it to the position she seeks.

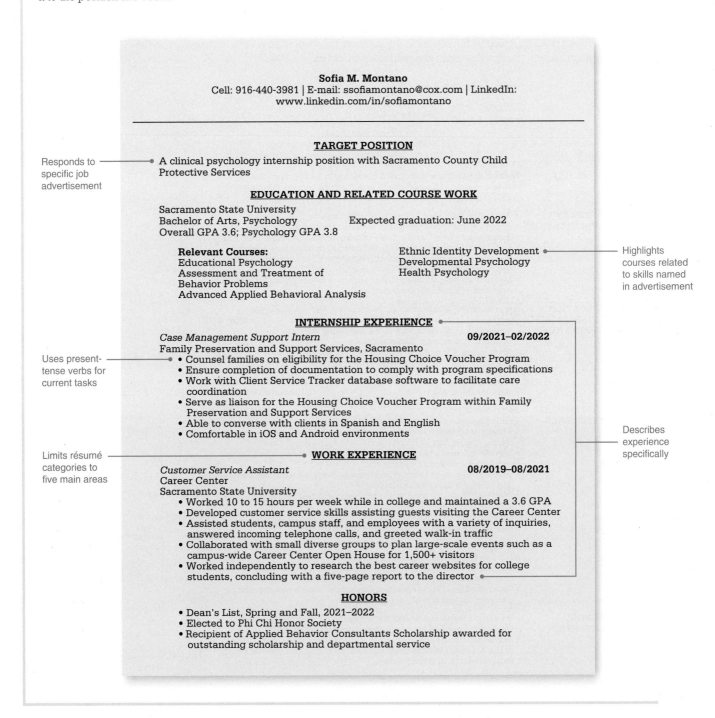

Responds to specific job advertisement

**Sofia M. Montano**
Cell: 916-440-3981 | E-mail: ssofiamontano@cox.com | LinkedIn:
www.linkedin.com/in/sofiamontano

**TARGET POSITION**

A clinical psychology internship position with Sacramento County Child
Protective Services

**EDUCATION AND RELATED COURSE WORK**

Sacramento State University
Bachelor of Arts, Psychology          Expected graduation: June 2022
Overall GPA 3.6; Psychology GPA 3.8

**Relevant Courses:**
Educational Psychology                Ethnic Identity Development
Assessment and Treatment of          Developmental Psychology
Behavior Problems                     Health Psychology
Advanced Applied Behavioral Analysis

Highlights courses related to skills named in advertisement

**INTERNSHIP EXPERIENCE**

*Case Management Support Intern*                09/2021–02/2022
Family Preservation and Support Services, Sacramento
- Counsel families on eligibility for the Housing Choice Voucher Program
- Ensure completion of documentation to comply with program specifications
- Work with Client Service Tracker database software to facilitate care coordination
- Serve as liaison for the Housing Choice Voucher Program within Family Preservation and Support Services
- Able to converse with clients in Spanish and English
- Comfortable in iOS and Android environments

Uses present-tense verbs for current tasks

Describes experience specifically

**WORK EXPERIENCE**

Limits résumé categories to five main areas

*Customer Service Assistant*                    08/2019–08/2021
Career Center
Sacramento State University
- Worked 10 to 15 hours per week while in college and maintained a 3.6 GPA
- Developed customer service skills assisting guests visiting the Career Center
- Assisted students, campus staff, and employees with a variety of inquiries, answered incoming telephone calls, and greeted walk-in traffic
- Collaborated with small diverse groups to plan large-scale events such as a campus-wide Career Center Open House for 1,500+ visitors
- Worked independently to research the best career websites for college students, concluding with a five-page report to the director

**HONORS**
- Dean's List, Spring and Fall, 2021–2022
- Elected to Phi Chi Honor Society
- Recipient of Applied Behavior Consultants Scholarship awarded for outstanding scholarship and departmental service

## Model Document 13.5 Functional Résumé: Recent College Graduate With Unrelated Part-Time Experience

Recent graduate Brody Mlodzik chose this functional format to de-emphasize his meager work experience and emphasize his potential in sales and marketing. This version of his résumé is more generic than one targeted for a specific position. Nevertheless, it emphasizes his strong points with specific achievements and includes an employment section to satisfy recruiters. The functional format presents ability-focused topics. It illustrates what the job seeker can do for the employer instead of narrating a history of previous jobs. Although recruiters prefer chronological résumés, the functional format is a good choice for new graduates, career changers, and those with employment gaps.

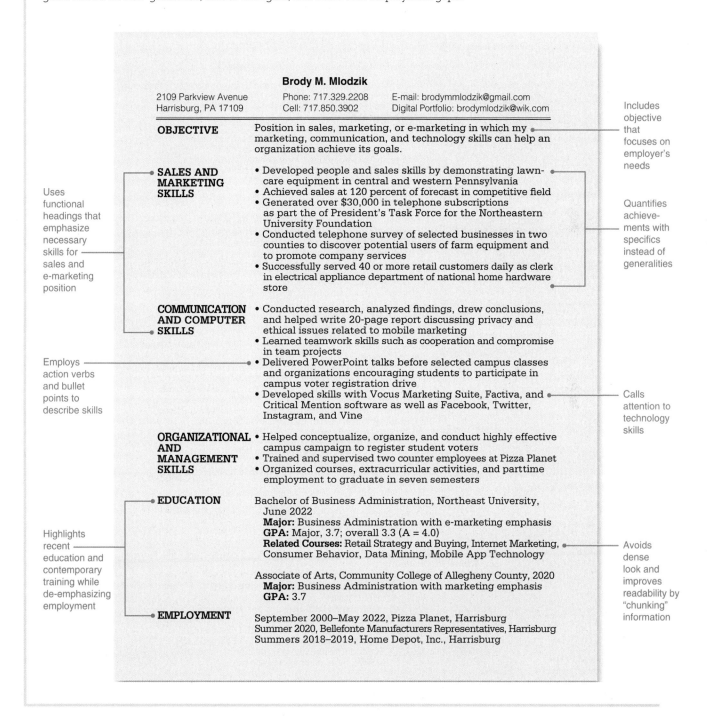

**Brody M. Mlodzik**

2109 Parkview Avenue
Harrisburg, PA 17109

Phone: 717.329.2208
Cell: 717.850.3902

E-mail: brodymmlodzik@gmail.com
Digital Portfolio: brodymlodzik@wik.com

*Includes objective that focuses on employer's needs*

**OBJECTIVE**
Position in sales, marketing, or e-marketing in which my marketing, communication, and technology skills can help an organization achieve its goals.

*Uses functional headings that emphasize necessary skills for sales and e-marketing position*

**SALES AND MARKETING SKILLS**
- Developed people and sales skills by demonstrating lawn-care equipment in central and western Pennsylvania
- Achieved sales at 120 percent of forecast in competitive field
- Generated over $30,000 in telephone subscriptions as part the of President's Task Force for the Northeastern University Foundation
- Conducted telephone survey of selected businesses in two counties to discover potential users of farm equipment and to promote company services
- Successfully served 40 or more retail customers daily as clerk in electrical appliance department of national home hardware store

*Quantifies achievements with specifics instead of generalities*

*Employs action verbs and bullet points to describe skills*

**COMMUNICATION AND COMPUTER SKILLS**
- Conducted research, analyzed findings, drew conclusions, and helped write 20-page report discussing privacy and ethical issues related to mobile marketing
- Learned teamwork skills such as cooperation and compromise in team projects
- Delivered PowerPoint talks before selected campus classes and organizations encouraging students to participate in campus voter registration drive
- Developed skills with Vocus Marketing Suite, Factiva, and Critical Mention software as well as Facebook, Twitter, Instagram, and Vine

*Calls attention to technology skills*

**ORGANIZATIONAL AND MANAGEMENT SKILLS**
- Helped conceptualize, organize, and conduct highly effective campus campaign to register student voters
- Trained and supervised two counter employees at Pizza Planet
- Organized courses, extracurricular activities, and parttime employment to graduate in seven semesters

*Highlights recent education and contemporary training while de-emphasizing employment*

**EDUCATION**
Bachelor of Business Administration, Northeast University, June 2022
**Major:** Business Administration with e-marketing emphasis
**GPA:** Major, 3.7; overall 3.3 (A = 4.0)
**Related Courses:** Retail Strategy and Buying, Internet Marketing, Consumer Behavior, Data Mining, Mobile App Technology

Associate of Arts, Community College of Allegheny County, 2020
**Major:** Business Administration with marketing emphasis
**GPA:** 3.7

*Avoids dense look and improves readability by "chunking" information*

**EMPLOYMENT**
September 2000–May 2022, Pizza Planet, Harrisburg
Summer 2020, Bellefonte Manufacturers Representatives, Harrisburg
Summers 2018–2019, Home Depot, Inc., Harrisburg

# Model Document 13.6 Chronological Résumé: University Graduate With Substantial Experience

Because Rachel has many years of experience and seeks executive-level employment, she highlighted her experience by placing it before her education. Her summary of qualifications highlighted her most impressive experience and skills. This chronological two-page résumé shows the steady progression of her career to executive positions, a movement that impresses and reassures recruiters.

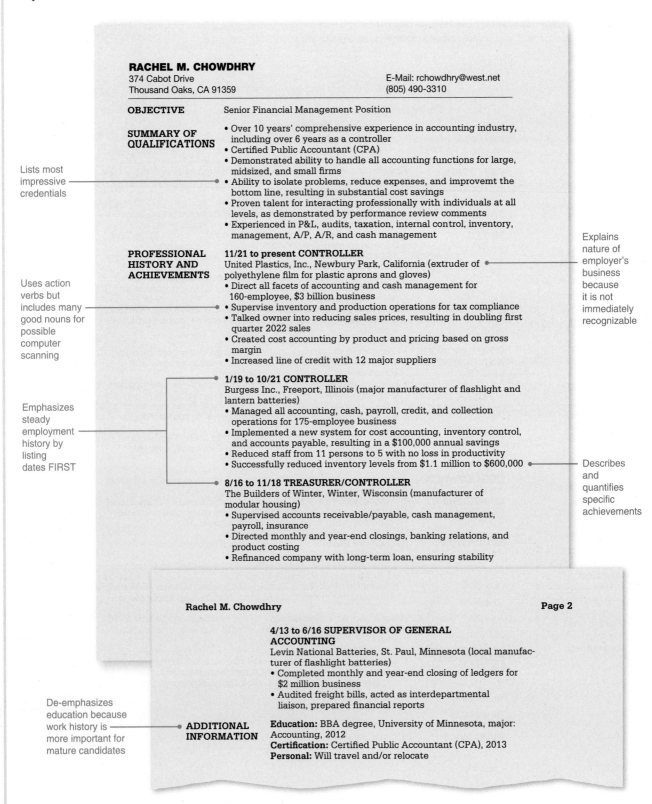

**RACHEL M. CHOWDHRY**
374 Cabot Drive
Thousand Oaks, CA 91359

E-Mail: rchowdhry@west.net
(805) 490-3310

**OBJECTIVE**  Senior Financial Management Position

**SUMMARY OF QUALIFICATIONS**
- Over 10 years' comprehensive experience in accounting industry, including over 6 years as a controller
- Certified Public Accountant (CPA)
- Demonstrated ability to handle all accounting functions for large, midsized, and small firms
- Ability to isolate problems, reduce expenses, and improvemt the bottom line, resulting in substantial cost savings
- Proven talent for interacting professionally with individuals at all levels, as demonstrated by performance review comments
- Experienced in P&L, audits, taxation, internal control, inventory, management, A/P, A/R, and cash management

*Lists most impressive credentials*

**PROFESSIONAL HISTORY AND ACHIEVEMENTS**

**11/21 to present CONTROLLER**
United Plastics, Inc., Newbury Park, California (extruder of polyethylene film for plastic aprons and gloves)
- Direct all facets of accounting and cash management for 160-employee, $3 billion business
- Supervise inventory and production operations for tax compliance
- Talked owner into reducing sales prices, resulting in doubling first quarter 2022 sales
- Created cost accounting by product and pricing based on gross margin
- Increased line of credit with 12 major suppliers

*Explains nature of employer's business because it is not immediately recognizable*

*Uses action verbs but includes many good nouns for possible computer scanning*

**1/19 to 10/21 CONTROLLER**
Burgess Inc., Freeport, Illinois (major manufacturer of flashlight and lantern batteries)
- Managed all accounting, cash, payroll, credit, and collection operations for 175-employee business
- Implemented a new system for cost accounting, inventory control, and accounts payable, resulting in a $100,000 annual savings
- Reduced staff from 11 persons to 5 with no loss in productivity
- Successfully reduced inventory levels from $1.1 million to $600,000

*Emphasizes steady employment history by listing dates FIRST*

*Describes and quantifies specific achievements*

**8/16 to 11/18 TREASURER/CONTROLLER**
The Builders of Winter, Winter, Wisconsin (manufacturer of modular housing)
- Supervised accounts receivable/payable, cash management, payroll, insurance
- Directed monthly and year-end closings, banking relations, and product costing
- Refinanced company with long-term loan, ensuring stability

---

**Rachel M. Chowdhry**  Page 2

**4/13 to 6/16 SUPERVISOR OF GENERAL ACCOUNTING**
Levin National Batteries, St. Paul, Minnesota (local manufacturer of flashlight batteries)
- Completed monthly and year-end closing of ledgers for $2 million business
- Audited freight bills, acted as interdepartmental liaison, prepared financial reports

*De-emphasizes education because work history is more important for mature candidates*

**ADDITIONAL INFORMATION**
**Education:** BBA degree, University of Minnesota, major: Accounting, 2012
**Certification:** Certified Public Accountant (CPA), 2013
**Personal:** Will travel and/or relocate

Most important, either practice can destroy a career. In the Communication Workshop at the end of this chapter, learn more about how to keep your résumé honest and about the consequences of fudging the facts.

## 13-4f Proofreading Your Résumé

After revising your résumé, you must proofread, proofread, and proofread again for spelling, grammar, mechanics, content, and format. Then have a knowledgeable friend or relative proofread it yet again. This is one document that must be perfect. Because the job market is so competitive, one typo, one misspelled word, or a single grammatical error could eliminate you from consideration.

By now you may be thinking that you'd like to hire someone to write your résumé. Don't! First, you know yourself better than anyone else could know you. Second, you will end up with either a generic or a one-time résumé. A generic résumé in today's highly competitive job market will lose out to a customized résumé nine times out of ten. Equally useless is a one-time résumé aimed at a single job. What if you don't get that job? Because you will need to revise and customize your résumé many times as you seek a variety of jobs, be prepared to write (and rewrite) it yourself.

# 13-5 Using Digital Tools to Fine-Tune Your Job Search

Technology is not only shaping the way applicants search for jobs, but also the way employers select qualified candidates. As discussed earlier, the first screener of your résumé may very well be an ATS. Nearly all large companies and scores of smaller and mid-size companies are now employing these systems.[30]

Why have ATS become so popular? Screening systems efficiently whittle down the applicant pool to just a handful of qualified applicants for the human hiring managers to review more closely. The sad truth for applicants, however, is that up to three quarters of résumés don't make it past the ATS screening.[31] Even after repeatedly entering the required information into clunky online forms, job seekers can't be sure that a human will ever review it.[32] Businesses run the risk of missing out on talented candidates who don't fit the standardized screening criteria or find the experience too daunting.

## 13-5a Maximizing the Rank of Your Résumé

The higher your résumé ranks when it is evaluated by an ATS, the more likely it will be reviewed by a recruiter or hiring manager. In the past candidates tried to game the system by stuffing their résumés with keywords. Newer screening systems are not so easily fooled. Although keywords are important, "the system looks for relevance of the keyword to your work history and education," advises job-search authority Quint Careers.[33] In addition to including the right keywords in context, your résumé must qualify in other ways to be selected. The following techniques, in addition to those cited earlier, can boost the probability that your résumé will rank high enough to qualify for review by a human reader.

- **Include job-specific keywords or keyword phrases in context**. Study carefully any advertisements and job descriptions for the position you want. Describe your experience, education, and qualifications in

**LEARNING OUTCOME 5**

Describe digital tools that can enhance your job search and résumé.

terms associated with the job advertisement or job description for this position. However, don't just plop a keyword into your résumé; use it in context to ensure ATS recognition (e.g., *collaborated within four-member team to create a pilot business plan*). In other words, offer a vivid snapshot of the activity or accomplishment.

- **Focus on nouns.** Although action verbs will make your résumé appeal to a recruiter, the applicant tracking system will often be looking for nouns in three categories: (a) a job title, position, or role (e.g., *accountant, Web developer, team leader*); (b) a technical skill or specialization (e.g., *Python, Java, C++*); and (c) a certification, a tool used, or specific experience (e.g., *Certified Financial Analyst, Chartered Financial Analyst*).

- **Use variations of the job title.** Tracking systems may seek a slightly different job title from what you list. To be safe, include variations and abbreviations (e.g., *occupational therapist, certified occupational therapist,* or *COTA*). If you don't have experience in your targeted area, use the job title you seek in your objective.

- **Concentrate on the Skills section.** A majority of keywords employers seek relate to specialized or technical skill requirements. Therefore, be sure the Skills section of your résumé is full of nouns that describe your skills and qualifications.

- **Keep the formatting simple.** Stay away from logos, pictures, symbols, and shadings.

- **Use conventional headings.** Include familiar headings such as *Skills, Qualifications,* and *Education.* ATS software may not recognize headings such as *Professional Engagement* or *Core Competencies.*

## 13-5b Showcasing Your Qualifications in a Career E-Portfolio

You have yet another tool to demonstrate your qualifications to prospective employers: the **career e-portfolio**. The professional electronic portfolio is a purposeful collection of digital files and documents showcasing the accomplishments of a students' academic career. Some e-portfolios are built like personal websites and feature sophisticated media.

**What Goes in a Career E-Portfolio?** A professional e-portfolio may include a copy of your career-specific résumé, reference letters, commendations for special achievements, awards, certificates, work samples, a complete list of your courses, thank-you letters, and other items that tout your accomplishments. An e-portfolio could also provide links to digital copies of your artwork, film projects, videos, blueprints, documents, photographs, multimedia files, and blog entries that might otherwise be difficult to share with potential employers.

Displaying a variety of resources in one place, e-portfolios offer many advantages, as seen in **Figure 13.9**. Once they are posted online, they can be viewed at an employer's convenience. Let's say you are talking on the phone with an employer in another city who wants to see a copy of your résumé. You can simply send a link to the Internet address where your résumé resides. E-portfolios can also be viewed by many individuals in an organization without circulating a paper copy. However, the main reason for preparing an e-portfolio is to show off your talents and qualifications more thoroughly than you can in a print résumé.

Some recruiters may be skeptical about e-portfolios because they fear that such presentations will take more time to view than paper-based résumés do. As a result, nontraditional job applications may end up at the bottom of the pile or be ignored. That's why some applicants submit a print résumé or e-mail a digital copy in addition to providing an e-portfolio.

**How Are E-Portfolios Accessed?** You have many options when you are ready for your e-portfolio to go live. Some colleges and universities make space available on their

**Figure 13.9** Making a Career E-Portfolio

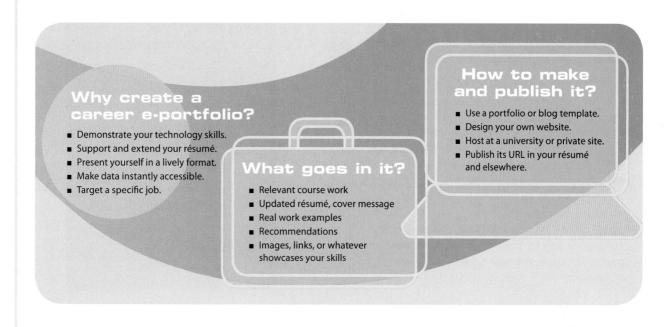

learning management systems to host student e-portfolios. In addition, academic institutions may offer instruction and resources for editing video, digitizing images, and preparing graphics. A few popular commercial platforms for hosting student e-portfolios are WordPress, Wix, and Weebly. Resourceful candidates may also simply provide employers with links to their e-portfolios stored in Google Docs, Box, or Dropbox.

## 13-5c Expanding Your Employment Chances With a Video Résumé

Still another way to expand your employment possibilities is with a **video résumé**. Video résumés enable job candidates to present their experience, qualifications, and interests in video form. This format has many benefits. It allows candidates to demonstrate their public speaking, interpersonal, and technical skills more impressively than they can in traditional print résumés.

Long before the COVID-19 pandemic nixed in-person interviewing, both employers and applicants were able to save recruitment and travel costs by using video résumés and, more commonly, by relying on virtual interviews.

Video résumés are becoming more prevalent with the popularity of YouTube, inexpensive but high-quality webcams, and widespread broadband. With simple edits on a computer, you can customize a video message to a specific employer and tailor your résumé for a particular job opening. In making a video résumé, dress professionally in business attire, just as you would for an in-person interview. Keep your video to three minutes or less. Explain why you would be a good employee and what you can do for the company that hires you.

Before committing time and energy to a video résumé, decide whether it is appropriate for your career field. Such presentations make sense for online, media, social, and creative professions. Traditional organizations, however, may be less impressed. Done well, a video résumé might give you an edge. Done poorly, however, it could bounce you from contention. Paper résumés still do a fine job of condensing your achievements. A video résumé, however, can show off strengths such as warmth,

Emily Vu, a computational physics student at the University of California, Irvine, created an unconventional résumé laser-focused on a product-manager position at Spotify that would require exceptional design skills. The senior with stellar credentials knew she had lots of competition: "I realized that my résumé was going into the void. . . . I had to do something a little bit different." When the Spotify listing suddenly vanished, she didn't give up. Instead, she posted her Spotify-themed résumé on Twitter and LinkedIn where it quickly trended. Many at Spotify, including CEO Daniel Ek, noticed. Emily landed a product-management opportunity. Her advice is to be authentic and "Just do the best with what you have."[34] What can you learn from Emily's example?

clear communication, charisma, humor, and conversational ability. Check out dazzling video résumé possibilities at **biteable.com**.

### 13-5d How Many Résumés and What Format?

At this point you may be wondering how many résumés you should make, and what format they should follow. The good news is that you need only one basic résumé that you can customize for various job prospects and format.

**Preparing a Basic Print-Based Résumé.** The one basic résumé you should prepare is a print-based traditional résumé. It should be attractively formatted to maximize readability. A hard-copy résumé is useful (a) during job interviews, (b) for person-to-person networking situations, (c) for recruiters at career fairs, and (d) when you are competing for a job that does not require an electronic submission.

You can create a basic, yet professional-looking résumé by using your word processing program. Our collection of résumé examples in this chapter provides ideas for simple layouts that are easily duplicated and adapted. You can also examine résumé templates for design and format ideas. Their inflexibility, however, may be frustrating as you try to force your skills and experience into a predetermined template sequence.

**Creating a Plain-Text Résumé for Electronic Submission.** After preparing a basic résumé, you can convert it to a plain-text résumé so that it is ready for e-mailing. Part of it will also be available to you for uploading to online submission forms. Many job boards and most government employers require job candidates to complete official application forms. Even if your résumé contains the same information, an application form is often required for legal and data processing as well as for employer convenience.

Some employers prefer that résumé information be submitted in **plain-text format**. This is a format that contains only standard keyboard characters—no special formatting such as bold, underlining, italics, and larger font sizes. Plain-text documents are sometimes preferred because they avoid possible e-mail viruses and word processing incompatibilities.

To create a plain, minimally formatted résumé, save your basic résumé document as *Plain Text* (*txt). Then, open the converted plain-text file with Word again, and continue to work with the no-frills document by following these guidelines:

- Use the default Courier font or select Helvetica or Arial. Don't revert to italics, boldface, and underlining, which could cause some scanners to misread text.

- In your plain-text file, only capital letters will remain after the conversion. Use caps for headings and to emphasize important words—but don't overdo the caps.

- Images, designs, tables, tabs, colors, and any characters not on a standard keyboard will have disappeared. Do not reintroduce them into your no-frills résumé.

- For bullets, use asterisks or plus signs.

- Use white space or a line of hyphens or equal signs to separate sections.

- If your original contained columns or tables, fix any jumbled text in your plain résumé.

- Information placed in a header or footer may appear at the bottom of the file after the conversion. Move your name and contact information to the top of the page.

- Paste a copy of your plain résumé into an e-mail message and send it to yourself to check its appearance and format. Also e-mail this embedded version of your résumé to a friend to try it out.

## 13-5e Submitting Your Résumé

The format you choose for submitting your résumé depends on what is required. If you are responding to a job advertisement, be certain to read the listing carefully to learn how the employer wants you to submit your résumé. Not following the prospective employer's instructions can eliminate you from consideration before your résumé is even reviewed. If you have any doubt about what format is desired, send an e-mail inquiry to a company representative, or call and ask. Most organizations request one of the following submission formats:

- **Word document.** Some organizations ask candidates to send their résumés and cover letters in hard copy by surface mail. Others request that résumés be submitted as Word documents attached to e-mail messages, despite the fear of viruses.

- **Plain-text document.** As discussed earlier, some employers expect applicants to submit résumés and cover letters as plain-text documents. This format is also widely used for posting to online job boards or for sending by e-mail. Plain-text résumés may be embedded within or attached to e-mail messages.

- **PDF document.** For safety reasons some employers prefer **PDF (portable document format)** files. A PDF résumé looks exactly like the original and cannot be altered easily. Converting your résumé from Word can be easily done by saving it as a PDF file, which preserves all formatting.

- **Company database.** Larger businesses and government organizations may prefer that you complete an online form with your résumé information. This enables them to plug your data into their template categories for rapid searching. You might be able to cut and paste the information from your plain-text résumé into the form. Some businesses may ask you to upload your résumé as a Word, PDF, or image file. To keep your formatting intact, opt for a PDF or image file.

Because your résumé is probably the most important message you will ever write, you will revise it many times. With so much information in concentrated form and with

**OFFICE INSIDER**

"The cover letter is often the product that a hiring manager will see once a candidate gets past the screening process. The cover letter is the opportunity to speak to the job in more intimate detail in ways a resume cannot. A candidate can speak to those intangibles through experiences and stories. And speak to why he or she is a fit for the company. It is an opportunity to speak directly to the hiring manager, get noticed, and is often the key talking point when folks get in a room and decide who to bring in for an interview."[35]

**Jon Christiansen,**
*CIO, Sparks Research*

so much riding on its outcome, your résumé demands careful polishing, proofreading, and critiquing.

# 13-6 Cover Letters—Do They Still Matter?

A cover message, traditionally known as a **cover letter** or **letter of application**, has always been a graceful way of introducing your résumé, and it remains relevant. The COVID-19 pandemic accelerated virtual recruiting and the use of AI-enabled ATS has skyrocketed, transforming the job search process. However, effective job-specific cover letters are still well worth the effort. In one survey, 87 percent of recruiters and hiring managers stated they do read cover letters, and 65 percent said they are influenced by them in their interview or hiring decisions. Applications accompanied by a well-tailored cover letter received a 53 percent higher interview callback than those without.[36] Even among tech companies of varying size, 48–65 percent require a cover letter, a study found.[37]

On the other hand, a recent survey by JobVite revealed that only 27 percent of recruiters prioritize cover letters in screening decisions.[38] Why? Recruiters may skip over cover letters because they are involved only with initial screening. Hiring managers, however, present a different story. They often seek as much information as they can obtain to avoid expensive bad hires. Cover letters may reveal key information missing in a résumé. Hiring managers are eager to learn whether the candidate will fit into the company culture.[39]

## 13-6a Creating a Customized Cover Letter

For new grads to compete in a job market saturated by degree holders, it's increasingly important to find a way to stand out.[40] Cover letters give you the opportunity to set yourself apart. A well-written cover letter can reveal to employers your ability to put together complete sentences and to sound intelligent. A cover letter also can be more personal and strengthen a weak résumé by showing how your special talents relate to the opening. "It's your opportunity to tell the world who you are, what you're about, and why you're qualified," says employment expert Dorie Clark.[41]

Although some hiring managers favor cover letters, they disagree about their length. Some prefer short messages with no more than two paragraphs embedded in an e-mail message. Other recruiters desire longer messages that supply more information, thus giving them a better opportunity to evaluate a candidate's qualifications and writing skills. These recruiters argue that hiring and training new employees is expensive and time consuming; therefore, they welcome extra data to guide them in making the best choice the first time. Follow your judgment in writing a brief or a longer cover letter.

Fizkes/Shutterstock.com

Regardless of its length, a cover letter should have three primary parts: (a) an opening that captures attention, introduces the message, and identifies the position; (b) a body that promotes the candidate and focuses on the employer's needs; and (c) a closing that requests an interview and motivates action. When putting your cover letter together, remember that the biggest mistake job seekers make when writing cover letters is being too generic.[42] You should, therefore, write a personalized, job-specific cover letter for every position that interests you.

**Gaining Attention in the Opening.** Your cover letter will be more appealing—and more likely to be read—if it begins by addressing the reader by name. Rather than sending your letter to the *Hiring Manager* or *To Whom It May Concern,* try to identify the name of the appropriate individual on LinkedIn or by studying the company's website. You could also call the human resources department and ask the name of the person in charge of hiring. If you still cannot find the name of any person to address, you might replace the salutation of your letter with a descriptive subject line such as *Application for Marketing Specialist Position.*

How you open your cover letter depends largely on whether the application is solicited or unsolicited. If an employment position has been announced and applicants are being solicited, you can use a direct approach. If you do not know whether a position is open and you are prospecting for a job, use an indirect approach. Whether direct or indirect, the opening should attract the attention of the reader. Strive for openings that are more imaginative than *Please consider this letter an application for the position of . . .* or *I would like to apply for. . . .*

Openings for Solicited Jobs. When applying for a job that has been announced, consider some of the following techniques to open your cover letter:

- **Refer to the name of an employee in the company.** Remember that employers always hope to hire known quantities rather than complete strangers.

  *Kennedy Harris, a member of your Customer Service Department, told me that Thompson & Associates is seeking a customer service trainee. The enclosed summary of my qualifications demonstrates my preparation for this position.*

  *At the suggestion of Tiffany Freed, in your Legal Services Department, I submit my qualifications for the position of staffing coordinator.*

  *Amarjit Singh, placement director at Southwest University, told me that Dynamic Industries has an opening for a technical writer with knowledge of Web design and graphics.*

- **Refer to the source of your information precisely.** If you are answering an advertisement, include the exact position advertised and the name and date of the publication. If you are responding to a position listed on an online job board, include the website name and the date the position was posted.

  *From your company's website, I learned about your need for a sales representative for the Ohio, Indiana, and Illinois regions. I am very interested in this position and am confident that my education and experience are appropriate for the opening.*

  *My talent for interacting with people, coupled with more than five years of customer service experience, make me an ideal candidate for the director of customer relations position you advertised on the CareerJournal website on August 3.*

- **Refer to the job title, and describe how your qualifications fit the requirements.** Hiring managers are looking for a match between an applicant's credentials and the job needs.

  *Ceradyne Company's marketing assistant opening is an excellent match with my qualifications. As a recent graduate of Eastern University with a major in marketing, I offer solid academic credentials as well as industry experience gained from an internship at Flotek Industries.*

  *Will an honors graduate with a degree in recreation and two years of part-time experience organizing social activities for a convalescent hospital qualify for your position of activity director?*

  *Because of my specialized training in finance and accounting at Michigan State University, I am confident that I have the qualifications you described in your advertisement for a staff accountant trainee.*

Openings for Unsolicited Jobs. If you are unsure whether a position actually exists, you might use a more persuasive opening. Because your goal is to convince the hiring manager to read on, try one of the following techniques:

- **Demonstrate an interest in and knowledge of the reader's business.** Show the hiring manager that you have done your research and that this organization is more than a mere name to you.

    *Because Signa HealthNet, Inc., is organizing a new information management team for its recently established group insurance division, could you use the services of a well-trained information systems graduate who seeks to become a professional systems analyst?*

    *I read with great interest the article in* Forbes *announcing the upcoming merger with CanMex Bank. Congratulations on this new venture and its notable $50 million in loans precharter! The possibility of helping your bank grow is exciting, and I would like to explore a potential employment match that I am confident will be mutually beneficial.*

- **Show how your special talents and background will benefit the company.** Human resources managers need to be convinced that you can do something for them.

    *Could your rapidly expanding publications division use the services of an editorial assistant who offers exceptional language skills, an honors degree from the University of Mississippi, and two years' experience in producing a campus literary publication?*

In applying for an advertised job, Tracy Karacia wrote the solicited cover letter shown in **Model Document 13.7**. Notice that her opening identifies the position advertised on the company's website so that the reader knows exactly what advertisement Tracy means. Using features in her word processing program, Tracy designed her own letterhead that uses her name and looks like professionally printed letterhead paper.

More challenging are unsolicited cover letters, such as the letter of Jared L. Chen shown in **Model Document 13.8**. Because he hopes to discover or create a job, his opening must grab the reader's attention immediately. To do that, he capitalizes on company information appearing in an online article. Jared purposely kept his cover letter short and to the point because he anticipated that a busy executive would be unwilling to read a long, detailed letter. Jared's unsolicited letter prospects for a job. Some job candidates feel that such letters may be even more productive than efforts to secure advertised jobs, because prospecting candidates face less competition and show initiative. Notice that Jared's letter uses a personal business letter format with his return address above the date.

## 13-6b Promoting Your Strengths in the Message Body

Once you have captured the attention of the reader and identified your purpose in the letter opening, you should use the body of the letter to plug your qualifications for this position. If you are responding to an advertisement, you will want to explain how your preparation and experience fulfill the stated requirements. If you are prospecting for a job, you may not know the exact requirements. Your employment research and knowledge of your field, however, should give you a reasonably good idea of what is expected for the position you seek.

It is also important to stress reader benefits. In other words, you should describe your strong points in relation to the needs of the employer. Hiring officers want you to tell them what you can do for their organizations. This is more important than telling what courses you took in college or what duties you performed in your previous jobs.

**Poor:**     *I have completed courses in business communication, report writing, and technical writing.*

**Model Document 13.7** Solicited Cover Letter

Uses personally
designed
letterhead

**Tracy R. Karacia**
_____

1770 Hawthorne Place, Boulder CO 80304
(303) 492-1244, smwilliams@yahoo.com

May 23, 2022

Ms. Sara Rose Belardi
Director, Human Resources
Del Rio Enterprises
4839 Mountain View Avenue
Denver, CO 82511

Addresses
proper
person by
name
and title

Dear Ms. Belardi:

Identifies job
and exact page
where ad
appeared

Your advertisement for an assistant product manager, appearing May 22 in the
employment section of your company website, immediately caught my attention
because my education and training closely parallel your needs.

According to your advertisement, the job includes "assisting in the coordination
of a wide range of marketing programs as well as analyzing sales results and
tracking marketing budgets." A recent internship at Ventana Corporation introduced me to similar tasks. Assisting the marketing manager enabled me to
analyze the promotion, budget, and overall sales success of two products
Ventana was evaluating. My ten-page report examined the nature of the current
market, the products' life cycles, and their sales/profit return. In addition to
this research, I helped formulate a product merchandising plan and answered
consumers' questions at a local trade show.

Relates
writer's
experience
to job
requirements

Discusses
schooling

Discusses
experience

Intensive course work in marketing and management, as well as proficiency in
computer spreadsheets and databases, has given me the kind of marketing and
computer training that Del Rio probably demands in a product manager. Moreover, my recent retail sales experience and participation in campus organizations
have helped me develop the kind of customer service and interpersonal skills
necessary for an effective product manager.

Asks for
interview
and repeats
main
qualifications

After you have examined the enclosed résumé for details of my qualifications,
I would be happy to answer questions. Please call me at (303) 492-1244 to
arrange an interview at your convenience so that we may discuss how my
marketing experience, computer training, and interpersonal skills could contribute to Del Rio Enterprises.

Refers reader
to résumé

Sincerely

_Tracy R. Karacia_

Tracy R. Karacia

Enclosure

**Improved:** _Courses in business communication, report writing, and technical
writing have helped me develop the research and writing skills
required of your technical writers._

In the body of your letter, you may choose to discuss relevant personal traits.
Employers are looking for candidates who, among other things, are team players, take
responsibility, show initiative, and learn easily. Don't just list several personal traits,
though; instead, include evidence that shows you possess these traits. Notice how in
the following paragraph the writer uses action verbs to depict a promising candidate:

# Model Document 13.8 Unsolicited Cover Letter

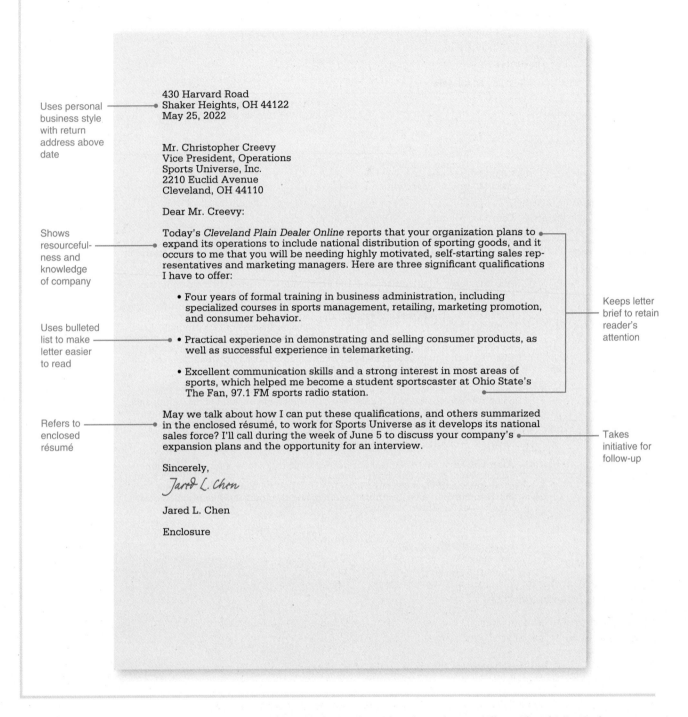

Uses personal business style with return address above date

430 Harvard Road
Shaker Heights, OH 44122
May 25, 2022

Mr. Christopher Creevy
Vice President, Operations
Sports Universe, Inc.
2210 Euclid Avenue
Cleveland, OH 44110

Dear Mr. Creevy:

Shows resourcefulness and knowledge of company

Today's *Cleveland Plain Dealer Online* reports that your organization plans to expand its operations to include national distribution of sporting goods, and it occurs to me that you will be needing highly motivated, self-starting sales representatives and marketing managers. Here are three significant qualifications I have to offer:

Uses bulleted list to make letter easier to read

- Four years of formal training in business administration, including specialized courses in sports management, retailing, marketing promotion, and consumer behavior.

- Practical experience in demonstrating and selling consumer products, as well as successful experience in telemarketing.

- Excellent communication skills and a strong interest in most areas of sports, which helped me become a student sportscaster at Ohio State's The Fan, 97.1 FM sports radio station.

Keeps letter brief to retain reader's attention

Refers to enclosed résumé

May we talk about how I can put these qualifications, and others summarized in the enclosed résumé, to work for Sports Universe as it develops its national sales force? I'll call during the week of June 5 to discuss your company's expansion plans and the opportunity for an interview.

Takes initiative for follow-up

Sincerely,

*Jared L. Chen*

Jared L. Chen

Enclosure

*In addition to developing technical and academic skills at Florida Central University, I have gained interpersonal, leadership, and organizational skills. As vice president of the business students' organization, Gamma Alpha, I helped organize and supervise two successful fund-raising events. These activities involved conceptualizing the tasks, motivating others to help, scheduling work sessions, and coordinating the efforts of 35 diverse students. I enjoyed my success with these activities and look forward to applying my experience in your management trainee program.*

Finally, in this section or the next, refer the reader to your résumé. Do so directly or as part of another statement.

**Direct reference to résumé:** *Please refer to the attached résumé for additional information regarding my education, experience, and skills.*

**Part of another statement:** *As you will notice from my enclosed résumé, I will graduate in June with a bachelor's degree in business administration.*

## 13-6c Motivating Action in the Closing

After presenting your case, you should conclude by asking confidently for an interview. Don't ask for the job. To do so would be presumptuous and naïve. In requesting an interview, you might suggest reader benefits or review your strongest points. Sound sincere and appreciative. Remember to make it easy for the reader to respond by supplying your telephone number and the best times to call you. In addition, keep in mind that some hiring officers prefer that you take the initiative to call them. Avoid expressions such as *I hope*, which weaken your closing. Here are possible endings:

**Poor:** *I hope to hear from you soon.*

**Improved:** *This brief description of my qualifications and the additional information on my résumé demonstrate my readiness to put my accounting skills to work for McLellan and Associates. Please call me at (405) 488-2291 before 10 a.m. or after 3 p.m. to arrange an interview.*

**Poor:** *I look forward to a call from you.*

**Improved:** *To add to your staff an industrious, well-trained administrative assistant with proven Internet and communication skills, call me at (350) 492-1433 to arrange an interview. I look forward to meeting with you to discuss further my qualifications.*

**Poor:** *Thanks for looking over my qualifications.*

**Improved:** *I look forward to the opportunity to discuss my qualifications for the financial analyst position more fully in an interview. You can reach me at (213) 458-4030.*

## 13-6d Sending Your Résumé and Cover Letter

How you submit your résumé depends on the employer's instructions, which usually involve one of the following methods:

- Send a short e-mail with both your cover letter and résumé attached (as a PDF preferably, to preserve your formatting).

- Send your cover letter as an e-mail and attach only your résumé (as PDF, Word document, or plain text).

- Submit both your cover letter and résumé by pasting them into the body of an e-mail. Convert both to plain text with minimal formatting first, as described earlier.

- Print your cover letter and résumé on quality stationary and send them by U.S. mail.

Serious job candidates take the time to prepare a professional cover letter. If you are e-mailing your résumé, use the same cover letter you would send by surface mail, but shorten it a bit, as illustrated in the incomplete **Model Document 13.9**. Just below your name, include your street address, e-mail address, and phone number.

## 13-6e Final Tips for Successful Cover Letters

As you revise your cover letter, notice how many sentences begin with *I*. Although it is impossible to talk about yourself without using *I*, you can reduce "I" domination with a number of thoughtful techniques. Make activities and outcomes, and not yourself, the subjects of sentences. Sometimes you can avoid "I" domination by focusing on the "you" view. Another way to avoid starting sentences with *I* is to move phrases from within the sentence to the beginning.

**Poor:** *I took classes in business communication and computer applications.*

**Improved:** *Classes in business communication and computer applications prepared me to . . . . (Make activities the subject.)*

**Poor:** *I enjoyed helping customers, which taught me to. . . .*

**Improved:** *Helping customers was a real pleasure and taught me to. . . . (Make outcomes the subject.)*

**Poor:** *I am a hardworking team player who. . . .*

**Improved:** *You are looking for a hardworking team player who. . . . (Use the "you" view.)*

**Poor:** *I worked to support myself all through college, thus building. . . .*

**Improved:** *All through college, I worked to support myself, thus building. . . . (Move phrases to the beginning.)*

### Model Document 13.9  E-Mail Cover Message

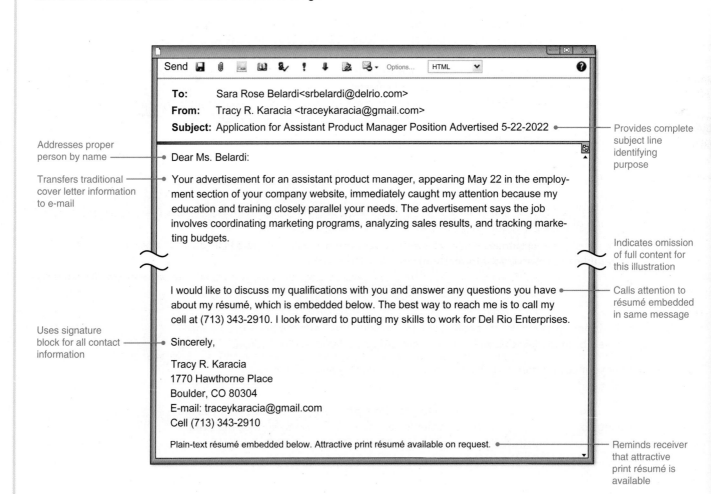

Addresses proper person by name

Transfers traditional cover letter information to e-mail

Uses signature block for all contact information

Provides complete subject line identifying purpose

Indicates omission of full content for this illustration

Calls attention to résumé embedded in same message

Reminds receiver that attractive print résumé is available

**To:** Sara Rose Belardi<srbelardi@delrio.com>
**From:** Tracy R. Karacia <traceykaracia@gmail.com>
**Subject:** Application for Assistant Product Manager Position Advertised 5-22-2022

Dear Ms. Belardi:

Your advertisement for an assistant product manager, appearing May 22 in the employment section of your company website, immediately caught my attention because my education and training closely parallel your needs. The advertisement says the job involves coordinating marketing programs, analyzing sales results, and tracking marketing budgets.

I would like to discuss my qualifications with you and answer any questions you have about my résumé, which is embedded below. The best way to reach me is to call my cell at (713) 343-2910. I look forward to putting my skills to work for Del Rio Enterprises.

Sincerely,

Tracy R. Karacia
1770 Hawthorne Place
Boulder, CO 80304
E-mail: traceykaracia@gmail.com
Cell (713) 343-2910

Plain-text résumé embedded below. Attractive print résumé available on request.

Strive for a comfortable style. In your effort to avoid sounding self-centered, don't write unnaturally.

Like your résumé, your cover letter must look professional and suggest quality. This means using a traditional letter style, such as block format. Also, be sure to print it on the same quality paper as your résumé. As with your résumé, proofread it several times yourself; then have a friend read it for content and mechanics. Don't rely on spell-check to find all the errors. Like your résumé, your cover letter must be perfect.

## Summary of Learning Outcomes

**1  Describe how digital age technology will enhance the four major steps in your job search.**

- The four steps in a job search include the following: analyzing yourself, exploring the open and hidden job markets, creating a customized résumé and cover letter, and knowing the hiring process.
- Recognize that searching for a job in this digital age now includes such indispensable tools as job boards, social networks, and mobile technologies.
- Emphasis today is on what the employer wants, not what the candidate wants.
- Start the process by learning about yourself, your field of interest, and your qualifications. How do your skills match what employers seek?
- To investigate career opportunities, visit a campus career center or its website, search for apps and virtual help online, take a summer job, interview someone in your field, volunteer, or join professional organizations.
- Identify job availability, the skills and qualifications required, duties, and salaries.

**2  List search strategies that explore the open job market.**

- In searching the open job market—that is, jobs that are listed and advertised—explore the big job boards, such as Indeed, CareerBuilder, Monster, and CollegeRecruiter.
- To find a job with a specific company, go directly to that company's website and social media to check its job openings and other possibilities.
- For jobs in specialized fields, search some of the many niche sites, such as Dice for technology positions or CoolWorks for seasonal employment.
- Take advantage of mobile apps to access and vet job openings as soon as they are listed.
- Protect yourself when using online job boards by posting privately, not revealing personal information, keeping careful records, and avoiding blind job postings.

**3  Identify job-search strategies that unlock the hidden job market.**

- Estimates suggest that as many as 80 percent of jobs are in the hidden job market—that is, never advertised. Successful job candidates find jobs in the hidden job market through networking.
- An effective networking strategy involves (a) developing a contact list, (b) reaching out to these contacts in person and online in search of referrals, and (c) following up on referrals.
- Because electronic media and digital tools continue to change our lives, savvy candidates use social media networks—especially LinkedIn—to extend their networking efforts.
- Invaluable in a job search, LinkedIn enables candidates to receive job alerts, leverage their networks, research companies, ask for recommendations, and help companies locate them online.
- Effective networking strategies include building a personal brand, preparing a professional business card with a tagline, composing a 60-second elevator speech that describes what you can offer, and developing a strong online presence.

**4  Explain how to organize your qualifications and skills into effective categories for résumés and an engaging LinkedIn profile.**

- Because of intense competition, you must customize your résumé to appeal to an applicant tracking system (ATS) as well as to a human reader.

- Chronological résumés, which list work and education by dates, rank highest with recruiters. Functional résumés, which highlight skills instead of jobs, may be helpful for people with little experience, those changing careers, and those with negative employment histories.
- Arrange your skills and achievements to aim at a particular job or company.
- Study models to effectively arrange the résumé main heading and the optional career objective, summary of qualifications, education, work experience, capabilities, awards, and activities sections.
- The most effective résumés include action verbs to appeal to human readers and job-specific nouns that become keywords selected by ATS.
- Prepare a LinkedIn page with a headline, photo, and profile, which includes information about your education, skills, and experience. Encourage your instructors and employers to post recommendations.

## 5 Describe digital tools that can enhance your job search and résumé.

- To maximize the rank of your résumé by an applicant tracking system, include job-specific keywords such as nouns that name job titles, technical skills, and tools used or relevant experience.
- Consider preparing a career e-portfolio to showcase your qualifications. This collection of digital files can feature your talents, accomplishments, and technical skills. It may include examples of academic performance, photographs, multimedia files, and other items beyond what can be shown in a résumé.
- A video résumé enables you to present your experience, qualifications, and interests in video form.
- Start with a basic print-based résumé from which you can make a plain-text résumé stripped of formatting to be embedded within e-mail messages or submitted to online application forms.
- Decide whether to submit your résumé as a Word, plain-text, or PDF document. You may be asked to enter your information into a company database.

## 6 Analyze the importance and construction of customized cover messages.

- Cover letters still play an important role in the job application process, especially to hiring managers.
- Cover letters help recruiters make decisions, and they enable candidates to set themselves apart from others.
- In the opening of a cover letter, gain attention by addressing the receiver by name and identifying the job. You might also identify the person who referred you.
- In the body of the letter, build interest by stressing your strengths in relation to the stated requirements. Explain what you can do for the targeted company.
- In the body or closing, refer to your résumé, request an interview, and make it easy for the receiver to respond.
- If you are submitting your cover message by e-mail, shorten it a bit and include your complete contact information in the signature block.

## Key Terms

## Chapter Review

1. Describe the challenges of the job market in the wake of the COVID-19 pandemic and the skills that will help you weather any economic climate. (L.O. 1)

2. List seven ways you can prepare for career opportunities in a dynamic job market while still in college (L.O. 1)

3. Although one may not actually find a job on the Internet, how can the big job boards be helpful to job hunters? (L.O. 2)

4. What is the difference between the open job market and the hidden job market, and how can candidates find jobs in each? (L.O. 2, 3)

5. In searching for a job, how can you build a personal brand, and why is it important to do so? (L.O. 3)

6. How do chronological and functional résumés differ, and what are the advantages and disadvantages of each? (L.O. 4)

7. Describe a summary of qualifications, and explain why it is increasingly popular on résumés. (L.O. 4)

8. What is a career e-portfolio? How can having one benefit you? (L.O. 5)

9. How can you maximize the rank of your résumé when it is going to be evaluated by an ATS? (L.O. 5)

10. Why is it smart to include a customized, job-relevant cover letter with all résumés you send, regardless of whether you send them by e-mail or expect them to be first read by an ATS? (L.O. 6)

## Critical Thinking

11. When asked whether they would take full-time gig work over a traditional job, 53 percent of Generation Z (born 1997–2012) respondents in a global study said yes.[43] Commissioned by the Workforce Institute of Kronos, this study, titled "Gen Z and the Gig Economy: It's Time to Gig in or Get Out," surveyed 3,400 individuals around the world. What is it about gig work that appeals to Gen Z people and others? What disadvantages do you see? (L.O. 1–4)

12. "If you are starting your job search with Monster.com, CareerBuilder, or similar search tools, then you are starting at the end of the chain," claims job-search author Ryan Guina.[44] What do you think he means? (L.O. 2, 3)

13. Why do you think some businesses avoid advertising job openings? If jobs are unlisted, how can candidates locate them? (L.O. 3)

14. Although it is highly recommended that new grads complete and maintain a LinkedIn profile, some critics charge that LinkedIn is a waste of time because it has become bogged down with spam connection requests, posturing, and users' attempts to market products instead of building relationships, as originally intended.[45] As a job candidate, will you post and maintain your résumé information on LinkedIn? Why or why not? How could candidates make better use of LinkedIn? (L.O. 4)

15. Phantom job listings are announcements for jobs that have already been filled through informal networking processes. The public job posting is necessary to comply with human resources department rules that mandate the advertising of open positions. Sometimes the job has been filled by an internal candidate who already had the position nailed down. Although not required by law, management policies and human resources departments at many companies demand that hiring managers list all openings on job boards or career sites. Often, hiring managers have already selected candidates for these phantom jobs. Do you believe it is ethical to advertise jobs that are not really available?[46] (L.O. 1–5)

# Radical Rewrites

**Note:** Radical Rewrites are available at the accompanying student site for you to download and revise. Your instructor may show a suggested solution.

## 13.1 Radical Rewrite: Poorly Written Résumé (L.O. 4)

One effective way to improve your writing skills is to critique and edit the résumé of someone else.

**YOUR TASK.** Analyze Elliana's poorly written résumé. List at least eight weaknesses. Your instructor may ask you to revise sections of this résumé before showing you an improved version.

**Résumé**
**Annalise Ortez-Villa**
1340 East Phillips Ave., Apt. D Littleton, CO 80126
Phone 455-5182 • E-Mail: Hotchilibabe@gmail.com | LinkedIn

**OBJECTIVE**

I'm dying to become an accounting associate in the "real world" with a big profitable company that will help me get the experience I need to become a CPA.

**SKILLS**

Microsoft Word, MS Outlook, MS Office, Powerpoint, Excel, spreadsheets Excel; experienced with QuickBooks, great composure in stressful situations; 3 years as leader and supervisor and 4 years in customer service

**EDUCATION**

Arapahoe Community College, Littleton, Colorado. AA degree Fall 2019

Now I am pursuing a BA in Accounting at CSU-Pueblo, majoring in Accounting; my minor is Finance. Completed 64 units of upper-division units. My expected degree date is June 2022; I recieved a Certificate of Completion in Entry Level Accounting in December 2019. GPA: 3.5

I graduated East High School, Denver, CO in 2015.

**Highlights:**

- Named Line Manger of the Month at Target, 10/2018 and 03/2018
- Obtained a Certificate in Entry Level Accounting, June 2019
- Chair of Accounting Society, Spring and fall 2021
- Dean's Honor List, Fall 2021
- Financial advisor training completed through Primerica (May 2020)
- Webmaster for M.E.Ch.A, Spring 2021
- Chair, American Accounting Association (AAA), Spring & Fall 2020

**Part-Time Employment**

Financial Consultant, 2020 to present
I worked only part-time (January 2020-present) for Primerica Financial Services, Pueblo, CO to assist clients in refinancing a mortgage or consolidating a current mortgage loan and also to advice clients in assessing their need for life insurance.

Target, Littleton, CO. As line manager, from September 2018-August 2019, I supervised 12 cashiers and front-end associates. I helped to write schedules, disciplinary action notices, and performance appraisals. I also kept track of change drawer and money exchanges; occasionally was manager on duty for entire store. Named line manager of the month August 2018 and March 2019.

Mr. K's Floral Design of Denver. I taught flower design from August, 2017 to September, 2018. I supervised 5 florists, made floral arrangements for big events like weddings, send them to customers, and restocked flowers.

## 13.2 Radical Rewrite: Inadequate Cover Letter (L.O. 6)

The following cover letter accompanies Annalise Ortez-Villa's résumé (**Radical Rewrite 13.1**). Like this applicant's résumé, the cover letter needs major revision.

**YOUR TASK.** Analyze each section of the following cover letter and list at least eight weaknesses. Your instructor may ask you to revise this letter before showing you an improved version.

To Whom It May Concern:

I saw your accounting position listing yesterday and would like to apply right away. It would be so exiting to work for your esteemed firm! This position would really give me much needed real-world experience and help me become a CPA.

I have all the qualifications you require in your add and more. I am a senior at Colorado State University-Pueblo and an Accounting major (with a minor in Finance) and have completed 64 units of upper-division course work. Accounting and Finance are my passion and I want to become a CPA and a financial advisor. I have taken eight courses in accounting and now work as a part-time financial advisor with Primerica Financial Services in Pueblo. I should also tell you that I was at Target for four years. I learned alot, but my heart is in accounting and finance.

I am a team player, a born leader, motivated, reliable, and I show excellent composure in stressful situation, for example, when customers complain. I put myself through school and always carry at least 12 units while working part time.

You will probably agree that I am a good candidate for your internship position, which I understand should start July 1. I feel that my motivation, passion, and strong people skills will serve your company well.

Sincerely,

## Activities and Cases

## 13.3 Opening Your Job Search With Self-Analysis (L.O. 1)

**E-Mail**

As you have seen earlier, the first step in a job search is analyzing your interests and goals and evaluating your qualifications. The following questions may help guide you to a satisfying career:

- What are you passionate about? Can you turn this passion into a career?
- Do you enjoy working with people, data, or things?
- How important are salary, benefits, technology support, and job stimulation?
- Must you work in a specific city, geographical area, or climate?
- Are you looking for security, travel opportunities, money, power, or prestige?
- How would you describe the perfect job, boss, and coworkers?

**YOUR TASK.** In an e-mail or a memo addressed to your instructor, answer the questions above that appear in the section "Starting Your Job Search With Self-Analysis." Draw a conclusion from your answers. What kind of career, company, position, and location have emerged from your self-analysis?

## 13.4 Taking Stock of Your Qualifications (L.O. 1, 4)

Before attempting to put together a winning résumé, take the following steps that will help you make the important task of creating a compelling job application easier.

**YOUR TASK.** Prepare four worksheets that inventory your qualifications in these areas: employment; education; capabilities and skills; and awards, honors, and activities. Use active verbs when appropriate and specific nouns that describe job titles and skills.

a. **Employment.** Begin with your most recent job or internship. For each position list the following information: employer; job title; dates of employment; and three to five duties, activities, or accomplishments. Emphasize activities related to your job goal. Strive to quantify your achievements.

b. **Education.** List degrees, certificates, and training accomplishments. Include courses, seminars, and skills that are relevant to your job goal. Calculate your grade point average in your major.

c. **Capabilities and skills.** List all capabilities and skills that qualify you for the job you seek. Use words and phrases such as *skilled, competent, trained, experienced*, and *ability to*. Also list five or more qualities or interpersonal skills necessary for success in your chosen field. Write action statements demonstrating that you possess some of these qualities. Empty assurances aren't good enough; try to show evidence (*Developed teamwork skills by working with a committee of eight to produce a. . .*).

d. **Awards, honors, and activities.** Explain any awards so that the reader will understand them. List campus, community, and professional activities that suggest you are a well-rounded individual or possess traits relevant to your target job.

## 13.5 Building Your Future by Choosing a Career Path (L.O. 1)
> Communication Technology > Web

Many people know amazingly little about the work done in various occupations and the training requirements.

**YOUR TASK.** Visit O*Net Online at **https://www.onetonline.org**, run by the U.S. Department of Labor's Bureau of Labor Statistics (BLS), to learn more about an occupation of your choice. This is the nation's premier source for career information. It provides detailed descriptions of the world of work for use by job seekers, workforce development and HR professionals, students, and researchers.

The career profiles featured cover hundreds of occupations and describe what people in these occupations do, the work environment, how to get these jobs, how much they earn, and more. The listings range alphabetically from Actuaries to Wind Turbine Service Technicians. Did you know that the median salary for a wind turbine technician is $56,230? Not bad, right?

Find the description of a position for which you could apply in two to five years. Learn about what workers do on the job, working conditions, training and education needed, earnings, and expected job prospects. Print or save the pages from the occupational listings that describe employment in the area in which you are interested. If your instructor directs, attach these copies to the cover letter you will write in **Activity 13.9**, or post them to your learning-management system (e.g., Canvas or Blackboard).

## 13.6 Discovering Salary Information (L.O. 1)
> Web

What salary can you expect in your chosen career? Wouldn't you like to know?

**YOUR TASK.** Visit **http://www.salary.com** and select an occupation based on the kind of employment you are seeking now or will be seeking after you graduate. In the text boxes below the heading Individuals (What am I worth?), enter the job title and desired location. What wages or salary can you expect in this occupation? Click on the job title to learn more about this occupation. Browse benefits, compare jobs, and find openings. Take notes on three or four interesting bits of information you uncovered about this type of job. Save the compensation information for easy access and sharing with fellow students, or bring a printout to class. Be prepared to discuss what you learned.

Alternatively, use **https://www.glassdoor.com**, a social network of company or industry insiders and current as well as past employees. The anonymous evaluations of businesses and their management on Glassdoor are candid. They provide a snapshot of companies' practices, culture, interview questions, regional median base salaries, CEO approval ratings, and other hard-to-find information. Glassdoor seems more comprehensive than Salary.com, even though its graphics are not as snazzy.

## 13.7 Exploring the Job Market (L.O. 1)
> Web

Where are the jobs? Even though you may not be in the job market yet, become familiar with the kinds of available positions because job awareness should be an important part of your education.

**YOUR TASK.** Save, clip, or print a job advertisement or announcement from (a) a social media site, (b) the job ad section of an online newspaper, (c) a job board, (d) a company website, or (e) a professional association listing. Select an advertisement or job listing describing the kind of employment you are seeking now or plan to seek when you graduate. Save this ad or job listing to attach to the résumé and cover letter you will write in **Activities 13.8** and **13.9**.

## 13.8 Writing Your Résumé (L.O. 4)
> Team

After taking stock of your qualifications and investigating career opportunities, you are ready to compile your résumé.

**YOUR TASK.** Using the data you developed in **Activity 13.4**, write your résumé. Aim it at the full-time job, part-time position, or internship that you located in **Activity 13.7**. Attach the job or internship listing to your résumé. Also prepare a list of references. Your instructor may assign a peer or small-group editing session. Revise your résumé until it is perfect.

## 13.9 Preparing Your Customized, Job-Relevant Cover Message (L.O. 6)

> **E-Mail** > **Team**

As we have seen, although some recruiters don't consider cover letters important, most hiring professionals (87 percent) *do* read them. The same study also found that higher callback rates (31 percent) and interviews (53 percent) resulted from applications with specific, job-relevant cover letters.[47]

**YOUR TASK.** Using the job listing you found for **Activity 13.7**, write a cover message introducing your résumé. Decide whether it should be a letter or an e-mail. Review the chapter discussion of cover messages. If your instructor directs, you may get help from your peers in editing and polishing your cover message. Again, revise until it is perfect.

## 13.10 Taking Your Job Search to LinkedIn (L.O. 2)

> **Social Media** > **Team** > **Web**

Despite criticism, LinkedIn is the acknowledged No. 1 site for job seekers and recruiters. It's free and easy to join. Even if you are not in the job market yet, becoming familiar with LinkedIn can open your eyes to the kinds of information that employers seek and also give you practice in filling in templates such as those that applicant tracking systems employ.

**YOUR TASK.** If you haven't done so already, set up a LinkedIn account and complete a profile. This consists of a template with categories to fill in. The easiest way to begin is to view a LinkedIn video taking you through the steps of creating a profile. Search for *LinkedIn Profile Checklist*. It discusses how to fill in information in categories such as the following:

- **Profile Picture.** Have a friend or a professional take a photo that shows your head and shoulders. No selfies! Wear work-appropriate attire and a smile.
- **Headline.** Use a tagline to summarize your professional goals.
- **Summary.** Explain what motivates you, what you are skilled at, and where you want to go in the future.
- **Experience.** List the jobs you have held, and be sure to enter the information precisely in the template categories. You can even include photos and videos of your work.

You can fill in other categories such as Skills, Endorsements, and Recommendations. After completing a profile, discuss your LinkedIn experience with classmates. If you already have an account set up, discuss how it operates and your opinion of its worth. How can LinkedIn help students now and in the future?

## 13.11 Deploying a Twitter Mini Résumé as a LinkedIn Alternative (L.O. 5)

> **Social Media** > **Team** > **Web**

Twitter may not be the first social media site you consider for posting your résumé. Savvy candidates, however, know that Twitter has one major advantage over more obvious sites such as LinkedIn and Facebook. Twitter is an unsaturated market where your brand and mini résumé could separate you from the crowd. Everyone wants to read less, including hiring managers. In up to 280 characters, your main selling points in a mini Twitter résumé would be an appealing, easy read.

The Twitter résumé teasers below present just enough information to tantalize a hiring manager looking for someone who fits her profile. In preparing a more professional Twitter résumé, include the job title you are seeking, your strongest and most relevant skills, and where you are now or wish to relocate. Use hyperlinks to refer readers to your full information on LinkedIn or your website. Use job-related hashtags for your desired position to attract employers seeking such a worker. To explore examples, conduct a Google search for *Twitter resumes*. Following are a few fun examples of content. Can you do better?

- Copywriter for print/online. Photo editor. Fashion/luxury market. #copywriter #fashionluxurymarket
- Recent grad. Intern experience in marketing/communication in NYC. Will relocate. #communicationinternship #marketingcommunication
- Data analyst. Coffee lover. Full-time cat mom. Database extraordinaire. Ref: Acct mgr @ABCLtd.#dataanalyst

**YOUR TASK.** Compose three possible mini Twitter résumés using your information. Your instructor may ask you to present them for discussion in class or in your chat/discussion group.

## 13.12 Analyzing and Building Student E-Portfolios (L.O. 5)

> **Communication Technology** > **E-Mail** > **Team** > **Web**

Take a minute to conduct a Google search on your name. Try enclosing your full name in quotations marks to lower the number of irrelevant hits. What comes up? Are you proud of what you see? If you want to change that information—and especially if you are in the job market—think about creating a career e-portfolio. Building such a portfolio has many benefits. It can give you an important digital tool to connect with a large audience. It can also help you expand your technology skills, confirm your strengths, recognize areas you need to develop, and establish goals for improvement. Many students are creating e-portfolios with the help of their colleges.

**YOUR TASK NO. 1.** Before attempting to build your own career e-portfolio, take a look at those of other students. Use the Google search term *student career e-portfolio* (try the phrase with or without quotation marks) to see lots of samples. Your instructor may assign you individually or as a team to visit specific digital portfolio sites and summarize your findings in a memo, an e-mail, or a brief oral presentation. You could focus on user and mobile friendliness, site design, page layout, links provided, software tools used, colors selected, or types of documents included.

**YOUR TASK NO. 2.** Next, examine websites that provide tutorials and tips on how to build career e-portfolios. Your instructor may have you individually or as a team write a memo or an e-mail summarizing tips on how to create an e-portfolio and choose the types of documents to include. Alternatively, your instructor may ask you to create your own career e-portfolio. Your college may even offer hosting. Inquire in your college of business or the career services department at your university.

## Grammar/Mechanics Checkup 13

## Number Style

Review Sections 4.01–4.13 in the Grammar/Mechanics Handbook. Then study each of the following pairs. Assume that these expressions appear in the context of e-mails, letters, reports, or memos. Write *a* or *b* in the space provided to indicate the preferred number style and record the number of the Grammar/Mechanics principle illustrated. When you finish, compare your responses with those at the bottom of this page. If your answers differ, study carefully the appropriate principles.

| | | |
|---|---|---|
| _____a____ (4.01a)____ | **EXAMPLE:** a. three new routers | b. 3 new routers |
| _____ | 1. a. thirteen club members | b. 13 club members |
| _____ | 2. a. Sixth Street | b. 6th Street |
| _____ | 3. a. thirty-two mini netbooks | b. 32 mini netbooks |
| _____ | 4. a. August 2nd | b. August 2 |
| _____ | 5. a. fifty dollars | b. $50 |
| _____ | 6. a. on the 18th of December | b. on the eighteen of December |
| _____ | 7. a. at 8:00 a.m. | b. at 8 a.m. |
| _____ | 8. a. 5 100-page proposals | b. five 100-page proposals |
| _____ | 9. a. more than twenty years ago | b. more than 20 years ago |
| _____ | 10. a. 9,700,000 unemployed workers | b. 9.7 million unemployed workers |

**1.** b (4.01a) **2.** a (4.05b) **3.** b (4.01a) **4.** b (4.03) **5.** b (4.02) **6.** a (4.03) **7.** b (4.04) **8.** b (4.07) **9.** b (4.08) **10.** b (4.10)

Every chapter provides an editing exercise to fine-tune your grammar and mechanics skills. The following résumé requires edits that address grammar, punctuation, capitalization, number form, and other writing issues. Study the guidelines in the Grammar/Mechanics Handbook (Appendix D), including the lists of Confusing Words and Frequently Misspelled Words.

**YOUR TASK.** Edit the following (a) by inserting corrections in your textbook or on a photocopy using the proofreading marks in Appendix C or (b) by downloading the message from the accompanying student site and correcting it at your computer.

---

### Sage W. Benton

1246 East 9th Avenue                                         swbenton@cybermw.com
Grand Rapids, Mich. 49510

**SUMMARY OF QUALIFICATIONS**

- Over three years experience working in customer relations
- Partnered with Assistant Manager to create mass mailing by merging three thousand customers names and addresses in ad campaign
- Hold AA Degree in Administrative Assisting
- Proficient with MS Word, excel, powerpoint, and the internet

**EXPERIENCE**

**Administrative Assistant,** Spencer Mold and Machine Company, Gran Rapids, Michigan
June 2021 to present
- Answer phones, respond to e-mail and gather information for mold designers
- Key board and format proposals for various machine Platforms and Configurations
- Help company with correspondence to fulfill it's guarantee that a prototype mold can be produced in less than 1 week
- Worked with Assistant Manger to create large customer mailings; enter data in Excel

**Shift Supervisor,** Old City Coffee Shop, Grand Rapids, Michigan
May 2020 to May 2021
- Trained 3 new employees, opened and closed shop handled total sales
- Managed shop in the owners absence
- Builded satisfied customer relationships

**Server, Hostess, Expeditor, Busser,** Roadside Girll, Toledo, Ohio
April 2018 to April 2020
- Helped Owner expand menu from twenty to thirty-five items
- Develop procedures that reduce average customer wait time from sixteen to eight minutes

**AWARDS AND ACHEIVEMENTS**
- Deans List, Spring, 2020, Fall, 2020
- Awarded 2nd prize in advertise essay contest, 2020

**EDUCATION**
- AA degree, Kendall Comunity College, 2021
- Major: Office Administation and Technology
  GPA in major: 3.8 (4.0 = A)

# Communication Workshop: Ethics

## Résumé Padding: Worth the Risk?

Given today's competitive job market, it might be tempting to pad your résumé. **Résumé padding** means adding false or exaggerated information to boost your credentials for a job. Unfortunately, this happens more often than we might think. A CareerBuilder survey of 2,500 hiring and human resources managers revealed that 75 percent have caught a lie on a résumé.[48] A Jobvite employer survey found that the five most common falsehoods involve technical skills (50 percent), experience (48 percent), competitive offers (35 percent), and salary history (31 percent).[49]

Candidates may embellish to qualify for a position, but it's a risky game. Background checks are easy thanks to the Internet and specialists who sniff out untruths. What's more, puffing up one's qualifications may be unnecessary. Another CareerBuilder survey revealed that 42 percent of employers would consider a candidate who met only three out of five key qualifications for a job.[50]

After they have been hired, candidates may think they are safe—but organizations often continue the checking process, incompetence may manifest itself, or the truth comes out by coincidence. If hiring managers find a discrepancy in a GPA or prior experience and the error is an honest mistake, they meet with the new-hire to hear an explanation. If the discrepancy wasn't a mistake, they will likely fire the person immediately.

No job seeker wants to be in the unhappy position of explaining résumé errors or defending misrepresentation. Avoiding the following actions can keep a job candidate off the hot seat:

- **Enhancing education, grades, or honors.** Some job candidates claim degrees from colleges or universities when in fact they merely attended classes. Others increase their grade point averages or claim fictitious honors. Any such dishonest reporting is grounds for dismissal when discovered.

- **Inflating job titles and salaries.** Wishing to elevate their status, some applicants misrepresent their titles or increase their past salaries. For example, one technician called himself a programmer when he had actually programmed only one project for his boss. A mail clerk who assumed added responsibilities conferred upon herself the title of supervisor.

- **Puffing up accomplishments.** Job seekers may inflate their employment experience or achievements. One clerk, eager to make her photocopying duties sound more important, said that she assisted the *vice president in communicating and distributing employee directives.* Similarly, guard against taking sole credit for achievements that required many people. When recruiters suspect dubious claims on résumés, they nail applicants with specific—and often embarrassing—questions during their interviews.

- **Altering employment dates.** Some candidates extend the dates of employment to hide unimpressive jobs or positions they lost. Others try to hide periods of unemployment and illness. Although their employment histories have no gaps, their résumés are dishonest and represent potential booby traps.

**CAREER APPLICATION.** Alyson finally got an interview for the perfect job. The big problem, however, is that she padded her résumé a little by making the gaps in her job history a bit smaller. Oh, yes, and she increased her last job title from administrative assistant to project manager. After all, she was really doing a lot of his work. Now she's worried about the upcoming interview. She's considering coming clean and telling the truth. On the other hand, she wonders whether it is too late to submit an updated résumé and tell the interviewer that she noticed some errors. Of course, she could do nothing. A final possibility is withdrawing her application.

**YOUR TASK.** In groups, discuss Alyson's options. What would you advise her to do? Why?

# Interviewing and Following Up

Shift Drive/Shutterstock.com

**Learning Outcomes**

After studying this chapter, you should be able to do the following:

**1** Explain current trends as well as the purposes, sequence, and types of job interviews.

**2** Describe how to prepare *before* a job interview.

**3** Describe what to do *during* a job interview.

**4** Describe what to do *after* a job interview.

**5** Prepare additional employment documents.

## 14-1 Sharpening Your Interview Skills

Whether you are completing your education or are in the workforce and striving to advance your career, a job interview can be life changing. Because employment is a major part of most people's life, the job interview takes on enormous importance. An excellent résumé, an engaging cover letter, and good references will help you secure an interview. None of these, however, will automatically get you hired. Only when you talk directly to the hiring manager will an organization be motivated to hire you.

Most candidates fear job interviews almost as much as making a speech or going on a first date. However, despite the importance of the interview, too many job applicants fail to prepare sufficiently. The truth is, though, that the more you learn about the process and the more prepared you are, the less stress you will feel. Moreover, a job interview is a two-way street. It is not just about being judged by the employer. You, the applicant, will be using the job interview to evaluate the employer. Do you really want to work for this organization?

To be successful in a competitive job market, you must keep up with the latest trends and techniques that recruiters use to select the very best candidates. **Figure 14.1** describes seven trends job candidates face today. This chapter offers the latest tips as well as traditional techniques that will improve your interviewing skills and boost your confidence.

## LEARNING OUTCOME 1

Explain current trends as well as the purposes, sequence, and types of job interviews.

**Figure 14.1  Latest Trends in Interviewing**

**Increasing use of artificial intelligence.** AI-powered psychometric assessment tests and games are designed to measure a candidate's strengths and weaknesses.

**Video interviewing.** Structured videos save time, reduce expenses, avoid travel, and improve consistency.

**Stretched-out sessions.** Employers take longer to hire as they seek the best cultural fit.

**Hiring for professional skills and potential.** Competencies such as creativity, adaptability, and ability to learn on the job are priorities.

**Group interviews.** Employers may interview many candidates together, or multiple hiring managers may interview one candidate individually.

**Project testing.** Job auditions test the abilities of candidates in real-world scenarios.

**Behavioral and situational questions.** Interviews include requests that begin with "Tell me about a time when you. . ." or questions that pose what-if situations about issues that could arise on the job.

ESB Professional/Shutterstock.com

Guffey, "Business Communication: Process and Product" Cengage Learning

Yes, job interviews can be intimidating and stressful. However, you can expect to ace an interview when you know what's coming and prepare thoroughly. Remember, preparation often determines who gets the job. First, though, you need to know the purposes of employment interviews, the typical sequence of events, and the types of interviews you might encounter in your job search.

## 14-1a  Purposes and Sequencing of Employment Interviews

An interview has several purposes for you as a job candidate. It is an opportunity to (a) convince the employer of your potential, (b) learn more about the job and the company, and (c) elaborate on the information in your résumé. This is the time for you to gather information to determine whether you would fit into the company culture. You should also be thinking about whether this job suits your career goals.

## Figure 14.2 Six Stages of the Hiring Process

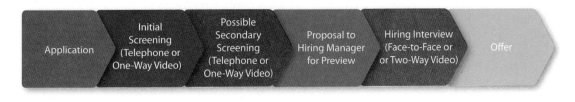

Application → Initial Screening (Telephone or One-Way Video) → Possible Secondary Screening (Telephone or One-Way Video) → Proposal to Hiring Manager for Preview → Hiring Interview (Face-to-Face or or Two-Way Video) → Offer

From the employer's perspective, the interview is an opportunity to (a) assess your abilities in relation to the requirements of the position; (b) discuss your training, experience, knowledge, and abilities in more detail; (c) see what drives and motivates you; and (d) decide whether you would fit into the organization.

The hiring process often follows a six-stage sequence, as illustrated in **Figure 14.2**. Following the job application, interviews proceed from screening to hiring interviews.

## 14-1b Screening Interviews

A **screening interview** does just that—it screens candidates to eliminate those who fail to meet minimum requirements. Companies use screening interviews to save time and money by weeding out lesser-qualified candidates before scheduling final face-to-face or video interviews. Although initial screening interviews may be conducted during job fairs or on college campuses, they usually take place by telephone or video.

During an initial screening interview, the interviewer will probably ask you to provide details about the education and experience listed on your résumé; therefore, you must be prepared to promote your qualifications. If you do well in the initial interview, you may be invited to a secondary screening interview. This interview may be conducted by a human resources specialist with more specific questions relating to the open position. It could be a telephone or a video interview scheduled on Zoom, Skype, or one of the many video interviewing platforms favored by HR professionals. The interviewer is trying to decide whether you are a strong enough candidate to be interviewed by a hiring manager.

## 14-1c Hiring/Placement Interview

The most promising candidates selected from screening interviews are invited to a **hiring/placement interview**. Hiring managers want to learn whether candidates are motivated, qualified, and a good fit for the position. Their goal is to learn how the candidate would fit into their organization. Conducted in depth, hiring/placement interviews may take many forms, such as the following:

One-on-One Interview. In a **one-on-one interview**, which is most common, you can expect to sit down with a company representative and talk about the job and your qualifications. If the representative is the hiring manager, questions will be specific and job related. If the representative is from human resources, the questions will probably be more general.

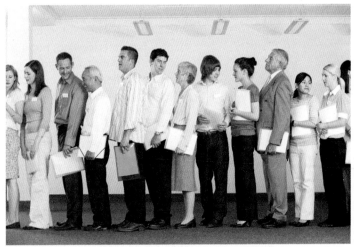

Group interviews can be stressful and frustrating for interviewees. However, employers who use this tool believe that "cattle-call" interviews allow them to rank candidates quickly in the categories of teamwork, leadership, and stress management.

**Panel Interview.** A **panel interview** is typically conducted by people who will be your supervisors and colleagues. Usually seated around a table, interviewers take turns asking questions. Panel interviews are advantageous because they save the company time and money, and they show you how the staff works together. If possible before these interviews, try to gather basic biographical information about each panel member. This information may be available on the company website or LinkedIn. When answering questions, maintain eye contact with the questioner as well as with the others. Expect to repeat information you may have given in earlier interviews. Take paper-and-pen notes during the interview so that you can remember each person's questions and what was important to that individual. Don't take notes on a laptop or other mobile device as interviewers may think you are checking incoming messages.

**Group Interview.** A **group interview** is one in which a company interviews several candidates for the same position at the same time. Some employers use this technique to evaluate leadership skills and communication styles. During a group interview, stay focused on the interviewer, and treat the other candidates with respect. Even if you are nervous, try to remain calm, take your time when responding, and express yourself clearly. The key during a group interview is to make yourself stand out from the other candidates in a positive way.[1]

**Sequential Interview.** In a **sequential interview**, you meet individually with two or more interviewers one-on-one over the course of several hours or days. It is not uncommon for a job candidate to endure three or more interviews over an extended period of time. For example, you may meet with human resources representatives, the hiring manager, and potential future supervisors and colleagues in your division or department. Listen carefully and respond positively to all interviewers. Promote your qualifications to each one; don't assume that any interviewer knows what was said in a previous interview. Keep your responses fresh, even when repeating yourself many times over. Subsequent interviews also tend to be more in depth than first interviews, which means that you need to be even more prepared and know even more about the company.

**Video Interview.** A **one-way video interview** is one in which a candidate responds to a list of scripted questions prepared by the hiring organization. When convenient, the candidate creates a video recording of the answers. The interviewer can view the job seeker, but the job seeker cannot see the interviewer. One-way interviewing benefits employers by cutting the time needed to meet lots of candidates. One-way interviewing also benefits candidates by enabling them to be interviewed at their leisure without traveling to distant locations. Candidates also can practice and perfect their responses by rerecording.

A **two-way video interview**, sometimes called a **live video interview**, is like regular face-to-face interviewing, but it is conducted by video call. A key advantage of two-way interviewing is that it provides an interactive forum enabling hiring companies to better assess a candidate's communication skills, body language, and personality. Preparing for either a one-way or a two-way video interview is extremely important; check out **Figure 14.3** for tips to help you succeed in video interviews.

No matter what type of interview you encounter, you will feel more comfortable if you know what to do before, during, and after the interview.

## 14-2 Before the Interview

**LEARNING OUTCOME 2**
Describe how to prepare *before* a job interview.

Once you have sent out at least one résumé or filled out at least one job application, consider yourself an active job seeker. Being active in the job market means that you should be prepared to be contacted by potential employers. As discussed earlier, employers often use screening interviews to narrow the list of candidates. If you do well in the screening interview, you will be invited to an in-person or video meeting. Screening interviews should be taken seriously.

**Figure 14.3   How to Ace a Video Job Interview**

| | |
|---|---|
| **Do your homework.** | Learn all that you can about the target company including its competitors, products, and goals. |
| **Plan your answers.** | For one-way interviews, questions provided in advance allow you to prepare perfect responses. For two-way interviews, practice answering typical questions until you can respond while looking into the camera. |
| **Check your tech.** | Ensure your webcam and microphone work. Position the camera at eye level. Close any unnecessary web browser tabs and applications. |
| **Adjust your lighting** | Place lights behind your computer and overhead so that your face is not in the shadows. |
| **Control your surroundings.** | Sit in a quiet room with a neat, neutral background. Avoid noise such as barking dogs, crying children, flushing toilets, or ringing cell phones. |
| **Dress to impress.** | Be well groomed. When applying for a professional position, wear a suit. Avoid distracting prints, disturbingly bright colors, and loud jewelry. |
| **Rehearse.** | Aim to be natural and comfortable in providing answers but avoid sounding mechanical. This requires lots of practice. |
| **Be the best you can be.** | Sit up straight. Don't let your eyes drop as if reading from a script. Don't mumble or fidget. Be upbeat and use positive words. Focus on answers and stories that show you match the skills listed in the job description. |

## 14-2a   Preparing for a Screening Telephone Call

Even with the popularity of texting and e-mail, most employers first contact job applicants by phone to set up interviews. Employers can judge how well applicants communicate by hearing their voices and expressions over the phone. Once you are actively looking for a job, anytime the phone rings, it could be a potential employer. Don't make the mistake of letting an unprofessional voice mail message or a lazy roommate or a sloppy cell phone manner ruin your chances. To make the best impression, try these tips:

- In your voice mail, make sure your outgoing message is concise and professional, with no distracting background sounds. It should be in your own voice and include your full name for clarity. You can find more tips for leaving professional telephone messages in Chapter 11.

- Tell others who might answer your phone at home about your job search. Explain to them the importance of acting professionally and taking complete messages. Family members or roommates can affect the first impression an employer has of you.

- If you have children, prevent them from answering the phone during your job search. Children of all ages are not known for taking good messages!

- If you have listed your cell phone number on your résumé and elsewhere, don't answer unless you are in a good location to carry on a conversation with an employer. It is hard to pay close attention while driving, even with hands-free equipment, or while eating in a noisy restaurant!

- Use voice mail to screen calls. By screening incoming calls, you can be totally in control when you return a prospective employer's call. Organize your materials and ready yourself psychologically for the conversation.

## 14-2b Making the First Conversation Impressive

Whether you answer the phone directly or return an employer's call, make sure you are prepared for the conversation. Remember that this is the first time the employer has heard your voice. How you conduct yourself on the phone will create a lasting impression. To make that first impression a positive one, follow these tips:

- Keep a list on your cell phone or near your landline of positions for which you have applied.

- Treat any call from an employer just like an interview. Use a professional tone and businesslike language. Be polite and enthusiastic, and sell your qualifications.

- If caught off guard by the call, ask whether you can call back in a few minutes. Take that time to organize your materials and yourself.

- Have the job description and your résumé available so that you can answer any questions that come up. Also have your list of references, a calendar, and a digital or paper notepad handy.

- Be prepared for a screening interview. As discussed earlier, the screening might begin with the first phone call.

- Take good notes during the phone conversation. Obtain accurate directions if necessary, and verify the spelling of your interviewer's name. If you will be interviewed by more than one person, get all of their names.

- If given a chance, ask for an interview on Tuesday at 10:30 a.m. This is considered the most opportune time. Avoid the start of the day on Monday and the end of the day on Friday.[2]

- Before you hang up, reconfirm the date and time of your interview. You could say something like *I look forward to meeting with you next Wednesday, May 18, at 11 a.m.*

## 14-2c Learning About the Target Company

One of the best ways to become a stand-out candidate during the hiring process is to investigate thoroughly the target organization. Once you have scheduled an in-person or video interview, you need to start preparing for it. Never enter an interview cold. Recruiters are impressed by candidates who have done their homework.

**Scouring the Internet for Important Company Data.** Search the potential employer's website, news sources, trade journals, industry directories, and social media presence. Follow the official company Twitter feed, and read the tweets of the firm's top managers and other industry influencers. Unearth information about the job, the company, and the industry. Learn all you can about the company's history, mission and goals, size, geographic locations, and number of employees. Check out its customers, competitors, culture, management structure, reputation in the community, financial condition, strengths and weaknesses, and future plans, as well as the names of its corporate officers or principals. A good place to start is the About Us section on an organization's website. In addition, look for company blogs. Blogs are excellent sources for company research. Finally, don't forget to google the interviewer.

**Analyzing the Company's Advertising.** In addition to its online presence, examine the company's ads and promotional materials, including sales and marketing information often available as PDF on the company website. One candidate, a marketing major, spent a great deal of time poring over such materials from an aerospace contractor. During his initial interview, he shocked and impressed the recruiter with his knowledge of the company's guidance systems. The candidate had, in fact, relieved the interviewer of his least-favorite task—explaining the company's complicated technology.

Locating Inside Information. To find inside information, check LinkedIn, Facebook, and Twitter. Follow and like the company on Facebook and Twitter. Comment shrewdly on the organization's status updates and other posts. Check out employee review websites such as Glassdoor to get the inside scoop on what it's like to work there. Learn about the organization's culture and values. Are opportunities for training and advancement important to you? How important is meaningful work? In one survey of American workers, nine out of ten reported that they were willing to earn less money to do more meaningful work. Are you in this group?[4] Try to connect with someone who is currently employed by the business—but not working in the immediate area where you wish to be hired. Be sure to seek out someone who is discreet.

As you learn about a company, you may uncover information that convinces you that this is not the company for you. It is always better to learn about negatives early in the process. More likely, though, the information you collect will help you tailor your interview responses to the organization's needs. You know how flattered you feel when an employer knows about you and your background. That feeling works both ways. Employers are pleased when job candidates take an interest in them.

## 14-2d Rehearsing Success Stories

To feel confident and be able to promote your qualifications, prepare and practice success stories. These stories are specific examples of your educational and work-related experience that demonstrate your qualifications and achievements. Look over the job description and your résumé to determine what skills, training, personal characteristics, and experience you want to emphasize during the interview. Then prepare a success story for each one. Incorporate numbers, such as dollars saved or percentage of sales increased, whenever possible. Your success stories should be detailed but brief. Think of them as 30-second sound bites.

Practice telling your success stories until they fluently roll off your tongue and sound natural. Then in the interview be certain to find places to insert them. Tell stories about (a) dealing with a crisis, (b) handling a tough interpersonal situation, (c) successfully juggling many priorities, (d) changing course to deal with changed circumstances, (e) learning from a mistake, (f) working on a team, and (g) going above and beyond expectations. Remember that you are being judged on your communication skills as well as your talents.

## 14-2e Cleaning Up Your Digital Presence

Potential employers definitely screen a candidate's online presence using Google and social media. One CareerBuilder survey revealed that 70 percent of hiring managers use social media to investigate prospective hires. Even more significant, 49 percent said they had found information that caused them not to hire a candidate.[6] What turned them off? The top reasons cited were (a) provocative or inappropriate photographs, videos, or information; (b) content about drinking or doing drugs; (c) discriminatory comments related to race, religion, and other protected categories; (d) criticism of previous employers or colleagues; and (e) poor communication skills.[7]

Teasing photographs and provocative comments about drinking, drug use, and sexual exploits make

Who hasn't had an "oops" moment after pressing Send? Similarly, some social media users are still oblivious to privacy settings and post inappropriate content that can sabotage their career plans. Before searching for a job, candidates should clean up their digital act.

Oakozhan/Shutterstock.com

students look immature and unprofessional. Think about cleaning up your online presence by following these steps:

- **Remove questionable content**. Remove any incriminating, provocative, or distasteful photos, content, and links that could make you look unprofessional to potential employers.

- **Stay positive**. Don't complain about things in your professional or personal life online. Even negative reviews you have written on sites such as Amazon can turn employers off.

- **Be selective about who is on your list of friends**. You don't want to miss out on an opportunity because you seem to associate with negative, immature, or unprofessional people. Your best bet is to make your personal social networking pages private. Monitor your privacy settings because they often change.

- **Don't discuss your job search if you are still employed**. Employees can find themselves in trouble with their current employers by writing status updates or sending tweets about their job searches.

## 14-2f   Dressing for, Traveling to, and Arriving at Your Interview

The big day has arrived! Ideally, you are fully prepared for your interview. Now you need to make sure everything goes smoothly. On the day of your interview, give yourself plenty of time to groom and dress.

**Deciding What to Wear and When to Arrive.** What to wear may worry you because business attire today ranges from ultracasual to formal suits. The best plan is to ask your interviewer what is appropriate, advises career counselor Liz Ryan.[8] Ask this when the interview is arranged, and you will be greatly relieved. However, if that request doesn't bring results, think about the research you have done on the company. What is its level of formality? Take a look at photos of its social media sites and notice what people wear at the office. For job interviews it's always safe to dress conservatively, even when conducted by video call.

Here's what you definitely should not wear, as reported on Monster.com: Flip flops, wedge sandals, ripped jeans or shorts, tank tops, halter tops, sandals, strapless tops and dresses, and athletic attire such as yoga pants and sneakers. Also avoid attire that is too casual, too ill-fitting, too uncomfortable, too different from the company culture, too scented, and too revealing.[9]

As part of your preparations for a face-to-face interview, make sure you can arrive at the employer's office without being rushed. If something unexpected happens that will to cause you to be late, such as an accident or bridge closure, call the interviewer right away to explain what is happening. Most interviewers will be understanding, and your call will show that you are responsible. On the way to the interview, don't smoke, don't eat anything messy or smelly, and don't load up on perfume or cologne. Arrive at the interview five to ten minutes early, but not earlier. If you are very early, wait in the car or in a café nearby. If possible, check your appearance before going in.

**Being Polite and Pleasant.** When you enter the office, be courteous and congenial to everyone. Remember that you are being judged not only by the interviewer but also by the receptionist and anyone else who sees you before and after the interview. They will notice how you sit, what you read, and how you look. Introduce yourself to the receptionist, and wait to be invited to sit. You may be asked to fill out a job application while you are waiting. You will find tips for doing this effectively later in this chapter.

**Greeting the Interviewer and Making a Positive First Impression.** If meeting the interviewer in person, make eye contact and smile warmly but don't extend your hand for a handshake. Although shaking hands was the standard greeting among

**OFFICE INSIDER**

Has the COVID-19 pandemic killed the handshake? The epidemiologist Anthony Fauci wishes for its demise to avoid respiratory-borne illness. Etiquette professionals believe the handshake may return after a delay. The neuroscientist Francis McGlone says that such welcome touching in work situations activates pleasure hormones, "drives more social behaviors and lowers a stress marker called cortisol, which helps establish bonding and trust."[10]

**Alex Williams,**
*reporter,* The New York Times

businesspeople in the past, following the COVID-19 pandemic, we have seen a profound shift toward touchless greetings. Instead of extending your hand, you could tilt your head or place your right hand on your heart or give a friendly wave and say, *I'm pleased to meet you, Mr. Roland. I am Faith Biondi.* If Mr. Roland, the interviewer, extends his hand, accept it graciously as a sincere greeting. Don't recoil or launch into a lecture on cleanliness and the history of handshaking. Afterwards, if you wish, you could wash your hands promptly.

## 14-2g Fighting Fear

Expect to be nervous before and during the interview. It's natural! One survey revealed that job interviews are more stressful than going on a blind date, being pulled over by the police, or taking a final exam without studying.[11] One of the best ways to overcome fear is to know what happens in a typical interview. You can further reduce your fears by following these suggestions:

- **Practice interviewing**. Try to get as much interviewing practice as you can—especially with real companies. The more times you experience the interview situation, the less nervous you will be. However, don't schedule interviews unless you are genuinely interested in the organization. If offered, campus mock interviews also provide excellent practice, and the interviewers will offer tips for improvement.

- **Prepare thoroughly**. Research the company. Know how you will answer the most frequently asked questions. Be ready with success stories. Rehearse your closing statement. Knowing that you have done all you can to be ready for the interview is a tremendous fear preventive.

- **Understand the process**. Find out ahead of time how the interview will be structured. Will you be meeting with an individual, or will you be interviewed by a panel? Is this the first of a series of interviews? Don't be afraid to ask about these details before the interview so an unfamiliar situation won't catch you off guard.

- **Dress appropriately**. If you have checked with the interviewer in advance and know that you are dressed properly, you will feel more confident. When in doubt, tend toward more formal, professional attire.

- **Breathe deeply**. Take deep breaths, particularly if you feel anxious while waiting for the interviewer. Deep breathing makes you concentrate on something other than the interview and also provides much-needed oxygen.

- **Know that you are not alone**. Everyone feels some anxiety during a job interview. Interviewers expect some nervousness, and a skilled interviewer will try to put you at ease.

- **Remind yourself that an interview is a two-way street**. The interviewer isn't the only one who is gleaning information. You have come to learn about the job and the company. In fact, during some parts of the interview, you will be in charge. This should give you courage.

## 14-3 During the Interview

**LEARNING OUTCOME 3**
Describe what to do *during* a job interview.

Throughout the interview you will be answering questions and asking your own questions. Your demeanor, body language, and other nonverbal cues will also be on display. The interviewer will be trying to learn more about you, and you should be learning more about the job and the organization. Although you may be asked some unique questions, many interviewers ask standard, time-proven questions, which means that you can prepare your answers ahead of time. You can also prepare by learning techniques to control those inevitable butterflies in your stomach.

## WORKPLACE IN FOCUS

Edvard Nalbantjan/Shutterstock.com

Don't take our word for it. Listen to what 2,600 hiring and human resource managers say are the top ten body language dealbreakers in interviews:[12]

1. Failing to make eye contact (67 percent)
2. Failing to smile (39 percent)
3. Playing with something on the table (34 percent)
4. Fidgeting too much in their seats (32 percent)
5. Crossing their arms over their chests (32 percent)
6. Having bad posture (31 percent)
7. Playing with their hair or touching their faces (28 percent)
8. Having a weak handshake (22 percent)
9. Using too many hand gestures (13 percent)
10. Having a handshake that was too strong (9 percent)

Review the section on nonverbal cues in Chapter 1. What messages might these nonverbal behaviors be sending? How can you ensure you master your mannerisms?

## 14-3a Sending Positive Nonverbal Messages and Acting Professionally

You have already sent nonverbal cues to your interviewer by arriving on time, being courteous, dressing appropriately, and greeting the receptionist confidently. You will continue to send nonverbal messages throughout the interview. Remember that what comes out of your mouth and what is written on your résumé are not the only messages an interviewer receives from you. Nonverbal messages also create powerful impressions. You can send positive nonverbal messages during face-to-face and video interviews by following these tips:

- **Control your body movements**. Keep your hands, arms, and elbows to yourself. Don't lean on a desk. Keep your feet on the floor. Don't cross your arms in front of you. Keep your hands out of your pockets.

- **Exhibit good posture**. Sit erect, leaning forward slightly. Don't slouch in your chair; at the same time, don't look too stiff and uncomfortable. Good posture demonstrates confidence and interest.

- **Practice appropriate eye contact**. A direct eye gaze, at least in North America, generally suggests interest and trustworthiness. If you are being interviewed by a panel, try to maintain eye contact with all interviewers.

- **Use gestures effectively**. Nod to show agreement and interest. Gestures should be used as needed, but not overused.

- **Smile enough to convey a positive attitude**. Have a friend give you honest feedback on whether you generally smile too much or not enough.

- **Listen attentively**. Show the interviewer you are interested and attentive by listening carefully to questions. This will also help you answer questions appropriately. Do not interrupt any speaker.

- **Turn off your smartphone and other electronic devices**. Avoid the embarrassment of having your smartphone ring, or even as much as buzz, during an interview. Turn off your mobile devices completely; don't just switch them to vibrate.

- **Don't chew gum**. Chewing gum during an interview is distracting and unprofessional.

- **Sound enthusiastic and interested—but sincere**. The tone of your voice has an enormous effect on the words you say. Avoid sounding bored, frustrated, or sarcastic during an interview. Employers want employees who are enthusiastic and interested.

- **Avoid empty words**. Filling your answers with verbal pauses such as *um, uh, like*, and *basically* communicates that you are not prepared. Also avoid irritating distractions or tics such as clearing your throat repeatedly or sighing deeply.

- **Be confident, but not cocky**. Most recruiters want candidates who are self-assured but not too casual or even arrogant. Let your body language, posture, dress, and vocal tone prove your confidence. Speak at a normal volume and enunciate words clearly without mumbling.

Naturally, hiring managers make subjective decisions based on intuition, but they need to ferret out pleasant people who fit in. To that end, some recruiters apply the so-called airport test to candidates, asking themselves the following: Would I want to be stuck in the airport for 12 hours with this person if my flight were delayed?[13]

## 14-3b Preparing to Answer Interview Questions

One way you can compensate for lack of experience is careful preparation and well-rehearsed responses to typical interview questions. In addition, the way you answer questions can be almost as important as what you say. Use the interviewer's name and title from time to time when you answer. *Yes, Ms. Yong, I would be pleased to tell you about. . . .* People like to hear their own names, but don't overuse this technique. Avoid answering questions with a simple *yes* or *no*; elaborate on your answers to better promote yourself and your assets.

Remember that your communication skills are being judged. Keep your answers positive; don't criticize anything or anyone. Strive to incorporate positive adjectives, appropriate inflection, and a confident voice tone.

During the interview don't be afraid to refocus or clarify vague questions. Some interviewers are inexperienced and ill at ease in the role. You may even have to ask your own question to understand what was asked: *By _____, do you mean _____?* Consider closing out some of your responses with *Does that answer your question, Mr. Singh?* or *Would you like me to elaborate on any particular experience?*

Always aim your answers at the key characteristics interviewers seek: expertise, competence, motivation, interpersonal skills, decision-making skills, enthusiasm for the company, excitement about the job, and a pleasing personality. Remember to stay focused on your strengths. Don't reveal weaknesses, even if you think they make you look human. You won't be hired for your weaknesses, only for your strengths.

As you respond, be sure to use good English and enunciate clearly. Avoid slurred words such as *gonna* and *din't*, as well as slangy expressions such as *yeah, like*, and *ya know*. As you practice answering expected interview questions, it is always a good idea to make an audio or video recording. Is your speech filled with verbal static?

You can't expect to be perfect in an employment interview. No one is. However, you can avert sure disaster by avoiding mistakes such as those described in **Figures 14.4** and **14.5**.

The following sections present questions that may be asked during employment interviews. To get you thinking about how to respond, we have provided an answer for, or a discussion of, one or more of the questions in each group. As you read the remaining questions in each group, think about how you could respond most effectively. For additional questions, contact your campus career center, or consult one of the career websites discussed in Chapter 13. If you rehearse success stories and anticipate interview questions, you will steer clear of the most common interview pitfalls shown in Figure 14.5.

When interviewing many candidates, recruiters may apply the airport test.

**OFFICE INSIDER**

"Practice interviewing out loud with mentors, adult fans, or even in the mirror. Most students have not done many (if any) job interviews—and definitely not when under pressure. It's important to hear the words you intend to speak, including the tone, emphasis, inflections and facial impressions, so that you don't blow it when it really counts. It's rare to get a second chance."[14]

**Andy Chan,**
*vice president for Personal & Career Development, Wake Forest University*

**Figure 14.4   The Ten Biggest Interview Mistakes**

**1.** Don't be late or too early. Arrive five to ten minutes before your scheduled interview.

**2.** Don't be rude or annoying. Treat everyone you come into contact with warmly and respectfully. Avoid poor eye contact, staring, and verbal tics such as *like, you know,* and *um.*

**3.** Don't criticize anyone or anything. Avoid saying anything negative about your previous employer, supervisors, colleagues, or job. The tendency is for interviewers to wonder if you would speak about their companies similarly.

**4.** Don't act unprofessionally. Don't discuss controversial subjects, and don't use profanity. Don't answer your cell phone or fiddle with it. Silence all electronic devices so that they don't even buzz, or turn them off completely. Don't bring food or coffee.

**5.** Don't emphasize salary or benefits. Don't address salary, vacation, or benefits early in an interview. Let the interviewers set the pace; win them over first.

**6.** Don't focus on your imperfections. Never dwell on your flaws or talk negatively about yourself.

**7.** Don't interrupt. Interrupting is not only impolite but also prevents you from hearing a complete question or remark. Don't talk too much or too little. Answer interview questions to the best of your ability, but avoid rambling as much as terseness.

**8.** Don't bring someone along. Don't bring a friend or relative with you to the interview. If someone must drive you, ask that person to drop you off and come back later.

**9.** Don't appear impatient or bored. Your entire focus should be on the interview. Don't glance at your watch, which can imply that you are late for another appointment. Be alert and show interest in the company and the position.

**10.** Don't act desperate. A sure way to turn off an interviewer is to act too desperate. Don't focus on why you need the job; focus instead on how you will add value to the organization.

## 14-3c  Warm-Up Questions

Recruiters usually start the interview with warm-up questions designed to get acquainted and put you at ease. They are also striving to gain an overview to see whether you will fit into the organization's culture. When answering these questions, keep the employer's needs in mind and try to incorporate your success stories.

1.  Tell me about yourself.
    Experts agree that you must keep this answer short (one to two minutes tops) but on target. Use this chance to promote yourself. Stick to educational, professional, or business-related strengths; avoid personal or humorous references. Be ready with at least three success stories illustrating characteristics important to this job. Demonstrate responsibility you have been given; describe how you contributed as a team player. Try practicing this strategy: *I have completed a _____ degree with a major in _____. Recently I worked for _____ as a _____. Before that I worked for _____ as a _____. My strengths are _____ (interpersonal) and _____ (technical).* Rehearse your response in 30-second segments devoted to your education, work experience, qualifications, and skills.

**Figure 14.5   How to Bomb a Job Interview**

**Instant Deal Breakers During Interview**

- 66% Caught lying about something
- 64% Answering a cell phone or text
- 59% Appearing arrogant or entitled
- 49% Dressing inappropriately
- 48% Blaming others for your mistake

Shutterstock.com

**Strangest Things Interviewees Have Done**

Took a family photo off the interviewer's desk and put it into her purse.

Said her main job was being a psychic/medium and tried to read the interviewer's palm.

Sang to a song on the radio playing overhead.

Started feeling the interviewer's chest to find a heartbeat so they could "connect heart to heart."

Ate a pizza he brought with him (and didn't offer to share).

Took the phone interview in the bathroom—and flushed.

Roman Samborskyi/Shutterstock.com

Source: CareerBuilder. (2017). CareerBuilder releases annual list of strangest interview and body language mistakes. CareerBuilder. (2021). Top 10 things NOT to do in an interview;

2. **Tell me what you know about us.**
   This is a killer question for those who haven't done their homework. An outstanding candidate will be able to present considerable information about the company. Primarily, however, this question eliminates clueless candidates who have not bothered to do even minimal checking.

3. **What are your greatest strengths?**
   Reread your résumé and cover letter to review what you want to promote. Stress your strengths that are related to the position, such as *I am well organized, thorough, and attentive to detail*. Tell success stories and give examples that illustrate these qualities: *My supervisor says that my research is exceptionally thorough. For example, I recently worked on a research project in which I . . . .*

4. **Do you prefer to work by yourself or with others? Why?**
   This question can be tricky. Provide a middle-of-the-road answer that not only suggests your interpersonal qualities but also reflects an ability to make independent decisions and work without supervision.

5. **What was your major in college, and why did you choose it?**

6. **What are some things you do in your spare time?**

### 14-3d Questions to Gauge Your Interest

Interviewers want to understand your motivation for applying for a position. Although they will realize that you are probably interviewing for other positions, they still want to know why you are interested in this particular position with this organization. These types of questions help them determine your level of interest.

1. Why do you want to work for [name of company]?
   Questions like this illustrate why you must research an organization thoroughly before the interview. The answer to this question must prove that you understand the company and its culture. This is the perfect place to bring up the company research you did before the interview. Show what you know about the company, and discuss why you want to become a part of this organization. Describe your desire to work for this organization not only from your perspective but also from its point of view. What do you have to offer that will benefit the organization?

2. What sets you apart from other people that might apply for this job?
   Although the answer to this is on your résumé, this is a chance to really promote yourself. Most interviewers will usually sit back and watch how well you can sell. This is when you review and expand on your summary of qualifications from your résumé.

3. Why are you interested in this position?

4. Why do you want to work in the _____ industry?

5. What interests you about our products (or services)?

### 14-3e Questions About Your Experience and Accomplishments

After questions about your background and education and questions that measure your interest, the interview generally becomes more specific with questions about your experience and accomplishments. Aim to show confidence when you answer these questions. If you are not confident in your abilities, why should an employer be?

1. Why should we hire you when we have applicants with more experience or better credentials?
   In answering this question, remember that employers often hire people who present themselves well instead of others with better credentials. Emphasize your personal strengths that could be an advantage with this employer. Are you a hard worker? How can you demonstrate it? Have you had recent training? Some people have had more years of experience but actually have less knowledge because they have done the same thing over and over. Stress your experience using the latest methods and equipment. Be sure to mention your computer training and Internet savvy. Emphasize that you are open to new ideas and learn quickly. Above all, show that you are confident in your abilities.

2. Describe the most rewarding experience of your career so far.

3. How have your education and professional experiences prepared you for this position?

4. What were your major accomplishments in each of your past jobs?

5. What was a typical workday like?

6. What job functions did you enjoy most? Least? Why?

7. Tell me about your technical skills.

8. Who was the toughest boss you ever worked for and why?

9. What were your major achievements in college?

10. Why did you leave your last position? *OR:* Why are you leaving your current position?

**OFFICE INSIDER**

"I was particularly impressed by a candidate who told me that although he goes into meetings with lists of questions to ask, he doesn't expect all of them will be answered. . . . [Instead,] he stays attuned to what the other person wants to talk about and finds creative ways to get at the key insights he is seeking."[15]

**David Priemer,**
*ex-Salesforce executive, entrepreneur*

## 14-3f  Questions About the Future

Questions that look into the future tend to stump some candidates, especially those who have not prepared adequately. Employers ask these questions to see whether you are goal oriented and to determine whether your goals are realistic.

1. What are your long-term career goals?
   Formulate a realistic plan with respect to your present age and situation, but keep your response fairly general. If you are considering different career paths, keep your options open. Show an interest in the current job and in contributing to the organization. Talk about the levels of responsibility you would like to achieve. One employment counselor suggests showing ambition but not committing to a specific job title. Suggest that you hope to have learned enough to have progressed to a position in which you will continue to grow. Keep your answer focused on educational and professional goals, not personal goals.

2. If you got this position, what would you do to be sure you fit in?

3. This is a large (or small) organization. Do you think you would like that environment?

4. Do you plan to continue your education?

5. What do you predict for the future of the _____ industry?

6. How do you think you can contribute to this company?

7. What do you expect to accomplish in the first 30, 60, and 90 days on the job?

8. How do you keep current with what is happening in your profession?

## 14-3g  Challenging Questions

The following questions may make you uncomfortable, but the important thing to remember is to answer truthfully without dwelling on your weaknesses. Be honest but pivot to the remedy you have targeted so that you can improve.

1. What is your greatest weakness?
   It is amazing how many candidates knock themselves out of the competition by answering this question poorly. The old cliché of turning a weakness into a strength (e.g., being a perfectionist or working too hard) no longer works. Instead, experts advise to be truthful but to carefully choose a weakness that you have been working to overcome and that won't sabotage your getting hired nor interfere with your job performance. Show you care about developing your skills and help the interviewer envision a positive outcome of your professional growth.[17] Mention a corrected weakness (*Because I was terrified of making presentations, I took a college course and also joined a speakers' club*). You could cite an unrelated skill (*I really need to brush up on my Spanish*). You could cite a learning objective (*One of my long-term goals is to learn more about coding and programming*).

2. What type of people do you have no patience for?
   Avoid letting yourself fall into the trap of sounding overly critical. One possible response is, *I have always gotten along well with others. But I confess that I can be irritated by complainers who don't accept responsibility.*

3. If you could live your life over, what would you change and why?

4. How would your former (or current) supervisor describe you as an employee?

5. What do you want the most from your job?

One of the best ways to fight fear before a job interview is preparing thoroughly. You can guess many of the questions that will be asked and prepare your responses in advance.

6. What is your grade point average, and does it accurately reflect your abilities?

7. Have you ever used drugs?

8. Who in your life has influenced you the most and why?

9. What should I know about you that is not on your résumé?

10. How do you define success?

## 14-3h Situational Questions

A **situational question** is one in which interviewers describe a hypothetical situation and ask how you would handle it. These questions help employers test your thought processes, problem-solving skills, and logical thinking. Situational questions are based on the type of position for which you are interviewing. Knowledge of the position and the company culture will help you respond successfully to these questions. Even if the situation sounds negative, keep your response positive. Here are a few examples with possible responses to the first two:

1. How would you respond if your fellow team members strongly resisted a proposal you made in a meeting?
You might explain the rationale behind your proposal with specific examples of the benefits that the recommendation could bring to the team. If the team continues to oppose your proposal, you should let it go and move on.

2. What would you do if you knew that your boss gave your team data that was totally wrong?
Let's say, for example, that in a team meeting your boss provided data that had not been updated, and you recognized the error immediately. Before responding, you should confirm that your figures are correct. Then you might tactfully share the correct data in a private conversation with your boss. You could suggest that the error was an oversight perhaps caused by figures that were released after an initial report and say you know that your boss would want to base the team project on accurate data. You would not correct your boss in front of the team, and you would try to understand how or why the mistake was made.

3. Your supervisor has just told you that she is dissatisfied with your work, but you think it is acceptable. How would you resolve the conflict?

4. Your supervisor has told you to do something a certain way, and you think you know a far better way to complete the task. What would you do?

5. Assume that you are hired for this position. You soon learn that one of the staff members is extremely resentful because she applied for your position and was turned down. As a result, she is being unhelpful and obstructive. How would you handle the situation?

6. A colleague has told you in confidence that she suspects another colleague of stealing. What would your actions be?

7. What would you do if an angry, disappointed customer confronted you? How would you resolve the customer's concern?

## 14-3i Behavioral Questions

Instead of traditional interview questions, you may be asked a **behavioral question** devised to prompt you to tell a story. The interviewer may say, *Describe a time when . . .* or *Tell me about a time when. . . .* To respond effectively, learn to use the storytelling, or STAR, technique, as illustrated in **Figure 14.6**. Ask yourself, what the **S**ituation or **T**ask was, what **A**ction you took, and what the **R**esults were.[18] Practice using this method to recall specific examples of your skills and accomplishments. To be fully prepared, develop a coherent and articulate STAR narrative for every bullet point on

**Figure 14.6  Using the STAR Technique to Answer Behavioral Interview Questions**

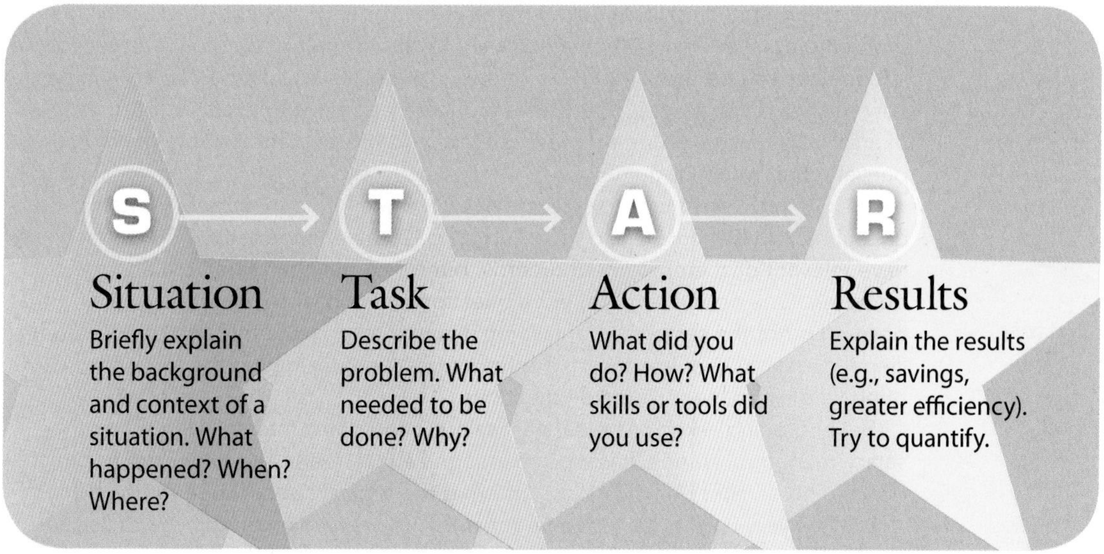

**S → T → A → R**

**Situation**
Briefly explain the background and context of a situation. What happened? When? Where?

**Task**
Describe the problem. What needed to be done? Why?

**Action**
What did you do? How? What skills or tools did you use?

**Results**
Explain the results (e.g., savings, greater efficiency). Try to quantify.

your résumé. One career coach has expanded this technique to form the acronym START. The second T stands for Tie, which means that interviewees should "connect the dots and tie the story to the company and position" for which they are interviewing.[19]

When answering behavioral questions, describe only educational and work-related situations or tasks, and try to keep them as current as possible. Here are a few examples of behavioral questions:

1. Tell me about a time when you solved a difficult problem.
   Tell a concise story explaining the situation or task, what you did, and the result. For example, *When I was at CyberTech, we continually had a problem of excessive back orders. After analyzing the situation, I discovered that orders went through many unnecessary steps. I suggested that we eliminate much of the paperwork. As a result, we reduced back orders by 30 percent.* Go on to emphasize what you learned and how you can apply that learning to this job. Practice your success stories in advance so that you will be ready.

2. Describe a situation in which you were able to use persuasion to convince someone to see things your way.
   The recruiter is interested in your leadership and teamwork skills. You might respond as follows: *I have learned to appreciate the fact that the way we present an idea is just as important as the idea itself. When trying to influence people, I put myself in their shoes and find some way to frame my idea from their perspective. I remember when I. . . .*

3. Describe a time when you had to analyze information and make a recommendation.

4. Describe a time that you worked successfully as part of a team.

5. Tell me about a time that you dealt with confidential information.

6. Give me an example of a time when you were under stress to meet a deadline.

7. Tell me about a time when you had to go above and beyond the call of duty to get a job done.

8. Tell me about a time you were able to deal with another person successfully even though that individual did not like you personally (or vice versa).

9. Give me an example of when you showed initiative and took the lead.

10. Tell me about a time when you were asked to complete a task you had never performed before.

## 14-3j  Salary Questions

Increasingly, state and local governments are adopting laws and regulations that prohibit employers from requesting salary history from job applicants. These laws are intended to ensure that employers offer equal pay for equal work rather than basing new salaries on past ones. Many have argued that a pay gap exists in part because of artificially lower starting salaries, especially for women and people of color, thus perpetuating wage inequity.

Despite new laws in some states, naïve or rogue hiring managers may still pose such questions. What should you do if asked for past salary information? New grads may not have relevant past employment records, but for career changers, a salary question can be tough. One option is to deflect a question about past salaries by explaining that this position is not the same as your last job. How to respond to this and other potentially illegal questions requires tact and forethought, as explained in the following section titled Illegal and Inappropriate Questions.

Beyond being asked to reveal past salary, candidates may still be asked other salary-related questions. It is wise to recognize that nearly all salaries are negotiable, depending on your qualifications. Knowing the typical salary range for the target position is very important in this negotiation. The recruiter can tell you the salary ranges—but you will have to ask. If you have had little experience, you will probably be offered a salary somewhere between the low point and the midpoint in the range. With more experience, you can negotiate for a higher figure. A word of caution, though. One personnel manager warns that candidates who emphasize money are suspect because they may leave if offered a few thousand dollars more elsewhere. See the Communication Workshop at the end of this chapter for dos and don'ts in negotiating a starting salary. Here are typical salary-related questions:

1. What salary are you looking for?

   One way to handle salary questions is to ask politely to defer the discussion until it is clear that a job will be offered (*I'm sure when the time comes, we will be able to work out a fair compensation package. Right now, I'd rather focus on whether we have a match*). If salary comes up and you are not sure whether the job is being offered to you, it's time to be blunt. Ask, *Are you making me a job offer?* Another possible response to a salary question is to reply candidly that you can't know what to ask until you know more about the position and the company. If you continue to be pressed for a dollar figure, give a salary range with an annual dollar amount. Be sure to do research before the interview so that you know what similar jobs are paying in your geographic region. As an expert negotiator said, "In business as in life, you don't get what you deserve, you get what you negotiate."[20] See the Communication Workshop for more tips on discussing salary.

2. How much do you think you are worth?

3. How much money do you expect to earn within the next ten years?

4. Are you willing to take a pay cut from your current (or previous) job?

5. What do you think is a reasonable salary for this position?

## 14-3k  Illegal and Inappropriate Questions

U.S. federal law states that "it is illegal to discriminate against someone (applicant or employee) because of that person's race, color, religion, sex (including gender identity, sexual orientation, and pregnancy), national origin, age (40 and

Salary negotiation during an interview is critical. If asked what you want for salary, a strategic response might be, "I know what I'd *like* to make, but I'm excited about working with your organization. What is the budget for this position?"

older), disability or genetic information."[21] Therefore, it is inappropriate for interviewers to ask any question related to these areas. Such questions become illegal, though, only when a court of law determines that the employer is asking them with the intent to discriminate.[22]

Many illegal interview questions are asked innocently by inexperienced interviewers. Shockingly, one survey revealed that 20 percent of interviewers admitted that they had unknowingly asked an illegal question.[23] Many interviewers don't know the law. Others are only trying to be friendly when they inquire about your personal life or family. Regardless of the intent, how should you react? If you find the question harmless and if you want the job, go ahead and answer it. If you think that answering it would damage your chance to be hired, try to deflect the question tactfully with a response such as *Could you tell me how my marital status relates to the responsibilities of this position?* or, *I prefer to keep my personal and professional lives separate.*

If you are uncomfortable answering a question, try to determine the reason behind it; you might answer, *I don't let my personal life interfere with my ability to do my job*, or, *Are you concerned about my availability to work overtime?* Another option, of course, is to respond to any inappropriate or illegal question by confronting the interviewer and threatening a lawsuit or refusing to answer. However, you could not expect to be hired under these circumstances. In any case, you might wish to reconsider working for an organization that sanctions such procedures.

Here are selected inappropriate and illegal questions that you may or may not want to answer:[24]

1. What is your marital status? Are you married? Do you live with anyone? Do you have a boyfriend (or girlfriend)? (However, employers can ask your marital status after hiring for tax and insurance forms.)

2. Do you have any disabilities? Have you had any recent illnesses? (But it is legal to ask if the person can perform specific job duties, such as *Can you carry a 50-pound sack up a 10-foot ladder five times daily?*)

3. I notice you have an accent. Where are you from? What is the origin of your last name? What is your native language? (However, it is legal to ask what languages you speak fluently if language ability is related to the job.)

4. Have you ever filed a workers' compensation claim or been injured on the job?

5. Have you ever had a drinking problem or been addicted to drugs? (But it is legal to ask if a person uses illegal drugs.)

6. Have you ever been arrested? (But it is legal to ask, *Have you ever been convicted of _____?* when the crime is related to the job.)

7. How old are you? What is your date of birth? (But it is legal to ask, *Are you 16 [or 18 or 21] years old or older?* depending on the age requirements for the position.)

8. Of what country are you a citizen? Are you a U.S. citizen? Where were you born? (But it is legal to ask, *Are you authorized to work in the United States?*)

9. What is your maiden name? (But it is legal to ask, *What is your full name?* or, *Have you worked under another name?*)

10. Do you have any religious beliefs that would prevent you from working weekends or holidays? (An employer can, however, ask you if you are available to work weekends and holidays or otherwise within the company's required schedule.)

11. Do you have children? Do you plan to have children? Do you have adequate child-care arrangements? (However, employers can ask for dependent information for tax and insurance purposes after you are hired. Also, they can ask if you would be able to travel or work overtime on occasion.)

12. How much do you weigh? How tall are you? (However, employers can ask you about your height and weight if minimum standards are necessary to safely perform a job.)

13. Are you in debt?

14. Do you drink socially or smoke?

15. Are you transgender or do you plan to transition in the future?

## 14-3l Asking Your Own Questions

At some point in the interview, usually near the end, you will be asked whether you have any questions. The worst thing you can do is say *no*, which suggests that you are not interested in the position. Almost as bad is using this time to continue to pitch yourself for the position. Instead, ask questions that will help you gain information and will impress the interviewer with your thoughtfulness and interest in the position. Don't forget that this interview is a two-way street. You must be happy with the prospect of working for this organization. You want a position that matches your skills and personality. Use this opportunity to learn whether this job is right for you. Be aware that you don't have to wait for the interviewer to ask you for questions. You can ask your own questions throughout the interview to learn more about the company and position. Here are some questions you might ask:

1. What will my duties be (if not already discussed)?
2. Tell me what it is like working here in terms of the people, management practices, workloads, expected performance, and rewards.
3. What training programs are available from this organization? What specific training will be given for this position?
4. Who would be my immediate supervisor?
5. What is the organizational structure, and where does this position fit in?
6. Is travel required in this position (unless mentioned in the job listing)?
7. How and by whom will my job performance be evaluated?
8. Assuming my work is excellent, where do you see me in five years?
9. How long do employees generally stay with this organization?
10. What are the major challenges for a person in this position?
11. What do you see in the future of this organization?
12. May I tour the facilities?
13. This job seems to be exactly what I'd really like to do. Do we have a fit here?
14. What is the next step in the hiring process?
15. When do you expect to make a decision?

Do not ask about salary or benefits, especially during the first interview. As a rule of thumb, it's best to let the interviewer bring those topics up first.

## 14-3m Ending Positively

After you have asked your questions, the interviewer will signal the end of the interview, usually by standing up or by expressing appreciation that you came. If not addressed earlier, you should at this time find out what action will follow. Career coach Don Georgevich recommends asking the interviewer when a decision will be made and whether you may follow up. "Interviewers always say yes," he reports, "and now you have permission to call them. In fact, they will expect your call."[25] This is not the time to be shy. Too many candidates leave the interview without knowing their status or when they will hear from the recruiter.

Before you leave, briefly summarize your strongest qualifications, show your enthusiasm for obtaining this position, and thank the interviewer for a constructive interview and for considering you for the position. Ask the interviewer for a business card, which will provide the information you need to write a thank-you message. Be sure to thank the receptionist. Departing gracefully and enthusiastically will leave a lasting impression on those responsible for making the final hiring decision.

## WORKPLACE IN FOCUS

How creepy is it to think that your voice, photo, and mannerisms may be ranked by bots to help organizations decide your employability? We're not fully there yet, but some organizations, mostly large employers, are increasingly relying on artificial intelligence tools to control the first round of video interviews. AI tools may compare a candidate's facial expressions, body language, voice, and verbal responses with algorithms that reflect ideal traits for the open position. Proponents claim that customized assessment algorithms are more accurate and less biased than human interviewers. How do you feel about being judged by AI?

Blue Planet Studio/Shutterstock.com

## 14-4 After the Interview

After leaving the interview, immediately take notes of what was said in case you are called back for a second interview. Write down key points that were discussed, the names of people you spoke with, and other details of the interview. Ask yourself what went really well and what you could improve. Note your strengths and weaknesses during the interview so that you can work to improve in future interviews.

### 14-4a Do I Really Need to Send a Thank-You Message?

Yes, you really should send a thank-you message after a job interview—if you want the job. One survey revealed that 80 percent of human resources specialists considered thank-you notes helpful following a job interview. However, only 24 percent actually received them.[26] When it's so easy to do, it's surprising that all serious candidates don't take advantage of this opportunity to show their good manners and genuine enthusiasm for the job. Promptness is key, though. Send your thank-you note no later than 24 hours after the interview.

Generally, you have three options for sending a thank-you message: a handwritten note card, a letter typed and printed on bond paper, or an e-mail. Handwritten cards are always impressive, but most managers today welcome e-mail. Not only that, but they also increasingly consider texting acceptable as a communication channel, particularly for scheduling interviews. Follow the employer's lead. If a recruiter texts you to schedule an interview (more than half do), sending a thank-you text message may be appropriate.[27]

Your preparation and knowledge of the company culture will help you determine whether an e-mail message or a traditional thank-you letter is more appropriate. Some experts even recommend sending both![28] Or you might text first and follow up with a note you send by snail mail. E-mails and texts have the advantage of enabling you to include a link to your e-portfolio, LinkedIn profile, or personal website. If you choose to send an e-mail or text, be sure to use professional language, standard capitalization, and proper punctuation. Whatever the format, double-check the correct spelling of your interviewer's name!

In your thank-you message, refer to the date of the interview, the exact title of the job for which you were interviewed, and specific topics discussed. Try to mention something you liked about the interview such as *Job interviews can be stressful, but you made me feel comfortable, and I am grateful for that*. Avoid worn-out phrases, such as *Thank you for taking the time to interview me*. Be careful, too, about overusing *I*, especially to begin sentences. Most important, show that you really want the job and

### LEARNING OUTCOME 4

Describe what to do *after* a job interview.

## OFFICE INSIDER

"Up until a few years ago, I was still advising people to cover their bases and send a quick same-day thank-you email (but not stalker-like from the elevator!), saying you have also dropped a note in the mail. But snail mail can take so long these days, and email thank-you notes are so common, you probably don't have to do both in many situations. Decide based on the age of the interviewer and the vibe of the place."[29]

**Kate White,**
*author, former editor-in-chief,* Cosmopolitan

that you are qualified for it. Notice how the letter in **Model Document 14.1** conveys enthusiasm and confidence.

If you have been interviewed by more than one person, send a separate personalized thank-you message to each interviewer.

## 14-4b Contacting Your References

Once you have thanked your interviewer, it is time to alert your references that they may be contacted by the employer. You might also have to request a letter of recommendation to be sent to the employer by a certain date. As discussed in

**Model Document 14.1** Interview Follow-Up Message

Uses customized letterhead but could have merely typed street and city address above dateline

**Thomas M. Taylor**

95 Grasslands Road, Valhalla, NY 10595
(914) 769-5002, thomastaylor@gmail.com

June 1, 2022

Ms. Victoria Sanchez
iDesign Marketing & Media
1055 Westchester Avenue
White Plains, NY 10604

Dear Ms. Sanchez:

Mentions the interview date and specific job title —

Talking with you Tuesday, May 31, about the graphic designer position in White Plains was both informative and interesting.

Thanks for describing the position in such detail and for introducing me to Ms. Mullins, the senior designer. Her current project designing an annual report in four colors sounds fascinating as well as quite challenging.

Personalizes the message by referring to topics discussed in the interview

Highlights specific skills for the job —

Now that I've learned in greater detail the specific tasks of your graphic designers, I'm more than ever convinced that my computer and creative skills can make a genuine contribution to your graphic productions. My training in design and layout using Photoshop and InDesign ensures that I could be immediately productive on your staff.

Shows good manners, appreciation, and perseverance— traits that recruiters value

You will find me an enthusiastic and hardworking member of any team effort. I'm eager to join the graphics staff at your White Plains headquarters, and I look forward to hearing from you soon.

Reminds reader of interpersonal skills as well as enthusiasm and eagerness for this job

Sincerely,

*Thomas M. Taylor*

Thomas M. Taylor

Chapter 13, you should have already asked permission to use these individuals as references, and you should have supplied them with a copy of your résumé and information about the types of positions you are seeking.

To provide the best possible recommendation, your references need information. What position have you applied for with what company? What should they stress to the prospective employer? Let's say you are applying for a job that requires a letter of recommendation. Professor Sindaha has already agreed to be a reference for you. To get the best letter of recommendation, help out Professor Sindaha. Write an e-mail describing the position, its requirements, and the recommendation deadline. Include links to copies of your résumé, college transcript, and, if applicable, the job posting or ad with detailed information about the opening. Or provide physical copies of these documents after the recommender agrees to write a message of support. You might refer to a positive experience with you that the instructor could use in the recommendation. Remember that recommenders need evidence to support generalizations. Give them appropriate ammunition, as the student has done in the following request:

*Dear Professor Sindaha:*

*Recently I interviewed for the position of administrative assistant in the Human Resources Department of Host International. Because you kindly agreed to help me, I am now asking you to write a letter of recommendation to Host.*

*The position calls for good organizational, interpersonal, and writing skills, as well as computer experience. To help you review my skills and training, I enclose my résumé. As you may recall, I earned an A in your business communication class last fall; and you commended my long report for its clarity and organization.*

*Please send your letter to Mr. Camden Singer at Host International before July 1 in the enclosed stamped, addressed envelope. You can also upload a scanned copy of your letter to the company's website. Follow the link below. I'm grateful for your support and promise to let you know the results of my job search.*

*Sincerely,*

In a reference request letter, tell immediately why you are writing. Identify the target position and company.

Specify the job requirements to help the recommender know what to stress.

Provide a stamped, addressed envelope or include a hyperlink to the upload website.

## 14-4c Following Up

If you don't hear from the interviewer within five days, or at the specified time, consider following up. Of course, if you have remembered to ask the interviewer when a decision is expected and whether you may follow up, you are all set. Otherwise, the standard advice to job candidates is to contact the interviewer with a follow-up e-mail or phone call.

An e-mail to find out how the decision process is going may be your best bet because such a message is less intrusive than a phone call or text. An e-mail also gives the interviewer time to look up your status information, leaves a written record, and eliminates annoying phone tag.[31] The following follow-up e-mail message would impress the interviewer:

*Dear Ms. Sanchez:*

*I enjoyed my interview with you last Tuesday for the graphic designer position. You should know that I'm very interested in this opportunity with iDesign Marketing & Media. Because you mentioned that you might have an answer this week, I'm eager to know how your decision process is coming along. I look forward to hearing from you.*

Inquire courteously; don't sound angry or desperate.

*Sincerely,*

If you follow up by phone, say something like, *I'm calling to find out the status of your search for the _____ position.* Or you could say, *I'm wondering what else*

**LEARNING OUTCOME 5**
Prepare additional employment documents.

*I can do to convince you that I'm the right person for this job.* It's important to sound professional and courteous. Sounding desperate, angry, or frustrated that you have not been contacted can ruin your chances.

Depending on the response you get to your first follow-up request, you may have to follow up additional times. Keep in mind, though, that some employers won't tell you about their hiring decision unless you are the one hired. Don't harass the interviewer, and don't force a decision. If you don't hear back from an employer within several weeks after following up, it is best to assume that you didn't get the job, and you should continue your job search.

## 14-5  Preparing Additional Employment Documents

Although the résumé and cover letter are your major tasks, other important documents and messages are often required during the job-search process. You may need to complete an employment application form and write follow-up messages. You might also have to write a letter of resignation when leaving a job. Because each of these tasks reveals something about you and your communication skills, you will want to put your best foot forward. These documents often subtly influence company officials to offer a job.

### 14-5a  Application Form

Some organizations require job candidates to fill out job application forms instead of, or in addition to, submitting résumés. This practice permits them to gather and store standardized data about each applicant. Whether the application is on paper or online, follow the directions carefully and provide accurate information. The following suggestions can help you be prepared:

- Carry a card or notes saved on your mobile device summarizing vital statistics not included on your résumé. If you are asked to fill out an application form in an employer's office, you will need a handy reference to the following data: graduation dates; beginning and ending dates of all employment; salary history; full names, titles, and present work addresses of former supervisors; full addresses and phone numbers of current and previous employers; and full names, occupational titles, business addresses, and telephone numbers of people who have agreed to serve as references.

- Look over all the questions before starting.

- If filling out a paper form, write neatly using blue or black ink. Many career counselors recommend printing your responses; cursive handwriting can be difficult to read.

- Answer all questions honestly. Write *Not applicable* or *N/A* if appropriate. Don't leave any sections blank.

- Use accurate spelling, grammar, capitalization, and punctuation.

- If asked for the position desired, give a specific job title or type of position. Don't say, *Anything* or *Open.* These answers make you look unfocused; moreover, they make it difficult for employers to know what you are qualified for or interested in.

- Be prepared for a salary question. Unless you know what comparable employees are earning in the company, the best strategy is to suggest a salary range or to write *Negotiable* or *Open.* See the Communication Workshop at the end of this chapter for tips on dealing with money matters while interviewing.

- Be ready to explain the reasons for leaving previous positions. Use positive or neutral phrases such as *Relocation, Seasonal, To accept a position with more responsibility,*

*Temporary position, To continue education,* or *Career change.* Avoid words and phrases such as *Fired, Quit, Didn't get along with supervisor,* or *Pregnant.*

■ Look over the application before submitting to make sure it is complete and that you have followed all instructions.

If asked to input data into fields on an online application, have a flash drive ready or access your cloud drive to retrieve digital records that you can carefully copy and paste into windows on electronic forms.

## 14-5b Application or Résumé Follow-Up Message

If your résumé or application generates no response within a reasonable time, you may decide to send a short follow-up e-mail or letter such as the following. Doing so (a) jogs the memory of the personnel officer, (b) demonstrates your serious interest, and (c) allows you to emphasize your qualifications or add new information.

*Dear Mr. Steinberg:*

*Please know I am still interested in becoming an administrative support specialist with Quad, Inc.*

*Since submitting an application [or résumé] in May, I have completed my degree and have been employed as a summer replacement for office workers in several downtown offices. This experience has honed my communication and teamwork skills. It has also introduced me to a wide range of office procedures.*

*Please keep my application in your active file and let me know when my formal training, technical skills, and practical experience can go to work for you.*

*Sincerely,*

> Open by reminding the reader of your interest.

> Review your strengths or add new qualifications.

> Close positively; avoid accusations that make the reader defensive.

## 14-5c Rejection Follow-Up Message

If you didn't get the job and you think it was perfect for you, don't give up. Employment specialists encourage applicants to respond to a rejection. The candidate who was offered the position may decline, or other positions may open up. A recent employer survey reveals that 77 percent of recruiters have gone back and hired a job seeker who was second or third on their candidate list. One shocking reason: 56 percent of recruiters have been ghosted by candidates who had *accepted* the job.[32] As you probably know, **ghosting** means rejection by cutting off all communication and vanishing. It's a rude and cowardly practice, depriving the other of closure.

In a rejection follow-up e-mail or letter, it is OK to admit that you are disappointed. Be sure to add, however, that you are still interested and will contact the company again in a month in case a job opens up. Then follow through for a couple of months—but don't overdo it. You should be professional and persistent, not annoying. Here is an example of an effective rejection follow-up message:

*Dear Mr. Mazahri:*

*Although disappointed that someone else was selected for your accounting position, I appreciate your promptness and courtesy in notifying me.*

*Because I am confident that you would benefit from my technical and interpersonal skills in your fast-paced environment, please consider keeping my résumé in your active file. My desire to become a productive member of your Transamerica staff remains strong.*

*Our interview on _____ was very enjoyable, and I especially appreciate the time you and Ms. Issapour spent describing your company's expansion into international*

> Subordinate your disappointment to your appreciation at being notified promptly and courteously.

> Emphasize your continuing interest.

> Refer to specifics of your interview.

*markets. To enhance my qualifications, I have enrolled in a course in international accounting at CSU.*

*Should you have an opening for which I am qualified, you may reach me at (818) 719-3901. In the meantime, I will call you in a month to discuss employment possibilities.*

*Sincerely,*

Take the initiative; tell when you will call for an update.

## 14-5d Job Acceptance and Rejection Message

When all your hard work pays off, you will be offered the position you want. Although you will likely accept the position over the phone, it is a good idea to follow up with an acceptance e-mail or letter to confirm the details and to formalize the acceptance. Your acceptance message might look like this:

*Dear Ms. Jackson:*

*It was a pleasure talking with you earlier today. As I mentioned, I am delighted to accept the position of project manager with Innovative Creations, Inc., in your Seattle office. I look forward to becoming part of the IC team and starting work on a variety of exciting and innovative projects.*

*As we agreed, my starting salary will be $55,000, with a full benefits package including health and life insurance, retirement plan, and two weeks of vacation per year.*

*I look forward to starting my position with Innovative Creations on September 19, 2022. Before that date I will send you the completed tax and insurance forms you need. Thanks again for everything, Ms. Jackson.*

*Sincerely,*

Confirm your acceptance of the position with enthusiasm.

Review salary and benefits details.

Include the specific starting date.

If you must turn down a job offer, show your professionalism by writing a sincere e-mail or letter. This message should thank the employer for the job offer and explain briefly that you are turning it down. Taking the time to extend this courtesy could help you in the future if this employer has a position you really want. Besides, it's plain courteous to say thank you for the job offer. Here's an example of a job rejection letter:

*Dear Mr. Glazier:*

*Thank you very much for offering me the position of sales representative with Bendall Pharmaceuticals. It was a difficult decision to make, but I have accepted a position with another company.*

*I appreciate your taking the time to interview me, and I wish Bendall Pharmaceuticals much success in the future.*

*Sincerely,*

Thank the employer for the job offer and decline the offer without giving specifics.

Express gratitude and best wishes for the future.

## 14-5e Resignation Letter

After you have been in a position for a while, you may find it necessary to leave. Perhaps you have been offered a better position, or maybe you have decided to return to school full-time. Whatever the reason, you should leave your position gracefully and tactfully. Although you will likely discuss your resignation in person with your supervisor, it is a good idea to document your resignation by writing a formal letter. Some resignation letters are brief, whereas others contain great detail. Remember that many resignation letters are placed in personnel files; therefore, you should format and write yours using the professional business letter-writing techniques you learned earlier. Here is an example of a basic letter of resignation:

*Dear Ms. Dowd-Garcia:*

*This letter serves as formal notice of my resignation from Allied Corporation, effective Friday, August 12. I have enjoyed serving as your project manager for the past two years, and I am grateful for everything I have learned during my employment with Allied.*

Confirm the exact date of resignation. Remind the employer of your contributions.

*Please let me know what I can do over the next two weeks to help you prepare for my departure. I would be happy to help with finding and training my replacement.*

Offer assistance to prepare for your departure.

*Thanks again for providing such a positive employment experience. I will long remember my time here.*

Offer thanks and end with a forward-looking statement.

*Sincerely,*

Although the employee who wrote the preceding resignation letter gave the standard two-week notice, you may find that a longer notice is necessary. The higher your position and the greater your responsibility, the longer the notice you give your employer should be. You should always give some notice as a courtesy.

Writing job acceptance, job rejection, and resignation letters requires effort. That effort, however, is worth it because you are building bridges that may carry you to even better jobs in the future.

## Summary of Learning Outcomes

**1 Explain current trends as well as the purposes, sequence, and types of job interviews.**

- Current trends in interviewing include (a) increasing use of AI and psychometric skills tests; (b) use of structured, one-way videos and video calls; (c) longer, multiple interviews; (d) hiring for interpersonal skills and potential; (e) project testing; (f) behavioral and situational questions; and (g) group interviews.
- As a job candidate, you have the following purposes in an interview: (a) convince the employer of your potential, (b) learn more about the job and the company, and (c) elaborate on the information in your résumé.
- From the employer's perspective, the interview is an opportunity to (a) assess your abilities in relation to the requirements of the position; (b) discuss your training, experience, knowledge, and abilities in more detail; (c) see what drives and motivates you; and (d) decide whether you would fit into the organization.
- Screening interviews, conducted by telephone or video, seek to eliminate less qualified candidates.
- Hiring/placement interviews may be one-on-one, panel, group, sequential, or video.

**2 Describe how to prepare *before* a job interview.**

- Prepare for telephone screening interviews by ensuring professional answering techniques and screening incoming calls.
- Make the first conversation impressive by using professional, businesslike language, and having your résumé, a calendar, and a list of your references handy.
- Research the target company by scouring the Internet and the company's advertising to learn about its products, history, mission, goals, size, geographic locations, employees, customers, competitors, culture, management structure, reputation in the community, finances, strengths, weaknesses, and future plans.
- Strive to locate inside information through social media.
- Rehearse 30-second success stories that demonstrate your qualifications and achievements.
- Scrutinize your online presence and strive to clean up any digital dirt.
- Decide what to wear to the interview by asking the interviewer what is appropriate.
- To reduce fear before an interview, practice interviewing, prepare thoroughly, and remind yourself that interviewing is a two-way street.

**3 Describe what to do *during* a job interview.**

- During your interview send positive nonverbal messages by controlling body movement, showing good posture, maintaining eye contact, using gestures effectively, and smiling enough to convey a positive, professional attitude.
- Listen attentively, turn off your cell phone or other electronic devices, don't chew gum, and sound enthusiastic and sincere.
- Be prepared to respond to traditional inquiries such as *Tell me about yourself.*
- Practice answering typical questions such as why you want to work for the organization, why you should be hired, how your education and experience have prepared you for the position, where you expect to be in five or ten years, what your greatest weaknesses are, and how much money you expect to earn.
- Be ready for situational questions that ask you to respond to hypothetical situations. Expect behavioral questions that begin with *Tell me about a time when you. . . .*
- Think about how you would respond to illegal or inappropriate questions, including questions about salary history that are prohibited in some states.
- Prepare your own questions about the job, the workload, training programs, your supervisor, and methods of evaluating job performance.
- End the interview positively by summarizing your strongest qualifications, showing enthusiasm for obtaining the position, thanking the interviewer, asking what the next step is, and requesting permission to follow up.

**4 Describe what to do *after* a job interview.**

- After leaving the interview, immediately take notes of the key points discussed.
- Note your strengths and weaknesses during the interview so that you can work to improve in future interviews.
- Write a thank-you e-mail, letter, or card including the date of the interview, the exact job title for which you were interviewed, specific topics discussed, and gratitude for the interview. If interviewers communicate with you by texting, follow their lead.
- Alert your references that they may be contacted.
- If you don't hear from the interviewer when expected, call or send an e-mail to follow up. Sound professional, not desperate, angry, or frustrated.

**5 Prepare additional employment documents.**

- When filling out an application form, look over all the questions before starting.
- If asked for a salary figure, provide a salary range or write *Negotiable* or *Open*.
- If you don't get the job, consider writing a letter that expresses your disappointment but also your desire to be contacted in case a job opens up.
- If you are offered a job, write a letter or e-mail that confirms the details and formalizes your acceptance.
- When refusing a position, write a sincere letter or e-mail turning down the job offer.
- Upon resigning from a position, write a letter that confirms the date of resignation, offers assistance to prepare for your departure, and expresses thanks.

## Key Terms

| | | |
|---|---|---|
| screening interview 453 | group interview 454 | live video interview 454 |
| hiring/placement interview 453 | sequential interview 454 | situational question 466 |
| one-on-one interview 453 | one-way video interview 454 | behavioral question 466 |
| panel interview 454 | two-way video interview 454 | ghosting 475 |

## Chapter Review

1. During a job interview, do the interviewer and the interviewee want the same thing? How do their purposes differ? (L.O. 1)

2. How can you reduce the amount of stress you might potentially experience while anticipating a job interview? (L.O. 1)

3. Career coaches warn candidates to never enter a job interview "cold." What does this mean, and how can a candidate heed the warning? (L.O. 2)

4. What are success stories, and how can you use them? (L.O. 2)

5. How should candidates handle questions about their weaknesses? (L.O. 3)

6. What are situational and behavioral interview questions, and how can you respond so that you impress the interviewer favorably? (L.O. 3)

7. List the steps you should take immediately following your job interview. (L.O. 4)

8. Why should you always send a thank-you message after a job interview, and what are your options for making your note impressive? (L.O. 4)

9. When filling out an employment application form, how should a candidate respond when asked the reasons for leaving previous positions? (L.O. 5)

10. Why is it a good idea to follow up after a job rejection? (L.O. 5)

## Critical Thinking

11. Put yourself in the shoes of an employment recruiter. You're impressed by a job candidate's résumé and references. During her interview, she responded well and asked insightful questions about the company. She's the best fit of all the applicants you have interviewed thus far. But, oh, no! She failed to send a thank-you after she met with you. Should you cross her off the list? Jessica Liebman, a publishing executive who has been hiring for ten years, did just that. Ms. Liebman followed her own simple rule: If someone doesn't send a thank-you e-mail, don't hire that person.[33] No thank-you, no job! She claims that a thank-you note differentiates the "bad eggs" from the "good eggs." Do you agree with this reasoning? Why or why not? (L.O. 4)

12. In a LinkedIn survey of over 5,000 talent professionals, respondents reported that they value so-called "soft skills" equally or more highly than hard skills.[34] Many recruiters, however, confess that they do not know how to measure emotional intelligence and other subjective job-readiness indicators. How do you think a hiring manager determines whether an interviewee has strong emotional intelligence? (L.O. 3)

13. Why is it a smart strategy to thank an interviewer, to follow up, and even to send a rejection follow-up message? Are any risks associated with this strategy? (L.O. 4, 5)

14. During a job interview, Cheryl was startled to be asked to provide her password and login credentials for her social media accounts. Is this request legal and ethical? (L.O. 3)

15. A recruiter for an organization has an outstanding prospect for a position. As part of his screening process, the recruiter checks the online presence of the candidate and discovers from her social networks that she is 18 weeks pregnant—and happily so. He knows that the target position involves a big project that will go live just about the time she will be taking maternity leave. He decides not to continue the hiring process with this candidate. Is his action legal? Ethical? What lesson could be learned about posting private information online?

## Radical Rewrites

**Note:** Radical Rewrites are available at the accompanying student site for you to download and revise. Your instructor may show a suggested solution.

### 14.1 Radical Rewrite: Lexie's Poor Interview Follow-Up Letter (L.O. 4)
**Team**

Lexie Tsuneshi has the right idea in sending a follow-up message after her interview for a marketing coordinator position in Bloomington, Indiana. However, her message could be more effective.

**YOUR TASK.** Based on what you have learned in this chapter, in teams or in a class discussion, list at least five weaknesses. Look for problems with punctuation, wordiness, proofreading, capitalization, sentence structure, and other writing techniques you have studied.

415 South Cory Lane
Sunny Slopes, IN 47401
June 14, 2022

Mr. Jared M. Rogers
Rasmussen Marketing
3205 East Covenanter Drive
Bloomington, IN 47402

Dear Mr. Rogers:

It was an exceeding pleasure and thrill to talk with you about the open position at Rasmussen Marketing. The position as you presented it seems to be a exceptional match for my marketing training and skills. The visionary approach to Account Management that you described, strengthened my resolve to work in a imaginative firm such as Rasmusen Marketing.

I would bring to the position strong organizational skills, and I have the ability to encourage others to work cooperatively within the department. My training in research and analysis of quantitative and qualitative data; as well as my experience as a marketing intern would enable me to help with the updating and management of the CRM system that you mentioned.

I certainly understand your departments need for strong support in the administrative area. I am definitely attentive to details and my organizational skills will help to liberate you to attend to more serious issues in the marketing arena. I was remiss in failing to mention during our very intriguing interview that I also have a minor in marketing despite the fact that it was on my résumé.

Thanks for giving me a chunk of your valuable time to interview me, and explain the goals of your agency along with the dutys of this position. As I am sure you noticed during the interview I am very interested in working for Rasmussen Marketing because I need to get a well-paying job to afford expensive rent and start paying off student loans; and look forward to hearing from you about this position. In the event that you might perhaps want additional info from me or facts about me, all you need to do is text me.

Sincerely,

*Lexie Tsuneshi*

Lexie Tsuneshi

## Activities and Cases

### 14.2 Mastering Scary Group Interviews (L.O. 1)
> Social Media    Web

Group interviews can be intimidating, and opinions on the practice are mixed. "Cattle-call" interviews can be stressful, shocking, even demeaning, some participants feel. One interviewee for an executive-level public relations position described being herded into a room with 200 other applicants where interviewers started bellowing questions at participants. Employers who like this tool say that cattle-call interviews are fair and efficient because they allow the quick ranking of candidates in categories such as teamwork, leadership, and stress management.

**YOUR TASK.** To deepen your understanding of group interviews, search the Web for articles and blog posts using the keywords *group job interviews* or *cattle-call interviews*. Job-search advice sites offer tips on coping with the anxiety of group interviewing. Collect the advice and report your insights in class or in a written document as determined by your instructor.

### 14.3 What Would Hiring Managers Find if They Researched You? (L.O. 1, 2)
> E-Mail    Social Media    Team    Web

An overwhelming majority (70 percent) of hiring managers rely on social media and Internet search engines to research job candidates. A significant CareerBuilder survey revealed that most hiring managers aren't intentionally looking for digital dirt. Six in ten employers say they are merely looking for information about candidates "that supports their qualifications for the job."[35]

Surprisingly, it may not be what they find but what is missing that matters. Almost 50 percent of hiring managers say "they are less likely to interview job candidates if they are unable to find information about that person online." Hiring managers who did find social media information online revealed that the following behaviors turned them off:

*Social Media Behavior Hurting Job Seekers*

| | |
|---|---|
| Provocative or inappropriate photographs, videos, or information | 40 percent |
| Information about candidate drinking or using drugs | 36 percent |
| Discriminatory comments related to race, religion, gender, etc. | 31 percent |
| Being linked to criminal behavior | 30 percent |
| Poor communication skills | 27 percent |
| Complaints about previous company or fellow employees | 25 percent |

Conversely, social media behavior that impresses recruiters includes the following: candidate's background information supported job qualifications (37 percent), candidate's site conveyed a professional image (33 percent), candidate's personality came across as a good fit with company culture (31 percent), candidate was well-rounded and showed a wide range of interests (31 percent), and candidate had great communication skills (28 percent).

**YOUR TASK.** Conduct a social media audit in your course. Armed with the knowledge acquired in this chapter and the information in this activity, critically evaluate fellow students' social media sites such as Facebook, Instagram, Twitter, and LinkedIn. In pairs or larger groups, look for positive attributes as well as negative qualities that may repel hiring managers. Report your findings orally or compile them in an e-mail or memo. If you identify negative behavior, discuss remedies such as how to remove offensive material.

## 14.4 Using Glassdoor to Prepare for Interviews and Find Salary Data (L.O. 1, 2)

> **E-Mail**   **Social Media**   **Web**

Many job seekers do not realize that the job and career site Glassdoor is a superb source of job-search information, postings, reviews, and salary data. Glassdoor provides anonymous posts by current and former employees revealing current information on company culture, salary comparisons, CEO approval ratings, interviews, and more. For authentic insider data about job interviews and other invaluable information, check out Glassdoor.

Let's say you wish to know what LinkedIn is like as an employer and how happy applicants are with LinkedIn's interview process. You would search for information about the company by its name and could refine your search by targeting a specific job title and location. You would see that at 4.4 (on a 5.0 scale), the career network has a high rating overall and that its CEO Ryan Roslansky has achieved an 86 percent approval rating—less than former CEO and current executive chairman Jeff Weiner, who had enjoyed 98 percent approval.

**YOUR TASK.** At the Glassdoor site, search for your dream employer. You can select from industries or search for companies by name. Examine the reviews and the interview modalities. How happy are interviewees and current workers with their employers? Share your results with the class, and, if asked, report your findings in a document—a memo, e-mail, or informal report.

## 14.5 How Much Are Your Skills Worth? (L.O. 2, 3)

> **Web**

Whether you are currently interviewing for a job or not yet in the market, it's good to know what your skills and education are worth. Salary research can give you a better idea of what salary figure you should expect or aspire to. Remember, too, that negotiating a beginning salary can make a huge difference in your overall lifetime earnings. Many salary research websites provide excellent salary information, and most are free. *Salary.com*, the most popular salary-specific job site, not only provides salary data but also offers information on cost-of-living calculators, comparison tools, and negotiating tips. Other notable salary research websites include Glassdoor, PayScale, Indeed, and Salary List. Also consider checking salaries for occupations at O*Net Online, which provides figures compiled by the Bureau of Labor Statistics.

**YOUR TASK.** For a job in which you are interested, consult three different salary research websites. Compare the salary information for a job if filled by a person with your qualifications, as well as your experience. Report your findings as your instructor directs.

## 14.6 Superwoman Conquers Stress Before Interview (L.O. 3)

> Web

In the hours before a make-or-break job interview, Emma Valentiner was a bundle of nerves. She wanted to do well, but she was petrified that she would stumble. To relieve her anxiety, she prepared herself by donning what she called ridiculous underwear adorned with perky pugs and prickly cactuses. As she approached the interview room, she stopped by the restroom, disappeared into a stall, and struck a Superwoman pose. With hands on hips, shoulders thrown back, and feet firmly squared, she breathed deeply for a few moments and told herself she could conquer this interview. This confidence-building trick worked to relieve her stress and helped her enter the interview poised and feeling self-possessed.[36]

**YOUR TASK.** Search news articles and Web blog posts for tactics or tips that new grads and others could employ to reduce anxiety before a job interview or a big test. Prepare a list of 10 ideas, including a few offbeat rituals such as Emma's. Write your list as a set of instructions and be ready to amplify if necessary. Report your advice in class or in a written document determined by your instructor.

## 14.7 Engaging Social Media to Investigate Potential Employers (L.O. 1, 2)

> Social Media  > Web

Valuable insider information about a company's culture, interview procedures, and day-to-day activities is available for those who take the time to search. Enterprising job seekers check YouTube videos, company and employee blogs, business Facebook profiles, LinkedIn pages, Indeed, Salary, Glassdoor, TikTok, and Twitter feeds.

**YOUR TASK.** Using Internet resources, examine the company's Facebook, Instagram, TikTok, and LinkedIn presence. Monitor any Twitter feeds for at least a week. Look for videos featuring the company on YouTube. Prepare a short report summarizing what you learned about the company through reading the blog posts, status updates, and tweets. Include a statement of whether this information would be valuable during your job search. After your review, are you more likely to apply for a job with this company or less so?

## 14.8 Preparing for Interviews With Worksheets (L.O. 2, 3)

Successful interviews require diligent preparation and repeated practice. To be well prepared, you need to know what skills are required for your targeted position. In addition to computer and communication skills, employers generally want to know whether you work well with a team, accept responsibility, solve problems, work efficiently, meet deadlines, show leadership, save time and money, and work hard.

**YOUR TASK.** Consider a position for which you are eligible now or one for which you will be eligible when you complete your education. Identify the skills and traits necessary for this position. If you prepared a résumé in Chapter 13, be sure that it addresses these targeted areas. Now prepare interview worksheets listing at least ten technical and other skills or traits you think a recruiter will want to discuss in an interview for your targeted position.

## 14.9 Telling Success Stories (L.O. 3)

You can best showcase your talents if you are ready with your own success stories that illustrate how you have developed the skills or traits required for your targeted position.

**YOUR TASK.** Using the worksheets you created in **Activity 14.8**, prepare success stories that illustrate the required skills or traits. Select three to five stories to develop into answers to potential interview questions.

For example, here is a typical question: *How does your background relate to the position we have open?* A possible response: *As you know, I have just completed an intensive training program in _____ . In addition, I have over three years of part-time work experience in a variety of business settings. In one position I was selected to manage a small business in the absence of the owner. I developed responsibility and customer service skills in filling orders efficiently, resolving shipping problems, and monitoring key accounts. I also inventoried and organized products worth over $200,000. When the owner returned from a vacation to Bermuda, I was commended for increasing sales and received a bonus in recognition of my efforts.* People relate to and remember stories. Try to shape your answers into memorable narratives.

## 14.10 Digging for Digital Dirt (L.O. 2)

> Social Media  > Web

Before embarking on your job hunt, you should find out what employers might find if they searched your personal life in cyberspace, specifically on Facebook, Instagram, TikTok, Twitter, and so forth. Running your name through Google and other search engines, particularly enclosed in quotation marks to lower the number of hits, is usually the first step. To learn even more, try some of the people-search sites such as MyLife, 123people, Snitch.name, and PeekYou. They collect information from a number of search engines, websites, and social media networks.

**YOUR TASK.** Use Google, MyLife, 123people, or another search tool to explore the Internet for your full name, enclosed in quotation marks. In Google, don't forget to run an *Images* search at **http://www.google.com/images** to find any photos of questionable taste. If your instructor requests, share your insights with the class—not the salacious details, but general observations—or write a short memo summarizing the results.

## 14.11 Talent Assessments: Reviewing Job Test Scenarios (L.O. 1, 2)
> Web

What do Foot Locker, Macy's, PetSmart, Neiman Marcus, Walmart, and Burger King have in common? They use pre-employment testing to identify applicants who will fit into the organization. Unlike classical aptitude tests that began in the military, today's online multiple-choice tests assess integrity, collegiality, and interpersonal skills in general.

To give you a flavor of these talent assessments, here are three typical scenarios:

1. *You have learned that eye contact is important in communication. How much eye contact should you have when conversing with someone in a professional environment?*

   A  At all times. You want to make sure the person knows you are paying attention.

   B  About 60–70 percent of the time

   C  Every now and then. You don't want to make the other person uncomfortable.

   D  About half the time

2. *You are attending an important meeting with colleagues who are more senior than you are. How much should you speak at the meeting?*

   A  You should look very interested but not speak at all unless they request it.

   B  You should speak only when the topic is in your area of expertise.

   C  You should try to talk as much as possible to show your knowledge.

   D  You should speak in the beginning of the meeting and every now and then.

3. *You just found out that people at work are spreading a bad rumor about you that is untrue. How would you respond?*

   A  Tell everybody that it is not true. You need to clear your name.

   B  Don't react to it at all. It'll blow over eventually.

   C  Find out who started it so you talk to them to make sure that they will never do it again.

   D  Talk to others about another coworker's rumor so people will forget about yours.

**YOUR TASK.** Answer the questions; then compare your answers with those of your classmates. Discuss the scenarios. What specific skills or attributes might each question be designed to measure? Do you think such questions are effective? What might be the best way to respond to the scenarios? Your instructor may share the correct answers with you. If your instructor directs, search the Web for more talent assessment questions. Alternatively, your instructor might ask you to create your own workplace (or college) scenarios to help you assess an applicant's interpersonal skills. As a class you could compare questions/scenarios and quiz each other.

## 14.12 Practicing Answers to Interview Questions (L.O. 2, 3)
> Team

Practice makes perfect in interviewing. The more often you rehearse responses to typical interview questions, the closer you are to getting the job.

**YOUR TASK.** Select three questions from each of these question categories discussed in this chapter: questions to get acquainted, questions to gauge your interest, questions about your experience and accomplishments, questions about the future, and challenging questions. Write your answers to each set of questions. Try to incorporate skills and traits required for the targeted position, and include success stories where appropriate. Polish these answers and your delivery technique by practicing in front of a mirror or by making an audio or video recording. Your instructor may choose this assignment as a group activity in class.

## 14.13 Anticipating Situational Interview Questions (L.O. 2, 3)
> Team    > Web

Situational interview questions can vary widely from position to position. You should know enough about a position to understand some of the typical situations you would encounter regularly.

**YOUR TASK.** Use your favorite search tool to locate typical descriptions of a position in which you are interested. Based on these descriptions, develop a list of six to eight typical situations someone in this position would face; then write situational interview questions for each of these scenarios. In pairs, role-play interviewer and interviewee, alternating with each question.

## 14.14 Examining Behavioral Interview Questions (L.O. 2, 3)

> Team   > Web

Behavioral interview questions are increasingly popular, and you will need a little practice before you can answer them easily.

**YOUR TASK.** Use your favorite search tool to locate lists of behavioral questions on the Internet. Select five skill areas such as communication, teamwork, and decision making. For each skill, find three behavioral questions that you think would be effective in an interview. In pairs, role-play interviewer and interviewee, alternating with each question. You goal is to answer effectively in one or two minutes. Remember to use the STAR(T) method when answering.

## 14.15 Negotiating a Salary (L.O. 3)

> Team

Negotiating an entry-level salary can be tricky. You want to get what you're worth, but you don't want to offend or scare off the recruiter—especially in a competitive job market. Worse yet, negotiating doesn't come naturally to most Americans.

**YOUR TASK.** To build your negotiating skills, read the Communication Workshop at the end of this chapter. Then, role-play a situation in which a hiring manager offers a candidate a starting salary of $49,500. The candidate wants $55,000 to start. The candidate responds to preliminary questions and negotiates the salary offer.

## 14.16 Creating a Digital or Paper Interview Cheat Sheet (L.O. 2, 3)

> Team

Even the best-rehearsed applicants sometimes forget to ask the questions they prepared, or they fail to stress their major accomplishments in job interviews. Sometimes applicants are so rattled they even forget the interviewer's name. To help you keep your wits during an interview, make a cheat sheet—either paper or digital—that summarizes key facts, answers, and questions. Review it before the interview and again as the interview is ending to be sure you have covered everything that is critical.

**YOUR TASK.** Prepare a cheat sheet with the following information:

- Day and time of interview:
- Meeting with [name(s) of interviewer(s), title, company, city, state, zip, telephone, cell, e-mail]:
- Major accomplishments (four to six):
- Management or work style (four to six):
- Things you need to know about me (three or four items):
- Reason I left my last job:
- Answers to difficult questions (four or five answers):
- Questions to ask interviewer:
- Things I can do for you:

## 14.17 The End of the Handshake? (L.O. 4)

> Web

As a result of the COVID-19 pandemic, people around the world have changed their greeting style. To reduce the risk of contracting the virus, many switched from the Western custom of shaking hands to a wide range of alternatives. Assume you have been asked by the editor of your school blog to post an article reviewing the history of the handshake and how the greeting has changed as the COVID-19 pandemic appeared and spread. What alternatives have emerged not only in your country but around the world?

Although most interviews during the pandemic were conducted by video call and a certain percentage of employers will continue the practice, eventually the handshake may come back once the pandemic wanes completely and face-to-face interviewing resumes.

**YOUR TASK.** Search the Web for current information about greetings that are considered polite, safe, and welcoming. What is the history of the custom of shaking hands? What alternatives have emerged to replace handshaking? Has the stigma of touching declined since the initial reaction to the pandemic outbreak? What advice would you give candidates who are being interviewed for jobs? Submit your findings in an e-mail or a format your instructor chooses. You may be asked to share your findings in a presentation illustrated with images.

## 14.18 Responding to Inappropriate and Illegal Interview Questions (L.O. 3)

Although some questions are considered inappropriate and potentially illegal by the government, many interviewers ask them anyway—whether intentionally or unknowingly. Being prepared is important.

**YOUR TASK.** Assume you are being interviewed at one of the top companies on your list of potential employers. The interviewing committee consists of a human resources manager and the supervising manager of the department in which you would work. At various times during the interview, the supervising manager asks questions that make you feel uncomfortable. For example, he asks whether you are married. You know this question is inappropriate, but you see no harm in answering it. Then, however, he asks how old you are. Because you started college early and graduated in three and a half years, you are worried that you may not be considered mature enough for this position. However, you have most of the other qualifications required, and you are convinced you could succeed on the job. How should you answer this question?

Alternatively, you are an older worker and are alarmed when the interviewer asks you about your age. Past 40, workers have some recourse against age discrimination although it's hard to prove. You worry that your mature age may unfairly put you out of contention. How should you answer this question under this scenario?

## 14.19 Asking Your Own Questions (L.O. 3)

When it is your turn to ask questions during the interview process, be ready.

**YOUR TASK.** Decide on three to five questions that you would like to ask during an interview. Write them down and practice asking them so that you sound confident and sincere.

## 14.20 Role-Playing Mock Interviews (L.O. 3)
> **Team**

One of the best ways to understand interview dynamics and to develop confidence is to role-play the parts of interviewer and candidate in a mock interview.

**YOUR TASK.** Choose a partner for this activity. Each partner makes a list of two interview questions for each of the eight interview question categories presented in this chapter. In team sessions you and your partner role-play an actual interview. One acts as interviewer; the other is the candidate. Prior to the interview, the candidate tells the interviewer the job he or she is applying for and the name of the company. For the interview, the interviewer and candidate should dress appropriately and sit in chairs facing each other. The interviewer greets the candidate and tries to put the candidate at ease. The candidate gives the interviewer a copy the résumé. The interviewer asks three (or more depending on your instructor's time schedule) questions from the candidate's list. The interviewer may also ask follow-up questions, if appropriate. When finished, the interviewer ends the meeting graciously. After one interview, partners reverse roles and repeat.

## 14.21 YouTube: Critiquing Interview Skills (L.O. 3)
> **Web**

The adage *Practice makes perfect* is especially true for interviewing. The more you confront your fears in mock or real interviews, the calmer and more confident you will be when your dream job is on the line. Short of undergoing your own interview, you can also learn from observation. YouTube and other video sites offer countless video clips showing examples of excellent, and poor, interviewing techniques.

**YOUR TASK.** Visit YouTube or search the Internet for interview videos. Select a clip that you find particularly entertaining or informative. Watch it multiple times and jot down your observations. Then summarize the scenario in a paragraph or two. Provide examples of interview strategies that worked and those that didn't, applying the information you learned in this chapter. If required, share your insights about the video with the class.

## 14.22 Table Manners on Display: Interviewing Over Meals (L.O. 3)
> **Team**   > **Web**

Although they are less likely for entry-level candidates, interviews over business meals are a popular means to size up the social skills of a job seeker, especially in second and subsequent interviews. Candidates coveting jobs with a lot of face-to-face contact with the public may be subjected to the ultimate test: table manners. Interviews are nerve-racking and intimidating enough, but imagine having to juggle silverware, wrangle potentially messy food, and keep your clothing stain free—all this while listening carefully to what is being said around the table and giving thoughtful, confident answers.

**YOUR TASK.** Researching tips can help you avoid the most common pitfalls associated with interviews over meals. Use your favorite search engine and try queries such as *interview dining tips, interviewing over meals*, and so forth. Consider the credibility of your sources. Are they authorities on the subject? Compile a list of tips and jot down your sources. Share the list with your peers. If your instructor directs, discuss the categories of advice provided. Then, as a class assemble a comprehensive list of the most common interview tips.

## 14.23 Thanking the Interviewer (L.O. 4)

> **Team**

You have just completed an exciting employment interview, and you want the interviewer to remember you favorably.

**YOUR TASK.** Write a follow-up thank-you letter to Meredith Murillo, Human Resources Development, Cybersecure, Inc., 4400 Legacy Drive, Plano, TX 75024 (or a company of your choice). Make up any details needed.

## 14.24 Following Up After Submitting Your Résumé (L.O. 4)

> **E-Mail**

A month has passed since you sent your résumé and cover letter in response to a job advertisement. You are still interested in the position and would like to find out whether you still have a chance.

**YOUR TASK.** Write a follow-up e-mail or letter to an employer of your choice that does not offend the reader or damage your chances of employment.

## 14.25 Refusing to Take *No* for an Answer (L.O. 5)

After an excellent interview with Meredith Murillo of Cybersecure, Inc. (or a company of your choice), you are disappointed to learn that someone else was hired. However, you *really* want to work for Cybersecure.

**YOUR TASK.** Write a follow-up message to Meredith Murillo, Human Resources Development, Cybersecure, Inc., 4400 Legacy Drive, Plano, TX 75024 (or a company of your choice). Indicate that you are disappointed but still interested.

## 14.26 Saying *Yes* to a Stellar Job Offer (L.O. 5)

> **E-Mail**

Your dream has come true: you have just been offered an excellent position. Although you accepted the position on the phone, you want to send a formal acceptance e-mail or letter.

**YOUR TASK.** Write a job acceptance e-mail message or letter to an employer of your choice. Include the job title, your starting date, and details about your compensation package. Make up any necessary details.

## 14.27 Demonstrating Your Growing Value to the Organization (L.O. 1, 4, 5)

Your boss has paid your tuition for this course. As you complete the course, the manager asks you for a letter about your experience in the course.

**YOUR TASK.** Write a letter to a boss in a real or imaginary organization explaining how this course made you more valuable to the organization.

## TOTAL REVIEW

This exercise reviews all of the guidelines in the Grammar/Mechanics Handbook as well as the lists of Confusing Words and Frequently Misspelled Words. Choose the correct option. When you finish, compare your responses with those at the bottom of the page.

_____c_____     **EXAMPLE**    a. The board have voted to give all employee's retroactive pay rises.
                                          b. The Board has voted to give all employees' retroactive pay raises.
                                          c. The board has voted to give all employees retroactive pay raises.

_____    1.   a. Our Human Resources Department provided a training session for my team and I, but rebuked us for Davids unexplained absence.
            b. Our Human Resources Department provided a training session for my team and me but rebuked us for David's unexplained absence.
            c. Our human resources department provided a training session for my team and me, but rebuked us for David's unexplained absence.

_____    2.   a. In the spring each of the families plans to improve its disaster preparedness.
            b. In the Spring each of the familys plan to improve it's disaster preparedness.
            c. In the spring each of the familys plan to improve its disaster preparedness.

_____    3.   a. About one-half of Pizza Hut's 8,000 outlets will make deliveries; the others focus on walk-in customers.
            b. About 1/2 of Pizza Huts 8,000 outlets will make deliverys, the others focuses on walk-in customers.
            c. About one-half of Pizza Hut's eight thousand outlets will make deliverys, the others focus on walk in customers.

_____    4.   a. The 6 branches of the United States military are: Army, Navy, Marines, Coast Guard, Air Force and Space Force.
            b. The six branches of the United States' military are: Army, Navy, Marines, Coast Guard, Air Force and Space Force.
            c. The six branches of the United States military are Army, Navy, Marines, Coast Guard, Air Force, and Space Force.

_____    5.   a. It's too close to the deadline of August 1 to rewrite the whole report.
            b. Its to close to the deadline of August 1 to rewrite the whole report.
            c. It's too close to the deadline of August 1st to rewrite the whole report.

_____    6.   a. If I was him, I would travel to Berlin, the German capital immediatly.
            b. If I were him, I would travel to Berlin, the German capital, immediately.
            c. If I was him I would travel to Berlin, the German capitol, immediately.

_____    7.   a. The company's insurance carrier inquired whether at this point in our contract it could change significant terms.
            b. The company's insurance carrier inquired whether, at this point in our contract, it could change significant terms?
            c. The companys insurance carrier inquired whether at this point in our contract, it could change significant terms?

_____    8.   a. The Accounting Director told Florian and I to address the 3 greatest difficultys of the new project.
            b. The accounting director told Florian and me to address the three greatest difficulties of the new project.
            c. The accounting director told Florian and I to address the three greatest difficultys of the new project.

_____    9.   a. If the Manager had seen the senders invoice, she would have payed it quickly.
            b. If the manager had saw the sender's invoice, she would have payed it quick.
            c. If the manager had seen the sender's invoice, she would have paid it quickly.

_____ 10. a. South Korean consumers buy there grocery in small quantitys; therefore, Walmarts sheer size overwhelmed and irritated them.

b. South Korean consumers buy their grocerys in small quantities, therefore, Walmarts sheer size overwhelmed and irritated them.

c. South Korean consumers buy their groceries in small quantities; therefore, Walmart's sheer size overwhelmed and irritated them.

## Editing Challenge 14

Every chapter provides an editing exercise to fine-tune your grammar and mechanics skills. The following interview follow-up message requires edits that address grammar, punctuation, capitalization, number style, concise wording, and other writing issues. Study the principles in the Grammar/Mechanics Handbook (Appendix D), including the lists of Confusing Words and Frequently Misspelled Words.

**YOUR TASK.** Edit the following (a) by inserting corrections in your textbook or on a photocopy using the proofreading marks in Appendix C or (b) by downloading the message from the accompanying student site and correcting it at your computer.

60 Mill Drive
Galloway, OH 43119
May 30, 2022

Mr. Terrell Pitts
Broad Street Associates
8350 West Broad Street, Suite 101
Columbus, OH 43222

Dear Mr. Pitts

It was extremely enjoyable to talk with you on Wenesday about the Assistant Account Manager position at Broad Street Associate. The position, as you presented it seems to be an excelent match for my training and skills. The creative approach to Account Management that you described, confirmed my desire to work in a imaginative firm such as Broad Street Associates.

In addition to an enthusiastic attitude I would bring to the position strong communication skills, and the ability to encourage others to work cooperatively within the department. My Graphic Arts training and experience will help me work with staff artists, and provide a understanding of the visual aspects of you work.

I certainly understand your departments need for strong support in the administrative area. My attention to detail and my organizational skills will help to free you to deal with more pressing issues in the management area. Despite the fact that it was on my résumé I neglected to emphasize during our interview that I worked for 2 summers as a temporary office worker. This experience helped me to develop administrative support and clerical skills as well as to understand the every day demands of a busy office.

Thanks for taking the time to interview me, and explain the goals of your agency along with the dutys of this position. As I mentioned during the interview I am very interested in working for Broad Street Associate, and look forward to hearing from you about this position. In the event that you might possibly need additional information from me or facts about me, all you need to do is shoot me an e-mail at lreid@buckeye.com or text me at 614 727 3893.

Sincerely,

*Lacey Reid*

Lacey Reid

## Money Talk: Salary Negotiations Dos and Don'ts

Negotiating a salary offer may not be the first priority for new graduates seeking entry-level positions. However, it does not hurt to try if you bring some special expertise or experience to the table.[37] Even at the entry level, most employers (75 percent) leave room to increase their first salary offer by 5 to 10 percent, and 84 percent of them say that candidates who negotiate are not risking their jobs.[38]

To discuss compensation effectively, though, you must be prepared for salary questions, and you should know what your skills are worth in your industry and geographic region. You also need to know basic negotiation strategies. Alas, negotiating doesn't come naturally to Americans. "Most people in our country are not used to bargaining," says salary expert Matthew Deluca. "But if you don't bargain, you are not going to get all you should."[39] The following negotiating rules, recommended by career experts, can guide you to a better beginning salary.[40]

### Rule No. 1: Postpone discussing salary for as long as possible in the interview process.

The longer you delay salary discussion, the more time you will have to convince the employer that you are worth what you are asking for. Ideally, you should try to avoid discussing salary until you know for sure that the interviewing company is making a job offer. The best time for you to negotiate your salary is between the time you are offered the position and the time you accept it. Wait for the employer to bring salary up first. If salary comes up and you are not sure whether the job is being offered to you, it is time to be blunt. Here are some things you could say:

*Are you making me a job offer?*

*What is your salary range for positions with similar requirements?*

*I'm very interested in the position, and my salary would be negotiable.*

*Tell me what you have in mind for the salary range.*

### Rule No. 2: Find out the typical salary range for similar jobs in similar organizations in your region.

Many job-search websites provide salary information. One of the best sources for salary and other candid insider information is Glassdoor. It allows you to search by region, so you know what similar jobs are paying in your area. The important thing here is to think in terms of a wide salary range. Let's say you are hoping to start at between $60,000 and $65,000. To an interviewer, you might say, *I was looking for a salary in the low to mid sixties.* This technique is called bracketing. In addition, stating your salary range in an annual dollar amount sounds more professional than asking for an hourly wage. Be sure to consider such things as geographic location, employer size, industry standards, the state of the economy, and other factors to make sure that the range you come up with is realistic.

### Rule No. 3: When negotiating, focus on what you are worth, not on what you need.

Throughout the interview and negotiation process, focus continually on your strengths. Make sure the employer knows everything of value that you will bring to the organization. You have to prove that your skills are worth what you are asking for. Employers pay salaries based on what you will accomplish on the job and contribute to the organization. When discussing your salary, focus on how the company will benefit from these contributions. Don't bring personal issues into the negotiation process. No employer will be willing to pay you more because you have bills to pay, mouths to feed, or debts to settle.

### Rule No. 4: Never say *no* to a job before it is offered.

Why would anyone refuse a job offer before it is made? It happens all the time. Let's say you were hoping for a salary of $60,000. The interviewer tells you that the salary scheduled for this job is $55,000. You respond, *Oh, that is out of the question!* Before you were offered the job, you have, in effect, refused it. Instead, wait for the job offer; then start negotiating your salary.

### Rule No. 5: Ask for a higher salary first, and consider benefits.

Within reason, always try to ask for a higher salary first. This will leave room for this amount to decrease during negotiations until it is closer to your original expectations. Remember to consider the entire compensation package when negotiating because benefits account for almost a third of your total compensation, according to the Bureau of Labor Statistics.[41] You may be willing to accept a lower salary if benefits such as remote work, insurance, flexible hours, time off, and retirement are attractive.

### Rule No. 6: Be ready to bargain if offered a low starting salary.

Companies are often willing to pay more for someone who interviews well and fits their culture. If the company seems right to you and you are pleased with the open position but have been offered a low salary, say, *That is somewhat lower than I had hoped, but this position does sound exciting. If I were to consider this, what sorts of things could I do to quickly become more valuable to this organization?* Also discuss such factors as bonuses based on performance or a shorter review period. You could say something like, *Thanks for the offer. The position is very much what I want in many ways, and I am delighted at your interest. If I start at this salary, may I be reviewed within six months with the goal of raising the salary to _____?*

Another possibility is to ask for more time to think about the low offer. Tell the interviewer that this is an important decision and you need some time to consider the offer. The next day you can call and say, *I am flattered by your offer, but I cannot accept because the salary is lower than I would like.*

*Perhaps you could reconsider your offer or keep me in mind for future openings.*

### Rule No. 7: Be honest.

Be honest throughout the entire negotiation process. Don't inflate the salaries of your previous positions to try to get more money. Don't tell an employer that you have received other job offers unless it is true. These lies can be grounds for being fired later on. They have a way of being revealed unexpectedly.

### Rule No. 8: Get the final offer in writing.

Once you have agreed on a salary and compensation package, ask for the offer in writing. You should also follow up with a position acceptance message—letter or e-mail—as discussed earlier in the chapter.

**CAREER APPLICATION.** You have just passed the screening interview and have been asked to come in for a personal interview with the human resources representative and the hiring manager of a company where you are very eager to work. Although you are delighted with the company, you have promised yourself that you will not accept any position that pays less than $60,000 to start.

**YOUR TASK.** With a partner, role-play the positions of interviewer and interviewee. The interviewer sets the scene by discussing preliminaries and offers a salary of $55,000. The interviewee responds to preliminary questions and to the salary offer. Then, reverse roles and repeat the scenario.

ArtBackground/Shutterstock.com

# Document Format Guide

Business communicators produce numerous documents that have standardized formats. Becoming familiar with these formats is important because business documents actually carry two kinds of messages. Verbal messages are conveyed by the words chosen to express the writer's ideas. Nonverbal messages are conveyed largely by the appearance of a document and its adherence to recognized formats. To ensure that your documents carry favorable non-verbal messages about you and your organization, you will want to give special attention to the appearance and formatting of your e-mails, letters, envelopes, memos, and résumés.

## A-1 E-Mail Messages

E-mail is an appropriate channel for short messages. Usually, e-mails do not replace business letters or memos that are lengthy, require permanent records, or transmit confidential or sensitive information. This section describes formats and usage. The following suggestions, illustrated in **Model Document A.1**, may guide you in setting up the parts of any e-mail. Always check, however, with your organization to ensure that you follow its practices.

**Model Document A.1** Typical E-Mail

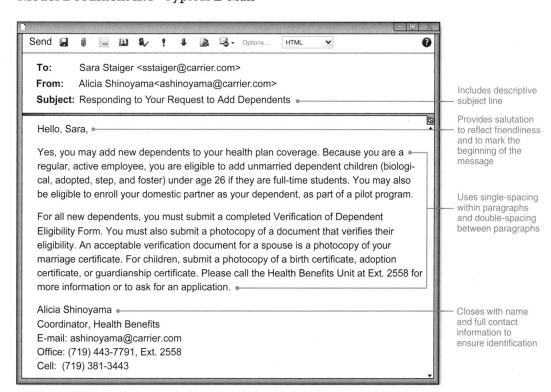

Send | Options... | HTML

**To:** Sara Staiger <sstaiger@carrier.com>
**From:** Alicia Shinoyama<ashinoyama@carrier.com>
**Subject:** Responding to Your Request to Add Dependents ●——— Includes descriptive subject line

Hello, Sara, ●——— Provides salutation to reflect friendliness and to mark the beginning of the message

Yes, you may add new dependents to your health plan coverage. Because you are a regular, active employee, you are eligible to add unmarried dependent children (biological, adopted, step, and foster) under age 26 if they are full-time students. You may also be eligible to enroll your domestic partner as your dependent, as part of a pilot program. ——— Uses single-spacing within paragraphs and double-spacing between paragraphs

For all new dependents, you must submit a completed Verification of Dependent Eligibility Form. You must also submit a photocopy of a document that verifies their eligibility. An acceptable verification document for a spouse is a photocopy of your marriage certificate. For children, submit a photocopy of a birth certificate, adoption certificate, or guardianship certificate. Please call the Health Benefits Unit at Ext. 2558 for more information or to ask for an application. ●

Alicia Shinoyama ●——— Closes with name and full contact information to ensure identification
Coordinator, Health Benefits
E-mail: ashinoyama@carrier.com
Office: (719) 443-7791, Ext. 2558
Cell: (719) 381-3443

**To Line.** Include the receiver's e-mail address after *To*. If the receiver's address is recorded in your address book, you just have to click it. Be sure to enter all addresses very carefully since one mistyped letter prevents delivery. Within your organization and in regular correspondence with external recipients, most e-mail systems will save previously used e-mail addresses and automatically replace them with the addressees' first and last names as you begin to type.

**From Line.** Most mail programs automatically include your name with or without the e-mail address displayed after *From*.

**Cc and Bcc.** Insert the e-mail address of anyone who is to receive a copy of the message. *Cc* stands for carbon copy or courtesy copy. Don't be tempted, though, to send needless copies just because it is easy. *Bcc* stands for blind carbon copy. Some writers use *bcc* to send a copy of the message without the addressee's knowledge. Writers also use the *bcc* line for mailing lists. When a message is sent to a number of people and their e-mail addresses should not be revealed, the *bcc* line works well to conceal the names and addresses of all receivers.

**Subject.** Identify the subject of the e-mail with a brief but descriptive summary of the topic. Be sure to include enough information to be clear and compelling. Capitalize the initial letters of main words. Main words are all words except (a) the articles *a, an,* and *the*; (b) prepositions containing two or three letters (such as *at, to, on, by, for*); (c) the word *to* in an infinitive (*to work, to write*); and (d) the word *as*—unless any of these words are the first or last word in the subject line.

**Salutation.** Include a brief greeting, if you like. Some writers use a salutation such as *Dear Erica* followed by a comma or a colon. Others are more informal with *Hi, Erica; Hello, Erica; Good morning;* or *Greetings*.

**Message.** Ideally, cover just one topic in your message, and try to keep your total message under three screens in length. Some experts recommend limiting e-mails to no more than one screen and instead suggest that writers attach letters or memos when sending longer, more intricate messages. Single-space your text and be sure to use both upper- and lowercase letters. Double-space between paragraphs.

**Closing.** If you choose to conclude an e-mail with a closing, you might use *Sincerely, Cordially, Thanks, Best wishes,* or *Warm regards,* followed by your name and complete contact information. Except for messages to colleagues, always include your contact information in the closing, called signature. Most e-mail programs allow users to create and automatically insert such a signature with each new message.

**Attachment.** Use the attachment window or button to select the name of any file you wish to send with your e-mail. You can also drag and drop most files and hyperlinks into your message.

## A-2 Business Letters

Business communicators write business letters primarily to correspond with people outside the organization. Letters may go to customers, vendors, other businesses, and the government. The following information will help you format your letters following conventional guidelines.

**Conventional Letter Placement, Margins, and Line Spacing.** Following are guidelines for formatting conventional business letters:

- For a clean look, choose a sans serif font such as Arial, Calibri, Tahoma, or Verdana. For a more traditional look, choose a serif font such as Times New Roman. Use a 10-point, 11-point, or 12-point size.
- Use a 2-inch top margin for the first page of a letter printed on letterhead stationery. This will place the date on line 13. Use a 1-inch top margin for second and succeeding pages.

- Justify only the left margin. Set the line spacing to single.

- Choose side margins according to the length of your letter. Set 1.5-inch margins for short letters (under 200 words) and 1-inch margins for longer letters (200 or more words).

- Leave from 2 to 10 blank lines following the date to balance the message on the page. You can make this adjustment after typing your message.

**Formatting Letters With Microsoft Word.** If you are working with Microsoft Word, the default margins are set at 1 inch and the default font is set at 11-point Calibri. The default setting for line spacing is 1.15, and the paragraph default is 10 points of blank space following each paragraph or each tap of the Enter key. Many letter writers find this extra space excessive, especially after parts of the letter that are normally single-spaced. The model documents in this book show conventional single-spacing with 1 blank line between paragraphs. To format your documents with conventional spacing and yet retain a clean look, we recommend that you change the Microsoft defaults to the following: Arial or Calibri font set for 11 points, line spacing at 1.0, and spacing before and after paragraphs at 0. Some organizations prefer serif fonts such as Cambria, Palatino, or Times New Roman for body text.

**Spacing and Punctuation.** In the distant past, typists left 2 spaces after end punctuation (periods, question marks, and so forth). This practice was necessary, it was thought, because typewriters did not have proportional spacing, and sentences were easier to read when 2 spaces separated them. Professional typesetters, however, never followed this practice because they used proportional spacing, and readability was not a problem. Influenced by the look of typeset publications, most writers now leave only 1 space after end punctuation. As a practical matter, however, it is not wrong to use 2 spaces, if done consistently.

## A-2a Business Letter Parts

Professional-looking business letters are arranged in a conventional sequence with standard parts. Following is a discussion of how to use these letter parts properly. **Model Document A.2** illustrates the parts of a block style letter.

**Letterhead.** Most business organizations in the United States use 8½ x 11-inch paper printed with a letterhead displaying their official name, street address, Web address, e-mail address, and telephone and fax numbers. The letterhead may also include a logo and an advertising message.

**Dateline.** If you are preparing a letter on letterhead paper, place the date 1 blank line below the last line of the letterhead or 2 inches from the top edge of the paper (line 13). If you are using plain paper, place the date immediately below your return address. Because the date goes on line 13, start the return address an appropriate number of lines above it. The most common dateline format is as follows: *June 9, 2022*. Don't add *rd, nd,* or *st* when writing the date. For European or military correspondence, use the following dateline format: *9 June 2022*. Notice that no commas are used.

**Addressee and Delivery Notations.** Delivery notations such as *VIA U.S. MAIL, E-MAIL, FAX TRANSMISSION, FEDEX, MESSENGER DELIVERY, CONFIDENTIAL,* and *CERTIFIED MAIL* are typed in all capital letters between the dateline and the inside address.

**Inside Address.** Type the inside address—that is, the address of the organization or person receiving the letter—single-spaced, starting at the left margin. The number of lines between the dateline and the inside address depends on the size of the letter body, the type size (point or pitch size), and the length of the typing lines. Generally, 1 to 9 blank lines are appropriate.

Be careful to duplicate the exact wording and spelling of the recipient's name and address on your documents. Usually, you can copy this information from the letterhead of the correspondence you are answering. If, for example, you are responding to *Jackson & Perkins Company*, do not address your letter to *Jackson and Perkins Corp.*

# Model Document A.2  Block and Modified Block Letter Styles

Letterhead

**Island Graphics**
893 Dillingham Boulevard
Honolulu, HI 96817-8817

(808) 493-2310
http://www.islandgraphics.com

↓ Dateline is 2 inches from the top or 1 blank line below letterhead

Dateline

September 5, 2022

↓ 1 to 9 blank lines

Inside address

Mr. T. M. Wilson, President
Visual Concept Enterprises
1901 Kaumualii Highway
Lihue, HI 96766

↓ 1 blank line

Salutation

Dear Mr. Wilson:

↓ 1 blank line

Subject line

Subject: Block Letter Style

↓ 1 blank line

Body

This letter illustrates block letter style, about which you asked. All typed lines begin at the left margin. The date is usually placed 2 inches from the top edge of the paper or one blank line below the last line of the letterhead, whichever position is lower.

This letter also shows mixed punctuation. A colon follows the salutation, and a comma follows the complimentary close. Open punctuation requires no colon after the salutation and no comma following the close; however, open punctuation is seldom seen today.

Complimentary close

If a subject line is included, it appears one blank line below the salutation. The word Subject is optional. Most readers will recognize a statement in this position as the subject without an identifying label. The complimentary close appears one blank line below the end of the last paragraph.

↓ 1 blank line

Sincerely,

↓ 3 blank lines

Signature block

*Mark H. Wong*

Mark H. Wong
Graphic Designer

↓ 1 blank line

Reference initials

MHW:pil

Modified block style,
Mixed punctuation

In the modified block style letter shown at the left, the date is centered or aligned with the complimentary close and signature block, which start at the center. Mixed punctuation includes a colon after the salutation and a comma after the complimentary close, as shown above and at the left.

Generally include a courtesy title (honorific) such as *Mr., Ms., Mrs., Dr.,* or *Professor* before a person's name in the inside address—for both the letter and the envelope. Although many women in business today favor *Ms.,* you should use whatever title the addressee prefers. Gender nonconforming individuals may ask to be referred to by pronouns such as *they/them/theirs, ze/zem/zir,* and other gender-neutral pronouns. They may also prefer honorifics that reflect their nonbinary identities, e.g., *Mx., Myr.,* or *Pr.* If you don't know the gender identity of a person, use the full name (first and last) without an honorific.

Spell out *Avenue, Street,* and *Company* unless they appear as abbreviations in the printed letterhead of the document being answered.

**Attention Line.** An attention line allows you to send your message officially to an organization but to direct it to a specific individual, officer, or department. However, if you know an individual's complete name, it is always better to use it as the first line of the inside address and avoid an attention line. Placing an attention line first in the address block enables you to paste it directly onto the envelope:

Attention Marketing Director
The MultiMedia Company
931 Calkins Avenue
Rochester, NY 14301

**Salutation.** For most letter styles, place the letter greeting, or salutation, 1 blank line below the last line of the inside address or the attention line (if used). If the letter is addressed to an individual, use that person's courtesy title and last name (*Dear Ms. Davis*). Even if you are on a first-name basis (*Dear Kim*), be sure to add a colon (not a comma or a semicolon) after the salutation. Do not use an individual's full name in the salutation (not *Dear Ms. Kim Davis*) unless you are unsure of gender or gender identity of the individual (*Dear Leslie Davis*).

It's always best to address messages to people. If, however, a message is addressed to an organization, consider these salutations: an organization of men (*Gentlemen*), an organization of women (*Ladies*), an organization of men and women (*Ladies and Gentlemen*). If a message is addressed to an undetermined individual, consider these salutations: a woman (*Dear Madam*), a man (*Dear Sir*), a title (*Dear Customer Service Representative*). Increasingly titles are preferred because they do not automatically assume a binary gender identity.

**Subject and Reference Lines.** Although experts suggest placing the subject line 1 blank line below the salutation, many businesses actually place it above the salutation. Use whatever style your organization prefers. Reference lines often show policy or file numbers; they generally appear 1 blank line above the salutation. Use initial capital letters for the main words or all capital letters.

**Body.** Most business letters and memorandums are single-spaced, with double-spacing between paragraphs. Very short messages may be double-spaced with indented paragraphs.

**Complimentary Close.** Typed 1 blank line below the last line of the letter, the complimentary close may be formal (*Very truly yours*) or informal (*Sincerely* or *Cordially*).

**Signature Block.** In most letter styles, the writer's typed name and optional identification appear 3 or 4 blank lines below the complimentary close. The combination of name, title, and organization information should be arranged to achieve a balanced look. The name and title may appear on the same line or on separate lines, depending on the length of each. Use commas to separate categories within the same line, but not to conclude a line.

Sincerely yours,

*Jeremy M. Wood*

Jeremy M. Wood, Manager
Technical Sales and Services

Cordially yours,

*Casandra Baker-Murillo*

Casandra Baker-Murillo
Executive Vice President

Some organizations include their names in the signature block. In such cases the organization name appears in all caps 1 blank line below the complimentary close, as shown here:

Cordially,
LIPTON COMPUTER SERVICES

*Shelina A. Simpson*

Shelina A. Simpson
Executive Assistant

**Reference Initials.**  If used, the initials of the typist and writer are typed 1 blank line below the writer's name and title. Generally, the writer's initials are capitalized and the typist's are lowercased, but this format varies. Dictation is increasingly becoming rare.

**Enclosure Notation.**  When an enclosure or attachment accompanies a printed document, a notation to that effect appears 1 blank line below the reference initials. This notation reminds the typist to insert the enclosure in the envelope, and it reminds the recipient to look for the enclosure or attachment. The notation may be spelled out (*Enclosure, Attachment*), or it may be abbreviated (*Enc., Att.*). It may indicate the number of enclosures or attachments, and it may also identify a specific enclosure (*Enclosure: Form 1099*).

**Copy Notation.**  If you make copies of correspondence for other individuals, you may use *cc* to indicate courtesy copy, *pc* to indicate photocopy, or merely *c* for any kind of copy. A colon following the initial(s) is optional.

**Second-Page Heading.**  When a letter extends beyond one page, use plain paper of the same quality and color as the first page. Identify the second and succeeding pages with a heading consisting of the name of the addressee, the page number, and the date. Use the following format or the one shown in **Model Document A.3**:

| Ms. Sara Hendricks | 2 | May 2, 2022 |

Both headings appear 6 blank lines (1 inch) from the top edge of the paper followed by 2 blank lines to separate them from the continuing text. Avoid using a second page if you have only 1 line or the complimentary close and signature block to fill that page.

**Plain-Paper Return Address.**  If you prepare a personal or business letter on plain paper, place your address immediately above the date. Do not include your name; you will type (and sign) your name at the end of your letter. If your return address contains 2 lines, begin typing so that the date appears 2 inches from the top. Avoid abbreviations except for a two-letter state or province abbreviation.

## Model Document A.3  Second-Page Heading

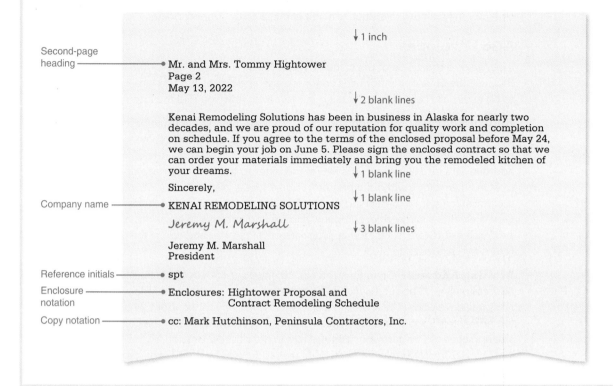

Second-page heading → Mr. and Mrs. Tommy Hightower
Page 2
May 13, 2022

↓ 1 inch

↓ 2 blank lines

Kenai Remodeling Solutions has been in business in Alaska for nearly two decades, and we are proud of our reputation for quality work and completion on schedule. If you agree to the terms of the enclosed proposal before May 24, we can begin your job on June 5. Please sign the enclosed contract so that we can order your materials immediately and bring you the remodeled kitchen of your dreams.

↓ 1 blank line

Sincerely,

↓ 1 blank line

Company name → KENAI REMODELING SOLUTIONS

*Jeremy M. Marshall*

↓ 3 blank lines

Jeremy M. Marshall
President

Reference initials → spt

Enclosure notation → Enclosures: Hightower Proposal and
            Contract Remodeling Schedule

Copy notation → cc: Mark Hutchinson, Peninsula Contractors, Inc.

---

580 East Leffels Street
Springfield, OH 45501
December 14, 2022

Ms. Ellen Siemens
Escrow Department
TransOhio First Federal
1220 Wooster Boulevard
Columbus, OH 43218-2900

Dear Ms. Siemens:

For letters in the block style, type the return address at the left margin. For modified block style letters, start the return address at the center to align with the complimentary close.

## A-2b Letter and Punctuation Styles

Most business letters today are prepared in either block or modified block style, and they generally use mixed punctuation.

**Block Style.**  In the block style, shown in Model Document A.2, all lines begin at the left margin. This style is a favorite because it is easy to format.

**Modified Block Style.**  The modified block style differs from the block style in that the date and closing lines appear in the center, as shown at the bottom of Model Document A.2. The date may be (a) centered, (b) begun at the center of the page (to align with the closing lines), or (c) backspaced from the right margin. The signature block—including the complimentary close, writer's name and title, or organization identification—begins at the center. The first line of each paragraph may begin at the left margin or may be indented 5 or 10 spaces. All other lines begin at the left margin.

**Mixed Punctuation Style.** Most businesses today use mixed punctuation, shown in Figure A.2. It requires a colon after the salutation and a comma after the complimentary close. Even when the salutation is a first name, a colon is appropriate.

## A-2c Envelopes

An envelope should be of the same quality and color of stationery as the letter it carries. Because the envelope introduces your message and makes the first impression, you need to be especially careful in addressing it. Moreover, how you fold the letter is important.

**Return Address.** The return address is usually printed in the upper left corner of an envelope, as shown in **Model Document A.4**. In large companies some form of identification (the writer's initials, name, or location) may be typed above the company name and address. This identification helps return the letter to the sender in case of nondelivery.

On an envelope without a printed return address, single-space the return address in the upper left corner. Beginning on line 3 on the fourth space (½ inch) from the left edge, type the writer's name, title, company, and mailing address. In MS Word and other word-processing software, select the appropriate envelope size and adjust the approximate return address location.

**Mailing Address.** On legal-sized No. 10 envelopes ($4\frac{1}{8} \times 9\frac{1}{2}$ inches), begin the address on line 13 about $4\frac{1}{4}$ inches from the left edge, as shown in Model Document A.4. For small envelopes ($3\frac{5}{8} \times 6\frac{1}{2}$ inches), begin typing on line 12 about $2\frac{1}{2}$ inches from the left edge. In MS Word and other word-processing software, select the correct envelope size and check to be sure your address falls in the desired location.

The U.S. Postal Service recommends that addresses be typed in all caps without any punctuation. This Postal Service style, shown in the small envelope in Model Document A.4, was originally developed to facilitate scanning by optical character readers. Today's OCRs, however, are so sophisticated that they scan upper- and lowercase letters easily.

**Model Document A.4  Envelope Formats**

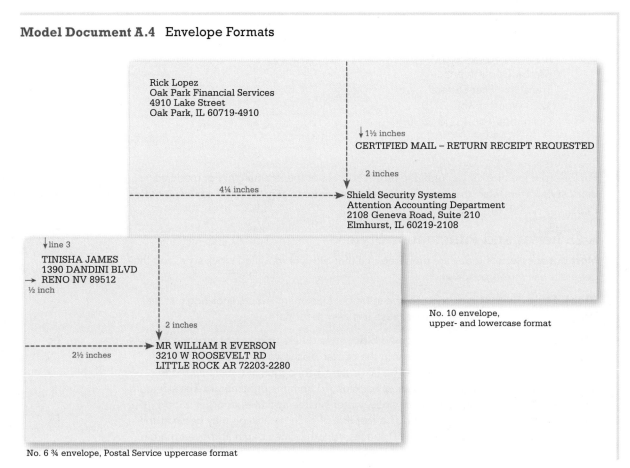

Rick Lopez
Oak Park Financial Services
4910 Lake Street
Oak Park, IL 60719-4910

↓1½ inches
CERTIFIED MAIL – RETURN RECEIPT REQUESTED

2 inches

4¼ inches → Shield Security Systems
Attention Accounting Department
2108 Geneva Road, Suite 210
Elmhurst, IL 60219-2108

No. 10 envelope,
upper- and lowercase format

↓line 3
TINISHA JAMES
1390 DANDINI BLVD
→ RENO NV 89512
½ inch

2 inches
MR WILLIAM R EVERSON
3210 W ROOSEVELT RD
LITTLE ROCK AR 72203-2280
2½ inches

No. 6 ¾ envelope, Postal Service uppercase format

Many companies today do not follow the Postal Service format because they prefer to use the same format for the envelope as for the inside address. If the same format is used, writers can take advantage of word processing programs to copy the inside address to the envelope, thus saving keystrokes and reducing errors. Having the same format on both the inside address and the envelope also looks more professional and consistent. For those reasons you may choose to use the familiar upper- and lowercase combination format. But you will want to check with your organization to learn its preference.

In addressing your envelopes for delivery in the United States or in Canada, use the two-letter state and province abbreviations shown in **Figure A.1**. Notice that these abbreviations are in capital letters without periods.

### Figure A.1  Abbreviations of States, Territories, and Provinces

| State or Territory | Two-Letter Abbreviation | State or Territory | Two-Letter Abbreviation |
| --- | --- | --- | --- |
| Alabama | AL | North Carolina | NC |
| Alaska | AK | North Dakota | ND |
| Arizona | AZ | Ohio | OH |
| Arkansas | AR | Oklahoma | OK |
| California | CA | Oregon | OR |
| Canal Zone | CZ | Pennsylvania | PA |
| Colorado | CO | Puerto Rico | PR |
| Connecticut | CT | Rhode Island | RI |
| Delaware | DE | South Carolina | SC |
| District of Columbia | DC | South Dakota | SD |
| Florida | FL | Tennessee | TN |
| Georgia | GA | Texas | TX |
| Guam | GU | Utah | UT |
| Hawaii | HI | Vermont | VT |
| Idaho | ID | Virgin Islands | VI |
| Illinois | IL | Virginia | VA |
| Indiana | IN | Washington | WA |
| Iowa | IA | West Virginia | WV |
| Kansas | KS | Wisconsin | WI |
| Kentucky | KY | Wyoming | WY |
| Louisiana | LA | **Canadian Province** | |
| Maine | ME | Alberta | AB |
| Maryland | MD | British Columbia | BC |
| Massachusetts | MA | Labrador | LB |
| Michigan | MI | Manitoba | MB |
| Minnesota | MN | New Brunswick | NB |
| Mississippi | MS | Newfoundland | NF |
| Missouri | MO | Northwest Territories | NT |
| Montana | MT | Nova Scotia | NS |
| Nebraska | NE | Ontario | ON |
| Nevada | NV | Prince Edward Island | PE |
| New Hampshire | NH | Quebec | PQ |
| New Jersey | NJ | Saskatchewan | SK |
| New Mexico | NM | Yukon Territory | YT |
| New York | NY | | |

**Folding.** The way a letter is folded and inserted into an envelope sends additional non-verbal messages about a writer's professionalism and carefulness. Most businesspeople follow the procedures shown here, which create the least number of creases to distract readers.

For large No. 10 envelopes, begin with the letter face up. Fold slightly less than one third of the sheet toward the top, as shown in the following diagram. Then fold down the top third to within ⅓ inch of the bottom fold. Insert the letter into the envelope with the last fold toward the bottom of the envelope.

For small No. 6¾ envelopes, begin by folding the bottom up to within ⅓ inch of the top edge. Then fold the right third over to the left. Fold the left third to within ⅓ inch of the last fold. Insert the last fold into the envelope first.

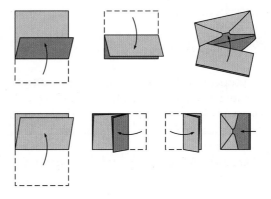

kenary820/Shutterstock.com

# B

# Citation Formats

Careful business writers properly cite the source of any data borrowed from others. Citing sources strengthens a writer's argument, as you learned in Chapter 10, while also shielding the writer from charges of plagiarism. Moreover, good references help readers pursue further research. As a business writer, you can expect to routinely borrow ideas and words to show that your ideas are in sync with the rest of the business world, to boost your credibility by invoking influential business authorities for support, or simply to save time in developing your ideas. To be ethical, however, you must show clearly what you borrowed and from whom.

Source notes tell where you found your information. For quotations, paraphrases, graphs, drawings, or online images you have borrowed, you need to cite the original authors' names, full titles, and the dates and facts of publication. The purpose of source notes, which appear at the end of your report, is to direct your readers to the complete references. Many systems of referencing are used by businesses, but they all have one goal: to provide clear, consistent documentation.

Rarely, business writers use content notes, which are identified with a raised number at the end of the quotation. At the bottom of the page, the number is repeated with a remark, clarification, or background information.

During your business career, you may use a variety of citation or documentation systems. The two most common systems in the academic world are those of the American Psychological Association (APA) and the Modern Language Association (MLA). Each organization has its own style for text references and bibliographic lists. The endnotes in this textbook represent a modified APA style. However, business organizations may use their own citation styles.

Before starting any research project, whether for a class or in a business, inquire about the preferred citation style. For school assignments ask about specifics. For example, should you include URLs and dates of retrieval for Internet sources? For workplace assignments ask to see a previous report either in a hard-copy version or as a soft copy (i.e., a digital file).

In your business and class writing, you will usually provide a brief citation in parentheses that refers readers to the complete reference that appears in a references or works-cited section at the end of your document. Following is a summary of APA and MLA formats with examples.

## B-1 American Psychological Association Format

First used primarily in the social and physical sciences, the American Psychological Association (APA) documentation format uses the *author-date citation system*. This method, with its emphasis on current information, is especially appropriate for business. Within the text, the date of publication of the referenced work appears immediately after the author's name (Rivera, 2021), as illustrated in the brief APA example in **Model Document B.1**. At the end of the report, all references appear alphabetically on a page labeled *References*. The APA format does not require a date of retrieval for online sources, but you should check with your instructor or supervisor about the preferred format for your class or organization. For more information about the APA format, see the *Publication Manual of the American Psychological Association,* Seventh Edition (Washington, DC: American Psychological Association, 2020).

## B-1a APA In-Text Citation Format

As you write, document each text, figure, or personal source that you borrow or reference with an in-text citation in parentheses. Following are selected guidelines summarizing the important elements of APA style.

- For a direct quotation, include the last name of the author(s), if available, and the year of publication; for example, *(Meadows, 2021, p. 32)*. If no author is shown in the text or on a website, use a shortened title or a heading that can be easily located on the References page; for example, *(History, n.d.)*.

- If you mention the author in the text, do not use the name again in the parenthetical reference. Just cite the date; for example, *According to Meadows (2021)*.

- Search for website dates on the home page or at the bottom of Web pages. If no date is available for a source, use *n.d.*

---

**Model Document B.1** Portions of APA Text Page and References

Cites book author (Rivera) and publication date ———

Peanut butter was first delivered to the world by a St. Louis physician in 1890 (Rivera, 2021). As discussed at the Peanut Advisory Board's website, peanut butter was originally promoted as a protein substitute for elderly patients (History, n.d.). However, the 1905 Universal Exposition in St. Louis truly launched peanut butter. Since then, annual peanut butter consumption has zoomed to 3.3 pounds a person in the United States (Barrons, 2020).

Uses first word of Web title (History); blog article has no author, no date

Cites journal author (Barrons) and date

Requires author's name (Meadows), date, and page number for direct quote ———

America's farmers produce 4.1 million tons of peanuts annually, about half of which is used for oil, nuts, and candy. Lisa Gibbons, executive secretary of the Peanut Advisory Board, says that "peanuts in some form are in the top four candies: Snickers, Reese's Peanut Butter Cups, Peanut M&Ms, and Butterfingers" (Meadows, 2021, p. 32).

### References

Scholarly journal with volume (23) and issue (3) numbers, page number, and DOI ———

Barrons, E. R. (2020, November). A comparison of domestic and international consumption of legumes. *Journal of Economic Agriculture, 23*(3), 45–49. https://doi.org/10-1058-0885-7974.30.6.678

Blog article without author, date, or page numbers ———

History of peanut butter. (n.d.). Alabama Peanut Producers Blog. https://www.alpeanuts.com/consumer_interest/article.phtml?articleID=102

Magazine article with volume (35) and issue (4) numbers ———

Meadows, M. A. (2021, May). Peanut crop is anything but peanuts at home and overseas. *Business Monthly, 35*(4), 31–34.

Book ———

Rivera, C. A. (2021). *The world's premier protein sources.* New York: HarperCollins Publishers.

## B-1b APA Reference Format

At the end of your report, in a section called References, list all sources alphabetically by author, or by article title if no author is available. To better understand the anatomy of an APA scholarly journal article reference, see **Model Document B.2**. As with all documentation styles, APA has specific capitalization, punctuation, and sequencing rules, some of which are summarized here:

- Include the last name of the author(s) followed by initials. APA is gender neutral, so first and middle names are not spelled out; for example, (Aten, K., & Thomas, G. F.).
- Show the date of publication in parentheses immediately after the author name(s). A magazine or newspaper citation will also include the month and day in the parentheses.
- Use sentence-style capitalization for all titles except journal article titles. Do not use quotation marks.
- Italicize titles of magazines, newspapers, books, and journals.
- Provide the source URL or the digital object identifier (DOI) when available for scholarly online periodicals. Copy and paste the URL or DOI from the source as a full hyperlink including http or https to avoid typos.
- Break a URL or DOI only before a mark of punctuation such as a slash. Omit period after URL or DOI.

For an expanded list of contemporary APA documentation format examples, see **Model Document B.3**.

# B-2 Modern Language Association Format

Writers in the humanities and the liberal arts frequently use the Modern Language Association (MLA) documentation format, illustrated briefly in **Model Document B.4**. In parentheses close to the textual reference, include the author's name and page cited (*Rivera 25*). At the end of your writing on a page titled *Works Cited*, list all the sources alphabetically. Some writers include all of the sources consulted. Include the URLs for Web references. For more information, consult the *MLA Handbook*, Ninth Edition (New York: The Modern Language Association of America, 2021).

## B-2a MLA In-Text Citation Format

Following any borrowed material in your text, provide a short parenthetical reference. Here are selected guidelines summarizing important elements of MLA style:

---

**Model Document B.2  Anatomy of an APA Journal Article Reference**

Authors · Year of publication · Article title · Volume number in italics, issue number in parentheses · Digital object identifier (DOI) as hyperlink for online retrieval · Journal title in italics · Page numbers

Aten, K., & Thomas, G. F. (2016). Crowdsourcing strategizing: Communication technology affordances and the communicative constitution of organizational strategy. *International Journal of Business Communication, 53*(2), 148–180. https://doi.org/10.1177/2329488415627269

## Model Document B.3  APA Sample References

**References**

Ajunwa, I. (2019, October 8). Beware of automated hiring. *The New York Times*. https://www.nytimes.com/2019/10/08/opinion/ai-hiring-discrimination.html

Alred, G. L., Brusaw, C. T., & Oliu, W. E. (2018). *The business writer's handbook* (12th edition). St. Martin's Press.

Bergeson, S. (2019, January 4). Really cool neutral plasmas. *Science, 63*(6422), 33–34. https://doi.org/10.1126/science.aau7988

Butman, J. (2013, May 29). *Becoming an idea entrepreneur.* Harvard Business Review (Producer). [Video]. https://hbr.org/video/2363618060001/becoming-an-idea-entrepreneur

Cengage Learning Holdings II, Inc. (2020). https://assets.cengage.com/pdf/Annual-Report-Fiscal-Year-Ended-March31-2020.pdf

Clifton, J. (2019, January). Investigating the dark side of stories of "good" leadership: A discursive approach to leadership gurus' storytelling. *International Journal of Business Communication, 56*(1), 82–99. https://doi.org/10.1177/2329488418796603

Decembrele, B. (2018, October 11). The job-hopping generation: Young professionals are on the move. *LinkedIn Blog.* https://blog.linkedin.com/topic/advance-your-career

Glass, I. (Host). (2021, May 30). Good grief! (No. 738) [Audio podcast episode]. In *This American Life.* WBEZ Chicago. https://www.thisamericanlife.org/radio-archives/episode/738/good-grief

How to start a business online. (2021). *Entrepreneur.* https://www.entrepreneur.com/article/17524

Marsen, S. (2020). Navigating crisis: The role of communication in organizational crisis. *International Journal of Business Communication, 57*(2), 163–175. https://doi.org10.1177/23294884|9882981.journals.sagepub.com/home/job

Merriam–Webster. (n.d.). Self-report. In *Merriam–Webster.com dictionary*. Retrieved July 12, 2019, from https://www.merriam-webster.com/dictionary/self-report

Riley, N. S. (2019, May 1). Birds, bees and bureaucracies. [Review of the book *Too Hot to Handle*, by Jonathan Zimmerman]. *The Wall Street Journal.* Retrieved 6 July 2016, from https://www.wsj.com/2Hlgjk3

U.S. Department of Commerce, Census Bureau. (n.d.) U.S. population clock. Retrieved August 9, 2020, from https://www.census.gov/popclock

Book → (Alred, G. L., Brusaw...)

Video → (Butman, J....)

Print journal article with volume (56) and issue numbers (1) as well as DOI hyperlink → (Clifton, J....)

Podcast episode → (Glass, I....)

Online journal article → (Marsen, S....)

Book review published in a newspaper online → (Riley, N. S....)

Online newspaper article → (Ajunwa, I....)

Online magazine article with DOI → (Bergeson, S....)

Annual report → (Cengage Learning...)

Blog post → (Decembrele, B....)

Online magazine article, no author → (How to start a business online...)

Dictionary entry (Retrieval date required for changing data source) → (Merriam–Webster...)

Webpage (Retrieval date required for changing data source) → (U.S. Department of Commerce...)

Note: Although APA style prescribes double-spacing for the References page in academic manuscripts, we show single-spacing to conserve space and to represent preferred business usage.

- For a direct quotation, enclose in parentheses the last name of the author(s), if available, and the page number without a comma *(Rivera 25)*. If a website has no author, use a shortened title of the article, blog, or journal heading that can be easily found on the Works Cited page *("History")*. MLA style requires that titles be enclosed in quotation marks.

- If you mention the author in the text, do not use the name again in parentheses, as *According to Rivera (27)*.

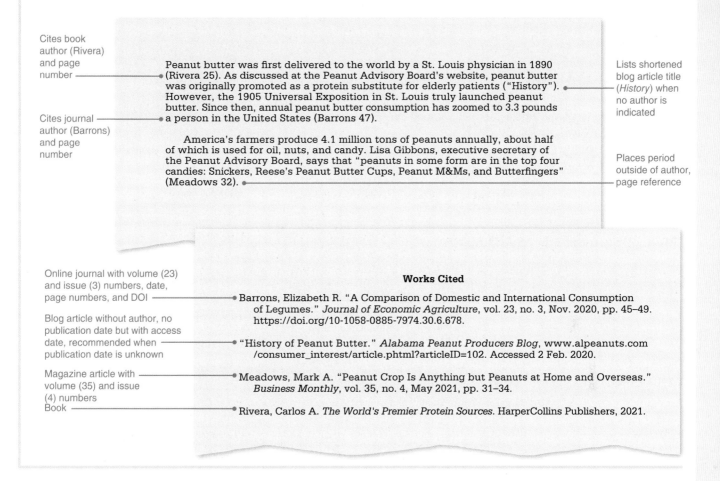

Cites book author (Rivera) and page number —

Cites journal author (Barrons) and page number

Peanut butter was first delivered to the world by a St. Louis physician in 1890 (Rivera 25). As discussed at the Peanut Advisory Board's website, peanut butter was originally promoted as a protein substitute for elderly patients ("History"). However, the 1905 Universal Exposition in St. Louis truly launched peanut butter. Since then, annual peanut butter consumption has zoomed to 3.3 pounds a person in the United States (Barrons 47).

America's farmers produce 4.1 million tons of peanuts annually, about half of which is used for oil, nuts, and candy. Lisa Gibbons, executive secretary of the Peanut Advisory Board, says that "peanuts in some form are in the top four candies: Snickers, Reese's Peanut Butter Cups, Peanut M&Ms, and Butterfingers" (Meadows 32).

Lists shortened blog article title — (*History*) when no author is indicated

Places period outside of author, page reference

**Works Cited**

Online journal with volume (23) and issue (3) numbers, date, page numbers, and DOI —

Barrons, Elizabeth R. "A Comparison of Domestic and International Consumption of Legumes." *Journal of Economic Agriculture*, vol. 23, no. 3, Nov. 2020, pp. 45–49. https://doi.org/10-1058-0885-7974.30.6.678.

Blog article without author, no publication date but with access date, recommended when publication date is unknown —

"History of Peanut Butter." *Alabama Peanut Producers Blog*, www.alpeanuts.com /consumer_interest/article.phtml?articleID=102. Accessed 2 Feb. 2020.

Magazine article with volume (35) and issue (4) numbers
Book —

Meadows, Mark A. "Peanut Crop Is Anything but Peanuts at Home and Overseas." *Business Monthly*, vol. 35, no. 4, May 2021, pp. 31–34.

Rivera, Carlos A. *The World's Premier Protein Sources*. HarperCollins Publishers, 2021.

## B-2b MLA Works-Cited Format

In a section called *Works Cited*, list all references alphabetically by author or, if no author is available, by article or post title. As with all documentation methods, MLA has specific capitalization and sequencing rules. Some of the most significant are summarized here:

- Include the author's last name first, followed by the first name and initial, as (*Rivera, Carlos A.*).
- Enclose in quotation marks the titles of articles, essays, stories, chapters of books, webpages, blog posts, individual episodes of television and radio broadcasts, podcasts, and short musical compositions.
- Italicize the titles of books, journals, websites, magazines, and newspapers.
- Include the URL for online references and provide the access date if no publication date is indicated.
- Do not identify the type of source (such as *Web, Podcast, Print, Video*) as required in the previous *MLA Handbook*.

To better understand the anatomy of the format of an MLA scholarly journal article reference, see **Model Document B.5**. For an expanded list of contemporary MLA documentation format examples, see **Model Document B.6**.

## Model Document B.5  Anatomy of an MLA Journal Article Reference

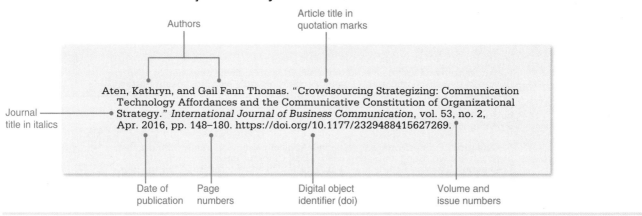

Authors

Article title in quotation marks

Journal title in italics

Aten, Kathryn, and Gail Fann Thomas. "Crowdsourcing Strategizing: Communication Technology Affordances and the Communicative Constitution of Organizational Strategy." *International Journal of Business Communication*, vol. 53, no. 2, Apr. 2016, pp. 148–180. https://doi.org/10.1177/2329488415627269.

Date of publication

Page numbers

Digital object identifier (doi)

Volume and issue numbers

## Model Document B.6  MLA Sample References

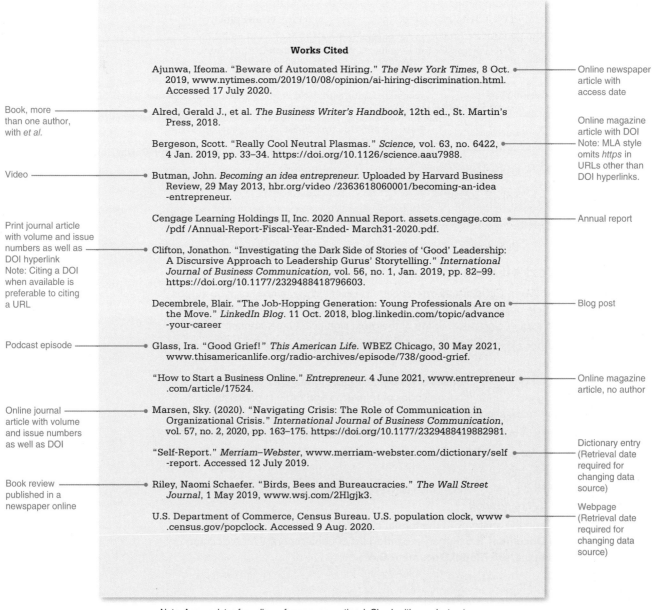

### Works Cited

Ajunwa, Ifeoma. "Beware of Automated Hiring." *The New York Times*, 8 Oct. 2019, www.nytimes.com/2019/10/08/opinion/ai-hiring-discrimination.html. Accessed 17 July 2020.

Alred, Gerald J., et al. *The Business Writer's Handbook*, 12th ed., St. Martin's Press, 2018.

Bergeson, Scott. "Really Cool Neutral Plasmas." *Science,* vol. 63, no. 6422, 4 Jan. 2019, pp. 33–34. https://doi.org/10.1126/science.aau7988.

Butman, John. *Becoming an idea entrepreneur*. Uploaded by Harvard Business Review, 29 May 2013, hbr.org/video /2363618060001/becoming-an-idea -entrepreneur.

Cengage Learning Holdings II, Inc. 2020 Annual Report. assets.cengage.com /pdf /Annual-Report-Fiscal-Year-Ended- March31-2020.pdf.

Clifton, Jonathon. "Investigating the Dark Side of Stories of 'Good' Leadership: A Discursive Approach to Leadership Gurus' Storytelling." *International Journal of Business Communication,* vol. 56, no. 1, Jan. 2019, pp. 82–99. https://doi.org/10.1177/2329488418796603.

Decembrele, Blair. "The Job-Hopping Generation: Young Professionals Are on the Move." *LinkedIn Blog.* 11 Oct. 2018, blog.linkedin.com/topic/advance -your-career

Glass, Ira. "Good Grief!" *This American Life.* WBEZ Chicago, 30 May 2021, www.thisamericanlife.org/radio-archives/episode/738/good-grief.

"How to Start a Business Online." *Entrepreneur.* 4 June 2021, www.entrepreneur .com/article/17524.

Marsen, Sky. (2020). "Navigating Crisis: The Role of Communication in Organizational Crisis." *International Journal of Business Communication*, vol. 57, no. 2, 2020, pp. 163–175. https://doi.org/10.1177/2329488419882981.

"Self-Report." *Merriam–Webster*, www.merriam-webster.com/dictionary/self -report. Accessed 12 July 2019.

Riley, Naomi Schaefer. "Birds, Bees and Bureaucracies." *The Wall Street Journal*, 1 May 2019, www.wsj.com/2Hlgjk3.

U.S. Department of Commerce, Census Bureau. U.S. population clock, www .census.gov/popclock. Accessed 9 Aug. 2020.

Labels (left): Book, more than one author, with *et al.* — Video — Print journal article with volume and issue numbers as well as DOI hyperlink Note: Citing a DOI when available is preferable to citing a URL — Podcast episode — Online journal article with volume and issue numbers as well as DOI — Book review published in a newspaper online

Labels (right): Online newspaper article with access date — Online magazine article with DOI Note: MLA style omits *https* in URLs other than DOI hyperlinks. — Annual report — Blog post — Online magazine article, no author — Dictionary entry (Retrieval date required for changing data source) — Webpage (Retrieval date required for changing data source)

Note: Access dates for online references are optional. Check with your instructor or organization about whether to cite URLs and dates of access.

# Correction Symbols and Proofreading Marks

In marking your assignments, your instructor may use the following symbols or abbreviations to indicate areas needing improvement. Studying these symbols and suggestions will help you understand your instructor's feedback. This information can also help you evaluate and improve your own e-mails, memos, letters, reports, and other writing. The correction symbols are keyed to the Grammar/Mechanics Handbook and to this text.

| | |
|---|---|
| **Adj** | Hyphenate two or more adjectives that are joined to create a compound modifier before a noun. See G/M 1.17e. |
| **Adv** | Use adverbs, not adjectives, to describe or limit the action. See G/M 1.17d. |
| **Apos** | Use apostrophes to show possession. See G/M 2.20–2.22. |
| **Assgn** | Follow the assignment instructions. |
| **Awk** | Recast to avoid awkward expression. |
| **Bias** | Use inclusive, bias-free language. See Chapter 2. |
| **Cap** | Use capitalization appropriately. See G/M 3.01–3.16. |
| **CmConj** | Use a comma before the coordinating conjunction in a compound sentence. See G/M 2.05. |
| **CmDate** | Use commas appropriately in dates, addresses, geographical names, degrees, and long numbers. See G/M 2.04. |
| **CmIn** | Use commas to set off internal sentence interrupters. See G/M 2.06c. |
| **CmIntr** | Use commas to separate introductory clauses and certain phrases from independent clauses. See G/M 2.06. |
| **CmSer** | Use commas to separate three or more items (words, phrases, or short clauses) in a series. See G/M 2.01. |
| **Coh** | Improve coherence between ideas. Repeat key ideas, use pronouns, or use transitional expressions. See Chapter 3. |
| **Cl** | Improve the clarity of ideas or expression so that the point is better understood. |
| **CS** | Avoid comma-splice sentences. Do not use a comma to splice (join) two independent clauses. See Chapter 3. |

| | |
|---|---|
| **CmUn** | Avoid unnecessary commas. See G/M 2.15. |
| **:** | Use a colon after a complete thought that introduces a list of items. Use a colon in business letter salutations and to introduce long quotations. See G/M 2.17–2.19. |
| **Dash** | Use a dash to set off parenthetical elements, to emphasize sentence interruptions, or to separate an introductory list from a summarizing statement. See G/M 2.26. |
| **DD** | Use document design (white space, margins, typefaces, bullets, lists, indentations, or headings) to enhance readability. See Chapter 4. |
| **Direct** | Use the direct strategy by emphasizing the main idea. See Chapter 3. |
| **DM** | Avoid dangling modifiers by placing modifiers close to the words they describe or limit. See Chapter 3. |
| **Filler** | Avoid fillers such as *there are* or long lead-ins such as *this is to inform you that*. See Chapter 4. |
| **Format** | Choose an appropriate format for this document. See Appendix A. |
| **Frag** | Avoid fragments by expressing ideas in complete sentences. A fragment is a broken-off part of a sentence. See Chapter 3. |
| **MM** | Avoid misplaced modifiers by placing modifiers close to the words they describe or limit. See Chapter 3. |
| **Num** | Use number or word form appropriately. See G/M 4.01–4.13. |
| **Ob** | Avoid stating the obvious. |
| **Org** | Improve organization by grouping similar ideas. |
| **Par** | Express ideas in parallel form. See Chapter 3. |
| **Paren** | Use parentheses to set off nonessential sentence elements such as explanations, directions, questions, or references. See G/M 2.27. |
| **Period** | Use one period to end a statement, command, indirect question, or polite request. See G/M 2.23. |
| **Pos** | Express an idea positively rather than negatively. See Chapter 2. |
| **PosPro** | Use possessive-case pronouns to show ownership. See G/M 1.07 and 1.08d. |
| **Pro** | Use nominative-case pronouns as subjects of verbs and as subject complements. Use objective-case pronouns as objects of prepositions and verbs. See G/M 1.07 and 1.08. |
| **ProAgr** | Make pronouns agree in number and gender with the words to which they refer (their antecedents). See G/M 1.09. |
| **ProVag** | Be sure that pronouns such as *it, which, this*, and *that* refer to clear antecedents. |
| **?** | Use a question mark after a direct question and after statements with questions appended. See G/M 2.24. |
| **Quo** | Use quotation marks to enclose the exact words of a speaker or writer; to distinguish words used in a special sense; or to enclose titles of articles, chapters, or other short works. See G/M 2.28. |

| | |
|---|---|
| **Redun** | Avoid expressions that repeat meaning or include unnecessary words. See Chapter 4. |
| **RunOn** | Avoid run-on (fused) sentences. A sentence with two independent clauses must be joined by a coordinating conjunctions (*and, or, nor, but*) or by a semicolon (;). See Chapter 3. |
| **Self** | Use *self*-ending pronouns only when they refer to previously mentioned nouns or pronouns. See G/M 1.08h. |
| **;** | Use a semicolon to join closely related independent clauses. A semicolon is also an option to separate items in a series when one or more of the items contain internal commas. See G/M 2.16. |
| **Shift** | Avoid a confusing shift in verb tense, mood, or voice. See G/M 1.15c. |
| **Sp** | Check misspelled word(s). |
| **Trans** | Use an appropriate transition. See Chapter 3. |
| **Tone** | Use a conversational, positive, and courteous tone that promotes goodwill. See Chapter 2. |
| **You** | Focus on developing the "you" view. See Chapter 2. |
| **VbAgr** | Make verbs agree with subjects. See G/M 1.10. |
| **VbMood** | Use the subjunctive mood to express hypothetical (untrue) ideas. See G/M 1.12. |
| **VbTnse** | Use present-tense, past-tense, and part-participle forms correctly. See G/M 1.13. |
| **VbVce** | Use active- and passive-voice verbs appropriately. See G/M 1.11. |
| **WC** | Focus on precise word choice. See Chapter 4. |
| **Wordy** | Avoid wordiness including flabby expressions, long lead-ins, unnecessary *there is/are* fillers, redundancies, and trite business phrases. See Chapter 4. |

**Figure C.1   Proofreading Marks**

# Proofreading Marks

| Proofreading Mark | Draft Copy | Final Copy |
|---|---|---|
| ⌒ Align horizontally | TO: Rick Munoz | TO: Rick Munoz |
| ‖ Align vertically | 166.32<br>132.45 | 166.32<br>132.45 |
| ☰ Capitalize | Coca-cola<br>sending a pdf file | Coca-Cola<br>sending a PDF file |
| C Close up space | meeting at 3 p. m. | meeting at 3 p.m. |
| ⊐⊏ Center | ⌉Recommendations⌐ | Recommendations |
| ℒ Delete | in my ~~final~~ judgement | in my judgment |
| ∨ Insert apostrophe | our companys product | our company's product |
| ⌃ Insert comma | you will of course | you will, of course, |
| ≈ Insert hyphen | tax free income | tax-free income |
| ⊙ Insert period | Ms Holly Hines | Ms. Holly Hines |
| ∨∨ Insert quotation mark | shareholders receive a bonus. | shareholders receive a "bonus." |
| # Insert space | wordprocessing program | word processing program |
| / Lowercase (remove capitals) | the Vice President<br>HUMAN RESOURCES | the vice president<br>Human Resources |
| ⊏ Move to left | ⊏I. Labor costs | I. Labor costs |
| ⊐ Move to right | A. Findings of study⊐ | A. Findings of study |
| O Spell out | aimed at 2 depts | aimed at two departments |
| ¶ Start new paragraph | ¶Keep the screen height of your computer at eye level. | Keep the screen height of your computer at eye level. |
| ⋯ Stet (don't delete) | officials talked ~~openly~~ | officials talked openly |
| ∼ Transpose | accounts recievable | accounts receivable |
| bf Use boldface | Conclusions bf | **Conclusions** |
| ital Use italics | The Perfect Résumé ital | *The Perfect Résumé* |

Tymonko Galyna/Shutterstock.com

# Grammar/Mechanics Handbook

## D-1 Introduction

In business, people are often judged by the way they speak and write. Communicating competently can mean the difference between success and struggle. Speakers may sound accomplished, but when they write, errors in language usage can hurt their credibility. As one wise student observed, "When I talk, I get by on my personality, but when I write, the flaws in my communication show through. That's why I'm in this class."

To help you upgrade or refresh your skills, we provide a condensed review of basic grammar and mechanics written just for you. This Grammar/Mechanics Handbook offers a rapid systematic review with these resources:

- **Grammar/Mechanics Test.** The 65-point pretest helps you assess your strengths and weaknesses. Your instructor will check your answers in class or give you an answer key.

- **Grammar/Mechanics Summary Profile.** The Grammar/Mechanics Profile reveals your strengths as well as pinpoints specific areas in which you need remedial instructions or study.

- **Grammar/Mechanics Test Online.** A parallel test is available at the accompanying student site. It covers the same principles as those in the textbook pretest, but with different content. The online test gives you immediate answers and feedback.

- **Grammar/Mechanics Review.** After taking the test, you can study the rules in the Grammar/Mechanics Review, which contains many checkup exercises to enable you to try out and reinforce your knowledge.

The first step in your systematic review of grammar and mechanics involves completing the following test.

## D-2 Grammar/Mechanics Test

***Guffey/Loewy, Essentials of Business Communication***    Name _____

This test is intended to reveal your strengths and weaknesses in using the following:

| | | |
|---|---|---|
| plural nouns | commas | number style |
| pronouns | semicolons, commas, and colons | confusing words, spelling |
| verbs | apostrophes | sentence structure |
| adjectives, adverbs | capitalization | |

The test is organized into sections corresponding to the preceding categories. Most of these topics are covered in the Grammar/Mechanics Handbook, although sentence structure is presented in the textbook. When you finish, check your answers with your instructor and fill out the Grammar/Mechanics Summary Evaluation at the end of the test.

## A. Plural Nouns

In sections A through F, each sentence is either correct or has one error related to the category under which it is listed. If a sentence is correct, write C. If it has an error, underline the error and write the correct form in the space provided.

_____ latches _____

**EXAMPLE:** The locksmith replaced several <u>latchs</u> that were difficult to operate.

1. Both of Andy's <u>brother-in-laws</u> managed fast food restaurants.

2. Several <u>attornies</u> in the Dallas office specialize in privacy law.

3. The new graduates discussed whether to move to rural areas, suburbs, or inner <u>citys</u>.

4. All job candidates are asked whether they can work on <u>Sunday's</u>.

5. Both the Richardsons and the <u>Gonzalez's</u> bought expensive graduation gifts.

## B. Pronouns—1

6. Just between you and me, only you and I know that she will be fired.

7. My colleagues and <u>myself</u> were praised by the client for our impressive pitch.

8. Whom did you ask to replace Omar and <u>I</u>?

9. Although <u>it's</u> cooling fan was too noisy, the laptop worked for Olivia and me.

10. Much of the project assigned to Heather and <u>I</u> had to be reassigned to Lee and Jax.

## C. Pronouns—2

11. Facebook often changes <u>it's</u> privacy settings without users' knowledge.

12. Was that elaborate strategic plan <u>her's</u>?

13. In an economic downturn, <u>us</u> new employees are let go first.

14. If you were <u>him</u>, would you consider resignation?

15. When I visit the company headquarters, for whom should I ask?

## D. Verbs—1

16. Because of the holiday, our committee <u>were</u> unable to meet.

17. This smartphone and its calling plan <u>costs</u> much less than I expected.

18. The list of payments <u>have</u> to be approved by the manager.

19. Neither the manager nor the employees in the office think the solution is fair.

20. A description of the property, together with several other legal documents, <u>were</u> submitted by my realtor.

## E. Verbs—2

21. Those reports have <u>laid</u> on his desk for more than a week.

22. If I <u>was</u> in charge, I would certainly overhaul the whole department.

23. If I could <u>chose</u> any city, I would want to live in Paris.

24. The antique car he wanted to restore has <u>set</u> in his garage for years.

25. Kira should have <u>went</u> to a college closer to home because she is homesick all the time.

## F. Adjectives, Adverbs

26. Until we have a <u>more</u> clearer idea of what is legal, we will not proceed. _____

27. Britney thought she had done <u>good</u> in her job interview. _____

28. The architects submitted <u>there</u> drawings a week after the original deadline. _____

29. Joyce felt <u>badly</u> that she couldn't help her colleague write the long report. _____

30. Our IT department monitors <u>peer to peer</u> file-sharing systems. _____

## G. Commas

For each of the following sentences, insert any necessary commas. Count the number of commas you add. Write that number in the space provided. All punctuation must be correct to receive credit. If a sentence requires no punctuation, write 0.

**EXAMPLE:** However because of developments in theory and computer applications, management is become more of a science. _____2_____

31. When you need service on any of your new equipment we will be happy to help you Mr. Greene. _____

32. For example  headquarters decides how tasks responsibilities and territories are assigned to our reps. _____

33. Emma Harvey who is the project manager at TeleCom suggested that I call you. _____

34. Your order Mr. Wong will be sent from Kansas City Missouri on September 1. _____

35. The construction of the U.S. interstate highway system began in 1956 and has spawned many new industries. _____

## H. Semicolons, Commas, and Colons

For each of the following sentences, insert any necessary semicolons, commas, or colons. Count the number of marks you add. Write that number in the space provided. All punctuation must be correct to receive credit. If a sentence requires no punctuation, write 0.

36. When doing research for your report consider these sources of information research databases the Internet books periodicals and government publications. _____

37. Jason Berry submitted his proposal however he forgot to enclose the budget. _____

38. Interest payments on bonds are tax deductible dividend payments are not. _____

39. We are opening a branch office in Tacoma and hope to be able to serve all your needs from that office by the middle of January. _____

40. As suggested by the committee we must first secure funding then we can consider expanding overseas. _____

In sections I–M insert the correct letters in the blank spaces.

## I. Apostrophes

For each of the following sentences, write the correct letter in the space provided.

41. One _____ moving testimony caused the jury _____ enough doubt to acquit. _____
    a. witnesses, members
    b. witness's, members
    c. witness's, members'

42. In just three _____ time, _____ transfer request was approved. _____
    a. week's, Evangeline's
    b. weeks', Evangelines
    c. weeks', Evangeline's

43. At the all-hands meeting of _____, the company's executive _____ were discussed.
    a. stakeholders, salaries
    b. stakeholders', salaries'
    c. stakeholder's, salary's

44. _____ likely that the old smartphone and _____ limited storage capacity won't work much longer.
    a. It's, it's
    b. It's, its
    c. Its, its

45. This _____ harvest of field crops was definitely more abundant than last _____.
    a. years, years
    b. years', year
    c. year's, year's

## J. Capitalization

For each of the following sentences, write the correct letter in the space provided.

46. The project manager and the _____ each received a new _____ computer.
    a. vice president, dell
    b. Vice President, Dell
    c. vice president, Dell

47. _____ Sanchez devised a procedure for expediting purchase orders from _____ warehouses.
    a. Vice President, area 5
    b. Vice President, Area 5
    c. Vice president, area 5

48. On a trip to the _____, _____ visited the Statue of Liberty.
    a. East Coast, uncle Hans
    b. East Coast, Uncle Hans
    c. east coast, uncle Hans

49. James Howe, _____ of _____ will give a keynote address at our shareholder meeting in the spring.
    a. the president/Kendrick, inc.,
    b. the President/Kendrick, inc.,
    c. the president/Kendrick, Inc.,

50. Jacqui enrolled in classes in _____.
    a. History, French, and Psychology
    b. history, French, and psychology
    c. history, french, and psychology

## K. Number Style

For each of the following sentences, write the correct letter in the space provided.

51. The bank had _____ branches in _____ suburbs.
    a. fifteen, three
    b. 15, 3
    c. 15, three

52. We set aside _____ for petty cash, but by _____ our fund was depleted.
    a. $40, December first
    b. forty dollars, December 1
    c. $40, December 1

53. In the past _____ years, nearly _____ percent of the population changed residences at least once.
    a. six, 16
    b. six, sixteen
    c. 6, 16

_____

54. Of the _____ viewer comments about our commercial we received, _____ were negative.
    a. 68, nine
    b. 68, 9
    c. sixty-eight, nine

_____

55. The meeting is scheduled for _____ at _____.
    a. May fifth, three p.m.
    b. May 5, 3 p.m.
    c. May 5th, 3 p.m. in the afternoon

_____

## L. Confusing Words, Spelling

For each of the following sentences write the correct letter in the space provided.

_____

56. Aliana gave Jason good _____ when she suggested he probe his _____.
    a. advise, consciense
    b. advise, conscious
    c. advice, conscience

57. First _____ must _____ to their payment obligations; then the office staff can admit them to see a doctor.
    a. patients, assent
    b. patients, ascent
    c. patience, assent

_____

58. The State _____ in Denver is the _____ government building in Colorado.
    a. Capital, premiere
    b. Capitol, premier
    c. Capitol, premiere

_____

59. Before we can _____ your property, we must _____ it.
    a. ensure, appraise
    b. assure, apprise
    c. insure, appraise

_____

60. The _____ of three companies met at _____ favorite restaurant in Hollywood.
    a. principals, they're
    b. principles, there
    c. principals, their

_____

## M. Sentence Structure

For each of the following options, write the letter of the correct sentence in the space provided.

61. a. I don't necessarily want to make allot of money, I want a pleasant workplace.
    b. I don't necessarily want to make a lot of money I want a pleasant workplace.
    c. I don't necessarily want to make a lot of money; I want a pleasant workplace.

_____

62. a. Once my visa is issued. I plan to work in China for a year.
    b. The message was meant to clarify the new guidelines, but it confused us instead.
    c. Send an e-mail to all staff, tell them our next all-hands meeting will be Monday.

_____

63. a. The deadline for the project was moved up three days. Which means that our team must work overtime.

_____

b. Tyrese supervises shipping, Gabriela manages the Legal Department.

c. No stock prices were available today; the market was closed for the holiday.

64. a. Let us help you develop your online résumé, visit us at Resume.org.

b. Many applicants responded to our ad, however only one knew C++, SQL, and Python.

c. Most job seekers must endure two kinds of interviews: screening interviews and hiring interviews.

65. a. Although Gianna will give him some tough competition, Rashad is confident he'll get the promotion.

b. The work ethic in America is not dead it is deeply ingrained in most people.

c. Leila thought she aced the interview, she was wrong.

## D-3 Grammar/Mechanics Test Summary Evaluation

Place a check mark to indicate the number of correct answers you had in each category.

| NUMBER CORRECT | | 5 | 4 | 3 | 2 | 1 |
|---|---|---|---|---|---|---|
| 1–5 | Plural Nouns | ___ | ___ | ___ | ___ | ___ |
| 6–10 | Pronouns—1 | ___ | ___ | ___ | ___ | ___ |
| 11–15 | Pronouns—2 | ___ | ___ | ___ | ___ | ___ |
| 16–20 | Verbs—1 | ___ | ___ | ___ | ___ | ___ |
| 21–25 | Verbs—2 | ___ | ___ | ___ | ___ | ___ |
| 26–30 | Adjectives, Adverbs | ___ | ___ | ___ | ___ | ___ |
| 31–35 | Commas | ___ | ___ | ___ | ___ | ___ |
| 36–40 | Semicolons, Commas, Colons | ___ | ___ | ___ | ___ | ___ |
| 41–45 | Apostrophes | ___ | ___ | ___ | ___ | ___ |
| 46–50 | Capitalization | ___ | ___ | ___ | ___ | ___ |
| 51–55 | Number Style | ___ | ___ | ___ | ___ | ___ |
| 56–60 | Confusing Words, Spelling | ___ | ___ | ___ | ___ | ___ |
| 61–65 | Sentence Structure | ___ | ___ | ___ | ___ | ___ |

Scale: 5 = You have excellent skills; 4 = You need a light review; 3 = You need a careful review; 2 = You need to study the rules seriously; 1 = You need serious study and follow-up reinforcement.

## D-4 Grammar/Mechanics Review

### Parts of Speech (1.01)

**1.01 Functions.** English has eight parts of speech. Knowing the functions of the parts of speech helps writers better understand how words are used and how sentences are formed.

a. **Nouns** name persons, places, things, qualities, concepts, and activities (e.g., *Kevin, Phoenix, computer, joy, work, banking*).

b. **Pronouns** substitute for nouns (e.g., *he, she, it, they*).

c. **Verbs** show the action of a subject or join the subject to words that describe it (e.g., *walk, heard, is, was jumping*).

d. **Adjectives** describe or limit nouns and pronouns and often answer the questions *what kind? how many?* and *which one?* (e.g., *red* car, *ten* items, *good* manager).

e. **Adverbs** describe or limit verbs, adjectives, or other adverbs and frequently answer the questions *when? how? where?* or *to what extent?* (e.g., *tomorrow, rapidly, here, very*).

f. **Prepositions** join nouns or pronouns to other words in sentences (e.g., desk *in* the office, ticket *for* me, letter *to* you).

g. **Conjunctions** connect words or groups of words (e.g., you *and* I, Mark *or* Jill).

h. **Interjections** express strong feelings (e.g., *Wow! Oh!*).

## Nouns (1.02–1.06)

Nouns name persons, places, things, qualities, concepts, and activities. Nouns may be grouped into a number of categories.

**1.02 Concrete and Abstract.** Concrete nouns name specific objects that can be seen, heard, felt, tasted, or smelled. Examples of concrete nouns are *telephone, dollar, Cadillac,* and *tangerine.* Abstract nouns name generalized ideas such as qualities or concepts that are not easily pictured. *Emotion, power,* and *tension* are typical examples of abstract nouns.

Business writing is most effective when concrete words predominate. It is clearer to write *We need 16-pound copy paper* than to write *We need office supplies.*

**1.03 Proper and Common.** Proper nouns name specific persons, places, or things and are always capitalized (*General Electric, Baltimore, Jennifer*). All other nouns are common nouns and begin with lowercase letters (*company, city, student*). Rules for capitalization are presented in Sections 3.01–3.16.

**1.04 Singular and Plural.** Singular nouns name one item; plural nouns name more than one. From a practical view, writers seldom have difficulty with singular nouns. They may need help, however, with the formation and spelling of plural nouns.

**1.05 Guidelines for Forming Noun Plurals.**

a. Add *s* to most nouns (*chair, chairs; mortgage, mortgages; Monday, Mondays*).

b. Add *es* to nouns ending in *s, x, z, ch,* or *sh* (*bench, benches; boss, bosses; box, boxes; Lopez, Lopezes*).

c. Change the spelling in irregular noun plurals (*man, men; foot, feet; mouse, mice; child, children*).

d. Add *s* to nouns that end in *y* when *y* is preceded by a vowel (*attorney, attorneys; valley, valleys; journey, journeys*).

e. Drop the *y* and add *ies* to nouns ending in *y* when *y* is preceded by a consonant (*company, companies; city, cities; secretary, secretaries*).

f. Add *s* to the principal word in most compound expressions (*editors in chief, fathers-in-law, bills of lading, runners-up*).

g. Add *s* to most numerals, letters of the alphabet, words referred to as words, degrees, and abbreviations (*5s, 2000s, Bs, ands, CPAs, qts.*).

h. Add *'s* only to clarify letters of the alphabet that might be misread, such as *A's, I's, M's,* and *U's* and *i's, p's,* and *q's.* An expression like *c.o.d.s* requires no apostrophe because it would not easily be misread.

**1.06 Collective.** Nouns such as *staff, faculty, committee, group,* and *herd* refer to a collection of people, animals, or objects. Collective nouns may be considered singular or plural depending on their action. See Section 1.10i for a discussion of collective nouns and their agreement with verbs.

## Review Exercise A—Nouns

Choose the correct option. Then compare your responses with the key at the end of the book.

_____

_____

_____

_____

_____

_____

_____

_____

_____

_____

_____

_____

_____

1. Several (a) *attornies*, (b) *attorneys*, (c) *attorney's* collaborated on the case.

2. In their e-mail the (a) *Metzes*, (b) *Metzs*, (c) *Metz's* said they wanted to buy the house.

3. The industrial park has recently lost five (a) *companys*, (b) *company's*, (c) *companies*.

4. The firm removed the (a) *benchs*, (b) *benches* to discourage smoking on the premises.

5. The economy is cyclical and (a) *up's and down's*, (b) *ups and downs* are normal.

6. Plant visits are possible only on (a) *Fridays*, (b) *Friday's*.

7. Many news (a) *dispatchs*, (b) *dispatch's*, (c) *dispatches* were released during the strike.

8. Several (a) *countries*, (b) *countrys*, (c) *country's* decided to nix the trade agreement.

9. Both my (a) *sister-in-laws*, (b) *sisters-in-law*, (c) *sisters-in-laws* paid a steep fine.

10. Some first graders have difficulty writing their (a) *b's and d's* (b) *bs and ds*.

11. The Albuquerque accounting firm employs two (a) *secretary's*, (b) *secretarys*, (c) *secretaries* for five CPAs.

12. Three competition (a) *runner-ups*, (b) *runners-up* claimed the judge was biased.

13. The Tudor-style home features several (a) *chimneys*, (b) *chimnies*, (c) *chimney's*.

14. Expensive camera (a) *lens*, (b) *lens'*, (c) *lenses* are no longer needed to create beautiful, professional photos.

15. Overseas exporters and shippers must include all (a) *bill of sales*, (b) *bills of sale*.

## Pronouns (1.07–1.09)

Pronouns substitute for nouns. They are classified by case.

**1.07 Case.** Pronouns function in three cases, as shown in the following chart.

| **Nominative Case**<br>(*Used for subjects of verbs and subject complements*) | **Objective Case**<br>(*Used for objects of prepositions and objects of verbs*) | **Possessive Case**<br>(*Used to show possession*) |
|---|---|---|
| I | me | my, mine |
| we | us | our, ours |
| you | you | your, yours |
| he | him | his |
| she | her | her, hers |
| it | it | its |
| they | them | their, theirs |
| who, whoever | whom, whomever | whose |

### 1.08 Guidelines for Selecting Pronoun Case.

a. Pronouns that serve as subjects of verbs must be in the nominative case:

   *He* and *I* (not *Him* and *me*) decided to apply for the jobs.

b. Pronouns that follow linking verbs (such as *am, is, are, was, were, be, being, been*) and rename the words to which they refer must be in the nominative case:

> It must have been *she* (not *her*) who placed the order. (The nominative-case pronoun *she* follows the linking verb *been* and renames its antecedent.)

> If it was *he* (not *him*) who called, I have his number. (The nominative-case pronoun *he* follows the linking verb *was* and renames its antecedent.)

c. Pronouns that serve as objects of verbs or objects of prepositions must be in the objective case:

> Mr. Andrews asked *them* to complete the proposal. (The pronoun *them* is the object of the verb *asked*.)

> All computer printouts are sent to *him*. (The pronoun *him* is the object of the preposition *to*.)

> Just between you and *me*, profits are falling. (The pronoun *me* is one of the objects of the preposition *between*.)

d. Pronouns that show ownership must be in the possessive case. Possessive pronouns (such as *hers, yours, ours, theirs,* and *its*) require no apostrophes:

> I bought a cheap cell phone, but *yours* (not *your's*) is expensive.

> All parts of the machine, including *its* (not *it's*) motor, were examined.

> The house and *its* (not *it's*) contents will be auctioned.

Don't confuse possessive pronouns and contractions. Contractions are shortened forms of subject-verb phrases (such as *it's* for *it is, there's* for *there is,* and *they're* for *they are*).

e. When a pronoun appears in combination with a noun or another pronoun, ignore the extra noun or pronoun and its conjunction. In this way pronoun case becomes more obvious:

> The manager promoted Jeff and *me* (not *I*). (Ignore *Jeff and*.)

f. In statements of comparison, mentally finish the comparative by adding the implied missing words:

> Next year I hope to earn as much as *she*. (The verb *earns* is implied here: … *as much as she earns*.)

g. Pronouns must be in the same case as the words they replace or rename. When pronouns are used with appositives, ignore the appositive:

> A new contract was signed by *us* (not *we*) employees. (Temporarily ignore the appositive *employees* in selecting the pronoun.)

> We (not *us*) citizens have formed our own organization. (Temporarily ignore the appositive *citizens* in selecting the pronoun.)

h. Pronouns ending in *self* should be used only when they refer to previously mentioned nouns or pronouns:

> The CEO himself answered the telephone.

> Robert and *I* (not *myself*) are in charge of the campaign.

i. Use objective-case pronouns as objects of the prepositions *between, but, like* and *except*:

> Everyone but John and him (not he) qualified for the bonus.

> Employees like Miss Gillis and *her* (not *she*) are hard to replace.

j. Use *who* or *whoever* for nominative-case constructions and *whom* or *whomever* for objective-case constructions. In making the correct choice, it's sometimes helpful to substitute *he* for *who* or *whoever* and *him* for *whom* or *whomever*:

For *whom* was this book ordered? (*This book was ordered for him/whom?*)

Who did you say would drop by? (*Who/He ... would drop by?*)

Deliver the package to whoever opens the door. (In this sentence the clause *whoever opens the door* functions as the object of the preposition *to*. Within the clause itself, *whoever* is the subject of the verb *opens*. Again, substitution of *he* might be helpful: *He/Whoever opens the door.*)

## 1.09 Guidelines for Making Pronouns Agree With Their Antecedents.

Pronouns must agree with the words to which they refer (their antecedents) in gender and in number.

a. Use masculine pronouns to refer to masculine antecedents, feminine pronouns to refer to feminine antecedents, and neuter pronouns to refer to antecedents without gender:

The man opened *his* office door. (Masculine gender applies.)

A woman sat at *her* desk. (Feminine gender applies.)

This computer and *its* programs fit our needs. (Neuter gender applies.)

b. Use singular pronouns to refer to singular antecedents:

Common-gender pronouns (such as *him* or *his*) traditionally have been used when the gender of the antecedent is unknown. Sensitive writers today, however, prefer to recast such constructions to avoid gender-biased pronouns. Study these examples for bias-free pronouns. See Chapter 2 for additional discussion of bias-free language.

Each student must submit *a* report on Monday.

All students must submit *their* reports on Monday.

Each student must submit *his or her* report on Monday. (This alternative is least acceptable since it is wordy and calls attention to itself.)

c. Use singular pronouns to refer to singular indefinite subjects and plural pronouns for plural indefinite subjects. Words such as *anyone, something,* and *anybody* are considered indefinite because they refer to no specific person or object. Some indefinite pronouns are always singular; others are always plural.

Somebody in the group of touring women left *her* (not *their*) purse in the museum.

| Always Singular | | Always Plural | |
|---|---|---|---|
| anybody | either | nobody | both |
| anyone | everyone | no one | few |
| anything | everything | somebody | many |
| each | neither | someone | several |

Either of the companies has the right to exercise *its* (not *their*) option to sell stock.

d. Use singular pronouns to refer to collective nouns and organization names:

The engineering staff is moving *its* (not *their*) facilities on Friday. (The singular pronoun *its* agrees with the collective noun *staff* because the members of *staff* function as a single unit.)

Jones, Cohen & Chavez, Inc., *has* (not *have*) canceled *its* (not *their*) contract with us. (The singular pronoun *its* agrees with *Jones, Cohen & Chavez, Inc.*, because the members of the organization are operating as a single unit.)

e.  Use a plural pronoun to refer to two antecedents joined by *and*, whether the antecedents are singular or plural:

> Our company president and our vice president will be submitting *their* expenses shortly.

f.  Ignore intervening phrases—introduced by expressions such as *together with, as well as*, and *in addition to*—that separate a pronoun from its antecedent:

> One of our managers, along with several salespeople, is planning *his* retirement. (If you wish to emphasize both subjects equally, join them with *and*: One of our managers *and* several salespeople are planning *their* retirements.)

g.  When antecedents are joined by *or* or *nor*, make the pronoun agree with the antecedent closest to it:

> Neither Jackie nor Kim wanted *her* (not *their*) desk moved.

h.  Use *they* with a singular antecedent if a person does not identify as male or female and wishes to be addressed as *they* (*their, them, themselves*, or the new form *themself*). To be gender neutral and inclusive, many users of modern American English respect the self-identified pronouns of gender nonbinary individuals as a matter of basic courtesy.

> Sam is unhappy with the feedback of *their* (not *his* or *her*) boss.
> (Sam wishes to be addressed using the plural pronouns *they, their, them*.)

> Ze thinks highly of hirself.
> (Common gender-inclusive pronoun in singular use; don't assume or guess gender identity based on pronouns alone. Ask what pronouns to use or share yours first.)

The Associated Press advises writers to reword sentences whenever possible to avoid gendered pronouns; in general contexts its guidelines recommend the use of plural antecedents with plural pronouns because they are not gendered:

> Each team member is responsible for *his* (*her, his/her, their*, etc.) team's success. (gendered, awkward, potentially excluding people who use other pronouns of identity)

> All team members are responsible for their team's success.
> (Preferred phrasing because the plural is gender neutral.)

To avoid awkward expression and confusion in people unfamiliar with gender-neutral pronouns such as *xe* or *ze*, the Associated Press suggests that writers use a person's name in place of a pronoun whenever possible. However, this can be awkward too:

> I was talking to Bryce Smyth and Bryce complained about high temperatures in Bryce's office.

American workers increasingly indicate their pronouns of identity in introductions, in their e-mail signatures, and other workplace situations.

## Review Exercise B—Pronouns

Choose the correct option. Then compare your responses with the key at the end of the book.

1.  The proposal was compiled by Jeremy and (a) *myself*, (b) *I*, (c) *me* last quarter.  _____

2.  (a) *Who*, (b) *Whom* did you say the boss has fired via text?  _____

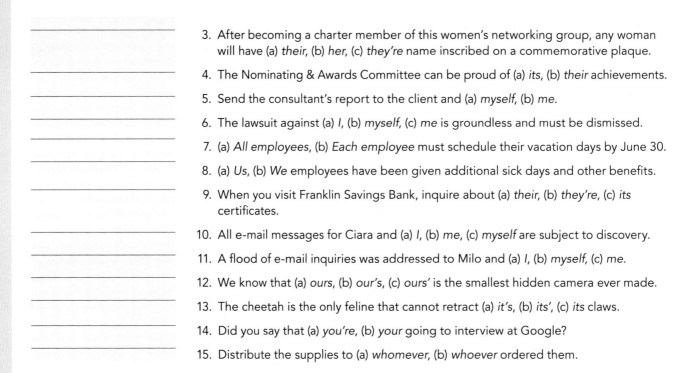

3. After becoming a charter member of this women's networking group, any woman will have (a) *their*, (b) *her*, (c) *they're* name inscribed on a commemorative plaque.

4. The Nominating & Awards Committee can be proud of (a) *its*, (b) *their* achievements.

5. Send the consultant's report to the client and (a) *myself*, (b) *me*.

6. The lawsuit against (a) *I*, (b) *myself*, (c) *me* is groundless and must be dismissed.

7. (a) *All employees*, (b) *Each employee* must schedule their vacation days by June 30.

8. (a) *Us*, (b) *We* employees have been given additional sick days and other benefits.

9. When you visit Franklin Savings Bank, inquire about (a) *their*, (b) *they're*, (c) *its* certificates.

10. All e-mail messages for Ciara and (a) *I*, (b) *me*, (c) *myself* are subject to discovery.

11. A flood of e-mail inquiries was addressed to Milo and (a) *I*, (b) *myself*, (c) *me*.

12. We know that (a) *ours*, (b) *our's*, (c) *ours'* is the smallest hidden camera ever made.

13. The cheetah is the only feline that cannot retract (a) *it's*, (b) *its'*, (c) *its* claws.

14. Did you say that (a) *you're*, (b) *your* going to interview at Google?

15. Distribute the supplies to (a) *whomever*, (b) *whoever* ordered them.

## Verbs (1.10–1.15)

Verbs show the action of a subject or join the subject to words that describe it.

**1.10 Guidelines for Agreement With Subjects.** One of the most troublesome areas in English is subject-verb agreement. Consider the following guidelines for making verbs agree with subjects.

a. A singular subject requires a singular verb:

> The stock market *opens* at 10 a.m. (The singular verb *opens* agrees with the singular subject *market*.)

> He *doesn't* (not *don't*) work on Saturday.

b. A plural subject requires a plural verb:

> On the packing slip several items *seem* (not *seems*) to be missing.

c. A verb agrees with its subject regardless of prepositional phrases that may intervene:

> This list of management objectives is extensive. (The singular verb *is* agrees with the singular subject *list*.)

> Every one of the letters *shows* (not *show*) proper form.

d. A verb agrees with its subject regardless of intervening phrases introduced by *as well as, in addition to, such as, including, together with*, and similar expressions:

> An important memo, together with several contracts, *is* missing. (The singular verb *is* agrees with the singular subject *memo*.)

> The president, as well as several other top-level executives, *approves* of our proposal. (The singular verb *approves* agrees with the subject *president*.)

e. A verb agrees with its subject regardless of the location of the subject:

> Here is one of the contracts about which you asked. (The verb *is* agrees with its subject *one*, even though it precedes *one*. The adverb *here* cannot function as a subject.)

There *are* many problems yet to be resolved. (The verb *are* agrees with the subject *problems*. The word *there* does not function as a subject.)

In the next office *are* several printers. (In this inverted sentence, the verb *are* must agree with the subject *printers*.)

f. Subjects joined by *and* require a plural verb:

Analyzing the reader and organizing a strategy *are* the first steps in message writing. (The plural verb *are* agrees with the two subjects, *analyzing* and *organizing*.)

The tone and the wording of the message *were* persuasive. (The plural verb *were* agrees with the two subjects, *tone* and *wording*.)

g. Subjects joined by *or* or *nor* may require singular or plural verbs. Make the verb agree with the closer subject:

Neither the memo nor the report *is* ready. (The singular verb *is* agrees with *report*, the closer of the two subjects.)

h. The following indefinite pronouns are singular and require singular verbs: *anyone, anybody, anything, each, either, every, everyone, everybody, everything, many a, neither, nobody, nothing, someone, somebody,* and *something*:

Either of the alternatives that you present *is* acceptable. (The verb *is* agrees with the singular subject *either*.)

i. Collective nouns may take singular or plural verbs, depending on whether the members of the group are operating as a unit or individually:

Our management team *is* united in its goal.

The faculty *are* sharply divided on the tuition issue. (Although acceptable, this sentence sounds better recast: The faculty *members* are sharply divided on the tuition issue.)

j. Organization names and titles of publications, although they may appear to be plural, are singular and require singular verbs.

Clark, Anderson, and Horne, Inc., *has* (not *have*) hired a marketing consultant.

*Thousands of Investment Tips is* (not *are*) again on the best-seller list.

**1.11 Voice.** Voice is that property of verbs that shows whether the subject of the verb acts or is acted upon. Active-voice verbs direct action from the subject toward the object of the verb. Passive-voice verbs direct action toward the subject.

Business writers generally prefer active-voice verbs because they are specific and forceful. However, passive-voice constructions can help a writer be tactful. Chapter 3 presents strategies for effective use of active- and passive-voice verbs.

| | |
|---|---|
| **Active voice:** | Our employees *send* many e-mail messages. |
| **Passive voice:** | Many e-mail messages *are sent* by our employees. |

**1.12 Mood.** Three verb moods express the attitude or thought of the speaker or writer toward a subject: (a) the indicative mood expresses a fact; (b) the imperative mood expresses a command; and (c) the subjunctive mood expresses a doubt, a conjecture, or a suggestion.

| | |
|---|---|
| **Indicative:** | I *am looking* for a job. |
| **Imperative:** | *Begin* your job search with the want ads. |
| **Subjunctive:** | I wish I *were* working. |

Only the subjunctive mood creates problems for most speakers and writers. The most common use of subjunctive mood occurs in clauses including *if* or *wish*. In such clauses substitute the subjunctive verb *were* for the indicative verb *was*:

> If he *were* (not *was*) in my position, he would understand.

> Mr. Simon acts as if he *were* (not *was*) the boss.

> We wish we *were* (not *was*) able to ship your order.

The subjunctive mood can maintain goodwill while conveying negative information. The sentence *We wish we were able to ship your order* sounds more pleasing to a customer than *We cannot ship your order*. However, for all practical purposes, both sentences convey the same negative message.

**1.13 Tense.** Verbs show the time of an action by their tense. Speakers and writers can use six tenses to show the time of sentence action; for example:

| | |
|---|---|
| **Present tense:** | I *work*; he *works*. |
| **Past tense:** | I *worked*; she *worked*. |
| **Future tense:** | I *will work*; he *will work*. |
| **Present perfect tense:** | I *have worked*; he *has worked*. |
| **Past perfect tense:** | I *had worked*; she *had worked*. |
| **Future perfect tense:** | I *will have worked*; he *will have worked*. |

**1.14 Guidelines for Verb Tense.**

a. Use present tense for statements that, although introduced by past-tense verbs, continue to be true:

> What did you say his name *is*? (Use the present tense *is* if his name has not changed.)

b. Avoid unnecessary shifts in verb tenses:

> The manager *saw* (not *sees*) a great deal of work yet to be completed and *remained* to do it herself.

Although unnecessary shifts in verb tense are to be avoided, not all the verbs within one sentence have to be in the same tense; for example:

> She *said* (past tense) that she *likes* (present tense) to work late.

**1.15 Irregular Verbs.** Irregular verbs cause difficulty for some writers and speakers. Unlike regular verbs, irregular verbs do not form the past tense and past participle by adding *-ed* to the present form. Here is a partial list of selected troublesome irregular verbs. Consult a dictionary if you are in doubt about a verb form.

**Troublesome Irregular Verbs**

| Present | Past | Past Participle *(always use helping verbs)* |
|---|---|---|
| begin | began | begun |
| break | broke | broken |
| choose | chose | chosen |
| come | came | come |

| Present | Past | Past Participle *(always use helping verbs)* |
|---|---|---|
| drink | drank | drunk |
| go | went | gone |
| lay (to place) | laid | laid |
| lie (to rest) | lay | lain |
| ring | rang | rung |
| see | saw | seen |
| write | wrote | written |

a. Use only past-tense verbs to express past tense. Notice that no helping verbs are used to indicate simple past tense:

> The auditors *went* (not *have went*) over our books carefully.
>
> He *came* (not *come*) to see us yesterday.

b. Use past-participle forms for actions completed before the present time. Notice that past-participle forms require helping verbs:

> Steve *had gone* (not *had went*) before we called. (The past-participle *gone* is used with the helping verb *had*.)

c. Avoid inconsistent shifts in subject, voice, and mood. Pay particular attention to this problem area because undesirable shifts are often characteristic of student writing.

| | |
|---|---|
| **Inconsistent:** | When Mrs. Taswell read the report, the error was found. (The first clause is in the active voice; the second, passive.) |
| **Improved:** | When Mrs. Taswell read the report, she found the error. (Both clauses are in the active voice.) |
| **Inconsistent:** | The clerk should first conduct an inventory. Then supplies should be requisitioned. (The first sentence is in the active voice; the second, passive.) |
| **Improved:** | The clerk should first conduct an inventory. Then the clerk should requisition supplies. (Both sentences are in the active voice.) |
| **Inconsistent:** | All workers must wear security badges, and you must also sign a daily time card. (This sentence contains an inconsistent shift in subject from *all workers* in the first clause to you in the second clause.) |
| **Improved:** | All workers must wear security badges, and they must also sign a daily time card. |
| **Inconsistent:** | Begin the transaction by opening an account; then you enter the customer's name. (This sentence contains an inconsistent shift from the imperative mood in the first clause to the indicative mood in the second clause.) |
| **Improved:** | Begin the transaction by opening an account; then enter the customer's name. (Both clauses are now in the imperative mood.) |

## Review Exercise C—Verbs 1

Choose the correct option. Then compare your responses with the key at the end of the book.

1. One workstation in our department, along with several on the second and third floors, (a) *is*, (b) *are* equipped with special ergonomic features.

2. Southwest Airlines (a) *is*, (b) *are* known for a fun culture that motivates employees.

3. Last week Ms. Knapp (a) *chosen*, (b) *choose*, (c) *chose* a new administrative assistant.

4. If he had (a) *saw*, (b) *seen* the company truck, he wouldn't have backed into it.

5. A set of guidelines to standardize procedures (a) *was*, (b) *were* developed.

6. One of the biggest headaches for bosses (a) *is*, (b) *are* dealing with workplace conflict.

7. Neither of the new interns (a) *are*, (b) *is* going to be hired at the end of the internship.

8. Addressing the conference attendees (a) *is*, (b) *are* slick McKinsey consultants.

9. You should have (a) *gone*, (b) *went* to lunch because now you're distracted and cranky.

10. Machine learning has (a) *became*, (b) *become* an integral part of our work lives.

11. If I (a) *were*, (b) *was* you, I would quit and look for another job.

12. No one but the HR director and a few managers ever (a) *talk*, (b) *talks* about work-life balance.

13. How long has the report been (a) *laying*, (b) *lying* on your supervisor's desk?

14. Have you (a) *broken*, (b) *broke* the contract accidentally or deliberately?

15. The office phone had (a) *rung*, (b) *rang* so frequently that someone unplugged it.

## Review Exercise D – Verbs 2

In the following sentence pairs, choose the one that illustrates consistency in the use of subject, voice, and mood. Then compare your responses with the key at the end of the book.

1. (a) You need to know technology, but you also must get along with coworkers.
   (b) You need to know technology, but one also must get along with coworkers.

2. (a) Leonard and Tyson were still motivated, but Steven hates his job.
   (b) Leonard and Tyson were still motivated, but Steven hated his job.

3. (a) Salespeople should know most prices; then you can provide quotes to customers.
   (b) Salespeople should know most prices; then they can provide quotes to customers.

4. (a) He was an enthusiastic speaker who always had a kind word for everyone.
   (b) He was an enthusiastic speaker who always has a kind word for everyone.

5. (a) Read all instructions first; then you deactivate and reset the old Apple Watch.
   (b) Read all instructions first, and then deactivate and reset the old Apple Watch.

## Adjectives and Adverbs (1.16–1.17)

Adjectives describe or limit nouns and pronouns. They often answer the questions *what kind? how many?* or *which one?* Adverbs describe or limit verbs, adjectives, or other adverbs. They often answer the questions *when? how? where?* or to *what extent?*

**1.16 Forms.** Most adjectives and adverbs have three forms, or degrees: positive, comparative, and superlative.

|  | **Positive** | **Comparative** | **Superlative** |
|---|---|---|---|
| **Adjective:** | clear | clearer | clearest |
| **Adverb:** | clearly | more clearly | most clearly |

Some adjectives and adverbs have irregular forms.

|  | **Positive** | **Comparative** | **Superlative** |
|---|---|---|---|
| **Adjective:** | good | better | best |
|  | bad | worse | worst |
| **Adverb:** | well | better | best |

Adjectives and adverbs composed of two or more syllables are usually compared by the use of *more* and *most;* for example:

> The Payroll Department is *more efficient* than the Shipping Department.
> Payroll is the *most efficient* department in our organization.

### 1.17 Guidelines for Use.

a.  Use the comparative degree of the adjective or adverb to compare two persons or things; use the superlative degree to compare three or more:

> Of the two plans, which is *better* (not *best*)?

> Of all the plans, we like this one *best* (not *better*).

b.  Do not create a double comparative or superlative by using -er with *more* or -est with *most*:

> His explanation couldn't have been *clearer* (not *more clearer*).

c.  A linking verb (*is, are, look, seem, feel, sound, appear,* and so forth) may introduce a word that describes the verb's subject. In this case be certain to use an adjective, not an adverb:

> The characters on the monitor look *bright* (not *brightly*). (Use the adjective *bright* because it follows the linking verb *look* and modifies the noun *characters*.)

> The company's letter made the customer feel *bad* (not *badly*). (The adjective *bad* follows the linking verb *feel* and describes the noun *customer*.)

d.  Use adverbs, not adjectives, to describe or limit the action of verbs:

> The business is running *smoothly* (not *smooth*). (Use the adverb *smoothly* to describe the action of the verb *running*. *Smoothly* tells how the business is running.)

> Don't take his remark *personally* (not *personal*). (The adverb *personally* describes the action of the verb *take*.)

> Serena said she did *well* (not *good*) on the test. (Use the adverb *well* to tell how she did.)

e.  Two or more adjectives that are joined to create a compound modifier before a noun should be hyphenated:

> The *four-year-old* child was tired.

> Our agency is planning a *coast-to-coast* campaign.

Hyphenate a compound modifier following a noun only if your dictionary shows the hyphen(s):

> Our speaker is very *well-known*. (Include the hyphen because most dictionaries do.)

The tired *child* was four years old. (Omit the hyphens because the expression follows the word it describes, *child*, and because dictionaries do not indicate hyphens.)

f.   Keep adjectives and adverbs close to the words they modify:

She asked for *a cup of hot coffee* (not *a hot cup of coffee*).

Patty *had only two days* of vacation left (not *only had two days*).

Students may sit *in the first five rows* (not *in five first rows*).

He *has saved almost* enough money for the trip (not *has almost saved*).

g.   Don't confuse *there* with the possessive pronoun *their* or the contraction *they're*:

Put the documents *there*. (The adverb *there* means "at that place or at that point.")

*There are* two reasons for the change. (The pronoun *there* is used as function word to introduce a sentence or a clause.)

We already have *their* specifications. (The possessive pronoun *their* shows ownership.)

*They're* coming to inspect today. (The contraction *they're* is a shortened form of *they are*.)

## Review Exercise E – Adjectives and Adverbs

Choose the correct option. Then compare your responses with the key at the end of the book.

1. Videoconferences can be productive, but for important negotiations, nothing beats (a) *face-to-face*, (b) *face to face* meetings.

2. If we had been more (a) *careful*, (b) *carefuller*, we could have foiled the ransom attack.

3. Why would we want to merge with (a) *they're*, (b) *there*, (c) *their* company?

4. The intern usually performed all assignments (a) *satisfactorily*, (b) *satisfactory*.

5. The team felt (a) *badly* (b) *bad* when it didn't win the contract.

6. The car dealer advertises a (a) *bumper-to-bumper*, (b) *bumper to bumper* warranty.

7. Of the two ideas the consultant presented, the first one is (a) *more*, (b) *most* feasible.

8. To avoid feeling overwhelmed, approach each task (a) *one-by-one*, (b) *one by one*.

9. The stock market performed (a) *worse*, (b) *worst* today than yesterday.

10. Some workers take feedback in performance appraisals (a) *personally*, (b) *personal*.

11. Our interviews proceeded (a) *slower*, (b) *more slowly* than we had hoped.

12. Newman's Own food company wanted to do (a) *well*, (b) *good* by donating all after-tax profits to charity.

13. Please set the boxes down over (a) *there*, (b) *their*, (c) *they're* until we can sort and distribute the goods.

14. When giving your presentation, avoid speaking too (a) *loud*, (b) *loudly*.

15. New York City is (a) *more close*, (b) *closer* to Europe than Chicago is.

# Prepositions (1.18)

Prepositions are connecting words that join nouns or pronouns to other words in a sentence. The words *about, at, from, in*, and *to* are examples of prepositions.

**1.18 Guidelines for Use.**

a. Include necessary prepositions:

> What type *of* software do you need (not *what type software*)?

> I graduated *from* high school two years ago (not *I graduated high school*).

b. Omit unnecessary prepositions:

> Where is the meeting? (Not *Where is the meeting at?*)

> Both printers work well. (Not *Both of the printers.*)

> Where are you going? (Not *Where are you going to?*)

c. Avoid the overuse of prepositional phrases.

| | |
|---|---|
| **Weak:** | We have received your application for credit at our branch in the Fresno area. |
| **Improved:** | We have received your Fresno credit application. |

d. Repeat the preposition before the second of two related elements especially when the second element is distant from the first:

> Applicants use the résumé effectively by summarizing their most important experiences and *by* relating their education to the jobs sought.

e. Include the second preposition when two different prepositions modify a single object:

> George's appreciation *of* and aptitude *for* computers led to a promising career.

# Conjunctions (1.19)

Conjunctions connect words, phrases, and clauses. They act as signals, indicating when a thought is being added, contrasted, or altered. Coordinate conjunctions (such as *and, or, but*) and other words that act as connectors (such as *however, therefore, when, as*) tell the reader or listener in what direction a thought is heading. They are like road signs signaling what's ahead.

**1.19 Guidelines for Use.**

a. Use coordinating conjunctions to connect only sentence elements that are parallel or balanced.

| | |
|---|---|
| **Weak:** | His report was correct and written in a concise manner. |
| **Improved:** | His report was correct and concise. |
| **Weak:** | Management has the capacity to increase fraud, or reduction can be achieved through the policies it adopts. |
| **Improved:** | Management has the capacity to increase or reduce fraud through the policies it adopts. |

b. Do not use the word *like* as a conjunction:

> It seems *as if* (not *like*) this day will never end.

c. Avoid using *when* or *where* inappropriately. A common writing fault occurs in sentences with clauses introduced by *is when* and *is where*. Written English ordinarily requires a noun (or a group of words functioning as a noun) following the linking verb *is*. Instead of acting as conjunctions in these constructions, the words *where* and *when* function as adverbs, creating faulty grammatical equations (adverbs cannot complete equations set up by linking verbs). To avoid the problem, revise the sentence, eliminating *is when* or *is where*.

| | |
|---|---|
| **Weak:** | A bullish market is when prices are rising in the stock market. |
| **Improved:** | A bullish market is created when prices are rising in the stock market. |
| **Weak:** | A flowchart is when you make a diagram showing the step-by-step progression of a procedure. |
| **Improved:** | A flowchart is a diagram showing the step-by-step progression of a procedure. |
| **Weak:** | A podcast is where a prerecorded audio program is posted to a website. |
| **Improved:** | A podcast is a prerecorded audio program posted to a website. |

A similar faulty construction occurs in the expression *I hate when*. English requires nouns, noun clauses, or pronouns to act as objects of verbs, not adverbs.

| | |
|---|---|
| **Weak:** | I hate when we're asked to work overtime. |
| **Improved:** | I hate it when we're asked to work overtime. |
| **Improved:** | I hate being asked to work overtime. |

d. Don't confuse the adverb *then* with the conjunction *than*. *Then* means "at that time"; *than* indicates the second element in a comparison:

We would rather remodel *than* (not *then*) move.

First, the equipment is turned on; *then* (not *than*) the program is loaded.

## Review Exercise F—Prepositions and Conjunctions

Choose the sentence that is expressed correctly or more effectively. Then compare your responses with the key at the end of the book.

1. (a) I hate it when my fitness tracker loses it's charge during a workout.
   (b) I hate when my fitness tracker loses its charge during a workout.

2. (a) All business documents should be concise, correct, and clear.
   (b) All business documents should be concise, correct, and written clearly.

3. (a) We don't know where the all-hands meeting is at.
   (b) We don't know where the all-hands meeting is.

4. (a) My boss's youngest son just graduated high school and is college bound.
   (b) My boss's youngest son just graduated from high school and is college bound.

5. (a) At the beginning of the consulting contract in the spring of the year at headquarters, we suffered staff shortages.
   (b) When the consulting contract began last spring, headquarters suffered staff shortages.

6. (a) A company-provided ombudsman investigates and resolves employee complaints.
   (b) A company-provided ombudsman is someone who investigates and resolves employee complaints.

_____

7. (a) We estimate that we will finish up the project well before the deadline.
   (b) We estimate that we will finish the project well before the deadline.

_____

8. (a) Volunteering is noble but also much more strenuous than I ever imagined.
   (b) Volunteering is noble but also much more strenuous then I ever imagined.

_____

9. (a) We need IT workers who can load software, monitor networks, and files must be duplicated.
   (b) We need IT workers who can load software, monitor networks, and duplicate files.

_____

10. (a) I don't know where to take this portfolio.
    (b) I don't know where to take this portfolio to.

_____

11. (a) What style of architecture should we consider for our second headquarters?
    (b) What style architecture should we consider for our second headquarters?

_____

12. (a) Algorithms recommend products to buy online and ads are also offered based on our interests.
    (b) Algorithms recommend products to buy online and offer ads based on our interests.

_____

13. (a) The new intern is more self-sufficient and independent than the previous ones.
    (b) The new intern is more self-sufficient and independent then the previous ones.

_____

14. (a) Net income results when all expenses are subtracted from total revenue.
    (b) Net income is when all expenses are subtracted from total revenue.

_____

15. (a) Where should we send the honorarium for your keynote address to?
    (b) Where should we send the honorarium for your keynote address?

## D-5 Punctuation Review

### Commas 1 (2.01–2.04)

**2.01 Series.** Commas are used to separate three or more equal elements (words, phrases, or short clauses) in a series. To ensure separation of the last two elements, careful writers always use a comma before the conjunction in a series:

Business letters usually contain a dateline, address, salutation, body, and closing. (This series contains words.)

The job of an ombudsman is to examine employee complaints, resolve disagreements between management and employees, and ensure fair treatment. (This series contains phrases.)

Trainees complete basic keyboarding tasks, technicians revise complex documents, and editors proofread completed projects. (This series contains short clauses.)

**2.02 Direct Address.** Commas are used to set off the names of individuals being addressed:

Your inquiry, *Mrs. Johnson*, has been referred to me.

We genuinely hope that we may serve you, *Mr. Lee*.

**2.03 Parenthetical Expressions.** Skilled writers use parenthetical words, phrases, and clauses to guide the reader from one thought to the next. When these expressions interrupt the flow of a sentence and are unnecessary for its grammatical completeness, they should be set off with commas. Examples of commonly used parenthetical expressions follow:

| | | |
|---|---|---|
| all things considered | however | needless to say |
| as a matter of fact | in addition | nevertheless |
| as a result | incidentally | no doubt |
| as a rule | in fact | of course |
| at the same time | in my opinion | on the contrary |
| consequently | in the first place | on the other hand |
| for example | in the meantime | therefore |
| furthermore | moreover | under the circumstances |

*As a matter of fact*, I wrote to you just yesterday. (Phrase used at the beginning of a sentence.)

We will, *in the meantime*, send you a replacement order. (Phrase used in the middle of a sentence.)

Your satisfaction is our first concern, *needless to say*. (Phrase used at the end of a sentence.)

Do not use commas if the expression is necessary for the completeness of the sentence:

Kimberly *had no* doubt that she would finish the report. (Omit commas because the expression is necessary for the completeness of the sentence.)

**2.04 Dates, Addresses, and Geographical Items.** When dates, addresses, and geographical items contain more than one element, the second and succeeding elements are normally set off by commas.

a. Dates:

The conference was held February 2 at our home office. (No comma is needed for one element.)
The conference was held February 2, 2019, at our home office. (Two commas set off the second element.)
The conference was held Tuesday, February 2, 2019, at our home office. (Commas set off the second and third elements.)
In February 2019 the conference was held. (This alternate style omitting commas is acceptable if only the month and year are written.)

b. Addresses:

The letter addressed to Mr. Jim W. Ellman, 600 Via Novella, Agoura, CA 91306, should be sent today. (Commas are used between all elements except the state and zip code, which in this special instance act as a single unit.)

c. Geographical items:

She moved from Toledo, Ohio, to Champaign, Illinois. (Commas set off the state unless it appears at the end of the sentence, in which case only one comma is used.)

In separating cities from states and days from years, many writers remember the initial comma but forget the final one, as in the examples that follow:

The package from Austin, Texas{,} was lost.

We opened June 1, 2010{,} and have grown steadily since.

## Review Exercise G—Commas 1

Choose the correctly punctuated item. Then compare your responses with the key at the end of the book.

1. (a) DelTech's two headquarters are in San Jose, California and Newton, Massachusetts.
   (b) DelTech's two headquarters are in San Jose, California, and Newton, Massachusetts.

2. (a) Hard hats on the contrary can lower the risk of head injury.
   (b) Hard hats, on the contrary, can lower the risk of head injury.

3. (a) Line workers, supervisors, and managers were offered vaccinations for COVID-19.
   (b) Line workers, supervisors and managers were offered vaccinations for COVID-19.

4. (a) Your new electric vehicle, Mr. Singh, is available for factory pick-up.
   (b) Your new electric vehicle, Mr. Singh is available for factory pick-up.

5. (a) The team members in the running for promotion are Sage, Kelsie, Zoey and Rory.
   (b) The team members in the running for promotion are Sage, Kelsie, Zoey, and Rory.

6. (a) During the warranty period, of course, all maintenance and repairs will be free.
   (b) During the warranty period of course all maintenance and repairs will be free.

7. (a) Can you think of any other ideas in addition to those that we have discussed?
   (b) Can you think of any other ideas, in addition to those that we have discussed?

8. (a) The town hall is scheduled for Friday, May 13 in the convention center.
   (b) The town hall is scheduled for Friday, May 13, in the convention center.

9. (a) The new publication explains how to obtain legal protection for ideas, trade secrets,copyrights, and patents.
   (b) The new publication explains how to obtain legal protection for ideas, trade secrets, copyrights and patents.

10. (a) In the meantime, please continue working on the account until we can find a replacement.
    (b) In the meantime please continue working on the account until we can find a replacement.

11. (a) As a rule, we do not allow visitors on the factory floor.
    (b) As a rule we do not allow visitors on the factory floor.

12. (a) I wonder, Ms. Fletcher, whether you could upload your recommendation letter directly to the foundation's website.
    (b) I wonder Ms. Fletcher whether you could upload your recommendation letter directly to the foundation's website.

13. (a) We have, no doubt, that your calculations are correct.
    (b) We have no doubt that your calculations are correct.

14. (a) The first Starbucks in New York City opened on April 22, 1994, at 87th & Broadway.
    (b) The first Starbucks in New York City opened on April 22, 1994 at 87th & Broadway.

15. (a) The production facility will move to 95 Maxess Road, Melville, New York, next spring.
    (b) The production facility will move to 95 Maxess Road Melville, New York next spring.

## Commas 2 (2.05–2.09)

**2.05 Independent Clauses.** An independent clause is a group of words that has a subject and a verb and that could stand as a complete sentence. When two such clauses are joined by *and, or, nor,* or *but,* use a comma before the conjunction:

> We can ship your merchandise July 12, but we must have your payment first.

> Net income before taxes is calculated, and this total is then combined with income from operations.

Notice that each independent clause in the preceding two examples could stand alone as a complete sentence. Do not use a comma unless each group of words is a complete thought (that is, has its own subject and verb).

> Our CPA calculates net income before taxes *and* then combines that figure with income from operations. (No comma is needed because no subject follows *and.*)

**2.06 Dependent Clauses.** Dependent clauses do not make sense by themselves; for their meaning they depend on independent clauses.

a. **Introductory clauses**. When a dependent clause precedes an independent clause, it is followed by a comma. Such clauses are often introduced by *when, if,* and *as:*

> *When your request came,* we responded immediately.

> *As I mentioned earlier,* Mrs. James is the manager.

b. **Terminal clauses**. If a dependent clause falls at the end of a sentence, use a comma only if the dependent clause is an afterthought:

> We have rescheduled the meeting for October 23, *if this date meets with your approval.* (Comma used because dependent clause is an afterthought.)

> We responded immediately *when we received your request.* (No comma is needed.)

c. **Essential versus nonessential clauses**. If a dependent clause provides information that is unneeded for the grammatical completeness of a sentence, use commas to set it off. In determining whether such a clause is essential or nonessential, ask yourself whether the reader needs the information contained in the clause to identify the word it explains:

> Our district sales manager, *who just returned from a trip to the Southwest District,* prepared this report. (This construction assumes that there is only one district sales manager. Because the sales manager is clearly identified, the dependent clause is not essential and requires commas.)

> The salesperson *who just returned from a trip to the Southwest District* prepared this report. (The dependent clause in this sentence is necessary to identify which salesperson prepared the report. Therefore, use no commas.)

> The position of assistant sales manager, *which we discussed with you last week,* is still open. (Careful writers use *which* to introduce nonessential clauses. Commas are also necessary.)

> The position *that we discussed with you last week* is still open. (Careful writers use *that* to introduce essential clauses. No commas are used.)

**2.07 Phrases.** A phrase is a group of related words that lacks both a subject and a verb. A phrase that precedes a main clause is followed by a comma if the phrase contains a verb form or has four or more words:

> *Beginning November 1,* Worldwide Savings will offer two new combination checking/savings plans. (A comma follows this introductory phrase because the phrase contains the verb form *beginning.*)

*To promote our plan*, we will conduct an extensive social media advertising campaign. (A comma follows this introductory phrase because the phrase contains the verb form *to promote*.)

*In a period of only one year*, we were able to improve our market share by 30 percent. (A comma follows the introductory phrase—actually two prepositional phrases—because its total length exceeds four words.)

*In 2019* our organization installed a multiuser system that could transfer programs easily. (No comma needed after the short introductory phrase.)

**2.08 Two or More Adjectives.** Use a comma to separate two or more adjectives that equally describe a noun. A good way to test the need for a comma is this: Mentally insert the word *and* between the adjectives. If the resulting phrase sounds natural, a comma is used to show the omission of *and*:

We're looking for a *versatile, error-free* operating system. (Use a comma to separate *versatile* and *error-free* because they independently describe *operating system*. *And* has been omitted.)

Our *experienced, courteous* staff is ready to serve you. (Use a comma to separate *experienced* and *courteous* because they independently describe *staff*. *And* has been omitted.)

It was difficult to refuse the *sincere young* telephone caller. (No commas are needed between *sincere* and *young* because *and* has not been omitted.)

**2.09 Appositives.** Words that rename or explain preceding nouns or pronouns are called *appositives*. An appositive that provides information not essential to the identification of the word it describes should be set off by commas:

James Wilson, *the project director for Sperling's*, worked with our architect. (The appositive, *the project director for Sperling's*, adds nonessential information. Commas set it off.)

## Review Exercise H—Commas 2

Choose the correctly punctuated item. Then compare your responses with the key at the end of the book.

1. (a) The distributor explained the supply dilemma point by point, and then proposed a solution to the problem.
   (b) The distributor explained the supply dilemma point by point and then proposed a solution to the problem.

2. (a) Corporations must register in the state in which they do business, and they must operate within the laws of that state.
   (b) Corporations must register in the state in which they do business and they must operate within the laws of that state.

3. (a) If you examine the costs you will see that our company offers the best product at the lowest price.
   (b) If you examine the costs, you will see that our company offers the best product at the lowest price.

4. (a) Kaylynn Wise, who recorded the highest sales, won a bonus trip to a luxury resort in Mexico.
   (b) Kaylynn Wise who recorded the highest sales won a bonus trip to a luxury resort in Mexico.

5. (a) If your computer runs more slowly lately, it may have picked up malware on the Internet.

(b) If your computer runs more slowly lately it may have picked up malware on the Internet.

6. (a) As soon as you return the completed form we will process your application.
   (b) As soon as you return the completed form, we will process your application.

7. (a) For the benefit of new-hires, we are offering a three-hour onboarding session.
   (b) For the benefit of new-hires we are offering a three-hour onboarding session.

8. (a) We hope that you will enjoy a prosperous year, and that we may have many more opportunities to serve you.
   (b) We hope that you will enjoy a prosperous year and that we may have many more opportunities to serve you.

9. (a) Rolando Lyons is a deeply committed, hardworking employee.
   (b) Rolando Lyons is a deeply committed hardworking employee.

10. (a) All our production processes are strictly confidential as I am sure you know.
    (b) All our production processes are strictly confidential, as I am sure you know.

11. (a) The salesperson, who collects the greatest number of sales points, will win a bonus trip to Hawaii.
    (b) The salesperson who collects the greatest number of sales points will win a bonus trip to Hawaii.

12. (a) Before sending any kind of message, remember that it will be stored practically forever.
    (b) Before sending any kind of message remember that it will be stored practically forever.

13. (a) Our company wants honest detail-oriented accountancy trainees.
    (b) Our company wants honest, detail-oriented accountancy trainees.

14. (a) Some of the challenges you describe in your report could be remedied with improved purchasing procedures.
    (b) Some of the challenges you describe in your report, could be remedied with improved purchasing procedures.

15. (a) Stacy Wilson, our new HR manager has come to us from our Atlanta office.
    (b) Stacy Wilson, our new HR manager, has come to us from our Atlanta office.

## Commas 3 (2.10–2.15)

**2.10 Degrees and Abbreviations.** Degrees following individuals' names are set off by commas. Abbreviations such as *Jr.* and *Sr.* are also set off by commas unless the individual referred to prefers to omit the commas:

> Anne G. Turner, *MBA*, joined the firm.

> Michael Migliano, *Jr.*, and Michael Migliano, *Sr.*, work as a team.

> Anthony A. Gensler *Jr.* wrote the report. (The individual referred to prefers to omit commas.)

The abbreviations Inc. and Ltd. are set off by commas only if a company's legal name has a comma just before this kind of abbreviation. To determine a company's practice, consult its stationery or a directory listing:

> Firestone and Blythe, *Inc.*, is based in Canada. (Notice that two commas are used.)

> Computers *Inc.* is extending its franchise system. (The company's legal name does not include a comma before *Inc.*)

**2.11 Omitted Words.** A comma is used to show the omission of words that are understood:

> On Monday we received 15 applications; on Friday, only 3. (Comma shows the omission of *we received*.)

**2.12 Contrasting Statements.** Commas are used to set off contrasting or opposing expressions. These expressions are often introduced by such words as *not, never, but,* and *yet*:

> The president suggested cutbacks, *not* layoffs, to ease the crisis.

> Our budget for the year is reduced, *yet* adequate.

> The greater the effort, the greater the reward.

If increased emphasis is desired, use dashes instead of commas, as in *Only the sum of $100—not $1,000—was paid on this account.*

**2.13 Clarity.** Commas are used to separate words repeated for emphasis. Commas are also used to separate words that may be misread if not separated:

> The building is a long, long way from completion.

> Whatever is, is right.

> No matter what, you know we support you.

**2.14 Quotations and Appended Questions.**

a.  A comma is used to separate a short quotation from the rest of a sentence. If the quotation is divided into two parts, two commas are used:

> The manager asked, "Shouldn't the managers control the specialists?"

> "Perhaps the specialists," replied Tim, "have unique information."

b.  A comma is used to separate a question appended (added) to a statement:

> You will confirm the shipment, won't you?

**2.15 Comma Overuse.** Do not use commas needlessly. For example, commas should not be inserted merely because you might drop your voice if you were speaking the sentence:

> One of the reasons for expanding our East Coast operations is that we anticipate increased sales in that area. (Do not insert a needless comma before a clause.)

> I am looking for an article titled "State-of-the-Art Communications." (Do not insert a needless comma after the word *titled*.)

> Customers may purchase many food and nonfood items in convenience stores *such as* 7-Eleven and Stop-N-Go. (Do not insert a needless comma after *such as*.)

> We have at this time an adequate supply of parts. (Do not insert needless commas around prepositional phrases.)

## Review Exercise I—Commas 3

Choose the correctly punctuated item. Then compare your responses with the key at the end of the book.

1.  (a) The business tycoon James Goldsmith said, "If you see a bandwagon, it's too late." _____
    (b) The business tycoon James Goldsmith said "If you see a bandwagon, it's too late."

2. (a) We expected Jan Collins, not Rogelio Rios to guide us through the restructuring.
   (b) We expected Jan Collins, not Rogelio Rios, to guide us through the restructuring.

3. (a) In short Steve Jobs was a visionary entrepreneur but also a tough task master.
   (b) In short, Steve Jobs was a visionary entrepreneur but also a tough task master.

4. (a) You lost a lot of money investing in cryptocurrency, didn't you?
   (b) You lost a lot of money investing in cryptocurrency didn't you?

5. (a) "An appeaser is one who feeds a crocodile, said Winston Churchill, hoping it will eat him last."
   (b) "An appeaser is one who feeds a crocodile," said Winston Churchill, "hoping it will eat him last."

6. (a) Gemma Marsh, MBA and Walker Schroeder, Esq. left the Chicago firm.
   (b) Gemma Marsh, MBA, and Walker Schroeder, Esq., left the Chicago firm.

7. (a) We are very fortunate to have, at our disposal, the best tax accountants in New York.
   (b) We are very fortunate to have at our disposal the best tax accountants in New York.

8. (a) The organic Michigan farm will expand into new crops such as, grapes and asparagus.
   (b) The organic Michigan farm will expand into new areas such as grapes and asparagus.

9. (a) In May customers opened 50 new accounts; in June, only about 20.
   (b) In May customers opened 50 new accounts; in June only about 20.

10. (a) Be self-confident, not arrogant in job interviews.
    (b) Be self- confident, not arrogant, in job interviews.

11. (a) No matter what, we will keep our restaurant open.
    (b) No matter what we will keep our restaurant open.

12. (a) "We have paralysis by analysis", said the chief operating officer.
    (b) "We have paralysis by analysis," said the chief operating officer.

13. (a) Most office-bound workers end their workday at 5 p.m.; home office workers as late as 9 p.m.
    (b) Most office-bound workers end their workday at 5 p.m.; home office workers, as late as 9 p.m.

14. (a) The better our advertising and recruiting, the stronger our personnel pool will be.
    (b) The better our advertising and recruiting the stronger our personnel pool will be.

15. (a) Mr. Bishop was named legislative counsel; Mr. Snyder, executive advisor.
    (b) Mr. Bishop was named legislative counsel, Mr. Snyder executive advisor.

## Semicolons (2.16)

### 2.16 Independent Clauses, Series, Introductory Expressions.

a. **Independent clauses with conjunctive adverbs**. Use a semicolon before a conjunctive adverb that separates two independent clauses. Some of the most common conjunctive adverbs are *therefore*, *consequently*, *however*, and *moreover*:

> Business messages should sound conversational; *therefore*, writers often use familiar words and contractions.

> The bank closes its doors at 5 p.m.; *however*, the ATM is open 24 hours a day.

Notice that the word following a semicolon is *not* capitalized (unless, of course, that word is a proper noun).

b. **Independent clauses without conjunctive adverbs**. Use a semicolon to separate closely related independent clauses when no conjunctive adverb is used:

> Bond interest payments are tax deductible; dividend payments are not.

> Ambient lighting fills the room; task lighting illuminates each workstation.

Use a semicolon in *compound* sentences, not in *complex* sentences:

> After one week the paper feeder jammed; we tried different kinds of paper. (Use a semicolon in a compound sentence.)

> After one week the paper feeder jammed, although we tried different kinds of paper. (Use a comma in a complex sentence. Do not use a semicolon after *jammed*.)

The semicolon is very effective for joining two closely related thoughts. Don't use it, however, unless the ideas are truly related.

c. **Series with internal commas**. Use semicolons to separate items in a series when one or more of the items contains internal commas:

> Delegates from Miami, Florida; Freeport, Mississippi; and Chatsworth, California, attended the conference.

> The speakers were Kevin Lang, manager, Riko Enterprises; Henry Holtz, vice president, Trendex, Inc.; and Margaret Woo, personnel director, West Coast Productions.

d. **Introductory expressions**. Use a semicolon when an introductory expression such as *namely*, *for instance*, *that is*, or for *example* introduces a list following an independent clause:

> Switching to computerized billing are several local companies; namely, Ryson Electronics, Miller Vending Services, and Black Home Heating.

> The author of a report should consider many sources; for example, books, periodicals, databases, and newspapers.

## Colons (2.17–2.19)

### 2.17 Listed Items.

a. **With colon**. Use a colon after a complete thought that introduces a formal list of items. A formal list is often preceded by such words and phrases as *these*, *thus*, *the following*, and *as follows*. A colon is also used when words and phrases like these are implied but not stated:

> Additional costs in selling a house involve *the following*: title examination fee, title insurance costs, and closing fee. (Use a colon when a complete thought introduces a formal list.)

> Collective bargaining focuses on several key issues: cost-of-living adjustments, fringe benefits, job security, and work hours. (The introduction of the list is implied in the preceding clause.)

b. **Without colon**. Do not use a colon when the list immediately follows a *to be* verb or a preposition:

> The employees who should receive the preliminary plan are James Sears, Monica Spears, and Rose Lopez. (No colon is used after the verb *are*.)

> We expect to consider equipment for Accounting, Legal Services, and Payroll. (No colon is used after the preposition *for*.)

**2.18 Quotations.** Use a colon to introduce long one-sentence quotations and quotations of two or more sentences:

> Our consultant said: "This system can support up to 32 users. It can be used for decision support, computer-aided design, and software development operations at the same time."

**2.19 Salutations.** Use a colon after the salutation of a business letter:

> Gentlemen:    Dear Mrs. Seaman:    Dear Jamie:

## Review Exercise J—Semicolons and Colons

Choose the correctly punctuated item. Then compare your responses with the key at the end of the book.

1. (a) Our branch in Pico Rivera specializes in commercial real estate; our branch in Newport Beach concentrates on residential real estate.
   (b) Our branch in Pico Rivera specializes in commercial real estate, our branch in Newport Beach concentrates on residential real estate.

2. (a) I arrived at the dealership very early; therefore I was first in line.
   (b) I arrived at the dealership very early; therefore, I was first in line.

3. (a) The restaurant has fantastic cooks; however, often they use too much salt.
   (b) The restaurant has fantastic cooks, however, often they use too much salt.

4. (a) The Chevy Bolt EV is available in three premium colors; bright blue metallic, silver flare metallic, and cherry red tintcoat.
   (b) The Chevy Bolt EV is available in three premium colors: bright blue metallic, silver flare metallic, and cherry red tintcoat.

5. (a) Four recruiting days have been reserved, August 1, August 15, September 1, and September 15.
   (b) Four recruiting dates have been reserved: August 1, August 15, September 1, and September 15.

6. (a) Many potential buyers live in Northern California; therefore, we will concentrate on that region.
   (b) Many potential buyers live in Northern California, therefore, we will concentrate on that region.

7. (a) Apply for a Platinum Plus Visa today, and we will waive the annual fee: in addition, you will earn 50,000 bonus miles.
   (b) Apply for a Platinum Plus Visa today, and we will waive the annual fee; in addition, you will earn 50,000 bonus miles.

8. (a) Big U.S. companies are discovering that hybrid work comes with plenty of complications; namely, Prudential, Expedia, and Twilio.
   (b) Big U.S. companies are discovering that hybrid work comes with plenty of complications, namely, Prudential, Expedia, and Twilio.

9. (a) For the executive retreat we are considering The Resort at Paws Up, Montana; Brush Creek Ranch, Wyoming; and Red Horse Mountain Ranch, Idaho.
   (b) For the executive retreat we are considering The Resort at Paws Up, Montana, Brush Creek Ranch, Wyoming, and Red Horse Mountain Ranch, Idaho.

10. (a) After the COVID-19 pandemic, most workers wanted a mix between remote and in-person work; many companies promised they would adopt a hybrid model.
    (b) After the COVID-19 pandemic, most workers wanted a mix between remote and in-person work, many companies promised they would adopt a hybrid model.

11. (a) The interviewees all asked about salary, next they inquired about benefits.
    (b) The interviewees all asked about salary; next they inquired about benefits.

12. (a) Most employees indicated that they enjoyed working remotely; but missed: the planning, ideation, and collaboration that takes place in person.
    (b) Most employees indicated that they enjoyed working remotely but missed the planning, ideation, and collaboration that takes place in person.

13. (a) Google is moving to a hybrid workweek; for example, employees work from the office three days a week and two days wherever they believe they work best.
    (b) Google is moving to a hybrid workweek, for example, employees work from the office three days a week and two days wherever they believe they work best.

14. (a) Google allows more workplace flexibility, a fifth of its staff can work from home permanently, and another fifth can shift to a different geographic location.
    (b) Google allows more workplace flexibility; a fifth of its staff can work from home permanently, and another fifth can shift to a different geographic location.

15. (a) The two most popular national parks in Utah are called Arches National Park and Canyonlands.
    (b) The two most popular national parks in Utah are called: Arches National Park and Canyonlands

## Apostrophes (2.20–2.22)

**2.20 Basic Rule.** The apostrophe is used to show ownership, origin, authorship, or measurement.

| | |
|---|---|
| **Ownership:** | We are looking for *Brian's keys*. |
| **Origin:** | At the *president's suggestion*, we doubled the order. |
| **Authorship:** | The *accountant's annual report* was questioned. |
| **Measurement:** | In *two years' time* we expect to reach our goal. |

a. **Ownership words not ending in s.** To place the apostrophe correctly, you must first determine whether the ownership word ends in an s sound. If it does not, add an apostrophe and an s to the ownership word. The following examples show ownership words that do not end in an s sound:

| | |
|---|---|
| the employee's file | (the file of a single employee) |
| a member's address | (the address of a single member) |
| a year's time | (the time of a single year) |
| a month's notice | (notice of a single month) |
| the company's building | (the building of a single company) |

b. **Ownership words ending in s.** If the ownership word does end in an s sound, usually add only an apostrophe:

| | |
|---|---|
| several employees' files | (files of several employees) |
| ten members' addresses | (addresses of ten members) |
| five years' time | (time of five years) |
| several months' notice | (notice of several months) |
| many companies' buildings | (buildings of many companies) |

A few singular nouns that end in s are pronounced with an extra syllable when they become possessive. To these words, add *'s*.

> my boss's desk   the princess's science background   Congress's summer recess

Use no apostrophe if a noun is merely plural, not possessive:

> All the sales representatives, as well as the assistants and managers, had their names and telephone numbers listed in the directory.

**2.21 Names Ending in *s* or an *s* sound.** The possessive form of names ending in *s* or an *s* sound follows the same guidelines as for common nouns. If an extra syllable can be pronounced without difficulty, add 's. If the extra syllable is hard to pronounce, end with an apostrophe only.

| Add apostrophe and s | Add apostrophe only |
|---|---|
| Russ's computer | New Orleans' cuisine |
| Bill Gates's business | Los Angeles' freeways |
| Mrs. Jones's home | the Morrises' family |
| Mr. Lopez's desk | the Lopezes' pool |

Individual preferences in pronunciation may cause variation in a few cases. For example, some people may prefer not to pronounce an extra *s* in examples such as *Bill Gates'* business. However, the possessive form of plural names is consistent: *the Joneses' home, the Burgesses' children, the Bushes' car*. Notice that the article *the* is a clue in determining whether a name is singular or plural.

**2.22 Gerunds.** Use 's to make a noun possessive when it precedes a gerund, a verb form used as a noun:

> Mr. Smith's smoking prompted a new office policy. (*Mr. Smith* is possessive because it modifies the gerund *smoking*.)

> It was Betsy's careful proofreading that revealed the discrepancy.

## Review Exercise K—Apostrophes

Correct any apostrophe errors in the following sentences. In the space provided for each item, write your correction. If a sentence is correct, write *C*. When you finish, compare your responses with the key at the end of the book.

1. All new depositors at our three bank branches qualify for free checking accounts.

2. Most graduates hope to repay their student loans in a few years time.

3. All departments occupy floors 1–5, but the CEOs office is on the sixth floor.

4. A patent provides protection for an inventors invention for 17 years.

5. Both companies campuses will be sold because employees now work from home.

6. Many chefs prefer to work with organic products.

7. The shipment of electronic components finally reached the plant after four weeks delay

8. Tyler dreamed of repaying all college loans in just one years time.

9. Only the CEO can change the councils directives.

10. The Floreses kids wanted to go to college in Florida because they loved the beaches.

11. Hackers stole thousands of customers account information.

12. All new customers qualify for three special perks during the first six months after signing up.

13. Psychologists and psychiatrists know that therapists notes are admissible evidence in court.

14. The United States' Treasury manages federal finances by collecting taxes and paying bills and by managing currency, government accounts, and public debt.

15. It was Mr. Humphreys signing of the contract that sealed our trading partnership.

## Other Punctuation (2.23–2.29)

**2.23 Periods.**

a. **Ends of sentences.** Use a period at the end of a statement, command, indirect question, or polite request. Although a polite request may have the same structure as a question, it ends with a period:

> Corporate legal departments demand precise skills from staff members. (End a statement with a period.)

> Get the latest data by reading current periodicals. (End a command with a period.)

> Mr. Rand wondered whether we had sent any follow-up literature. (End an indirect question with a period.)

> Would you please reexamine my account and determine the current balance. (A polite request suggests an action rather than a verbal response.)

b. **Abbreviations and initials**. Use periods after initials and after many abbreviations.

| | | |
|---|---|---|
| R. M. Johnson | c.o.d. | Ms. |
| p.m. | a.m. | Mr. |
| Inc. | i.e. | Mrs. |

The latest trend is to omit periods in degrees and professional designations: BA, PhD, MD, RN, DDS.

Use just one period when an abbreviation falls at the end of a sentence:

> Guests began arriving at 5:30 p.m.

**2.24 Question Marks.** Direct questions are followed by question marks:

> Did you send your proposal to Datatronix, Inc.?

Statements with questions added are punctuated with question marks:

> We have completed the proposal, haven't we?

**2.25 Exclamation Points.** Use an exclamation point after a word, phrase, or clause expressing strong emotion. In business writing, however, exclamation points should be used sparingly:

> Incredible! Every terminal is down.

**2.26 Dashes.** The dash (constructed at a keyboard by striking the hyphen key twice in succession) is a legitimate and effective mark of punctuation when used according to accepted conventions. As a connecting punctuation mark, however, the dash loses effectiveness when overused.

a. **Parenthetical elements**. Within a sentence a parenthetical element is usually set off by commas. If, however, the parenthetical element itself contains internal commas, use dashes (or parentheses) to set it off:

> Three top salespeople—Tom Judkins, Tim Templeton, and Mary Yashimoto—received bonuses.

b. **Sentence interruptions**. Use a dash to show an interruption or abrupt change of thought:

> News of the dramatic merger—no one believed it at first—shook the financial world.

> Ship the materials Monday—no, we must have them sooner.

Sentences with abrupt changes of thought or with appended afterthoughts can usually be improved through rewriting.

c. **Summarizing statements**. Use a dash (not a colon) to separate an introductory list from a summarizing statement:

> Sorting, merging, and computing—these are tasks that our data processing programs must perform.

**2.27 Parentheses.** One means of setting off nonessential sentence elements involves the use of parentheses. Nonessential sentence elements may be punctuated in one of three ways: (a) with commas, to make the lightest possible break in the normal flow of a sentence; (b) with dashes, to emphasize the enclosed material; and (c) with parentheses, to de-emphasize the enclosed material. Parentheses are frequently used to punctuate sentences with interpolated directions, explanations, questions, and references:

> The cost analysis (which appears on page 8 of the report) indicates that the copy machine should be leased.

> Units are lightweight (approximately 13 oz.) and come with a leather case and operating instructions.

> The latest laser printer (have you heard about it?) will be demonstrated for us next week.

A parenthetical sentence that is not embedded within another sentence should be capitalized and punctuated with end punctuation:

> The Model 20 has stronger construction. (You may order a Model 20 brochure by circling 304 on the reader service card.)

**2.28 Quotation Marks.**

a. **Direct quotations**. Use double quotation marks to enclose the exact words of a speaker or writer:

> "Keep in mind," Mrs. Frank said, "that you must justify the cost of networking our office."

> The boss said that automation was inevitable. (No quotation marks are needed because the exact words are not quoted.)

b. **Quotations within quotations**. Use single quotation marks (apostrophes on the keyboard) to enclose quoted passages within quoted passages:

> In her speech Mrs. Deckman remarked, "I believe it was the poet Robert Frost who said, 'All the fun's in how you say a thing.'"

c. **Short expressions**. Slang, words used in a special sense, and words following *stamped* or *marked* are often enclosed within quotation marks:

> Jeffrey described the damaged shipment as "gross." (Quotation marks enclose slang.)

> Students often have trouble spelling the word "separate." (Quotation marks enclose words used in a special sense.)

Jobs were divided into two categories: most stressful and least stressful. The jobs in the "most stressful" list involved high risk or responsibility. (Quotation marks enclose words used in a special sense.)

The envelope marked "Confidential" was put aside. (Quotation marks enclose words following *marked*.)

In the four preceding sentences, the words enclosed within quotation marks can be set in italics, if italics are available.

d. **Definitions**. Double quotation marks are used to enclose definitions. The word or expression being defined should be underscored or set in italics:

The term *penetration pricing* is defined as "the practice of introducing a product to the market at a low price."

e. **Titles**. Use double quotation marks to enclose titles of literary and artistic works, such as magazine and newspaper articles, chapters of books, movies, television shows, poems, lectures, and songs. Names of major publications—such as books, magazines, pamphlets, and newspapers—are set in italics (underscored).

Particularly helpful was the chapter in Smith's *Effective Writing Techniques* titled "Right Brain, Write On!"

In the *Los Angeles Times* appeared John's article, "E-Mail Blunders"; however, we could not locate it online.

f. **Additional considerations**. In this country periods and commas are always placed inside closing quotation marks. Semicolons and colons, on the other hand, are always placed outside quotation marks:

Mrs. James said, "I could not find the article titled 'Cell Phone Etiquette.'"

The president asked for "absolute security": All written messages were to be destroyed.

Question marks and exclamation points may go inside or outside closing quotation marks, as determined by the form of the quotation:

Sales Manager Martin said, "Who placed the order? (The quotation is a question".)

When did the sales manager say, "Who placed the order?" (Both the incorporating sentence and the quotation are questions.)

Did the sales manager say, "Ryan placed the order"? (The incorporating sentence asks a question; the quotation does not.)

"In the future," shouted Bob, "ask me first!" (The quotation is an exclamation.)

**2.29 Brackets.** Within quotations, brackets are used by the quoting writer to enclose his or her own inserted remarks. Such remarks may be corrective, illustrative, or explanatory:

Mrs. Cardillo said, "OSHA [Occupational Safety and Health Administration] has been one of the most widely criticized agencies of the federal government."

## Review Exercise L—Other Punctuation

Choose the correctly punctuated item. Then compare your responses with the key at the end of the book.

1. (a) Was it hairstylist legend Vidal Sassoon who said that the only place success comes before work is in the dictionary.

(b) Was it hairstylist legend Vidal Sassoon who said that "the only place success comes before work is in the dictionary."

(c) Was it hairstylist legend Vidal Sassoon who said that the only place success comes before work is in the dictionary?

2. (a) The Latin phrase "nota bene" is used to draw the attention of an audience to something and means "note well, take notice."

   (b) The Latin phrase *nota bene* is used to draw the attention of an audience to something and means "note well, take notice."

   (c) The expression nota bene is used to draw the attention of an audience to something and means note well, take notice.

3. (a) Economists wondered whether the sharp rise in inflation would be temporary?

   (b) Economists wondered whether the sharp rise in inflation would be temporary.

4. (a) Unbelievable! Our sales are through the roof!

   (b) Unbelievable. Our sales are through the roof.

5. (a) You should set up for your 4 p.m. video meeting at 3:45 p.m..

   (b) You should set up for your 4 pm video meeting at 3.45 pm.

   (c) You should set up for your 4 p.m. video meeting at 3:45 p.m.

6. (a) Was it Oscar Wilde who said, "Always forgive your enemies. Nothing annoys them more"?

   (b) Was it Oscar Wilde who said, "Always forgive your enemies. Nothing annoys them more?"

7. (a) "Artificial intelligence, shouted the IT manager, is no match for natural stupidity." (b) "Artificial intelligence," shouted the IT manager, "is no match for natural stupidity!"

8. (a) The actor Bette Midler said, "The worst part of success is to try to find someone who is happy for you."

   (b) The actor Bette Midler said "The worst part of success is to try to find someone who is happy for you".

9. (a) The journalist's employment article was titled "How to Ace That Job Interview."

   (b) The journalist's employment article was titled How to Ace That Job Interview.

10. (a) Marvin wondered whether he had taken enough units for his BA degree?

    (b) Marvin wondered whether he had taken enough units for his BA degree.

11. (a) You did update the daily cash sheet, didn't you?

    (b) You did update the daily cash sheet, didn't you.

12. (a) Our questionnaire—see Appendix A, had only 20 questions.

    (b) Our questionnaire (see Appendix A) had only 20 questions.

13. (a) Savanna scored a perfect 180 (can you believe it) on the LSAT exam?

    (b) Savanna scored a perfect 180 (can you believe it?) on the LSAT exam.

14. (a) Our basic operating costs (rent, utilities, and wages) have risen 5 percent over last year.

    (b) Our basic operating costs: rent, utilities, and wages—have risen 5 percent over last year.

15. (a) The team seemed "psyched" before the important match.

    (b) The team seemed psyched before the important match.

# D-6 **Style and Usage**

## Capitalization (3.01–3.16)

Capitalization is used to distinguish important words. However, writers are not free to capitalize all words they consider important. Rules or guidelines governing capitalization style have been established through custom and use. Mastering these guidelines will make your writing more readable and more comprehensible.

**3.01 Proper Nouns.** Capitalize proper nouns, including the *specific* names of persons, places, schools, streets, parks, buildings, holidays, months, agreements, websites, software programs, apps, games, historical periods, and so forth. Do not capitalize common nouns that make only *general* references.

| **Proper nouns** | **Common nouns** |
|---|---|
| Instagram, Flixster, WorldMate | popular mobile apps |
| Mexico, Canada | U.S. trading partners |
| El Camino College | a community college |
| Sam Houston Park | a park in the city |
| Phoenix Room, Statler Inn | a meeting room in the hotel |
| Memorial Day, New Year's Day | two holidays |
| Google, Facebook, Wikipedia | popular websites |
| George Washington Bridge | a bridge |
| Consumer Product Safety Act | a law to protect consumers |
| PowerPoint, Photoshop, Excel | software programs |
| Will Rogers World Airport | a municipal airport |
| January, February, March | months of the year |

**3.02 Proper Adjectives.** Capitalize most adjectives that are derived from proper nouns:

| | |
|---|---|
| Greek symbol | British thermal unit |
| Roman numeral | Freudian slip |
| Xerox copy | Hispanic markets |

Do not capitalize the few adjectives that, although originally derived from proper nouns, have become common adjectives through usage. Consult your dictionary when in doubt:

| | |
|---|---|
| manila folder | diesel engine |
| venetian blinds | china dishes |

**3.03 Geographic Locations.** Capitalize the names of *specific* places such as continents, countries, states, mountains, valleys, lakes, rivers, oceans, and geographic regions:

| | |
|---|---|
| New York City | Great Salt Lake |
| Allegheny Mountains | Pacific Ocean |
| San Fernando Valley | Delaware Bay |
| the East Coast | the Pacific Northwest |

**3.04 Organization Names.** Capitalize the principal words in the names of all business, civic, educational, governmental, labor, military, philanthropic, political, professional, religious, and social organizations:

Genentech

*The Wall Street Journal**

New York Stock Exchange

United Way

Commission to Restore the Statue of Liberty

Board of Directors, Midwest Bank

San Antonio Museum of Art

Securities and Exchange Commission

National Association of Letter Carriers

Association of Information Systems Professionals

**3.05 Academic Courses and Degrees.** Capitalize particular academic degrees and course titles. Do not capitalize general academic degrees and subject areas:

Professor Bernadette Ordian, *PhD*, will teach *Accounting* 221 next fall.

Mrs. Snyder, who holds *bachelor's* and *master's degrees*, teaches *marketing* classes.

Cole enrolled in classes in *history, business English*, and *management*.

**3.06 Personal and Business Titles.**

a.  Capitalize personal and business titles when they precede names:

Vice President Ames

Board Chairman Frazier

Governor G. W. Thurmond

Professor McLean

Uncle Edward

Councilman Herbert

Sales Manager Klein

Dr. Samuel Washington

b.  Capitalize titles in addresses, salutations, and closing lines:

Mr. Juan deSanto
Director of Purchasing
Space Systems, Inc.
Boxborough, MA 01719

Very truly yours,

Clara J. Smith
Supervisor, Marketing

c.  Generally, do not capitalize titles of high government rank or religious office when they stand alone or follow a person's name in running text:

The president conferred with the joint chiefs of staff and many senators.

Meeting with the chief justice of the Supreme Court were the senator from Ohio and the mayor of Cleveland.

Only the cardinal from Chicago had an audience with the pope.

d.  Do not capitalize most common titles following names:

The speech was delivered by Robert Lynch, *president*, Academic Publishing. Lois Herndon, *chief executive officer*, introduced him.

e.  Do not capitalize common titles appearing alone:

Please speak to the *supervisor* or to the *office manager*.

Neither the *president* nor the *vice president* could attend.

---

*\*Note*: Capitalize *the* only when it is part of the official name of an organization, as printed on the organization's stationery.

Appendix D: Grammar/Mechanics Handbook

However, when the title of an official appears in that organization's minutes, bylaws, or other official document, it may be capitalized.

f.  Do not capitalize titles when they are followed by appositives naming specific individuals:

We must consult our *director of research*, Ronald E. West, before responding.

g.  Do not capitalize family titles used with possessive pronouns:

| | |
|---|---|
| my mother | your father |
| our aunt | his cousin |

h.  Capitalize titles of close relatives used without pronouns:

Both *Mother* and *Father* must sign the contract.

**3.07 Numbered and Lettered Items.** Capitalize nouns followed by numbers or letters (except in page, paragraph, line, and verse references):

| | |
|---|---|
| Flight 34, Gate 12 | Plan No. 2 |
| Volume I, Part 3 | Warehouse 33-A |
| Invoice No. 55489 | Figure 8.3 |
| Model A5673 | Serial No. C22865404-2 |
| State Highway 10 | page 6, line 5 |

**3.08 Points of the Compass.** Capitalize *north, south, east, west,* and their derivatives when they represent *specific* geographical regions. Do not capitalize the points of the compass when they are used in directions or in general references:

| **Specific regions** | **General references** |
|---|---|
| from the South | heading north on the highway |
| living in the Midwest | west of the city |
| Easterners, Southerners | western Nevada, southern Indiana |
| going to the Middle East | the northern part of the United States |
| from the East Coast | the east side of the street |

**3.09 Departments, Divisions, and Committees.** Capitalize the names of departments, divisions, or committees within your own organization. Outside your organization capitalize only *specific* department, division, or committee names:

The inquiry was addressed to the *Legal Department in our Consumer Products Division.*

John was appointed to the *Employee Benefits Committee.*

Send your rèsumè to their *human resources division.*

A *planning committee* will be named shortly.

**3.10 Governmental Terms.** Do not capitalize the words federal, government, nation, or state unless they are part of a specific title:

Unless *federal* support can be secured, the *state* project will be abandoned.

The *Federal Deposit Insurance Corporation* protects depositors from bank failure.

**3.11 Product Names.** Capitalize product names only when they refer to trade-marked items. Except in advertising, common names following manufacturers' names are not capitalized:

| | |
|---|---|
| Magic Marker | Dell computer |
| Kleenex tissues | Swingline stapler |
| Q-tip swab | ChapStick lip balm |
| Levi 501 jeans | Excel spreadsheet |
| DuPont Teflon | Canon camera |

**3.12 Literary Titles.** Capitalize the principal words in the titles of books, magazines, newspapers, articles, movies, plays, songs, poems, and reports. Do not capitalize articles (*a, an, the*), short conjunctions (*and, but, or, nor*), and prepositions of fewer than four letters (in, to, by, for) unless they begin or end the title:

Jackson's *What Job Is for You?* (Capitalize book titles.)

Gant's "Software for the Executive Suite" (Capitalize principal words in article titles.)

"Performance Standards to Go By" (Capitalize article titles.)

"The Improvement of Fuel Economy With Alternative Fuels" (Capitalize report titles.)

**3.13 Beginning Words.** In addition to capitalizing the first word of a complete sentence, capitalize the first word in a quoted sentence, independent phrase, item in an enumerated list, and formal rule or principle following a colon:

The business manager said, "*All* purchases must have requisitions." (Capitalize first word in a quoted sentence.)

Yes, if you agree. (Capitalize the first word in an independent phrase.)

Some of the duties of the position are as follows:

1. *Editing* and formatting Word files
2. *Arranging* video and teleconferences
3. *Verifying* records, reports, and applications (Capitalize first words in a vertical enumerated list.)

One rule has been established through the company: *No* smoking is allowed in open offices. (Capitalize a rule following a colon.)

**3.14 Celestial Bodies.** Capitalize the names of celestial bodies such as *Mars, Saturn,* and *Neptune.* Do not capitalize the terms *earth, sun,* or *moon* unless they appear in a context with other celestial bodies:

Where on *earth* did you find that manual typewriter?

*Venus* and *Mars* are the closest planets to *Earth.*

**3.15 Ethnic References.** Capitalize terms that refer to a particular culture, language, or race:

| | |
|---|---|
| Asian | Hebrew |
| Caucasian | Indian |
| Latino | Japanese |
| Persian | Judeo-Christian |

**3.16 Seasons.** Do not capitalize seasons:

In the *fall* it appeared that *winter* and *spring* sales would increase.

## Review Exercise M—Capitalization

Choose the sentence with correct capitalization. Then compare your responses with the key at the end of the book.

1. (a) The president and the vice president of Parker Fasteners flew to Los Angeles to meet with Northrup Grumman executives.
   (b) The President and the Vice President of Parker Fasteners flew to Los Angeles to meet with Northrup Grumman executives.

2. (a) Your Flight 506 on United Airlines is leaving from Gate 104.
   (b) Your flight 506 on United Airlines is leaving from gate 104.

3. (a) My aunt and I created a simple TikTok video featuring our cat.
   (b) My Aunt and I created a simple TikTok video featuring our cat.

4. (a) Leilani took classes in Sociology, German, Marketing, and Economics.
   (b) Leilani took classes in sociology, German, marketing, and economics.

5. (a) Experts believe that robots will soon take over routine human tasks all over the world.
   (b) Experts believe that Robots will soon take over routine human tasks all over the World.

6. (a) We reserved the Dragonstone room at the Omni hotel and resort for our Fall conference.
   (b) We reserved the Dragonstone Room at the Omni Hotel and Resort for our fall conference.

7. (a) When working on engineering equations, Isaias switches the keyboard on his Apple computer to Greek symbols.
   (b) When working on Engineering equations, Isaias switches the keyboard on his Apple Computer to Greek symbols.
   (c) When working on engineering equations, Isaias switched the keyboard on his Apple Computer to greek symbols.

8. (a) After taking the Marina freeway, we drove North to Venice Beach.
   (b) After taking the Marina Freeway, we drove north to Venice Beach.

9. (a) The Federal government promised our State funds to rebuild its infrastructure.
   (b) The federal government promised our state funds to rebuild its infrastructure.

10. (a) The Boston Marathon is an annual Sporting Event hosted by the City of Boston on Patriot's Day.
    (b) The Boston marathon is an annual sporting event hosted by the city of Boston on Patriot's day.
    (c) The Boston Marathon is an annual sporting event hosted by the city of Boston on Patriot's Day.

11. (a) Last fall it appeared that sales would pick up in the spring and summer months.
    (b) Last Fall it appeared that sales would pick up in the Spring and Summer months.

12. (a) My Uncle Jeffrey purchased a Subaru Forrester for his trip from Chicago to Los Angeles along the Route 66 this Summer.
    (b) My uncle Jeffrey purchased a Subaru Forrester for his trip from Chicago to Los Angeles along the route 66 this Summer.
    (c) My uncle Jeffrey purchased a Subaru Forrester for his trip from Chicago to Los Angeles along the Route 66 this summer.

13. (a) Martin Cooper, a general manager at Motorola, created the first true cell phone.
    (b) Martin Cooper, a General Manager at Motorola, created the first true Cell Phone.

14. (a) The Fishing Industry in the Pacific Northwest is reeling from the impact of Government regulations.
    (b) The fishing industry in the Pacific Northwest is reeling from the impact of government regulations.
    (c) The fishing industry in the Pacific northwest is reeling from the impact of Government regulations.

15. (a) A federal judge in San Francisco ruled that businesses must make their websites accessible to people with disabilities.
    (b) A Federal judge in San Francisco ruled that businesses must make their Websites accessible to people with disabilities.

## Number Style (4.01–4.13)

Usage and custom determine whether numbers are expressed in the form of figures (e.g., *5*, *9*) or in the form of words (e.g., *five*, *nine*). Numbers expressed as figures are shorter and more easily understood, yet numbers expressed as words are necessary in certain instances. The following guidelines are observed in expressing numbers in written sentences. Numbers that appear on business forms—such as invoices, monthly statements, and purchase orders—are always expressed as figures.

### 4.01 General Rules.

a. The numbers *one* through *ten* are generally written as words. Numbers above *ten* are written as figures:

> The bank had a total of *nine* branch offices in *three* suburbs.

> All *58* employees received benefits in the *three* categories shown.

> A shipment of *45,000* lightbulbs was sent from *two* warehouses.

b. Numbers that begin sentences are written as words. If a number beginning a sentence involves more than two words, however, the sentence should be revised so that the number does not fall at the beginning.

> *Fifteen* color options are available in our latest smartphone lineup.

> A total of *156* companies participated in the promotion (not *One hundred fifty-six companies participated in the promotion*).

**4.02 Money.** Sums of money $1 or greater are expressed as figures. If a sum is a whole dollar amount, omit the decimal and zeros (whether or not the amount appears in a sentence with additional fractional dollar amounts):

> We budgeted *$300* for a digital camera, but the actual cost was *$370.96*.

> On the invoice were items for *$6.10*, *$8*, *$33.95*, and *$75*.

Sums less than $1 are written as figures that are followed by the word *cents*:
By shopping carefully, we can save *15 cents* per unit.

**4.03 Dates.** In dates, numbers that appear after the name of the month are written as cardinal figures (*1, 2, 3*, etc.). Those that stand alone or appear before the name of a month are written as ordinal figures (*1st, 2nd, 3rd*, etc.):

> The Personnel Practices Committee will meet *May 7*.

> On the *5th* day of February and again on the *25th*, we placed orders.

In domestic business documents, dates generally take the following form: *January 4, 2015.* An alternative form, used primarily in military and foreign correspondence, begins with the day of the month and omits the comma: *4 January 2015.*

**4.04 Clock Time.** Figures are used when clock time is expressed with *a.m.* or *p.m.* Omit the colon and zeros in referring to whole hours. When exact clock time is expressed with the contraction o'clock, either figures or words may be used:

> Mail deliveries are made at *11 a.m.* and *3:30 p.m.*

> At *four* (or *4*) *o'clock* employees begin to leave.

**4.05 Addresses and Telephone Numbers.**

a. Except for the number *one*, house numbers are expressed in figures:

> 540 Elm Street                     17802 Washington Avenue
> One Colorado Boulevard             2 Highland Street

b. Street names containing numbers *ten* or lower are written entirely as words. For street names involving numbers greater than *ten*, figures are used:

> 330 Third Street                   3440 Seventh Avenue
> 6945 East 32nd Avenue              4903 West 23rd Street

c. Telephone numbers are expressed with figures. When used, the area code is placed in parentheses preceding the telephone number:

> Please call us at *(818) 347-0551* to place an order.

> Mr. Sims asked you to call *(619) 554-8923*, Ext. 245, after 10 a.m.

**4.06 Related Numbers.** Numbers are related when they refer to similar items in a category within the same reference. All related numbers should be expressed as the largest number is expressed. Thus if the largest number is greater than *ten*, all the numbers should be expressed in figures:

> Only *5* of the original *25* applicants completed the processing. (Related numbers require figures.)

> The two plans affected *34* employees working in *three* sites. (Unrelated numbers use figures and words.)

> Exxon Oil operated *86* rigs, of which *6* were rented. (Related numbers require figures.)

> The company hired *three* accountants, *one* customer-service representative, and *nine* sales representatives. (Related numbers *ten* and under use words.)

**4.07 Consecutive Numbers.** When two numbers appear consecutively and both modify a following noun, generally express the first number in words and the second in figures. If, however, the first number cannot be expressed in one or two words, place it in figures also (*120 70-cent* stamps). Do not use commas to separate the figures.

> Historians divided the era into *four 25-year* periods. (Use word form for the first number and figure form for the second.)

> We ordered *ten 30-page* color brochures. (Use word form for the first number and figure form for the second.)

> Did the manager request *150 100-watt* bulbs? (Use figure form for the first number since it would require more than two words.)

**4.08 Periods of Time.** Seconds, minutes, days, weeks, months, and years are treated as any other general number. Numbers above *ten* are written in figure form. Numbers *ten* and under are written in word form unless they represent a business concept such as a discount rate, interest rate, or warranty period:

> This business was incorporated over *50* years ago. (Use figures for a number above *ten*.)

> It took *three* hours to write this short report. (Use words for a number *ten* and under.)

> The warranty period is limited to *2* years. (Use figures for a business term.)

**4.09 Ages.** Ages are generally expressed in word form unless the age appears immediately after a name or is expressed in exact years and months:

> At the age of *twenty-one*, Elizabeth inherited the business.

> Wanda Tharp, *37*, was named acting president.

> At the age of *4 years and 7 months*, the child was adopted.

**4.10 Round Numbers.** Round numbers are approximations. They may be expressed in word or figure form, although figure form is shorter and easier to comprehend:

> About *600* (or *six hundred*) stock options were sold.

> It is estimated that *1,000* (or *one thousand*) people will attend.

For ease of reading, round numbers in the millions or billions should be expressed with a combination of figures and words:

> Facebook estimates that it has *1.98 billion* users.

> More than *163 million* viewers watched last year's Super Bowl game.

**4.11 Weights and Measurements.** Weights and measurements are expressed with figures:

> The new deposit slip measures *2* by *6 inches*.

> Her new suitcase weighed only *2 pounds 4 ounces*.

> Toledo is *60 miles* from Detroit.

**4.12 Fractions.** Simple fractions are expressed as words. Complex fractions may be written either as figures or as a combination of figures and words:

> Over *two thirds* of the stockholders have already voted.

> This microcomputer will execute the command in *1 millionth* of a second. (A combination of words and numbers is easier to comprehend.)

> She purchased a *one-fifth* share in the business.*

**4.13 Percentages and Decimals.** Percentages are expressed with figures that are followed by the word *percent*. The percent sign (%) is used only on business forms or in statistical presentations:

> We had hoped for a *7 percent* interest rate, but we received a loan at *8 percent*.

> Over *50 percent* of the residents supported the plan.

---

*Note: Fractions used as adjectives require hyphens.

Decimals are expressed with figures. If a decimal expression does not contain a whole number (an integer) and does not begin with a zero, a zero should be placed before the decimal point:

> The actuarial charts show that *1.74* out of *1,000* people will die in any given year.

> Inspector Norris found the setting to be *.005* inch off. (Decimal begins with a zero and does not require a zero before the decimal point.)

> Considerable savings will accrue if the unit production cost is reduced *0.1* percent. (A zero is placed before a decimal that neither contains a whole number nor begins with a zero.)

### Quick Chart—Expression of Numbers

| Use Words | Use Figures |
|---|---|
| Numbers *ten* and under | Numbers *11* and over |
| Numbers at beginning of sentence | Money |
| Ages | Dates |
| Fractions | Addresses and telephone numbers |
| | Weights and measurements |
| | Percentages and decimals |

## Review Exercise N—Number Style

Choose the option that is correctly expressed. Then compare your responses with the key at the end of the book.

1. Only (a) *five*, (b) *5* of the 350 Constant Contact messages were undeliverable.

2. A new department store opened on (a) *5th Avenue*, (b) *Fifth Avenue*.

3. Our retreat was scheduled for (a) *August eight*, (b) *August 8th*, (c) *August 8*.

4. The new library bookshelf measures (a) *eight by ten*, (b) *8 by 10* feet.

5. The meeting starts at (a) *9 a.m.*, (b) *9:00 a.m.*, (c) *9 o'clock a.m.*

6. The hotel has (a) *68*, (b) *sixty-eight* rooms with ocean view.

7. One soccer game drew (a) *two*, (b) *2* million viewers.

8. The coffee machine cost (a) *sixty dollars*, (b) *$60 dollars*, (c) *$60*.

9. Our company was founded (a) *21*, (b) *twenty-one* years ago.

10. We were lucky to obtain a (a) *two*, (b) *2* percent interest rate for our business loan.

11. The prepaid vehicle maintenance plan extends to (a) *3*, (b) *three* years.

12. A (a) *30-day*, (b) *thirty-day* return policy covers all electronics.

13. Kohl's offers (a) *$20*, (b) *twenty dollars*, (c) *$20 dollars* off with every Amazon return.

14. The shipment arrived on the (a) *22nd*, (b) *twenty-second* of June.

15. She owned (a) *3*, (b) *three* tablets, each a different generation of Apple device.

## D-7 Key to Grammar/Mechanics Handbook Review Exercises

### Review Exercise A—Nouns

**1.** b (attorneys) **2.** a (Metzes)
**3.** c (companies) **4.** b (behes)
**5.** b (ups and downs) **6.** a (Fridays)
**7.** c (dispatches) **8.** a (countries)
**9.** b (sisters-in-law) **10.** a (b's and d's)
**11.** c (secretaries) **12.** b (runners-up)
**13.** a (chimneys) **14.** c (lenses)
**15.** b (bills of sale)

### Review Exercise B—Pronouns

**1.** c (me) **2.** b (Whom) **3.** b (her)
**4.** a (its) **5.** b (me) **6.** c (me)
**7.** a (All employees) **8.** b (We)
**9.** c (its) **10.** b (me) **11.** c (me)
**12.** a (ours) **13.** c (its) **14.** a (you're)
**15.** b (whoever)

### Review Exercise C—Verbs 1

**1.** a (is) **2.** a (is) **3.** c (chose) **4.** b (seen)
**5.** a (was) **6.** a (is) **7.** b (is) **8.** b (are)
**9.** a (gone) **10.** b (become) **11.** a (were)
**12.** b (talks) **13.** b (lying) **14.** a (broken)
**15.** a (rung)

### Review Exercise D—Verbs 2

**1.** a **2.** b **3.** b **4.** a **5.** b

### Review Exercise E—Adjectives and Adverbs

**1.** a (face-to-face) **2.** a (careful)
**3.** c (their) **4.** a (satisfactorily) **5.** b (bad)
**6.** a (bumper-to-bumper)
**7.** a (more feasible) **8.** b (one by one)
**9.** a (worse) **10.** a (personally)
**11.** b (more slowly) **12.** b (good)
**13.** a (there) **14.** b (loudly) **15.** b (closer)

### Review Exercise F—Prepositions and Conjunctions

**1.** b **2.** a **3.** b **4.** b **5.** b **6.** a **7.** b **8.** a
**9.** b **10.** a **11.** a **12.** b **13.** a **14.** a **15.** b

### Review Exercise G—Commas 1

**1.** b **2.** b **3.** a **4.** a **5.** b **6.** a **7.** b **8.** b
**9.** a **10.** b **11.** a **12.** a **13.** b **14.** a
**15.** a

### Review Exercise H—Commas 2

**1.** b **2.** a **3.** b **4.** a **5.** a **6.** b **7.** a **8.** b
**9.** a **10.** b **11.** b **12.** a **13.** b **14.** a
**15.** b

### Review Exercise I—Commas 3

**1.** a **2.** b **3.** b **4.** a **5.** b **6.** b **7.** b **8.** b
**9.** a **10.** b **11.** a **12.** b **13.** b **14.** a **15.** a

### Review Exercise J—Semicolons and Colons

**1.** a **2.** b **3.** a **4.** b **5.** b **6.** a **7.** b **8.** a
**9.** a **10.** a **11.** b **12.** b **13.** a **14.** b **15.** a

### Review Exercise K—Apostrophes

**1.** C **2.** years' **3.** CEO's **4.** inventor's
**5.** companies' **6.** C **7.** weeks' **8.** year's
**9.** council's **10.** Floreses' **11.** customers'
**12.** C **13.** therapists' **14.** States
**15.** Humphrey's

## Review Exercise L—
## Other Punctuation

**1.** c **2.** b **3.** b **4.** a **5.** c **6.** a **7.** b **8.** a
**9.** a **10.** b **11.** a **12.** b **13.** b **14.** a
**15.** a

## Review Exercise M—
## Capitalization

**1.** a **2.** a **3.** a **4.** b **5.** a **6.** b **7.** a **8.** b
**9.** b **10.** c **11.** a **12.** c **13.** a **14.** b **15.** a

## Review Exercise N—
## Number Style

**1.** b (5) **2.** b (Fifth) **3.** c (August 8)
**4.** b (8 by 10) **5.** a (9 a.m.) **6.** a (68)
**7.** b (2 million) **8.** c ($60) **9.** a (21)
**10.** b (2 percent) **11.** a (3) **12.** a (30-day)
**13.** a ($20) **14.** a (22nd) **15.** b (three)

# Notes

## Chapter 1

1. Smith, N. (2020, December 9). We may be exactly wrong about technology and inequality. *Bloomberg*. Retrieved from https://www .bloomberg.com; Manyika, J., Lund, S., Chui, M., Bughin, J., Batra, P., Ko, R., & Sanghvi, S. (2017, November). Jobs lost, jobs gained: What the future of work will mean for jobs, skills, and wages. McKinsey Global Institute. Retrieved from https://www.mckinsey.com

2. World Economic Forum. (2020, October). The future of jobs report 2020, 16. Retrieved from https://www3.weforum.org

3. Hart Research Associates. (2018, July). Fulfilling the American dream: Liberal education and the future of work. Selected findings from online surveys of business executives and hiring managers conducted on behalf of the Association of American Colleges & Universities, 14–15. Retrieved from https://www.aacu.org

4. National Association of Colleges and Employers (NACE). (2020, January 16). The top attributes employers want to see on resumes. Job Outlook 2020. Retrieved from https://www.naceweb.org; NACE. Job Outlook 2019, 2018 Internship & Co-op Report, and 2017 Recruiting Benchmarks Survey. Retrieved from https://www.naceweb.org; Hart Research Associates/Association of American Colleges & Universities. (2015, January 20). Falling short? College learning and career success. Retrieved from https://www.aacu.org

5. Burrow, G. (2020, September 4). Resilient skills to succeed in a post-COVID world. Emsi. Retrieved from https://www.economicmodeling .com. See also National Association of Colleges and Employers. (2016, December 16). Job outlook: Hiring for U.S. jobs expected to be flat. Retrieved from https://www.naceweb.org

6. Quoted in Zipkin, N. (2017, June 23). What skills will you need to succeed in an uncertain future? *Entrepreneur*. Retrieved from https://www .entrepreneur.com

7. Duxbury, L., & Lanctot, A. (2017, April 20). Carleton University. Retrieved from https://newsroom.carleton.ca

8. Hart Research Associates. (2018, July). Fulfilling the American dream: Liberal education and the future of work. Selected findings from online surveys of business executives and hiring managers conducted on behalf of the Association of American Colleges & Universities, 14–15. Retrieved from https://www.aacu.org

9. Rios, J. A., Ling, G., Pugh, R., Becker, D., & Bacall, A. (2020, January 21). Identifying critical 21st-century skills for workplace success: A content analysis of job advertisements. *Educational Researcher, 49*(2), 80–89. doi: 10.3102/0013189X19890600; Watanabe-Crockett, L. (2016). The critical 21st century skills every student needs and why. Global Digital Citizen Foundation. Retrieved from https://globaldigitalcitizen.org

10. Kehaulani Goo, S. (2015, February 19). The skills Americans say kids need to succeed in life. Pew Research Center. Retrieved from https://www .pewresearch.org

11. Manyika, J., Lund, S., Chui, M., Bughin, J., Woetzel, J., Batra, P., Ko, R., & Sanghvi, S. (2017, November). Jobs lost, jobs gained; What the future of work will mean for jobs, skills, and wages. McKinsey Global Institute. Retrieved from https://www.mckinsey.com; Elliott, L. (2016, January 24). Fourth industrial revolution brings promise and peril for humanity. *The Guardian*. Retrieved from https://www.theguardian.com; Greenfield, R. (2016, December 7). Forget robots—people skills are the future of American jobs. *Bloomberg*. Retrieved from https://www.bloomberg .com; Deming, D. J. (2016, August). The growing importance of social skills in the labor market. Harvard University and National Bureau of Economic Relations (NBER). Retrieved from https://scholar.harvard.edu

12. Schwantes, M. (2017, June 13). These 3 billionaires agree: You need this skill to be successful. Inc. Retrieved from https://www.inc.com

13. Rios, J. A., Ling, G., Pugh, R., Becker, D., & Bacall, A. (2020, January 21). Identifying critical 21st-century skills for workplace success: A content analysis of job advertisements. *Educational Researcher, 49*(2), 80–89. doi: 10.3102/0013189X19890600

14. Davidson, K. (2016, August 30). The "soft skills" employers are looking for. *The Wall Street Journal*. Retrieved from https://blogs.wsj .com; National Association of Colleges and Employers (NACE).

15. Doyle, A. (2020, July 21). You can get fired for what you post online. The Balance Careers. Retrieved from https://www.thebalancecareers .com; Madell, R. (2015, June 15). The 3 biggest social media snafus that can cost you the job. *U.S. News & World Report*. Retrieved from https:// money.usnews.com

16. Loten, A. (2020, November 19). People skills a plus for tech job seekers. *The Wall Street Journal*. Retrieved from https://www.wsj.com

17. Satell, G. (2015, February 6). Why communication is today's most important skills. *Forbes*. Retrieved from https://www.forbes.com

18. Solomon, G. (2018, August 9). Why mastering writing skills can help future-proof your career. *Forbes*. Retrieved from https://www.forbes .com

19. Belkin, D. (2017, June 5). Exclusive test data: Many colleges fail to improve critical-thinking skills. *The Wall Street Journal*. Retrieved from https://www.wsj.com

20. Hart Research Associates. (2018, July). Fulfilling the American dream: Liberal education and the future of work. Selected findings from online surveys of business executives and hiring managers conducted on behalf of the Association of American Colleges & Universities, 14–15. Retrieved from https://www.aacu.org

21. Manyika, J. (2017, May). Technology, jobs, and the future of work. McKinsey Global Institute. Retrieved from https://www.mckinsey.com

22. Friedman, T. L. (2017, May 24). A road trip through rusting and rising America. *The New York Times*. Retrieved from https://www.nytimes.com

23. Yang, D. (2016, May 24). Who are you calling soft? The value of soft skills in a tech-obsessed economy. *The Huffington Post*. Retrieved from https://www.huffingtonpost.com

24. Jones, J. M. (2018, October 9). Confidence in higher education down since 2015. Gallup blog. Retrieved from https://news.gallup.com

25. Abel, J. R., & Deitz, R. (2019, June 5). Despite rising costs, college is still a good investment. Federal Reserve Bank of New York. Retrieved from https://libertystreeteconomics.newyorkfed.org; Cook, L. (2015, August 17). Seriously, go to college. *U.S. News & World Report*. Retrieved from https://www.usnews.com

26. Beach, G. (2018, June 26). Hard-pressed by soft skills, CIOs face talent challenge. *The Wall Street Journal*. Retrieved from https://www.wsj.com

27. National Association of Colleges and Employers. (2017, November). Job outlook 2018: Career Readiness, 32; Davidson, K. (2016, October 4). Soft skills give workers a big edge. It's time to start focusing on them in school, report says. *The Wall Street Journal*. Retrieved from https://blogs .wsj.com

28. Brenan, M. (2020, October 13). COVID-19 and remote work: An update. Gallup. Retrieved from https://news.gallup.com; PwC. (2020, June 25). When everyone can work from home, what's the office for? PwC's US remote work survey. Retrieved from https://www.pwc.com

29. PwC. (2020, June 25). When everyone can work from home, what's the office for? PwC's US remote work survey. Retrieved from https://www .pwc.com

30. Kitchen, M. (2018, October 5). How to disconnect from "always on" work culture. *The Wall Street Journal*. Retrieved from https://www.wsj.com

31. Gottschalk, S. (2018). *The terminal self: Everyday life in hypermodern times*. New York: Routledge, 14.

32. Robinson, B. (2020, June 19). Is working remote a blessing or burden? Weighing the pros and cons. *Forbes*. Retrieved from https://www .forbes.com

33. Landrum, S. (2017, March 17). Millennials driving brands to practice socially responsible marketing. *Forbes*. Retrieved from https://www .forbes.com; McGregor, J. (2019, May 15). More CEOs were forced out for ethical lapses in 2018 than poor financial performance. *The Washington Post*. Retrieved from https://www.washingtonpost.com; Punishing CEOs for bad behavior: 2017 public perception survey. Stanford Graduate School of Business. Retrieved from https://www.gsb.stanford.edu

34. Thoughts on the business of life. (n.d.). *Forbes* Quotes. Retrieved from https://www.forbes.com

(2016, December 7). The attributes employers seek on a candidate's resume. Job Outlook 2017. Retrieved from https://www.naceweb.org

35. Zenger, J., & Folkman, J. (2020). *The new extraordinary leader: Turn good managers into great leaders* (3rd ed.). New York: McGraw-Hill, 168.

36. Crockett, R. O. (2011, March 14). Listening is critical in today's multicultural workplace. *Harvard Business Review*. Retrieved from https://hbr.org

37. Dean, S., & East, J. I. (2019). Soft skills needed for the 21st-century workforce. *International Journal of Applied Management and Technology, 18*(1), 17–32. doi: 10.5590/IJAMT.2019.18.1.02. Retrieved from https://search-proquest.com; Boyle, D., Carpenter, B., & Mahoney, D. P. (2017, Fall). Developing the communication skills required for sustainable career success. *Management Accounting Quarterly, 19*(1), 1–9. Retrieved from https://search-proquest.com

38. Riordan, C. M. Three ways leaders can listen with more empathy. In: *Emotional intelligence: Mindful listening*. (2019). Boston: Harvard Business Review Press, 29–37.

39. Treasure, J. (2020, September 18). The future of listening. Julian Treasure blog. Retrieved from https://www.juliantreasure.com

40. International Listening Association. (n.d.). Listening and speech rates. International Listening Association. Retrieved from https://listen.org

41. Murphy, K. (2019). *You're not listening*. New York: Celadon Books, 70.

42. Stibitz, S. (2015, January 30). How to really listen to your employees. *Harvard Business Review*. Retrieved from https://hbr.org

43. Colbert, A., Yee, N., & George, G. (2016, June). The digital workforce and the workplace of the future. *Academy of Management Journal, 55*(3), 733. doi.org/10.5465/amj.2016.4003

44. Doubek, J. (2016, April 17). Attention, students: Put your laptops away. NPR. Retrieved from https://www.npr.org

45. Mehrabian, A. (2017/1972). *Nonverbal Communication*. New York: Routledge, 39.

46. Watzlawick, P., Beavin Bavelas, J., & Jackson, D. D. (2011). *Pragmatics of human communication: A study of interactional patterns, pathologies and paradoxes*. New York: W. W. Norton, 30.

47. Birdwhistell, R. (1970). *Kinesics and context*. Philadelphia: University of Pennsylvania Press.

48. Kinsey Goman, C. (2018, March 7). On National Women's Day, don't look less than you are. *Forbes*. Retrieved from https://www.forbes.com; Burton, V. (2016). *Successful women speak differently: 9 habits that build confidence, courage, and influence*. Eugene, OR: Harvest House Publishers, 65.

49. Hall, E. T. (1966). *The hidden dimension*. Garden City, NY: Doubleday, 107–122.

50. St. Louis, M. (2017, June 8). Research shows that the clothes you wear actually change the way you perform: Here are some good reasons to always "dress the part." *Inc*. Retrieved from https://www.inc.com

51. Kinsey Goman, C. (2016). Body language tips for women who mean business. American Marketing Association. Retrieved from https://www.amanet.org/training/articles/Body-Language-Tips-for-Women-Who-Mean-Business.aspx

52. Jacob, L. (2018, May 22). Who has the most tattoos? Dalia Research. Retrieved from https://daliaresearch.com

53. Broussard, K., & Harton, H. (2017, September). Tattoo or taboo? Tattoo stigma and negative attitudes toward tattooed individuals. *The Journal of Social Psychology, 158*(1). doi: 10.1080/00224545.2017.1373622

54. Hotson, E. (2020, January 14). More people are getting tattoos—So workplaces must be keeping up, right? Well, it's a bit more complicated than that. BBC.com. Retrieved from https://www.bbc.com

55. Figure based on Chaney, L. H., & Martin, J. S. (2011). *Intercultural business communication* (5th ed.). Upper Saddle River, NJ: Prentice Hall, Chapter 5; J. Chung's analysis appearing in Chen, G. M., & Starosta, W. J. *Foundations of intercultural communication*. Boston: Allyn and Bacon, 1998, 51; and O'Hara-Devereaux, M., & Johansen, R. (1994). *Globalwork: Bridging distance, culture, and time*. San Francisco: Jossey-Bass, 55.

56. Davis, T., Ward, D. A., & Woodland, D. (2010). Cross-cultural and international business communication—verbal. *National Business Education Association Yearbook: Cross-Cultural and International Business Education, 3*; Hall, E. T., & Hall, M. R. (2000). Key concepts: Underlying structures of culture. In M. H. Albrecht (Ed.), *International HRM: Managing diversity in the workplace*. Hoboken, NJ: Wiley-Blackwell, 200–202; Hall, E. T., & Hall, M. R. (1990). *Understanding cultural differences*. Yarmouth, ME: Intercultural Press, pp. 183–184.

57. Chaney, L. H., & Martin, J. S. (2011). *Intercultural business communication* (5th ed.). Upper Saddle River, NJ: Prentice Hall, 93.

58. Beamer, L., & Varner, I. (2011). *Intercultural communication in the global workplace* (5th ed.). Boston: McGraw-Hill Irwin, 143.

59. Chen, M.-J., & Miller, D. (2010, November). West meets East: Toward an ambicultural approach to management. *Academy of Management Perspectives, 24*(4), 19ff. Retrieved from https://search.ebscohost.com; Sheer, V. C., & Chen, L. (2003, January). Successful Sino-Western business negotiation: Participants' accounts of national and professional cultures. *The Journal of Business Communication, 40*(1), 62.

60. Salehan, M., Kim, D. J., & Lee, J.-N. (2018, September). Are there any relationships between technology and cultural values? A country-level trend study of the association between information communication technology and cultural values. *Information & Management, 55*(6), 725–745. doi: 10.1016/j.im.2018.03.003; Rowley, C. (2017). Whither globalization and convergence? Asian examples and future research. *Asia Pacific Review, 23*(1), 1–9. doi: 10.1080/13602381.2016.1238602; Vargas, J. H., & Kemmelmeier, M. (2013). Ethnicity and contemporary American culture: A meta-analytic investigation of horizontal-vertical individualism-collectivism. *Journal of Cross-Cultural Psychology, 44*(2), 208–209. Retrieved from https://wolfweb.unr.edu

61. Beamer, L., & Varner, I. (2011). *Intercultural communication in the global workplace* (5th ed.). Boston: McGraw-Hill Irwin, 312–316.

62. Lam, L. W., & Xu, A. J. (2019). Power imbalance and employee silence: The role of abusive relationship, power distance orientation, and perceived organizational politics. *Applied Psychology, 68*(3), 513–546. doi: 10.1111/apps.12170.

63. Copeland, L., & Griggs, L. (1991). *Going international*. New York: Penguin, 94. See also Beamer, L., & Varner, I. (2011). *Intercultural communication in the global workplace* (5th ed.). Boston: McGraw-Hill Irwin, 340.

64. Beamer, L., & Varner, I. (2011). *Intercultural communication in the global workplace* (5th ed.). Boston: McGraw-Hill Irwin, p. 350; Copeland, L., & Griggs, L. (1991). *Going international*. New York: Penguin, 12.

65. Roeder, A. (2020, January 6). Social media can be positive for mental health and well-being. Harvard T. H. Chan School of Public Health. Retrieved from https://www.hsph.harvard.edu; Limbu, M., & Gurung, B. (2014). *Emerging pedagogies in the networked knowledge society: Practices integrating social media and globalization*. Hershey, PA: IGI Global, 72.

66. Ducharme, J. (2020, May 8). COVID-19 is making America's loneliness epidemic even worse. *Time*. Retrieved from https://time.com; Murphy, K. (2020, January 9). Talk less. Listen more. Here's how. *The New York Times*. Retrieved from https://www.nytimes.com; Whitley, R. (2020, January 29). Loneliness in young adults: A growing mental health issue. *Psychology Today*. Retrieved from https://www.psychologytoday.com; Cigna. (2020). 2020 U.S. Report: Loneliness and the workplace. Retrieved from https://www.cigna.com; Cigna. (2018). 2018 Cigna loneliness index: Survey of 20,000 Americans examining behaviors driving loneliness in the United States. Retrieved from https://www.multivu.com

67. Vinnakota, R. (2017, January 24). How social media divides us. The Aspen Institute. Retrieved from https://www.aspeninstitute.org

68. Shao, G. (2019, August 16). Social media has become a battleground in Hong Kong's protests. CNBC. Retrieved from https://www.cnbc.com

69. Girard, J. (2019, September 25). Visual color symbolism chart by culture. Lifewire. Retrieved from https://www.lifewire.com; Cousins, C. (2012, June 11). Color and cultural design considerations. Web Designer Depot. Retrieved from https://www.webdesignerdepot.com

70. Kapur, A. (2019, November 1). The rising threat of digital nationalism. *The Wall Street Journal*. Retrieved from https://www.wsj.com

71. Delaney, R. (2014, October). Voluntourism will boost your career. *Consulting—Specifying Engineer*. Retrieved from https://search.proquest.com

72. Fish, J. M. (2014, February 25). Tolerance, acceptance, understanding. *Psychology Today*. Retrieved from https://www.psychologytoday.com

73. Tress, L. (2017, January 23). In the barren south, Israelis and Arabs work to green the Middle East. *The Times of Israel*. Retrieved from https://www.timesofisrael.com; Blumberg, A. (2015, April 21). In the Middle East, Muslims and Jews work in unison to care for the environment. *The Huffington Post*. Retrieved from https://www.huffingtonpost.com

74. Frey, W. H. (2018, March 14). The US will become "minority white" in 2045, Census projects. The Brookings Institution. Retrieved from https://www.brookings.edu

75. Older people projected to outnumber children for the first time in U.S. history. (2018, September 6). United States Census Bureau. Retrieved from https://www.census.gov

76. Xavier, J. (2014, March 31). Diversity defines our global economy. Do you speak the language? *Entrepreneur*. Retrieved from https://www.entrepreneur.com

77. Boykiv, Y. (2015, June 3). How to build and sustain a diverse team. *Fast Company*. Retrieved from https://www.fastcompany.com

78. Ibid.

79. Hunt, V., Yee, L., Prince, S., & Dixon-Fyle, S. (2018, January). Delivering through diversity. *McKinsey Report*. Retrieved from https://www.mckinsey.com

80. Bush, M., & Peters, K. (2016, December 5). How the best companies do diversity right. *Fortune*. Retrieved from https://fortune.com

81. Krawcheck, S. (2017). *Own it: The power of women at work*. New York: Crown Publishing, 37.

82. Meakin, L. (2019, June 14). BOE's Carney calls for diversity to stop groupthink in banking. *Bloomberg*. Retrieved from https://www.bloomberg.com

83. Molinsky, A., & Jang, S. (2016, January 20). To connect across cultures, find out what you have in common. *Harvard Business Review*. Retrieved from https://hbr.org; Pfau, B. N., & Kay, I. T. (2002). *The human capital edge: 21 people management practices your company must implement (or avoid) to maximize shareholder value*. New York: McGraw-Hill, 72–73, 75.

84. Schooley, S. (2019, August 12). Lost in translation: 19 international marketing fails. *Business News Daily*. Retrieved from https://www.businessnewsdaily.com

85. Siegel, R. (2019, October 29). Tweens, teens and screens: The average time kids spend watching online videos has doubled in 4 years. *The Washington Post*. Retrieved from https://www.washingtonpost.com

86. Branson, R. (n.d.). Tony Hsieh remembered. Richard's Blog. Retrieved from https://www.virgin.com

87. Treasure, J. (2020, September 18). The future of listening. Julian Treasure blog. Retrieved from https://www.juliantreasure.com; Heitler, S. (2011, November). The art of listening: How open are your ears? *Psychology Today*. Retrieved from https://www.psychologytoday.com

88. Stibitz, S. (2015, January 30). How to really listen to your employees. *Harvard Business Review*. Retrieved from https://hbr.org

89. Heitler, S. (2011, November). The art of listening: How open are your ears? *Psychology Today*. Retrieved from https://www.psychologytoday.com

90. Pannell, N. (2018, June 26). 6 common types of body language that don't mean what you think. *Insider*. Retrieved from https://www.insider.com

91. Based on Smith, J. (2014, December 15). 26 annoying phrases you should stop using at work. *Business Insider*. Retrieved from https://www.businessinsider.com

92. Rai, S. (2018, November 20). Twitter CEO gets trolled after wading into India's caste debate. *Bloomberg*. Retrieved from https://www.bloomberg.com

93. British minister in cultural gaffe after giving Taipei mayor "taboo" watch. (2015, January 26). *The Guardian*. Retrieved from https://www.theguardian.com

94. Špaček, L. (2008). *Nová velká kniha etikety*. Prague: Mladá Fronta, 260.

95. Fifty-six percent of hotels in Japan bar visitors with tattoos from bathing facilities. (2015, October 22). *Japan Today*. Retrieved from https://japantoday.com

96. Unless attributed otherwise, the scenarios are based on Richards, K. (2018, December 19). 5 major brand fails of 2018—And what every marketer can learn from them. *Adweek*. Retrieved from https://www.adweek.com

97. Schneider, E. (2020, January 10). 4 lessons from WW's unfortunate promoted tweet that ran while WWIII was trending: How to be nimble when the unexpected happens. *Adweek*. Retrieved from https://www.adweek.com

98. Fired Vancouver waiter: I'm not rude, just French. (2018, March 26). *BBC News*. Retrieved from https://www.bbc.com; Bachega, H. (2018, March 28). Fired Vancouver waiter case: Are the French really rude? *BBC News*. Retrieved from https://www.bbc.com

99. Fluker, D. (2020, June 4). 20 Companies hiring entry-level positions for college grads now. Glassdoor. Retrieved from https://www.glassdoor.com

100. Aslam, S. (2020, November 3). LinkedIn by the numbers: Stats, demographics & fun facts. Omnicore. Retrieved from https://www.omnicoreagency.com; Barnes, N. G., Mazzola, A., & Killeen, M. (2020, January 9). Oversaturation & disengagement: The 2019 Fortune 500 social media dance. Center for Marketing Research, University of Massachusetts Dartmouth. Retrieved from https://www.umassd.edu

101. Osman, M. (2020, October 19). Mind-blowing LinkedIn statistics and facts (2020). Kinsta. Retrieved from https://kinsta.com

# Chapter 2

1. Casten, S. quoted in Zweig, J. (2019, October 19–20). Time for advisors to speak in plain English. *The Wall Street Journal*, 32.

2. Silverman, D. (2009, February 10). Why is business writing so bad? *Harvard Business Review*. Retrieved from https://hbr.org

3. Arnold, V. (1986, August). Benjamin Franklin on writing well. *Personnel Journal*, 17.

4. Bacon, M. quoted in Business writing: One-on-one speaks best to the masses. (1988, April). *Training*, 95.

5. Clark, B. (2020, November 9). The two most important words in blogging, persuasion, and copyediting. *Copyblogger*. Retrieved from https://www.copyblogger.com

6. Riesterer, T. (2019). You vs. we: Which is the best way to phrase a campaign? *Adweek*. Retrieved from https://adweek.com

7. Google. (2012, January 30). Personal communication with Mary Ellen Guffey.

8. Lahey, S. (2018, February 16). Emojis at work: The good, the bad, and the legally binding. Zendesk. Retrieved from https://relate.zendesk.com; Mims, C. (2019, July 20). Yes, you actually should be using emojis at work. *The Wall Street Journal*. Retrieved from https://www.wsj.com

9. Geraghty, L. (2017). *Positive tone: It's how you say it*. Wavelength. Retrieved from *https://wavelength.training*

10. Be positive. Adapted from Brandi, J. (2009, March). Winning at customer retention. *Communication Briefings*, 5. Retrieved from https://www.customercarecoach.com

11. Opelka, G. (2017, September 26). I've got a problem: "No problem." "You're welcome" is much more civilized, thank you very much. *The Wall Street Journal*. Retrieved from https://www.wsj.com

12. Link, S. (2012, May 2). Use "person first" language. [Letter to editor]. *USA Today*, 6A.

13. Carrick, R. (2018, July 9). Why it's not your fault it's so hard to understand investing. *The Globe and Mail*. Retrieved from www.theglobeandmail.com

14. Davies, S. (2020, October 6). Access for all: Plain language is a civil right: An unmissable global virtual conference. Shelly Davies Blog. Retrieved from https://www.shellydavies.co.nz; Plain writing is a civil right. (2009). E-WRITE. Retrieved from www.ewriteonline.com

# Chapter 3

1. LaFleur, C. (2015, October 20). Why write? The relevance of good writing in the Internet age. LaFleur Marketing. Retrieved from https://lafleur.marketing

2. Greenfield, R. (2014, July 29). *Fast Company*. Brainstorming doesn't work; try this technique instead. Fast Company. Retrieved from www.fastcompany.com

3. Wiens, K. (2012, July 20). I won't hire people who use poor grammar. Here's why. On Harvard Business Review Blog. Retrieved from https://hbr.org

4. Johnson, L. G. (2011, January 12). Avoid this simple "comma splice" error. Retrieved from https://www.businesswritingblog.com

5. Wylie, A. (2009). How to make your copy more readable: Make sentences shorter. PRsay. Retrieved from https://comprehension.prsa.org; Goddard, R. W. (1989, April). Communication: Use language effectively. *Personnel Journal*, 32.

6. A message to our fans. (2016, March 17). *SeaWorld cares*. Retrieved from https://seaworldcares.com

7. O'Conner, P. T. (2019). *Woe is I: The grammarphobe's guide to better English in plain English*. (4th edition). New York: Riverhead Books/Penguin Random House, 217.

8. Bernoff, J. (2016, September 6). Bad writing is destroying your company's productivity. *Harvard Business Review*. Retrieved from https://hbr.org

9. PayScale. (2016, May 17). Leveling up: How to win in the skills economy. [Press release]. Retrieved from https://www.payscale.com

# Chapter 4

1. King, S. (2000). *On writing: A memoir of the craft*. New York: Scribners, 13.
2. Reh, F. J. (2019, November 20). Writing for business. The Balance Careers. Retrieved from https://www.thebalancecareers.com
3. Notable & quotable: William Zinsser. (2015, May 22). *The Wall Street Journal*. Retrieved from https://www.wsj.com
4. Whitmore, J. (2017, February 7). Don't underestimate how much spelling matters in business communications. *Entrepreneur*. Retrieved from https://www.entrepreneur.com
5. Adams, S. (2015, April 27). 10 tips for better business writing. *Forbes*. Retrieved from https://www.forbes.com
6. Bernoff, J. (2016, September 6). Bad writing is destroying your company's productivity. *Harvard Business Review*. Retrieved from https://hbr.org
7. McClusky, B. Quoted in Gausepohl, S. (2016, July 11). These 10 buzzwords are annoying your employees. *Business News Daily*. Retrieved from https://www.businessnewsdaily.com
8. Sword, H. (2012, July 23). Zombie nouns. *The New York Times*. Retrieved from https://opinionator.blogs.nytimes.com
9. Twain, M. (1888, October 15). Letter to George Bainton. Retrieved from https://www.twainquotes.com
10. Levitt, A. (2020, February 3). Mutual funds are still keeping secrets. *The New York Times*. Retrieved from https://www.nytimes.com

# Chapter 5

1. The Radicati Group. (2019, April). Email market, 2019-2023. Retrieved from https://www.radicati.com; Clement, J. (2019, August 9). Number of e-mail users worldwide 2017-2023. Statista. Retrieved from https://www.statista.com
2. Tschabitscher, H. (2019, June 27). 19 fascinating email facts. Lifewire. Retrieved from https://www.lifewire.com; Lynkova, D. (2019, April 22). The surprising reality of how many emails are sent per day. Techjury. Retrieved from https://techjury.net
3. The Radicati Group. (2018, March). Email statistics report, 2018-2022. Retrieved from https://www.radicati.com
4. Madrigal, A. C. (2014, August 14). Email is still the best thing on the Internet. *The Atlantic*. Retrieved from https://www.theatlantic.com
5. Duffy, J., & Moore, B. (2019, December 12). The best business messaging apps for 2020. *PC Magazine*. Retrieved from https://www.pcmag.com; Feintzeig, R. (2014, June 17). A company without email? Not so fast. *The Wall Street Journal*. Retrieved from https://www.wsj.com
6. Elgan, M. (2018, March 31). Why email is the best social network. *Computerworld*. Retrieved from https://www.computerworld.com
7. Clement, J. (2019, August 9). E-mail usage in the United States—Statistics & facts. Statista. Retrieved from https://www.statista.com
8. Dean, J. (2016, October 25). Slack CEO Stewart Butterfield on the future of communication. *The Wall Street Journal*. Retrieved from https://www.wsj.com
9. Connley, C. (2018, June 5). Suzy Welch: 4 email mistakes that make people hate you. CNBC. Retrieved from https://www.cnbc.com
10. Gillett, R. (2017, February 21). 21 unprofessional email habits that make everyone hate you. *Business Insider*. Retrieved from https://www.businessinsider.com
11. La Roche, J. (2019, March 16). Goldman Sachs CEO reveals the valuable job skill he's finding "less and less." Yahoo Finance. Retrieved from https://finance.yahoo.com
12. Abramovich, G. (2019, September). CMO by Adobe. Retrieved from https://cmo.adobe.com
13. Koren, M. (2018, June 11). The most honest out-of-office message. *The Atlantic*. Retrieved from https://www.theatlantic.com
14. The Radicati Group. (2019, April). Email market, 2019-2023. Retrieved from https://www.radicati.com; Clement, J. (2019, August 9). Number of e-mail users worldwide 2017-2023. Statista. Retrieved from https://www.statista.com
15. O'Conner, K. (2016, July 25). Email is forever. *Houston Chronicle*. Retrieved from https://www.chron.com
16. Vaughan, A. (2018, January 16). BP's Deepwater Horizon bill tops $65bn. *The Guardian*. Retrieved from https://www.theguardian.com; Vance, A. (2014, December 4). The eight most expensive e-mail snafus in corporate history. *Bloomberg Business*. Retrieved from https://www.bloomberg.com

17. Nagele-Piazza, L. (2018, June 15). Tips for managing workers' after-hour use of mobile devices. SHRM. Retrieved from https://www.shrm.org; Brandeisky, K. (2016, July 22). 5 things you didn't know about using personal email at work. *Money*. Retrieved from https://time.com
18. Bell, J. D. (2018, August 24). Firing for online behavior. SHRM. Retrieved from https://www.shrm.org; Brandeisky, K. (2016, July 22). 5 things you didn't know about using personal email at work. *Money*. Retrieved from https://time.com
19. Lamb, S. E. (2015). *Writing well for business success*. New York: St. Martin's Griffin, 139.
20. Bohns, V. K. (2017, April 11). A face-to-face request is 34 times more successful than an email. *Harvard Business Review*. Retrieved from https://hbr.org
21. Jaffe, E. (2014, October 9). Why it's so hard to detect emotion in emails and texts. *Fast Company Co.Design*. Retrieved from https://www.fastcodesign.com
22. Turk, V. (2020). *Kill reply all: A modern guide to online etiquette*. New York: Plume, Penguin Random House, 9–10.
23. Mobile fact sheet: Mobile phone ownership over time. (2019, June 12). Pew Research Center. Retrieved from https://www.pewresearch.org
24. Gottsman, D. (2017, September 27). 10 professional texting etiquette rules. *HuffPost*. Retrieved from https://www.huffpost.com
25. Strasburg, J. (2017, January 13). Deutsche Bank bans widely used text-messaging programs for business use. *The Wall Street Journal*. Retrieved from https://www.wsj.com; Bit, K. (2014, June 9). Cohen's Point72 bans instant messaging for some managers. *Bloomberg Business*. Retrieved from https://www.bloomberg.com; Rushton, K. (2013, December 15). JP Morgan to ban staff from instant messaging services. *The Telegraph*. Retrieved from https://www.telegraph.co.uk
26. Campbell, D. (2019, March 27). Wall Street is losing its battle against encrypted apps like WhatsApp and WeChat as it tries to police employee communications—and even regulators are stumped. *Business Insider*. Retrieved from https://www.businessinsider.com; Keller, L. J. (2017, March 30). Wall Street's new favorite way to swap secrets is against the rules. *Bloomberg*. Retrieved from https://www.bloomberg.com
27. Motor vehicle safety at work: Distracted driving at work. (2019, September 30). Centers for Disease Control and Protection. National Institute for Occupational Safety and Health. Retrieved from https://www.cdc.gov
28. The Emily Post Institute. (2017). Texting at the dinner table. Retrieved from https://emilypost.com; The Emily Post Institute. (2017). Texting manners. Retrieved from https://emilypost.com
29. Fischer, M. (2017, May 1). What happens when work becomes a nonstop chat room. *New York Magazine*, Intelligencer. Retrieved from https://nymag.com
30. Warren, T. (2019, July 11). Microsoft Teams overtakes Slack with 13 million daily users. *The Verge*. Retrieved from https://www.theverge.com
31. Peer review for Slack. (2019). Gartner Peer Insights. Retrieved from https://www.gartner.com
32. Scott, C. L. (2020, March 5). So, you got Slack for your employees. Make sure you're ready for it. *The Wall Street Journal*. Retrieved from https://www.wsj.com
33. Moses, E. R. (2019, October 11). Viewpoint: The legal risks of digital workplace apps. SHRM. Retrieved from https://www.shrm.org
34. Scott, C. L. (2020, March 5). So, you got Slack for your employees. Make sure you're ready for it. *The Wall Street Journal*. Retrieved from https://www.wsj.com
35. Based on Akhtar, A. (2019, September 4). Your guide to workplace Slack etiquette. *Inc*. Retrieved from https://www.inc.com
36. Richter, F. (2019, March 7). The steady rise of podcasts. Statista. Retrieved from https://www.statista.com; Smith, A. (2015, April 1). U.S. smartphone use in 2015. Pew Research Center. Retrieved from https://www.pewinternet.org
37. Winn, R. (2020, February 7). 2020 podcast stats & facts (new research from Jan 2020). Podcast Insights. Retrieved from https://www.podcastinsights.com
38. Comedy, news, society and culture podcasts most listened-to genres in podcasting. (2019, December 16). Edison Research. Retrieved from https://www.edisonresearch.com
39. Yonchev, O. (2019, December 31). 7 social media trends to watch out for before 2020 hits. PR Daily. Retrieved from https://www.prdaily.com

40. Beyond the Iron: The Caterpillar podcast. Retrieved from https://www.caterpillar.com

41. Walmart Radio. (n.d.). Apple Podcast Preview. Retrieved from https://podcasts.apple.com

42. Orman, S. (n.d.). Women & Money. Retrieved from https://www.suzeorman.com

43. Day, M. (2018, March 27). The fraud and the four-hour workweek. *Jacobin*. Retrieved from https://jacobinmag.com; Schein, M. (2019, January 17). Tim Ferriss is everything that's wrong with the modern world (and why you should follow his lead). *Forbes*. Retrieved from https://www.forbes.com

44. Podcast Directory. (2020, February). TED Radio Hour. Retrieved from https://www.npr.org

45. P&G, GEICO love advertising on podcasts. (2019, June 6). Radio Ink. Retrieved from https://radioink.com

46. Rose, J. (2020, February 26). 14 reasons to not listen to Suze Orman. Good Financial Cents. Retrieved from https://www.goodfinancialcents.com

47. Dekmezian, G. (2016, September 23). Why do people blog? The benefits of blogging. *HuffPost*. Retrieved from https://www.huffpost.com

48. Barnes, N.G., Mazzola, A., & Killeen, M. (2020, January 9). Oversaturation & disengagement: The 2019 Fortune 500 social media dance. University of Massachusetts Dartmouth. Retrieved from https://www.umassd.edu

49. Ibid.

50. Snyder, B. (2016, January 29). Here's why Doritos is ending its "Crash the Super Bowl" contest. *Fortune*. Retrieved from https://fortune.com

51. Pulse: Our teams, our stories, our careers. Target. Retrieved from https://pulse.target.com

52. Smith, R. A. (2020, January 2). Work clothes, reimagined for an age of wearable tech. *The Wall Street Journal*. Retrieved from https://www.wsj.com; Gage, D. (2018, September 16). Wearable health monitors: Do they work? *The Wall Street Journal*. Retrieved from https://www.wsj.com; Schatsky, D. (2018, September 11). Wearables: The new workforce superpower. CIO Journal, Deloitte. *The Wall Street Journal*. Retrieved from https://deloitte.wsj.com

53. Rayson, S. (2017, June 26). We analyzed 100 million headlines. Here's what we learned (new research). BuzzSumo. Retrieved from https://buzzsumo.com

54. Plourde, D. (2020, January 30). Do you have what it takes? Top 20 most rugged jobs in America. Direct2Dell. Retrieved from https://blog.dell.com

55. Chartrand, J. (n.d.). Do you have useless website content? Men With Pens. Retrieved from https://menwithpens.ca

56. Spencer, J. (2019, November 25). How to start a blog: A really simple beginners guide on how you can create your own blog in just 20 minutes. MakeAWebsiteHub. Retrieved from https://makeawebsitehub.com

57. Abramovich, G. (2019, September). CMO by Adobe. Retrieved from https://cmo.adobe.com

58. Barnes, N. G., Mazzola, A., & Killeen, M. (2020, January 9). Oversaturation & disengagement: The 2019 Fortune 500 social media dance. Center for Marketing Research, University of Massachusetts Dartmouth. Retrieved from https://www.umassd.edu

59. More than half of employers have found content on social media that caused them NOT to hire a candidate, according to a recent CareerBuilder Survey. (2018, August 9). CareerBuilder. Retrieved from https://www.prnewswire.com

60. Social media fact sheet. (2019, June 12). Pew Research Center. Retrieved from https://www.pewresearch.org

61. Vogels, E. A. (2019, September 9). Millennials stand out for their technology use, but older generations also embrace digital life. Retrieved from https://www.pewresearch.org

62. Desilver, D. (2019, August 29). 10 facts about American workers. FactTank. Retrieved from https://www.pewresearch.org

63. Perrin, A., & Anderson, M. (2019, April 10). Share of U.S. adult using social media, including Facebook, is mostly unchanged since 2018. Pew Research Center: FactTank. Retrieved from https://www.pewresearch.org

64. Quesenberry, K. A. (2018, January 2). The basic social media mistakes companies still make. *Harvard Business Review*. Retrieved from https://hbr.org

65. Frier, S., & Wagner, K. (2020, February 27). TikTok marketers chase billions of views in uncharted terrain. *Bloomberg*. Retrieved from https://www.bloomberg.com

66. Zhan, L. (2019, November 12). Will TikTok become the next Huawei? *Business Insider*. Retrieved from https://www.businessinsider.sg

67. Cardon, P. (2015). Enterprise social networks (Internal social media platforms). *NBEA 2015 Yearbook: Recent and Projected Technology Trends Affecting Business Education*, 37.

68. Better serving members using one social spot. (n. d.). Yammer Success Story: Featured Customers. Retrieved from https://cdn.featuredcustomers.com

69. Wall, M T. (2015, June 8). After employee disagrees on internal social network, IBM changes travel policy. LinkedIn. Retrieved from https://www.linkedin.com

70. Gillett, F. (2017, December 14). Harrods sells out of luxury £950 Aspinal of London bags at bargain £8 after a "website pricing blunder." *Evening Standard*. Retrieved from https://www.standard.co.uk

71. Neubert, S. (2016, February 11). Goodyear brings spirit of innovation to every facet of product development and delivery. Microsoft 365. Retrieved from https://www.microsoft.com

72. Carley, S. (n. d.). Empowering employees for improved customer service and a better bottom line. Yammer Success Story: Featured Customers. Retrieved from https://cdn.featuredcustomers.com

73. Brin, D. (2017, July 18). Agility, willingness to pivot are key for transforming companies: IBM's Gherson. SHRM. Retrieved from https://www.shrm.org

74. The compliance risks of social media. (n.d.). Thomson Reuters. Retrieved from https://legal.thomsonreuters.com

75. Samuel, A., & Marquez, S. (2018, May 29). Should companies let employees use social media at work? *The Wall Street Journal*. Retrieved from https://www.wsj.com

76. IBM social computing guidelines: Blogs, wikis, social networks, virtual worlds and social media. (n.d.). IBM. Retrieved from https://www.ibm.com

77. Bizzi, L. (2018, May 17). Employees who use social media for work are more engaged—but also more likely to leave their jobs. *Harvard Business Review*. Retrieved from https://hbr.org

78. 66% of U.S. employees are working remotely at least part-time during the COVID-19 pandemic. (2020, April 16). Cision PR Newswire. Retrieved from https://www.prnewswire.com

79. Chang, E. (2017, November 30). Why halting social media use in the workplace fails. *The Street*. Retrieved from https://www.thestreet.com

80. Anderson, J., & Rainie, L. (2017, October 19). The future of truth and misinformation online. Pew Research Center: Internet & Technology. Retrieved from https://www.pewresearch.org

81. Thompson, S. A., Warzel, C. (2019, December 19). Twelve million phones, one dataset, zero privacy. *The New York Times*. Retrieved from https://www.nytimes.com

82. Altschuler, G., & Tarrow, S. (2019, October 20). Combatting fake news on social media will take a village. *The Hill*. Retrieved from https://thehill.com; Shearer, E., & Matsa, K. E. (2018, September 10). News use across social media platforms 2018. Pew Research Center: Journalism & Media. Retrieved from https://www.journalism.org

83. Schmidt, A. L., Zollo, F., Del Vicario, M., Bessi, A., Scala, A., Caldarelli, G.,

84. Stanley, H. E., & Quattrociocchi, W. (2017, January 31). Anatomy of news consumption on Facebook. *Proceedings of the National Academy of Sciences, 114*(12), 3035–3039. Retrieved from https://www.pnas.org

85. Anderson, J., & Rainie, L. (2017, October 19). The future of truth and misinformation online. Pew Research Center: Internet & Technology. Retrieved from https://www.pewresearch.org

86. Silverman, C., & Singer-Vine, J. (2016, December 6). Most Americans who see fake news believe it, new survey says. *BuzzFeed News*. Retrieved from https://www.buzzfeednews.com

87. Flood, A. (2016, November 15). "Post-truth" named word of the year by Oxford Dictionaries. *The Guardian*. Retrieved from https://www.theguardian.com

88. O'Sullivan, D. (2016). When seeing is no longer believing. CNN Business. Retrieved from https://www.cnn.com

89. Bell, C. (2018, February 1). The people who think 9/11 may have been an "inside job." BBC News. Retrieved from https://www.bbc.com

90. Harris, S. (2019, February 5). Making sense with Sam Harris—Jack Dorsey. Podcast episode #148. Retrieved from https://www.stitcher.com

91. Stephens, B. (2019, May 3). Facebook's unintended consequence. *The New York Times*. Retrieved from https://www.nytimes.com

92. Social media firms "failing" to tackle cyber-bullying. (2018, February 26). BBC News. Retrieved from https://www.bbc.com

93. 2020 Businesses @work: Most popular factors. (2020). Okta.com. Retrieved from https://www.okta.com

94. Vogels, E. A., & Anderson, M. (2019, October 9). Americans and digital knowledge. Pew Research Center: Internet & Technology. Retrieved from https://www.pewresearch.org

95. 2020 Businesses @work: Most popular factors. (2020). Okta.com . Retrieved from https://www.okta.com

96. Jurkowitz, M., & Mitchell, A. (2020, January 29). An oasis of bipartisanship: Republicans and Democrats distrust social media sites for political and election news. Pew Research Center: Journalism & Media. Retrieved from https://www.journalism.org

97. LaFrance, A. (2016, January 6). The triumph of email. *The Atlantic*. Retrieved from https://www.theatlantic.com

98. Based on Samuel, A. (2020, March 6). The tech habits of co-workers that drive us crazy. *The Wall Street Journal*, R1–R3.

99. Martin, G. (2019, April 18). Is a podcast right for every business? CO. U.S. Chamber of Commerce. Retrieved from https://www.uschamber.com

100. Clark, D. (2014, October 28). How to launch a successful podcast—fast. *Forbes*. Retrieved from https://www.forbes.com

101. Montoya, M. (2012, October 16.) 5 ways Twitter can get you fired. Examiner.com. Retrieved from https://www.examiner.com

102. Connected leadership. (2019). Brunswick Group. Retrieved from https://www.brunswickgroup.com

103. Gravier, E. (2019, June 26). The top 10 most "connected" CEOs on social media—and where you can follow them. CNBC.com. Retrieved from https://www.cnbc.com

104. Shanbhag, A. (2016, March 2). What happens when you quit social media? I found out. *Makeuseof*. Retrieved from https://www.makeuseof.com; Gaddis, B. (2016, February 9). Here's what happened when I quit social media. *The Huffington Post*. Retrieved from https://www.huffingtonpost.com; Hempel, J. (2015, August 2). I'm quitting social media to learn what I actually like. *Wired*. Retrieved from https://www.wired.com; Sparkes, M. (2013, April 11). Twitter and Facebook "addicts" suffer withdrawal symptoms. *The Telegraph*. Retrieved from https://www.telegraph.co.uk

105. Moeller, S. D. (2010). 24 hours: Unplugged. A Day Without Media. Retrieved from https://withoutmedia.wordpress.com; The Associated Press. (2009, September 6). Center tries to treat Web addicts. *The New York Times*. Retrieved from https://www.nytimes.com

106. Allcott, H., & Gentzkow, M. (2017). Social media and fake news in the 2016 election. *Journal of Economic Perspectives*, *31*(2), 211–236. doi: 10.1257/jep.31.2.211

107. Komando, K. (2020, April 23). The great 5G coronavirus conspiracy. *USA Today*. Retrieved from https://www.usatoday.com

108. Cox, C. (2020, December 17). Fact check: Syringes with RFID technology track vaccines, not recipients. *USA Today*. Retrieved from https://www.usatoday.com

109. Horton, A. (2020, July 20). John Oliver on coronavirus conspiracy theories: "People are going to get burned." *The Guardian*. Retrieved from https://www.theguardian.com

# Chapter 6

1. Internet usage statistics: World Internet users and 2020 population stats. (2019, December 31). Miniwatts Marketing Group. Retrieved from https://internetworldstats.com

2. Pulcinella, S. (2017, August 30). Why direct mail marketing is far from dead. *Forbes*. Retrieved from https://www.forbes.com

3. Whittaker, Z. (2019, September 26). DoorDash confirms data breach affected 4.9 million customers, workers and merchants. *TechCrunch*. Retrieved from https://techcrunch.com; Carson, B. (2019, September 26). DoorDash data breach compromises 4.9 million people. *Forbes*. Retrieved from https://www.forbes.com

4. Based on Emily Post Institute. (n.d.). Effective business letters. Retrieved from http://www.emilypost.com

5. Perkins, B. (2016, January 13). Are we clear? Writing well can be key to your career. *Computerworld*. Retrieved from http://www.computerworld.com

6. Dwoskin, E., & Timberg, C. (2018, April 23). How merchants use Facebook to flood Amazon with fake reviews. The Washington Post. Retrieved from https://www.washingtonpost.com; Trust and influence on online reviews. (2019). BrightLocal. Retrieved from https://www.brightlocal.com;

7. Harrison, K. (2019, May 7). 10 companies that totally rock customer services on social media. Business News Daily. Retrieved from https://www.businessnewsdaily.com; Banjo, S. (2012, July 29). Firms take online reviews to heart. *The Wall Street Journal*. Retrieved from http://online.wsj.com

8. Gibbons, S. (2018, September 20). Why businesses need to see customer feedback as make-or-break. *Forbes*. Retrieved from https://www.forbes.com

9. Statista. (2020, November 4). Expected response time for social media questions or complaints in U.S. & global 2018. Retrieved from https://www.statista.com

10. Klemp, N. (2017, March 31). 10 rules of engagement: How to respond to social media complaints. Salesforce Blog. Retrieved from https://www.salesforce.com

11. Stum, L. (2017, November 1). Seven reasons people don't read instructions. Learning Stream. Retrieved from https://www.learningstream.com

12. Bernstein, E. (2015, August 10). Don't hit send: Angry emails just make you angrier. *The Wall Street Journal*. Retrieved from https://www.wsj.com

13. Cox, K. (2016, March 14). The 8.5 steps to making an effective complaint that gets a solution. *Consumerist*. Retrieved from https://consumerist.com; Johnston Taylor, S. (2014, December 30). The best ways to file a consumer complaint. *U.S. News & World Report*. Retrieved from http://money.usnews.com; Torabi, F. (2011, July 28). Bad customer service? 3 smarter ways to complain. CBS News. Retrieved from http://www.cbsnews.com

14. Tran, T. (2020, March 3). What is social listening, why it matters, and 10 tools to make it easier. Hootsuite. Retrieved from https://blog.hootsuite.com; Morrison, K. (2016, March 18). 5 tips for using social listening to understand customers. *Adweek*. Retrieved from https://www.adweek.com

15. Hoopfer, E. (2019, March 3). Social media LUV: How Southwest Airlines connects with customers online. *Dallas Business Journal*. Retrieved from https://www.bizjournals.com

16. Doyle, A. (2020, January 29). You can get fired for what you post online. The Balance Careers. Retrieved from https://www.thebalancecareers.com

17. Warren, K. (2018, April 11). 18 unbelievable things people did at work that got them fired immediately. *Insider*. Retrieved from https://www.insider.com

18. Huddleston, T. (2019, October 10). Can you get sued over a negative Yelp review? Here's what you need to know. CNBC. Retrieved from https://www.cnbc.com; Posting a negative review online can get you sued. (2019, July 22). CBS News. Retrieved from https://www.cbsnews.com

19. Local consumer review survey. (2019, December 11). BrightLocal. Retrieved from https://www.brightlocal.com

20. Gurchiek, K. (2018, February 23). Saying "thank you," "I'm sorry" is simple but meaningful. SHRM. Retrieved from https://www.shrm.org

21. Mau, E. (2019, December 18). Study examines the effectiveness of apology laws on reducing medical malpractice liability. Borden Ladner Gervais LLP. Retrieved from https://www.blg.com; State apology laws may not reduce risk of liability. (2017, February 15). ECRI. Retrieved from https://www.ecri.org

22. Molinsky, A. (2016, November 25). The 4 types of ineffective apologies. *Harvard Business Review*. Retrieved from https://hbr.org; Hollis, L. (2014, February 27). Sorry seems to be the hardest word. *Management Today*. Retrieved from http://www.managementtoday.co.uk

23. Keltner, D. (2016, May 22). The power of saying thank you. *The Guardian*. Retrieved from https://www.theguardian.com

24. Sanchez, C. (2019, July 16). Nine ways to turn a customer complaint into a valuable lesson; 4. Stay focused on solutions and forego scripts. *Forbes*. Retrieved from https://www.forbes.com; Baer, J. (2015, June 24). How asking for help can turn haters into brand advocates. *Inc*. Retrieved from http://www.inc.com

25. The Emily Post Institute. (n.d.). Advice: Sympathy notes and letters. Retrieved from http://emilypost.com; Heathfield, S. M. (2016, December 28). How to write a sympathy letter. *The Balance*. Retrieved from https://www.thebalance.com

26. The Emily Post Institute. (n.d.). Advice: Sympathy notes and letters. Retrieved from http://emilypost.com

27. A case for the dwindling art of letter writing in the 21st century. (2014, June 5). Radio Boston WBUR. Retrieved from http://radioboston.wbur.org

28. Carrera, M. (2019, September 5). Diesel mocks "wardrobing" phenomenon with fall ad campaign. WWD. Retrieved from https://wwd.com

29. Based on Klemp, N. (2017, February 9). 10 rules for responding to customers on social media. Appirio. Retrieved from https://hub.appirio.com

30. Based on Buddy Media. (2011). How do I respond to that? The definitive guide to Facebook publishing & moderation. Retrieved from https://christinastallings.files.wordpress.com

31. Scenario based on Glazer, E. (2016, June 3). J.P. Morgan says employees don't always have to wear suits. The Wall Street Journal. Retrieved from https://www.wsj.com; Eisen, B., & Glazer, E. (2016, June 3). The Wall Street Journal. Retrieved from https://www.wsj.com

32. J.P. Morgan dress code leaves women guessing. (2016, June 7). Finews.com. Retrieved from https://www.finews.com

33. Binkley, C. (2016, June 3). Business casual can be complex, especially for women. The Wall Street Journal. Retrieved from https://www.wsj.com

34. Smith, C. (2020, February 21). 80 interesting Yelp statistics and facts (2020); by the numbers. DMR Business Statistics. Retrieved from https://expandedramblings.com

35. Barnes, C. M. (2018, August 27). You know you need more sleep. Here's how to get it. Harvard Business Review. Retrieved from https://hbr.org

36. Ibid.

37. Weinberger, M. (2018, December 1). Read the sweet letter that Microsoft sends to the newborn children of its employees. Business Insider. Retrieved from https://www.businessinsider.com

# Chapter 7

1. Creelman, V. (2012). The case for "living" models. Business Communication Quarterly, 75(2), 181.

2. Veltsos, J. (2012). An analysis of data breach notifications as negative news. Business Communication Quarterly, 75(2), 198. doi: 10.1177/1080569912443081

3. Krzanich, B. (2016, April 19). E-mail to employees. Intel. Retrieved from https://newsroom.intel.com

4. Canavor, N. (2012). Business writing in the digital age. Thousand Oaks, CA: Sage, 62.

5. Joyce, C. (2012, November). The impact of direct and indirect communication. International Ombudsman Association. Retrieved from https://www.ombudsassociation.org

6. Kashtan, M. (2013, May 20). Saying "no" without saying "no": How to say "no" to someone so they know they still matter to us. Psychology Today. Retrieved from https://www.psychologytoday.com

7. 5 ad trends to be wary of in 2020. (2020, January 7). Truth in Advertising. Retrieved from https://www.truthinadvertising.org

8. When responding to customer complaints online, answer with deliberate speed. (2017, July 31). Forbes. Retrieved from https://www.forbes.com

9. Schweitzer, M. E. (2006, December). Wise negotiators know when to say "I'm sorry." Negotiation, 4. Retrieved from https://search.ebscohost.com

10. Bentley, J. (2018). What counts as an apology? Exploring stakeholder perceptions in a hypothetical organizational crisis. Management Communication Quarterly, 32(2), 207. doi:10.1177/0893318917722635

11. Racine, M., Wilson, C., & Wynes, M. (2018, October). The value of apology: How do corporate apologies moderate the stock market reaction to non-financial corporate crises? Journal of Business Ethics, 1–21. doi:10.1007/s10551-018-4037-5. Retrieved from https://search.proquest.com; Chance, D., Cicon, J., & Ferris, S. P. (2016, January). Poor performance and the value of corporate honesty. Journal of Corporate Finance, 33. doi:10.1016/j.jcorpfin.2015.04.008. Retrieved from https://search.proquest.com

12. Daskal, L. (2018, April 23). 4 impressive ways great leaders handle their mistakes. Inc. Retrieved from https://www.inc.com

13. Ross, M. (2018, November 22). 4 reasons why empathy is good for business. Entrepreneur. Retrieved from https://www.entrepreneur.com

14. Parmar, B. (2016, December 1). The most empathetic companies, 2016. Harvard Business Review. Retrieved from https://hbr.org

15. Zaki, J. (2019, May 30). Making empathy central to your company culture. Harvard Business Review. Retrieved from https://hbr.org; 2019 state of workplace empathy. (2019). Businessolver. Retrieved from https://www.businessolver.com

16. Zhang, H. (2020, February 4). The New York Times increases digital subscription price for the first time. CNN Business. Retrieved from https://www.cnn.com

17. Zimmerman, E. (2012, April 7). Accentuating the positive to angry customers. The New York Times. Retrieved from https://www.nytimes.com

18. Houlihan, M. (2012, September 21). Oops, my bad! 5 ways your business can improve by admitting to mistakes. Entrepreneur. Retrieved from https://www.entrepreneur.com

19. When responding to customer complaints online, answer with deliberate speed. (2017, July 31). Forbes. Retrieved from https://www.forbes.com

20. The Zendesk customer experience trends report 2019. (2019). Zendesk. Retrieved from https://www.zendesk.com

21. Wolfe, J. (2018, November 20). Want faster airline customer service? Try tweeting. The New York Times. Retrieved from https://www.nytimes.com; Guliani, B. K. (2016, February 15). Twitter's greater revenue is due to its faster responses. Digital Vidya Blog. Retrieved from https://www.digitalvidya.com

22. Armano, D. (2017). Digital transformation journey: Brands' secret weapon to combat marketing disruption. Edelman Digital. Retrieved from https://edelmandigital.com

23. Ahmed, M. (2017, January 13). Social media customer service statistics and trends. SocialMediaToday. Retrieved from https://www.socialmediatoday.com

24. Gibbons, S. (2018, September 20). Why businesses need to see customer feedback as a make-or-break. Forbes. Retrieved from https://www.forbes.com

25. Wolfe, J. (2018, November 20). Want faster airline customer service? Try tweeting. The New York Times. Retrieved from https://www.nytimes.com

26. Josephs, L. (2018, January 9). Between five minutes and five hours: How long airlines take to respond to your complaint on Twitter. CNBC. Retrieved from https://www.cnbc.com

27. Forbes, M. (1999). How to write a business letter. In K. Harty (Ed.), Strategies for business and technical writing. Boston: Allyn and Bacon, 108.

28. Forbes Coaches Council. (2017, July 17). 14 ways to approach conflict and difficult conversations at work. Forbes. Retrieved from https://www.forbes.com

29. Heathfield, S. M. (2019, June 25). How to fire an employee with compassion and class. The Balance Careers. Retrieved from https://www.thebalancecareers.com; Browning, M. (2003, November 24). Work dilemma: Delivering bad news a good way. Government Computer News, 41; Mowatt, J. (2002, February). Breaking bad news to customers. Agency Sales, 30.

30. Prossack, A. (2018, October 28). How to have difficult conversations at work. Forbes. Retrieved at https://www.forbes.com; Gallo, A. (2015, March 30). How to deliver bad news to your employees. Harvard Business Review. Retrieved from https://hbr.org; Ensall, S. (2007, January 30). Delivering bad news. Personnel Today, 31. Retrieved from Business Source Premier database.

31. McCartney, S. (2018, April 24). At Southwest Airlines, the minutes after disaster struck. The Wall Street Journal. Retrieved from https://www.wsj.com

32. Vozza, S. (2015, February 2). When companies stop excusing bad behavior. Fast Company. Retrieved from https://www.fastcompany.com

33. Bies, R. J. (2013, January). The delivery of bad news in organizations. Journal of Management, 39(1), 136–162. doi: 10.1177/0149206312461053

34. Bergh, C. (2018, July–August). The CEO of Levi Strauss on leading an iconic brand back to growth. Harvard Business Review. Retrieved from https://hbr.org

35. Rand, B. (2019, January 23). University mistakenly emails 430 acceptance letters, blames "human error." ABC News. Retrieved from https://abcnews.go.com

36. Reeves, M. (2019, January 22). Never mind: "Big mistake" cited as USF St. Pete takes back 430 admission letters. Tampa Bay Times. Retrieved from https://www.tampabay.com

37. Rand, B. (2019, January 23). University mistakenly emails 430 acceptance letters, blames "human error." ABC News. Retrieved from https://abcnews.go.com

## Chapter 8

1. Morgan, H. R. (2018, March 28). 3 reasons being aggressive in sales is an outdated and harmful tactic. *Forbes*. Retrieved from https://www.forbes.com

2. Carter Hartley, L. (2019). *Persuasion: Convincing others when facts don't seem to matter.* New York, NY: TarcherPerigee, 37.

3. Perloff, R. M. (2020). *The dynamics of persuasion: Communication and attitudes in the 21st century* (7th ed.). New York: Routledge, Kindle edition, Chapter 1.

4. 4 Cialdini, R. B. (2021). *Influence: The psychology of persuasion.* New York: HarperCollins, xiv.

5. Page, D. (2018, May 15). How to complain constructively (and get results). NBC News Digital. Retrieved from https://www.nbcnews.com

6. Brandon, J. (2014, December 12). 20 leadership experts share their best leadership tip. *Inc.* Retrieved from https://www.inc.com

7. Kumar, A. (2018, June 5). As Howard Schultz retires, will his impact on labor be one of his core legacies? *Forbes.* Retrieved from https://www.forbes.com

8. Grainger, B. (2017, December 5). Surviving the open office (really, it's not so bad). Evernote Blog. Retrieved from https://evernote.com

9. Lucas, S. (2019, September 16). Employee buy-in to promote workplace engagement. The Balance Careers. Retrieved from https://www.thebalancecareers.com; Gleeson, B. (2017, October 15). 5 powerful steps to improve employee engagement. *Forbes.* Retrieved from https://www.forbes.com

10. Gupta-Sunderji, M. (2014, July 22). The art of persuasion. *HRVoice.* Retrieved from https://www.hrvoice.org

11. Taute, M. (2015, January 19). Disney creative director Will Gay: How to sell your ideas. The Creative Group, Robert Half. Retrieved from https://www.roberthalf.com; Pollock, T. (2003, June). How to sell an idea. *SuperVision*, 15. Retrieved from https://search.proquest.com

12. Office of Inspector General. (2015, June 15). Enhancing the value of mail: The human response. United States Postal Service. Retrieved from https://www.uspsoig.gov; Lee, K. (2015, May 22). Seven reasons to make direct mail part of your digital marketing. ClickZ. Retrieved from https://www.clickz.com

13. Pulcinella, S. (2017, August 30). Why direct mail marketing is far from dead. *Forbes.* Retrieved from https://www.forbes.com

14. Compton, J. (2015, March 4). Direct mail goes digital. Direct Marketing. Retrieved from https://www.dmnews.com; Direct mail statistics show B2B mailings are still effective. (2011, March 8). *Minuteman Press.* Retrieved from www.deerpark.minutemanpress.com; Hartong, B. (2011, March). Revitalize your direct mail strategy. *Customer Interaction Solutions*, 10. Retrieved from https://proquest.umi.com

15. Ward, S. (2016, January 4). The B2B marketing mix: Direct mail campaigns. Pardot. Retrieved from https://www.pardot.com; Macleod, I. (2013, October). Infographic: Consumers more likely to deal with direct mail immediately compared to email. The Drum. Retrieved from https://www.thedrum.com; DMA releases 2010 response rate trend report. (2010, June 15). Target Marketing. Retrieved from www.targetmarketingmag.com

16. Paikin, L. (2020, April 23). Direct mail retargeting: Evolution and overcoming obstacles. *Forbes.* Retrieved from https://www.forbes.com

17. Tweh, B., & Patel, S. (2020, January 14). Google Chrome to phase out third-party cookies in effort to boost privacy. *The Wall Street Journal.* Retrieved from https://www.wsj.com

18. Pulcinella, S. (2017, August 30). Why direct mail marketing is far from dead. *Forbes.* Retrieved from https://www.forbes.com

19. Jones, R. (2020, March/April). Facing the consequences: A look at some lesser-known costs of distracted driving. *Westways*, 16.

20. Ziglar, Z. (2006). *Secrets of closing the sale.* Grand Rapids, MI: Revell/Baker Publishing, 57.

21. Kruse, K. (2016, December 19). 5 subtle ways to persuade and influence others. *Forbes.* Retrieved from https://www.forbes.com

22. Haskel, D. (2015, April 14). 2015 DMA response rate report: Direct mail outperforms all digital channels combined by nearly 600%. IWCO Direct. Retrieved from http://www.iwco.com

23. Gallo, C. (2019, July 15). The art of persuasion hasn't changed in 2,000 years. *The Harvard Business Review.* Retrieved from https://hbr.org

24. Verblow, B. (2019, January 2). You've still got mail. Forrester. Retrieved from https://go.forrester.com

25. Patel, S. (2016, January 4). 5 easy ways to build more business relationships as an entrepreneur. Entrepreneur. Retrieved from https://www.entrepreneur.com; *Harvard Business Review on reinventing your marketing.* (2011, May 7). Boston: Harvard Business Press Books.

26. Musil, S. (2019, February 26). FTC settles its first case over fake paid reviews on Amazon. CNET. Retrieved from https://www.cnet.com; Dvorak, J. C. (2015, October 21). Write an Amazon review, go to jail. *PC Magazine.* Retrieved from https://www.pcmag.com

27. Berger, L. L., & Stanchi, K. M. (2018). *Legal persuasion: A rhetorical approach to the science.* New York: Routledge, 5.

28. Larson, C. U. (2013). *Persuasion: Reception and responsibility* (13th ed.). Boston: Wadsworth, Cengage Learning, 17.

29. Based on Yu, R. (2009, 13 March). Hotels take action to pare down food, restaurant expenses. *USA Today*, 3D.

30. Kokalitcheva, K. (2016, March 21). These 8 employers will pay you to volunteer. *Fortune.* Retrieved from https://fortune.com

31. Loveday, S. (2020, February 28). The cheapest electric cars for 2020. *U.S. News & World Report.* Retrieved from https://cars.usnews.com; Demuro, D. (2015, January 20). 8 least expensive electric vehicles. *Autotrader.* Retrieved from https://www.autotrader.com

32. Stillman, J. (2017, August 25). Here's how to spot fake online reviews with 90 percent accuracy, according to science. *Inc.* Retrieved from https://www.inc.com

33. Broida, R. (2019, March 4). How to spot fake reviews on Amazon, Best Buy, Walmart and other sites. CNET. Retrieved from https://www.cnet.com; Cohen, J. (2019, June 26). How to spot a fake review on Amazon. *PCMag.* Retrieved from https://www.pcmag.com

34. Stillman, J. (2017, August 25). Here's how to spot fake online reviews with 90 percent accuracy, according to science. *Inc.* Retrieved from https://www.inc.com

35. Cohen, J. (2019, June 26). How to spot a fake review on Amazon. *PCMag.* Retrieved from https://www.pcmag.com

36. Scenario based on Federal Trade Commission. (n.d.). FTC fact sheet: It looks good . . . but is it true? Retrieved from https://www.consumer.ftc.gov

37. McGinley, L. (2019, February 11). FDA launches tougher oversight of supplements. *The Washington Post.* Retrieved from https://www.washingtonpost.com

38. Tchekmedyian, A. (2018, September 4). Gwyneth Paltrow's Goop to offer refunds over "unsubstantiated" claims about health benefits. *Los Angeles Times.* Retrieved from https://www.latimes.com

39. Upadhyaya, K. K. (2019, January 23). "Iron Chef" Cat Cora awarded $565k in lawsuit against shuttered Meatpacking restaurant. *New York Eater.* Retrieved from https://ny.eater.com

40. Saad, N. (2019, September 3). Ariana Grande sues Forever 21 over failed deal and lookalike model. *Los Angeles Times.* Retrieved from https://www.latimes.com

41. Fair, L. (2016, July 15). It's no longer business as usual at Herbalife: An inside look at the $200 million FTC settlement. Federal Trade Commission. Retrieved from https://www.ftc.gov

42. Trying to lose weight? Watch out for false promises. (2019, August). Federal Trade Commission. Retrieved from https://www.consumer.ftc.gov; Daller, J. A. (2017, June 22). Muscle stimulators, do they work? On Health. Retrieved from https://www.onhealth.com

43. Electronic muscle stimulators. (2019, August). U.S. Food & Drug Administration. Retrieved from https://www.fda.gov

44. Hiltzik, M. (2016, January 6). If you weren't smart enough to know Lumosity was making bogus claims, the FTC has your back. *Los Angeles Times.* Retrieved from https://www.latimes.com

45. Wischhover, C. (2019, October 22). Skin care brand Sunday Riley got in trouble for writing fake reviews. It just settled with the FTC. *Vox.* Retrieved from https://www.vox.com

46. Musil, S. (2019, February 26). FTC settles its first case over fake paid reviews on Amazon. CNET. Retrieved from https://www.cnet.com

## Chapter 9

1. Hawkins, A. J. (2019, April 12). Electric scooters may not be around for long. The Verge. Retrieved from https://www.theverge.com; Korus, S. (2019, February 19). Electric Scooters: The unit economics may spell trouble. Retrieved from https://ark-invest.com

2. Sweet, K. (2017). Writing in third person in APA style. *The Pen and the Pad.* Retrieved from http://penandthepad.com

3. Spotify reports second quarter 2019 earnings. (2019, July 31). Spotify. Retrieved from https://newsroom.spotify.com

4. The Bridgespan Group. (n.d.) How to talk about finances so non-financial folks will listen. Retrieved from https://bridgespan.org

# Chapter 10

1. Policies for action: Public policy research to advance racial equity and racial justice. 2020 Call for proposals. (2020, September 30). Robert Wood Johnson Foundation. Retrieved from https://www.rwjf.org

2. City of Hermosa Beach. (2020, April 15). Bids and proposals (RFPs & RFQs). Retrieved from https://www.hermosabeach.gov

3. Center for the Advancement of Science in Space. (n.d.). Unsolicited proposals. Retrieved from http://www.iss-casis.org

4. Moses, S. (2018, June 27). How to create impossibly good project proposals. Retrieved from https://www.workamajig.com

5. Ouellet, D. (2020, January 7). What to do when an RFP asks for resumes. Retrieved from https://www.echelonone.ca

6. Elliott, M. (2010-2013). Writing. Retrieved from http://marianne-elliott.com

7. Hutchinson, O. (2018, May 7). 4 key questions on primary vs secondary research. *Euromonitor*. Retrieved from https://blog.euromonitor.com

8. Linton Weeks cited in O'Neill, C. (2018, April 9). 10 ways academic libraries are leading change. The Wiley Network. Retrieved from https://www.wiley.com

9. Neil Gaiman cited in O'Neill, C. (2018, April 9). 10 ways academic libraries are leading change. The Wiley Network. Retrieved from https://www.wiley.com

10. urveyMonkey. (2017). Customers love SurveyMonkey. Retrieved from https://www.surveymonkey.com

11. Peltz, J. F. (2019, July 28). How Starbucks has picked up steam again. *The Los Angeles Times*. Retrieved from https://www.latimes.com

12. McGuire, P. (2014, August 10). Perilous plagiarism. *Huffpost*. Retrieved from https://www.huffpost.com

13. Stuart, E. (2016, January 19). ASU professor resigns amid plagiarism accusations. *Phoenix New Times*. Retrieved from http://www.phoenixnewtimes.com; Iyengar, R. (2015, November 25). 200 South Korean professors charged in massive plagiarism scam. *Time*. Retrieved from http://time.com; McCabe, F. (2014, December 2). UNLV fires professor accused of "serial plagiarism." *Review Journal*. Retrieved from https://www.reviewjournal.com; McGuire, P. (2014, August 10). Perilous plagiarism. *Huffpost*. Retrieved from https://www.huffpost.com

14. Kuratko, D. F. (2020). *Entrepreneurship: Theory, process, and practice*. 11th ed. Cengage Learning, 45–46.

15. Code of student rights, responsibilities, & conduct. G: Uphold and maintain academic and professional honesty and integrity. (2021). Indiana University. Retrieved from https://studentcode.iu.edu

16. U.S. Census Bureau. (2019, May 23). Fastest growing cities primarily in South and West. Census Bureau press release. Retrieved from https://www.census.gov

17. Evans, C. L. (2018). *Broad band: The untold story of the women who made the Internet*. Portfolio/Penguin, 204.

18. Frozen Fire. (2019). 5 tips for creating effective infographics. Retrieved from https://frozenfire.com

19. Bandy, J. (2017). What is service learning or community engagement? Retrieved from https://cft.vanderbilt.edu

20. Cohen, N. (2021, January 30). Anti-vaxxers posing as victims has a history. Look at Andrew Wakefield. *The Guardian*. Retrieved from https://www.theguardian.com; Park, A. (2011, January 6). Study linking vaccines to autism is "fraudulent." *Time*. Retrieved from https://healthland.time.com

21. Quick, J. D., & Larson, H. (2018, February 28). The vaccine-autism myth started 20 years ago. Here's why it still endures today. *Time*. https://time.com; Haberman, C. (2015, February 1). A discredited vaccine study's continuing impact on public health. *The New York Times*. Retrieved from https://www.nytimes.com

22. Perry, S. (2015, April 7). "Plagiarism, fraud, and predatory publishing" are polluting science, says bioethicist Arthur Caplan. *Minnpost*. Retrieved from https://www.minnpost.com

23. Iyengar, R. (2015, November 25). 200 South Korean professors charged in massive plagiarism scam. *Time*. Retrieved from https://time.com

24. Piper, K. (2019, January 9). The American public is already worried about AI catastrophe. Vox. Retrieved from https://www.vox.com

25. Edelstein, S. (2016, April 27). Now, finally, the Germans are getting scared of Tesla? Green Car Reports. Retrieved from https://www.greencarreports.com

26. Fung, E. (2019, October 26). Save the American mall? *The Wall Street Journal*, B5.

# Chapter 11

1. Rainie, L., & Anderson, J. (2017, May 3). The future of jobs and jobs training. Pew Research Center. Retrieved from http://www.pewinternet.org

2. Manyika, J., Lund, S., Chui, M., Bughin, J., Woetzel, J., Batra, P., Ko, R., & Sanghvi, S. (2017, November). Jobs lost, jobs gained: What the future of work will mean for jobs, skills, and wages. McKinsey Global Institute, 78, 80, 90. Retrieved from https://www.mckinsey.com

3. Workplace etiquette offenses. Politeness accelerates career advancement. (2018). [Slideshow.] Robert Half/Accountemps. Retrieved from https://www.roberthalf.com/blog

4. Zwilling, M. (2015, August 7). 6 keys to a positive online presence and reputation. *Entrepreneur*. Retrieved from https://www.entrepreneur.com

5. Wells, A. (2017, January 9). The cost of workplace incivility. *Insurance Journal*. Retrieved from https://www.insurancejournal.com/magazines/editorsnote/2017/01/09/438162.htm; Porath, C. (2015, June 19). No time to be nice at work. *The New York Times*. Retrieved from ttps://www.nytimes.com

6. Mitchell, H. (2018, February 19). The big impact of a little rudeness at work. *The Wall Street Journal*. Retrieved from https://www.wsj.com

7. Taylor, S. G., Kluemper, D. H., Bowler, W. M., & Halbesleben, R. B. (2019, July 10). Why people get away with being rude at work. *Harvard Business Review*. Retrieved from https://hbr.org; Wallace, J. B. (2017, August 18). The cost of workplace rudeness. *The Wall Street Journal*. Retrieved from https://www.wsj.com

8. Porath, C. (2016, December). The hidden toll of workplace incivility. *McKinsey Quarterly*. https://www.mckinsey.com; Porath, C., MacInnis, D., & Folkes, V. (2011, April 17). It's unfair: Why customers who merely observe an uncivil employee abandon the company. *Journal of Service Research, 14*(3). doi: 10.1177/1094670511404393. Retrieved from https://jsr.sagepub.com/content/early/2011/04/15/1094670511404393

9. Simons, J. (2017, November 15). Companies wake up to the problem of bullies at work. *The Wall Street Journal*. Retrieved from https://www.wsj.com

10. Porath, C. (2016, November 23). Civility at work helps everyone get ahead. *The Wall Street Journal*. Retrieved from https://www.wsj.com

11. Forni, P. M. (n.d.). Dr. Forni's civility web site. Johns Hopkins University. Retrieved from https://krieger2.jhu.edu

12. Genzlinger, N. (2018, December 7). P.M. Forni, who argued for "choosing civility," dies at 67. *The New York Times*. Retrieved from https://www.nytimes.com

13. Porath, C. (2015, June 19). No time to be nice at work. *The New York Times*. Retrieved from https://www.nytimes.com

14. Martin, J. (1991, December 11). Wearing a bib to dinner is a hard habit to digest. *Chicago Tribune*. Retrieved from Proquest.

15. Asghar, R. (2014, May 27). Dining etiquette: The business meal as a test of character. *Forbes*. Retrieved from https://www.forbes.com

16. Albrecht, K. (2009). *Social intelligence: The new science of success*. San Francisco: Jossey-Bass, 3.

17. Alvino, N. (2018, September 11). What working for Enron taught me about corporate ethics. *Entrepreneur*. Retrieved from https://www.entrepreneur.com

18. Chismar, D. (2001). Vice and virtue in everyday (business) life. *Journal of Business Ethics, 29*, 169–176. doi: 10.1023/A:1006467631038

19. Hughes, T. (2008). Being a professional. Wordconstructions. Retrieved from https://www.wordconstructions.com; Grove, C., & Hallowell, W. (2002). The seven balancing acts of professional behavior in the United States: A cultural values perspective. Grovewell. Retrieved from https://www.grovewell.com

20. Elan, P. (2021, March 14). Teen Vogue: Controversy continues after editor-in-chief apologizes for anti-Asian tweets. *The Guardian*. Retrieved from https://www.msn.com

21. DeMers, J. (2015, January 29). Communication in 2015: Text, voice, video or in-person? *Inc.* Retrieved from https://www.inc.com; Plantronics. (2011). How we work: Communication trends of business professionals. [White paper]. Retrieved from https://www.idgconnect.com

22. Mediation techniques for conflict resolution: Using online mediation. (2017, February 20). Harvard Law School Program on Negotiation. Retrieved from https://www.pon.harvard.edu; Brenner, R. (2007, October 17). Virtual conflict. *Point Lookout*, Chaco Canyon Consulting. Retrieved from https://www.chacocanyon.com; Drolet, A. L., & Morris, M. W. (2000, January). Rapport in conflict resolution: Accounting for how face-to-face contact fosters mutual cooperation In mixed-motive conflicts. *Journal of Experimental Social Psychology*, 26.

23. Moss, T. (2017). *Speaking out: A 21st-century handbook for women & girls.* New York: Harper Collins; Hotz, R. L. (2014, December 1). How to train your voice to be more charismatic. *The Wall Street Journal.* Retrieved from https://www.wsj.com; Borkowska, B. (2011). Female voice frequency in the context of dominance and attractiveness perception. *Animal Behaviour, 82*(1), 55–59; Niculescu, A., van Dijk, B., Nijholt, A., Haizhou, L., & See, S. (2013, March 31). Making social robots more attractive: The effects of voice pitch, humor and empathy. *International Journal of Social Robotics, 5*(2), 171–191; Derrick, D. C., & Elkins, A. C. (2012, November 30). The sound of trust: Voice as a measurement of trust during interactions with embodied conversational agents. *Group Decision and Negotiation, 22*(5), 897–913.

24. Moss, T. (2017). *Speaking out: A 21st-century handbook for women & girls.* New York: Harper Collins.

25. Grose, J. (2015, July 23). From upspeak to vocal fry: Are we "policing" young women's voices? Fresh Air. NPR. Retrieved from https://www.npr.org

26. Smith, J. (2013, December 20). How to use your 2013 mistakes to build a better 2014 at work. *Forbes.* Retrieved from https://www.forbes.com

27. Heathfield, S. M. (2021, February 28). 10 things you should never do when firing an employee. The Balance Careers. Retrieved from https://www.thebalancecareers.com

28. Rosenberg McKay, D. (2016, June 20). You had me at hello: Getting to know proper telephone etiquette. *The Balance.* Retrieved from https://www.thebalance.com

29. Popescu, A. (2018, January 25). Keep your head up: How smartphone addiction kills manners and moods. *The New York Times.* Retrieved from https://www.nytimes.com

30. Mobile fact sheet. Mobile phone ownership over time. (2019, June 12). Pew Research Center. Retrieved from https://www.pewresearch.org

31. Popescu, A. (2018, January 25). Keep your head up: How smartphone addiction kills manners and moods. *The New York Times.* Retrieved from https://www.nytimes.com

32. The Nielsen total audience report. (2019, October 2). Retrieved from https://www.nielsen.com

33. Rainie, L., & Zickuhr, K. (2015, August 26). Americans' views on mobile etiquette. Pew Research Center. Retrieved from https://www.pewinternet.org

34. Hutchinson, A. (2018, September 11). Smartphone etiquette 2018 [Infographic]. SocialMediaToday. Retrieved from https://www.socialmediatoday.com

35. Lakey, D. M. (2007). *The board building cycle: Nine steps to finding, recruiting, and engaging nonprofit board members.* 2nd ed. Washington, DC: BoardSource, 10.

36. Shellenbarger, S. (2018, July 23). You could be too much of a team player. *The Wall Street Journal.* Retrieved from https://www.wsj.com

37. Gallup. (2017). State of the American workplace, 131. Retrieved from https://www.gallup.com

38. Gensler. (2019). U.S. workplace survey 2019. Retrieved from https://www.gensler.com

39. Haas, M., & Mortensen, M. (2016, June). The secrets of great teamwork. *Harvard Business Review.* Retrieved from https://hbr.org

40. Jones, A. (2019). The Tuckman model implementation, effect, and analysis & The new development of Jones LSI model on a small group. *Journal of Management, 6*(4): 23–28. doi: 10.34218/JOM.6.4.2019.005; Robbins, H. A., & Finley, M. (2000). *The new why teams don't work.* San Francisco: Berrett-Koehler, Chapter 29.

41. Desilver, D. (2020, March 21). Working from home was a luxury for the relatively affluent before coronavirus—not any more. Pew Research Center. Retrieved from https://www.weforum.org

42. Parker, K., Menasce Horowitz, J., & Minkin, R. (2020, December 9). How the coronavirus outbreak has—and hasn't—changed the way Americans work. Pew Research Center. Retrieved from https://www.pewresearch.org; Courtney, E. (2020, December 21). Remote work statistics: Navigating the new normal. Flexjobs. Retrieved from https://www.flexjobs.com

43. Gensler. (2020, Summer/Fall). U.S. workforce survey 2020. Retrieved from https://www.gensler.com

44. Upwork study finds 22 percent of American workforce will be remote by 2025. (2020, December 2020.) Retrieved from https://www.upwork.com; Castrillon, C. (2020, December 27). This is the future of remote work in 2021. *Forbes.* Retrieved from https://www.forbes.com

45. Economist Nicholas Bloom in Wong, M. (2020, June 29). Stanford research provides a snapshot of a new working-from-home economy. Stanford News. Retrieved from https://news.stanford.edu; Haag, M. (2021, March 29). Remote work is here to stay. Manhattan may never be the same. *The New York Times.* Retrieved from https://www.nytimes.com

46. *Virtual collaboration.* (HBR 20-minute manager series). (2016). Boston: Harvard Business Review Press, 2–3.

47. Chavez-Dreyfuss, G. (2020, October 22). Permanently remote workers seen doubling in 2021 due to pandemic productivity: survey. *Reuters.* Retrieved from https://www.reuters.com; Castrillon, C. (2020, December 27). This is the future of remote work in 2021. *Forbes.* Retrieved from https://www.forbes.com; Birkinshaw, J., Cohen, J., & Stach, P. (2020, August 31). Research: Knowledge workers are more productive from home. *Harvard Business Review.* Retrieved from https://hbr.org; The business case for remote work—for employers, employees, the environment, and society. Cost and benefits. (2021). Global Workplace Analytics. Retrieved from https://globalworkplaceanalytics.com

48. Johnson, J. (2016). Collaboration next: Planning for the way we work now and into the future. Insight to the Point, Allsteel. Retrieved from https://www.allsteeloffice.com

49. The value of teamwork in the workplace. (2017). Robert Half. Retrieved from https://www.roberthalf.com; Romero, L. E. (2016, January 20). What everyone should know about teamwork. *Forbes.* Retrieved from https://www.forbes.com; Scudamore, B. (2016, March 9). Why team building is the most important investment you'll make. *Forbes.* Retrieved from https://www.forbes.com; Mattson, D. (2015, February 19). 6 benefits of teamwork in the workplace. Sandler Training. Retrieved from https://www.sandler.com

50. Katzenbach, J. R., & Smith, D. K. (2015). *The wisdom of teams: Creating the high-performance organization.* Boston: HBR Press, 182; Chinnery, K. (2010, May 13). At the end of the day. BRW. Retrieved from https://global.factiva.com; Ruffin, B. (2006, January). T.E.A.M. work: Technologists, educators, and media specialists collaborating. *Library Media Connection, 24*(4), 49. Retrieved from EBSCO.

51. Anderson, K. (2015, September 13). Why and how to cultivate conviviality at work. *Forbes.* Retrieved from https://www.forbes.com; Ferrazzi, K. (2013, December 18). To make virtual teams succeed, pick the right players. HBR Blog Network. Retrieved from https://blogs.hbr.org; Holtzman, Y., & Anderberg, J. (2011). Diversify your teams and collaborate: Because great minds don't think alike. *The Journal of Management Development, 30*(1), 79. doi: 10.1108/0262171111098389; Katzenbach, J., & Smith, D. (1994). *Wisdom of teams.* New York: HarperBusiness, 45.

52. Hern, A. (2018, April 24). The two-pizza rule and the secret of Amazon's success. *The Guardian.* Retrieved from https://www.theguardian.com; Pratt, E. L. (2010). Virtual teams in very small classes. In R. Ubell (Ed.). *Virtual teamwork: Mastering the art and practice of online learning and corporate collaboration.* Hoboken, NJ: Wiley, 93.

53. Haas, M., & Mortensen, M. (2016, June). The secrets of great teamwork. *Harvard Business Review.* Retrieved from https://hbr.org

54. Househ, A. A. (2018, September 14). Tradeswomen enter the male-dominated construction industry. *Workforce.* Retrieved from https://www.workforce.com

55. Ferrazzi, K. (2015, March 27). How to run a great virtual meeting. *Harvard Business Review.* Retrieved from https://hbr.org

56. Accountemps, Robert Half. (2018, July 30). Time spent (and wasted) in meetings. Retrieved from https://www.roberthalf.com; Feloni, R. (2015, December 19). 7 reasons why your work meetings are a waste of time—and how to fix them. *Business Insider UK.* Retrieved from https://uk.businessinsider.com; Shellenbarger, S. (2015, July 7). Don't be the office schedule-wrecker. *The Wall Street Journal.* Retrieved from https://www.wsj.com

57. Fox, J. (2018, June 26). CEOs have to go to lots of meetings, too. *Bloomberg.* Retrieved from https://www.bloomberg.com; Ferrazzi, K. (2014, December). Getting virtual teams right. *Harvard Business Review.* Retrieved from https://hbr.org

58. Rogelberg, S. G., Shanock, L. R., & Scott, C. W. (2012). Wasted time and money in meetings: Increasing return on investment. *Small Group Research, 43*(2), 237. doi: 10.1177/1046496411429170

59. Fisher-Yoshida, B. (2018, October 3). 3 tips to make the most out of your next meeting. *Inc.* https://www.inc.com

60. Krieger, L. M. (2021, February 23). New Stanford research: Why Zoom meetings can wipe you out. *The Mercury News.* Retrieved from https://www.mercurynews.com

61. Axtell, P. (2018, June 22). The most productive meetings have fewer than 8 people. *Harvard Business Review.* Retrieved from https://hbr.org; Shellenbarger, S. (2016, December 20). A manifesto to end boring meetings. *The Wall Street Journal.* Retrieved from https://www.wsj.com

62. One day, a community transformed—Serv-a-palooza 2018. (2018). Timberland. Retrieved from https://www.timberland.com

63. Shellenbarger, S. (2015, July 7). Don't be the office schedule-wrecker. *The Wall Street Journal.* Retrieved from https://www.wsj.com

64. Owens, K. (2014, June 11). How to get employees to plug in to your meeting and not their devices. *Fast Company.* Retrieved from https://www.fastcompany.com

65. Haag, M. (2021, March 29). Remote work is here to stay. Manhattan may never be the same. *The New York Times.* Retrieved from https://www.nytimes.com

66. *Running virtual meetings: Test your technology, keep their attention, connect across time zones.* (2016). Boston: Harvard Business Review Press; Schlegel, J. (2012). Running effective meetings: Types of meetings. Salary.com. Retrieved from https://www.salary.com; Cohen, M. A., Rogelberg, S. G., Allen, J. A., & Luong, A. (2011). Meeting design characteristics and attendee perceptions of staff/team meeting quality. *Group Dynamics: Theory, Research, and Practice, 15*(1), 100–101; Schindler, E. (2008, February 15). Running an effective teleconference or virtual meeting. *CIO.* Retrieved from https://www.cio.com

67. Knowles, K. (2018, June 27). How to boss it like: Katharina Borchert, Chief Innovation Officer at Mozilla. *Forbes.* Retrieved from https://www.forbes.com

68. Blackburn, C. (2021, February 2). Virtual board meetings—Are they here to stay? KPMG. Retrieved from https://home.kpmg; Five reasons why your company needs to embrace video conferencing now. (2017). *Forbes.* Retrieved from https://www.forbes.com; Fox, J. T. (2014, October 8). Why virtual conferences will not replace face-to-face meetings. *International Meetings Review.* Retrieved from https://www.internationalmeetingsreview.com

69. Newport, C. (2016). *Deep work: Rules for focused work success in a distracted world.* New York: Grand Central Publishing, 52.

70. Davidson, K. (2016, September 8). Soft skills in short supply? Says one reader: "Give up on the snowflakes. *The Wall Street Journal.* Retrieved from https://blogs.wsj.com

71. Friedman, J. (April 1, 2021). How remote work helped us move past old-school "professionalism." *Fast Company.* Retrieved from https://medium.com

72. Hollon, J. (2007, November 13). Meeting malaise. *Workforce.* Retrieved from http://www.workforce.com

73. Zipkin, N. (2018, April 19). Why Elon Musk hates meetings. *Entrepreneur.* Retrieved from https://www.entrepreneur.com

74. Jackson, A. (2017, October 3). Elon Musk has reportedly used a brutal tactic to keep from wasting time in meetings. *Business Insider.* Retrieved from https://www.businessinsider.com

75. Scenario based on Shellenbarger, S. (2017, November 7). Can you keep your meeting to five minutes? *The Wall Street Journal.* Retrieved from https://www.wsj.com

76. Zetlin, M. (2015, ). 8 smart ways to stop people from checking their smartphones during meetings. *Inc.* Retrieved from https://www.inc.com

77. Nauen, R. (2017, June 29). Are smartphones killing productivity in the workplace? CareerBuilder. Retrieved from https://www.careerbuilder.com

78. Rosenberg McKay, D. (2020, September 17). Rules for using cell phones at work: Etiquette Tips for using your phone on the job. The Balance Careers. Retrieved from https://www.thebalancecareers.com

79. Simons, J. (2018, May 16). "I lost it": The boss who banned phones, and what came next. *The Wall Street Journal.* Retrieved from https://www.wsj.com

# Chapter 12

1. Bughin, J., Hazan, E., Lund, S., Dahlström, P., Wiesinger, A., & Subramaniam, A. (2018, May). Skill shift: Automation and the future of the workforce. McKinsey Global Institute. Retrieved from https://www.mckinsey.com; 2020 Workplace learning trends report: The skills of the future. Udemy for Business. Retrieved from https://info.udemy.com

2. Leveling up: How to win in the skills economy. (2016). PayScale. Retrieved from http://www.payscale.com

3. Key attributes employers want to see on students' resumes. (2020, January 13). National Association of Colleges and Employers. Retrieved from https://www.naceweb.org; Job outlook 2020 survey. (2020, January). National Association of Colleges and Employers. Retrieved from http://www.naceweb.org

4. Nakano, C. (2016, June 15). Presentation habits presenters don't like to admit. Prezi Blog. https://blog.prezi.com; Gallo, C. (2014, September 25). New survey: 70 percent say presentation skills are critical for career success. *Forbes.* Retrieved from http://www.forbes.com

5. Gallo, C. (2014, September 25). New survey: 70% say presentation skills are critical for career success. *Forbes.* Retrieved from https://www.forbes.com

6. Booher, D. (n. d.) 5 tips for executives who become public speakers. Booher Research Institute. Retrieved from http://www.booherresearch.com

7. Dhu, P. (2016, August 16). 9 tips for quickly building rapport with your audience. LinkedIn. Retrieved from https://www.linkedin.com

8. Medina, J. (2014). *Brain rules: 12 principles for surviving and thriving at work, home, and school.* Seattle, WA: Pear Press, 191–192.

9. Medina, J. (2014). *Brain rules: 12 principles for surviving and thriving at work, home, and school.* Seattle, WA: Pear Press, 233, 239.

10. Gallo, C. (2020, January 6). What it takes to give a great presentation. *Harvard Business Review.* Retrieved from https://hbr.org; Medina, J. (2014). *Brain rules: 12 principles for surviving and thriving at work, home, and school.* Seattle, WA: Pear Press, 233, 238–239.

11. Howder, R. (n.d.). About Prezi. Retrieved from http://prezi.com/about

12. Tufte, E. (2003). *The cognitive style of Powerpoint.* 2nd edition. Graphics Press; Duarte, N. (2008). *Slide:ology: The art and science of creating great presentations.* Sebastopol, CA: O'Reilly Media; Atkinson, C. (2018). *Beyond bullet points: Using PowerPoint to tell a compelling story that gets results.* (4th ed.). Pearson Education.

13. Atkinson, C. (2018). *Beyond bullet points: Using PowerPoint to tell a compelling story that gets results.* (4th ed.). Pearson Education.

14. Reynolds, G. (2019). *Presentation Zen: Simple ideas on presentation design and delivery.* 3rd ed. New York: New Riders/Pearson Education, 308.

15. Booher, D. (2003). *Speak with confidence: Powerful presentations that inform, inspire, and persuade.* New York: McGraw-Hill Professional, 126; Morr, K. (2016, July 5). How to choose the best colors for your presentations. Prezi Blog. Retrieved from https://blog.prezi.com; Ciotti, G. (2016, April 13). The psychology of color in marketing and branding. *Entrepreneur.* Retrieved from https://www.entrepreneur.com

16. Wakefield, J. (2015, December 18). How to avoid "death by PowerPoint." *BBC News.* Retrieved from http://www.bbc.com

17. Hearn, H. J. (2017, December 11). 6 PowerPoint presentation tips. American Express. Retrieved from https://www.americanexpress.com; Bates, S. (2005). *Speak like a CEO: Secrets for commanding attention and getting results.* New York: McGraw-Hill Professional, 113.

18. Gallo, C. (2020, January 6). What it takes to give a great presentation. *Harvard Business Review.* Retrieved from https://hbr.org

19. Johnson, D. (2021, February 25). How to give better PowerPoint presentations and improve your slides to keep an audience engaged. *Business Insider.* Retrieved from https://www.businessinsider.com; Sommerville, J. (2019, May 30). The 7 deadly sins of Powerpoint presentations. The Balance Small Business. Retrieved from https://www.thebalancesmb.com

20. Hedges, K. (2014, November 14). Six ways to avoid death by PowerPoint. *Forbes.* Retrieved from https://www.forbes.com

21. Miller, T. (n.d.). She's 22, from rural Zimbabwe, and a mogul in the making. Kiva. Retrieved from https://www.kiva.org

22. Dray, K. (2017, March 27). Adele emotionally explains why she may never tour again. *Stylist.* Retrieved from https://www.stylist.co.uk

23. Fleming, R. (2004). *The inner voice: The making of a singer.* New York: Viking, 109.

24. Surprising celebrities with stage fright. (2020, August 20). MSN.com. Retrieved from https://www.msn.com; Britt, B. (2017, May 15). Adele, Van Halen among musicians who battle stage fright. Grammys. Retrieved from https://www.grammy.com; Enright, P. (2007). Even stars get stage fright. NBC NEWS. Retrieved from http://www.nbcnews.com

25. Quoted in Reynolds, G. (2014, January 20). Coping with presentation anxiety & "stage fright." Presentation Zen. Retrieved from http://www.presentationzen.com

26. Eaton, K. (2016, June 8). Getting over stage fright with the help of your smartphone. *The New York Times.* Retrieved from https://www.nytimes.com

27. Booher, D. (2011). *Speak with confidence.* AudioInk. GooglePlay.

28. Whitmore, J. (2017, January 10). 5 tips to reduce presentation anxiety. *Entrepreneur.* Retrieved from https://www.entrepreneur.com

29. Search YouTube or search the top 100 speeches at American Rhetoric: http://www.americanrhetoric.com

30. Nisen, M., & Guey, L. (2013, May 15). 23 of the best pieces of advice ever given to graduates. *Business Insider.* Retrieved from http://www.businessinsider.com

31. Duarte, N. (2008). *Slide:ology: The art and science of creating great presentations.* Sebastopol, CA: O'Reilly Media, 64.

32. Reynolds, G. (2020). *Presentation Zen: Simple ideas on presentation design and delivery,* 3rd ed. Berkeley, CA: New Riders/Pearson Education, 68.

33. Mackey, S. W. (2012, November 4). Step up: Be an ambassador. Retrieved from http://sarahwmackey.com

34. How will you take part? (n.d.). Heal the Bay. Retrieved from https://healthebay.org

# Chapter 13

1. Blake, S. (2020, July 10). The class of 2020 is getting a crash course in pivoting—changing their career outlook, delaying graduation—whatever it takes. CNBC. Retrieved from https://www.cnbc.com

2. Rosenberg, E. (2020, September 4). College tuition vs. investing: Is it worth it? Investopedia. Retrieved from https://www.investopedia.com; Gundersen, H. (2020, August 6). What is the ROI of your college degree? Bankrate. Retrieved from https://www.bankrate.com

3. Gray, K. (2021, April 19). The attributes employers seek on students' resumes. NACE. Retrieved from https://www.naceweb.org

4. Bureau of Labor Statistics. (August 22, 2019). Number of jobs, labor market experience, and earnings growth: Results from a national longitudinal survey summary. Retrieved from https://www.bls.gov

5. National Association of Colleges and Employers. (2021). Internship & co-op report 2021. NACE. Retrieved from https://www.naceweb.org

6. Shellenbarger, S. (2019, May 7). Job advice for grads: A tricky proposition. *The Wall Street Journal,* A11.

7. Doyle, A. (2020, January 30). What is the hidden job market? The Balance Careers. Retrieved from https://www.thebalancecareers.com; Laumeister, G. (2015, June 2). The hidden job market and what to do about it. DailyWorth. Retrieved from https://www.dailyworth.com

8. Maurer, R. (2017, June 23). Employee referrals remain top source for hires. SHRM. Retrieved from https://www.shrm.org

9. Doyle, A. (2019, August 2). Top 6 best free job search apps. The Balance Careers. Retrieved from https://www.thebalancecareers.com; McCullum, K. (2019, April 21). 12 best job search apps to find your career. Retrieved from https://www.learnhowtobecome.org

10. Bennett, M. (2020, October 7). The power of an employee referral. Johnson Service Group. Retrieved from https://jsginc.com

11. Ibid.

12. Maurer, R. (2017, June 23). Employee referrals remain top source for hires. SHRM. Retrieved from https://www.shrm.org

13. Bump, P. (2021, March 22). 31 LinkedIn stats that marketers need to know in 2021. HubSpot. Retrieved from https://blog.hubspot.com; Schomer, A., & Carnahan, D. (2020, September 25). US digital trust study: Which social media platforms have the highest levels of digital trust among US social users. *Business Insider.* Retrieved from https://www.businessinsider.com; Statistics. (2021). LinkedIn. Retrieved from https://news.linkedin.com

14. Barnes, N. G., Mazzola, A., & Killeen, M. (2020, January 9). Oversaturation & Disengagement: The 2019 Fortune 500 social media dance. Center for Marketing Research, University of Massachusetts Dartmouth. Retrieved from https://www.umassd.edu

15. Statistics. (2021). LinkedIn. Retrieved from https://news.linkedin.com

16. Garriott, O. (2015, February 6). 10 LinkedIn tips for students and new grads. Retrieved from https://www.linkedin.com

17. Better Team Facebook. (2019, October 2). How to post a job on Facebook. Retrieved from https://www.betterteam.com; Mauer, R. (2018, July 31). How to get started with recruiting on Facebook. Retrieved from https://www.shrm.org

18. Ward, M. (2017, September 8). Why you should be creating a unique resume for each job application. CNBC Make It. Retrieved from https://www.cnbc.com

19. Qu, L. (2019, November 7). 99% of Fortune 500 companies use applicant tracking systems. Jobscan. Retrieved from https://www.jobscan.co

20. Doyle, A. (2017, April 5). How many pages should a resume be? *The Balance.* Retrieved from https://www.thebalance.com; Ryan, L. (2016, May 2). How long should my resume be? And 15 other resume tips. *Forbes.* Retrieved from https://www.forbes.com; Isaacs, K. (n.d.). How long should my résumé be? Monster. Retrieved from http://career-advice.monster.com

21. 75% of HR managers have caught a lie on a resume, according to new CareerBuilder survey. (2017, September 14). CareerBuilder. Retrieved from http://press.careerbuilder.com

22. Indeed Career Guide. (2020, January 27). How to write a summary of qualifications. Retrieved from https://www.indeed.com

23. Malacoff, J. (2019, August 27). 10 résumé tips you haven't heard before. Glassdoor. Retrieved from https://www.glassdoor.com

24. LinkedIn for Volunteers. (n.d.). Use your skills to make a positive impact. Retrieved from https://volunteer.linkedin.com

25. Jalan, A. (2017, March 14). LinkedIn profile photo tips: Introducing photo filter and editing. LinkedIn. Retrieved from https://blog.linkedin.com

26. Hehman, E., Flake, J. K., & Freeman, J. B. (2015). Static and dynamic facial cues differentially affect the consistency of social evaluations. *Personality and Social Psychology Bulletin,* 1–12. doi: 10.1177/0146167215591495

27. Fisher, C. (2015, January 21). Brand YOU year: How to brand yourself without sounding like everyone else. LinkedIn Official Blog. Retrieved from http://blog.linkedin.com

28. Adams, S. (2015, April 23). Seven ways to make LinkedIn help you find a job. *Forbes.* Retrieved from http://www.forbes.com

29. Kreps, L. (2015, June 25). The legal risks of lying on your résumé. Shake Law.com. Retrieved from http://www.shakelaw.com

30. Qu, L. (2019, November 7). 99% of Fortune 500 companies use applicant tracking systems (ATS). Jobscan. Retrieved from https://www.jobscan.co/blog [Copyeditor: Yes, this is a correct URL.]

31. Skillings, P. (2015, March 1). How to get the applicant tracking system to pick your résumé. Big Interview Blog. Retrieved from http://biginterview.com

32. Florentine, S. (2016, February 1). Why your ATS may be killing your recruiting efforts. *CIO.* Retrieved from http://www.cio.com

33. Applicant tracking systems 101 for job-seekers: Understanding the ATS technology that dominates online job search. (n.d.). Quintessential Careers. Retrieved from http://www.quintcareers.com

34. Kidwai, A. (2021, April 27). Read the résumé a college senior used to land her dream internship at Spotify and praise from CEO Daniel Ek. *Business Insider.* Retrieved from https://markets.businessinsider.com

35. Caprino, K. (2019, March 23). How to write a resume that passes the artificial intelligence test. *Forbes.* Retrieved from https://www.forbes.com

36. Yang, P. (2020). Cover letters: Just how important are they? ResumeGo. Retrieved from https://www.resumego.net; Pohle, A. (2021, January 21). How to write a cover letter that stands out. *The Wall Street Journal.* Retrieved from https://www.wsj.com

37. Do cover letters still matter? Here's what data shows. (2019, June 19). The Ladders. Retrieved from https://www.theladders.com

38. 2020 Recruiter nation survey report. Jobvite, 19. Retrieved from https://www.jobvite.com

39. Scivicque, C. (2017). Are cover letters still relevant? Ivy Exec Blog. Retrieved from https://www.ivyexec.com

40. Tanzi, T., and Dmitrieva, K. (2020, February 20). The job market is hot. So why are half of U.S. grads missing out? *The Los Angeles Times.* Retrieved from https://ww.latimes.com

41. Pohle, A. (2021, January 21). How to write a cover letter that stands out. *The Wall Street Journal.* Retrieved from https://www.wsj.com

42. Caprino, K. (2019, March 23). How to write a resume that passes the artificial intelligence test. *Forbes.* Retrieved from https://www.forbes.com

43. Gig in or get out. (2019, September 18). Retrieved from https://www.businesswire.com

44. Guina, R. (2019, January 22). The hidden job market—How to find a job that isn't advertised. Cash Money Life. Retrieved from https://cashmoneylife.com

45. Mateo, A. (2020, January 15). Is LinkedIn a waste of time? *The Wall Street Journal.* Retrieved from https://www.wsj.com

46. Kolakowski, M. (2018, October 12). Phantom job postings. Retrieved from https://www.thebalancecareers.com/phantom-job-postings -1287159; Weber, L., & Kwoh, L. (2013, January 9). Beware the phantom job listing. *The Wall Street Journal,* B1 and B6.

47. Pohle, A. (2021, January 21). How to write a cover letter that stands out. *The Wall Street Journal.* Retrieved from https://www.wsj.com

48. 75% of HR managers have caught a lie on a resume, according to new CareerBuilder survey. (2017, September 14). CareerBuilder. Retrieved from http://press.careerbuilder.com; West, T. (2020, March 27). The lies we tell at work—and the Damage they do. *The Wall Street Journal.* Retrieved from https://www.wsj.com

49. 2020 Recruiter nation survey report. Jobvite, 8. Retrieved from https://www.jobvite.com

50. Employers reveal biggest résumé blunders in annual CareerBuilder survey. (2015, December 31). CareerBuilder. Retrieved from http://www.careerbuilder.com

# Chapter 14

1. Cobert, A. (2017). Standing out from the crowd: How to nail a group interview. *The Muse.* Retrieved from https://www.themuse.com

2. Rueff, R. (2018, July 14). 5 tips: Best time to schedule an interview. Glassdoor. Retrieved from https://www.glassdoor.com; Smith, J. (2016, November 9). The perfect time to schedule your job interview. *Business Insider.* Retrieved from http://www.businessinsider.com

3. Deloitte. (2017). Interview tips: From preparation to follow-up we offer seven tips to ensure a strong interview. Retrieved from https://www2.deloitte.com

4. Schor, S. (2018, November 6). 9 out of 10 people are willing to earn less money to do more meaningful work. *Harvard Business Review.* Retrieved from https://hbr.org

5. McIntosh, B. (2013, April 30). How to ace an interview with job success stories. Retrieved from http://www.biospace.com

6. Career Builder. (2018, August 9). More than half of employers have found content on social media that caused them not to hire a candidate. Retrieved from https://www.prnewswire.com

7. CareerBuilder. (2016, April 28). Number of employers using social media to screen candidates has increased 500 percent over the last decade. Retrieved from www.careerbuilder.com

8. Ryan, L. (2015, March 21). What to wear to a job interview. *Forbes.* Retrieved from https://www.forbes.com

9. Ashford, K. (2020). 7 interview looks that say "Don't hire me." Retrieved from https://www.monster.com

10. Based on Williams, A. (2020, August 20). Will we ever touch (professionally) again? *The New York Times.* Retrieved from https://www.nytimes.com

11. Active listening for interview success: How your ears can help you land the job. (2008, August 13). BioSpace. Retrieved from http://www.biospace.com

12. Lorenz, M. (2021, January 18). Top 10 things NOT to do in an interview. CareerBuilder. Retrieved from https://www.careerbuilder.com; CareerBuilder releases annual list of strangest interview and body language mistakes. (2017, January 12). Retrieved from http://press.careerbuilder.com

13. The airport test: What it is and why employers use it (with tips). (2021, April 15). Indeed. Retrieved from https://www.indeed.com

14. Chan, A. (2013, June 14). Top 10 interview tips for new college graduates. *The Huffington Post.* Retrieved from http://www.huffingtonpost.com

15. Stillman, J. (2019, ). The 3 best interview questions to gauge a candidate's EQ. *Inc.* Retrieved from https://www.inc.com

16. Martin, C. (n.d.). List of strengths and weaknesses: What to say in your interview. Monster. Retrieved from http://www.monster.com

17. Rebecca Horan, personal branding expert, cited in How to talk about your weaknesses in an interview. (2021, February 10). CareerBuilder. Retrieved from https://www.careerbuilder.com

18. Tigar, L. (2020, January 30). What is the Star Method and why it will help you ace your next interview. Ladders. Retrieved from https://www.theladders.com; Tyrell-Smith, T. (2011, January 25). Tell a story that will get you hired. *Money/U.S. News & World Report.* Retrieved from http://money.usnews.com

19. Elliott, K. (2021, March 2). How to prepare for a job interview in 2021. *Forbes.* Retrieved from https://www.forbes.com

20. Karrass, C. L. (n.d.). *In business as in life, you don't get what you deserve, you get what you negotiate.* Beverly Hills, CA: Stanford St. Press.

21. U.S. Equal Employment Opportunity Commission. (n.d.). Prohibited employment policies/practices. Retrieved from https://www.eeoc.gov

22. Heathfield, S. M. (2020, June 10). Illegal interview questions and what you need to know. The Balance Careers. Retrieved from https://www.thebalancecareers.com; Doyle, A. (2019, September 20). How to handle illegal or inappropriate interview questions. The Balance Careers. Retrieved from https://www.thebalancecareers.com; Illegal interview questions and female applicants. (2018, December 10). FindLaw. Retrieved from https://employment.findlaw.com

23. Grasz, J. (2015, April 9). 1 in 5 employers has unknowingly asked an illegal interview question. CareerBuilder. Retrieved from http://www.careerbuilder.com

24. Glassdoor. (2020, February 23). 8 inappropriate interview questions and how to tackle them like a pro. Retrieved from https://www.glassdoor.com; Common interview questions: What you can ask and when it is legal. (n.d.). Monster. Retrieved from http://hiring.monster.com; Gerencer, T. (2019, February 12). Illegal interview questions an employer cannot ask [So don't answer!]. Zety Resume Builder. Retrieved from https://zety.com

25. Georgevich, D. (2016, June 10). Career coach. Personal communication with Mary Ellen Guffey.

26. Accountemps. (2017, November 17). A little thanks goes a long way. Retrieved from https://www.roberthalf.com; Belli, G. (2017, January). Should we still be sending thank-you notes after interviews? PayScale. Retrieved from http://www.payscale.com

27. 2021 Job seeker nation report, 12. Retrieved from https://www.jobvite.com; 2020 Recruiter nation survey, 3. Retrieved from https://www.jobvite.com

28. Ryan, L. (2016, February 22). Send the perfect post-interview thank you note. *Forbes.* Retrieved from https://www.forbes.com

29. Manning, K. (2016, March 4). Here's what to write in your thank-you note after a job interview. *Fast Company.* Retrieved from https://www.fastcompany.com

30. Smith, J. (2016, November 8). Here's exactly how many times you should follow up after a job interview. *Business Insider.* Retrieved from http://www.businessinsider.com

31. Owens, Y. (n.d.). 3 rules for following up with a recruiter. *The Muse.* Retrieved from https://www.themuse.com

32. 2020 Recruiter nation survey, 10. Retrieved from https://www.jobvite.com

33. Wilkie, D. (2019, April 10). No thank-you note? No job. Retrieved from https://www.shrm.org

34. LinkedIn. (2019). Global talent trends 2019. Retrieved from https://business.linkedin.com

35. More than half of employers have found content on social media that caused them NOT to hire a candidate. (2018, August 9). CareerBuilder. Retrieved from http://www.careerbuilder.com

36. Shellenbarger, S. (2019, October 22). Find your job interview Zen. *The Wall Street Journal,* A12.

37. How to negotiate salary after you get a job offer. (2020, October 8). Robert Half. Retrieved from https://www.roberthalf.com; Vogt, P. (n. d.). Entry-level salary (probably) isn't as negotiable as you think. Monster. Retrieved from http://career-advice.monster.com

38. Connley, C. (2018, September 4). 4 tips for negotiating your first salary when you have zero industry experience. CNBC. Retrieved from https://www.cnbc.com

39. DeZube, D. (n.d.). Ten questions to ask when negotiating a salary. Monster. Retrieved from https://www.monster.com

40. Salary negotiation: How to ask for a higher salary. (2021, March 25). Program on Negotiation, Harvard Law School. Retrieved from https://www.pon.harvard.edu; How to negotiate your first salary (with tips). (2021, April 1). Indeed. Retrieved from https://www.indeed.com; How to negotiate an entry-level salary. (2021, March 8). Indeed. Retrieved from https://www.indeed.com; Zucker, R. (2020, December 16). 9 compensation negotiation strategies that work. *Forbes.* Retrieved from https://www.forbes.com; How to negotiate salary after you get a job offer. (2020, October 8). Robert Half. Retrieved from https://www.roberthalf.com; Connley, C. (2018, September 4). 4 tips for negotiating your first salary when you have zero industry experience. CNBC. Retrieved from https://www.cnbc.com; Reshwan, R. (2016, June 6). 3 strategies for salary negotiations. *U.S. News & World Report.* Retrieved from http://money.usnews.com

41. Connley, C. (2018, September 4). 4 tips for negotiating your first salary when you have zero industry experience. CNBC. Retrieved from https://www.cnbc.com; Hamilton, K. (2017, January). The careful art of negotiating your first salary. PayScale. Retrieved from http://www.payscale.com

# Index

*Italic page numbers indicate illustrative information in figures.*